jansculion

KAY BOYLE
Author of Herself

KAY BOYLE

Author of Herself

JOAN MELLEN

Farrar, Straus & Giroux

NEW YORK

Library of Congress Cataloging-in-Publication Data
Mellen, Joan.
Kay Boyle : author of herself / Joan Mellen. — 1st ed.
p.   cm.
Includes bibliographical references and index.
1. Boyle, Kay, 1902–92—Biography. 2. Women authors,
American—20th century—Biography. 3. Women political activists—
United States—Biography. I. Title.
PS3503.09357Z78   1994   813'.52—dc20 [B]   94-654 CIP

The author is grateful to the following for their kind permission to use material in this book:
Elizabeth Barnett, literary executor of the Estate of Edna St. Vincent Millay, for the poem
"Conscientious Objector," by Edna St. Vincent Millay, from Collected Poems, copyright © 1934,
1962 by Edna St. Vincent Millay and Norman Millay Ellis (HarperCollins).
Ian Franckenstein, for quotations from the published and unpublished writings of Kay Boyle.
Unpublished materials copyright © 1993 by Ian Franckenstein.
Special Collections, Morris Library, Southern Illinois University at Carbondale, for material from the
Kay Boyle Papers; the Philip Kaplan Expatriate Papers; the Caresse Crosby/Black Sun Press Archives;
the Herman and Fay Rappaport Collection of Kay Boyle; and the Erich and Evelyn Kahler Kay Boyle
Papers, VFM 29, Ernest Walsh letters to Kate Buss.
ARS, for the photo of Kay Boyle by Man Ray, copyright © 1993 by Man Ray Trust—ADAGP-ARS.
The Henry W. and Albert A. Berg Collection, The New York Public Library, Astor, Lenox,
and Tilden Foundations.
The Ernest Hemingway Collection (#6250-A), the Alfred Kreymborg Collection (#6561), and the
R. W. Stallman Collection (#6778) of the Clifton Waller Barrett Library, Manuscripts Division,
Special Collections Department, University of Virginia Library.
The Samuel Beckett Estate, for quotations from the letters of Samuel Beckett to Kay Boyle.
Box 1 of the Harold Loeb Collection, Manuscripts Division, Department of Rare Books and Special
Collections, Princeton University Libraries.
The Harold Nemerov Papers, Washington University Libraries.
The David Rattray Collection of the East Hampton Library.
The Authors League Fund for quotations from the letters of Djuna Barnes, copyright © the Authors
League Fund, 234 West 44th Street, New York, New York 10036, as literary executor of the Estate of
Djuna Barnes.
Marianne Craig Moore, literary executor of the Estate of Marianne Moore. Papers of Marianne
Moore, V:6:45, the Rosenbach Museum & Library, Philadelphia.
The Newton Arvin Papers, Smith College Library Rare Book Room.
KPFA Radio, for radio transcripts copyright © 1988 by KPFA Radio, Berkeley, California.
Harry Ransom Humanities Research Center, the University of Texas at Austin.
Yale Collection of American Literature, Beinecke Rare Book and Manuscript Library, Yale University.
The Newberry Library for material from the Malcolm Cowley Papers, copyright
© Estate of Malcolm Cowley.
New Directions Publishing Corporation for material by William Carlos Williams, copyright © 1994
by William Eric Williams and Paul H. Williams.
Paula Scott, for gracious permission to quote passages from the letters of Evelyn Scott.
Isabel Bayley, literary trustee for the Estate of Katherine Anne Porter, for material copyright © 1993
by Isabel Bayley.
The Estate of Edward Dahlberg.
The James T. Farrell Papers, Special Collections, Van Pelt Library, University of Pennsylvania.
Elaine Sproat, for material from the Lola Ridge Papers, Sophia Smith Collection, Smith College.
Berenice Abbott/Commerce Graphics Ltd., Inc.
And to: Dorothy Bryant, Gwen Davis, Kathleen Fraser, Doris Grumbach, Faith Gude, James G.
Hietter, James Laughlin, Margaret Nemerov, Stan Rice, Katherine Vail, and Deborah L. Zike.

FOR
RUTH PRAWER JHABVALA
AND C. S. H. JHABVALA

Acknowledgments

Of all writers, the biographer indulges in no hyperbole by insisting that writing a life is a collaborative effort. I could not have offered this impression of Kay Boyle's life were it not for the generosity of spirit of many people and their willingness to offer historical testimony. My deepest appreciation must go first to David V. Koch, curator of Special Collections at the Morris Library at Southern Illinois University, which houses the majority of Kay Boyle's papers, for his integrity, his intelligence, his patience, and his friendship. It is a truism that librarians are by no means by definition friends to the researcher. David Koch redeems his calling. I would also like to thank Sheila Ryan, formerly Curator of Manuscripts and Shelley Cox, Rare Books librarian.

My gratitude goes as well to Kathe Vail and Faith Gude, Kay Boyle's daughters, for whom no question was too trivial (now, what breed of dog *was* Diane, and how did you spell her name?). My intrusions into their lives were met every time with graciousness and a desire to help. No less am I grateful to Kay Boyle's son, Ian Franckenstein, who acts on the stage as Ian Swift, for his many, many kindnesses. For personal hospitality I am grateful to Kathe Vail, Faith Gude, and Sharon Cowling.

Among Kay Boyle's friends, and my fellow biographers, I would like to single out in particular James Laughlin, Tania and the late James Stern, Jacqueline Ventadour Hélion, Jerome M. Garchik, Hugh Ford, and Elaine Sproat for their goodwill, patience, and generosity.

They were not alone. I will simply name some of the people without whose assistance, sometimes in large ways, sometimes in small, I could not have written a life of Kay Boyle. I am indebted to each of them: Daniel Aaron, Edward Albee, Ethel Alexander, Roger Angell, Charles Amirkhanian, Beverly Axelrod, Deirdre Bair, Isabel Bayley, Simon Michael Bessie, Coburn Britton, Andreas Brown, Dorothy Bryant, John Bunzel, Carolyn Burke, Luise Caputo-Mayr, Richard Centing, Arthur Chandler, Blair Clark, Paul Coltoff, Liadain O'Donovan Cook, Robert

Coover, K. Smokey Cormier, Marc Cote, the late Muriel Cowley, Rob Cowley, John Cowling, Sharon Cowling, Gary Crowdus, Peter Cunningham, Gwen Davis, Joan Boyle Detweiler, Bruce Detweiler, Alexina Duchamp, Bob Dunn, Dr. Helga Einsele, Irving Falk, Benjamin B. Ferencz, Lawrence Ferlinghetti, Peggy Fox, Kathleen Fraser, Christine Friedland, Arnold Gates, John Gerassi, Joan Givner, Herbert Gold, Ted Goeser, Doris Grumbach, Padraic Gude, Yvonne Hagen, the late Susan Hager, Jim Hietter, Joseph Illick, Russ Jennings, David Cay Boyle Johnson, Juliet Judge, the late Evelyn (Lily) Kahler, Ted Keller, H. T. Kirby-Smith, Kenneth Koch, Myrine Kuhn, Nancy LaPaglia, Mabel Lilienstein, Leo Litwak, Helen Major, Reginald Major, Anne Martindell, Eva Mayer, Jennifer McCord, Howard McCord, Anne McCormick, Ken McCormick, Cyra McFadden, Hank McGuckin, Jackie McGuckin, Stuart Creighton Miller, Jessica Mitford, Kate Moses, Donald W. Muntz, the late Howard Nemerov, the late George Novack, Philip O'Connor, Joshua Odell, Father Gerry O'Rourke, Selden Osborne, Ron Padgett, Charlotte Painter, Grace Paley, William R. Patton, Jane Platt, Andrew N. Poliakoff, the late George Popper, the late David Rattray, Stan Rice, Donald Richie, Ariel Rosenblum, Sidney Rosenblum, Sandro Rumney, Maryellen Rump, Sonia Sanchez, Andrew Sarris, Duane Schneider, Michel Sciama, Martin Scorsese, David Shapiro, Donna Sharer, the late William L. Shirer, Jack Shoemaker, Elaine Showalter, Eric Solomon, Donald Staples, Dr. Tom Stone, Fraser Sutherland, Tree Swenson, Studs Terkel, Olga Titelbaum, Marsha Giegerich Torkelson, Robert Treuhaft, Diana Trilling, Victor Turks, Julia Vail, Amos Vogel, Burton Weiss, Jacqueline Bograd Weld, Nancy Wilner, Brenda Wineapple, Manfred Wolf, Shawn Wong, Noel Young, and Deborah Linton Zike.

I would like to thank the University Committee of Temple University for very graciously awarding me two study leaves during the period that I worked on this book.

For its support and encouragement, I would also like to acknowledge the Biography Seminar sponsored by the English department of New York University, and in particular Aileen Ward, who invited me to be a member, and Kenneth Silverman, who offered sustenance and encouragement to this book by inviting me to share a chapter with the members.

Many librarians and their staffs have aided me richly. In particular I would like to mention Cathy Henderson and her staff at the Harry Ransom Humanities Research Center of the University of Texas at Austin; Patricia Willis and her assistant Daria Ague at the Beinecke Library at Yale University; Kevin Ray, the curator of manuscripts at the Olin Library of Washington University at St. Louis; Michael Plunkett at the Alderman Library of the University of Virginia at Charlottesville; Cathy Meaney and her staff at Temple University's Paley Library; Stephen Crook and Philip Milito at the Berg Collection of the New York Public Library; Ruth Mortimer at the William Allan Neilson Library at Smith College; Blanche T. Ebeling-Koning, former curator for rare books and literary manuscripts at the McKeldon Library of the University of Maryland; Anne Goddard at the National Archive of Canada, the National Library of Canada at Ottawa; Stephan Chodorov at Camera 3 Productions, Inc.; Josefine Justic at the Stadtmagistrat Innsbruck (Stadtarchiv) and Dr. Franz-heinz Hye, director of the Archives at the Senatrat University, in Austria; Laura Chase at the Cincinnati Historical Society; Allisa Wiener, the reference librarian at the Minnesota Historical Society; Dorothy

King at the East Hampton Library; and Marilyn A. Duncan, the assistant librarian, and the staff of the National Society of the Daughters of the American Revolution. I would also like to thank John Kennedy of Temple University's Paley Library.

I am grateful as well to the Charles Patterson Van Pelt Library at the University of Pennsylvania; the Firestone Library at Princeton University; the Poetry Center at San Francisco State University; the George Arens Collection at the Syracuse University Library; the Bobst Library at New York University; the Berks County Historical Society, Pennsylvania; the Blegen Library of the University of Cincinnati; the Newberry Library in Chicago; and the National Book Foundation.

For their graciousness and patience, I am especially indebted to the librarians at the Hopewell Branch of the Mercer County Library in New Jersey, in particular to Hope Sudlow and Jean Chen. No book was too obscure for them to locate, no task too formidable.

No less must I express my gratitude to Virgil W. Dean, the research historian at the Kansas State Historical Society, for his extraordinary interest in this project.

Gallant friends stood by through the seven years of this undertaking, offering help, advice, moral support, and I must name them: Louise Collins, Pat Gartenberg, Carole Klein, B. J. Lifton, Marion Meade, Mayumi Oda, Michael Pakenham, Carl Rollyson, Mya Shone, who is such a good friend that she went to take pictures of Kay Boyle's birthplace in St. Paul, Rosalie Siegel, Dorothea Straus, and Francine Toll. To Dan Tooker, former student of Kay Boyle's and friend, I owe a special debt of gratitude.

I was assisted in this undertaking by assistants of considerable dedication and ability: Frank Walgren and Donald Dingledine. Without them, this work would have been immensely more difficult.

I thank Karen Ibach for her competence and effort, Jane Gelfman, my agent, and Daniel J. Kornstein for his generous support.

Not least, showers of gratitude to my exacting and gracious editor, Jack Lynch, and to indefatigable Elisheva Urbas, who did all the editorial work at Farrar, Straus, and Giroux.

Finally I must offer my deepest gratitude to my teacher, the late Irving Howe, at the City University of New York, for the grace of mind which he brought to the study of literature, and for teaching me to read the relationship between literature and politics; to David Rieff, for his faith in this project; to Bob Knight for the intelligence and courage with which he has inspired me from the first day I made his acquaintance; and to Ralph Schoenman, of course, my best friend, for such support and kindness as few are lucky enough to find, and who has been there for me, in all seasons.

Contents

. . . I'll never
Be such a gosling to obey instinct, but stand
As if a man were author of himself
And knew no other kin.

WILLIAM SHAKESPEARE
Coriolanus, V, iii, 34–37

CONSCIENTIOUS OBJECTOR

I shall die, but that is all that I shall do for Death.

I hear him leading his horse out of the stall; I hear the
*   clatter on the barn-floor.*
He is in haste; he has business in Cuba, business in the
*   Balkans, many calls to make this morning.*
But I will not hold the bridle while he cinches the girth.
And he may mount by himself: I will not give him a leg up.

Though he flick my shoulders with his whip, I will not tell
*   him which way the fox ran.*
With his hoof on my breast, I will not tell him where the
*   black boy hides in the swamp.*
I shall die, but that is all that I shall do for Death; I am
*   not on his pay-roll.*

I will not tell him the whereabouts of my friends nor of my
*   enemies either.*
Though he promise me much, I will not map him the route
*   to any man's door.*
Am I a spy in the land of the living, that I should deliver
*   men to Death?*
Brother, the password and the plans of our city are safe
*   with me; never through me*
Shall you be overcome.

EDNA ST. VINCENT MILLAY

(Read by Kay Boyle on KPFA San Francisco
on the occasion of her eighty-fourth birthday.)

KAY BOYLE
Author of Herself

Introduction:

Place Names

*I do not believe there is any past, because if you believe in the
past nothing else any longer exists, and if you believe in what is
to come it does come, like a miracle . . .*

I'm going to write a record of our age.

Her white hair is waved and swept dramatically up from her face,
pristine, impeccable. Her scarlet lips remind us of the belles of the twenties
in Greenwich Village and Paris some seventy years ago. Large white earrings in the shape of flowers tell us who she is. Now she proceeds from
her book-filled studio apartment, which is as spartan, as neat as she,
although it is dotted with photographs of her third husband, once the Baron
von und zu Franckenstein, a tall, blondish, handsome man with a look of
shy vulnerability in his eyes. Alongside rests a framed portrait of craggy-
faced Samuel Beckett. There are also photographs of a young Apple, the
daughter now dead.

She makes her way to the elevator, ascending to the cafeteria for
lunch. Two women join her, but they will not say "Good afternoon," nor,
they have given her to know, do they wish her to join them in the dining
room.

Today she does not need them, for she has a guest, a publisher who
is about to reissue one of her fourteen novels. This one, *Gentlemen, I
Address You Privately*, was her third, first published in 1933. The passionate
physical love at the heart of this novel is between men, and it's treated as
natural and with dignity, without a trace of self-consciousness or condescension.

"Why do so many old people get mean?" Kay Boyle inquires of her
companion, Noel Young, who is of a certain age himself, if some twenty
years her junior.

The other women at The Redwoods, a retirement community in Mill
Valley, California, do in fact have grounds for their irritation with the
famous writer who lives among them. For Kay Boyle has garnered an

admirer, Dr. Tom Stone, recently retired, who comes frequently to take her to lunch or dinner. And although Dr. Stone attended these other women as well, it's only Kay Boyle he now returns to see.

"You have to be over eighty and write thirty books," Kay Boyle says sardonically. The indignities of old age have never led her to forget who she is.

For she's frail now, her hands so gnarled by arthritis that it has become painful for her to write. She's eighty-eight, and if her hair is still impeccably arranged, her signature white earrings in place, and her lips scarlet, she is also shrunken and unsteady on her feet; she is no longer the tall, imperious, black-haired, misty blue-eyed figure of drama and authority, "the writer Kay Boyle," whose fame her mother, born in 1874 on the Kansas prairie, had dreamt of since her "Katherine" was only six years old. But if she is the survivor of many losses and unrelenting illness—the second of her six children, Apple, died two years ago—she remains, emphatically, Kay Boyle.

In October of 1990 another operation, one for abdominal surgery, weakens her. She has survived nearly every ailment to which the species is heir: cerebral meningitis, disease of the gallbladder, pneumonia, diverticulitis, breast cancer twice, a hysterectomy, broken bones late in life, angina, crippling arthritis, increasing deafness, incipient blindness, and all the weakening of age. Her hearing is poor and she finds it difficult to read anything except the newspaper. But she decided to move back to her studio from the hospital wing. She'll hold out a little longer, she tells her son, Ian, who visits her every day.

But there remain proofs to edit, revisions still to be made, for she is not satisfied with *Gentlemen, I Address You Privately*. She must expunge it now of its "youthful excesses." There are far too many adjectives, for one thing. The flap copy too must succumb to her blue pencil. "Had stolen some goods" is so awkward. From her bed Kay Boyle dictates to an assistant; that phrase must be changed to "was wanted for theft."

It's 1991, and then 1992. Quietly resigned, she tells Kathe, one of her French daughters, and Ian, that she is ready to die: "it's too long."

Kay Boyle has been one of the most accomplished American short story writers of this century, as well as a poet, novelist, memoirist, foreign correspondent, and political activist. Born in St. Paul, Minnesota, in 1902, six years after that town's most famous author, F. Scott Fitzgerald, into a rich upper-middle-class family, she grew up quickly, in Philadelphia, Atlantic City, Washington, and Bryn Mawr. Her culture-minded mother considered her a genius, a prodigy, certain to go far. In a hurry as her youth drew to a close in Cincinnati, where the Boyle family had retreated after the loss of its fortune, Kay at twenty made her break with the past. She moved to New York and never looked back.

At twenty-one, as she disembarked in France, Kay Boyle was already a published poet. She had served as the assistant to the revolutionary anarchist poet Lola Ridge, the New York editor of Harold Loeb's short-lived yet superb literary magazine, *Broom*. Having married a French engineer named Richard Brault, Kay alighted in Brittany, where she began her lifelong autobiographical chronicle in prose and verse. From Les Brossis, Pleudihen, the Côtes du Nord, Le Havre, La Chartreuse, Harfleur, Cannes, Grasse, and Annot, with a hiatus in Stoke-on-Trent, England, she found her way to Paris—just in time.

In drama and intensity, her life rivaled her work, while her work reflected the life not only in its emotional truths, but in plot. Kay Boyle herself became the central figure of most of her novels. "I have put only my talent into my works," Oscar Wilde, the sly mentor of Boyle's Paris friends Harry and Caresse Crosby, once declared. "I have put all my genius into my life." By her mid-twenties, the same could be said of Kay Boyle.

The year 1926 found her in the South of France, having escaped the dull Brault to become the lover of the dashing Irish-American poet-editor of *This Quarter*, Ernest Walsh. They knew each other because Walsh had sought for his magazine, along with those of Pound, Joyce, and Hemingway, the poems and stories of twenty-four-year-old Kay Boyle.

Kay and the wild, handsome, dying Irish poet are in Grasse in March. Already he has entered the final stages of consumption. May places them in Mougins; in June they move to a mountain village called Annot, where they remain for July and August. The man whom fifty years later Kay Boyle would still call "the love of my life" dies in Monte Carlo in October. A few months later she bears his child, Sharon, the first of her six.

In 1927 Kay Boyle, impoverished and alone, demands that *This Quarter* survive. "It's been wound up by a fierce integrity and it ought to keep going," the twenty-five-year-old asserts, as if she could will it to happen. Words like "fierce integrity" and "courage" are already coin of the realm for her life as for her art. By her mid-twenties she has achieved what Dickens's David Copperfield hoped for himself when he wondered whether he would "turn out to be the hero of my own life, or whether that station will be held by anybody else." No supporting player, she has become the heroine of her own life.

Only in 1928 does Kay Boyle reach Paris. Eugene Jolas has already published her in *transition*. Instantly she becomes the golden girl among the expatriates, among her new friends not only Harry and Caresse Crosby but James Joyce, Marcel Duchamp, Brancusi, Picabia, Hart Crane, and Robert McAlmon. If not the friend, she is the acquaintance of Gertrude Stein, whose *Tender Buttons* echoed through her youth. For much of 1928 she is prey to the self-styled guru Raymond Duncan, brother of Isadora. From him she must effect a dramatic escape.

The place names multiply: they are now Paris street names: 17 rue

Louis-David, 59 rue Notre-Dame-des-Champs, the rue de Courcelles, the rue d'Alésia. At Le Moulin du Soleil, outside Paris, the mill Harry and Caresse Crosby bought from Armand, Comte de la Rochefoucauld, the pipes freeze in winter and they all drink 1811 brandy. Crosby with his Black Sun Press will be the publisher of Kay Boyle's first book, called *Short Stories*. He draws a line down through literary history: "Sappho Jane Austen Kay Boyle." Before she is thirty, Kay Boyle will have invented a new form for the short story which will become the signature for one of the most important American magazines of the second half of the century.

She was a great beauty, Kay Boyle, tall and angular, elegant, and always the one pursued, not the pursuer. Only two men whom she loves fail to take her to their hearts, one because his predilections forbid, the other mistakenly believing that in her early sixties she was on the threshold of old age. Many of the artists and writers of her generation fell for her and they didn't forget her: Archibald MacLeish, and William Shirer, and James T. Farrell, and Nelson Algren. "Kay," Farrell scrawls in 1958, nearly thirty years after their first meeting, "you are gentle / And I have loved you / Down the years . . . know chéri Kay / You were loved since 1931. . . ." Requited and unrequited, love multiplies.

As lover of the brilliant, madly flamboyant painter and surrealist Laurence Vail, former husband of Peggy Guggenheim, again a pregnancy ahead of her next marriage, Kay perfects her craft at Sainte-Aulde outside Paris, and then once more in the South of France, at the Villa Coustille, at Col-de-Villefranche. Growing rich in stories, poems, and novels, as the wife of Vail she lived in Vienna, witnessing the rise of fascism and writing about it, her great theme of the thirties. From snowy Kitzbühel in the Tyrol, the Vails flee to Devon for a year of respite in England.

Always she dramatized the unlikely and inhospitable places where she plied her writer's trade. Kay Boyle would remember "a room in a run-down Paris hotel in the Latin Quarter, a room that looked out on a cluttered courtyard in which pigeons complained all day and drunken drifters cried all night." Her "remote corner of a terrace in the South of France" turned out to be a place where "French invalids came for a sight of the Mediterranean shining somewhere below." Her room in Austria was "bare as a monk's cell, in a mountain hut ten thousand feet above sea level, with the wide avenue of a glacier passing outside in total silence." Wherever she was, she wrote.

In the summer of 1936, a chalet in Mégève in the Haute-Savoie in France became home for the Vails. Kay Boyle was raising Vail's children, Sindbad and often Pegeen, as well as her own four. The German invasion brought new place names: Cassis-sur-Mer, Marseilles, and then Lisbon, gateway to the land she had not seen for eighteen years. Having fallen in love with a refugee Austrian baron named Joseph von und zu Franckenstein, an antifascist nearly eight years her junior who has been the children's tutor, Kay masterminds his escape to freedom. It is *Jane Eyre* in reverse, the woman artist as heroine in a real-life romance rivaling *Casablanca* in drama and intensity.

Kay Boyle's sojourn in Europe seemed over. She had published four novels, three novellas and three collections of short stories, a volume of poetry, a ghostwritten memoir, a ghostwritten thriller, three translations, and one children's book, as well as a good number of the entries in a compendium called *365 Days*. She was among the finest American artists who had gone to Europe.

By 1941, apart from Gertrude Stein, Kay Boyle was considered by some to be the foremost woman writer of her generation. Katherine Anne Porter called her "among the strongest" to have emerged from the shadows of Stein and Joyce. "Hemingway's successor," pronounced Mary Colum. And then a chain of misfortune, injustice, tragedy became midwives to Kay Boyle's artistic failure of nerve.

There are now in 1941 less glamorous places where she must exercise the habit of her craft. Colorado is the scene of her third marriage, to the Austrian baron, soon to become a war hero. Alone in America, Kay Boyle shuts herself in the toilet with her typewriter while two new babies sleep. As never before, she must now write for money. After a wartime interlude in New York, Europe once more beckons.

Foreign correspondent for *The New Yorker*, Kay Boyle in 1946 is back in Europe at the Hôtel de France et Choiseul in Paris, or at the Château de Nesles, Nesles, par Rosay-en-Brie, or at Le Vésinet, France; she is in Germany at Marburg, at Frankfurt am Main, at Bad Godesberg when McCarthyism extends its arm abroad, as Cohn and Schine, vicious twins of iniquity, find their way to her door. Branded traitors, Kay and Joseph wearily make their way home, he demoralized, she ready to fight.

They retreat to Connecticut, to a cottage at West Redding, and then to Rowayton, and a house on the grounds of a girls' school on an inlet of Long Island Sound. Kay Boyle hurries away mornings to a rented room to write. Her youngest daughter, Faith, beautiful and haughty and clever, the image of the young Kay Boyle, recalls her mother in the fifties as "a Queen in exile."

Something happens to the work, to Kay Boyle's reputation, as she continues to enact her life on a cosmopolitan stage, the stage of world history. Audiences are bewildered by Kay Boyle's characters, Europeans moving in unfamiliar landscapes, people facing the unrelenting demands of history in overwhelming times of upheaval. They suffer life under fascism; they break their hearts in the French resistance; they must survive the betrayals of the Spanish Civil War. They are people about whom few in America wish now to read. At the height of her hard-earned and unmistakable achievement as an artist, Kay Boyle begins to become—unknown.

Once more the place names change. Betrayed by the adopted country to which he had given his heart, Joseph Franckenstein sickens and dies. And yet in the 1960s here is the widowed Kay Boyle, in her sixties, emerging in San Francisco. She takes up residence in the Haight-Ashbury in a gaudily gingerbread Victorian house recalling the century against which her mother had so vociferously rebelled.

A political activist now, Kay Boyle becomes once more a figure of legend, of myth, as she immerses herself in the struggles for civil rights and against the Vietnam War, for student rights, against injustice in America, in Iran, in the Soviet Union. The sixties are her sixties as her life spans the century. Ageless in the ferocity of her beliefs, and in the stalwart integrity of her commitments, Kay Boyle for the next three decades will redefine what it means to be a "woman of age."

New place names chart her path: Hollins and Boston and Roxbury, and the Ho Chi Minh Trail. She is incarcerated at Santa Rita prison. She moves to Oregon, to Washington, and finally to Oakland, where in her eighties she sits writing at a simple white-painted kitchen table, as serviceable a desk as any she has graced. In her trademark white carved plastic earrings, her back straight with indignation, a great beauty through the ninth decade of her life, she carries on.

The unbending enemy of self-pity, unrelentingly dedicated to her art, she is now the author of forty-five volumes. Nearly ninety, she settles at Mill Valley, Marin County, California, where at a retirement community she organizes what surely must be her last chapter of Amnesty International. Emotional and romantic, she has survived illness, death, and betrayal, a stranger to tears.

For this most unapologetically autobiographical of writers, her work has been the story of her life. The life to which she devoted her genius provided ample, worthy venues for literature. But there were literary pitfalls, turbulent zones of which she took too little heed. The life for Kay Boyle, as for Oscar Wilde, sometimes so imitated the art that it seemed even as if she were living her life as a dress rehearsal for coming fiction. Truth resided in the work; in her life she adhered to lesser standards. There were times too when the work abounded in mannerisms, in posturing; her stories and especially her novels became self-justifying, as if they suffered for being apologias for the life.

With the passing years, Kay Boyle felt increasingly committed to values beyond the perfection of her craft. Unlike Wilde in this, she concluded that the artist must be a force for social and political good. With a warrior mentality, an epic heroine now, she cleaved her way through so that her style carried her militance. Fierce in the defense of her convictions, thriving on outrage, even as the years weakened her, Kay Boyle, in her work as in her life, welcomed risk, and never blinked. Unintimidated from her earliest youth, when she stood up to "Puss," her grandfather, a man rooted in bourgeois respectability, she was never daunted by convention.

Citizen of the planet, Kay Boyle lived the history of the century, bearing arms. "Isn't Vail a Jewish name?" Ezra Pound is said to have inquired of her husband's origins. Howsoever much she liked him, Kay Boyle left Ezra Pound behind.

"My dear fellow, do what you feel," Bertrand Russell once advised parliamentarian R. H. S. Crossman, who was plagued over whether to leave his wife to marry the woman he loved. Kay Boyle required no one's sanction when she left her first husband, Richard Brault, to follow Ernest Walsh, nor when she left Laurence Vail to begin life anew with her Austrian baron. "You're just like Mama!" her older daughters, still angry twenty years after the breakup of the Vail marriage, accused her youngest, Faith Franckenstein, who would live by her own lights, modeling herself, she would say, after her mother. In her family Kay Boyle became not "Grandma" but an institution, a figure.

Like Chaucer's Wyf of Bathe, Kay Boyle has had her world "as in my tyme." She chose a full authentic life before feminism would give it a name. Never would she allow herself to be tagged a "woman writer." From the age of twenty, learning from her mentor Lola Ridge, Kay Boyle stood up for "the liberation of all people, both women and men." Kay Boyle's has been many lifetimes: an American life, a French life, a Paris life, an Austrian life, a wartime American life, a German life, a Connecticut life, a California life, all these place names of her fiction.

Those who would revive the silenced reputations of American women writers have strangely ignored her. In a 1990 *New York Times Magazine* article, Mary Gordon, attempting to overturn the "overwhelmingly male" canon, invokes the familiar names of Edith Wharton, Willa Cather, Flannery O'Connor, Katherine Anne Porter, and Eudora Welty. Kay Boyle has been too international, too little susceptible to easy definition to be useful. She has situated the relationships of men and women amid the drumrolls of history and politics. Harry Crosby might have linked her to Jane Austen, but she was never domesticated. And she eschewed latter-day feminism as too narrow a politics for one who had been familiar since her youth with socialists no less than with suffragettes.

The years honed her character, this woman of manifold contradictions. Cold and pale, her white hair alive with indignation, she was both imperious and self-deprecating, honest yet given to exaggeration and mythologizing. A writer who exquisitely anatomizes suffering and failures of love, she was never given to introspection either in her life or in her art. Modest and yet vain, she appeared as the political radical in a Paris suit carrying a fine leather briefcase and a fountain pen to class at tumultuous San Francisco State. Desirable to men, a conqueror of the male heart, she was sexually puritanical. A woman of great moral and physical courage, she imparted to her children many fears: of water, of mountains, of those horses which stampede through the pages of her fiction with such defiance.

"My life can be known through my work," she dismissed one would-be biographer. Rich in love, in work, in commitment, the life of Kay Boyle has been a personal chronicle of the century which it spans. This, then, is a biographical impression of that life, as, inevitably, it becomes as well a story of our time.

1

A Little Girl in a Hat

*I force myself to contradict myself so as to avoid conforming to
my own taste.*
MARCEL DUCHAMP

I was there to kill what was not dead, the 19th century.
GERTRUDE STEIN

On a cold winter day in 1913 they marched up to the entrance of
the monumental 69th Regiment Armory on Lexington Avenue, in New York,
a tiny mother and her two young daughters. As always, they were dressed
to meet the demands of fashion, the mother in either her fine velvet hat
with its rolling moleskin brim or, perhaps, even the hat with the blue
ostrich feathers, which little Kay would remember as "drooping like ferns
across the deeper azure of her eyes." From the time they were three, Kay
and her sister wore hats—to the movies in Atlantic City, on summer
afternoons in Mount Pocono. One of Kay's hats was made from old neckties,
another of patent leather. Still another was so buoyant, Kay Boyle was to
remember in 1967 as she composed her chapters for the memoir *Being
Geniuses Together*, that it floated on water.

"Where are the girls' hats?" Katherine demanded of whichever servant
was responsible for dressing her daughters. Tiny, gentle, and frail, she
never raised her voice, but she was strong of will. Little Kay was her
mother's daughter, her alter ego. Having heard from her Grandma Evans
the story of how her mother as a little girl had tried to keep a lamp chimney
from falling by carrying the searing-hot object across a room to a table
where she could set it down, Kay examined the deep scar on her mother's
palm and felt protective, sharing her mother's pain. Katherine's hands were
so "weak, so useless, the bones in her slender, nervous fingers . . . ready
to break in two."

Katherine Evans Boyle was thirty-nine years old on that day, although
no one in the family knew it, certainly not her youngest daughter and
namesake. A woman's age belonged to the realm of mystery, and was
something so deeply forgotten that the woman herself lost all sense of the

reality. Katherine might have been telling the truth when she pleaded that she herself didn't know how old she was.

Now Katherine, "no bigger than a hummingbird," as her writing daughter Kay would describe her, led her two girls determinedly into the ugly building. She had traveled to New York from Philadelphia, where next season the family would rent the Bryn Mawr house of the painter John Singer Sargent, an irony not wasted on Katherine, already a fervent devotee of the new "modern art." Sargent, master of an academy-style art ("the apotheosis of an ostrich plume," Van Wyck Brooks called him), was a target of scorn for the forward-looking men who had planned the Armory Show which introduced the great modernist painters of Europe to America. Sargent "turned everything he painted into satin," Ashcan realist John Sloan contemptuously dismissed the Master. To make way for the new, the old must retreat.

Although she was born in the 1870s, Katherine was no Victorian herself. What appealed to her were innovation, imagination, and the liberal sensibility born at the turn of the century. Two years before Kay's birth, Eugene V. Debs had run for President as the candidate of the Social Democratic Party, and Katherine became a fervent supporter. She believed in labor's right to organize and, with her artist sister Nina, in women's suffrage. Katherine knew that as art rejected the privileged, hidebound past, so politics meant change, even the change demanded by Debs, who, when asked by Lincoln Steffens what *he* would do with the trusts, replied, "Take them!" Debs's 1908 campaign for the presidency had been waged in direct opposition to capitalism because "it's wrong. It's inherently unjust, inhuman, unintelligent—and it cannot last."

John Sloan, one of the prime movers of the Armory Show, called Eugene Debs "one of the most Christ-like men I had ever met . . . he would share his clothes or his last crust of bread with any man poorer than himself." When years later Debs went to prison for violating the Espionage Act by opposing World War I, he decorated his cell with a drawing by John Sloan. Art and politics, Katherine agreed, were inseparable. "There can be no life without change, as there can be no development without change," Frederick James Gregg wrote in the preface to the catalogue of the Armory Show, "to be afraid of what is different or unfamiliar, is to be afraid of life."

Katherine encouraged the budding artists in her charge, the painter Janet and the writer Kay, to eschew the Victorian past. Always an admirer of the new modernism, Katherine became a friend of Alfred Stieglitz, honorary vice president of the Armory Show. He had been the first American to show Cézanne, Picasso, Matisse, and Rousseau at his Fifth Avenue gallery "291." Predicting a storm of abuse, Stieglitz had attempted to prepare the community for the invasion of Duchamp and the others. "The dry bones of a dead art are rattling as they never rattled before . . . they're breathing the breath of life into an art that is long since dead," he wrote in the New York *American* a month before the opening of the Armory Show. But few were prepared for the prediction that this exhibition would be like "a great fire, an earthquake, or a political revolution." Katherine was one of a minority which did understand.

Since before her marriage, she had loved to take pictures. Her dream was to become a professional photographer. When she met Stieglitz through her sister Nina, and Nina's friends the painters Charles Sheeler and Morton L. Schamberg, Stieglitz had encouraged her in this ambition.

"Set up your own darkroom and develop your photographs yourself!" Stieglitz urged her. Then Katherine's father-in-law, Jesse Peyton Boyle, the patriarch of the Boyle household, had laid down the law. Such a profession was neither proper nor appropriate for any daughter-in-law of his. Katherine had transferred her ambitions to her daughters, carrying their crayon drawings off to Stieglitz so that he might offer his verdict, certain he would detect budding genius in at least one of her offspring. Katherine told Stieglitz she would not hire an art teacher. Under systematic instruction, she believed, something "precious" might be lost. Spontaneity, fidelity to the unconscious, alone produced art. The discipline of formal education could only be destructive. "To permit them to be themselves," Katherine wrote Alfred Stieglitz, is "the greatest good I could render them." It was Stieglitz himself, Katherine told him, who had fortified her belief that her daughters should be allowed "to work out their ideas unconsciously," and it was "291" and Stieglitz, Katherine said, in her flattering way, which had provided her with "a firm foundation for my belief."

"I am frankly anxious over their future," Katherine confided. "They require more than I have to give them." So she attempted to enlist the great man in her scheme of making artists of her daughters.

Stieglitz responded. "Have the young ladies done any drawing of late, and writing?" he wrote Katherine when they had ceased to be children. The final exhibition of the 1911–12 season at Stieglitz's "291" had been devoted to the works of artists aged two to eleven, among them Janet Boyle, aged eleven, and Kay Boyle, nine. Katherine told Stieglitz she was "honored" when he said he wanted to keep some of Kay's and Janet's drawings in his permanent collection. Janet was the better painter, Janet painted all the time, while Kay preferred to write poetry. They were bitter rivals, these sisters, bitter competitors as legatees of their mother's lost ambition.

Two years older, Janet had more power. One day she decided not to speak to little Kay at all, so enraged was she by their mother's obvious favoritism.

"Get down on your hands and knees and beg!" Janet ordered. Kay, of course, complied.

"I'll speak to you if you give me five cents!" Janet declared. And so Kay scrounged, searching for the pennies to pay her older sister to talk to her.

Awaiting Katherine, Janet, and Kay inside the Armory building this cold winter day were five oils by Morton L. Schamberg, as well as six oils by Charlie Sheeler, another favorite of Katherine's, another of those "hungry young men," as Janet Boyle would later call them, invited to dine with the Boyle family at Katherine's invitation, and whom she would address as "son." Hot summer days in Atlantic City Sheeler pushed little Kay in a rolling chair along the boardwalk. Both Sheeler and Schamberg had made their obligatory pilgrimages to 27 rue de Fleurus, where they had met the literary model Katherine Evans Boyle set for little Kay, Gertrude Stein. Gertrude and her brother Leo had both been wearing the brown corduroy and leather sandals popularized by Raymond Duncan with his "simple life movement," to which little Kay would one day subscribe. In a year Katherine would be reading aloud to Janet and Kay from Gertrude's new book: "a little monkey goes like a donkey." Katherine knew that Gertrude Stein was a pioneer who had set as her task "to kill what was not dead, the 19th century," who was trying to achieve in writing what the Cubists had done in painting. No book more than *Tender Buttons* delighted Kay Boyle as a child.

In the gallery, the 69th Regimental Band serenaded luminaries from Enrico Caruso to Mrs. Astor, to Frank Crowninshield, the famous publisher, who would arrange for little Janet to work as an artist for *Vogue* in less than a decade. There too was William Carlos Williams, "giddy with joy," who would one day grant Kay Boyle her first important review, heralding her as a major figure in American literature when she was only twenty-seven years old, a modernist like himself.

The three Boyle women proceeded into the crowded room honoring the Cubists, the "chamber of horrors," as it was dubbed. There Kay Boyle saw the painting which was the crowning glory of the Armory Show, Marcel Duchamp's "Nude Descending a Staircase." "I laughed out loud when first I saw it, happily with relief," Williams said. But if the philistines called it a desecration of womanhood, a threat to the sanctity of the family, and a vicious attack on the moral fabric of society, this "explosion in a shingle factory" excited little Kay Boyle.

As *The New York Times* rightly perceived, the "Nude" was "contradicting itself." Few perceived that contradiction was the essence of the new art, Duchamp's nude disappearing only to reemerge, transcending its own fragmentation. "I force myself to contradict myself so as to avoid conforming to my own taste," Duchamp declared. In the defiance of consistency lay the potential for artistic growth. "Art is the only form of activity in which man shows himself to be a true individual," he said.

Little Kay felt the shock of wonder, understanding even at eleven what her mother's friend Alfred Stieglitz called "the battle cry of freedom." At that moment, as she gazed at the swellings suggesting breasts, the vertical form which might or might not be a leg, saw a foot with only one round toe and one pointed toe, saw buttocks turned inside out, saw the nude erupting out of nowhere, Kay Boyle might have begun to formulate her own art. Later she would write stories which also plunged headlong into an action, preceded by no exposition, no explanations. This is art, Kay Boyle decided, as she fell in love with a painting. No less a moment or so later was she enchanted by Brancusi's "Mademoiselle Pogany," a giant marble egg-shaped disembodied head.

It was fortunate that her grandfather Jesse Peyton Boyle had not accompanied them, for it may have been on this very day that Theodore Roosevelt visited the Armory Show. Roosevelt, who had been President when Kay Boyle was born, in the very month of her birth had brought suit for the dissolution of the Northern Securities Holding Company under the Sherman Antitrust Act. Like many, Jesse Peyton Boyle believed Roosevelt was the enemy of business. Now Roosevelt was demanding to be taken to see the "Nude Descending a Staircase." "Where's that woman!" Roosevelt shrieked.

"That's not art! That's not art!" Roosevelt bellowed. "He's nuts and his imagination has gone wild!" So he dismissed the work of the man to whom Kay Boyle would one day dedicate her poetry, and who, one drunken evening in Marseilles, would save her life. It may even have been that Kay Boyle had heard the name of the clean-shaven, knife-slim, thin-lipped, narrow-eyed ironical Frenchman at the dinner table one night from Charlie Sheeler, who described Duchamp as a man "built with the precision and sensitiveness of an instrument for making scientific machinery." Certainly she never forgot the painting, for as she would describe herself as a young woman alighting in 1923 in France in *Being Geniuses Together*, each morning "in the French family's closed, finite world, Duchamp's nude descended the staircase with me as I carried the *pot de chambre*, like a chalice, raised in my two hands."

From Stieglitz, from Sheeler, from Schamberg, from her mother, who brought these men to her dinner table, Kay Boyle learned that art substitutes for logic an atmosphere of continuous invention. Art shocks. Art inspires. And those who make art are unique individuals. Critics shouted that the new modernism was ugly, childish, revolting, absurd, indecent, immoral, and decadent. Kay Boyle already knew that she too would rebel against bourgeois taste. It was the great Armory Show of 1913 which more than any other single event sent the most adventurous spirits of Kay Boyle's generation to Europe a decade later. Before long she would join them.

That precocious little eleven-year-old in her hat had been born on February 19, 1902, at 900 Goodrich Avenue in the fashionable Crocus Hill section of St. Paul, Minnesota, where the rich people lived. It was a two-story Victorian clapboard house set among avenues of mansions, not far from the stately residence of the railroad magnate James J. Hill, who had built the Great Northern Railway. Matthew Josephson, later to be one of Kay Boyle's antagonists, dubbed Hill a "robber baron." Even President Roosevelt called both Hill and J. P. Morgan, his confederate, "malefactors of great wealth." In that vast mansion only a few blocks from the house where Kay Boyle drew her first breath no servant was allowed to look into Hill's face, lest he be fired on the spot; the one-eyed "robber baron" was, in fact, short, fat, bald, and ugly.

Jesse Peyton Boyle, Kay's grandfather, had also prospered by America's unbridled laissez-faire capitalism. Buttressed by his Wall Street investments, the Boyles lived well, served by a maid and a cook, who were paid five dollars a week. He had been born in Philadelphia on June 4, 1849, to a prosperous Irish Catholic family. The family was rich and ambitious enough to send Jesse Peyton Boyle, nicknamed "Puss" (short for "Grandpuss"), to school near London, where he developed a lifelong love of Shakespeare. When he was eighteen, Peyton Boyle returned to England on a sojourn designed to prepare him for the priesthood. He was living in a cottage in the English countryside when one day he was accosted by a beautiful woman eight years his senior, who told him she was looking for her cousin. Puss fell in love. By the time he returned to America, Puss not only was no longer a candidate for the priesthood but had become an agnostic, which amounted to his being an atheist in the eyes of his horrified family. At once he was disowned and disinherited.

That didn't matter, because Jesse Peyton Boyle went on to marry his spirited cousin Jennie, who lied to him about her age, the 1880 census listing them both as thirty-one; he became a Philadelphia lawyer. They had a son named Howard Peterson, born in November of 1874, who would be Kay Boyle's father, and a daughter named Margaret, whom they called Madge, born in January of 1876, who would live all her life under her father's rule. Jesse Peyton Boyle and his family moved west. He practiced law, and then joined the fledgling law book publishers West Publishing Company, where he became editor-in-chief, and created the *Decennial Digest or Corpus Juris*, a legal dictionary, which all his life he would claim as his greatest achievement. When West Publishing was incorporated, Puss contributed no small share of the capital and became a partner. But he had a fiery Irish temper and by 1902, the year of Kay Boyle's birth, he had so quarreled with his partners that he left West, still today a leading law book publisher, pulled up stakes, and moved the family back to Philadelphia.

Although later in her life Kay Boyle would wrap herself in a mantle of Irishness, in her youth as Katherine's favorite, she defined herself by her mother's ancestry. Far from being Irish, her maternal great-great-great-grandfather was General Jacob Bower (or Bauer), who had served on the staff of General George Washington. Rising to the rank of major general, he put all his money at the service of the American Revolution and in 1783 was one of the officers who formed the Society of the Cincinnati. At fifty-five, he commanded a brigade of the Pennsylvania militia during the War of 1812, dying a poor man in 1818. In homage, his local newspaper, the *Berks & Schuylkill Journal*, wrote that "he sacrificed at the Shrine of Liberty a large patrimony . . . like many of the Veterans of the Revolution, he was doomed to feel the stings of adversity in his old age." In middle age, when disgrace and poverty overtook Kay Boyle, she thought of him, "proud he made that choice."

Jacob Bower's oldest son, George, married Catherine Cameron, whose grandfather, George Scott, was a first cousin of General Winfield Scott, "Old Fuss and Feathers" himself, the hero of the war of 1812. Catherine and George named one of their daughters Catherine. In 1844, this Catherine, Kay Boyle's great-grandmother, married Dr. Cyrus C. Moore. In 1854 they had a daughter, whom they named Evangeline. Everyone called her Eva and it was this Eva Moore who was to be Kay Boyle's grandmother. One day, Cyrus and Catherine decided to move to the Kansas prairies and promptly set forth by covered wagon.

Kay Boyle wrote a memoir years later for Gale Research's *Contemporary Authors Autobiography Series* in which the heroine was Catherine's little daughter Eva, whom Kay depicted as setting out alone in the mornings ahead of the wagon train, dancing ahead of the horses, singing at the top of her lungs, "fearless of Indians, of anything else in life." This was her ancestry, proof that she came from a long line of spirited women. In fact, it had happened, but not to Eva Moore. Art, Katherine had insisted to Kay, was sacred, life its pale shadow. Why not, then, invent the life, fictionalize it, even as truth was reserved for fiction? Kay Boyle heard the story of a little girl running ahead of the wagon train at a boring dinner party in 1960 when she was a resident at the MacDowell Colony. At dinner, "a very ancient grandmother who remembered Indian days in the West," Kay Boyle confided to her friend poet Howard Nemerov, speaking "in a very thin distant voice" had described her mother walking ahead of a caravan of covered wagons, "starting out two or three hours before they did in the early morning, walking so far ahead that at times they did not catch up with her until noon and she was not afraid." The story so captivated Kay Boyle that ever after she spoke as if this were the experience of her own grandmother.

Eva Moore did exist, however, a beauty with creamy white skin and thick auburn hair. At sixteen she had become a schoolmarm on those Kansas prairies, where every night she watched Indian fires burning along the horizon. For a time she made her peace with the untamed land. Less than two years later she married David J. Evans, the superintendent of schools, a nondescript man five feet ten inches tall with blond hair and grey eyes, who at nineteen had enlisted in the Union Army, only to be kicked by a horse; when he was discharged, his arm was covered with sores and ulcers. One gunshot wound in the left side and this experience with the horse comprised his less than heroic Civil War experience, hardly suitable fare for a romanticizing granddaughter. Settling after the war in Auburn, Kansas, he was first employed on a sheep ranch. He became an editor and an attorney and finally superintendent of public instruction for Shawnee County, Kansas. Although Kay Boyle in her long life spoke only of her grandmother and never of David Evans, in fact he was an active public figure who was president of the Kansas State Teachers Association and an earnest educator. When he married Eva Moore on February 26, 1871, he was twenty-five and she seventeen. The bride's father, listed as the Reverend C. C. Moore, officiated at the ceremony.

Family gossip had it that the marriage was doomed because David Evans was "a good deal older" than his wife, although the eight-year difference was not unusual for the time. It was said too that David Evans was an alcoholic. Preferring to believe that this marriage had been nothing short of subjugation and betrayal, Kay Boyle depicted it as a tragedy in her 1930 story "Episode in the Life of an Ancestor," which, she told her mother, was to be about "Grandma."

Eva Evans is seventeen and about to be given in bondage to a lowly schoolmaster by her widower father, an insensitive man who wants only to domesticate his wild freedom-loving daughter. He resents her staunch sense of independence and would tame her as a wild horse had to be tamed. Kay Boyle imagined her grandmother in a sunbonnet, her wide skirts "hullabalooing out behind her in the wind." Her fingers had rarely seen a needle, no matter that she knew Eva Evans was a fine seamstress and that the story was intended to be part of Kay Boyle's family history. In the story, Cyrus Moore cares more for his future son-in-law than he does for his daughter, whom he accuses of having a "hard heart."

Eva and David Evans set up housekeeping in young and booming Topeka, and by the time he was twenty-nine, mild-mannered or not, David Evans had accumulated three thousand dollars' worth of real estate. In 1880, the family, which had grown to include Inez (Nina), born on Christmas Day 1873, and Katherine, born in December of 1874, moved to Great Bend, Kansas, where David practiced law.

Certainly it was true that Eva Evans was unhappy. Her husband drank too much; they had nothing in common and she wanted better lives for her girls. One day in 1881 she took as radical and risky a decision as a woman of her time and social station could make. With her two daughters, eight and six years old, she drove in a hired buggy through the early dawn to the southern edge of Great Bend near the Arkansas River. She caught the Atchison, Topeka, & Santa Fe, pulling into Great Bend at 5:03, and set off for Washington.

But Eva Evans never looked back, or regretted leaving David with his drinking, his self-pity, his weakness. At the age of twenty-seven, she became one of the first women to be hired by the federal government, in charge of the Land Grant Division of the Department of the Interior. Opposite her desk hung a huge map of the western states, dotted with many colored thumbtacks. When she received a settler's claim, Eva climbed up on a stepladder and marked it on the map with a colored tack.

"They're really only squatters," Eva Evans confided to her grand-daughter Kay years later. "But I prefer to call them pioneers." And she showed little Kay the primitive sketches, picturing trees and cabins, a creek, a hill curving up toward a mountain, drawn on birch bark, on newspaper, which had been rolled up and mailed to her, a scene Kay Boyle would re-create in another story about her grandmother called "The Man Who Died Young," published in 1932.

Eva Evans was paid seven hundred and twenty dollars a year, enough to support her and her daughters. Her boss, a hunchback, fell in love with her, but she did not divorce David, who made his way to Washington by 1892. A broken man whose wife refused to live with him, he worked as a clerk in the Bureau of Provisions and Clothing of the Department of the Navy. As a direct descendant of Jacob Bower, Eva was eligible for membership in the Daughters of the American Revolution, but declined to join an organization whose conservatism offended her. For thirty years she worked for the government. When her auburn hair turned grey, believing a woman who had a job did not have white hair, she donned an auburn wig, from which little white hairs occasionally peeked.

One Christmas morning, Kay and Janet rushed to open their visiting grandmother's door only to stand frozen in horror as she clapped both hands over her totally bald head. Later Kay Boyle's mother explained. Grandma Evans had lost her hair through worry and the necessity of working to support herself and her daughters. Now she had always to wear her auburn "transformation." Indeed, as the years passed, Eva visited her younger daughter's household as often as she could, sewing clothes for Kay's Paris china dolls, trimming their coats with feathers, "to remind them of Paris," she told Kay.

In Washington, Eva had joined the Christian Scientists, and while Janet hated to be dragged to the long services at the Church of Christ Scientist, Kay didn't mind. What Kay remembered most about Eva Evans was how she would turn affectionately to kiss the Boyles' black servants, the cook and the chambermaid, while the Boyle men glared in disapproval, and even Kay and Janet were a bit shocked.

Eva Evans had been ambitious for her two daughters, as Katherine Evans Boyle would be for her own. Nina Evans became a career woman, Kay's disagreeable "Tante" who brought the world of the arts to her sister Kate. Nina studied at the Corcoran Art School in Washington, at the Pennsylvania Academy of Fine Arts in Philadelphia, and in Bruges, Belgium. Financed by her sister Kate's father-in-law, Jesse Peyton Boyle, she even studied in Europe with Robert Henri, Charles Sheeler, and Morton Schamberg. Later she became, as Nina Allender, the chief cartoonist for *The Suffragist* and *Equal Rights*, having joined the National Woman's Party. In the 1921 edition of *Who's Who in the Nation's Capital*, Nina Allender omitted her age: it was a family trait. Indeed, her niece Kay most of her life listed the date of her birth as 1903, and told her own children she never knew how old she was, although in fact Dr. B. Hogden, who delivered her, dutifully mailed the required postcard to the St. Paul Department of Health on February 22, 1902, four days after her birth, announcing that she had been born on the nineteenth, no secret to anyone.

Mythologizing among the women of Kay Boyle's family was the norm. Nina Allender called herself a "widow," although she had in fact been abandoned by her handsome English husband, Charlie Allender, who embezzled thousands of dollars from the bank where Puss got him his job. Then he ran away with another woman. Still later the Boyles learned that he had originally fled from England to escape a jail sentence for embezzlement and forgery.

Tante, whom Kay termed "a total, total egoist," nonetheless, devoted herself to the struggle of American women for the vote and had become the only woman political cartoonist in the country. Nina Allender was the first artist to depict the suffragette as an attractive, smartly dressed and feminine young woman, erasing the image of those sexless maiden ladies, dowdy and in spectacles, who had previously symbolized woman's suffrage to male cartoonists. Nina's best-known drawing was of Susan B. Anthony herself with a red shawl about her shoulders, a pretty young woman mounting the steps of the Capitol, in her hand a scroll petition previously signed by twenty thousand Americans demanding that an amendment to the Constitution award women the right to vote. In 1936 this drawing would be made into a U.S. postage stamp, as Tante's cartoons became part of the permanent collection of the Library of Congress.

Nina Allender rang doorbells, to the point of exhaustion. One door was opened by a minister whose response was short and brutal, as Kay Boyle would later recount the incident as a family legend.

"A woman's place is in the home!" he declared.

Poor Tante was tired and hungry. She had been out for two hours of canvassing, with only one signature to show for her night's work, and that was a woman's signature.

"Whose home do you suggest I stay in?" Nina Allender demanded of the man with dignity as she choked back her tears so that, as he shut the door in her face, he would not observe that she was crying.

A visit to Grandma Evans and Tante in Washington produced in a teenaged Kay Boyle's diary the following line: "the vote, equal rights, these words mean to me the grace and courage of my grandmother, and of my mother, and of my aunt who sought to follow in every act of their lives where Susan B. Anthony led." Eva Evans and Nina Allender both had demonstrated that women could make their own way, apart from the security of marriage. Their men proved themselves to be domineering or weak, feckless or disloyal.

So Kate, Nina's sister, discovered as she settled into life as the privileged daughter-in-law of rich Jesse Peyton Boyle. She had married Howard

Peterson Boyle, a slim, dapper man with a wide black mustache, a weak and ineffectual man under the thumb of his reactionary father. A man without work, or, it seemed, ambition, convictions, or energy, he moved as a shadowy figure through Kay Boyle's childhood. Son of an aggressive father and an unloving mother, Howard suffered from a deep sense of inferiority and weakness. He grew up to be a mild, docile man, who left the University of Pennsylvania Law School after two years, terrified that he might fail his final exams. His daughter Janet believed he might have been happy as a professor, but his domineering father would never allow him to construct a life outside of his control.

Certainly he loved Katherine Evans and was an ardent suitor in their early days as she taught him how to take photographs. When she denied she was beautiful, he reassured her. "I won't have you running down your chin to me in such a fashion as you did today!" Howard wrote. "Just you put it down that there are half a dozen kisses due me for those remarks."

Unlike his father, Howard encouraged Katherine in her photography, pleading only that the frail young woman not "try to do more than you ought in the printing line." His love letters continued after their marriage. "No, little wife," Howard wrote, "don't go at all but stay with me in my dreams all night, your arms about me, soothing me to sleep on that dearest of all sweet pillows. Kiss me now before you put me to sleep and tell me that you feel my love and are giving me all of yours in return." He signed his letters "your loving 'boy,' Howard." They began their marriage in his father's household in St. Paul, with Howard being employed as well by West Publishing, as an assistant manager in the editorial department. Puss could bear no male rival, and it did not take long before he effaced his son from the marital scene.

Indeed, whatever gainful employment Howard managed was owing to his father. When in 1902 the Boyles moved to Philadelphia, Puss financed Howard in a bookshop, which soon failed. "It was not that he did not know about books, or that he was not a polite, if rather ill-at-ease salesman," Kay Boyle remembered. "It was quite simply that he knew he would fail in whatever he undertook to do." Finally Howard "worked" on the advisory board of the Philadelphia Children's Homeopathic Hospital, for which he received no salary, to which he commuted every day by train from their suburban residence. Asked what sort of work her father did, Kay Boyle would reply, "Nothing." As she grew up, she saw him as a "frustrated person who couldn't communicate his feelings," silent and introverted. He was so overshadowed by his father that he could make no decision on his own and could not even respond to one of Kay's requests without saying, "Just as soon as I speak to Puss," escaping then into his father's office.

Later Kay Boyle would sum up the influence of them both: "I knew from my father and grandfather what I didn't want to be, and the kind of person I really didn't have any respect for at all."

Puss ruled the household, moving the family between Philadelphia and Bryn Mawr, Washington and Atlantic City's Beach Haven, and Mount Pocono, always holding the purse strings tight. His own daughter Madge got an allowance, but Katherine was dependent on him for every penny; he even accompanied her on shopping expeditions, flirting with the saleswomen while he waited for his beautiful daughter-in-law to emerge from the fitting rooms so that he could pass judgment on every hat, dress, and coat. He could be generous, and he could charm, although his rule was a "rigid one," as Kay observed. Janet Boyle, later Jo or Joan as she chose to be called, was more forgiving, seeing her grandfather as a generous and cultured man given to quoting Shakespeare, his temper and Irish wit down-to-earth.

"What do you want for Christmas?" Puss demanded of Kay one year. "A diamond ring? A diamond surrounded by sapphires?" To Kay's amazement, he then rang up his Wall Street broker, murmuring, "I need some money," and it was done. Most of the jewelry, however, he bought for his daughter-in-law, with whom he was in love, one day even purchasing blue enamel earrings, which turned out to be fake when the enamel peeled off like paper.

As her autobiographical stories of the 1930s were to reveal, Kay Boyle's childhood was dominated by her diminutive grandfather, hiding his baldness beneath a black silk skullcap, padding around the house in soft doeskin slippers, his "belly pouting in his dove-grey clothes." There were ponies and pony carts and horseback riding on the beach. There were also rules as Puss taught Kay manners and morals and skills. In keeping with his role as family patriarch, Puss appropriated for himself a room at the top of the house where he seated himself behind a rolltop desk.

"Come in!" Puss replied to the tentative knock of a child. "Come in, come in, whoever you are! Come in!" To Kay he liked to dictate letters, teaching her "neatness and order," a compulsive orderliness which was to remain with her for the rest of her life. One day Kay arrived with the news that she had lost her doll's white shoe. Puss pinched his glasses on his nose.

"Go up to the attic and find box number . . . ," Puss instructed his black servant, Ben. Everything was catalogued and ordered and marked.

Puss took Kay for rides in the rolling chairs pushed by "colored boys" along the boardwalk. He peered at the sand drawings on the beach, sending a shower of coins down upon an artist who depicted the likeness of George Washington; Puss rained insults on one who drew the big face of Theodore Roosevelt with his grinning teeth, the trustbuster who dared talk of "a moral standard for business." (Puss, of course, was wrong. Despite Roosevelt's bluster and bravado, the most rapid growth of trusts took place during his administration. His successor, William Howard Taft, did more to curb their power than he ever did.)

"As a capitalist," Puss informed the waiter at the Atlantic City hotel where he took Kay to tea, "I've labored all my life, and I'm partial to the merits of the system." If the waiter had the temerity to ask what system, he was told in short order.

"The capitalistic system, by God!" Puss blustered.

Toward his black servants, Puss was condescending, and so Kay imitated him. When the black servant Ben got down on his hands and knees to make the fire at night, Kay and Janet patted him on the head as if he were a dog, believing that this made him happy. (In the 1930s Kay Boyle wrote some of her best stories excoriating the racism Puss imposed on the Boyle household: "White As Snow," "Ben," and the brilliant "Black Boy," in which Puss hires a skinny black boy to push their rolling chair, a boy little Kay discovers is homeless and whom she befriends, to her grandfather's displeasure. At the story's close, little Kay is thrown from her horse and is comforted by the black boy, his sympathy earning him a stinging, vicious slap "square across the mouth" administered by her grandfather.

But both Kay and her sister preferred Puss to his wife, Jennie, "Mother Boyle," a strict Presbyterian and churchgoer, who never wore lip rouge, never drank wine, and detested the Evans women, insisting they call her "Mother Boyle," while she called them "Eva," "Nina," and "Kate." Kay was her favorite. Janet, the more rebellious of the two children, was punished by being made to sit for hours in a dark leather-cushioned chair without moving. In particular, Mother Boyle hated her daughter-in-law Kate, sexual jealousy her obvious motive, for she could not help but notice how the frail Katherine with her black hair waved low on her cheeks and her wasp waist and full, loving lips captivated Puss, how appealing he found her deep-set azure eyes, and how gifted she was at flattery, a skill she practiced no less on Puss than on such luminaries as Alfred Stieglitz. Never raising her voice, Katherine knew how to make people do things for her. "You're a wonderful cook," she'd say, or "You do it, you're the better seamstress." Mother Boyle and her daughter Madge both resented Katherine, but, as Kay Boyle remembers, "there was nothing they could do about it."

When Kay was still young, Mother Boyle died. Puss then was free to turn his attentions on his daughter-in-law unimpeded. Forbidden to exercise his sexual impulses directly, Peyton Boyle entered into a tantalizing outwardly adversarial relationship with his daughter-in-law. And Katherine seems to have played along. One day she went so far as to invite him to join her at lunch with the suffragette Alice Paul, who had founded the National Woman's Party in 1916. Whether she resented his domination and her own financial dependence or whether it was an act of sexual cunning, Katherine brought together the reactionary opponent of Theodore Roosevelt and Woodrow Wilson and the brusque Alice Paul, a revolutionary feminist. Perhaps Katherine even thought that Puss, who fancied himself a connoisseur of women, might come to admire the fiery Paul with her piercing eyes and abundant shining brown hair piled on the top of her head.

That evening, as Kay Boyle recounts the incident in her 1977 essay "Report from Lock-up," Kate asked Puss what he thought of Alice Paul, prefacing her question with a litany of Paul's accomplishments.

"She wrote her doctor's thesis on the status of women," Kate said, speaking so softly you could scarcely hear her. "She wanted firsthand experience about the position of women in industry, so she became a factory worker in England."

"Very interesting," Puss allowed.

"And then she became involved in the women's militant movement in England. How I wish you'd been there as her lawyer to plead her case!" Katherine soon enough had resorted to her customary flattery.

At this Puss shook his head and smiled his most gracious smile.

"You know my judgment of a woman doesn't depend on what she thinks or what she does," Puss reminded his flirtatious daughter-in-law, "but on whether or not she has a kissable mouth. Alice Paul does not have that attribute!"

If Katherine had invited the evocation of her own "kissable mouth," if she allowed the sexual innuendo, the sexual play, it was because she was a thwarted woman, not only in her artistic ambitions, but in her disappointment over the man she married, Howard Peterson Boyle, whom Kay Boyle would remember as "just completely negative in our lives." So absent as husband and father was Howard that Kay once wrote a letter to the "advice to the lovelorn" column of one of the Philadelphia newspapers. "How can I help my father and mother like each other more than they do?" she inquired.

One day Kay put the question of her father's passivity to Mother Boyle.

"Why doesn't Dad speak very much?" Kay demanded of the still beautiful and cruel Jennie Peterson Boyle.

"Your father doesn't have a temper the way his father has," she explained, "and I'll tell you why." Then Mother Boyle recounted how when Howard was three years old and had not put away his toys as she had ordered him to do, but flew into a rage, she grabbed a bucket of icy water from the stable boy and threw it over his head.

"And that fixed that!" Mother Boyle told Kay.

Little Kay became her mother's daughter, feeling what Katherine felt. Katherine clung to her daughter, confiding in her, as if she were an adult, "all that enchanted her, all that stirred her deeply . . . explaining, gossiping, laughing." Giggling together, the two became conspirators against grandfather and father, the Boyles. Katherine devoted herself to expanding her daughters' horizons, the visit to the Armory Show but one example of her stalwart efforts. Determined that they see her as a role model, she told them how she smoked in public, to Puss's chagrin. She never inhaled. She just liked to shock people. One day, informed by the maître d' at the

Philadelphia Arts Club that women were not permitted to smoke in the hotel, Katherine and her friends bravely lit up again.

"The gentlemen at the next table are smoking," Katherine remarked in her soft voice. Hearing her so defiantly demand equal treatment, the men at the next table, as Kay Boyle was told the story, "rose and snapped open their monogrammed cigarette cases before her in homage."

By the time she was six years old, Katherine had convinced Kay that she was a poet and a writer. Little Janet looked on jealously, and when she was eighty-seven years old would remark bitterly, "It was not until years later that our little mother was granted her claim to fame. That magic phrase 'my daughter Kay Boyle' really indicated her own triumph which gave substance to those long-gone dreams."

2

Mother and Daughter

Mother's untroubled and intuitive knowledge about books and painting, theatre and music, people and politics, was my entire education. The bits and pieces of formal schooling I was later subjected to came to nothing at all.

Katherine never went to school because of a curvature of the spine so severe she had to be locked into a contraption hanging from a door for long hours; she received little formal education. Neither would Kay spend much time at school. As her mother had been ill, so as a child Kay Boyle soon welcomed illness as a means of gaining her own way. An attack of whooping cough at the age of three so incapacitated her that she had to learn to walk all over again. At four, she contracted typhoid fever, and all her hair fell out. Already vain, she never appeared now without her tan silk cap. A three-week bout with measles followed the typhoid. On New Year's Eve that year, as Kay lay in her bed recovering, she listened to the sound of the bells and vowed to live until New Year's Eve 1999 so that she could welcome in the new century. Katherine worried about this sweeter of her two daughters, the one whom she always said had been born laughing. She thoroughly approved of Kay's increasingly strong will and indulged her in whatever she wanted.

Endlessly, Katherine photographed her favorite, producing a portrait of Kay at four in white high-button shoes and a rabbit mask complete with ears thrust through her inevitable bonnet, which is tied with a fancy satin ribbon under her chin. Kay's expression is grave. "This is Kay when she was four," Katherine told anyone who would listen.

Leaving her mother to spend a day at school came as an unwelcome shock. On her first day at kindergarten, some nasty little boys locked her into the cloakroom, where she scrambled among jackets, sweaters, and rubbers until she was rescued by the teacher. Katherine was sympathetic. There would be time in the years ahead for education; Kay need not go to school just yet. To make her point, little Kay refused to walk down the side of the road where the kindergarten was located, even when Katherine held her hand. Katherine made her the companion she sorely needed as she developed an increasing contempt for her husband so emasculated by his father.

Summers the Boyles took their daughters to Europe, to France, England, Scotland, and Germany; the first of these trips occurred in the summer of 1902, when Kay was just six months old. Later Katherine photographed a tiny Kay in her stiff black patent-leather hat. Then they were off, walking hand in hand through the gardens of the Tuileries on their way to the Grand Guignol.

Not surprisingly, Kay was slow in learning to read, and it became something of a family disgrace as by six she stopped even making the effort. It didn't matter to Katherine, who wrote down the "poems" her daughter spoke aloud. Evenings after supper Kay and Janet sat up in their beds in their nightgowns armed with pencils and drawing paper. Attired in her blue velvet dressing gown, her tiny feet in silver mules, Katherine sat in an armchair between the four-poster beds of her daughters reading from *The Wind in the Willows* or *Alice in Wonderland* or *The Secret Garden*. Puss, when he read, chose Conrad and Kipling. Howard preferred Robert Louis Stevenson and Sir Walter Scott. These Kay pronounced "dull." As time passed, whatever her father and grandfather did was wrong, whatever Katherine did, right. "My grandfather was too outspoken, my father closed it all in . . . I didn't like Father," Kay Boyle as an adult exaggerated, at least as far as the grandparent was concerned, for there were also moments of real tenderness between Kay and Puss. But as the little girl realized that Puss, and hence Howard, insisted on opposing Katherine's unconventional views of politics and art, Kay became determined to set herself against both of them.

As Katherine read, the girls illustrated the story, and they were made by their mother to feel guilty if they so much as dropped their pencils for an instant to stretch their fingers. When Katherine went out for the evening, Kay, as soon as she had begun to read and write, would pin a poem to her pillow so that she would immediately discover it on her return. For her mother's birthday, for Christmas, Kay's present was always a poem, or a story illustrated in watercolors, then bound in a book.

That Kay Boyle grew up amid luxury was reflected in her watercolor paintings of "ladies of fashion," turn-of-the-century fashion plates in jackets trimmed with ermine. Katherine and Eva Evans taught Kay and her sister that women of substance never appeared in the world unless they were perfectly turned out, their exquisite costumes windows into their orderly souls. "Tango Tea" in Kay's 1913–14 notebook depicts "ladies" in floor-length fur-trimmed costumes of tangerine, pale jade, and pink. One holds a big black fur muff. The ladies doing their Christmas shopping wear hats defiant with feathers. A woman with an ermine muff walks a white-and-liver-spotted dog as snowflakes descend around her. Kay's caption reads:

"I'm so afraid of hurting him." If Puss was the giver of material objects, Katherine could be pleased only by a gift of creative expression.

No one was more skilled a propagandist of her daughter's creative efforts than Katherine Evans Boyle. "Have you read this one of Katherine's?" Katherine would write to a friend, copying one of Kay's poems into her letter. A particular favorite was "When I Sprinkle the Tennis Court," in which the child-poet bemoans the fate of the trees "all dying and dusty." When she was twelve, Kay was permitted to join the Boyle dinner guests. After dinner, Katherine might read not only from *Tender Buttons* but from one of Kay's youthful compositions. So one night, as Kay sat "dying of shame," Katherine read aloud from her diary of their crossing to Europe on the SS *Rotterdam* in 1912, a story about Kaiser Wilhelm II riding down Unter den Linden. Little Kay had produced a romantic tale in which the crowd is shocked when the Kaiser's horse chooses the wrong gate through which to pass, rather than the one reserved for royalty. Kay Boyle remembered her mother asserting that the only difference between Gertrude Stein's writing and her own was that while Miss Stein's was true, Kay's was as original as Miss Stein's, while being allegorical and humorous as well.

At every opportunity Katherine Evans Boyle insisted that Kay was an artist. Kay's ideas came from her mother: Katherine taught generosity, as behind Puss's back she gave away the exquisite clothes he bought for her to the black maid Fanny, who was her size. She gave Puss's fur-lined gloves to a blind man on a Philadelphia street. Whenever she could, she preached that labor should organize, as she did to the mailman who sat in her kitchen and told her he had five children whom he couldn't afford to support.

At the Meadowside in Mount Pocono, Katherine confronted the proprietor, Smithy, who was none too pleased when Katherine invited the shy painter Morton Schamberg to lunch. Other guests had complained that she had invited a Jew to lunch, Katherine was told. "Tomorrow I'll have to talk to everyone on the porch about the differences in religious beliefs," Katherine told Kay that night as she recounted the incident. Katherine was also an inveterate writer of letters, and taught Kay to do the same. Teaching, as always, by example, Katherine wrote to Kenneth Grahame, the author of *The Wind in the Willows*, offering Janet's view that he might write a sequel in which Mr. Toad would be seen in a more favorable light.

As their years in the East passed, as they moved from suburban Philadelphia to Bryn Mawr, to Washington, to Atlantic City and Beach Haven, Kay continued to avoid school. Janet went to Madeira in 1912, the year the family lived in Washington. Falling "desperately ill," Kay dropped out after a few weeks. At the Friends School in Atlantic City, Kay managed a few games of basketball and a few rounds of "thee" and "thou" and "thine" before dropping out. She did sympathize with her teacher, who seemed as tired and miserable as she was.

"Maybe at vacation time she'll get rested and meet a nice young man and get married," Kay confided to Katherine. However progressive Katherine's views, Kay Boyle grew up in an America where being a woman meant marriage and children, first and foremost. At what Kay Boyle remembers as "Miss Shipley's School" (the Shipley School) in Bryn Mawr, where Janet excelled, Kay used as her excuse to drop out that she had killed "an enormous and beautiful night moth" under her shoe. School was not only unnecessary but immoral. Bad things happened there. Katherine acquiesced. It was her mother who made everything right. When, sledding one winter at the Meadowside, Kay smashed into a telegraph pole, she was comforted by Katherine placing a kiss in each of her palms. Kay then closed her hands tight, so that she might hold her mother's kisses fast until morning.

The lessons of Kay Boyle's privileged childhood were all learned outside of school. At the Meadowside she was taught horseback riding by Alexander, the seventy-year-old son of slaves, who, as Kay later remembered it, taught her that "to be disciplined and to struggle patiently for excellence were not obligations you honored once or twice a week, but at every waking moment." When Kay was thrown from her horse, Alexander told her he was "ashamed at what you let him do." Little Kay tried to stand up, but could not. The world spun before her dazed eyes. But Alexander showed her no mercy.

"You get right back on him!" he repeated. Only when she couldn't get her foot into the stirrup and began to cry did Alexander relent. "I don't like to see people forgetting their standards," he added. Then they rode in silence back to the Meadowside.

A willful little girl, at Beach Haven Kay took to grabbing from behind and holding onto the belt of the local policeman, whose name was Primrose. Then she remembered herself zooming along on her roller skates, block after block.

It was the Boyles' black maid, Fanny, who reprimanded Kay then. "If you were colored, there wouldn't be any tomorrow afternoons for you children, you know that, don't you? Old Primrose, he'd send for the wagon and have you locked up. You know there wouldn't be any tomorrow afternoons if you weren't white. You know that, don't you?"

Katherine continued her forays into high culture as long as the family remained in the East. When a young professor whom she met at the Meadowside confessed that he longed to meet the famous English lecturer, poet, novelist, and critic John Cowper Powys, who toured even the most obscure of American cities, and invite him to lecture before his class, Katherine attended one of Powys's lectures herself. A tall, handsome, sensitive-looking man with a square jaw and a hawklike profile, as well as a full head of curly hair and a full-bodied British accent, Powys appealed to women like Katherine. With his talk of the "individual" and "creativity," with his insistence on language as a "sacred trust" through which human "souls" communicated, he won her over. Powys began his lecture on *Coriolanus* with the concept of the hero standing alone, launching at once into quotation as he utilized his considerable talent as an actor, which in no small measure accounted for his great popularity:

> "*As if a man were author of himself*
> *And knew no other kin.*"

For Katherine, Powys represented the culture for which she was starved in what she insisted was the philistine atmosphere presided over by Jesse Peyton Boyle. Powys saw literature—and life—in terms of great men, of heroes. Katherine subscribed to the same view, her own pantheon populated by powerful men from Stieglitz to Debs. This hero worship she passed on as a legacy to Kay. Powys allowed Katherine to believe as well that the only real religion was art, and as she refused to have her daughters baptized and did not allow them to belong to any church as children, she passed these ideas on to Kay Boyle as well. Only at the end of her life was Kay Boyle to repudiate these views of Katherine's and become converted to Roman Catholicism.

After one of Powys's lectures in Philadelphia, Katherine Evans Boyle strode up to the platform. With her azure eyes firmly making contact with those of the great man, she invited him to dinner. Not surprisingly, John Cowper Powys accepted.

"Dinner is served!" Nettie, wearing her best starched apron, called out.

Katherine had organized the meal with great care: cream of artichoke soup was followed by the main course, a broiled salmon surrounded by miniature snowballs of new potatoes garnished with parsley. Nettie poured the white wine into the long-stemmed glasses and passed the elaborately decorated salmon first to Katherine and then to the guest of honor. John Cowper Powys decided to pass up the salmon, however.

"I think I'll wait for the meat course," he announced.

Another of Katherine's conquests was the singer Mary Garden, from whom a note garnered her and a singer friend named Marie Lawall an invitation to lunch in New York. Later Katherine took Kay to Philadelphia to hear Mary Garden sing in Massenet's *Le Jongleur de Notre-Dame*. When she returned home, Kay decided that just as the juggler had paid homage to the Virgin, she would do the same for her little statue of the Buddha and would write a poem for him.

By now Kay and her sister were publishing their works in their own magazine, which they called *The Blue Heron*. Puss arranged for fifty copies to be run off every month. By the time she was ten years old, Kay Boyle had her own typewriter, and the magazine was her first outlet for her stories and poems, whose titles ranged from "Merry Christmas" and " 'Tis Spring" to "The Velvet Curtain," about a little girl who refuses to open her Christmas presents unless her grandfather is present. If later Kay Boyle was to depict

Jesse Peyton Boyle as the enemy of her youthful freedom, the evidence of that moment reveals that she was devoted to him.

Yet the carefully cultivated spell of culture and art created by Katherine was forever being broken by the interventions of the grandfather. Under the eyes of Kay and her sister, Katherine and Puss waged their sexually tinged warfare until she fell ill and he grew too old. But during Kay Boyle's early years, Puss and Katherine acted out their impossible struggle. He submitted a serial about his Catholic education at boarding school for publication in *The Blue Heron*. Katherine became so angry she stopped speaking to him, encouraging his hopeless pursuit of her in the face of her tantalizing near distance. He would pursue, she would remain forever unattainable, the pattern Kay Boyle would adopt in all her relationships with men for the rest of her long life. As Katherine had to remain inaccessible, so Kay would remain cool and aloof with all her suitors, husbands, and lovers, heightening their desire all the more. It was one more of Katherine's tendencies, along with her hero worship, her socialist views, and her exaltation of art and the "individual," from which Kay Boyle would never deviate.

Katherine's provocative disapproval of his article for *The Blue Heron* only incited Puss. He sent Katherine flowers; he sent her candied marrons. Holding herself apart, knowing her power resided in holding out as long as she could, Katherine made no acknowledgment of her father-in-law's efforts to woo her. As Kay watched, she learned from the interaction between her grandfather and her mother the way women were to deal with men. Finally Puss appeared at the door of Katherine's second-floor retreat, where she shut herself away to avoid the sounds of his quarrels with his daughter Madge, who did not know how to woo him as she did. When Puss screamed at Madge, Kay rushed to her room, kneeling down before her little statue of the Buddha, praying that he might intervene on her poor aunt's behalf. Later Kay Boyle came to believe that Puss was so hard on his daughter because she was plain, in such sharp contrast to his beautiful, azure-eyed, and unattainable daughter-in-law.

Katherine spoke to Puss now, but only to continue their combat, the only acceptable outlet for their strong and obviously sexual feelings for each other.

"You were attacking Catholic teachings," Katherine accused her father-in-law. "Why must you force these poor children to print it? They don't know what you're doing. They don't understand that there is propaganda, and that is one thing—and then there is art." Art was Katherine's refuge against the tangle of feelings she did not know how to explore: her disappointment with her pale shadow of a husband, the frustration of her failed marriage. What drove her now was Kay and Janet's pursuit of art, which she must protect at all cost. Katherine Evans Boyle adopted many causes; among them was Margaret Anderson's trial for the obscene act of having serialized James Joyce's *Ulysses* in *The Little Review*, as she sent

Anderson, whom she did not know, a message of solidarity. But foremost was her need that her daughters, and Kay in particular, fulfill her own failed dream of being an artist.

"If my writing is good," Puss continued the debate, glad of the opportunity to engage with his daughter-in-law, "then it is literature. It is art. Good writing makes it possible for a man to write interestingly, stirringly, on any subject, any subject in the world. As it happened, I chose my early education. I might just as well have chosen . . . the habits of the flea."

"That's where you made your mistake," Katherine retorted, savoring the excitement as much as Puss did.

With Kay and Janet as witnesses, and collaborators, Puss used the children and their magazine to make his male presence felt in all their lives. He offered to print one hundred copies of *The Blue Heron* every month, mimeographing the covers in full color. So he evoked little Kay's gratitude as she threw her arms around her little grandfather and gave him a big hug. Then she stroked his brow as he liked it stroked. "My heart was shaking for joy inside me," she later remembered in "Security," the story she wrote in 1936 about the incident. As a child she lived as a writer, flourishing with literary success. Immediately Kay and Janet published Puss's new parable without even reading it first.

The piece was signed "Grimm Anderson" and was about a neighbor who refused to assist a friend being beaten up by a robber. "There is such a thing as being too proud to fight," this neighbor declares as he allows the violence to continue unabated. Europe was at war now and, according to the adult Kay Boyle, Puss was outraged that pacifist Woodrow Wilson insisted on keeping America out of the fray, refusing to help the citizen besieged by the robber. Nothing more than their conflicting political views brought Katherine and her father-in-law into combat. Puss became apoplectic with rage whenever Katherine played Mozart or Schubert on the phonograph, so bitter were his anti-German sentiments. Mozart and Schubert were Austrian, not German, Kay depicts Katherine as haughtily informing her father-in-law, as if Austria then were any less the enemy. But it made a good story. Kay has Puss seize the metal arm of the phonograph, toss the record aside, and replace it with "Keep the Home Fires Burning." At such moments in Kay Boyle's imaginary re-creation of her childhood which she insisted was autobiographical, Katherine retreated to her bedroom and closed the door behind her. While Kay sat knitting scarves for the *poilus* in the trenches, and made bandages according to Red Cross specifications, Puss placed an index finger in each corner of his mouth, stretched it wide under his white mustache, and hissed loudly in movie theaters whenever the image of Woodrow Wilson appeared in a newsreel.

As Kay Boyle recounted the scene in "Security," Katherine had been sitting in her room wearing a blue silk dressing gown, an evening gown spread out on the bed awaiting her, when she read Puss's parable. At once, clutching the offending story, she grabbed Kay's hand and rushed down the stairs.

Downstairs in the library, Puss sat eating cheese straws by the fire, waiting for the cocktails to be brought in on the cocktail cart.

"Cad! Hypocrite!" Katherine launched her attack.

"To what, if I may ask, am I indebted for this outburst?" Puss slyly inquired. His courtesy concealed the passion his daughter-in-law aroused in him.

"You, reading your *Wall Street Journal*, playing your market, you the head of a family—the patriarch!—making two little girls responsible for your militaristic views!"

Puss wiped his delicate fingertips on a pure-white handkerchief, which had been so carefully laundered by Fanny. "I fail to grasp your meaning," he insisted. "I am in no sense a militarist. You are making a preposterous statement, my dear Kate."

As eager a participant in their warfare as her father-in-law, Katherine kept it going as long as she could.

"Too cowardly to put your own name to it! Signing it 'Grimm Anderson'! I should think you would be ashamed."

Then, as always, Katherine turned to her favorite child, to Kay.

"You should keep clear of such issues. You shouldn't get into politics in your paper," Katherine told her daughter. "You don't know about war and peace. You don't know the kind of horror and wholesale death words like these would lead us to!"

"As backer of this publication," Puss declared, "I see no reason why indisputable common sense should have no place in its pages."

"You should get rid of him!" Katherine declared hotly, addressing Kay. "You should let him have nothing to do with your magazine! Bring it out as you used to, on your own typewriters, paint it with your own brushes! Don't let him print it if he's going to use you as a mouthpiece for his views!"

At this, Katherine marched back upstairs, past the busts of Dante and Beatrice which adorned either side of the stairway landing. This time she locked herself into her room for three days. Nettie brought her meals up on a tray. To keep her interested, Puss hired a carpenter to work on the second-floor moldings. Amid the hammering and the racket, he stood outside Katherine's door arguing with the carpenter about the importance of America's entering the war.

Kay listened and Kay chose her side. She would be with Katherine against Howard and Puss, against the men of the family, for whom by now she had "no respect at all." Later she marched up to the third floor and knocked once more at Puss's door. No man, not even her grandfather, must gain control over her. Puss sat behind his rolltop desk, smoking a cigarette.

"We owe you for the publication of this number," she haughtily told Puss, a hauteur she learned from Katherine and which would forever characterize her relations with everyone, male and female, adults and children.

"I wish you would take over to your account my Union Iron and Steel, Preferred."

Having transposed the wartime context of 1916 onto a childhood scene in 1913, when she was eleven, Kay has Puss give her the following February, on her eleventh birthday, another Union Iron and Steel Preferred bond, "for security's sake." Once more she was in his debt. But whatever the story's historical discrepancies, Kay Boyle revealed that she had learned her lesson. Men like Puss who exerted their wills over you, and challenged your freedom, were to be watched carefully. Weaker, more passive men whom you might control at least did not so seriously threaten your becoming who you wanted to be. The little girl who shared his rolling chairs on the boardwalk of Atlantic City felt real affection for Jesse Peyton Boyle. But when increasingly he came into conflict with Katherine, her loyalty went to her besieged mother.

During World War I, Howard Boyle left the family to spend most of his time with his cousin Merritt Boyle, an engineer whose education at Penn had been financed by Puss. Merritt's plan was to found an "engineering company" in Cincinnati. Once more Puss paid to create an occupation for his hapless son. Kay and Janet, Katherine and Puss, were in Atlantic City when suddenly Puss fell ill, so crippled with rheumatism that he spent the better part of a year in bed. Howard took over the management of his investments.

Every day Katherine sat in Puss's room and read *The Wall Street Journal* to him. Every day Kay, now nearly fourteen, sat at a little table in Puss's room writing on a lined pad the letters he dictated to her. Puss pronounced each syllable distinctly, spelling out the words he believed she might not know, for Kay's obstinate refusals to attend school had left her deficient in grammar and spelling. Fondly, Puss called Kay his "amanuensis," as on her personal typewriter she typed away at his letters, each centered on the page, each margin measured with a ruler and marked in pencil. Kay did not miss her father, nor was she told what the "Boyle Engineering Company" did.

One afternoon, following a visit Howard had made from Cincinnati, Kay discovered on the floor, near the wastebasket, two crumpled halves of a torn letter. Retrieving the fragments, she recognized her father's handwriting. "Dear Mary," the letter began, "I cannot tell you how much less than nothing my life would be without you in it. . . ."

Kay kept her father's secret, persuading herself that this was not so much a letter to a woman named Mary as one left there for her to read, "asking for something none of us could give." Later she dramatized the incident in her 1932 story "Three Little Men," in which the daughter is portrayed as strong, and the father one of three weak, "little" men who inspires nothing so much in his daughter as "silent anger."

The dark truth of her father's misery, her grandfather's debilitating illness, and the war found expression in Kay Boyle's poetry, which now evinced a growing social consciousness. At fourteen she wrote about the exploitation of child labor and working women, and the suffering of slaves, poems written in a twenty-five-cent office ledger record book with a hard black cover. "The Working Girl's Prayer" begins: "My heart is sad / And yet the sky is blue." As a young poet Kay Boyle saw her duty to sympathize with the downtrodden; the poet's role was to expose and reform an unjust world where the innocent suffer, a view she was to hold all her life. The artist searches out the pain of those who cannot speak for themselves, even an "Art School Model" who sits immobile yet "struggles to master her tears." Two fine poems in the 1916 notebook are "At the Cathedral Hospital" and "The People's Cry," both responses to the carnage of war.

Nine months passed. Suddenly Puss's doctors ordered that he have all his teeth extracted. Mysteriously the rheumatism disappeared. But just as he left his sickbed, the news came that Howard had ruined him. The Boyles were now penniless. These financial reverses meant that the servants had to be dismissed and the family had to move to Cincinnati.

Katherine had hoped to take Kay and Janet to New York, the better to set them on the path to greatness. This was not to be. As her dream that Kay would one day become a great writer seemed to be in jeopardy, Katherine was consoled by her own mother, Eva. "The girls are so well grounded," their grandmother was convinced, "that one year will not make a great difference. We have rejoiced that they have always had the best." For Eva Evans, for Katherine Evans Boyle, women disappointed in their husbands, everything revolved around the children. During these years, Eva told Katherine she drew "long breaths of joy and relief" that she had lived to see Kay and her sister grown so that she would "always mean something to them."

In Cincinnati, Puss rented an entire floor of a boardinghouse. Janet, who now changed her name to Joan, and Kay were enrolled in both Miss Kendrick's School for Girls and in the Cincinnati Conservatory of Music, where Joan studied piano and Kay the violin. At Miss Kendrick's, Kay became notorious for circulating a petition about the poor food. She was temporarily suspended, thus postponing another foray into formal education. Puss bought season tickets to the Cincinnati Symphony to distract them from their painful discovery that the Boyle Engineering Company was nothing more than a garage for the repair and parking of the city's mail trucks. Located in a huge, dark warehouse, it occupied two city blocks in the industrial section of Cincinnati.

Nineteen sixteen marked the final year of Kay Boyle's childhood as her poems grew dark. "Everything is so silent and lonely this Christmas eve," she wrote. Joyous people existed in the world, but she was not one of them. The very word "friends" now grated "harshly" on her ears. The sudden move to Cincinnati caused Kay Boyle to grow up more rapidly than she would otherwise have done. Katherine struggled to reestablish her cultural interests; Puss was intent on restoring some financial stability to the family. Kay and her sister were left on their own.

At fifteen, Kay took up with a car salesman who lived on the third floor of their boardinghouse. He told her he was "recently divorced," and seemed a romantic figure as he sang "a little love, a little kiss, / I would give you all my life for this" on the boardinghouse piano. His favorite poet was Robert W. Service. Wearing a raccoon coat, he picked Kay up in the afternoons outside Miss Kendrick's in his Stutz convertible with its wire-spoked wheels. Soon Kay considered herself engaged to be married. But one day the man's wife arrived, threatening to press charges as she packed Kay off home. Gently, Katherine confronted Kay's suitor, who assured her that Kay remained a virgin.

Of course, he did not tell Katherine that he and Kay were engaged and planned to marry; Kay was mortified when Katherine told her the man had failed to claim her as his next bride. Kay did not allow herself to cry, however. She had never seen her mother cry, and for the moment Katherine remained her model. Kay told herself she was happy that her mother and sister at least believed that she did not go to bed with the man. Puss and Howard did not ask. "They did not want to know," Kay Boyle remembered years later with bitterness. Recounting the incident to her own daughters, Kay's sister Joan revealed that her sympathies were entirely on the side of the "poor man."

By 1917, Kay had become a flapper, a premature twenties woman with her rolled stockings and bobbed hair, smoking cigarettes, drinking, and making what passed for love in the back seats of automobiles. The car salesman vanished from the scene, but a legion of young men quickly took his place. Kay bemoaned her looks, not least a skinny body which made her look like a "telegraph pole." Katherine's aura of unattainability, with which she had for years tantalized Puss, her hauteur and coolness, now became Kay's own as she prided herself on being a fast young woman, her goal a date every night of the week.

Her sister remained her rival. Jealously, according to Kay Boyle, Joan attempted to sabotage her relationships with men, lying to them when they called and chasing them away, or, as Kay accused her, grabbing them for herself. Joan offered her explanations: "I'm sorry but he called and I told him . . ." Kay decided her sister and her mother could not get along with each other because Joan was as belligerent as Mother Boyle herself.

Kay had become a highly strung, overly emotional young woman who professed to weep at the sight of recruits marching down the streets to the troop trains bound for England and France: her 1917 poetry combined her two passions: hatred of the war and her infatuation with romantic love. One of the poems in the 1917 notebook was dedicated to one R.B., for Kay had a new beau. His name was Richard Brault, pronounced "Bro," and he was a French exchange student at the University of Cincinnati, studying electrical engineering. He spoke fractured English, saying "for a half a sock" instead of "for heaven's sake" and he called friends and enemies alike "you son of a peach."

But, to Kay Boyle, Richard Brault cut a fine figure in his sky-blue French uniform, a beret perched jauntily over one ear. Tall and dark, with handlebar mustaches, he was a war hero, decorated with the Croix de Guerre. Now he sang French war songs with "biting venom," was a rebel against the hypocrisies of the Catholic Church, and was contemptuous of his father's army career. He could be fun as he danced the cancan and appeared in a musical comedy singing "Madelon." Kay's first poem to Brault was written when she was fifteen years old. Brault had his "great heart and soul . . . murdered / By life and not by death." Kay Boyle had found a hero.

One day in 1918 Kay was walking home from the Conservatory of Music when the ground began to wave under her feet. For two weeks she lay unconscious, suffering from the influenza to which many soldiers in the American Army in Europe had already succumbed. Then one morning she awoke feeling refreshed, a feeling "of great clarity" about her. Her father was no longer sitting in his customary place. Joan was still asleep. Suddenly the bathroom door opened, and a man dressed in white appeared. Kay was not afraid. Kay knew the man. It was the painter Morton Schamberg.

"I came to tell you that you're going to be all right," Schamberg said. "Just forget about these three weeks that you've been so ill." Kay fell back to sleep clutching Schamberg's hand. In the morning Katherine seemed moved when she heard the story, not yet telling her daughter she had just received a telegram from Charlie Sheeler informing her that Morton Schamberg had died in Philadelphia of the flu. Superstitious all her life, nearly seventy years later, Kay Boyle at eighty-five, in every respect mentally capable, remained convinced that Morton Schamberg had actually visited her in her bedroom that morning. "Isn't that wonderful," she exclaimed. "He came!"

In September of 1918 Kay enrolled at the Ohio Mechanics Institute, a technical school with some liberal arts courses, the better to learn some skills (she took mechanical drawing), since the Boyles had fallen into even more dire straits. From the little house to which they had moved from the boarding establishment, they had been forced to move to a small apartment and to sell some of their furniture. Kay was accepted, although she had to write an "I" for "incomplete" under "high school grade." Kay proved to be as indifferent a student as she had in Philadelphia. From 1918 to 1920, she was a frequent truant, often absent from algebra, English, freehand drawing, and even French. Her major was "architectural design."

Kay and Joan studied at the Parsons School of Fine and Applied Arts in New York in the fall of 1919, only to be sent home when once more the money ran out. It was Howard Peterson Boyle who was sent to New York to break the news, and he cried, the first time Kay had ever seen her father show any emotion. But even as she tried to console him, Kay was angry. "You should be crying because of your failures as a father and not because the service station isn't making any money," she thought bitterly.

Back in Cincinnati, to Kay's chagrin, the Boyles were reduced to living on the second floor of the Boyle Engineering Company in rooms permeated by the smell of gasoline from the shop below and beset by the roar of accelerating car engines. To appease Kay, Puss purchased a used Model T Ford, which she was allowed to drive. But Kay had also to work as switchboard operator at the garage and to ring up the customers' bills. Joan said she could make money designing newspaper ads for department stores, and did. But Kay sat at the switchboard, being paid eighteen dollars a week, eight of it going back to Puss for her room and board. Her half-hour lunch she took with her mother. Otherwise, as she sat at the switchboard she wrote poems and stories, trying to be cheerful, deciding, as she was to remember in her memoir of 1984, that lightness of heart was a form of high courage and pessimism "the shiverings and shakings of bleak cowardice." On her days of truancy from the Ohio Mechanics Institute, she did the housework, sardonically dubbing herself "the little fairy in the home."

As Kay entered her young womanhood, Puss proved far more repressive than he ever had. When she and her sister put on white dresses and went out to collect money for the Red Cross on the streets of Cincinnati, Puss exploded. When Kay was out late with one of her many boyfriends, Puss paced up and down the room. "You know what's happening now in the back seats of those cars, don't you?" he demanded of Katherine.

"You're sending these beautiful girls out and you're making prostitutes of them," Puss accused his recalcitrant daughter-in-law.

Indeed, Kay, now a tall, slender young woman with misty deep-set blue eyes and black hair, was a true beauty. Richard Brault in his "horizon-blue" uniform was by no means her only suitor. A medical student took her to the movies and naughtily put the tip of his tongue in her ear. An assistant architecture instructor at the Mechanics Institute pursued her, as did an aspiring writer named Coppy, who dubbed her "Trilby." Men for Kay Boyle during her Cincinnati years were to be manipulated and managed, teased and cajoled. It was always advisable to add one more to your "string" of admirers. To make Brault jealous, she recounted her exploits at a marshmallow roast with Coppy where she lost both her garters and her stockings slid down her legs as if, Kay said, she were a "Mack Sennett bathing girl." What could a poor girl do, she implied, but remove both shoes and errant stockings and go wading? Coppy swooned that she had "the most perfect foot in the world." She was already a haughty, self-confident woman contemptuous of people she deemed her inferiors. To Brault, she reported that at the end of the evening of the marshmallow roast she had kissed each member of the group good night, "males and females impartially." Behind their backs she mocked her erstwhile companions. "You would have laughed at the expression of these dumb German faces," she told him.

Kay broke with a suitor named Ralph because he did not understand her, for she did not "act in the manner of the other girls you have known." Not as great a fool as Kay would have him, Ralph called her bad-tempered. "If I loved you," she retorted, "NOTHING would make any difference. But of course I don't and you don't either." Ralph had another girlfriend and this Kay could not abide. Haughtily Kay told him that when he realized "what a splendid precious thing love is," he would not "cheapen it by momentary whims." She expected nothing short of total devotion from each of her many suitors, viewing the slightest opposition as treason and sufficient cause for a young man to be banished.

Kay allowed each of her gentlemen callers to believe she cared for him only, even as Brault persisted in his stolid courtship. An uneasy flirt, she flitted from a dance with Shelley to a walk with George, theater with the hangdog Ralph, promises from Bill, whose only fault was that he didn't like to write letters, and visits from the inevitable Brault. Only occasionally was she "rather down on myself" because it was not "the square thing to do." Sometimes she was discovered in her emotional duplicity. One day she told one of her suitors how sorry she was that he was ill and couldn't see her.

"You don't sound sorry at all," the young man bitterly retorted. "You don't care anything about me at all . . . I am a fool to even think of you." When he told her he would never love anyone, Kay dismissed this as "baby talk." One night she dreamed she married Bill, and went to live in Central America with him, only to abandon him, while Bill, even as an estranged husband, remained "on the string," telling her he would call her up on Monday. That marriage was not what she really desired, the example of her mother's unhappiness firmly in her mind, is conveyed in her escape from Bill, even as consciously she was considering only whom and not whether to marry.

According to Kay Boyle, Katherine's preference for her was a young man named Lewis Browne, who was studying to be a rabbi at the Hebrew Union College. Admiring Browne's intellect, and pitying him because he was crippled, Katherine promoted the relationship. Browne may well have been another of those needy young men whom Katherine called "son," and with whom she obviously enjoyed surrounding herself as unthreatening admirers. For evidence that she actually hoped Kay would marry Lewis Browne, we have only Kay Boyle's later word. But Katherine's defense of Morton Schamberg at the Meadowside suggests that she at least may well have been free of the prevailing anti-Semitism.

Kay, however, was repelled by both Browne's mind and his flesh. The days of Katherine's authority over Kay Boyle were long gone. In fact, however, Kay's case against Browne was a good one. Although he could not dance and his complexion was a "disaster," what troubled her more was his lack of moral fiber. Browne became upset when his friends criticized him for taking Kay, a Christian, to Sunday-afternoon synagogue dances. Young Kay Boyle was appalled by this intolerance, her reaction a legacy of Katherine's influence. Simultaneously Kay herself expressed anti-Semitic sentiments: at one restaurant party she attended with her best friend, Ann Penn, and her cousin, Kay described the new husband of one of their mutual friends as "a little vile looking jew with a bald head. I don't know whether to pity her or not."

Kay Boyle had become a young woman full of bravado and irony, believing herself to be the superior person her mother had always claimed she was. Catching herself crying at a movie, she could not resist observing that "everyone in the near vicinity was touched by my extreme humanness. It was almost amusing in its absurdity." Kay bragged that she felt as if she were "about a century old, as though everyone else were mere babes in comparison."

Sexuality, however, remained a problem. Good women had to remain virgins even as they had to arouse their suitors to keep them. Young Kay Boyle accepted the physical advances of her men. George, for one, expected to kiss her. "If I object," she reasoned, like every American girl of her time, "he'd get his feelings hurt and never return." Ralph was more pliant; it was easier for her to "keep him in order." Brault she had yet to kiss, as she feared he would put her in the class of "the other kind" and "that I do not want."

For all her bravado, Kay remained a conventional woman of her time, wary of rebelling against the double standard dividing women into good girls or whores, that standard which turned the good girls into teases. Should Richard ever discover her promiscuity, Kay feared, he "would only be right in supposing me heartless, brainless and fickle." Women, Kay believed, were the inferiors of men. "Why should pretty, vain, little women be able to rule great, fine men?" she pondered. At the same time, as she now viewed marriage as a means of escape from the restrictions of Puss's household, she decided that a dull, steady man would best suit her independent spirit. "I suppose one must marry a sort of common-place man in the long run," she decided.

Certainly she was not in love with Richard Brault, who seemed immature to her despite his having spent four years in the trenches. But the more he hesitated about proposing, the more she saw him as her only hope. Katherine was now forty-six years old, and had fallen victim to chronic depression, sometimes sleeping the entire afternoon away. One morning in the kitchen Kay tried to tell Puss that Katherine might do better in a sanitarium, so totally had she succumbed to neurasthenic ailments.

"For God's sake what do you want me to do? What can I do? You're dragging me to the poor-house, every one of you," Puss shouted in a rage of Irish temper. Then he eyed Kay.

"And you're the worst. You make conditions, conditions, conditions! You say you stay home to be with your mother and then you suggest sending her away and not taking care of her. You want to get her off your hands!"

At this Kay took umbrage.

"You can swear at anyone in the world you want to," Kay told her grandfather, "but I have never been sworn at and I won't stand for it!"

Kay stoutly insisted that she was "willing to give up anything" for her mother—"she is so dear and sweet and I love her so." She professed it to be "very wonderful to be able to sacrifice all one can for another person —that is truly happiness." In fact, leaving home was her first priority as she devoted herself to extracting a marriage proposal from a man, if not Brault, then another of her suitors. "He either flops or fizzles," she decided of Brault, "he either pops the fatal question" or she would marry Bill. She considered her strategies: tears in her voice, babbling incoherently.

Kay listened intently as Brault spent two hours trying to explain the difference between a socialist and a Bolshevik. She loosened and lost a bright yellow garter and her stocking fell tantalizingly about her ankle. Brault was so often "grumpy" that Kay had to wonder "how one can loathe those whom they love best." At the evening party with Ann and her cousin Colonel Penn, Kay made a point of allowing the colonel to kiss her three times, getting her lipstick all over his white mustaches while Richard glowered. On the way home they did not speak a word to each other. Kay insisted on standing in the pouring rain while Richard went up to his room for the umbrella he had borrowed from Puss.

As they walked back to the Boyle Engineering Company, Brault's irritable mood changed. He helped Kay over puddles. Sensing her advantage, Kay, in her typical mode, drew away.

"What in hell is the matter?" Brault now demanded.

"Nothing."

This indeed worked. Soon Richard Brault was telling Kay Boyle what a wonderful companion she was, so sweet, so gentle, so understanding. Kay at once seized her advantage.

"Dick, forgive me. I love you," Kay murmured.

At this poor Brault grabbed her and hugged her and kissed her and said he adored her. Before the evening was out, Kay had put her head down on her knees while, as she later described it, "hot little tears oozed" from her eyes. Female submissiveness, she knew, was required. "How could you have hurt me so?" she whispered. At this sign of her vulnerability, Brault took her into his arms and kissed her for what she described as at least five minutes. Brault, she secretly believed, was "nothing but a big kid with a kid's humors and whims and tempers." But she had discovered how to manage him. By the end of the evening they were engaged.

Now Brault had only to be converted to a hero, to be worshipped as Katherine worshipped her heroes. Brault's "vile disposition" Kay attributed to his being a "genius." His poetry was "marvellous," his dreams "remarkable." She called him "a god" and insisted she was overjoyed to have found such a man in "this rather sordid world of ours." So also as she marched toward marriage had she bettered her recalcitrant older sister. "They made one perfect man in the whole, wide world," Kay announced to Joan, now nicknamed Jo, her old competitor, "JUST ONE! And I got him!"

Jo, however, managed to escape to New York, and a job on *Vogue* magazine, leaving Kay behind in Cincinnati, where she sold her violin to pay for a night course at a secretarial school, and worked by day, in her words, for a "Rotarian" wholesale jeweler. In stenography class, Kay had to copy the line "We feel that we can count on your support to help us to fight the growth of Socialism in this country and absolutely exterminate their unsound principles." Kay said she was "becoming more radical every day, absolutely *red*," and was repelled, even as she laughed at a woman acquaintance who refused to utter the word "anarchist" in company. Kay pronounced herself "too amused." At the moment of the anti-red Palmer Raids, motivated as they were by fear of organizing labor, which Attorney General A. Mitchell Palmer and cohorts like J. Edgar Hoover deemed synonymous with Bolshevism, Kay Boyle was calling the Bolshevik Revolution "a great and glorious experiment."

Now, in the spring of 1921, radical politics revived Katherine, who became a supporter of the Farmer-Labor Party, a coalition of socialists, workers, and farmers. Soon Kay and Katherine were joined at the Boyle dinner table by union organizers and members of the American Civil Liberties Union and the Women's Peace Society. A friend of ACLU founder Roger Baldwin persuaded Katherine to run for the Cincinnati Board of Education on the Farmer-Labor ticket. Puss and Howard at once opposed the idea, but they kept quiet. Katherine, however, was too timid to make the obligatory public speeches and she lost. One night she brought home to dinner a young labor organizer named Duane Swift, whom she had met at a Farmer-Labor meeting. Although she was engaged to Richard Brault, Kay Boyle promptly fell in love with Swift.

Indeed, Swift was a more romantic figure than the irritable Brault. He had been a conscientious objector in the war and had gone to jail for his beliefs. Soon Kay was driving Swift to political meetings in the family Model T Ford and from one union local meeting to another, venturing as far as Kentucky. Kay joined Swift's Federated Press and distributed membership blanks and literature. She called Swift "Tommy," and managed to lure him away one afternoon to a picnic, where she read him her poems, which Swift later remembered as being "delicate and gentle," about the sky and the rain and the spring. Kay planned to continue in her seductive aims by reading Sara Teasdale to Swift: "But oh, to him I loved, who loved me not at all, I owe the little gate that led thru Heaven's wall." When he proved recalcitrant, finally mailing her a rejecting postcard, she reacted with her habitual hauteur: "he is SO romantic: a penny postal ant type."

Alas for Kay, Swift preferred Katherine, with whom he had become infatuated. Indeed, they were a threesome on most of their outings: Kay, Katherine, and Swift. After the three went out dining and dancing, with Swift about to return to Chicago, they returned to their car only to find the side of the Ford bashed in. Katherine at once kissed Swift goodbye, and pushed him into a taxi. "Forget us," she said in her gentle way. "We can take care of ourselves." So she endeared herself to one more man forever. It was typical of Katherine in these years self-effacingly to make such gestures. The children (with their mothers) of the "Children's Crusade" passed through Cincinnati on their transcontinental walk to Washington to demand freedom for their political prisoner fathers who had refused to fight in World War I. Like Debs, they viewed the war as a conflict between rival capitalist powers in which it was not in the interest of workingmen to sacrifice their lives; Katherine generously invited a group to stay overnight at the Boyle apartment.

Kay became politically active for the first time herself, as she served as head of the women ushers at the mass meetings for Lincoln Steffens and William Z. Foster, urging support for Farmer-Labor candidates. Kay sold badges and collected money. (A steelworker who had participated in the strikes of 1919, Foster was being attacked as a Bolshevik; he was to become the leader of the American Communist Party after Stalin's consolidation of power.)

In the Model T, with her mother, Kay shepherded muckraker Lincoln Steffens around Cincinnati, although when he came to dinner Puss and Howard retreated in protest to their rooms. That they chose silence rather than active disapproval allowed Kay to drive Steffens to his lecture. During the fall political campaign of 1921, Kay drove Farmer-Labor speakers, running for local office and urging protection for farmers and members of labor unions, government ownership of some industry, and social security laws, from street corner to street corner, distributing literature. After work at the jeweler's, she knocked on doors for radical candidates and collected several hundred signatures asking for the immediate release from prison of Eugene Debs. Debs, indeed, was freed in 1921 by President Harding, who invited him to the White House. "I have heard so damned much about you, Mr. Debs," Harding told the socialist, "that I am very glad to meet you personally."

Katherine continued to brag about Kay to her political friends. Kay was a prodigy, she said. She won literary prizes at school and she wrote stories which sold—fantasies of Katherine's unrelenting ambition for this daughter. Katherine's union friends viewed Kay as a "free spirit" and a "flaming youth." They thought she was a worry to her mother, while Katherine excused her everything because, she told everyone, Kay was a "genius." Kay occasionally showed up at one of the picket lines on which her mother was marching, a tall, blue-eyed, black-haired girl who looked so much like her mama. In tow was her dashing French army officer boyfriend, still an engineering student, but obviously reluctant to discard his blue uniform and blue beret.

For the most part, however, Kay thought of Cincinnati as a "refuse heap" and longed for the day when she could join her sister in New York. Meanwhile she began her first novel, which she called *You Were Born Laughing*, an autobiographical book, of course, later to be called *The Book of Cincinnati*. She wrote poetry and even dreamed of making movies, her first hero to be Jesus, "a weather-beaten rugged type of man, nervous and highly strung to the nth degree," as, like many before her and since, she would demythologize Christianity. Fastidious as ever in her appearance, she shaved her arms until Brault complained that they were "too bristly." They went to the movies after her typing class to see Norma Talmadge, and necked in the back of the Model T Ford, until one night they were stopped by a local cop horrified to see a respectable young woman smoking in public.

"This is my wife," Richard told him nervously. "Yes," said Kay hysterically, "Mrs. Brault." The cop persisted in wanting to know why Kay was smoking, so indecent an act; she told him it soothed her nerves since she had "recently lost a very dear sister."

So Kay Boyle at this tense moment unconsciously revealed the depth of her jealousy, her longing to be rid of her more beautiful, more accomplished sibling rival. Kay and Joan—they were destined to become virtually lifelong rivals and competitors. As Kay was to outstrip her sister in achievement, later it would be Joan who would exhibit the greater hostility.

It was only when he learned that Kay was the granddaughter of Jesse Peyton Boyle, who had bought tickets to the policemen's ball, that he relented. "Let 'em do what they please," he now told his cohort. "Young, ain't they?"

The following day the cop called Kay for a date. "We're engaged," she told him icily. Then she hung up.

Kay's plan to move to New York included Richard Brault, whom she would immediately marry and accompany to France to visit his "adorably impossible" family in Brittany. Puss vehemently opposed Kay's marriage to so poor a man, a strategy which led her in turn to persuade herself that she did in fact love Richard. "We have been talking for three years without stopping and we haven't said it all yet," she stoutly declared. Kay feared Puss might say something disastrous to Richard. She felt that she and Brault were "being pressed down by sheets of iron" whenever they visited the Boyle apartment. Whenever Richard even telephoned, Puss stared at Kay as if, she said, she had committed murder. "You're only with him because of the uniform he wears and the medals pinned on his chest!" Puss told her. In November of 1921 Kay and Richard chipped in to pay for what she hoped would be her last month at secretarial school.

That same month produced a landmark in the life of Kay Boyle. She had at last broken into print with a letter to the editor of Harriet Monroe's *Poetry* magazine. Under the headline of "Reactionary Composers," Kay writes demanding that music catch up with the other arts and join the modernist movement. Already a polemicist at the age of nineteen, she attacks not only "the reactionaries among the composers and critics" but audiences stubbornly demanding "that our operatic, song and orchestral compositions should remain more than a little antiquated, scented with lavender." Even as a teenager, Kay Boyle insisted that people take sides. "Unless there is a tendency in the arts to reflect the spirit of the age," she lectured the readers of *Poetry*, "they are without constructive value." Nor was the language of the young Kay Boyle temperate. "Meanwhile," she writes, "music stands like a Boston bas-bleu, her skirt a little shortened because of the influence of Korsakov and Dvorak, but still wearing her New England rubbers." The moderns, Kay concludes, "*are* ourselves, our explanation, the story which the future generations shall read of us." Music had better catch up with poetry.

"You with your Crowninsheild [sic] and I with my Harriet Monroe!" Kay wrote her older sister in jubilation, aligning their mutual mentors. "Anyway, we strike high."

But Harriet Monroe turned down her poem "Gautama," as did *The Nation*, along with a poem called "The Poet's Lady." "I'm not discouraged yet," Kay declared as she begged her sister to ask "Crownie" to help her find a job in New York. The sisters remained antagonists, however, and when Jo burst into print with some reviews, Kay responded with faint praise ("they have more that stamp of utter professionality which, to some extent, your earlier things lacked"). Kay, after all, was the writer, as she criticized her sister's grammar, misspelling words in the process: "I am very urgently against unnecessities in writing just as I am in everything else," she wrote Jo pompously. For her part, Joan demanded of Katherine, "WHAT IS Kay planning to do? Is it still architecture? Why not domestic science or sewing? Dressing would come in very usefully—even in Paris, n'est-ce-pay?"

Miserable in Cincinnati, Kay lamented: "I am losing all my sweetness and good will toward men." Stubborn silence reigned at the Boyle dinner table. Puss had forbidden politics as a subject of conversation, none of Katherine's talk of Indians dying like cattle in boxcars or miners being killed in Virginia. Every time Katherine opened her mouth now, Kay reported, "a sweet and forbearing silence" fell upon "the masters of our house." Puss talked about Fatty Arbuckle's trial with its "amusing features."

"You make me sick!" Puss accused his increasingly fragile daughter-in-law. "You're simply BURSTING with virtue."

One night, Puss, after gorging himself on what Kay counted as three bananas, five pastries, and many doughnuts, sat back in his chair and patted himself on his round belly.

"Do you know, Howard," he said provocatively, deliberately ignoring those bleeding hearts, his daughter-in-law and her daughter, "I think there must be people starving in America today."

Kay's eyes flashed. "Think?" she interjected. Then, before anyone could reply, she rushed to the sanctity of her bedroom.

Kay knew that Howard, at least, wanted her to remain in Cincinnati. But here she would suffocate; here all her dreams would die. One day Howard asked what her ambition was, but all Kay could tell him was "I want to get married." She tried to say more, then burst into tears. There were fresh scenes. Her alienation from Puss and Dad was now complete.

"I hate the name of Boyle like I hate poison!" Kay cried in frustration. At twenty she finally fled Cincinnati for New York, never to lay eyes on either Puss or Howard again.

3

She Was a Role Model

I'd give a year of France for one evening with Lola.

In New York, Jo did help. At once she provided Kay with letters of introduction to several magazine editors provided by her dashing mentor, *Vanity Fair* editor Frank Crowninshield, that worldly sardonic gentleman who had become the soul of Condé Nast's new magazine; Crowninshield had also been one of the organizers of the great Armory Show of 1913.

Albert Jay Nock, editor of *The Freeman*, was happy to go for a walk in Central Park with the tall, striking, black-haired young woman with her high aristocratic nose and deep-set blue eyes. But instead of offering Kay Boyle a job, he told her to go back to the Midwest and work on a small-town newspaper.

Burton Rascoe, literary editor of the *New York Tribune*, did give her a test—only to ridicule her flowery metaphors. Brusquely, he told her not to bother him again. In the fictionalized memoir of her early life, *Being Geniuses Together*, Kay pictured herself shortly after her arrival in New York marching into the offices of *New Masses*, a magazine which would not begin publishing until four years later, in May of 1926. But in her lilac suit, carrying her black imitation-leather briefcase crammed with juvenilia, no doubt she did make her way to the receptionist's desk of some political magazine.

"I believe in the world they are making. I believe in it very much," Kay Boyle remembered herself saying, only to be treated with scorn by the receptionist, who, staring at her waved hair, high heels, and purple suit, doubted, Kay surmised, that she could possibly be a socialist. But Kay was not going to be defeated so easily. Franklin P. Adams read her poems at his desk and put an item about them and the lilac suit in his New York *World* column.

Then Gilbert Seldes at *The Dial* gave Kay Boyle a real assignment. Among the books strewn about his office, he offered her the chance to pick some out and review them. When Seldes saw her selections, he pronounced her a "discriminating young lady!" Two unsigned reviews by twenty-year-old Kay Boyle were published in *The Dial* under "Briefer Mention," one in August of 1922, a review of Remy de Gourmont's *Mr. Antiphilos, Satyr*, and, in October, one of Sidney Dark's *An Outline of Wells*. "The words of a connoisseur of women," Kay wrote of *Mr. Antiphilos, Satyr*, "voiced by an experimenter with civilization who hides his hoofs in provincial horns and secretly polishes his horns." Writing for *The Dial*, Kay could not resist showing off a bit.

Alone without her namesake, this daughter who was to be everything she was not, Katherine fretted, so that Kay wrote reassuringly, "Would I be writing reviews, or poetry, or stories, or anything, if it wasn't for you?" Katherine longed to leave Puss and Howard and move to New York to be with her daughters. "You will be with us soon," Kay promised her languishing mother. Meanwhile she went to the theater, swam at the Y, and signed up for a short story writing course at Columbia University, only to be told she had first to take a prerequisite English course, which turned out to be filled with immigrants learning English. One night Kay and Jo sat up all night on a grimy train bound for Washington so that for one last time they might see their grandmother, who had suffered a stroke. "My, my, my," Eva Evans repeated over and over again. She died in October of 1922.

Kay's first steady job in New York was as secretary to a wholesale dress manufacturer. Then Jo used her *Vogue* connections and Kay was hired as part-time secretary to fashion writer Marjorie Welles. Richard Brault arrived armed with his degree in electrical engineering. But his irritability did not translate into effectiveness and with his still deficient English the only job he could get was as a meter reader for Edison Electric.

Poor as they were, Kay Boyle married Richard Brault on Saturday morning, June 24, 1922, at City Hall in New York. Joan Boyle was their witness. Their first home was one room on the first floor of a brownstone on East Fifteenth Street. Bedbugs had already taken up residence. Kay cooked their meals on a hot plate in the windowless bathroom. It was an inauspicious beginning. On their first morning as a married couple, they were awakened by a special delivery letter from Howard P. Boyle. Kay was absolutely forbidden to marry Richard Brault until he was in a position to support her.

Seeing themselves as rebels against bourgeois convention, Kay and Richard had cards printed up reading: "Kay Boyle and Richard Brault announce their marriage . . ." By so appropriating the conventional parental function, Kay believed she was committing an act of outrageous rebellion, and she enjoyed it. Two weeks later, a cable arrived from Brittany from Richard's former army officer father. Unless Kay and Richard were immediately married by a priest, the Braults would never lay eyes on Richard again. Hardly rebels now, the young couple complied. But because Kay was not a Catholic, the priest insisted on marrying them in the little chapel in the rear of the French church. Richard stood there grimly, refusing even to look at the priest as he read the service.

Kay brought the first of many kittens into her life, wrote poems, one of which, "Monody to the Sound of Zithers," appeared in the December 1922 *Poetry*, and did her typing for Marjorie Welles. Kay Boyle's talent, her promise, were immediately recognized, and this first published poem was anthologized a year later in a volume edited by one William Stanley Braithwaite.

Even more significant to her literary career was that in early November Kay went to work as business correspondent and advertising manager for Lola Ridge, the revolutionary socialist and feminist poet, who was New York editor of Harold Loeb's literary magazine, *Broom*. Loeb's "clean sweep" signified his publishing the new modernists—William Carlos Williams, Gertrude Stein, Marianne Moore, Hart Crane, and Sherwood Anderson—as well as reproducing the paintings of Picasso, Matisse, Juan Gris, Léger, Klee, and Kandinsky. Kay, who had declared herself in Cincinnati for "l'art pour l'art," could not have managed a more perfect venue for her apprenticeship.

Ridge recommended Kay Boyle to Loeb, who was working out of Berlin, as "a good stenographer and rapid typist, and has a good business training." Kay worked at *Broom* for six months, wheedling advertisements, even selling the magazine on street corners herself. She wrote to Loeb constantly, urging him to apologize to *Arts and Decoration* for using the word "inferior" in connection with them, and so avoid a lawsuit; she organized subscription lists, ordered an Addressograph machine, and wrote letters to potential advertisers. As she had once distributed union literature, now during performances of *Six Characters in Search of an Author*, which had been serialized in *Broom*, she sold copies of the magazine in the lobby, earning forty-eight dollars on one Saturday alone. Often their letters crossed, and while Loeb wrote that he could not understand why they were out of money in New York, Kay worried about how they were going to pay for the tea for their Thursday-afternoon gatherings. Misunderstandings accumulated.

But it was all worthwhile for Kay Boyle, who found in Lola Ridge the mentor to supplant Katherine. A tiny, frail woman with a long, pale, thin face, an aquiline nose, and dark hair pulled tightly back, Ridge was a friend of the anarchist Emma Goldman, having written for Goldman's magazine, *Mother Earth*. She believed that the rights of women could not be won without a social revolution, and she opened to Kay Boyle a world of progressive ideas: the urgency of contraception as a means of liberating women, the acceptance of homosexuality, the insistence that women be acknowledged as writers rather than as "women writers," ideas which would percolate through Kay Boyle's work for the rest of her life.

Lola Ridge was also an Irish patriot, who, like Yeats, had written a poem about the Easter rising of 1916. "Censored lies that mimic truth," Ridge begins "The Tidings," "censored truth as pale as fear." And she closes with a self-flagellating cry against her own inexcusable absence from the barricades: *They are fighting to-night in Sackville Street, / And I am not there!*

Like Katherine Evans Boyle, Ridge was a supporter of Eugene Debs. Socialism was the new dawn, Lola believed, as she wrote a poem dedicated "To Alexander Berkman." "Woman is not and never has been man's natural inferior," Ridge asserted in her essay "Woman and the Creative Will." Living by her feminist principles, she encouraged younger women, like Kay Boyle and Evelyn Scott. To Evelyn, already a published poet and novelist, Lola recommended Kay Boyle's writing. Lola also urged her friend Marianne Moore to read Kay's poetry. "I shall watch for Kay Boyle," Moore promised. When Lola Ridge suggested to Kay that she read the poems of Emanuel Carnevali, the Italian poet, who, working on the staff of *Poetry* in Chicago, had fallen ill with encephalitis and returned in 1922 to Italy, Carnevali at once became important to her. But Kay Boyle and Emanuel Carnevali were not to meet for a decade.

Kay, whether in response to the bossiness of her older sister, or to a culture which so valued men over women, generally preferred male company. She justified herself by accusing women of being ever in search of affectation in other women, while "there is nothing to discover in me," as if she too were not schooled in duplicity and in parading behind a persona. But Lola was different. "She has a personality of enormous charm and grace which puts her beyond sex," Kay thought. "She is made for everyone to worship—and she doesn't really give herself to or actually NEED anyone."

As Kay had observed in the dance Katherine had performed with Puss, so now from Lola she learned how distance could be liberating, acquiescence a form of enslavement. Kay and Lola Ridge drew close. Sometimes they even danced together, with Kay assuming the male role and leading the frail, sickly Lola. When Ridge was ill, Kay cooked for her. Always she showed Ridge her poems, hoping for praise. In the fiery, opinionated Lola Ridge, a woman dedicated to principles, a woman willing to act on her beliefs, Kay Boyle discovered the woman artist on whom she could model herself. As Lola Ridge had always written under her maiden name, so Kay too would always publish as "Kay Boyle."

Kay had only two good dresses and one pair of shoes. But Joan gave her a strawberry-red chiffon scarf. Too poor to buy makeup, she had to burn a cork to produce eyeliner, and she blackened her lids so heavily people in the streets would sometimes stare, excessive makeup a failing which also would remain with her for all her life. But her days at *Broom* were exhilarating, and the sour temperament and disappointments of Richard Brault receded as she dedicated herself to the well-being of Harold Loeb's magazine. Indeed, Loeb was so impressed by Kay's dedication that he asked her to keep an informal log for him, including "the petty gossip, who was in, what suggestions they make, and what they think of *Broom*."

Before long Kay had doubled the advertising, and handled with aplomb and her characteristic hauteur a brouhaha created by the post office over a *Broom* contest, a drawing accompanied by the question "Which Prominent American Does This Represent?" The chief objection offered by the post office, which had accused *Broom* of running an illegal lottery, Kay reported to Loeb with sarcasm, was that "it doesn't look like any American they ever saw, and if it's Babe Ruth, why such a funny mouth?" By January of 1923 the *Broom* stationery bore Kay Boyle's name below that of Lola Ridge: "Kay Boyle, Business Manager."

Every Thursday afternoon and one evening a month Lola held a party at the *Broom* office on East Ninth Street. Kay served the tea with lemon and milk cakes, and here she met Marianne Moore and John Dos Passos, Waldo Frank and Babette Deutsch, Laura Benét, Edwin Arlington Robinson, Elinor Wylie, Glenway Wescott, and William Carlos Williams. Most of the time Kay remained silent, shyly listening, happy simply to be there. Of all the writers she met at *Broom*, she was most impressed with William Carlos Williams, for, she said, "his modesty, his simplicity, his generosity." A flirtatious man with a reputation for seducing young women, despite his being married to Florence, or "Floss," Williams took a liking to eager, intelligent young Kay Boyle, inviting her and Richard to visit him in Rutherford, New Jersey, where, chivalrously, he complimented Kay on her blue challis dress with the little red roses printed all over it.

Among the American writers who refused to attend Lola's teas because her left-wing politics repelled him was one Robert McAlmon, who with Williams had started a magazine of his own called *Contact*. Lola in turn dismissed McAlmon as a poet, arguing that he drank too much. Kay read McAlmon's work in *Poetry* and liked it. But it was the man who appealed to her romantic imagination. Lola had described McAlmon as "wild and daring and as hard as nails." McAlmon wore one turquoise earring, which matched his ice-blue eyes. Not only a poet, he had been a cowboy, and an aviator in the war. Kay regretted that he would not attend Lola's parties. (Indeed, in his novel *Post-Adolescence*, McAlmon satirized Lola Ridge's New York evenings. Lola appears as Dora, a woman who "evangelizes" with her verse, "spouting with a super trance look in her eyes about the perspiring moon or the hot belly of that illegitimate child of industrialism, the city." McAlmon wrote that what Dora needed was "a few good meals," except that "she'd still be pathetic." As for her politics, she was only "pretending to be revolutionary.")

Ridge was opinionated and strong-willed. She resigned from *Broom* ostensibly in protest against Gertrude Stein's being included in an issue to be devoted to American writers, sending off a telegram to Loeb: "Resign on inclusion of Gertrude Stein in American number." "Gertrude Stein has only an occasional gleam," Ridge insisted to a skeptical Loeb, "it is mostly blah! blah!" Ridge was adamant, her prejudice perhaps political, perhaps feminist, perhaps solely literary. "In a few years," Ridge was certain, "her work will be on the rubbish heap with the rest of the literary tinsel that has fluttered its little day and grown too shabby even for the columns of the daily." *Broom* was to print new writers, discover new talent, Ridge insisted. In fact, her resignation as Loeb's American editor had as much to do with Loeb's reluctance to grant her the autonomy he had promised, editorial control over which American writers were to be included in *Broom*.

For a while things seemed to be patched up between Lola and Loeb, and she threw a party for him in the two basement rooms when he came to New York. "Eyes shining above her scimitar nose," Loeb wrote of the occasion, "Kay Boyle helped Lola make the guests welcome." Loeb was surprised when Kay Boyle submitted "some excellent verse" to be included in *Broom*. He had thought of her only as "a businesswoman." Indeed, two more poems by Kay Boyle made their way into print in January of 1923, "Old Burden" in *Forum* and "Morning" in *Broom* itself, its having been submitted to Loeb with a handwritten endorsement by Lola Ridge. "Kay Boyle, young, unprinted," Lola scrawled, "her poetry reveals much promise." "I am afraid / That I am loving things with pain," the poet cries out in "Morning." And still she was just approaching her twenty-first birthday. Kay Boyle's two exquisite lyrics mark the close of her apprenticeship, and a triumph for which Katherine Evans Boyle had so long yearned.

Kay stayed on at *Broom* after Lola's departure, writing to thank her for "that comradeship which has brought me to the many realizations—or rather the confirmation of my individual convictions." Although Kay Boyle had admired Gertrude Stein's writing for years, she wrote Lola consolingly that she shared with her the ideal of a magazine which would "truly be the articulation of youth," indicating that she supported her rejection of Gertrude Stein for the American number. It was far more important to ingratiate herself with Ridge than to defend Gertrude Stein. Kay told Lola her dream was that the two of them might start a magazine of their own "in the spirit of the conscientious objector, the Irish nationalist, the students of Germany, the Indian tribes," all movements in which youth had set itself against "the dimmed false sentiment of age."

Kay Boyle's own last days on *Broom* were frustrating. When she learned that Simon Guggenheim had written to Loeb on behalf of the uncles, withdrawing their financial support, Kay cabled Loeb that she and Lola would like to take over the magazine. Loeb seemed to have agreed, only to change his mind. Kay worked on into March without pay. Ever the mistress of detail, competent to the end, she informed Loeb that he could legally mail the March *Broom* directly from Germany as "printed matter." She sent him the names of the American bookdealers selling *Broom*, with whom he should now deal directly. Kay also arranged with *The Dial* to take over the *Broom* subscribers list.

Kay was bitter, believing that the demise of this magazine of the avant-garde was unnecessary. "I am sorry you felt you had to let *Broom* die," Kay wrote Loeb. "This assisting at the burial of a yet living thing is not one of the happiest things in the world."

Then young Kay Boyle was granted her first lesson in the duplicities of literary politics. Suddenly Loeb informed her that the New York office was not to be closed after all. Expatriate poet Matthew Josephson, who had settled in Berlin close to Loeb, was coming to New York to take over. Josephson was a proponent of the view that art should adapt itself to the tempo of the machine age, a view antithetical to that of the young Kay Boyle deeply under the influence of Lola Ridge. We ought, Josephson wrote in the November 1922 *Broom*, "to plunge hardily into that effervescent, revolving, cacophonous milieu . . . where the billposters enunciate their wisdom, the cinema transports us, the newspapers intone their gaudy jargon."

Kay had to race over to the *Dial* offices to retrieve the list of *Broom* subscribers. Luckily she found that the business manager, Samuel Craig, was nice about it. Then she had to write to all the dealers informing them that *Broom* would continue. "I am not entering any of the March shipments in the books on this side," Kay wrote Loeb coldly. "You will keep track of that over there and then whoever takes charge here can transfer the charges to this ledger. The books are all in perfect order so it will be a simple matter." Her tone was icy as she signed her letter, not "Kay," as she had been doing, but "Kay Boyle."

Matter-of-factly, she asked Loeb whether he planned to publish two poems she had submitted to *Broom*, "Portrait of a Poet" and "Prize Fight." "I'm rather hard up," she told him. However angry Kay Boyle was over Loeb's failure to keep his promises to Lola Ridge, she was not about to burn her bridges behind her. When Loeb wrote back that he did plan to use "Portrait of a Poet," Kay accepted his revisions, changing "his" to "the" in the first line and "expressions" to "completions."

Kay Boyle did not appear again in the pages of *Broom*. Her final communication from Loeb took the form of a note from Berlin on March 26, in which he thanked her for having continued to work all through March without pay. He praised Kay for the *Broom* ads he had discovered in some recent issues of *The Dial*, which were "splendid." Without referring either to Lola Ridge or to Matthew Josephson, who was coming with another expatriate writer, Malcolm Cowley, to take her place, Loeb sounded a final infuriating note: "I am ever so grateful to you."

Kay and Richard decided that spring to go to France for three or four months to visit his family in Brittany. When Kay became pregnant, she decided at once to have an abortion. Appearing before the Braults pregnant seemed deeply undesirable.

In 1923, of course, abortion was neither legal, safe, nor simple. Lola Ridge sent Kay to a Dr. Mary Halion, at whose hands Kay endured a series of half-hour treatments designed to result in a "miscarriage." Kay described the series of daily half hours as "torture," after each of which she expelled some of the offending fetal tissue. Then she would rush home and into bed until the next session. Not only cooking but eating became an ordeal. Each of these visits cost an exorbitant five dollars and it seemed for a while as if they would go on indefinitely. Lola Ridge paid Dr. Halion's fees.

Meanwhile William Carlos Williams had accepted two of Kay's poems for *Contact*. "The idea of contact simply means that when one writes they write about something," plain-talking McAlmon had declared when he named the magazine. Kay still had not met the man with the turquoise earring and the ice-blue eyes. But he was now publishing her.

Broke, Kay had to borrow two hundred and fifty dollars from Harold's estranged wife, Marjorie Conant Loeb, to pay for their journey to Europe. Kay would repay the debt, she said, by selling her novel, *The Book of Cincinnati*. The advance, Kay was certain, would also be enough to pay for their return passage home. This was to be a vacation, not exile and not expatriation.

On their way to the French line pier Kay and Richard stopped at Childs for pork sausages and pancakes with maple syrup. Still weak, Kay was in severe pain from her abortion. She also felt some trepidation at the prospect of meeting Richard Brault's parents. But she had made her choices. When she had married Richard Brault, according to the law then, Kay Boyle had automatically relinquished her American nationality. She had become solely a citizen of France.

They sailed on the SS *Suffren*. Eating well, sleeping well, Kay said she had begun to feel more like "the brave spirit" Katherine expected her to be. Happily she wrote letters daily, including one to Harold Loeb announcing her arrival in Europe. He would be a contact indispensable to her ambitions, the key to literary Paris, even as she prepared to meet the Braults in the provincial countryside. "I shall hope to see you for a moment then—to tell you how much I dislike Matthew Josephson," Kay wrote, preserving her independence even as she kept up with Loeb.

Already her marriage was far from idyllic. When Richard was not irritable, he became taciturn. Only when he drank wine did he become animated. Heavy, gloomy, and pessimistic, he was a stranger to gaiety, to the lightness of being. Nonetheless, from the start he was a kind, generous, and solicitous husband. When Kay remained in so much pain from the abortion that she couldn't sit on a hard chair, Brault managed to procure for her a choice sofa seat at dinner. On the *Suffren* he had their cabin changed to an outside one by paying an additional one hundred and fifty francs so that Kay could sit up in bed and read in a more pleasant environment. She read her Aunt Nina's going-away present, *The Judge* by

Rebecca West and *Women in Love*, which Kay haughtily pronounced lacking in the "certain strokes that are so completely Lawrence." Aunt Nina had criticized her poetry and had the temerity to disagree when Kay said that "there is NO time but YOUTH." Already Kay Boyle would brook no opposition. Now she was so angry that she was unable to write her aunt the required "dutifully profuse letter."

Touchy, opinionated, and haughty, Kay Boyle decided that her mother and Lola were her only allies. She and Lola were both "rebels" and people who "really live." The spiritual unit of her life was Katherine, Lola, and herself, with Richard Brault, like Howard Peterson Boyle before him, outside the circle. Indeed, Brault had been jealous of Kay's New York friends. Now he was delighted that "there'll be only each other to really care about for several months and it'll make us need each other so much more." Outside America, Brault hoped, they would grow closer, casting everyone else "outside the thing that makes our lives real."

Kay was lost in her own thoughts. Only the moonlight and the romantic atmosphere on board ship made her feel as if she "could embrace the entire Brault family." She feared that they would judge her, that they would not perceive her as she truly was, "an uncertain person who loves her mother more than life." So Kay Boyle alternated between self-doubt, shyness, and timidity and the formidable self-sufficiency, hauteur, and arrogance with which she had manipulated her passel of suitors in Cincinnati and admonished Harold Loeb for the fecklessness with which he managed *Broom*.

Toward the end of the journey, Kay began to bleed, and the ship's doctor ordered her to keep off her feet. Mere bleeding, however, did not prevent her from attending the *bal costumé* on the final evening on board. Kay wore one of Richard's suits and appeared as Alfred de Musset. Richard she pronounced "gorgeous" in a turban and girdle.

To meet the Braults, Kay decided to wear the blue challis dress with the little red roses so admired by William Carlos Williams. Packed in her trunk as well was a fur coat, but her wardrobe was limited. On June 5, the young couple stood on the deck of the *Suffren* as it made its way into the slip at Le Havre. On the quay stood five Braults: Papa and Maman, two of Richard's sisters, Charlotte and Marguerite, and a child Richard didn't recognize. Six years his senior, Charlotte was married to a rich man named Jean, who, alas, was crippled and walked with two canes.

"Any rain on the voyage?" twenty-year-old Marguerite called up to them.

"My God, I'd forgotten how much talk there will be about the weather," Richard moaned.

The three Brault women were all wearing grey suits, and hats. Hatless, Kay had only the strawberry-red chiffon scarf. At once it was clear that Kay's appearance was not acceptable. As they moved through customs, Maman told Kay a change of costume was in order. Did Kay have *un tailleur gris* somewhere among her luggage? Although they were driving to the

Brault home in Brittany in Charlotte's limousine, and no one would see her, Kay still must be dressed in a formal grey suit for travel. Kay could not speak French at all, despite a few childhood lessons. Meanwhile Richard attacked his family in her defense: "So if you don't have a grey suit, then you just don't take trips? . . . If a girl hasn't got a *dot*, she can forget about marriage, isn't that so? And now this farce about grey suits! I swear the whole society over here . . ."

Now Maman had joined the customs inspector who was pawing through Kay's trunk. There was a copy of *Sun-up* by Lola Ridge, first editions of T. S. Eliot, Ezra Pound, and William Carlos Williams, *The Brook Kerith* by George Moore, and a photograph of Katherine Evans Boyle tucked inside a catalogue from Stieglitz's "291." But there was no grey suit.

Soon the party began the two-day journey to Pleudihen on the Côtes du Nord *en famille* in the black chauffeur-driven limousine. Kay was squeezed into the back seat with Maman and Marguerite. "We'll have to get her a hat of some kind in Rouen," Maman whispered. "Otherwise it's impossible for her to go inside the cathedral with us." At Rouen in the square, Jean turned to his wife, Charlotte, and said, "It must have been about here that La Pucelle burned!" Kay winced. She had landed in the lap of the bourgeoisie, a nastier, less generous French version of Puss, from whose subservience to convention and obeisance to "respectability" she had fled.

Finally Maman bought her a preposterous white straw hat which didn't fit, but sat perched on the top of her head. Richard couldn't resist translating his father's negative remarks. "Ladies don't put paint on their mouths, and they don't wear earrings as big as cartwheels. On certain occasions ladies wear small diamonds or seed pearls in their ears. Tell her to take those white loops off and to wipe the red paint off her mouth." As Kay Boyle later remembered in *Being Geniuses Together*, at that moment she recalled the words of Glenway Wescott, who had told her at one of the *Broom* gatherings that the "great white hoops of [her] Woolworth earrings were worth coming from uptown down to East Ninth Street to cast an eye on." But the heady days of the literary life at *Broom* had ended for Kay Boyle. The next morning she appeared without either lipstick or earrings.

As soon as they arrived at the Brault home in Brittany, Kay took to her bed, pleading fatigue and nerves. Still she endured the effects of the abortion. Kay hung her photograph of her mother opposite her bed and worked on her novel, in which she portrayed Cincinnati as a "nest of reactionary stagnation."

The Braults did make an effort. They washed her underwear and stockings and carried up her breakfast tray. Every morning Maman stood in the garden and called up, "Good morning, Kay," so that Kay would hear English when she awakened and not be homesick. They were "dear and devoted," she wrote back home. At first it seemed their only sin was that they were "boring." Kay believed they would despise her if they knew what she was really thinking, so she dissembled. "They love me because I don't look, perhaps, like what I am," she concluded.

Most men succumbed to Kay Boyle's combination of feminine help- lessness and iron will, her elusiveness and her flattery, and Richard Brault's father was no exception. Soon he was preparing Kay's breakfast coffee by himself, beating an egg into the cup so that she might regain her strength, something he had never done for anyone in his life. In the evening he took Kay in to dinner on his arm, and when her rouge wore off, naively he told Richard he must take her up to bed because she was growing pale. At dinner one night she relaxed enough to talk politics, almost, she thought, making "a red" out of one of her sisters-in-law with talk of the injustices of the American government and the lies of the Associated Press. As French chauvinists, the Braults were entirely at home with Kay's belief that the American press was owned by England.

"I think I should be most awfully good-natured if I could spend my life in bed," Kay purred. "The situation is all primed for good production," she wrote Lola Ridge, "and I expect to write a lot." Menstruation time, however, produced nothing but white mucus, and considerable pain. Kay was examined by Richard's doctor brother, Pierre, who urged her to get away from the family as much as possible. Kay was to give herself warm douches every day, and a huge douche arrangement was bought so that she could cleanse herself every morning—lying down. "How it is to be done we don't yet know, as it would most certainly soak everything in bed," she wrote Katherine, confident that her mother eagerly awaited news of virtually every breath she took. Pierre, she reported, also prescribed a tonic to keep her bowels open and build her up. He had told her she would be much better once she had children, as if childbearing were a woman's sole function.

Pierre's implication that her purpose was to add children to the Brault clan at once made them antagonists. "He is the only one of the family who realizes the futility of the family," Kay concluded, "and yet we are op- posed." His advice she would turn into fiction in her satire of the Brault family, *Plagued by the Nightingale*, published in 1931. Kay herself was determined not to have children for years, and she was well schooled in the means of preventing conception. Literature was what motivated her, as the most important people of her time continued to publish her. In June "Shore" appeared in *Contact*. A passerby surprises a girl bathing. "I had lost the meaning of progression," he says. The image of beauty is its own justification.

Once the Braults stopped pampering her, however, Kay concluded that life in Brittany was narrow, stultifying, and alien. Everything about the Braults now irritated her, not least their unfailing morning ritual of flinging sheets and blankets onto the windowsill as if "to purify linen and

soul and flesh of whatever sinful memories lingered of the night before."
As soon as she was well enough, Kay had to carry her chamber pot down
two flights of stairs, a towel discreetly laid over it, and empty it into the
one toilet in the house. She and Richard had not been married under
French law, and this worried the Braults. But they did not insist that Kay
and Richard remarry because then the banns would have to be published
in St.-Malo and friends and neighbors would "raise their dogmatic eyebrows" at their having lived "in sin" up to this point. It was all in sharp
contrast even to the mildly progressive views held by Eva Evans, who had
been born in the middle of the nineteenth century, let alone to those of
the revolutionary Lola Ridge.

Kay spent all her time with Richard, even taking photographs of him,
just as Katherine had done of Howard. In the walled town of St.-Malo, Kay
left her clothes in a public bathing cabin only to emerge with a headful of
lice. Scandalized, Maman produced a comb and a bottle of turpentine,
warning Kay to keep her disgrace from Papa. His entire summer would be
ruined should he learn that his daughter-in-law had lice in her hair. "American lice," Maman called them.

A woman must be schooled in the domestic arts, and Kay was expected
to darn linen, make fresh mayonnaise, and milk the goat. Privacy was a
rarity and Papa strolled into the room while Kay was in bed with Richard,
ostensibly to close the windows. Every Sunday, Kay and Richard were
expected to attend High Mass in the village. Politics led to more bad feeling.
Richard fought bitterly with his father over the Dreyfus case. Kay, more
diplomatic, kept quiet this time. For her tact, Richard irritably rebuked
her. "You're a fine figure of a rebel!" he complained. "You get on damned
well with every one of them!"

"What time is it in New York now?" Kay would ask Richard longingly.
Penniless, they were trapped, as Richard failed to find a job among the
French, who were suspicious of his American degree. When Lola Ridge
offered to take up a collection to pay for their return passage to America,
Richard refused, unwilling to go back to work for Edison Electric. In
Plagued by the Nightingale, Richard is called Nicolas, a petulant, grumpy,
and weak man who blames his wife for their descent into the bourgeoisie.
"It's mostly your fault too that we're here," he accuses Bridget (Kay). "It
was your idea that we come to France . . . well, now it's up to you to get
us away."

"Darling, darling, I love you," Bridget tells Nicolas in this romantic
novel. "I am so happy to be alive with you that I could die with joy!" Her
excessive protestations tell the reader that the Brault marriage was already
in trouble.

On the August day when Kay contracted the lice, she had purchased
a novel on the station platform. It was short enough for her to read line by
line with her dictionary, as French continued to evade this most unsystem-

atic of students. "I am stumbling along slowly with this painful language," she had written in July to Nina Allender.

The novel was *Le Diable au Corps*, a first work by a young writer named Raymond Radiguet, and Kay found it spellbinding. Like herself, young Radiguet had been trapped among the French bourgeoisie. But he points a way out, the road to freedom from the narrow-minded complacency of the provincial French, as he discovers that sexual obsession leads directly to indifference to the object of one's desire. The boy hero is perversely pleased to discover that "nothing makes us less sentimental than passion." Youth lives by its own laws, Radiguet, Jean Cocteau's lover, preached to a Kay Boyle in need of just this encouragement, and these are perverse, unpredictable, subversive, and, inevitably, self-destructive. Chafing under the strictures of living among the Braults, Kay recognized in *The Devil in the Flesh* the truth by which she longed to live. She too wished to cast her lot with the instinctual, welcoming contradiction, as Marcel Duchamp had advised, as a badge of authenticity. She had married into the French bourgeoisie for which both she and Radiguet had considerable contempt; his declaration of the superiority of irrationality to reason was balm to her restless spirit.

In Radiguet's youthful defiance, Kay Boyle saw open wide the avenue to her own escape from a husband she had begun to view as "a separate entity." Evenings, she flirted now with one of Pierre's friends, a doctor named John, who would be the model for Luc in *Plagued by the Nightingale*. To John, Kay's amorous intentions were obvious. He told her flatly "he had had two cases of abortion in the last year, and wanted to avoid a third!"

Although she had obviously led the man on, Kay affected indignation. "The conceit of him," she sputtered, as she had been caught out in her own game, "he judged by my amorous glances and because I called him 'darling' occasionally." She managed to so ridicule the doctor that Richard even joined her in the joke and they both became "incapacitated with laughter." But it seems that Kay already felt something less than passion for her husband.

As Brault remained unemployed, the news from the family in America was less than encouraging. Aunt Madge was killed by an automobile in Cincinnati. Howard failed at one more business, and Katherine, now living in New York with Jo, considered rushing back to Cincinnati to help. "Poor defeated Dad," Kay wrote Lola Ridge, "who never recognized the adventure in life and will feel so keenly that he is fifty and looking for any kind of work to keep him and mother and my grandfather, and any number of clinging old aunts and uncles in their respective boarding houses." Kay had not altered in her dislike of the Boyles, of Dad, who was "drifting mercilessly," and of Puss, who was "wearing his so-needed philosophy completely thin." Kay wished she could help, but in 1923 she earned a total of twelve dollars from her writing. "Oh, I want a million dollars," she moaned helplessly.

But even in Brittany she had not lost contact with the literary world. Glenway Wescott wrote her that in Paris Robert McAlmon was publishing all the good books through his publishing house, Contact Editions. Wescott arranged for Kay to earn a little money by copy-editing the proofs for a long poem by Marianne Moore called "Marriage" being published in booklet form by Monroe Wheeler through his publishing venture "Manikin." The renewal of contact with people from her days at *Broom* served Kay as an elixir. Meanwhile, she compiled a list of potential subscribers and book-dealers for the magazine she still hoped to produce with Lola Ridge. Several times she wrote Ridge for Emanuel Carnevali's address so she could send him copies of *The Liberator* and *The Nation*, which Katherine was forwarding from America. Kay practiced her French, moving on from Radiguet to Apollinaire.

Through that long summer of 1923 Brault searched for employment. In August at St.-Malo, Kay met a Dr. Christian on the promenade and so charmed him that he developed "a most convenient deafness which prevented him from hearing anything Richard said." But this was no longer flirting for the sport. Kay bemoaned her fate. Kay lamented "the unequal chance of youth against pull and graft and capitalism." Playing along, Dr. Christian announced he had a contact in Switzerland who might help Richard. "All Brault need do is stick by you and let you run him and he's bound to come out all right," the good doctor said, perceiving how much more powerful was the wife than her whining husband.

Indeed, Kay felt well now and by August her menstruation was back to normal, "more flowing than before the 'miscarriage,' " she let Katherine know. Kay's medical innocence, however, was profound. Did Katherine believe that getting her feet wet before the return from Mont-St.-Michel, just two days before her period was due, held it back for two weeks? Kay wanted to know.

New York ever beckoned as Kay fantasized renting the old *Broom* office, scene of her triumphs, from Marjorie Loeb, now divorced from Harold and living there. But Richard Brault would participate in none of these dreams. Kay Boyle stayed on in Europe only for her husband's sake. "As long as we've thrown in our lot together on a basis of mutual sacrifice and understanding, sworn to hold together until the relationship holds no further inspiration, I feel that something else should be considered before we take a step toward New York," she wrote Jo, obviously struggling to believe it.

Paris, Kay insisted that August of 1923, held no appeal for her. "If it is a choice between Paris and a miserable salary—and New York," Kay declared, they would return to America. But Kay had a personal motive too for not yet going home. "You will love me so much the better and my capacity to love you will be infinitely widened," Kay promised the older sister whose love she doubted, whom she found it so difficult to love. She would come home only once she had triumphed as an artist and fulfilled Katherine's ambitions for her.

When she did go back, Kay now asserted, unconsciously demonstrating her intuition that she would not be loved merely for herself, but only for who she could become, her return would be "laden with brilliant paintings, portfolios of work," for she had not yet given up painting. She would be fluent in "at least two foreign languages." So it would happen, if not with paintings, then with stories, poems, and novels. But it would take her eighteen years.

4

Buttocks and Thighs

*Paris doesn't mean for me 'The Dôme' and the hot fierce
arguments across liquor . . .*

At thirty I'll be dead.

Richard Brault's sister Charlotte contributed three thousand francs
so that Kay and her brother could go to Paris. There, certainly, Richard
would be able to find a job.

"We will go away and be ourselves again," Kay said.

"Ourselves? Who are we? Who in the name of God ARE we? Answer
me that!" Richard snapped at his wife.

Unlike her irritable husband, Kay Boyle knew exactly who she was
and who she wanted to be, knew that in Paris she would find "surprisingly
many people . . . to see." At once she wrote to Harold Loeb asking for
the name of a cheap hotel. "Richard is to be job-hunting and I getting my
last look at civilization before we're off to the Congo or Central Africa,"
she wrote. Meanwhile, she viewed her own prospects in terms of New York,
still hoping to start a magazine with Lola Ridge. "I'm ready to work like
a dog," she wrote her mentor, "anything, *anything*, only there must be an
open wide tremendous magazine started."

Kay's Paris plan was to confront Harold Loeb and attack "the cheap
cheap cheap criticism of Jean Toomer, Matthew Josephson, Malcolm Cowley" appearing in *Broom* while keeping secret her and Lola's plan. The
Braults rode third-class to Paris. To save money, Kay pleaded she was
trainsick and couldn't possibly eat.

Clothes were a problem. With Paris in mind, a New York friend had
made her an ankle-length black silk dress, which was far too tight. Kay
added the strawberry-red chiffon scarf, the big earrings, and the lip rouge
forbidden at Chez Brault. The day after her arrival in Paris, Kay knocked
at Loeb's door. He and his mistress, Kitty Cannell, were asleep. Loeb

finally opened the door wearing a silk dressing gown. He was clearly annoyed, but he did invite Kay and Richard to tea.

Shyness was no obstacle as with "heat and bitterness" Kay Boyle told Harold Loeb exactly what she thought of the way he had handled the New York operation of *Broom*. Kay knew her career depended upon her asserting herself, and she did. Abjectly, Loeb apologized, denying he even had a role in Lola's being refused the opportunity to take over the magazine. Loeb told her he was surprised she and Lola had been willing to get out the March *Broom*. Challenging Lola Ridge's sincerity, he said he believed they "would not do another thing as long as his name was connected with it, so that was why Lola offered to buy his name off it."

No timid ingenue, Kay hotly declared that the issue was "much more grave" than whether Loeb's name was on *Broom*. It "was a question of making good the promises to subscribers in the quickest way we could."

"I should never have sent that first cable," Loeb apologized. "I never understood that you were willing to send out March *Broom*." Yet Kay had his letter thanking her for offering to work without a salary throughout March. When he invoked Josephson and Cowley as opposed to "sky-scraper primitives," Kay summoned the temerity to demand, "But *must* we be thrown into camps? Can't we stand without cliques?"

Whatever her quarrel with Loeb, Kay Boyle's ambition was never at rest and she had brought her poems with her. Loeb promised they would be published in the next New York number of *Broom*. But Kay was not appeased. Loeb should have been a traveling salesman, she decided. "One has no belief in him and yet . . . there is that appealing dependency in him that one simply responds to and sympathizes with beyond all else." Her judgment was that she liked Loeb "without having the slightest respect for him." As for his mistress, Kay decided that Kitty Cannell was not at all pretty.

Kay agreed to meet Loeb again at four o'clock one afternoon at the Café de la Paix. She wore the ill-fitting black silk dress and a broad-brimmed black hat she had unearthed in the Brault attic. To pass the time, she wandered around the Left Bank to the rue de l'Odéon and Shakespeare and Company, where she hoped to catch a glimpse of James Joyce. Should Richard find a job in Paris, she plotted, she would ask Sylvia Beach for a job.

Kay arrived at the Café de la Paix a half hour early, only to hover until Loeb arrived. She watched as he made his way across the crowded terrace to a table where a man in a grey suit sat drinking an aperitif. Suddenly Kay Boyle felt hopelessly inadequate, her timidity reasserting itself. She saw herself as thin as a rail, "smeared with make-up like a whore," in an absurd hat and a dress which might split up the seams at any moment. It took courage to whisper the name Harold Loeb and then to make her way to the table and accept a Pernod. The name of the man drinking the aperitif escaped her. But now she did notice his steel-blue eyes, and his handsome profile, which was not unlike John Barrymore's. Yet he was aloof, frightening, even as he directed acrimonious laughter toward the religious cultist and mystic Gurdjieff, seated a few tables away.

"God's got to be a good poet or a good composer before I'll genuflect," Robert McAlmon declared. In comparison, Kay thought, Loeb "had no more personality than a clean expensive blanket lying folded across the café chair." No doubt Loeb knew what McAlmon really thought of him, that "the *Broom* outfit (descending upon Paris) meant to be literary at all costs," but were in fact as naive as children. Suddenly, McAlmon fixed his ice-blue eyes on Kay Boyle. Abruptly, he demanded to know who she was and what she was. Kay could not manage to utter a single word in reply.

Returning to her cheap hotel, drunk on Pernod, Kay collapsed on the rayon chrome-yellow bedspread. She hated her life, hated the "wasted months at St.-Malo" which kept her from literary Paris. Most she hated being the outsider, a frightened child in an outlandish black dress bursting at the seams. Richard returned, jobless still. Obliquely, Kay tried to suggest that their marriage may have been a mistake. But all she could manage was "we must find our people and commit ourselves to them; we must cast aside all others" without delay. Time was short. Unable to tell her French husband directly that she wanted a life different from the one she shared with him, Kay rushed off into the night.

Still drunk, in tears, she found herself at the Bois de Boulogne, where she spent the night on a park bench. In the morning she was determined to go to Shakespeare and Company and ask for McAlmon's address. Then she would ask him for a job typing, taking dictation, and reading proofs for his Contact Editions. To pass the time, as Kay Boyle relived the scene years later in *Being Geniuses Together*, she bought a copy of George Moore's *The Lake* at a quayside stall along the Seine. She read the line: "There is a lake in every man's life, and he must ungird his loins for the crossing." Once more she was being urged to summon the courage to go forth in life. Once more she hesitated.

It was still too soon. When Kay returned to her hotel, she learned that Brault had gotten a job—in Le Havre as an engineer with the local electric company. They fell into each other's arms. Then they celebrated with a good dinner on the Boulevard des Capucines. Kay chose not to consider that they would be poor "as the French were poor, and the mere fact of this would define our meaning and our geographical place."

By October of 1923 Kay found herself in the ugly port city, condemned to a ground-floor two-room furnished apartment, dark and grimy, with neither electricity nor running water, a far cry from the stately households of her childhood. When Kay opened the kitchen cupboards, she discovered every dish was caked with rotting food. The stove was filthy. The toilet was a dirty bucketlike object in the courtyard which they had to share with two other families. In the bedroom they found a chamber pot encrusted with urine, which Kay began at once to scrape off with a knife. When she tossed into the sink a pan of water, fetched by Richard from a pump in the street, it reappeared on the floor: there wasn't even a pipe.

Baths had to be taken at a public bathhouse, where Kay brought the week's dirty underwear to wash in a stone sink. Then she hung it to dry in one of the rooms, where it dripped onto the cracked linoleum floor. When Richard's brother-in-law Jean's chauffeur arrived bearing fruits and vegetables from the Brault garden, the wet clothes dripped on his head, and Kay "burst into tears." The location of this abode was the "rue des Jardins."

"It's my fault we took this place," Kay blamed herself, even as she dubbed them "members of the proletariat." But Richard demurred and insisted, "No, it's mine." Richard's sister Charlotte died that autumn of complications of pregnancy, having been too Catholic to use contraception, although her health was delicate and she had been warned. Kay blamed her brother-in-law Pierre, whom she did not like, rather than Charlotte's husband, Jean. "If he could have unbent his ego" with an abortion, she believed, he might have saved his sister's life. (Kay would dramatize this incident in the best section of *Plagued by the Nightingale*.) Worse for Kay was that Charlotte had promised to help her and Richard with a large check; now she had died without a will.

Living under such primitive conditions in a damp harbor town where it rained every day, Kay fell ill. First came "chilblains." Her toes hurt; she couldn't sleep at night for the pain. A sore throat followed. Kind and attentive as ever, Richard heated water for her to wash in bed and cooked breakfast. One night he bicycled home from work with pink toenail polish and a brush and Kay painted her toes, a lifelong habit. In a filthy environment without hot water, blackheads popped out on her face and she scrubbed them hard with a nail brush twice a day until they were gone. The elegant young flirt of Cincinnati had been brought low indeed.

Housework took up so much time that little was left for writing. "You can't be free and yourself if you do your own housework," Kay learned. Under no circumstances, she told herself, must she become pregnant. "I just don't want any protruding personalities—no babies or anything like that," she wrote Katherine. In the absence of legal abortion, threatened by poverty, Kay lived in terror of pregnancy. Only her brash, haughty attitude saved her. "I know how to have my next miscarriage," she bitterly joked in another letter to Katherine. "Sunday, while spiking the roast for the rotisserie, I poked the handle of the rotating bar savagely into me and spurted anew my menstruation—later I was pulling the cork of a bottle, the bottle clasped between my legs, pulling and pulling, and I almost flooded the kitchen." When Jo in New York became pregnant, Kay advised her to "try something playful on this order."

Kay Boyle had grown up a spoiled young woman and now she petulantly compared her sister Jo with Charlotte, who had been generous to her and Richard. "Joan will never think of it," Kay complained to her mother, as if her sister owed it to her to help support them. Meanwhile, she regaled Katherine with details of how there were no canned soups, no ice, no meat, and she had to boil a "sea-spider" or eat mussels, which were sometimes poisonous because they had clung to the copper cables of a buoy.

When Kay and Richard couldn't afford to pay a twelve-franc gas bill, they fled, giving the landlady a false address. (Months later the woman spotted Kay in the street and pursued her for blocks until Kay ducked into the post office and escaped.) At one pension where she inquired about room and board, she was bitten on the thigh by a police dog.

At last the young Braults found a new home—one tiny room facing the sea, with electricity. But again there was no bath. They did eat in the adjacent restaurant, allowing Kay afternoons to write. At first she enjoyed the solitude of Le Havre. But by December she was plunged into loneliness. "How I *loathe* it without a companion-soul to talk with," she wrote Katherine. She had discovered she did not feel alive "unless I am in action." Still, Kay insisted she possessed resilience of character. She was proud that "no matter *what* has come, I've been able to meet it and sustain it." For hours she walked along the seawall, collecting driftwood on the beach, appalled as the French fishermen shot down sea gulls for sport. Everywhere there were stray cats, and on one of her walks she spied a man, as she put it in one of her long letters to Katherine, "masturbating" the strays, which "at first seemed most horrible to my limited nature." Never for long without a cat of her own, she adopted Felix, a female. Little boys followed her in the street because she was so different.

The marriage survived as Kay tried to take comfort in the goodness of her husband. "If it wasn't that Richard is Richard I should not be bearing it," she wrote Lola. "But he is so utterly right, so understanding and complete that I couldn't go on without him." She tried to persuade herself that her marriage didn't "limit anything," even as she knew it did. One Sunday after an outing in the countryside, and returning home muddy and soaked, they looked up "romanticism" in the dictionary. "It's what we appear to build our lives on, and it's probably no good to anyone. Maybe we ought to try something else for a change," Richard told Kay. The moment was sobering.

Still, companionably, they marketed together. Kay knitted Richard a sweater while he sat reading. Only occasionally did her discontent surface. One night, spitefully, she bit into a huge perfect apple she knew he wanted. As she related the incident, "the table crashed over and I broke a dish." But Richard Brault was an enthusiastic supporter of Kay Boyle's work. A letter she was writing to *The New Republic* he pronounced "wonderful."

Ever mindful of her ambition, she wrote so many letters that she couldn't afford the postage and had to wait for Richard's next paycheck to mail them. Loeb wrote her he had severed all relations with *Broom*, and she surmised this meant Matthew Josephson had refused to serialize Loeb's own novel. Now she expected Josephson to return the poetry she had submitted. When Lola sent her Carnevali's address, Kay mailed him all her old copies of *The Dial*, *The New Republic*, and *The Liberator*. Receiving no answer, Kay persisted in her effort to link herself with the literary life of her time. She wrote Carnevali again.

This time he replied, describing a visit from Robert McAlmon, who had promised both to pay for a year at a private sanitarium and to publish Carnevali's stories in his Contact Editions. Carnevali praised their mutual friend, Lola Ridge, as "one of the most beautiful signs we have of woman's emancipation." Of young Kay Boyle, Emanuel Carnevali had two questions: was she beautiful and of what was she proud in her ancestors?

No, I am not beautiful, Kay replied. She was "thin as a rake and had a broken nose." Of her ancestors, she said nothing. As Kay later put it, "It was difficult to set down the names of my ancestors and what they had accomplished, the reason being that I disliked the look pride gave the features of a man's or woman's face."

Kay knew now that literary success would come neither quickly nor easily. "I have lost a very peculiar sort of faith I had in circumstances," she wrote Lola Ridge, "and I have shed a final skin. And since the final skin has dropped, I feel that I am at last able to write."

She wrote a poem about Le Havre which she called "Harbour Song" and submitted it to every journal she could. A poem based on her *Book of Cincinnati* also went out, to be rejected by *The Nation* and *The Freeman*. "Portrait of a Poet," once destined for *Broom*, went to a twenties magazine called *Double Dealer*, publishing out of New Orleans and taking William Faulkner's work. *Double Dealer* turned it down with an infuriating "Let us see others." Kay began the novel *Plagued by the Nightingale*, its title suggested by Glenway Wescott from a poem by Marianne Moore.

"I am almost speaking real French now!" Kay suddenly discovered. "Oh, I'm so seething to the teeth with energy." Now she wished to return to America, the better to sell her work. On the strength of her "radical activities" in Cincinnati, "a specific and clear stroke of protest" about labor conditions, she applied for a grant to the left-wing Garland Fund, whose director was Roger Baldwin and its secretary Elizabeth Gurley Flynn, then an anarcho-syndicalist. Freda Kirchwey, later editor of *The Nation*, was on the board. Kay received a recommendation from Mary D. Brite of the Cincinnati branch of the American Civil Liberties Union, who remembered the Boyle car and its "willing driver," how they all "used to pile into that car to the breaking point," and how Kay "was so willing to put aside her own work at all hours." But the Garland Fund turned her down.

When Kay heard from Puss, who suggested she ought to be paid properly for work like copy-editing the proofs of Marianne Moore's "Marriage," Kay said she was glad she wasn't returning to America. "Puss is the actually *poor* one among us," she insisted. "It is difficult not to be unkind when one thinks of him . . . I am sorry, sorry, sorry but he smothers it all with his dreadful, dreadful, dreadful philosophy. His soft clinging dreadful philosophy." The slightest criticism provoked her invective. "Wouldn't I rather shiver and write what I want about life and the capitalistic system than have my remarkable 'earning power' amazing three continents?" she unburdened herself to Jo. "Understanding must come through actual suffering and so few people can actually suffer."

But Kay seemed incapable of imagining what others might feel. When Puss fell ill, she still refused to write to him. "I really want to write," she pleaded with her ally, Katherine, "my understanding is with them, but I have nothing to say."

At Christmas, Lola sent a check which Kay put away toward a future trip to America. Katherine sent Evelyn Scott's novel *Escapade* and Waldo Frank's *Holiday for Christmas*. One of those she met at Lola's parties, Frank had written Kay from Paris: "I wonder why you choose to winter in Le Havre," to which Kay replied, "Of course no one would choose to 'winter' in Le Havre any more than one would choose to do one's own washing." Of Evelyn Scott's writing, Kay professed herself to be enamored: "I love her."

Katherine also sent Kay her favorite author D. H. Lawrence's newly published *Studies in Classic American Literature*. She had begun to address her envelopes again to "Miss Kay Boyle," without Kay's having suggested it, so deeply were mother and daughter in harmony. With the dollar Katherine sent, Kay and Richard decided to buy two "good books," rather than the pint of champagne and quart of liquor they had considered. Katherine also included that most welcome of gifts, "two gorgeous bunches of paper." Tante sent five dollars, which would cover either a week of food or more than half the rent or a badly needed overcoat for Richard. They decided to pay the dentist and buy two pairs of shoes for Kay, oxfords for everyday wear and fur boots, new soles for Richard's shoes, and some coal.

William Carlos Williams wrote he would be passing through Le Havre on his way to Paris. He would have only an hour to visit with Kay on the dock. But certain she could enlist her feminine wiles to lure him for the entire day, she arranged for a fancy lunch. The boat docked on a cold Tuesday in January of 1924. Williams emerged wearing a grey tourist cap. His wife, Floss, appeared in a brown checked suit and a bell-shaped hat which almost covered her eyes. Kay proposed the lunch and a visit to their little room, where she had simulated a window with shards of colored glass. Kay pleaded her loneliness. She knew only her grocer, she told Williams, certain he was susceptible to her charms.

McAlmon was waiting for them in Paris, Williams told her. McAlmon is waiting, Floss repeated, so that Kay took an instant dislike to both Florence Williams and the steely-eyed McAlmon, blaming them both for Williams's refusal to stay the night in Le Havre. "Poor girl," Williams thought. She "would gladly have followed us." Devastated, Kay fell into despair, later insisting that she had learned her bitter lesson: "People of dignity are not to be dragged by the hair of their heads into the precincts of one's life," although many years later she was to attempt the same ploy with Samuel Beckett.

Kay Boyle turned twenty-two that February. In protest, perhaps, against wasting her life in damp Le Havre with Richard Brault, she lied about her age. "Tomorrow I shall be twenty-one," she wrote David Lawson, Lola's husband. At home, Katherine sold the Boyles' Oriental rugs to keep Dad and Puss alive. Finally Howard went into the business of brake liners. "I think you splendid in your resourcefulness and courage and wish that I were nearby to help you out," Kay wrote her father. She was happy, she insisted, "although isolated." Paris, where everyone knew she was bound, remained "in the far future." Meanwhile she remained mired in domesticity with Richard Brault. Felix gave birth to four kittens: two were offered homes; two Kay and Richard dropped into the ocean.

In April of 1924, as Kay and Richard planned to move, not to Paris, but to neighboring Harfleur, Kay Boyle announced for the first time her expatriation from America. "I do not want to come to New York," she now told Lola. America was bourgeois and capitalist. She had done well to escape from a culture grounded upon "the business of money-making, money-spending, money-saving." If she had her choice, Kay said, she would go to Paris and join Raymond Duncan's back-to-nature colony. There Isadora's brother presided over a commune where the acolytes wore togas and sandals, and made their own clothes and food, free of materialism and petty greed—or so Kay Boyle believed.

"He seems to me very fine," Kay enthused, "he isn't afraid of anything and his one law is beauty." Buried in Le Havre, Kay saw Raymond Duncan as "living a remarkable denial of this system" in those "pure and simple robes that he weaves and makes himself." His theater in Paris, she thought, was "wholly free from false tradition." Burdened as she was by grinding poverty and household chores, the idea of a commune seemed seductive, as Kay thought they all could go: Lola, Katherine, and even Lola's protégée Evelyn Scott. "We could live in sandals and smocks and be free to escape each other when bitter moods were upon us." As if Richard Brault had been obliterated from the planet, Kay spoke of a community of the women artists she admired, "subsidized" by "someone." Such a commune, of course, had to be in France, where one was "free." For Kay Boyle now subscribed to the expatriate cant that Europe represented freedom, and America, enslavement. What had begun as a vacation in Europe for Kay and Richard Brault was now "the assertion of a new faith and the beginning of a new tradition."

"I shall be free!" Kay added for good measure, somewhat prematurely.

In the late spring of 1924 Kay and Richard moved to a drafty stone house which had once been a monastery in a rural village across the harbor from Harfleur. The toilet this time was an outdoor privy with at least a wooden seat and a cement floor. There was also a garden with rabbit hutches and chicken coops, which Kay was expected to stock. Amid tears of frustration and much ripping out of her efforts, Kay made her own clothes, or wore ill-fitting hand-me-downs which hung on her rail-thin body. Much of her time went to working in the garden, planting turnips, potatoes, and cabbages, which she sold at a stall in *les halles*, traveling to market twice a week with a farmer who claimed most of her profits for the privilege of the ride and rental of the space.

Her neighbors, farm women, taught her how to cook and preserve green beans, salt away butter, and even "how to remove with my thumbnail the scab on the underside of an ailing chicken's tongue, so that it need not die of the pip." Dinner invariably meant soup, salad, soft-boiled eggs, and radishes. "I see my husband rarely," Kay reported, "he comes in for meals and then is swallowed up in the garden." For company she now had a dog named Charlot. Kay Boyle indeed had begun to think of herself as a Frenchwoman, even as her French remained heavily American-accented. "I don't think I ever want to see America again," she repeated. "Not for years." The disparity between how she lived and how she defined herself, as an artist, remained enormous.

It rained often, as at Le Havre, and it was cold. In June, afflicted with neuralgia and dysentery, Kay sat wrapped in sweaters day and night. If there was an intellectual life across the harbor at Harfleur, meetings and debates, the Braults were too isolated even to find out the schedules. "Once I wrote a book," Kay mourned at a low moment. Now she had "lost the spirit." Kay even professed to miss her sister. When Jo resigned from her job, Kay was encouraging, however. "I want you wholly free—as wholly as one can be—doing . . . things as they come to you," she wrote Jo. Katherine visited that summer of 1924, her trip supplemented by a gift of one hundred dollars from Lola Ridge.

Social life for Kay now consisted of time spent with friends of Richard's, notably a couple named Paul and Yvonne, who arrived on Bastille Day eve. The drunken evening began with Pernod, progressed to the point where Kay was unable to distinguish between Paul and Richard, and included Kay's sprinkling handfuls of hot mussels on her freshly waxed floor, only to fall into bed with Yvonne: "Yvonne's lovely long dark hair was unwound and covering us both as we lay clasped in each other's arms on mother's bed. Oh, dark, subtle, odorous hair. It was a cool dark curtain over my mind." The bisexual moment ended when Paul, who had collapsed prostrate on the floor clad only in Richard's peacock-blue wrapper, came over and kissed Kay deeply. This embrace in turn was interrupted as Richard emerged out of the darkness.

As for the French, Kay decided, as she surveyed the crowds on Bastille Day, relaxing in a café after the departure of Paul and Yvonne, they were "such hideous people, such vile voices, such lewd clothes." The beach was "swarming with unbeautiful bodies, [like] Annette Kellerman's hairy arm-pits and agitated Adams apples—I was sick." Kay decided that she and Richard "were the only attractive people this side of the Atlantic." Indeed, Kay Boyle later said that "in France, all those years in France, I never had any neighbors who became friends."

But if Kay complained that she was no longer writing, this was not true. She revised "Harbor Song," spelled in the American way, which combined prose and verse, and was a poem in paragraph form, consulting with Lola Ridge by mail, even over the excessive use of exclamation points. "I knew that because I felt it necessary to put them in here . . . there is something wholly wrong with the words," Kay shrewdly assessed her work. Katherine, who had made her an artist, Kay no longer took seriously; she had left her mother behind as she now saw their relation as "too personal, too super-personal, to make me feel that there is any unprejudiced belief in what I can do." "You," Kay wrote Lola Ridge, "whom I love stands alone in my life as the one person who has any depths of faith in me." But, as Kay sought confirmation from everyone, even Howard was sent a copy of "Harbor Song." "I don't understand it, but don't give me up yet," Howard Peterson Boyle replied, anxious to remain in contact with his daughter.

Kay Boyle's first major success as a writer came when Harriet Monroe at *Poetry* accepted "Harbor Song." There were, however, conditions. Kay must remove two sections: "Labor Horses," which depicted horses with eyes like wounds, "threads of blood" across their hoofs, and "Whore Street." These images of violence and sexuality were far too extreme for the staid Miss Monroe. In the line reading "I call you comrade, you who strip the wind, leaping deliriously to slap her naked buttocks," Kay was asked to remove the word "buttocks." Miss Monroe suggested that "shoulders" replace "buttocks." Miss Monroe would not "risk" either "Whore Street" or "buttocks." As for "Labor Horses," it was entirely too "outspoken" and also had to go.

Kay haughtily replied that from the moral standpoint she was wholly unable to judge. But from an aesthetic perspective "shoulders" was completely "wrong." Miss Monroe, in reply, suggested that "thighs" replace "buttocks." This was as far as she would go. Kay Boyle, needing desperately the acceptance of this, her first long poem, and also needing the money, chose not to reply to the "thighs" suggestion. She assumed, correctly, that Miss Monroe would interpret her silence as agreement that "thighs" replace "buttocks." When Kay sent Evelyn Scott "Harbor Song," she was gratified to be praised for one of the passages Harriet Monroe had censored.

With much trepidation, Kay sent her novel about her youth in Cincinnati, now called *The Imponderables*, to Lola for comments. "My people are not real," she feared. "I have fundamentally failed." Scott too received some chapters, only to write Lola Ridge that Kay was capable of "a sense

of definition" that "no other similar prose immediatist of her type does show
. . . if she'll only hold fast . . . why she'll be great." Scott believed Kay
was destined to be "one of the great artists of her generation," and admitted
she "had not expected her to be that good." To Kay herself, Scott wrote,
"You are, or you ought to be, our coming novelist—our very best." Bol-
stered by the faith in her of the established poet Lola Ridge and the younger
novelist Evelyn Scott, Kay typed the final draft of the Cincinnati novel,
calling it now *Process*.

Shrewdly, Kay surveyed what she considered her most immediate
female competition. Women writers were far inferior to men, she believed,
while "it was an actual pain in the heart when they failed to be what they
themselves had given their word that they would seek to be." Evelyn Scott's
Escapade, she decided, lacked vision. Katherine Mansfield's gaze was "too
constricted." Rebecca West at least did not "whimper." Only Lola Ridge
was safe from Kay Boyle's scorn of her female competitors. Mostly she put
as much distance as possible between herself and women writers, unless
the woman had sufficient influence to help her.

Jo did help by sending Kay and Richard money to go to Paris, where
Jo was now working drawing the models at couture openings. Through
Vogue, she had become friends with a woman named Pauline Pfeiffer.

"I'd love to introduce you to a young writer named Ernest Hemingway,"
Pauline said after she learned Kay was a writer too.

Hungry for connection with other writers, Kay was at once enthusiastic.
"Oh, I've read his first book," she gushed, referring to the collection of
short stories *In Our Time*, published by Robert McAlmon's Contact Editions. "I'm crazy about it." After Pauline departed, Jo remarked that Pauline
was Hemingway's lover, although she was also his wife Hadley's best friend.
But Hemingway was tired of living with Hadley in poverty, and Pauline
had a lot of money.

That summer Kay felt as if she had been stuck in the outskirts of Le
Havre "for infinity." A September visit to the Braults did nothing to lighten
her spirits. "I weep profusely every night after having been tranquil as an
angel all day," she wrote Katherine. Winter arrived, "cold and sunless."
By January, Kay was in bed with a raging fever, vomiting and wretched.
She learned of a rich patroness of the arts who had descended upon Paris;
"a strong labor woman" was how Kay cryptically described to Lola Ridge
this "lady in Paris who is veritably the sixth richest woman in America."
Kay sent her a copy of her novel about Cincinnati. But nothing came of
it.

When Kay thought of Paris now, it was as a place she would go by
herself, without Richard Brault. Her Paris would not be "the Paris of Harold
Loeb and the Cowleys." Nor, she insisted, was she interested in "new
contacts." However Evelyn Scott had praised her, Kay had no interest in
meeting "Evelyn Scott or anybody." Defensive now about having been
excluded from the literary feast as the twenties passed, Kay asserted that

the glamorous Paris of expatriate license was not necessary to her. "Paris doesn't mean for me 'The Dôme' and the hot fierce arguments across liquor—," she said hotly, "not Harold Loeb's Paris, nor Cowley's, nor Gorham Munson's!" Meanwhile, she began what would be a third novel. Its title was *March Minot*, its hero was homosexual, and it was set in Le Havre and Harfleur.

But Paris beckoned and in May it was Evelyn Scott who generously sent Kay and Richard enough money for a two-day visit. At last the two protégées of Lola Ridge would meet face to face. Kay decided at once that she did not like Scott, whom she found hectic, uncontrolled, and unfocused. "One was aware at every instant of the nervous complexities of Evelyn's marital, and sexual, and professional lives," Kay complained later. To Kay Boyle, always sensitive about her lack of a formal education, Evelyn seemed "desperately intellectual." Scott also made the mistake of telling Kay that she did not like Robert McAlmon. He was "alien and cold," she said, "remote, like a homosexual." Having met McAlmon only that once at the Café de la Paix, but having been romantically intrigued by him since New York, Kay at once took umbrage.

"No, that I don't believe," she said coldly.

"Well, I didn't believe it either," Evelyn replied. But how then was one to explain that "no fire ever struck between them" as it had with Bill Williams? Later, having no idea of how uncharitably Kay viewed her, Evelyn said she liked Kay Boyle, finding her "a sensitive, intelligent and talented girl." Yet some instinct led Scott to qualify her praise: "just how much of a rapport for friendship that would constitute I couldn't tell in those two days." To Lola, Kay sent a sanitized assessment of Evelyn Scott. "Evelyn is very fine," Kay wrote Lola. "I had not visualized her as simple and as untouched." In short, Kay neither trusted nor liked Evelyn Scott.

But in Scott's smoke-filled hotel room, Kay met Louise Theis, who with her husband, Otto, edited the English weekly *The Outlook*, which was publishing many Paris-based American expatriates. This was an important contact. With a further twenty-five-dollar contribution from Jo, Kay and Richard soon visited the Theises in London, where they lived in Norman Angell's flat in Temple Bar.

One night the Theises took their young friends to a party. Kay wore an evening dress of gold silk which she had sewn from an old portiere Katherine had sent. It was raining that evening, a soft English rain. On the way Kay broke her shoe and walked barefoot. But at the party a handsome man with blond hair and a ruddy complexion asked her to dance. Immediately he took his date home and returned. Would Kay like to go for a walk? He had the key to the private garden at the square. Flirtatious Kay Boyle did not hesitate for an instant. To keep her company, the handsome blond man removed his own shoes and the two disappeared together into the night, barefoot.

Alone in the rain in the garden they picked the flowers and tossed them joyously at each other. Climbing into the trees, they hung from the limbs, pitching more flowers as they sang what they remembered of arias from Mozart and Puccini. Then they sat down in the wet grass and talked all the night through.

Perhaps to this beautiful, sympathetic young woman with her misty, deep-set blue eyes who looked so piercingly into his own, who listened so sensitively, the handsome blond man unburdened himself. Perhaps he spoke of his own embarrassing shyness, although he didn't feel shy with her, and of how difficult it was for him to make friends, how he always had to be explained, apologized for, so that he was always more at ease with women than with men. Perhaps Vyvyan Holland told Kay Boyle how until the age of eighteen he did not know with what offense his father, Oscar Wilde, had been charged.

Indeed, perhaps thirty-eight-year-old Holland shared with twenty-two-year-old Kay Boyle during those hours they spent together what few visual memories he had of the "smiling giant, always exquisitely dressed, who crawled about the nursery floor with us and lived in an aura of cigarette smoke and eau de cologne." And perhaps out of his lifelong anguish, he spoke of his father's fine character, "his great humanity, his love of life and of his fellow men and his sympathy. He was the kindest and gentlest of men, and he hated to see anyone suffer." And, as the dawn came up, perhaps he even remembered how as a boy he had felt as if, had he himself died, no one "would shed a single tear, or, indeed, give [him] another thought." And yet, although his mother's family kept him in the dark, his father had been alive. "I was," Vyvyan Holland may have told Kay Boyle, "constantly in my father's thoughts, but, as I was given to understand that he was dead, I could not know about that."

At dawn, hand in hand, they made their way back to the house. Richard was furious, but there was nothing he could do. Back in Harfleur, Kay began a correspondence with Vyvyan Holland. They pressed flowers into their letters. Although they were never to meet again, the incident touched a need Kay Boyle had long repressed. That night in an English garden with Vyvyan Holland prefigured the end of the Brault marriage.

Increasingly now, Richard was irritable and Kay observed him ever more critically. He was a negative person who was quick enough to speak out loudly against government, against the use of force, against the Army, against capitalism. But it was all words. He was a *rouspéteur*, Kay concluded, one of those people who simply grumble all the time.

What kept Kay Boyle going now was her work, and praise from expected quarters. Emanuel Carnevali wrote to tell her "Harbor Song" was "the best I have read in years. You go a mile a minute, beating Villon and Rabelais on your impetuous way. Its sensuality blossoms forth like peonies in the sun, like some terrific tropical flowers. You, like Lola Ridge, are a crucible of great fires." At the dawn of 1925, Kay had also received a letter from Ernest Walsh, an American poet living in Europe, who had read her poems in *Broom*, in *Forum*, and in *Contact*. He was particularly impressed with "Harbor Song." Walsh wrote he was starting a new literary magazine himself, the first issue to be dedicated to Ezra Pound. Would Kay Boyle contribute some of her own work? At once Kay wrote back and sent Walsh some poems, an excerpt from *March Minot*, and a story. Their correspondence had begun. Its theme was art and literature. Soon Walsh sent Kay Boyle some of his own poetry.

Ernest Walsh accepted Kay's short story "Passeres' Paris," an arch, mannered mood piece about an American tourist in Paris, for his magazine, *This Quarter*, paying her immediately one hundred and twenty francs. He also decided to publish a revised version of "Harbor Song," to be called "Summer," restoring the sections Harriet Monroe had censored. "Whore Street," in which "breasts swing in slow delirious rhythm . . . a white arm lifted, odor from the pit staining the sagging mattress of the sea," would soon find its way into print. In "Summer" the "buttocks" are replaced by "the empty-caverned loins open parched mouths, gape wearily away." "Summer" closes on the dramatic "Whore Street" section, which includes such startling images as "bed, baring firm iron limbs, scars the approach of darkness," and "memory dangling hot tongues . . . behind his eyes the white ripe fruit, the wine that crouches at the core."

Thomas Seltzer, the New York publisher of Evelyn Scott's *Escapade*, had rejected *Process*, calling it "the hectic outburst of untrammeled youth." But it didn't matter. Kay Boyle knew she was now on her way.

Walsh was so taken with Kay's account of her correspondence with Harriet Monroe over "Harbor Song" and the "buttocks" and "thighs" that he wrote an open letter to Monroe in the second number of *This Quarter*, using her censorship of Kay Boyle's poem to differentiate his magazine from hers. "I notice you changed the word 'buttocks' in Kay Boyle's poem to 'thighs,'" he wrote. "Or perhaps she did to get accepted . . . it spoiled the poem. 'Thighs' is simply in bad taste and no amount of moral reasoning or sensitiveness can change that. . . ." Ernest Walsh had risen to the defense of the writer Kay Boyle before he ever met her, as Evelyn Scott had done before him.

That Autumn/Winter (1925) number of *This Quarter* also carried "Flight," the excerpt from *March Minot*. The delicate nature of a solitary homosexual artist in Le Havre is contrasted with the rough sexuality of the local seamen. The strong influence of D. H. Lawrence in Kay Boyle's early work was already apparent. Like Lawrence, Kay Boyle described feelings as palpable entities, as the man, a homosexual, puts to rest his female pupil's sexual longing: "his voice in firm and muscular retreat from her, flushing her cheeks and eyes." The same issue of *This Quarter* included cantos by Ezra Pound, an extract from Joyce's "Work in Progress," and Ernest Hemingway's "The Undefeated." The taste of Ernest Walsh was clearly impeccable.

"I feel I grow ten years older every year," Kay complained to Katherine as she faced still another season in Harfleur. In October, she broke a tooth and lacked the one hundred thirty francs to get it fixed. Another sore throat attacked her. Richard waited on her hand and foot, providing oysters which slid easily down her throat. In her isolation, Kay tried to remain intellectually alert. She spoke of supporting the Bolshevik experiment. "Russia is the eclectic creator of a pragmatic philosophy of economics . . . this applied communism is the natural growth and result of accumulated economic activity," she wrote Katherine, confident still that her mother would devour her every word uncritically.

To Louise Theis, she admitted how lonely she was. "You don't realize, Louise," Kay pleaded, "what it is to have no one, *no one*, to talk amusingly or merrily with all day long—nothing but the price of gigot and boudin blanc . . . and amiable Richard on whom to vent my impatience after seven." Kay counted on *The Outlook* buying a sonnet so she could get her fur coat out of hock. Self-pity stalked her. "At thirty I'll be dead," she proclaimed melodramatically.

But stimulated by Ernest Walsh's belief in her, Kay Boyle now wrote every day. In contradiction to her many laments, she professed herself even glad she didn't "know anyone within a thousand miles." She was looking for a New York agent who might take on her short stories, as diligently she kept up her correspondence with Lola, Evelyn, Glenway Wescott, and Carnevali, who now urged her to visit him in Italy, although she must "prepare herself to see a very sick man."

Then Kay fell ill again. Her health had deteriorated drastically in the dank, moist air, and she lost weight she could ill afford to lose. She coughed incessantly now and grew so weak that a local woman was enlisted to do the chores. "I am not myself, whatever myself may be," she wrote sadly to Katherine. Too tired to eat, she coughed. Subject to drenching night sweats, she could not sleep. Perpetually recurring fevers kept her from doing any writing. From childhood she had loved animals, and there was always a cat in her life. Now, annoyed by the yowling of her cat in heat, one of the farmers drowned it in a cesspool. Kay began to dream every night of the cat's final death struggle as it sank into the filthy bog. What could she do but write to Ernest Walsh, telling him she was too sick to work? She was giving up.

Richard Brault was neither exciting, talented, nor ambitious. Although by March of 1924 he had applied for an "efficiency job" with the electric company, which Kay hoped would be "much more interesting work for him," he was passed over. Brault loathed the work he did, which had involved his first going through a "working-man stage," wearing overalls and being confined to a part of the plant which was not even steam-heated and had dirt floors. He was appalled by his salary of three hundred fifty francs a month. Neither advancement nor his hoped-for transfer to Paris ever materialized.

Yet he was good to his wife. Now he did all the cooking. He cleaned the house, the rabbit hutches, and the chicken coops. He also continued to work his six-day week, pedaling in the rain to work every morning on his bicycle. When he returned in the evening, he put glass jars with flaming cotton in them on Kay's sore chest.

When Kay did not recover, Richard became alarmed. "Is there any place you think it would be good for you to go?" he asked her. The Braults sent money and told Kay to think about going south. Evelyn Scott invited her to Perpignan. "But into the intellectual and sexual turmoil of her life" Kay refused to venture. Being rescued by a woman did not appeal to Kay Boyle's imagination.

"I don't want to go ahead," Kay murmured helplessly. "I want to go back to where I was a long time ago!" Trapped by the daily drudgery of a provincial Frenchwoman's life, by an intellectually barren environment, by grueling isolation, and by a kind, well-meaning husband, Kay could only long like a child for the nurturing of her childhood. Chronically ill and weak, depleted of energy, she could no longer take solace in writing.

Twisting and turning, she slept fitfully, at odd angles. At Christmas, Richard and the neighbors tried to "spoil" her with boxes of candy, an "elaborately hideous perfume sprayer," and a bottle of "quelques fleurs." A big dinner was planned, but Kay could not rise from her bed. She felt a little better on New Year's Day, when Richard bought a quarter of a turkey and some snails. Nothing ever tasted so good to his malnourished, feverish wife.

Then, on January 2, 1926, a letter arrived from the South of France which would transform Kay Boyle's life forever.

5

The Man She Loved

*And I, who had preached fidelity and denounced betrayal,
accepted faithlessness as if it were the one thing I had
been waiting for.*

*She talked about him as the most incredible thing that
ever happened to her.*
FAITH GUDE

The letter was from "that angelic Ernest Walsh," a man Kay had
yet to meet. But already generous to Kay Boyle, not only was he publishing
her work, but he sent her a thousand-franc advance on the serialization of
Plagued by the Nightingale, even before paying the contributors to the
second number, swearing her to secrecy. Once he learned she was sick,
Walsh swiftly took charge, relieving Kay of the responsibility of the decisions he now told her she must make. She must not even type the remainder of *Plagued by the Nightingale*, because that would risk a serious
breakdown. And she must escape at once from the storm belt. He himself
had failed to go south to recover thirteen years before, "hence my present
condition," Walsh confided.

Tubercular himself, Ernest Walsh feared that Kay was suffering from
the same disease. Walsh then formulated a plan: Kay must visit the South
of France to recover, stopping in Paris on her way. There he had provided
for a free consultation with his own specialist, Dr. Ducasse. Then she was
to come to Grasse and stay at a pension near the Château Simon, the villa
he occupied with Ethel Moorhead, his patroness, the woman who was
financing *This Quarter* and taking care of him. Walsh promised to meet
Kay at the station either at Grasse or at Cannes. He had arranged everything.
Gracious, elegant in his manners, he reassured her that she would not be
imposing on them. It is dull and lonely for us, he told her. He and Ethel
had been too busy working on *This Quarter* to have made any friends.

Kay Boyle, accepting, was overwhelmed by Walsh's generosity. He
was, she decided, "the most humane person I've ever heard of." The
deprivations under which she had lived since October of 1924 when the
Braults moved to Le Havre had taken their toll on her health and on her

appearance. Every morning now as she rose in the cold to make the fire, she saw in the mirror a long, thin face and eyes "burning out of her head." She knew this wasn't "the way you get tuberculosis." But neither she nor anyone else knew what was wrong with her either.

For the journey, Kay rummaged among her clothes. Most were hand-me-downs. There were two knitted silk dresses which had belonged to one of Richard's aunts. There was the grey dress that had belonged to Jo, a black coat from someone else, and the old fur coat she had taken with her on the *Suffren*. But she had lost so much weight that nothing fit. "Everything hangs largely on me," Kay lamented. Dad and Puss had sent her five hundred francs for Christmas and with this money she had purchased a new suit for Richard. For herself, there was money remaining only for a few pairs of stockings, having her mother's umbrella re-covered and her typewriter repaired. All this she packed in a big trunk, most of which was taken up with her books and papers.

Sad at leaving Richard and her beloved dog Charlot, that ebullient personality, who was so fond of swimming in the cold northern sea, she persuaded herself that she would die should she remain at Harfleur. "I *hate* to leave R., nothing on earth but absolute physical inability to stay here would induce me to go off," she wrote her mother. She spoke, however, as if she were leaving for good, and not for the month, or six weeks, which was the plan. Indeed, even as she would not admit that she was escaping from a way of life no longer tenable, Kay cried on the train half the way to Paris. Or perhaps she cried because she knew she had decided to change her life and the decision was irrevocable.

As he had promised, Ernest Walsh was there waiting when Kay's train pulled into Grasse. Kay Boyle saw a man "tall and slender and ivory-skinned, with bold, dark, long-lashed eyes." His black eyebrows met "savagely" above his nose. He had an air of fragility about him too, "accentuated by his pallor and height," as Kay would describe him. But "his head was beautiful, drooping a little as if it were too heavy for his body." Walsh had a high brow, heavy dark hair, a gentle look in his eyes, and an air of gaiety. He wore grey flannel pants and brown suede shoes. A soft light-colored wool coat was thrown casually over his shoulders.

Standing beside him on the station platform was a woman in her forties, at least ten years his senior. She was dressed in a clan plaid suit and had short bobbed greying hair; on her nose was perched a pince-nez, giving her "an air of authority." She had a lean, stiff figure and a long nose, and what writer Edward Dahlberg would later call "an acrimonious mouth." This was Ethel Moorhead.

However illness had marred Kay Boyle's appearance, Ernest Walsh saw in Kay, soon to celebrate her twenty-fourth birthday, a beauty, a tall, slender woman with misty, heavily lidded blue eyes, black hair, and rosebud lips, her prominent irregular nose adding character to her face. Bone-thin now, she seemed fragile, vulnerable. Perhaps he had fallen in love with her before they ever met, for Ernest Walsh was as much a romantic as Kay Boyle.

In the combination of weakness and iron strength that formed so much of her appeal, Kay for a moment hesitated. Then she began to move forward. More than anything else she wanted to be courageous. Timidity would not serve her well here.

Almost as soon as he began to speak, Walsh told her he was carrying in his pocket a copy of Emanuel Carnevali's *A Hurried Man*, which Robert McAlmon had just published. He was writing a review, Walsh said. In his effort to help Kay Boyle overcome her shyness, he talked only of Carnevali.

"For heaven's sake, wait until the poor girl has caught her breath," Ethel Moorhead admonished him.

Born seven years before Kay in 1895, in Detroit, Ernest Walsh, like Kay Boyle on her father's side, was of Irish extraction. His father had been a tea and coffee merchant and he was raised on a plantation in Cuba which his father managed. He grew up to be a wild young man, impetuous, emotional, and given to dark moods. At seventeen he had contracted tuberculosis. Back in America, he assumed a devil-may-care life, ignoring his illness. He studied at Columbia University and managed a cafeteria. When World War I beckoned, he managed to enlist in the fledgling Air Corps despite his tuberculosis. At a Texas flight school, his plane crashed and one of his ribs penetrated a lung. From then on Walsh was to suffer from repeated hemorrhaging and he spent the next four years in and out of hospitals.

During his illness, Walsh began to write poetry. Harriet Monroe accepted four of his poems for the January 1922 number of *Poetry*. Released from the hospital as an "incurable consumptive," never having seen combat, although Kay Boyle was later to dramatize him otherwise, Walsh lived on a pension as a "totally disabled War Veteran." Soon people concluded that his suffering had left him "unbalanced," which meant extravagant. Walsh liked to check into hotels without being able to pay, then frantically tried to raise the money. In New York, he was held hostage at the Ambassador Hotel, where the cheapest room went for eight dollars a day. Harriet Monroe came to his rescue.

When he was twenty-seven, Walsh decided it was time for Paris. His doctors warned he would never return alive. But such advice this gay, spirited young man was not about to heed. It was March of 1922 and he was armed with an introduction to Ezra Pound from Harriet Monroe. Almost immediately he landed in the American hospital. Pound visited. Thinking Walsh "a little mad," Pound offered some instruction in poetry and wrote him a note of introduction to Brancusi. It was a not altogether inauspicious beginning.

Released from the hospital, Walsh checked in at the Claridge Hotel, not, of course, the elegant London hostelry, but a Paris establishment with its own cachet. The Veterans' Bureau did not know his address; his pension had not yet caught up with him. But that he was virtually penniless did not cramp his style. One day Ernest Hemingway ran into Walsh at Ezra Pound's studio. Walsh was accompanied by two women in long mink coats. They had all arrived in a chauffeured limousine straight from Claridge's. Hemingway saw a man "dark, intense, faultlessly Irish, poetic and clearly marked for death." But Hemingway at once liked Walsh and before long he was calling him, affectionately, "Ernesto della Walsha."

Soon enough the Claridge, in lieu of Walsh's unpaid bill, seized his luggage. Disaster seemed imminent. Then Walsh was rescued by a woman he met at the Claridge bar. His voice emerges in Kay Boyle's autobiographical 1932 novel, *Year Before Last:*

> *In Paris I bought five suits and a chamois cape and I lived at the Claridge like I had money, he said. I ate soup and bread and soup and bread in a café for a month . . . and sometimes the Claridge people got sorry and let me come and look at the four other suits they were keeping for me and the nice pigskin bags until I could pay the bill. And then Eve came along. . . .*

His rescuer, whom Kay Boyle would call Eve, was Ethel Moorhead, daughter of a general in the British Army, and a woman of means. Ethel was also a painter and a militant suffragette who had gone to prison for her beliefs, a strong-willed, formidable woman, as Kay Boyle describes her in *Year Before Last:*

> *. . . the woman who could go to prison for a thing, who could close her mouth to food and water, and who could bite the torture instruments by which they tried to feed hunger-strikers in British jails . . . when they let her out of prison she bought a red wig and burned British churches. . . .*

Ethel showed Walsh her paintings; he read her his poems. She paid his overdue hotel bill. It was July and Paris was stifling. They traveled from Switzerland to Algiers, to Capri until it became cold, from hotel to hotel, fleeing innkeepers who, fearing Walsh's consumption, were anything but welcoming. On these travels, Walsh wrote more poems, seventeen going off to Harriet Monroe. One or two were good, Walsh believed. Toward Moorhead, he was profoundly grateful: "My debt to her is too great to ever repay," he said. It was now 1923, the year of Kay Boyle's arrival in Europe.

Sometimes Walsh would hemorrhage and have to lie on his back for weeks. Then Ethel read to him aloud from Dickens, omitting the sad parts. When he was no longer well enough to travel, she transported him to her home in Edinburgh, where he lay in bed for one whole month, hemorrhaging. He went on a milk diet, drinking nine quarts of milk a day and eating no solid food. Nothing helped. But Harriet Monroe accepted ten more poems.

In Scotland, life was not easy between Walsh and Moorhead. He quarreled with her suffragette friends. Wild, expansive, affectionate, intense, and dashing, ill or not, he made his conquests, among them the nurse Ethel hired. Ethel yearned for him sexually, and was fiercely jealous of the women with whom he slept.

"It's bad for your health to be falling in love. The doctor warned you," she told him.

"She was a damned pretty girl, which is more than can be said about your feminist friends," Walsh retorted.

Having just accepted some of Walsh's poems, which he was now submitting to magazines other than *Poetry*, Ford Madox Ford's *Transatlantic Review* failed. Marianne Moore at *The Dial* rejected one of Walsh's poems which was written in the quasi Middle English he favored. Ironically, it was Mike Gold, the guardian of the proletcult, who accepted a group of Walsh's poems for *New Masses*.

But rejection did not daunt Ernest Walsh, who considered himself an original and a genius, as he later made clear in an essay called "What Is Literature?": "To be a genius the original mind requires . . . nerves and force. Pressure. Force and pressure . . . Behind the mind is all that a man has resisted from the day of his birth. This creates the pressure." In Paris, Ethel was approached to finance a successor to the *Transatlantic Review*, only for Walsh not to be invited to contribute his poetry. It didn't matter, because Walsh now dreamed of editing his own literary magazine, in which he would publish unknown poets and showcase his own work. Enthusiastically, Moorhead agreed at once to make his dream a reality.

Among the first stories Walsh published in *This Quarter* were Hemingway's "Big Two-Hearted River" and "The Undefeated," which had been rejected by *The Dial* as too "strong." Grateful for the thousand francs Moorhead paid for "Big Two-Hearted River," Hemingway shepherded the first issue through production in Paris. The hot-tempered Walsh became Hemingway's enemy when Hemingway pleaded that he couldn't both write and help edit the magazine, which involved endless trips to the printer. "I haven't written one single thing since I first started going down to Clarke's," Hemingway wrote Walsh apologetically in March of 1925. Walsh accused Hemingway of extortion when he recommended an American friend named Bill Smith to do the work for a thousand francs a month (Hemingway had done it for free). "Don't trust Hemingway," Walsh scrawled on a note which Ethel found among his papers after his death.

At the time all the hard feeling was on Walsh's side. About to sail for New York in February of 1926, Hemingway expressed his regret at being unable to visit Walsh and Moorhead at Grasse, and so Kay Boyle missed one more opportunity to meet him. When she arrived, it is likely Walsh vented his rage at Hemingway's ingratitude, probably accounting for her own lifelong dislike of him, a more plausible motive than her frequently repeated outrage that he had been having an affair with Hadley Hemingway's friend Pauline, and which was absurd given the free sexual life she was to lead. (Hemingway's revenge was to come years later in a scathing portrait of Ernest Walsh in *A Moveable Feast.*)

In 1925 Ethel Moorhead and Ernest Walsh visited Emanuel Carnevali in Bazzano, Italy. Walsh had brought cigarettes and a phonograph. He sat down by Carnevali's bed and wiped his brow with eau de cologne. The Italian poet, trembling with encephalitis, was overwhelmed by Walsh's generosity. "There is no death in either of us," Walsh told him. "Poets are the holy men, the principal worshippers at every religion, the prophets, the great soldiers . . . artists are the salt of the earth."

"Where there is beauty is no death," Walsh told Carnevali. To Carnevali, it seemed the American's pale face was glowing and "suffused with poetry," and he seemed a man who loved life, a man full of joy. Inspired by the encounter, Walsh went on to write a homage to Carnevali which he published in *This Quarter*: "I felt he had become ill not because he was weak but because he was strong. I never felt death in him." So Walsh and Kay Boyle were linked by their both having been drawn close to Carnevali, even before they met.

For 1926 Moorhead and Walsh leased the Château Simon and here Kay Boyle arrived, settling in a cheap pension within walking distance. She had money enough only for a six-week stay. Dinner awaited at the château on Kay's first night in Grasse. Amid wine and good talk, Walsh was neither solemn nor pretentious. Every ten minutes, the second-floor toilet flushed of its own volition. Full of gaiety, Walsh got up each time and danced a little jig to the music of the flushing toilet. Kay mentioned the figure of St. Michael on the spire of Mont-St.-Michel, which had been struck by lightning thirteen times.

"That's me!" Walsh cried, still dancing.

He read poetry out loud, McAlmon, Joyce, Carnevali. He read a letter from Hemingway. It was clear from his talk that he had known his share of women, among them Hildegaard Flanner, the sister of writer Janet Flanner (Janet had settled in Paris in 1922 and that year, 1926, would publish her novel *The Cubical City*).

"Fidelity!" Ethel Moorhead snorted. "That's one thing you never knew anything about!"

Mornings, Kay worked on *Plagued by the Nightingale* at her pension. Still unsure of whether she had tuberculosis, she awaited Dr. Ducasse's report from Paris. Her letters to Richard Brault were passionate protestations of her devotion. "I *wish* you were here, I adore you, I love you," she wrote her husband, "I was so happy to have your letter, my darling. I think of you every minute. Tears came to my eyes when I thought of you as I read." Kay pictured herself eating a lonely lunch at a café, consuming by herself a bottle of "*vin du pays.*" But with Walsh and Moorhead, Kay feasted on American food for the first time since she left home: shredded wheat, Heinz baked beans, and tomato soup.

Almost immediately Kay was caught up in a life with Walsh, whom his friends called Michael, and Ethel. They talked of going to Italy, where Kay could meet Carnevali and Ezra Pound. As victims of a common disease, it seemed, Kay and Ernest Walsh shared cures and regimens of cod-liver oil, pills, and other "poisons," as Kay put it. To the family back home, Kay reported that Walsh and Moorhead were "charming people," who "treat me like a very little Katherine." Mindful of the puritanical attitudes of Katherine no less than of Puss, Kay identified Moorhead as Walsh's "aunt."

One morning there was a knock on Kay's pension room door. She was sitting up in bed over her *café au lait* as Walsh entered, his light-colored overcoat draped over his shoulders. Ethel's moved out, Walsh announced. She saw what was happening to me, and perhaps to you. I don't know how you'd feel about taking me on. Kay Boyle chronicled the moment in the novel *Year Before Last*. Richard is Dilly, Walsh is Martin, and she is called Hannah:

> *Yes, you were nice as Dilly's wife, said Martin. Or you might do as mine. I'm not so sure about that. But she doesn't like you this way. I can't wait, I told her. Maybe I'll be dead to-morrow or the day after, I told her. And off she went with this idea.*
>
> *Did she call me a lot of pretty names? said Hannah.*
> *It doesn't matter if she did, he said.*

Kay Boyle at once embraced the risk. She followed her heart, casting her lot with the passionate, handsome, wildly romantic, doomed poet. She was asserting her womanhood for the first time; she was in love, and into this perfect union she would admit no barrier, legal, psychic, physical, or moral. In Le Havre, in Harfleur, she had been determined that there be no babies. If at first in France she had been suffering the complications of her New York abortion, subsequently she had seen to it that there would be no children, no obstacle to her work. Now Kay Boyle and Ernest Walsh made love without contraception, embracing the consequences in a commitment that was total and irrevocable.

So Kay Boyle at last shed the skin of her youth; so she lived the truths Radiguet had discovered in *The Devil in the Flesh*, as the emotions triumphed over logic, reason, and bourgeois morality. As Kay Boyle later remembered, at the moment she accepted Ernest Walsh, she "gave not a thought to what would become of Richard or whom Ethel would turn to now, for nothing mattered to me except Michael's beauty and his courage, and I wanted to pay homage to what he was for all my life."

To justify so unconventional a choice, Kay Boyle needed to elevate Ernest Walsh to a pantheon of heroes, as her mother had done with Alfred

Stieglitz. William Carlos Williams had been an inaccessible idol, Lola Ridge of the wrong sex. The worship of heroes was a feature of Kay Boyle's youth, as in these years before the ascendancy of fascism the notion of the poet as prophet, and the Nietzschean concept that some men were superior to others and so were not subject to the same laws, took root among Kay Boyle's set.

As Walsh saw himself as a genius, a poet-hero, so now he told Kay Boyle that her role in life was to be that of "homage-giver to the great." No feminist, he did not view her, as Lola Ridge and Evelyn Scott had done, as a potentially great artist herself to whom others would pay homage; that was a role he offered only to men. And Kay Boyle did not mind. She was no defender of the rights of her sex, despite the influence of Tante, unlike Evelyn Scott, who refused to believe in prophets and cast an ironic eyebrow upward at Kay Boyle's view that the "divine fire" belongs to only a few. What Walsh admired was Kay Boyle's soft womanliness, and in *Year Before Last* he calls Hannah "patient, quiet, possessed."

Moorhead had gone. But she remained nearby in Monte Carlo, where she frequented the casinos, reminding Walsh that all the money for *This Quarter* came from her. Periodically she threatened to withdraw her support. Often she tried to awaken his guilt at having abandoned her. Walsh wrote a poem to Moorhead during these days called "Anger and Silence," in which he called her the "faithful" one and himself "unfaithful," as if they had been lovers. Acutely aware of her importance to him, and not ungrateful, he longed to bridge "this damnable space between you and me." But he had made his life with Kay Boyle and that was not negotiable.

Kay was ecstatic. She refused to believe that Walsh was dying, so vital, flamboyant, so full of life did he seem. She believed one day he would miraculously take a turn toward health, for he was an ardent lover, an intense and committed artist. As they both had sacrificed other people, so they were bound to each other. The one certainty of their lives became that they could not bear to be apart.

"A great fear gives courage," Ernest Walsh wrote in one of his best poems. Indeed, all of his finest work was done during his time with Kay Boyle. Most of these poems were testaments to their love for each other, a love heightened by daily intimations of mortality:

> *Fear and not love held us, but I*
> *Remember our fear as a thing of beauty*
> *And to know beauty is to know love.*

Walsh now called Kay Boyle his "wife." In her role as one who was to "pay homage," she took dictation on the typewriter, answered correspondence, and returned manuscripts, as if her time on *Broom* had been in preparation for this. She also did the shopping, cooking, and cleaning, tasks which now seemed not at all onerous, as they had in Le Havre and

Harfleur. And there were luxuries: a hot bath every day no less than the comfort of being in love. When she hung the laundry out to dry, Kay sang Michael's favorite songs. Many of the moments of their intimate time together are chronicled in *Year Before Last:*

> *We must make some promises to each other, he said. We must promise each other never to die and go away, he said. The taste of the soap and water was running into Hannah's mouth. Martin rubbed her face dry with a towel and stuck a point of it in to clean her ears. . . .*
> *Your neck, he said, is black.*

To Puss and Katherine both, Kay wrote that as soon as Brault was settled in a new job she would join him. When Richard was hired by the Michelin tire people, Kay reported that soon she would be moving to Clermont with him; they would be reunited by summer. Now she remained in the South only because her chest still tightened up and she coughed and spat on the first poor day. "When one is ill, solitude is not a virtue," Kay wrote disingenuously, as she tried to justify her behavior, as if being with Brault had been tantamount to being alone.

Love and guilt both softened her now and she wrote loving letters to her grandfather. "It is a long time that I have not heard from you," she said. "I do love your letters so much." However oppressive she had found her grandfather in her young womanhood, a glowingly happy Kay Boyle was now warm and gracious to the aging Puss. He forwarded an old letter he had sent her when she was a child in Mount Pocono, with a photograph. Kay replied she had discovered "a profound contentment which, without you, actually and psychically, could not have been." She reported she had read parts of his letter out loud to Michael, who exclaimed that Puss must be "another great Irishman like himself." Making an effort to cheer up the lonely old man, Kay told him Michael wished he could drop in on Puss of an evening to talk. In love, she had grown wiser, and kinder.

Kay also wrote so often to Richard Brault that Walsh became angry and jealous:

> *When are you going to give up letters and realize? he said suddenly. He threw his cigarette away in irritation.*
> *What part of your life or your vanity or what is it that you must be having letters every day from everywhere? he said. Can't you get over the past, or what is the matter with you that you can't leave your husband alone, for instance? Even if I have friends, there's nothing I can find to say every day in a letter to them.*

Kay did fret. That Brault was even "spasmodically" pining for her diminished her happiness somewhat. She insisted her heart wept for her dog Charlot, "to whom the end of the world has come." Jo planned a visit to Cannes and Kay wrote to the family about her dog ("my heart weeps for him"), hoping "Jo won't be too much the grand demoiselle to bring him with her."

Meanwhile Kay worked well, and Harriet Monroe continued to accept her poetry. She had abandoned writing the socially aware poems she had favored since her adolescence, and years later would speculate that she had been "living the dream of protest" in her unconventional life with Walsh, the "dream of Debs and McSwiney," the latter a labor leader she had known in Cincinnati. She and Walsh were outcasts, she committing adultery, he stigmatized by his illness. Their very lives were protest enough.

Kay Boyle's writing continued to attract attention as Edward J. O'Brien listed her in his "Honor Roll" of short story writers for the year 1925. Dutifully, Brault forwarded O'Brien's letter. News from Brault about a possible job in Madagascar produced a cold reaction from Kay's lover. "The climate is not good for people with tendencies like yours," he told her.

After a month in the South, Kay's health had improved. Her cough was gone and she had gained four pounds. But fresh colds, difficult to shake, still seized her, or so she wrote Puss: "I take to my bed, lose my voice and become unbearable." Living alone with Howard now in Cincinnati, isolated and lonely, Puss wrote Kay some of that sententious philosophizing she had always abhorred ("Truly time and space are like the mist in the morning and the sound of the wind") and sent her a check. Kay accepted the money. Walsh and Miss Moorhead, she wrote her ever-generous grandfather, were providing her with free room and board, so that she would be able to remain in the South until the summer. But with his check, she would be able to pay for her own laundry and buy a new pair of shoes. Brault did not send her any money, nor did Kay ask for any.

By March of 1926, Kay was ready openly to justify her affair with Ernest Walsh. That she could be a victim of tuberculosis also made her want to squeeze every drop from life. Brault, of course, knew nothing. All that mattered to Kay now was how happy Ernest Walsh made her. "Martin," Hannah whispers in *Year Before Last*, "I am drunk with heaven." They adopted a kitten and named it Ezra. But when Walsh wrote Pound that he had fallen in love, an ungracious response followed: "Corresponse suspended herwith until without'er of (pssb. ?) yu cummup fer air."

No matter, the young couple talked of buying a house where the chickens would eat in the kitchen. They would weave their own linen; Kay had not forgotten Raymond Duncan's "back to nature" cult. Then the communal ideal seemed preposterous and they laughed at "such two wrecks of humanity getting back to the soil." Walsh insisted he had five years to live. To the lovers, that seemed an eternity.

At last Kay heard from Dr. Ducasse. She did not have tuberculosis after all. Deep scars from a childhood bout with whooping cough had weakened her lungs, rendering her susceptible to respiratory infections. But that was all. Romantically, Walsh invoked what even Kay Boyle called "slop" about the healing power of love. He insisted that since Kay had arrived, he had become "a bigger and better man."

Jo, as promised, now came to visit, accompanied by Pauline Pfeiffer. For a week prior to their arrival a letter every day had arrived for Pauline from Ernest Hemingway. He had written only to request that Pauline purchase perfume from Grasse and lingerie in Cannes as gifts for Hadley, Kay was told. The subterfuge irritated her, as the name Hemingway had to have annoyed Walsh. Pauline haughtily claimed she planned to convert Hemingway to Catholicism. To Walsh's annoyance, she spoke of the Church with what Kay interpreted as "unshaken moral certainty." Siding with Pauline in all the arguments which flared, Jo made it plain she did not like Ernest Walsh at all. Nor, despite Kay's pleas, had she brought the dog, Charlot. But when she departed, knowing Kay was penniless, and entirely dependent on Walsh, Jo left Kay one hundred francs.

Kay tried to help Walsh with *This Quarter* by inviting Alfred Stieglitz to contribute. Her letter is as embarrassing in its flattery as once Katherine's were: "You are what there is to beleive [sic] in," Kay gushed. "That I have accepted you fundamentally through mother's love and emotion makes you no less real to me." Kay wrote Stieglitz she felt about him the way she did about Lola Ridge and Georgia O'Keeffe, a new name for her. She also exalted the importance of Ernest Walsh: "you and he are going in the same direction—important in a fourth dimensional sense." Her statement both offers a preposterous comparison and is a lesson in the art of flattery. When she met Picabia and his wife, Gabrielle Buffet, Kay dropped Stieglitz's name. Afterward, airily and in her still faulty French she dismissed the Picabia residence as "rather too Arts Décoratif, and an atmosphere of prosperous complacency." But she had moved into the world of artists, one to which she had long aspired, one of which she had dreamed as she languished in Le Havre and Harfleur by the side of her irritable engineer husband.

Most of the time, Kay and Walsh were alone together. The life they shared is chronicled in Ernest Walsh's 1926 poems. Walsh describes himself as "a traveller abroad," a man who passes "through cities as a thief." His "wife" is "the most beautiful woman in our city and for that / matter / In all the cities of our exile." Yet despite Kay's perfection, he remains a man for whom domesticity is too constraining. He looks out the window "while my wife's thighs grow cooler and cooler." At last poor Kay "turns / Her face to the wall and falls asleep without me."

Kay, Walsh finds, is too possessive. "She wants to know my thoughts," he writes, depicting her as "peep[ing] under my eyelids." Yet she is blissfully content, peeling potatoes while Walsh is "always somewhere else." Then he forgives her: if she wants to know everything, it's "because she loves me and cannot be alone." Like the most conventional woman of her time, Kay Boyle in love was subservient, willing, dependent. Indeed, in her own version of their time together, Kay Boyle pictured herself as endlessly watching, admiring the man she loved:

But whenever he opened his lips to smile, a veil of understanding and beauty fell over his features; he lifted his proud face in pride and two black lanterns of wisdom sprang to light in his eyes.

Yet when Kay revealed a hint of her independent spirit, Walsh became frantic to know *her* thoughts: "what is there to be done with a woman who must be alone to / Feel and who being left alone is pleased with herself. . . ." The next line contains the title of the novel originally called *March Minot*: "Gentlemen, I address you privately."

In the poems, sharp eroticism reveals the high sensuality of their life together. Kay Boyle aroused great physical passion in her man. She puts on her nightdress singing, and laughs as she comes to bed. Each part of her body is a source of wonder to him: "She. Her. Hair in places. Breasts in places. Thighs soft." In the morning he stares at her in the mirror, so that she tries to hide her "pretty buttocks."

Largely forgotten, these fine love poems of Ernest Walsh deserve to be better known. Kay Boyle is so beloved that "the house is full of her in / Every corner." His love for her makes her so happy she smiles at the landlord and even has a good word for the man who delivers their coal. She is so much in love she wakes Walsh up to ask for a drink of water to keep him with her a few more moments. In the poems Kay Boyle is twenty-two, perhaps because she had lied to Walsh too about her age. But he loves everything about her, how she murmurs in her sleep "like the lake of Killarney," as their shared Irishness became one more link between them. Kay's physical beauty makes other men envy Walsh, she whose "breasts are as white as before the kitten came and / People bow to me in the streets with all the respect / due a husband." Their eroticism grows more fierce with increasing reminders of Walsh's mortality. He wishes he were a normal, healthy "jealous husband," rather than the "old fellow" his ill health has made him:

The way her breasts meet is hidden from me
By her lips asking my lips if I am here and
The flight of her thighs to her belly is
Too swift for my eye that lingers her love is too
Swift for a lover in love. . . .

Kay bragged to her sister about her "moral turpitude," as if it were a badge of honor, of sexual liberation. Then she had to admit she had "lied." Walsh was only the second man with whom Kay Boyle, a woman emerging from Victorian times, had slept. He was also the first she had truly loved.

By March 16, they were penniless. Walsh's pension check, their only source of income, had failed to arrive. Amid much laughter, they jumped into the car and rode out into the countryside, feasting on one hard-boiled egg, rice, and peanut butter. Walsh sets one of his poems on St. Patrick's Day, picturing Kay in her apron with the "big orange blocks" cleaning birds for dinner. Her face is pale because his child is "in her belly." In reality, Kay Boyle was not pregnant. So strong was Walsh's love, however, even as he was mortally ill, that he and Kay were obviously trying to have a child. If Kay Boyle was going to bear a child not her husband's, an unthinkable act for a respectable woman of her time, it was going to be a conscious and voluntary act, no accident.

Yet Walsh could not forget how much he owed Ethel Moorhead, and how unhappy the advent of his young lover had made her. Without Ethel, whom he loved for having given him his magazine, he felt himself "alone." He also desperately needed her financial help. Ezra, the cat, broke a huge Japanese vase and Kay and Ernest Walsh could not afford to replace it. They asked the Picabias for help, with no success. Meanwhile, a betrayed Moorhead sulked nearby. In April, Walsh decided to drive to Hyères to see her. His plan was to see her alone, only to be unable to bear to leave Kay behind. Both Kay and Ernest Walsh rendered the moment in their writing:

> But if you did come . . . I couldn't very well open the door of the car and say get out, move on, could I? I couldn't very well say if you wait long enough here on the roadside somebody else will come along and cherish you. You are easy to cherish. Nobody could pass you by.

In Walsh's account in his poem "Night Before Journey," he asks himself why "he is leaving his wife alone in the bed / though her breasts and buttocks are as good as any other." Yet he chooses to rise early for the journey to Ethel, "to one my wife has betrayed."

While Walsh spent three days with Moorhead, Kay remained in their hotel room, knitting, annoyed he was out in his "smoking" being wined and dined. When he returned, Walsh was silent. All Kay could learn was that Ethel had given him all the money she had in her possession. "I'm as unhappy as hell," Kay wrote Jo. As they were about to head for Grasse, their car broke down, adding an enormous garage bill to their other debts.

On the first of May, unable to pay the rent, Kay and Walsh got into the broken-down car and fled from Grasse. Now began their life "on the run," the title Kay Boyle gave to an excerpt from *Year Before Last* she was to publish as a short story in the June 1929 issue of *transition*. The isolated penniless couple began a doomed wandering up and down the South of France in search of a hotel which would accommodate the nighttime coughing of the obviously tubercular man. For a while they stayed at the Hôtel de France in Mougins, near where Picabia lived, since Walsh planned to include reproductions of his paintings in the next issue of *This Quarter*.

Increasingly irritable, Walsh sought compromise, a way to make peace with Moorhead, even if it meant Kay's leaving. Distressed by his obvious horror at the prospect of losing *This Quarter*, Kay decided to free him. She would go back to Brault; she could not be responsible for his losing the magazine. In the novel it is only an accidentally missed train, and Ethel's petulant capitulation after inadvertently witnessing their farewell embrace, which keeps them together. When the fictional Walsh urges her to go back to Brault and make him happy, Kay lifts her hand and strikes him under the mouth.

Late in May of 1926, Ernest Walsh suffered a severe hemorrhage which kept him in bed until the middle of June. The Hôtel de France would have them no longer, and they moved on to Annot, a hill town near Cannes. Here Kay settled down to help on *This Quarter*, writing to Lola that this was the magazine they had dreamed of, "the most exciting and authentic publication America has had since *Soil*." To these modernists, that they reached only a tiny audience, a "happy few," testified to their artistic virility. *Broom*'s paid subscribers had numbered only one thousand, and *This Quarter*'s had to be considerably less. "I think Michael is with Steiglitz [sic] and Carnevali and Robert McAlmon one of the great men of this America," Kay declared to Lola, as she requested the subscriptions lists of *The Dial* and *Broom* to bolster the circulation of *This Quarter*.

In June, Kay at last became pregnant. From the start she and Walsh imagined the child she carried as a boy. "Iffe I cude have a sonne I wude want his mother to / Be a beutiful happye ladye," Walsh wrote in his quasi Middle English. Men, boys, Kay also believed, were preferable to women and girls. To fulfill Katherine's ambition for her, now her own, Kay Boyle had to ally herself with men. So too, as if she were an Irish peasant woman needing sons to protect her in her old age, Kay Boyle wanted a male child.

One day in July, thin and pale, both of them hollow-eyed and mal-nourished, their clothes shabby, Kay and Ernest Walsh were sitting on the terrace of the Hôtel Grac in Annot when an eager, foppish young man tentatively approached their table.

"I have the first number of *This Quarter* in my room," he said. "I know every word of it by heart." Turning to Walsh, he told the ailing poet, "I recognize you from your photograph."

His name was Cedric Harris, although he published his poetry under the name Archibald Craig. He was in Annot to visit his cousin, Gladys Palmer, an heiress of the Palmer biscuit family; the Princess of Sarawak was a title she retained since she had been married to the brother of the British Rajah of that area of northern Borneo still under British protection. Craig joined Kay and Michael for a Pernod. Chattily he told them his cousin was George Meredith's goddaughter, and that she had known Oscar Wilde. "A delightful Monroe Wheelerish fairy," Kay thought, referring to her

Broom acquaintance, the printer and publisher Monroe Wheeler. By 1926 Wheeler was printing his friend Glenway Wescott's books, among others, from nearby Villefranche.

As bored and ambitious socialites then as now collected literary people, Gladys Palmer arranged for Kay and Walsh to have a room at the back of the hotel where his coughing wouldn't be heard. They found her spontaneous, kindly, rich, and generous. Conversationally, she was, of course, as Kay put it, "rather dull and commonplace." But Kay Boyle and Ernest Walsh were in desperate need of friends.

That July, with Kay pregnant, the couple decided they must settle with Richard Brault. Having been hired by Michelin tire in Clermont-Ferrand, Brault innocently wrote his wife that they would be eligible for a company house. He sent her the money to meet him for a day "to decide what we were going to do with our lives," promising to bring Charlot along. Kay remembered how he had tended her in her illness, bathed her face, fed her. But she loved another man now. As she described her final assessment of Richard Brault in *Year Before Last*, he had become too small a man for her, one with "no wild need for the sound of other men's might, or fame, or wonder":

> *She saw him with sorrow, a dark sallow man in his corduroy riding breeches . . . pedalling down the road away from her, smaller and smaller, with his shoulders humped in discontent and the small of his back drawn in with irritation. He hated the rain on his face and the mud on his heels four times a day.*

Brault had offered too circumscribed a life for the ambitious Kay Boyle. Any man she loved, she was now certain, must be a poet, a man with "wild" desires, even as she blamed herself for the cruelty of abandoning Brault, and saw herself as "a hard woman."

Early one morning, Walsh put Kay on the train, seeming to have acquiesced in the meeting. Then he drove along the narrow winding road, like a madman racing the train for fifteen minutes. Kay met Richard Brault at Digne, northwest of Cannes in the mountains, then a day's journey away. In separate rooms, they spent the night in a hotel. If Jo couldn't be bothered, Richard had the kindness to bring Charlot. But it did him no good. Kay asked for a divorce. Brault refused on the ground of the Catholicism of "Maman and Papa and the sisters." He had not, he said, told the family about Kay and Ernest Walsh.

"Maybe one day everything will change," Brault said.

Divorce laws in France decreed that one partner accuse the other of adultery, ensuring a scandal. But Kay had other concerns, her pregnancy and that Walsh might suffer another hemorrhage. She did not argue with Brault. "I'll go back with you, just to the station," he offered.

At a little mountain station shortly before Annot, a noisy entourage, among them the Princess of Sarawak, boarded the train and seized Kay's and Richard's bags. Walsh waited in his car until he saw Kay through the train window. Then he leapt up the steps of the railway car and dragged her to the door. The conductor pulled the alarm. The train whistle blew. To calm the conductor down, Walsh invited him and the engineer for a quick *pastis*. The champagne soon flowed. Then they all, including Richard, piled into the car and returned to Annot, stopping on the way for more champagne.

That night the Princess gave a dinner for her young poet cousin Archibald Craig. Kay was pleased that Richard had so amusing an evening on what would be the first night of his "vacation." He had brought with him a picture of Jo cut out of *Vogue* magazine. Jo looked very much fatter, Kay thought, jealous of the attention awarded her childhood rival, whom she had always believed was more beautiful than she. The Princess praised the wonderful quality of Jo's skin. No one was told that Richard was Kay's husband and he took a room by himself. During these July days a calm settled over the group. Brault and Walsh behaved cordially toward each other.

But the parties, and the stimulation, had taken their toll. In the middle of one night, Walsh awakened with a far more severe hemorrhage than the one he suffered in Mougins, although he could still administer his own injection. While everyone was told he had to remain in bed with a stomachache, Richard Brault went off to have the hemorrhage prescriptions filled, pretending they were for himself.

The next night, Walsh had another hemorrhage. For the first time he was too weak to give himself an injection, and so now Kay had to do it. "Good as a doctor," Walsh praised her. Kay sterilized the needles and kept the ice pack on his chest filled, watchful as he coughed up virtual tumblerfuls of blood. She was unable to stop the bleeding for four hours.

For the remainder of his stay, Richard waited on Walsh, allaying suspicion and cheering Kay up. Kay refused to leave her lover's bedside for a moment. Two days passed. Walsh seemed to be recovering. Then, one afternoon as Kay and Richard sat having tea while Walsh slept, the sick man suddenly sat up and began to bleed. Kay used the one remaining injection. Then, frantic over where to get more ice and more ampoules, Kay turned to her husband once more for help.

Richard raced out in search of a chauffeur who might drive him to Monte Carlo. There he was to buy several dozen ampoules, and deliver a letter to Ethel, urging her to come to Annot at once. Brault was gone the entire night, making self-sacrificing efforts Kay Boyle omitted from her chronicles of Ernest Walsh's illness, both *Year Before Last* and *Being Geniuses Together*. Only in 1974 was Kay Boyle ready to acknowledge how "solicitous" and "understanding" Richard Brault had been.

"He *Must* Be Perfect"

I'll never look at another man again.

Ethel Moorhead arrived at five that morning. Walsh was glad to see her. But when he didn't bleed again, Moorhead grew suspicious. Had she been summoned on a ruse? Kay quickly left for the villa of an American novelist of Australian origins named James Francis Dwyer, who wrote frequently for *The Saturday Evening Post* and *Redbook*, to get more ice. Then she would wait for the train from Nice, bearing their daily supply. Almost as soon as she was gone, Walsh became agitated. He was certain, he told Moorhead, that Dwyer had designs on Kay.

When Kay Boyle returned, it was to face Moorhead's jealous rage. But this time Kay screamed back at her so loudly that Ethel had no choice but to slam out of the room. Kay was beautiful and young. She was carrying Walsh's child. It was she who had been nursing him. Now she seized her advantage. The next morning, Walsh tried to reconcile the two women, both of whom he needed. You always somehow find excuses for her, Ethel complained. Then Ethel departed. And even now Kay wrote her mother that she planned to join Richard Brault in Clermont for the winter, something she had no intention of doing. Her pregnancy remained a secret.

When Ethel next visited, ostensibly to discuss the new number of *This Quarter*, Kay fled at once and spent the day with the Princess of Sarawak. Now Ethel told Ernest Walsh she was removing his name from the magazine, which she and Robert McAlmon would edit together without him. Then she demanded that Walsh give her all the manuscripts which had been submitted. Enraged, Walsh grabbed a carafe of water from his bedside table and flung it at Moorhead. The shattered fragments still littered the floor when late that night Kay returned. The sick man raged out of control, and it was Kay who had to bear the brunt of his anger.

As the days passed, Walsh's strength waned, and with the depletion of his vitality, his anger also dissipated. He hoped, he told Kay, that the three of them could live together harmoniously under one roof. In one of the most affecting passages of *Year Before Last*, Kay Boyle renders this moment of opposition between the lovers. Martin asks Hannah whether Eve could want her too, to which Hannah replies that "love is narrow as a coffin. It is not wide and warm . . . it casts everyone out. It is sharp and pointed, like a thorn." But Martin is not persuaded. "I believe that Eve can want us both," he insists.

The stress, the abrupt changes in their living conditions, poor diet, and lack of medical care took their toll on Kay's pregnancy. She began to experience a frightening vaginal discharge, which was not soft, but came in hardened lumps. The entire vaginal area had become inflamed. A doctor prescribed daily douches and vaginal suppositories. Her novel, however, was to focus not on her own poor health, but on the pathos of the failing Walsh hoping he might be a "good father."

At last the demon of Ernest Walsh's disease overtook him. Pregnant and ailing herself, young Kay Boyle had to summon every fragment of her energy to help him. Semi-delirious, he became paranoid, accusing Kay of rejecting him because she was repelled by his illness. No longer using ether, for which there was no time, Kay administered the injections without an anesthetic and as rapidly as she could. At night she slept on the hard wooden floor so that her movements on the bed would not "start the blood again spilling from his body." Finally she summoned Moorhead.

Even more terrible scenes ensued. *Year Before Last* has Moorhead calling Kay a whore, while Kay forces herself to reason that "a lady with a background could never be a whore." At one insane moment Moorhead confiscated Walsh's medicines to make him dependent on her. Meanwhile, if Kay remained out of his room for too long, Walsh grew frantic and began to sob bitterly, inciting Moorhead's jealousy all the more. You don't go mad when I'm out of the room, she accused him. Then she attacked Kay for having been too squeamish to give him a hypodermic needle.

From the middle of September into October, Kay Boyle presided over the sickbed of Ernest Walsh, arranging for oxygen to be sent up to Annot from Nice every day. Then the coughing stopped and he entered the final stage of his illness. That he was aware of what was happening to him made the moment even more horrifying: "a thread of blood ran suddenly from his mouth," she was to write. "I'm dying, he said."

Finally Kay and Ethel agreed that he should be moved from the hotel. When Walsh was carried out on a stretcher, he seemed so thin and shrunken as to be scarcely recognizable. Gladys Palmer and Archibald Craig stood watching as he was placed in the waiting ambulance. "I'll see you in Monte Carlo!" Walsh called, startling them because his voice was so strangely strong. Then the ambulance roared off to Moorhead's villa in Beausoleil,

Monte Carlo. In the ambulance, the oxygen tube was placed in his mouth once more. It was the eleventh day of October.

For five days Walsh continued to bleed, suffering two hemorrhages every day. No one could help him. That month the *Calendar of Modern Letters* published a section of Kay's novel-in-progress, *March Minot*, which she called "Collation," another mannered piece strongly influenced by D. H. Lawrence. But she was entirely focused on the sick man. Moorhead remained petulant, her emotions out of control. She dropped things, and knocked against Walsh's bed whenever she came near it, as if still to punish him for his defection to this other woman. Once she spilled some water down his neck. When the sick man chided her for being so clumsy, she became enraged.

Together, Kay and Ethel watched at Ernest Walsh's bedside. Each in her turn promised him that *This Quarter* would continue. They were at their vigil when he at last choked and died. Ethel then sat down and made sketches of the dead man's face.

Those torturous two weeks when Ernest Walsh, Kay Boyle, and Ethel Moorhead suffered together are not depicted in *Year Before Last*. Instead Kay closes her novel on Walsh in the ambulance, deliriously believing he is once more flying at aviation school, clinging to his last thread of life, as he would remain alive for her for more than a half century to come.

Ernest Walsh was buried on Saturday, October 16, 1926, in a Monaco cemetery facing the sea and the Prince's palace. He was thirty-one years old.

Kay told herself her life had ended. Eight days after the funeral, she wrote an elegy to the man she would always call the love of her life. "You have danced with your hard feet backward, as an Indian dances," she wrote in "For an American." The poem closes on a "Lament" spoken by his solitary "wife," pregnant, but utterly bereft of consolation:

> *"Here I sit quiet and blind in the sun*
> *With new leaves coming wet on the boughs in the light*
> *And in darkness and the dark sap singing. . . ."*

At four o'clock in the morning of the day of Ernest Walsh's death, Ethel Moorhead had asked Kay Boyle, "What will you do now, you poor forlorn girl?" Kay hoped to return to New York, where Katherine, Jo, and Lola Ridge might help her through the five remaining months of her pregnancy. If, with her customary bravado, at Harfleur she had announced her expatriation, Kay, no stranger to contradiction, now said she had no hesitation about leaving "this rotten France." She invited Ethel to join her in New York, where together the two would edit the third number of *This Quarter*, which was to be a memorial issue dedicated to Walsh and contain the first installment of Kay's short novel *Plagued by the Nightingale*. Ethel agreed, suggesting that Kay be named editor, a proposal Kay says she rejected. With Ethel now somewhat strapped for money, Kay planned to persuade the American consul that, as Walsh's widow, she was entitled to passage back home, as well as his monthly war pension of about two hundred dollars a month.

When Kay wrote Katherine of her plans, her mother's response came as a thunderbolt. Katherine went on and on now about the horrors of Ellis Island, which Kay would have to face as a French citizen. Kay must not return because she would have to endure the unpleasantries of immigration. Kay Boyle had no trouble deciphering this message. Katherine was refusing to accept a daughter pregnant out of wedlock, whose child could not even be given her legal husband's name because Kay was adamant about registering him as "Walsh."

For the first time in her life, Kay dropped completely out of touch with her mother. Instead, she wrote a defiant letter to Howard. "My kid will have his own family," she asserted. "Miss Moorhead who wasn't afraid to give me what she could ill-afford to give; Carnevali who is dying of paralysis in Italy; Lola Ridge who is ill in New York. There's the blood, and the tradition and the future of my kid." Summoning her full romantic powers, Kay spoke of her coming son as "a Christ." He would have three godfathers: Picabia, Carnevali, and the French doctor, Kent-Monnet, who had attended Ernest Walsh. The baby would be called Michael Kent. Moral support came from what should have been an expected quarter. A new woman herself, Evelyn Scott reminded Kay she was "a rare artist" and should be "damned glad of the kid . . . you're carrying a whole microcosm of Michael's universe."

But Kay was not "glad of the kid." Living at the mercy of Moorhead, she lapsed into self-pity, insisting that she didn't want a baby, but Michael "re-born." If she could have her lover back, she would gladly sacrifice the child, since "he was something to have gone on with and a child is sad because it is an ending of something beautiful even though it is the beginning of itself." Kay saw her baby as a bitter reminder of all she had lost.

Never one to remain idle for long, Kay threw herself into work on the third issue of *This Quarter*. For a "New York letter," she turned to Lola Ridge, since "no one in America has the energy and vision and power. Everyone busy being homosexualists or the other thing. Everyone else occupied with movements or sects." So in the late twenties Kay Boyle took her stand for modernism, rejecting the socialist realist aesthetic demanded by American critics close to the Communist Party. "I don't believe anything would make me feel like agreeing with Michael Gold," Kay valiantly declared. Her ambition to become the writer Kay Boyle intact, despite her break with her mother, Kay vowed to "do great things" once "this beastly birth is done with." Once she had achieved success, she would "thumb [her] nose at the Boyle family."

Literary success was not far off for Kay Boyle now. A few weeks after

Walsh's death, Kay heard from an obscure poet who had been writing the literary column of the Paris edition of the *Chicago Tribune*. His name was Eugene Jolas, and he was starting a magazine which, he told her, had something in common with *This Quarter*. It would be called *transition* and he was inviting Kay Boyle to contribute to the first number.

But Kay's gratification was spoiled by Ethel's rancor. Jolas, Ethel complained, should have written directly to her as Walsh's co-editor and not to a "fly-by-night . . . who had sought to usurp her place." One day Ethel virtually tore the knitting out of Kay's hands. "You don't have to walk down the street the way you do, d'ye hear me?" she sputtered. "There's absolutely no necessity, none, for you to stick your stomach out so everyone can see!"

Sexual jealousy fueled Moorhead's rage, Kay's pregnancy a constant reminder of what she had shared with Walsh. One day Ethel even entered the bathroom while Kay was in the tub. There she stood, studying the younger woman's breasts, thighs, and belly. "I'll never understand it," Moorhead said. "You're really not that beautiful, you're really not." When Picabia offered to do a portrait of Walsh for the magazine, even as he continued to befriend Kay, that rankled in Ethel's heart too.

Kay Boyle concentrated on surviving. She attempted to make her peace with the lonely older woman, accompanying her to the casino in Monaco, where Ethel taught her *trente et quarante* and roulette. She wrote to Brault, who obligingly shipped some of her furniture and rugs to Monte Carlo from Harfleur. So challenged, she willed herself not to succumb to the "abstract tradgedy [sic] in being without a husband, an income, or a future." She tried to borrow money from Marjorie Loeb and Lola Ridge; in haughty tones bred of fear and defensiveness she told her friends that such gifts would be "for the sake of literature and the future and history." Bits of money dribbled in. Kay now ate more than she ever had, and felt herself growing immense, even as the ugly vaginal discharge disturbingly continued.

At Christmas, Richard Brault visited Kay. He slept on the couch in the living room and brought Kay a phonograph with a record of the Charleston, and new clothes. Kay wept in gratitude. On Christmas Eve, Richard told her he had been appointed manager of the Michelin branch in Stoke-on-Trent in England. In Harfleur, he had been having an affair with a sweet woman named Mary, he confided. Noticing how much he was drinking, Kay urged that he marry Mary.

But Brault was still in love with Kay, and he invited her to join him in England as soon as the baby was born. They could lead separate lives, Brault promised. Kay hesitated. She told herself she detested the English, "the Righteous, the God's brightest spot, the Superior Mind." Still, she was pregnant and penniless. She was not ready to burn this bridge behind her.

After he returned to Harfleur, Brault began to send money every week for Kay and her unborn baby. "He approaches the divine," she acknowledged. But accepting his offer was problematic. "When a thing is done it is done," Kay knew. Returning his affection was out of the question. "I want never to forget that Michael was the greatest and most exciting person alive," Kay Boyle declared. If Brault remained in her life, it was because with him she would not be betraying her love for Ernest Walsh: "with Richard I can do this more simply than with anyone else."

At the New Year, not having heard from Katherine even at Christmas, and learning from Jo that she had been ill, Kay wrote to her mother. "I feel that I have lost you," she said sadly, "and it is a wound all the way down in me that we are so apart." At Monte Carlo, however, Kay affected a new persona, embodying both careless bravado and a nihilistic appetite for risk. She began by insisting that she planned to enjoy the pain of childbirth since it was "one experience I've not had." She was glad she didn't have the "dry regret" of not having given herself wholly to Ernest Walsh. She admired Carnevali for opening his heart to Walsh, having "given him everything at once," since had he not, she and Carnevali would not now share their love of the dead poet.

Kay Boyle had become a woman voracious for life's bounty. "First impressions," she decided, "are the only ones of any value." Having been through "a worse hell than anything that can ever happen to me," she would courageously plunge headlong into living, eschewing all consequences. "You should have eloped with your Italian," Kay lectured Katherine, suddenly reminding her mother of a missed opportunity for love, a solitary reference amid their many letters and Kay Boyle's later memoirs, "and left us to be Boyles."

There would be no regrets in her own life, not now and not ever. She had made Walsh happy, something, she believed, no one else had done. "All he wanted was to live with someone he loved and have a child," she now said. "And he did for me what no one can ever take away from me. It is there solid and sharp in me like love or pain but it is something better than these." As a restless "flaming youth" chafing at the restrictions of Puss's household, Kay Boyle had grown hard in Cincinnati. Now she grew harder. "I'll have a sharp hard edge," she wrote of herself during this period in *Year Before Last*.

Pregnant or not, Kay devoted herself to being glamorous. She borrowed a scarlet Chinese robe from Moorhead, blacked her eyelids, put on long jet earrings, tossed black jet over her hair, and went out on the town, no matter that her escort was only the Princess's cousin Archibald Craig, whom Kay called "the fairy who is all kinds of comfort." To men, she appeared to be beautiful, helpless, spirited, ambitious, and in need. Dr. Kent-Monnet invited her to luncheon, as did the American consul. Unaware that she was a married woman, Kent-Monnet then offered Kay Boyle "the home and devotion of a distinguished and elderly man." He praised her poetry for its "perfect euclidian harmony" and introduced her to his daughter, who was Kay's age. They drank "side-cars," lethal concoctions of brandy and triple sec. But this was one offer Kay could refuse.

Finally, exhausted by life with Ethel, Kay moved to the Clinique Ste.-Marguerite at Nice, registering as Mme. Walsh. Ignorant as ever of medical science, Kay had to be reassured that the baby could not inherit Walsh's disease. "He *must* be perfect," Kay said fiercely of her son. "What can I feed his son to give him too a taste of that fiery spirit?" she wrote Lola, viewing the baby still as the second coming of his father. The child had to be a boy, not, of course, because Kay knew that to be so, and not only because he would inhabit Ernest Walsh's spirit. A woman steeped in Victorian prejudice as much as she epitomized twenties bohemia, Kay Boyle believed then, and later, that only a male child could sufficiently express the force of her love. Women were the devalued sex; against this bigotry Kay Boyle never in her long life would protest.

Meanwhile, she set up her room, with books all around her, and on the walls Picabia's watercolors, including his portrait of Walsh. She tore out the photographs from Paul Rosenfeld's book *Port of New York* and hung them as well: Alfred Stieglitz along with John Marin, Marsden Hartley, Sherwood Anderson, and Georgia O'Keeffe. She had her own bidet, hot water, perfume, powder, eau de cologne, a pleasant nurse, and frequent callers, among them Picabia himself. Kay had to change her baby's name now. He would not be Michael Kent, but Michael Francis, for Picabia, who promised her the Picabia family cradle. No longer was she frightened or depressed. "I think the world is good to me," Kay Boyle decided that March of 1927.

Her routine was orderly. A morning douche was followed by milk and cake at a café. Then Kay walked down the Promenade des Anglais, where she joined Ethel and Archie, who were living temporarily at the Princess's apartment, overlooking the sea. Afternoons, they worked on *This Quarter*. At seven, Kay was back at the clinic for dinner and to write letters. "Do you realize that you are the most important man in America?" she now wrote Stieglitz. Lola she praised as "a signal to us," as opposed to Harriet Monroe and Marianne Moore, people of far less significance. To others, however, Kay scoffed at the "schemes and philosophies" of both Stieglitz and Ridge: "one can't accept labor as the torch or New York as the promised land," she said. But flattering Stieglitz was essential because she wanted him and O'Keeffe to help distribute a leaflet Archibald Craig had written about *This Quarter*, and even to solicit subscriptions. "You are a poet, you are a great believer," Kay shamelessly appealed to Stieglitz, "for the fourth number will you write something?" Name-dropping her way through the letter, she reported that Brancusi was on his way to carve the stone for Ernest Walsh's grave.

Stieglitz was also enlisted to be part of the family she was creating for her son. "To whom else could I be turning?" she appealed to the old

man she scarcely knew. "You are my family, you and Davy," she wrote
Lola Ridge, who sent a check. To Puss, however, Kay wrote that "one
cannot ask it of strangers—and to whom else could I turn now that I am
alone—but to you who have known so much of me?" She was coming home,
she told her grandfather, so he could know the great-grandson who would
be "a true Irishman." Only with Archibald Craig and Brault was Kay able
to "weep and be weak," to reveal her real feelings.

On the day before her son was to be born, Kay sat typing a story she
planned to dedicate to Puss. She wore a little pink-and-white jacket Jo had
made for her. Writing was her priority; that she knew. "He must be able
to speak and reason and discourse at once or I shall be bored to death
with him," she half joked. "And unless it be a perfect baby I shall turn
my face to the wall and die."

Even as the baby's head had "well descended," as she put it, Kay
walked down the Promenade des Anglais to mail her usual packet of letters
at the Place Grimaldi and then indulge in tea and a smoke. At one in the
morning she went into labor, making, she later bragged, "enough racket
to wake the town of Nice." Grandly she refused even "a whiff of chloroform."
Through Kay's seven hours of labor, Ethel Moorhead sat by her side, holding
her hand. At 8:20 the following morning, an eight-and-one-half-pound baby
appeared. As soon as Kay was stitched up, she summoned breakfast, while
Ethel rushed out to cable Katherine the news.

Alas, the baby, Kay said, was everything she "didn't want." It didn't
resemble Ernest Walsh with his flashing dark eyes and dark hair. This
child was blond and blue-eyed. Worse, it could not be named either Michael
Francis or Michael Kent or Michael anything, for it was—a girl! Perhaps
Frances, for Picabia, Kay mulled, trying to reconcile herself. Then together
with Ethel she chose Sharon for the rose of Sharon from the Song of Solomon.
"I like the sound of Sharon Walsh," Kay said. "It sounds as Irish as it
should—and then it has a real meaning." Five days later, Kay Boyle,
suffering from "beastly" hemorrhoids, was reclining on a chaise longue
correcting the proofs of *Plagued by the Nightingale.*

Legally, the baby was "Sharon Brault." Ethel took her down to the
Mairie de Nice and registered her as Ernest Walsh's legitimate child,
producing Walsh's passport and swearing that Kay and Walsh had been
legally married at her own family home in Edinburgh. In the anachronistic
French patriarchal manner, the child could be registered legally only as
her father's, not her mother's.

Picabia soon visited, bearing a blue silk-and-lace dress and bonnet.
"She's the image of Stieglitz!" he teased. Kay introduced Ethel as "Miss
Moorhead," only to be attacked as soon as Picabia was gone. "In Europe
every woman over twenty is a madame, not a mademoiselle!" she told Kay
angrily. At this, Kay burst into tears. Soon Kay learned Ethel had accused
her of spreading the tale that she was sole editor of *This Quarter.* With
Archie Craig, she giggled hysterically over imaginary advertisements: "*This*

Quarter—Ethel Moorhead 'sole' editor—accept no substitutes!" Craig and Kay now decided to edit an annual poetry anthology, in contrast to the "girl-girly off-moments of Harriet's crew or the mouthings of Eliot." They, however, would "discover our own great men."

But Ethel's erratic behavior, and Kay's total dependence on her, soon exacted their price. Baby Sharon, as if aware of the conflict swirling around her, fell ill, vomiting up her milk, succumbing to diarrhea, and crying incessantly. The nurses, trying to speak English, pronounced "baby" as "bobby," and so Sharon received the name by which she would be called all her life: Bobby. Kay returned home with Ethel because she had nowhere else to go.

She tried to sympathize with Ethel, who got "so little credit" for what she did. But she dreaded having always to explain herself "when there is nothing to explain." When Richard Brault told his mother baby Sharon was his child, according to Kay Boyle the Braults dispatched a friend to call on her to discover where the child had been baptized. Kay lied, making up the name of a church, only for the emissary to confront her with the discovery that there was no such place. Meanwhile, she kept up her writing, although Bobby was "a damned noisy affair." Carefully Kay examined the baby's nose to be certain Bobby had not inherited her high prominent beak. "Her nose seems small," she ventured. To Stieglitz, she wrote mournfully: "I did want a son."

In April, Kay's tenuous isolation with Moorhead was broken by a sudden three-day visit from—Robert McAlmon. Kay longed to talk with him alone, about Walsh and Carnevali, and Eugene Jolas's new magazine, *transition*. But as she had at the Café de la Paix, she "quailed before his icy gaze" and sat dumbly listening. She did ask him to help with her "living poetry" anthology. But McAlmon told her that once his rich wife, who wrote under the name Bryher, got her divorce decree, he would be penniless. Kay could only lament that she was always meeting people five years too late.

If Kay had indulged in romantic fantasies about Robert McAlmon from the time she first heard about him from Lola Ridge, only to be disillusioned at their first meeting, she liked him better now. Ernest Walsh had praised him extravagantly in his essay "What Is Literature?," calling McAlmon "the most honest and authentically American of our writers, and the only man writing who can seriously compete with Joseph Conrad and James Joyce." McAlmon, she knew, had befriended and published Carnevali, who, in turn, had praised McAlmon as "a youth, agile and attractive, passing by without taking his hat off to anybody." They were all bound, Kay and Walsh, McAlmon and Carnevali.

Now in Monte Carlo, Kay found McAlmon "honest and sensitive . . . the real thing." He drank endless bottles of gin. As always, he talked incessantly. But, Kay thought, his "hard, obdurate, stubborn and insensitive manner" did not conceal his being "keenly sensitized to the subtleties of truth." Sharon watched, mesmerized, as McAlmon waved his cigar. In her scorn, Ethel spoiled McAlmon's visit for Kay. And one evening she launched a full-scale attack.

"Ask her opinion on anything, and she simply doesn't know," Ethel said nastily. "Ask her what she as an American thinks of Negroes."

"I'm not interested in what she thinks of Negroes," said McAlmon.

"Very well, I'll ask her what she thinks of Negroes," Ethel persisted, with a smile which froze poor Kay's heart.

"I don't know—I don't know what I think of them!" Kay cried. "I only know I like them! I've always liked them!"

"You see," Ethel leered. "She likes Negroes! Isn't that kind of her? Isn't that really wonderful."

At another meal, Ethel advised McAlmon to take his leave lest Kay ruin a third man's life. Later she maliciously told McAlmon that Richard Brault was paying for Sharon's keep.

"So that," Ethel laughed cruelly, "should give you a hint of whose baby it is!"

Despite all this, Kay was cheered by McAlmon's visit. She proposed to Archie that they open the poetry anthology with McAlmon's "North American Continent." It was as if McAlmon's very presence, his "perfectly peeled eye," had given her new courage. Indeed, the day after his departure, she received a note from St.-Tropez. "You don't belong there," McAlmon told her. "You haven't asked me, but I would say get out." Should Kay need money to engineer her escape from Ethel, she should write to him in care of Sylvia Beach at Shakespeare and Company. Shortly thereafter Ethel had visitors from Scotland, who warned her they feared Moorhead might "inadvertently" harm the baby. Kay must not leave Ethel alone with Sharon since she was capable even of dropping the baby out of the window "in error." Ethel's "mad" and "unreasonable" suspicions gave credibility to the threat.

Kay idly wished she could go "off somewhere by myself with Sharon, beginning over again." But she was penniless and jobless, without the academic degrees employers were likely to demand, and saddled with an illegitimate child. Only her own "arrogant pride," she knew, prevented her from facing the reality that her sole option was the protection and financial support of a man. Richard Brault was her lifeline and she seized it. In the middle of one more hot argument with Ethel, she rushed out of the apartment, telephoned Richard, then wired McAlmon for fifty dollars to get herself and the baby to England. Within twenty-four hours the money had been deposited in the bank at Monte Carlo.

"I'll spend the rest of my life paying him back," Kay vowed. It was a promise she kept.

Kay set her departure for the last week of May 1927. Overflowing with ambition, she hoped that with her "obstinacy to believe in my own importance," that obstinacy Katherine had so encouraged, she would find time to write. She was to be a housewife, and she feared that role, writing Evelyn Scott that housework should be blotted from existence. "You and Lola and me doing that is a sin against our own holy ghosts," she asserted. But she was exhausted, and all she desired for the moment was "to be neither right nor wrong, but simply to be." So anxious was she to escape from Moorhead that she made no arrangement to send on her furniture and rugs.

Ethel accompanied her to the train station in Monaco.

"Tell the baby's father that its resemblance to him is striking," Ethel called out maliciously.

The trip was an ordeal. In Paris, carrying baby Sharon and her cat Tout Petit, Kay was met by Richard's sister Marguerite, the Braults once more, as Richard saw to it that Kay would not have to spend the night in a hotel alone. Jo was on assignment in London. Katherine was with her. There Kay faced with trepidation her disapproving mother and sister.

She was destitute, with no home of her own, while Jo was already taking care of their mother, a role she saw as her own. So Kay Boyle made the harshest of judgments against herself: "there was not a promise to myself I had not broken, not a vow to others I had not betrayed." Then she set off for the barren industrial landscape of England where Arnold Bennett had set his Five Towns novels. It's only for the summer, she whispered to herself. At night, she dreamed of Ernest Walsh, Michael coming back to life, "and the color coming back in his face, and his laughter, and saying to me—it isn't true, it isn't true, it isn't true."

In Stoke, Kay and Brault slept in the same bed, but they did not make love. Was she sponging on Richard? Kay knew she was, as she called herself, a "hard" and "unmoving" woman who believed that "because one person is dead . . . everything else is a makeshift." Kay dressed in black, and vowed never to make love to another man. When her trunk arrived from Monte Carlo, it contained Walsh's clothes, and, at its bottom, his photograph, its glass shattered. Kay decided to wash the clothes and send them on to Carnevali. Proclaiming her "chastity," she turned to her work.

Among the community of Michelin workers in the French enclave of Stoke-on-Trent, Kay befriended the black-haired, black-eyed vivacious wife of another engineer. Her name was Germaine Garrigou, and, like Kay, she was living with a man she did not love. Germaine helped Kay wash Walsh's clothes and together they packed them up and carted the heavy parcel down to the shipping office. So it became that with Germaine, Kay could satisfy her strong need to talk about Ernest Walsh. With Germaine as her witness, ceremonially Kay would remove Walsh's photograph from its hiding place at the bottom of a suitcase.

Before long Germaine insisted that, for baby Bobby's sake, Kay cast off her black garments for clothes "the color of spring." Thus encouraged, Kay frivolously purchased green kid slippers with straps across the instep and high-heeled black patent-leather shoes, her love of clothes firmly intact after all. Germaine taught her how to apply tinted pencils to her eyes and suggested she wear a white mantilla over her black hair to add drama to her appearance.

More important was the fact that the childless and generous Germaine assumed the role of Bobby's babysitter so that Kay could write. Katherine had sent her a typewriter, and as soon as she unpacked it, Kay sat down and wrote a poem. Then she took up *Plagued by the Nightingale*, although she doubted that Ethel would continue the serialization. Her thoughts turned to New York publishers who might do a volume of her stories along with "the nightingale." (Indeed Ethel not only refused to publish the second installment, but even rejected two of Archibald Craig's poems because they "show the Boyle influence." She told McAlmon she and Kay had "disagreed on the subject of motherhood," and so had decided to separate.)

In exchange for her help, Kay helped Germaine conceal a lover from her husband, even one night when the husband returned home too soon quick-wittedly jumping into the lap of the salesman lover as if he belonged to *her*. Germaine, Kay soon discovered, was having affairs "all over the place." Tall, lean, imperious, with her air of inaccessibility and her hooded blue eyes, Kay soon garnered her own share of admirers. An Englishman living at the local "club" invited her to "walk the continent" and Kay fantasized going, leaving Bobby behind, "anything to escape the stolidity of this settlement."

From the start, Kay plotted to leave Stoke-on-Trent, where she was bored and "dementalized." But there were no jobs, either there or in London, although Kay pleaded to Louise Theis that she was "willing to be an anything which pays enough to keep me fed and clothed." Her assets she listed as "boundless energy and health and a vivacious manner," as well as a "cultivated wit." Another of her virtues, Kay said, was that she "believed in . . . humility." When Jo failed to produce a job for her in London, Kay complained that "my sister is about as much help as Sharon." Before long she had written to Sylvia Beach asking for a job as a secretary or saleslady. But no job was forthcoming at Shakespeare and Company. Three months in Stoke, subjected to "entangling" teas and dinners for Brault's colleagues, rendered her desperate. Even having a maid named Appleby, who, dressed in a white lace cap and apron, freed her to return to her typewriter, didn't help enough.

"Why Richard selected Stoke and me, instead of Clermont and a lady who wanted to sleep with him, I don't know," Kay said. It became increasingly difficult to sleep in the same bed with Richard while denying him sex. "I cannot inflict a platonic wife upon Richard for the rest of his existence," she realized. Nor could she "live on someone else all my life." It irritated her to see Richard acting as a father to Bobby, not so much because it was disloyal to Ernest Walsh's memory, Kay was honest enough to acknowledge, as because she wanted to have Bobby "for my own." She was as possessive a mother with her first child as she would be with her last. She did plan to tell Bobby that her father "was the gayest, the bravest, the simplest and the most gallant of poets."

Temporarily reconciled to one of those "inevitable times when one must try to start all over again," she studied German and shorthand. That August, encouraged by Germaine Garrigou, Kay was to write, she took an old American flag and wheeled Bobby's carriage down to the American consulate in Stoke, where she planned to burn the flag in protest against the impending execution of the anarchists Sacco and Vanzetti. As she recalled the incident many years later, she changed her mind and went home because America, the country she loved, did not belong either to Judge Thayer or to the governor of Massachusetts or even to the President of the United States, Calvin Coolidge, who had refused the shoemaker and the fish peddler clemency. (In none of the correspondence for these months of 1927 does her aborted protest appear, although she chronicles every detail of her life, and every mood; the incident may well be apocryphal, part of Kay Boyle's fictionalizing of her life which would lead her to such fabulizing as appropriating the story of an old pioneer woman for Eva Evans's own.)

It was *transition* which was now bringing Kay Boyle the writer to people's attention. On the suggestion of one of its editors, the publishers Boni and Liveright in New York wrote wishing to consider her novel *Plagued by the Nightingale*. It was the first anniversary of Ernest Walsh's death, "a sad month, a terrible month," as Kay saw her eyes turn "red with crying endlessly which is something I never do." But preparing the manuscript allowed her "no time for sorrow although the heart is filled with it." One consolation was that Bobby had turned pink and white, dimpled and blond, a beautiful baby out of Renoir.

From Stoke, Kay engaged in a bitter quarrel with Evelyn Scott on the subject of McAlmon, toward whom Scott accused her of maintaining an "emotional prejudice." More, perceiving Kay Boyle's hero-worshipping propensities, Scott found herself incredulous at Kay's participating in the "aura of bowed and humbled love" which surrounded the person of Alfred Stieglitz. Nor did Scott admire Carnevali much as a writer. Unwilling to evaluate hero worshipping as a mode of thought, Kay chose instead to defend herself.

"If I considered Carnevali a sick, weak, unfortunate and pity-craving wop," she wrote Scott hysterically, "I'd not insult him by shoving my money at him." And her very humanity demanded that she flatter Stieglitz. Why not, Kay reasoned, if it gives "a comfortable feeling to an old man who has done damn good work." But it was Scott's renewed attack on McAlmon which now led Kay Boyle to decide that Evelyn had "ceased being an honest writer." "You are a cold brute," Kay wrote her. Ernest Walsh's enthusiasms were now her own, as she had taken literally his decree that her role in life was to offer homage to the great.

Of course she confided the whole incident to McAlmon himself. "Hasn't Mrs. Scott perhaps an emotional prejudice herself," McAlmon replied wickedly, "not only against me, but against ideas?" Clearly McAlmon could defend himself. "I'm so tough and hard that I not only chew nails for breakfast, but I distrust idealism with a friendship-breaking clause included," McAlmon told her. By January of 1928 Kay Boyle was effusive in her protestations of friendship—for Scott. "I'd walk a million miles if there were no sea attached to it," she wrote Evelyn, "could I come upon you in a white sweater, talking despite a red nose and fever." Scott was a "literary saint," who never mentioned her "own struggles and achievements," unlike Kay herself, who recognized that she was unable to "get away from mine."

Richard Brault spent Christmas Eve with Katherine in London on his way to St.-Malo, where Papa Brault had died. In Stoke, Bobby had her first tree. Germaine Garrigou dressed up as Santa Claus while Bobby good-naturedly relinquished her toys to more aggressive babies without a tear or a protest, Kay proudly noted. Unlike the other children, she was not afraid to kiss Santa Claus, perhaps because she recognized her friend Germaine behind the disguise. But Bobby would allow no one to hold her but her mother.

Every time Kay spoke to her, Bobby smiled.

And, for all her woes, 1927 was a banner year for Kay Boyle as she published ten poems, that first part of *Plagued*, five short stories, a review, and even a short list of her pet peeves. Increasingly in both her poetry and her prose she turned to her own life. "Do you think I could write a story about Grandma?" she asked Katherine. So she conceived of "Episode in the Life of an Ancestor," which would appear in the fall 1930 issue of *Hound and Horn*, making Edward J. O'Brien's Honor Roll.

The February 1927 issue of *Poetry* carried three lyric poems which Kay referred to as "Richard's poems," the series ending with a solitary Brault walking "with the rain on his shoulders / Like a loose mantle." These were Kay Boyle's gifts to her first husband, having been mailed to him autographed from Monte Carlo. Her "pet peeves" were in *This Quarter*, and they included such localisms as "The Tall Man with Black Moustache at the Hôtel Cosmopolite in Monte Carlo," as well as the Hôtel de France at Mougins, where she and Walsh had been treated so unkindly.

Ezra Pound, who had declined to contribute a tribute to Walsh, also made her list, not surprisingly, as Ethel took the opportunity to undedicate the first number of *This Quarter* on the ground that Walsh "was disillusioned about Ezra Pound before he died." (Nor was Pound alone in his skepticism about Walsh: Wyndham Lewis that year in his *Time and Western Man* not only mocked the cult of *This Quarter* but attacked Walsh ["big rough hairy dark-browed Mr. W-sh"] as an "ideal fool," a "romantic," and a schoolboy "sick for things he has never experienced." Foremost among Lewis's complaints was Walsh's championing "Bud Macsalmon" as "one of the most astonishing writers since the fathers of English literature.")

More significant for Kay Boyle were her five poems in *This Quarter* dedicated to Walsh, among them "To America" and "For an American." Sexual imagery predominates. "You shall try to gather his seed when it is blown from the stalk," Kay writes, as the sea moves "thick in my blood." In "Comrade" she promises to abide by his inspiration: "We shall follow in the tread of his heart beating." All are elegiac, all leave the poet bereft: "the clay of his bones is a hard famine."

Kay Boyle's prose in the late twenties already tended toward the mannered and the *précieuse*. Its best feature is sensual imagery, as in the installment from *Plagued* the Kay figure washes the face of her husband: "his face soft and defenseless in her hands, his fine nostril threaded with hair." The Brault character, Nicolas, in this early version of her later novel, is already afflicted with a hereditary bone disease, Kay's analogue for what she saw as the weakness of Richard Brault. As he emotionally abandons Christine (Kay), Kay Boyle argues for the spiritual necessity of her having abandoned Brault for a positive and life-renewing relationship. From the start, in her stories and novels, Kay Boyle not only reenacted her actual experiences but enlisted her fiction as the arena where she could justify her moral choices.

Immediate praise came to her for the segment of *Plagued by the Nightingale* published in *This Quarter*. Lola told her it was "full of a running sap and the words are luminous with a light that shines from within." William Carlos Williams told her it was "superbly written." Calling her prose "feminine," he quickly added that it was "fully equal to the best male stuff." These were times when a woman's writing had always to be compared with that of men, as if it couldn't be considered alone. "No man could write like you," Williams went on, unable to view Kay Boyle but as a "woman writer." "This is what I have always looked for from a woman. I am happy now, permanently happy to know you can do this good work."

"Here's to the next ten years!" Williams saluted Kay Boyle, not at all prematurely, as in 1927 her stories began to appear in rapid succession. "Summer," in *Calendar: A Literary Review*, chronicled her love for Walsh from the point of view of a young woman observing them at their hotel. A repressive old woman, the girl's guardian, views Kay and Walsh with horror, as "decency" forbids their sexuality: "what could any good, good people be at in the hills all day, all day that way?" But Kay Boyle in the twenties had embraced sexual freedom, as she had refused to abide by bourgeois conventions, which included burying oneself in a dead marriage. Even as it reveals Kay's early stylistic dependence on D. H. Lawrence, the imagery of "Summer" is dazzling in its intensity; Walsh coughing is compared to "a trapped fox barking in frenzy to get out of the room, and flinging down with its soft, gasping belly on the young man's belly, its worn, thin bark snapping its teeth at his chest."

"Theme," in the April *transition*, evoked old age so convincingly that years later Kay Boyle would say she, a "woman of habits" like her own character, became the woman of her own story written when she was twenty-five years old. She wrote "Theme" as she awaited what she was convinced was the birth of her son, and the story is about a woman frightened of losing her male child, frightened he will abandon her. In that same issue, returning the favor, Kay reviewed Williams's *In the American Grain*. Correctly, Kay acknowledges that this was Williams's most important work to date; wisely too she recognizes that Williams in his "approach to America" had transcended outworn notions of the truth: "There is nothing left over from another age." It was the claim of twenties Paris, what Kay, no less than Ernest Walsh, strove for, and what Gertrude Stein had meant when she asserted that she was there to kill what was not dead, the nineteenth century.

Except for July, October, and November, Kay was published in every succeeding issue of *transition* in 1927. Her two poems also evoked her grief over Walsh's death. "My blood is a long lament for you," Kay writes in "And Winter." January of 1928 brought "A Sad Poem," in which Kay summons "Jesus Jesus [to] remember this man," and pictures herself with the homely image of "wiping my nose on the back of my hand." It was as if her grief were inexhaustible, fuel for a lifetime of laments.

From the start, Kay's relations with Jolas were prickly. In September of 1927 he assigned her to review Hart Crane's *White Buildings* for the January issue. "I've been waiting for months to tell the world what a horse's patoot I think Hart Crane is," Kay exulted. If he were challenging the place in American literary history Ernest Walsh might occupy, she would demolish the usurper. Hart Crane, Kay announced, "is done with life and with civilization, presumably with human emotions, with human ambition." Worse, his poetry was "doomed to failure because it is false . . . dull and humorless . . . a lot of words hiding a human fear." His grandmother "was probably a better bet than he," Kay wrote. Clearly Crane's intellectual poetry touched a nerve, evoking her lifelong sense of inferiority about her lack of education, and indeed her anti-intellectualism. Art, she wrote Theis, "seems to me to be a much simpler thing than critics make it. I mean simpler to honour and to know."

Jolas was appalled. For Jolas, "after Crane America has no poets." *White Buildings* was an "immense" book. At once he assigned Laura Riding, a friend of Crane's, to write a counter-review to be published in the same issue. Riding was given the advantage of responding to Kay Boyle's text, while the reverse was not true. "A poet can go about his job in many different ways," Riding lectured Kay, as she defended Crane's use of artifice as "something heroic, moving, beautiful." Correctly, she perceived that passion lay behind Crane's intellectual poetry, even if it was "theatrical."

Crane himself took note of "Kay Boyle's explosive boil." Obviously distressed, he wrote his friend Isidor Schneider that Kay Boyle had made a wholesale condemnation of both "my grandmother and her grandson's poems": "We were damned together—for trying to 'climb up onto another plain' or something." Kay meanwhile was furious that Jolas had dared append Riding's defense of Crane to her own review. "And as for Hart Crane!" she sputtered. "And Laura Riding!! Who is she? Does she possibly sully the name of our fair states?" This was Kay Boyle at her most imperious. Jolas was now an upstart who had dared suggest he was picking up where *This Quarter* left off.

Kay warned Evelyn Scott not to deduce by her being published in *transition* that the magazine "means anything to me." The editors were "horses' asses, the critics as feeble and bloodless as the *Dial*'s." She also said she found "the hero-worship business of Stein and Joyce simply appalling." Neither Stein nor Joyce was a god of hers, hence her objection to Jolas's assertion that he would publish anything Stein sent him. "Even Jesus Christ gets repetitious sometimes though I think as an artist he was more sensitive than Gertrude," Kay crowed. Louise Theis received the same tirade. "Don't talk *transition* to me," Kay warned. "It's a horse's patoot as far as I'm concerned."

What remained apparent was that by the end of the twenties Kay Boyle had mastered the short story form, and *transition* was the vehicle in which she did it. "Portrait," dramatizing her struggle with Ethel Moorhead during the last moments of Walsh's life, was anecdotal. "Polar Bears and Others" moved toward psychological development as it pictures, this time, Kay and Richard Brault. Brault informs her a woman is coming to Le Havre whom he wants her to meet, only to be unable to acknowledge that he really wants the other woman. When he chooses not to meet her, the heroine has only contempt for him: "I'll be something more than sacrifice and bitterness to you . . . go on, get out!" For this sin against his soul, Kay considered Brault "lost to all old dignities."

Each story represented an advance in technique and development. "Bitte Nehmen Sie die Blumen," the most fully developed of Kay Boyle's early *transition* stories, pictured Kay pushing Bobby's baby carriage, while in a stream-of-consciousness mode the author plumbs the mysteries of sexual attraction: "I took a cigaret from him, and when he lit it for me he was so close to me that I felt his body alive through the bars of the fence." Unique for a woman writer of her time, Kay Boyle boldly conveys how the object of sexual desire need not be, often is not, worthy: "I was waiting to hear his voice singing God save the king with an arrogance I despised, but which ran in beautiful rivers down his throat."

From the start, out of narcissism, out of Katherine's having made so much of her, Kay Boyle placed herself, or a thinly disguised surrogate, at the center of her fiction. The woman in "Bitte Nehmen Sie die Blumen" has turned into an "old maid," as Kay in Stoke-on-Trent described herself. When she meets a man, she longs only to "wound him." Sexuality, "all that," has "dried up" in her. She makes herself look unattractive, brushing her hair "back straight as a board" from her face, while her grief is causing it to turn grey. She is like Kay Boyle in all respects but one: she has a boy child.

As it was for Kay Boyle now, her grief has made her reckless, a theme Kay realizes by freeing the story from traditional grammar, eliding the sentences and abandoning punctuation. She is a woman, as Kay Boyle saw herself, who would change her entire life on a whim: "for a turn of his body I would be leaving Peleser and making a new life with this man I would be doing this for no reason at all except that he was beautiful to me."

At the end, the man loses her out of his abjectness, "the sad proud humility of his heart." Indeed, tempted as she was by the real-life offer that she "walk the continent" with her admirer, Kay Boyle did not escape from Stoke-on-Trent with the Englishman whose attentions she had described in letters to Katherine. She had another life in mind.

7

At Last, Paris

The abandoning of Bobby for a fortnight or so until the job
developes [sic] seems unavoidable.

I used them for toilet paper!

In the middle of March of 1928, Kay Boyle at last left Stoke-on-Trent for Paris. The only job she could find was as ghostwriter for Gladys Palmer, the Princess of Sarawak, who wanted her memoirs published. Kay would be paid five hundred francs a month (the franc then being worth two cents), plus room and board. There was only one condition. The Princess, who had been deprived of her own children by her husband, was not about to tolerate the presence of Bobby in her apartment on the rue Louis-David. Bobby would have to live elsewhere.

Kay was desperate. She had failed in her efforts with the American consul to be renaturalized as an American citizen, and had failed to receive an allowance for Bobby as part of Walsh's war pension. Kent-Monnet sent a letter swearing Ernest Walsh had told him he had "every intention of being present at the birth of his son," thus demonstrating that he considered himself to be the child's father. But this was not accepted as sufficient proof. The consul also insisted that since Kay had lived more than two years abroad, she had permanently lost her American nationality.

Indeed, America seemed remote, and the idea of looking for a job in America "appall[ed]" her, Kay said. Boni and Liveright had rejected *Plagued by the Nightingale*, and Kay was bitter, certain that "it's fresher than a lot of stuff they print." When Louise Theis tried to console her, saying that "someday" she would write great things, she took umbrage: "That to me means that I must have failed to write authentically what was happening to me now. I don't believe in the future, the me own or anybody else's."

Kay accepted the Princess's offer even as she maintained that she hated to "abandon" her child even for a fortnight. But it was "unavoidable."

Kay believed that Gladys Palmer's intention was "to weed Bobby for a time out of my life so that I can devote my energies to Archibald." She called the Princess's "counting Bobby out . . . a definite snag." Having insisted "I want my kid all the time," Kay left Bobby behind in London and went to Paris. It was her only alternative, she felt, and a better one than remaining dependent on Richard Brault.

The most important thing for a woman, Kay Boyle had learned the hard way, was "to have one's own work, making independent one's life, and that is what I want my daughter to know." Never before or later would Kay Boyle sound so feminist a note. "If women have children," she declared, "they should be able to support them themselves, or else refrain from having them." It took considerable courage for Kay Boyle to sacrifice the protection of the one man available to help her. There were other women in the bohemian Paris of the 1920s who lived in defiance of society's norms: one was Caresse Crosby, soon to become Kay Boyle's closest woman friend among the Paris expatriates. But unlike Caresse, whose children were not illegitimate, Kay had neither an inheritance nor a husband.

Leaving Bobby in London with her mother, Kay went to Paris to become the amanuensis and secretary to Gladys Palmer, a buxom woman six feet tall and weighing over two hundred pounds, whose blond hair had turned white, she told Kay, virtually overnight when her husband took her six children away from her and made them wards of the court. Her face, according to one observer, was "at once wise, sad, petulant, surprised and infantile." Her eyes were a faded periwinkle, and her wide mouth seemed to suggest generosity, although in fact she was extremely stingy. Gladys Palmer chain-smoked through a long cigarette holder and talked constantly about her desire to convert to Roman Catholicism, even as she seemed really to care only about getting her name in the newspapers and finding a new husband. She was a woman without purpose or convictions, another of those who had come to Paris to live for pleasure.

At once Kay Boyle's circumstances altered dramatically. She resided among the overstuffed chintz chairs and sofas and the thick carpets of the Princess. A life-sized bronze of Gladys Palmer's dead Aberdeen terrier reclined on a hearth rug. Kay had her own room, where every morning the English maid drew her bath; at nine a French maid brought her breakfast, which included caviar, on a silver tray. Once a week the Princess weeded unwanted garments from her closet, and Kay was given to wear the mistress's hand-me-downs, dresses by Lanvin, Poiret, and Molyneux. These were altered by a dressmaker, with whom Bobby was put to board when she was finally brought to Paris.

Kay's first task was to locate the son of one of Gladys Palmer's mother's friends. The son turned out to be Vyvyan Holland. Kay failed to track down her old acquaintance. But she was no secretary punching a time clock. At once Paris opened itself to her, she the author of so many poems and stories in *This Quarter* and *transition*. Kay Boyle was also already notorious—as the woman who had won Ernest Walsh away from Ethel Moorhead.

Archie Craig, who also lived on the rue Louis-David with the Princess, at once took Kay to meet the man she had denounced as a "horse's ass." His wife, Maria, a rather large and plain woman, poured tea from a silver teapot. Maria sensed a rival in this tall, slender young woman with the heavy-lidded blue eyes, white skin, and black hair whose prominent nose added only importance to her face and who was such an accomplished flirt. Eugene Jolas was immediately charmed. At once Jolas had eyes only for Kay Boyle.

A few days later, Archie escorted Kay to her first Paris party, at the Jolases', who were about to depart for Colombey-les-Deux-Eglises, where they had rented the house which one day would be bought by General de Gaulle. Kay wore an orange panne velvet dress borrowed from Joan and a black velvet cloak belonging to the Princess. The tiny elevator was out of service, and so Kay and Archie began to climb the winding staircase up the four flights. They went slowly because Archie was weak with tuberculosis. Soon they observed a slender, handsome man in a tweed jacket and grey flannel slacks, obviously an Englishman or an American, mounting the stairs slowly behind them, slowing down so as not to overtake them. Once he stopped to tie his shoelaces. Kay and Archie were amused, as he seemed so determined not to arrive at the Jolases' door at the same time as they did.

It was at this party that Kay Boyle met James and Nora Joyce. Nora professed admiration for Kay's dress, which could not possibly be English. Which Paris collection did it come from? she inquired. Joyce wanted to talk about pensions and restaurants in Switzerland once he learned that Kay had already seen some of Europe, and was a "traveller . . . like our friend McAlmon." Kay later said she was too shy to tell Joyce she was a writer. Nor had she read his work. When she was twenty, she had tried to read some of *Ulysses*, but had given up after the first paragraph. She was not much of a reader. She did tell Joyce she was "visiting" with the Princess of Sarawak, inspiring a story about the present white Rajah. Kay Boyle would say the one subject the Paris writers avoided in social conversation was writing. (Harold Loeb complained that Joyce didn't seem to be interested in anything until the subject of French provincial cooking came up.)

Kay was astounded when a hush descended upon the room and Maria Jolas led Gertrude Stein, all in purple silk, into her salon. Kay remained with the Joyces, who, Kay remembered, pretended nothing had happened. Sylvia Beach joined them, and Nora introduced Kay as an "Irish colleen, with her dark hair and her misty blue eyes." Two glasses of champagne had paralyzed Kay Boyle, who could only interject, "What about my broken nose?" Tediously, then, Kay recounted that accident on her sled in a Pocono blizzard.

Several times during the evening, Kay searched the room for Robert

McAlmon. He was not there. But she did attract admirers on this first evening out in Paris. Men were at once drawn to this black-haired, blue-eyed beauty in stunning orange panne velvet who seemed so down-to-earth and vulnerable, so approachable. First the surrealist poet Philippe Soupault asked if he might see her home. But he had a rival in the diffident young man in the tweed jacket who had followed her and Archie up the stairs. Smitten with Kay Boyle, he had escorted his wife, Ada, who must have met him there, home, only to return to offer his company to Kay Boyle. His name was Archibald MacLeish, he said, and having been a war veteran and having earned a law degree at Harvard, he had come to Paris to be a poet. He did not bother to tell Kay Boyle that he was married.

Kay spent most of her time with Archie Craig on both the ghostwriting and their *Living Poetry* anthology, as they hung announcements in the Montparnasse cafés. Archie called Bobby "the kidney" and scrupulously avoided touching her, no father substitute he. Kay and Archie planned in their anthology to challenge "the machine," as they bemoaned how industrialization had threatened the wellsprings of art. A more difficult assignment was the memoir, since the Princess, vague and passive, seemed unable to remember much about her childhood. Kay and Archie concocted the story as they went along, keeping in mind that their purpose was to gain revenge against Gladys's husband. To aid them, a young Canadian expatriate named John Glassco, nicknamed "Buffy," was hired to type the finished product.

Kay used *Relations and Complications (Being the Recollections of)* by H. H. the Dayang Muda of Sarawak to advance her own causes. She has the Princess call *This Quarter* "undoubtedly the greatest quarterly of the arts ever printed," and she has her praise Ernest Walsh: "his poetry, and his vigorous prose radiated belief and vitality." If Gladys Palmer didn't have much to say, Kay Boyle had words which had to be said. So she has Palmer proclaim that the influence of Ernest Walsh was immeasurable: "the young artists of the world realized that at last a prophet worthy of their faith had come to them." Kay also penned a description of herself on the terrace of the hotel in Annot: "Kay Boyle was twenty-three; arrogant, self-contained, but with the indescribable Irish charm that is so hauntingly reflected in her work." Modesty did not forbid.

Oblivious or heedless of the jealousy of his wife, Eugene Jolas opened Paris to Kay Boyle. He took her to lunch at Ferrari's on the avenue Rapp, where they were joined by James and Nora Joyce. Once they encountered Laura Riding and Robert Graves, who together in Majorca had founded the Seizin Press. At the sight of this rival, who had chastised her in the pages of *transition*, Kay, by her own admission, haughtily stalked off to another table, where she ate her lunch alone.

Unfazed, Jolas introduced her to Robert Desnos, André Breton, Tristan Tzara, André Derain, and Louis Aragon, and even Ezra Pound. She learned to like such bohemian fare as *tête de veau*, ears and brains. Mostly she listened to the talk of "art," of surrealism and the logic of dreams. Jolas and André Breton took her once to a Russian fortune teller. At a party Gertrude Stein sang "On the Trail of the Lonesome Pine" and "On a Bicycle Built for Two," accompanying herself on a banjo. And always Kay Boyle made conquests. Newspaperman Jay Allen thought she held her head in such a way that she resembled "a Hittite princess." Kay Boyle was learning to strike the memorable pose, using her female attributes as if she believed, knew, it wasn't enough to be a fine writer for a woman to succeed. If Gertrude Stein, the model Katherine had set before her, had discovered her particular style, Kay Boyle knew she had to find her own.

"They're madder than hatters and freer than the wind," Jolas told Kay of Harry and Caresse Crosby, the golden couple of twenties Paris, known for pushing hedonism to its limits. Harry was a nephew of J. P. Morgan and a poet; Caresse, a descendant of the *Mayflower*'s Governor Bradford, had invented the backless brassiere. Together they had founded the Black Sun Press, while seeking ever more bizarre experiences, ever raising the ante required for the frisson of pleasure they sought. Harry painted his fingernails black, dressed in black, and subscribed to Oscar Wilde's view that the only things one never regrets are one's mistakes. Style substituted for convictions, genius was applauded, and sex with an ever wider variety of partners was something Harry expected of himself, in the Crosby apartment at 19 rue de Lille in the giant marital bed, and elsewhere. "I like girls when they are very young before they have any minds," Harry said as he and Caresse together made love to an eleven-year-old Tunisian child on a trip to North Africa.

Sometime between two and three in the morning on May 19, 1928, Kay and her ever-available escort Eugene Jolas entered the Bal Nègre, a club which featured black jazz musicians. Jolas led Kay up to the balcony, where Harry and Caresse Crosby were laughing and drinking champagne. Harry, his head skull-like and severe, welcomed Jolas and Kay to the "mad party," which included that night, as he reported in his diary, "Ganay Little Rock Face Armand de la Rochefoucauld the Crouches and Frans and May." Frans de Geetere was a Dutch painter who lived on a houseboat and gave wild parties, where drugs and sex abounded, parties which lured Harry, invariably without Caresse. Caresse looked up and met the eyes of the black-haired woman whose eyes seemed "silver-green," a woman, Caresse remembered, built "like a blade," a woman "neat as a needle," a woman as self-possessed as a "Seminole maiden." Kay Boyle's beauty astounded everyone she met.

Having met the notorious Crosbys, Kay directed her attentions largely to Harry. "How good of you both to refuse to allow me to continue in my intention not to drink," she wrote coyly, as she set out fiercely to cultivate this relationship. Flattery beckoned. "If you wrote out what is there churning about inside of you," she told him, "there'd be something else again." Kay also used the *Living Poetry* anthology politically, as a means of making friends. "Nothing but the Testament of the Sun," she told Crosby, referring to *Shadows of the Sun,* his diary published by Black Sun in 1928, "has the conviction and despair of originality."

Flattery invariably worked. By June, Harry was proclaiming that Kay Boyle was one of the few great writers of her generation, and the only woman he would name: "(Saint Léger James Joyce T. S. Eliot—and perhaps Cummings and perhaps Kay Boyle and perhaps Hart Crane and perhaps MacLeish)." He called her "the best girl writer since Jane Austen." When Kay later read Harry and Caresse part of her attack on Stephen Vincent Benét's *John Brown's Body,* which she called "a dull book," both Crosbys offered their approval. There was even, according to Kay Boyle's niece Susan Hager, a ménage à trois one night in the great Crosby bed—Harry and Caresse and Kay.

"McAlmon is in Paris," Archie told Kay one day. But she couldn't find him. He never had a fixed address, she learned, but moved from hotel to hotel, restless, discontented, anguished.

Jolas liked Lipp's, that brasserie at St.-Germain-des-Prés favored by the journalists, and there one night Kay met William L. Shirer, who was reporting for the foreign edition of the *Chicago Tribune.* Kay was in a group. Fresh out of Iowa, and "corn-fed," Shirer was at once overcome by the haughty, vivacious beauty. Kay Boyle seemed to Shirer "terribly sophisticated"; she was already famous. Overcome with shyness, he was too timid to make an overture.

Kay was engrossed in conversation with the besotted Shirer when into Lipp's walked . . . Robert McAlmon at last, the man Kay had been yearning to see since Monte Carlo. Lean and apart, his thin line of a mouth revealing nothing of his feelings, McAlmon with his ice-blue eyes scanned the banquettes at Lipp's. He made no sign that he recognized Kay Boyle, but walked over to the bar and ordered a beer. At once Kay rose, and leaving Jolas and Shirer and everyone else behind, joined McAlmon.

"Bob," she began.

McAlmon slapped the money for the beer down on the bar. "Come on," he said. "Let's go up to Le Grand Ecart. There may be some lively people there." They hailed a taxi bound for Montmartre, where at once McAlmon began to attack Jolas as a phony, along with the portentous language in which the *transition* writers too frequently indulged. McAlmon laughed his hard dry laugh.

"How can you sit for hours listening to the talk about the 'revaluation of the spirit in its intercontinental relations' and the 'destruction of mechanical positivism'?" McAlmon demanded of Kay Boyle. "Maybe it's time you stopped putting things between yourself and reality."

Kay admitted her reality wasn't doing very well. She was subdued, as awed by McAlmon's brilliance as she had been at their first meeting.

At Le Grand Ecart they drank gin fizzes. The son-in-law of the *patron* invited the glamorous Kay to dance, since McAlmon would not dance with her. When she returned to the table, McAlmon had switched to harder refreshments. Suddenly a black-nailed dirty hand appeared from behind the green curtains of a window behind them. Without a word McAlmon placed his glass of whiskey into the stranger's hand. The image remained in Kay Boyle's mind for years: McAlmon generous, bitter, grand, and mysterious, but always lucid.

"You're a provincial!" McAlmon suddenly confronted her, fixing on her his cold gaze of steel. "You and Bill Williams are the two small-town people who should never have hit Montparnasse." Kay wondered if he meant that she was drunk and couldn't hold her liquor.

"You've got here too late," he went on. "The good days are finished."

Admiring his muscular body and air of inaccessibility, so parallel to her own, Kay fell in love with Robert McAlmon, even as she knew the truth about his homosexuality. John Glassco has the character based on Kay Boyle in his *Memoirs of Montparnasse* tell him, after he has told her McAlmon had offered to publish his book, "By God, I think he's crazy enough about you to do it." McAlmon told Kay he had been deceived by his wife, Bryher, implying that he had not known that she was a lesbian, for in denying that he had made a marriage of convenience, he was simultaneously denying that he was homosexual, an admission he was not ready to make, then or later. Kay did not allow herself to perceive the subterfuge.

That night McAlmon, ever in search of fresh distraction, took Kay to Bricktop's, and then to the new Coupole presided over by Bob Lodewyck, who, as Kiki, Man Ray's model and mistress, put it, "knew everything, saw everything, and said nothing." He introduced Kay Boyle to other Paris habitués, like Flossie Martin, a former New York chorus girl sent to Paris to develop her voice but who chose to spend her days on the Dôme *terrasse* and her nights at the Dingo, and to Kiki and to Hilaire Hiler, a painter and stage designer who played jazz piano.

To Kay's distress, McAlmon remained bored. His mood that night is conveyed in Kay Boyle's autobiographical story "I Can't Get Drunk," which was published in 1932 in *Contempo*. It was an homage to the man she had loved: "to see him with his lean mouth closed like a wallet, his eye like iron and as cold as, would it ever come into your head that the mouth of his heart was open," she wrote. Kay's McAlmon remains on the surface, perpetually waiting for something to happen, knowing only that something is wrong. "I don't know what's the matter with me he said. I can't get drunk." Ever on his guard, this fictional McAlmon complains to Kay Boyle about "that paint all over your face," her usual excessive makeup. She is clearly in love with him, as she reminds him of a moment when he kissed her good morning. But McAlmon is as unable to reciprocate her affection as he is to acknowledge his true sexuality. Most men found Kay Boyle enchanting. Yet that night, as on others, all McAlmon wanted to do was talk about other women.

"If only Djuna Barnes or Mina Loy turned up," McAlmon lamented to Kay, "the evening might be saved." Kay felt empty, unattractive. I'm just zero with him, she thought miserably. Later Nancy Cunard, the dashing writer and publisher, told her about "the nights Bob and I spent looking for you all over Paris." Needing to make each woman feel inadequate, McAlmon had made Kay feel he wanted only Nancy, and Nancy that he wanted Kay.

That same night, now bored with the Coupole, McAlmon led Kay across the boulevard du Montparnasse to the Sélect. There he introduced her to Harold Stearns, the racetrack tout "Peter Pickem" in the Paris edition of the *Chicago Tribune*, who would be the model for the hero of her novel *Monday Night.* One minute McAlmon was drunkenly singing "Me and My Shadow," assuming his habitual "cold hilariousness." The next he was gone.

Yet Kay did not give up hoping that McAlmon would declare his love for her. They went to the Joyces', where Joyce wanted to talk only about his daughter Lucia and her dancing. McAlmon took Kay to Brancusi's studio, where they talked about Ernest Walsh. He took her to a party given by Hilaire Hiler, where Kay did a "wild ring-around-a-rosy" and McAlmon pretended to be Nijinsky. He even took her away for a weekend to Clairefontaine, near Rambouillet. She longed for them to become lovers, but they did not. Kay had to content herself with diverting McAlmon by proposing that he submit poetry to Jolas under the pseudonym "Guy Urquhart," Urquhart being his mother's maiden name. Jolas indeed fell for it, as Kay Boyle proved McAlmon to be what she needed him to be: a poet.

Kay waited for McAlmon to reach out to her as a man, a yearning she converted to fiction in "Spring Morning," one of the few of her short stories which did not find magazine publication. In the quasi-stream-of-consciousness style of this period, she cries out for a McAlmon who could never heed her call: "I have waited so badly I have waited but so badly I have waited so badly for you what are you going to do?" She loves him and would say yes should he ask her to marry him. But he was still married to Bryher and it did not come up. "If I had money I would buy him I thought body and soul," Kay writes, alluding to why McAlmon had married the heiress. McAlmon appears in "Spring Morning" only in a photograph: "I was putting the rouge and the black on my eyes it is the poor bugger's fault I said that he is purpose and pride when everything else is rejected through a sewage of emotion."

Kay persisted in believing McAlmon was in love with her, that only some force beyond his control prevented him from expressing his real feelings for her. But late that spring of 1928 McAlmon betook himself to Le Canadel, near Villefranche, where he was frequently entertained at a villa rented by Peggy Guggenheim and Laurence Vail, the surrealist writer and painter. Here McAlmon befriended a handsome blond Texan named Edwin Lanham, whose book *Sailors Don't Care* McAlmon would publish under his Contact imprint. Years later, Joan Boyle, then Lanham, laughed at Kay's lifelong belief that Robert McAlmon had been in love with her and, if unencumbered, would have married her.

"You know, that's just another example of her egomania," said Kay's salty, down-to-earth sister who saw Kay as forever, narcissistically, believing various men were in love with her. "I know whom McAlmon was in love with. He was in love with my husband Eddie Lanham!"

On Sundays, Kay visited Bobby at the dressmaker's. When it was time for her to leave, Bobby, now fourteen months old, wept bitterly, throwing herself on the floor in a wild tantrum. Each week she felt as if she were being abandoned anew. Richard invited Kay to return to Stoke, but that dead end had no appeal. When the peripatetic Princess suddenly made plans to forsake Paris for one of her watering places, Kay was faced with the need to find another situation.

One day Archie took Kay to tea at Gertrude Stein's salon on the rue de Fleurus. Stein ignored her and Kay sat talking with Alice B. Toklas about recipes. Later Archie reported to Kay that Toklas requested that he not bring Kay there again, Gertrude Stein having pronounced her as bourgeois, as middle-class as Hemingway. Kay wondered if it was true, or if Archie, jealous of his friendships, simply wanted to keep Gertrude Stein for himself.

Archie had in turn invited Gertrude to tea at the Princess's. One day a rattling of the windows of the apartment on the rue Louis-David heralded the approach of a fawn-colored two-seater Ford bumping over the cobblestones. Kay watched from the window as Gertrude Stein alighted in her vicar's hat, thick stockings, and heavy boots. She was wrapped in a thick raglan overcoat.

At tea, intimidated, Kay could find nothing to discuss but the weather. The Princess lit one cigarette after another in her long cigarette holder. Obviously bored, Stein ate a chocolate éclair, followed by a baba au rhum. Kay thought Stein could only have been willing to come because the Princess, the "Dayang Muda," had a title.

Suddenly the doorbell rang. Into the room swept a grey-haired man of about fifty. His long hair was pinned in silky braids in a crown around his small eaglelike head. His bare feet, in thonged sandals, were immaculate despite the mud of the inclement day. The man removed his outer cloak, revealing his odd costume: a low-necked tunic of a coarse white material, secured around the waist by a cord, from which hung a leather bag, his purse.

At once the man began to talk very fast about his old battles with his sister's lawyers. "If only she had stuck to dancing," he wailed. "But she had to be a businesswoman as well, although she didn't know her mind from one day to the next. She was not consequent. That is why she could never establish anything in one place."

"I knew you when you drank sherry and smoked cigars," Gertrude said, laughing, restored to equanimity by the sudden appearance of an old friend.

"You have an excellent memory, Gertrude," the man answered, "probably due to the fact that you keep repeating things over and over."

"Raymond," Gertrude replied, "I knew you when you worried about the crease in your trousers."

Raymond Duncan came twice to dinner at the apartment of the Princess of Sarawak. He described his colony, that experiment in healthful living in which Kay had been interested since Le Havre when she fantasized moving there with Lola and her mother. The children drank only goat's milk, Duncan told her. They wove their own cloth; they made their own sandals. There was even a hand printing press. At this Kay and Archie exchanged glances, thinking of the *Living Poetry* anthology, still without a publisher, but which might be printed on Duncan's press. Now here was Raymond Duncan offering Kay and her child a place among his communards.

"All your troubles will be ended," Duncan promised. "Sharon will be with other children and you'll be there too."

Penniless and alone, frightened by the impending departure of the Princess, Kay seized her opportunity and joined Raymond Duncan's group. Bobby remained a responsibility with which she had no means of coping. Now the baby would be cared for by a community of people and Kay could spend time on her writing. Motherhood itself, however it authenticated a woman's femininity, was no attractive way of life to the women of twenties Paris. Nora Joyce lavished most of her attention on her husband, and Caresse Crosby even housed her children in an icy toolshed so that Harry would not have to endure their company. As for Kay Boyle, her art would always come first.

By May 8, Bobby had already been moved to the Duncan establishment, even as Kay remained chez the Dayang Muda. There wooden benches served as beds. In the garden the disciples painted on cloth, while Duncan passed from one to another, commenting. With bare legs and feet and flimsy tunics, young girls took dance class in the salon. Kay would, she believed, take over the printing press on the first of June and do Duncan's publishing for him. "We hope to make a big thing of it," she confidently wrote Puss. Knowing full well the harsh conditions of life at the Duncan colony, the Princess rented an apartment for Kay across the street from the commune at 47 rue Chardon-Lagache in the sixteenth arrondissement, a fashionable part of town even then, on the right bank and not far from the Bois de Boulogne, so that Kay would not have to live with Raymond "in his community conditions."

Raymond Duncan was now a hale fifty-three. His wife had died and the colony was run by his mistress Ayah, who enforced the rules. In particular, there were rigid dietary requirements. The theory was that you need never defecate if you ate healthy food, since you would burn it all up. Little Bobby was at once punished for unnecessary bowel movements. When Kay finally arrived, she was relieved that despite her long absence, Bobby had "far from forgotten me." Every night Kay returned to her apartment to write. It seemed a good life. She was paid four hundred francs a month, and told herself adopting the toga meant saving money on clothes; she never wore stockings anyway. Kay even had time to take dance classes with Raymond's other sister, Elizabeth, a class where the "expression" of Isadora Duncan was propounded. Another student was Lucia Joyce.

So enthusiastic was Kay Boyle about Raymond Duncan's "cult," a term he used, that she invited Richard Brault to come over from England and join. "If only he would join the Duncan colony it would be a much more interesting life for him than what he is doing—and nothing eccentric about it at all," Kay went on. More and more of her time was spent in the apartment, however, while Bobby remained across the road. The idea of living as a single mother without people to help her remained virtually inconceivable to Kay Boyle.

"I shall do great things and you will be proud of me," Kay wrote her grandfather.

Kay's entrance into the commune was celebrated by a party where McAlmon spiked the punch with brandy and Duncan pretended not to notice. Kay perceived that he must have viewed her friends as potential customers for the togas and sandals and so looked the other way. Kay herself wore a golden tunic, and promptly perched on the lap of Bill Bird, publisher of Three Mountains Press. "McAlmon is the third corner in every triangle," Bird remarked. But as he tried to explain what he meant, Kay had turned to chat with poet Robert Desnos about Jacques Baron, reputed to be the youngest poet in Paris.

From the start, Kay Boyle had her doubts about Raymond Duncan's colony. "I am interested—with qualifications—in what he is doing," she said. Soon she was ordered to limit her contact with Bobby, who belonged to the colony now and no longer to her exclusively. The words "mother" and "father" were forbidden, confusing little Bobby more. Worse, Kay was not allowed to cuddle her child. Nor would Kay be seeing Bobby during the day. If Kay believed she was there to run the printing press, Duncan had other ideas.

Kay was assigned to sell togas and sandals and scarves at the Duncan shop on the boulevard St.-Germain, where she had to squat down to use the filthy toilet in the courtyard. When Kay returned to the commune at night, she found Bobby lying filthy in her crib, unattended to, perhaps punished for having performed the forbidden function. The commune itself was filthy and disorderly. No one had enough to eat. The only clean person was Duncan himself, as Kay revealed in her satiric portrait of Duncan as Sorrel in her fourth novel, *My Next Bride*, published in 1934.

The colony members were supposed to be weavers. But no weaving was carried on. They were supposed to be making sandals, but no sandals were made. One day a week Kay had to remain at the colony to prepare lunch for the seven or eight adults and an equal number of children. Otherwise she had to use her four-hundred-franc salary for subway fare and her lunch of goat cheese, yogurt, and fruit, which she was expected to eat in the back room of the shop so that it could remain open all day. Meanwhile, as she reveals in *My Next Bride*, Duncan frequented Rumpelmayer's, where he indulged himself with ice cream and cakes.

Kay Boyle attempted to continue her own Paris life. She dined with Brancusi, discussing the design for Walsh's tomb. Brancusi smelled of red wine and garlic. When Kay asked about critics who attempted to place him in a "school," Brancusi replied, "*Je ne suis pas sculpteur. Je suis polisseur.*" Kay also continued to write for *transition*, which carried her "Letter for Archibald Craig," a poem whose title she later changed to "A Letter to Francis Picabia." From the twenties on, Kay Boyle used dedications and poem titles as a means of flattering friends or winning new admirers. Having fallen out with Archie Craig, she simply renamed the poem, its content never having had anything to do with its ostensible recipient. This "Letter," in fact, was another of her laments for Walsh, those poems Archibald MacLeish would call her finest poetry. "I am sick for a sight of him," Kay cries, "for whom my tears fall." Kay remained one of Jolas's most frequent contributors, as he ran her "The United States," an overwritten poem dedicated to William Carlos Williams, and "Written for Royalty," a fragment from *Year Before Last*. (In the same issue Jolas also published "The Silver Bull" by "Guy Urquhart," as well as a jingle called "Wanton Prejudice": "I'd rather live in Oregon and pack salmon / Than live in Nice and write like Robert McAlmon." Jolas obviously still had no idea who Urquhart was.)

Six days a week, by nine in the morning Kay was at the Duncan shop. First she washed the sidewalk with a brush and a bucket of water. Then, waiting for her first customer, she wrote bits of poems and stories on the backs of envelopes, sometimes using as scrap paper poetry manuscripts which had been submitted to the *Living Poetry* anthology. Visitors came, however: Harry Crosby, George Davis, Harold Stearns, and Germaine Garrigou. Even James Joyce dropped in one day to discuss whether he should allow Lucia to go to Salzburg to study at the Duncan school of dance there. When Joyce asked about the looms, Kay covered for Duncan.

Despite the drudgery of her life as a member of the cult, Kay remained a belle of Paris. One Saturday night she went off with Hilaire Hiler to view

Chartres at dawn. Upon her return, she jumped from the front seat of Hiler's moving car, spraining her ankle. At once Raymond Duncan gathered her up into his arms and carried her into the house, where he offered a bath and massages, binding her ankle himself. You can rest tomorrow, he told her. On Monday morning, however, Kay was expected to be at the shop.

Late in June, Richard Brault stopped off in Paris on a business trip. Kay took him to the Coupole, where they ran into McAlmon. Disapproving of her having joined the Duncan colony, disapproving as well of seeing her with Brault, McAlmon walked over and ripped the notice for *Living Poetry* from the wall. Looking straight into Kay's eyes, he tore it to shreds.

"That's what I think of your crazy, senseless undertakings," he shouted. "That's what I think of your taste in poetry!" At this, Kay grabbed a stein of beer and hurled it in McAlmon's direction. Missing its intended target, the glass bounced off the bar as its contents splashed in Buffy's face. Kay and Richard took their leave to the sound of McAlmon's mocking laughter. He must be jealous of my being with Richard, Kay concluded. He must be in love with me.

The next day McAlmon left Paris. The Princess and Archie had already gone. Eugene Jolas was at Colombey. Then, in the middle of July, Kay was informed that Raymond and Ayah would be taking the whole colony to Nice for six or seven weeks. Bobby would be going along with the other members of the commune.

So began Kay Boyle's Paris summer of dementia. Later she remembered herself during that time as having been "mad with despair." Wearing a midnight-blue cape, she hit a different Montparnasse bar every night, sleeping with whomever she encountered. The short story "Vacation-Time," published in the fall issue of *transition*, reveals that she entered her first bar right after the train departed. Her black makeup running down her face, she introduced herself to "a Jewish fellow, fat like a mother" (possibly Hilaire Hiler), saying, "I just sent my little girl off to the south." The man spoke to her through a cocaine haze. That she didn't like him perversely qualified him as a sexual partner and she went off to have sex with him in his shabby room.

After such nights, Kay slept on the floor of the Duncan shop on the boulevard St.-Germain. In the morning, she faced her guilt, as revealed in "Vacation-Time": "if you had kept the kid with you it would have had the whole world against it if it had turned out unnatural and refused to give love to its own momsy-womsy." (Disapproving, McAlmon later discounted Kay Boyle's nakedly raw autobiographical stories of the late twenties. "In those days," he wrote, "events for Kay were too hectic for the soundest writing.")

One night Harry Crosby brought Kay to the barge of that louche couple Frans and Mai de Geetere, the *Vert Gallant*. The scent of opium filled the cramped space as music blared, champagne flowed, and people had sex in front of each other. Kay joined in. Kay even had an affair that summer with seventeen-year-old John Glassco, its progress recounted in the manuscript version of his autobiography, *Memoirs of Montparnasse*. Kay appears as May Fry, who was "modelled after you," Glassco wrote Kay Boyle years later, being "beautiful, brilliant, sensitive, witty, charming and footloose." That was how men perceived Kay Boyle that summer of 1928. On Bastille Day, May (Kay) sat in a crowded car, on Buffy's lap, kissing him. Twenty-six-year-old Kay easily seduced Buffy. "You are sweet, and you look so Olympian tonight," she told him. Soon, in a carriage of their own, they became lovers, May crying out, "Oh, this is heavenly. Only think, we're both so young." Afterward, they looked into each other's eyes "with rapture."

Kay and Buffy found it difficult to find a place to make love, the studio Buffy shared with McAlmon hardly being appropriate. Yet in bed they performed "wonderful feats of inventiveness and endurance." Meanwhile, Buffy had also become the lover of Gladys Palmer's latest houseguest, Lord Alfred Douglas, the slimy nemesis of Oscar Wilde. Buffy had been McAlmon's lover too. He was, in fact, primarily homosexual. No wonder that making love to May (Kay) gave him "the impression of being a kind of phonograph needle which produced a music audible to her alone: her loins still rotated, thrust and withdrew—occasionally with such violence as to make me skip a groove." But Buffy received "little pleasure to myself" because if he viewed sex as a source of pleasure, Kay Boyle did not.

Soon John Glassco began to suspect that Kay was trying to get pregnant again: "the solemn and rather alarming thing about May Fry was . . . that for her the real purpose of the act of love was not pleasure but procreation. The very idea froze the blood in my veins." Indeed, as flirtatious as Kay Boyle was, she was not driven by sexual desire. Sex meant claiming men, and, later, having more babies, and not primarily the mutual giving of pleasure. When Kay accused John Glassco of "distortion," he changed her name in the published version of *Memoirs of Montparnasse* to Diana Tree, who, still resembling Kay Boyle, is a tall, haughty name dropper. Diana Tree is pretentious, and self-dramatizing, as she asserts, melodramatically, "I'm not going to be serious about any man again, ever." She wears Kay's midnight-blue cape and, like Kay, changes "her lovers with bewildering rapidity." Buffy asks if she knows Joyce, and she replies, guardedly, "as well as I know anyone else." All her life Kay Boyle would make exaggerated claims of her closeness with James Joyce, and later with Samuel Beckett. Diana Tree defends Raymond Duncan as "sincere" until a small handsome man sets her straight: "he's an exhibitionist with nothing to show. He's trying to prove he's something besides being Isadora's brother, and he's not. His milieu is the bourgeoisie." That voice is obviously McAlmon's.

As that summer dragged on, Kay took more lovers, among them Robert Sage, the *transition* editor. Sage took her only copy of her still unpublished autobiographical novel, *The Book of Cincinnati*, and sent it off to a Chicago publisher friend of his, who promptly and permanently lost it. Hilaire Hiler was another of Kay Boyle's lovers; his father wrote Kay Boyle a letter demanding to know whether she intended to marry his son. Kay flushed the old man's letter down the toilet. Her lovers were invariably people for whom she felt contempt, as she admitted to writer Hugh Ford in 1978. "With anyone I liked, it didn't happen. I didn't want it to." It was a madness, getting drunk, searching for someone she didn't hate as much as she hated the one before. If she had to choose between being with someone all night and going home alone, Kay chose the someone.

Nor did Kay feel any guilt when one day Maria Jolas stormed into the Duncan shop. George Davis was there keeping her company, but Maria was determined to speak her mind even before a third party.

"I've come here for one reason and one reason only," Maria Jolas told Kay Boyle. "May I have my husband back?"

"I don't understand," Kay demurred.

"Yes, you do. Now don't lie to me. You do!"

Caresse Crosby also suspected that Kay was sleeping with Harry Crosby because he seemed always to be in her shop. Later Kay said she dedicated *My Next Bride* to Caresse "because I wanted her to understand." She did not sleep with Harry Crosby, although in the novel Antony does kiss Victoria and tell her he's in love with her. But it's his wife, Fontana (Caresse), he sees while he kisses Kay.

One day that August, Kay was distributing fliers advertising Duncan's togas and sandals and scarves when she became so thirsty she went off at four in the afternoon to the Coupole. There she sat talking with Gaston, the barman. Suddenly a red-faced man fiercely puffing on a cigarette, accompanied by a hideous-looking woman, in Kay's judgment, approached her.

"Do you know who I am?" he demanded drunkenly.

"I have no idea," Kay answered, her hauteur intact.

"Well, you better know," the man belligerently replied. He had submitted some poems to the *Living Poetry* anthology only to receive no reply. "Why didn't you send them back?" he stormed.

"I used them for toilet paper!" Kay retorted.

"Who *were* those people?" Kay asked Gaston as soon as they were gone.

Gaston knew them well. They were the heiress Peggy Guggenheim and Laurence Vail.

Kay now discovered that she was pregnant. The father could have been any one of many. Harry and Caresse Crosby at once contributed five thousand francs for an illegal abortion, to be done on the avenue de Wagram. Kay went accompanied by the Princess. You have saved me "from eternal damnation," Kay told the Crosbys gratefully. "Without you," Kay thanked Caresse a second time, "I'd have been preparing a Jewish cradle and braziers and misery." The reference suggests her belief that Hilaire Hiler was the father, and reveals, of course, the lurking anti-Semitism to which all of her set subscribed; when Laurence Vail married Peggy Guggenheim, his susceptibility to that particular bigotry surfaced frequently.

Almost immediately, Kay returned to the shop. Condemned to remain all day, she had no alternative but to use the "deep fecund green" privy in the courtyard, from which issued "the myriad, dark smells of the earth's bowels." One hot August night Kay felt so dizzy, was so overtaken by a headache, that she said she must have fallen into a depression over Bobby's absence. But the next morning, she kept pressing her back downward while stretching herself up onto the headboard of the bed. Then she fainted. Katherine was visiting and she summoned an ambulance, which roared its way to the American Hospital at Neuilly.

Eleven days of delirium were followed by the spinal tap which saved Kay Boyle's life as she became one of the few adults to survive the epidemic of cerebral meningitis in Paris in the late twenties. The doctor agreed that the filthy outdoor toilet had bred the disease in its stagnant water. Informed of Kay's illness, the Duncan cultists were annoyed that Ayah had to open the shop herself. Nor did Ayah bother to visit Kay.

When Kay left the American Hospital, she was walking with the aid of two canes. She returned not to the grimy apartment across from the commune, but to Eddie Lanham's studio on the rue d'Alésia. Kay was nursed back to health by Katherine, who had been staying there. Kay must have considered Lanham one of her beaux, because she seethed when she discovered that in her absence Jo, in Paris now for *Vogue*, had fallen in love with him, just as she had stolen Kay's boyfriends during their adolescence. Jo paid the bills for Kay's three weeks in the hospital and took care of all the living expenses of Kay and Katherine at the rue d'Alésia. "You've never been a sister to me!" Jo accused Kay angrily when Kay complained about her stealing Lanham.

Even as she knew Bobby needed her, Kay refused to return to the commune. At the studio, Katherine cooked for her, and coddled her as she had in her childhood. The meningitis was followed by a cold and a cough. Another week passed without Kay's coming over from her apartment to sleep a single night at the commune.

When she finally appeared, Duncan treated her coldly. He insisted her illness had been psychosomatic, the result of her mother's appearance in Paris. Kay produced a paper from the hospital certifying that she had cerebral meningitis. But Duncan wouldn't even look at it, as he launched into a lecture about the prison of the nuclear family and the "psychological disorders" it breeds. Then, suddenly, Duncan made his first sexual overture to Kay Boyle. Taking her into his arms, he crooned, "You are the honey which draws men and women to the beehives. I would like to be privileged to taste that honey."

Although she did not succumb, Kay did not break with him. Still she told people that Bobby's growing up in the Duncan commune would be "a sane and healthy living and one in which I believe, for I am not yet tired of rebellion and Bobby grows more stalwart at it every day." To Stieglitz, Kay wrote that "the beautiful Sharon is growing up in a tunic and sandals and expressing herself in French."

In a feature, the autumn issue of *transition* inquired of some Americans why they chose to live in Europe. (Editor Jolas too, although he was raised in Lorraine, the son of a French father and a German mother, was an American citizen who had been born in New Jersey.) The magazine's questionnaire inquired: "Why do you prefer to live outside America? How do you envisage the spiritual future of America in the face of a dying Europe and in the face of a Russia that is adopting the American economic vision? What is your feeling about the revolutionary spirit of your age, as expressed, for instance, in such movements as communism, surrealism, anarchism? What particular vision do you have of yourself in relation to twentieth century reality?"

Gertrude Stein replied that "America is now early Victorian, very early Victorian, she is a rich and well nourished home but not a place to work . . . moreover a young man casts his lot with that which is ascending, not descending. Europe is upon the ascent." Kay Boyle's reply is high-flown and haughty. "Explanations," she asserts, as apologies for an action are a "collection of words as important as a lace handkerchief in a slaughter-house," a line Harry Crosby loved. Still angry at Matthew Josephson for having taken over *Broom*, she labels him the "American intellectual" in a land where "each citizen functions with pride in the American conspiracy against the individual." The only admirable figures were members of her personal pantheon: Stieglitz, composer George Antheil, whom Walsh had published, Charlie Sheeler, and Man Ray. "To what can one return?" Kay Boyle demanded, fearing conformity, fearing her countrymen, who were certain to "impose their achievements upon what is going on in my heart and in my soul." She was now the writer Kay Boyle, a person "too proud and too young to need the grandeur of physical America which one accepts only at the price of one's own dignity." She may have been poor, but she was herself, a writer "too proud to find nourishment in a situation that is more successful than myself."

Having resolved "to be a saner person and a more simple and generous person because my way of disintegrating is completely disastrous and wrong," in October Kay returned once more to work at the Duncan shop on the boulevard St.-Germain. Not wanting to leave her mother home alone all day, she urged Katherine to come with her.

8

Kay and Laurence

I felt when I walked down the street with him that he might
suddenly fly away—he had so little connection with
ordinary behavior.

PEGGY GUGGENHEIM

One day in November of 1928 two rich American women marched into the Duncan shop ready to purchase enough of the master's creations to fill a "Raymond Duncan wing" of a Kentucky museum. Once more Kay lied for Duncan. She did not reveal that he was a complete fraud, the creator of none of the artifacts. And she had her reasons. She hoped that with the money Duncan would buy a decent printing press so that she could at last publish her poetry anthology. She also believed she would earn a commission for inducing the foolish women to buy Duncan's fakes. Instead, Duncan spent most of the $25,000 on a grand American automobile. He did receive a discount for attaching a banner to the side of the car. It read: "Raymond Duncan Drives a Chrysler."

At last Kay decided to separate from the commune for good. The Crosbys had gone to America with letters of introduction written by Kay to Stieglitz and William Carlos Williams. They left Kay their chauffeured limousine, which she used to take her to the shop and to Elizabeth Duncan's dance class. Now Kay used the automobile to remove her possessions to the basement of the apartment house on the rue Louis-David, where the Princess was back in residence.

Like any cult leader, Duncan did not take kindly to Kay's announcement that she was leaving. "Bear with me," he pleaded, attempting to take her into his arms. "Everything will change." Kay even thought she saw tears on his lashes. Ayah took a more direct approach.

"*You* may go," she shouted at Kay, "but not the child." The cultists had paid for Sharon's vacation. Kay had virtually abandoned her anyway. Now the little girl belonged to the commune.

Alarmed, Kay remained, even working with Duncan on the catalogue for the Kentucky museum, writing imaginative descriptions of each worth-less object the witless Americans had purchased, an incident she recounts both in the novel *My Next Bride* and in her memoir *Being Geniuses Together*. She was worried because Sharon had been illegally registered at Nice when Ethel lied to the consul, swearing that Kay and Ernest Walsh had been legally married. Kay had no way of proving that Sharon was her daughter.

One snowy night just before Christmas, Kay closed the shop at six o'clock and headed for the Coupole, where she was to meet Robert McAlmon to discuss how she might escape from the Duncan colony. On the way she bought some mistletoe, as if she still harbored some hope for McAlmon and herself. She was very thirsty, she longed to give way, but the doctors had forbidden her to drink alcohol in the wake of her meningitis.

At the Coupole, amid the columns painted by artists for their supper—the bare-breasted woman, the man playing the flute with a black dog/cat on his shoulder, the sexy Josephine Baker look-alike swaying with her eyes closed—people were eating at the banquettes that circled the dome at the center of the room: *cassoulet*, oysters, *choucroute*. At one of the tables, Kay spotted McAlmon.

Suddenly, from another table, a man, sitting with a woman, yelled, "Come and have a drink and supper with us. We've just ordered oysters and white wine!" Kay and McAlmon moved toward the table, and as the man rose to greet them, Kay recognized him. It was that red-faced person whom she had told she used his poems for toilet paper! The man was slender and of medium height with streaky yellow hair and a beaklike Roman nose. Without a word, he seized the mistletoe from Kay and held it over her head. With mock courtliness, he kissed her nose, her eyelids, and then her mouth. When he seemed in no danger of ceasing, Kay looked helplessly toward the man's companion.

"Kay, don't take it seriously," said the woman, who was as blond as the man and had the same beaky nose. "That's the way he is. Just tell him to go away."

When still the man would not release her, his companion ordered, "Laurence, stop!"

"I'll sit between you and my brother so he won't eat the mistletoe," Clotilde Vail said. Kay ordered buttermilk, to Laurence Vail's amusement.

After the Vails departed, McAlmon outlined his plan. Kay must kidnap Bobby from the Duncan entourage and take her to the Crosbys' country retreat, Le Moulin du Soleil, at Ermenonville, an hour from Paris, where they had gone for Christmas. The Princess of Sarawak would invite Kay and nine colony children to lunch on December 31 in honor of the New Year.

On the morning of the thirty-first it snowed again. Kay ordered two taxis, and with the children shivering in their tunics and sandals, they all headed for the rue Louis-David. As soon as they rolled up, the children rushed into the warm building. Kay and Sharon lingered in their taxi. Then they raced toward McAlmon's hotel.

It was noon and McAlmon was still asleep. Laurence Vail was about to arrive to drive them out to Le Moulin. But as if he hadn't a care in the world, McAlmon got up and ordered coffee and croissants. While he showered and shaved, Kay and Bobby fell asleep together in his bed.

"You'd better wash her feet before we go," McAlmon said, taking one look at the bedraggled Sharon Walsh.

Kay had escaped but she inadvertently left behind a trunk, never to be returned, which contained one of her most valued possessions: her volume of Ezra Pound's poetry which she had brought from America. But that was small enough price to pay for her daughter's liberation, and her own.

It was New Year's Eve at Le Moulin as Bobby, Kay, McAlmon, and Laurence arrived. The noise was deafening. Frightened, Bobby began to wail.

"My god, what a nursery!" Harry Crosby shouted. Then he raced out the door, in search of Constance Crowninshield Coolidge, the niece of Frank Crowninshield and the particular beautiful young woman presently accommodating him. Crosby's diary for that day reports a drunken embassy man snoring "and a squeaking (Kay Boyle's child)." There were ten bedrooms in the tower of Le Moulin, each painted a different color, but never enough room for Harry when children were present; he wouldn't return until Sharon and Billy and Polleen, Caresse's children, were back in Paris. On this New Year's Eve at Le Moulin, Bobby, along with Billy and Polleen, slept in a farm building with the servants.

Laurence had gone home. Kay had lost sight of McAlmon when suddenly he emerged.

"It's too damn depressing, so depressing that I can't even get drunk," he complained. "They're wraiths, all of them. They aren't people. God knows what they've done with their realities." The moral chaos, the lascivious brawl, the emptiness appalled good Bob McAlmon on this New Year's Eve.

Kay tried to humor him as they walked around the grounds, not holding hands, but as friends. Kay suggested that the Crosbys' Black Sun Press might publish his poems, quoting the one she thought should open the volume.

"For Christ's sake, six years saying the same poem? When are you going to grow up, kid?" McAlmon turned on Kay Boyle, who was fond of quoting McAlmon's "Wall Street Chant." His self-hatred predicted his coming obscurity now that his days as a small publisher of "unknowns" like Hemingway were over.

"The God-damned fucking, quivering pieces of me! Good enough to be flushed like you know what down the drain! Stinking enough to be tacked on the barn door in warning to the young! Fouled up enough for—what? You finish it! I'm fed up with whatever it is I'm carrying around inside this skin, rattling around inside these bones!"

It seemed as if his pain were bottomless.

"For Christ's sake, don't care about me! Stop it, will you? Let the God-damned pieces fall apart!" They parted then, Kay and her best friend, the man who had rescued her and Bobby, first from the neurotic Ethel Moorhead and today from the wily Duncan.

In the morning when Kay collected Bobby from the servants' quarters, she learned that McAlmon had departed, just as the snow began once more to fall. He sensed that his day was done. Gertrude Stein had already stolen the entire edition of *The Making of Americans*, which McAlmon and Bill Bird had published together through the Three Mountains Press. Nor would Hemingway, whose first book McAlmon had published, remain a friend. Obscurity awaited poor Bob McAlmon as the snow began to fall on the first morning of the new year 1929 at Le Moulin du Soleil, the pleasure palace of Harry and Caresse Crosby.

Fleeing south now, Robert McAlmon was never to bestow upon Kay Boyle his physical love, for that no woman would be truly offered. But, as she was later to discover, he had left her his typewriter. Within months Kay was paying McAlmon homage in two poems, "Confession to Eugene Jolas" and "Dedicated to Guy Urquhart," both appearing in *transition*. "O pretty papa so much have you done for me that my spirit falters," she writes, picturing herself in borrowed clothes with heavy powder and rouge, Bobby on her knee, knowing that there would be no "provider to take us home." There is only "one man I see the skin of his lips and his eyes rocking . . . and his sad words and his blame on me." No matter that she "thought of somebody else every minute," McAlmon meant more to her than any lover.

As for Kay, as we leave her at the dawn of this new year, she had to relinquish at last her struggle to win McAlmon's love. But there was a man who did want her and he wanted her very much.

"I suppose one must marry a sort of commonplace man in the long run," Kay had written to her sister Jo in 1921. The yellow-haired man with the beaky nose now entering her life, however, was assuredly not commonplace. Born in 1891 in France of an American father and mother, he was an American. Unlike the grumpy Brault, he shared Ernest Walsh's gaiety. If Brault had little sense of humor, Laurence Vail was a veritable soul of wit. Constantly amazed at life's contradictions, he was forever alert to the absurd. He was worldly, ironic, sophisticated, mischievous, and no fool, although utterly impractical about money. No wonder, what with his rich Rhode Island mother, Gertrude Mauran, a member of the Daughters of the American Revolution, he had never had to work a day in his life.

Like Walsh, Laurence Vail was an artist, practically a requirement in a man for Kay Boyle during her Paris years. He was given to tantrums, brawls in cafés and elsewhere, great outbursts, and a deep nihilism which admitted the wildest amorality. But Kay found Laurence's spontaneity and joie de vivre exhilarating. Laurence was as well an emotionally dependent man, weaker of will than she, another requirement for Kay, who had learned to be jealous of her freedom from the time Katherine had suffered under the tyranny of Puss.

But if Kay was recapitulating Katherine's experience in choosing a weak man, Laurence, unlike Howard Peterson Boyle, was never predictable or conventional or dull. With Laurence, who had gone to Oxford, Kay received the education in literature and art she had missed as that willful little girl who had refused to go to school. In the twelve years she spent with Laurence Vail, Kay Boyle was to do her best work.

In 1922, Laurence, then thirty-one years old, married Peggy Guggenheim. But the central relationship of his life was with his sister Clotilde, with whom as a child he had shared the nightmarish emotional outbursts of his painter father Eugene, who periodically took to his bed and threatened to die and leave them all behind. *"Le Maître Noir"* he was called. As Eugene viewed life as forever precarious, so Laurence learned that all effort must be ultimately futile. And after so many mornings of awakening to find his father still alive after all, Laurence discovered he was unable to believe in anything; the absurdity of existence paralyzed him.

Neither Eugene nor Gertrude offered Laurence and Clotilde the affection they craved. When Kay Boyle met Laurence Vail, she found him locked in a lifelong alliance with his sister which had been formed in childhood against their cold martinet of a mother with her chilly New England soul and their neurotic father. As a young man, Laurence had decided that Clotilde must always be with him, "whomever I live with and marry." Clotilde came first, and as a condition of his marrying Peggy Guggenheim, Laurence had even demanded that Clotilde join them on their honeymoon on Capri. "They gave one the feeling that they were made for incest," Peggy said later, "and by not indulging in it they augmented their frustrated passion."

The trauma for Laurence of Clotilde's marriage is depicted by Kay Boyle in her story "Wedding Day." Uncompromisingly, Kay Boyle reveals the strong erotic bond between brother and sister with their "yellow manes" and "the proud arch in their noses." On this day both are beset by grief at the thought of being parted. Kay drew, as always, from reality. On the night before Clotilde's marriage to a French soldier and vintner named Alain Le Merdie, Laurence ran to her apartment, banging frantically on the door and yelling, "I'm here to save you. I'm here to save you." So Laurence pleaded until the early hours of the morning.

In Kay's story, as brother and sister go rowing, both mourn the loss: "Suddenly their hearts fled together and sobbed like ringdoves in their bosoms. This was the end, the end, the end, this was the end." At a student

forum sponsored by Southern Illinois University in 1964, Kay Boyle insisted, "It was just a brother and sister relationship. A great many people
have thought this was an incestuous story, but it was not." Thus, apparently
for reasons of propriety, she obfuscated, contradicting what she had
achieved and what she knew. "She was always a liar," Laurence would
say, but that was much, much later. At the time, even Kay's mentor William
Carlos Williams depicted the incestuous feelings between Laurence and
Clotilde. In his *A Voyage to Pagany*, he has the sister tell the brother,
who is based on Laurence, "I shall never love anyone as I love you." And
in Laurence's own 1923 novel, *Piri and I*, he creates a fantasy of incest
rewarded as he and Piri look alike, share a love of mountain climbing (as
did Laurence and Clotilde and all the Vails), and even marry.

By 1929, when Kay entered Laurence's life, his marriage to Peggy
Guggenheim was over. Knowing well Laurence's history, as Peggy put it,
of throwing "bottles about if he's drunk too much pernod on an empty
stomach," Kay planned to add order to his life. They would move to the
country, Kay decided, along with Bobby and Laurence's son Sindbad, age
five, of whom he had custody. (His daughter Pegeen, three, to Laurence's
distress, went with Peggy.) Laurence would give up drinking and write and
paint his surrealist collages. He would take his art seriously, as he never
before had done. Side by side the two of them would live as artists together.

Kay indeed could call herself an author now, for in 1929 Black Sun
was to publish her first book, a collection of short stories. She stood at the
threshold of a brilliant career, with few women competitors among American
modernist writers. She was fiercely ambitious, and, living with Laurence
Vail, she had the financial security of a home. Laurence offered Kay and
her illegitimate child the "security of family life," the freedom to pursue
her unrelenting ambition. After her bout with meningitis, the doctors at
the American Hospital had forbidden Kay to have sexual intercourse for
several months. Laurence was patient, and understanding. He is lovely,
Kay thought, as at first they spent time together without making love.
Proudly Kay presented Laurence to the Dayang Muda. When on January
8 of the new year Harry Crosby turned up at the rue Louis-David, he found
Kay reclining on a chaise longue. There Harry met, for the first time, that
"unpredictable fellow" Laurence Vail.

Kay Boyle now was ready to take full advantage of her beauty, for at
the age of twenty-seven she was so dazzling a figure that everyone wanted
to photograph her, including Man Ray. She was known for her sexy eyes.
But, intimidated by Man Ray, she became so nervous that she dropped
her eyelids.

"Can't you keep your eyes open?" Man Ray demanded, while Laurence
stood roaring with laughter. Man Ray's Kay Boyle in a beret, her hand on
her chin, her eyelids, indeed, slightly drooping, is a paradigm of woman's
mystery and would be the finest photograph of her ever taken. Maurice

Grosser and Henry Varnum Poor both painted her portrait in these years, and, not long after, Henry Miller, having read *Year Before Last*, wrote her, "Your breasts must be made of diamonds and your womb of platinum."

As the twenties drew to their close, Kay and the Crosbys and Laurence remained immune to the gathering social passions of the thirties. "Your murder of Max Eastman good job," Kay telegraphed the Crosbys. "I drink to Harry Crosby in cocktails." So Kay dismissed the stalwart socialist editor of *The Masses* and *The Liberator*. Anything was better than "the poetry of social comment," Robert McAlmon thought in 1929 as the decade of proletarian literature dawned. "Balls to all that social stuff." Kay agreed.

With her cool head, Katherine Anne Porter saw through Eugene Jolas as "a wooly-brained incoherent posturing fraud," aware that Kay "had a weakness for that sort." (Twelve years Kay Boyle's senior, Porter was her major rival as an American woman writer of short stories. In 1929 Porter would publish her masterpiece, "The Jilting of Granny Weatherall," in *transition*, and in 1930 "Flowering Judas" in *Hound and Horn*. Only in 1932, however, would she make her way to Paris.)

Indeed, Kay and Jolas and the Crosbys continued to talk of "genius," and considered liberation from bourgeois convention an end in itself, even in the face of the world depression, even in the face of the socialist experiment in Russia. For Kay and her friends, artifice remained all. "Come hell or high water," an exasperated McAlmon remembered in his 1934 memoir, *Being Geniuses Together*, Kay "had to romanticize every situation."

The last year of the twenties was a happy one for Kay. She enjoyed Laurence Vail, even as his rages may have reminded her of the excitement Puss's emotional outbursts brought to the households of her childhood. So she duplicated her mother's responses to the sensuality of her father-in-law's explosions. "I am so happy I feel as though my heart would break open," Kay confided to Caresse Crosby. Unwilling to acknowledge what she had felt for Robert McAlmon, she said she hadn't "been in love for two years, and I suddenly am and I feel all dazzling and speechless and stardust and wind and wild horses and perrier water." Kay also became a propagandist for Laurence's paintings, inducing Jo to order one of his screens. "I think you'd like Laurence Vail's paintings," Kay wrote Stieglitz, promising to send him photographs.

Having learned the lesson of dependence, and the need for women to attain some measure of economic self-sufficiency, Kay was determined to assume financial responsibility for herself and Bobby. In March of 1929 she took a job with an American fashion writer named Bettina Bedwell. Kay's articles, published in the *Paris Tribune*, an offshoot of the Chicago paper, were signed Bettina Bedwell, and she was paid one hundred dollars a month to write twice a week about the shops which advertised there. For additional articles she would receive fifty dollars more. Harry Crosby objected, declaring she should "write and write and write about guts instead of about fashions." Insisting upon her financial independence, Kay pleaded, "But I'm going to. You'll be proud of me yet."

Kay stayed close to the Crosbys. Indeed, should they not invite her often enough, Kay let them know her disappointment.

On one occasion in February of 1929 at Le Moulin, Kay and Laurence arrived to discover Hart Crane in residence working on *The Bridge*. Kay and Laurence feasted on goose and red wine amid a mob described by Harry Crosby later as "poets and pederasts and lesbians and Christ knows who." Hart Crane had, of course, not forgotten Kay's devastating review of *White Buildings*. Spotting her talking with Eugene Jolas, Crane at first ignored her. Later, with Crane "magnificently intoxicated," as Caresse Crosby put it, Kay provoked him; "makes fun" of him, Harry noted in his diary. Furious, Crane threw one of the Crosbys' magazines into the fire because it had one of Kay Boyle's stories. That it also contained one of his own poems didn't matter. Then they made up, and when Crane recounted how he had seduced a count on the eve of his marriage, his action, he later reported, was thoroughly approved by all, "(including Kay Boyle and Laurence Vail)." By the spring Hart Crane's list of the most impressive people he met in Paris included "Kay Boyle (who has decided she likes me)." Indeed, when a brawl at the Sélect landed him in jail, it was Kay who came to his rescue by searching for Harry Crosby, whom she located basking in the sun on the *Vert Gallant* with Frans and Mai de Geetere. Crosby at once supplied the money to pay Hart Crane's eight-hundred-franc fine.

Kay and Laurence frequently saw the Crosbys, driving back and forth between Paris and Le Moulin drinking rum grogs on the way; or Kay and Laurence entertained the fast couple at Laurence's Paris studio, where one day Laurence presented Caresse with "a marvelous picture called Explosion." On Valentine's Day, Kay and Laurence sent a valentine to the Crosbys, a painting by Laurence, a poem by Kay. One night at Le Moulin, when Kay and Laurence were in bed, English publisher Jonathan Cape's wife Gretchen appeared and got into bed with them. Kay took the middle and just lay there, incapable of moving. But sometime during the night Gretchen managed to embrace Laurence. Cape later had his revenge as he bragged to Caresse that he had sexual intercourse with his wife's corpse.

If there was a cloud over Kay Boyle's happiness in her early days with Laurence Vail, it was Peggy Guggenheim with her money and her claims on Laurence's children, Sindbad and Pegeen. It rankled with Kay that Laurence was living in part on three hundred dollars a month in alimony from Peggy. "I loathed her and she loathed me," Peggy remembered. "Oh, my God! How she loathed me!" According to Peggy, they hated each other on sight. Kay professed that her meetings with "Peggy Vail" always began well but ended "disastrously." Kay made Peggy the demon, and told people she and Laurence were "both nervy and peculiar and worried about his Guggenheim wife and whether she'll throw the babies over the roof as her sister did," a nasty allusion to Peggy's sister Hazel. The year before, in 1928, on the eve of her husband's defection, Peggy's sister Hazel had tossed her two toddlers, one four years old, the other one, off the roof of the Hotel Surrey in New York. The ubiquitous Guggenheim uncles at once stepped in, seeing to it that no criminal charges were issued. Hazel was spirited away for "recovery" in a European sanitarium.

In his effort to gain custody of the children, Laurence plotted to prove "the family is insane," using the Hazel episode as evidence. Laurence succeeded in gaining legal custody of Sindbad only, even as he tortured himself for having stupidly left Pegeen behind when he left Peggy.

It took Kay Boyle only a short time to discover that Laurence was indeed "nervy and peculiar." Attributing his violence and mania, incorrectly, to the breakup of his marriage with Peggy, Kay decided to care for him "in every way." With her, Laurence would drink less. Rational behavior would follow.

From the start, Kay dominated Laurence in a way Peggy never could. Whenever she sensed that he was about to make a scene, she made one herself instead. Observing, Peggy remarked to her mother, Florette, how frightened Laurence seemed to be of Kay. "Too bad he wasn't frightened of you, frightened of you, frightened of you," Florette told her. Kay also accomplished what Peggy never could; she managed to limit Laurence's contact with Clotilde, so that Bobby was scarcely to remember her Aunt Coco. Meanwhile Kay stirred Laurence up against Peggy, telling him he must be wary lest Peggy kidnap Sindbad. Kay spoke even of going to Russia, anywhere to escape his ex-wife. "We can't fight her," Kay said, "but we can clear out." Meanwhile Kay and Laurence both did all they could to alienate Sindbad from his mother. "You lead such easy rich lives while Kay and Laurence have to work so hard," Sindbad was to accuse his mother; for years Kay and Laurence concealed from him that Peggy was supporting them. Many years later Sindbad Vail was to tell his mother's biographer, Jacqueline Weld, that both Kay and Peggy were "perfect bitches."

In March, four years away from marrying Laurence Vail and having ignored her doctors' instructions, Kay became pregnant, a pregnancy complicated by the side effects of her meningitis. Now she did resign as Bettina Bedwell's assistant. That she was extremely ambitious, that money might indeed become a problem, could not compete with Kay Boyle's need to express being a woman by bearing children. Toward fulfilling her biological function, Kay Boyle proved to be the most conventional of women, and indeed, very much like John Glassco's May Fry, for whom the aim of sexual intercourse was procreation. That she was not married to the baby's father, that she ever more purposefully defied bourgeois convention, did not bother Kay Boyle, although Puss was told only that she alone had rented a house outside of Paris with three thousand francs she received for a book. It is wonderful "that I have a roof over my head all paid for for a year to come," Kay wrote Puss, without mentioning Laurence Vail. Puss was distressed, and not fooled. "I think a great deal these days of Kay," he wrote Jo, "and wonder as to the details of her life; and it all sounds a bit too self-dependent and very lonely." Soon they dropped out of touch for good. "Her unconventional life seems a barrier to our present intimacy," Puss decided. "I could wish it otherwise."

In fact, of course, Kay and Laurence had left Paris together, settling in a village on the Marne called Ste.-Aulde, two hours away. Harry Crosby suggested Kay translate the first chapter of *Babylone*, a work by the surrealist René Crevel, to be called "Mr. Knife, Miss Fork," which would appear first in *transition* and a few years later in a Black Sun Press edition. At a long table Kay and Laurence sat translating together, collaborators. Having been born in Paris, Laurence wrote perfect French. Their points of view, however, were decidedly different. Kay's impulse was to adapt, add her own flourishes. Laurence insisted on a translator's remaining faithful to the original.

"But that's not exactly right," Laurence would object.

"It's more poetic" was always Kay's reply. Her foreword, "An Open Letter to René Crevel," is a masterful homage. "The mystery is not mine to touch," Kay writes, "it cannot be translated." Addressing herself directly to Crevel, she tells him he has "revived an aristocracy of the emotions, and if the wind of it blow in a few isolate places, it is enough."

Paris beckoned often. Leaving little Bobby, now two, and Sindbad, six, in Ste.-Aulde with the servants, Kay and Laurence drove into Paris regularly. Kay admitted she chose a place "within easy motoring distance . . . so that it will not be too far to see the children often." Restless in the country, Laurence dragged Kay into town whenever he could. Once he encouraged her to leave Bobby behind in Ste.-Aulde—with scarlet fever. Kay rationalized, and then did as she pleased. Bobby was with "trained nurses and doctors"; she "couldn't be better taken care of." That she felt guilty about leaving her "poor baby alone in the country," that she would have no "peace of mind," didn't result in her changing her mind. Off Kay went to Paris to see Caresse. The children did not come first for either Laurence or Kay and soon Kay was spending only three or four days a week in the country.

Success beckoned too. When Harry Crosby had promised to publish her short stories with the Black Sun Press, Kay had laboriously copied them out by hand. "There's nothing better calculated to bring on a swell case of neurosis than laboriously copying out things one wrote once upon a time," she quipped, clearly ecstatic. As well she might have been. *Short Stories*, which appeared in March of 1929, was an exquisite volume, a work of art with its gorgeous gold lettering and fine paper. Seven of Kay Boyle's stories were included: "Theme," "Bitte Nehmen Sie die Blumen," "Summer," "Uncle Anne," "Portrait," "Vacation-Time," and "Spring Morning." One hundred and sixty-five copies were printed. The dedication read: "For Laurence Vail." In the copy Kay signed for Harry and Caresse, she wrote a poem ending "I shall be there when the wave has gone by." Always one to return favors, Kay soon wrote a *Paris Tribune* paean to Harry Crosby.

Short Stories received the review of a lifetime from Kay's mentor William Carlos Williams. It was called "The Somnambulists," appeared in *transition*, and heralded Kay Boyle's arrival in literary history. As Harry Crosby compared her to Jane Austen ("Sappho Jane Austen Kay Boyle," he repeated in his diary that August), Williams said Kay Boyle picked up where Emily Dickinson left off. Kay Boyle's short stories, Williams proclaimed, "assault our sleep." Presciently, however, Williams feared for Kay Boyle, predicting that she would fail to be successful and appreciated in America, not only because she was a modern and an experimentalist, as she then was, but also because she was a woman. "Few women have written like this before," Williams claimed, "work equal in vigor to anything done by a man but with a twist that brings a new light into the whole Sahara of romanticism." Kay had written with an honesty sufficient to enrage the "corrupt puritans" back home. She would not be easily forgiven.

Eugene Jolas sounded no less enthusiastic a note in a review which called Kay Boyle's first book "a turning point in the evolution of American literature"; in *Blues*, Charles Henri Ford wrote that Kay Boyle's stories "amaze and cut and make one cry out because of their beauty." A fan letter about Kay Boyle and *Short Stories* came from Archibald MacLeish to Harry Crosby. "I believe in her absolutely when she writes," MacLeish wrote. Kay was "grand." The world, MacLeish believed, "was her oyster," and "all she has to do is open it." He feared only that Kay might not open that precious oyster because she was "afraid of not being modern." Even as she burst upon the literary scene, warnings were addressed to Kay Boyle which she would have done well to heed. Nor was honest Bob McAlmon, who always told the truth about writing, so enthusiastic about this first volume of Kay Boyle's short stories. Later he wrote they "were by no means as good" as those she did later, although they did help her "get recognition from more commercial publishers."

But Kay Boyle was feeling a sense of her power as a writer. In the *Paris Tribune* that spring she reviewed *transition* No. 15, bizarrely comparing the magazine which had ensured her reputation with *The New Yorker* back home, in her eyes its most significant competitor. *The New Yorker* left "no field for revolt, for mystery," Kay asserted, insisting on the comparison although the two magazines had virtually nothing in common; it was shallow and predictable compared with the "fantasy" *transition* provided. Listing *transition*'s contributors, the "experimental vocabulary of James Joyce" no less than the "intense and direct prose of Robert McAlmon," and "Harry Crosby's hymns," Kay concluded that "any one of these contributions is more than a comment upon what New Yorkers will say over the teacups this week." As contradiction and inconsistency were to sound the prevailing note in Kay Boyle's life and work, so she was soon to be applauded and achieve her greatest notoriety as the author of one astoundingly accomplished short story after another, published in—*The New Yorker.*

That June, *transition* published a manifesto written by Harry Crosby and Eugene Jolas which they called "The Revolution of the Word." Inaccurate in its literary history, pretentious, and essentially superfluous, it insisted that there had been a "revolution in the English language" among the Paris modernist writers who now disregarded "existing grammatical and syntactical laws." Jolas and Crosby declared their freedom from "the propagation of sociological ideas" and, in their final precept, added, "the plain reader be damned," an obvious attempt to gain attention. Rewriting, mythologizing Paris as she did her own life, Kay Boyle would later assert that "The Revolution of the Word" called for acceptance of a uniquely American, as opposed to a British, syntax and vocabulary. In fact, the document says nothing of the sort; in any case, it was Mark Twain and Walt Whitman who had already forged that revolution.

"The Revolution of the Word" hardly signaled a literary movement, as Kay Boyle was also later to claim. There was never even a meeting of the signers of the document, or a moment when they felt they were participating in a call to arms. Among those who agreed to sign when Jolas mentioned it to them were Harry, of course, and Caresse, Laurence Vail, Hart Crane, and Kay Boyle.

"Mumbo Jumbo," said McAlmon, the ice in his blue eyes glinting, his thin lips tight with bemusement. *transition* prose, he had long ago decided, was "a constant example of how not to write." Ashamed of having signed "The Revolution of the Word," which he soon realized was both pretentious and rather silly, Hart Crane pleaded that he had been drunk. Laurence Vail in a surrealist piece published in *transition* called "Gaspar Loot" mocked the document: a newsboy cries "Paper Sir REVOLUTION MISTER WORD HINSURRECTION my l'awed WORD DEFIED." Even Kay had to admit, "I probably didn't even read it before I signed it, probably had three or four Pernods and said, 'Well, that sounds great,' and then put my name to it." But William L. Shirer, who was there, remembers her as a Jolas enthusiast, as Katherine Anne Porter had noticed, and a camp follower. "She loved the stuff," he says.

In later years, Kay Boyle was to picture herself in Paris writing pamphlets on the subject of the revolution of the word which "we" distributed "in the sidewalk cafés." She would talk of trying to make a "wholly grand experimental school of writing . . . come to life." She reported that T. S. Eliot and Henry James were burned in effigy on the boulevard du Montparnasse, an event unrecorded in any of the memoirs of the time, including her own. "The American language was just beginning," Kay later decided, a success for which "we certainly cleared the way for people to go ahead with what we had begun." Ironically, the writer she would attack all her life, Ernest Hemingway, was the one who most fulfilled the demand of the proclamation as she defined it, who, taking Twain as his model, was to insist upon colloquial speech and a clean language. "No one pays attention to Hemingway anymore," Kay Boyle would say in the 1980s as she persisted in her efforts to consign Ernest Walsh's tormentor to literary oblivion.

Predicting that her baby would be born by the end of November, Kay's doctor told her to move to Paris by the fifteenth. Laurence was delighted. They moved first to the Prinkania on the rue Notre-Dame-des-Champs, where Kay registered as Mme. Vail, although she was still Mme. Brault. (Only in September of 1930 would she go to the South of France to await Brault's divorce papers, which were then served on her, and only on January 9, 1931, was she actually divorced from Brault.) When the baby showed no signs of appearing, they moved to the Hôtel Verdun on the rue de Courcelles. Lola Ridge passed through Paris but made no attempt to locate Kay. Jo married Eddie Lanham. Shouldering the responsibility for Katherine once more, Jo gamely took her mother along on her honeymoon.

In early December, Kay moved to the Maison de Santé on the rue Borghese at Neuilly-sur-Seine. It was here, on December 18, that at last she bore—another daughter. Having threatened to name the child Apple-Jack, Laurence settled on Apple-Joan; Kay later insisted that he chose the name for Sharon's sister from the Song of Songs: "I am a rose of Sharon . . . as the apple tree among the trees of the wood."

If Kay was disappointed at the appearance of a second female child, Laurence was elated. He had lost Pegeen. Apple, as she herself later put it, would be "a girl for Papa," as they all called Laurence. At once Laurence transferred his affection to his new daughter, for which her half sister Pegeen never forgave her. Later Kay would tell people Laurence so took over Apple that at times she wasn't even allowed to be near her.

In 1929, Laurence was still married to Peggy, as Kay was to Brault. And so once more the legal parentage of one of Kay Boyle's children was thrown into question. In the French manner, once more the father went to court to declare for the child. "I recognize her as Vail, mother *inconnu*," Laurence said. A while later, having learned that Apple had at last arrived, and was being aired afternoons in the Jardin Luxembourg, Peggy headed for the park, where she hid in the bushes to get a look at Laurence's new baby.

In New York, with a pearl-handled Belgian revolver, a week after Apple was born to Kay and Laurence, Harry Crosby shot first his mistress, one Josephine Rotch Bigelow, and then, mysteriously, four hours later, himself. He chose for the venue of his suicide a borrowed apartment at the Hotel des Artistes on the West Side. The *Chicago Tribune* wrote that he had "lived more fully than any man of his generation."

The June 1930 number of *transition* was a memorial issue in honor of Harry Crosby. In addition to carrying Kay Boyle's most powerful antiwar poem, "The Only Bird That Sang," which invokes Eugene Debs, who had died in 1926, it contained her "Homage to Harry Crosby." "There was no one who ever lived more consistently in the thing that was happening then," Kay wrote. Harry had "courage," and "no consistency except the consistency of his own choice, and always the courage to match it." Harry was a loving man, Kay added, "his heart . . . open like a door, so open that there was a crowd getting into it." She showed the text to Caresse first; she asked Caresse whether she might wish to send any of Harry's things to Carnevali.

That same year Kay published her "Valentine for Harry Crosby" in *Blues*, the magazine edited by Charles Henri Ford, after it had been rejected by *Hound and Horn* as "not a poem to appear in print." Now Harry joined Kay Boyle's immortal dead, Eva Evans in Washington "forgotten / In the government office with a wig on" and her paternal grandfather: "What man who speaks in Jury Trial today does not remember / The law books Jesse Peyton Boyle compiled . . ."

"I am proud of everything Harry ever did," Kay went on in this, the year after Harry's death, "I am proud of every tear that falls out of my eyes for him because they are the tears for a man who could never fall below his own high self." One day Harry had inscribed an edition of *transition* stories to Kay Boyle: to "a big writer, an immense writer, a such a good writer to the greatest in America, Kay Boyle." Now Kay returned the compliment. That same spring of 1930, in a "Paris Letter for Charles Henri Ford," Kay once again eulogized Crosby, contrasting him with that enemy of promise, her bête noire, Ernest Hemingway. "Because Harry Crosby took each day as a new challenge," Kay wrote, "his work is a testament where Hemingway's is a blasphemy."

Harry was "healthy," Hemingway "blasted," the passion of her invective belying her later assertions that she didn't like Hemingway only because he had been unfaithful to Hadley with her best friend, Pauline. Catherine of *A Farewell to Arms* was a "wonderful woman," Kay had to grant, even as she added spitefully, "perhaps he made her up because he knew he could never have anyone so wonderful." Caresse had to apologize to Kay Boyle for even considering a reprint of Hemingway's *The Torrents of Spring* for the Crosby Continental Editions.

A few years later, when perhaps it was no longer politically necessary or desirable publicly to exalt Harry Crosby, Kay changed her mind. In an unpublished preface to Crosby's diary, *Shadows of the Sun*, Crosby was now "not one of us . . . in no sense a modern, having no place, no interest, no taste for experiment in modern life." Nor was he the openhearted man of her original homage: "People were the enemy; his intimates were such things as a superb collection of old keys, illuminated manuscripts, stained glass windows." Kay disapproved now of Crosby as a selfish man, "the only person alive in a confusion of many days and objects."

By 1973 the man who had published her first book became "a very cruel and heartlessly self-centered man" who immersed his wife in "a terrible, terrible hell of his own making," a man motivated by money, a frequent accusation Kay Boyle was to make in her later years against those of whom she disapproved. But six days after Harry Crosby's death, Kay Boyle said, "I loved him from the depths of my heart." His suicide was a mere "emotional blunder" rather than "a choice he made." But that "he had the courage to meet it should shame us all."

Harry rose, a phoenix out of the ashes of his miscalculation, the hero of the romance they were all living. Kay and Laurence welcomed a bereft Caresse back to Paris as Kay sent her friend, whom she admired as "a fiery little steed," three letters on the cold winter day of her return alone.

9

The Writer Kay Boyle

If she goes the right way, she ought to be first rate. Or she may just fall into the egotistical self-exploitation that some very clever writers . . . fall into.
KATHERINE ANNE PORTER

I think that I write my short stories too quickly.

As Kay Boyle moved into the thirties, the decade of her greatest accomplishment as a writer, she and Laurence left Paris and its environs for good. They settled in one of the "runaway colonies" of the Paris expatriates, first at Villefranche-sur-Mer, and then at Col-de-Villefranche, on the Riviera near Nice. Paris was, most of them agreed, finished. "It marks an epoch," Kay wrote in her increasingly supercilious tones, "when Kiki too writes her memoirs."

From the villa of Mary Reynolds, now living with Marcel Duchamp, where the roof leaked, they moved to the Villa Coustille, a red stone house hidden in a thick grove of pine trees high above the old town on the Moyenne Corniche. There was a terrace and a garden, where they ate lunch under a medlar tree. Col-de-Villefranche was also only half a day's drive to the Maritime Alps, where Laurence could ski in winter and climb in summer. Unlike Peggy, who wanted nothing to do with Laurence's mountain-climbing obsession, Kay made herself a willing companion, although always she preferred to remain at her typewriter. The family consisted of Kay and Laurence, Sindbad, Bobby, Apple, occasionally Pegeen, a white bitch named Lulu, and a maid named Hélène, who was suffering from tertiary syphilis.

Although Kay affected to be "worried" by Cagnes-sur-Mer, the "in" place where there were "so many people . . . so many people at tables, talking, people I don't know, people I find confusing," and professed to reject "café society," never even meeting F. Scott Fitzgerald, who was in the neighborhood, in fact she and Laurence were very social. They formed their own coterie, which included former Wall Street speculator and writer Robert Carlton Brown, author of the pulp Nick Carter detective novels, and inventor of a "reading machine," which he insisted would permit you to read a full-length book in ten minutes. When Kay met him, Brown was already a veteran of a colorful career, having published magazines in South America; he boasted that he had written one thousand stories. Later he would write about cookery.

Close by as well were Mary Reynolds and Duchamp as well as the great anarchist exiles Emma Goldman and Alexander Berkman. The poet Alfred Kreymborg lived next door. Allan Ross MacDougall, nicknamed "Dougie," a Paris habitué who had written *A Gourmet's Almanac*, visited often. One evening at a hillside restaurant above Nice, Kay began to praise a story she had read in Whit Burnett's new *Story* magazine, only for a member of the company, a young Anglo-Irish writer, thin, purposeful and direct in his demeanor, to remark, "I wrote that story." So Kay Boyle began a lifelong friendship with James Stern.

Kay drew so close to Bob Brown, who lived up the coast at Cagnes-sur-Mer, that they began to write to each other at least once a day. "I like your energy, your lustiness, and direction," Kay had replied to Brown's invitation for her to write a "Readie" for his machine, thus inaugurating their friendship. (Kay's "Readie," called "Change of Life," was, appropriately enough, in her stream-of-consciousness mode: "Sat smoking cigarettes thinking change coming over him . . .")

If by day Kay wrote, by night she indulged in the heavy drinking that became such a norm that in one of her letters to Brown she spoke of being "perfectly sober and inspired," as if this indeed were the exception. At one party Kay got drunk and, babbling, announced she had coined a new verb based on the name of one of the more notorious of the expatriates, Abraham Lincoln Gillespie, a flamboyant character famous for his outrageous use of language: "I gillespie, you gillespie, we gillespie," Kay recited. "Links was gillespieing me at the time I made it up!"

Overwhelmingly, Kay preferred men to women as friends. The major exception was Caresse Crosby, who, with her many publishing enterprises, could still provide publication opportunities. To Caresse, Kay wrote in the flattering tones she had reserved for such as Alfred Stieglitz. It was Caresse, Kay told her friend, who had given *her* the strength to go on. Kay insisted she had given up, would no longer "write, or care anymore, but just . . . give up and go to America," only to be "boiling over with determination and conviction" at the return of her friend from New York.

One day in August of 1931 Caresse and a lover visited Kay and Laurence at Col-de-Villefranche. It was seven in the evening when they arrived, and the sun had not yet set. Kay was laying the table in the garden overlooking the bay, Pegeen and Bobby beside her. She radiated happiness and an aura of electricity, Caresse thought. Her "fine humor" shone in her blue eyes. Admiringly, Caresse noted she was as slim as ever, "tirée-à-quatres-épingles." The little girls, Caresse saw, "adorned" their mother.

When Caresse awoke the next morning, she heard the tap-tapping of

Kay's typewriter, even as she could smell coffee laced with chickory in the kitchen. Wandering out, she discovered her hostess in the middle of a maelstrom, so that it seemed as if she were tap-tapping the typewriter with one hand and bathing baby Apple in the kitchen sink with the other, while, at the same time, scrambling eggs on the driftwood-burning stove. Competence, energy, ambition—these defined Kay Boyle from her earliest years as a woman combining life with a man, and the raising of many children, with the writer's life.

Caresse had also come to provide work, and before the visit was over, she had hired Laurence to translate *Bubu de Montparnasse* by Charles-Louis Philippe and Kay to do Raymond Radiguet's *Le Diable au Corps*. "Oh, darling," Kay wrote after Caresse had gone, "I shall die if you don't let me do this one! It is one of the greatest, simplest books . . . Please, take anything else from me, but let me translate that!"

If Kay could be frank and confessional with Bob Brown, she reserved her admiration for Alexander Berkman, whom she called "a great and courageous man." "I've been in prison too," Kay joked one night early in their acquaintance, alluding to the fourteen years Berkman served in prison for his attempted assassination of Henry Clay Frick, chairman of Carnegie Steel, in the wake of the bloody Homestead strike in Pennsylvania when Berkman was twenty-two years old. Kay's "prison experience" amounted to one wild night at Cagnes-sur-Mer when she had called a *commissaire de police* a "*cochon*" because she deemed that he had "insulted" Laurence Vail, no doubt well launched into one of his fiery brawls.

Emma Goldman and Sasha Berkman had both been deported from America in December of 1919 to the Soviet Union, victims of the Palmer raids—only to be disillusioned by the abuses of the socialist ideal they discovered there. At Kronstadt, they had been horrified when they heard Trotsky threaten to "shoot like pheasants" all who dared to "raise their hand against the Socialist fatherland."

"Anarchism is more demanding of the individual than Communism," Sasha told Kay. "Communism actually doesn't demand much of the individual." He was gentle, forbearing, and compassionate. As for Berkman, he was at once enamored of Kay, even as, at sixty, he appeared with a young mistress named Emmy Eckstein.

Kay was generous and sympathetic toward Berkman. She did not extend the same compassion to his fellow exile Emma Goldman, whose patron was none other than the hated Peggy Guggenheim. For years she would tell people that Emma Goldman "didn't seem to me to have the integrity that Sasha had . . . it was no great privilege to have known Emma Goldman, who was one of the most self-righteous people I've ever known." Emma lacked "integrity" because she was living on Peggy's generosity. That Kay herself was doing the same thing, living on Peggy's money, only reflected her habitual inconsistency. Kay Boyle liked to have her men friends to herself, and it could hardly have pleased her when at a celebration for Emma's birthday at the apartment of Frank and Nellie Harris, she had to watch as Emma and Sasha, lovers once, comrades forever, waltzed in each other's arms.

Emma Goldman, of course, was a feminist, and Kay was not. One night at one of the many dinners they shared, the differences between the two women emerged. Women ask deeper and more enduring things of sex, Sasha began, initiating the argument. The sex urge was the impulse of women's highest activities, the source of their painting, writing—and their politics. Kay Boyle at once concurred. But Emma Goldman shook her head. Emma laid down her fork.

"You know, dearest comrade," Emma told Sasha, "you are a very sentimental man, especially where women are concerned. As for this theory about the sex urge, I've yet to be convinced that any woman, Kay here for instance, who has two of her own and two step-children, actually wants a large flock of children." Kay, who believed in a woman's perpetual fulfillment of her biological function, and in the creativity of bearing children, kept silent.

"Let Kay speak for herself about that," Sasha said, rushing to Kay's defense. Emma ignored Kay's silence.

"There's another sign in the sky about the awakening of women in American society," red Emma predicted, not at all perturbed by Kay's unwillingness to debate the merit of a woman's gaining fulfillment through her biological function. "A large minority of American women are refusing to have children." In the work of her friend Margaret Sanger, Emma saw a harbinger of revolutionary change, a liberation of women from biological enslavement.

"You can't have a 'large minority,' " Sasha quibbled, unwilling to abandon Kay, whose debating skills were no match for those of Emma Goldman. While Emma talked on, Kay continued to turn a deaf ear.

"There is Kay and there are other friends," Sasha always said. If Kay remained envious of Emma Goldman, she professed to like Sasha's lover Emmy Eckstein, who was no competitor, hence a "grand girl." Kay even said she enjoyed Emmy's fractured English, in which "shriek" meant "shrink." Emmy, Kay decided, was "Stein, Carnevali and her own sweet self all rolled into one."

Emma and Sasha both lived precarious lives as exiles in Europe. Berkman, lacking papers, was subjected virtually every three months to expulsion orders from the French government. Kay Boyle at once devoted herself to helping Berkman evade the authorities. The telephone rang very early one morning that summer of 1931; it was Emmy Eckstein telling Kay and Laurence that the police had already visited. Driving at once to Nice, they found Sasha sitting up in bed eating a croissant and drinking *café au lait* from a tray on his lap. He had been ordered out of France for having created an "antimilitarist" propaganda campaign in Toulon, no matter that he hadn't been in Toulon for two and a half years.

Kay soon wrote up a petition to have the expulsion order permanently annulled, persuading Caresse Crosby to gather signatures of "viscounts and princes," as Kay put it, like the Comte de Rochefoucauld. Kay then asked Caresse to enlist Roger Vitrac, whose work Lola had published in *Broom*. When they learned that Vitrac was unavailable, Kay suggested that Caresse go to see André Breton and take him with her to see Gaston Bergery, a deputy from the Radical Socialist Party and an influential member of the government.

A naive Caresse Crosby reported that Sasha's attempted assassination of the president of United States Steel, as she put it, made him "in their eyes . . . a dangerous character as it comes under the act of anarchism." But she and Bergery did visit the Ministère des Affaires Etrangères, where they met with Michel Hauser, who was in charge of Berkman's case. Eventually Kay and Caresse were victorious in their efforts. As long as Sasha remained in Nice, his permission to reside in France would automatically be renewed every three months. To celebrate this victory, Kay Boyle organized a grand dinner for eleven guests, which Emma Goldman attended, and great, Kay later reported, was "the rejoicing." Kay then began to urge Caresse to publish Sasha's autobiography, which he was calling *I Had to Leave*.

That summer of 1931 Robert McAlmon turned up in the "runaway colonies" with the news that he had extracted the manuscript of Ernest Walsh's poems from Ethel Moorhead. Toward the man Kay repeatedly called the love of her life, the man who was the hero of the autobiographical novel she was writing, and whose poems she was obsessed with getting published, Laurence Vail took a detached view. There was no point in being jealous of a dead man, Laurence thought. And, in any case, who could compete with a martyred poet? Kay's friend Bessie Breuer, an editor at Harcourt, Brace in New York, wanted to publish Walsh's poems. Kay said she was pleased "because he would have loved it so," but also "for Bobby's sake so she will have something tangible of him." Bobby, however, at five, assumed Laurence Vail was her real father, and no one bothered to tell her otherwise.

That summer too, it appears, Kay was faced with more evidence of Robert McAlmon's homosexuality. Even as for years she had been working on a novel which would be one of the most sensitive and sympathetic ever written on the subject, first called *March Minot*, and then *Gentlemen, I Address You Privately*, she seems to have been repelled that McAlmon had so completely repudiated the fantasy she had long cherished. "All the filth about McAlmon . . . has so turned my stomach that I can't be civil to him," Kay asserted, yielding to full moral outrage. "As far as being friendly with him ever again—that's finished!" Receiving a note from McAlmon, she replied "in trembling and fury," writing two closely typed pages of invective. "I have been seething and boiling and tearing my hair at his superior, stupid, dishonest, crooked, unimaginable mind, soul and temperament," she fumed, vowing to rush to Cagnes and hit him in the eye. She had thought she would never say anything but good things about McAlmon. Now all that had changed.

The frenetic pace Kay lived in these early years with Laurence Vail left little time for attention to the children. Kay called Bobby "happy." In fact, this was far from the case. In October of 1931, Bobby was sent to Blanche de Castille, a Catholic school, where she behaved badly and suffered abuse from the other children. "I'm always a victim," Bobby began to think after the nun put *her* in the corner to be punished. One night shortly after her fifth birthday, when Kay and Laurence were out as usual, Bobby set fire to the dining room, burning up an armchair, a curtain, and a cupboard, an obvious cry for attention. Never one to delve into psychology, into motives, her own or anyone else's, Kay reacted sardonically. "Fortunately the whole house didn't go, nor any of the children," she quipped.

The children had already begun their lifelong habit of courting Kay, competing for her attention. After Bobby uttered her first dirty words in French, and Kay washed out her mouth with soap, she found forlorn little Pegeen weeping.

"You never wash my mouth out with soap," Pegeen complained through her tears. "I'm only your stepdaughter, so you don't . . ."

And yet, proving Emma Goldman wrong, and despite how little time she actually gave the children, what with the frequent trips to Paris, and their nightlife, Kay longed for another baby, "to keep us company at home all day." Meanwhile there were now always a maid and a cook, and the constant hirings and firings of servants were all that took her away from her work. Kay and Laurence hired immigrant Italian girls illegally in France to take care of the children in exchange for their food and a roof over their heads. Servants did the cooking, washed the dishes, took care of the laundry, and cleaned the house. In 1931 Kay added an Alsatian to her staff. Still, she complained of having to work "hard at baby love."

On a Paris foray, at a party given by the poet Walter Lowenfels, Kay Boyle found herself seated on a fragile yellow-and-black-striped sofa beside a slim, handsome young man with an aquiline nose, light blue eyes, and fair hair. He was attractive, even as, with his direct gaze, he could seem severe. The man began to tell Kay about the play he had seen the night before, Machiavelli's *Mandragola*, which he pronounced the most "powerful" play in the Italian language. But if, to Samuel Beckett, Kay seemed bored, in fact she was distracted. Finally she told him that Lucia Joyce had just been committed to a mental institution. When Kay told Beckett that she didn't believe in madness, "not for a minute, not under any guise," and that "love is the missing element," expressing once more her antipathy to psychology, Beckett spoke of "an abyss, and when a person goes over that abyss, love can't bring them back." Beckett, recounting how he had visited Bethlehem Royal Hospital in Kent, spoke of a bridge being constructed to lure back those who crossed over. It would be many years before Kay Boyle was to see again the man she was later to claim was her oldest and best friend.

Link Gillespie had told Kay Boyle of a writer in Paris so poor he and his wife could not afford to buy clothes for their coming baby. Kay sent Apple's old baby clothes to Paris. That Christmas, Kay and Laurence headed once more for Paris, this time taking Sindbad and Bobby, but leaving Apple behind in Nice. It was freezing, and, as Kay Boyle was to tell the story years later, she was standing near the potbellied stove in Laurence's studio when a forlorn figure with a cap pulled down over his eyes, carrying a parcel, appeared at the door. "I brought back the baby clothes," the man said. At this, the group of celebrating friends burst into a collective laughter, only for the woebegone man to explain that his baby had died. So Kay Boyle became friends with James T. Farrell, who wrote the story "Studs" in 1929, but would not publish *Young Lonigan*, the first volume of the *Studs Lonigan* trilogy, until 1932. At least that's how she recounted it. In fact, it was in a letter that Farrell informed her of the death of the baby. They did become friends in Kay Boyle's usual manner. She wrote paeans of praise to Farrell: "everything I have ever read of yours I have liked very much, and it will make me very happy to talk to you and read more." Meeting the flirtatious Kay Boyle, Farrell was at once enamored, announcing he wanted to be "Kay's bodyguard" and "follow her everywhere." He was one of many.

Loyalty was Kay Boyle's credo. She lobbied for Peter Neagoe to include Ernest Walsh and Emanuel Carnevali in his influential anthology *Americans Abroad*. Having forgiven McAlmon, she urged Caresse to publish a volume of his stories. Since McAlmon was certain to "leave out all the sentimental, childish ones which are among the best," Kay offered herself to make the selections. Enemies, of course, were to be dealt with mercilessly. Kay was incensed when she discovered that Ethel Moorhead had sold the name "This Quarter" to a publisher named Edward Titus, husband of cosmetics mogul Helena Rubinstein. When Titus announced a poetry contest, only to deem no entry worthy of honor, Kay became even angrier at Titus with his "pompous decision that there is no living poetry worthy of his little Jewish hundred dollars!" In obvious anti-Semitic ridicule, she imagined Titus "obsequiously rubbing his hands saying 'Miss Boyle, someday you will be begging me to publish you!' "

In the early thirties, the moral culture of fascism was in place, as Kay Boyle subscribed to both hero worship, with its dark overtones of *Übermenschen*, and to a glorification of the Aryan physical ideal. "I wish you could see Bobby and Apple," Kay wrote William Carlos Williams, "such nice blonde Germanic babies." Kay Boyle's stories and novels were soon to become populated by blond, physically powerful, Germanic heroes. It was a time when Kay Boyle cultivated Ezra Pound, urging him to "leave that gay Rapallo and come to Paris soon." His views and hers throughout most of the thirties were much the same. She remained a modernist in the manner of D. H. Lawrence, Pound, and T. S. Eliot, and no more than Laurence Vail was she interested in issues of justice, history, or politics, which she left to the proletarian novelists at home. Kay Boyle remained the pupil of Ernest Walsh, who, in an open letter to *New Masses* written shortly before his death, had argued that "organized opinion and emotion can never be right" and that " 'good labor' and 'bad capital' was an absurdity." Editor Mike Gold's response was that Walsh would have made a "wonderful writer in time had he broken through the professional esthetic group in which he came to live." Had he been aware of Kay Boyle, Gold might easily have said the same of her. Indeed, Kay Boyle lived to make just that breakthrough.

It was at the very moment that she began to be widely recognized that Kay Boyle began to apologize for the inadequacies of her work, and to argue that having to earn so much money to support the family prevented her from producing art of the highest quality. In fact, she was not paying most of the bills; Laurence was. But Kay spoke as if all the financial responsibilities were hers. Completing her translation of *Babylone*, working on *Le Diable au Corps*, which Caresse would publish in 1932, she wrote Caresse she was "at a terribly low ebb" because she was unable to pay the rent. Sacrificing herself with wearying translations which "swallow one whole" was demoralizing. Exaggerating, as was her perpetual mode, she announced that she "had better be a stenographer again."

In part, Kay Boyle's obsession about money was related to her obsession with Peggy Guggenheim and everything related to her. Kay told people that Peggy hated it when she earned money which might be used to support Sindbad. Every four or five months, Kay insisted, Peggy asked Laurence how much money Kay made so she could add the equivalent to Sindbad's support. When Peggy came to take Sindbad for the weekend, Kay melodramatically reported she was searching for somewhere to go "for consolation." Kay also let it be known that Laurence suffered in his continued contact with Peggy. "I'm afraid Laurence won't get over this week," Kay confided to Bob Brown in early February of 1932, "for his ex-wife is arriving on Friday or Saturday for the weekend to take Pegeen back." It was as if Peggy populated an area of Laurence's life she could not control, and Kay did not like it. Kay also insisted that Peggy's lover, John Holms, so lusted after *her* that once he pursued her right into the ladies' room of a restaurant. Kay said the same thing of Jonathan Cape, insisting that he told her, "I think you and I were meant to be together." As far as Kay was concerned, they were both "sons-of-bitches." Anyone associated with

Peggy, of course, had to be a scoundrel. Cape, however, could be forgiven for *his* lascivious ways since he was her publisher. "There is something human about him, for all his inhuman self," Kay decided.

Cushioned by Laurence's allowance from his mother and his alimony from Peggy, Kay and Laurence rode out the Depression with enough ease to make them virtually oblivious to the economic disaster devastating the planet. Kay could even consider refusing a check her sister Joan sent her. It was only when Laurence told her it was just the sort of thing Peggy would do when her sister Hazel sent *her* a check that Kay reconsidered. They were also able to lend money to Bob Brown when he needed it.

Out of her long-programmed and inescapable need to achieve her mother Katherine's dream for her, Kay unrelentingly drove herself to write. If she had to do translations, she worked nonstop until they were done. One day Kay bragged that she had beat her own record by typing eleven pages an hour for five hours helping Laurence complete his translation of Robert Neumann's *On the Make*. "If only I can work hard and long enough," Kay told herself, "things will go beautifully before very long." She developed the habit of working on her writing until midnight every night. When she injured her eye, and had to wear an eye patch, still she worked on, protesting that she was "doing the best I can." If she was sick over anything, Kay said, it was losing "days of work when I need to finish things for the sake of money."

Mrs. Vail arrived for a visit and pronounced Kay and Laurence "going to hell and rack and ruin." But it didn't matter to Kay Boyle what her prospective mother-in-law thought. One evening she celebrated the completion of the day's work by drinking two Pernods without leaving her worktable. Work made Kay Boyle feel most herself, as if she could relax only by fulfilling Katherine's dream. More than anything she loved to sit at that table overlooking the calm blue bay of Villefranche surrounded by flowers and her blue and red pencils.

Kay Boyle was now represented by a New York literary agent named Virginia Rice. From the start, Rice exerted pressure on her to write "women's fiction." Kay must set her stories in England and deal with themes of marriage and love. At once Kay perceived the danger and protested vigorously. She was no "woman writer" confined to themes comfortable to middle-class housewives. At once, in defiance of her agent's attempt to consign her to a ghetto of "female" writers, Kay took to calling Rice "Vagina." "Vagina," Kay said, was "most aggravating and more like a woman than any woman has a right to be." Moreover, Kay added, "she farts!"

But as she longed for sons and not daughters, and respected male rather than female friends, Kay Boyle also seemed to believe, in conformity with the dominant cultural norm of her time, that women were more trivial people than men, herself included. "The speech that suits my ear and mouth," she wrote in her lyric "A Glad Day for Laurence Vail," "is talk of cloth or keys or bread. A man's mind should be elsewhere. By climbing higher he pursues the sun." Evelyn Harter interviewed her for the first major article about her life and work in *The Bookman,* one of the most important literary journals of the day, published out of London. Women writers, Kay told Harter, with the sole exception of Gertrude Stein, whom she had taken to praising in contradiction to her earlier disparaging remarks, weren't worth reading. "Tact and complacency have long been women's attributes," she argued, "and I think they prove a drawback to good reading." Women writers did "not write simply or violently enough for my taste," she said. Yet as contradiction defined her thinking, she was irritated when an article in the New York *Telegram* entitled "Men the Best Writers" named Virginia Woolf and Vita Sackville-West and "Kay Boyle in America" as "excellent examples of how women miss being great." Kay's all too rare sense of humor came to her aid then. "I miss in high society so it's all right," she wrote Brown.

From the start Kay Boyle demanded that she be seen as a writer, not as a woman writer. When Brown, who read the manuscript, called *Gentlemen, I Address You Privately* the work of a "lady writer," Kay promised her next novel would be "hot from the heart and there ain't no ladies in it." Under no circumstances, she ordered, must Brown call her a "lady novelist." Such words would only lead her "back to the gutter . . . expiring in a drain with an empty bottle of gin in my hand." Kay Boyle had become a hard-talking thirties woman, no victim and no second-class citizen of literature.

Far from dealing with domestic themes, Kay Boyle vowed to "write a record of our age." With characteristic bravado she prepared to be misunderstood by reviewers. "The present day reader," Kay declared, "is not worth a ha'penny bit." She would write not for women readers or for critics, or to please "Vagina." She was writing "for posterity."

Kay Boyle was published commercially for the first time when in 1930 Jonathan Cape brought out *Wedding Day and Other Stories.* As would be the case with every one of her books, the reviews were mixed. In *The Nation,* Gerald Sykes wrote it was now time for Kay Boyle to be considered not as a "mere lower case revoltée," but as "more enterprising, more scrupulous, potentially more valuable than nine-tenths of our best-known authors." Her strength, he believed, was in her depiction of female sexuality, in her understanding of "feelings which could have been generated in no other place than a woman's body." Kay Boyle "put to shame nearly every other emancipated woman writer who has attempted to deal with this subject." *The New York Times Book Review* praised Kay Boyle for being one of the *transition* experimenters who had succeeded in letting "the subconscious out." From the outset, however, critics warned, as Sykes did, that "her work abounds in mannerisms." E. B. C. Jones in *The Adelphi* cautioned that "the impression made is of too much affectation." It was her greatest weakness as a writer, and it characterized her personality as well: Kay Boyle seemed addicted to striking a pose, succumbing to the haughty gesture, the arch mannerism.

In 1931, Cape and Harrison Smith in New York, then partners, published *Plagued by the Nightingale*. In its longeurs, it suffered from Kay Boyle's evident preference for and mastery of the short story form. With little forward plot movement, episodes curl back on themselves, and interpolated tales, ravaging chronology, grind the action too often to a halt. The concept of a marriage doomed by a hereditary disease strains credulity. At twenty-nine, Kay Boyle was no Ibsen.

Kay dedicated *Plagued by the Nightingale* to Katherine Evans Boyle ("For My Mother and Her Undying Flame"). In the text she contrasts Katherine's approach to raising children with that of the Braults. For Katherine and her family, "everyone was an individual, with his own individual way to go." Autobiography colors the whole. Where once Kay rejected Carnevali's question about her ancestors, now she has her surrogate, Bridget, regret not having "heroes behind me with which to have shamed" the Braults. "I should like to have had successful ancestors," Kay writes. There is also an homage to Puss. "Whether I could live with him or not he was a fine man," she writes.

In this the final version of her *This Quarter* serial, the character based on Richard Brault is so unpleasant that the novel reads as if Kay were justifying having fled from Brault into the arms of Ernest Walsh. The doctor named Luc, not in the serial, seemed to Kay finally like an afterthought. "It was a better book before I dragged in a love interest," she realized.

Predictably, the reviews for this first novel were mixed. Hart Crane generously sent word from Mexico that "Kay's novel, *Plagued by the Nightingale*, impressed and delighted me immensely." But if the New York *American* pronounced the novel as powerful as Edith Wharton's *Ethan Frome* ("there is the splendor of the stars in her writing"), *The New York Times Book Review* wrote, "one cannot complain of the surface of her book. What one does complain of is that there isn't enough below it." The writing suffered from "prettiness" and "daintiness." *The Spectator* in Britain complained that Kay Boyle was "at present too self-conscious," while "her style pirouettes stiffly before a looking glass."

To her good fortune, *The New Republic* assigned Katherine Anne Porter to review *Wedding Day and Other Stories* and *Plagued by the Nightingale* together. Porter agonized over her review. "They are very gorgeous," she confided to her friend Josephine Herbst about the short stories. Yet, Porter thought, "there is something a little off somewhere in this talent, or maybe it is just that she is a little shrill and noisy because she isn't quite certain." In 1931, Katherine Anne Porter perceived that Kay Boyle was already at a crossroads in her quest for literary excellence. "If she goes the right way," Porter predicted, "she ought to be first rate." But she feared that Kay was as likely to "fall into the egotistical self-exploitation that some very clever writers . . . fall into." Her autobiographical obsession, so exclusively grounding her work in her own experience, marked a real danger. Yet Porter was on her side. "I hope Kay Boyle gets over her toughness that is just a thin layer over what seems perilously like apple-sauce beneath," Porter said, "and that the inner fiber strengthens and warms a little. Then she's going to be grand."

When it came time to write the actual review, Porter suppressed her reservations, deciding to praise the author as "good almost in spite of herself." There remained "that suspicion of taint that keeps cropping out," which made it difficult to write the piece. "I have fiddled all around it," Porter confided to Herbst, "trying to do that girl justice, and I am having a hard time." Kay Boyle was "gorgeous and irritating, sharp as a whip and mean as the devil, and a vitality that is like a sock on the snoot." But it continued to bother Porter that it was "almost impossible to get her disen-tangled from her work." She had "that kind of personality that *is* her work, and comes very near sometimes to simple self-exploitation, that is the bane of too many literary women and some men." No more astute analysis of Kay Boyle would ever be penned. The final printed review, however, was so favorable ("a magnificent performance" if also "only a beginning") that Kay at once wrote Porter that every sentence she had ever written made her want to "shout and wave and cry."

Now, in July of 1931, she published her first story in *The New Yorker*, "Kroy Wen." It was a story which she recycled from a little magazine called *Front* out of Amsterdam, which had printed it in 1930. If he knew, Harold Ross didn't mind. From the early thirties and for the next twenty years, Kay Boyle published one distinguished story after another in the pages of this magazine, so that she redefined the short story form, inventing a major version of what came to be known as the "New Yorker story." As Vance Bourjaily was to sum up Kay Boyle's achievement as a writer of short stories in 1980 in his Sunday *New York Times* review of her major collection, *Fifty Stories*, she "invented techniques we still practice, and introduced themes that still concern us."

The typical Boyle story began "in medias res," smack in the middle of things, with no exposition to introduce the reader to the characters, no explanation of their situation. One dramatic situational moment replaced the old-fashioned imperatives of plot, rising action, and resolution; she invariably offered none. Like the other modernists of her generation, she had developed her craft virtually at the moment of the publication of Hei-senberg's "uncertainty principle" with its rejection of the Newtonian idea that the behavior of matter and energy could be reliably predicted. She startlingly wrote about characters under emotional duress as if the future need not invariably, indeed would not, bear any relationship to the definable past. As she drew her art from her life, her short stories stalwartly rejected the biographical approach to character. Nor in the thirties and forties, the decades of her ascendancy as a craftsman of the short story, was there so much as a hint of moralizing judgment. As Evelyn Harter put it in her appreciation in *The Bookman*, her characters "simply live before us for a few terrible moments." There were few happy endings. "All human misery can be seen as the failure of love," the romantic Kay Boyle then believed. That became her great theme.

In 1931, Harold Ross published two more stories, "One of Ours" in October and "Christmas Eve" in December. Ross became Kay Boyle's strongest literary advocate in America. When "Black Boy," her brilliant story of Puss, herself as a child, and the black boy on the beach at Atlantic City, a story excoriating American racism, was rejected that year by *Harper's*, *Forum*, and *Scribner's*, so that Kay feared it might end up at *The American Mercury*, Harold Ross had the courage to buy it for *The New Yorker*. "Maybe they aren't going in for magic this season," Kay said sardonically when *Harper's* disingenuously rejected "Black Boy" despite some "magical" passages.

"One of Ours," a little-known story, and one she did not choose herself later to anthologize, was nonetheless the writer at her youthful best. An Englishwoman's stroll through an exhibition depicting life in the colonies offers a biting satiric exposé of British racism toward Britain's colonial subjects. At first Mrs. Umster is repelled by images of black Africans "like a knot of black gleaming serpents." Then, in a surreal moment, with the appearance of a Nigerian, she falls prey to the repressed sexual desire at the root of her bigotry: "When he stretched up his arms and yawned, she could see down, down into the fathomless pit of his belly." Kay Boyle's reputation as a short story writer was immediately so strong that T. S. Eliot requested a story from her for *The Criterion*. He rejected "One of Ours," however, as too "indelicate" to print in England, although he professed to have "derived considerable pleasure and amusement from its perusal."

The two hundred dollars Harold Ross paid her for that first story, "Kroy Wen" (New York spelled backwards), led Kay to an orgy of short story writing, to a feeling that she was so infallibly strong a writer that she could afford to take shortcuts. She began to write much too rapidly, cranking out a new story on July 8 and another on July 9 of 1931 as she sat opposite Laurence at their worktable. Some indeed followed Virginia Rice's prescription. "Pretty English," Kay admitted. "I hope they're English enough to sell." She knew she was writing her stories "too quickly, in the stress of wanting to make a little money," knew it was "a lamentable idea." Yet she kept on doing it, kept sabotaging her own talent, even at the very moment she was coming into her own. Sometimes she made a joke of what seemed to be her uncontrollable impulse to write too rapidly. "I'm going to drink myself under the table," Kay mocked herself, "and then I'll write something decent."

At other times, out of some hubris long ago cultivated in her by a mother so determined to believe she would become the writer Kay Boyle, she seemed to believe her talent was so strong that there was nothing she could do to damage it. "I want to be a prolific writer and write tomes and tomes," she wrote Bob Brown, as if Katherine's ambition for her itself accounted for her frantic productivity. "I could write ten novels with one hand and five epic poems with the other," Kay Boyle said when she was twenty-nine, and she believed it. At the same time she mistakenly under-valued the genre in which she most excelled. "I *have* to write short stories whether I want to or not," she said. She spoke of keeping "the ship afloat with short stories."

Kay Boyle from the start devoted most of her time and the best of her energy to her writing. If she took a trip, riding up the Basses Alpes on a mule, with baby Apple before her in the saddle, it was only to return to the worktable renewed. Painful wisdom teeth did not delay her. In her spare time she read her literary mentor, D. H. Lawrence, pronouncing *The Rainbow* "too dark loinsy and utter depthsy." A sore eye sent her to bed, where she read Bob Brown's book *You Gotta Live*. Then, denying that she was "an intellectual or something," she wrote him a critique. It was Kay who suggested that Brown end his book with the line "I'll say you do." All she wanted in return was not to be called a "lady novelist." Then she was back at her worktable, as if someone had chained her to a wheel to produce. When Rice reported two rejections of short stories now, Kay could see what was wrong with them. But she continued to write too rapidly, too carelessly.

By October of 1931 Kay had begun still another novel, *My Next Bride*. Meanwhile she seethed over her publisher Harrison Smith's complaint that her "fairy book," *Gentlemen, I Address You Privately*, was such a disap-pointment that she would do well to let it "hang over" so that it would not damage her growing reputation. She worked days and nights, fleeing to bed two nights in a row that October in tears "out of pushing all day and half the night." This, she insisted, was "the only way to get things done."

Suspecting that Harrison Smith was right about *Gentlemen, I Address You Privately*, Kay instructed Virginia Rice to sell her novel about her time with Ernest Walsh, *Year Before Last*, first. She had become a skilled manipulator, by no means content to leave decisions to her agent. Although she called Cape "sly and foxy and obscene, and I don't doubt dishonest," although she said she "felt like taking cold douches after a day with him," she signed with him to publish *Gentlemen, I Address You Privately*. But when Harrison Smith, no longer Cape's partner, suddenly cabled that he would offer a thousand-dollar advance for *Year Before Last*, Kay was ready to back out of her agreement with Cape. That "Vagina" didn't want "that horrid Cape to have it," and refused to send Cape the manuscript, preferring Smith, made Kay Boyle determined to do the opposite of whatever her agent advised.

"Vagina" and her partner seem like "a couple of half-wits," Kay Boyle declared, with all their "lovey-dovey" business over Harrison Smith, although they also seemed to be frightened of asking him for the thousand-dollar advance he had promised for *Year Before Last*. Harper's was also interested and Kay plotted to use the initiatives made by Harper's to force Harrison Smith to award her a contract of one hundred dollars a month. Kay communicated with Harper & Brothers in London without bothering to tell Rice.

Finally, when Smith came up with the better terms, Kay dropped Cape. Publishers were fickle, recalcitrant, and stingy. "What's a girl to do?" Kay pleaded disingenuously. "I'm as ignorant, as ignorant as can be." When Smith suddenly insisted that if *Year Before Last* failed to earn back its one-thousand-dollar advance within a year, the deficit should be subtracted from royalties on future books, Kay, on the advice of her neighbor Frank Scully of *Variety*, struck the clause from the contract. Rice had urged Kay to "pay back the advance if the book doesn't sell." Her days now as Kay Boyle's agent were numbered. Strong-willed, and confident in her future, Kay mailed back Rice's check. The deal was off unless Smith paid the thousand dollars "with no strings attached." When Kay learned that Harrison Smith had turned down Laurence's novel *Murder! Murder!*, Kay became even angrier at "Vagina."

Bob Brown knew of an agent named Ann Watkins, and Kay authorized him to speak to Watkins on her behalf. "Tell her I'm not satisfied," Kay suggested, "or don't tell her anything, maybe." Kay and Brown both were now disillusioned with Virginia Rice. "She's a bad businesswoman," Brown egged Kay on. "You should be getting more money." Ann Watkins would "do much better and not be half so grasping and lecturing" as Virginia Rice. Indeed, Ann Watkins became an indefatigable agent for Kay Boyle, energetically calling magazine editors and offering them twenty-four hours to make a decision on a story. Soon Kay concluded she liked this "hard-boiled baby" very much.

With three novels sold, and a fourth begun, Kay returned to her translation of Radiguet's *Le Diable au Corps*. She told Caresse she was fortunate not to have agreed to allow Radiguet's former lover Claire Perlmutter do the translation, "unless you had wanted it done in very quaint Polish-Jewish." Kay also began to write an epic poem about the history of aviation, for which she applied for a Guggenheim fellowship, her distaste for Peggy no obstacle. Poetry remained her first passion, Kay told William Carlos Williams. The aviation poem was in fact Laurence's idea, and one to which Kay warmed as she discussed it with the painter Pierre Matisse one night.

In her usual flirtatious manner, recounting the story years later and sounding very much like the "fictionalizing" of reality of which her sister Joan all her life would accuse her, Kay asked Matisse's advice; what should she do in her depiction of an Englishman "gliding out of a balloon over

London" regarding the weather since she didn't know whether it was raining or the moon was out?

"Have the moon shine and the rain fall at the same time," Matisse told her. This was truly revolutionary, Kay thought. But the words of famous, successful male artists were always gospel to her.

10

"If It Were Not for the Children"

I'll never forget a picture in the Paris paper—the wedding of Larry Vail and Kay. And here were the three of them, they were standing there with the preacher, and the three of them are surrounded by four children.

WILLIAM L. SHIRER

In April of 1932, Kay and Laurence decided to get married at last, choosing the Nice City Hall for the ceremony. Kay stated that they were taking this step only so they could "travel on the same passport." Technically, however, she remained a citizen of France, and marrying Laurence would not automatically restore her American citizenship. She talked now of moving to Austria, where the exchange rate was so much better and Laurence would have mountains to climb. Never did she express any concern about Apple's legitimacy. Rather, she treated having borne her two children out of wedlock as a badge of honor, proof of her freedom from bourgeois convention.

If Mrs. Gertrude Vail, no rebel, approved of this marriage, Maria Jolas thought it was shocking, since there were so many children. "Just do it privately, without any public notice," she advised Kay, letting her know she thoroughly disapproved of how she had been living. She's always telling me what to do, Kay thought, irritated. But even Sasha Berkman thought it was "stupid to make a special celebration because of her wedding two years after the fact." The old anarchist sent a telegram: "MAY LOVE LAST IN SPITE OF LEGAL BONDS AND SANCTION."

"Wedding bells for Kay Boyle and Laurence Vail," Wambly Bald wrote in the Paris edition of the *Chicago Tribune* on March 22. "We hear that among those present will be Peggy Guggenheim, Vail's first, but we haven't received word about the intentions of M. Brault, Kay's first, who lives in London. Montparnasse is quite goggy about the coming event."

Laurence surprised Peggy by inviting her to the wedding. He had asked her "for some morbid reason," Peggy thought. She hated Laurence's attempts to throw her together with Kay, whom she now was calling a second-rate writer. Peggy came with the man for whom she had left Laurence Vail, John Holms. Bettina Bedwell attended, as did Mrs. Frank Harris and Hilaire Hiler. Caresse, Dougie, and Emma Goldman failed to appear, but Sasha, despite his telegram, was there.

"Laurence Vail and Kay Boyle Wed in Simple Ceremony," read the unsigned notice in the *Paris Tribune*, for April 3, 1932, "but the knot was tied just the same. Moreover, the principals in the matrimonial venture were accompanied at the wedding by a ready-made family of four children."

The bride stood reed slim, tall and full-breasted in a silky tea-length gown ruched at the hem. A big cloche hat concealed the right side of her face. Her cap of black curls was cut short; her heavy black eyebrows, which had not been plucked according to current fashion, stood guard over her deep-set, heavily lidded blue eyes. Her skin was creamy white, her dark red lipstick in sharp contrast, as she stood ramrod straight for the photographer. Kay Boyle was surrounded by her "flower girls," Pegeen, Bobby, and Apple, who wore bonnets, the bottoms of their silky dresses ruched in just the way Kay's bridal dress was. In the photographs, Sindbad holds a pistol, which made everyone laugh.

Kay was given away by Bob Brown. He and Clotilde were their witnesses as Kay and Laurence signed the register. The company then made its way to the Villa Coustille to party. Ever after, whenever she saw a wedding party, Pegeen would ask Kay, "Where are the children? Why aren't the bride's little girls there?"

Continuing her astounding productivity, in 1932 Kay published not only the translation of *The Devil in the Flesh* and the novel *Year Before Last* (dedicated to Carnevali) but also two poems, eight short stories, and a piece called "Writers Worth Reading," in which she had the temerity to review both her husband-to-be and her best friend, Bob Brown. "You'll only make a fool of me because everyone knows we're living together," Laurence had protested. Kay ignored him. In the pages of *Contempo* that July she compared Laurence Vail to William Faulkner, while praising Brown for his personality: his "mind and heart are wide, wide open, open and shining like an open door at night." As always in these years, Kay Boyle made virtually a political issue of her distrust of reason and logic. "It has always been left to the poets to water the emotions," she asserted, "and when they sharpened their wits instead, it left the appetite high and dry."

She began now to devote herself to cultivating her image in America. For an autobiographical sketch which was to accompany (but never did) her short story "The Man Who Died Young" in the *Yale Review*, she described herself sardonically as a French citizen. "If allowed to enter New York," she wrote, "I must recite the names of the presidents and prove that I can write my name." She professed herself happy in Europe, which she preferred to America. And she lied about her age: being thirty was unacceptable, so Kay said she was born in 1904. Later, ashamed, she was to tell her daughters she never knew how old she really was, another lie, since Dr. B. Hogden had, of course, dutifully recorded her birth four days after the fact.

That February day at the turn of the century, Hogden had mistakenly written in the year as 1901. Now, in 1932, even as she was saying she was born in 1904, Kay wrote to the Division of Public Health in St. Paul to change that date to the correct 1902. Her letter was indeed recorded on February 3, 1932. (In "The Man Who Died Young," as if still she could not forget Carnevali's urging her to praise her ancestors, Kay depicts her grandmother Eva Evans actually meeting George Washington when he was still a general, a meeting that "gave a dignity to the heart, a pride to the bearing." Like Kay Boyle, Eva Evans in this story longs not for a child, or a daughter, but for a son who "would be a pride to any woman.")

In story after story, all autobiographical in impulse, Kay Boyle rewrote her life, more often than not fabulating. In "Friend of the Family," published in *Harper's*, Katherine appears as married to a rigid, unsympathetic man, a composite of Puss and Howard. Her joie de vivre is restored through the visit of an opera-singing baron, even as Katherine had been sustained by such admiring young men as the union organizer Duane Swift. "Mother" smokes, as Katherine did, and her voice is "soft and filled with love" for her little girls. When the baron is finally banished by the father, the mother, renouncing the Italian admirer who might have made her happy, lies on her bed and moans "like a woman crying all night." So Kay viewed her mother's marriage, and so she determined that, unlike Katherine, whom she had chastised in 1927 for not going off with her Italian, leaving "us to be Boyles," she would follow love wherever it led. "Three Little Men," which T. S. Eliot accepted for *The Criterion*, retold the story of Howard as a man "too eager for love," as Kay vowed never to show eagerness, always to withhold herself, always to be the object sought and never completely at the mercy of any man. That moment when Kay found the fragment of the letter Howard had written to "dearest Mary" is dramatized only to show her anger at a father who had not seized the possibility of happiness when it came to him.

With Laurence Vail in their early years Kay Boyle believed that she had found happiness, so much happiness that she almost rebelled against Katherine's stricture that her success as a writer come first. "I simply cannot, will not, don't want to, get back to work," she wrote Brown. Kay wished she could read and sit in the sun, play with the children and the dogs, and then wander off to the market to purchase dinner. She would like to have a corset fitted, pluck her thick black eyebrows. "The Riviera's fine for everything but work," she complained in a short-lived rebellion.

In these first years of her marriage, Kay devoted herself to encouraging Laurence to take his work seriously, to reject his habitual view that aristocrats like himself did not engage in commerce. Laurence, some thought, acted as if he were an eighteenth-century aristocrat who had landed in the twentieth century by mistake. Laurence "behaved" as if success was vulgar and it was wrong to sell your art. As when during his marriage to Peggy he had tossed the manuscript of his novel *Murder! Murder!* into the fire and had to begin all over again, so with Kay he destroyed his works of art invariably on the night before they were to be taken away for an exhibition.

An American Legion show was rejected by Laurence as an unsuitable venue for his screens and paintings. At this, Kay "willfully," as she put it, "kidnapped" two screens and put them in the show without his knowledge. "I don't think it matters much where one shows as long as people see the things," Kay argued. Kay tried to please her eccentric husband, who drank heavily and had been given to tantrums and scenes since his childhood, when, emulating his father, he threw a plate of boiled endives on the floor in a rage, and developed the habit of throwing the crockery to express his displeasure. When it snowed, Kay accompanied Laurence to Beuil for skiing. Upon their return on one occasion, Laurence, restless and agitated, complained that "the cries of the offspring" were too much for him. Kay agreed that he should rent a room across the road for his work. Kay then protested that they were "both lonely for the sound of the other's machine."

Mostly the servants kept "the cries of the offspring" to a minimum. Bobby screamed in pain one day. That no one could ignore, and Kay waited for her daughter to undergo the ghastly mastoid operation so commonplace in those years. "I wish I could give a leg or an arm or anything so that it would not have to be," she declared melodramatically. When Bobby recovered, Kay and Laurence took the children to Italy and Austria, Laurence having determined that Sindbad was ready for a three-hour climb.

Sindbad, Pegeen, and Bobby were able to manage the mountains, but not Apple, still only two years old. Kay agreed to leave Apple behind in Cortina d'Ampezzo at the Hotel Venezia with an English nanny, while the others went off for an overnight expedition. When the car rolled up a few days later, Apple stood on the hotel steps, hopelessly waiting. Suddenly she began whirling and spinning, whirling like a dervish, spinning out of control. Something awful must have happened in these forty-eight hours, Kay thought. Then she banished the incident from her mind.

Back home, they resumed their social life, getting "pie-eyed" often. "You have no sex appeal," Bob Brown suddenly told Kay one night. His words stung. She saw herself as glamorous and exciting to men. She continued to believe that most men she knew were in love with her.

Kay told people Laurence had been jealous as she wrote about her love affair with Ernest Walsh. In fact, throughout their years together, Laurence functioned as Kay Boyle's editor and mentor, as he had been for Peggy. Laurence worked out the chapter divisions for *Year Before Last*. When he found the ending too abrupt, Kay rushed off to get Bob Brown's opinion, carelessly pitting the two men against each other. But Kay was proud of this novel, which she believed was "infinitely better than either of the other two." Finding it "an ordeal" to write, Kay Boyle even momentarily doubted her autobiographical approach to fiction. "What the literary value of stripping oneself naked may be," she wrote Caresse, "God alone knows." Then, and for the rest of her life, she went on doing it.

T. S. Eliot rejected *Year Before Last* for Faber and Faber in London as being too "sexually frank." In her arrogance Kay told everyone that Eliot had refused to recommend the book, which subsequently Faber and Faber did publish, because in one scene Martin (Ernest Walsh) calls "The Waste Land" a "minor" poem. She received rave reviews when the novel appeared from expected places like *Contempo* and the *Paris Tribune*, where Waverley Root, a friend, wrote that *Year Before Last* was "as near perfect as any novel which has been discussed on this page since William Faulkner's *Sanctuary*."

There were, however, many negative reviews. In *The Nation*, Robert Cantwell made proletcult demands, insisting, inaccurately, that the novel was not about Kay's love for Ernest Walsh, but about "the predicament of the exile, more or less isolated in a society he can only partially understand." Socialist realist demands were already being made of writers, as *The Booklist* minimized the novel's value as being "limited to readers of literary tastes." Most of the Marxist critics chose not to notice her. If Granville Hicks had decided that André Malraux's *Man's Fate* failed as a revolutionary novel because there weren't enough workers in it, Kay Boyle's stories about love and family were not even worthy of consideration. Willfully, the Marxist critics ignored her powerful exposés of racist America in such stories as "Black Boy," "White as Snow," and "Ben," all published in *The New Yorker*. Meanwhile the formalist "New Critics," who preferred poetry, did not take her up because her poetry was topical, dealt with antiwar themes, and invoked such figures as Eugene Debs, while the poet refused to view art as divorced from history and circumstance. That she had stayed on too long in Europe and had ceased to be an "American" writer, depicting American scenes, further alienated the Marxist critics. That she was a woman made it easier for them all to ignore her.

Kay Boyle could dismiss reviewers who were uncomfortable with her modernism. But the renewed charges of her self-consciousness, artificiality, and mannered prose warranted her attention. Myra Marina, an admirer, nonetheless complained of her "near preciosity." That she ignored these early warnings about the arch and mannered quality of her prose was one important reason why Kay Boyle was unable to sustain her early fine reputation. By 1940 Philip Rahv would accuse her of lacking "a subject which is organically her own . . . something more tangible than a fixed interest in certain abstract patterns of emotion and behavior." Her "elaborate technique" only underscored the weakness of her writing. She had not taken the point.

Unfortunately, Kay Boyle could ignore the warnings she received in the early thirties because there were so many accolades. "If this writer goes on being ignored," E. B. C. Jones wrote in *The Adelphi*, "the critic may well despair." In *The Saturday Review of Literature*, Gladys Graham hoped that with *Year Before Last* Kay Boyle would "reach the larger public she deserves."

"I have not seen such beautiful writing in a very long time," Clare Boothe Brokaw (later Luce) wrote of the short stories, requesting for *Vanity Fair* "something in the style of the sketches which you have had in *The New Yorker*." Kay sent an ill-conceived story called "Lydia and the Ring-Doves," which did appear in *Vanity Fair*, although it had been rejected by Kay's friend Louise Theis for *The Everyman*. The story returned to the ancestor theme Carnevali had unloosed upon Kay Boyle, as Lydia wants "dead great men to give her balance and background for her single life . . . the dignity of knowing what her people had been." Kay Boyle was not published again in *Vanity Fair*.

Determined to secure her literary reputation, while hurriedly making as much money as she could, a potential contradiction she failed to acknowledge as such, Kay Boyle decided no longer to waste her time on translations. Caresse asked her to translate André Breton's *Nadja*. Kay turned down the two thousand francs. The Vails, Kay pleaded, "live too much from hand to mouth, with absolutely nothing set aside, to be able to let down for even a month." A dentist fractured Kay's jaw while pulling a tooth and pieces of bone worked their way out, so that her face was swollen with abscesses; still she did not alter her frenetic writing schedule. Finishing *Year Before Last* had caused her to lose so much time she must "keep at short stories all summer long to make life possible here." She would take time out only to work on selecting stories for the McAlmon anthology.

But if she had once been worshipful toward McAlmon, if in the past she had accepted his literary judgments, Kay Boyle had become her own woman. McAlmon had doubts about a young writer named William Faulkner. "I don't see why he should be expected to give a photographic view of the South," Kay argued. "Faulkner does get more power and a kind of physical despair I like into his things more than anyone."

When McAlmon complained about her selections, Kay lectured him. "Do you think I picked out the ones I wanted for my own book or even selected the name?" she demanded. "If one depends on one's living on getting printed, it's the kind of thing one has to swallow." Kay admitted that the price of selling her stories to *The New Yorker* was that she had to include "what they feel is necessary for the readers to have clarified." She would have been more elliptical, less realistic, had she her own way. McAlmon was being lectured at the same time from another quarter. "People too lazy to examine the facts are not intelligent enough to write interesting books (reduced to bulls and memoirs depending on personalities)," Ezra

Pound wrote him in an apt comparison with Hemingway, referring on the one hand to *Death in the Afternoon* (1932) and on the other to McAlmon's *Being Geniuses Together.*

Always gentle now with her old friend who seemed headed down the road to oblivion, Kay begged McAlmon not to "think I'm trying to be important, but you know how much I like your work and so does everyone else." When Waverley Root gave the McAlmon collection, *The Indefinite Huntress and Other Stories,* a title Kay Boyle chose, a negative review, Kay wrote an impassioned letter to the editor. Root had compared Hemingway's "stripped sentences," which worked, with McAlmon's, which "cut away all the feeling as well." Kay was indignant. "If there be really any debt owed," she wrote, it was one "owed by Hemingway to McAlmon, who wrote these tales long before Hemingway had written any at all." Passionately wrong, Kay Boyle was also uncompromisingly loyal. "Something rather grand ought to be done about McAlmon—something that would fix him without confusion in the minds of the younger writing-men and in the American scene," she argued. When H. G. Wells came to lunch at Col-de-Villefranche and spoke admiringly of McAlmon's writing—"what an unusual and vigorous feeling for the language he has"—Kay was elated.

She was working frantically herself, but apparently was never too busy to pick up the sword on behalf of one of her pantheon. When critic Austin Warren dared attack William Carlos Williams in the *New English Weekly,* Kay produced a scathing denunciation of Warren for his "insensitive dismissal of the work and value as poet, critic, and editor of William Carlos Williams." Williams in turn then wrote an important essay on poetry in the form of a letter addressed to Kay Boyle. It began with a statement she once made to him: "Some kind of poetic form has to be found or I'll go crazy."

When Lola Ridge persisted in evading her, although she was again in Paris, Kay asked Evelyn Scott to tell her "how sad I am that she does not write . . . she is always for me one of the rarest and most beautiful persons alive." Loyal to her youth, Kay was genuinely distressed to learn that Hart Crane had jumped from the *Veracruz* into the sea. "He was a dear and extraordinary soul," she remembered, even as, with her characteristic naiveté regarding matters of psychology, she asked Caresse, "Do you think it possible that he did it himself? . . . why do all the good gay ones have to go so early?"

Nor, when Sasha Berkman's permission to remain in France was once more interrupted, did Kay abandon this friend. Caresse must once more see Gaston Bergery. Sasha had despaired. "Do you think Bergery will be too busy now to be bothered by such things as my future life?" he wrote Kay. She redoubled her efforts and now began to urge Caresse to publish Sasha's translation of a volume of Russian short stories in the Crosby Continental Editions. "The poor darling is almost destitute," Kay pleaded.

Kay herself rewrote Sasha's synopsis for the volume as well as his auto-biographical statement, which she found "too non-committal." When she spotted flaws in Berkman's translations, Kay offered to rewrite the stories herself. "I would give you anything," Kay pleaded with Caresse, *"My Next Bride*, the aviation poem, if it would only mean that you could go on with your planned list and take Sasha's book." Berkman needed "some hope and courage." Kay promised to "write like a maniac," to "work night and day," as if she weren't doing so already, "for Sasha to have a book." When Caresse declined, Kay begged her to consider Berkman for any translating job that came along. To Evelyn Scott, whose help Kay also enlisted, Kay wrote, "I'd like to do something for Sasha more than anything in the world." At such times Kay Boyle gave new meaning to the ideal of friendship.

Even as she had announced herself content, already strains began to develop in her new marriage. Laurence was a jealous man, an emotion fueled by alcohol. In particular, he was jealous of Kay's friendship with Bob Brown and those letters flying over the hills of the South of France. That Kay had written "A Comeallye for Robert Carlton Brown," describing Brown as a rebel whose "heart is like a hawk's flight," as her contribution to Peter Neagoe's anthology, added to Laurence's distress.

Laurence also began to be irritated by Kay's increased success and her devotion to worldly acclaim. The praise that came so frequently to her exacerbated his own feelings of worthlessness, which had always led him to sabotage his own efforts. So envious was he that he took to forcing her into the car for trips to Italy, to anywhere, interrupting her work. On these excursions Laurence was at last in control. Years later Kay Boyle was to tell an interviewer that "the thing that was very wonderful about Laurence Vail was that he would decide, maybe once every two or three months, that we should go off for a week at Capri or somewhere like that. Then I would have time to write and think about things." So Kay Boyle mythol-ogized. Always she struggled against Laurence's cruel and jealous com-pulsion to stop her from writing.

Sometimes when Laurence got drunk, he became mean, so that later Bill Shirer would call him "a son of a bitch." He went on four-day binges of drinking, demanding that Kay accompany him. He would pick up Kay's typewriter and throw it against the wall. Once he followed her into the women's room, suspecting that she was about to have sexual intercourse with someone. "I have done nothing," Laurence's surrogate, another Martin, wails in the 1931 novel *Murder! Murder!* "I am a nobody. A nothing." Kay's growing notoriety reminded Laurence of the paltry recognition he had received, the limited audience he himself had conspired to keep small.

Kay began to write her letters to Bob Brown by hand late at night so that Laurence would not hear the typewriter and think she was working. One night, with scant provocation, Laurence hurled a candelabra at Brown.

On another occasion, at their favorite beer-and-sausage place, Laurence erupted ferociously. He grabbed Bob Brown by the throat and nearly choked him to death.

Kay expected Bob and his wife, Rose, to be understanding and forgive Laurence this outrage, as she indulged Laurence in the mad, self-destructive excesses which indeed were the source of much of his sexual attraction. She was aroused by seeming danger; she enjoyed the frisson of incipient violence. But for that frightening attack, Bob Brown was unwilling to forgive Laurence Vail.

"To know that you and Rose doubt Laurence in any way," Kay haughtily wrote Brown, "is something I cannot bear." That Brown had recounted the incident to "a relative stranger" has "hurt me terribly," Kay told him. Laurence had been "wounded by the things you said." Laurence had been such a "devoted" and "sensitive" friend.

When she was in the wrong, Kay Boyle invariably became aggressive. "You have done him more harm than he could ever have dreamed of doing you," she informed Brown. That Brown had accused Laurence of worrying about whether Brown would pay him back the hundred dollars he had borrowed was insupportable. "If you need it, he will send you more," Kay said, in full hauteur. "Of the lot of us, he is the most honest, the staunchest, the gentlest, and in the last analysis, the one each of us can count on for the real thing."

Her friendship with Robert Carlton Brown now ground to a long halt. Kay had ruled that Brown was "disloyal." Now he had to be banished. "It is a great, great, great daily sadness," she said sententiously, "but it is so . . . nothing can be changed."

With the loss of her amiable confidant, life in the "runaway colonies" at once soured. Kay went to see the movie *The Blue Angel* and, romantic that she was, wept throughout, feeling "lost and homeless and cheerless." Kay and Laurence both now vowed that by the new year 1933 they would be gone.

Ann Watkins indeed turned out to be a "hard-boiled baby." Immediately perceiving Kay Boyle's strength in the short story, she suggested that Kay at once publish another collection. The title story would be Kay's first O. Henry Memorial Award winner. *The First Lover and Other Stories* appeared in March of 1933 under Harrison Smith's imprint. Smith finally had agreed on a hundred-dollars-a-month deal, and for a time Watkins personally paid Kay Boyle an additional hundred. Of the fourteen stories in the collection, only four had never before been published; of those, only "The Meeting of the Stones" was up to Kay Boyle's highest standard. Kay dedicated this volume to Eugene Jolas: "Follow the voice that booms in the deepest dream, deeper go, always deeper."

Reviewers in America saw quickly enough that this was a hastily conceived volume, in particular Louis Kronenberger in *The New York Times*

Book Review, too influential a critic to be ignored. In a three-column review befitting the hopes held for Kay Boyle as a writer, Kronenberger noted that "Miss Boyle has not yet quite mastered her art, and sometimes she hasn't very much to communicate." The insufficiency of Kay Boyle's ideas stood in stark contrast to her jewel-like prose and unique imagery. Indeed, calling for greater "toughness," Kronenberger echoed Katherine Anne Porter. He too believed Kay Boyle had it in her to "become as significant as she already is individual."

The "taint" Porter had perceived was identified by most of Kay Boyle's reviewers. Kronenberger said she "comes close at times to being precious." *Forum* used the terms "precious" and "attenuated." *The Nation* called it "artifice." *The New Republic* begged her to "match her manner more surely with its material, for then she will be greatly significant."

Heedless, and in full hubris, Kay Boyle chose once more not to take this very constructive criticism to heart. Instead, her stance became to turn anyone who challenged her into an enemy. Haughtily questioning the worthiness of some of Edward J. O'Brien's Honor Roll selections, she challenged O'Brien to a debate on the future of the short story. When he did not reply, she asked Milton Abernethy, the editor at *Contempo*, to print her letter and one of O'Brien's, and "then have O'Brien's remarks left blank, and I argue with him as if being answered." Such a "debate," Kay thought, "would be really funny." When George Davis, her old admirer who had frequented Raymond Duncan's shop, offended her, Kay ordered Caresse to "never, never, never write the name of George Davis again on a piece of paper . . . it's like touching *merde*."

Kay and Laurence both were skilled backbiters, vicious gossips, even as Kay flattered the notorious. They indulged this appetite in the pages of the friendly *Contempo* in a dialogue which was ostensibly a review of Peter Neagoe's anthology *Americans Abroad*. "I believe that exile bathes the vision clear," Kay wrote eloquently, "perhaps for the tears shed in it, or perhaps not." She praised her pantheon: Sasha Berkman and even Emma Goldman, Jolas ("one of the true poetic explorers of our time"), and Gertrude Stein ("each word she writes is a stone cast after you"). As she had in *The Bookman* interview, so now she felt confident enough to praise Stein for her achievement and for the influence Stein had been in her youth.

That done, Kay laced into Samuel Putnam, a literary workman of Paris and a prolific translator. Putnam's sin was that he had been associate editor for the hated Edward Titus on his revival of *This Quarter*. "Mr. Putnam," Kay wrote, "is another hack who has leeched such a long time on the extremest members of the literary corpse that he is now able to write sentences . . . but it has not yet been required of him to use his mind." Laurence then joined her in comparing Putnam's work to "a platter of wilted *hors d'oeuvres* which you would not hesitate to wave away."

In May, Abernethy published Putnam's reply. He preferred translation (his passion was Rabelais, but he translated Kiki's memoirs too), he wrote, with as much dignity as he could muster, "to wangling advances out of publishers on wishy-washy schoolgirlishly sentimental novels such as Miss Boyle's." The weak link, of course, was Laurence. "In conventional circles, such as those frequented by Miss Boyle and Mr. Vail," Putnam declared, "I believe that it is customary for the husband at least to try making the living." Laurence Vail had in his blurb called himself a translator without naming any of his translations. "Possibly," Putnam asked nastily, gaining the last word, "Mr. Vail is a translator who does not translate?" (In fact, Laurence was to publish three.) Kay Boyle's only reply was a glowing review of her short story collection *The First Lover* which appeared in the same issue of *Contempo* as Putnam's letter. "I wondered why you printed Putnam's libel," Kay wrote Abernethy haughtily from Florence, where the Vails had traveled. "It wasn't amusing or interesting, and although I think each side should have its say, his was too refutable."

Kay's short story "Convalescence," published in 1933, offers a glimpse into the Vail ménage in the early thirties. The heroine has two stepchildren and two natural children. But the only ones she loves, the only ones worthy of her love, are the two boys, her stepson, Bindy (Sindbad), and her own fantasized son, Rolly. The little girls have "stone hearts . . . like those of perverts, in a privy world of their own." "You're not my *real* sister," one of the little harpies taunts the other, "Bindy's not your *real* brother." So Bobby and Apple and Sindbad squabbled, their childish quarrels exacerbated by Kay Boyle's obvious favoritism. "Where's my father?" little Midge asks; she is told he is dead, something Bobby still had not been told. Kay Boyle was far more honest in her fiction than in her life, where she continued to allow Sharon "Vail" to believe that Laurence was her natural father. The last words of the story go to the beloved stepson, Bindy, who passes judgment on the ugly little girls who don't love their mother enough: "You fools!"

"Life Being the Best," which appeared in *Harper's* in November of 1933, introduced her great theme of the thirties: how the idea of fascism took hold in the minds of the educated and well-meaning. The setting in this first attempt is Italy, where carabinieri shadow the townsfolk, and Palavicini, an innocent, takes refuge for his survival in the growing fascist movement. Tentatively, she had begun to write that "record of the age" she had promised. Both "Life Being the Best," and "Keep Your Pity," which Ann Watkins could place only in the *Brooklyn Daily Eagle*, were weak, hastily written pieces. But Kay Boyle was now groping for the myth, and the voice to tell the story of the erupting political catastrophe to come.

Her other great and persistent theme of the thirties was homosexuality. Her point of view, rare for her time, rare for a woman writer, despite exceptions like Sappho and Radclyffe Hall, appeared in the novel *Gentlemen, I Address You Privately*, but also in poems and stories. Her poem "In Defense of Homosexuality," published in the *New Review* in April of 1932, refuses any absolute definition of gender. Homosexuality, far from being a "passing fad," was a mode of experience timeless and inevitable. "I speak of it as a thing with a future," Kay writes, "at present badly done by amateurs." In her tolerance, in her perception that homosexual experience may be a way station toward heterosexuality, or that the reverse may be true, that the two forms of sexuality may be "complements," Kay Boyle was a Bolshevik at the barricades of enlightenment. (The poem itself landed her in one of her many literary quarrels. When she originally submitted it in 1928 to Ezra Pound's journal *Exile*, Pound rejected it because of "an utterly unwarranted paragraph about me in a number of T. Quarter." This, of course, was Ethel's removal of Pound's name from the dedication of the first number of *This Quarter* after Walsh's death. Pound interpreted Kay's poem "In Defense of Homosexuality" as a "personal attack." In the *New Review*, along with the poem, Kay published Pound's nearly four-year-old letter to her without his permission. Pound at once demanded that his name be removed from the *New Review*'s masthead, a moot point since that April issue was the *New Review*'s last.)

But the theme of homosexuality was far more important to Kay than as a mere weapon in her literary skirmishes. It reflected her pain at the revelation of McAlmon's homosexuality, an anguish which, as she did with all the important experiences of her life, she converted into deeply felt fiction. "The Meeting of the Stones" is about a young woman, as Kay had been with McAlmon, who becomes attracted to a man only to discover him running his tongue along his lip in lust for a young man. Out of her own humiliating, yet profound desire for a man who preferred men, Kay Boyle granted homosexual characters a major place on the stage of her fiction, from minor efforts like "To the Pure," which *Scribner's* published, to her novel *Gentlemen, I Address You Privately*, brought out by Harrison Smith and his new partner, Robert Haas, in November of 1933.

The final rewriting of this, Kay Boyle's third published novel, proceeded after she had relinquished her hope that she and McAlmon might make a life together. That it meant a great deal to her is reflected in her choosing for its title that line by Ernest Walsh. The best character is the ex-priest, Munday, in whom Kay Boyle discovers "the womanly" in a man; his lover, Ayton, a callow, wayward sailor, is the kind of man Hart Crane had described to her when he recounted his many love affairs. But that Ayton is unworthy doesn't prevent Kay Boyle from depicting with tender acknowledgment the beauty possible in the physical love between two men. Kay draws the connection between being a homosexual in her time and being an outcast. If she faults Ayton, it is not for his homosexuality, but for his casual amorality, a behavior that transcends gender.

The years of constant revision somehow did not help; the novel is shapeless, and the ending, as Ayton impregnates a peasant woman and Munday stays on to care for her, belies the point. So confusing was that ending that critics concluded that Munday had come over to the side of heterosexuality, an interpretation she then had publicly to reject. That she separated her homosexual characters at the end represented a failure of nerve, almost as if she had forgotten whose story she was telling. Sixty years later, acknowledging the problem, she added a new last line making clear that the ex-priest Munday and the woman, Leonie, were together not as potential sexual partners, but as "sole survivors of a ship that had foundered."

As would always be the case, Kay Boyle used her fiction to tell the truth about her life, to rationalize it, to mirror it, to reflect the unconscious unresolved yearnings with which she never came to terms. The emotional landscape of her life appears in Munday's violence "that bubbled like a hemorrhage," as Ernest Walsh is resurrected. The Le Havre fishermen are here to shoot down sea gulls for sport. Ayton goes to Sarawak, where Gladys Palmer was marooned. And there is also a passage about Howard Peterson Boyle, along with Kay Boyle's personal vow that her life would be different from his no matter what it took, one which explains her penchant for taking risks. As the years were to reveal, she was to make enormous sacrifices in her effort to seize whatever bounty, whether for literary advancement or sexual gratification, circumstances offered:

> *My father never had any anger. He had no interest or heart for anything, and there must be some explanation for it. Someday he was going to start to live . . . and before he knew it the poor man was dead. He had no idea that one thing set on top of the other makes the monument . . . in spite of himself, although he'd had none of life, there was the monument piling up and there it was in the end. My father was nothing on earth, he was no one at all, but there was his terrible monument of privation erected.*

Kay Boyle determined early to spend her life "freely wherever I happen to be," as her character Munday says. He chose a dissident sexuality; she would put her own instincts and needs before those of any other human being. In the risk of homosexual choice, she discovered the metaphor for her own relentless drive to demand her personal freedom, whatever the cost.

The critics were swift to discover the flaws in *Gentlemen, I Address You Privately.* Kronenberger complained of "undue theatricality" in the Munday-Ayton relationship, and found the novel lacking in "any real centre." As Kay Boyle resisted reason, logic, and causality, so her novels all suffer from incoherence of structure and plot. "Ornament," as Kronenberger put it in his *New York Times* review, was "substituted for architecture." *The Nation* called the novel "another of those orgies of sensibility with which she has been providing us for some time."

Certainly it was true in the early thirties that Kay was being attacked by Mike Gold's literary thought police for failing to produce proletarian literature. Robert Cantwell in *The New Republic* accused her, along with

Hemingway and Henry James, of the flaw of presenting "a world made up of insulated groups having only the thinnest contacts with the social life of their environment." Kay Boyle could afford to ignore all that, but not the complaints about what Cantwell, and others, called her "labored and artificial eloquence." Henry Seidel Canby in *The Saturday Review of Literature* warned that "virtuosity is this writer's curse." Clifton Fadiman, in *The New Yorker*, one of the few to succumb to an antihomosexual slur, complained that "Kay Boyle's style is more perverse than her subject matter, if possible."

Not surprisingly, the novel did poorly. When Macy's ran an advertisement for men's underwear in *The New York Times* under the heading "Gentlemen, we address you privately," however, that "hard-boiled baby" Ann Watkins promptly threatened legal action, and came away with sixty dollars. If Harrison Smith were "more commercial and did something about it," Kay Boyle complained, he might make some money from her books. But even she knew better. "Or then he mightn't," she had to admit.

Even as she had already begun a new novel, *My Next Bride*, and was still working on her "air epic," Kay now began to assemble pieces of Emanuel Carnevali's prose to make up an autobiographical book to be called *The First God*. Caresse must publish both Carnevali and Sasha Berkman. That Caresse was having an affair with Richard Simon, publisher of Simon & Schuster, seemed to make these projects more likely.

June of 1933 was Kay and Laurence's last month at the Villa Coustille in Col-de-Villefranche. No matter that on the thirtieth of January that "decorator's man," that student of Karl Marx from Braunau on the Inn, had taken his oath of office as Chancellor of Germany. The Vails saw no reason to alter their plans. Nice was "abominable." Kay longed for "a cheaper and more difficult country," she announced, one full of "cold mountains and calmer physiognomies." Nor would Kay miss Paris, she said. Paris was best to visit "at long intervals as we do, once a year." They were moving to Austria. Their maid, Gina, refused to accompany the Vails, the proximity of Hitler being too much for her, if not for them.

Working at her usual breakneck speed, Kay developed a fever, even as Bobby contracted the mumps. Still, Kay with her usual competence packed the trunks and hired movers to send the Vails' furniture on to its destination in what would become "the Greater Reich." Irate, their landlady stood smoking a monogram-tipped cigarette, surveying the scene. Bobby still had the mumps. Kay felt as if she hadn't slept for two weeks. But she packed her "two blond-headed infants," as she dubbed Bobby, at seven hardly an infant, and Apple, into the battered Renault, and the Vails were on their way.

Their route would take them to Italy, and then through mountains and glaciers. But Kay told herself she would write some quick short stories on the way to "keep the pennies dribbling in." During the second week of

July of 1933, as she traveled to Austria, Kay Boyle at last met Emanuel Carnevali. It's "the first time!" she wrote Abernethy, to whom she submitted Carnevali's poems since he couldn't afford to send them himself. "I am in an unbeleivable [sic] state about it."

On a blazing-hot day in their beat-up Renault, they drove across the Italian plain, which Kay pronounced as near to hell as any place could be. At last they arrived at Bazzano, on a dead white square covered with dust, surrounded by mountains, with its castle: "which one of these country towns hasn't a castle to boast of?" Carnevali would write. There was a little café, above which, they had been told, Carnevali lived. It took a quarter of an hour before a woman at last led Kay and Laurence into Carnevali's little room.

The cell-like room, which faced the square, was filthy, and so tiny it was barely big enough to hold the narrow iron bed and the cupboard from which books tumbled. On a tin washtable sat an old typewriter. On the floor sat the gramophone Ernest Walsh had once brought, while on a hat tree in the corner hung a few shreds of clothing, grey with the dust of the hot Italian town. White moths flew about, visible in the sunlight.

Carnevali lay on the bed, shaking uncontrollably. He was, Kay thought, "like a pinned butterfly," and her heart went out to him. His face was big and strong, framed by black locks of hair, dotted by black eyes. His skin was as pure and clean as ivory. He was a well-made man, with a great chest bare in the relentless July heat.

His shaking never stopped, not at night, not at all, Carnevali said, although Kay felt as if his "endless agitation" would surely cease at any moment. Carnevali said he typed by holding one hand still with the other, then striking the typewriter keys. Now he held fiercely on to the bars of his bed, behind his head, trying to stop the shaking. Later Kay was to call Carnevali the gayest person she had ever met, gay as Harry Crosby and Ernest Walsh were gay. Taking a good look at her, Carnevali would write: "if we were to detach Kay Boyle's head from the body, it would drop down and then bounce back to its owner. It is elastic. But if mine fell from my body it would drop down and stay wistfully there."

Kay and Laurence had brought two bottles of champagne. With their help, Carnevali managed, she later recounted, to set the glasses one on top of the other to make a tower so that the champagne brimmed over from the first into the second and then into the third in a yellow torrent. To Kay, it was sickeningly sweet. Suddenly she burst into tears. Quickly composing herself, she read aloud to Carnevali Caresse's letter in which she said she liked the portion of his *The First God* which Kay had sent her.

"Perhaps," Carnevali said, "they will print it out of charity."

At this, she began to cry again. Slightly drunk, she decided she would leave Laurence and the children and remain here to care for the man Ernest Walsh had also loved. Meeting Carnevali brought back all the pain of the

(above left) Grandma Eva Evans at the age of twenty-seven; *(right)* Nina Allender ("Tante"): "Whose home do you suggest I stay in?"; *(below)* Howard and Katherine Evans Boyle: "How can I help my father and mother like each other more than they do?"

(opposite, top to bottom) Jesse Peyton Boyle with Katherine, Kay, and Janet: "a kissable mouth"; the Boyle family: Howard, Katherine, Janet, and Kay; Puss, when he read, chose Conrad and Kipling. With Kay, *right*, and Janet (1905); *(above)* Janet and Kay at Mount Pocono; *(below)* Kay, *center*, a belle of Cincinnati, c. 1917 *(Morris Library)*

(*above left*) Richard Brault: "He was a *rouspéteur*" (*Morris Library*); (*right*) Ernest Walsh: "the love of her life" (*Morris Library*); (*below*) Graeme Taylor, John Glassco, and Robert McAlmon in Nice, 1928 (*Morris Library*)

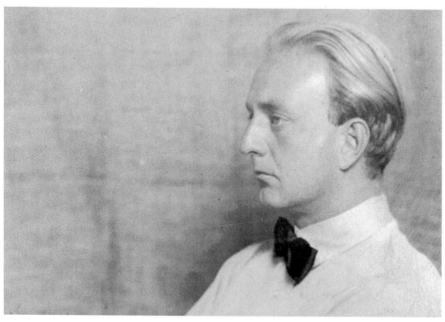

(above) Laurence Vail climbing the "Nomatterhorn"; *(below)* Laurence Vail: "no commonplace man"

(above) Kay Boyle photographed by Man Ray, c. 1930; *(opposite top)* Clotilde Vail; *(bottom)* Wedding Day, 1932: Kay with Pegeen Vail, *left*, and Sharon (Bobby) Brault Vail *(Morris Library)*

(above left) Kay Boyle in the Alps (Morris Library); (right) Kathe and her nurse, Cilli, in Austria: "I've never met a Jew!"; (below left) The chalet Les Six Enfants; (right) Kurt Wick: "I have promised Kurt I will not leave him here"

loss of Ernest Walsh, before which her feelings for Laurence Vail seemed paltry, less than nothing. With Walsh's death, Kay suddenly knew she had lost the possibility of loving any man. She believed, even later, that she was faced with a real decision, for so romance overwhelmed reality.

"I don't know what to do," she wrote Caresse, "for I do know that every day I live will be a rebuke to me, for I should be with him, and I have not the courage to say that everything else is a contortion except being with him. It is not as easy as explaining this as love—it is a necessity, for if the thing he is did not exist and had never existed, there should be no reason to live at all." The sight of Carnevali brought Walsh back to life and at that moment it was as if nothing else mattered for Kay Boyle.

Kay did not, she says, tell Laurence Vail then that she believed it was her duty to remain at Bazzano to care for the dying poet. But, she insists, Laurence knew. "You do not need to tell me," Laurence said at last. "I know if it were not for the children what you would do." Kay had promised as she departed that she would return to see Carnevali in three weeks. In fact, she was never to make her way back to Bazzano again despite all these protestations.

After she left Bazzano, Kay told people Carnevali would die should she not get his book published. Caresse must "move heaven and earth, you must, my darling," Kay wrote. "It is not because he is ill, but because he is one of the last survivors of our faith." Caresse wrote a check and crossed her fingers. Even as Carnevali, inspired by Kay's confidence that *The First God* would be published, renewed his efforts, forwarding pages to her as soon as he completed them, Kay wrote Caresse the book had to be placed "or I will never write again."

But in New York that hot summer of 1933 Caresse was told by Clifton Fadiman at Simon & Schuster that while he wouldn't mind publishing Kay Boyle, both Crevel and Carnevali were out. The interview ended with Caresse Crosby rushing in sobs from the room. Finding Dick Simon in his office, she grabbed an inkwell and threw it at him with all her might. So ended not only any chance of Simon & Schuster's publishing Emanuel Carnevali but also Caresse's love affair with Dick Simon.

Kay was too shrewd to have depended on Caresse Crosby. She asked Caresse to give the Carnevali manuscript to Ann Watkins, who, for her part, was perfectly willing to sell Simon & Schuster Kay Boyle's next novel, *My Next Bride*, should they want it. Kay did not forget Carnevali, and when André Breton and Paul Eluard sent her a questionnaire, "*Pouvez-vous dire quelle a été la rencontre capitale de votre vie?*" Kay replied that the most important encounter of her life had been with Carnevali, the paradigm of the poet, "isolate in himself," who expressed "the chastity of his power." Still enslaved by the dime-store romanticism of John Cowper Powys, imbibed by Katherine Evans Boyle all those long years ago, Kay said she believed in "the mysticism of the flesh and the miracles of its passion."

In her most high-flown tones, she wrote, "I have sought to eliminate the errors and stupidities of chance by the brutal and pitiless demand that what I can give homage to be there or else be damned."

Following Ernest Walsh's observation that she existed to pay "homage," Kay Boyle redoubled her efforts to help Carnevali, "if I die in the attempt," she wrote William Carlos Williams. She would never forget "the solitude, the loneliness, the absolute poverty." She urged Abernethy to devote an entire number of *Contempo* to Carnevali. "I could get you enough to fill it with marvellous smashing stuff," Kay promised.

"I hope your high hopes about my novel will never fall to pieces for I need money more than ever," Carnevali wrote Kay. After he received a second check from Caresse Crosby, he again wrote Kay, "Is it possible that I am, after all these years of privation, suddenly to be a rich man?"

As soon as she received this letter, Kay instructed Ann Watkins that she would sign only with a publisher who would do Carnevali and Ernest Walsh as well. And then it seemed that against all odds Ann Watkins had pulled it off. Harcourt agreed to publish all three: the Walsh poems, Carnevali's novel with a five-hundred-dollar advance—and Kay's *My Next Bride*, paying fifteen hundred dollars. Better yet, Harcourt would add two thousand more as soon as they received Kay's manuscript.

11

Nazis as Heroes

*She had a sneaking admiration for fascism. She was
impressed a bit.*
TANIA STERN

*The gods of the North have proved after all to be
her kind of material.*
MARK VAN DOREN

Kay and Laurence arrived in Vienna late that summer of 1933
without having made any advance arrangements. They took two rooms at
the Hietzingerhof, Hauptstrasse 22, facing dreary backyards, in a city where
darkness seemed to descend early in the day and rain fell perpetually. Kay
soon succumbed to the grippe, hating Vienna, hating the food, the globs
of cream and the inevitable dark pork.

Immediately she perceived that the Austrian people were sad and
desperate, "without hope or promise." The friends she made were plotting
to abandon Austria as soon as they could. But Kay, graduate of the school
of Eugene Jolas, approached politics impressionistically and emotionally,
and she had only a fragmentary understanding of the forces churning in
Austria that summer and autumn of 1933. In fact, while Marxists and
socialists in Vienna were bent on preserving the parliamentary democracy
of the republic, in the provincial Tyrol a paramilitary right-wing group
known as the Heimwehr, an organization dedicated to the creation of a
fascist Austria, was flourishing, dominating both police and army. Their
natural rivals were the Nazis, the committed adherents of National Socialism.

Kay and Laurence arrived just as these contending forces were beginning to clash in their dress rehearsal for the inevitable. As Marxists,
socialists, and trade unionists still spoke for the working people in Vienna,
as in the wings waited those indigenous fascists, the Heimwehr, the National
Socialists, fueled by conviction, unity, and an undeviating faith in their
destiny, were increasing in number. The ineffectual Christian Socialist
government of Chancellor Engelbert Dollfuss, part of the "Fatherland
Front," less a political party than "an Austrian club with a Viennese coffee-

house character," teetered precariously, offering no redress to an economically devastated Austria. Antisocialist and Catholic, Dollfuss remained hostile to both socialists and National Socialists, flirting all the while with the Heimwehr, as he relied on the support of his ally in Italy, Mussolini.

As Kay took up her writing, her subject was not yet Austria moving to the fulfillment of Hitler's prophecy of *Anschluss* on the first page of *Mein Kampf*, but twenties Paris and Raymond Duncan. If, she kept insisting, the dedication to Caresse Crosby of her new novel, *My Next Bride*, was meant to persuade her friend once and for all that she had never slept with Harry Crosby, her motive was much more practical. The many letters full of effusions of love and devotion which Kay wrote to Caresse during her early weeks in Vienna were motivated by a very different concern. Kay was laying the groundwork for severing their professional connection.

The unsatisfactory progress of their publishing collaborations was very much on Kay's mind as she wrote Caresse of her "bewildering love," and spoke of Caresse's "gaety [sic]" no less than her "pride," her "nose," and "the kind of perfume you have." She urged Caresse to forget the past, to believe in "what is to come," for then it would, "like a miracle." The final scene of *My Next Bride* portrays Victoria (Kay) in bed with Fontana, the Caresse character, Caresse's arm around Kay's neck. So gratuitous did this ending seem that critics later concluded that the author was depicting a lesbian relationship. But this was not so. As always, Kay Boyle was articulating the demands of her life through her art, attempting to explain to Caresse that although their business relations had come to an end, their friendship, she hoped, had not.

"I wish you would write to me that things between you and me will never change," Kay pleaded with Caresse, inviting her to Austria, "where life is good and the snow ready to fall." Life, of course, was hardly "good"; Kay Boyle found Vienna scarcely bearable. But she feared Caresse would not forgive her for so abandoning their arrangement that Ann Watkins had proposed to Dick Simon that Kay and Laurence do some translations for *him*.

Indeed, Caresse was upset. Kay professed herself to be "absolutely heartbroken that there should be these difficulties between you and me about it," even as she went on to blame Caresse for not having written to her soon enough from America with the news that Clifton Fadiman had refused to publish Carnevali's autobiography. She offered Caresse the opportunity to publish a limited edition of *My Next Bride*—in Europe only —as a Black Sun book, and went her own publishing way.

Winter descended swiftly upon Vienna. The streets were covered with ice, the air damp with the murderous *Föhne*, those southern winds out of Africa which ripened the corn and the vines of the Alpine valleys yet also brought such depression, such despair that hospitals in Austria wouldn't operate on patients when those warm winds blew. Kay Boyle saw people barefoot, shivering in doorways, silently dying of hunger as Vienna bowed to the aftermath of the world depression.

Kay and Laurence welcomed a visit from James Stern and the novelist Ethel Mannin. One night the four ducked into a *Weinstube* to avoid what Kay described as the omnipresent poor, "destitute, barefooted families, the mothers with half-starved babies wrapped in their shawls, standing with lowered heads, begging for coins or for bread." The Austrian people, Kay saw, as the seeds of her writing about the moment of the rise of fascism in Austria germinated, were living in hell. "The breath of the white horses of Vienna was smoke on the air of the indoor arena where they danced," Kay wrote years later in a birthday letter to James Stern, "and our type-writers were silent as we looked the other way." Through the darkness rang now the booming voice of Adolf Hitler promising economic recovery—jobs!—and a renewal of national pride and self-esteem for all German-speaking citizens of the Greater Reich. Kay Boyle's typewriter would not be silent for long.

Kay was momentarily distracted by news from Robert McAlmon that Ethel Moorhead, having read *Year Before Last*, which she called libelous, was threatening to prevent Harcourt from publishing Ernest Walsh's poems. "I was more to him than she ever was," Moorhead raged. So jealous did she remain of Kay Boyle that McAlmon thought she was ready to accuse *him* of having fathered Bobby. McAlmon called Moorhead a "lonely sex-starved and thwarted old gal," and offered to serve as intermediary.

Moorhead feared the manuscript had been tampered with, and indeed Kay had retyped the poems and secretly added some that had appeared in the memorial issue of *This Quarter*. When Ethel asserted that should Kay have anything to do with the publication, she would scuttle it at once, Kay was ready to "fight it out" with her. McAlmon advised subterfuge, although Ethel, despite having been named literary executor in Walsh's will, did not hold a legal copyright because the will had never been through probate.

"The moment she knows you're involved," McAlmon told Kay, "she'll shoot herself or you before she'll sign anything, and it'd be you first." Moorhead's hatred for Kay Boyle was now an "obsession." Kay and McAlmon first chose Ford Madox Ford to write the introduction. When he declined, they invited Archibald MacLeish. Reading MacLeish's text, Kay asked him to omit a reference to Walsh's "being loved by a beautiful and gifted woman." MacLeish ignored her, and when Ethel read his introduc-tion, she tore the manuscript into shreds and demanded that Harcourt cease publication at once. Meanwhile, alarmed, Kay threatened to withhold her manuscript of *My Next Bride* from Harcourt until she was absolutely certain they would honor their obligation and bring out Walsh's poems. *Poems and Sonnets* by Ernest Walsh was published by Harcourt, Brace & Co. in 1934—"with a Memoir by Ethel Moorhead."

In December, the Vails ended their three "frightful" months in Vienna. Bundling children, cat, and a St. Bernard puppy into the ramshackle Renault, they drove through a "magnificent blizzard" to Kitzbühel, a "deep snowy place," with its enchanting Tyrolean houses, inns, and bars and long ski runs. Only in climbing did Laurence Vail feel free; he had described himself in his novel *Piri and I* as a "superficial hero straddling a razor-like ridge somewhere between earth and sky . . . pleased to regard himself on the uppermost pinnacle of the earth's wrinkled crust. Perhaps he is prince of the world." In the mountains, climbing, skiing, Laurence need not compete, need not believe in anything, need not descend into earnestness and grow bored, need not fail. Kay too learned to enjoy climbing, which she was to describe in her story "Maiden, Maiden" as a spiritual experience where there was "no talk, for the lips are closed to save the breath for better things."

In Kitzbühel, Kay and Laurence lived at the Kaiserhof, a pension where meals were taken *en famille*, at a level of luxury few Austrians could now afford. The provincial Tyrol remained the stronghold of the paramilitary right-wing group, the Heimwehr. Amid the exquisite snowy landscapes, the Heimwehr prepared to do battle with their National Socialist rivals. Politically innocent, Kay professed herself "ecstatic" at her new surroundings. From her window at the Kaiserhof her view was so magnificent, she wrote to everyone, that it was like "being born again." Kay hired a "country girl" to take care of the children and went to work.

Kay was also pregnant once more. That the size of her family forced her to write for money did not prevent her from procreating, a role she continued to view as a woman's natural destiny. Her children "adorned" her, as Caresse had said. Kay also believed that her motherhood was diminished by her not having a male child. "Send me some names of boys," she wrote Evelyn Scott. "I want it to be a boy and can't think of any good-sounding ones." To others she boasted of how easy her pregnancies were, a mark of her womanliness. In fact, she was not well gynecologically. Suffering from "queer inward feelings," she took to her bed whenever she could.

Simultaneous with this new pregnancy came a fresh need for money, so that it seemed as if having babies for Kay Boyle was an unconscious rebellion against fulfilling her mother's ancient dream for her. Art must give way to commercialism because there wasn't enough money. Bettina Bedwell arrived in Kitzbühel to collaborate with Kay on a melodramatic potboiler, a thriller with a fashion setting, which would be written by Kay and published under Bedwell's name. Having agreed, Kay complained, hating every minute of the writing, "to the point of tears and rage." She longed to "write my own pretty things." But Bedwell was paying her an advance of two hundred and fifty dollars, Kay to receive 50 percent of the royalties. "I'm in a state of nerves and ready to kill anyone on sight," Kay wrote Ann Watkins after weeks of work with Bedwell.

What emerged was *Yellow Dusk*, a conventional thriller about a rich widow in Paris nearly fleeced of her fortune and an ingenue nearly kidnapped into the "white slave trade." Yet even in this ghostwritten romance Kay Boyle managed to interject not only her own voice but her biography. "I'm going places, I'm going places fast," the ingenue Abigail announces, talking as Kay Boyle talked. The hero has, alternately, Kay's and Ernest Walsh's voices. "You make me believe in simplicity," Andrew Rake tells Abigail. "You are gentle. You are tender. Some strong man will show you how to live a life." So Ernest Walsh's ghost was summoned to see Kay Boyle through her vulgar task. *Yellow Dusk* was published in 1937 with jacket copy which announced that "Miss Bedwell is a writer with a nice idea of how to serve up a story." Inside, the publishers, Hurst & Blackett in London, printed their spring 1937 list, which included the English translation of a German work called *My Struggle* (*Mein Kampf*).

Kay also continued to work on her history of aviation in verse, undeterred by having failed in her first effort to win a Guggenheim fellowship. An epic poem about aviation was another act of defiance as she struggled against Virginia Rice's old insistence that she write "nice girlish novels and short stories about the English." Emotional loyalty also kept her at her task. Harry Crosby had taken up aviation near the end of his life. "Harry's spirit will supply the wind," Kay had grandly claimed, "books of reference will supply the facts."

Kay applied again for a Guggenheim, with recommendations from Evelyn Scott, Archibald MacLeish, and Padraic Colum; Scott predicted, quixotically, that Kay as a poet would "go much further than she has in prose." This time Kay was successful. She would receive $1,800, but only if she produced a doctor's note testifying that she was fit to start work at once. Ann Watkins must conceal, Kay said, that she was pregnant, her baby due in June. "The baby can come at any time," Kay declared, "but I can carry on with my work. That's not going to slow me down!"

"Being pregnant makes little difference to me in the work line," Kay insisted. Having babies, rather, was "a nice kind of relaxation" after all the writing and typing, as she revealed indeed that bearing children was a form of rebellion against being the writer Kay Boyle. Once her children were born, however, others would see to their needs.

Kay planned to split her Guggenheim money three ways. Laurence would receive a third because the aviation epic had been his idea. Kay had also decided to give a third to her friend Dougie, Allan Ross MacDougall, a man she found witty, catty, and great fun. One day in Col-de-Villefranche she had said she hoped Dougie would "stay forever," so fond of him was she. Dougie was to do all the research on aviation history. Not unreasonably, MacDougall asked for money in advance before he began his arduous task. Kay blanched.

"Why don't I pay you so much an hour?" Kay suddenly suggested, altering their agreement. Furious with her for what he viewed as duplicitous behavior, Allan Ross MacDougall vowed never to speak to Kay Boyle again.

It was in the Tyrol that Kay began to observe the political scene with literary interest. Financed by Austria's industrialists, who backed them as the best alternative to parliamentary democracy, the Heimwehr now began to purge the Tyrol of both Nazis and socialists. But if they were relatively lenient toward the National Socialists—indeed, Heimwehr leader Prince Ernst Rüdiger von Starhemberg admired Adolf Hitler and declared, "we were fascists, we are fascists, we will remain fascists"—that February the Heimwehr mobilized for the brutal destruction of the democratic left of Vienna.

In February of 1934 civil war erupted in the capital. A general strike failed. The Dollfuss government, fearing socialists more than fascists of any stripe, then ordered a vicious massacre of the workers in the tenement named for Karl Marx. Deaths of scores of women and children were followed by the systematic executions of many socialists, as Hitler's work was done for him by the Heimwehr. Meanwhile, continuing to support Dollfuss, the Heimwehr was losing ground to the National Socialists. In the Tyrol, the Heimwehr stamped out fires set in the shape of swastikas on the mountainsides, fires lit by despairing Austrians hearkening to the call from across the frontier. Dissident youths, doctors, teachers, shopkeepers, all future characters in Kay Boyle's fiction set in Austria, listened intently to the call to all German-speaking folk of the Fatherland.

In Austria, Kay worried even more about Laurence's idleness than she had in France. It was Laurence, however, who came up with the idea of compiling a three-volume symposium about life on the planet as it would unfold in 1934. At once he enlisted Kay's superb organizing help. Secretly miserable over this new interruption of her writing, Kay felt she had no choice but to lend herself wholeheartedly to Laurence's new scheme. "It's awful for him to have not a single word of encouragement or a penny coming in," Kay wrote her sister Joan. Kay told people that Laurence's "1934" would make money. But, in fact, much more was at stake and she knew it: her husband's entire sense of self-esteem was involved. "I'd give five years of my life (which sounds darn little)," she said with her usual hyperbole, "to see Laurence working with the assurance that what he wrote was going to see the light of day." She insisted that "his industry would put to shame half the businessmen in the world today." Privately, however, she called him "lazy-go-lucky" and was well acquainted with the demons that denied him worldly success. Laurence in Austria clearly needed "a new lease on life," and Kay, about to bear their second child, was still committed enough to the marriage to see that he got it.

Eventually Laurence's project would contract into one volume. Called *365 Days*, it would present a three-hundred-word sketch or short story for each day of the year based on an actual event of significance which had occurred on that day in some country. Kay was the one who wrote to their friends for contributions: Evelyn Scott, William Carlos Williams, Robert McAlmon no less than her sister, her mother, and even her father, who contributed a piece from Cincinnati. She wrote William Saroyan, who sent an enormous package containing three hundred and sixty-five short stories and a huge picture of himself; James T. Farrell, still the good Marxist, reserved May 1. When the contributors ignored the three-hundred-word limit, Kay did the cutting, mailing the rewrites from her room at the Kaiserhof. It was at this time that forty-three-year-old Henry Miller sent Kay his manuscript for *Black Spring*. Kay replied that when he matured, Miller would no longer need to write exclusively about his sexual experiences, would no longer "equate . . . sexuality with vulgarity." (In 1977 Kay regretted that admonition, calling it "the kind of puritanical, or twi-lighty romantic hang-up I had then, and still have, but to a lesser degree.")

Obsessively neat as always, following Puss's example, Kay was appalled as Laurence filled their hotel rooms with accumulated newspapers. A prince of the old school, he never cleaned up, never did any chores whatsoever. Meanwhile everyone kept sending more newspapers. Kay's friend Nina Conarain arrived from London to help. When people sent stories without including the original clipping, no doubt because they had made their stories up, Kay and Nina and Laurence invented them.

Before long, Laurence's interest in *365 Days* flagged. He grew bored and restless, and Kay wound up writing a third of the entries herself, sometimes under her own name, sometimes under a range of pseudonyms, including the "Reverend Clarence Wimley, Ph.D.," or "Larry Boyle," as she reflected her unconscious longing for the son she hoped would soon be born to her. From "Moscow," Kay wrote about the lonely, neglected wife of the chairman of a Komsomol cell whose husband divorces her for being "too undeveloped socially and politically to comprehend the happiness of Komsomol family life." Veteran of those long evenings with Sasha and Emma, she was well aware of how the socialist ideal had been undermined by the Stalinist state. In her pieces on Stavisky, Japanese nationalism, Sir Oswald Mosley's fascists, and political prisoners in Ireland, she revealed how far she had moved beyond that "girl writer" who had exasperatedly dubbed her agent "Vagina" because Rice was ready to consign her to a ghetto of woman writers. Kay Boyle's pieces in *365 Days* reveal a liberal, forward-looking politics and a contempt for injustice, racism, and class snobbery.

She was working well, producing one brilliant sketch after another as she awaited the birth of her third child. All that marred Kay's spring was a visit from her nemesis, Peggy Guggenheim, mourning the sudden death of her lover, John Holms. Peggy gladly joined Laurence in all-night drinking expeditions, to Kay's intense annoyance. One night Kay stubbornly sat fuming in the old Renault as Laurence and Peggy and the entourage they collected rushed from one hot, noisy, smoky *Weinstube* to another.

As the National Socialists planned a putsch against Chancellor Dollfuss in Vienna, Kay and Laurence headed for Innsbruck, where Kay was to bear her much-longed-for son. They stopped at the elegant Hotel Hellenstainer on the Andreashoferstrasse; as usual, Kay's endless concerns about money did not keep them from living well. In one of the best rooms with a glass-enclosed balcony overlooking the hotel's *Biergarten*, Kay and Laurence settled to await the birth of their child.

Next door to the Hotel Hellenstainer were the offices of an anti-Nazi newspaper, the *Tyrolia*. On the night of June 28, 1934, while Kay and Laurence slept, a constable watched over the printing works of the *Tyrolia*. At 12:30 a.m., the constable spotted a suspicious-looking figure darting from the courtyard adjoining the printing works building. At once he called the night porter, and together the two men searched for the suspect. They found no one. But they did spy a package the size of a shoebox lying on the roof of the one-story building where the newspaper's rotary press was housed. Smoke poured from the package, which was wrapped in brown paper.

Swiftly now the constable and the night porter scampered out onto the roof. The constable seized the smoking package and threw it as hard as he could. It landed in the *Biergarten* of the Hotel Hellenstainer.

Suddenly there was a ferocious explosion. Kay and Laurence were awakened to the sound of shattering glass as their balcony gave way. In the midnight dark they crawled out of their beds, Kay heavily pregnant, across a carpet of glass. When the lights finally came on, they could see shreds of the manuscript of *365 Days*. As she later wrote in her novel *Primer for Combat*, "they drifted slowly down around us, like flower petals in the smoke."

In the morning, looking down on the *Biergarten*, Kay and Laurence saw a shambles. On the ground where the bomb had exploded was a hole two and a half feet wide and a foot and a half deep. The bowling alley had been destroyed; the tabletops and chairs had been tossed up into the remaining branches of the chestnut trees. Even the iron parts of the chairs and tables in the *Biergarten* had been twisted out of shape. All the windows of the glass veranda were broken. At the *Tyrolia* next door, a hundred windowpanes were shattered, but the printing press was undamaged. The constable and the night porter became heroes, for they had saved the rotary press, the most valuable piece of machinery. Modestly, prudently, the constable insisted on remaining anonymous. It was the most powerful act of sabotage up to that time in the Tyrol. With the *Tyrolia*'s support of labor and its anti-Nazi views, there was no doubt in anyone's mind who was responsible. The National Socialist offensive was well underway. That same night in Innsbruck, Nazis seem to have materialized everywhere.

Soon the Heimwehr took over, and men of the Heimwehr interviewed Kay and Laurence. They scrutinized pages of the torn manuscript, filled with Laurence's arrows and dates. "1934" was circled, as well as "February." The Heimwehr wondered whether this was a reference to the February events when the Heimwehr had destroyed the left opposition to fascism. Even as Kay and Laurence were on their hands and knees collecting the fragments of newspaper cuttings, the Heimwehren wondered whether Laurence, indeed the most unpolitical of men, might not be a suspicious character.

On July 7 in Innsbruck, Kay Boyle bore her third child. She was named Kathe, after the proprietress of the Kaiserhof, but legally Katherine, her mother's name. Blond and blue-eyed, with the Vail beaky nose, Kathe resembled Laurence and her Aunt Clotilde. She grew up trying to please Kay and Laurence both, a straightforward, if melodramatic human being, generous and emotional, a middle child who learned early that her father preferred her sister Apple, her mother, sometimes Bobby, sometimes Apple. She was no one's particular favorite.

It took her mother four months to be reconciled to Kathe's gender. "We wanted a boy to balance things a bit," she wrote to Bob Brown, with whom she was back in touch, adding, finally, "She's too lovely to want to exchange for anything imaginable."

On July 25, with Kay and Laurence safely back in Kitzbühel, men of the Austrian SS donned army uniforms and occupied the chancery. If their putsch failed, they did manage to shoot little Chancellor Dollfuss as he tried to flee the building. Unable to mark the significance of this event, Kay pronounced Kitzbühel quiet. "Everything much exaggerated in the Paris papers," she insisted. "I suppose," Kay wrote with more bravado than sense, "the American papers are working up intense feeling too. Everyone is *convinced* that Dollfuss was double-crossed and put out of the way by the Heimwehr."

Of the double-dealing role Dollfuss had played, Kay Boyle seemed unaware, for neither in her autobiographical fiction nor in her letters did she refer to how Dollfuss had used the Heimwehr to destroy the social democratic and left opposition, the sole real alternative to National Socialism.

One night the only shop in Kitzbühel owned by Jews was burned to the ground.

"Oh, well, that's the way it is," Laurence told Kay. "You never had any education in history. These things go by in cycles." Laurence remained cynical. History repeated itself. "There's no use getting worked up about it," Laurence said.

Kay burned with indignation. Laurence didn't believe in himself or anything else. When in December of 1934 Kay went to Paris and witnessed antifascist labor protests, she didn't even bother to discuss them with Laurence when she returned.

They had two servants to help, Fanni and Cilli. At night while Cilli washed diapers and Kay nursed the baby, they discussed politics. A member of the Austrian Nazi Party, Cilli admitted that several nights a week she defied the law of the Tyrol by participating in the lighting of fires in the shape of swastikas high on the mountains surrounding Kitzbühel. Having once worked in the Soviet Union as the nanny for Paul Robeson's son, Cilli, according to Kay, saw a real resemblance between the revolution in Russia and the one taking place in Germany now.

"I've never met a Jew," Cilli proudly told Kay one evening. "I would be incapable of being in the same room with a Jew and I hope I never have to meet one." Kay resumed reading the essays of Bertrand Russell to Sindbad then. Happy that "A." was in power across the frontier, Cilli listened.

That summer the Vails entertained again that most ambiguously welcome of guests, Peggy Guggenheim. She had brought Pegeen to Kitzbühel for her vacation and was planning to take Sindbad to Italy. Innocently, Cilli sat down at the table and had dinner with Kay and Laurence—and Peggy.

After Peggy's departure, Kay informed Cilli that not only had she been in the same room with a Jew but she had actually eaten a meal with one. Never again, Kay Boyle insists, did Cilli speak to her employers about the unbearable qualities of Jews. But a year later, when Kathe was a fat, blond, sunburned little girl, someone suddenly came into the room where she was in her crib. At once Kathe stood up and raised her arm in the "*Heil Hitler*" salute. Cilli had taught her well.

Now the paramilitary Heimwehr uneasily shared power with the remnants of Dollfuss's "Fatherland Front," relying still on Mussolini's support, even as Hitler and Mussolini were moving closer together. On the gates of the disintegrating, fragile republic, despite the failure of their putsch of July of 1934, the Nazis banged for entry. With great pride did Kathe's nanny, Cilli, continue to help in the lighting of those twisted crosses. In the Tyrol, remote from Vienna, where the left-wing movement of workers' and soldiers' councils had been shattered, Kay Boyle picked up her pen to chronicle the death throes of the Austrian republic.

Having completed *My Next Bride*, leaving Paris behind forever, Kay began to write about how Nazism was seizing the souls of Austria's best and brightest. Her first pieces about how fascism in Austria and Germany had taken hold were for *365 Days*. For January 29, she wrote "Austrian Nazis Continue to Demonstrate Despite Warning by Pocket Chancellor." For the first time, Kay Boyle made a literary decision that would prove fateful for her; she decided to write about fascism in Austria from the point of view of the Nazi, the better to reveal why good people might be attracted to such a force. In this piece she becomes the Nazi sympathizer lighting candles, as Cilli had on the mountains, to create a burning swastika. Only with the word "monstrous" does the author intervene, differentiating her point of view from that of her characters.

In "Austria," for February 20, Kay follows a protest demonstration as schoolchildren object to the dismissal of their Nazi teacher, Fräulein Moeller. Depicting a community where "the heart had been starved" since the war, Kay reveals the spiritual malaise of an impoverished Austria where 400,000 people were unemployed, an Austria squeezed by the West on one side and Germany on the other. Fräulein Moeller is so poor she wears the same sweater and skirt to work every day and owns only one dress. So, Kay Boyle writes, intellectuals in Austria saw in Nazism "an end to the misery in the cities, to the want in the country, to the armies of penniless men who roved back and forth, year after year, across the mountains of the land." Uniquely, by temporarily withholding authorial judgment, Kay Boyle was able to dramatize amid the intolerable circumstances of Austria how fascism might be seen as a means to self-respect by ordinarily moral, indeed virtuous, people.

In "National-Socialists Clean Up Notorious Den of Perverts," a homosexual club is raided by Nazis, tear gas thrown in upon women dancing with women, men with men. So Kay Boyle believed that the loss of the choice of sexual preference prefigures the loss of all freedoms. The Nazi saboteur is "shy," with a "delicate face," as she reveals how Nazism had reached into every corner of Austrian society. (Kay Boyle's 1935 *Harper's Bazaar* story "Count Lothar's Heart," about an Austrian aristocrat, also returned to the theme of homoerotic love.) Cilli's dinner with Peggy Guggenheim was fictionalized in the story of a Jewish woman who goes to bed with a storm trooper only to leave him a note informing him of her national origins: "I fear that being defiled you'll have to shoot yourself." And for July 25, the day of Dollfuss's death, Kay produced the first sketch of her brilliant story "The White Horses of Vienna," as a doctor is interrupted in the middle of a puppet show mocking the ineffectual Chancellor which he is staging for his children and guests. If now the Heimwehr have the power to arrest *him*, Kay makes it clear that the Heimwehr's days are numbered. In another of her antifascist sketches, Kay describes a widowed Mrs. Dollfuss foolishly requesting sympathy from an unsympathetic Mrs. Mussolini.

Residing in what she called "the powder chest of European politics" until the spring of 1935, Kay Boyle produced some of her best and most controversial work. That sketch about the doctor which became "The White Horses of Vienna," published in *Harper's* in April of 1935, was a first-prize winner of the O. Henry Memorial Awards. Eloquently, recalling Thomas Mann's masterpiece "Mario and the Magician," she captures the moment at which fascism takes hold of the minds and hearts of good people. Kay Boyle's fascist doctor is a beautiful man, with golden hairs on his thighs. He is also a good man, ministering to the sick. Kay Boyle calls him only "the doctor," as if he were defined by the nobility of his calling.

When he injures his leg lighting swastika fires, a young Jewish assistant is dispatched from Vienna. With great courage Kay Boyle describes the virtues of the Nazi doctor through the eyes of this Jewish observer. Nor is the doctor anti-Semitic, as Kay Boyle perceived that it wasn't always anti-Semitism which drew Austrians to Nazism, that indeed many fascist movements became racist only as they collaborated with their Nazi occupiers.

From her original sketch, Kay retained the puppet show, elaborating a dialogue between the "monstrously handsome grasshopper," the Nazi, and a clown. The grasshopper is called "The Leader." "The cities are full of churches," he says, referring in part to Dollfuss's religiosity, "but the country is full of God." He speaks with "a wild and stirring power," and for him the clown with his paper flowers is no match. When the doctor is jailed by the Heimwehr at the end, his assistant, called Dr. Heine, so sympathizes that he determines to toss peaches through the bars of the doctor's prison window. For her perception of the spiritual, no less than the emotional, power of fascism, Kay Boyle would not be easily forgiven.

In October of 1934, Bobby was stricken with diphtheria and had to be quarantined at the Innsbruck *Infektionshaus*, where she remained for three weeks. Yet when Caresse Crosby arrived, Kay and Laurence, leaving a barely convalescent Bobby behind, took off for Munich for "an October-Fest fling." In her memoirs Caresse Crosby fabulates a scene which could hardly have taken place. The entire company barges innocently into an inn hosting the German high command wearing brown shirts, where "at the head of the table sat a gimlet-eyed man with a Charlie Chaplin moustache who didn't miss a *Heil*." "One didn't know they were 'Nazis' then," Caresse writes coyly. In Munich they decided to look up Thomas Mann's son Klaus. On the phone at a hotel where they stopped, Kay refused to reply in kind to the telephone operator's *"Heil Hitler."*

"Guten Tag," Kay said in her most imperious tones. Soon they were being lectured by the hotel proprietor about the inadvisability of attempting to talk with Jews!

Kay Boyle had published novels in 1931, 1932, and 1933. Now, in 1934, she brought out *My Next Bride*. "It's a history of women," Kay wrote Ann Watkins, "and of that nameless and nonsexual thing that can bind women to each other closer than can any relationship with men." Later she would insist that its theme was "material inequality," with the Harry Crosby character suffering "the misery of too much wealth," while the Raymond Duncan surrogate exhibits "hideous greed." Kay was rarely an apt critic of her fiction, although she perceived when slipshod work resulted from hasty writing. In her retelling of life at the Duncan commune in *My Next Bride*, the themes of the friendship between women and of economic injustice scarcely emerge at all.

In America reviewers were impatient with one more novel about Paris. In *The New Yorker* Clifton Fadiman yawned and called *My Next Bride* "the last expatriate novel." *The Christian Century*, unimpressed by Kay's tale of those sexy nights on the houseboat of Frans and Mai, and of Raymond Duncan trailing about Paris in his toga and sandals, said it "dates hopelessly." Edith Walton in *The New York Times Book Review* called it "trivial material." The novel's style was attenuated and critics had lost their patience. It was a young and brilliant Mary McCarthy writing in *The Nation* who summed up the novelist's weakness. Kay Boyle, McCarthy perceived, with her "exaggerated attention to detail" and "pretentious intensity," lacked sufficient ironic distance from her subject matter. Her "heavy, yearning seriousness" suggested that Duncan, Crosby, and Caresse "were people of some importance." They obviously were not.

But if she had only damaged her reputation as a novelist with *My Next Bride*, her stories continued to be welcome in America throughout the thirties, and in the best places. Despite the weaknesses of "Lydia and the Ring-Doves," George Dangerfield at *Vanity Fair* wrote Kay Boyle, "I need hardly tell you how glad we should be to see anything you might care to submit." Planning the first issue of the *Southern Review* for June of 1935, Cleanth Brooks tracked Kay Boyle down through the Guggenheim Foundation, "extremely anxious" to have her work. For "Maiden, Maiden," appearing in *Harper's Bazaar* in December of 1934, Kay was paid a substantial three hundred and fifty dollars. Janet Flanner, who had met her in Paris in the late twenties, had been outraged to learn *The New Yorker* was paying Kay two hundred and fifty, more than she was getting, and launched a protest on her own behalf. Meanwhile Kay Boyle and Ann Watkins cleverly recycled Kay's work so that the sketches from *365 Days* were dispatched as original stories, even to *The New Yorker*.

As always, Kay Boyle's life was her work. The children were sent to bed at seven, and Bobby now felt as if Kay were someone "way above, distant"; there were no mother-daughter talks. Most of Kay's attention went to Sindbad, whose illness at Christmas occasioned a visit from Peggy and Pegeen. An uneasy truce had been declared; Peggy allowed Laurence and Kay to stay in her unoccupied house in Paris, and Peggy visited with her lovers, one of whom was the Communist Douglas Garman. Peggy watched with irritation as Kay played the part of the "efficient nurse," taking care of Sindbad, and doing everything she could to make *her* feel *de trop*. Worse, Garman, who in 1926 had published one of Kay's earliest stories, "Collation," in his magazine *Calendar of Modern Letters*, seemed to have fallen prey to Kay Boyle's charms. Fortunately, as soon as they were alone, Garman confided that he no longer admired Kay's writing, that her novels were not very good. One night at dinner Peggy announced that Garman and his daughter Debbie, who was Pegeen's age, were coming to live with her.

"How can you possibly take on the responsibility of looking after Debbie?" Kay haughtily demanded, with her usual implication that Peggy was the incompetent, she the nurturing mother.

On Christmas Eve, Kay dressed as Santa Claus, donning a long white beard, a red robe, and a red hat. From her childhood with Katherine, she had learned to turn family holidays into rituals, dramatic with significance.

"I didn't know Santa Claus was so thin!" Bobby whispered to Pegeen. "It looks like my mother!"

"You idiot!" Pegeen whispered back.

That Christmas of 1934 Katherine was in Cincinnati, lonely and depressed. Kay instructed Ann Watkins to send her a check for thirteen dollars. Katherine lived now only for news of her writer daughter.

Nighttime in Kitzbühel that January of 1935: Although it was against the law to listen to "A." on the radio, Kay and Laurence sat up listening in secret to Hitler. They wondered whether the Saar would vote in the January 13 plebiscite to be reunited with Germany. Captivated by the emotional appeals, Kay Boyle said she found it "strangely thrilling" to hear the officials give their directions to the inhabitants of the Saar on how to "make their mark" on the ballots. Kay found Hitler's appeal to all German-speaking people to return to the Fatherland "really moving." As always, she succumbed to emotion, in contrast, for example, to her later account of how Cilli had learned tolerance by dining with Peggy Guggenheim. The French radio speeches she labeled "disgusting—all finance and big promises and wide arguments and assurances by slick-tongued diplomats." Her views, in fact, were remarkably similar in language and point of view to those of Ezra Pound, who was equally appalled by the machinations of British finance capital. Kay and Pound and many of their friends shared a sense of hopelessness before the inadequacies of the democracies to meet the crisis of the world depression; many believed that had England and France given Austria the loans that might have kept her democracy alive a little longer, Mussolini might not have had so free a hand in her politics.

Culturally, now, Kay Boyle stalwartly rejected America. "We are not *against* America," she said, "but against the kind of check they like to put upon one's personal living and upon general living." America was inhospitable to the artist, Kay believed. When early in 1935 D. H. Lawrence's patroness, Mabel Dodge Luhan, invited her to join the artists' colony in Taos, New Mexico, Kay replied that should she ever return to America, and she had no intention of so doing, she would avoid New York and "go directly to the west or south." America meant mindless Babbitry, blandness, and the absence of intensity.

"I prefer the emotional thing," Kay declared, "and the Germans have it in Hitler anyway." In the snowy Tyrol, as Cilli taught baby Kathe the "*Heil Hitler*" salute, Kay Boyle too hearkened to the Nazi appeal. Fifty years later, revising her life, Kay Boyle declared, "I could not believe my ears when Eugene Jolas just before the *Anschluss* told me he had been so stirred by Hitler's appeal to all German peoples to return to the Fatherland that he had actually wept." But in her letters of the period, Kay Boyle responded exactly as he did to the populist, anticapitalist rhetoric of the

Nazis. Emotional, a romantic, and a person with little systematic under-standing of history, Kay Boyle at the dawn of 1935 was also caught up in the storms of sentiment fueled by the tyrant in Berlin.

Kay Boyle's novel about Austria, *Death of a Man*, reflects the degree to which emotionally she not only understood but finally had come to participate in the feelings that drove so many Austrians to National So-cialism. Its characters were based on people Kay met at the *Infektionshaus* where first Bobby and later Apple and Laurence had been quarantined. Two lay sisters, one a hunchback, would appear in her novel, while the doctor would be its hero.

Learning in March of 1935 that the sisters were leaving the *Infek-tionshaus*, being too old any longer for service, Kay came to take them out for a meal. Then she watched carefully as they seemed "ready to faint," while the "sweet one's eyes filled with tears at the thought of all they couldn't eat going back to the kitchen!" Wrapping the leftover chocolate cake, veal chops, chicken, and bread in a napkin, Kay observed Laurence offer the hunchback a cigarette only for her to "sit there puffing away grimly." Sarcastically, Kay wrote her mother that the hunchback was the only person in the hospital who owned a mirror, although "she is so re-pulsive, like a monster, like a toad, that one has to look the other way at table."

Kay Boyle could dispassionately tell the story of the good man who turns to fascism in a short story like "The White Horses of Vienna," since in this, as in many of her stories, she refrained from narcissistically in-cluding herself as a character. *Death of a Man*, with its Kay Boyle surrogate, a woman named Pendennis, greedily admiring of, indeed falling in love with the fascist doctor, prevents the author from telling the story without participating in the doctor's own emotional responses to Hitler and his cohorts. In *Death of a Man* she exhibits so narrow a political understanding that she fails even to mention the socialist and democratic opposition to fascism which had distinguished Vienna upon her arrival, and the novel suffers from deep confusions. Although later she criticized Jolas for being stirred by Hitler's appeals, Kay at the time dedicated her novel to him.

If *Death of a Man* fails as a novel, it offers, as did all of Kay Boyle's long fiction, mirrors into the author far more accurate than anything she might have said about herself then or later. Pendennis shows us a Kay Boyle haughty and imperious, who tears up a letter from her father, de-claring, "That's what I do with orders!" as Kay had on the morning after her wedding to Richard Brault torn up Howard's letter. She offers as well a visual image of herself at thirty-three: thin-legged and slender, with "long lovely tapering limbs." Pendennis is proud of her slender body, as Kay Boyle was of hers. She is also a flirt, certain of her power to control men. "If I'm living with you then I'm not sitting waiting in a grand hotel for you to do what you have to do and then come back," Pendennis says, as Kay Boyle might well have done. She is also full of Kay Boyle-like hyperbole as she declares she's "been divorced twelve times and I've come to Europe to find a title." Pendennis does, however, as Kay may well have done on her trip to Germany, say "*Grüss Gott*" instead of "*Heil Hitler.*" And everyone falls in love with her, her English husband no less than the "dark and hot-eyed young Nazi doctor," Prochaska.

What Kay Boyle does best is capture the tonalities of the environment—Austria before the *Anschluss.* She dramatizes the explosion at the Hotel Hellenstainer from the point of view of its Nazi proprietor; she reveals how only the Nazis had confidence in the future as the young doctor lights those swastika fires, and she includes a silly young woman like Cilli who sees "A." as a sexual object, "as women of another less desperate country might speak of an actor of whom they dreamed at night." Cilli's mother is like the real-life Cilli, saying she "wouldn't sit at a table if I knew a Jew were sitting at it."

In passionate language Kay Boyle conveys how in this fallen land Nazism represents a triumph over despair, "part of something thriving, not doomed." Prochaska receives a full hearing as the author shows how Austrians chose National Socialism not to be conquerors, not to be rich, and not because they were anti-Semites, which they had been, in any case, for centuries. They longed to remember their history "without shame" and to live normal lives once more, with "new shoes," young love, and wine in the evening. Prochaska listens to music "from Berlin or Munich or from Mozart's town," and is restored to his culture, so that his flesh becomes "clean," his "power abundant."

So deeply, however, does Kay Boyle immerse herself in the consciousness of the young Austrians attracted to National Socialism that when she attempts to portray two Jewish women, with no ironic distance and in her omniscient voice, she makes them "bovine," with "heavy flesh and slow sulky eyes," women with black mustaches. Once more she reveals herself to be partaking of the fascist aesthetic, as she had done in 1931 when she boasted to William Carlos Williams of her "blonde Germanic babies." Neither Dr. Prochaska nor any Nazi appears in the scene to take responsibility for the anti-Semitic point of view.

At the end Pendennis abandons her passionate Nazi lover not because she perceives an alternative to National Socialism, but out of a tired individualism. It is true that she objects to Prochaska's condoning a Jew's exclusion from an athletic competition. But her perspective then falters, the result of Kay Boyle's having in all her writing about Austria focused only on Dollfuss, the Heimwehr, and the Nazis, as if these were the only political forces in existence. Pendennis leaves Prochaska (only to change her mind at the very end anyway) not because she perceives what's wrong with being a Nazi, let alone what it would have taken to defeat Hitler, but because he isn't free not to take orders. As Thomas Mann revealed in "Mario and the Magician," it's not enough not to want to do something; the will falters before the absence of a viable alternative with which to combat evil. So Kay Boyle's most political novel, and potentially her most powerful, succumbs to her limited political and historical understanding of what was happening to Austria.

When *Death of a Man* was published by Harcourt in 1936, her reputation as a novelist was damaged even further. "Novelist she is not, nor ever will be," Helen Moran wrote in the *North American Review*. American reviewers concluded from her sympathetic Nazi characters that Kay Boyle must be something of a Nazi herself. Her obvious admiration of blond and blue-eyed characters had to mean that she had failed to distance herself from Nazi culture. Clifton Fadiman, who had voted against giving the 1935 O. Henry Memorial Award to "The White Horses of Vienna" because the story was pro-Nazi, saw her as having been influenced by Hitler's decadent romanticism. Most reviewers concurred.

"The glamour which Miss Boyle casts over the National-Socialist movement seems anything but true," *The Times Literary Supplement* of London wrote. *Time* magazine in America called *Death of a Man* a "Nazi Idyll," while Mark Van Doren in *The Nation* accused her of trying "to hypnotize the reader into a state of what may be called mystical fascism." In *The New Republic* Otis Ferguson called *Death of a Man* a "case for the Nazi spirit" and "special pleading," as he pointed out that "those who plot in the wine cellars and keep the swastikas burning on the mountains at night are the outstanding characters; the author's sympathy and understanding are theirs."

Had Kay Boyle not entirely omitted from her panorama of Austria the defeat of the workers' and socialists' struggle against fascism, most of these criticisms would have been nullified; by not contrasting her Nazis with those who knew better—and they existed—she produced a maddening book. Or, as Ferguson put it, she got in "absolutely over her head in all this land, ancestors, mysticism and kraut."

If in a short story like "The White Horses of Vienna," she need not have offered a complete vision of the panoply of forces at work, in a novel about Nazism such an omission was unthinkable. Whatever opposition to "A." existed before February of 1934—or after—Kay Boyle was obliged to give it a hearing, or so her reviewers unanimously believed. Some indeed perceived what Kay Boyle's conscious intention was, as Alfred Kazin in *The New York Times Book Review* praised her for offering so clear a view "of the impulses that have driven so many plain folk to Hitlerism." But Kazin had to conclude as well that "the story is built on sand." Ferguson was in the majority, however, as he called *Death of a Man* "a weak thing to be coming from such talents," and urged the author to come home where she would find "AUTHENTIC COUNTRY COMPLETE WITH PEOPLE HUNGER STRIFE."

Kay Boyle never perceived what went wrong with *Death of a Man* and would acknowledge only that the fault lay in her repeated insistence upon including an "agonized American girl" at the heart of her novels. "She is disguised," Kay Boyle thought, although of course she was not, "but she is really me, and she is very boring." But much more was at stake than "that virtuous American woman stalking the pages," as Kay Boyle put it.

"She's sympathetic to the Nazis!" her sister Jo declared after reading "The White Horses of Vienna." Shrewdly, Jo discerned how the sexuality of the blond, blue-eyed, golden-thighed Aryan male aroused the author. At this time Jo and Katherine were living together, and according to Kay, Jo's comments kept her mother and her sister from exchanging a word for a whole year.

Katherine, of course, defended her writer daughter. Distressed over the plethora of hostile reviews accusing her of being a Nazi sympathizer, Katherine wrote Kay in sympathy that "the true artist presents; he does not judge." Any effort Kay Boyle might have made to develop as an artist and a thinker was blunted by her mother's unqualified endorsement of everything she said, everything she did.

12

Kitzbühel-Devon-Mégève

*I would not give in, nor did she of course—how could she, she
knew she knew best, that she did things well.*
LAURENCE VAIL

*She said "his father" as though talking of someone who had
passed by in the street.*
Monday Night

Kay Boyle and Laurence Vail left Austria not because of fear of the
restless Heimwehr, or the growing ascendancy of National Socialism and
the inevitability of *Anschluss*, but because Sindbad had become chronically
ill with bronchitis, which led finally to pleurisy. For their new home, Kay
chose England, where Sindbad would go to boarding school. To get the
family to Paris, and then to England, she borrowed money from Ann Watkins. Movement between countries was a constant problem because neither
Apple nor Sharon had been legally registered. Kay had been too busy when
Apple was born; Laurence had never taken the trouble to adopt Sharon.
Grandly Kay called baby Kathe "my first legitimate child and very smug
about it." At such times she sounded as if she still had not grown beyond
the Paris reflex of taunting the bourgeoisie.

On April 27, 1935, she packed her family into the Renault and headed
for Paris. They stopped in Switzerland to visit James and Nora Joyce, who
were also entertaining the Jolases. Maria and Kay were surrounded by
children, but both succumbed when Joyce enlisted them to take turns as
his typists. Idly, Nora sat watching. Nor was she bothered when the ever-
outspoken Mrs. Jolas demanded, "Kay and I are not professional typists.
It seems to me that you could help us out on this a bit."

"To tell you the truth, Mrs. Jolas," Nora answered, "I was never much
interested in me husband's work."

One night, as James Stern entered the Deux Magots in Paris, he noticed
a basket just inside the entrance with a seemingly abandoned baby lying
in it. Suddenly Stern spotted an old friend he had not seen since Vienna,
and so he learned that the name of the baby lying in the basket near the
door was Kathe.

From Paris, Kay and Laurence brought the children to Devonshire. From her vantage at Yew Tree Cottage, her home in South Harting, Peggy took note as Kay and Laurence left "all their many little daughters" in a local pub and then drove by themselves down to Devon. They rented a house at Seaton high above the sea; Sindbad was enrolled at Bedale's, a progressive boarding school permeated with Fabian socialist views.

"I want to become a boarder, like Sindbad," Bobby told Kay and Laurence. But they said no, and Bobby thought: I never get what I want.

Kay Boyle was to remain a year in England. As she had been miserable in Stoke-on-Trent, so she hated every moment she spent in the English countryside. It was "a good place for work," but it was "depressing." And it was far from cheap. Kay was convinced that because they had rented the house high on a hill called "The Mount," their neighbors believed they had more money than they did, and they were charged high prices for everything. Contradictory, full of bravado as always, in defiance of the reality, Kay professed herself unwilling to own a radio, insisting that she had "always avoided them like the plague," as if she and Laurence had not sat spellbound by Hitler's broadcasts all those nights in Kitzbühel.

Kay's complaints multiplied as she excoriated "the utter dullness of the country, the faces, the lives, the drinks, the streets." It was all "enough to make one want to die." "Life's too short to spend it in the U.K.," she moaned as she immediately began to search for some "livable place," one presumably free of the impending political conflicts. "Even the typewriter ribbon is soaking from the general misery of an English October afternoon. What a country!" Kay exaggerated.

To pass the time the family played Authors, a card game Katherine had sent. Soon Laurence invented a game of their own called Family. Kay bought plain white cards and she and Laurence and Bobby sat drawing and painting by the fire as they listened to Bach on the radio she had insisted she would not purchase. Each family member was depicted on his leading card: the four other cards of his suit were also listed on that leading card. Mrs. Vail, Grandma Coco as she was called, had one card picturing a string of minute climbers since she had been one of the first women to reach the summit of Mont Blanc. Another depicted thirty-one of her trunks, which were filled with feather boas and feather muffs, brocaded gowns with bustles and solid-silver tea and coffee sets, and knee-high button shoes. The first card of Katherine Evans Boyle's suit depicted Alfred Stieglitz, to whom she even now continued to send adoring paeans: "It is good for me to know that you are—and that O'Keeffe continues to produce things that are beautiful."

Bobby's education had suffered. Now at nine she spoke French and German, but her spelling and writing in English left something to be desired. Kay satirized her daughter's difficulties in a *New Yorker* story called "Education," in which Bobby is perplexed when a teacher assigns her a composition about "Christopher." Martha (Bobby) knows so little about

America, the homeland of both her parents, that she thinks Christopher must be someone who died of a broken heart at sea. Mercilessly, Kay Boyle transcribes in scarcely literate prose Bobby's description of how she had set their house at Col-de-Villefranche on fire: "I got a stik and bushed it in the fire and wen it was alite I put it to the curdens and the curdens all cought alite. . . ." The mother in the story remains cool, amused, and indifferent. If she is troubled by her daughter's problem with spelling, she is too self-absorbed to do anything about it. At the end Martha writes a letter to Emperor Haile Selassie inviting him to come live with the Vail family. So in her art, as in her life, Kay proudly insisted that formal education meant little, that the Vail children had been educated in what counted, no matter that their schooling was so erratic that they could scarcely write or spell.

Kay, of course, took off for London whenever she could. She dined with Jonathan Cape, even asking him to publish a historical novel Howard Peterson Boyle had written. One night in London, Kay and Laurence found themselves at the Fitzroy Pub, where a stocky young man with burning eyes had climbed up onto the bar and was reciting poetry no one wanted to hear. Kay was fascinated; she was certain she had discovered another Irish poet. A brawl soon erupted.

"Let's save him from British violence!" Kay urged Laurence, who needed no encouragement to become involved in barroom turbulence.

Only hours later, when they had gone off together into the night, did the poet finally ask Kay Boyle her name. And only then did Kay ask Dylan Thomas his.

Illness assailed Kay's family that English year. Apple's bronchitis began it. Then in America, Katherine developed cancer. All her needs were now supplied by Joan, who earned the gratitude of Howard for "the wonderful home you are making for Mother." Kay wrote she felt "desperate that I cannot be generous as I want to be." Sentiments had to suffice. On Thanksgiving Day of 1935, Clotilde suffered an appendix attack and was rushed to the American Hospital at Neuilly-sur-Seine. But the ether was administered too rapidly, congesting her lungs, and she died. From this death, Laurence Vail would never recover. On Christmas Day, Eugene Vail died, and, soon after, his brother George, an ice-skating champion and man-about-town.

It was this last death which changed their lives. Laurence was his Uncle George Vail's sole heir. With his inheritance, they were now able to plan their escape from England in earnest. They considered Grenoble. Annecy, in the French Alps, with its "snow and sports," seemed enticing. France it would certainly be.

Never idle, Kay filled her last months in England with her usual preoccupations. She reestablished contact with Ezra Pound, who, she hoped, would help get money into fascist Italy for Carnevali, "the lily-souled Emanuel," as Pound had called him in a letter to Harriet Monroe. Kay wanted Pound to give her the name of a shop in Bologna where she might purchase a radio for Carnevali, which she hoped Pound would deliver. And Pound responded, willing to deliver the "instrument" to Bazzano. He could not resist adding a few political sentiments along the way: "the same bank swine who have been starving England want to extend the famine and widen the distressed areas. All USURY / all part of infamy to CURTAIL consumption, make famine, money famine that prevents USE of the plenty that exists."

Pound was right, for the English made it difficult to get the money to Italy. Kay wanted to endorse a check for more than a thousand francs which she had received from the *Revue de Paris* over to Pound to buy the radio. "The sanctions thing is part of the whole, filthy scheme," she wrote Pound, agreeing with his views. "I'd like to meet some exciting English who believe in something, and with energy." When the bank refused to tell Kay the rate of exchange for the lira, she sent Pound a check for ten pounds, hoping the Italians would cash it.

Disaster pursued Carnevali, even as Pound managed to get him transferred to the encephalitis wing of a Rome hospital as a free patient. First the radio, which Pound had supplied, was confiscated by the owner of the bistro to settle Carnevali's bill: a fact Kay learned from "this pederast," as she put it, the slur suggesting that her politics may even then have been one thing, her real feelings another, as her remembered defense of Jews to Cilli was contradicted by the anti-Semitic portraits in *Death of a Man*.

Then Carnevali reacted badly to one of the drugs he was given; his sexual appetites became exaggerated, and he wrote violent letters, to Kay and to Pound. He also sexually attacked several nurses and was banished from the hospital. After one unpleasant note too many from Carnevali, Pound bailed out. "Good God," Kay pleaded, "haven't we all had them?" When Pound didn't reply, Laurence scraped the money together to get Carnevali back to Bazzano. Kay wrote to McAlmon for help; there was no more she could do. (Sometime during the war, Carnevali, alone in his room, choked on a piece of bread caught in his windpipe and died.)

The winter of 1936 found Kay Boyle at the peak of her powers as a writer of short stories. She celebrated her thirty-fourth birthday with a grand party at which she boasted that twenty-nine different types of hors d'oeuvres were served, including a dill pickle stuffed with cream cheese. That February a new collection, *The White Horses of Vienna and Other Stories*, was published to much praise. In *The Saturday Review of Literature* she was called "a consummate artist," as beside the review stood a poem by Archibald MacLeish dedicated to Kay Boyle and picturing her as a "sea bird" who sang unhalted. (The major dissenting review came from Edith Walton in *The New York Times Book Review*, which called the stories Kay Boyle "at her near-best," but still "not good enough to allay one's fears for her.")

Book-length studies of major twentieth-century figures now discussed her respectfully, as Harlan Hatcher in *Creating the Modern American Novel*, published in 1935, called her the "most interesting" of the writers engaged in "poetic realism." Hatcher, like Kay's journalistic reviewers, also noticed that "she has been writing too much and too hurriedly to develop the power that would make her great." But Kay Boyle continued to write "short stories that make me blush with shame." It was as if she had to sabotage herself; Uncle George Vail's money made no difference. Her unconscious rebellion against the path Katherine had determined she walk continued, even as she was doing some of her best work.

From the mid-thirties on, critics noticed as well that Kay Boyle was the antithesis of the feminist. In a feminist literary study published in 1936 called *The School of Femininity: A Book For and About Women as They Are Interpreted Through Feminine Writers of Yesterday and Today*, author Margaret Lawrence included Kay Boyle in a chapter called "Helpmeets." Her women characters, Lawrence found, were "self-effacing" and "un-ambitious for themselves." Nor was the critic much taken with the Kay surrogate Hannah in *Year Before Last*, the "little girl pal," who helps a man and even tries to resemble him, but remains "a talented second-fiddle person." So early feminists objected to Kay Boyle's depiction of women as inferior to men. Lawrence, writing in the tradition of Kay's Aunt Nina Allender, urged women writers to reject romantic myths, not least "the desire innate in the gentlewoman to lean against the protection of a man who loves her." But Kay was no more interested in portraying strong self-defined women in her fiction—women who had achieved as much as she had—than she was in heeding the critics who urged her to slow down, write less, and perfect her craft.

Romantic as she was, as unable as she was to depict women characters with the courage to do more than further the talents of their men, Kay Boyle herself was fiercely ambitious for literary fame. She remained one of the American writers in the thirties who kept at a safe distance from politics. "I am not a Communist," she insisted. "I am not convinced that Russia has solved anything at all." Her credo remained that of John Cowper Powys: her convictions ended with the supremacy of the "individual" at any cost. "I cannot follow the present trend—the literary trend . . . of beleiving [sic] in that as a solution . . . which, if followed out to the end, would make the individual an anachronism," she declared, emphasizing her distance from any form of Marxism. She and McAlmon both would have nothing to do with "the prevalent Red fad." Whatever Senator McCarthy might say about her later, she stood in the thirties firmly against those who saw some solution in Stalinism. She had listened too long to Emma and Sasha for that. (Kay lost her great friend when Alexander Berkman, calling his life "useless," suffering from cancer, killed himself in the winter of 1936.)

Kay even said now she was "filled with rage against such Communists as Bob Brown who turned red because they lost all in Wall Street and now exploit ignorant travellers to Russia." But politics remained for Kay Boyle, always, a matter of the personal. James T. Farrell, that most political of men in the thirties, was "perfectly sound," not because he understood what was happening in Russia, which he did, but because he had "been through the mill." She herself stood apart. "I just don't believe," she said.

At the end of July the Vails packed up and left England. On their way, they visited Nancy Cunard at her farmhouse in La Chapelle-Réanville, about sixty miles from Paris. Kay was dedicating to Nancy a long poem she had begun about the Scottsboro boys, who had been falsely accused of rape in the American South, and whose case had become a *cri de coeur* for the Communist party in America.

They were moving to Mégève, a storybook village of gabled farmhouses and chalets nestled beneath Mont Blanc, in the Haute-Savoie, a village of snow where horses pulled sleighs through the streets in winter. With Laurence's inheritance from, as Kay put it, "miserly" Uncle George Vail, they bought a chalet, which they named Les Cinq Enfants. It was, the children would later remember, an enchanted chalet, all stone and wood, three stories, with a wooden balcony all around carved with hearts and other fanciful decorations, and a dining room big enough for a banquet—although there was only one bathroom. Kay said she welcomed the idea of becoming "a country housewife" since everyone seemed "drunk and actively miserable in cities."

In Mégève, Kay Boyle quickly organized her household. On the inside door of every cupboard she tacked a list of its contents, shelf by shelf. On the evening before, the maids set the table for the children's breakfast, which they ate downstairs in the black-and-white-tiled kitchen with the servants. Older children could eat with Laurence and Kay and their unceasing houseguests, but they were not encouraged to join in the conversation. "Children should be seen and not heard," Mrs. Vail told them. Kay did not disagree.

The numerous servants were supervised by Josephine, the family retainer, who had begun with Mrs. Vail as an accolyte out of a convent. Cilli and Fanni had come with the Vails from Austria, although soon Fanni would return to honor her obligation and bear children for the Reich. Kay neither cooked, cleaned, shopped nor did laundry. She did draw up the menus; Josephine then ordered the food and supervised its preparation.

Occasionally Kay tried to persuade her daughters to be as neat as she, but with small success.

"Yes, Kline," Apple would answer obediently, "Kline" pronounced "Klin" being her special name for her mother. Kay called Apple "Pudie." Kathe called Kay "Mimi." Kay called Kathe "Pussy Kat" or "Kat." Her loneliest daughter, Bobby, called Kay "Mumsy," while her desolate step-daughter, who admired her so much, but felt she was less loved by Kay than the others, had to call her plain "Kay."

Kay threatened. Half gaily, almost singing, with a characteristic little tilt of her head, Kay might call out, "No skiing today, Pudie, 'til you've cleaned your room." A half hour later, still singing, Kay might sweep into the room and, exasperated by her daughter's slowness and inefficiency, take over herself, busy as she was. "The only way to get things done is to do them yourself," Kay said again and again.

Kay threw extraordinary energy into her neatness, Laurence observed: "You can doze off in a zephyr, but not in a mistral." Kay believed there was only one way of being neat, her way. Laurence's efforts to help, as he put it, "riled her like opposition."

They had begun to fight, and fight they did. Neither Laurence nor Kay would give in. "How could she," Laurence was to remember some years later, "she knew she knew best, that she did things well . . . well, this made me feel I could not do things well." To her husband and children, she behaved as if she were a goddess now, perfect, more a myth in action than a real person. Always weaker, dependent, helpless, neither Laurence nor any of the children would ever be as capable as she, as right about things, as in control.

In her ruthlessly organized life at Mégève, Kay placed her writing first, now more than ever. In the very early morning you could hear the tap-tapping of her typewriter. That tap-tapping was the last thing you heard at night when you fell asleep. No one, even when there were guests, saw Kay Boyle before lunch. Then, between lunch and five or six, she disappeared again to her study. Every day the big black family dog, Diane, headed for Kay's workroom. Kay opened the door and Diane entered. Quietly Kay then closed the door against all further interruptions. From her window, out beyond the pine trees and the ravine, Kay could see Mont Blanc. But she must not be distracted. Kay drew the curtains and sat down at her typewriter, Diane at her feet. Years later Apple remembered standing outside her mother's closed door, listening to the tap-tapping of the type-writer. She longed to knock; she longed to see her mother. But she was afraid, and so she stood there, immobilized.

If Kay's heart was in her work, Laurence's was in the mountains, as he organized expeditions all seasons of the year. Occasionally Kay might accede to Laurence's pleas and be lured away from her typewriter, although she avoided these interruptions whenever she could. Laurence said he preferred climbing to just about everything "except that one woman in ten, my children and pipe," and the children, if not always Kay, had to join him. "I'm fed up with mountain climbing!" Bobby muttered one day. But if you could walk, you had to go, in foul weather as in fair. When Kay joined them, she decked herself out in an elaborate Austrian climbing costume and boots, a skirt rather than trousers, unlike her mother-in-law, who in her heyday had climbed in knickerbockers, her face blackened with charcoal against the sun.

When he was not out on the mountains, Laurence could be found in his studio on the floor above Kay's. In that studio there was a single photograph, of his sister Clotilde. At dinner Laurence would invariably find a way of introducing Clotilde's name into the conversation. Then he would burst into tears.

If it seemed to the outside world that Kay Boyle was so extraordinary a woman that she could combine a brilliant literary career with being a wife and a mother of many, while entertaining on a grand scale and maintaining many strong friendships, the reality was less sanguine. As a mother she had little time to be affectionate or personal, or engage in long conversations with children about their feelings. What she did, as her own mother had done, was demand that they all be creative—and that they never oppose her, but, rather, worship her as if she were, indeed, a goddess.

They should never be idle, she told them. "Use your imagination!" The children of Kay Boyle had to sing and act and write poems and paint pictures, which were exhibited three times a year in children's art shows, just as Katherine had sent Kay's and "Janet's" creations to Mr. Stieglitz. When Peggy Guggenheim, following Stieglitz, mounted a show of child artists at her London gallery in the autumn of 1938, all the Vail children were represented.

It was Kay who came up with the idea of the *Vails' Family Almanach*, which resembled the scrapbooks and "birthday books" of her own childhood. Endlessly energetic, Kay did all the typing; Peggy Guggenheim even designed one of the covers. Inside were Kay's own poems and stories written for children, as well as the children's productions. "Child, thou art loving" was one of her own poems, and a frequent theme in the children's books she was to write for money in the coming years. Their mother also fascinated, seduced the children with her humor, her great storytelling flair, as she did with her elusiveness and inaccessibility. The most charming of her poems was "Advice to Children," a symphony of irony in which she urges her children to do everything she wishes they would not:

> *I pray you, dears, do not agree—*
> *The shock would be too much for me—*
> *But hold your own as children must*
> *Against those crumbling into dust.*

In great good humor Kay urges them all to do their worst, from chewing gum and reading books at the dinner table to frolicking out into the snow in lacy dresses, without socks "when the temperature is six below." Equally fanciful was Kay's serial for the *Almanach* "Something Wrong with the

Wind," a takeoff on Margaret Mitchell's novel, with a fourteen-year-old heroine named Bobeen who "suffers spiritually over things she simply couldn't tell a soul about." Her favorite line is "Mother, you can't make me," and her favorite film is *Wuthering Heights*. As Kay Boyle demanded protestations of devotion from her children, Bobby obliged with poems about motherhood, including "That Lovely Saint," in which her mother appears as a woman whose mouth "had a power / of saying words of / Truth and only truth."

Kay was a marvelous storyteller, but the children soon learned that she didn't always tell the truth. When Giles, the brother of Pegeen's best friend, Jacqueline Ventadour, visited, Kay made him take a nap. As soon as she was gone, Giles climbed out the window and joined the other children for a smoke, only to slip back into bed just before Kay returned. "See, you did sleep," Kay told him. "I came in when you were asleep and I saw you. You were fast asleep." Neither Giles nor Jacqueline told her that she had been found out.

Thirteen-year-old Jacqueline had grown close to Kay, for if she faltered in day-to-day devotion, Kay could be a stalwart friend. Kay seemed to worry if you had a cold. As busy as she was, she noticed. But Jacqueline had far greater cause to be grateful to Kay Boyle. When a psychoanalyst friend of Maria Jolas's had persuaded Jacqueline's mother, Fanny, to send her to what amounted to an asylum for children because she was too high-spirited, Kay and Laurence found out. On their next trip to Paris they visited Jacqueline in her lonely exile. Then they persuaded Fanny to set her free. The Vails invited Jacqueline to Mégève every summer and holiday in 1937, 1938, and 1939. "They're the happiest family I've ever seen," Jacqueline thought then.

In these formative years of her daughters' lives, Kay Boyle continued to insist that their creativity was enough. The formal education that might discipline and train their minds as well as render them capable of earning their own livings did not interest her, although she and her sister both had found themselves at times in their lives without the financial protection of men. Kay Boyle was not a parent who considered making sacrifices so that her children might do better in life than she had done.

Instead, she treated them as pale reflections of herself, cultivating the romantic illusion that since they were her children, they had to be artistically talented. So she insisted that they perform for guests in the basement of Les Cinq Enfants, where the piano was kept along with the boots and skis. The one child who genuinely liked her studies was Bobby, who talked at eleven of wanting to become a veterinarian. But Kay Boyle never did anything—then or later—to help her pursue that ambition. Guggenheim heirs Pegeen and Sindbad attended boarding schools. "Pegeen can scarcely spell her own name," Kay snidely remarked one day with her usual haughty, defensive scorn of formal education. Their daughters' creativity was an adornment Kay and Laurence vaguely assumed they would bring to advantageous marriages, no matter that Kay Boyle herself had never made such a marriage—and never would. Certainly Laurence's allowances from Vail mother and Guggenheim wife seemed never to be enough.

On January 27, 1937, Kay went to Geneva, where she took the oath of repatriation and registered as a United States citizen, according to a new law dating from June of 1936 allowing a native-born American woman who had lost her citizenship by marriage to an alien to get it back.

There was a steady influx of guests at Les Cinq Enfants, sometimes so many that Kay Boyle would melodramatically shut herself up in her room indefinitely with Diane, waiting, she announced, "for rain." Emmy Eckstein came with stomach trouble and an unfinished autobiography, which Kay volunteered to help her rewrite. Kay wanted the book to be called *The Death of Alexander Berkman*. Meanwhile, for they could be generous, Kay and Laurence shepherded Emmy from one doctor to another in a futile search for a cure for her illness.

James Laughlin, that young Harvard student of means who had corresponded with her, met Kay for the first time when he came to Mégève to ski; he announced he had used part of a schoolboy prize at Choate to purchase *Year Before Last*. He was starting his own publishing company, he said, which he would call New Directions, and he wanted to be the first to publish a collection of her poetry. Ever the businesswoman, before long Kay had sold Laughlin three pieces from *365 Days* for his journal, *New Democracy*.

Mary Reynolds and Marcel Duchamp never made it to Devon, but they did come to the Alps, which Marcel insisted on climbing in bicycle racer's shoes instead of boots. Dedicating poems to friends had now become an obsessive mode of flattery. Kay wrote "A Complaint for M and M," opening with a rebuke because Reynolds and Duchamp had not accepted her invitation to the opening night of the 1937 Paris Exposition, an event living in Mégève would not cause her to miss. James Stern brought his new wife, Tania, and they braved Laurence's erratic driving. One day Laurence drove them all into Chamonix, only to be hit by a bus. Kay did not criticize Laurence's always dangerous driving or belittle him in public. But she had a way of taking charge, and it was obvious that her efficiency annoyed her husband. Wherever Laurence went, an atmosphere of disarray followed him; clearly he was frustrated to have so perfect a wife.

There was another side to Kay's frequent entertaining at Les Cinq Enfants in these prewar years. If she could be hospitable, she could also be mean and insensitive. And always she was predictably vicious toward anyone who dared oppose one of her icons. She had lunch in Paris with her old adversary Laura Riding, who had dared mock William Carlos Williams as a "worshipper of Poe"; Kay attacked Riding as "a vindicative [sic] bitch . . . vicious and looking for a fight." The purpose of the lunch had been to hate "her pretentiousness, hate her work, hate her face." Kay

Boyle had garnered enough acclaim now to behave as if she were a queen, a law unto herself.

A favorite sport of Kay and Laurence, and whoever was at table with them, was to savage absent friends. There was also another unwholesome habit they developed. On their frequent trips to Paris, Kay and Laurence would end a conversation by inviting acquaintances to visit them at Mégève. When the innocent guests arrived, they were told by Kay Boyle exactly what generous sums they were expected to tip Josephine and the other servants. These were exorbitant amounts of money, as much as the people would have paid for a hotel in elegant Mégève. Sometimes the guests didn't have that much with them, and, more than once, softhearted Sindbad slipped them some money. Then, as soon as these "guests" departed, they were subjected to scathing, cutting remarks. The older children were appalled. (Years later Kay would even complain that "poor as church-mice" as they were, Jay Laughlin never contributed so much as a bag of groceries.)

Kay could also be touchingly considerate. She and her surrogate, Apple, who was sent to the post office every day, to the child's distress, were the postmistress's best customers. Later, after the Germans had invaded France, and foodstuffs, let alone chocolate, were scarce, Kay purchased a huge box of candy in Geneva for the postmistress in gratitude for her help. The postmistress thanked her.

"Oh, it was nothing," Kay demurred.

"That's all right. It's the thought that counts," the postmistress most inappropriately replied. Kay turned that into one of her funniest stories: the unheard-of gift of a gigantic box of chocolates being treated as if it were nothing at a time when there was no cooking oil, gasoline, sugar— or chocolate.

When Howard Peterson Boyle died in October of 1936, Kay behaved as if she were inconsolable, throwing herself in tears into Bobby's arms. The child was startled to be so chosen, and Bobby later concluded, "I was the only bastard, so she felt I was more hers." "My father died and I haven't talked to him since I married Brault," Kay wept, surprising Bobby still further since she had no idea what Kay's relations with her father were. The poor man, Laurence sympathized, crushed by Puss on one side and by his wife on the other.

Laurence knew Katherine Evans Boyle well by now, for she had become a frequent visitor at Les Cinq Enfants, at sixty-three a wizened, weak old woman, forever flattering her granddaughters, although all she found to praise was their physical appearance. Otherwise Katherine was a name dropper, invariably invoking Alfred Stieglitz and her other hero now, Franklin Delano Roosevelt. Languid and a hypochondriac, she occasionally roused herself and went off to Geneva to work at the headquarters of Alice Paul's new World Woman's Party. She preferred, however, to dress herself elegantly in Jo's hand-me-downs, her favorite a black silk dress with a big yellow plaid stripe (which Kay was soon to appropriate for herself), and mix with Kay's guests. Katherine liked James Stern, "such a slender, fastidious looking person," no wonder that Kay Boyle remained bone thin all her life.

Late in 1938 Katherine found herself scrutinizing another guest. It was writer Djuna Barnes, who had been Laurence's mistress when he lived in Greenwich Village in 1919–20. At forty-seven, Barnes, who had completed her masterwork, *Nightwood*, published in 1936, thanks to Peggy Guggenheim's hospitality, remained a beauty.

Bored, Djuna cast a predatory eye on James Stern.

"I wonder how I can get rid of Tania," she remarked to a shocked Katherine, who immediately conveyed her words to Kay.

"Do you know Henry Miller?" Djuna asked the company one cold December day as she huddled on a divan to keep warm. "Isn't he a shit? Look at his picture! He surely must be a Jew!" Few of Kay's circle were free of the prevailing anti-Semitism, and few bothered even to conceal it.

"To grow old is the greatest horror," Djuna confided on another day to Katherine. "When men no longer fall for you and want to fuck you."

"Djuna is not an intellectual at all," Katherine reported to her daughter, "and this is the source of her trouble." For her part, Djuna decided she did not like Kay. She "feigned an affectionate nature to get by," Djuna concluded, penetrating that show of affection which had attracted young Jacqueline Ventadour. But she was really "hard as flint inside." No doubt aware that she had not won over this particular "hard-boiled baby," Kay dedicated a poem to her, "Angels for Djuna Barnes," invoking Djuna's omnipresent fear: "Maidened by constant springtime, angels refluent go / Towards youth, not age, and purer shyer grow."

Meeting Kay Boyle for the first time in a Paris café in 1938, Henry Miller's writer-patroness, the diarist Anaïs Nin, echoed Djuna Barnes's reaction. It was clear that Kay Boyle could not tolerate beautiful women. If, among the female expatriates, they were rival writers, it was so much the worse. Kay greeted Anaïs Nin with her coldest hauteur. When Nin pleasantly remarked how fitting it was that they should be meeting on a Monday night, the title of Kay's most recent novel, Kay remained "inexpressive," her "bird profile" a mask. Kay had succeeded in making Nin feel "anonymous." When Nancy Cunard arrived for a visit at Les Cinq Enfants in 1938, Kay felt undermined by Cunard's strong political commitments, her support for the Loyalists in Spain. Kay self-righteously declared that she would lose her identity were she "to join or enter into a framework of any kind." She did, however, complete her poem dedicated to Cunard about the Scottsboro boys. Kay aligned herself in this, one of her best poems of the thirties, with the outcast, including as victims the girl accusers:

Not girls or men, Negroes or white, but people with this in common:
People that no one had use for, had nothing to give to, no place to offer
But the cars of a freight train careening through Paint Rock, through
*   Memphis . . .*

With Kay either working, traveling to Paris, or entertaining guests, the children ever more frequently fended for themselves. When they read Margaret Kennedy's 1925 novel *The Constant Nymph*, about a family called "Sanger's circus," in which the father, an opera composer, brings up a huge brood "most shockingly" in a chalet in the Austrian Tyrol, they assumed the book had been written for them. So the big girls enjoyed reading about "the sacredness of Sanger's room," which so reminded them of Kay's workroom, equally forbidden territory, where, as Kennedy writes, "no child ventured . . . without express permission." Like the Sanger daughters, the Vail girls even wore Tyrolean dress, an affectation Kay cultivated as she made regular trips to Lanz's in Salzburg for these Heidi-like dirndls and black embroidered sweaters and embroidered blouses. In Munich in 1939, amid the gathering storm, Kay managed to purchase for Kathe a red peasant dress with a matching hat which very much pleased the five-year-old, vain of her beauty and her blond curls, if not of her beaky Vail nose.

Indiscipline bred individuality, that highest value of all, Kay Boyle believed, and she encouraged her children to indulge in the spontaneous expression of their creative gifts. When they read in *The Constant Nymph* that the "noisy geniuses" who were Sanger's children received "no sort of regular education," but were "ignorant of obedience, application, self-command or reverence," Kay's daughters identified at once with these children. They too were periodically neglected.

Kay found the time to praise Sindbad for his developing antifascist consciousness; indeed, in Austria, Sindbad had created his own little news-paper. But her daughters began to feel the strain of her inconstant attention. "She gave us symbols," the most generous, Kathe, later remembered, thinking of her sixth-birthday chair laid with ferns and flowers and of the elaborate Christmases, the tree always sparkling with ornaments. But it was Apple who suffered most under the strain of trying to grow up in so emotionally chaotic a household.

On the eve of one of Kay and Laurence's frequent departures for Paris, where they were to spend a week, Apple fell ill with chicken pox. Laurence generally hated to leave the children when they were sick. But this time even he agreed that they would go anyway. Small for her age, with a "vivid little face," Apple was lying quietly in her bed when Kay entered to say goodbye. Apple's eyes were closed. She made no sound as the tears rolled down her cheeks. Apple felt as if she were dissolving, as if she no longer existed. But still Kay would not postpone her trip.

One summer day they were on one of their mountain walks, Kay ahead holding the hands of two of the children, Apple trailing behind. It was a moment Apple was to remember all her life: Kay holding the hands of these two other children, but not hers.

Nor was it only Apple who would look back on the hothouse of their years at Mégève with pain. Bobby had grown up to be a Pre-Raphaelite beauty with burnished gold hair, so that Laurence would call her a "Tyrolean Gretchen." Warmhearted, loyal, stubborn, loving books, loving animals, Bobby was also shy, withdrawn, and very sensitive. Like all the other children, of course, she called Laurence "Papa."

Kay and the girls were sitting in a group together when suddenly, speaking to eleven-year-old Bobby offhandedly, Kay said "your father," and she was not speaking about Laurence Vail. She was talking about some Irish poet named Ernest Walsh!

What's she talking about? Bobby wondered. She was confused and upset, for surely Laurence Vail was her father. What could her mother have meant? Wasn't she Bobby Vail, the name by which everyone knew her? Shattered, Bobby turned to the only person she, no less than any of the children, could talk to. Bobby sat down and wrote a note to Laurence. "I now know that you're not my father. You can't love me as much as the others." Then she slipped the note under Laurence's studio door.

After a while Laurence emerged from his studio. His face was wet with tears. "You must know I consider you my daughter," Laurence told Bobby. "I love you as much as if you were my own daughter."

Even then there was no talk between Kay and Bobby over this startling revelation. Kay turned to the only place where she truly communicated, to her fiction, where she promptly incorporated the entire incident. In *Monday Night*, published in 1938, a little *boy* suffers the same experience Bobby did, inadvertently learning his father's identity.

Now Bobby hung Ernest Walsh's picture in her room. He was an unrecognized Irish poet, she told visitors. Walsh suddenly became a romantic figure for all the big girls. When Jacqueline wrote a poem about him for the *Vails' Family Almanach*, Kay said she was touched; this pleased Jacqueline as they all continued to vie for Kay's approval. Still Kay did not talk to Bobby about why she had kept that secret so long. She was so self-involved, the child concluded, as to seem heartless and yet not even to realize it, a pure narcissist. She was not maternal, not nurturing. The Sterns, sympathizing, thought Bobby had an "inferiority complex" and viewed her as a person who felt "as if she didn't belong anywhere."

While Kay's typewriter tap-tapped into the night, Laurence took over the roles of both mother and father. At night he tucked the children in, and engaged in long talks on such topics as where the moon and stars ended, or if they ever did. "Never," Papa told Kathe one night. "One galaxy after another." It was terrifying to think there was no roof over the universe. But Papa reassured you.

"Strictly speaking," Laurence Vail was to write in his 1945 memoir, *Here Goes* (never to be published), "Bobby is not my daughter." Yet "since Bobby has spent the greater part of her life with me, and she appeared to like it, and I liked it, I consider her entirely my daughter."

Now it was out in the open.

The following Christmas, Grandma Coco, Gertrude Mauran of the DAR, of the strong puritan stock of New England, hung cellophane stockings filled with money for each of her grandchildren on the Christmas tree at Les Cinq Enfants. You could see right into the stocking. She had given all the children ten dollars, except for Bobby, who received only five.

It's because I'm not a Vail, Bobby knew.

"I refuse to accept this money," Bobby, hurt and incensed, told Laurence. Kay didn't figure into the discussion at all.

"Take it for my sake," Laurence urged.

Laurence had been good to her. Bobby decided to swallow her pride, however it rankled.

"All right. I will. But I find it very humiliating," Bobby replied quietly.

Then Laurence laced into his mother for her insensitivity, for her cruelty. Laurence threw a full-scale tantrum, making everyone afraid he would tear down the Christmas tree and smash to bits every ornament on it.

13

"Dostoievsky in a Ski Suit"

*Liked him more than I ever have and was spell-bound by talk on
social credit and Chinese—I loved listening to him and wanted to
stay hours.*

If, in America, Kay Boyle was rapidly becoming known as the glamorous expatriate who stayed on, a woman who had reached fulfillment in
every aspect of her life, at home in Mégève her marriage was foundering.
For Kay, Laurence's outrageous joie de vivre, his emotionalism, and the
high excitement which might erupt at any moment had begun to pall. All
too ready to admit that "self-control was never my forte," Laurence flew
into rages not only in cafés but at family meals. His scenes, he knew,
flourished in the home atmosphere, where they were directed, as he himself
later put it, "at a woman, preferably at one of my wives or at my mother."
Yet for all his flamboyance Laurence was a weak man, like Brault, and
Kay's father, a man with a will weaker than her own.

Kay kept up appearances. For one of her book jackets, she wrote, "I
always take my husband's judgment on wines, ski-runs, mountains, and
writing, and would not send out a word without having his opinion of it."
At the time she was writing those words the marriage was already in serious
trouble.

Often now, exasperated by Kay's insistence on doing things her way,
Laurence would slam out of the house, muttering, "If she does things so
well, let her do them, hell." He threw Kay's typewriter against the wall
and broke more crockery. It also soon became apparent that Kay took a
cruel delight in provoking him, as if his loss of control enhanced her own
cool competence. And all through these Mégève years Kay talked often in
Laurence's presence about Ernest Walsh, the man she *really* had loved.

Laurence was even more provoked by Kay's unrelenting productivity.
"She's a writing machine," he complained. He laughed at her "romantic
novels." Sometimes his irritation took the form of a joke as he pictured

her writing on two chairs or in bed with the typewriter digging into her stomach, her face so close to the page that the paper tickled her chin. When Kay, typically, claimed that the very smell of carbon paper excited her, Laurence retorted, "Just a whiff and she's at it, typing merrily for hours."

At six in the evening Laurence wanted his wife to lay off work and join him for an aperitif. As the tap-tap of her typewriter continued, Laurence indulged in a solitary drink. After dinner, Kay was ready to begin again. "Not for long," she promised. "Just to finish a page and take it out of the typewriter." When she failed to reappear, then he might storm in and hurl the typewriter against the wall. Laurence stopped his own writing and stuck to painting and decorating screens and bottles so as not to compete with his writer wife. But soon he began more actively to ridicule her work, as if by proving that her efforts amounted to little, he was demonstrating as well that he hadn't fallen all that far behind. Laurence began to equate Kay's writing obsession with what he called Peggy's "peddling."

Meanwhile Kay continued to use their desperate need for more and more money as her excuse for nonstop writing. They were spending eight hundred dollars a month to run Les Cinq Enfants, she told people, while their income was less than five hundred. To make up the difference, they sold off Uncle George Vail's remaining securities, although the market was not favorable. Kay compared herself to the mother in D. H. Lawrence's story "The Rocking Horse Winner," as she even moaned about Sindbad's school fees, which were paid for by Peggy! Listening, people thought she exaggerated the need for money. "It was an idée fixe," Jimmy Stern concluded. Indeed, Kay worked frenetically to fulfill Katherine's ambition for her; the excuse about money fooled no one.

As Laurence began to turn to his daughters for emotional comfort, even taking baths with them in their childhood, he was not yet ready to give up on Kay. But the scenes became nastier. Every morning a maid brought Kay and Laurence breakfast in bed: jam and toast and tea. They lay there naked one morning when, Kay having been particularly provocative, Laurence grabbed the jam pot and rubbed its entire sticky contents into her pubic hair, coating it with the thick jam as once he had rubbed jam into Peggy's hair when he became exasperated with her. On another occasion Kay locked herself in the bathroom with her typewriter balanced on her lap, sitting on the toilet, just to have a door to lock against Laurence. But Laurence gained entry and dragged her to the foot of the mountain he was determined to have her climb with him. Kay longed then to leave Laurence and the children and escape to Paris for the peace and quiet she needed to write.

They had not ceased to live as man and wife, however, and in July of 1938, as they set off on one more trip, Kay was pregnant again. Heedless of the *Anschluss*, which had occurred earlier in the year, they took Cilli home to Kitzbühel; at Lanz's, Kay stocked up on Alpine costumes; she visited Elizabeth Duncan in Munich, and in Zurich endured lunch with James and Nora Joyce at a health-food restaurant, a "depressing little place where cold oatmeal was moulded into the shape of pork chops and then sprinkled with breadcrumbs and fried; and beefsteaks were fashioned out of some other substance, and tinted red." Laurence had to be content with cranberry juice. Ever the inveterate correspondent, Kay had kept in touch with Joyce, inscribing a copy of *The White Horses of Vienna* to him, and quibbling with this great man over the word "*sagt*," which she had got into her head Joyce had coined. Patiently Joyce explained to Kay Boyle that it meant "said."

In September, with Jonathan Cape, Ira Morris, the meat-packing heir from Chicago, and his wife, Edita, the Vails drove to Rapallo to visit Ezra Pound. Laurence liked Cape. Kay, however, could not forget how Cape had boasted to Caresse that he had sexual intercourse with the corpse of his wife, and liked him no better than she had in earlier years. Ezra Pound, Kay Boyle enjoyed. Far from being appalled by his views, as she later insisted, Kay endorsed most of them. Monetary reform seemed necessary to her too as she wondered whether it might not be able to "effectively do what the other systems have not done." If Pound was an anti-Semite, so still was she, if one less virulent. "The awful thing is that one can see only the rich Jews," Kay lamented, "who are pretty terrible in any country— and cannot find out anything about the penniless ones who can't get out of the country. They are the ones I want something done for." The friend with whom she was traveling, Ira Morris, was himself one of those "rich Jews," although she may well have had her nemesis, Peggy Guggenheim, in mind.

Announcing he was studying Japanese poetry, Pound was in the company of two Japanese poets. The Japanese were the finest practitioners of modern poetry, he said. Pound declared that "the Japanese are justified in taking anything they can from the Chinese" since it had long been the Chinese who were stealing and copying Japanese culture.

When she returned to Mégève, Kay received some pamphlets from Ezra Pound, along with a postcard invoking her to "Read these!" At once she ordered *Natural Economic Order*, one of the works Pound recommended, and wrote him that she would purchase *Two Nations* and *Economic Democracy* as soon as she could get to Brentano's in Paris. "Liked him more than I ever have," Kay reported enthusiastically to Pound's American supporter Jay Laughlin, "and was spell-bound by talk on social credit and Chinese—I loved listening to him and wanted to stay hours." Laughlin replied sympathetically; during Pound's spring visit to America, he confided to her, everybody "loved him except the professional anti-fascists. They all expected an ogre and found a very delightful raconteur instead." (Again in her 1942 autobiographical novel, based on her diary for 1940, *Primer for Combat*, Kay described Pound fondly: a character looks "the typical American hayseed for a change—like Ezra Pound the last time in Rapallo.")

Far from having been offended by Pound's views, or having ceased communication with him after the one visit, as she later told the FBI, Kay wrote to Ezra Pound in November of 1938. She requested that he read the manuscript of an article she was writing about William Carlos Williams. "Just a few straight words from you as to whether I've made anything clear . . . if you could just say this-this-this-this, the way you do, I'd be grateful to you. I don't want to send it over to Laughlin if you think it hopeless and bad." Pound had been a mentor to so many people, Kay Boyle might have reasoned: why not to her as well? And far from being offended by his political pamphlets, Kay reported to Pound that she was following up on his recommendations.

Later Kay denied she liked Pound, insisting that she had been "appalled" by his views as he ranted "over and over" not only about Mussolini but also about Hitler; he had declared himself "in full accord with *all* their policies, including the annihilation of the Jews." She decided he had been "almost hysterical on the subject of the international Jewish conspiracy," having been slighted by "Jewish editors and publishers," his work minimized by "Jewish critics."

But if Pound said all these things, it did not bother her at the time. "I disliked him then," Kay Boyle rewrote the history of their 1938 meeting in Rapallo, "long before he embarked upon his venomous broadcasts on the Italian radio in praise of Mussolini and Hitler whom he described as the two greatest statesmen of our time." By 1987 Kay Boyle had completely rewritten history. In the forties she may have thought it dangerous to admit to the FBI that she had been Pound's admirer; later it suited her image to have opposed him from the start.

When Harcourt backed out of their agreement to publish Carnevali, having already paid three hundred of the five-hundred-dollar advance, arguing that the book was libelous and "obscene," Kay offered first to rewrite it. Then she begged Jay Laughlin to publish it. "I'll feel obliged to do it if nobody else will, just because you want me to," Laughlin pleaded. "But I'm scared to death of it." Kay threatened to withdraw her attentions. Laughlin's refusal, she told him, "alters every feeling I had about you." But Laughlin would not jeopardize his fledgling publishing house, not even for Kay Boyle.

That December of 1938 a young English poet named David Gascoyne was received at Les Cinq Enfants by Kay Boyle wearing a "blue maternity gown." She appeared to be "middle-aged, quiet, gently reserved," with scarcely any connection "between her personality and her high-flown ardent prose." Indeed her sixth pregnancy made her unwell and by the next time Gascoyne visited she had taken to her bed.

She now longed obsessively for a son. She attributed her feelings to a minor character, a swineherd's pregnant wife in her 1938 novella "The Bridegroom's Body," published in the fledgling *Southern Review*. "If he hasn't a son this time then it's probably the last time," Lady Glourie, the protagonist, says, referring to the custom that the swinery could not continue in a family without a male heir; in her fiction, in which she tried to be loyal to the truth, Kay Boyle thus objectified her own irrational need for a male child, a need which went far beyond the general cultural preference for boys over girls. When Jo bore a second daughter in 1938, Kay commiserated, hoping Jo's new husband, a prosperous lawyer named Frank Detweiler, "isn't too disappointed about it not being a boy. Perhaps you will have another." More than ever Kay Boyle at thirty-seven prayed for a son. Before long, as always, she took her fantasy for truth and convinced herself the child was a boy.

He would have to be born in Switzerland, so he "won't have to be French and go fight Hitler in a year or two," she quipped. "Stumped" for boys' names, she thought of something Spanish, although the names of the Loyalist heroes were "all so long." Meanwhile, Laurence, who enjoyed having daughters, decided to keep the name Clover in reserve.

By March of 1939 Kay and Laurence were at the Hotel Eden in Lausanne, "waiting in the garden of Eden for Cain or Abel," as Kay put it. As she waited, she endured a last unpleasant communication from Ethel Moorhead, who pronounced herself "dying" in Cannes and requiring Kay to come at once to take over as Ernest Walsh's literary executor. Neither Kay's report about Bobby's progress nor the news that she was about to have a baby appeased Moorhead. In response to Kay Boyle's failure to rush to her side, Moorhead replied that she had named a "writing friend" to be Walsh's literary executor, someone, presumably unlike Kay Boyle, who would see "that full justice be done to his genius."

"You should never have told her you were about to have a baby," Laurence remarked shrewdly. Kay had to agree.

When the baby was finally ready to be born, its head was twisted in a "peculiar" position, or so Kay described it; the doctor had first to turn the head completely around and then remove the baby with forceps. As this, Kay Boyle's fourth child, entered the world, she wasn't even breathing.

"Of course it's a girl," Kay bemoaned her fate to McAlmon shortly after that March 29 when Clover Vail made her appearance. "The Boyle girls can't seem to bring anything else off." To Laughlin, she complained that it was "hard to bear . . . it was rather a blow having another girl." She envied her old Paris friend Bill Bird because his daughter had been "luckier and had a boy." Kay had to resort to her fiction for the satisfaction of bearing a son; in *Primer for Combat* Kathe appears as Catherone, born on Kathe's actual birthday, July 7, 1934, and Apple is called Pudie, and is undergoing extensive dentistry, as Apple was. But the one-year-old child who is obviously Clover's counterpart is a boy named Jerry.

Kay had assumed childbirth would become easier each time. But not only had this been a difficult birth. The doctor told her that she needed an operation since her vagina had descended "in some queer fashion and the rectum all mixed up with it." And he was adamant that there be "no more children." It appeared that she had sacrificed with this "small and gentle" baby her last opportunity for a son. Kay tried to count her blessings. On her twelfth birthday, Bobby had won a big silver cup for the jump, slalom, and downhill race, "all of which sounds manly enough," Kay conceded. But no accomplishments of a daughter could compensate for her need to bear a male child.

They were all at dinner at the newly renamed Les Six Enfants one evening.

"Where's the baby?" Laurence suddenly demanded.

"She's downstairs," Kay said indifferently, referring to the black-and-white-tiled basement where the small children ate and Josephine had her room.

"Bring her up! I want to see her!" Laurence persisted.

"Josephine's with her," Kay, annoyed, put him off. "She's all right."

By June, Kay was getting in six to eight hours of "typing" a day. "I've so many months to make up for," she explained, what with having the baby, recuperating, and getting servants settled.

Kay had another problem to deal with now, and that was her increasingly neurasthenic mother, who had decided she didn't like Alice Paul and that "the women [wore] her out." Kay planned to send Katherine back to America with Mrs. Vail, who irritated her for a different reason: Kay thought Mrs. Vail had spent enough money honoring her husband's memory and ought now to help her and Laurence financially. Mrs. Vail seemed to think she was "making millions," Kay complained.

Kay Boyle went on to satirize both her mother and her mother-in-law in two short stories: "War in Paris," published in *The New Yorker* in 1938, and "Major Engagement in Paris," in *The American Mercury* in 1940. Neither portrait is flattering. Mrs. Hodges (Vail) has a "sharp, icy Boston eye," and in "War in Paris" is a bully who cares only about getting her seventeen-year-old cat out of town before the hostilities begin. Katherine is Mrs. Peterson (Puss's wife Jennie's maiden name), a timorous, wailing, uncertain woman, "faltering" and "tentative" with a "frail, fading voice." She is no help whatsoever to Mrs. Hodges. Mrs. Peterson bears no resemblance to the figure Kay would later mythologize as her mother, the stalwart embodiment of culture and determination who had stood up with such moral authority to Puss.

Throughout the thirties Kay Boyle had stayed clear of political involvement. With war inevitable, however, such disinterest could not continue. In 1939 a manifesto was circulated by the *Partisan Review* urging American artists, writers, and intellectuals to oppose American intervention in Europe's growing hostilities. Its perspective was revolutionary and socialist, as it viewed the war as an impending conflict between imperialist powers, much as World War I had been. Indeed the statement had been drafted by Leon Trotsky and amended by the surrealist André Breton. In contrast, at that moment before the Hitler-Stalin pact of August 1939, the Communists supported American intervention, viewing Hitler as a threat to Russia.

A group was formed calling itself the League for Cultural Freedom and Socialism, and under its banner the statement was published in the Summer 1939 *Partisan Review*. Unlike the Communists, it supported the continuation of strikes at home, even as it denounced those under the sway of the Communist Party, who were in fact no more than "apologists for the Kremlin dictatorship." Among the signers were James T. Farrell, James Laughlin—and Kay Boyle. Having seen Laughlin's signature on the petition, Kay said, she endorsed it immediately, so allying herself with the Marxists of the independent left.

Kay may well have signed "in large part," as she put it to Laughlin, "because I saw your name there as well." At the time she was doing whatever she could to please him in the hope that he would still publish Carnevali. When Dylan Thomas seemed unwilling to come to terms with New Directions "because they're not offering me enough money," she wrote him he should be "proud and pleased" to be published by James Laughlin. But as the friend of Alexander Berkman and Emma Goldman, who had rejected Lenin's Bolshevism, no less than Stalin's, Kay Boyle would not have been expected to link progressive views with an endorsement of Stalin; in signing the *Partisan Review*'s anti-Stalinist document she would seem indeed to have been following her own beliefs. Throughout the thirties she had stood her ground against "the tendency to confuse literature and party politics," despising Mike Gold and his bullying insistence on proletarian literature. On August 23, 1939, the very day of the Hitler-Stalin pact, Kay Boyle reassured her friend Charles Henri Ford that she had signed the manifesto, adding that she thought the *Partisan Review* "a very excellent magazine." The League statement insisting on the political independence of writers expressed her own views.

After the Hitler-Stalin pact, the League continued to urge strong opposition to any American involvement in the hostilities in Europe. Still it seemed that the new conflict resembled the earlier war, in which, people like Eugene Debs had believed, workers shouldn't have to kill each other in defense of the interests of the ruling class. A second manifesto reiterated this position even as it expressed its loathing for "fascism as the chief enemy of all culture, all real democracy, all social progress." Among the signers of the second statement were William Carlos Williams, Charles Henri Ford—and Kay Boyle.

By the time the statement was published, however, France had been invaded by Germany. Seeing her signature in print, Kay Boyle dashed off a letter repudiating the *Partisan Review*'s second antiwar statement, insisting she had not seen the text. "As the war had not then been declared in Europe," she wrote, "it is patently impossible that I signed the document which you publish in this issue." Indeed, as Kay Boyle said, it was "a most questionable policy to place anybody's signature after a document which he had not had the opportunity to read." Printing her letter, Dwight Macdonald pointed out, not entirely unreasonably, that he had concluded she would agree since she had signed "the general manifesto of common political aims."

But emotion for Kay Boyle always took supremacy. Macdonald had assumed she understood that France's being at war with Germany did not alter the issue: the war still seemed to these socialists a conflict between contending capitalist and imperialist powers.

Not then and not later, however, was Kay Boyle a political woman who placed events in a historical context. Nor had she any interest in the struggles of the working class, or those of socialism. Moreover, consistencies of logic, of principle, eluded her. That she could endorse a socialist view committed to the idea of world revolution one day and take it back the next did not trouble her. When Germany went to war against France, Kay at once supported American intervention.

It wasn't politics that interested Kay primarily during those years in Mégève, but her career. Her novels and stories of this period were noticeably devoid of either social or political concerns. In 1938 she published her most unified novel to date, *Monday Night*, and *The Crazy Hunter: Three Short Novels*, all set in England. Correctly, she called "The Crazy Hunter" "the best thing I've ever done," although most critics preferred the equally powerful "The Bridegroom's Body." Where once D. H. Lawrence had been the dominant influence on her work, now it was Faulkner. "I am sure *Monday Night* would never have been written as it was had I not read with enormous enthusiasm Faulkner's *Pylon*," Kay Boyle said later. (This was equally true for her underrated novel *1939*, which remained unpublished until 1948.) Kay had begun to write book reviews for American publications, producing an eloquent endorsement of Faulkner's *The Unvanquished* for *The New Republic*. In a compassionate reading she found Katherine Mansfield's "unhappy little stories" redeemed "on every page . . . by the speechless confession of her own inadequacy." She liked Kafka "exceedingly," couldn't "see the sense in Henry Miller," but preferred Céline, and out of personal animus found T. S. Eliot "over-rated." Ever since he had congratulated her on her "great" book, *Year Before Last*, Kay said sarcastically, "I knew how incompetent a critic he was." (She neglected to add in this peroration to McAlmon that Eliot had recommended to Faber and Faber that they not publish *Year Before Last*.)

Monday Night was one of the few novels Kay Boyle wrote in which she did not make a personal appearance. Her hero is an alcoholic newspaperman wandering around Paris in search of a story, a man based obviously on Harold Stearns, whom, like all the Montparnasse crowd, Kay knew well. She calls him Wilt, gives him a book idea to pursue, and adds a mystery-story element, a quest for the truth about a sinister toxicologist.

Wilt's crony Bernie has come to Europe in search of "a hero," as Kay cleverly turns her own relentless insistence on paying "homage" to great men to its appropriate satiric purpose. Harold Stearns had once called Paris "the greatest testing-ground of character in the world for the young American." From this statement Kay developed the theme of this quirky novel about one night in night-town Paris, a novel which demythologized the Paris that Hemingway had so romanticized in *The Sun Also Rises*.

Like all of her long fiction, *Monday Night* offers its share of brilliant imagery. Even as feminism held no attraction for her, as a woman writer she could convey in heartbreaking prose what it felt like to be a woman of a certain age. A middle-aged barwoman who plays no role in the plot comes alive through her "wondrous triumph in being over forty and still as radiant as this, the blood still pounding powerfully, the limbs still sweet with lust." The author, of course, was also approaching forty.

Autobiography for Kay Boyle ruled even in a novel in which she refrained from interpolating a personal surrogate. As all her life she distrusted the claims of science and reason, so she makes the scientist-toxicologist, Sylvestre, a fraud. That defining moment of Bobby's life is here, as a little *boy* discovers the identity of his real father, as if Kay somehow believed that the cruelties of life could be redeemed if only they were rendered into art; the scene recapitulating Bobby's trauma is so powerful that Kay was able to market it to *Harper's Bazaar* as a short story called "Life Sentence." Finally, *Monday Night*, while remaining a minor work, is dashing in its tone as Wilt unmasks Sylvestre, yet is cheated of the opportunity of breaking the story. The novel is poignant in its implicit homage to Stearns and impeccable in its evocation of nighttime Paris. There is even a cameo appearance by Kay's friend "Bob la Coupole," who during one of Kay's 1938 trips to Paris sent Bobby a plastic replica of the White Horse used to promote the whiskey. Seemingly without politics, the novel does offer one scene in which a Frenchman, anguished over the fate of Loyalist Spain, chastises an Englishman: "It is you who could stop it if you, your country, really cared."

Dylan Thomas wrote Kay a fan letter, calling *Monday Night* "a very grand book indeed." Most critics in America, however, dismissed this novel, reflecting the culture's vestigial loyalty to the norms of the proletcult. Alfred Kazin scolded her for focusing on abnormal characters, "manikins who walk through her books as on hot beds of coal." Otis Ferguson complained that "all the people here are from the deep fringe of the oddly formed and cruelly dealt with," while *Time* called them "puzzling neurotics."

At the dawn of the forties, both for *Monday Night* and for her *The Crazy Hunter: Three Short Novels*, Kay Boyle was attacked for the absence of ordinary people in her work and for her modernist style. Her fellow signer for the League for Cultural Freedom and Socialism, and certainly no Stalinist, Philip Rahv nonetheless objected in *The Crazy Hunter* to the "fragility of her themes and their detachment from substantial experience and convincing locations"; euphemisms aside, Rahv is obviously suggesting that she should have depicted workers in cities. Her modernism was equally suspect. In his *New Republic* review of *Monday Night*, Ferguson blamed Eugene Jolas for having corrupted her: "the average Transition [sic] wonderboy can be turned over to the more advanced psychiatry, and nobody the worse." When Jay Laughlin told her that Carnevali in America would be "hard to sell because there is prejudice among the intellectuals against that generation of expatriate and foreign writers," he might just as well have been talking about Kay herself.

Indeed, the critics were letting Kay Boyle know that it was time to come home. Even as in her review of *The Crazy Hunter: Three Short Novels* Mary Colum pronounced Kay Boyle "the most talented of contemporary American novelists," she added that what the writer did best was depict "the American psyche." The implication was that with her "peculiar American power of depicting loneliness and frustration," she would do well to go home and focus on American subjects.

"The Crazy Hunter" and "The Bridegroom's Body," two of the "three short novels," remain examples of Kay Boyle at her finest. This stunning volume helped establish her reputation among young writers immune to the social realist strictures of thirties critics. Howard Nemerov fifty years later remembered the impact "The Bridegroom's Body" had made on him as an adolescent. In *The New York Times Book Review* at the time, Peter Monro Jack wrote that Kay Boyle had to be "one of the best short-story writers in America," as she was. In *The New Yorker*, prickly Clifton Fadiman pronounced "The Bridegroom's Body" "very beautiful indeed."

There were, as always, powerful autobiographical resonances. Laurence Vail appears as Candy in "The Crazy Hunter," as Kay chronicled the growing strains in her marriage. If "the Mother" is a coldhearted woman, Candy is Laurence as a disillusioned wife then viewed him, a man whose wife gives him "the tail-end of a career or an occupation because he never had one of his own." He is a man who weeps after he's made a mistake, as Laurence was given to extremes of emotionalism, a self-pitying, aging dilettante. Pitilessly, Kay included even the sexual element of Laurence's attachment to his daughters. As Laurence took those baths with his girls, so that years later Apple remembered unhappily the image of his penis in the water, and Clover would think "it was sexual, the way Laurence looked at us," so Candy puts his arm in his daughter's sleeve "and drew her against him until he felt the ribs and the breast under the sport shirt moving against his squire's cloth." (Many years later Clover would confront her mother: "Didn't you see the way he looked at us?" "I don't think that was true. But why didn't you say anything at the time?" Kay replied mildly. Yet that she was, of course, perfectly aware of the incestuous sexual element between Laurence and his daughters is demonstrated in "The Crazy Hunter," written during her Mégève years.)

At the same time Kay Boyle chronicled her daughters' growing emotional alienation from her. The young woman Nan observes her mother free a fishhook from a bird's throat and reflects that her mother "can touch these things, you can touch death and wipe it off in your handkerchief afterwards and touch pain without shrinking from it but you cannot take me in your arms any more." Nan goes on to fall in love with an Ernest Walsh surrogate, an Irishman named James Sheehan with thick dark lashes just like Walsh's.

Kay had written both "The Crazy Hunter" and "The Bridegroom's Body" more for art than money, and the superb results are unmistakable. In "The Bridegroom's Body," she created one of her strongest woman characters in Lady Glourie, tough, independent, sensitive, passionate, sexual, and uncompromising, if lonely because her son has gone off to school, as Kay obviously was drawing on how she missed Sindbad in England. Like Kay, she knows the love of men. So much more remarkable, then, was Kay's evocation of the nurse Miss Cafferty's frankly lesbian confession of love for Lady Glourie, a surprise to the reader, who is led to believe that the nurse must want either Lord Glourie or the farmer Panrandall.

No less than in *Gentlemen, I Address You Privately* are the impulses of homosexual passion depicted as understated, delicate, and natural. Homosexual desire appears unimpeded by the author's moral judgment or dime-store psychology. Miss Cafferty is a woman loving another woman in all the ways human beings can love. The swans, who are the metaphoric analogues of the people in this very Lawrencian story, also at times become homosexual, Kay Boyle reveals; homosexuality arises in nature as in society. That Lady Glourie kills the awful predatory male swan does not make *her* a lesbian. But that Miss Cafferty feels otherwise is clear: "Let me say it!" she cried in sudden passion. "Let me say it! I came out to think about you here alone where there might be something left of you somebody hadn't touched."

Lady Glourie cannot share the feeling, but she understands: "You mustn't speak like this." (As earlier she had denied that incest motivated the characters in "Wedding Day," so in 1981 Kay would deny that lesbian feeling motivated Miss Cafferty at the climax of "The Bridegroom's Body." Sternly she declared that she "never for a moment" suggested that "a lesbian affair" would be "a solution to the problems of the loneliness of the women involved." All she meant, she insisted, was that the two women could offer each other "comfort and solace." Since only one of her characters was a lesbian, the point is somewhat moot.)

The persistence with which Kay Boyle was later to deny the homosexual themes in her early work requires some understanding. In *Gentlemen, I Address You Privately*, in "In Defense of Homosexuality," in "The Meeting of the Stones" and "To the Pure" and "Count Lothar's Heart," she revealed original and unbiased depictions of homosexual feeling. That she later denied that she had done so might be attributed, critic Donald Richie suggests, to a fear of her themes being categorized and vulgarized, or rendered unacceptable because they evoked taboo feelings in a culture in which she was struggling for recognition. That she had never been given credit by critics for her original depictions of homosexual feeling might also have contributed to the older Kay Boyle's devaluing this contribution. Yet no writer of her day wrote with such sensitivity about the love between two people of the same sex.

That she saw her work as a record of her life also interfered with her own assessment of its value. When in the early 1980's a young professor named Sandra Whipple Spanier suggested that there were lesbian conclusions in both *My Next Bride* and "The Bridegroom's Body," Kay replied irrelevantly that homosexuality was "an aspect of love that I was never moved to experiment with . . . none of my very deep and enduring relationships with women had any lesbian undertones or overtones," as if the life were the ultimate text for the art, the two interchangeable. Spanier had spoken of the work, not the life; but in Kay Boyle's mind there was no distinction between the two, and since she was not a lesbian, there could be no lesbian consciousness in her art.

She continued to write poetry, although it had become increasingly didactic and declarative, full of well-meaning rhetoric. James Laughlin published her first collection, *A Glad Day*, in October of 1938 in a five-hundred-copy edition. Kay tackled the proofs fiercely. "I've truly never seen such carelessly done setting in my life," she complained to Laughlin. Like her pristine workspace, like those well-ordered cupboards at Les Six Enfants, perfection in every aspect of life was Kay Boyle's norm. Always scrupulous about money obligations, even as she spent freely, she told Laughlin that since she had not included the dates for each poem, she would pay extra for the new setting; since inadvertently she had included an "old copy" of "In Defense of Homosexuality," she would also pay for the resetting of that poem herself. Otherwise, Laughlin was responsible for the "APPALLING" typesetting. But when Laughlin told her he would lose money even if he sold every copy, Kay graciously refused any royalties.

The reviews of *A Glad Day* were mixed. *Time* wrote: "as much as a woman can, Kay Boyle swaggers." Not unfairly, the reviewer said that "her brilliance dissipates itself in smarting, useless pictures." But Louise Bogan, writing in *The New Yorker*, praised her "great talent for language, sharp sense and . . . rich subconscious," even as she concluded that she was a better poet in her love poems and less good in works like her poem about the Scottsboro boys. (Two months later Bogan went on to write a devastating parody of Kay Boyle's *prose* in *The Nation* as she skewered Kay for indulging in mannerisms out of all proportion to sense: "Thick blood-filled livers, cut off from their source," hang up on the streets of Marseilles, while a train "sighs" like "a saint" amid "the ecstasy of the long silent shining monogrammed rails" and "the courage" runs out of a man "like grease.")

Kay herself had no illusions about her poetry. Of the early ones, she concluded, "I never had an idea at all." They were, as Reuel Denny was to write in *Poetry*, "imagist" and "without a crisis." She had told Laughlin that were he to include an introduction, it should "dwell on my sensibility." Shrewdly, she remarked, "I think the intellect had a terrific struggle to leave some mark on these romantic wails, and didn't succeed."

"My book on flight ought to be far, far better," she wrote Laughlin; in fact, the air epic was never published, but for a few fragments that appeared in an anthology edited by Eugene Jolas called *Vertical*, which was put out by the Gotham Book Mart in New York.

Even as she did some of her best work in the late thirties, Kay Boyle continued to devote much of her time to writing for money. Generous to a fault, after Germany invaded France she gave away hundreds of francs to friends and neighbors in need. Meanwhile she alternated between being the "born writer" Louise Bogan and so many others were confident she was, and subverting her talent. She would no longer write novels, she decided, because no publisher would give her a contract like the one she had for *365 Days*. "I simply haven't sold," Kay admitted. She had only written the novels "for the advance because we had to have it to make ends meet." She confessed that she preferred the short story: "I always loathed writing novels."

Yet she was also writing formula short stories, including one she called a "cheap story which I hope the *New Yorker* will want to buy." So in addition to such works as "The Crazy Hunter" (Harcourt paid her a paltry three hundred dollars as the advance for *The Crazy Hunter: Three Short Novels*), she wrote such romantic, silly stories also set in England as "How Bridie's Girl Was Won," "The King of the Philistines" and "The Herring Piece." Kay Boyle's reputation as a short story writer was now so secure that she managed to sell the first to *Harper's* and the other two to *The New Yorker*, where Harold Ross himself was her admiring editor.

She determined to "stick to short stories and stick to them hard if we are to continue living in this house." It was "the magazines" which had to help her; she was now making two hundred fifty to five hundred dollars on each story, and so couldn't "afford to put a year's labor into a novel." Indeed, between 1936 and 1941 Kay Boyle sold twenty-four stories to *The New Yorker*, including "Defeat," which won first prize in the 1941 O. Henry contest. *Harper's* published two stories, *Harper's Bazaar* five plus one non-fiction piece, *The Saturday Evening Post* one, and even *Reader's Digest* an "unforgettable character" vignette.

Money was now determining most of Kay's literary decisions. As a wedding present for forty-four-year-old Caresse, who had married a twenty-seven-year-old dilettante named Selbert Saffold Young in March of 1937, Kay offered her friend an "aviation" novelette. Misunderstanding, Caresse, who had begun an arrangement with the Dial Press, concluded she had garnered Kay for a multi-book contract. Kay demurred; she was bound to Harcourt, which had already lost money on her. It was for money as well that in 1939 she published her first children's book, *The Youngest Camel*, based on a piece she wrote for the *Vails' Family Almanach*.

Its predictable theme is the love between an aging mother camel and her little *boy*, the youngest camel. Father is gone, having left no life insurance, as Kay revealed once more her increasing irritation with Laurence's fecklessness, his never having worked a day in his life, his leaving her with all the burdens. The son, of course, is creative; he sings such beautiful songs that the mother wipes the tears from her face with the leaves of a banana tree. The mother camel is also an ideal mother, as through her art Kay pleaded with her children for understanding and tolerance. The youngest camel is separated from his mother and must develop the moral stamina and courage to find his way home, as if Kay were exhorting her children to forgive her for the scanty attention she gave them. The youngest camel must learn how to live without his mother, as the Vail children had so often to discover other sources of solace.

In *The New Yorker*, Clifton Fadiman pronounced *The Youngest Camel* "a good book and a charming one," likely to be read by "nice, intelligent, rather mature and polite young ladies of thirteen and fourteen." Indeed, Kay dedicated this book to Pegeen, now fourteen; Bobby, twelve; Apple-Joan, ten; Kathe, five; and Clover, less than a year old.

By the late thirties Kay was viewed in America as a glamorous writer out of Paris. If the reviews of her work were mixed (*Newsweek* bluntly called *Monday Night* "one of her failures"), the woman herself was emerging in the American popular cultural imagination as a figure of romance, mystery, and drama: as Alfred Kazin put it, "our own little Dostoievsky in a ski suit." Others had returned to America; Kay Boyle had remained in Europe, "stuck it out," and, Kazin thought, "won." Kazin imagined Kay Boyle as "our last real tie with the Hitler-darkened Europe," standing "gloomy as life, wonderful as ever, impervious to hecklers." She had become a work of art in her own right.

Kay now consciously cultivated that image. She favored big white earrings in the shape of edelweiss ("so nice when you are sunburned after skiing or mountain climbing"), no matter that she preferred her writing table to Laurence's expeditions. She announced that she dedicated all her poems to friends, neglecting to mention that these recipients were always notorious themselves. "When I like someone very much I feel like making them something," she said coyly, "and because I can't paint I make them something to hang up where they want to see it or carry around if they feel like it." Being the mother of a large, handsome brood had become part of the image, as if the children were no more than extensions of their mother's ego, as Clover came to believe. Three months after Clover's birth, Kay redesigned her stationery to read

Les
Six
Enfants.

Kay Boyle had become the stuff of drama, like a movie star about whom stories could be concocted, as *Newsweek* decided she was "a frail girl from Minnesota," a place she had not seen since she was six months old. Her "frailty" was another myth; Kay Boyle was closer to the "flint" Djuna Barnes had noticed.

She had now reached her height as a literary celebrity. Her reputation was further boosted when Mary Colum decided she was "Hemingway's successor." Colum insisted that these two alone, Boyle and her lifelong adversary, remained originals, having created "a new genre of fiction," part journalism, part meditation on life.

Kay Boyle had indeed become "the writer Kay Boyle," beautiful girl expatriate, photographed on the mountains on skis with a long line of children behind her. *Newsweek* claimed she was "one of the few women who can avoid the so-called feminine approach to writing without sounding phony or artificial." As war descended, as the forties approached, few reviewers bothered to mention that this was a *woman* writer. "She does not merely write," Clifton Fadiman said, "she is a writer. There aren't many around these days."

14

Bronzed Apollo

I thought of him and I couldn't work any more.

That spring and summer of 1939 after Clover was born, Kay Boyle cut an impressive figure in Mégève. Straight-backed and model thin, impeccably groomed, and fashionably attired, thanks to her sister Jo, she was a woman of grace, elegance, and intensity. She also evidenced that considerable hauteur born of a deep sense of pride in the reputation she had earned through hard work and determination. Her conversation was mesmerizing, peppered as it was with self-dramatizing. Yet Kay could also be attractively self-deprecating, with that ingratiating way she had of poking fun at herself. Those heavily lidded, deep-set blue eyes looked directly into yours as you spoke to her, for she was a listener whose attentiveness made people feel good.

In the year that war came to France, Kay Boyle was the mother of four, and the stepmother of two, emotionally needy young people. But she herself was only thirty-seven, still a young woman, and, now, sexually restless. She longed for a romantic relationship with a man, a man unlike Laurence Vail, an idealist, or so she would later claim. In fact, the type of man to whom she was attracted, an attraction that appeared first in her stories, and then surfaced publicly in her life, was the tall, blond Aryan, golden hair on his thighs, his eyes a hard, cold blue, his hair white-blond. "The gods of the North have proved after all to be her kind of material," Mark Van Doren noticed in his review of her novel *Death of a Man*. From the mid-thirties on, one can read sexual longing in Kay Boyle's descriptions of the men of Austria, some of whom, like Dr. Prochaska, were turning to fascism. In Kay Boyle's fiction of the thirties, her women yearn to be enveloped by these men and to be obliterated by their own passion.

In the 1934 "Maiden, Maiden," Willa not only longs for her tall, blond

Aryan guide but is also deeply disenchanted, even irritated, with her long-standing partner. She speaks for Kay, as she too trudged along on mountain-climbing expeditions with a man who no longer fulfilled her: "We keep on climbing so as to get away from each other. There used to be some reason for us being together but there isn't any more."

In *Death of a Man*, the woman who is the writer's surrogate, who is her mirror image, casts off her pallid English husband for the virile Dr. Prochaska. In "The Baron and the Chemist," written in 1937 and published a full year before Clover was born, a restless, unhappy wife living in a chalet feels as if she must change her life or cease to exist, so urgent is her need for sexual renewal. Were she not to "see other people's faces" she would "come to hate the one man's that she had to look at, or hate the sight of her own caught frozen in the glass before her." Into town sweeps a mysterious baron in Tyrolean stockings. If this particular baron turns out to be a fraud, a man in trade, and no aristocrat at all, what we remember is that wife yearning for a passion long gone from her marriage.

Such Aryan sexual ideals leap from the pages of Kay Boyle's writing of the thirties, even in the poem dedicated to Marcel Duchamp and Mary Reynolds, "Complaint for M and M," where we meet Hubert, whose "German makes the edelweiss grow colder sharper purer in my heart." Kay Boyle all her life insisted to her children and potential biographers alike that "enough of my life can be known through my work," and indeed her work of the late thirties provides a virtual record of her emotional life. The most explicit account of her growing need appeared in "Anschluss," published in *Harper's* in April of 1939, only a month after Clover's birth, and an O. Henry prize winner. Nowhere more dramatically, more explicitly, does she reveal her need for a man very different from Laurence Vail.

Merrill, an American fashion editor working in Paris, goes on vacation to the Tyrol. She is thirty and panicked at the prospect of growing old, as Kay Boyle, a beautiful woman, would feel intensely the loss of her physical powers. "This is the way life goes on," Merrill mourns, "and now I am old and nothing wonderful can ever happen."

Then Merrill meets Toni, whose broad shoulders and yellow hair recall the doctor of "The White Horses of Vienna" and Dr. Prochaska. Toni too is put in jail for lighting fires in the shape of swastikas, and he's equally beautiful. Sexually enthralled, Merrill watches Toni, the sports organizer at the lake, dive into the water: "the heels lifted, the calves small as fists with muscle, the knees flat, the thighs golden and slightly swollen for the movement not made yet but just about to come." We are, of course, at the *piscine* in Mégève, watching a real-life man dive.

In the story, Merrill loses Toni, her "animal and golden-flanked Apollo," to Hitler. But Kay had already found her own "bronzed flat-bellied Apollo," as she would describe this man in her novel about him, *1939*, right there in Mégève. His name was Kurt Wick, and he was a tall, blond, blue-eyed athlete with a dramatic deep cleft in his chin—the local ski instructor and the swimming instructor in summer. Dazzlingly hand-some, with a quick smile, Kurt Wick was in his late twenties, ten years her junior, as Kay Boyle now began her pattern of pursuing, of choosing, much younger men, men who would idolize her and court her and worship her.

Tall, blond Kurt Wick had come to Mégève to teach skiing to the French, and he was having a considerable success. He was a good teacher, a perfectionist, demanding that his students precisely place their arms and legs. "You've got the legs of a good skier," he encouraged a less than promising beginner. Others thought he was not such a nice man. Teaching little Kathe to ski, he hit her with his pole whenever she made a mistake. But many women of Mégève were infatuated with Kurt Wick. A pregnant Kay Boyle was one of them, for in April Kay had already written to Jay Laughlin of the *German* refugee who would be the hero of the ski novelette she was writing, "a darling man . . . beautiful on skis."

Wick opened a school with a shop attached where he sold ski equip-ment and an inn where he was assisted by his French wife, Hélène, whose father was ambassador to Belgium and whose uncle was none other than Marshal Pétain. Mégève was a very small village. Kurt Wick soon became a frequent guest at Les Six Enfants. Tall, blond, and sunburned from long hours on the slopes, his hands broadened by skiing, he often casually dropped in for a drink. Later people were to whisper that he was a Nazi sympathizer and, still later, that he was not bothered by the Germans because of his connection with Marshal Pétain. But Kurt Wick had no interest in politics. He was a philanderer, and that he was attached didn't impede his romantic exploits as he moved from a liaison with a Polish woman to Kay. Nor did the presence of a house full of children inhibit Kay, who had felt deeply her father's wasted, thwarted life, who was willing to take the risks.

For Wick, it was not a question of winning Kay away from Laurence, who perhaps had thrown one too many pieces of crockery, whose violence when, as Laurence put it in his novel *Murder! Murder!*, he was "full of gin" was no longer exciting. A deep sense of his own inferiority had settled over Laurence. He was essentially a kind man who meant no harm, whose excesses undoubtedly stemmed from a sense of his own powerlessness and failure as an artist. "It is better to be anything, even a murderer, than a sick weak thing who rages very often and talks a lot," as Laurence described himself in *Murder! Murder!* With murder, of course, out of the question, Laurence pleaded in an effort to be understood, people succumb to a catalogue of vices. He then proceeded to list his own: "they argue, sulk; raise their voice, slam a door; join the army, write a play, bite their nails; break china, weep, repent; go in for drink, or women, or exploration; buy flowers, collect stamps; get old, go far away, ruin their health and dispo-sition." Nor would Laurence blame Eugene and Gertrude, and his irregular childhood, for "they too had parents . . . and they, my grandparents, had parents too." There was a dark nightmarish side to Laurence closed to himself, and to his wife. Certainly what was once eccentric and wild good fun no longer amused Kay.

For a time they lived in symbiosis, Laurence spending time with the children, Kay working, working so obsessively that later, when Josephine went to Paris for ten days and Kay herself had to take full responsibility for baby Clover, she was not pleased at all. "I shall miss her very much," Kay purred to the returning Josephine as happily she relinquished Clover, "although it is impossible for me to get enough work done with so much time given to her." Laurence was wistful. Kathe and Clover were different children when their mother took care of them, he remarked. But all he could do was wish that Josephine had not returned at all.

In the politically charged days now before them, Kay began to revel in political discussion while Laurence increasingly drew back. He disdained do-gooders, and Kay's proliferating causes irritated him. "People overrate principles," Laurence would say, "they can do a great deal of harm." Kay insisted one must take sides; Laurence was skeptical, countering: "People aren't what they say they are and they aren't what they do. They are what they are." Given the irrationality of human nature, he reasoned, it didn't matter which causes people chose: "red ties, blue shirts and black shirts," it all amounted to the same thing.

No longer loving her husband as a man, Kay was further irritated as, with Hitler about to invade Poland, she heard Laurence laughing, quoting his pet phrase, "Mooslini-Hoodini"—it was all the same. He called "the Individual," that sacred entity for Kay and Katherine Evans Boyle and her long-ago mentor John Cowper Powys, "that joke of jokes." In 1939 Laurence surveyed the scene and would not choose between "the Radicals, the Communists, the anarchists. The Radical-Anarchists, the Communist-anarchists, the radical-Communists. The socialist-Radicals, the Radical-Socialists . . ." Observing what he called this "supreme *dégringolade* of the human species," Laurence threw up his hands in dismay, while Kay's irritation grew.

Why did you leave Papa? the children later asked. Always, and in print as well, Kay blamed Laurence's politics, his belief, as she put it in 1984, "that individuals could not affect the unending cycle of circumstances." Her words conveyed a partial truth. But Laurence had not changed, was the same man she had married. Laurence had always believed that "the individual" was no more than someone scratching a pimple on a "large bare posterior in full sight of others." There was no such thing as a hero, Laurence thought, because "there is not a single person whose conduct is entirely above suspicion." Daunted by his wife's productivity, Laurence had the better mind: "I must think of something to do which will keep me from thinking. But I can't think of a way to stop thinking without thinking," he once wrote. Only in one respect had he changed; he was no longer a mentor and supporter. By the late thirties he had taken to mockery of her "romantic novels" and had become a saboteur of her grueling work schedule.

For her part, Kay was a different person from the young woman Laurence had met in Paris. She was now one who was not beyond using their ostensible political differences to mask her need to address her long-repressed romantic and sexual needs. For all his fascination with "whores and prostitutes," Laurence had been a faithful husband. It was Kay Boyle now in 1939 who crossed the line in search of romantic love and sexual renewal. For despite her later explanations about how her marriage disintegrated because of Laurence's politics, she chose a man who had no principles at all.

The man on whom she set her heart, the man for whom she decided to break up the Vail family, was the tall, blond, blue-eyed Don Juan of Mégève, Kurt Wick. Far from offering a passionate sense of justice to counter Laurence's skepticism, he was a man whose only topic of conversation at table was—skiing. James and Tania Stern, still frequent guests at Les Six Enfants, observed it all, and it seemed to them so unjust. Laurence still loved Kay, and was in every way superior to Kurt Wick. But Kay craved danger, and excitement. Her self-dramatizing was now particularly suspect, so that even her causes began to seem more like self-aggrandizement than real commitments. In 1939, appalled, the Sterns left for America, abandoning Kay and Laurence to the final moments of their drama.

By now Kay's writing was suffused with images of Kurt Wick. She commemorated their first meeting in "Diplomat's Wife," published in February of 1940 in *Harper's Bazaar*. "Effortlessly," he skis down the slopes "with his strong slender legs held close, one knee locked fast but limber a little behind the other." He is so blond that whatever the weather, "the snow falling or the rain, it seemed a strong sun were shining on him." His eyes are ice blue, his hair the color of spun gold, and he is so beautiful that the author makes it seem inconceivable that any woman would not fall in love with him. And in this fantasy of longing, Wick is unattached. Those "shamelessly painted women" of Mégève who pursue him mean little, for he wants only a woman "tall and lean with black hair worn longish," a woman with earrings which are "big ivory flowers blooming like home and country and the forgotten outline of other mountains," a woman with a "boy-like body," so thin is she, a woman who makes a "swift, arrogant stop" as she arrives at his terrace.

So necessary was it to Kay Boyle to make this woman herself, as if she were living her sexual fulfillment through her own story, that she describes not only her mirror image but her experiences. She must greet an Austrian with "*Grüss Gott*," as Kay had done on that visit to Hitler's Germany with Caresse Crosby, refusing to utter the words "*Heil Hitler*," even in irony. She must have a daughter who calls her Mimi, as Kathe did. And if this character is French, with a *maréchal* for a grandfather, as Wick's wife was Marshal Pétain's niece, this is Kay Boyle feasting her eyes on Kurt Wick, "tall and radiant against the timber like a god of the pre-Christian world." If Kay Boyle were to love a man, he must be a god, a hero, as Ernest Walsh had been. Her character has a cold man for a husband, a man her father's age. As Kay Boyle had rationalized her adultery with Ernest Walsh by making Richard Brault ill and unattractive in *Plagued by the Nightingale*, so now she excuses her liaison with Kurt Wick by depriving her heroine's husband of any redeeming qualities.

Laurence was convinced that Kay did not like sex all that much, as Buffy had also discovered in Paris. But as Kay described herself at the moment she fell in love with Kurt Wick, her voice "swoons in her throat" as he kisses her. Nowhere more powerfully had she written of the joy of sexual transport, not even about Ernest Walsh in *Year Before Last*, and never about Laurence Vail. As evocations of a woman's raw physical desire for a man, both "Diplomat's Wife" and Kay Boyle's novel about Kurt Wick, *1939*, are unrivaled in the literature of their day, and perhaps second only to that major influence on her early work, D. H. Lawrence's writing about women in sexual ecstasy.

In *1939*, Kay Boyle described Kurt Wick as the man with whom she wanted to spend the rest of her life. So autobiographical was this novel that when it was published almost a decade later, it was with a long disclaimer insisting that the characters were "imaginary." In fact, it was all drawn from life.

Kay appears as Madame Audal, looking like an "empress" with her "high-boned" cheeks and arrogant spirit. She wears Kay's signature "white earrings in her ears like flowers," and she is committing adultery with a blond, sunburned ski instructor named Ferdl Eder, her "blond-wristed . . . fawn-eared boy." He is the object of Madame Audal's lust and she is obsessed by him: "Ferdl stripped to the waist . . . or Ferdl playing chess against the cone of Mont Blanc in the window." This was, in fact, exactly Kay Boyle's view from her workroom at Les Six Enfants. In Faulknerian cadences Kay chronicles her reawakened sexuality: "Physical beauty or physical courage or even physical love were not the words of explanation for the legend, for in the end there is no name for the fabulous power (like the sign of the cross made on the air confounding evil) which is the heart's passionate, unblemished sign."

For a long time Laurence suspected nothing. Kurt Wick was constantly at Les Six Enfants, and it seemed everyone in Mégève knew about Kay and him but Laurence. One hot August day, Wick, as usual, was flaunting his blond splendor before Kay and a host of others at the Mégève *piscine*. In the crowd was one of his friends in town, another tall, blond Austrian refugee. This Austrian observed carefully the tall, fair-skinned, black-haired, blue-eyed American, so elegant a figure that you would never have known she had given birth to her fourth child only five months earlier. Radiantly beautiful, she talked with great animation. She laughed. This Austrian could not take his eyes off her. He hovered nearby. As for Kay, she had eyes only for Kurt.

But this was a love affair that had to be played out against a historical scenario. A few weeks after that day at the *piscine*, Hitler invaded Poland, and France, honoring her pledge, immediately declared war against the Reich. Later Kay would describe the war as an "eloquent background" to her "own personal and violent revolution"; at the time it was not so romantic. Before long in Mégève there was no regular mail, movies, fish, soda water. The French had mobilized and there were no longer men in the shops, streets, or cafés. Kay collected bundles of warm clothing for the refugees from Franco's now fascist Spain, who were turned back when they arrived helplessly at the borders of France. An ominous stillness settled over the little village of Mégève.

Kay and Laurence stayed on. "Life only seems possible in this place," she had written ambiguously to Jay Laughlin, "and I should hate to give it up." Even as she feared censorship might prevent her from mailing her work back to America, she had no intention of going home and leaving Kurt Wick behind. "It is interesting to be here and live through it all," she wrote her sister, omitting any mention of Kurt Wick. It was obviously time to return to America, as so many had done, but Kay was accumulating reasons not to do so. "I feel I've been here so long that it is the only place to be while living is possible here. I feel a bit too old to begin again in America now. And how live? I doubt if we could." France, she insisted, was her "essence and her intelligence." She named all those who were remaining: the Joyces, Maria Jolas, Fanny Ventadour, Kitty Cannell, whom she had never liked, Mary and Marcel. "Half the world is ski-ing while the other half dies," she commented with her usual bravado, "and the night-clubs are open until three in the morning." By February of 1940, soap and oil were scarce in Mégève. Soon sugar, oil, pâtés, and rice would be rationed. Only baby Clover was eligible for the seven hundred and fifty grams of sugar.

In interviews, to most friends, Kay Boyle spoke as if her life were proceeding normally. She told one reporter she prided herself on three things, "her house, her cooking, and her varied menus," although she was never much of a cook; there had always been others to perform that function. "Everything is very quiet here," she wrote James T. Farrell, "and we work on and the children go to school, and the new one is eight months old." There was only one ambiguous clue to her having found a young lover: "our hair gets grayer and grayer."

With France at war with Germany, Kurt Wick, who, along with all Austrian exiles, after the *Anschluss* had become a citizen of the Third Reich, was now in trouble. Austrian nationals in France had become "enemy aliens," and the French authorities decided that their declarations of loyalty could not be trusted. That autumn of 1939 they were all shipped off for internment in those early concentration camps, where rat meat soon became a much-sought-after delicacy. Dysentery and typhoid were endemic, and lice and fleas and bedbugs so pervasive that the men preferred to sleep on the damp sand ground.

Kay Boyle fictionalizes the moment when Kurt Wick was declared an enemy of France in "Effigy of War," published the following year in *The New Yorker*. Here he is a *Danish* swimming teacher, but immediately recognizable, "sun-blacked, blond-head" with arms "as thick and smooth as taffy." He is no match for the Greek who roars, sadistically, "France for the French!" as Kurt Wick's enemies in Mégève similarly denounced him. In "Diplomat's Wife," the Wick character is imprisoned, leaving the Kay Boyle surrogate to sit alone in a café fortifying herself against the growing cold with a cognac. She has risked all for love and she does not regret it. In *1939*, Ferdl, having torn up his Nazi passport and thrown it into the sea, is ordered to "training camp," glaring at the authorities "in casual, arrogant grace."

The real-life Kurt Wick, along with his Austrian friend who had suffered a *coup de foudre* at the sight of Kay at the *piscine*, was shipped off to an internment camp near Lyons. Kay wrote to him often. She sent him packages, and at his suggestion she sent packages to his Austrian friend, who was, she learned, the Baron Franckenstein. The Baron had no socks; he was constipated. Kay Boyle sympathized. She sent Kurt and the Baron old copies of *Life* magazine, and even some packets of the toothpicks favored by her mother-in-law, which she had satirized wickedly in "Major Engagement in Paris." In her diary-novel *Primer for Combat*, Kay tells us she sent Kurt Wick three Sulka handkerchiefs and whiskey in empty cologne bottles, along with her many letters.

The Baron had no idea that the packages came from the woman he had fallen in love with at the *piscine*; in his thank-you note, he wrote as if his benefactor were a man. But even when Kay informed him of her gender, he had no idea of who she was.

Before long all enemy aliens interned in France were given a choice; they could remain in a concentration camp or join the Foreign Legion. The Baron decided to remain interned. But Kurt, an outdoor man, an athlete, hated to be confined. He was also worried about anonymous letters denouncing him as a Nazi. Kurt chose the Foreign Legion. Those letters calling Kurt Wick a Nazi, those "monstrous charges," as Kay put it, so upset her that she stopped speaking to the man who owned the hotel next door to Les Six Enfants, who she was certain had been behind the denunciations.

To bid Kurt Wick farewell before he left for North Africa, a group from Mégève planned to visit him at the concentration camp at Lyons.

Among them were the innocent Laurence, and Kay, and, of course, Kurt's wife, Hélène. The night before this journey, Laurence was irritated by an unexpected visit from his brother-in-law, Alain Le Merdie, now a captain in the French Army.

Laurence, who had never had much sympathy for his sister's husband, was bored. "Bored people are heavy," he thought. He endured the visit, further annoyed that Kay had vanished somewhere upstairs and had refused to help him entertain the stolid Le Merdie, no doubt to work on one of her "romantic novels."

When at last Le Merdie departed, Laurence went up to the bedroom. Pinned to his pillow was a note. As Kay Boyle had pinned her childish poetizing to Katherine's pillow, now she used the same method to send a message to Laurence.

"I've left for Lyons to see Kurt Wick," Kay wrote. Now Laurence knew. Heartbroken, he got drunk. When he told Hélène what had happened, however, she was not surprised, for Kay Boyle was hardly the first. Hélène raised an eyebrow. Hélène was more bemused than angry.

"What's the matter with her?" Hélène could not resist commenting. "Doesn't she realize who he is?"

Hélène's assertion that Kurt Wick was a flagrant womanizer did not console Laurence. He clung now to Bobby, and cried. "You know where she's gone," he moaned. Only thirteen, Bobby was swept up in the sexual trauma of Kay and Laurence, as Laurence made her his confidante and, he hoped, his advocate with Kay.

As for Bobby, she couldn't stand Kurt Wick. He was a vulgar Don Juan, she thought, this married ski instructor with whom every woman in Mégève was infatuated. What could her mother see in him? Bobby's sympathies were entirely with Laurence.

As Kay arrived at Kurt's cell in Lyons, the door was left half open for an instant; the sentry stepped aside, and that other Austrian, Kurt's friend, the Baron, caught a glimpse of Kay before the door closed. Now he knew that Kurt's lover was the woman at the swimming pool with whom he had fallen in love.

That night signaled the end of Kay's marriage to Laurence Vail. These were twenty-four hours, as she chronicled in *Primer for Combat* which "brought to an end everything except sorrow and anger between Benchley and me." Except for the changed names, the story and its emotions are entirely autobiographical. Kay Boyle had fulfilled all her romantic yearnings. They go for a walk, Kurt allowed this freedom now that he was bound for the Foreign Legion, and "Wolfgang kept saying that everybody was looking at us because his hair was too bright and his face too black from skiing to go with it, and also because we looked too happy."

Back in Mégève, everyone was furious, not least Pegeen, who loved and admired her stepmother.

"You think my mother is so terrible. Look at yours!" she lashed out at Bobby. Bobby was even more embarrassed when she overheard the elegant Mme. Wick finally tell Laurence, "It's about time this thing stopped!"

In June, the Germans marched into Paris. "Not a nation but a class has won," Kay Boyle said in *Primer for Combat*, revealing that she did indeed understand the perspective of the League for Cultural Freedom and Socialism. Her solution for France, for Europe, however, was not a working-class struggle against capitalist rulers, but "*un chef*," a strong leader, indeed a hero. What France needs, Kay thought, is "a direction, a faith, a belief, even if only in one man, to bind it together." It was, of course, a typical view of her time, if also one she had imbibed at Katherine's knee. Politics was comprised of the acts of certain individuals, as she blamed the French government, "those men who might have been expected to know and must have known there was no possibility of declaring war with any hopes of winning it."

France had fallen. But Kay had a plan. She and Kurt would move to some mountainous region of America. He would run a ski establishment there, just like the one in Mégève. Kay informed only Katherine that she and Kurt had "decided to make a life together," had spoken to "NO ONE but you" about this. Neither Laurence nor the children had yet been told. "This more or less happy family life goes on," Kay wrote her mother, "with this great thing around us and this other personal thing ahead." She had cast her lot with Kurt without even having discussed the details with Laurence; she had no idea of "what arrangement Laurence will come to with me with the children."

The children were of secondary importance to Kay now. "I only know that we will have to get to America, and I have promised Kurt I will not leave him here," she revealed to Katherine. At first she considered the possibility of Laurence and the children going to America first, to be followed by Wick and herself. But she had made her choice: "This is the one completely definite thing I know about my life and that it will have to work out one day," she told her mother. She and Kurt had made "elaborate plans, down to the last detail." In one of her romantic fantasies, she pictured herself and her lover living for a time in Portugal, with Kurt fishing for a living until his papers were in order.

Kay was preoccupied now with securing a visa to America for Kurt. She enlisted Caresse Crosby and Jay Laughlin—without telling them what her relationship was to the refugee she was determined to help. It was no small matter in 1940 to arrange the emigration to America of a legal citizen of the Reich; and a German alien refusing Nazi documents became a man without a country. "He is financially independent," Kay reassured Laughlin, stretching the truth, "a great skier," which was, of course, true, "and a fine guy." "He isn't a Jew," she added, "and he is a very solid, good person and nobody in the world could ever have any doubts about him in any way."

Kay Boyle had lived well most of her life, with the exception of her time in Cincinnati and in Le Havre and those months at the hands of Raymond Duncan. "You know the kind of life I like," she wrote Laughlin, as she outlined what Kurt Wick would need. "Where is Sun Valley you talked about?" she asked. Kay had not set foot in America since 1923 and knew little of her native land. "You almost make America sound good and right—as if one could live high," she told Laughlin, "and make enough money to meet the prices of even over there." All Kay could think about was getting Kurt Wick to America "QUICKLY." When Dylan Thomas wrote to ask her for a blurb, she instructed Jay Laughlin to write one for her.

Kay knew the matter was urgent not only because of the difficulties of emigration to America but also because Kurt's wife, Hélène, with two children to bind him, had every intention of using her connection to Marshal Pétain to keep Kurt with her. "Can't you work a miracle for me?" Kay begged Laughlin in July of 1940. In exchange for his help, she promised him "a miracle . . . in the way of writing if you want it some day."

But progress on Wick's visa moved slowly. Long-standing bank deposits, bank references, were required. Laughlin offered to sign an affidavit certifying that Kurt Wick would be employed by New Directions, only for the American consul in Lyons to tell Kay that she should not use such an affidavit since this would suggest work was being taken away from a needy American. Caresse was to provide a bank affidavit. Kay told her, "Laurence and I will take care of the money side of the question."

"I'm obsessed by this matter of the civil status of these ex-Poles, ex-Austrians, ex-Czechs in France. I literally beat my head and scream all day and night about it," Kay told Laughlin, implying that she had no personal stake in Kurt's visa. Rather, it was her cause. "Some country must do something about the situation of these men," she pleaded, "they must be given papers which will enable them to live as human beings, not as outcasts, and I wish I could see the way to it being done." Kay seemed also to believe that she could liberate Kurt Wick from the Foreign Legion without much trouble—or, perhaps, that his wife would do it for her.

While Kay waited and attempted to influence the fate of her lover, life for the Vail family in Mégève grew more difficult. Kay doubted now that her large family could survive another winter in Europe. Although Mégève remained in the "free zone," unoccupied by the Germans, travel became difficult and food even more scarce; ration tickets permitted only one egg a month. In restaurants you had to show your ration ticket and only then would they weigh your piece of meat. Wine and tobacco were no longer available in the cafés. At night Kay listened to De Gaulle on the radio. By day she planned for a future with Kurt Wick. "I do feel that if anyone wants anything as badly as I want this and will work for it as hard as I am prepared to do, that it simply has to go through," she believed.

She was determined not to leave him behind. Her writing was suffering now, although for public consumption she blamed the war, which had "changed so much in the things I had begun to write and now I cannot go back to them for my heart and mind are filled with newer problems." She talked about making "a lot of money—and I MUST do so." On the verge of leaving Laurence Vail, for the first time she did indeed need to earn money on her own.

While Kurt languished in North Africa, the Foreign Legion hardly to his liking, Kay bicycled to Lyons to see the American consul. She decided next to go to America to obtain the visa. Sindbad would be her excuse. Sindbad was now ready for college, and since Peggy had refused to take him home, she would accompany Sindbad to America and enroll him at Dartmouth. Meanwhile she could visit the banks and scout for a ski resort for Wick. "Sindbad has never been to America so it would be too cruel to send him to work it all out for himself," Kay said. She would be back in a month.

Then she hesitated. She decided she needed legal assurance that she would be able to return to France; none was forthcoming. Although in 1937 she had reestablished her American citizenship, she remained simultaneously a French citizen as well. Still, the thought of being denied reentry into France alarmed her. Her love for Kurt remained "the one completely definite thing I know about my life." Indeed, to live out her fantasy with her "bronzed flat-bellied Apollo," she was ready to abandon her family. For the moment she remained in France.

The outcome of the affair is chronicled in *Primer for Combat*. An idealized Laurence stands by watching the folly of his wife, who pleads with the consuls to save her lover. If later Kay would dismiss Laurence as a man insufficiently opposed to Hitler, writing in 1940 she saw him as a man who was deeply liberal, a man with a strong sense of justice and an "instinctive faith" in the French willingness to oppose Germany. Not surprisingly, this Laurence is both bewildered and devastated by her affair: "I'll never understand it. A Don Juan, a cheap lady-killer, an Austrian yodeler—and you falling for it, you being taken in!"

But no less does she chronicle her own sexual renewal. Kurt had taught her "what the flesh could be." She implies that she was sexually complete for the first time in her life.

And then things began to go wrong. The visa did not materialize. In the novel Wolfgang falls ill and is tended to by his wife, who, unlike Kay, is free to travel to North Africa.

The real-life Kay Boyle did not give up easily. Even when it was apparent that Hélène had Wick firmly in hand, Kay persisted in trying to obtain the visa, telling herself that all she wanted was her lover's freedom. Laurence could only watch in dismay as Kay, called Phyl in the novel, receives a nasty telegram from Wolfgang's wife ordering her not to meddle. Benchley, Kay was able to write when it was all over, was appalled: "For

God's sake, don't tell me what makes you look like that. I'm sick of romance, shattered or otherwise. I simply don't want to know."

At the end Kay Boyle learned what everyone else already knew: "Is it possible . . . that the successful ski teacher can have affiliation only with the successful cause?" Suddenly, when he had given her up, Kay concluded that Wick was no more than "the unconfused and perfect athlete." Suddenly he became what he always was, a man who had come to the Haute-Savoie to make money because times were hard in Austria, and not because he opposed Hitler, something she had always known. She writes that should it have suited him, had Marshal Pétain not been there to come to his aid, he might easily have become a collaborator: "one thing in one woman's language and another thing in another woman's language, and perhaps he is nothing in anybody's language." Her language is that of the woman scorned. Kay Boyle's fiction was sacrosanct, and in it she was honest; so she admits in *Primer for Combat* that the entire connection with Kurt Wick was based on mere lust, he in "his tight little black sweater . . . and his wrists out, blond and bare."

In the novel they meet one last time at a ski refuge on the mountainous Mégève landscape. He is still sexually desirable to her, even as she lies to herself, tells herself she is seeing him again only so that "there wouldn't be a bad taste left." Weakly, Wick tells her nothing has changed. But angrily Kay Boyle accuses him of wanting to be an "honored citizen" of Vichy, "teaching swimming in summer, flirting with girls next winter on skis," all he ever was. She calls him a "trapped" man, as indeed Wick was the perfect tool. Extricated from the Foreign Legion by his well-connected wife, the real-life Kurt Wick lived out the war in France, having made his peace with Vichy.

The affair had ended. But Kay Boyle knew she could never again make things right with Laurence. Rationalizing, she told herself that the marriage could not have continued in any case, that Kurt Wick, "through accident," became "the name for the separation." Near the end of *Primer for Combat* she pleads for Laurence Vail's forgiveness and his understanding. One last time they climb a mountain, as they had climbed so many mountains in their eleven years together. But Kay had set out on a journey that excluded Laurence, one peopled by what Benchley in the novel calls "strangers" and "intruders." She longs to take Laurence's hand, to say, "Let it be another year, and another country . . . let me not be the woman I am, I wanted to say, but I could not say it."

Another epoch of Kay Boyle's life had come to an end.

15

My Baron

It's so easy to be unselfish when you're not in love.

*I have not the endurance for regret. I refuse regret because it is
the admission that I have ignored somewhere and at some time
the singleness of the choice that is offered.*

One should change one's life every ten years.

During the summer of 1940, Kurt Wick's friend, the Baron von und
zu Franckenstein, having rejected the option of the Foreign Legion and
escaping from camp, returned to Mégève, where he resumed teaching at
the Collège Florimontane. One day, wishing to thank Kay Boyle for the
English-language magazines and other items she had sent to him in the
concentration camp, he arrived at Les Six Enfants. Unaware of the Baron's
romantic fantasies about her, Kay extended the Vails' hospitality.

Joseph von und zu Franckenstein was as handsome a man as his
countryman Kurt Wick, but without the vanity of his friend. He was twenty-
nine years old, and nearly six feet tall, with dark blond hair, soft hazel
eyes, and broad shoulders. His nose was prominent, reflecting his aristocratic origins. There was also a weather-beaten look about this man, and
he was awkward in his movements. But when he spoke, he revealed a
certain delicacy and sensitivity, if also an abiding shyness. In contrast,
his laugh was loud, unselfconscious, and roaring, one few could forget.
His English was flawless.

In the company of Kay Boyle at last, Joseph spoke with great animation
of the things he loved best: Mozart, Dostoyevsky. As he talked, he lit one
cigarette after another, inhaling in a strange way that the observant writer
would describe in *Primer for Combat*, where he appears as Wolfgang's
friend Sepp: "The smoke hovers an instant just inside his lips, and then
it is licked suddenly back, like a sly white serpent on his tongue, and the
mouth and the air are wiped absolutely clean."

As a frequent visitor at Les Six Enfants, Joseph revealed how his
ancestors had for centuries been barons of the Holy Roman Empire. He
had been born into the highest ranks of the Austrian nobility, his complete

name: "Baron Joseph Maria Casimir Konrad Michael Benedictus Maurus Placidus Aloysius Hieronymus von und zu Franckenstein." His Hapsburg fathers had come to Austria in 1273, people, as one writer characterized them, "manipulative, industrious, strangely modest, inexorable, decent, stodgy, staunch." Joseph too was industrious, modest, and even a little stodgy, a man out of the baroque and hieratic Hapsburg court. He was also passionate, ineffectual, romantic, impractical, and obsessed indeed by Mozart. His father, Baron Conrad, dead of a stroke, had been a staunch Roman Catholic, who listed his occupation as "landowner" and was an active member of the Monarchist Party. Joseph had kept his own Roman Catholic faith. One of Joseph's brothers, Ludvig, was in the Wehrmacht, having become a Nazi after the *Anschluss.*

His mother was a Countess Esterházy, her ancestry even more aristocratic than his baron father's. On her side Joseph was related to Emperor Franz Joseph, and he was a great-great-great-great-grandson of Maria Theresa, Empress of Austria and mother of Marie Antoinette. There was one odd note to Joseph's ancestry; much later it would emerge that he and Richard Brault were distant cousins.

The most distinguished member of the family in 1940, however, was Joseph's cousin Sir George Franckenstein, who had been Austrian ambassador to the Court of St. James's. After Hitler annexed Austria, von Ribbentrop invited Sir George to return to the Fatherland as chief of all the former Austrian embassies and ministries. Sir George not only refused but requested British citizenship, thereby sacrificing his title. King George VI at once knighted him, and so he became "Sir George."

It was a romantic story, full of idealism and high-mindedness which Joseph related to the captivating Mme. Vail. He had grown up in a castle, which his father had been forced to sell after World War I. But his education—at *Gymnasium* in Germany and later at St. Andrew's University in Scotland—had made him a cosmopolitan man. He had also received a doctorate from the University of Innsbruck for a thesis which compared the Stuarts in Scotland with the House of Hapsburg, for one of the Stuart princesses had married one of the Hapsburg princes.

His scholarly, mild-mannered exterior masked in this young Austrian, not yet thirty years old, firm and idealistic principles. In the little town of Heiligkreuz in the Tyrol, where he came of age, he had been known as the "Red Baron" because he did not adhere to the conservatism expected from his title. Unlike his father, he was a liberal, a democrat, an admirer of American democracy. If he had joined the Fatherland Front, which had supported Chancellor Dollfuss, it was because he believed it was committed to strengthening Austrian independence from Germany. By 1937, Joseph was writing anti-Nazi pamphlets and articles for the local press, immediately arousing the hostility of the Nazis. Even as he was completing his doctoral dissertation, he was addressing peasant rallies at meetings, where he sought, as he explained, "to arouse the Tyrolean people to an awareness of their own independence as Austrians, and to convince them that *Anschluss* with Nazi Germany would be the greatest disaster which could befall our country." Having received his degree, he fled to France, to Mégève, where he took a job as Professeur des Langues Etrangères at the Collège Florimontane; he taught Latin and Greek no less than English and German, and also trained his pupils in elementary rock climbing. His ambition was to emigrate to England and become a political journalist.

As soon as France and Germany were at war, Joseph had offered his services to the military authorities at Mégève. Instead, on September 3, 1939, he was declared, like his friend Kurt Wick, an enemy alien and sent to Camp Chambarand, near Grenoble, and then to St.-Savin, near Lyons. Sir George Franckenstein had arranged a visa to England, but Joseph had no permission to travel and had to remain incarcerated. He had brought *Hamlet* with him and he read it to the other prisoners in both English and German during that hard cold winter. After four weeks the interned men had been segregated according to religion. Joseph declared that he was a Roman Catholic, twenty years later to berate himself for cooperating with the authorities even to this extent. "I've never forgiven myself that I told them my religion," he told fellow internee George Popper. "I should have refused to say what religion I have. It was none of their business."

In January of 1940, Joseph was one of the prisoners selected to serve the French Army as a *prestataire*, a laborer put to work building fortifications, roads, barracks, and railroads behind the front. Then, in April, he was cleared of being either a Nazi or a Communist, and assigned as a civilian laborer with the British Expeditionary Forces at Nantes. Dressed in a makeshift uniform, he continued to perform manual labor. With the fall of France in June, and Dunkirk, Joseph escaped from the concentration camp with the help of a French officer who had requisitioned one of the trucks supplied by the Royal Air Force. He longed to join the Free French or English forces even as he feared, as did all these interned men, that he would be returned to Germany according to the Compiègne armistice France had signed with Germany in June of 1940, which provided for the "surrender on demand" of all German refugees living in France—in practice, anyone the Germans found politically undesirable. Joseph made it to the Pyrenees, but failed to get into Spain. When he learned that Mégève would be in the Unoccupied Zone, he returned to the Collège Florimontane to figure out what to do next.

Teaching languages paid little, however, and Joseph tutored private pupils as well, among them Bobby and Apple and Pegeen, and even Sindbad when the war prevented him from returning to school. As her children's tutor, Joseph saw Kay Boyle more often now; he played chess with her. He spoke of his collection of Mozart records back in Austria, of his stamp collection, and of his dreams.

Kay was at once mesmerized. Here was a handsome young Austrian who was the antithesis of Kurt Wick, a principled man who was ready to risk his life for his beliefs, a man of great physical courage. In his willingness to risk his life in defense of the democracies against Nazi Germany, Joseph was unlike not only Wick but also Laurence. Even as she was still trying to get Wick into America, Kay made helping the young baron her newest cause. He was a man, she would write in *Primer for Combat*, with nothing "but a pair of climbing boots and a Tyrolian jacket and a hearty laugh and a knowledge of Mozart to take with him wherever he goes."

After listening to one of his stories about his time on a road gang as a *prestataire*, Kay wrote a short story about him called "Men," its hero a young baron, a "strong man" who protects an innocent young girl. Writing stories, writing poems was a form of seduction for Kay Boyle, as she charmed Joseph at once by portraying him as the hero of his own life. As Kay translated his life into her prose, Joseph became a hero of romance, this man descended from Emperor Rudolph Hapsburg, whose nose, she wrote, is "fine enough for any member of royalty to have worn with pride." Nor in her description did she ignore his physical attractiveness, his being tall and big-boned with "a longish, weather-flushed face and shy, strained, rather prominent green eyes." Kay also gave her fictional baron Joseph's laugh, "so pure and hearty, so entirely without venom." "Men" would appear in *Harper's Bazaar* in February of 1941.

In *Primer for Combat*, where Joseph is called Sepp, Kay Boyle chronicles the moment when she moves from one Austrian to the other; she chooses to open Sepp's letter before Wolfgang's. In the novel it is she who has sent him the five hundred francs to buy a bicycle so that he might return to Mégève.

That summer of 1940, as Kay was preoccupied with her Austrians, Peggy Guggenheim rented a house on Lake Annecy. Bobby and Pegeen and Sindbad were in the process of losing their innocence. "Are you still a virgin?" Sindbad demanded one day of Apple, still only ten years old and so tiny that she looked like a very little boy. One day Kay discovered Pegeen and Bobby flirting so shamelessly in the village that as they all walked back up to Les Six Enfants, Kay accused them of acting like "little whores." In her remaining innocence, Bobby thought she heard her mother call her a "little horse," and she took it as a great compliment, knowing as she did how her mother loved horses. Kay must have been telling Bobby that she loved her too. Pegeen surrendered her virginity that summer to a boy named Edgar Kuhn, whose father was an American in the movie business. Peggy was busy pursuing the local hairdresser.

But when at the end of the summer Peggy settled in a hotel in Mégève, she soon caught sight of the handsome young Austrian baron. Joseph was in despair. The woman he loved, Mme. Vail, was inaccessible, no doubt, he thought, still in love with Kurt Wick. He was in a state of *traumatisme* when Peggy came upon him. Peggy consoled the desolate young baron, even as she knew about his involvement with Kay. One night Peggy at last gained her revenge on the woman who had always behaved as if she were so superior, who in her insolence had even bought her a subscription to *Time* magazine. Now forty-two and in her prime, Peggy enticed Joseph to her bed.

Bitter at Kay's betrayal of his father, Sindbad was not sorry when he learned that Peggy had seduced Kay's "lily-white prince." Nor did Joseph's title impress Sindbad, even if it did his stepmother. "Austrian barons are a dime a dozen," Sindbad said. Kay, of course, thwarted any designs Peggy might have had on Joseph Franckenstein. She's trying to marry him because the one thing she doesn't have is a title, Kay told people.

Still Joseph had not declared himself to Kay and still she hung back. But they spent every moment they could together, discussing politics, such questions as whether Italy would make a separate peace with England. Joseph carried Kay's rucksack on his back; he pushed her bicycle up the steep roads of Mégève. Sometimes when they climbed, he sang to her, in his strong clear voice, Don Giovanni's "Reich mir die Hand, mein Lieben." The feeling between them grew. When Kay wrote to Kurt Wick that she had heard Joseph sing, Wick jealously accused Joseph of being a man "guilty of certain activities in his own country," referring to anti-Nazi activities. Soon after she received that letter, Joseph informed Kay that Kurt Wick was back in Mégève. It was then that Kay had her last fateful meeting with the ski instructor.

And soon after that Joseph gave an assignment to Pegeen and Bobby and Apple. They must write an essay in German describing—their mother. "*Bleue Augen, schwarze Haar, so schön . . .*," Bobby struggled. Overcome by emotion as he read these words, Joseph looked up to see Kay Boyle standing at the top of the stairs, tall and straight, her eyes staring into his as if she were a queen. Suddenly Joseph dropped all the schoolbooks he was holding, and they tumbled everywhere about his feet.

This man is in love with me, Kay now knew. Her heart was filled with joy. She smiled then, and Joseph's heart surged with hope.

Free now to confess how long he had loved her, Joseph recounted how he had seen her at the *piscine*; he had measured the time he had known her from that day when they said nothing to each other, when he had not known she was Kurt's lover. But at the train station at Annecy as he waited to go off alone to the concentration camp, he had given a boy on the platform ten francs to wave to him and say "*au revoir*" through the window. As the train pulled away, and the boy ran along waving his hand, Joseph, sitting inside between the gendarmes, had told himself, I am going south for the season. That is Mme. Vail outside waving to me. "Goodbye, Mrs. Vail," Joseph had said aloud, thinking that the gendarmes must find him completely mad.

"The day your first letter came, and my name was called out, everybody burst into laughter because in the months I had been there, no one had ever written me before," Joseph confessed. He had replied, writing her about a day in the autumn of 1937 when he had taken his horse out and crossed the railway tracks where Mussolini's train was scheduled to come through. During the long nights in the internment camp he had written her imaginary letters, full of what he called "stupid, idiotic things" he felt he couldn't say to anyone but her. Now he declared a love that was so simple and so sincere that it took Kay Boyle's breath away.

For years she had longed for just such a declaration. Now it had come. At last Kay Boyle had the lover with whom she could live out her passion against the backdrop of history. Kay immediately returned Joseph's affection. He became "my Baron." He was the man she loved. It was as if Kurt Wick had never existed.

She felt at that moment as if she had come through some crucible which redeemed her character. She soon stopped drinking so much; she said she was learning "not to want to see things in an exalted way," as she revealed how well aware she was of her tendency to romanticize. She had become a better person because of her love for Joseph. The man she loved, Kay thought, was more even than a human being. She saw him as a "symbol, the figurehead for the kind of persecution and destruction of what is." She had met this kind of nobility only once before, in the person of Alexander Berkman, whose *Prison Memoirs* Kay now gave Joseph to read.

Indeed, Joseph was a sensitive man. He took home the revised version of Kay's story about him, "Men," and when he came to the last page he wept, wept, he later told her, in the way he had not since his father had died, wept in a way he had not since he lost his country. Joseph told Kay he had found "the one woman . . . the one person in the world." She alone understood him. "Men" revealed to the young baron that Kay Boyle was "more me" than he was himself. From his room right there in Mégève he wrote her that he hoped when he saw her next she would be neither haughty nor conventional. He longed only for her to smile at him.

Were she just to smile, Joseph wrote, she would turn "this rotten, rebellious professor of the young into his old dry-eyed self again." In his love letters, Joseph described being with Kay Boyle as "heaven on earth." In keeping with his classical education, his letters were laced with allusions to Greek and Roman goddesses, Diana (not the lovely black one, he joked, referring to Kay's beloved dog) and Aphrodite and Juno and Artemis. He named them all. Kay Boyle was all of these to him. She was also, Joseph wrote, "more aware of what any of us went through than I ever was myself." And then his romantic side took over:

And Ysel can be honey or nectar or ambrosia or whatever old Jupiter and his goddesses drank up there in Olympus or Ossa, and a crocodile can turn into manna or into Proserpine's horn or was it Ceres or both, or Diana . . . and you are all three of them together and Aphrodite on top of it, and Helena and Cytherea and Cypris, born just as Aphrodite was born out of the white horses in the Mediterranean by Jupiter's will . . . or Juno or Artemis or like my immaculately cellophaned "Fairy Queen."

Kay Boyle could count on only one person to endorse this new relationship. So she pleaded with Katherine to acknowledge "my Baron." Katherine must not view Joseph as the mere successor to Kurt Wick. This was the real thing. "My Baron is something that scarcely ever happens once, and certainly not twice," Kay wrote her mother. Nor was their relationship based primarily on sex. It was rather that they thought the same things instantly. They laughed together. Joseph, moreover, was the ideal man, the epitome of "courage," which Kay Boyle now defined as "a matter of being gay enough and unegotistical enough and knowing enough about history, and liking Shakespeare and Mozart and Greek and Latin and horsebackriding enough to feel a separate being without any feeling of sacrifice or persecution or criticism in one's bones."

As always, Katherine approved, fretting all the while, as Kay's sister Jo observed, that "Kay Boyle" might be "out of white thread and soap." Jealously Jo pictured their mother frantically praying for the fall of the British Empire "because the letters of Kay Boyle to her mother and vice versa were held up for weeks by those imperialistic bastards." It rankled still that Katherine had chosen Kay as the vessel through which to fulfill her creative aspirations. Unperturbed by her older daughter's disapproval, Katherine picked up her pen and wrote a letter to Joseph's mother, the Baroness von Franckenstein, in Austria, as was only proper.

As Kay Boyle elaborated on her fantasy, on images of Joseph as the ideal man and lover, it was almost as if she were virtually inventing him. Joseph had to be noble and perfect because for him, as so recently for Kurt Wick, she planned to risk all, leaving her family behind. Kay, of course, was still living with Laurence and the children. But now nothing mattered but Joseph. Soon, inevitably, everyone knew. So smitten was Kay that she played an old gramophone record over and over every night from five o'clock until dinnertime. The rag contained the line "Joseph, Joseph, won't you make up your mind?" This refrain echoed through the rooms of Les Six Enfants, so that everyone grew sick of it. The big girls exchanged looks. Laurence, of course, heard it too. But Kay didn't care.

Now Kay sought to procure a visa for *Joseph*. He refused to allow her to help him. She became "impatient with his humility." Mont Blanc stood "blue with snow in the high, clear evening light" as Kay played chess with her baron, the man she needed to see as a hero, a fighter for freedom, and a symbol of all the oppressed of Europe. Everything in her life shrank to insignificance before her love for this man. Later she wrote to Ann Watkins, "I am terribly, hopelessly in love. What would have become of me had I never found him? He is absolutely a miracle."

There were twelve days when Kay and her baron spent all their time together. Kathe fell ill with mastoid disease, as Bobby had before her. But it was Laurence, even as he was suffering, knowing that this time he had lost Kay for good, who was present at the operation, Laurence who skied to the hospital every day to help his daughter with her therapeutic exercises. Kay was arguing with the American consul in Lyons, who was uneasy about Joseph despite his being the cousin of the Austrian ambassador who had refused to return when the Nazi government summoned him home after the *Anschluss*. It all seemed farfetched, Joseph's attempts to sneak into Spain, no less than his having claimed to be an Englishman when he produced the number of the English visa Sir George had in fact procured, a ploy which had failed. Matters seemed even more urgent when Joseph, as a foreigner, even in the "*zone libre*" had to register once more. He still wanted to join the Free French, but the British were afraid that such a man must be a German agent.

Kay and Joseph began now to make plans to leave Mégève. There was a day when Kay confronted Laurence with the finality of her decision. Although Joseph was much larger than he, Laurence took a swing at this man who had invaded his home, and who, as the teacher of his children, had stolen his wife away.

Indeed, Laurence succeeded in knocking Joseph down. Believing that his very life depended upon his being with Kay, Joseph did not retaliate. All Laurence could do was fire him as the children's tutor and banish him from the house whose hospitality he had so grievously violated.

"Get out. Just get out," Laurence said with dignity.

Kay Boyle set her date. In January of 1941 she would leave Laurence and move to Cassis-sur-Mer, just outside Marseilles in the South of France, where she would work to obtain Joseph's visa to America. She would take baby Clover, Kathe, and the maid Josephine with her. "I cannot work in the atmosphere that is here, and I cannot see the proper people about Joseph's visa, stuck here in Mégève," Kay said matter-of-factly. Even Katherine was not told the whole truth. "This is not a breaking up of the home," Kay wrote, although of course it was. But if Kay was given to dramatizing, this time reality surged to meet her exaggerations: the Gestapo were roaming the Unoccupied Zone, providing the collaborationist Vichy government with the names of *apatrides*, those men without countries, destined for concentration camps.

During her last days in Mégève, Kay took Apple for a haircut and permanent wave, announcing that her daughter now looked like movie star Danielle Darrieux. She consoled Kathe, who burned her finger in a saucepan of clay, and read *Crime and Punishment* aloud to Pegeen. On Joseph's recommendation she herself read Aldous Huxley's *Ends and Means*. She even went out skiing and with her usual exaggeration announced she had attempted a double somersault, only to sprain foot, knee, and shoulder. No matter, she pronounced her skiing now "presentable."

"What do you think of her going?" Laurence asked Joseph one cold snowy day in January shortly before Kay's departure for Cassis.

Joseph could not find a word to say, a single sound to make. He just sat there thinking that if anyone told him he would be shot the next morning it would have been possible to keep on thinking and talking and eating. But this other thing made him cease to be a man. He was as romantic as Kay. But he was also a timid, diffident man fearing that he would be unable to survive even this separation: he in Mégève, uncertain of his future, Kay in Cassis. Facing life in Mégève without her, all he could see was absolute darkness. He felt as if he had loved her for a very long time. She was a worldly woman with six children under her care. He was unable to imagine a future with this "mad American writer," as he had described her to a fellow internment camp inmate. She had spoken to him of New York. Joseph imagined the two of them meeting furtively at a drugstore on Forty-second Street. Would it be any more satisfying than their furtive meetings at the Petite Taverne here in Mégève? Wouldn't Mme. Vail have to rush away? In love letters before her departure, Joseph expressed his terror of a future without her:

When I'm with you I believe in everything, even my own vision of what I have sought to be, but when you go it will all go blank again, because if I am the stone effigy of the Ostrogoths' king, then you are Guinevere who simply breathed on me by passing and once you have passed I shall have to put my shield down by my side again and my spears and my dog beneath my feet and turn to stone again forever—because I love you and when you ask me to understand your going away I cannot because I can understand nothing but this.

She will abandon me sooner or later, Joseph feared. She won't know what to do with me in the end. "I only know how to say 'I want,' " Joseph told her, "and you always say 'I will' or 'we will' and perhaps you can teach me to say it." Once more Kay Boyle was the stronger partner in the relationship. But this much younger man was ready to worship her, even to describe her as a queen. Once more Kay Boyle seized life's bounty, doing what Howard Peterson Boyle had not done for himself, what Katherine, thwarted in an impossible triangle with husband and father-in-law, had not done; she would live for herself.

Leaving Mégève, Kay sounded an old note. She would write books and stories to make her mother and her children "proud" of her, presumably so that she would be forgiven for what she was about to do. Bobby, she told herself, could not be proud of her were she just another Mégève unfaithful wife meeting young men in cafés and trying to look young and maybe even succeeding for another four or five years.

To the end, Laurence pleaded with Kay not to go. Then, on the night before her departure, as her suitcase lay open on the bed, filled as it was with her lovely clothes, Laurence grabbed a tube of Duco cement glue and in fury squeezed the ugly yellow paste all over his wife's immaculate dresses. And still she would go.

With milk, meat, and coal unavailable, with the schools open only three hours a day, and all the restaurants closed, and arrests now frequent, it was clear that the Vail family would have to leave France. But Kay's mind was focused solely on making "a permanent and good thing for Joseph" in America, "a good lovely life for Joseph." She would remain at Cassis for two or three months, and then leave for America. She told the children she was leaving behind in Mégève that she would make the fourteen-hour train journey from Marseilles every two or three weeks, and perhaps she even believed that she would. Joseph would join her at Easter.

To American friends back home, Kay described Marseilles as the liveliest city in France, a place where there was "lots of material for short stories." In fact, Marseilles was a perilous place. New laws granted the police the right to arrest all foreign Jews and intern them in concentration camps, placing in jeopardy even Peggy and her latest paramour, surrealist painter and sculptor and veteran of Dada Max Ernst, who was in Marseilles and had already been taken once by the police for questioning. Joseph stood in great peril as Kay Boyle took his future into her very capable hands.

She moved to Cassis, leaving three bewildered, indeed devastated children behind. Apple would talk to no one, not even Bobby. She refused to comb her hair, so that it soon became tangled and unruly. Apple seemed to be crying all the time, weeping for her mother. Bobby wrote Kay many letters, announcing, in her hope to win her mother's interest, that she decided to spend her life writing poetry. When Kay sent a batch of post-cards, but neglected to send one particularly to Bobby, her oldest daughter fell into a new depression. That March, Bobby lamented that she was spending her first birthday without her mother. Kay sent her a nightgown that was much too big. Bobby then read *Plagued by the Nightingale*, writing her mother that she was "so wonderfully poetical when you write," and condemning her own "stupid poetry."

Pegeen thought she understood Kay's decision. But even to Pegeen, who loved Kay so much, it was an "ugly sad subject." Nor could Pegeen refrain from begging Kay to return. "Oh, Kay do come back, please do," she wrote.

Now Laurence sought consolation from his daughters, lying in bed with little Apple as they cuddled. Laurence was to confide in Apple most, telling her that he wanted to marry her since a daughter would surely never leave him. Still they took baths together. Frightened, Apple made sure not to look at "that thing."

In Kay's absence, Peggy Guggenheim burst upon Les Six Enfants, so that Kay's daughters feared that Peggy had come to replace their mother. Feeling abandoned, Bobby could not bear to see Peggy at the head of the table serving the soup. Then, when Peggy and Laurence were at Lyons applying for transit visas for the family to Spain and Portugal, Max Ernst arrived, a romantic figure in a black cape with a voracious appetite. "I guess there's nothing to eat in Marseilles," Bobby concluded.

Kay Boyle's daughters scrutinized Max and Peggy, debating about whether they were lovers. One day Pegeen walked into Peggy's room to discover Peggy with her breasts naked and Max Ernst standing there. That was news. That Bobby and Apple were disturbed by Peggy only made them miss Kay all the more, while Bobby was convinced that Peggy hated them. "She's so stupid, stupid, stupid," Bobby wrote to Kay, knowing that any criticism of Peggy would please her mother. Even Peggy's vanity irritated Bobby: "the way she talks about her thin ankles!" Peggy was always talking about sex, asking about sex, something Kay would never do.

In Cassis and in Marseilles that spring of 1941, Kay Boyle worked frantically to find a means of getting Joseph to America. She tried the Jewish Rescue Committee, which wouldn't help her because Joseph wasn't a Jew. Making the rounds, she ran into her old friend Germaine Garrigou from Stoke, now with a French soldier lover. As Kay Boyle was to recount the moment, history repeated itself as Germaine's husband arrived "looking daggers." Kay then grabbed the French soldier's cap and gazed affectionately into his eyes to deceive the suspicious husband, just as she had done in Stoke fourteen years earlier. The coincidence sounds like fiction; with Kay life and art were ever interchangeable.

It was no small matter for Joseph even to make his way to Marseilles, for he lacked the safe-conduct pass issued by the military authorities which would have permitted him to travel in France. A foreigner lacking such a document could be shipped at once to a concentration camp. But Kay learned that you could avoid the police checkpoint at the Gare St.-Charles by entering the service corridor for the station restaurant of the Hôtel Terminus. If anyone asked where you were going, you could say you wanted to use the telephone, or to wash your hands. Once you were in the hotel, you could walk out into the street, like any hotel guest. Under the noses of the Gestapo, who guarded every doorway now at the railway station, Kay spirited Joseph through the restaurant and to safety.

The news that Joseph had joined Kay and his children in Cassis filled Laurence with rage and he boarded a train for Marseilles. Clover, he explained to people, wouldn't understand what was going on. But Kathe, now nearly seven, would. Laurence decided to take Kathe home with him. Nor did the little girl mind. She didn't like Joseph; as soon as he arrived she had kicked him in the shins. Nor would she call him anything but "*celui-là*."

One night that spring an unlikely group gathered in a Marseilles café: Kay and Laurence, Marcel Duchamp and Mary Reynolds, Peggy Guggenheim and Max Ernst. Laurence had invited Kay to the café off the main street for a drink. Fearing that Laurence might make a scene, Kay did not bring Joseph with her, but left him at Cassis-sur-Mer.

"The boat on which you've shipped all your paintings to America has sunk," Kay taunted Peggy. Then Laurence got to the point of the meeting, attacking Kay for refusing to return to Mégève to help pack up the family's possessions. So selfish was she, so preoccupied with Joseph, that she neglected her family, putting her lover first. In a temper, Laurence began to throw the crockery. Then the shouting began.

Haughtily, Kay rose from her seat. She had to catch the bus back to Cassis, she announced.

Drunk and furious, Laurence grabbed the marble top off the table and raised it high over his head. He was going to smash it down on the head of this impossible woman who so callously was destroying the life they had built, who was bringing so much pain to their children. He was so angry that he wanted to smash her to bits, with her white earrings, those imperious blue eyes, that hauteur.

Suddenly, terrified that Laurence might indeed kill Kay, for never had he seen him so out of control, Marcel Duchamp jumped up and interposed his body between them. Later, disbelievingly, Duchamp said, "It was the only brave act I ever performed in my life. I even ran away from being conscripted into the Army because I hated violence." The artist whom little Kay had first heard of at the Armory Show in 1913 had become the instrument of her survival twenty-seven years later.

Weeping, Kay bolted for the door, rushed out of the café, and ran down the street. In mad pursuit, Laurence followed her. Marcel sped out the door as well, running along one side of Kay while Laurence ran along the other. Marcel shouted the name of his hotel and his room number, or it might have been Peggy's room.

"If she goes to that hotel, I'll kill both of you," Laurence screamed.

Breathless now, they kept running down the main avenue of Marseilles.

"We have to talk," Laurence cried at last.

"I think I have to settle this with Laurence," Kay told Marcel Duchamp.

It was to Peggy Guggenheim's hotel room at the De Noailles facing the sea that Kay and Laurence now repaired to unravel their tangled relations. There were two single beds. Man and wife, each lay down on a bed, as they stayed up all night working out with whom the children would live once they reached America.

"Why must you leave me?" Laurence asked one last time. But Kay Boyle had not been in love with him for years, and for a long time she had yearned for a romantic love forever lost to them.

In the middle of the night there was a hard knock on the door. Terrified, Kay opened the door to discover men from the Gestapo. But the Vails produced their American passports and the Germans retreated.

Leaving Kay and her baron and baby Clover in Marseilles, Laurence took Kathe and Josephine back to Mégève. On the way home, Laurence slept with Kathe, who wet the bed. When Josephine reprimanded her, Kathe denied it. "I hugged my father so hard that we sweated so much and that's why the bed is wet," Kathe said. "I didn't do wee-wee."

On April 5, the American consul at Marseilles granted Joseph a quota immigration visa on the basis of an "affidavit in lieu of passport." Now all Kay had to do was find a place for him on one of the ships which left every four or five days bound for Martinique, a colony under the sway of Vichy. Kay approached Varian Fry, who ran the Emergency Rescue Committee in Marseilles, a group organized to help German refugees caught in France, spiriting artists and intellectuals in danger from the Gestapo to America. For thirteen months Fry worked, unaided by the American consulate, which had scant sympathy for this effort to rescue German poets and social democratic politicians, some of them even socialists. The American embassy, Fry discovered, was conspiring with Vichy, refusing to help with the exit visas required to get the refugees into Spain and Portugal. Both Kay and Peggy Guggenheim were members of the *comité de patronage* set up to help Fry and on which André Gide also served.

Varian Fry could not help but admire Kay Boyle, an "intense, emotional, and very finely wrought" woman who had come in quest of a visa for her lover. Each time she came to the Emergency Rescue Committee office she wore those white bone earrings Fry later described as "cut in the form of the many-petaled flowers of the edelweiss." But when Fry seemed not to be giving the Baron Joseph von und zu Franckenstein sufficient priority, Kay Boyle lashed out at him in fury. At that moment Fry was engrossed with helping Rudolph Breitscheid, leader of the Social Democratic bloc in the Reichstag, and the writer Franz Werfel. But Kay Boyle was concerned only about Joseph, Joseph whose case was so urgent because, unlike the others, having escaped from an internment camp, he didn't dare pass through Spain, but had to board one of the ships carrying French Army officers and functionaries to Fort-de-France.

Twenty-four hours before a ship called the *Erica* sailed, Fry told Kay that Joseph and his friend George Popper should come to Marseilles with their bags. Kay was to accompany them to the Emergency Rescue Committee office on the boulevard Garibaldi.

It was Easter weekend. On Saturday morning, Kay and Joseph arrived with his luggage only to find the offices at 18 boulevard Garibaldi shut tight. Fry had obviously taken off for his country refuge, the Villa Air-Bel, dubbed the "Château Espére-Visa" by Russian novelist Victor Serge.

Furious with Fry for having failed to keep what she insisted had been a promise, Kay accused him of an "undeniable form of cruelty." In a rage, she resigned from the committee, calling Fry completely irresponsible. By this time she had discovered that Fry had failed to cable Joseph's biographical data to the Emergency Rescue Committee headquarters in America, although she had offered to pay for the cable. Even the American consulate was more humane, and less evasive, Kay chastised Fry: "To be the great humanitarian you must learn to be ruthless as well, for the anguish such evasion can inflict is truly incalculable." In fact, Kay Boyle had rushed to judgment only later to discover that Fry had not betrayed her, that the *Erica* had taken no passengers.

Told at the boulevard Garibaldi office that there were no more places on the *Winnipeg*, a second ship sailing that week for Martinique, Kay decided to trust no one but herself. She headed for the Transatlantique offices, where she was in fact able to purchase two tickets! Nervously Joseph had insisted that Kay be sure that his friend George Popper travel with him. He feared still that once the ship passed the Straits of Gibraltar, the Germans would come on board and pick him out as a fugitive.

Kay Boyle and her young lover spent one last night in Marseilles. They stayed at a hotel where the proprietress preferred a transient trade, sleeping on perfumed sheets under a satin coverlet. Finally, on May 6, Joseph sailed away from his Nazi tormentors on the SS *Winnipeg*, bound for Martinique. In whatever direction the wind blew, the romantic young Austrian baron wrote the woman he loved, he smelled the "violent perfume" of the sheets of their last night together.

16

Going Home

*She deserted a great number of children who had been
the center of her life. I can never forgive her for that.*

JAMES STERN

She was a bitch to leave Papa.

SINDBAD VAIL

*So you see even I, Bob darling, have done the thing I swore I
would never do at middle age . . . fall in love with a man seven
years my junior who will probably fall in love with Bobby or
another of my daughters in the end.*

Kay had at first arranged ten places on one of the forty-one-ton Pan
American Clippers, which had begun transatlantic crossings only in the
summer of 1939. But Laurence had steadfastly refused to travel on the
same plane with his wife's lover, although traveling with his ex-wife and
his soon-to-be ex-wife did not bother him at all. Passage for everybody,
except Joseph, would be paid by Peggy Guggenheim, who withdrew from
her account at the Banque de France in Marseilles five hundred and fifty
dollars for each, the amount a person was entitled to take out of the country.

As the group, which included the Vails, Peggy, and Max, traveled
through Marseilles to Spain and on to Lisbon to await Clipper passage to
America, the Vichy-registered *Winnipeg* carrying Joseph to the Americas
ran into trouble. After being harassed by a bomber sent out by the governor
of Martinique, who was no friend of Vichy, the ship was captured by a
Dutch gunboat, which diverted it to Trinidad, where it was delivered over
to the British, the Allies needing ships. The British were also certain
German spies were aboard. Joseph was fortunate. As a result of the *Winnipeg*'s being captured, Vichy canceled all future sailings. Kay Boyle had
saved him at the ultimate moment. And at the end of June of 1941, only
a month later, the American consulates in France were forbidden by Washington to grant any visas at all without specific authorization from the State
Department. Had it not been for Kay's valiant and diligent efforts, there
might have been no way for him to be accepted into the United States.

In Trinidad all the passengers were quarantined. The British interrogated each one separately. Joseph was questioned about composer Hanns
Eisler, a German Communist and fellow passenger. He told them he had
never spoken to Eisler, and requested that Sir George Franckenstein be

contacted. The next day a cable arrived. If Joseph would join the British Army at once, Sir George would have a bomber from England sent to pick him up.

But for Joseph there was Kay Boyle to consider, the woman he loved. To return to Europe now would be to lose her. Joseph chose to make his way to America, where he would wait for Kay, although he didn't have a penny to his name.

In Lisbon, to relieve the tension, to escape from the company of Laurence and Peggy, Kay checked into a clinic on the pretense that she had "sinus trouble." Meeting the beautiful English surrealist painter Leonora Carrington, Max Ernst's former lover, Kay advised her to cast her lot with her current paramour, a Mexican journalist. That Carrington had not seen Ernst since the spring of 1940, when he had been detained by the French police, had not lessened his ardor. By thus intervening, Kay incurred Ernst's lifelong enmity.

After the first two weeks, with no immediate prospect of a Clipper becoming available to transport the unhappy company to America, Laurence and all the children and Peggy and Max moved from scorching Lisbon to a hotel by the sea at Monte Estoril, where they occupied an entire floor. Late into the night you could hear the sound of Laurence weeping. Meals were taken at a huge table in the middle of the dining room, elaborate eight-course meals at which emotions ran high as Laurence, as was his way, used the dinner table as a forum for emotional expression. Peggy sat at the head of the table, with Max and Laurence on either side. The long line of children sat facing each other.

When Laurence visited Kay at her clinic on one of his train trips into Lisbon to check on the Clipper passages, Kay had a request to make. She had learned that Joseph had been detained in Trinidad. He could not be admitted into the United States without five hundred dollars being deposited in a bank in his name. Kay had already contacted Henry Varnum Poor and Bessie Breuer as well as Grace Flandrau in St. Paul to vouch for the fact that Joseph would not become a public charge.

Kay now requested that Laurence send telegrams, including one to Joseph, telegrams costing hundreds of *escudos*. Generously, Laurence complied. Kay wanted him as well to ask Peggy to lend her the money so that Joseph could fly from Trinidad to Miami. This Peggy refused. Kay next approached her soon-to-be ex-mother-in-law Mrs. Vail for the money to allow Joseph to complete his journey to America. On Laurence's advice, his mother agreed. Later Kay told people she had paid Mrs. Vail back for this extraordinary favor out of her first short story sale in New York. But Laurence told Kathe she never did. (In Laurence's memoirs he offers Peggy's reactions: "No, I'll never forgive Daze [Kay] for the way she acted . . . And you stood for it. You let her walk all over you. Why you even lent her money so she could get her lover out of France . . . you were an angel to that fiend.") On June 7, Joseph flew to Miami, where he was denied entry into the United States and detained by the FBI at an airport hotel for days. Finally, Henry Varnum Poor and Bessie Breuer sent him the fifty dollars which all aliens had to possess before they could be admitted to America.

Unwilling to subject herself to the "high tension," which would only be intensified by her presence, Kay remained in Lisbon, seeing the children only on Sundays. Kathe had diarrhea on her birthday; Clover, now two, was afflicted with boils. Kay was not there. One night Apple was walking along the balustrade of the terrace when she caught a glimpse through his open room door of Max Ernst, stark naked, adding blue coloring to his white hair. The moment was traumatic, as was Laurence's having taken up with a local prostitute. "I hope now you'll marry a nice, fat Italian cook," Apple later told her father.

Even in Kay's absence tempers flared. Ernst made clear his hatred of Kay once Leonora followed her advice and married her Mexican in Lisbon; Peggy attacked Kay, while Pegeen infuriated her mother by rushing to Kay's defense. Laurence confided his pain over Kay's defection to his daughters.

"She's a monster," Laurence told Bobby.

"No, she's not," Bobby staunchly defended her mother. Suddenly Laurence became so angry that he lifted the top off the café table and threw it wildly in Bobby's direction. Luckily he missed. Appalled, the restaurant proprietor pushed the whole group out the door. "Before I call the police," he told them. Secretly Bobby despaired. She had learned that in America she would be separated from her sisters Apple and Kathe, who would be living with Laurence. She would have to go with Kay to take care of little Clover.

At last, after five weeks, Pan American made a Clipper available for the eleven bedraggled souls: Kay and Laurence, soon to be divorced, Peggy and Max, soon to be married, six children, and a wistful, forlorn Jacqueline Ventadour, the only one for whom Peggy didn't have to pay. There was no room for Diane, who had boarded the American Export liner *Exeter* to make the journey alone, which she accomplished without incident. And so they boarded, Kathe already carrying American comic strips, Apple with Edgar Allan Poe and *Little Women*, Bobby with her Hemingway. It was July, but this family's luggage included eight pairs of skis. Sindbad bet Kay there would be no wine on board and won the bet. He was by no means pleased with his stepmother, however.

"You're the only mother I've ever had," Sindbad was to tell her scathingly. "You haven't only ruined one man's life. You've ruined two!" He would never forgive her. Taking up the cause of the Austrian baron, Jimmy Stern thought, she had made many people very unhappy. For a person of such supposed idealism, with all her causes and principles, always trying to help people in need, she had done the most devastating thing to the people closest to her. Maybe she should have taken other people a little more seriously than herself, Stern believed. She was arrogant and she lacked humility. And the man she had chosen was so conservative, so what was it all about?

The Clipper bumped its way through other turbulent zones, and the children began to vomit in their paper bags. Apple's braces flew off. Max and Pegeen went to war over the one remaining berth. In this universe where children were granted no special consideration, Max emerged victorious and Pegeen had to share Peggy's sleeping compartment. In lieu of wine they drank scotch, and before the journey ended Max let Kay Boyle know how much he detested her for interfering in his romance with Leonora Carrington.

At last the Clipper descended to Long Island Sound and was towed to the landing of the La Guardia Marine Air Terminal. On Bastille Day, July 14, 1941, Kay Boyle returned to the homeland she had not seen for eighteen years. Reporters and photographers besieged this illustrious group. Among those who interviewed Kay Boyle that day was one Sonia Tomara, a metro reporter for the *New York Herald Tribune*, who would later figure importantly in Kay Boyle's life. But none of them seemed to know quite what to make of this odd collection of human beings. Their interest in the painter Ernst and the entrepreneur-heiress Peggy palled, however, before their fascination with the elegant, majestic woman at the center of all these children. Someone remarked, "She looks as though she were answering a challenge," this reed-slim, straight-backed woman with those heavily lidded blue eyes sparkling with interest in her new surroundings.

Kay, called "Mrs. Katherine B. Vail (Kay Boyle)" in the New York *World-Telegram* of July 15, told the assembled reporters she was writing a novel based on the lives of German refugees in French concentration camps, where conditions were "dreadful." The family planned, she announced, to move to Providence, Rhode Island. Indeed, divorce remained a stigma in America at the turn of the forties; that Kay Boyle was about to be divorced a second time could harm her image, and even cause her to lose some of her audience. Truly in need of money now, her target audience had to be the middle-class housewife, reader of the women's magazines and *The Saturday Evening Post*, and divorce might endanger her appeal there. And so it was a happy, unified family which she presented as having come to America, because they didn't have enough food in France.

The Associated Press photographed the Vail family seated on a couch in the airport terminal. At the extreme left, glassy-eyed and staring straight ahead, clutching her father's walking stick, while sitting on his knee, is Apple-Joan Vail. Laurence's beaky nose is prominently in profile; his thin lips are pursed, his legs crossed as he looks toward the others seated beside him. Next to Laurence is his daughter Pegeen, who has placed her hand on her stepmother Kay's shoulder, as if for support. Pegeen's face is turned so that she looks at Kay, seeking direction.

Leaning on Kay Boyle's knee is a frightened-looking toddler in a dress with a white collar and cuffs, Clover, while at the extreme right sits a glaring, suspicious young woman, Bobby. Seated on Bobby's lap is a pretty blond little girl, Kathe. Behind, to the far right of this uneasy group, is a young man with his father's thin lips and his mother's bulbous nose, dashing nonetheless, in his dark suit, white shirt, and tie. It is that young man of the world, Sindbad Vail.

Only one figure in this group seems serene. It is Kay herself, an impeccably groomed figure in a light jacket and dark dress ensemble. She smiles straight ahead at the photographer, totally oblivious of the others. Her dark hair is perfectly arranged, her signature white earrings firmly in place. She is bone thin, even gaunt, yet at ease with herself, clearly a woman of consequence. Her expression is affable, even open, as if she would reply frankly to any question a reporter might pose.

"Kay Boyle's Was the Largest Family to Arrive on One Clipper" reads the caption affixed to this family portrait. The *World-Telegram* called them "the biggest family ever to arrive on a transoceanic ship."

"Story of the Family," Kay wrote on a page of her notebook for 1941: "Divided into two groups. The outsiders (Pegeen, Kathe) and those who have a secret, inexplicable part." Pegeen and Kathe, Kay considered "outsiders." They were the blondes, the "stupid ones," as years later she would admit to her daughter Clover. Honest and direct, they did not complicate Kay's life. Nor did they interest her, as did Bobby, Ernest Walsh's child, who bore her grievances silently, and Apple, mysteriously unapproachable, so tiny and undeveloped for her years, and seemingly without gender. Toward Bobby, with whom she had been less than honest, and toward Apple, whose needs she had so flagrantly ignored when she ran off with Joseph, Kay bore her own secret, irremediable guilt.

In America, the returned celebrity at once put her European years behind her. She found herself psychologically incapable of even writing to anyone she had known in France. It wasn't that she didn't care, she insisted. It was that she "simply cannot do it." Until the autumn of 1942 letters could still get through to Vichy France. But Kay, eschewing self-examination, put the context of her life with Laurence behind her.

Instead she threw herself into the role of the returned celebrity. As if she were a fashion model, she was photographed by Louise Dahl-Wolfe for *Harper's Bazaar*. Reporters described her clothes. People talked about Kay Boyle as a romantic figure, one associated with chauffeured limousines and suites at the George Cinq or the Savoy. Kay went shopping at proletarian S. Klein on Union Square, where she purchased an aqua-and-white print dress for two dollars, occasioning a "photo opportunity." Ingratiatingly, she confessed to reporters that in the melee at Klein's she had lost a frightened two-year-old Clover Vail for a good thirty-five minutes.

Later Kay was photographed in the two-dollar aqua dress, to which she had added a wide black picture hat, purchased on Fifty-seventh Street, with a black veil. The outfit was completed by long black gloves, a black clutch purse, and black suede platform shoes which, she revealed, she had purchased in Lisbon. Her ears were adorned with her trademark ear-rings in the shape of the edelweiss. As if she were a movie star, her clothes were scrutinized in the press; enjoying the attention, Kay Boyle revealed that her platform shoes were the rage in Spain and Portugal, where women wanted to appear taller, and that the platforms were made not of cork, but of nickel. For evening, she said, she favored tailored white clothes. To write, she wore a *robe de chambre*. With a trace of hauteur she added, "I couldn't possibly concentrate in a dress."

But Kay Boyle was no mere decorative object. She represented the glamour and the achievement of the Paris expatriates. Her mystery was made all the more piquant by her confessions of how difficult life had been in war-torn Europe, where there had been no milk and no meat for her children. Famous writer, wife, mother, she returned to America bearing witness to history, to a Europe already deep in the vortex of war.

One day she met the press in the Park Avenue offices of her agent, Ann Watkins. As she submitted to the reporters' questions, she smoked a cigarette down to the last half inch. "We'd stand in line for a half-hour or more for a packet of matches. And cigarettes were even harder to get," she confided. She portrayed her experience in terms of high drama. "Rich refugees literally pushed us aside—big rolls of money in their pockets," Kay said dramatically. People who had bought platinum which they con-verted to automobile tools were able to cross the frontiers, she insisted improbably.

Nor had Kay arrived in America without a cause. She was determined to defend the French against the accusation that they had "lain down on the job" against the Germans. They were "men without arms," she ex-plained. The German military machine easily overcame them. Kay also acknowledged that she had been called a Nazi for writing *Death of a Man*.

"Perhaps I was at fault," Kay Boyle said disarmingly. "The emotions were there and I put them down and the picture was not thoroughly rounded—it couldn't be in a novel of that kind. But I am not a Nazi." Then she diverted the conversation to those men who had fled Germany— she did not say Austria—only to be thrown into French concentration camps. Always she portrayed the Vail family as intact. She invoked the "Vails' Family Almanach," for which, she said, "Papa makes the covers."

Ever mindful of reaching the widest audience possible, she asked, "Does my style seem involved?"—only to answer her own question: "It doesn't to me." Meanwhile as part of her legend, she invoked how much she liked "the smell of carbons." Her image, however, was of the woman who had it all—family, career, marriage. She confided that during her first week in New York she had visited the Central Park zoo every afternoon, where her children ate frankfurters and went on the merry-go-round, as if at once they had become typical Americans.

Belying her descriptions of life with her children was the writing routine she outlined: she rose at seven, tended to household duties until eight-thirty, wrote until lunch, rested, might play a game of chess—this a veiled reference to Joseph, who loved the game—worked again until teatime, had friends to dinner, and went to bed by ten: no mention of the children in that. Kay Boyle was too honest, however, to praise her domestic skills. She could cook, she admitted, "only in a haphazard way." She also added, mysteriously, that she planned to move to a ranch out West.

Sultry, exquisite, Kay soon sat for a spread in *Town and Country* to be photographed by George Platt Lynes. Her heavily lidded eyes stare straight ahead as she perches on a brocade chair. Her expression is brooding, as if she has lived long and hard. On her ears are the edelweiss, while she wears a "two-piece suit of grey wool, pin-striped with white and trimmed with snakeskin," a suit which could be purchased in New York at Jay Thorpe, a shop which catered to the very rich. Casually thrown over her black hair is a crocheted veil-like black shawl, in her hand black gloves. A slim gold wedding band circles her finger. The caption describes "Mrs. Laurence Vail," who had returned to America from Europe after an absence of *twenty* years.

On that hot Bastille Day the Vails had proceeded to the Hotel Great Northern on Fifty-seventh Street, where Mrs. Gertrude Vail had reserved the rooms. Joseph awaited Kay Boyle; almost immediately he applied for American citizenship. When the group dispersed, Kay headed for Nyack and the home of the painter Henry Varnum Poor and Bessie Breuer, his wife, taking Joseph, Bobby, and Clover with her. Laurence took Apple and Kathe to Matunuck Beach in Rhode Island, where he described himself mournfully as "deep in domestic smash-up." The first friend he contacted was Djuna Barnes, recognizing as he did that "Djuna with her maternal quality likes people when they're down." Eventually Laurence found his way, with the help of Malcolm Cowley, to Sherman, Connecticut. Soon Laurence was teaching seven-year-old Rob Cowley a limerick:

> *There was a young man from Thistlehurst*
> *Who when he peed had to whistle first.*
> *One morning in June*
> *He lost his tune.*
> *His bladder burst.*

In Connecticut, Laurence confided to Malcolm Cowley about how Kay withheld sex all the time. It was clear that he was bitter. "The last time I saw her, her hair was dyed the color of hen-shit," he told Muriel Cowley sometime later. Eventually Laurence met English writer Cyril Connolly's ex-wife Jeannie, and life became more tolerable.

When Diane's ship docked, Laurence fought Kay bitterly over the custody of the dog, as bitterly as he had for Apple and Kathe. "She's mine!" he cried. Diane moved in with Laurence, Kathe, and Apple. But whenever she caught a glimpse of Kay, whenever Diane spotted her dear friend, who had written so many novels and poems and stories by her side, Diane howled as if in great pain. Diane missed Kay so much. It was obvious to everyone, even seven-year-old Kathe, who wrote her mother from Connecticut: "Diane wants you I think so."

Another ship docked that hot summer of 1941, but Nancy Cunard was forbidden to disembark in Brooklyn because she had no visa. Kay took precious time away from her writing to join Janet Flanner and Solita Solano to take the subway to Brooklyn. Somehow the women persuaded an officer to relax his rules, and there was beautiful Nancy dancing down the gangplank. The four women sat on crates on the wharf and drank beer, sharing all their many adventures.

Kay returned to Nyack and her financial dilemma. Unable to find a job, Joseph was tutoring the Poors' sixteen-year-old son, who was about to enter Andover, and doing some translating. After registering at the Cooperative Bureau for Teachers on Broadway, all he was offered was a job in Bermuda. Meanwhile, Kay left the Poors, renting first some rooms and then a house in Nyack for fifty dollars a month, a price which included bed linen and silver. Frantically she tried to sell some short stories. Nearing completion of *Primer for Combat*, to depict Kurt Wick's life accurately she wrote to West Point for information on the Foreign Legion and a "Régiment de Marche des Volontaires Etrangères."

By now Kay really was the sole breadwinner of her family, as she opened her first checking account. When, by October, Joseph remained unemployed, they agreed that he should go off to California to work on a citrus-fruit ranch managed by an Austrian he had met at the internment camp. Once more the lovers would be separated.

In California, Joseph found his Russian boss something of a Simon Legree. The work, planting trees in the San Bernardino Mountains, was grueling. But his Austrian friend, a man named Karczag, promised that Joseph might soon be able to take over one of the ranches as its manager. Joseph stayed on.

Endorsing the fantasy of their running a ranch together—so similar to her earlier dream of managing a ski resort with Kurt Wick—Kay announced it to reporters and discussed it with Bob McAlmon, who had returned to America in the fall of 1940 to work in Phoenix at the Southwest

Surgical Supply Co. owned by his brothers George and Bert. Her ambition was "to get a ranch and raise horses, since Joseph rides well and knows a lot about them . . . where would you suggest we go—New Mexico or Arizona?" For all her indignation in her letter to the *Partisan Review* about the need for American intervention in the war in Europe, it seems not to have entered her personal calculations that autumn of 1941 that it might actually happen.

In Nyack, Kay Boyle plunged into a busy existence. Frantic for money, she decided to enter the lecture circuit, and did, speaking before audiences of two and three hundred. The publicity surrounding her return had helped. Letters from admirers arrived. The young writer Warren Miller wrote that she "and Carlos Williams are the only American writers who know what prose is or what it should be."

In November, Kay won her second O. Henry prize for best short story of the year. "Defeat" had appeared in *The New Yorker* in May, a recycled chapter from *Primer for Combat*. Kay Boyle's personal favorite of all her stories, it amply succeeds in its own right. A narrator begins by passionately chronicling the fall of France, when the "men of that tragically unarmed and undirected force which had been the French army once but was no longer" came "trickling" back home. Moral witness contrasts the German "blond demigods" with their "rustproof tanks and guns, the chromiumed electric kitchens, the crematoriums," with the resources of the shabby, unprepared, yet heroic French.

In particular, one short dark Frenchman returns to Pontcharra (Mégève), a seemingly unheroic figure who reveals the true French spirit. He is given no name, only "bus driver." Yet he articulates the truths Kay believed in. Not only had the officers and politicians betrayed their countrymen, but the French people themselves—the women—had been corrupted; "if you're one kind of woman any kind of uniform looks all right to you after a certain time" is his bitter discovery. Having been rescued by a French schoolteacher who cut up French flags to serve him and his friend as a disguise, having concluded that "a country isn't defeated as long as its women aren't," he is bitterly disillusioned. On Bastille Day, the French women in the town where he is hiding, seduced by pastries and chocolate and lemonade and beer, dance with the Germans. Nowhere more vividly had Kay depicted the sting of moral defeat.

For her lectures, Kay drew on similar anecdotes to show what was happening in France. She spoke out against "the State Department, and the Fascist element in every country." She insisted that she spoke "absolutely non-politically." She was not advocating any particular policy, she said, but only reiterating a moral truth: that nothing matters "except the individual resistance and the individual protest."

On the day before the bombing of Pearl Harbor, Kay Boyle insisted that "my talk is neither for intervention nor against it—it's simply a talk about the way I, and a great many other people, feel about the situation over there." Conscious always of public opinion, she took a circumspect, an apolitical stance. Often she described the concentration camps in which Kurt Wick and Joseph Franckenstein had suffered. Kay Boyle was in demand: Chicago and Cincinnati were added to her schedule. In New York, she spoke in French at the Alliance Française, announcing to an unaware public that there was indeed a French resistance.

In Cambridge, Kay spoke at the Institute of Modern Art to raise money for refugees. Wearing black slacks, fortified with scotch and caviar, Kay was the first speaker; Roger Fry, André Masson, Marc Chagall, and Jacques Lipchitz would follow her.

Trembling and cold, Kay Boyle stood there "hating" the faces looking up at her, even as she described the situation of the political refugees stranded in Marseilles. She said that, like the Free French, whom she impressionistically invoked, she was for a "European democracy," not a return to the old order, that class conflict in France was more significant than the superficial political issues. But these Americans didn't seem to understand.

Repelled by having to ask for contributions, she did so anyway. Chagall's manner she found "obsequious." Lipchitz was the best of the lot. Artists and writers were in the process of dragging money, dollar by dollar, from their bourgeois audience when the chairman stopped the program so that everyone could listen to President Roosevelt on the radio. After a paltry $750 was collected, Kay was further irritated that she was expected to go off "to the flat of a poetess," where they all sat on "soap boxes." Other events were more successful. Six thousand dollars was raised at a lunch at the Commodore where she spoke, and four thousand in Baltimore.

In Nyack, Kay ferreted out every opportunity to earn money. She taught writing at the adult night school, published stories in *Vogue* and *Harper's Bazaar*, modeled clothes for *Town and Country*, and did everything she could to cash in on her notoriety. She accepted every book-reviewing assignment she could garner. In *The New Republic* she hectored two young writers: "just or unjust I am far too much concerned with what they both have failed to do."

Kay Boyle spoke now as a judge of both political morality and literature. Meanwhile she never missed an opportunity to return a favor, as she did for Katherine Anne Porter, whose introduction to Eudora Welty's *A Curtain of Green* she praised as offering "as good a set of standards to bring to the evaluation of writers and writing as any I have seen." Even when Porter praised Welty for having been spared a "militant social consciousness," hardly her own view, Kay Boyle kept silent. Only when Porter doubted whether Welty would do as well writing novels as short stories did Kay Boyle demur, this judgment hitting too close to home: "I foresee no way of failure for her written or unwritten novel."

As busy as she had made her life, Kay missed Joseph. She tried to arrange lectures out West so that she could "see my love" for a few idyllic days at Elsinsore Lake in California. But she was unsuccessful. Nor was Joseph doing well. Lonely, he complained of the hard manual labor. He seemed also to be suffering a loss of confidence in this new country. Joseph's descriptions of how hard he was working at the Rancho Rayo de Sol made Kay so frantic that one midnight she telephoned George Popper, who lived nearby, to come over to commiserate. Then she unburdened herself about how Joseph was being mistreated.

Kay knew, for both their sakes, that she had to see Joseph, "and he feels he must see me, before spring." Indeed, it was as difficult for her as it was for him. She said she could not "keep sane under the present circumstances if this continues any longer." She had hoped to make *Primer for Combat* a mutual diary, a collaboration in which Joseph wrote the political and military record, and she the emotional and personal side; this was now impossible.

Meanwhile she worked obsessively, writing in bed, writing every spare minute. "I am writing hard—I must write hard," she said. Laurence visited, bringing Kathe and Apple. As Kay pondered the form her diary *Primer for Combat* was to take, together over whiskeys he and Kay discussed the function of a diary as opposed to a novel. With his taste for the fragmentary, so in keeping with his peripatetic personality, Laurence preferred the immediacy of a "brief, quick record."

But as she readied *Primer for Combat* for publication, Kay Boyle did not take his advice; she fictionalized; she developed. She changed the names because "I am completely against this sort of dishing up of one's private life and loves," as if this book were not a roman à clef of her affair with Kurt Wick and the beginnings of her relationship with Joseph.

On December 7, as soon as he heard the news of the bombing of Pearl Harbor, Joseph wrote to his draft board in New York: "In case you need my service, I am ready." After Pearl Harbor, Kay Boyle gave no more lectures. America had other things on its mind than the plight of refugees in France.

Around Christmastime, Pegeen ran into Leonora Carrington in Manhattan at Peggy's housewarming party. When Carrington spoke warmly of Kay Boyle, Pegeen began to cry uncontrollably, the tears streaming down her face. "I hate thinking of you now, Kay," Pegeen wrote her stepmother, "it makes me miserable; and when I see you, which isn't often, I hardly talk to you. Kay I miss you, I miss you so much, you can't imagine." Pegeen even praised Kay's little house in Nyack, "so sweet and cozy," not "impersonal and big" like her mother's new home. Wanting desperately to stay close, Pegeen befriended Bobby. Proudly she informed Kay that the baby, Clover, had "at last accepted me as a sister. She talks to me and calls me E . . . een. I'm so pleased about that."

In England, Nina Conarain received a Christmas card signed "Laurence and Kay Vail." "I think of them all the time and wonder how it really is with them," Nina echoed the concerns of many of the couple's old friends.

At last Joseph decided to return to Nyack. But just as he was boarding the bus, he was detained by FBI agents who told him "enemy aliens" were forbidden to leave one town for another. Now Kay really became frantic. She mobilized friends to write to the U.S. Attorney in Los Angeles, and tried to enlist Archibald MacLeish, who had become Librarian of Congress. Kay was disgusted by what she considered MacLeish's ineffectuality: "he is—perhaps completely—a poet, and has no place in the world of taking decisions and doing acts." Joseph was confined for three more weeks before he was granted permission by the FBI to go to Los Angeles to make the journey East. Kay had to borrow the sixty dollars for his bus ticket.

Living in Rockland County during these early years of the war, Kay Boyle cultivated her gift for friendship. She renewed her ties with William Carlos Williams, and with Ann Watkins, and her husband, Roger Burlingame, analyzing page by page one of Burlingame's manuscripts. One day she spotted a letter in the newspaper written by one Heinz Pol on the subject of the internment camps in France. At once Kay invited Pol and his wife to dinner. Carson McCullers was a neighbor, and if McCullers at first looked askance at Kay's "hybrid ménage," they soon became friends. McCullers in turn introduced Kay to Muriel Rukeyser, who was not above telling Kay that sometimes Carson would get so drunk that she'd have to follow her into the bathroom and pull up her underpants.

Worried about Marcel Duchamp still in Europe, Kay tried to arrange his visa for America, an effort complicated by Duchamp's reluctance to come. "Marcel remains for all of us one of the symbols of what life should be," Kay wrote Charles Henri Ford in the high-minded tones she ever more frequently affected, "the absolute individual and the right to be." Soon she was accusing several people of not having done enough for Duchamp. Charles Henri Ford found this infuriating, as he told William Carlos Williams, "It seems to be stupid and presumptuous to say nothing has been done." Those who had tried to help had met with Duchamp's resistance.

Stern and judgmental, Kay would rarely admit she was wrong about anything or back down from a position, however hastily it had been taken. Instead, she defended her actions, as she even defended the recalcitrant Duchamp's refusal to accept what she called "the indignity of an immigrant's visa." When Duchamp finally arrived, Kay found him unchanged, "one of the dearest people I have ever known." Together they attended art exhibits, and Duchamp visited her often.

Thursday night became "Marcel's night" as he made his way to Westchester County when she moved there to report on the decadent life in Manhattan. Having long since stopped painting, still Marcel did not look for a job, but found a way of being supported by other people. He did advise Peggy about exhibitions at her new gallery.

"This is my purifying evening," Marcel told Kay as Kathe climbed up on his lap and touched the mole under his chin. "*Arrête! Arrête!*" he ordered then. On Wednesday nights, Duchamp visited the Sterns, Jimmy having become the art critic for *Time* magazine.

"This is my purifying evening," Duchamp told Jimmy and Tania.

Kay also found the time to help and encourage young writers, like Lorraine Catheron, whose name she used in *Primer for Combat* as Kathe's. Kay personally sent Catheron's poems to Alfred Kreymborg, who suggested that she show them to Frederick Lewis Allen at *Harper's*, who accepted one. By now Kay defined part of her responsibility as an established figure to help young and unknown writers.

By January 20, 1942, Joseph had returned. But unemployment stalked him. Bill Shirer tried to arrange for him to broadcast anti-Nazi propaganda to Germany. He did write a few political scripts for CBS radio, but mostly he tutored private students for two dollars and fifty cents or three dollars an hour. Joseph failed a medical examination for a factory job because he had a hernia from lifting rocks at the ranch. His teeth were so decayed that eight immediately had to be extracted. Finding employment was additionally difficult because of his draft status. From the start America proved to be inhospitable to this gentle, scholarly man, who lived so completely inside himself and his dreams.

Kay Boyle redoubled her efforts to write short stories for money, now with an eye toward the movies. She began to tailor her stories to fit the model—long on romanticized characters and melodrama, short on imagery, and rushing headlong to a happy ending—favored by *The Saturday Evening Post*. She continued to teach at Nyack High School; one evening sitting in the back row of her evening writing class for high school teachers were Caresse Crosby and Henry Miller. Kay and Joseph also began to drink heavily together, and George Popper was shocked by one wild ride in Ann Watkins's car while Kay and Joseph drank and the whole group searched for the Palisades Amusement Park, which turned out to be closed. Popper found it difficult to visit Kay and Joseph now because he did not drink at all.

At high school in Nyack, Bobby, now fifteen, missed Apple. One day after school, frustrated by a writing assignment, Bobby asked Kay to help her. In half an hour, Kay wrote the essay, one so full of humor, and so exquisitely written, that for the first time Bobby appreciated her mother's great abilities. It was too rare an occurrence, however, for either to be bothered by the scam. Kay received an A for that piece of work. On another occasion Kay took the time to show Kathe how to use a dictionary. This unusual circumstance of her mother taking so much interest in her was a special moment which Kathe would long cherish, no matter that Kay had always airily told the girls that "spelling doesn't matter," ensuring indifferent spelling from them all.

In April of 1942, Kay Boyle, still married to Laurence Vail, found herself once again pregnant. Loving a man meant, indubitably, bearing him children, no matter that it was wartime and they had little income. Once more she hoped for a son as she moved to Mount Vernon to be closer to Manhattan and to the Jolases, who lived nearby. Kay hung a ski poster in her new kitchen to give the visiting children a feeling of the landscape they sorely missed, and hung it alongside De Gaulle's June 18, 1940, address to the French people: "I, General de Gaulle, now in London, call upon the French officers and soldiers who are on British soil. . . ."

As summer approached, Joseph began to answer newspaper advertisements for jobs as a "camp counselor." With the help of the daughter of an English friend, a director of the Bank of England, and one of Sir George Franckenstein's friends as well, he landed a six-week stint at the Nature Friends of America camp at Midvale, New Jersey, for which he would be paid seventy-five dollars. Joseph was the swimming and hiking instructor for boys aged five to twelve. He slept in the dormitory, keeping order, and on weekends met the visiting parents. He had accepted the job subject to being called by the draft board. Indeed, a physical examination on Governors Island revealed that spots on his lung which had been detected a year earlier were gone; in July of 1942 Joseph was pronounced physically fit for service.

That summer the children were torn between Laurence and Kay. Wistful and stoical, Apple, now twelve, never mentioned Kay to the other children. In the enclave of eccentrics at Sherman, Connecticut, there were frequent parties. One Saturday evening, during one of these occasions, Apple climbed an old maple tree only to fall and break her shoulder. Then she had to sit with her face set against the pain, her arm in an improvised sling, until the party was over and Laurence would take her to the doctor in New Milford. It turned out to be a nasty injury and Apple was confined to a hospital in New York, where Kay visited her twice a week.

Kathe responded to the family trauma by becoming more tempestuous, raucous, and ebullient. She wrote her mother news of every detail of her life, even that Clover took "ages washing"; she had also learned to ask after Joseph. Kay's "Pussy Kat" was now reading *The Youngest Camel*, which she pronounced "very very nice." Her letters began: "Dear Mimi, I love you."

They had all been taught the habit of writing letters, that tradition handed down from Katherine Evans Boyle, even Pegeen. Should Peggy ever say a word against her beloved stepmother in her presence, Pegeen continued to grow angry. "Darling Kay," Pegeen's letters began. What Kay felt, Pegeen and Bobby felt, as the big girls tried still to live in emotional symbiosis with Kay Boyle. After visiting the Vail group, Bobby told Kay how sad she was that her mother had to remain in so hot a place as Mount Vernon all summer; it was "terrible" that Kay had to work so hard.

"You must be so lonely all alone in Mount Vernon, Kay," Pegeen sympathized. "I hate to think of it. You must be working *so* hard." If Kay

Boyle needed consolation, she certainly had it from this lonely girl, who added a PS: "I love you always very very much." No less than Sindbad had Pegeen long viewed Kay as the only mother she had known.

It's been a year, Pegeen lamented, since "we arrived in this huge dump." Like her father, like Apple, Kathe, and Bobby too, Pegeen hated America.

17

Babies

*My own darling went over the beginning of this month, and the
last news I had of him he was dodging robombs in London. Oh,
God, if only it would be over quickly.*

B_y 1942 Kay Boyle was one of the best-known writers in America.
The Sacramento Bee put her face at the center of its July 2 crossword
puzzle with the clue: "O. Henry Prize Winner." *Current Biography* for
1942, in a four-page article, noted that she had been compared to "artists
as dissimilar as Jean Cocteau and Turgenev, Ernest Hemingway and
D. H. Lawrence." Acknowledging that "many critics seem to feel that she
has never quite fulfilled her early promise," *Current Biography* added that
"few have denied either the fastidiously morbid power of her style . . . or
her subtleties of insight." Frances Steloff of the Gotham Book Mart requested of a group of authors and critics "The Ten Books Which Have
Most Influenced Me" and Kay responded:

> *A Hurried Man* by Emanuel Carnevali
> *The Brook Kerith* by George Moore
> *The Lake* by George Moore
> *Anna Karenina* by Tolstoy
> *Crime and Punishment* by Dostoevsky
> *The Eternal Husband* by Dostoevsky
> *The Brothers Karamazov* by Dostoevsky
> *The House of the Dead* by Dostoevsky
> *Light in August* by William Faulkner
> *Pylon* by William Faulkner

A curious omission was D. H. Lawrence, the writer who had most influenced
her early style, replete as it was with bird, beast, and flower analogues to
human emotions and with its descriptions of characters' unconscious yearn-

ings. But it would be characteristic of Kay Boyle to omit the writer whom she had most closely imitated, the better to have seemed an original herself.

If the children worried that Kay in Mount Vernon required consolation because she was alone and without Joseph, they needn't have been. Never had she worked harder, or more rapidly. She did what she called her "propaganda bit," writing broadcasts for the Office of War Information, wrote stories for *The Saturday Evening Post*, finished turning her "Armistice Diary" into the novel *Primer for Combat*, and kept up her correspondence. She urged Jay Laughlin to publish a new collection of her stories—this time with an advance because she was "pretty broke" and "working harder every minute trying to make ends meet." Nowadays, she referred to her writing as "typing." "Typing like mad," she wrote Caresse.

She pursued large-scale book reviewing not only for *The New Republic* but for *The New York Times Book Review*, the *New York Herald Tribune Book Review*, and *The Nation*. The assignments she received were usually about twenties Paris or the fall of France. In her reviews, as in her many letters to the editor, Kay Boyle's mission was to set the record straight. To *The Nation* she wrote endorsing André Schwob's exposé of Pétain. Despite our "policy of appeasement," Kay said, we "were never at any time dealing with a well-intentioned if rather decrepit French military gentleman but with a traitor."

These reviews were passionate, personal, uncompromising, and hard-hitting. She knew of what she spoke, and came either to praise or to blame—with considerable emotion. She did give an evenhanded review to Elliot Paul's *The Last Time I Saw Paris*. Kay takes Paul to task for the superficiality of his description of the French people: "he has managed to serve them only as clever make-up man, and their true substance has nowhere been set down." Warming to her attack, she writes: "we become acquainted with sixty or more French women and men in the pages of this book, and they are all very droll and recognizably 'froggy' figures, rigged out, it might be, for the Hollywood conception of a typical little-street-in-Paris scene. They are so picturesque and so quaint that they end by being grotesque." Yet she praises Paul for his "great capacity for responding with warmth to the needs of mankind." As early as 1942 Kay Boyle rejected the notion of mythologizing twenties Paris. So she notes that Paul, "to his everlasting credit," refrains from including "an anecdote about Joyce, Gertrude Stein, Picasso, or Ernest Hemingway." Her private opinion was that it was "the worst book ever written about France," as she wrote McAlmon. But in the end she did not give it "the filthiest review" which she bragged to McAlmon she would.

If she praised Vladimir Pozner's novel of the fall of France, *The Edge of the Sword*, for bearing "unmistakeably" the "exciting accents of truth," she wrote scathingly of its sequel, *First Harvest*, which she found a "heedless little volume." Nor did Kay Boyle reserve her respect for the well known. She was quick to pay homage to all writers who believed in something beyond themselves. For its depth of vision, she praised *A French Officer's Diary* by D. Barlone, a major in the Free French forces. His, she wrote, was a story of "courage, of unshaken loyalty, of stubborn hope." She preferred Dr. Charles Odic's *Stepchildren of France*, an eyewitness account of what happened to the Jews in France, to "the cautious subtleties of Gide." With the clandestinely printed pseudonymous pamphlet about a supposedly artistic-minded German officer billeted in 1941 in a French château, *The Silence of the Sea*, however, she fell short; she foundered before a work in which the point of view was not obvious and direct, but subtle and satiric. (The pseudonymous author, "Vercors," turned out to be a resistance leader satirizing the hypocrisy by which "sensitive" Germans justified the occupation of France, and by 1948 *The Silence of the Sea* had sold more than a million copies in seventeen languages.)

She was on safer ground with *The Truth About De Gaulle*, where she could praise one of the "uncompromising patriots of our time," while chastising the Americans living in a country "founded on the principles of liberty" who required a book to perceive our own principles "translated into concrete terms before we can acknowledge their veracity." At such times an intolerance crept into her tone, that hauteur she had cultivated since her adolescence. That same censorious spirit appeared in her denunciation of Jean Malaquais's *War Diary*; Malaquais was "not a Frenchman in any sense of the word," as his diary was a mere "complaint of the frustrated and assaulted individual." Activism in the service of an ideal had become Kay Boyle's credo. In her review of *War Diary*, she compared Malaquais unfavorably not only with her old friend Alexander Berkman but with a painter named Jean Hélion, who had written a book called *They Shall Not Have Me*. Indeed, no one would have known that Hélion, an unlikely name for her to have invoked, was the much older man whom Laurence would persuade to marry a now wild, distraught, and unhappy Pegeen.

As she had always done, Kay reviewed friends like the German poet Walter Mehring. Even in her review of Nabokov's *The Real Life of Sebastian Knight*, published by New Directions, she focused more on New Directions and on James Laughlin's "Note" than on the book itself, so that *The New Republic* had to cut most of it. Personal and arbitrary, in her review of a novel called *Victory Was Slain*, she took umbrage at the author's point of view: "The Austrian aristocracy is libelously and ludicrously represented by a drooling half-wit and a Hollywood conception of a *Herr Exzellenz*." She wrote as if she were responding to a personal attack, but without, of course, informing the reader that her excessive language stemmed more from a defense of Joseph than from the flaws of the book in question.

If once Kay Boyle had counted herself among the modernists, her preference now veered to the once-despised social realism. As in her life she shunned self-examination and introspection, so in her literary taste she now preferred the socially grounded to the psychological. She wrote a paean to Upton Sinclair, whom she compared with H. G. Wells, praising both for "their attack on popular prejudice and the retarded mind." She was particularly hard on women writers, producing a meanspirited attack on Elizabeth Bowen for creating "imaginary people" and for failing to "absorb virility from the class whose problem she defines."

It was as if she had seized the tail end of the proletcult, which she had for so long shunned. Suddenly now, she was attacking Bowen for offering the "proud bitter lesson—that only the unrecorded, unuttered, wholly clandestine communion with one's own ego is the answer offered by the years." At the very moment when the anguish of her fractured family would seem to require self-examination and attention to the suffering and confusion of her children, Kay assumed the stance that only by one's action in the world is one revealed. Focus on the self represented a denial of truth, justice, and salvation. Conveniently, the world was at war: who then could insist on the luxury of looking inward?

In August of 1942, Joseph was drafted. His farewell party was hosted by Joan Detweiler in New Rochelle. "Just a simple party with a glass of punch and a slice of cake, and a few people in," Kay urged Caresse. "PLEASE do come."

Joseph was sent first to Camp Upton in New York. But he had already through friends contacted the National Ski Patrol and requested that he be assigned to the ski troops. Indeed, he was almost immediately placed with the 87th Mountain Infantry Regiment, then stationed at Fort Lewis, in Washington State on Mount Rainier. From there he was transferred to Camp Hale in Colorado, where he did his basic training, and then was assigned to instruct the troops for winter warfare. Before long Kay was "wild" to join him.

But she was six months pregnant now, and she had to stay home to finish more stories and the "damnable" serial she had undertaken for *The Saturday Evening Post*. For the second time she would bear a child in the absence of its father to whom she was not married. When Apple and Kathe visited now, Kay devoted herself to telling them what to do, how to become industrious, and she always had to be right. "Always coming out smelling like a rose," Apple would say after one of her visits. If Laurence increasingly seemed helpless and dependent, even now that he was more deeply involved with Jeannie Connolly, Kay was cold and perfect, clean, angelic, justified in whatever she did, and never to be challenged. As Joseph worshipped her, so must her children.

Primer for Combat was published by Simon & Schuster on November 2, dedicated to Ann Watkins and Roger Burlingame. The book jacket was a patriotic red, white, and blue; on the back cover Kay Boyle urged her readers to buy War Bonds: "it is now a matter of the survival of ourselves as individuals, and of the survival of that freedom, honor, and human dignity which can be lost if we refuse to recognize our country's needs."

At once *Primer for Combat* sold 2,500 copies, which cheered Ka if this was modest by the standards of the time. Descriptive no, excerpts appeared in *Harper's Bazaar* ("The Eternal Train") and *moiselle* ("The Statue's Face"), while Kay also mined from its pages se . eral short stories, presented as original works: not only the prize-winning "Defeat" and "Men" but "They Weren't Going to Die," "This They Carried with Them," and "T'en Fais Pas." *The things they carried?*

The reviews were more respectful than for any of Kay's other novels, not only because the style was more direct and less mannered but also because she had become so familiar a figure on the American literary landscape. Marianne Hauser in *The New York Times* was dazzled by Kay's "incisive portrait of France after her defeat," illuminated "from a hundred different angles." In *The Atlantic*, Raoul de Roussy de Sales wrote that "nothing better has been written on France since the Germans got there." Perceptively, he did wonder why "exceptional women" like Phyl (Kay) and Corinne (Hélène Wick) "waste so much love over this ineffectual hero . . . whose outstanding feature seems to be his remarkable golden hair." So indeed had Laurence, Bobby, Jimmy Stern, and many others wondered. When Josephine Herbst in the *Sun* praised *Primer for Combat*, and Kay Boyle's themes of "the cold determined need to participate" and "this urge to share the common fate," Kay Boyle wrote to her appreciatively.

Primer for Combat proved to be an unequivocal success for Kay Boyle. But at her New York book party she revealed herself to be no more kindly to fellow women writers in person than in print. Anaïs Nin found her as coolly impersonal as she had been in Europe: "again the bird profile, words one cannot remember, no human expression of recognition." Again Kay Boyle made Anaïs Nin feel "anonymous."

"I want a son so badly," Kay said as she awaited the birth of her fifth child. "It *can't* be another girl." Robert McAlmon was ordered to "pray for a boy." Her son, Kay this time decided, would be named Carson, after her new friend Carson McCullers; Kay had chosen her to be the child's godmother. "Think of it!" McCullers exclaimed in admiration of the indefatigable Kay working on another book, writing her many letters, even as the baby was due over the weekend.

In the hospital Kay persisted in her correspondence, writing a note of sympathy to Peggy Guggenheim's sister Hazel, whose husband had died. When Hazel called to thank her, Peggy became infuriated, and doubly so when Hazel pronounced Kay Boyle "*so* nice."

"That's a long-distance call," Peggy told her sister. "Please pay me back!"

Faith Carson Franckenstein was born at Doctors Hospital on East End Avenue on December 3, 1942. Kay and Joseph had decided to call their new little girl Fay, a combination of Kay and Franckenstein. But the Countess Esterházy from Austria managed to make known her objection; no saint had ever been named Fay. Since this child was to be baptized in the Catholic Church, she must bear a saint's name. "Felicitas," suggested the Countess, and so the child was named.

"Incredible as it may seem," Kay told Jay Laughlin, "I've produced another girl." But bearing the child of a man she loved, Kay Boyle was not nearly so disappointed at having another daughter as she had been three years earlier when Clover was born. "I'm counting on her," Kay said graciously, "as my most gentle and devoted daughter." Faith Carson, as she came to be known, was indeed tiny and "doe-like," as Kay reported, "sort of like a small, trusting hand placed in one's own forever." It was as lovely a statement of a new mother as one could imagine, if manifesting little prescience of the strong, forceful woman Faith Carson would become. With even less prescience would Kay award Faith her special name. This most beautiful of her daughters would be called for years "Mousie." Carson McCullers had just suffered the loss of a woman she loved named Annemarie. "I want you to let me love you always," she told Kay Boyle, seeing a "connection between Fay Carson and Annemarie."

That Christmas of 1942, despite the presence of a new baby and her frenetic writing schedule, Kay Boyle had a special present for her oldest child. Earlier she had arranged for Bobby to do some translating for Caresse. Then, as Katherine Evans Boyle had sent Kay's own childish poems to friends and neighbors, Kay sent one of Bobby's to Alfred Kreymborg with a note: "I think it very beautiful."

Now, for Bobby's special Christmas present, Kay saw to it that one hundred copies of *Four Poems* by Sharon Vail be printed by Anaïs Nin's Gemor Press in New York. The heavy green paper cover with its red lettering was impressive; the dedicatory poem, not surprisingly, was "to Mama": "one, the only one, / One and all." One of the poems bore homage to the only father Bobby had ever known: "Papa, I love you."

Scarcely recovered from childbirth, Kay planned to take baby Faith and Clover to Colorado to visit Joseph. From Colorado, she would move on to Reno, where she would settle for the six weeks required for her to gain a divorce from Laurence. In February, Joseph would be eligible for a furlough and they would be married. As her wedding present, Jay Laughlin offered Kay a two-week vacation at his ski lodge in Utah. Kay said she might as well get some skiing in before returning East.

Kay wanted Laurence, who could so easily afford it, to pay for her trip to Nevada. But Laurence had not forgiven her; certainly he would not finance a divorce he opposed. Kay had to wait for a thousand-dollar advance from *The Saturday Evening Post* for her serial about France, which she was calling *Avalanche*. Spitefully, Kay talked about how much she disapproved of Laurence's apparent indifference to the war, which stood in such sharp contrast to Joseph's heroism. Self-righteously, she told people Laurence would be much happier if he were involved, like her friend Bessie Breuer's husband, Henry Varnum Poor, who had been appointed by the

War Department to cover the Alaskan front as an artist-correspondent. "I should think Laurence would *want* to," Kay insisted, "not from any high falutin' ideas of patriotism . . . but because it's a thing that's going on and it can't very well be ignored." Clearly she had chosen the superior man. Clearly the breaking up of the Vail family had been justified.

January of 1943 found Kay already in Reno. The autobiographical aspects of *Primer for Combat* had been obvious to everyone who knew her, but many people thought Kay was already married to "my Sepp," the father of her child. Rather than admit that she had borne the child out of wedlock, Kay announced she was heading for Hollywood, and even asked Bob Brown to mail some of her letters from Los Angeles so that the postmarks would confirm her fabrication. In Reno, Kay's lawyer was relieved that Faith had been registered under Joseph's name, making adoption proceedings unnecessary. Kay's marriage to Joseph would make the baby "fully legitimate."

Kay's long absence hurt Bobby most, as her daughter in a letter obsequiously thanked her mother for the "love and confidence in me which I hope I shall never have occasion to lose." Bobby wrote as if she did not believe she was loved unconditionally for herself, but must ever prove herself worthy, must ever reassure her mother that she worshipped her: "I don't think many people have such mothers as you and I don't think many children love their mothers as I do," Bobby pleaded. Bobby even apologized for writing so often, as if she were the unworthy suitor, and her mother higher, better, and forever unattainable, the "marvellous brilliant lady reading this who takes such wonderful, wonderful interest in me and to whom I love telling all my stupid thoughts."

Kay left Bobby in Westchester with her mother, but Katherine Evans Boyle took no interest in her granddaughter. She didn't even bother to sit down to meals with Bobby, but closed her door, as so often she had done in Puss's household. It was Maria Jolas who served as Bobby's surrogate mother in Kay's absence, while Katherine complained about all she had to do, creating chaos in her wake. Kay was irritated by her mother, who, fully capable, yet increasingly self-pitying, did nothing to help her.

Still, Kay did not break the pattern of confiding all her troubles and complaints in her mother. Predictably, Katherine replied with an endorsement of whatever her younger daughter did: "I'm glad you're coming out on top of everything," Katherine wrote. "You always do." Yet this time the mother's words further infuriated the daughter. Burdened by her responsibilities, albeit ones she had freely chosen, she resented her mother's self-centeredness. Yes, Kay thought, she managed, but only "by typing until three in the morning and looking fifty years old!" Her peace of mind did not improve when she received an unpleasant letter from Laurence containing his lawyer's bill for three hundred dollars, which he asked Kay "please to pay." Down to her last hundred dollars, Kay borrowed the money from Ann Watkins.

In Reno, Kay Boyle set herself the goal of writing eight pages of *Avalanche* a day, no matter what. Grinding out her serial, she said she couldn't stop work "for an instant." She wrote so rapidly that at times she lost track of the plot. By February 7, she had written fifty-two thousand words with twelve thousand to go. Only when Clover and baby Faith fell ill at the same time did her productivity fall from eight to four pages a day. And always she was exacting. At one of the hotels where she stopped during the war, she proudly would recount, one of the chambermaids remarked, "It's such a relief to have you here, because most women leave piles of dirty diapers in the corridor."

Although Kay Boyle was later to tell interviewers she had servants to help her only in Europe, in fact during the war years the children were taken care of by others. In Reno she had "my biddy," a woman she called "strange" and "a mental case" whose presence nonetheless allowed her to work ten hours a day. Kay made Faith's formula and took Clover to school in the morning. There her duties ended.

Kay's divorce from Laurence Vail was granted on February 19, 1943, her forty-first birthday. The grounds were "extreme cruelty," the property settlement sealed. At nine-thirty in the morning, Kay received her divorce; by seven in the evening she and the children were on a train bound for Salt Lake City. There, at the Newhouse Hotel, Joseph saw his baby daughter for the first time. In Salt Lake City, with a marriage license on which she listed her age as forty, Kay Boyle at last married her baron, who was now thirty-two years old.

It was on the day of her marriage to Joseph Franckenstein that the FBI began its long pursuit of Kay Boyle. FBI agents suddenly materialized to interview her about her visit to Rapallo to see Ezra Pound in 1938. Someone in New York had told them she had had an affair with the notorious Pound, now broadcasting for Mussolini, before World War I! That she was twelve years old in 1914 did not occur to the FBI agent who added this piece of "information" to her file.

There was a honeymoon at Jay Laughlin's Alta, Utah, ski lodge, as planned. "She's as quiet as a mouse," Kay reported of her newest daughter. "She has the loveliest nature of any child I ever knew." Whether it was hubris, whether it was that she could not separate herself from the view that full womanhood meant bearing children, whether it was a means of binding her much younger husband more closely to her, or simply that bearing children was one more act of fulfillment of her bountiful creativity, or out of some darkly secret rebellion against Katherine's early dreams for her writer daughter, Kay Boyle now did nothing to prevent becoming pregnant again.

Joseph, for his part, was increasingly worried because his American citizenship had repeatedly been delayed. One day, after he had returned to Camp Hale, some federal agents handed him a German document to read aloud, which Joseph began to do, only to discover that he was reading the oath of allegiance to the Führer.

"What the hell is this?" Joseph shouted angrily. Ordinarily a mild man, he could manifest considerable temper when provoked.

"It was to see if you could read German easily," Joseph was told. He replied that he had his Ph.D.

In April of 1943, Private First Class Joseph Maria Franckenstein finally became an American citizen. Kay Boyle began a long poem called *American Citizen: Naturalized in Leadville, Colorado*, which Simon & Schuster was to publish in book form in 1944 with a curious dedication to Carson McCullers: "her husband, like mine, is serving overseas." At the time the poem was published, not only were Carson and her husband, Reeves, divorced, but at no time during their marriage had Reeves served overseas. Kay, however, could always draw others into her mythology, and why not her closest friend, who was something of a legend herself? Indeed, the speaker in the poem addresses her refrain to a Carson, who, like herself, is waiting out the war in the absence of the man she loves: "Carson, the days are long this year."

Rhetorical, prosaic, poetry of statement, *American Citizen* pays that form of homage to Joseph which Ernest Walsh had suggested was her role:

> *He has done what the men of Europe have done,*
> *Done it quietly as the drawing of breath, done it waltzing and cursing,*
> *Done it in chain gangs, done it laughing out loud,*
> *Done it crying when the cold of the season exacted*
> *That homage be paid it . . .*

For the women left behind, life demanded bravery: "Carson, turn your coat collar up, throw the cigarette / from your hand / and dance with me," Kay implores. Women must prove themselves worthy of men like Joseph, who "crossed my own mountains into others because / It was asked of me." The real-life Carson indeed marveled. "Kay," she wrote, "you have more life and vigor and courage in you than anyone I know . . . I try to take courage and patience from the knowledge that you are in this world."

Kay returned home briefly, to take Katherine and Bobby back out West with her. At Grand Central Station, Katherine, lighting a cigarette, set her veil on fire. The flames shot upward, turning the white roses on her hat brown. Finally the hat was snatched from her head, and Gene Jolas, who had come to see them off, stamped out the fire. Baby Fay, as Kay still called her, screamed at the top of her lungs. Passing through Chicago, Kay picked up her aunt Nina Allender, who joined the group.

They stopped in Colorado at the Brown Palace Hotel in Denver, where Kay could be near Joseph. Writing ever more rapidly, hastily, Kay continued to spurn birth control and any concern about the emotional, financial, or health risks childbirth at her age might incur. Now she was pregnant *again*, in quest of the son who had eluded her since 1927.

Vomiting, suffering from diarrhea, Kay was annoyed that Katherine offered so little assistance. Her mother had promised to "take charge." Instead she went off sightseeing with her sister Nina. Kay was bitterly disappointed in Katherine during these claustrophobic months in hotel rooms. Katherine Evans Boyle, who had endured the philistinism of her father-in-law and her husband to nurture Kay's every talent, had aged into a self-indulgent, distant woman who seemed to believe that Kay was ungrateful for all she had done for her. On the day Kay completed *Avalanche*, Katherine took to her bed with one of her convenient colds.

"Mother has been incredibly selfish—increasingly so, I feel," Kay wrote Jo. Where once Katherine had seemed a paragon with her letter writing, now Kay was disgusted that her mother did "*nothing* but write cards or letters *all* day." When Kay had an opportunity to eat dinner with Joseph at camp, Katherine refused to cook for the baby, who was ill with a temperature. Kay had to delay her departure to arrange lunch for Bobby and Clover and her mother, feed the baby, and then wash the dishes. All this, Kay sarcastically reported to her sister, so that Katherine could "write to Julia about the church's architecture or the flowers on the altar."

When Katherine's old friend, Grace Flandrau, who had contributed to *365 Days*, visited, Katherine took out a photograph of her mother, Eva Evans.

"Is Kay anything like her?" Grace asked.

At such a suggestion, Katherine was shocked.

"Oh, no!" she protested. "Mother and I have the same natures—sweet and gentle and self-sacrificing. Jo and Kay are just the opposite—they're the *hard* members of the family."

"I never heard such maudlin self-worship!" Kay replied tartly. Bobby burst out laughing.

In May, Joseph was transferred from Camp Hale to Fort Ord in California, to participate in preparations for retaking the Japanese-occupied Aleutian Islands. Kay followed, children in tow, sharing a house in Carmel for a while with another army wife. She wrote at the kitchen table. She closed herself into a room. Spotting the seals sunning themselves on the rocks, she invented stories of Japanese spies swimming ashore. But always she worked. Sometimes there was a knock at the door, and there was Joseph, whose visits could never be wholly predicted.

On August 5, Joseph shipped out for Kiska in the Aleutians, although by the time he landed the Japanese had gone. In the Aleutian theater, with Henry Moscow of the *New York Post*, he edited the regiment's daily newspaper, which he named *The Rucksack*. The other men, who had at first been suspicious because he was a refugee, found in his happiness their own loneliness relieved. Joseph also turned out to be a great raconteur, recounting stories of how he was busted from the rank of corporal when he served with the British and how he had thrown a group of Nazis out of an Austrian beer hall.

In a letter written to Kay in June of 1944, Burton Pierce, one of Joseph's army buddies who came to "admire and respect him and to want his companionship," brought to life Joseph Franckenstein among the men on the lonely Aleutian Islands:

> *One night Joe and Peter and Stan Feld and I sat in a tent out of the rain and wind playing rummy by candlelight. Joe was in excellent spirits with a force to his happiness that infected all of us. Suddenly he burst into an operatic song. I don't know the song. I don't know opera. I don't know the language of it. But it was wonderful for the man in it. It didn't need the language nor a sense of the culture of the song's people nor the song's story. The manner by which the man sang the song said it all, told the great compassion the man had for living, his faith in being alive and in being able to break into this strong song.*
>
> *Joe went from one song to the next and I knew none of them but forgot about being ignorant. I have never seen a face such as his then, so full of feeling, joy, and raw strength—happy in this moment, with the moment, and beautiful with it.*
>
> *Then he broke off and laughed, an excited warm strong laughter.*

Now back in New York, Kay settled at the Sevilla, an apartment-hotel. Louise Dahl-Wolfe photographed mother and children at table. Bobby is still dressed as the "Tyrolean Gretchen" Laurence had dubbed her. In a striped apron, Kay holds baby Faith Carson, feeding her from a spoon, while seated around the table are impeccably dressed Clover, Kathe, and Apple observing the mugs of milk and the basket of bread which they had been cautioned not to touch. The photograph was published in the November 1943 *Harper's Bazaar*, the image of the author as, they wrote, "talented mother." Later, Kay dressed the children in cowboy hats and cowboy shirts and was again photographed amid a crowd of clean, beautiful, happy children.

In fact, the summer of 1943 had been another troubled time for the children. Apple was afraid to go down to Candlewood Lake to swim for fear she might embarrass Peggy Guggenheim lying naked, sunbathing. Laurence embarrassed her too. Laurence told his daughters that both Peggy and Kay had left him because he had a small penis. Still they took baths together.

Pegeen, now seventeen, was not with them, but in Acapulco. Her first adventure was being picked up by Errol Flynn and spending time with him aboard his yacht docked in Acapulco Bay. Then she fell in love with one of the Acapulco divers, going so far as to move in with him and his family in their dirt-floor hut. Pegeen refused to come home, announcing that she planned to marry her Mexican diver. Laurence, alarmed, hurried down to Mexico to escort a daughter suffering from a venereal disease back to America, with Pegeen pleading all the while that she wanted only to go back to Acapulco and get married.

Back at Camp Hale, Joseph applied to the psychological warfare combat unit of the Office of Strategic Services (OSS). "I am willing and eager to accept any mission, no matter how hazardous," he wrote.

In October, the first installment of Kay's wartime serial, *Avalanche*, was published in *The Saturday Evening Post*, along with an essay called "World Harmony," in which she discovered a silver lining in the war's "mixing up of people," Americans and Europeans, and so creating a vast public ("such as yours," she added, praising the hand that fed her). She confided that three of her daughters attended the Lycée Français in New York and that she and her husband, "Joseph von Franckenstein"—no matter that Joseph had renounced his title in becoming an American citizen—would run a "serious ranch" after the war. Her husband sang Mozart, she said, claiming that "it is far better to sing than to sit around talking about one another, and it makes one look far younger." Looking younger was increasingly a concern for Kay Boyle, now in her forties with a younger husband.

That November of 1943 Kay fulfilled her dream; at last she bore a son. He was baptized Jan Sanin, and alas, he was not a healthy baby. Jan, first called Johnny, then Ian, had a windpipe which didn't open completely and he could not swallow. At once he was placed in an incubator. Kay was beside herself. Finally the doctors devised a means of opening his esophagus and the baby could take sustenance. This baby was so skinny and ugly, like a bat, that Kay nicknamed him "the bat" or "batsy," which later became "Boostie."

By January of 1944 Kay was living at 117 West Fifty-eighth Street with Clover, Bobby, Faith, and baby Boostie, who remained chronically ill. The biographical note for a radio appearance called her the "mother of several children and considered by her friends to be a curious mixture of advance guard [sic] intellectual and patient homebody." Busy as she was, Kay took the time to write a letter to her stepdaughter, Pegeen, who had taken a job as a body model for artists. Kay suggested that she devise a plan for her independence. If in the raising of her own children Kay Boyle had never stressed the practical need for them to earn their own livings, she now, ironically, advised the young heiress to get some "training." Pegeen should try drama school or commercial school.

"Making yourself free financially is the very first step in happiness and pride," Kay wrote the bewildered young woman, revealing that even if she might never formally ally herself with women's groups and although she would never apply the term to herself, she was a feminist in her understanding of how crucial it was for a woman to be economically independent. "You have exactly one life to lead," Kay wrote her stepdaughter, "and it is within your power and yours alone to decide to lead it well."

The letter was compassionate, intelligent, and gentle, but it was too little and too late. Within months, Pegeen went to live with the painter Jean Hélion, a married man twice her age; on August 18, 1944, Pegeen turned nineteen. Kay's attentions, so limited since her writing came first, had to be divided among Apple, Kathe, Bobby, Clover, Mousie, and Boostie. There was neither time nor energy for Pegeen.

Without informing Joseph of Ian's fragile health, lest he object, Kay decided to rejoin him in Colorado, where he remained a private first class at Camp Hale. Her trip to Leadville was paid for by Carson McCullers, who had received, unexpectedly, a five-hundred-dollar royalty check from Sweden. The entire journey was a nightmare, with Ian vomiting and coughing all the way. The train from Denver did not stop at Leadville. They were put off in a raging blizzard at a siding at six in the evening with all their luggage. The wind blew in gales. Nothing could be seen for miles but fields of snow. Wrapped in his blue bunting, Ian coughed as they waded through snowdrifts to a bus stop. Trudging along, Mousie lost one of her shoes, which disappeared in the rapidly falling snow.

A five-mile bus trip to Leadville followed. It was a Sunday and the bus was filled with soldiers and Wacs, two of whom, Kay disapprovingly observed, were hideously drunk, "the most revolting sight I have ever seen." But Kay Boyle was never one to make allowances for the vagaries of women.

By the time they arrived at the Hotel Vendome in Leadville, Ian had a temperature of 102 degrees. Kay started a steam kettle in the hotel room and telephoned the doctor in New York. After Ian recovered, Kay found a tinsmith in Leadville who lent her his scales so that she could weigh this dangerously thin baby regularly.

Every night it snowed in Leadville, but no hardship seemed too great for Kay, who wanted to be near her young husband. She washed the baby's diapers in the sink and dried them on the radiator, irritated, as always, by the slowness of her servant, this time a Mrs. Ruminoff. Meanwhile she had her share of adventures: a drunk pursued her amorously; another man in a Stetson sat down at her table in the restaurant to renew their acquaintance, which, he told her, "had begun at the Red Wing," a bordello opposite the Brown Palace Hotel in Denver.

As the certainty of Joseph's being sent overseas loomed, he managed to spend every night with his wife at the Hotel Vendome. Some weekends he arrived in time for Saturday lunch, remaining until Monday morning. Ian slept soundly in bed with his parents. On weekday mornings Joseph rose at six to depart as Kay awakened the baby for his feeding.

These desperately snatched wartime visits became the precious apogee of their relationship. In the army, Joseph was proving himself, if not yet by rank, then by example, to be a leader of men. His confidence in his manhood during these years nourished Kay's respect for him, as they nurtured their passion free of the tedium of routine domestic settings.

For the third time in three years, with Ian scarcely six months old,

Kay Boyle became pregnant. It was now as if, completing one book and moving immediately on to the next, so she kept on bearing children. The bibliography grew as did the family. She was fulfilling an image of herself as a woman surrounded by a crowd of beautiful, creative, well-behaved children, reflections of her own exceptional self. Always there must be a baby. Unconsciously too Kay Boyle had discovered the one acceptable means of sabotaging Katherine's ambition for her, which had been burnt into her psyche in childhood. It was a device she seemed indeed compelled to adopt as long as her health permitted.

As Kay went West so frequently in the early forties, her children suffered increasingly. Spending her seventeenth birthday in the absence of her mother, Bobby combated depression. Apple reported severe headaches, and had become self-deprecating, as if she didn't deserve the attention she craved. "I suppose you are too busy to write," Apple wrote her mother. During those winters of 1943 and 1944 Kay sent many gifts, from Indian tents and moccasins to bracelets, feathers, and swans. "I wish I could hear your voice," Apple replied. "I would not mind being your husband for the rest of my life." Kathe had become maddeningly out of control; "fiendish," Bobby called her. She too tried to remind her mother of the life they had once known together. On one of her letters was a circle, Diane's "*museau.*" "Diane just kissed you," Kathe wrote imploringly.

When Kay Boyle filed her income-tax return for 1943, she was able to list her income at a healthy $26,761.67, with royalties from *Avalanche* at $9,357.95. Among her dependents she listed her husband, Pvt. Joe Franckenstein. She was ambitious for her young husband, however, and was distressed when Joseph was denied special privileges he had been promised. Joseph had been one of an "especially picked group which was returned from Kiska," Kay wrote Jay Laughlin in March, "a couple of months before the others to form the Mountain Training Group. As you doubtless know, they had all kinds of special privileges, were to get ratings, and were all very pleased with themselves." Rumor had it as well that this Mountain Training Group would be kept in America to train further regiments. Then, in the middle of March of 1944, Kay learned that the Mountain Training Group "would no longer exist in its present form, but would be combined with the 10th Reconnaissance."

Kay lamented. "Joseph is so perfect for that kind of work," she said. Instead he was "put as radioman in the 3rd Battalion Headquarters of the 87th," scheduled for overseas duty in April. Ambitious always for her husband, Kay justified herself: "to have him just an infantryman going up a beach somewhere instead of doing something he is fitted for seems practically too much." In preparation, Joseph's battalion went off on maneuvers for three to five weeks. Uncertain of whether to remain in Leadville, Kay returned to New York.

One night in May of 1944, almost immediately upon her return East, Kay suddenly discovered that she was bleeding, bleeding so profusely, so quickly that she feared for her life. She had ignored the warning of doctors after Clover's birth that, should she want any more children, corrective surgery was necessary. With her usual hubris, she had gone on to have two more, and had become pregnant with a third.

Now at one in the morning, unable to stop the bleeding, and alone with the children, Kay raced to telephone the one person she felt she could turn to. Although he had not forgiven her, and never would, Laurence came to her rescue. Calmly he told her to elevate her feet up onto the baby carriage. Then he rushed to her apartment.

Finally the ambulance arrived. Seeing that much blood, the drivers at once lined the stretcher with newspapers. By the time they reached the street, the newspapers were heavily soaked through with blood. And even as she was being carried to the hospital, Kay called out instructions about how Ian, sick again, and Mousie were to be taken care of.

The baby who would have been Kay Boyle's seventh child was gone. She was forty-two years old and was firmly warned by her doctor that there should be no more children. All the while Kay was certain that her doctor, Hans Lehfeldt, was in love with her. Too weak this time to carry on her correspondence, from her hospital bed Kay dictated her daily stream of letters to Jay Laughlin and others, which she requested be typed at Simon & Schuster.

Joseph almost failed in his effort to be accepted by the OSS for espionage work. When the FBI investigated him for intelligence clearance, one "M-3" vetoed him on moral grounds: "Subject is morally weak in character, as he lived in adultery and had a child prior to his marriage." This anonymous source was also offended by the fact that Joseph was "not averse to accepting money for his support from women without making a genuine effort to consider the same as loans and attempting to liquidate his obligations." It was from Mrs. Vail, from Kay, from Bessie Breuer, and even indirectly from Peggy that he had accepted such support.

But there were many positive recommendations, testifying to Joseph's "personality, his dignity, his absolutely flawless knowledge of past and present history, and the directness of his approach to every subject." The OSS accepted Joseph, who after ten weeks of training in Washington, was transferred to England, where he called on Kay's old friend English journalist Nina Conarain, with whom she and Laurence had worked on *365 Days*.

He looks just like Kay, Nina thought. A look of Kay seemed to come over his face every now and then. Sunburned from his outdoor training, Joseph was grateful for the gin he had missed, Nina wrote Kay, and at one point he "burst into the French Sailors' songs of the Maquis" he had heard at Maria Jolas's Second Avenue canteen, Le Marseillais. Proudly he produced photographs of Mousie and Boostie. "He's the most comfortable understanding person," Nina reported to Kay. "You don't have to explain a thing to him—he just knows; and he laughs at the same kind of things you and I laugh at." With his weather-beaten look, Joseph didn't even seem to be younger than his wife, but ideally matched with her.

Kay moved to 124 East Seventy-fourth Street, where she entertained friends, like Natalia Murray, who marveled at how serene she was, working at the kitchen table while children swarmed restlessly about. Kay read García Lorca that summer, and Rimbaud, and was told by an old friend named Bill March, who had analyzed her handwriting, that she had "moral courage to a degree . . . but physical courage to a much greater extent." In retelling the story of their afternoon together, Kay Boyle stressed that she was much more interested in the fact that that was the day Boostie pushed his mother's arms away and took his first three or four tottering steps.

That spring of 1944 Carson McCullers brought a German refugee to one of Kay's dinner parties, a man she introduced as "Mr. Kantor," a news monitor on the German desk of CBS in charge of listening in on foreign broadcasts. Luise Rainer, the actress, was there, as well as the Heinz Pols. A chill at once descended on the evening when Kantor and Pol were introduced.

At dinner, Kantor denounced Arthur Koestler, with whom he had been in a concentration camp in France. Koestler had a private room and special favors because he denounced German Communists to the French authorities, Kantor said.

After dinner, Pol took Kay aside. He had known Kantor in an internment camp in France in 1939 and 1940, where Kantor had been exposed as a Communist Party operative attempting to influence young French writers. Might not he have the same assignment in America? Pol suggested that Kay warn Carson McCullers. "Don't make too much of it because it will reflect on me," Pol nervously cautioned Kay Boyle. "But I think she should be warned."

In the morning, Kay telephoned Carson. When she would not name her source, however, Carson became indignant. When Kay finally named Pol, Carson promised not to tell "Mr. Kantorovich," as she called him. Then she did. At once Kantorovich called Pol and accused him of slander. (In 1946 Kantorovich surfaced in East Berlin, working for the propaganda ministry. Nor would this be the last Kay Boyle was to hear of the incident.)

Kitty Cannell, whom she had first met as Harold Loeb's mistress, Kay decided, was "a worse bitch than any of us imagined." In response to Cannell's "Goebbels-inspired" article in the *Reader's Digest*, called "France Without Law," Kay authored a letter of protest, which was signed by Mary Reynolds, Janet Flanner, Solita Solano, and Elsa Maxwell and was printed in September. Kay accused Cannell of speaking on the Vichy radio and of writing her Paris fashion articles for *The New York Times* from Paris with the city under German rule. To Cannell's charge that "the moral fiber of the French people has crumbled," Kay angrily retorted that "the moral fabric of Miss Cannell has crumbled." Anyone who did not recognize that France was "a fallen but undaunted country" had to be a collaborationist.

That summer too Kay heard from the Dayang Muda of Sarawak, waiting out the war in Bombay. She offered Kay fifty pounds to rewrite a book Kay described as being "about the gremlins" which a boyfriend had written. Archie was now in a sanitarium in Scotland. Kay said she tore up the letter.

In 1944 Jacqueline Ventadour returned to France to join the resistance. Kay was invited to a reception at the Waldorf in honor of "Le Général de Gaulle," "Président" of the "République Française." The essays she published, "Vocabulary of Courage" in *Harper's Bazaar* and "Battle of the Sequins" in *The Nation*, were about what it felt like to be a wartime wife left behind to wait. In "Battle of the Sequins," surreal department-store mirrors reflect not the women haggling for blouses with sequins, but the fighting women in Russia, in England, and in the Maquis.

While Kay Boyle did whatever she could for the war effort, Peggy wrote her memoirs, *Confessions of an Art Addict*, as did Laurence, who in his *Here Goes* named Kay "Daze O'Connor," and Peggy, anti-Semitically, "Pigeon Peddleheim." With the children, Laurence pored over photographs of Les Six Enfants and promised that after the war they would return to Mégève. Laurence imagined himself finding Mégève lonely. Jeannie, with her lack of vitality and her laziness, was the opposite of Kay; she was so indolent that once she had been in Mégève and had a letter of introduction to Kay and Laurence, yet never did anything about it. Laurence wondered whether Jeannie might return to France with him.

Laurence thought they might start by sharing a house in Amagansett that summer of 1944. Then came the incident that Laurence was never to forget and that would henceforward be known as "Laurence's tragedy."

One day the sea was heavy and turbulent. But obstreperous Kathe, never to be denied, insisted on going swimming and taking the cook's son with her. Before long, they were screaming for help. At once Laurence plunged into the sea to rescue his precious daughter, now drowning. He swam forcefully out into the ocean. But before he could get to Kathe, he came upon the outstretched hand of the cook's son. There wasn't an instant to spare. I'll come back for him afterwards, Laurence decided, as he swam frantically out toward ten-year-old Kathe. But Jeannie had already saved Kathe. By the time Laurence went back for the boy, he had drowned.

For years Laurence was plagued by nightmares. Drunk, he would relive the horrible incident. "It wasn't my fault, was it?" Laurence would plead. "Would *you* have saved him first? What would you have done?"

18

Simulated Captain

I hope my dreams will sometime leave me so that I can dream only of you again.
JOSEPH FRANCKENSTEIN

I picked out Kay Boyle's Avalanche *in the hope of finding a novel worth reading, and have been somewhat taken aback to get nothing but a piece of pure rubbish.*
EDMUND WILSON

Late in 1944, Kay Boyle was invited by the Army Air Forces to join a group of thirteen writers who would tour American air bases in Europe and North Africa. After returning to America, they were to write and give lectures about how impressed they had been. The trip would last three months. Determined to seize whatever opportunity for adventure and advancement might come her way, Kay accepted.

Boostie, still chronically ill, was only fourteen months old. Mousie was two, Clover six. But the chance of seeing Joseph, if only briefly, in England, no less than the glamour of being accredited by Washington as a war correspondent (she never wrote a single article or story about the junket), overrode any concerns about the children. The older ones, who had still not recovered from her having broken up the family for her young lover, were so upset over her decision to absent herself for three months that they all refused to see her off at Grand Central Station on the first leg of her journey, except for ten-year-old Kathe.

Traveling in her Wac officer's uniform as a "simulated captain," having been taught how to salute properly, Kay Boyle, along with Roger Burlingame, *Ladies' Home Journal* columnist Dorothy Cameron Disney ("Can This Marriage Be Saved?"), and the others, including two *Journal* editors, left in early January of 1945. Upset by the flourishing black-market dealing he observed, according to Kay Boyle, Burlingame left the group early in the tour.

But it appealed to Kay's romantic spirit to stay up late each night to be briefed on plans for the next day's bombings and in the morning to share coffee with pilots before they took off. She did spend two weeks in

England close to Joseph and in London she encountered Nancy Cunard in a British uniform.

"How in the world did we get on the side of authority?" Nancy laughed.

In Paris, the group was put up at the Ritz, which had been requisitioned by the American Army. Kay rang up her old friend "Bob la Coupole"; before she even identified herself, he replied, *"Bon soir*, Madame Boyle!" perhaps recognizing Kay's tentative French accent. One morning at the Ritz, Kay was chastised by the maître d'hôtel for choosing the wrong table for breakfast.

"I'm sorry, but you can't sit at this table. That's for Mr. Hemingway," Kay was told. If Hemingway and his wife, Martha Gellhorn, were to discover someone sitting at "their" table, Gellhorn was sure to make one of her terrible scenes.

Kay Boyle suffered other trying moments. She had to listen, she said, recounting her trip in her later years, to an Army Air Forces general reveal that he viewed the entire French nation with contempt. Her attempts to visit Free French air bases were also frowned upon. At the Press Club she met Bill Bird, now a war correspondent. Amid the singing of songs of the French Resistance with CBS correspondent David Schoenbrun, they found a moment to reminisce about their mutual friend Robert McAlmon.

"He deserved better, much better," Bird said. "I wanted you to do something about him then, but I didn't know how to tell you what I meant." They agreed McAlmon had never received credit for his achievements as publisher and major catalyst for the renaissance of American writing in Paris in the twenties. Now in Paris in 1945, Kay considered her options, even as she garnered material she needed for a second serial about France, which she hoped to sell to *The Saturday Evening Post* and which she would call *A Frenchman Must Die*.

For years Kay Boyle enjoyed recounting one particular incident. One cold February day Kay was at Verdun in the mess hall when she suddenly needed a toilet; she wandered through cavernous rooms until she found herself in a room where troops were readying themselves for battle the next morning. In this freezing place, heated by only one wood-burning stove, she was rescued by a black soldier, who led her to a bathroom with the words: "You look like a lady looking for a place to go." It pleased Kay when the man said he would stand outside and see that nobody came in. (In 1986, when she recounted the incident, this time to her hostess in Bowling Green, where she was teaching, and the woman remarked, "I suppose he insulted you," Kay sputtered with indignation. "How do people get that way?" Kay pronounced her disapproval.)

After a visit to American intelligence headquarters in Caserta, Italy, where Kay met Colonel Thornton Wilder, and a last-minute foray into North Africa, the group returned to America. It was late March. For twenty-four hours, Boostie had no idea who this woman was. He did not recognize his mother.

By February, having made a number of parachute drops into Occupied France, Joseph began his most dangerous mission. Disguised in the uniform of a German Wehrmacht sergeant of the Reichs Sicherheits Hauptamt, armed with OSS-forged German papers, he began to make his way to Austria. As he pretended to examine a German's papers at the Milan railroad station, an observant German officer thought him suspicious; Joseph's answers persuaded the officer that he was a deserter from the Wehrmacht. Suddenly the man loudly placed Joseph under arrest and began to march him to Gestapo headquarters, taking a route that led them down an alley. As soon as they were out of sight of passersby, Joseph pulled out his gun and shot the officer dead. Then he escaped into the crowds.

Making his way to Innsbruck, the center of Austrian resistance in the Tyrol, Joseph contacted Dr. Karl Gruber, head of the local underground (and later to be Austrian ambassador to the United States). He was operating under the code name "Horneck," after Count von Horneck, one of his ancestors, whose name was emblazoned on the Countess Esterházy's silver. With fellow OSS officer Fritz Molden, Joseph's goal was to create the first liberated zone in western Austria.

But information was difficult to come by. At the end of April, Joseph, with the help of the Austrian resistance forces, succeeded in infiltrating the Gestapo. They accepted Joseph as one of them and assigned him to an Austrian ski battalion stationed near Innsbruck. It was during this time that a secret meeting was arranged between Joseph and his mother. The Countess was told only that there was someone waiting in a remote mountain hut who wanted to see her. When she arrived, Joseph stepped from his hiding place behind the stove. He was dressed, as always now, in his German uniform.

The Countess took a good look at her son in his Nazi uniform. She did not greet him. She expressed no relief that he was alive. The Countess had only one thing to say.

"You too?" the Countess declared with disgust, believing that, like his brother Ludvig, Joseph too had become a Nazi.

One day one of his Nazi comrades announced to Joseph with great pleasure: "*Das Schwein ist tot.*"

"Who's dead?" Joseph wanted to know.

"Roosevelt, he died!" the German told him.

Joseph's eyes so filled with tears that he had to turn his head away.

Unbeknownst, of course, to the Gestapo, Joseph continued in his resistance work, posing as a Nazi yet working all the while as a partisan. As a member of the OSS's "Homespun" mission, Joseph and a former Wehrmacht private named Lothar Koenigsreuter set up a training camp for partisans in the mountains near Innsbruck.

The "Homespun" mission ended in late April. Joseph and Karl Novacek, a fellow partisan, and Fritz Molden awaited a shipment of machine guns, explosives, and radio sets as they readied themselves for a last stand against the surrounding Nazis. Joseph remained cheerful, optimistic, and good-humored. According to Fritz Molden's account, he began each morning by singing "Heimatschutz! Let's do 'em, get yer knives out quick. Stick 'em in and twist 'em round, cor, lads, what a kick!" Life seemed to be fulfilling all his expectations. Evenings he could be discovered reading poetry; often he quoted Rilke. "Only a couple of days," Joseph promised, "and the Ivans'll be in Vienna and the Yanks in Salzburg." If the Germans still controlled the Tyrol, with two SS panzer divisions approaching, the American Seventh Army was on its way.

On April 26, Joseph arrived at the Kemater Alm with a fellow OSS operative. At five in the morning of April 28, acting on information extracted from a captured intelligence officer, convinced he was a deserter, the Germans came after him. He was ordered out of his bed and his room was searched. Joseph was told to dress while SS guards kept watch.

Before long Joseph was resisting, giving the Germans "as good as they got." Then his ammunition ran out. He ordered his partisan trainees to make a run for it, while he remained behind to hold off the SS for what he hoped would be ten more minutes. At first the trainees refused. At last they went. Finally, tossing their remaining hand grenades at the Germans, Joseph and Karl Novacek ran out of the building. When the Germans opened up with machine-gun fire, Novacek was hit. Joseph turned back, knelt down, and took the dying man in his arms. Immediately SS men grabbed him and Joseph was sent to the Reichenau concentration camp outside Innsbruck. He had been behind enemy lines almost one month.

In their efforts to discover the identity of this deserter in his SS Abwehr uniform (after the July 20 attempt against Hitler that failed, the Abwehr, which was the German counterespionage unit, was transferred and became part of the SS Abwehr), the Germans tortured Joseph, hanging him upside down and beating him. Then they stood him up against a wall and trained their machine guns on him. He would not talk and again he was hung upside down and beaten. Unconscious, he was thrown into a cell so small he could not stand up, where the only object was a bucket filled with excrement. In their final torture attempt, the Germans put his thumbnail in the doorjamb and then slammed the door on his fingers so that the nails turned blue at the base. But Joseph never confessed or revealed his true identity.

On May 1 at Reichenau, he was sentenced to death as a deserter: a death warrant was signed. Just as the Germans were about to carry out the sentence, there was a commotion. Fearing, mistakenly, that an American helicopter had landed, the Germans rushed outside. Quickly Joseph grabbed a Luger off the wall, and still wearing his German uniform, ran out and headed for the barbed-wire fence. A guard stopped him. "I'm an American. You take care of me and I'll take care of you," he declared as he negotiated his way to freedom.

Joseph's heroic wartime efforts concluded as he and men of the Austrian resistance captured Nazi barracks and arrested the SS officers. They
also removed the mines from the roads so that the American troops could
enter Innsbruck safely. Joseph and Gruber created a Tyrolese government;
by the time the Americans arrived, the American flag flew along with the
Austrian flag and the red-and-white flag of the Tyrol. Fritz Molden was
reunited with Joseph at the Dollinger Inn, where they drank to the fallen
Karl Novacek. It was May of 1945 when Joseph was finally able to communicate with a frantic Kay Boyle, who had not had any news of her
husband for two months.

According to Fritz Molden, after he and Joseph had placed flowers
on the mound of earth where Karl Novacek lay, they took the funicular up
to the top of the Patscherkofel. Looking down on Innsbruck, Joseph mentioned that he might like a professorship at the university in Vienna after
the war, that he might like to return to Austria. But he lacked the right
connections, not having joined any political party. He knew, Molden wrote,
neither the Minister of Education, a Communist, nor the member of the
Austrian People's Party who succeeded him, nor the Socialist Minister of
the Interior. Joseph was told that he was an American citizen and that his
future lay with the Americans.

Remaining in Austria working for the Americans, Joseph helped to
identify war criminals and to establish postwar courts, schools, and universities. He was so busy in denazification work that he managed to sleep
only three nights in his mother's house during these months. Wild Bill
Donovan had promised that OSS wives would soon be allowed to join their
men, and Joseph wanted Kay to fly to Switzerland at once, "bringing all
the babes along."

But Kay remained in New York. Her favorite political figure was, by
1945, Henry Wallace, who, she wrote Caresse, was "the answer . . . to
all our hopes and prayers." She gave many parties at her brownstone with
the help of her maid, Edie Mae. One night Maria Jolas organized a dinner
at Kay's house at which Marcel Duchamp would be the host and Jean-Paul
Sartre the guest of honor, only for Marcel to cancel. "Tell Sartre not to
come because I don't know him," Kay told Duchamp.

The group, which included William L. Shirer and Dick Simon, now
her publisher, were in the middle of dinner at the long table in the basement
kitchen when the doorbell rang. Kay opened the door to a tiny man. Kay
could not imagine who this might be.

"I think you must have made a mistake. This is Kay Boyle's house,"
she told him haughtily.

"*Oui, oui, je suis Jean-Paul Sartre*," the man replied. When he asked
for Duchamp, Kay told him that Marcel was in Chicago. When she invited
him to join the others, however, he accepted with apparent reluctance.
Sartre took a place at the table, where he drank a Pernod, and chatted in

French with the children. Suddenly he announced he was leaving and abruptly, without another word, headed for the stairs.

Five days later, Sartre's assistant invited Kay to a cocktail party in his honor. But Kay had taken offense: Sartre had been rude to her guests, and she would not attend his function.

Her junket as a "simulated captain" did bring her assignments from *The Ladies' Home Journal* to write two articles for their series "How America Lives." For each piece the writer would spend twenty-four hours with a family, examining everything about their lives, down to their bank accounts. Kay's 1946 pieces featured an Irish Catholic family and one of Belgian refugees. Both were *apologiae pro vita sua*, more about Kay Boyle's own life than that of her subjects.

The kitchen of Kitty Quinn is "gleaming," "immaculate," and "scrubbed clean," with the canned goods neat and orderly in the closet, exactly like Kay's own ruthlessly tidy kitchens. "I guess children are my art," says Kitty, mother of nine, as Kay offers a hint at why she had so many herself. One of the Quinn daughters has a "delicate heart-shaped face," exactly like Apple's. And once more, ostensibly invoking the Quinns' family history, the writer gives us that scene with the covered wagons moving across the prairies, although this time Kay seats the woman "erect, steady-eyed, intrepid in the driver's seat," rather than having an Eva Evans surrogate dancing before the convoy.

The Belgian lawyer turns out to be a scholar of Latin and Greek like Joseph, while the family's flight across France echoes Kay's own; one of their favorite wartime commentators turns out, coincidentally, to be Kay Boyle's own close friend William L. Shirer. She otherwise complied with *The Ladies' Home Journal*'s demands, even listing Kitty Quinn's waist, bust, and hip measurements.

As Bobby approached her high school graduation, she posed a challenge to Kay Boyle. Having excelled as a student, Bobby wished now to go to college.

"I can't afford it," Kay Boyle told her abruptly. Her attitude remained that since *she* had no diploma yet had been so successful, her children ought to be able to do the same thing. Distracted, even dismissive, Kay did not even consider how Bobby's goal might be accomplished. Instead, Kay asked Caresse to get Bobby a job at what Caresse called "the Mellon Gallery's French Cultural Division" in Washington, with the possibility of a transfer to France. Caresse replied that she hoped Bobby could type.

So Bobby fell finally into the cracks of her disrupted family. Kay's thoughts were with Joseph and her two younger children. A tearful Bobby, wearing her "Forever France" uniform, sailed for France alone on September 15 to make her own way as best she could. All her life she would regret her lost education.

Kay did find time, however, during that summer of 1945, to head for Grand Central Station to welcome Carson McCullers back from the upstate

Yaddo colony and take the manuscript of her new book, called *The Member of the Wedding*, home to read. The next day Kay called to tell her friend she loved the book, but wished only that Carson had shown greater compassion and rendered a sharper characterization of the soldier. You have "deliberately turned your face away," in this "evasive" episode, Kay said. But when Truman Capote argued that the soldier had to remain on the "outward fringes of the dream" or the whole story would be unbalanced, McCullers left it as it was.

Kay tried relaxing at her sister Joan Detweiler's Plainfield, New Jersey, farm, where she found life so hectic "with babes, animals, housework, farmwork" that she couldn't even attend to her regular correspondence. Laurence had taken a house at Truro on Cape Cod in Massachusetts, where, on flipping on the radio and learning that Japan had surrendered, he decided Hirohito was "too good to lose. I'd keep him." Laurence agreed with Douglas MacArthur. "You don't find Gods every day; they don't grow on bushes," was Laurence's shrewd perception. No man in Kay Boyle's life would ever rival Laurence for his wit, gaiety, literary education, sophistication, irrepressible spirit, and pure intelligence, which made him forever an enemy to cant, vulgarity, hypocrisy, and sentimentality.

When Laurence asked his daughters whether he should marry Jeannie Connolly, they agreed. Even Peggy endorsed this marriage. "She's the only wife or girlfriend you ever had I can get on with," Peggy told him. "I don't hate her at all."

On his way to Strasbourg, Joseph stopped in Paris, where he was offered dinner at Fanny Ventadour's. Jacqueline admired the attractive Joseph, so that it was a virtual *coup de foudre*. Kay Boyle's fear that Joseph would fall for one of the girls might have come true had he not been so absolutely loyal and devoted to her. No other woman existed for him then. All he wanted to talk about with Jacqueline were old times at Mégève.

Bearing the medals that testified to his heroism during the war, Joseph returned to America in December of 1945. Often he had thought of Mousie, his blonde, blue-eyed "Fairy Princess," as he called her. Eagerly Joseph rushed into the bedroom, anxious to see his daughter.

"Run over and hug him," Kay urged her three-year-old.

Mousie burst into tears. He was so big, and so loud. Mousie couldn't imagine who this frightening man might be.

Both during the war and in its aftermath, Kay Boyle publicly expressed her views about America's international role. In 1944 she declared that Germany must be broken up and then policed. America had "an important role in postwar reconstruction." All her stories now chronicled the European conflict, as she continued to select themes unusual for women writers. From 1941 on, she was no longer writing the psychological mood pieces familiar to readers of *This Quarter* and *transition*. Both her style and her themes underwent a complete transformation.

If, during World War II, Kay Boyle wrote masterpieces like "Defeat," she also published many potboilers, like "Frenchman's Ship" and "The Ships Going to Glory" for *The Saturday Evening Post* and "The Last Aviator Left Flying" for *American Magazine*. But in both her finely crafted stories and her commercial fiction, her characters' lives are played out against the entrapments of history. In 1939, she had inaugurated this approach in "Listen, Munich." A young American woman suffers the first quarrel of her fresh marriage, not in the luxury of psychological isolation, but against the raucous background of ascendant Nazism. Even in the slight piece "Wanderer," published in *Accent* in 1942, a story dedicated "to Pegeen Vail," the fourteen-year-old heroine is swindled not on an ordinary day, but on September 2, 1939, as her father sits reading *Time* to discover "if there was going to be a war or if there wasn't."

Kay Boyle brought to American readers fictions from the front, the experiences of people of whom they had never heard; in "They Weren't Going to Die" (1940) she tells the story of the Senegalese imported into France to serve as *chair à canon*, cannon fodder for the Germans. Here and in the charming high-toned soap opera "Hilaire and the Maréchal Pétard" (1942), she exposes the class loyalties forged between upper-class French and Germans, who had more in common with each other than with the lowly recruits who were to do the fighting. In many of her stories she told of the refugees caught in France, men who hated fascism yet were not trusted by the French to fight. They were "the tattered, exiled army of despair still undespairing," and they appear in "Poor Monsieur Panalitus," in "Men," in "Their Name Is Macaroni" and in "This They Carried with Them."

Autobiography informs all these stories. In "Let There Be Honour," when the Kurt Wick character, a former Heimwehr, kisses the heroine, she dismisses him in the same cold angry words Laurence spoke to the usurping Joseph Franckenstein: "Now, just get out." When her heroine falls in love, she feels what Kay did when she met Joseph: "I couldn't believe I'd ever meet anyone again who was everything I wanted him to be." The man she loves, an Englishman here, in turn speaks words remarkably like those Kay had Ernest Walsh use to describe her in *Year Before Last*: "you were so beautiful that men never stopped trying to get there just to look at your face."

In "Hilaire and the Maréchal Pétard," the American heroine gets up and leaves a café terrace when German officers sit down at the next table, as Kay had done. The hero is Sindbad, who starts a newspaper about "the war," as Sindbad had done. Even Ernest Walsh makes a fictional appearance, if only in the sentimental "The Last Aviator Left Flying" (1943), an obvious call to patriotism. With his black hair and albeit blue eyes, "the lashes smeared black along the lids," he is tender toward the fatherless ten-year-old of the heroine, who had once, like Kay's own children, "done the Matterhorn with Papa." In this instance, the man, called Michael, adopts one of the Laurence figure's children; in real life Laurence had failed to adopt Ernest Walsh's daughter.

"Some were written for love, and some for money," Kay Boyle admitted of her wartime stories, in the foreword to her collected *Thirty Stories*, published in 1946. Most of the time, however, she was writing romantic claptrap for the slick glossies, although occasionally a slight effort like "Nothing Ever Breaks Except the Heart" (1941) found its way into the pages of *The New Yorker*, undoubtedly because Harold Ross was such a close friend and admirer. If between 1940 and 1946 she published seven stories in *The New Yorker*, she also had seven in *Harper's Bazaar* and twenty appearances in *The Saturday Evening Post*, counting her serials, as well as two in *Woman's Home Companion*. She also appeared in *The American Mercury*, *Mademoiselle*, *American Magazine*, and *Reader's Digest*. Of all these forty-two short stories in general magazines, only two were of the very first rank, "Defeat," and "Winter Night," which was published in *The New Yorker* in January of 1946. The latter was an exquisite vignette of a privileged little American girl who learns from her survivor babysitter how other little girls had suffered. Eschewing moralizing, Kay Boyle never enlists the words "death," "Jew," "Nazi," or "concentration camp" in a story with brilliant artistic economy.

But most of Kay Boyle's wartime stories were potboilers, loose and baggy indulgences, deadened by long didactic moments, and peopled by flat characters moving through plots laden with coincidence and improbability. Putting aside literary aims, she turned her artistry to such jingoistic pieces as "The Little Distance" (1943) and "Luck for the Road" (1944). Kay Boyle always knew the difference. Acknowledging the literary weakness of these hasty efforts, she argued that since everyone in America was criticizing France for lying down on the job, she was bringing the truth to the widest possible American public. By the end of the war, she was writing so hastily that she didn't bother even to fictionalize her message. In "Hotel Behind the Lines" (1945), she has an Italian newspaperman say, "We need you, you Americans. Do not leave us yet."

Kay Boyle actually wrote two types of potboilers during the war. One group, suffering as it did from romantic sentimentality, did at least throw light into the corners of a political reality to which few in America had access. Among these were "Nothing Ever Breaks Except the Heart," about refugees waiting in Lisbon, and "Their Name Is Macaroni," about the persecuted Italian residents of Mégève, who hadn't become French citizens yet hated the fascists. The archly romanticized "The Canals of Mars," the story of Kay and Joseph's last night before he leaves for the front, powerfully evokes wartime America.

At the same time, Kay Boyle was writing stories utterly lacking in nuance of character, among them a melodrama like "Frenchman's Ship," which she wrote, she admitted, for Jean Gabin, in the hope of a movie sale, to the delight of Pegeen, who told her, "Bobby and I worship him beyond measure." "The Little Distance," "The Ships Going to Glory," "Luck for the Road" (sold to NBC for one hundred dollars), and "The Last Aviator Left Flying" bore little of the subtlety that distinguished Kay as a master craftsman of the short story. "Frenchman's Ship" offers a mysterious French horse trainer with "the look of romance on his flesh and in his eye." The burning ship represents France awaiting American rescue. In "The Last Aviator Left Flying," a Rosie the Riveter heroine, a war widow, falls in love with her Walsh-surrogate instructor, "a broad shouldered, dark, square-browed man" who talks Hemingway-style: "There's a war on. It might be advisable to win it." She replies, female-Hemingway-style: "I know. That's why I'm here." Magically he appears to light her cigarette on a ferry, as if she were Lauren Bacall or Veronica Lake.

Avalanche was advertised as the first novel written in America about the French resistance; it eliminates the nuanced view Kay offered in *Primer for Combat* and "Defeat," to insist that most of the French supported the resistance, that collaborators were few. Kay Boyle herself called *Avalanche* "this blasted serial," and admitted to Bob Brown that she had to force herself to "stop being a precious, careful writer" in order to "get the rough copy hacked out somehow."

Avalanche, which became Kay Boyle's only best-selling novel, appeared in seven installments in *The Saturday Evening Post* between October and December of 1943. It was published by Simon & Schuster and featured as an alternate by the Book-of-the-Month Club; the Armed Forces bought 250,000 copies so that airmen bailing out over France might be aware of the resistance and its dynamics. On January 30, 1944, *Avalanche* appeared as number twelve on *The New York Times*'s list of "Best Selling Books," where it remained for the first three weeks in February and, skipping one week, for two weeks in March.

The Saturday Evening Post had insisted that the heroine be half American and so Kay made her Fenton Ravel, the daughter of a French father and an American mother; the Simon & Schuster jacket copy refers to her as "a young American girl." The serial format demanded that the French resistance hero, Bastineau, reappear often; Kay admitted that she "dragged him in every twenty pages, and . . . left it that way when it was published as a book." Fenton Ravel, in fact, is modeled on Bobby. At fourteen she falls off a white horse and into the arms of Bastineau, who sings as he climbs, as Joseph did. Joseph also appears as another character, a fleeing Austrian with hollow cheeks, "all the courage in the world," and an Oxford accent. A Frenchman who has a sport shop is Kurt Wick, not the callow opportunist he was, but a secret member of the resistance. Everyone is romanticized, even Les Six Enfants, the scene of much of the action with its "sloping eaves and balconies running the house's length and oil-stained railways carved in the shape of lifted stag heads with the antlers edged with snow." There is high-minded talk of "national pride," and some clever use of detail; a Gestapo spy is scented with "fresh, fragrant soap" in a land where soap is a rarity. And there are masterful descriptions of the ice, the glaciers, the fissures, and the icefalls, which Kay Boyle had long been skilled in depicting.

At the end Fenton is captured at gunpoint by a Gestapo agent named de Vaudois, a Swiss with a white scar slashed across his cheek, for whom the villagers, long-suffering in the France which has become a "great penitentiary," are no match. As Fenton is about to be shot, Bastineau jumps "down the chimney's broad, wooden shaft, his arms spread like a diver's, his eyes and teeth pure white and savage in his face." As if his jumping down the chimney were not absurd enough, Bastineau accomplishes this feat singing, "wondrous and loud and wild," the song *"L'In-fant'rie Alpin-e, voilà mes amours!"* Conveniently the village priest arrives to marry Fenton and Bastineau, who will now fight together in the resistance.

Forty years later, the author was to defend *Avalanche* as "written with greater simplicity of style than anything I had written before," as she seems to have forgotten *Primer for Combat* with its fine direct style. Nor would she concede its stylistic inadequacies. "It was not for an instant 'propaganda,' " she angrily insisted. Nor later would she admit that writing for money produced *Avalanche* as much as did serving the cause.

But with money obviously her goal, she tried to repeat her success in the pages of *The Saturday Evening Post* with *A Frenchman Must Die*, another serialized potboiler, in February and March of 1946. The hostilities had ended, but Vichy collaborators and former members of the "Milice," the French storm troopers, still stalked the countryside, Kay Boyle reported, a threat to a democratic postwar France. Her hero, another half American, is called Guy Mitchie, a man whose underground exploits had made him a legend. Kay's propensities for hero worship perfectly suited these serial romances. The heroism of the protagonist even absolves the author of the need for character development. Guy Mitchie's best exploits occur before the serial even begins, freeing Kay Boyle from the exigencies of plot, a task before which she always faltered. At the end, Mitchie is involved in a classic chase through the Haute-Savoie, as he tracks down a rich industrialist named Pliny, who had been a collaborator, and brings him to justice in swashbuckling style.

Of course, there is a girl with whom Mitchie must fall in love, Pliny's secretary. She's another Kay Boyle look-alike, slender and arrogant, if with the dark auburn hair of Grandma Eva Evans. And, of course, it is love at first sight. Even more embarrassing is the rhetoric on behalf of the resistance: "It was part of a singular romance not with a woman but with a country." Other autobiographical notes include Mitchie's French mother, a countess, like Joseph's, remarking that a grey suit was "the only outfit that Frenchwomen of the decenter class will put their foot outside the door in," as if the Braults too had to make an appearance in a Kay Boyle romance. The cardboard characters of *A Frenchman Must Die* and its melodramatic flourishes place it a rung below even *Avalanche* as a piece of writing.

Some, of course, were delighted with this new Kay Boyle now writing for a mass audience. In *The Ladies' Home Journal* in a notice for *A Frenchman Must Die*, Bernardine Kielty applauded Kay Boyle, "the intellectual, whose books used to be distinctly of the long-haired variety," and who had been "one of the small esoteric group of literary experimenters who appeared regularly in Transition [sic], the Paris-American Little Magazine." But Kay Boyle had seen the light. Having returned to "easygoing, unexacting, wholesome America," she now sold "to an increasingly large public." Kay was not so fortunate, however, with the arbiters of literary taste and reputation.

On January 1, 1944, Edmund Wilson succeeded Clifton Fadiman as the book reviewer for *The New Yorker*. The first book he chose to review was Kay Boyle's *Avalanche*. Poised to establish his voice and authority, Wilson found in Kay an easy target, a writer with a considerable reputation now producing work worthy of a Daphne Du Maurier. Wilson concluded that Kay Boyle had been corrupted by greed, having fashioned a work obviously "with an eye to the demands of Hollywood."

Wilson easily made his case. He blanched at the "terrific" climax of *Avalanche*, where "the hero leaps down through a large open chimney" singing. Bastineau, Wilson thought, "combines the glamor of Charles Boyer with the locomotive proficiency of Superman." For years critics had warned Kay to rid her work of the *précieuse*, those arch mannerisms. Now Wilson accused her of tones of "false solemnity," of the "bad romantic habit of making foreign conversation sound translated," and of employing "the idiom of a feminized Hemingway."

If in the past, Wilson continued, Kay Boyle had tried "to produce something of serious interest," her current writing for *The Saturday Evening Post* canceled forever that possibility. Always the enemy of all forms of cant, Wilson admitted that he had found *This Quarter* and *Transition* [sic] "full of nonsense," as indeed they were. Now, so "depressed" was he by Kay Boyle's fall from grace, her having revealed herself to be no better than "women writers for the popular magazines," that he found himself thinking of those magazines with "a longing that it would have surprised me in that period to be told I should ever feel." Wilson said he simply could not "see how a writer with a really sound sense of style could have produced this book even as a potboiler." With that sentence he sounded the death knell for Kay Boyle's reputation as a writer of merit.

While *Avalanche* was decidedly not literature, and Wilson had every right to judge the work on its own terms, his review amounted to overkill. *Avalanche*, and the later *A Frenchman Must Die*, together occupied a very small place in the large body of work Kay Boyle had produced. But Wilson decided not only that *Avalanche* was "nothing but a piece of pure rubbish" but that Kay Boyle's entire oeuvre had at once to be called into question. As far as Wilson was concerned, and his review would reverberate for the remainder of her career, Kay Boyle could no longer be taken seriously.

Had he been alone in this judgment, perhaps Kay Boyle could have escaped the long-lasting effects of Wilson's devastating review. But many echoed his dismay. What annoyed Diana Trilling, reviewing *Avalanche* for *The Nation*, was that by introducing "italicized passages of literary exaltation and by the parade of her whole familiar bundle of literary mannerisms," the author was pretending "to more and better than pot-boiling." *Time* began its review of *Avalanche*, entitled "Pot-Boyler," with "Kay Boyle has sold the Left Bank down the river." Struthers Burt in *The Saturday Review of Literature* insisted that "a person like Miss Boyle hasn't a right to do this." Catherine Maher in *The New York Times Book Review* likened Kay Boyle to romance writers Martha Albrand and Helen MacInnes. "And now that 'Avalanche' is on its way to enjoyable reading by devotees of Martha Albrand and Helen MacInnes," Maher wrote, "let the rest of us hope that Kay Boyle's next novel will take up the thread where 'Primer for Combat' left off."

In England, equally appalled, *The Spectator* cast Gary Cooper rather than Charles Boyer in the role of Bastineau. Nor could her reputation have been helped by the publication the following August of an interview in the New York *World-Telegram* in which she said she adored Faulkner, dismissed Aldous Huxley, and asserted that "while she can understand people seeking escapist reading, it is not for her." Predictably, the reviews of *A Frenchman Must Die* in 1946 were equally dismal. *The Saturday Review* dismissed it as "plain melodrama," *The New York Times Book Review* wondered at its "clichés," and *The Booklist* called it "very slight."

Simon & Schuster published *Thirty Stories* in 1946, a volume that should have been considered entirely separate from Kay Boyle's wartime melodramas. It included much of her best work from "Black Boy" and "Wedding Day" and "The White Horses of Vienna" to "Defeat" and "Winter Night." Indeed, many critics acknowledged her achievement. Forgetting about *Avalanche*, Struthers Burt called her "one of the best" storytellers now living and "by and large, the best in this country." *The New York Times* praised the stories for their "unmistakeable honesty."

But now she suffered a second major attack on her work. Echoing Edmund Wilson's dismissal two years earlier, Margery Barrett, under the headline "Tour in Technicolor," attacked *Thirty Stories* in the pages of the Stalinist *New Masses*. Reinventing the proletcult, Barrett upbraided Kay Boyle for insufficient appreciation of the working class, for romanticizing Hitler as a "revolutionary idealist," and for racism in depicting the Senegalese in "They Weren't Going to Die" as "happy, cruel black children." As if Kay Boyle had not written paeans to the resistance in *Avalanche* and *A Frenchman Must Die*, Barrett attacked her for presenting those French women who danced with the Germans in "Defeat" as her last word on the French response to the Germans.

Worst for Barrett was the writer's choice of heroes, all upper-class, all "tall, handsome, slim, Nordic (British, or more frequently Austrian), reticent, often titled, usually officers and always gentlemen." Barrett was not responsible for knowing that Kay Boyle was depicting men she loved rather than indulging in upper-class elitism. "If she has tears for life erased, youth corrupted, labor enslaved or learning prostituted," Barrett went on, "she doesn't shed them here." The serials, she acknowledged, were "contributions to the war effort . . . but Miss Boyle's slick efforts and her 'serious' work appear to have become one, and the result is the sorry spectacle of a first-rate talent converted into cash."

Four months later, Kay replied to Barrett in the columns of *New Masses.* She dutifully listed all her working-class characters, "fishermen, soldiers, exploited servants, refugees, mountaineers." She foolishly challenged Barrett's view that "Wedding Day" was a "study in incest" by replying that it was no more a "study in incest," which it is, than "The White Horses of Vienna" condoned fascism, which it did not. She even insisted, oddly, that the main character of "The White Horses of Vienna" was "a professional man of Jewish faith seeking to make his living in the Austrian Tyrol in 1934." That was plainly untrue; the hero is the Nazi doctor and not the Jewish assistant. Either Kay had not reread her story or in her effort to be politically correct she deliberately fabricated.

Finally Kay was reduced shrilly to flaunting her extraliterary credentials. The Nazi ministry of education had banned her books for translation. She had been attacked on the Vichy radio as "a Communist writer inciting the French to revolution." Weren't these facts ample demonstration that she was on the right side? She closed with some ill-advised name dropping: Alexander Berkman had urged her, Kay Boyle said, to "continue in your indictment of the ordinary individual, and in your insistence upon each of us taking the responsibility of being an extraordinary individual."

Barrett, given the final word, lectured Kay tellingly on her failure in all her writing about the rise of fascism to treat its serious opposition, indeed a major flaw in her work. Easily, Barrett dismissed Berkman as a "romantic anarchist," and taking the high ground informed Kay in the true spirit of the proletcult that "the world is not for extraordinary individuals but for all individuals." Didn't fascism indeed, Barrett said, offer "as one of its philosophic bases the superman, the 'extraordinary individual'?" The invocation of anarchist Berkman, whom the Communists considered a renegade, had to have inflamed the pro-Soviet *New Masses.*

According to Kay Boyle, she was forced by Simon & Schuster to read Edmund Wilson's review of *Avalanche* because she had to defend herself in a radio interview against an attack by Bennett Cerf. Once more she argued that in *Avalanche* she had been trying to reach as many Americans

so that they might understand "how all that was simple and
~~rable in France had been betrayed. The French had not laid~~
b." The French people themselves, she argued, had been
g business interests—French big business which was hand
ɢᴏ̯ᴜᴠ̯ᴇ with German big business." Kay felt she came off very badly on
that radio program because "I didn't know who Edmund Wilson was, and
I thought him exceedingly stupid for not understanding what I was trying
to do in that book." But as Barrett wrote in her equally damaging review,
good intentions in literary matters are never enough.

Damage had been done to Kay Boyle the writer, and her later acknowledgment that *Avalanche* "was simply not literature, and it didn't need
a critic to point that out," did not help. Her argument, that she had written
potboilers to persuade a mass audience to change its mind about the French,
failed to take into account that cardboard characters and rhetorical sol-
emnities never convinced anyone of anything; it failed as literature of
persuasion as it failed as literature. That she had written "without apology"
for *The Saturday Evening Post* did not prevent later critics from concluding
that Kay Boyle was no longer the person Mary Colum had called "Hemingway's successor." Kay's argument, which she continued to advance as
late as 1981, that had *Avalanche* not been written, Air Force men para-
chuting from disabled airplanes into France would not have understood the
political situation, was also beside the point, and amounted to special
pleading. Nor did *Avalanche*'s dedication to Marcel Duchamp and Mary
Reynolds, as "Monsieur and Madame Rrose Sélavy," after Duchamp's
pseudonym (*Eros c'est la vie*), do anything to redeem this book as literature,
as Kay Boyle may have intended with this lofty choice.

The sole support of her burgeoning household in the forties, Kay had
squandered her considerable literary goodwill. Rather than develop her
skills to match the challenging wartime themes, to which she had such
unique access, she trivialized them. Mistakenly, or out of some sense of
hubris, she behaved as if she could have it both ways. Kay Boyle the
heroine come home with her beautiful family would continue to write serious
fiction. At the same time, unimpeded, she could write commercial fiction
peppered with some of her old descriptive flourishes to remind readers that
this was, after all, the writer Kay Boyle.

The returned expatriate Kay Boyle, in love with her young war hero
husband, a romantic and a fantasist, approached her work as she did her
life. As she seemed to believe that Sindbad and Pegeen and Bobby and
Apple and Kathe and Clover would not be seriously scarred by the dismantling of the "Sanger circus," that she need not devote considerable
time to her foundering daughters, so she wrote as if she would inevitably
be forgiven for prostituting her talent. A stranger to introspection, she
concluded only that Wilson and Barrett and her other detractors had been
unfair.

A holder of grudges as well, Kay Boyle never forgave Edmund Wilson.

Nearly fifty years after his review of *Avalanche* appeared, she attacked him as "a dry-as-dust intellectual who could never in his entire lifetime have responded to the courage and commitment and contemporary reality of a resistance movement." By 1946 Kay was ready to return to Europe, decidedly leaving behind an America where her literary reputation had taken a downward turn.

19

Foreign Correspondent

*She was like some bright beautiful herald of coming happiness
. . . it was a beautiful thing she left with me and it
changes everything.*

KATHRYN HULME

K ay Boyle was to leave America with her reputation scarred. Yet she remained after World War II among the most prolific and frequently published American writers. With both *Thirty Stories* and *A Frenchman Must Die* out in 1946, Simon & Schuster postponed the publication of *1939*. Its salesmen pleaded that they could not sell three Kay Boyle books in one year. Meanwhile both *Three Short Novels* and *Monday Night* were about to be reprinted. Kay was also completing three ski novelettes about Joseph, which she hoped would be serialized in *The Atlantic Monthly*, and which she was calling "Enemy Detail." Indeed *The Ladies' Home Journal* called her "a good person to remember when we think we're being overworked." At the height of her notoriety, she could shrug off her depiction as "Ray Soil" in Peggy Guggenheim's now-published memoirs. Kay denied that she had read them and so felt, she said, "undefiled." Then she added: "things like that are of no importance at all."

Indeed, she now turned her attention to the political situation in postwar Europe. While she was still in New York, she had befriended Julio Alvarez del Vayo, Foreign Secretary of the Loyalist government, now living in exile. "If a political man no longer stands on his own country's soil, he is maimed and mute," the pro-Soviet Del Vayo told her over tea and cake at Longchamps, "and he must be a great believer in a great faith in order to survive."

Her *Nation* article describing this meeting oddly does not mention Del Vayo by name, but refers to him only as "the Spaniard," perhaps for security reasons, perhaps for purposes of high drama. Her piece reveals as well that she had little understanding of the Spanish Civil War, but viewed it in absolutes of good and evil, fascism against freedom. Apparently she had not even read George Orwell's 1938 *Homage to Catalonia*, which chronicled Stalin's betrayal of the anarchists, syndicalists, and Trotskyists. She would travel as a foreign correspondent to Spain unprepared for any but the most emotional of responses.

In New York too in those last days, Kathe finally accepted *"celui-là,"* Joseph, introducing him to the game "Touchy," which Laurence had invented. "Touchy" required players to touch the sleeve, the collar, the cap of soldiers, or, best of all, the red pompon of French sailors in New York. But when they returned to the brownstone on Eighty-seventh Street, Kay was horrified that her husband should behave in so undignified a manner in public. People who knew them now whispered that she wore the pants in the family. "Poor man," Laurence began to say, "she's bossing him around."

In November of 1946, Harold Ross hired Kay to be *The New Yorker*'s staff correspondent in Europe, accredited by the War Department to travel in Germany and Austria. Under their agreement, Kay was to write a minimum of six pieces a year, what Ross hoped would be "fiction out of Germany." Rightly, Ross believed life in Occupied Germany was exactly the subject matter for which Kay Boyle's talent and experience had prepared her. Kay also agreed to give *The New Yorker* "first reading" rights on all her fiction. Receiving a retainer of one hundred and seventy-five dollars a month, she now found herself free of the burden of having to write for money for the glossies.

Laurence, Apple, and Kathe returned to Les Six Enfants, along with Diane, who was a different animal now. The family upheavals had apparently destroyed her equanimity forever and she had grown wild and uncontrollable as well as inconsolable. One day shortly after their return, Diane killed a kitten. Kathe raced about the mountainsides, followed by Diane and her other dog, Réma, while Apple, now seventeen, worried about what would happen to her since she had been given no real education. Clover visited Les Six Enfants only under protest, a fact her sisters tried to conceal from Laurence so as not to hurt his feelings. All Clover could think of was her mother. When Apple took her on an excursion up a mountain and produced some Kleenex, Clover kissed the tissues. "Oh, Mama's Kleenexes!" she exclaimed.

Kay had given Apple a particular mission; she must burn all of Kurt Wick's letters. The romance was no secret to any of Kay's daughters, as she cultivated the habit of confiding in her children as if they were contemporaries. Wick was still in Mégève when they arrived. Immediately Laurence readmitted him to Les Six Enfants as if nothing had happened, and that winter hired him to teach Jeannie to ski. In the summer he was engaged as Clover's swimming instructor and even took her riding on his motorcycle.

When Joseph took a job as a civilian employee of the Army, aiding in the "reconstruction of Democratic Germany," and was to be stationed in Offenbach, Kay was not pleased. She had hoped that he could get a job with UNESCO in Paris. She herself steadfastly refused to move to Germany. Three of her children were in school in France, she demurred, which was not exactly the case. Kay Boyle also said that her "strong feelings" about the German people made it impossible for her to live among once and present Nazis.

Whether or not the shine had gone off her new marriage, Kay Boyle chose separation this time. Indeed, she and Joseph were more accustomed to living apart than together. If, as Buffy had surmised so long ago, sexuality in Kay's mind was associated with procreation, she could no longer participate in the creative act of bearing children. At forty-four, her hair now grey, and her ambition as strong as ever, her priority seemed not to be domestic togetherness. Joseph was practiced in worshipping her from afar, and he would continue to do so.

Having received the press one last time, attired flamboyantly in narrow black frontier pants and a black Western shirt, which she called her "cowboy outfit," Kay Boyle, foreign correspondent, sailed back to France. Joseph, Bobby, now a secretary for French radio, and Marcel Duchamp met her train. She set up housekeeping in Paris at the Hôtel de France et Choiseul on the rue St.-Honoré, a former convent, where in 1905 Eleanor and Franklin Roosevelt had honeymooned.

Cooped up in a hotel room with Mousie, not yet four, and Boostie, not yet three, and seven-year-old Clover, Kay typed away at night. Fellow residents kept awake cleared their throats in protest, protests which Kay heard through the paper-thin walls. Three nights a week electricity cutbacks put an end to any work at all. Milk ration cards had been distributed and Kay resented having to waste six hours one day obtaining hers. One of her trunks had gotten soaked during the ocean crossing and her clothes were in ruin. In no respect was life easy for a mother with three children in her care in Paris in 1946. Food shortages necessitated Kay's enlisting Ann Watkins, who sent condensed milk, canned orange juice, toothpaste, toilet paper, and extension cords from America.

Nor were the children happy in Paris. Particularly miserable was Ian, who missed his nurse, Edie Mae, and whimpered, "I want to go home," it seemed to his mother, twenty times a day. Kay also had to nursemaid Carson McCullers, now in Paris in an apartment Kay had arranged at the Hôtel de France et Choiseul. She tended to come down to breakfast with a water glass filled with gin in her hand. Nor was Kay pleased when Reeves had an affair with Bobby. Finally, because of a dispute over who would spend the summer of 1947 at Rosay-en-Brie, the country château of Ira and Edita Morris, the friendship between Kay Boyle and Carson McCullers cooled permanently.

Having begun at a salary of $2,644.80, Joseph was rising in the ranks of the Occupation. By October, he had been promoted to the rank of instructor, coordinating a training program in censorship operations. In Paris, Kay renewed her old friendships—with Mary Reynolds, who invited her to a dinner party, where she saw Samuel Beckett, whom she had not met in nearly two decades, and Bill Bird, with whom once more she talked about how Robert McAlmon had been "exploited, betrayed, neglected, deceived, and imitated beyond recognition."

With Janet Flanner, Kay arranged dinner with Archie MacLeish, now a United Nations representative. As they began with drinks in the MacLeish hotel room, it seemed that every few minutes the doorbell rang and another dress was delivered for his wife from one of the couturiers. Kay and Janet exchanged disapproving looks. At dinner Kay and Janet launched into a discussion of all the positive things MacLeish could do with the United Nations. MacLeish, indeed, seemed so receptive that Kay was stunned when in the newspaper the next morning she read that he had resigned his post. Out of Kay Boyle's moral indignation this friendship also soured.

In December, Kay Boyle joined the Overseas Press Club of America; by January of 1947 she was ready to don her uniform and begin her work as a foreign correspondent in Germany. To her postwar journalism, she brought her considerable gifts as a writer of fiction, a keen interest in politics and history, and great sympathy for the survivors of this war-torn landscape. With the children settled in Paris, and poor Clover struggling in a public school without knowing a word of French, Kay departed for Germany.

On the cold January day Kay boarded a train from Paris to Frankfurt, where she would meet Joseph, she found herself surrounded by drunken American soldiers of the Occupation, troops so dissipated and unruly that she believed the rumors of German girls being raped by GIs, their bodies then tossed from jeeps. Joseph met her, shaggy and unkempt, and her first act was to give her husband a haircut. Later someone said she must have put a bowl on his head.

Her goal was to reach Wildflecken, a camp for Polish displaced persons. Traveling in a rented jeep taxi across the icy landscape from Frankfurt toward Hanau, she passed the ruins of houses and factories, and was overcome by what she called "the German bitterness, the German misery . . . the cold hated life of a country in the bleak dawn." It took her and her black American driver from Georgia six hours to find the camp, once one of the largest SS training camps, now housing, among others, fifteen thousand uprooted Poles. One of Kay's objectives was to write a children's book about a little girl DP.

Kay arrived at two in the afternoon, only to find Wildflecken in turmoil over forced nationality screenings of the Poles. Many were upset, convinced that there would be forced repatriations back to Poland. Four men had almost been killed by a mob of fifteen hundred. Epidemic disease was rife among the children. When Kay burst into deputy director Kathryn Hulme's office, she was the first correspondent to set foot in this godforsaken place.

"If you knew me, you'd have known I'd have got through somehow," Kay told an astonished Hulme. Hulme felt her entire outlook turn brighter as she beheld Kay Boyle, a beautiful, gracious woman with perfectly coiffed grey hair which belied her long journey. Warm and friendly, Kay confided that she had to return immediately to Offenbach to be with her husband. But she took the time to meet Hulme's animals, whose names she at once learned. "And that's Lummel," Kay said, introducing herself to the dog. "And Framboise," she added, patting Hulme's cat.

Kay also found material for her morally outraged pen. She learned that "unaccompanied children" were being given the choice of being repatriated to Poland in a special children's train or traveling in boxcars with their DP guardians. Although at least half had witnessed their parents being murdered by the Nazis, a Polish officer attempted to cajole them into returning by promising, "Your parents are awaiting you in Poland." She wrote in *The Nation* about a nursing mother who sold her milk on the black market, and a German nurse who told her, "Hitler and the others wouldn't recognize their beautiful place now." Although Kay wanted to write a DP story that would "revolutionize" the world, instead she would chronicle what she saw at Wildflecken in a short story entitled "The Lost," published in 1951 in a magazine called *Tomorrow*, and leave it to Hulme to tell the story of the displaced persons in her own book, *The Wild Place*.

"I'll simply die until I know the end of this," Kay said as she prepared to depart the next morning, referring to the dispute among the inmates regarding the election of a new Polish committee, on which the antireparation faction demanded representation, an election further complicated by the issue of whether only Poles were to be eligible to vote. She told Hulme, "It's the duty of people like us to try to make America understand." A Polish DP drove her back to Offenbach in the confiscated Cadillac of a Nazi general. "Nazism has not been destroyed," he told her. "It is as strong in the people's hearts now as it ever was."

"She was like some bright beautiful herald of coming happiness," Hulme thought after she had said goodbye to Kay. "It was a beautiful thing she left with me and it changes everything. I have expectancy now, every time I look toward the West." Kay Boyle had insisted upon hope; she had disdained premature defeat and self-pity, and the moral and physical courage she seemed to possess in such abundance left many inspired.

In April, Kay went to Spain, as she had promised Julio Alvarez del Vayo, who, "very like Alexander Berkman," had assumed the role of hero in her life. In Paris, Del Vayo had founded an organization called Fighting Spain, in which Kay was ready to take part, as she invited Del Vayo to help celebrate Bobby's twentieth birthday. But when Kay produced an article about the trial of a group of nine teenagers in Madrid accused of terrorism, a study of the political persecution of intellectuals under Franco, Harold Ross rejected it as "too far outside our usual fact, or article treatment." "Isabelita Has Lost Her Reason" went to *The Nation* instead. In June, Kay returned to Spain, where she pictured the homeless living in caves, a fate they preferred to swearing they had never carried arms against Franco. "Faces of Spain" also went to *The Nation*. The fictional product of these trips to Spain was a long short story called "Passport to Doom" when it first appeared, but republished under Kay's original title, "Decision," in the 1958 reissue of *Three Short Novels*, where it replaced "Big Fiddle."

To the story's great detriment, Kay Boyle once more makes a gratuitous autobiographical appearance in her white earrings, leaving "Decision" only ostensibly about an anti-Franco intellectual who must decide whether or not to go into exile. Kay admitted to Ann Watkins, who was perplexed by the piece, that "Decision" was as much about herself, the author-narrator, as about her character Manuel; the title "Decision" referred equally to her "own to write" and to the Spaniard's. In fact, there is no real "decision" at all; Manuel's commitment to remain to oppose Franco has been a foregone conclusion from the start.

Kay Boyle called "Decision" "one of the most interesting things I have written," as she compared it to *Monday Night* and "The Crazy Hunter." Defensive about having written so many potboilers during the war, she asserted that "Decision" proved that she could "still write—and not in an emotional, overwrought way, but in a matured, disciplined way." She also predicted that it would be difficult to sell. But in fact *The Saturday Evening Post*, changing the title, wisely, to "Passport to Doom," bought it at once, recognizing it as their kind of material and of a piece with Kay Boyle's wartime romances.

Indeed, in 1947 and 1948 she continued to publish slick fiction for a mass audience, stories marred by excesses of sentimentality, stories populated by children and animals. "Miracle Goat," published in *Woman's Home Companion*, evokes one day when Kay at her sister Joan's New Jersey farm by herself delivered a kid, to the amazement of the entire family. In the story, the veterinarian appears as another of those men of reason and science Kay so scorned. Another autobiographical resonance is apparent: as the goat proves not to be too old to bear children, so Kay validated her own bearing of children into her forties. The alcoholic writer father, who lies down on his daughter's bed and confides his loneliness, is of course Laurence, who here conveys to Apple Kay Boyle's own credo: "Books are wrong and doctors are wrong because they've forgotten about the mystery."

Even more slight were "One Small Diamond, Please" and "The Searching Heart," which also went to *Woman's Home Companion*, and "Dream Dance," about Kathe as a ballerina, published in *The Saturday Evening Post*. No less trivial an effort was "Evening at Home," in which the writer depicts herself in her New York brownstone taking in for the night a drunken woman who for no apparent reason echoes Henry James by calling herself Mrs. Daisy Miller, a deed of charity which goes unrewarded. Somehow this story found its way into *The New Yorker*, although Harold Ross did reject a story Kay wrote about boy mascots of the American troops being sent to America—on the ground of its implausibility. *The New Yorker*, having done its fact check, still "didn't want to take a chance."

But even as she continued to publish such sentimental stories for easy money, she simultaneously began to write some of her finest fiction, at first in France and later in Germany. On the basis of the harrowing train ride from Paris to Frankfurt, she produced "Army of Occupation" for Harold Ross. The story remains powerful despite its autobiographical self-indulgences; even as Kay often amazed people by insisting that men were in love with her, here a corporal takes one look at the (still) black-haired, slender war correspondent, modest, shy, and vulnerable, now being harassed by drunken American soldiers, and at once not only falls in love with her but proposes marriage. Published in *Tomorrow* in May of 1948, Kay's fine "French Harvest" depicts war-torn France, where shopkeepers wonder whether "it might have been better if the Germans had won," and sodden GIs straddle a statue of Jeanne d'Arc. Harvests are still being brought in by unrepatriated German prisoners, who greet each other in the darkness of night with "*Heil Hitler!*"

Anti-American feeling runs rife. As in the 1966 reprise "Fire in the Vineyards," which would mark Kay Boyle's final appearance in the pages of *The Saturday Evening Post*, she tells of how Americans were despised because their country did not suffer as others had. Americans don't help matters by insisting on condemning France for sitting "on a corner holding a tin cup out." By the time "Fire in the Vineyards" was published, America was at war in Vietnam, and Kay Boyle used the earlier postwar moment to suggest that later time: "What are we doing in uniform in every European country? What are we doing here?" an American woman asks.

It was unfortunate for Kay that her fine novel *1939* was not published in America until February of 1948 with Edmund Wilson's review still reverberating among critics. Where, earlier, reviewers might have emphasized the fine level of craftsmanship, now they acknowledged Kay Boyle's mastery of technique only to zero in on her failure to distance herself as an author from her callow hero, the Kurt Wick figure, Ferdl. *The New Yorker*, her own magazine, found him "an improbably picturesque figure" whose "struggles with his political conscience seem pretty glossy"; in *The New York Times Book Review*, Nona Balakian called Ferdl "little more than a glamor-boy athlete and lover." Both Margery Barrett and Wilson had attacked Kay Boyle for her excesses of romanticism. Now *Time* began its review: "Why is it that Kay Boyle's novels so often disappoint?" Accurately, *Time* noted that her characters "don't stand a chance of survival between the same covers with Author Boyle's high-tension consuming prose." Indeed, having written *1939* at the height of her affair with Kurt Wick, and never having taken the time to revise it, she was guilty of insufficient irony, toward the man no less than toward her woman character who is so un-questioningly susceptible to him.

Even before these reviews appeared, Richard Simon had decided he could no longer keep pace with the stream of novels and reprints Kay Boyle always expected to have published immediately. Simon & Schuster, he wrote, "hasn't done for you the sort of job that your work deserves." Kay Boyle was still considered a literary figure to be reckoned with, and Ann Watkins at once enlisted as her editor Edward Aswell, editor-in-chief of Whittlesey House, the trade division of McGraw-Hill. He had succeeded Maxwell Perkins as Thomas Wolfe's editor when the author left Scribner's for Harper & Brothers.

Their first project would be the ski stories Kay had called "Enemy Detail," a title to which Aswell at once objected. American audiences were tired of the war and books about the war, he thought. Kay immediately changed the title of this novel about Joseph in the ski troops to *His Human Majesty*. Admiring, unceasingly encouraging, Aswell proved to be a publisher who would be the envy of any author. When by January of 1948 he still did not have his manuscript, he wrote to Kay Boyle: "My faith in you is unwavering, and will not waver. I have known all along that you were working very hard on this new novel and have suspected that you were having some trouble making it come right. But it will come right, and I know that just as you do." By February, after he had read one hundred and forty-one pages, Aswell was ecstatic. "This is a great book," he pro-claimed. In March, he told her she had entered "a new period" in her writing. He felt "immense pride" to have "some small share, some iden-tification, with what I am convinced is to be your period of greatest real-ization and fruitfulness as an artist." For Aswell, it was as if Kay Boyle were starting over.

Kay tried to meet the challenge, complaining all the while about "12 million interruptions and demands and frustrations a day." In 1947 she had developed such severe stomach pain that she thought she must have ulcers. She tried to persuade Joseph "to resign his foul job in Germany" so that they could move to the French countryside, as once she and Laurence had done. Having completed an assignment as a translator in the office of the chief counsel for war crimes at Nuremberg, Joseph had come to France in September of 1947 and applied for a job with the United Nations, only to be told that the quota for Americans had been filled. Unable to get a job, Joseph studied under the GI Bill of Rights at the Ecoles des Hautes Etudes Internationales Sociales et du Journalisme. Then he returned to Wiesbaden to work for the military government of Hesse.

In addition to her usual responsibilities, Kay had also to entertain her mother-in-law, the Countess Esterházy, who attended Mass twice a day, and began a campaign for Kay to have her marriage to Richard Brault annulled so that she and Joseph could be married in the eyes of the Catholic Church. One of the conditions for such an annulment was for Kay to swear that she had never consummated her marriage to Brault.

"Any one of those conditions would be a lie," Kay protested.

"*Ma chérie*," the Countess persisted, "couldn't you lie just this one time?" Kay held firm and there was no annulment. She was even amused by the Countess, who returned home from church one day dissolved in tears over a war criminal who had committed suicide in his Paris jail cell.

"But, Momi," Kay demurred, "he sent hundreds of thousands of Jews to their deaths."

"Yes, *ma chérie*," said the unflappable Countess. "But he was a baron!"

If Kay Boyle had truly remained in Paris to be near all her children, the decision was not an unqualified success. About to join her mother at Le Vésinet in a rented house with a yard, Kathe was reluctant to leave her dog, Réma, behind in Mégève. But Kay insisted. Her response to willful children who challenged their mother's wisdom was that they must not love her enough.

"Don't be angry and please understand me and my feelings," Kathe, now thirteen, pleaded with her "Mimsy" as she tried to get her mother to understand how she felt about Réma: "I love her so much, even better than ballet, so if it is very impossible for her to come I should prefer to stay here." Kathe feared that Réma would forget her and that the dog was too young to have puppies in her absence.

"Amazing," Kay replied. "A daughter who prefers her dog to her mother!"

Kathe capitulated. In great sorrow, leaving Réma behind in Mégève, she went to live with her mother in Paris.

"Where's Réma?" Kay asked as soon as Kathe arrived.

"You told me not to bring her," Kathe answered.

"Oh, did I?" Kay airily murmured.

Kay had told Kathe everything had been arranged about school. In fact, it had not. She had still to take an entrance exam. On a hot summer day while the rest of the family relaxed at the Morrises' place in Rosay-en-Brie, Kathe went alone to take her exam. Her mother cared more about her work than about them, Kathe thought, unlike Laurence, who was human, who never let you down. When a medical examination revealed Kathe suffered from incipient tuberculosis, she returned to the mountains of Mégève and her beloved Réma.

In these postwar years none of Kay's children were happy. Lonely and disoriented, Apple, seventeen and young for her years, lived with Bobby. One night, a cast-off boyfriend of Bobby's crawled into her bed and she lost her virginity. Frightened, she became sexually frigid for years to come. Mousie and Boostie huddled together in a school where they were taught by nuns who did not allow them to speak English. The two became virtually inseparable, so that Mousie refused even to go to the dentist because it meant hours of separation from her brother.

One day Kay picked Clover up from school. Suddenly, impulsively, Clover bent down and kissed her mother's hand on the seat beside her. At once, repelled, hating to be confronted by this child's overwhelming need for her, Kay pulled away.

"Don't ever do that again!" she said harshly. It was a moment Clover would remember all her life, her own act of subservience and her mother's rejection and failure to appreciate the depth of her love.

Between January and May of 1948, while Kay remained in France at Le Vésinet, Joseph continued at Wiesbaden, reporting on the progress the Germans were making toward democratization. He moved on to Marburg, where he reorganized the local newspaper on an American model, news in one place, opinions in another, while trying to make sure that Nazis weren't restored to their old positions of authority.

In Marburg, Joseph's closest colleagues were a man named Gerhard Gerber and Franz Borkenau, a lecturer in modern history at Marburg University and former Communist and member of the West European section of the Presidium of the Comintern. Borkenau spent most of his time in classrooms inveighing against Communism. When he indicated he expected time off to prepare for his lectures, Joseph was firm. "You're working first for us," he told Borkenau. "Whenever you get through with your work here, I have no objection to your doing anything else."

"I can spot a Nazi or a Communist anywhere," Borkenau boasted.

"Did this man [a Nazi suspect] actually tell you he had been a member of the Nazi Party?" Joseph would persist. Borkenau asserted that he could tell by the way the man looked at him, the way he screamed at him, that he had been a Nazi.

"What about me?" Joseph ironically asked Borkenau one day. With his idealist's faith in American democracy, with his having looked death by the Gestapo in the eye, and with his years of service bringing democracy to the benighted former Reich, surely he was immune to Borkenau's accusations.

"You are not a Communist," Borkenau told him. But Borkenau had heard Joseph praise the Soviet Union for having abolished the death penalty and say he hated the talk of Communists being "enemies." Now behind Joseph's back, Borkenau sneered: "He's pro-Soviet." Already the House Un-American Activities Committee had begun its hearings on the Hollywood Ten. Joseph, however, whose loyalty to America had been demonstrated by his having risked his life on its behalf, went on innocently expressing his democratic beliefs. When Borkenau took a three-week leave, Joseph seized the opportunity and fired him.

That April of 1948, Joseph had to contend with a junior military government officer named Ernest Knoblauch, who was as virulently anti-

Communist as Borkenau. In addition, Knoblauch freely expressed his disdain for Jews and Negroes.

"The entire British Labour government is run by Jews," Knoblauch declared one day. Joseph objected.

"You're a Communist, aren't you?" Knoblauch finally sized up Joseph Franckenstein. McCarthyism was settling over Occupation Marburg; only a year later the government would refuse to allow black writer and ex-Communist Richard Wright to speak at Amerika Haus because he was "politically undesireable."

Joseph was a hero to most of his colleagues, like young Donald Muntz, who was in charge of the local Amerika Haus, one of eighteen or nineteen U.S. Information Service Centers with open-shelved libraries, music rooms, English-language programs, film showings, and a constant stream of lecturers which had been established in every major city and university town of the former American zone. Joseph was kindly, quiet, scholarly, and an egalitarian who insisted on being called plain "Joe." (He revealed, however, that he was a bit irritated that Mary Shelley had expropriated his family name.) His dark hair now covered a bald spot, but he was tall and slim and handsome, despite his prominent Esterházy nose, and his manners were courtly. None of the male members of his family had lived past the age of forty-six, Joseph liked to say, and he was convinced he would die young of cancer, as they had.

Another of Joseph's colleagues had been an American named Ted Goeser. When he said he was going to Paris, Joseph suggested he look up Kay. Soon Goeser found himself escorting Bobby and Apple out on the town. For once a man preferred the younger sister, Apple, whom Katherine Evans Boyle had taken to comparing to herself. Apple, her grandmother had concluded, was a person who "could not thrive on introspection, trying to conceal the feeling of inadequacy," and was of a lonely nature and "retiring," like herself.

To Ted, Apple confessed that Laurence had made her feel sexual, and that she was both afraid of him and afraid of denying him anything for fear of losing his love. It was clear to Ted that Apple had been alienated from her mother for some time. Apple told Ted how, as a child, she had listened outside Kay's door to the sound of the typewriter and been afraid to enter. "She wrote potboilers during the war," Apple said scornfully.

In May of 1948 Joseph came to Paris and escorted Mousie, Boostie, Clover, and Kay to Marburg. If Kay appreciated the medieval university town presided over by its eleventh-century *Schloss*, Germany still repelled her. Its ramparts were "flung far and wide," she wrote in her 1960 novel about Occupation Germany, *Generation Without Farewell*, "and its breast and bulwarks and heart made of the coldest stone." Kay described the children as "speechless at the sight of the destroyed cities, and everything still seemingly so recently bombed, with the radiators and bits of bed-steads still hanging from the twisted rafters."

The Franckensteins moved into a big five-bedroom house with bal-conies on the second story. It was on the Georg Voigtstrasse, on the side of a hill, and it had been confiscated by the Occupation government from a Nazi. But Kay had three servants, and, all the time they lived in Germany, Mousie and Boostie and Clover never did any chores; they dropped their pajamas on the floor knowing a maid would retrieve them, and they didn't have to make their beds.

Privilege in this context made Kay Boyle uneasy. She said she felt like "a conqueror, well-fed, well-housed, in a defeated but still bitterly defiant country." Surrounded by a "hard bitter population," she served her family American food purchased at the commissary and drove an American car. And she found the Americans serving the Occupation so insensitive that she feared her children would "turn into rude aggressive little Amer-icans"; there was "no possible gentleness or graciousness in life in this atmosphere." It was not a good combination, Kay found, the American "with the cold north German thing." If Nazism seemed alive and well, dismaying too was the callous disregard for ordinary German people she found among snobbish Americans who served with the Occupation. These Americans were so intolerant toward anything different from themselves that nine-year-old Clover's red bloomers worn under her skirt earned her the sobriquet "Stinky."

Nothing in Germany pleased Kay Boyle. If there was a "democratic force" at work in the trade union movement, it was weak and ineffectual. In local elections, old Nazi politicians were being reelected, and at a reception for one of the victors, Kay Boyle learned, the swastika was quickly removed from the parlor when an American intelligence officer entered the room. Kay typed Joseph's reports of interviews he did with local political leaders and noticed that not once did the words "liberty" and "freedom" appear in their dialogue. Instead they spoke of a "united German culture" and a "united Germany." Meanwhile she resented being told to be "tactful, to be careful, not to judge people too harshly, too indiscriminately," as was always her way, and to believe that people had been forced to join the Nazi Party. "What is this conspiracy which decrees that we must not be too brusque with the Germans . . . that they are not 'ready for the truth'?" she demanded.

Nor could Kay sympathize when people remarked on what a hard time the Germans were having. The Germans had higher bread rations than the French, Kay pointed out, and were already becoming better dressed. She was appalled by "the stubborn refusal to admit that the bones in exter-mination camps are bones and the human hair actually hair," the refusal of the Germans to believe "that millions were deliberately annihilated by design and plans." Kay Boyle said she feared that "the most monstrous national crime in history" would soon "become a mere incident in history." The writer who had promised to provide "a record of her age" was doing just that.

One night shortly after her arrival, after too many whiskeys with Gene Jolas, who was also serving with the Occupation, Kay concluded that what Germany needed was "the appearance of a figure as alien to them, and as strange to tradition as Gandhi." Jolas at once observed that such thinking was reminiscent of Hitlerism. But she remained too much a hero worshipper not to insist, "Why not a leader, a fuehrer if it be a leader who would teach Germany, as Gandhi did India, to strive for the dignity of freedom without succumbing to hatred or violence?" Contradicting herself, she maintained her hope that freedom would come to the Germans, although it could not be imposed on them: "it must come from their inner conviction."

From Kay Boyle's point of view, the Americans offered no more than a "show of uniforms." What was really needed was "an occupation by intellectuals" which "would give the Germans an awareness of their past monstrosities, a hatred of brutality, a realization of what a new future might be." Kay Boyle, gathering material for what would be among her strongest collections of short stories, *The Smoking Mountain*, one which in 1991 would find its way onto the German best-seller lists, forty years after its original publication, was appalled as she watched the Occupation impart to Germany the worst characteristics of home. Racism was rife, a racism endorsed by the locals, so that Kay's German cook spoke of "all these niggers you see around Marburg now." When Colonel Marcus Ray, General Clay's black adviser on "Negro affairs," arrived to study how black soldiers were being treated in the Occupation, Ernest Knoblauch and others let him know he was not welcome to dine at the club where officers were billeted. Joseph himself had been told they opposed "sitting down at table with a nigger." Ray ate with the Franckensteins on the Georg Voigtstrasse.

Some American officers were equally contemptuous of German intellectuals. At a gathering at Amerika Haus, the rector of Marburg University, who was a Kantian philosopher and a very old man, got up to lecture about education as the "road that all free men must share." He was shouted down by "Sonny" Jim Newman, the Land Commissioner for Hesse, who yelled that the old professor should speak English. Liberal Americans like Donald Muntz shifted uneasily in their seats. Kay described the incident exactly as it happened in *Generation Without Farewell*, where she gave Sonny Jim the name General Roberts.

Kay and Joseph had one more encounter with Ernest Knoblauch, whom Kay would depict as the intelligence officer Overstreet in *Generation Without Farewell*. Overstreet is a sly, insidious, black marketeer always on the lookout for dissent, which he interprets at once as "Communism." "I thought I detected a rosy tinge," Overstreet threatens the Donald Muntz character, Seth Honerkamp. By the novel's close, Overstreet has removed John Hersey's *Hiroshima* from the library as subversive, and has had Seth Honer-kamp fired.

Sometime later Kay and Joseph committed the unpardonable sin of refusing to attend Ernest Knoblauch's housewarming party.

Knoblauch, who no doubt wanted to show off the famous writer to his friends, was furious. The Franckensteins simply had to attend his party. Suddenly Knoblauch invoked a "list" he had made. Gesturing toward his inner breast pocket, he seemed to imply not only that he would show Joseph the list if he agreed to attend the party *but* that should Kay and Joseph not attend, they might find their own names on "a list" as well.

"You don't want to be put in such a spot," Knoblauch threatened, insinuating that the list contained names of people willing to testify against him. When Joseph looked dubious, Knoblauch became more specific.

"Do you want to see the list?" he taunted. "If you agree to go to the party, I'll show you the list. Otherwise I won't."

"I'm not interested in seeing any list," Joseph said coldly. "We're not going. I don't care." Then he demanded that Knoblauch, whom he despised, leave his office at once. Knoblauch was eventually given a bad efficiency rating and asked to resign.

Hating the well-fed smug Americans, housebreakers, thieves, and bandits preyed on the easy-living Occupation officers. After their house was robbed while they were sleeping upstairs, Kay no longer felt safe at night when Joseph was away hunting. It was a pastime he enjoyed despite his singular lack of success in killing animals.

20

The Smoking Mountain

I have done a book, and in it I have made clear, I think, my feelings about this wretched country—and its tragic people.

Married to a young husband, Kay was careful never to allow Joseph to see her without makeup. She always dressed up, even to shop for groceries. She said it was gratifying for Joseph to be able to support his family for the first time, although in fact they spent all they had and there was never enough money. But Kay insisted it was a relief not to be making all the household decisions herself. It was a relief, she said, "to be considered (by Germans and Americans alike) as a 'dependent woman' and therefore of no real importance." It had been a long time since she had been bothered by crises of identity, when being considered "dependent" could have damaged her strong sense of her own importance. As for Joseph, he worshipped his returned wife, fondly calling her "Fifi."

Old friends like Jimmy Stern and Robert McAlmon remained dubious and concluded her new marriage was a terrible mistake. McAlmon's opinion was that Kay was unhappy, even miserable, if relieved that her oldest children were now "on their own," with Laurence responsible for them. "What's the cause of Kay Boyle's misery?" McAlmon wrote Stern in October of 1948. "Is she suffering a marriage split up or disillusion about herself as a writer and less success?"

Her writing schedule was now, however, even more demanding than it had been at Mégève. In Germany, Kay Boyle rose at five in the morning, even if she and Joseph had stayed up until four at a party. By the time she joined the family for breakfast she had written for three hours. When she learned that her editor, Edward Aswell, had four children himself, she said she knew he would understand "what it is to have the interests, the demands, the love, of six pulling at one's time, one's capacities, one's heart." It was her old complaint about having to work hard at "baby love," which she had made twenty years earlier in the South of France. In fact, no one was permitted to interfere with her work for long. Soon in Germany people began to realize that you didn't dare tell her anything or you'd wind up in print and be surprised because she never told you she was doing it.

As always, of course, Kay Boyle's social life was full. There was a dinner with a judge who told her, "In my position, unfortunately, it was never possible for me to know what the common man was thinking." Afterwards Kay said she shuddered thinking of the dozens of common men who must have passed before that judge "in their moments of greatest trouble and distress." Such tones of high-minded moral indignation were ever more customary with her now. At lunch with Thornton Wilder on the day after he spoke at the university, Kay asserted, melodramatically, "I'd rather be dead than Swiss."

"But, madam, a fine distinction!" Wilder replied. They agreed it was better to live in Europe, "the actual problems nearer to truth," than in America. But sometime later when Kay traveled to Berlin and ran into Wilder on the train, he snubbed her. "Silly man," she pronounced him, one of the few she had not succeeded in charming.

As she published more nonfiction in *The Nation*, Kay became known as much as a social commentator as a writer of fiction. From America she was constantly sought to sign petitions for a host of causes. However pressed the family was for money, Kay Boyle could always be counted on for a small contribution to a good cause, like the Girls' Vacation Fund, to send a child to camp. Many petitions must have come to Kay Boyle, either directly or indirectly, from Freda Kirchwey and *The Nation*, because during her stay in Germany she put her signature to several documents ostensibly issued by independent groups which were in fact sponsored by the Communist Party. Unknowingly, Kay lent her name, her prestige, and sometimes her money to groups whose politics were far from what she would have found acceptable.

Too quickly reading these texts, she believed only that she was supporting worthy causes. When an appeal went out to American writers on behalf of eleven executive board members of the Joint Anti-Fascist Refugee Committee, who had been convicted of contempt of Congress for refusing to open their books and records to the House Un-American Activities Committee, Kay Boyle signed her name. In March of 1949, she allowed her name to be used to sponsor the Call to the Cultural and Scientific Conference for World Peace, known as the Waldorf Conference, another Communist-sponsored event. In July, she was listed as a sponsor of a Bill of Rights Conference; in September, of the American Continental Congress for World Peace held in Mexico City. Ten dollars went to the National Conference Against Deportation Hysteria, sponsored by a dubious organization called the American Committee for the Protection of the Foreign Born. Ann Watkins had forwarded the appeal along with her other mail, and to Kay Boyle it seemed perfectly acceptable to provide legal representation for foreign-born men and women who couldn't afford lawyers. In the same spirit she sent fifteen dollars to the American Association for the United Nations and some money to the Boys' Brotherhood Republic, a boys' camp for poor children. If hidden agendas were being served, Kay Boyle certainly had no time to inquire into what they might be.

It was not only Communist Party surrogates to whom Kay gave her support. She inspected the book collection at Amerika Haus, and wrote to Joseph's superior Fred Leonard suggesting that the library include more southern writers, like Faulkner, Erskine Caldwell, Carson McCullers, and Katherine Anne Porter. She noticed that her friend James T. Farrell's *Studs Lonigan* trilogy was absent, and recommended that. And she wanted German students to be afforded access to all the library's services.

She was always in search of material. One night Gerhard Gerber brought Nazi aviatrix Hannah Reitsch to dinner at the house on the Georg Voigtstrasse. Kay served shrimps ("little crabs," Reitsch called them) while Hannah told her how throughout the war she had dreamed of saving human lives. "It was the young I cared about," Hannah Reitsch said as Kay listened in disgust. Meanwhile Reitsch had succeeded in inventing a way for German planes to cut through the cables of the London barrage balloons. She spoke too of hers having been the last plane to take off from Berlin at the end of the war.

As for the Jews, Hannah Reitsch knew nothing. "You see, I was a flying woman, a birdwoman," she told Kay. "I only knew what was taking place in the sky. I was not even a member of the Nazi Party." Kay Boyle had been in search of "another face of Germany." In Hannah Reitsch she did not find it, as she continued what she called her "painstaking and almost completely loveless search" for "good" Germans. Kay now concluded they had either been exterminated or become refugees. Remnants of Nazism seemed to be everywhere. Later in Frankfurt, when she emerged from her house, the street cleaner on Kay's block would salute, standing completely rigid, holding his broom straight up, in the fascist style.

When polio broke out in Germany during the summer of 1948, Joseph and Donald Muntz organized a campaign to purchase iron lungs for the Marburg hospital. Kay asked friends in America like Ann Watkins for donations, and professed herself delighted that the Germans "in this bigoted little town are acting really democratic—all working for a common purpose in which the common-weal is concerned." This event was worked into Kay's novel *Generation Without Farewell*. "All this had never before taken place in Hesse," Kay was to write, "perhaps never before in Germany."

The polio scare induced Kay to send Clover off to Laurence and to board Mousie and Boostie at a farm in the country. Terrified, the children huddled together at night in a big feather bed, which they unfailingly wetted.

"Why do we pee in our bed?" Mousie asked Kay when she came to visit over the weekend.

"You pee in bed because you've been left alone here and you're unhappy," Kay told her youngest daughter. The explanation seemed to help. But that night Mousie wet the bed once more.

Laurence that summer took Kathe and Clover to Italy. Kathe told Clover to conceal how many letters she was writing to her mother lest his feelings be hurt. But Clover seemed always to be insisting on staying in her room to write one more letter. Long hours she wept in misery because she missed Kay so much. Nor could Clover bear the slightest criticism of her mother. When Clover accused Kathe of pulling her hair while combing it and Kathe remarked that Kay pulled it much more, Clover leapt to her mother's defense. "She does not. Mommy's nice!" Clover insisted.

At every opportunity Clover brought Kay's name into the conversation. Even when someone noted that the restaurants in Florence did not open until seven-thirty in the evening, Clover couldn't resist pointing out that "Mommy has dinner at six." Jeannie was hurt because, as they explored exotic new places, all Clover would talk about was what Mousie and Boostie had done, or what "Doday," which was Joseph's name with the children, said when he went hunting, or how Mommy's dog ran away. Kay was always on her children's minds, as Kathe too, during a fierce electric storm in Rimini, could think only of how terrified Mama, who was so afraid of storms, would have been.

"I like Venice a lot, but I like home best," Clover said at the end of the trip.

"Where is home?" Laurence asked his youngest gently. But having been instructed by Kathe to hide her tears, not to reveal how much she missed Kay, Clover did not speak the words which rose to her heart: Where Mama is, that's home.

In October, Kay left for Paris to attend Bobby's wedding to Michel Sciama, a young teacher who had been a hero in the French resistance, which he had joined when he was seventeen. Sciama had been captured and incarcerated for two years at Buchenwald. Clover cried for five days without stopping. Joseph seemed unable to assume a parental role toward his stepdaughter. He was kindly but distant, and didn't seem to pay much attention. When her mother was gone, Clover felt as if she herself no longer existed, and Kay seemed always to be absent; as an adult Clover would remember of the years in Germany Kay forever going to the "prisons," which had become one of Kay Boyle's causes.

"I don't know why you're always crying," Kay told Clover in exasperation one day, "you're the worst child." Fearing her disapproval, the children learned to conceal their feelings. Kay was prone to treat an angry child as a personal affront.

In the autumn of 1948, Kay and Joseph moved to Frankfurt, where Joseph had been appointed deputy chief of the Press Branch of the Military Government. The six daily newspapers in the Frankfurt region were his responsibility. It was in late November as she was packing for the move that Kay Boyle heard rumors that during the past summer she and Joseph had been investigated as Communists. "This is the kind of evil, of madness, one has to deal with," Kay Boyle said impatiently.

Kay called the move to Frankfurt "as near to living in suburbia as possible—if you turn your head from the ruins." But she had a fine stone house covered with ivy, a house with the luxury of two bathrooms, where she created a salon. Eugene Jolas was now editing the *Neue Zeitung*, the Occupation's German-language daily newspaper, and was working closely with Joseph. Evenings Maria Jolas came to play the piano and sing her mildly bawdy, slightly racist songs of the American South.

Finally, in the women of Frankfurt Kay found occasion for hope. At Christmas the German women marched in protest against the war toys Americans had put in the Frankfurt toy stores. When Kay requested from the editor of the *Frankfurter Rundschau*, an anti-Nazi who had been in a concentration camp during the war, a list of prominent women who had been antifascists, she was referred to one Helga Einsele, the director of the Frankfurt Women's Prison and a lawyer. Introducing herself as a reporter, Kay interviewed Einsele about the prison. She was astonished to discover that the women prisoners were living in virtual solitary confinement, not because Dr. Einsele wanted it that way, but because the prison had been built a century before and lacked common rooms. At once Kay offered to give English lessons to the prisoners. Soon she was appearing once and sometimes twice a week.

She threw herself into teaching the prisoners, accepting all comers. The only English the prisoners knew was what they had learned from their GI boyfriends. Kay at once instructed Ann Watkins to ship two copies of *Alice in Wonderland* for her "life-termers." Kay helped her students write a play based on "Der Rattenfänger von Hameln," and it was performed for the assembled prison population—with Mousie and Boostie in the cast. Einsele had no budget, and so Kay provided all the props herself, as well as the pencils and paper for the English lessons, along with sweets for the prisoners. Christmas of 1950 Kay dressed Mousie as an angel with great white wings and a silver crown and the child sang "O Little Town of Bethlehem" before weeping inmates.

When Einsele visited the Franckensteins at home, she was received by her hostess dramatically attired in a long black dress, with her inevitable white earrings. Einsele watched admiringly as Kay danced with her handsome husband. Later when Kay gave a speech in Heidelberg about the personality of a woman in a free country, a speech based on her grandmother Eva Evans, Helga Einsele served as her interpreter. Einsele anticipated that there would be a small audience, with the event taking place at the local Amerika Haus. She was amazed to discover the university campus at Heidelberg filled with fancy cars and an audience in evening dress come to hear her unassuming friend Kay Boyle, who was introduced as "one of the greatest living writers in the world."

Kay Boyle said she enjoyed writing *His Human Majesty*, "perhaps because Joseph is one of the principal men in it." Although she had begun it at the time of the novel's action, in 1943, she completed it only in the late forties in Germany. Indeed, she admitted it felt "really ridiculous" to be in Germany "writing this novel about the issues of 1944." Then she added with her now customary exaggeration: "with a revolution taking place around us." Her only hope was that *His Human Majesty* would be perceived as addressing universal issues of "truth and loyalty—and fidelity."

Although *His Human Majesty* was written with serial sale in mind, each chapter ending on a little climax, *The Atlantic*, its intended home, rejected it for serialization. Joseph is idealized as Fennington, singing as he skis. He sucks in the smoke of his cigarette as Joseph did, and speaks in the voice of Kay Boyle: "the capacity for lightness and gaiety is courage, and the capacity for depression, cowardice." One revealing moment comes when Kay uses the pages of her novel to chide her husband for worshipping her as much as he did, as if, yielding to truth in her fiction, she felt a certain discomfort with not being loved for herself as a real woman with all the flaws and inadequacies that go with being human. "Perhaps there's no woman high enough, pure enough for you, except in dreams," someone tells Fennington.

Not surprisingly, despite some routine praise, the reviewers were skeptical. In *The Saturday Review*, Nathan Rothman complained of Kay Boyle's "signal failure . . . to bring her visionary art to terms with reality," and Nona Balakian in *The New York Times Book Review* worried that "her characters become simply projections of her highly emotional responses." Peter White in *The Commonweal* doubted "if any good publisher would have accepted this as the first novel of an unknown author."

Even as *His Human Majesty* sold few copies, Kay Boyle enlisted her now standard defense: that high-minded themes should compensate for less than well-wrought fiction. She was insisting that her work be judged for the nobility of her sentiments and for her politically impeccable intentions. "I probably write to escape a feeling of guilt," she was quoted as saying in the same issue of the *Times* which ran Balakian's review. "I feel guilt for every act of oppression that has been committed in my time, and the older I grow the more I want to write about those commonplace things that we all accept which lead to acts and eventually to states of official oppression." It was ironic that the novel which occasioned these ringing words was, perhaps, her weakest.

At the same time as she was completing *His Human Majesty*, Kay began to write some of her most powerful short stories, inspired by her experiences in Occupied Germany. "I want to write stories madly—the feeling of the people—and have made copious notes," she told Ann Watkins. There was no American better placed to chronicle that historical moment. If no two writers at that point in Kay Boyle's career had less in common than she, now a social realist, and Henry James, ever turning inward, they did share their internationalism. Both defined what it meant to be American by confronting their characters with denizens of the Old World, in Kay Boyle's case American postwar culture with its European counterpart in all its vestigial fascism.

Jean Stafford arrived to work on a piece about Germany for *The New Yorker*. Competitively, Kay took Stafford to task for her "superficiality": "I believe it a real tragedy that you did not go down and talk to the young men beside the Neckar spitting at Americans and at American cars." Stafford was wrong in her belief that the Occupation workers lived "in comfort, wealth and beauty," in contrast to the Germans. And she had spent only three days.

At a furious pace, Kay now began to write stories on two themes. She tackled the Occupation itself with its "departmental intrigues, the defeat of all idealism, the total absence of any understanding of why we are here." At the same time she would "try to articulate all the despair, the absolute hopelessness" she felt about the Germans. In 1949 *The New Yorker* published five of Kay Boyle's finest stories, all to be collected in *The Smoking Mountain*, her next book with Edward Aswell at McGraw-Hill, which she dedicated "to Harold Ross who wanted fiction out of Germany."

Kay Boyle's best German stories are free of her earlier tendencies toward mannerism and arch and precious set pieces of description. She wrote plainly and yet ironically, as if she were an anthropologist in quest of discovering how the atrocities of Nazism could have happened. As Helga Einsele put it, in Germany the "devastating fire had been extinguished, but the mountain went on smouldering for a long time after." From this insight Kay produced masterpieces like "The Criminal," set in Marburg, where the "criminal" is not the Nazi who turned in the names of neighbors whom he caught listening to Allied broadcasts, but a starving German who breaks into houses at night to steal food, as a robber had done at Kay Boyle's own house. She shows us the peanut butter, "as thick as clay," which she purchased for Mousie, Boostie and Clover, and even the "Walther" (in reality a Luger) which Joseph had "liberated" from the Germans in May of 1945 as he escaped from the Gestapo.

The equally powerful "Begin Again" depicts the Kay figure on the autobahn picking up hitchhikers. A young girl with bleached hair and "Post Exchange" nylons says, "I don't see how a white girl can go out with a nigger." A one-legged veteran recalls "the good years"; a former judge confides he is certain Franklin Roosevelt "had Jewish blood." Wisely the author refrains from commenting, allowing her German characters to indict themselves. In "Fife's House," a chilling story, Fife is Ian, whose mother sits forever typing on her bed, while his friend Horst, a ten-year-old miniature Nazi, steals his watch, and finally sets fires in the garbage cans. But Kay Boyle is equally hard on the officers of the American Army of

Occupation for their callous disregard of German suffering in the fine "Summer Evening."

In 1949, in a harbinger of what was to come, *The New Yorker* rejected one of Kay Boyle's stories. "Frankfurt in Our Blood" was less a story than a little dialogue between two women on a train, one Jewish, one Kay Boyle. *The Nation* published it. But it seemed that Kay had lost some of her power as a writer of fiction. Increasingly now she was writing essay-like didactic passages into her stories, and she began to have real trouble selling them.

By December of 1949 she was begging Ann Watkins not to lose faith in her as a writer of fiction, not to conclude that she was "not going to write stories that sell anymore." Admitting that her writing was not going well, Kay pleaded that she was facing a "re-adjustment to life on occupation terms." Once this was over, she would do better. But "The Lovers of Gain," which in June of 1950 only *The Nation*, a magazine largely of political journalism, would buy, revealed an exhausted writer.

The best writing she did in 1950 was her reportage of the trial of a Nazi named Heinrich Baab, who had participated in fifty-six acts of murder in Frankfurt between 1938 and 1943. "A Reporter in Germany—The People with Names" was published in *The New Yorker* and became the "Introduction" to *The Smoking Mountain*. Kay at once perceived the significance of the Baab trial. It was not an American-ordered denazification, but a German being condemned by Germans, in a German courtroom, before German judges and a German jury. Here she was confident she had at last discovered "the *other* face of Germany." It was about "the good Germans" realizing that the "punitive stage" could not cease until every German "realizes and acknowledges what took place here less than a decade ago."

Before Hannah Arendt made the same point about Adolf Eichmann, Kay discovered in Baab, sitting in the dock compulsively shelling and eating peanuts, the "mediocrity" of such men. Lacking the political and philosophical range of Arendt, she is not very successful when she attempts to analyze what made Baab, whose father was a member of the Social Democratic Party, develop his taste for "uniformed prestige." For her overview, she relies on a quote her friend Heinz Pol had sent her: "We Germans have never fought on the barricades for freedom . . . we have never tried and condemned one of our own kings, or presidents, or leaders."

Where Kay Boyle excels in "The People with Names" is in her dramatic powers as a novelist, in her novelistic portraits of Baab himself, of his surviving victims and those witnesses who have come to testify against him, and of prosecuting attorney Kosterlitz, whom she describes with the "French word *fin*, which means that he is subtle and quick of mind, and exact and light of speech." When Kay showed her manuscript to Kosterlitz, the only Jew involved in the trial, he told her that "it does not seem humanly possible that anyone not born in this country could have done such a job both in comprehension and in accuracy." Indeed, when *The Smoking Mountain* was reviewed, the *New York Herald Tribune Book Review* called her reportage of the Baab trial "a terrifying document," and several critics compared her to Rebecca West.

Kay had been irritated when *The New Yorker* demanded from McGraw-Hill a permissions fee of fifty dollars for each of the eleven stories published in *The Smoking Mountain* which had first appeared in its pages. They had invoked her 1946 contract, which gave them full copyright, a condition she had accepted to lessen her income-tax burden. But Aswell's advance had been a respectable fifteen hundred dollars. Each year, from 1946, when their contractual relationship began, Kay Boyle was, nonetheless, eager to renew her arrangement with *The New Yorker*. It gave her press credentials to travel in the East and access to such events as the Baab trial. She told Ann Watkins she felt "very strongly" about remaining on a correspondent basis. "I love Ross—and I feel closely allied to the whole outfit," she said. In May of 1950 her press accreditation had got her to East Berlin, where "NO ONE is being allowed in or out this week unless one has press accreditation." She had hoped then to write a piece about a Communist rally, an article that never materialized.

In the spring of 1951 Joseph was given home leave. Kay Boyle took her family to America in time for the publication of *The Smoking Mountain*, and she gave interviews on what she had discovered in Germany. Invoking Hans Jahn, the head of the Railway Workers Union, whom she had portrayed in an article in *The Nation*, she told *The New York Times* that the American Occupation was not "giving enough support to what is good in Germany," like the democratic trade union movement, "the only anti-Communist force that is absolutely adamant in its anti-Communist position." Dissident and democrat she might be, but she made it abundantly clear that she was not a Communist.

What with the publication of another powerful collection of her short stories this would seem to be a moment of triumph. But it was now, at the beginning of the fifties, that Kay Boyle's stories stopped selling in America. Never again would she sell another story to *The New Yorker*. Before long even an old standby like *The Nation* could no longer be counted on to print her fiction. There were many reasons why her fiction was no longer easily salable, some of them her fault, others a reflection of the state of literary culture in America, and still others resulting from the historical moment.

Harold Ross had fallen ill with cancer, and the decisions about Kay Boyle's fiction at *The New Yorker* were being made by Gus Lobrano, with whom she shared no personal ties. Lobrano clearly did not like her work. Rejecting a story, he agreed to consider revisions, but nothing she did satisfied him. Until 1952 Kay's contractual arrangement giving *The New Yorker* the right of first refusal to four stories a year continued, but they simply stopped buying. For this reason even she was reluctant to sign the

1952 renewal. Then she concluded that it "would be the wrong time to make a break" and renewed the arrangement.

Although her increasing didacticism, and the hastiness with which she was turning out story after story, contributed to her dilemma, it was not the case that all of Kay Boyle's stories were so weak that they were no longer publishable. A typical example of her problems with Lobrano involved one of her most interesting stories, originally called "The Dancing School," which was based on a day in the life of a well-meaning and liberal servant of the Occupation—namely, Donald Muntz. Rejecting it, Lobrano said he doubted whether semi-starvation was still common among the Germans. "Our impression," he wrote Ann Watkins, "is that it belongs pretty much to a past era," no matter that Kay Boyle knew otherwise. Lobrano's complaint that there was "no element which binds the various episodes of the piece into a significant whole" was more valid. She rewrote "The Dancing School," only for Lobrano to reject it again as still lacking "a sharp focus." In fact, the story, published in *The Smoking Mountain* as "Aufwiedersehen Abend," is one of the best in the collection.

A more significant reason why Kay Boyle had lost her American audience was that she was attempting to address an America which had little sense of what was happening in Europe—and didn't care. It was the fifties, when Americans wanted to forget the agonies of the previous decade and to believe that everything was right with the world. The very fact that Kay Boyle continued to set her stories in Europe made them difficult to sell in America. Even Ann Watkins was reluctant, she said, to send "The Dancing School" to *Harper's* because she believed it showed "the German people nostalgic for the Nazi regime," as if this weren't the case. Overruled by her client, Watkins submitted it and *Harper's* bought it. (They paid, however, only three hundred dollars, a far cry from the thousand she had been getting from *The New Yorker*.)

The fifties were also a time when Americans were turning inward, cultivating their own gardens. The renewal of interest in psychoanalysis and Freudian psychology demanded a preoccupation with self and home. Writers for the popular magazines were exalting the virtues of domesticity, reflecting a cultural taste for isolationism of which Kay would never again be capable. France and Germany, where her stories were set, were now part of a distant bad dream. Then the Korean War intervened, further diverting America's interest away from the aftermath of World War II. With a new war in the newspapers, no one wanted to buy stories about that earlier conflict which were not leavened by Cold War imperatives.

Kay Boyle had also to confront still another adversary. McCarthyism by the early fifties had so pervaded the culture as to frighten magazines away from printing anything with the remotest suggestion of political, let alone dissident, content. In such a cultural climate they censored themselves. Kay's stories out of Germany attacking racism among Americans in the Occupation were enough to be interpreted as disloyalty, as were her other criticisms of the Occupation. It didn't even require that she and Joseph were now being investigated in earnest by the FBI. As story after story was now rejected, Kay could only suffer in dismay.

Meanwhile her financial obligations seemed to be multiplying geometrically. She was helping to support Katherine, now in a nursing home in California, her mother-in-law, the Countess Esterházy, her own grown children, and Joseph's widowed sister-in-law's children, as well as her immediate family of Clover, Mousie, and Boostie. Joseph's minimal government salary made scarcely a dent. Soon Kay Boyle found herself "typing ten and twelve hours a day nearly every day," typing through increasingly painful gallbladder attacks, and toothaches, neglecting her teeth so badly that an infection rotted part of her jawbone away. She herself had known that "The Dancing School" was "a bit rambling and filled with stuff I simply had to get off my mind." She knew too that stories with European settings were almost impossible to sell.

Then she underestimated the problem of selling her stories in America. *Harper's* had "wonderful foreign coverage," she thought. And indeed they did buy not only "Aufwiedersehen Abend" but also "Home," a story about an African-American GI who falls for a scam enacted by a German woman using her children to fleece innocent soldiers. His need to be "the dispenser of white-skinned charity" has rendered him vulnerable. (In 1955 *Harper's* also bought "The Kill.") Lobrano had rejected "Home" because, he said, "it isn't really clear why the G.I. in this case is a Negro." But it was also rejected by *The Saturday Evening Post* before *Harper's* took it. Kay Boyle had been fortunate in selling this story to *Harper's*, as she and Watkins both underestimated her dilemma. Indeed, Watkins continued to submit Kay Boyle's stories to Gus Lobrano at *The New Yorker*.

But Lobrano also rejected a story called "Famine," a hunting story which had no politically sensitive themes. This time Stuart Rose at *The Saturday Evening Post*, an editor who admired Kay, came to her aid, paying her a much-needed three thousand dollars, and changing the title to "A Disgrace to the Family." "So much for Lobrano's criticism that it was more writing than story," Kay told Ann Watkins, "for writing certainly does not sell to 'The Post.' " If her work no longer pleased the serious arbiters of fiction, at least she was making money.

Lobrano rejected "Cabaret," a riveting vignette of young actors at a *Gaststube* attempting to confront a middle-class German audience with its Nazi past, only for the unregenerate Nazis to laugh uproariously at the anti-Nazi skits. It was "too cumbrous to be wholly effective," Lobrano said, and it went to *Tomorrow*. "The Lost," her story about Wildflecken, and in particular about an American Army "mascot" who believes a black American GI will adopt him and take him to America, seemed virtually impossible to sell. At *The New Yorker* it was rejected by William Maxwell because "this is the sort of story we should have published in 1947, at the latest." *Today's Woman* told Ann Watkins that "the subject of European orphan children is a somewhat familiar one to us at this point." Kay Boyle, they implied, had become passé. Knox Burger at *Collier's*, who professed to be very interested in her writing, rejected "The Lost" on the ground of its improbability: "I think that it is unlikely that a boy who is as responsive, as quick to learn and mimic Americans, would, at this stage of the game, be unaware of the fact that prejudice toward the Negro exists in America."

"I know how futile is the argument that it really happened," she helplessly told Watkins, "but still, it really did." That she was writing so hastily also contributed to her many rejections. Lobrano patiently told Watkins he was rejecting "The Kill" because he wasn't sure "what Kay had in mind making the boy's father an American Indian. The father's background seems to have very little to do with the essential theme of the story, and somehow he didn't come out clearly as an Indian." Such a response reflected the carelessness with which the story was composed, and "The Kill" was also rejected by *The Reporter* and *The New American Mercury*, which told Watkins that "most of us feel that Miss Boyle is going backwards in this one; it reads so much like the things she used to do in the 30's." It is difficult to tell whether this invocation of the politically charged thirties masked current self-censorship since Kay's stories were now being turned out so rapidly that often indeed they lacked shape and focus.

Kay was helping fuel her detractors by continuing to repeat herself and by producing fiction that was less than polished. "Autobahn, 1951" was an attempted reprise of "Begin Again," the fine story in which she had pictured herself picking up hitchhikers. "If you don't sell it to 'The New Yorker' I shall utter piercing screams," she melodramatically wrote Watkins.

But *The New Yorker* rejected it immediately and predictably, as "a good deal less effective than the similar piece Kay did about the Autobahn a couple of years ago." Whit Burnett rejected it for *Story* because it was "almost only a sketch." *The Reporter* rejected it as "not up to her usual level." Even Carey McWilliams at *The Nation* couldn't help her this time, admitting only that "this particular story just doesn't fit our needs at present."

To save face, and in a desperate attempt to return to the fold, Kay sent *The New Yorker* "A Christmas Story for Harold Ross," stipulating that it was Ross's private property and could not be shown to anyone else. But it too was rejected. It was around this time, according to Joan Givner's biography of Katherine Anne Porter, that Porter revised her view of Kay Boyle. "How I was deceived in this talent," she said, remembering the praise she had lavished on *Plagued by the Nightingale* and on the *Wedding Day* collection. "It rotted very early. But it *was* talent."

Despairingly now, Kay was ready to give up on the short story, the form in which she had most excelled. When Ross had bought her piece on the Baab trial for *The New Yorker*, she had hoped this "might break the spell" of the magazine's "psychosis now about my things." Still in the hope of another *New Yorker* sale, Kay had turned her attention to writing about a trial involving animal poisoning at the Frankfurt zoo. The director appointed in 1945 had been a member of the Nazi Party, a fact he concealed. Meanwhile the head keeper was accused of poisoning animals, only for the poisonings to continue while he was in jail.

Ross had responded enthusiastically to the idea. Although he had "a rather vast amount of German stuff on hand," he encouraged her to go forward, promising too that if they decided to cover the Ilse Koch trial, Kay Boyle would be "the girl for it from our standpoint." But Ross had to tell Kay that "with this country's mind on another war now, we are doubtful about covering still another Nazi trial." Kay Boyle waited impatiently for the animal poisoning case to be resolved. The trial dragged on, she feared libel implications, and the piece was never completed.

"Summer Evening" was selected for the 1950 O. Henry Memorial Award volume. But from then on it was only Stuart Rose, one of the progressives remaining at *The Saturday Evening Post*, who truly welcomed her writing. In September of 1951, he bought a sentimental story called "The Woman in the Glass" (later titled "Diagnosis of a Selfish Lady"). As if she were unaware of how tenuous her publishing future in America was becoming, Kay Boyle complained that Rose was paying only 2,250 "berries," while the *Post* had given her three thousand for "A Disgrace to the Family." Watkins, who now had a keener appreciation of her client's precarious situation, said she was "glad to have it."

Never introspective about either her life or her art, Kay Boyle seemed not to understand why her stories no longer sold. "God knows what's happened," she told Watkins early in 1951. She concluded she didn't have enough time to work. "All I seem to do is shop for food, get passports renewed, go to the cleaner," she complained. Joseph typed his reports late into the night, disturbing her sleep. When Watkins gently suggested that their European settings alone were making her stories difficult to sell, Kay argued that "the background HAS to be German because that's my area now. There's no reason why love shouldn't hold up just as well in Germany as anywhere else, and love seems to be what they want." And yet she knew, even as she wrote "The Woman in the Glass," that it was little more than another "character sketch," like "Autobahn, 1951." "I suppose it's having everything rejected recently which makes me uncertain about things," she wrote Watkins. When *The Saturday Evening Post* finally bought "The Woman in the Glass," it was Kay Boyle's first sale anywhere in fourteen months.

When she had read the proofs for *The Smoking Mountain*, she had perceived in another moment of self-knowledge how the autobiographical element weakened her fiction. "I hate the figure which emerges—the eternal 'I'—from these pages, and I hope to efface her wholly in all the future writing that I do," she promised. Then she could not free herself from this literary narcissism. Watkins tried to help. *The Post* wanted "a story of action out-of-doors of strong men and strong women," she told Kay.

Frightened now, Kay tried consciously to fashion her work to sell. If earlier, however, she was able to distinguish between what she called the "cheap sordid stories" she wrote strictly for money and good solid work, the distinction seemed to blur in her mind. "I'm your baby for bad stories again," she told Watkins. She persisted in believing that she could "write down," produce romantic potboilers one day and serious fiction the next. In fact, she had written her last well-crafted story, her last focused novel.

As always, she cultivated the image of the writer Kay Boyle, one who did not accept "invitations to lunch or tea, or cocktail parties, or dinner"—hardly the case. On her 1951 visit to New York, she did refuse to do any radio programs, and spoke to the *Herald Tribune* of how she detested "expensive places in any country or mak[ing] small talk with expensive people." She pictured herself working "in a small room where no current of air can disturb my papers or the heart's precarious flame." There was truth in that confession. "If I must go away from my little room," Kay admitted, "I am impatient. I want to be closed in there, feeding the fire in peace."

Through these darkening times, Kay wrote twice a week to Ann Watkins, who handled her money, supplied her with books, and even purchased Christmas presents for the children, like a "Tiny Tears" doll for Mousie. So emotionally symbiotic was Watkins with her author that she even dreamed one night of Kay riding by in a "surrey with a fringe on top," waving to her agent "in a very cavalier way," only for Watkins to board a bus and chase after her. When Watkins overtook the surrey, the writer got out and fell into her agent's arms, the two weeping "copious tears." Kay pronounced the dream "lovely." Undaunted by the many rejections, Watkins kept circulating the manuscripts, and recirculating them in revised form. It was Watkins who saw to it that each year *The New Yorker* renewed Kay's contract.

"I'll have to write another novel quick," Kay decided, "and one that has some sort of public, for I don't want to be eased off to another publisher again." Neither *His Human Majesty* nor *The Smoking Mountain* had earned out their advances. But Edward Aswell agreed to give her a contract for a novel to be set in Germany; Kay promised him "a big love story." Aswell told her that it should not have the word "German" in the title because "it arouses in many a certain latent hostility." Kay changed her working title from "The German Summer" to "The Foreign Summer." This was the novel which would be published as *Generation Without Farewell*.

With money ever on her mind, needing to accumulate as many projects as she could, Kay thought of translating René Crevel's surrealist work *Babylone*, mythologizing herself as "one of the last people to talk with him before he died." She pondered moving to Hollywood to work for Samuel Goldwyn. "I would leave for Hollywood at any time, provided the dough offered was worth it," she told Watkins. "I could leave the children with Joseph." She sent Goldwyn story suggestions—with German settings. No offer came from Hollywood.

Desperate for money, and with Stuart Rose still in her camp, Kay Boyle decided to try for another *Saturday Evening Post* serialization. They had paid her $25,000 in 1946 for *A Frenchman Must Die*. Now she hoped for a comparable sum for a serial set in contemporary France. "I'm running on too close a margin financially to devote four or five months (or more) to this serial unless it's going to mean real money," she told Watkins. She wanted a commitment before she would start. The hero, she said, would be Bobby's husband, Michel Sciama, who had now been decorated by both the French and British governments for his work with the resistance. Kay decided to move to Cassis, in France, near where Bobby and Michel lived, for three weeks to get started. She would return to Germany, and then be back in Cassis for the summer of 1952.

Under such pressure, Kay Boyle found herself pondering old themes. Once more she would redeem France in American eyes: "the romance, the fire, the sense of justice, the logic." Michel was both anti-Communist and anti-De Gaulle, a perfect hero for the political moment which both bewildered and challenged Kay Boyle now. Michel stood for the best of present-day France and the serial would be his biography. Rose, however, hesitated. He decided not to commit himself to another Kay Boyle serial until he saw the completed work.

In April of 1952, Kay Boyle admitted to Ann Watkins that she hadn't written a word in three months. She feared she could no longer consider herself a writer. Harold Ross had died that past December, and she knew *The New Yorker* was decidedly unfriendly to her. Because it was her habit, her raison d'être, her identity, Kay Boyle insisted that nothing would interfere with her writing: "I'm just NOT going to let everything take my time except the important thing, which is writing," she insisted. She made this vow at a moment when her personal life had turned toward disaster, and she was facing a far greater threat than the mere rejection of her stories by American magazines.

"It became necessary within the past few weeks for us to defend ourselves against unspecified charges," Kay Boyle wrote Stuart Rose in May of 1952. A worse nightmare was racing toward its climax.

21

Guilt by Marriage

Regarding KAY BOYLE FRANCKENSTEIN, ——— *described her as*
a temperamental and impulsive woman who was prone to lend
her name to causes which allegedly were in the interest of the
common man, whether they were or not.

FBI FILE OF KAY BOYLE

A s the Palmer Raids and the Red Scare followed upon the end of
World War I, seizing in their tenacious grasp Emma Goldman and Kay
Boyle's beloved Sasha Berkman, so McCarthyism followed the end of World
War II. In both cases demobilization without immediate rearmament meant
the threat of massive unemployment. With unemployment would come
discontent and demands for radical change from the labor movement now
that, with the war over, strikes could no longer be forbidden as endangering
"national security." A militant labor movement might even draw on the
political legacy of the thirties, as post-World War I radicals had looked to
the Bolshevik example. A "Cold War" would ensure that the economic
problems of the Depression, which had been deferred by World War II,
would not recur.

Long before the conflict had ended, those who sought the remilitari-
zation of America, and the intensification of rivalry with the Soviet Union,
knew that such a policy would entail silencing those who would talk,
instead, of peace. That those urging social change after the war would be
accused of disloyalty to the United States was a tour de force in political
manipulation. That a class of professional informers would be created, who
would lie shamelessly about people's "membership" in the Communist
Party, revealed how dead in earnest were those intent upon policing America. By the mid-forties, any criticisms of rearmament, or doubts about
whether a Cold War was really in America's best interests, were considered
treason, indeed "un-American."

Now "loyalty" and "security" were invoked to intimidate, as even
intellectual independence was equated at once with sycophancy toward
Stalin and the Soviet Union. The result was the persecution of hosts of

people who were mere liberals, people who talked about "peace," and were vaguely anticapitalist. Many of the victims were, in short, not former members of the Communist Party, or even "fellow travelers," but people like Kay Boyle and Joseph Franckenstein. After its original 1943 interview, the FBI had continued to investigate her. When in 1949 Joseph Franckenstein was appointed news editor of the *Neue Zeitung*, which was part of the State Department's Voice of America effort, J. Edgar Hoover, under the Federal Employees Loyalty Program, instructed the Washington field FBI to investigate his "character, reputation and loyalty." Ironically, Joseph had already dismissed a writer named Ludwig Delhees for his Stalinist politics when the investigation began. Kay Boyle was warned by Heinz Pol: "you can not imagine how reaction, bigotry, hatred, pro-fascist feelings and war propaganda have grown here since you have left." But Kay was too distracted to listen.

The FBI at once uncovered the original OSS investigation in which Joseph had been accused of moral turpitude for living with "a popular fiction authoress" out of wedlock and for borrowing money from women which he did not repay. Kay Boyle had borne his child out of wedlock. The conclusion in 1944 had been that while Joseph was "somewhat unconventional," he did not possess "disloyal tendencies." Now in the summer of 1949, with these old files in hand, Hoover directed agents in Denver, St. Louis, New York, Salt Lake City, New Haven, Washington, D.C., Newark, and San Diego to renew their investigations of both Kay Boyle and Joseph Franckenstein.

A May 2, 1947, FBI report had concluded that "there is no identifiable adverse information concerning Kay Boyle." That conclusion was ignored as Kay Boyle's file grew rich in evidence of "subversion." Meanwhile Joseph's files revealed that he had been employed in 1942 by that Nature Friends of America camp at Midvale, New Jersey, which now appeared on the Attorney General's list of subversive organizations. But most people praised Joseph as a "fine individual" whose loyalty to the United States could not be questioned.

The FBI focused its attention instead on Kay's behavior. The New Haven field office revealed that she had been "a follower of Henry Wallace" and "a strong supporter of all Mr. Wallace's policies." (Wallace, of course, had been endorsed in his bid for the presidency by the Communist Party, and constantly called for harmonious relations with the Soviet Union.) In addition, as one informant told the FBI, Kay Boyle was "of a Bohemian nature." Kay, the Paris expatriate, had been divorced not once, but twice, and had borne three children out of wedlock.

Like anyone, she had her share of detractors, and the FBI found them. Nyack neighbors contributed the observation that the Franckensteins were "careless in dress and appearance," although this is difficult to believe of the impeccable author who never appeared anywhere without her makeup.

Someone also accused the Franckensteins of "not [being] attentive to the
whereabouts of their children."

What friends may have considered Kay Boyle's eccentricity, proof of
her individuality and distinction, was now converted to proof of her dubious
loyalty to America. "Impulsive" was an adjective which kept recurring.
She was "a highly intelligent person, but one who is inclined to be impulsive
and easily swayed to interest herself in the cause of the underdog," someone
said. Another informant called her "a temperamental and impulsive woman
who was prone to lend her name to causes which allegedly were in the
interest of the common man, whether they were or not." Kay, a less than
friendly acquaintance revealed, seldom "looked into the cause for which
her name was given to ascertain as a fact that the cause was what it claimed
to be." This was true. Indeed, she had professed herself to be "shocked"
to discover after David Greenglass was arrested for treason that he had
been executive secretary of the American Committee for the Protection of
the Foreign Born, to which she had sent ten dollars in 1949.

It wasn't long before the FBI uncovered all the petitions Kay Boyle
had signed for organizations which appeared on the Attorney General's list
and discovered her name mentioned in the *Daily Worker*. She had Communist friends, like Nancy Cunard, and another figure of whom the FBI
took a dim view, Heinz Pol.

In October of 1949, as Joseph signed his "Appointment Affidavit,"
swearing he was "not a Communist or Fascist," Hoover extended the investigation to Germany. Joseph's name was now placed by military intelligence on a "grey list," on the basis of "an unevaluated allegation that
one, Franckenstein, first name unknown, employed by ISD at Marburg,
was a fellow traveller." By April of 1950 the FBI's field investigation had
been sent to the Loyalty Security Board for consideration under President
Truman's "loyalty program." General Conrad E. Snow, chairman of the
Loyalty Security Board, recommended that the Department of the Army
now conduct a further investigation "of the activities of subject and wife
in Germany."

For Kay and Joseph, life continued as before. In March of 1950 Bobby
bore her first child, Guillaume, whom Kay described to Jay Laughlin as a
"beautiful son." It was Kay's first grandchild.

In July of 1950, Joseph was promoted and left the *Neue Zeitung* of
which he had been the news editor, to become deputy chief of intelligence
for Hesse.

Kay and her sister Joan began to squabble about the financial arrangements of caring for Katherine, with Joan ripping up Kay's checks or
returning them to her in the mail, as Kay put it, "when I try to regulate
our accounts." Katherine, in the aftermath of a severe stroke, was comforted
by thoughts of her daughter the writer. A friend told her that Kay was

"filled with light, strength, and vitality," and this thrilled Katherine. "Be well," Katherine wrote Kay, "you are so important."

Joan wanted Katherine to come to her New Jersey farm to recuperate. Jealously, Kay insisted that her mother remain in California, and, with the money she received from *The New Yorker* for her report on the Baab trial, she promised to send Katherine five hundred dollars at once and another five hundred later. "Please do not be persuaded to go to New Jersey," she begged the ailing Katherine, "under no conditions should you go there. As long as I am able to take care of you, I want you to have independence." Melodramatically, Kay told Ann Watkins it would be "the death of my mother" should Katherine go to live with Joan.

Continuing to address her letters to her sister as "Dearest Jo," Kay bitterly told Ann Watkins that "it makes me too furious that Mother has to be treated like a spendthrift in her last years, poor lamb." To Jo, Kay wrote only, "I feel Mother is far better off where she is than either with you or me." Meanwhile, as always, Katherine sided with Kay, her favorite: "and you had helped her in so many ways (other than financial), and I know that you will continue to do so," she wrote Kay of Jo.

Kay visited her mother in California during the spring of 1951. "I think her courage, wit, and endurance are beyond all belief," she said after seeing Katherine, who still smoked and who still enjoyed the chocolates with which the admiring Puss had plied her all those long years ago. Katherine told Kay how moved she had been by the preface to *The Smoking Mountain*. "My feelings are steady and deep and I love and admire you," Katherine said. "The precious book" was "a serious joy." Katherine told Kay she knew "Jo is jealous of you. I know she was in the past," Katherine admitted, "but there's no use in digging up the past." Neither mother nor daughter would engage in introspection, even now. When Kay left after seeing her very frail mother, she cried long and hard, "a real flood," as she described it. "How close you and I are," Katherine wrote to Kay after her departure.

In January of 1952, facing death at last, Katherine sent a message for Kay not to grieve. She would be nearer to Kay than she ever had been, always standing ready even after death to help her in any way she could.

In Paris, Jeannie Connolly died of a brain hemorrhage suffered while she was vomiting. Her alcoholism had become so severe that she had a big glass of gin when she awakened in the morning and at night Laurence had virtually to carry her up to bed. She was thirty-nine years old. Laurence, Kay pronounced, took it well. Jeannie's illness had rendered him "quite sober and very worried," and, Kay added maliciously, "almost a human being again." As for Kay's alcoholic friend Carson McCullers, Kay wrote Ann Watkins that "she and Reeves are apparently drinking gin, and wine, and so consider themselves completely on the water wagon."

Even as her gallbladder erupted ever more frequently, as her stories were not selling, as the government continued its investigation, Kay Boyle seemed to be increasing her obligations. There was time for the nursing of her pet dachshund named Honey Chile, whom Kay fed milk with an eye-dropper. Kay Boyle now took in strays, first animals, and then, for a while, even German orphan children. It seemed an odd thing to be doing, and so Kay had to create a rationale. "In giving all this attention to Honey Chile," she argued, she "was fighting for Mary too." But Mary Reynolds had died of uremia in 1950 in Paris anyway.

It was as if Kay Boyle, still resenting having to live her mother's dream, was finding new ways to sabotage, to resist, the unconsciously assumed burden. If a host of new outside forces were conspiring against her, and this time they were, she was continuing to create circumstances which made it impossible for her to return with full concentration to her craft. The "senseless interruptions" Kay complained of, the interruptions she had engineered, "confuse the continuity even of one's soul," she said. So her unconscious mind continued to wage warfare against what her mother had determined that she be.

In November of 1950 Apple married Ted Goeser, with Joseph as best man. To make the trip to Paris for the wedding, Kay Boyle had to borrow one hundred dollars from Ann Watkins. After Kay departed, Clover cried so hard that the room began virtually to spin around her. Yet even when her mother was there, it seemed as if she wasn't there for her at all. Kay made a great fuss when in January of 1951 Clover made her first journey alone to Paris from Germany to visit Laurence. Kay said she found it "dreadful" to see "her little rain-and-tear streaming face at the window of the sleeping compartment." That she contributed to the little girl's pain by making such a drama of Clover's departure for a visit to Laurence did not occur to her. On a subsequent visit, after Clover had insisted that she hated Laurence and didn't want to go, Mousie offered to go with her. "I just hate Mousie going there with him, to Mégève," Kay confessed to Ann Watkins, suggesting once more that she was well aware of Laurence's overly physical closeness toward his daughters. On that visit, as Clover sat in stony silence, refusing to sit on Laurence's lap, while he beckoned her, Mousie thought she would love to sit on Laurence's lap. Her own father was so remote, so refined. But Laurence didn't want her. He wanted Clover.

Kay had, of course, by now long known that she was being investigated. But she continued to express her views, the views of any well-meaning liberal. She was "absolutely heart-sick, crushed, outraged by the catastrophe in Korea." In the midst of McCarthy's rampages, she talked of peace and joined the American Association for the United Nations. When the American government made a loan to Franco's Spain, Kay Boyle spoke, in melodramatic style, of "making some kind of really violent and meaningful protest—like renouncing my American citizenship." "I know that in our country we can speak our protest aloud on every subject that we wish," she wrote Jay Laughlin, "and I want to be a part of a country of which this is true."

Laughlin wrote back as an advocate of Cold War hysteria, speaking of how the Russians were bent on conquering the world, and if they "start marching to the Atlantic, the only place where we can expect to keep toeholds are in England and Spain." Unintimidated, Kay Boyle fired off an indignant reply. "I didn't know anyone—except McCarthy—still believed that the Russians intend to march across Europe to the Atlantic," she wrote Laughlin.

She did add that "the Russian strategy is far more subtle and deadly than that." But Kay went on deploring America's commitments to "regimes we can only despise." She was for recognition of Communist China, and no deals "with Franco, the puppet regime in Greece, and Indo-China." America, Kay Boyle said, had no business making "ignominious treaties with tyrants." Nor was she in favor of "bolstering up the non-realistic government at Bonn." As 1950 drew to its close, Kay Boyle behaved as if, in keeping with the American Constitution, she enjoyed every freedom to express her views. Meanwhile U.S. Army investigators were learning of Joseph's encounters with the anti-Communist Franz Borkenau and the anti-Semitic and anti-Communist, Ernest Knoblauch.

Borkenau, however, did not confine his attack to Joseph and his "Communism." He accused Kay Boyle of being "a pink," with definite "Communist sympathies." Worse in these puritanical times, she "wore the pants in the family." The insidious suggestion was that if her views were subversive, so indeed must be Joseph's, since she controlled him. They were "misfits in so far as their marriage is concerned." The investigators listened.

The investigation of Kay and Joseph continued through 1951 as long lists of potential American informants were compiled, from Roger Burlingame to Richard Simon, to Joseph's superior in Marburg, Fred Leonard, to Eugene Jolas, Bessie Breuer, William L. Shirer, and Stuart Rose. Members of the American press in Germany who knew Kay and Joseph were interviewed. By the end of May of 1951 Franz Borkenau had appeared at the New York office of the FBI to denounce Joseph as "one hundred per cent pro-Soviet." As for his wife, Kay Boyle, she was nothing less than an "organized Communist."

Many of those interviewed spoke favorably of the couple. Kay was called "pro-French," a person who feared a resurgence of Nazism in Germany. Kay Boyle was "a Liberal," and "a kind person who goes out of her way to help others." Joseph was called "a Liberal who would probably vote for a candidate in the Democratic party if he were in the United States." If he was "slightly left of center," he remained "a strong believer in freedom of the press and is against racial prejudice." None of this would matter.

And still Kay had no idea of how deep and prolonged the investigation had become. When she had received no mail from Ann Watkins for two weeks in February of 1951, she joked, "I can only conclude that the air mail service has been disrupted by the bad weather, or that I am under another Communist cloud and my mail is being stopped and read. (This latter suspicion is intended to be humorous.)" Even when Joseph was taken off intelligence work and brought back to the *Neue Zeitung*, Kay was not overly alarmed. But at the end of September of 1951 Joseph was relieved of his duties at the newspaper again and made "chief assistant" in the Office of Public Affairs.

Robert McAlmon, James Stern, and indeed Laurence appear to have been correct in their assessment of the Franckenstein marriage. For even as great trouble brewed around them, Kay and Joseph had settled into an uneasy arrangement. Kathe visited her mother in March of 1951. She enjoyed practicing acting with Kay (she had been accepted into the Paris Conservatoire, where she would study with a famous Comédie Française teacher). But she was astonished at how firmly and dominantly Kay Boyle ruled the household. She did indeed, as that informer had suggested, "wear the pants" in the family. Kathe was only sixteen and it shocked her as Kay badgered and carped at and criticized and humiliated Joseph.

One night they were all at dinner, Kay and Joseph, Clover, Mousie, Boostie, and Kathe. Joseph had been having trouble with his dentures, which weren't tight enough. Kay made a cutting, sarcastic remark at his expense. The children laughed. Kathe was appalled.

After dinner she confronted her mother.

"Why do you talk to him like that?" Kathe demanded.

Now Kay burst into tears. It was the first time Kathe had ever seen her mother cry. "I don't know if he really cares," Kay wept. When Kathe still pressed her about picking on Joseph so mercilessly, she replied, "I think he likes it."

Returning to Paris, Kathe described the incident to her father. Laurence drew on his pipe. "He's too nice," Laurence remarked. "Kay shouldn't have someone like that. He's gotten himself into a mess." But Apple offered no such sympathy when Kathe told her that "Kay is terrible to him."

"I hate Joseph Franckenstein," Apple said. "He's a nothing. Poor Mama. How could she do anything with someone like that?" Kathe herself concluded that the marriage was "a fiasco."

Nor was Kay finding it easy to raise her young family. On her home leave to America that spring, on the subway Mousie and Boostie had been so obstreperous that a stranger had reprimanded them. "Be nice to your granny, now," she told them, pitying the grey-haired woman for whom the high-spirited children were obviously too much.

That April, while Kay was still in New York, an ominous article appeared on the front page of the *Herald Tribune*, under the headline "Judy Holliday and Jose Ferrer Named on House Red-Front List." The House Un-American Activities Committee had released a report listing the names of "alleged Communist fronts and their sponsors." It was, they said, "the most dangerous hoax ever devised by the international Communist conspiracy." The *Tribune* article also included a list of people "affiliated with various 'peace' organizations or Communist fronts." Foremost among them was Kay Boyle.

Frank Detweiler's secretary spotted Kay's name in the newspaper that morning. At once Detweiler rang up his sister-in-law. "It's preposterous," he told her. But when Kay later lunched with Roger Baldwin, he advised her to write to the *Herald Tribune* and demand a retraction. Even this she did not take seriously. When Edward Aswell asked if she wanted McGraw-Hill to intervene on her behalf, Kay told him no. She did not believe it was necessary.

So oblivious to danger did Kay Boyle remain that when Vincent Sheean asked if she would add her name to an open letter requesting that President Truman bar American military aid to the Franco regime, a letter sponsored by the Joint Anti-Fascist Refugee Committee, she said yes. On May 17, her name appeared in the *Daily Worker*, along with those of the other signatories. (Well aware, of course, that the letter had been sponsored by a Communist front organization, the *Daily Worker* omitted its name.) On June 1, a right-wing magazine called *Counterattack* explained that Moscow did not want Spain strengthened, because that would "make Stalin's job of taking over Western Europe more difficult." It reported that the Communist Party had been "whipping up anti-Franco sentiment," and listed the signatories. Among other innocuous causes to which Kay contributed now was the Kenneth Patchen Fund, to help the paralyzed poet, the National Wildlife Federation, and the Pyramid Lake Paiute Indian tribe. "She'll just jump on any bandwagon if it seems like an interesting thing to do," Joan remarked of her sister.

On a visit to Paris, Kay thought Nancy Cunard was cold to her, "because I'm not a Communist." Grace Flandrau, in Paris, extended an invitation, proof for Kay that her old friend "does not believe I am a Communist after all!" When Kay wrote Heinz Pol of her indignation that Ethel and Julius Rosenberg had been found guilty of treason and been sentenced to death for having passed atomic bomb secrets to the Soviets, rhetorically demanding, "Have we become so frightened that we are afraid to speak out in defense of wrongfully convicted people as we did in the days of Sacco and Vanzetti?" Pol tried to explain the new cultural climate in America. People were "so frightened that they would probably not rush to the defense of people like the Rosenbergs [unless] there was a reasonable degree of suspicion that there had been a frame-up," Pol told her.

On June 19, 1951, Louis Budenz, that most ubiquitous of the FBI's informants, appeared to denounce Kay Boyle as a Communist. Once a member of the Central Committee of the Communist Party, and an editor of the *Daily Worker*, in 1946, Budenz, at the age of fifty-three, had taken it as his mission to wage warfare against "Communism." He had denounced Owen Lattimore, an adviser to the State Department for Far Eastern affairs, and would go on to denounce scores of people as Communists or fellow travelers. Budenz insisted that it was more dangerous to sponsor Communist Party front organizations than even to be an open party member. "Stalin's most effective representatives," Budenz argued, were those unsuspecting people who signed the petitions Kay Boyle had signed. Fellow informant Harvey Matusow later confessed he had been paid by the government to give false testimony under oath; Budenz too may have been paid to lie. That he did lie there is no doubt.

"Sometime in the early 1940's," Budenz now told the FBI, Kay Boyle had been a Communist. In about 1944, he declared, she "showed hesitancy concerning her Communist Party allegiance and wished to be relieved of all obligations in that respect." Ruth McKenney, who had written *My Sister Eileen*, had then been assigned by "the Cultural Commission of the Communist Party to see her in New York and straighten the matter out." McKenney and Alexander Trachtenberg, whom Budenz described as the "Red cultural commissar for America" in charge of "manipulating the intellectuals," later told him, Budenz reported, that Kay Boyle "had straightened out her relations with the Party at that time." Several times up to 1945, Budenz insisted, "he officially heard Miss Boyle referred to as a member of the Communist Party in connection with Communist front organizations." During his testimony, Budenz also described an encounter in which he discussed Kay Boyle with Ruth McKenney outside the Communist Party headquarters. Like Franz Borkenau, Budenz declined to testify against Kay Boyle before a Loyalty Security Board, rare for him. Before he was through, Budenz would testify at sixty such hearings, and that he would not publicly denounce Kay Boyle suggested that his lies about her were simply too blatant even for a hearing where the normal rules of evidence did not apply. But the damage had been done.

That July of 1951 an FBI agent in Buffalo was told that "Kay Boyle" was a "CP member or CP sympathizer." Revealing that he knew little of Kay Boyle, this informant called her a "well-known writer for *Collier's* magazine," a publication which had never bought one of her stories. But the individual did know that Kay Boyle was in Germany. "Kay Boyle is an active CP member," the informant insisted, and an "international courier."

In the midst of all these troubles, of most of which Kay Boyle had no idea, her sister Joan, faced with a faltering marriage, decided she wanted to adopt two young children. Because she was past fifty, Joan knew it would be difficult to find children to adopt in America. Now she enlisted Kay to find two German war orphans to be sent to her. Kay told her children that Joan would not come to Germany herself because she would have to apply for a new passport and so everyone would know her true age. Once Kay had snatched her photograph album away from Joan's daughters, Brooke and Susan, so that they would not know that Joan was in fact the older sister. "You must never tell the cousins the truth," Kay told Kathe. "She looks ten years younger than I do anyway."

Passing through Paris on his way to Frankfurt, Frank Detweiler purchased an exquisite sexy nightgown as a present for Kay. Bobby and Kathe exchanged glances; it didn't seem to be an appropriate present for your wife's sister. Indeed, one night while Detweiler was staying in the house in Frankfurt, Kay awoke to discover "Frankie," as she called him, in bed with her. Quickly she got up and headed for the bathroom. But when she returned to bed, once more he got into her bed and positioned himself on top of her. Then in the morning he apologized.

Frank Detweiler returned to America without having selected German war orphans for his wife to raise. This task was left to Kay. Beset by crises—the continuing government investigation, the constant rejections of her stories by magazines which had published her in the past, the needs of a growing family now that Bobby had a second child, a daughter, Emanuelle—still Kay kept searching for orphans. "I've been dashing between hospital, school, prison, and orphan asylums for the past week," she wrote Ann Watkins in March of 1952. Sometimes Kay took Mousie with her to the orphanages, where the little girl was overwhelmed by the rows of cribs filled with abandoned children. It was an experience Mousie would never forget.

At last Kay found eleven-month-old little Manfred, not a war orphan, but "so very much our kind of child—blond and blue eyed." Kay was so taken with him that she was tempted to adopt him herself. There was also a little girl named Erica. But Manfred must be considered first, Kay said, since should it not work out, "I would like to have him myself, whereas Erica . . . would mean just one more girl." Recognizing that this seemed irrational, she added, "Boostie wants a baby brother." She had just celebrated her fiftieth birthday.

Amid all this excitement surrounding the adoption and arrival of foster children, Clover suffered all the more from her mother's seeming inaccessibility. Sadly she now requested that she go to America to live for a year with the Detweilers. Kay had wanted her mother's watch, which had been one of her many birthday presents from Puss, for Clover. But such sentimental gestures could not fill emotional voids. Clover chose to live with her aunt and uncle.

Finally Kay located little Wolfgang, aged three and a half. At once she welcomed him into her household, all the while professing "many misgivings as to my qualities as a foster mother." For Wolfgang, Kay Boyle expressed boundless enthusiasm. He was "of a gentleness which cannot be described . . . affectionate, gay, quiet, sensitive, eats everything one gives him, sleeps like a top." She managed to find the time to go to the American Clothing Store and indulge herself in an "orgy of spending" for him. At night, little Wolfgang sang his dolls to sleep. I realized, Kay Boyle said, "all I have missed in not having such a young one around for so long a time." She wrote "Frankie dear" that she wanted to rush out and show Wolfgang off to her friends. "He has not a selfish bone in his body," she declared.

Wolfgang's daily companion, the person who took care of him, however, was Mousie, now ten years old, who had persuaded the local taxi drivers to take her and Wolfgang to the zoo. Some time later when a few taxi drivers greeted the little girl, Kay asked Mousie, "How come those men know you?" So to her horror she learned the truth. In June, when Kay went off to visit Bobby in Cassis, she left her "handsome little Wolfgang" behind with the very busy Joseph. Wanting a little one around again did not extend to sustained care.

Finally Wolfgang and a little girl named Heidi were sent to America to be adopted by the Detweilers. But they did not fare well. Joan decided not to tell them they were adopted, incredibly, and the children were forbidden to speak German to each other, although they did it secretly. Wolfgang, of course, had been too old to be deceived, and remained dubious when Frank Detweiler told him he had learned German on a family trip to Germany. "I remember only one plane ride," he protested. Later he whispered to Heidi, "I think you're German. But I'm from Paris." The first Christmas Wolfgang sneaked downstairs and set fire to the Christmas tree. "I was sorry I hadn't kept them," Kay Boyle remembered, regretting all her life that she had not adopted Wolfgang herself. And he, who did not find love or affection with the Detweilers, regretted it all his life too.

That spring in Frankfurt in the gathering storm Mousie and Boostie were ready for their first Communion, which they celebrated, as they did all things, together. Kay Boyle was honoring her commitment to her mother-in-law, and to Joseph, that the children be raised as Roman Catholics. Kay privately remained appalled. "Of all farcical things, in white veils and what-not," she confided to Ann Watkins, she who as a child had been excused from church, "the dishonesty of it makes me physically ill." It was one more factor in her growing alienation from Joseph.

Laurence at sixty-one remained angry at Kay for ending *their* marriage. "Why did she do such a thing?" he still was asking, this time of his friend Yvonne Hagen, an art critic for the *Herald Tribune*. "She broke up the family. It wasn't my fault." Now he accused Kay of turning Clover against him. Yvonne noticed that Laurence needed to be needed and enjoyed it when his daughters came and told him their troubles, as always he sided with them against their husbands. Laurence might kiss the necks of his daughters, or even touch their bosoms. But it was more appreciation than lasciviousness, Yvonne thought. A while later when Laurence was sued for breach of promise by a woman who insisted he had promised to marry her, Peggy gave him the twelve thousand dollars to pay her off. "I got out of my marriage most infamously," Laurence confided to Kay, for they were never wholly lost to each other. "All the Vail batteries came to my assistance, and I felt very sorry for the poor woman having nobody but enemies to whom she could complain about my most horrible awfulness . . . well, that nightmare's over."

In 1952 the nightmare was beginning in earnest for Kay and Joseph even though in January the Loyalty Security Board had actually dropped their charges against him. Simultaneously, they cleared Kay Boyle, who they finally seem to have been persuaded was no more than "a liberal interested in the 'under dog' " whose books did not "indicate communist sympathy." Like her husband, they concluded, Kay Boyle was "anti-communistic." It would seem that the problem had gone away.

Foolishly, Kay had presented two letters from her friend Heinz Pol to the Public Affairs officials in Germany in the hope of clearing herself. Because of these letters, dating from 1950 and 1951, the Loyalty Security Board once more went into action and renewed its investigation of Joseph. In his letter of March 6, 1950, Pol had admitted that in the years prior to Hitler's putsch, he had worked with the Communists. He noted that he had never been a "fellow traveller," and pointed to the records which proved he wrote against the Nazis years before the Communists took up their fight against them.

But Pol also described the Waldorf Conference as having been picketed "by some hundred fascists and dopes, mostly organized by Catholic Veterans and White Russians, nicely protected by thousands of policemen." He wrote as well that he was "very happy" to see Kay Boyle "among the sponsors." Then, unwittingly, Pol made a distinction which in the hysteria of the fifties, and the organized intimidation running rampant, served only to damage Kay Boyle, and himself, immeasurably. "The future belongs to Socialism," Pol went on. He continued to recognize "genuine Socialism or Communism as the legitimate forces to bring about a better tomorrow." He admitted, in fact, that he was a Communist, but one of the anti-Stalinist variety, retaining his faith in the ideal by distinguishing between it and its deformation in Stalin's Soviet Union.

That Kay Boyle could offer this letter as proof of her innocence of guilt by association with the Marxist Pol was extraordinarily naive. Her situation was further exacerbated by the second letter, in which Pol thanked her for getting him free-lance work with the *Frankfurter Rundschau*. Included were Pol's suspicions about a man named Kurt Hellmer, who must have been the informant who told the FBI that Kay Boyle had helped him. ("Nobody knows about it but you and I and the editors of the FR.") Fearlessly for the times, or with monumental naiveté, in May of 1951, having received Pol's letter, Kay Boyle had written an indignant letter to Kurt Hellmer, one of the German editors of *Aufbau* in New York, demanding that he formally apologize to Heinz Pol for denouncing him as a Communist who wrote "anti-American" articles for the *Frankfurter Rundschau*.

Taken together, the Pol letters suggested that Kay Boyle had gotten a job on a German newspaper for an avowed Communist. Perhaps had Kay Boyle not brought these letters to the government's attention, there would have been no security hearing. Untold misery might have been avoided. In all likelihood her literary reputation would have been vastly higher than it was in the next thirty years of her life. But in helping Heinz Pol find work, she was, as always, standing by a friend. She would not be ashamed of such an action; nor would she conceal it. Guilt by association was not a concept she would ever acknowledge.

On March 17, Joseph's case was forwarded to the Loyalty Security Board for reconsideration. The reopening of his case, it soon became clear, was based solely on what amounted to his guilt by marriage to Kay Boyle. Now, not the Pol letters, but the old denunciation by Louis Budenz, which had been in Kay's file back in January when Joseph was cleared and Kay termed a "liberal" and "anti-communistic," was invoked as the rationale for superseding Joseph's earlier security clearance. The memo reopening the case reads: "Subject's wife is stated by a confidential informant of known reliability to have been a member of the Communist Party as late as 1945." Moreover, there had been "no evidence to indicate that she had terminated this membership."

At once Dean Acheson, Truman's Secretary of State, ordered the High Commission in Bonn to remove Joseph from handling any classified information, an action which itself virtually terminated his career in the Foreign Service. Joseph was transferred to the *Amerika Dienst* program of the Public Affairs office and limited to work of a routine nature, such as translating articles from the German daily newspapers. By April, Kay already feared the worst, that "out of the blue may come the word that he is relieved of all his duties—or else he will be cleared."

Knowing nothing of Budenz's denunciation, Kay believed that her trouble had begun when she had been named in that *Herald Tribune* article. She also suspected that her friendship with Heinz Pol might be contributing to her dilemma. "I know Pol is not, and never was, a Communist," Kay told Ann Watkins in April of 1952, forgetting that in his 1950 letter to her, Pol had declared his faith in a Communism different from the Soviet model, but in Communism nonetheless. Meanwhile Kay worried about Pol's ability to gain American citizenship. As always, she acted from her heart and from her personal beliefs. When Clement Greenberg wrote a letter to *The Nation* complaining about "the consistently pro-Soviet coloration" of Julio Alvarez del Vayo's columns, and questioning his fitness to be foreign editor, Kay angrily defended her friend.

It appears that Kay had little understanding of either Pol's or Del Vayo's politics, which were in turn very different from each other; one was a democratic socialist, the other a Soviet sympathizer. But they were both people she liked, and in whom she believed, and she rose to their defense. She was "defending all writers from irrelevant and irresponsible attack." Never having joined any political party herself, Kay Boyle, out of her old hubris as out of her old integrity, continued to behave in the eye of McCarthyism as if she had nothing to fear from expressing her beliefs loudly and openly. She knew she was not a Communist. Why should she then have anything to fear?

22

Loyalty Hearing

It has taken me a long time to believe that only the Communists can use the word "peace."

On May 8, 1952, the Loyalty Security Board voted to hold a formal hearing to determine whether Joseph Franckenstein was a Communist disloyal to America. Kay and Joseph dropped everything to collect character references from friends and colleagues. Kay sought the support of her editors, Stuart Rose at *The Saturday Evening Post* and Edward Aswell at McGraw-Hill. But more crucial to her case was an endorsement from *The New Yorker*, to which she had been accredited as a foreign correspondent since 1946 and for which she had written often since 1931. Kay requested from William Shawn, from her particular editor, Gus Lobrano, and from Katharine White that they make some statement declaring that they believed she was a loyal American.

Immediately Kay received endorsements from Aswell and Rose, from Roger Burlingame, from Janet Flanner, and even from Carson McCullers. From *The New Yorker* editors she was not so fortunate. Kay Boyle was long to quote Katharine White's reaction: "Kay darling, you could never be a member of the Communist Party. How ridiculous! Why don't you forget about the whole thing?"—although no such words appear in either of Katharine White's June 1952 letters to her. White, rather, wrote Kay that she hoped "that the many fine letters from newsmen who have been seeing you and your husband in Germany and from your editors in this country will soon straighten the matter out." As for *The New Yorker*, Shawn would represent them.

Shawn delayed responding to Kay's request for weeks. At last he sent her a cable which she found "encouraging." But Shawn's actual letter to Shepherd Stone at the Bureau of German Affairs of the Department of State was flat and evasive. Although he had been asked to speak only about Kay

Boyle, gratuitously he began by declaring, "I do not know Mr. Franck-enstein, and can say nothing about him." Admitting that Kay Boyle had indeed been accredited as a *New Yorker* correspondent, Shawn pleaded that he scarcely knew her since she had dealt with his predecessor, Harold W. Ross. "I have had practically no first-hand dealings with her," Shawn said, "nor have I ever discussed politics with her." He closed by ambig-uously saying he had always taken "her loyalty for granted."

In October, Gus Lobrano finally wrote Kay Boyle a letter. But it contained so many qualifications that it could be read as much as an attack as an endorsement. Lobrano confessed that he had heard Kay Boyle "make critical comments about our government," and although he added he had heard General Eisenhower do so as well, it was Kay Boyle's and not Dwight Eisenhower's loyalty that was in dispute. Even more damaging was Lo-brano's suggestion that Kay Boyle, "out of an extraordinarily sensitive sympathy for the human race, combined with what seems to me political naiveté, might be cozened and imposed upon." So Lobrano suggested how Kay Boyle might have been a Communist dupe, without indicating any faith that her beliefs rendered her disloyalty impossible.

In contrast to such pusillanimity were Roger Burlingame's assertion that Kay Boyle was "unable to betray her country or her government by any deed, word or thought" and Stuart Rose's terming her "a true patriot." Aswell, after calling Kay Boyle a person whose very existence "makes one proud . . . to belong to the human race," added that "as an American," he denounced those who made such charges. From *The New Yorker* circle only fellow correspondent Janet Flanner spoke positively about Kay as "a courageous American liberal," someone loyal "to the best and rarest kind of democratic idealism."

Together in Paris that May, Flanner and Kay Boyle had attended the First Congress of Cultural Freedom, later to be exposed as CIA-funded, where they listened to Faulkner and Malraux; on that trip too Kay attended the funeral of Eugene Jolas. Obviously distressed, Kay was irritated with Bobby, whom she accused of writing her vague, uncommunicative letters. "You told me your letters were opened, so I had to be careful about what I said," Bobby defended herself. But her mother's unjust attack stung.

On September 8, in Bad Godesberg, General Conrad E. Snow informed Joseph that the hearing would take place on October 20. The specific charge against him was nothing Joseph Franckenstein had done, thought, or said, but his guilt by marriage. What occasioned this hearing was that his wife "Kay Boyle Franckenstein has endorsed or sponsored the activities of various Communist front organizations in the U.S. during recent years and has reportedly held membership in the Communist Party." Regarding Joseph, they were interested in his 1942 employment with the Nature Friends of America, an organization on the Attorney General's list, and in his relationship with Gerhard Gerber.

Joseph's reply to Snow was drafted with the help of his friend William

Clark, Chief Judge of the Allied High Commission Courts, who was married to Sonia Tomara, that reporter who had been among those to interview Kay in 1941 on her return to America. Indignantly Joseph compared his having been "charged" with his wife's opinions to "the criterion of guilt by association so much favored by the Nazi and Communist dictatorships." At once Joseph denied that Kay Boyle had "held membership in the Communist Party." And he demanded that if she indeed had endorsed or sponsored Communist front organizations (which she had), the State Department must prove that "she knew the organizations were on the Attorney General's subversive list."

Joseph also attempted to answer the charges against himself. Gerber had been awarded a security clearance before Joseph hired him as an investigator. He himself so believed in the principles of democracy that he had left Austria because he was unwilling to live under a dictatorship. He ended by defending his wife, "a distinguished writer, whose devotion to her country is not only a matter of private, but of outspoken public record."

Judge Clark could not represent them. But he recommended a young lawyer in Germany named Benjamin B. Ferencz. At the age of twenty-seven, Ferencz had been chief prosecutor at the Nuremberg trial of the Einsatzgruppen commanders, twenty-two elite Nazi SS officers responsible for the deaths of one million Jews. He had been part of the War Crimes Division attached to General Patton's Third Army and had been present at the liberation of Buchenwald, Matthausen, and Dachau, where he interrogated Nazi officers. Now Ferencz was working out of Nuremberg as counsel for the Jewish Restitution Successor Organization. He was quick-witted, highly intelligent, and a young man with a strong moral sense. When the diminutive Ferencz had arrived at Nuremberg, Judge Clark, a large man, had told him, "I'm going to have to lean on you," to which the brash young attorney retorted immediately, "Don't lean too hard, Judge." Kay and Joseph drove the seven hours to Nuremberg. They were not disappointed.

At once Ferencz agreed to take the case as his patriotic duty. He would accept no fee. Kay Boyle liked him enormously, finding him an "energetic, soft-spoken, extremely intelligent, clear-headed young man," one of the "compensations" of the "whole sad affair." "A tiny little Hungarian Jew," Janet Flanner was to call Ferencz. "Brilliant. Kind. Gentle."

Ferencz realized at once that Kay must call character witnesses of her own since she was the one "more gravely accused—accused of being a Communist Party member," and involved with six subversive organizations. On October 6, Kay wrote Janet Flanner. Could Flanner produce any letters Kay had written over the years in which she had denounced Communism? Flanner could not, and Kay did not remember that in 1936 she had written to Jay Laughlin most unequivocally: "I am not a Communist—I am not convinced that Russia has solved anything at all."

Already burdened with an inflamed gallbladder, Kay's health now declined further. She worried about the five thousand dollars of expenses the case would entail—even with Ferencz working without a fee. When 'Janet Flanner saw her on October 10, Kay already looked "ghastly," having lost fourteen pounds. Kay revealed that for Joseph's sake she would not return to the United States. Sadly disillusioned with America, the country in which he had such faith, whatever the outcome of his hearing, he had decided to spend the rest of his life in Europe.

"He is forty (certainly fifteen years, if not more, her junior then)," Flanner decided, "has made his only career in the department, has no training except to ski all year for which he is now old even at that junior age." But Kay had so aged that at fifty she looked many years older than she was. When Kay told Flanner that she had made another sale to *The Saturday Evening Post*, Flanner, like many of Kay Boyle's friends, lamented her having turned her talent to crass commercial ends. "Oh, alas, alas, her need for money," she remarked. But she thought Kay was "a wonderful woman," and agreed at once to come to Bad Godesberg to testify for her beleaguered friend.

As Ferencz perused Kay's file, he was appalled by the equivocating letters from Shawn and Lobrano. He knew he would be asked at the hearing for a response from her employers. Yet these letters were either so weak or so damning that he couldn't introduce them. Ferencz suggested that Kay write to Shawn again and request a different wording. But Kay was too upset to ask for a more unequivocal letter. Later she wrote Shawn, "How could one ask for warmth and belligerent defense . . . when cautiousness was the only thing that had been offered?" A man of irony, Ferencz found Lobrano's letter humorous, particularly his statement that he had not found any disloyal statements in Kay's "fiction" writings, implying that in her nonfiction Communist propaganda might reside. But so crucial did Ferencz believe it was for *The New Yorker* to be represented in Kay Boyle's defense that he considered using a portion of the Lobrano letter nonetheless.

Other than the generalities in Conrad Snow's letter, none of the evidence against the Franckensteins had been made available. Ferencz immediately paid a visit to High Commissioner James B. Conant in Bonn, demanding the evidence. But Conant refused to tell him anything. "I'm sorry. I can't stop it," he told Ferencz helplessly. Ferencz told him he had even given the SS extermination squads, the Einsatzgruppen, all the documents which existed against them, and in keeping with Constitutional principles, every benefit of the doubt. Now in the "case" against Kay and Joseph he wasn't told who the informants were—or even what the charges were.

Indefatigable Ferencz next visited Houston Lay, who would serve as the Loyalty Security Board counsel. Again he reminded an officer of American justice how he had provided the defendants at the Nuremberg trials with every shred of evidence against them in order that they might prepare a defense. Again he was stonewalled. Lay told him only that Joseph had "associated with persons of Communist tendencies" in the late thirties. "Someone" had denounced Kay Boyle as a member of the Communist Party. Ferencz was given a list of the organizations she had allegedly sponsored so that she could refer to her files and checkbooks.

Kay racked her brain to discover the identity of the "special C.P. functionary" assigned to bring her back to Communism. All she could recall was that evening in 1944 when Carson McCullers had introduced her to that "Mr. Kantor," who Heinz Pol warned her was a Stalinist agent.

Three days before the hearing, Ferencz, Kay, and Joseph met with Houston Lay. Since this was his first loyalty case, Ferencz said, he wished to have an assistant counsel. Disarmed, Lay told him he could have anyone that he desired. At once Ferencz replied that he wished to have Kay assist him.

Joseph said hardly a word at this meeting. It was Kay who angrily denied she ever attended meetings of the Communist Party and demanded that the sources of the charges against her be revealed. When Lay replied that the government had to keep its sources confidential, Kay defiantly threatened that journalist Drew Middleton, a friend, had assured her that the story would be spread across the front page of *The New York Times*.

Undaunted, Lay told her that "a display of temper at the hearing would probably not be to her advantage." Then as soon as the Franckensteins and Ferencz were gone, Lay sent a classified telegram to John J. Sipes, the legal officer for the Loyalty Security Board at the Department of State in Washington: "Have learned Franckenstein intends demand wife sit as co-counsel. Is there basis for refusal?"

Kay Boyle's FBI file reveals that Sipes was told Kay Boyle might "raise questions of civil liberties" at the hearing. She is a "very well-known writer" with "many contacts among newspapers," Sipes discovered. One of the government's main concerns would be to see that publicity was avoided so as not to expose the degree to which Americans were being deprived of their normal constitutional rights and protections. Meanwhile the Loyalty Security Board operating out of Bad Godesberg prepared shamelessly to violate those rights.

The hearing against Kay Boyle and Joseph Franckenstein began at ten in the morning on Monday, October 20, at Mehlemer Aue in Bad Godesberg. Kay and Joseph faced a three-member panel, presided over by La Verne Baldwin, the consul general at Düsseldorf. Joining him were Zinn B. Garrett and Clarence A. Wendel. Houston Lay was present as the Loyalty Security Board's legal adviser, along with Herbert L. Sultan, his assistant. On this first day of the hearing Kay sat beside Benjamin Ferencz, the State Department not yet having found grounds to bar her from the proceedings.

It was a "hearing" and not a trial, and so the normal constitutional protections did not obtain, even as neither Joseph nor Kay had been charged with any crime. Gossip and innuendo provided by unnamed accusers not required to be present or to have signed affidavits were treated as "evidence." Normal privacy protections were violated; Joseph was asked to prove he attended church regularly; Kay Boyle had to testify that she had applied to the Roman Catholic Church to sanction her marriage. The separation of church and state was only one of a host of laws disregarded. A 1947 Executive Order by President Truman charged the Secretary of State with the responsibility to dismiss employees about whose loyalty there is "a reasonable doubt." That was all the law the government seemed to believe it needed.

Kay Boyle retained her composure. But she was so harassed and pressured that she was reduced to pleading that all her life she had been an anti-Communist. Her First Amendment right to believe what she wished was violated along with the Fifth Amendment protection that one need not incriminate oneself. Kay and Joseph immediately swore they were testifying voluntarily, as if they had any choice.

Into this hall of mirrors marched little Benjamin Ferencz, his task to prove a negative: that his client, Joseph Franckenstein, and his wife, Kay Boyle, were not Communists. Indeed, Joseph's superiors and colleagues at once testified to his loyalty. Cleverly Ferencz had his own witness, Apple's husband Ted Goeser's brother John, reveal that it was Franz Borkenau, who had "denounced other people before of the same thing," who had accused Joseph "falsely." Werner Dietrich, an intelligence officer, named the former Resident Officer at Marburg, Ernest Knoblauch, as a person likely to have denounced Kay and Joseph Franckenstein. It was Dietrich who recalled that Joseph had immediately dismissed Ludwig Delhees from the *Neue Zeitung* when he discovered Delhees was a member of the Communist Party.

The questions put to Ferencz's witnesses were either ill-informed, irrelevant, unconstitutional, absurd, or insidious. Baldwin asked Goeser whether there was much Communism in Marburg in 1948. Denazification, the ostensible aim of the Occupation, was treated as an unnecessary nuisance and a bore, and by their attitude the panel revealed they infinitely preferred Nazis to Communists. "Denazification or de-Communization action?" Goeser had to inquire of Baldwin at one point. Then he tried to explain that when Joseph had been in Marburg, weeding out Communists was not an American priority. Baldwin's committee didn't want to hear it.

Ferencz's strategy was to remove any possible doubt about Joseph's loyalty before he called Kay. But before that, he established that every superior under whom Joseph had served was prepared unequivocally to swear to his loyalty. Among those who also testified for Joseph was Sonia Tomara, a known anti-Communist and a White Russian, who revealed how much suffering the Bolsheviks had brought upon her family. Had Kay Boyle any "pro-Communist sympathies," Ferencz suggested, Tomara would never have praised her as "a person interested in human rights and democratic principles."

Chairman Baldwin's first question to Tomara revealed how ill-prepared the committee was.

"You say that Mrs. Franckenstein was a member of the resistance in France?"

Zinn Garrett wanted to know whether Kay Boyle had appeared to be "more enthusiastic about the Russian Army than the average anti-Nazi person was at that time."

Tomara was too clever for him. Asked whether Kay had made a distinction between "Russia as a nation," the "Russian people," and "Communist Russia" during the anti-Nazi struggle, she smiled. She was "very much in favor of the Russian nation," but not at all in sympathy with those who would have joined the Germans in the hope that they might liberate Russia, was Tomara's reply. Antifascism had been the issue, she reminded them.

Judge Clark was called next, a figure with considerable prestige in the Occupation. Having been the youngest federal judge in American history, he was a maverick with the aplomb and self-confidence born of his being a scion of privilege and inherited wealth (he was a Clark Thread Company heir). Clark could be obstreperous even as he enjoyed twitting fellow members of the bar, particularly those less intelligent than he. (In 1932, in one of his more flamboyant legal gestures, he had declared the Eighteenth Amendment unconstitutional.)

Clark cited two recent Supreme Court decisions which challenged the entire legality of the present hearing, one decreeing that membership in supposedly subversive organizations was not sufficient cause for the State Department to terminate an employee's service. The other demanded hearings to determine whether these organizations were, indeed, "subversive."

An extraordinarily handsome man, even at the age of sixty-one, his blue-grey eyes flashing, Clark quickly stole the show. He confided to the panel that there was so much "malicious gossip" around HICOG, the high command in Germany, that should anyone have accused the Franckensteins of being pro-Communists, he would have known it. As for anything said against Kay Boyle, Clark lectured the panel members as if they were schoolboys. "After all," he told them, "all of us have people who don't like us."

Nor would Judge Clark accept as dangerous even the Joint Anti-Fascist Refugee Committee. "If you want my free legal advice," he confided with feigned intimacy, "it clearly seems rather peculiar to charge people with belonging to an organization which the Supreme Court says has not been properly classified." When one of the panel members stoutly advised Clark that the board could not deal with the right of the Attorney General to place certain organizations on his list, Clark replied:

"No, you would be then taking the place of the Supreme Court of the United States, as you no doubt are well qualified to do, but it might be considered a little impudent."

Clark ended his testimony as forcefully as he had begun it. Certainly he had no acquaintance with the organizations Kay Boyle was accused of sponsoring, other than through his "learned research." He did recall that one had to do with the Bill of Rights, a subject on which he had written about fifty opinions. "I have always held that everybody, no matter how unpleasant they are, is entitled to the Bill of Rights," Judge Clark told the panel.

Joseph testified that afternoon, determined, he said, to prove every charge "not correct and false." Terrified that he might lose his American citizenship, he was now in poor health; his replies were earnest and without guile as he explained how at that nature camp he had tried to keep the children from "stepping into poison ivy." In true McCarthyite fashion, Lay at once asked Joseph, preposterously, for the names of the campers, their parents, and those organizations to which the woman who had recommended the job to Joseph belonged.

"I would gladly submit any if I knew them," Joseph answered.

"Your English is so good now that one would think you had been born to it completely," Lay accused him.

"I thank you very much for the compliment," Joseph replied. "I was partly educated in England and held various posts in England." Joseph remained, ill at ease as he was, true to his principles: what had bothered him about Gerhard Gerber, he revealed, was not any suspected Communism, but that he had not dissociated himself sufficiently from Nazism.

Since Ferencz had been shown none of the denunciations, Joseph did not know Borkenau had accused him of having objected to the Communists being called "enemies." "What would have been your reaction had he referred to the Nazis or Communists as being enemies?" Lay demanded slyly. Indeed, Joseph became confused. Obviously distressed, he was too honest to deny he had ever made such an objection.

"I would have—my idea would be that," he rambled, "I mean, it was understood that both Nazis—I mean, enemy as a term applied during war, naturally the Nazis were enemies, but the war was over, and by the same token the Communists who had only recently been our allies. . . ." Finally, under Lay's unrelenting questioning, Joseph admitted that the Communists were our ideological enemies. During the questioning about Ernest Knoblauch's "list," even board member Zinn Garrett became confused. "I didn't understand what sort of list he was speaking of," he said.

Finally, Ferencz asked Joseph about his wife. Had Kay Boyle been a member of the Communist Party, Joseph replied with dignity, he certainly would have known it because she was not in the habit of keeping anything from him. His wife was "very generous," he said as he offered the committee a list of the many donations Kay Boyle had made. Only a Houston Lay would have had the heart to confront this obviously simple and good man with the accusation that his wife was a politically naive dupe who might have been used by the Communists and then drawn him into her web of deception. Lay asked Joseph whether Kay, had she received a letter "which made up a pretty good story of a legitimate cause," might have made a contribution "without inquiring as to what the organization was itself." Joseph had to reply in the affirmative. Questioned about their checkbook and whether he would have been aware of contributions "within a short time [after] they had been made," Joseph had to admit that although they had a joint account, Kay Boyle was in charge of it.

With a fine sense of drama, Ferencz reserved for last the story of Joseph's life, his internment during the war as an "enemy alien," and how he had infiltrated the Gestapo disguised as a Wehrmacht sergeant, only to be captured, tortured, and sentenced to death. Escaping, he had "put all the Nazi big-wigs in the jug," Joseph explained, liberating Innsbruck before the arrival of the American troops. When finally the lawyer asked the panel whether they had any special questions regarding Joseph's army career, not even Houston Lay could challenge Joseph's indubitable integrity.

Late in his testimony Joseph explained that he was bringing up his children as Catholics. "I wanted my children to also believe in this life hereafter," he explained. Faith's Holy Communion keepsake was passed around, along with her Certificate of Baptism as "Felicity Franckenstein." Joseph also testified that he knew the stand the Catholic Church took against Communism.

On Tuesday morning, before the board could resume its questioning of Joseph, Chairman Baldwin made an announcement. He now had the grounds to remove Kay Boyle from the hearing room. Invoking paragraph 395.32 of the Regulations and Procedures Manual, he insisted that only the officer or employee and "his counsel or representative, and the witness who is testifying" could be present. Since Ferencz was there as his counsel, Joseph had no need of a "personal representative." Baldwin now deemed it "improper" anyway that Kay Boyle be her husband's representative since she was "an interested party." Kay Boyle's "proper role," Baldwin declared, was "as a witness to be present only during her own testimony." When Lay stated for the record that Kay Boyle was not an attorney, and hence the right of an accused to counsel and co-counsel did not apply here, Ferencz quickly replied that no requirement existed that either his representative or counsel be a lawyer. But this was one battle Ferencz lost, and Kay Boyle had to sit for the remainder of the hearing outside in the anteroom.

The remaining questions directed to Joseph were snide. Baldwin challenged even his having applied for a job with the United Nations. Could it have been that Joseph thought this would have enabled him to continue to live in Europe? Loyal Americans, it was implied, stayed home. Those with nefarious motives roamed the planet. Joseph replied that he wanted to contribute to the "reconstruction of Democratic Germany." Asked why his wife had chosen to reside abroad virtually since 1923, Joseph was at a loss. After all, when Kay Boyle left America for Europe, he had been thirteen years old.

At the end, Joseph stated his credo. Passionately he declared himself "opposed to any type of totalitarian government, be it of the fascist, be it of the Nazi, be it of the Franco, Tito, or Lenin or Stalin brand." He had believed when he emigrated to America, Joseph said, that "true democracy functions more perfectly and with greater consistency" in the United States than anywhere else. But his present experience had shocked him "profoundly." The charges by "nameless" and "irresponsible" persons had distressed him more than he was able to say.

"My faith in our American democracy is strong enough to carry me through this present ordeal," he declared with dignity, "and I assure you that I shall remain a loyal citizen regardless of the outcome of this hearing."

In keeping with his strategy, Ferencz called a witness for Kay Boyle before he would allow her to appear. Edwin Hartrich of *The Wall Street Journal* addressed the issue of the incriminating article in the *Herald Tribune* of April of 1951 by pointing out that so politically biased was that paper that it even ran a special column on Sundays written by the FBI and the son of the publisher on the subject of Communism. The panel focused on Kay Boyle's suspicious failure to demand that the *Herald Tribune* retract her name.

Just before noon on that second day, Kay took the stand. Immediately Ferencz put the question: had she ever been a member of the Communist Party or "knowingly joined any party or group" which she knew "advocated the overthrow of the United States Government. . . ." Before Ferencz could finish, Kay Boyle replied. "Never." But Ferencz did finish: "by force or violence?"

"Never, never," said Kay Boyle. Nor did any member of the panel challenge this statement. It was almost as if they either didn't believe Louis Budenz or actually knew that he had lied.

Much time was spent on whether Kay had sponsored or endorsed those Communist front organizations. She did not remember having supported the Joint Anti-Fascist Refugee Committee or the American Continental Congress for Peace or the New York Bill of Rights Conference on behalf of twelve jailed Communists. She did produce from her papers "a summary of the Bill of Rights Conference," but no proof she had sent them a message or a check, although she granted that it was "conceivable." Nor did she admit she had sent ten dollars to the National Conference Against Deportation Hysteria. When Lay called the sponsoring organization, the American Committee for Protection of the Foreign Born, "subversive and Communist," Ferencz replied by reading from their letterhead the names of six reverends, two bishops, seven "honorables," and a slew of doctors and professors.

Ferencz was aided by Kay Boyle's political innocence no less than by his belief in the law. That the Joint Anti-Fascist Refugee Committee was pervaded by Communists was true. That Kay Boyle was unaware of this fact was also apparent. Nor would Ferencz accept that people should have known which organizations were on the Attorney General's list of subversive organizations.

"Would you say there were hundreds or thousands of such organizations?" Ferencz finally inquired. Told by Houston Lay that there were four pages of names, Ferencz mischievously demanded, "Is that fine print?" When Ferencz asked Kay Boyle whether she had been among the hundreds of thousands of people who supported organizations without being aware of their subversive character, she admitted that she had. What astonished Kay Boyle was the emphasis on her position on the Spanish Civil War; she was asked not only whether she associated with Spanish refugees in Mégève but, absurdly, whether she had visited an exposition in Geneva of paintings from the Prado, an exhibition held under the auspices of the Loyalist government.

Obviously frightened, and confused by the implication that supporting the Loyalists meant supporting Communism, Kay said she had not contributed to Spanish refugees. Had she known the Soviets were supporting the Loyalists, Kay said—and she may have been dissembling here—she would not have supported them. "It has taken me a long time to believe that only the Communists can use the word 'peace,' " Kay Boyle said pointedly as she was asked to account for having been a sponsor of the Waldorf Conference. (When Lay mistakenly called the organization of the Waldorf Conference the Cultural Conference for Peace, instead of the Cultural and Scientific Conference for World Peace, Ferencz could not resist exposing the absurdity of Lay's obsession with the Attorney General's list: "Is that a new organization other than the one listed here?")

Lay forced Kay to agree that "on the basis of [her] present knowledge," it was indeed advisable to make inquiries "because these things have been infiltrated by elements with which we are not in sympathy." When Lay asked her whether she knew of any time when her name had been used wrongly, and she had objected, Kay Boyle said she did not, neglecting to mention, or forgetting, her angry letter in 1939 to the *Partisan Review* objecting to her name on a petition opposing the coming capitalist war. It was just as well, of course, since the board might well have demanded why she did not dissociate herself from the Communist organizations presently under discussion.

Throughout, Kay Boyle conducted herself well. She faltered only when Lay trapped her into saying she never considered the House Un-American Activities Committee "an official thing." "I thought it was a hysterical committee, attacking people, smearing right and left without any responsibility," she said. When she called HUAC "a self-appointed thing by McCarthy and others," Lay informed her it was an official committee of the United States government. When one of the members asked whether she had ever been asked to appear before them, Kay Boyle replied, "I would gladly have welcomed the opportunity to appear before them at the time." As for her work, Kay Boyle had her reply ready:

"I have always written in defense of the individual and any infringements of the rights of any individual as completely opposed to the totalitarian system; I have always written against concentration camps; and I have written many stories outspokenly against the Communist system."

The last part of her statement was not quite true. Only in the past year, as she was being investigated, did Kay Boyle write a long two-part story, "The Daring Impersonation," explicitly against Communism, for *The Saturday Evening Post*. And throughout Kay Boyle demonstrated her considerable political naiveté. Asked to outline the principles of the Communist Party, she replied: "suppression of free enterprise, all individual expression or freedom of thought, speech; freedom of the press completely suppressed; any enemies of the Communist Party to be liquidated or to die in concentration camps." But she was saying what was politically correct. She agreed that the courts had jurisdiction over the twelve Communists convicted under the Smith Act, and even agreed that their civil rights were not being violated, although of course they were, since they were convicted of exercising their First Amendment right to believe what they wished and had never advocated violent overthrow of the government.

Kay Boyle had to believe that if she said the right things, she could save herself and Joseph. So she even denied that there was a distinction between "Communism" and "Sovietism," although on the strength of Heinz Pol's 1950 letter to her alone, she had to have known better. Lay even got her to deny that she believed in "absolute freedom of speech," although at first she said that she did believe in it. What if such speech encouraged rebellion or violent action against the government? Lay demanded.

Finally Kay Boyle had to prove not only that she was not a Communist but that she was a fierce anti-Communist as well. She mentioned her support of the United Nations. This wasn't good enough since the Soviets were also members. She invoked the Red Cross. Nor did this suffice. Kay Boyle was asked to refer "specifically" to something she had done that would prove she had "anti-Communist tendencies." Luckily, it was lunchtime and a forty-five-minute recess was called.

In the afternoon Lay zeroed in on the petition Kay Boyle had signed requesting that no aid be given to Franco. When Kay called Vincent Sheean, who had brought the petition to her, a "completely reliable individual from the ideological point of view," Lay informed her that Sheean had been a Communist Party member!

Only after hours of such grueling questioning was Ferencz able to lead Kay Boyle through the story of her life and her work. As usual, she lied about her age, giving 1903 as her date of birth. She told of the "American" prizes she had won for her work, and how the Army Air Forces had invited her to Europe in 1944. She stretched the truth by describing "The White

Horses of Vienna" as being about "the anti-Jewish feeling in Germany at that time." Ferencz invoked one of the *Ladies' Home Journal* pieces on "How America Lives" which was broadcast on the radio by a Catholic organization, and how Kay Boyle had been attacked in 1947 by the Communist *New Masses* as a "plush lady writer." If the Communists disliked her, surely she must be an anti-Communist.

Kay now described two stories she planned for *The Saturday Evening Post* as proof of her opposition to Communism. One was her serial about Michel Sciama, who, Kay told the panel, was "always violently anti-Communist." The other was "The Daring Impersonation," about a corporal's wife who finds herself kidnapped to East Berlin in an industrial diamond smuggling scam, another of her potboilers. Written as she was being investigated, "The Daring Impersonation" shows the Communist side as a "nightmare" as Soviet agents kidnap the leaders of the "anticommunist underground." This time Kay Boyle would write not only to put money in the Franckensteins' diminishing coffers but also to establish her political reliability to the McCarthyites.

Ferencz, knowing the weak link would be *The New Yorker*, focused as much as he could on the other magazines for which she was writing. He read from one of her letters to Stuart Rose: "the French don't want war and they don't want Communism," and he had her declare that no one had ever accused *The Saturday Evening Post* of being a subversive publication. Kay even read from two unpublished stories, "Autobahn, 1951," and her story about Soviets who come to DP camps and lie to the children that their parents were still alive to make them return to Eastern Europe, based on her long-ago visit to Wildflecken. (At Wildflecken, of course, these were not Soviets at all, but Polish officers.)

Ferencz had Kay name all the magazines to which she had sold her work, from *The New Yorker* to *Woman's Home Companion*. Unimpressed, Lay wanted only to know whether she had ever written for *In Fact* or any anti-Communist magazines. Shrewdly he asked whether the role the Communists had played in the French resistance had been reflected in *Avalanche*. Kay told him "there were no politics at all except the politics between the Allies and the Germans." What weakened that novel here worked in her favor, as she admitted *Avalanche* was "a romanticized account."

Indeed, well-meaning liberal that she was, Kay Boyle was *au fond* a profoundly unpolitical person. If Houston Lay had thought he was dealing with a sophisticated political operative, he was sorely mistaken. Her politics were highly emotional, founded on, as one informant had said, "sympathy for the underdog," and little more. "Intuition" guided her. Even an attempt by the panel to connect her sympathy with labor to Communist ideology fell flat, because Kay Boyle did not perceive even the thrust of the argument.

But notwithstanding his youth, Benjamin Ferencz was no innocent. Wisely he took his client through the list of donations she had made to those children's camps, the Indian tribe, the wildlife fund, the iron lung campaign in Marburg, the United Nations. "I might add for the record that this does not appear to be one of the organizations on the Attorney General's list, certainly, by looking at the names of some of the presidents and vice-presidents," Ferencz allowed himself. Under committee questioning, Kay asserted that *The Nation* "is known as a very strong anti-Communist paper." The only reason she didn't write for it more, she went on, was that it didn't pay enough money "to help my children." This latter was the only part of this statement that was true. Lay may have been too astounded at this characterization of *The Nation* even to bother to follow up.

Ferencz remained convinced that he could not introduce all the many affidavits on her behalf without offering anything from the magazine which had actually employed her, *The New Yorker*. After Stuart Rose's generous statement, he read the sentence in Lobrano's letter in which Lobrano declares himself incapable of believing Kay Boyle would do anything to further the designs of the Communist Party. Swiftly he then moved on to the strongest letter they had, the one from Edward Aswell. But the panel asked that the entire Lobrano letter be copied for them. There was nothing Ferencz could do but oblige.

As Ferencz had feared, the panel quickly seized on it. Garrett wanted to know why Lobrano considered her politically naive. "It seems strange for a publisher and writer of political fiction to say you were naive," he said, as if Lobrano rather than Kay were the author of her stories. Disoriented, Kay replied that her "great friend" at *The New Yorker* had been Harold Ross, who, she was certain, would have made a stronger statement in her defense had he been alive. Lay too seized on Lobrano's statement. Kay Boyle was obviously not the "organized Communist" Franz Borkenau had accused her of being. But if she had been used by the Communists, they might be able to prove Joseph Franckenstein was a security risk after all.

Kay's testimony ended on a flat note. She repeated that she had stopped making contributions, once she knew "these seemingly innocent organizations were Communist infiltrated." So frequently was she approached, Kay revealed, that only last night she had received a request for a contribution. Ferencz at once asked, "*Did* you contribute to it?"

Kay motioned disdainfully. The appeal turned out to be from the Federation of German-American Women's Clubs, which had been "sponsored" by none other than the American high command itself!

But so rattled was Kay Boyle that by the end of her testimony, to her own chagrin, she "meekly," as she later put it, told Chairman Baldwin that she and Joseph were hoping eventually to be married in the Catholic Church. As for the politics of her former husband, Laurence Vail, about which she was also questioned, Kay was blunt: "he is a reactionary, a man who always had money."

23

The Nineteenth Floor

*Our whole investment, yours & mine, of trust in the 19th floor
has undergone a kind of bankruptcy because of Godesberg.*

JANET FLANNER

At three in the afternoon of the second day of the Loyalty Security
Board hearing, a car came for Janet Flanner at her inn on the Rhine. In
the anteroom of Room I-208 on the second floor Flanner found Kay looking
"nervous, white and thin." Flanner was led at once into the hearing room,
where she sat with Joseph at her left, and Benjamin Ferencz between them.
Having found Kay and Joseph both in a state of "paralyzed melancholy,"
Flanner planned to be in her testimony "quick, strong, and light as possible,
to counteract the gloom, to give a shock of differentness from Joseph and
Kay." At once she would establish a complicity with the "judges." She
and they were loyal Americans and anti-Communists who as decent people
had to share a disdain for unfair denunciations.

Ferencz began by asking Flanner whether she had a reputation as "an
anti-Communist writer." Good-humoredly, Flanner, known to them all as
Genêt, author of *The New Yorker*'s letters from Paris, replied that she had
been informed "on good authority" that she was included on a "list" kept
by the Communist press in Paris. She was "a known and writing, functioning
anti-Communist." This established, she could launch into encomiums of
praise for the uprightness of Kay Boyle and her commitment to democratic
principles. Kay, Flanner testified, possessed "a kind of American democratic radiance" and was a person who would "always tell you what she
thought." So, cleverly, Flanner established that should Kay Boyle have
harbored pro-Communist sentiments, she would not have kept silent about
them. Flanner bragged that she could spot any Communist, unless he was
trained by the Moscow Art Theater and hid behind "false mustaches." Kay
Boyle was not one of them.

Kay Boyle could not have been defended by a more persuasive witness.

Flanner was self-confident, knowledgeable, and formidable, as she compared Kay to herself. Having been born in the Midwest, they shared, Flanner said, the same "core of Lincolnianism." Her friend possessed "an illuminating, obstinate, strong core of downright Middlewestern democratic Americanism." Moreover, Flanner added, she was extremely generous. "If you were in trouble, go to Kay Boyle Franckenstein," Flanner said. "Tell her a hard luck story and she digs into her pocket." Her contributing to so many spurious organizations could be attributed to her "maternal" side as the mother of six children.

Flanner also did for Kay what neither William Shawn nor Gus Lobrano would do. She spoke for *The New Yorker*. Without informing Shawn that she would be testifying, Flanner confirmed Kay's importance to the magazine. She also verified Kay's statement that the previous editor, Harold Ross, had believed in her. Judging from the "empty faces" of the panel, suddenly Janet Flanner realized that they had never heard of Harold Ross! Flanner also denied that *The New Yorker* could have been influenced by Kay's name having appeared in that *Herald Tribune* article. She described her colleagues as "an extremely loyal editorial group" which "would never consider that anyone connected with them had been besmirched by a thing like that." Idealized view as it was, it helped.

Flanner at once perceived that Chairman Baldwin was both "wooden" and not nearly so dangerous as Houston Lay, whom she found to be a man of "cement." It was Baldwin who asked whether Kay had "an acute political intelligence." Stoutly, Flanner said she did, although she focused her response more on Kay's actions than on her thinking. "I think she has a high degree of the best interpretation of the political sensibility, living by it, and making it work, and practicing it," Flanner said, her awkward language revealing her discomfort with the question. Reaching for American colloquialisms, Flanner kept to her objective of creating a camaraderie between herself and Kay's accusers.

"I don't think that Kay Franckenstein buys any pigs in the poke," Flanner said. "Oh, no, she knows what she is up to."

Flanner brought logic and shrewdness to the defense. When Lay told her it was a "matter of historical record" that the Loyalists had received aid from Russia, Flanner informed him they received aid from democratic people as well. When Garrett once more invoked Lobrano's harmful letter, asking Flanner whether Kay might have been naive enough to embrace Communism out of her "conscientious opposition to the Nazis and Fascists," Flanner was firm. "She is no milksop," Flanner said, or "somebody you wind around a little finger like a bandage." When Garrett wondered whether Kay was the kind of person who might lead a double life, Flanner burst into laughter, and all the judges laughed with her. Only Houston Lay kept his cement face intact. "There wasn't any mollycoddle, lollipopping around her," Flanner repeated.

Ferencz was elated. He had found Flanner's testimony "moving and

358]   KAY BOYLE / *Author of Herself*

superb." But Flanner herself was worried. She and Kay and Joseph were all "semi-Europeanized, semi-Americanized." The judges, "all utterly American," might not understand them.

At ten of five, on this the final day of the hearing, Ferencz recalled Kay Boyle to tell the story of "Mr. Kantor." Then it was over. Ferencz requested that the board permit her to remain in the room by her husband's side for his closing statement. But without missing a beat, Baldwin refused him. Kay rose and returned numbly to the anteroom.

Ferencz's closing statement was brilliant. He asserted that the Franckensteins had been denied basic rights: to subpoena witnesses, to have counsel of their choice, to have their counsel paid should they not have been able to afford to pay him, to examine the evidence against them, or to cross-examine those nameless, faceless informants who had denounced them.

"Both of these people have been subjected to an ordeal and the type of humiliation which they have not earned in America," he said ardently. "We run the danger now of identifying loyalty with orthodoxy. We don't want to stifle criticism in the United States." As for the most serious charge against Joseph, his association with his wife, his "guilt by marriage," Ferencz was indignant. "We haven't relied on two lines in a newspaper story. We haven't relied on the *Daily Worker*. We haven't relied on anonymous pamphlets and we haven't relied on anonymous informants.

"Although you don't have the power to sentence a man to death or to sentence a man to prison," Ferencz said passionately, "you do have the power to deprive him of the means of living not only for himself but for his family as well."

By the time Ferencz had finished, Lay's assistant, Herbert Sultan, who, it turned out, was not made of "cement," broke down and wept.

It was Lay, however, who closed the hearing. He announced that it would be a matter of public record only "if Mr. Franckenstein chooses to make it public." This, of course, was not so, for people with as little authority as Roy Cohn would gain access to these documents. On the matter of Joseph's having had the opportunity to choose his own counsel, which Ferencz had raised since the board had refused to change the date allowing General Edward Greenbaum, their original choice of counsel, to come from America to Germany to represent the Franckensteins, Lay was acerbic. He wished to declare for "the record" that he thought Kay and Joseph had "been extremely well represented."

As indeed they had been.

When Benjamin Ferencz asked Kay how she felt the next morning, he discovered that she had recovered her spirits. "For the first time in my life I feel like joining something," she said. "I feel I must have something to protect me so that this kind of thing cannot happen again. For the first time in my life I feel that being an American is not enough." A colleague under similar duress called to tell Joseph he was resigning as "the best way out." But such a course was not open to Kay Boyle or any husband of hers. Two weeks after the hearing, she and Joseph sent Houston Lay a long list of typographical errors in the transcript.

As Kay was ready to fight on, Houston Lay was "not too well satisfied" with the hearing. He regretted not delving "into the relations between the two in respect of the child born before their marriage, while she was another man's wife." Then he could have undercut the argument that Joseph's Catholicism made it impossible for him to be a Communist. Lay also feared Kay's threat that "she was going to get us or fix us." HICOG gossip revealed that Kay Boyle planned now to argue for her rights in the press. Lay and Sipes searched the Foreign Service Manual for a means of silencing her.

On December 6 a one-word telegram came to Kay and Joseph from Benjamin Ferencz: "Cleared." This indeed was a victory. Joseph had been exonerated, as Chairman Baldwin had, it turned out, been persuaded by the "outstanding and heroic character" of Joseph's military service. The panel had indeed been troubled that there had been no "documentary proof or support" for Louis Budenz's assertion that Kay had been a member of the Communist Party. They had been fair. Whatever the pressure from Houston Lay, they had refused to be guided by undocumented denunciations by nameless people, however "reliable" the FBI insisted they were. But no official notice of Joseph's being cleared came, either from Washington or from the office of the High Commissioner at Bonn. A bit worried, Kay and Joseph waited.

Houston Lay was not only disappointed. He was not finished. He believed that Kay Boyle was at least a "parlor pink." Were she the employee, he was certain, "she would be a security risk." Had he a vote, Houston Lay thought, he would have cleared Joseph on loyalty, but voted against security on the ground of his being married to Kay. Now he attributed the panel's favorable decision for the Franckensteins to Kay's "personality" and "the personality of some of the employee's witnesses." Indeed, one of the panel members had gone up to Janet Flanner after her testimony to tell her how much he enjoyed her Genêt columns in *The New Yorker*.

Lay knew that Joseph desired a permanent Foreign Service appointment. He decided now to do everything in his power to thwart that ambition. Lay had powerful allies in Washington. Not only was John Sipes his counterpart across the seas, but he could also count on Scott McLeod, the administrator for the Bureau of Security and Consular Affairs and, as Kay Boyle would learn, "McCarthy's man." Walter J. Donnelly remarked that a person who "was a little bit sympathetic toward a Communist or disloyal group was like a man who made a little pass at another man's wife." Joseph may have been cleared by the security panel in Germany. But this decision still had to be "administratively reviewed" in Washington by the security branch of the State Department, and again by the President's Loyalty Review Board. Lay's first victory was that Joseph would never receive official notice of the board's decision to clear him.

From Washington, the decision was made to continue to deny Joseph access to classified information "until the security administrative review has been completed." On December 12, at the Department of State, Deputy Under Secretary Carlisle H. Humelsine informed General Snow that Houston Lay's comments questioned the entire competency of the panel in Joseph's case.

Lay next put in motion a strategy designed to silence Kay Boyle. He had found a clause in the Foreign Service Manual which prohibited not only employees but also their families from writing or speaking on "political or controversial subjects" without State Department approval. In Washington, bureaucrats busied themselves over whether Kay's writings since 1946 had received clearance, since she had been the wife of a government employee. The State Department's Committee on Unofficial Publication, shades of George Orwell, borrowed a copy of *The Smoking Mountain* from the Library of Congress and Kay was requested to submit "for clearance" a speech she was announced to be giving.

But Robert L. Thompson, the State Department's chairman of the Committee on Unofficial Publication, pronounced *The Smoking Mountain* "good fiction" which "in no way undermines United States policy or the implementation of that policy in Europe now or at the time the material was published." In fact, that clause in the Foreign Service Manual had never been enforced. Fearing Kay's outrage, Lay decided it would be unwise to ask her for copies of her writings. In his papers he noted that she was "a highly sensitive and volatile personality who reacted strongly to her husband's difficulties with the Loyalty Security Panel." Kay Boyle had beat him again. But still Lay was not done.

As Robert Thompson showed, as the panel in Bad Godesberg had demonstrated, the government was not entirely bereft of good and fair people. Indeed, on the last day of 1952, General Snow himself, undaunted by pressure from the State Department's security office, endorsed the findings of the panel. He preferred Kay Boyle's testimony, he said, which he found "consistent and credible," to the "somewhat vague, second-hand information of an informer who is to the panel anonymous." Snow ruled that the case should not be referred to a new panel. The unanimous decision in Joseph's favor should stand.

But even General Snow could not prevail over a McCarthyite bureaucracy once it had the scent of a vulnerable victim. Sacrifices of the innocent were required to keep the population in America intimidated, and dissent in abeyance. Houston Lay and his powerful friends were not about to release a prey whom they had already cornered, one whose wife had been involved with all those Communist front organizations. The State Department's security office now refused to recommend "clearance of Mr. Franckenstein on security." The FBI was dispatched to reinterview Louis Budenz, who was to reveal the source of his information about Kay Boyle's being a member of the Communist Party. The FBI was also ordered to locate Ruth McKenney, who, according to Budenz, had been put in charge of monitoring the loyalty of her alleged fellow party member, Kay Boyle.

Kay left "depressing" Bad Godesberg at the end of December for Paris to attend Kathe's wedding to a handsome Yugoslav actor, who performed under the name Charles Millot. Kathe was just eighteen, but Laurence had worried that this daughter, were she not to marry early, "would be in bars, on the streets, in a hotel room a great part of the night." Laurence encouraged Kay to accept the marriage. "I do believe," he wrote, "as much as one can believe anything, that she is in good hands."

Kathe, now grown, still sought her mother's blessing, which she did by accepting Kay's own views, her mother's very formulations, as her own. "I know that one must live one's entire life, every single minute and gesture of it must be done in the way one believes, and one must try as much as possible not to compromise," she wrote, echoing Kay's own sentiments. All the children believed that to win their mother's love, they must obliterate any distinction between themselves as individuals and her.

When Kay Boyle returned to Germany from Paris, she found in her mail the standard form she received each year from the Heidelberg Military Post which was to be signed by *The New Yorker* confirming her press accreditation. Indeed, at the same time a year before, in February of 1952, *The New Yorker* had signed the same document, "officially" confirming for the government Kay Boyle's press credentials. It was a matter of form since her contract with the magazine ran until November of 1953. Kay Boyle's Department of Defense "certificate of identity," a laminated card with her photograph on it, read: "Press Representative for *The New Yorker*, expiring November 1, 1953."

Kay feared there might be trouble. Since her report on the Baab trial, which had appeared in September of 1950, the editors on the nineteenth floor had rejected every Kay Boyle story which Ann Watkins sent them. In January of 1953, *The New Yorker* rejected one more, "The Young Man of the Morning," as "kind of flat and implausible." Kay communicated her alarm to Watkins. "Inasmuch as the *New Yorker* does not accept anything I write, perhaps they will not wish to accredit me for another year." But Kay instructed her agent to "try it, anyway."

Promptly *The New Yorker* telephoned the Watkins office. They would not be signing Kay's accreditation form. They were willing to offer her one of their "first-reading fiction agreements." But they would not officially acknowledge a relationship with Kay by confirming that she was accredited until November. (According to Kay's later recollection, upon Flanner's return from Bad Godesberg, she had received a cable from William Shawn accusing her of having "jeopardized the reputation of *The New Yorker*" by her appearance as a character witness for Kay. Solita Solano later told Kay that Janet had "wept for hours.")

"Have I been completely mistaken in the character of Bill and of the magazine too?" Janet Flanner wondered. It was one thing for the "Notes & Comments" columns of the magazine to bemoan "the curse of our time —witchburning." It was another to act. "When it comes to acting, proving, & bearing witness, what did the magazine DO when Kay was in trouble?"

Kay immediately wrote to Shawn. Her letter was temperate. She acknowledged that *The New Yorker* had not published her work for several years. But, she told Shawn, she could not help but conclude "that this sudden action on the part of *The New Yorker* is in some way related to the recent loyalty and security hearing to which my husband and I were subjected." Her suspicion, Kay added, was confirmed by the fact that no one at the magazine had written her inquiring as to its outcome. Pained, Kay wrote Shawn that she accepted his dismissal, but could not help but feel that "Harold would have done it in a different way."

Although in her letter Kay had refrained from mentioning her own and Benjamin Ferencz's disappointment with Shawn's and Lobrano's caviling letters, Shawn immediately invoked his letter—but only to complain that Kay had not acknowledged it. This excused him, he implied, from inquiring about the hearing. Defending Lobrano's letter, Shawn argued that "its obvious honesty and forthrightness" were precisely what made it effective.

Now, Shawn said, he was refusing to sign the Heidelberg Military Post form on the ground that Kay was "not active as a correspondent for us and for several years had not, in fact, written anything we published." So he could not justify signing the form which amounted, he jesuitically argued, to a "renewal" of her accreditation (which it did not). "WE have withdrawn nothing," Shawn said. "We simply refused whatever it was the Watkins office requested."

Nor would Shawn admit the obvious: his not signing the form amounted to an open repudiation of Kay. In any case, there would be no public act of solidarity with this longtime *New Yorker* writer now in trouble, and no silent agreement of first refusal of her stories could compensate for that. What further hurt Kay was Shawn's passing comment in his letter that Harold Ross in 1951, the year of his death, had "misgivings" about renewing her accreditation because of her "relative inactivity." (Katharine White supported Shawn by simultaneously telling Janet Flanner that Ross had renewed the accreditation only because Kay Boyle had "so goddam many kids.")

In his explanation to Janet Flanner of why he had refused to sign Kay's routine Army form, Shawn offered a new explanation, one he must have concocted after the fact. Suddenly Shawn insisted that it was illegal for him now *or ever* to have signed the Heidelberg form, as it had been illegal for the magazine to have accredited Kay from the start. Only full-time employees were entitled to be accredited! Shawn was therefore "constitutionally" prevented from signing the Army form. Katharine White told Flanner, justifying *The New Yorker*'s repudiation of Kay Boyle, that it would be a "deception of our government" for them to have signed the paper.

It was easy for William Shawn to dismiss a writer who, he obviously had decided, no longer belonged in the pages of *The New Yorker*. It required greater sophistry to deal with the determined Janet Flanner, who remained indefatigable in her defense of Kay's rights, no matter that she shared none of her liberal politics. Perhaps assuming that Flanner was as anti-Communist as he, and hence willing to sacrifice the civil liberties of those who had not embraced this ideology, Shawn wrote Flanner in April of 1953 that he believed in the McCarthy committee's right to punish those accused of "disloyalty." He had not been an "intimate friend" of Kay Boyle's, he said. He certainly had not been about to "testify falsely to somebody's innocence for fear he might later be proved innocent." Kay Boyle, Shawn slyly implied, might indeed have been guilty.

Bewildered, yet refusing to acknowledge defeat, Kay Boyle mailed another Heidelberg form to Ann Watkins in the hope that *The New Yorker* would reconsider. The least they could do, Kay thought, was "write to Heidelberg and tell them that they have had reason to suspend me as their correspondent. People over there don't realize how things like this are looked on here where everything is under army or official control of some kind." She would in turn agree that in November their association would automatically come to an end. Kay hoped Lobrano, if not Shawn, might sign the form "to protect my reputation over here . . . it seems to me that after all these years of association they could do this final thing for me." Despite the icy letter she had received from Shawn, Kay Boyle still found it inconceivable that *The New Yorker* should abandon her so completely.

Kay replied to Shawn in a five-page single-spaced letter, typing out portions of the testimony of the Loyalty Security Board hearing to demonstrate how damaging Gus Lobrano's letter had been to her case. She answered each of Shawn's arguments with grievances of her own, beginning with Shawn's tardiness in writing a letter on her behalf. Now she told Shawn that his letter had been so harmful that her lawyer dared not use it at the hearing.

In this second letter to Shawn, Kay begged him to reconsider his decision. She had heard twice more from the Heidelberg Military Post, which had requested that *The New Yorker* inform them one way or the other without delay what their intentions were. They had asked her for "an explanation as to why the accreditation was being withdrawn." It was "a grave matter" when "sponsorship is withdrawn" in this environment, Kay said. As for her "relative inactivity," she had certainly submitted stories to *The New Yorker* "regularly."

Replies came from Katharine White and William Shawn—not to Kay Boyle, but to Janet Flanner. White now defended Shawn's and Lobrano's honesty, in contrast to the "weakening over-statement" of Kay's other letters. As for Lobrano's calling Kay "politically naive," Shawn endorsed that view. Shawn, Flanner was told, attributed her own testifying for Kay Boyle neither to her courage nor to her political astuteness, but to her "warm-heartedness," and so he forgave her for this breach of discipline.

Liberal in her defense of democratic principles—especially when they were under siege—Janet Flanner was not appeased by the attempts of Shawn and Katharine White to retain her goodwill. She also was politically astute enough to recognize the damage Shawn's betrayal would cause Kay Boyle. Flanner told Kay that the public "would think that the *New Yorker* really had a reason for not aiding you & if so what was it?"

"I have always felt married to *The New Yorker*," Flanner said sadly. "Now it is like having fallen out of love." Her friend Solita Solano scrawled on one of Flanner's letters to Katharine White, under Flanner's signature: "who broke a lance for Kay Boyle." Flanner believed it was her duty to resign from *The New Yorker*. But she could not. "You have a husband, six children, and a distinguished writing career," Kay Boyle says Flanner pleaded. "I only have *The New Yorker* as husband, children, career." From that day on, according to Kay, she and Flanner never again spoke of how *The New Yorker* had treated her.

As late as April 16, Ann Watkins begged Shawn to reconsider and sign the press form. But he would not. Army headquarters withdrew Kay's name from the list of accredited correspondents in Germany, adding to her demoralization. "This is a fine thing to have happen now when we are accused of everything," Kay said, burning with indignation. "My own magazine backs out."

Bitterly, she instructed Ann Watkins to telephone Shawn and tell him that one "*cannot withdraw* accreditation from an old-timer like me at the moment that old-timer is being accused of being . . . a Communist Party member by the McCarthy Committee." Watkins was to tell Shawn that Kay Boyle "was through . . . if *The New Yorker* doesn't need me, I certainly don't need *The New Yorker*. As far as I'm concerned, my last piece has appeared in its pages. And you know I don't change my mind." Indeed, never again was a piece by Kay submitted to *The New Yorker*.

Years later she would be even angrier when she learned how Shawn was explaining why he had withdrawn her accreditation: "What could I do? I had to withdraw her accreditation. She said she didn't want her words to appear anymore in *The New Yorker*." The chronology, of course, was the reverse. In a *Nation* article in October of 1987, Shawn is quoted by Natalie Robins as explaining that "if Kay Boyle had actually written an article or some articles for *The New Yorker* as a correspondent, even though not a staff correspondent, it is possible that the magazine would have been in a better position to ask for a renewal of her accreditation." Yet even if Kay Boyle had stopped being published by the magazine in 1950, *The New Yorker* had published seven of her short stories and the long nonfiction piece in the four years after 1946 when their agreement began. And she was not requesting a "renewal of her accreditation," only that William Shawn sign the form attesting to the fact that she was already accredited to them contractually until the coming November.

Meanwhile Joseph remained in limbo, neither fired nor fully reinstated with normal access to classified information. Worried about her demoralized husband, Kay Boyle feared that *The Saturday Evening Post* might back out of their agreement to publish "The Daring Impersonation." When, in 1953, the *Post* did publish both "The Soldier Ran Away" and "The Daring Impersonation," Kay urged Ann Watkins to do everything she could to sell them to Hollywood. But Watkins could not.

More rejections followed. In February, *Harper's Bazaar* rejected "Fear," because they were "unconvinced of the woman's identification with the emotional landscape of France," a subject with which Kay Boyle should have had no trouble. In March, *Collier's* rejected a story because it was "too much a woman's point of view." In June, MacLennan Farrell was blunt in his rejection of a story for the same magazine: "her characters are dreadful dopes. The child-woman is as irritating as any character I've encountered in some time. The husband is neither man, woman, nor character." Kay told Watkins she found it almost impossible to concentrate now, and her work suffered. Nor was Edward Aswell pleased by what he saw of her serial about Michel Sciama. "I shall keep a completely open mind and shall read the revision when it comes as though I had never seen a draft of it before," he said generously.

But if Kay Boyle wasn't certain before, she was now. "I imagine the big magazine market will be closed to me from now on," she told Watkins. Then with a trace of self-pity she announced that she could "get a job as someone's secretary . . . (although I'm not so young anymore)."

For some months the government had been silent. "All indications are that all is well," Kay wrote Watkins. She was unaware of the new FBI investigation. In February the FBI reinterviewed Louis Budenz on the matter of Kay Boyle's membership in the Communist Party, only to be told by Budenz that his memory had deserted him with the passage of time and that he had nothing to add to his statement of June of 1951. In March the FBI had found Ruth McKenney in Paris only for McKenney to tell them she had never met Kay Boyle, exploding Budenz's now obvious lie. Meanwhile Kay and Joseph clung to the hope that he would be reinstated so that he could apply for a long-overdue promotion.

Kay Boyle remained outspoken in her beliefs, although she had added a distinctly anti-Communist theme to her statements. So she concluded that French anger toward America was felt "not ONLY by the Communists" but also by "the real believers in democracy." She opposed our "senseless policy" in building up Germany, "which has every reason to make trade and military and every other kind of agreement with Communist Russia rather than with us." She had also begun frequently to dissociate herself from the Soviet Union. Any intelligent person, Kay Boyle said, should oppose "the alliance of a strong, military Germany with the East."

In May of 1953 Kay considered a visit to America since Joseph was entitled to "statutory leave." But she was warned that if he went home before the official security clearance arrived, he might not be permitted to return. Joseph was advised to hang around Bad Godesberg as long as possible so as not to be fired. Looking into the future, and into the eyes of her depressed, embittered husband, Kay knew Joseph had to have something "to build on when the employment ends here." She feared the "added ordeal of facing zero in the way of a job and future when we get back." But there were no prospects, and the future seemed dim.

That spring Houston Lay had been assigned to fire unnecessary personnel, which meant anyone who had had a loyalty and security hearing and was hence "suspect," whether or not they were cleared. Joseph was indeed in serious trouble. Kay now instructed Ann Watkins to send lawyer Edward Greenbaum one hundred dollars to pursue Joseph's clearance in Washington. With money scarce, Kay considered cashing in War Bonds she had taken out in the names of her six children.

Kay was affected physically by the case against Joseph. "Thin as a rake" as she had been all her life, by now she had lost twenty pounds and was skeletal. She suffered from low blood pressure and gallstones from her dysfunctional gallbladder. Dispirited, she waited for the ax to fall.

In a letter dated April 2, Joseph received notice that his "limited-service appointment" would be terminated as of May 8. A "permanent replacement" had become available. He was being dismissed not because he was a loyalty or security risk, however, but "as a result of the reduction program." Bitterly Joseph replied that he was "unable to accept the terms" of his dismissal. He declared now publicly that he was not convinced that he had been told the real reasons why he had been fired. Meanwhile he tried to buy time, requesting that he be permitted to remain at his post in Germany until June, when the school year ended. He had been the first man to be dismissed in his division, although he was senior to four others who should have been fired first in any reduction program. Since he was a veteran, nonveterans should have been dismissed first as well. On the advice of his attorneys, he told reporters, he would continue to report for work and remain in his government quarters.

Three days after Joseph received his letter of dismissal, Joseph McCarthy's chief counsel, Roy Cohn, and his friend G. David Schine arrived in Bad Godesberg as part of their tour of U.S. Information Service libraries in quest of Communist books—and Communists. In Paris, Cohn had removed one of Kay Boyle's books from the shelves of the U.S. Information Service library. Ben Bradlee, then press attaché at the American embassy in Paris, and later the editor of *The Washington Post*, observed that this "outraged a lot of the old libs to whom Kay Boyle was kind of a symbol."

Joseph had been dismissed before Roy Cohn got to Bad Godesberg.

(above) Kay in the late thirties; *(below)* Kay and her baron, Cassis, 1941 (*Morris Library*)

(above) The Vail family arrives in America, Bastille Day, 1941: Apple-Joan, Laurence, Pegeen, Kay with Clover, Bobby with Kathe, Sindbad; *(below left)* Kay in the aqua-and-white print dress, summer 1941 (*New York Post*); *(right)* "Mrs. Laurence Vail" photographed by George Platt Lynes

(above) Kay in New York, c. 1945: "radiant to men, to children too" (*Morris Library*); *(below)* "talented mother": Kay with Sharon (Bobby), Clover, Faith, Apple, and Kathe in New York, 1943 (*Louise Dahl-Wolff*)

(left) Kay and Joseph in 1944: "He is absolutely a miracle"; *(below)* Kay and Ian, Kathe, Clover, Apple, and Faith, with Belle, *left*, in Central Park, c. 1945 *(Berenice Abbott)*; *(opposite, top left)* simulated captain Kay Boyle and Free French aviator in France, February 1945 *(Morris Library)*; *(top right)* reunion in France, 1946: Apple, Kay, and Kathe; *(bottom)* Kay and Joseph, c. 1959: "like brother and sister"

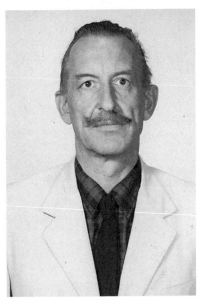

(above) Kay with Robert Frost, c. 1955 *(Morris Library)*; *(below left)* Kay in Connecticut, 1960; *(right)* passport photo of Joseph Franckenstein, 1962: "I feel lonely . . ."

(above left) Robert Gessner, painted by Brenda Moore: "last love"; *(right)* Faith Gude with children of the commune; *(below)* 1975 march from Delano to Modesto. *From left:* Joan Baez, senior; Kay; Jackie McGuckin; and Eric McGuckin

(above) Kay and Ian in Oakland, 1987: "I don't want you to live without me";
(below) Kay Boyle at eighty-eight (Marin *Independent Journal*)

But ever the mythologizer, Kay began to tell interviewers that Cohn and Schine, on orders from McCarthy, had gone through the files and themselves terminated anyone who had had a Loyalty Security hearing, including Joseph Franckenstein. Joseph's dismissal, Kay Boyle told Sandra Whipple Spanier, who was revising a dissertation about her, was "brought about by Cohn and Schine, acting for Senator McCarthy." Kay repeated this distortion to a writer working on a book about Katharine White: "McCarthy's assistants, Cohn and Schine, were sent by McCarthy to look through the files of those employees who had Loyalty-Security Hearings, and within twenty-four hours my husband was fired." It was more dramatic for Joseph to have been fired by the notorious "distempered Jackals," as perhaps it was more melodramatic to have Katharine White callously dismiss Kay Boyle's troubles by declaring, "You could never be a member of the Communist Party," while refusing to write a letter in her behalf. The facts, however, were dramatic enough and required no such embellishment.

Increasingly disoriented, Joseph was now placed on "leave without pay" status. He was offered an "unclassified" letter declaring that his dismissal "was not due to any security or loyalty considerations." Even now when defeat loomed, Joseph refused to accept either the letter or the dismissal. Repeatedly he insisted that he could not be fired because he was a veteran and senior in service. Moreover, he could not be considered "surplus" because he remained one of the few serving in Germany who were truly bilingual. He demanded "openly to prove my loyalty" and complained that he still had no official notification that the Loyalty Security Board had cleared him.

Joseph knew that the American presence in Germany was moving toward a permanent Foreign Service, one to which he had wanted to apply. But he insisted upon being dismissed only after his security clearance came through. Kay stood behind her husband, knowing as she did that were he not cleared before he was fired, he "would never get a decent job anywhere again—certainly not in government service, and perhaps not anywhere." Meanwhile, in a bureaucratic misstep, Joseph actually received a letter from Washington stating he had been "designated" as a possible permanent Foreign Service employee and asking him to fix the date for his examination. Privately, even Janet Flanner grew irritated with Kay as her troubles multiplied. "Kay shouldn't have got herself into this mess," Flanner sputtered.

Newspapers all over the world now reported that Joseph Franckenstein had been fired. An editorial appeared in *The Washington Post* on May 25 headlined "The Easy Out." "Mr. Franckenstein is entitled to a clearcut verdict on the security charges," the *Post* wrote; "as the situation stands now, there is ground for suspicion that Mr. Franckenstein has been thrown as another human sacrifice to the graven image of McCarthyism." The *Post* called for an investigation and intervention by High Commissioner James B. Conant, the very official who had refused all help to Benjamin Ferencz.

Even as Kay feared that in early May they would be evicted from their government apartment, she defiantly threw a party on April 13 on the occasion of the tenth anniversary of Joseph's American citizenship. It was to be a surprise. Robert Lochner, the *Neue Zeitung*'s first editor, who had hired Joseph, took him to his home while Kay set out an elaborate buffet dinner. She had invited twelve people who she believed really loved this honest upright man. One big table was filled with flowers and gifts from admirers. Cables arrived from old friends like Dorothy Disney, who wrote, "We wish we could celebrate tonight with one of our favorite citizens."

When the Lochners brought Joseph up the stairs into the apartment, the assembled company, Mousie and Boostie among them, sang "America the Beautiful." When they came to the line "America, America, God shed his grace on thee," many wept openly. Among them were Joseph's former secretaries, along with the Lochners and Ted Kaghan, who as chief of the Information Division of the Office of Public Affairs had been Joseph's overall superior officer in Germany since 1949; Kaghan himself was accused of Communism and forced to resign from Occupation service.

In May, with Apple and Ted and the Countess Esterházy present, Mousie and Boostie were confirmed in the Catholic Church. With nine people staying in the tiny apartment, Kay typed legal documents for Joseph. She concealed from her mother-in-law that Joseph had been dismissed and that May 8 had been his last day of work.

Back in Washington, John Sipes was delighted that Joseph had refused to accept the "unclassified" letter, the deal that in exchange for his not challenging his dismissal he was granted written reassurance that his being fired was not a matter either of his loyalty or of security considerations. Now the entire record could be reviewed. Sipes decided that Joseph need not be offered another hearing. The State Department's security division now ruled formally that Joseph was a security risk, his continued employment likely to "result in his knowingly or unknowingly taking actions which could be inimical to the interests of national security." Washington recommended that Joseph be fired for security reasons. Houston Lay had won at last.

In Germany, Joseph fought on. He read in the April Foreign Service newsletter that those fired for "reduction in force" would be dismissed on or about April 18. He had been dismissed on April 2. Wasn't his dismissal, then, illegal? The newsletter also indicated that years of service and veteran's status would be taken into consideration. Joseph wrote a final pleading letter to James B. Conant, addressing Conant as a man with a record of "moral courage." But all he gained was an extension of his leave-without-pay status to August. Finally, on General Greenbaum's advice, Joseph agreed to leave Germany, although his instinct was to refuse to leave his post in what amounted to a sit-down strike and to refuse to vacate government housing until justice was done.

Defeated now, and bitter toward his adopted country, Joseph wanted to remain in Europe and make his life there. But Kay Boyle was determined to fight. "This is one of the times in history when one must go back and speak out with those of the other America clearly and loudly enough so that even Europe will hear," she wrote in a "Farewell to Europe," in *The Nation.* "Ah God, how one must fight the evil that has spread like a disease throughout America!" she wrote Nancy Cunard. She was on the side of the "brave and the free." There were, she insisted, "strong forces at work on our side in America," and she was "eager to ally myself with them when we get back."

Packing her trunks, Kay discovered many letters from Harold Ross. "I didn't fail him in life anyway," she told herself sadly, "even if I'm failing him now." But in this time of great trouble, her sense of humor, sporadic as it was, had not entirely deserted her; she confessed to Ann Watkins that she had a sexual dream about Ann's husband, Roger Burlingame, in which he was cut high in the groin and as he bled, Kay made him a bandage while Ann gave him a drink.

On one of her last evenings in Germany, Kay visited Helga Einsele at her little house near the Frankfurt Women's Prison. A group had gathered. "Write to us about the other America," Einsele said, hoping to encourage her battered friend, "it must be there." Einsele was eloquent as she bid Kay Boyle farewell. "Tell them when you get back that we had our demagogue too!"

Whatever his "moral courage," James B. Conant told John Foster Dulles back in Washington not to worry about Joseph Franckenstein's insistence upon remaining in Germany. HICOG had every authority to evict Kay and Joseph from government-owned housing. It turned out not to be necessary. On June 23, the Franckenstein family sailed home from Le Havre, on a ship ironically called *America.*

Virtually penniless, homeless, and at the end of their resources, Kay and Joseph pondered where they might settle. Kay considered her sister Joan's farm in Plainfield, New Jersey, where they went first. But then, in one more extraordinary act of generosity and friendship, Ann Watkins offered the Franckensteins her cottage in West Redding, Connecticut, as a "temporary refuge."

Even as she was repaying an old loan to Grace Flandrau, Kay had to ask Frank Detweiler for money; Detweiler at once gave her a thousand dollars, and then a second thousand. Kay continued to write frantically, producing a new anti-Communist short story called "The Carnival That Came to the West," published as "Carnival of Fear" in 1954 in *The Saturday Evening Post.*

The hardest years for Kay Boyle had only just begun.

24

Land of the Free

I'll go back when I'm old, maybe, and it will be like going to a
new country because there's nothing waiting for me.
—My Next Bride

"Thin, old, and nerve-wracked" was how Janet Flanner described Kay when they parted in Paris. Kay's emotional distress was only exacerbated in America. The fighting began almost as soon as they returned. The children had never heard their parents fight. Now they seemed to be fighting all the time.

Joseph would grab a suitcase, storm out of the house, and get into the car. In tears, Kay raced out after him onto the driveway. "I hate you, I hate you, I hate you," she screamed after her mild-mannered, now bewildered husband. Mousie and Boostie screamed at him too, "I hate you," so mad at him were they for making their mother cry. All three children sided with their mother.

They fought continuously, about money, about work. Kay thought Joseph should find a job as a teacher, a professional. Beyond despair, Joseph insisted that it didn't matter. For a while he worked as a short-order cook frying eggs in a Danbury diner until he was fired for incompetence. Kay was disappointed in the man who had once appeared to her as so noble and heroic. Now he seemed to lack initiative, drive, ambition, and aggressiveness. He was not the man she had invented.

Returning to America in 1953 under the cloud of McCarthyism, Kay Boyle discovered herself married to a man with no more practical sense, no better able to take care of his family, than Howard Peterson Boyle had been. Laurence too had been emotionally dependent. But Joseph, with neither friends nor acquaintances of his own, was far more dependent on his wife. Kay's friends, like Howard Nemerov, found Joseph charming and agreeable, a man with a very upright carriage, Prussian in manner, and a bit of a martinet. Few got to know him well.

It had begun in Germany. But now ever more emphatically Kay took to bullying Joseph into living up to the fantasy she had fashioned. If she had been critical of him before, as Kathe had discovered in Germany, it seemed she never ceased criticizing him now: the way he drove the car, how much he smoked, how sloppy his study was, what he wore. She was always at him, and he said nothing. Only when Kay needled him too much would he fight back.

No more from her husband than from her children could Kay tolerate opposition. They all must worship her. As the fifties dragged on, she grew increasingly depressed, overemotional, and weepy. As always, she complained that she didn't have enough time for her work, and that writing for money made it impossible for her to accomplish the serious writing she intended.

The fights sometimes focused on Joseph's case. "It's hopeless, it's a waste of time," Joseph bitterly concluded. Kay's stance was different. A glamorous woman still in her prime, wearing wide silver bracelets and white earrings, a presence, she would not allow the world to desert her, and she insisted that Joseph do everything in his power to gain vindication. It was in the fray that she seemed to flourish.

Joseph began to deteriorate, physically, spiritually, and emotionally. He retreated into his private world. Numb and silent, he behaved as if something terrible had happened to him, as indeed it had. William L. Shirer visited them and found he couldn't sit down and talk with Joe about the hearing because he was "so goddamned ashamed."

Joseph spent a week in Washington, learning only that he would be investigated *again*. When he tried to see Allen Dulles at the CIA, the director had his secretary tell Joseph there was "nothing he could do for him." Even Benjamin Ferencz had to wonder at Kay and Joseph's determination that he clear himself so as to be able to work again for the government. "By this time I think I would have been very tempted to tell the administration to go run the country themselves," Ferencz said with his characteristic irony.

Chronically ill with her infected gallbladder, which she tried to control by diet, Kay found herself without household help for the first time in twenty-five years. Immediately she sat her three children down. "Your entire life will change now," she told them. "I've got to work and the three of you will start taking care of everything." Fourteen-year-old Clover would do the shopping; Faith, eleven, would clean the house. "None of you have ever taken care of anything in the house and you're going to learn now," Kay said. When Mousie cooked a good dinner, her mother complimented and encouraged her.

Every morning Kay would put half a grapefruit with a cherry on it before Joseph's place in the kitchen. When he came in, if everyone did not turn at once and say, "Good morning," he became grumpy. "Nobody around here says, 'Good morning,' " Joseph would say. In the evenings he retreated into his own world, not even asking the children how they had spent their days. It was Kay who talked to them, endlessly telling them stories of the past, of how Laurence had poured glue onto her clothes, of how Laurence had cut his arm in a frenzy as he destroyed his paintings one night, the blood shooting up to the ceiling, and Kay had put the tourniquet on the wrong arm, of how Joseph had fallen in love with her at the swimming pool, and of how Laurence had told him to "just get out."

Always when Joseph wasn't home, Kay had taken Clover into her bed with her for comfort. When Joseph returned, and Clover showed no inclination to leave, Kay had to tell her, "This is Joseph's and my bed." Clover had become increasingly possessive, unwilling to share her mother with others. When now Kay often had to leave to give lectures to earn money, Clover would throw herself into her mother's closet and hug the clothes perfumed with Kay's signature Chanel No. 5.

Frank Detweiler's generosity had saved Kay, but now, as always, the sisters could not tolerate each other. Kay hated Jo for being hard on her dogs, so that whenever she'd ask about a dog, she'd be told it had been put to sleep. There was so much tension between the sisters that Kay's small children almost always broke something when Jo was present. It galled Kay to have to borrow money from the Detweilers and still there was never enough.

Kay wrote in bed, way into the night as she had in Mégève. She rose early and began again. Deluded that there was sufficient "organized and passionate resistance" to McCarthy, Kay hoped to write a book about the loyalty hearing, together with Joseph. But Ann Watkins was unable to sell the idea.

By the end of August, Kay had arranged for scholarships for the three children at the Cherry Lawn School in Darien. That November, Kay found herself unable to meet her payments because the scholarships couldn't cover tuition and board. To make amends, she presented a copy of *The Youngest Camel* to the school library.

All three children hated being separated from their mother, and Boostie cried himself to sleep every night. Mousie worried about her mother's health: "Please, please don't work!" she begged Kay. Nothing was kept from the children and they all worried about money and about Kay's health. Mousie didn't care about whether she would be receiving any birthday presents; all she wanted was to "come home."

Yet when Kay visited the Cherry Lawn School and found Mousie happy to run off and play as soon as her mother was ready to depart, Kay was upset. "Mousie doesn't miss me," she complained, as if the child's homage were insufficient, no matter that Mousie had written her, "I wish you were a little girl here in Cherry Lawn . . . you could be my partner in swimming." Clover left her mother no doubt. Once when Kay was leaving, she threatened to throw herself under the wheels of the car. Finally, when Mousie was attacked by a janitor, Kay took her out of the hated school.

Kay Boyle tried to raise this second family as she had her first in Mégève, encouraging them to dabble in the arts and little more. Kay had Clover read her poetry out loud for guests, and Clover concluded, as her sisters had before her, that if you were not interesting and artistic in Kay Boyle's household, "you were not tolerated." When Kay went out at night, Ian would pin a poem to her pillow, just as his mother had done for Katherine. Mousie and Boostie put on plays, and Kay invited guests to come over and watch. It was Mégève all over again. Once, when Mousie and Boostie were sitting on the porch listening to the radio, their mother found them and demanded, "How can you just sit there listening? Go read a book!"

Honoring her commitment, Kay did not interfere with Joseph's taking Boostie and Mousie to church on Sundays, although he himself never went to confession or took Communion. At church he would sit looking at his watch the whole time. Their mother's children, neither Faith nor Ian was to become a Roman Catholic. Meanwhile the Countess Esterházy, still determined to sanctify Kay and Joseph's marriage in the eyes of the Church, wrote to Monsignor Sheen, who received them in his New York office. Joseph knelt down and kissed the Monsignor's ring. It was an act Kay Boyle had never seen him perform before, and she was amazed. But the visit produced no sanctification of their marriage.

At last Joseph found work—as assistant headmaster and language teacher at the Thomas School, a "young ladies' school" in Connecticut. Immediately he had told ancient Miss Thomas that he was considered "a security risk." Valiantly, she hired him anyway for three thousand dollars a year, which he supplemented with a Latin seminar for graduate students at Columbia University on Saturday mornings, and classes in Greek, French, and German at the Norwalk Adult Education program. His Ph.D. from Innsbruck could not get him an academic job in America now, and he enrolled in a Master's Program at Columbia.

But the Franckensteins were able to live in Rowayton in one of the two houses on the grounds of the Thomas School. Living rent-free, they would occasionally be compelled to move from one house to the other, so that Kay Boyle kept them both scarcely furnished; to each, however, she brought her precious keepsakes from Europe.

At Greycote, an old converted boathouse on Long Island Sound, Kay and Joseph slept in a ground-floor bedroom which opened out over the cove, in two single beds. Her undemonstrative parents had seemed so much more like brother and sister than husband and wife that Mousie was once astonished to open a bureau drawer—and discover condoms.

At Greycote, Joseph retreated to a study with windows overlooking the saltwater cove. His large desk was piled high with books in Latin and Greek, crumpled bits of paper, and overflowing ashtrays. Through the gauzy white curtains of the French doors, the children made out his form, sitting at his desk, lost in his own world. He always held a lit cigarette and a cloud of smoke surrounded him, a homeless scholar, uprooted and alone.

"Get your father to help you!" Kay would say, sending the children to Joseph when they needed assistance with their homework. But Joseph would yell at Mousie when she was slow to learn. He was impatient with his students no less than with the children at home, and when the Thomas School girls would read their Latin translations aloud in class, the atmosphere would be thick with tension. Invariably one of them would burst into tears. When no one could conjugate a verb correctly, and no one volunteered, Joseph would say sarcastically, "*La silence de la mer.*" His unhappiness was apparent to his students.

As the case dragged on, it seemed at times that Kay had grown hard, even bitter. It was as if life had denied her something. Increasingly she was away from home, teaching, lecturing, at lunches. By the late fifties she had discovered the MacDowell Colony as a refuge. Home in America, Kay Boyle had swiftly begun to forge her own life. One winter in the late fifties she left the family at Greycote and spent her weekdays at Ann Watkins's West Redding cottage to be alone to work in peace.

Whether it was Edmund Wilson's old attack, her own long absence, the fact that her great form had been the short story, or that she had for a long time subverted her talent by writing for the glossies, Kay found now that she was virtually forgotten in America. In an article in *College English*, Professor Richard C. Carpenter wrote that despite her considerable achievement, Kay Boyle was "singularly little known." In a generous appreciation, Carpenter insisted that "Miss Boyle has done much excellent work and should be better known," as he pointed to her "mastery of her own kind of fictional technique." In a 1952 study, *The Short Story in America*, Kay Boyle was quoted as explaining her lack of notoriety by describing her writing as "of so unnational a character that, for me, the question of 'roots' in any particular soil or tradition is not of any moment."

Settling permanently in her native land, even as she began to be lauded by academics like Carpenter and Harry T. Moore of Southern Illinois University as one of the most important short story writers of the century, Kay continued to be unable to get her stories published, and she slid deeper into obscurity. It wasn't quite a blacklist, because she had been having trouble getting into print long before the hearing. And Knopf published *The Seagull on the Step*, her Michel Sciama story, in 1955, and *Generation Without Farewell*, her Marburg novel, in 1960.

In fifties America, Kay Boyle determinedly remained an internationalist in provincial times. "Is one not to write about foreign countries and current history because someone in America is not conversant with foreign news?" she later asked rhetorically. The problem had begun when she was in Europe and it persisted. In 1955 she published only one old story, "The Kill," in *Harper's*, although four of her short pieces appeared in *The Nation*. In 1956 and 1957 she could not sell a single magazine story. That her problem went beyond blacklisting was reflected in the fact that by 1957 she was regularly reviewing books for *The New York Times Book Review.* In 1958 she wrote only for *The Nation* and *The Progressive.* Although her internationalism and her politics may have been contributing factors, the most compelling reason now why she could no longer publish her stories was that her habit of subverting her talent had caught up with her for good. "Writing down" for money had finally so damaged her work that she had lost the craft, not only that distinctive style which had graced her early *New Yorker* stories, and those first stories she wrote for Harold Ross out of Germany, but even the facility which pleased *The Saturday Evening Post.* The Kay Boyle who wrote those stories was no more.

In place of nuance, she had chosen didacticism, as she did in the serial she was calling a sequel to *Avalanche,* which revived a now passé theme. "France was never more greatly in need of our understanding and our confidence," Kay asserted in the mid-fifties as she completed her *Scaffoldings of France,* which would be called *The Seagull on the Step.* Fearful of being misunderstood, knowing this was far from her best writing, she explained the allegory to Edward Aswell. The story should be read, Kay Boyle said, as a parable of "Innocence and Corruption, Labor and Capital, Artist and Bourgeois." Meanwhile the idealized hero, Michel Vaillant (Sciama), would speak "for no party," but for a revitalized democratic France.

Just before Christmas of the torturous year 1953, Aswell rejected *Scaffoldings of France.* "The characters seem to be stock figures, and I think you will agree that the attempt to write a sort of international political parable is a very difficult one," he told her. With Ann Watkins, Aswell was more blunt: "Frankly, if this book is published, I do not think it will do Kay's reputation much good." At the same time Stuart Rose rejected it as a serial for the *Post* on the ground that there was not enough "physical action."

Although, happily, Knopf bought the novel, even as Alfred Knopf and his wife invited Kay and Joseph to lunch at their home in Purchase, New York, Kay Boyle feared that Aswell had been right. If *Seagull* contained much of what she believed, it had also been "written to sell," was another of her "writings down." She predicted it would fail "to be satisfactory from anyone's point of view," and she felt "badly." She explained that she had written it for *The Saturday Evening Post,* "thinking hard of my accumulation of debts and the grocery bill." After the *Post* rejected it, she lacked "the income or the time to do it over." When Knopf wanted to buy it, she "could not afford to say no to his advance" of $2,500. The novel would appear, as she instinctively knew, "in all its lack of balance, offering man stature at the same time that its contrived plot reduces him to the size of the magazine page."

The Seagull on the Step was indeed a hybrid, revealing its melodramatic origins as a serial. Sciama is the victim of the heroine's hero worship, a Bobby-like character in her mother's silver bracelets. The characters are all stereotypes: a corrupt trio of bourgeois doctor, mayor, and realtor is joined by an aristocrat, a Third World victim, and the heroine's rejected fiancé, who stands for purblind America. Meanwhile Sciama stands for the workingman, and is compared to both Jeanne d'Arc and De Gaulle.

Kay Boyle's own political views are spoken by many, including a soldier who says, "They can fight their war in Indo-China without me being there," a prescient moment indeed. Vaillant himself would be a political force, but must await help from an American woman who "knew the American constitution and its amendments," as Kay now demonstrated her own patriotism. Other reflections of her travail under McCarthyism appear as a local priest says, "There's nothing to fear for a country where every man speaks his own mind out," and there is a gratuitous reference to corrupt, bribe-taking Communist councilmen.

Glaring as well is her old denigration of women. Madame Marceau, the aristocrat, tells the heroine, Mary, "We need men to speak to the working people for us, because we don't know what to say to them ourselves." Mary's *father* is a veterinarian, as Kay Boyle transposes Bobby's thwarted childhood ambition onto a male character. Indeed, such professions were available to none of her daughters, who could be artists, painters, actresses, dancers, or poets, pale reflections of their mother, but not doctors, lawyers, or even teachers, just as, like their mother, they would all marry men who did not achieve worldly success. By the fifties, as Kay Boyle assumed the role of grande dame, women as a group were held at a distance in both life and art.

From Michel Sciama's real-life experiences, Kay Boyle borrowed anecdotes such as how resistance men helped American fliers who had been shot down. As a fifteen-year-old who had staged a demonstration on Armistice Day against the German invasion of France the previous June, and had spent eighteen months in prison, he was exactly the kind of man she would idealize. But for the most part, Vaillant is not Sciama, but a heroic abstraction. "She liked me the way she liked Joseph," Sciama concluded.

The real-life Sciama lacked Vaillant's political ambitions, and became a schoolteacher. Nor did he even play the game of *joute*, at which Vaillant excels and in which men violently knock each other out of boats. He was an ungainly fellow who once at dinner, out of nervousness, seized one of Kay's ubiquitous white gloves and mistakenly used it as a napkin.

Kay laughed then, a regal woman surrounded by young children. When she had passed Mousie to Sciama, that he might carry her, Sciama was touched by the grace of her gesture. He saw Kay Boyle as a woman of contradictions, a person who believed in the resistance and working-class struggles, yet who complained about the defects of French plumbing. "She liked me before Bobby did—and after," Sciama would remember. Indeed, Bobby had married a person whom her mother might have chosen. When in 1959 Bobby and Sciama were divorced, Kay, to Bobby's chagrin, kept on telling people, "She has the most marvelous husband, Michel Sciama," doctoring her daughter's biography no less than her own.

Sciama visited Kay in Connecticut, where he and Joseph exchanged war stories. But he could not help noticing how Kay bossed her husband. In Germany on the rare occasions when she allowed Joseph to drive, she had been the quintessential backseat driver, criticizing his every move. Joseph had made a joke of it then. But now Sciama found Kay's browbeating of Joseph harsher.

So too did Fanny Ventadour, who came to visit Kay in Connecticut only to be astonished when Kay prevented her husband from removing their bags from the car. "Oh, Joseph will get those!" Kay said, summoning Joseph from the house, and treating him, Fanny thought, like a servant. Joseph had been a schoolteacher. The accident of the war had made him a hero. But now he returned to being what he had always been, a quiet, academic-minded man, and it was clear to many that Kay was disappointed.

The Seagull on the Step, one of her weakest books, nonetheless received a rave review from Paul Engle in *The New Republic*. Engle called it a "wonderful story," and closed on an homage to Kay Boyle suggesting, perhaps, coming as it did during her travail under McCarthyism, that the review was as much an act of political solidarity as it was an assessment of the novel. "There is only one Kay Boyle," Engle wrote, "whose elegant English, idiomatic French, imaginative energy and personal creativeness are a common glory shared by France and America." Lewis Gannett too sang her praises, calling *The Seagull on the Step* a "love letter to France and to the United States . . . told with tough wit and sensitive poetry." Bearing no grudge, William Shawn printed a review calling the writing "exact and true." Others were less charitable, as Sidney Alexander in *The New York Times Book Review* found "the parable . . . too self-conscious" and the "sharp poetic realism" too soon congealing "into symbolism more literary than alive."

Alfred Knopf was pleased as he immediately went into a second printing, and ran a full-page advertisement in the Sunday *Times*.

Kay had written this book under great stress, some of it during her last miserable days in Germany when she and Joseph were holding out in their Bad Godesberg apartment, and the rest in Ann Watkins's tiny cottage in Connecticut. Staunchly, Janet Flanner praised the book highly to its besieged author. "Your intensity is probably too great for most American readers," Flanner told her, "since emotions are a human quality we are running dry of, like a creek in the middle west in the summer." Flanner thought that the "very fine reviews" were a sign that Kay's bad luck was over and that times were changing for her and Joseph.

Money was still a great problem. Then a businessman named Herman Rappaport, who collected rare books of modern British and American literature, came to Kay's aid. In 1951 Rappaport had written her requesting an autographed picture. By 1954 he and his wife were regularly sending the Francksteins parcels of clothing and books for the children, which Kay tried to repay with manuscripts of short stories and poems. One winter, she related, only a warm coat from the Rappaports stood between Clover and the elements.

In April of 1954 Joseph was officially suspended from the Foreign Service as a security risk. Within a month the State Department filed new charges. Joseph was informed that "your associations, behavior and activities tend to show that you are not reliable or trustworthy, and furnish reason to believe that you may be subject to coercion, influence, or pressure which may cause you to act contrary to the best interests of the national security." Once more Kay set to work collecting affidavits attesting to her own and Joseph's loyalty to America and their abhorrence of Communism. The nightmare had resumed.

Again the charges against Joseph focused primarily on Kay Boyle. Joseph was not "reliable or trustworthy" because *she* had been a member of the Communist Party and had "endorsed or sponsored various Communist front organizations or projects." It was entirely her influence on him which was likely to cause him to "act contrary to the best interests of the national security." Budenz's attack was revived, as was Borkenau's innuendo that she was an "organized Communist." This time Kay was also charged specifically with having "maintained contact and association with one Heinz Pol." That Ruth McKenney had told the FBI she had never met Kay Boyle did not prevent the State Department from repeating that she had been Kay's Communist Party contact.

Kay Boyle's unconventional behavior, her bohemianism, was as much a part of the new attack as her purported Communism. Explicitly the State Department accused Joseph of the charge that "during the period July 1941 through February 1943" he had conducted himself "in an immoral manner in your association with Kay Boyle Vail." If he wasn't a Communist, that he had committed adultery was unquestionable. That Kay and Joseph had not "made any substantive reply" to this charge at the earlier hearing was now considered an admission.

Frantically, Kay Boyle combed her stories again for proof of her anti-Communism. She told her lawyer, General Greenbaum, that she had never written a pro-Communist story, and copied her *Nation* interview with union leader Hans Jahn, and two selections from *365 Days*, "Siberia" and "Moscow," which proved that she harbored no romanticized sympathy for Stalin's Soviet Union. "Autobahn, 1951" had characters who had fled from Communism. *The Saturday Evening Post* stories "The Daring Impersonation" and "Carnival of Fear," written precisely for the purpose of clearing her name, denounced Communist tyranny in the eastern zone of Berlin. Since "Carnival of Fear" had yet to be published, Kay submitted a newly set printed version to the State Department. Indeed, in "Carnival of Fear" the Soviets are portrayed as truly sinister and Russia as a place where they "kill you for politics." The author of such a story could not possibly be a Communist sympathizer, let alone a party member.

Throughout this period, as she tried to defend herself, Kay Boyle spoke only of "the individual" and the "moral responsibility" of the writer. Remaining profoundly unpolitical through the late thirties and forties, she had demonstrated no awareness of the findings of the Dewey commission, which revealed Stalin's systematic murders of leading Bolshevik figures, never knew what really happened in Spain, and manifested little insight into Stalin's regime, despite all those evenings on the terrace of her house at Col-de-Villefranche with Emma Goldman and Sasha Berkman. She remained an emotional, good-hearted sympathizer with the downtrodden, who befriended James T. Farrell, who belonged to the anti-Stalinist left, and Heinz Pol, an anti-Stalinist Marxist. At the same time, she sought advice from Freda Kirchwey and Carey McWilliams of *The Nation*, which was decidedly unsympathetic to the anti-Stalinist left. Gus Lobrano had called her "naive." However coldhearted such a response had been during her time of trouble, he was essentially correct.

The State Department ruled that Joseph would be afforded no new hearing, on the technicality that he had been a "temporary" rather than a permanent Foreign Service officer. No one was sanguine about their ability to clear their names now. "There is nothing that can be done until the country wakes up from this nightmare in which we are living," journalist Joe Alsop told Kay. Only Kay's brother-in-law, Frank Detweiler, sounded a cheerful note: "First you were cleared by the Democrats, and now you'll be cleared by the Republicans!" Hoping publicity might help, Greenbaum planned to release Kay Boyle's statement to the press, while demanding an open hearing from the House Un-American Activities Committee. With money scarce, and Kay and Joseph in debt for ten thousand dollars, Joseph took a job at a summer camp for boys in Vermont for four hundred dollars.

Kay Boyle had always been a loyal friend, and now many of her friends helped her: Jay Laughlin, William L. Shirer, Nina Conarain, Sonia Tomara, Ann Watkins, Roger Burlingame, and Maria Leiper of Simon & Schuster, whose moving testimonial made Kay weep. Eva Mayer, with whom Kay had shared that house in Carmel while their husbands were both at Fort Ord, wrote she had never once met a Communist in Kay's house.

Kay even asked Laurence to write on her behalf. Laurence pleaded, ineffectually, that anything he would write would be inadequate. "When I have had a set task to write," Laurence wrote his ex-wife, "I get a sort of writer's cramp." Laurence did remember that Kay had angrily once told a young man he wasn't worthy of an American passport because he had made derogatory statements about the United States. But Laurence did not "want to mention Sindbad's name." Finally, even as he dreaded having to appear before a consular official to get his signature "legalized, and red tapes," Laurence asked Kay to draft the letter for him. Of course, she would not.

Ira Morris feared that "an affidavit from another subversive" and

Wallace supporter like himself would not help, but at once generously offered money. And later Caresse Crosby gave Kay a group of Matisse lithographs to sell. The only truly sour note came from the poet Walter Mehring, who told Kay he could not swear that he had never met Communists at her house because he had encountered both Kantorowicz (or "Kantor") and Heinz Pol there. Kay called Mehring "cruel" and loyally insisted that "were Pol a Communist, I can assure you that he would not still be one of my closest friends." Granting that Pol did not believe "that the capitalistic system has solved all of mankind's economic ills," she demanded of Mehring, "do you?" Then courageously she added, no matter the hazardous times, "I certainly don't."

General Greenbaum had the statements and affidavits, along with Kay's and Joseph's statements and some of her writings, printed up and bound in a tidy booklet. She was in some disagreement with her lawyer because she had insisted on declaring her political sympathies, which included a statement of support for the Loyalists and her opposition to Franco. Lacking nothing in grit, she insisted it was better to be defeated "on a strong, fearless statement rather than on one which sins by its omissions." But Greenbaum deleted her endorsement of the Loyalists: "that the Communists made propaganda of this conflict does not affect the essential rightness of the Loyalists' cause." He also deleted a reference to Faith's and Ian's having been baptized in the Catholic Church.

Greenbaum also removed the history of her friendship with Heinz Pol, and her attack on Ernest Knoblauch, whom Kay had called "a tragically neurotic man, unbalanced, unhappy, striving for ease," a man who climbed the hills surrounding Marburg every night with his police dog on the trail of political revolutionaries. Gone too were some of her rhetorical excesses: "Where is the record of these things? In what distorted mind have they taken shape?" From Joseph's statement, Greenbaum removed his regret that he and Kay had not been married in the Catholic Church, and how his mother, "with full cooperation from my wife, is attempting to procure an annulment of my wife's first marriage in the Church."

Kay's final statement is a sad document. Defensively, she denies that she ever knew Ruth McKenney, her husband Richard Branstein, or the Communist apparatchiks Alexander Trachtenberg and Victor Jerome, her association with the latter two being the only new charge which had been brought against her. (In his second interview with the FBI, Budenz had vaguely mentioned Jerome.) Kay asserted she believed in "the principles of American democracy." All her works opposed "any infringement on the rights of the individual, which were anathema to the Communist creed."

Kay goes on to relate her family history, invoking Jacob Bauer, who was on George Washington's staff, her great-grandfather Moore who migrated to Kansas, and her aunt Nina Allender, who was still alive, and who had fought for "the American woman's franchise." Pathetically Kay repeats how in 1937, as soon as the law allowed, she had applied for her

American citizenship to be restored. Greenbaum did allow her to suggest it was Kantorowicz or "Kantor" who had named her and Pol to the FBI as Communist Party members. It would be more than twenty years before Kay Boyle would have access to the several thousand pages of her and Joseph's FBI file and so learn that it had been Louis Budenz who had denounced her.

Kay's conclusion was eloquent. "Were it not for my pride in all that America is," she wrote, "and my conviction that that great wrong done my husband will be undone, I must say quite simply that my heart would break." Nervously Joseph wrote a separate letter to John Sipes, pleading that his conduct with his wife before their marriage was "purely personal." As if privacy rights had not long been eroded, Joseph declared that "it has been a tradition of the political life of America that the private lives of public men are their own concern."

As they reveal in their internal documents, what Sipes and his underlings feared more than anything was that Joseph or, worse, his friend the obstreperous Judge Clark might attempt to "publicize the Department's action." Yet General Greenbaum nervously decided not to release the statements and to rely on "high level" political pressure. Kay fell victim to depression and increased physical malaise as she and Joseph waited for the State Department's response. A rumor that her passport might not be renewed depressed her even more. Driving down a Connecticut road, Kay composed a poem. "October, and the month fills me with grief," she wrote, contrasting herself as the girl she once was, with her heart "light as a leaf," with what she had become: "a witch . . . in fury . . . grey-haired and brooding."

Late in October, John Sipes released an eleven-page "opinion," ruling that Joseph's written answer to the new charges had been "insufficient." Joseph's reinstatement was "not clearly consistent with the interests of national security." The cause was "adverse information regarding his wife and the influence which she may be expected to exert over him." The dupe, the puppet of his wife, Joseph was deemed a security risk. As for Kay, the State Department ruled that her "admitted contributions to Communist front organizations" belied her denial that she had been a member of the Communist Party. Once more the government used the charge of sexual immorality as its excuse. Joseph had conducted himself "in an immoral manner" with "Kay Boyle Vail," who had "borne illegitimate children to two men to whom she was not married and while she was still married to someone else." (In fact, Kay Boyle had borne *three* children out of wedlock: Bobby, Apple, and Faith.)

Finally it was Kay's "adulterous living" which rendered Joseph "a man of weak morals and character." Sipes also resurrected the old complaint that Joseph had lived "on the earnings of his women acquaintances." Gratuitously, the report concluded that Joseph's Catholicism was "the most superficial of religious beliefs." As for his war record, Sipes declared that

Joseph's service in the Army "is not of such a nature or sufficiently out-standing to have any particular bearing on the case at hand." It was as if Joseph had to have died to demonstrate his loyalty.

Kay called the ruling "a kick in the teeth." *The Saturday Evening Post* had requested that she inform them when her clearance came through. Now, justly, she feared that her last commercial outlet would be gone. Publicizing their dilemma might make any public-school teaching for Joseph impossible. Nor would it render Kay any more acceptable "to the commercial writing markets" which she desperately needed. Never one to yield to defeat, she urged that her friends write to President Eisenhower requesting a new hearing for Joseph. General Greenbaum too had run out of alternatives. Finally, in desperation, he advised Kay to bring the matter to a head by applying to have her passport renewed.

The Nation was now Kay Boyle's only magazine outlet, and she published in January "A Declaration for 1955," in which she introduced what would be her most important theme for the rest of her life: "it is the writers, the intellectuals of a country who bear the full weight of moral responsibility . . . when the histories are written it is only the poets, and those who read them who remain." *The Nation* also published a Kay Boyle short story called "A Puzzled Race," in which a man, obviously Joseph, must leave Germany to testify at a hearing in America. Joseph appears as a paradigm of loyalty: "his wife was his established love, and he needed no other, and America was his country."

Kay Boyle would reiterate the theme of the need for artists and writers to speak out in a long essay called "Intellectuals Are Failing America," which appeared in the *St. Louis Post-Dispatch*. Invoking Jean-Paul Sartre and Simone de Beauvoir, who had condemned the Soviet Union's "brutal suppression of the Hungarian people's fight for liberty," she urged American writers to reject "contemporary standards." "Each isolated in his own conviction, quite alone," Kay wrote, invoking her feelings of abandonment in a society where too few voices had been raised in defense of McCarthy's victims.

In January of 1955, Kay Boyle successfully renewed her expired passport. But when in late February Joseph tried to renew his, he was refused on the ground that he was married to a member of the Communist Party.

At ten-thirty on the morning of April 5 there was a knock at Kay Boyle's door in Rowayton. Joseph was out teaching at the Thomas School. Kay was in bed, still recovering from an attack of pneumonia. Mousie answered the door.

"It's the American government, you've got to come down," the man boomed. Kay appeared in an empire-style dressing gown and found a man who introduced himself as Maurice J. Magner, a Special Agent of the New York Passport Division of the State Department.

"Do you hold passport number 2079?" he asked.

"Yes," Kay Boyle admitted, insisting at once on seeing his credentials.

"May I see it?" Magner wheedled.

"No," Kay Boyle told him quickly, "but you may talk to my lawyer about it." At once she produced Greenbaum's address.

Magner was unhappy. He had been ordered to confiscate her passport and had been briefed that if she should ask why, he was to tell her that if she wanted to know the reason, she should communicate with the passport office. Kay had apparently foiled him.

When Magner complained that he had driven all the way from New York, Kay told him he "could have telephoned and the State Department could have written a letter saying they'd made an error in renewing my passport. I would have done the proper thing. But this isn't the way you take people's passports from them."

"We figured you wouldn't answer the telephone," Magner, obviously rattled, replied. Then Kay Boyle became emotional as she told him how she had been ill with pneumonia and that this was her first day out of bed.

"This is additional persecution!" she said. "Oh, how my poor husband is suffering!" Then her anger surfaced once more. "Justice will be done!" Kay Boyle dismissed the intruder.

"Imagine such methods to track people down in their homes like murderers," Kay Boyle told people afterward. "One might as well be living in Russia."

A week later, Kay Boyle received a letter from the State Department requesting that as an "alleged Communist" she return her passport. But there was dissension within the State Department and some functionaries stood up for Kay's continued freedom to travel. After Kay and Joseph submitted new affidavits swearing they were not Communists, and General Greenbaum mailed the passport office a review of *The Seagull on the Step* along with Knopf's *New York Times* advertisement, they received new passports. At one point Frances Knight, the notoriously paranoid director of the passport office, even asked the Assistant Attorney General to investigate Kay to determine whether there was enough evidence for criminal proceedings to be instituted against her for lying on her passport application. But a cooler head replied that there wasn't enough evidence that Kay had been a party member.

Still encouraging her beleaguered friend, Janet Flanner pronounced the passport victory a "good sign . . . that yr bad luck is over, that times are changing for you & Joseph & that you have emerged on the other side of this period of cruel limbo where you have been impaled." Indeed, that October Dean Harry Ransom of the University of Texas talked with Joseph about his becoming a professor of classical languages at the university.

Believing that the tide was at last turning, Kay Boyle wrote to the National Council of the Arts, Sciences, and Professions to discover whether they had ever asked her to sponsor the Waldorf Conference, and whether, indeed, she had done so. Receiving no reply, Kay wrote directly to Harvard astronomer Dr. Harlow Shapley, who had originally contacted her. She requested a letter stating that she had not been connected with the planning of the Waldorf Conference, nor had she been a member of the Council. Kay pleaded that her family's "personal liberty" was at stake. But she got no reply from Shapley either.

25

Vindication

*I have simply lived . . . in passionate defense of the rights of
the individual, which is certainly the antithesis of
the Communist dogma.*

*Our moral tradition proclaims the right of the individual to argue
even with God, but here Mr. Franckenstein has not been allowed
to argue with his human judge!*
SENATOR THOMAS C. HENNINGS, JR.

With America's need in 1953 to get Germany into the alliance as part of Cold War realpolitik, the Occupation courts were hastily turned back to the Germans. Even as he was working on important cases that remained to be resolved, Judge William Clark was abruptly ousted from his post as Chief Judge of the Allied High Commission courts. On vacation in the Canary Islands, he was suddenly given a passport allowing him admission only to the United States, preventing him from returning to Frankfurt. Back home, he at once brought suit against the government, demanding that he be given a passport good for travel anywhere abroad. His lawyer was Morris Ernst, General Eddie Greenbaum's partner. Now, in 1955, Clark was sixty-four and living in retirement in Princeton, New Jersey.

Once more Judge Clark came to Kay and Joseph's rescue. Roger Baldwin was dubious and told Kay Boyle that William Clark was a "lone operator, too eccentric to work in harness . . . and too irascible when he gets aroused to have good judgment." But Clark acted decisively and effectively on the Franckensteins' behalf when no one else would. He began by writing to Under Secretary of State Robert Murphy exposing the absurdity of the charges against Joseph, beginning with his having "been a swimming instructor (God save the mark!)." Fearlessly, Clark challenged the McCarthyite ploy that personal morality had anything whatever to do with either loyalty to America or the national security. "If there was any truth in the morals charge," Clark wrote Murphy, "under the Kinsey report 90% of the American men would be disqualified and that this further would include President Cleveland and President Eisenhower."

Next, Judge Clark brought Joseph's case to Senator Thomas C. Hennings, Jr., a Democrat from Missouri, who was chairing the Senate Judiciary Committee's Subcommittee on Constitutional Rights, investigating the abuse of the rights of American citizens who had been fired on political grounds by the federal government. With a flair for the dramatic, Senator Hennings had decided to hold his hearings in the same chamber where Joseph McCarthy had reigned.

Late in November of 1955, Kay and Joseph went to Washington to testify before the Hennings committee. They had at last reached the turning point in their long travail. Years later Kay Boyle wrote that "to be able to speak in a public forum . . . was in itself like a release from prison." The Hennings committee could not change the government's ruling against Joseph. But it could offer recommendations to the Secretary of State.

Under oath, once more Joseph recounted the story of his life. By now he had an endorsement from the former head of the Innsbruck resistance movement, Karl Gruber, serving as Austrian ambassador in Washington. Gruber wrote for the record that Joseph "was completely anti-Communist in his thinking and was fully aware of the danger which had arisen due to the Soviet attempt to force Austria into the Communist camp."

Kay Boyle testified that the State Department itself had published her work in the *Neue Zeitung*, even after Joseph's 1952 security hearing. Despite Roy Cohn's zealous efforts, her books remained in U.S. Information Service libraries. Abruptly, but begging her forgiveness, Lon Hocker, the Hennings committee legal counsel, broke in to ask, "Are you or have you ever been a Communist?"

"No, I never have been," Kay replied. Nor had she ever been a member of any organization. Rail thin, still elegant, her makeup a touch too heavy, in her cultivated accents she described how agent Magner had invaded her home demanding that she surrender her passport.

The hearings of the Hennings committee broke the ice. The State Department had sent as its observer Orson W. Trueworthy, who, when asked by Hocker if he wished to reply, mumbled that the State Department did not wish to "make any comment at this time." It was revealed that three quarters of those fired hadn't even been informed that their loyalty had been in question. Only Joseph McCarthy didn't like what was happening, as he called the Hennings hearings "a disgrace to the Senate" which posed "a grave threat to the security of the United States." (That very Senate had censored McCarthy a year earlier.)

The press now felt free enough to take up the cause of truth and justice. Photographs of Kay Boyle and Joseph Franckenstein suddenly were published in newspapers throughout the land. Kay appears as a smiling woman in late middle age wearing a severe buttoned-up suit and flamboyant white earrings. She stands beside a smiling, rumpled, and very weary-looking gentleman with a mustache. His hair is thinning, and his expression suggests bewilderment; his forehead is lined with furrows of anxiety.

Reporters particularly enjoyed the irony of the government's labeling

Kay Boyle a "Red" while including her books in its "anti-Communist Overseas Information program." Joan Detweiler wrote to her local newspaper, the *Plainfield Courier-News*, to point out that Kay Boyle and Joseph Franckenstein were not standing trial for their "subversive connections," but were among 9,605 "security" cases being reconsidered. Meanwhile at press conferences Kay vented her frustration. "We don't want to sound vindictive, but it is ridiculous and absurd for my husband to have suffered this injustice, never even allowed to defend himself," she told the *New York Post.*

Joseph had defended himself, but at a new cost. Dean Harry Ransom of the University of Texas, who had promised Joseph a salary of seven thousand dollars a year, and Kay Boyle a period of serenity "so that my life as a writer would be more or less undisturbed," was suddenly out of touch. There would be no academic job in America for Joseph Franckenstein. "It must be the publicity about us which has made us controversial in the eyes of the university," Kay told Caresse Crosby. Later Ransom denied he had ever offered Joseph a position; loyally Caresse at once canceled a speaking engagement she had accepted at Texas.

Senator Hennings was personally outraged by the injustice suffered by Kay and Joseph. "Your case is one of the most flagrant violations of constitutional rights by the State Department," he told them. By December 5, he had sent John Foster Dulles, the Secretary of State, a copy of the Franckensteins' transcript, requesting a comment "particularly on the question of guilt-by-kinship." It all came back to John Sipes, who immediately decided that the State Department must not place itself "in a position of apologizing." The majority of those terminated, he well knew, had involved "the issue of personal associations," the "kinship factor." Should Joseph be cleared, they would be inundated with similar cases.

But Senator Hennings kept up his pressure. When by January 10 Dulles had not replied, Hennings wrote to him again, "anxious to have the department's views on the issues of the Franckenstein case, particularly on the issue of 'guilt by kinship.' " The very next day Hennings received a caviling letter from Assistant Secretary of State Thruston Morton, dated December 23 (!). In his best doublespeak, Morton refused to discuss Kay and Joseph's case on its merits. "The matter of an employee's association is often one of the factors in determining his security reliability," Morton evaded. After all, he added, a figure out of some Kafkaesque nightmare, "guilt in the legal sense" was not involved, only "whether a person is suitable for Governmental employment."

But Hennings would not be stonewalled. Bypassing the underling Morton, on January 23 he wrote to Dulles yet again. Hennings complained that Morton's reply raised "grave doubts in the mind of any disinterested observer as to whether the Department actually achieved fairness in its handling of this case." Kay and Joseph were now in the hands of a powerful advocate for their rights. Hennings went back to the original letter which

Joseph had been offered in Germany and according to which he would agree to be terminated on the condition that he accept a letter stating that he was not a security risk. This only proved, Hennings wrote, that Joseph never had been a "real loyalty or security risk." Even in *Adler v. Board of Education*, a case Morton himself had invoked in his letter to Hennings, teachers fired as security risks had hearings. Nor was guilt by association ruled to be constitutional.

Hennings then played his most powerful card. Unless Joseph's case was reconsidered "on its merits," he threatened, "public confidence in the procedures of the whole government security program" would be eroded. In short, he would drown the State Department in unfavorable publicity. At the same time, Judge Clark wrote again to Robert Murphy. Only "unfavorable publicity for the Department," he reiterated, awaited them should they not act.

Kay and Joseph had considered litigating their case through the courts, only to conclude that they could not afford such a suit. But Judge Clark threatened anyway; he would represent them himself, he said, bringing not only his "legal skill" but "also my heart." Judge Clark was fond of Kay, their flirtatious relationship egregious enough to upset his wife, Sonia Tomara. But this was nothing new. Even now, men continued to be susceptible to Kay Boyle.

Meanwhile Hennings in one more letter challenged the technicality that since Joseph had been only a "temporary" employee, he had not been entitled to a second hearing. "The fact remains," Hennings reminded Dulles, "that he has not been allowed even to discuss the merits of his case with the person or persons responsible for making the decision of dismissal."

Sipes had lost and he knew it. Finally Dulles appointed a Special Assistant, John W. Hanes, to meet with General Greenbaum. "A very great wrong" has been done "two extremely fine people," Greenbaum told the neophyte. Knowing that Houston Lay, Loy Henderson (another Deputy Under Secretary at State), Scott McLeod, and Sipes were now on the defensive, Greenbaum allowed himself some rhetorical indignation. The State Department's refusal to talk with Joseph "face to face," he told Hanes, "smacked of Soviet Russia rather than the United States." At a loss, Hanes pleaded he knew little about the case.

Now the security group plotted its damage control. Henderson told McLeod to cut off all communication with both Greenbaum and Hennings. Under no circumstances would they agree to a new hearing, although Joseph's was the only security dismissal under Executive Order 10450 on which no hearing had been held. They feared publicity ("possible public relations difficulties") and embarrassing themselves by reversing their earlier ruling.

The cleverest of the pack, Sipes came up with the idea that they need only "vacate" the judgment; they need not "clear" Joseph of the charges themselves. Why not allow Joseph's record to be restored to its status on May 8, 1953, when he was terminated as part of the "reduction in force" program? Then they need never address the merits of the charges. In return, Joseph would have to waive all rights and benefits which may have accrued to him between 1953 and 1954 when he was on "leave without pay."

Sipes and his sidekick Hanes now put pressure on Edward Greenbaum to accept the deal. There would be no new hearing. Self-righteously they claimed no additional information had been offered pointing to "the incorrectness of the original decision." By now, lying was a matter of course. Joseph would do well, they said, to petition to "vacate the proceedings which resulted in the adverse security finding," and go away.

Greenbaum, of course, didn't like it. He wanted a complete "vindication . . . an affirmative statement by the Department that it entertained no doubts as to the Franckensteins' loyalty." But anxious to have it over, and knowing Kay and Joseph could not afford to litigate, Greenbaum compromised. He agreed that "additional intervention" from the Hennings committee would only jeopardize the Department's efforts. Kay and Joseph would not "push the matter in that forum at this time."

Kay was by no means pleased. Ted Kaghan urged her to "fight the bastards and make them pay." It was all right to accept the letter. But then they must "sue . . . a humdinger of a suit for material redress for years of difficulty and financial embarrassment caused by the government's hasty action based on misinformation, now admitted." Speaking out of his own pain at having been fired from government service for his political views, Kaghan told Kay, "I would not be silent. I would not compromise. I would not make deals. You have everything to gain by raising the biggest goddamned stink you can." Knowing Greenbaum now had a stake in his "gentleman's agreement" with Sipes, Kaghan still urged Kay and Joseph on. "These bastards ought to be kicked in their administrative balls at every opportunity," he said.

Kay tried to get her friend Rowland Watts to enlist the ACLU to sue on their behalf. "Only litigation can bring about full clearance," Joseph wrote to Watts. When the ACLU would not take the case pro bono, Joseph tried Benjamin Ferencz. But Ferencz said the organizations he worked with provided funds for victims of *Nazi*, not American persecution. In 1956 Kay and Joseph could not even afford to pay Greenbaum his nine hundred dollars of disbursements for the year.

Finally Kay and Joseph bowed to necessity. In the letter they agreed to accept, for the first time they would be given the official verdict of the 1952 Bad Godesberg security hearing, which had cleared Joseph. Joseph's "security status had been favorably resolved," it read, "by action of the Loyalty Security Board." Nor did Joseph's termination from government service bear any relationship to either his or his wife's "loyalty." The State Department finally mailed this letter of vindication to Kay Boyle and Joseph Franckenstein on April 1, 1957.

Sipes and company agreed among themselves never to reveal why they had gone even this far. They were further infuriated when they received a letter from Joseph, obviously written by Kay, acknowledging receipt of the letter "vacating" the judgment that Joseph had been terminated for disloyalty to America. Joseph wrote he was pleased that "the Department has finally recognized the injustice of the charges of disloyalty which were brought against me and my wife and has honorably withdrawn them."

Of course, Sipes had done no such thing; all along he had been adamant that the 1954 charges be allowed to stand uncorrected. He had "withdrawn" nothing said or done after May of 1953. Joseph praised his adversaries for "correcting a great injustice" and expressed his gratitude for "this official clearance for which we have fought, and hoped, and waited for nearly five years."

Apoplectic at this insinuation that Joseph had been given "official clearance," rather than clearance as of May 1953, Sipes and Hanes decided that the government would make no reply to Joseph's letter with all its "factual inaccuracies." Any acknowledgment which failed to point out the factual errors, they thought, deep in doublethink, might "constitute acquiescence by the Department." Instead, they would file Joseph's letter, together with a memorandum to the file reasserting that "no charges have been withdrawn." Under the current security program, Joseph in their eyes still had not been cleared, and if Sipes had anything to say about it, he never would be.

But on April 22, 1957, the Hennings Subcommittee on Constitutional Rights announced that the State Department had indeed "cleared" Joseph of "four-year-old security charges." Hennings insisted on a sweeping interpretation of the term "cleared," with no limitations on the time of the clearance. He insisted on his own vindicating language, as the legislative branch of the government dared the executive now to challenge its jurisdiction over Joseph and Kay's fate.

The press at once responded, choosing to ally itself with Hennings's valiant efforts. A *Washington Post* editorial on April 23, headlined "Franckenstein," evoking, of course, Mary Shelley's story, applauded the government for at last making "grudging and inadequate reparation to a citizen irreparably injured by a clearance system which imputes guilt by association and relies on 'anonymous' information." The *Post* and *The New York Times* both agreed now that something had to be done to save other "innocent victims of the monster created in the name of national security."

As far as the press was concerned, there was no ambiguity about Joseph's having been cleared. As the *Chicago Tribune* put it, "security risk charges against him and his wife have been wiped off" the State Department's records. Late in April, indefatigable Judge Clark, in this the year of his death, testifying now against Scott McLeod, thus found a way to read the editorials supporting Joseph from the *Christian Science Monitor* and *The Washington Post* into the *Congressional Record*.

Alfred Knopf, one of the few to publish Kay during all of this turmoil, immediately sent her a note expressing his delight "at your and your husband's final clearance . . . the right ending to a disgraceful business." Kay herself viewed the moment as indeed a "new beginning." To her agent's assistant, Sheila St. Lawrence, she wrote, "Isn't it a glorious day to be cleared of loyalty and security charges?"

Now Kay was supporting eight people, including Joseph's mother in Austria and his brother's virtually destitute family in Istanbul. Bobby, with three small children, had left Michel Sciama and had contracted tuberculosis; she sorely needed her mother's help. Kay was listing Bobby as a "part-time dependent."

Knopf published *Generation Without Farewell*, Kay's novel set in 1948 in Marburg, in 1960. Its hero, Jaeger, was drawn so extensively upon her German journalist friend Siegfried Maruhn that the novel became virtually a work of nonfiction. Over a four-year period, Maruhn patiently read the growing manuscript for accuracy. When Kay wrote he hated his father because he beat his children, as the teachers did, Maruhn corrected her. This was, he said, "a very popular misconception of German education." In their extensive correspondence, Maruhn detailed not only the facts of his life, including his years in the Hitler Youth (he called Hitler his "*Garant der Zukunft*," the guarantor of his future), but how he felt when he was captured by the Americans in 1944, and his evolving admiration of America. Maruhn even described for the author what he wore when he returned to Germany from an American POW camp in 1946: an American Army uniform with a black "POW" stenciled on it.

Maruhn corrected spelling errors and factual mistakes, such as her point that the pensions of the old and the blind had been devalued by the currency reform, which they had not. But reading the completed work, Maruhn praised Kay Boyle for having "pictured the spirit of the time remarkably well." Indeed, her evocation of Occupation Marburg is the great strength of *Generation Without Farewell*. Kay wanted, appropriately, to dedicate this novel to Siegfried Maruhn. Modestly he told her it seemed "an honor undeserved" and suggested she use only his initials. The dedication of *Generation Without Farewell* reads: "For Siegfried."

The appearance of Kay Boyle's thirteenth novel was treated as a publishing event. Entering a local bookstore, Kay discovered her face on the cover of what she called "Book Buyers' Weekly"; and Knopf had raised the advance from thirty-two hundred to four thousand dollars. There were, as Kay put it, "public songs and dances" to improve sales as Kay Boyle, victorious over McCarthyism, received her most consistently fine reviews.

"You must immerse yourself completely in her glancing prose to absorb its subtleties of meaning," John Barkham wrote, not at all bothered by what *Newsweek* had called its "paralysis of plot." In the *Herald Tribune Book Review*, Gene Baro called *Generation Without Farewell* "difficult but fascinating" and "one of her best." Martha McGregor wrote in the *New York Post* that "Kay Boyle's distinguished prose . . . has never seemed more lovely and less mannered," in contradistinction to Granville Hicks's complaint in *The Saturday Review* that the prose was "too mannered"—the old charge. In the all-important Sunday *New York Times* Virgilia Peterson wrote, "Kay Boyle has never written more poignantly, never come closer to absolute pitch than in this new novel." Kay also received letters of praise from George Steiner, who told her that her "voice has been one of the few to beat against the wind," and from William Carlos Williams, who called *Generation Without Farewell* "an interesting novel abreast with the times in this troubled age of postwar Germany."

Generation *Without Farewell* was the most widely reviewed of any of her novels, receiving even a notice in *McCall's*, which said it was "a very meaningful story of the aftermath of war." *Newsweek* printed a "Chat with the Author" in which Kay, "statuesque and elegant," called Germany "terrifying" and said she hoped "I never have to set foot in that country again." *The New York Times Book Review* ran a feature calling attention to its own "glowing" review of *Generation Without Farewell* and to the "phenomenal feat" that Kay Boyle had accomplished in writing twenty-two books while simultaneously being "engaged in bringing up children." An accompanying cartoon pictured a writer with a pencil behind her ear carrying a typewriter and knocking on a door while children raise a rumpus in the background, one banging on a drum. Harry T. Moore, now one of her strongest supporters, wrote in the *Kenyon Review* that he hoped *Generation Without Farewell* might "bring her some of the recognition she deserves and will help to place her among the fine women authors of our time who do not write like men."

Desperate for money, in 1958, unbeknownst to Knopf, who was waiting for the manuscript of *Generation Without Farewell*, Kay had quietly contracted with Edward Aswell, who had moved to Doubleday, to write a history of Germany for "The Mainstream of the Modern World" series edited by John Gunther. The subject seemed logical, and the advance would be a then generous eight thousand dollars, to be paid over three years, with fifteen hundred dollars on signing; the manuscript would not be due until April of 1961. "I don't know a damn thing about history," Kay told Joseph. But he reassured her. "We'll do it together. It will be all right," he said.

Alfred Knopf learned of this contract only in 1960 when *Generation Without Farewell* was published, and he was offended by Kay's "lack of candor." But she could not worry about the delicacies of her publishing relationship with Knopf. The financial failure of *Generation Without Farewell*, despite all those fine reviews and all that publicity, meant that she had to forgo her hope of paying off all the family debts and going to Europe the following summer. She was worried about Bobby's tuberculosis. Indeed, it had been seven years since Kay had seen either Bobby or Kathe.

Joseph had been cleared, but he was still teaching at the Thomas

School. Meanwhile Kay earned from her writing in 1961 only $4,255.24, and in 1962, $3,306.04. When Frank Detweiler was unable to lend her any more money, she feared being unable to "pay grocer, milk, rent, telephone, electricity, or income tax" and turned to Kathryn Hulme, Howard Nemerov, and Ann Watkins for loans. She tried to sell one of the numbered "valises of all his works of art" which Marcel Duchamp had once given her. There were sales of the foreign and British rights of Kay Boyle's books—Faber and Faber bought *The Seagull on the Step* for one hundred and twenty-five pounds; in 1960 there was an Italian sale of *Monday Night*; in America an anthology called *The Face of Prejudice* gave her fifty dollars for "Black Boy." But with so many dependents, the money slid through her fingers as quickly as she earned it.

And as always there were serious health problems. After an ugly bout with vomiting, and pain "so violent that I didn't care if I lived or died," she concluded she must make time for a gallbladder operation. Frequent visits to the dentist brought her the additional pain of not being able to pay her bill. In 1956 "active colitis" had joined the gallbladder trouble, her doctor telling her it "comes more from worry and over-work than anything else." Exploratory surgery was necessary to free her from a cancer scare.

If she had had a grueling writing schedule in Mégève and in Germany, now Kay worked "so hard I'm dizzy." One Christmas, she decided, she would treat "like any other day, and type steadily through it." She continued in her ill-advised strategy of quickly sketching a story, and then having the Watkins agency submit it. Then she would wait for a reaction, agreeing to revise according to the editor's suggestions. It was a poor approach because the editor's mind was invariably set against a story and the revisions failed to satisfy. Elliot W. Schryver of *Woman's Home Companion* wrote: "getting a story by Kay Boyle made me feel almost nostalgic." Her old supporter Stuart Rose at *The Saturday Evening Post* had to reject a story called "Destination: Hurricane" because it "seems to have no real reason for being." A story called "The Wristwatch" was rejected by *Collier's, Good Housekeeping, Redbook,* and the *Ladies' Home Journal*. The *Journal* did publish a poem called "Spring" in 1957, one which had previously been rejected eight times; it reflected Kay Boyle's travail under McCarthyism: "each man is a country, with both north and south, loyalty, treason / Passion and its repudiation, in / Him."

Through these hard years of the fifties and the early sixties, Kay Boyle was producing hasty and ill-conceived work, and it did not help that admirers like Harry T. Moore talked of creating "a Kay Boyle vogue," telling her "these writings of yours are so good they will not go unrecognized forever." Moore now told her that *The Seagull on the Step*, which had fallen a thousand dollars short of earning out its advance, failed because "the personal relationships are too intense." He neglected to add that this book, as even Kay Boyle knew, would have profited from greater care.

When Rust Hills, fiction editor at *Esquire*, rejected "Should Be Considered Extremely Dangerous" as relying too greatly on melodrama, Kay Boyle still would not accept that it was primarily her frantic pace which was deeply damaging her work. "A hex on Rust Hills," Kay told Ann Watkins. "What does he think we are, wholesale dealers in stories?" But the same story was rejected by Katherine Gauss Jackson at *Harper's*: "it's as if she were trying to say so many things that no one of them comes through." A feud with Edward Weeks added *The Atlantic* to her "blacklist," headed, of course, by *The New Yorker*. "Nobody's jumping up and down with joy over the things I write," Kay lamented. It was not until 1964, with the acceptance of "The Ballet of Central Park" by *The Saturday Evening Post*, that she would sell another short story.

Living an increasingly independent existence, Kay Boyle went by herself to New York frequently, for lunches with television executives, dinner parties, and the theater. Franchot Tone was determined to play the lead in a film version of *Monday Night*, as he told Kay Boyle that "this way of story-telling makes me tingle." Kay's name never appeared in *Red Channels* and her many radio and television sales in the mid-fifties belied her later contention that her stories didn't sell because she was "blacklisted." "Carnival of Fear" was sold to television for $1,250. Gore Vidal in 1954 wrote requesting permission to adapt "The Soldier Ran Away" for television, and the program appeared on October 23, 1955. Calling her "a distinguished and representative writer of our time," Jerry Wald at Columbia Pictures wrote requesting material or ideas "published or not" from Kay. Henry S. White at Screen Gems searched for a Kay Boyle property for his "Filmed Anthology" series. In 1956, before Joseph had been officially cleared, NBC produced "Diagnosis of a Selfish Lady" on its *Five Star Matinee*, and in December of 1958 CBS used "The Crazy Hunter" on its *Desilu Playhouse*, paying Kay three thousand dollars and giving Franchot Tone his opportunity to star in a Kay Boyle story. (The *Herald Tribune* called the production "a soggy plodding drama," and Kay herself concluded, "I guess authors shouldn't look at their own works distorted in other mediums.") What annoyed her even more, she who hated to be consigned to any ghetto of "women writers," was that WNYC radio in 1958 broadcast "White as Snow" in its *For the Ladies* program.

The sales went on. Sapphire Films chose "How Bridie's Girl Was Won" for its "Women in Love" series, paying the author fifteen hundred dollars for this potboiler set in England. Far from having been forgotten, Kay could boast of a large coterie who knew about her and held her in high respect.

In January of 1958 Kay Boyle was elected to the National Institute of Arts and Letters; it was another sign that she was recognized as a major literary figure of her day. At once she became obsessively involved in internecine Institute politics as she struggled to have her friends elected, and forged relationships with those who might second her nominations in

exchange for her endorsing theirs. By February she had successfully nominated Samuel Beckett for an honorary award. By June she had proposed
her friend Howard Nemerov. When Nemerov was not elected the first time,
Kay persisted, and became the seconder for his second nomination.

Institute dinners became the scene of political confrontations. "I'm
going to go over and tell Langston Hughes exactly what I think of him,"
Lillian Hellman told Kay Boyle at one such evening, determined to embarrass someone who she believed had not stood up to McCarthy. Em-
boldened by Hellman's activism, Kay replied, "Well, I'm going to go over
and tell Lionel Trilling what I think of him.

"Why did you say you wouldn't attend a dinner party if Kay Boyle
was present!" she demanded of Trilling. Trilling demurred. He said he had
been told Kay wanted him to promote her books.

"I don't function like that!" Kay said indignantly.

By 1960 she had been selected as a jury member for fiction for the
National Book Awards, another measure of the respect she was accorded
during these years. But to her fellow members of the committee, Brendan
Gill, Alexander Laing, William Peden, and Charles J. Rolo, she was a
trying colleague. So annoyed was Kay Boyle by the vote that she threatened
to blackball "the big function." She had to be persuaded that "it would be
a childish thing to do, and an insult to a nice young man, who was flown
back from Rome to be awarded," Philip Roth, who won for *Goodbye,
Columbus.* Dramatizing herself, as always, Kay Boyle described the encounter: "it was suggested that I be thrown out the window," until, finally,
she "threw in the sponge—or is it the towel?" As soon as it was over, she
sold her reading copies to the Gotham Book Mart and her friend Frances
Steloff. In 1961 *Generation Without Farewell* was a nominee, but it failed
to win.

Kay Boyle navigated her aging with as much aplomb as a beauty can.
Laughingly she called herself a grey-haired grandma. When John Glassco
in 1958 suggested that they return together to Paris, she wrote Bob Brown,
"Wouldn't it be a shock to him if grandma should take him at his word!"
Meanwhile "grandma," elegant to a fault, sacrificed none of her glamour.
If her clothes were sometimes hand-me-downs from the generous Rappaports (Jimmy Stern took to calling Herman Rappaport the "Magician from
Brooklyn"), Kay Boyle remained, as Marianne Moore called her, "an enchanter." Kay had begun to teach, and Malcolm Cowley told her students
would take her course just to see what sort of clothes a famous novelist
wears. No matter her elegance, Kay Boyle waxed indignant then. "How
like a man, when I have no clothes with which to impress them at all,"
she said, clearly regretting the fact. To Cowley, she pleaded, "My God,
what a shock they'll get! I haven't bought a rag since our Foreign Service
hey-dey in 1953."

But as an old white raincoat from the Rappaports became an evening cloak, with her hair as carefully arranged as always, with silver and white scarves, she was as glamorous as ever. Kay Boyle easily garnered admirers in her fifties, among them Judge Clark, Harry T. Moore, Eric Kahler at Princeton, and old standbys like William L. Shirer and James T. Farrell. Nelson Algren took to calling her "dearest Argie-Bargie" after a line in one of her reviews, signing his letters "Arfy-Dorfy." "Blessing on your pointy pen, your pointy house and your pointy precious head," he wrote to Kay in 1958.

Since her youth, Kay Boyle had been a connoisseur of friendship, and her financial problems, her health problems, and her family problems of the period did not cause her to neglect her friends. When Robert McAlmon had been out of touch for a year and a half, Kay tried to track him down with a note: "Where are you?" McAlmon died in February of 1956 of pneumonia. When in 1959 a professor named Robert E. Knoll wrote a monograph on McAlmon, which Kay found "inadequate," she decided then to "write my own book about him one day."

In 1962 Kay reviewed for a little magazine called *Prairie Schooner* Knoll's anthology of McAlmon's selected prose, *McAlmon and the Lost Generation*, exalting her old friend. "There was never anyone quite like McAlmon around," Kay wrote, calling him "one of the most fascinating figures of his generation." Her goal was to spare McAlmon oblivion, and it became as important to her as reviving her own reputation. That August she began a long effort to get McAlmon's memoir, *Being Geniuses Together*, published in America. Thinking she would write an introduction, she drove up to Yale to examine his papers. She found it a depressing experience. "It seemed disturbingly wrong, somehow, for all these papers, letters, etc. to be exposed and fed on, preyed on by others," she decided, feeling she could "not write a word about him, ever." A woman of contradictions, Kay not only would write about McAlmon within six years, eloquently, but would sell her own "papers, letters, etc." to first one library and then another.

Bob Brown died in 1959 and Kay wrote a loving memorial, published in *The Village Voice*. She described her friend of thirty years as "the unjudging, undamning, unbigoted, inexhaustible artist and friend that he never ceased to be." Nancy Cunard and Evelyn Scott had reentered her life. As she sought to help them with publishers, she reviewed William L. Shirer's *The Rise and Fall of the Third Reich* for the *New York Post*. When Princeton professor Gordon A. Craig dared to write a negative review in the *Herald Tribune*, Kay fired off an indignant letter, insisting Shirer had written "a vitally important contribution to the history of our time." Meanwhile to Shirer she wrote a satiric poem venting her rage at the "pedagogue" who dared: "A curse on Gordon Abominable Craig / Efface him, erase him, and give him the plague."

Sometimes in her efforts to help her friends, Kay Boyle overreached.

In the same issue of *The New York Times Book Review* in which her review of Bessie Breuer's *The Actress* appeared, Kay Boyle's blurb graced the publisher's advertisement. Kay pleaded she had not known she would be assigned the review when she wrote the blurb; she insisted she had expected the publisher, Harper's, to write to the *Book Review* editor, Francis Brown, explaining.

She also wrote a poem to Roger Burlingame: "For a Friend Whose Eyes Were Operated On in May." "A Poem of Gratitude" for Caresse Crosby was published in *Poetry* in March of 1959. Indeed, Caresse was still helping, sending Kay a check for her share of a reprint of Kay's translation of *The Devil in the Flesh*. In its March 1960 number, *Poetry* would print "Two Twilights for William Carlos Williams" and "A Dialogue of Birds for Howard Nemerov," and in 1961 "Two Poems for a Poet," the poet, again, Nemerov. When Kenneth Rexroth wrote negatively about Nemerov's poetry in *The New York Times Book Review*, Kay Boyle shot off an angry poem to the editor: "Kenneth Rexroth makes me wax wrath / Whenever he happens to cross my path." As an "Addendum" to a letter from Nemerov, and Rexroth's reply, Francis Brown ran the poem. When Hayden Carruth in his *Nation* review dared write that Nemerov's poems are not the kind that one returns to for rereading, a letter from Kay went off at once. Kay and Nemerov would remain devoted to each other until Nemerov's death in 1991.

Kay rediscovered her old acquaintance Marianne Moore in the fifties. Moore was now a celebrity, and Kay courted her, accompanying her 1958 Christmas card with a poem dedicated to Moore, with a line for each letter of Moore's name, which included "Irreplaceable As Treasures Are Your Eclogues" and closed with "endless homage with good reason." Kay defended Moore just as she did Nemerov. When Karl Shapiro was not properly respectful of Moore's poetry, she lectured him that he should have learned from Robert McAlmon, who "had an instinctive and belligerent loyalty to exceptional accomplishment which made betrayal of the exceptional writer an outrage." Shapiro pleaded he wished only to "put an end to all that petrified poetry and theory which poor Marianne Moore is a victim of." Nor did she find a supporter for her defense of Moore in William Carlos Williams, who believed Moore had "descended into orthodoxy in which she resembles the back-slider of our age the notorious T.S.E." Williams added: "much as we both loved Bob McA. he was not often a good writer." Kay Boyle, who never permitted a word to be spoken against Robert McAlmon in her presence, let the matter rest.

Even as she was writing more poetry now, Kay knew she wasn't a very good poet. "One of the main things wrong with my poetry is that I am a prose writer, and therefore over-explicit," she admitted to Nemerov. But Williams assured her she had "progressed a lot in the art," even if, as she frankly acknowledged, she knew nothing of "poetic metres or feet—that's one reason why my poetry is so unreliable. Sometimes it turns out, but most times not." As in her politics, so in her poetry, Kay increasingly relied on intuition.

By the late fifties too she had divided the world into heroes and villains, the legacy of her old hero worshipping. Freely she took up the sword for friends, and against foes, and there was little middle ground. "What a hypocrite she is," Kay wrote to Ann Watkins of Katherine Anne Porter, when she learned Porter had revised her estimate of Kay Boyle's writing, "every bone of her body is false." There were few patches of grey. Kay waxed indignant when Walter Lowenfels, who had been out of touch since the late twenties and was now under siege by McCarthyism, suddenly listed her name on a brochure as one of his admirers without first requesting her permission. When Frank O'Connor called James Joyce "a crashing bore" and a "sponger," in his *Times* review of a book by Mary and Padraic Colum, Kay wrote a vitriolic denunciation of the reviewer. "Mr. O'Connor's ill-mannered arrogance and insufferable conceit, as well as his envy of other Irish writers of fame, have long been a source of amusement." This time Francis Brown chose not to run her letter.

Often she was plain unfair. She objected to Knopf's not quickly publishing a collection of her short stories so that she could earn some extra money, unwilling to grant that they had cause to hesitate since she had not yet turned in the manuscript of *Generation Without Farewell*, which was long overdue. She said she hoped they would do it "as a gesture." Nor would she admit, as Knopf editor Herbert Weinstock had told Ann Watkins, that her later stories were "marred by her tendency to preach and to worry about world affairs."

Kay Boyle replied that she thought "a lot of preaching needs to be done if publishers can't discriminate between the writers who are struggling like mad to get their writing done and meet their commitments, and those who pick up advances and live gaily and carelessly." It was as if her poverty was sufficient cause for her to be published. "We don't drink, partly because we can't afford it," Kay complained to Ann Watkins, "and we don't have guests, because we have neither the time nor money."

In the late fifties Kay and Ann Watkins were clever at mining Kay Boyle's earlier body of work. Kay revised *The Youngest Camel* and sold the new version to Harper's for a thousand dollars. Jay Laughlin agreed to reprint a paperback edition of *Thirty Stories*. Harry T. Moore searched for someone to write the introduction, and they considered Diana Trilling— until Philip Rahv told one of Laughlin's editors that he thought "Mrs. Trilling was opposed to the kind of writing that Kay Boyle represents and violently frightened by the political point of view that she thinks Kay Boyle has." Indeed, Trilling believed that by signing all those petitions set forth by Communist front organizations, by lending her name to the Waldorf Conference, Kay Boyle had become one of those "advocates of a regime which not only denied every freedom to which liberalism is presumed to be dedicated but also murdered more people than were murdered by the Nazis." Finally David Daiches wrote an introduction, only to succeed in irritating Kay. It was too cool. "He did say you were one of the best writers of the short story," Moore tried to console her.

At Christmastime in 1956 there was only twenty dollars in the bank as Kay rushed to New York to meet with a man from MCA to discuss recording one of her stories. In 1957 Moore arranged for Thomas A. Bledsoe at Beacon Press to reprint *Three Short Novels*, with Kay substituting "Decision" for "Big Fiddle," and earning another five hundred dollars.

By 1957 Kay Boyle could offer more measured assessments of her own work. When the critic R. W. Stallman wanted to read her works, she urged that he begin not, as he intended, with *My Next Bride*, which was "just about the worst book of mine for anyone to begin on or end with," but with *Year Before Last*, to be followed by *Monday Night*, *Thirty Stories*, *The Smoking Mountain*, and finally "The Crazy Hunter." (As always she omitted the very fine *1939* because she had so changed her mind about its hero, and perhaps as well because the reviews had been quite harsh.) It was as if Kay Boyle knew her best work was now long behind her.

26

Abandoned

*I should be grateful for this great love—that I can love anyone
at my age so tremendously.*

When Kay Boyle discovered that she couldn't support her large family with her writing, she turned to teaching. She began in 1954 with creative writing courses at the Thomas School where she offered her students such imaginative assignments as writing from the point of view of a white wolf being pursued by hunters in the Arctic—or of Marie Antoinette on her way to the guillotine. She assigned Dylan Thomas to teach her pupils "that words have a shape."

Even as she began a career which would span more than two decades, she spoke of her lack of qualifications. Indeed, as always, behind her bravado about the meaninglessness of formal education lay a deep sense of insecurity about her own lack of it. She could neither spell nor parse a sentence, she said, and she had no advanced degrees, or any degree. Gallantly, she made up her own rules. She would never use a red pencil, she decided, and stuck to it even with her graduate students later: "the difference between the black of a student's writing and the red of the teacher's comment implies a difference in language and status." Meanwhile, to help the family, for two summers Clover and Mousie ran a six-week "play school" at the Thomas School Farm, teaching painting, modeling, ballet, and drama to students aged four to ten, who each paid thirty-six dollars. In the fall of 1957 Kay Boyle taught a ten-week course in the history and analysis of the short story one afternoon and one evening a week.

Kay had looked for other paying jobs, but none materialized. She read manuscripts for New Directions for a small reader's fee, and enlisted Caresse to find an organization which might employ her. "I can edit manuscripts, type, meet people, do a lot of things," Kay said. Theodore H.

White recommended her to be a fiction editor at *Collier's*, but they didn't want another woman. She also read manuscripts for Robert Smith at the Magazine Institute for seventy-five dollars a week. The work was torture, and she let Smith know it, while he complained that Kay "obviously considered" she was "going slumming" when she associated with him. Ever competitive, how Kay envied Katherine Anne Porter who, she imagined, was turning down "thousands in readings and recordings, and nobody ever offers me thousands for anything."

The turning point came when she lectured at the Bread Loaf writers' conference. After ten days at Bread Loaf, Kay decided to edit a "series of pamphlets, written by thinking, feeling, caring writers on what they believe." As she approached Richard Wright, simultaneously she let him know that she knew he was "working with the State Department, or the FBI . . . and that you gave information about other Americans to these powers in order to keep your own passport and be able to travel." It was part of the wide swath she cut with her sword now, ferreting out the villains as she glorified the heroes. "A pamphlet would stop such a rumor," Kay told Wright.

No pamphlets appeared. But as a consequence of her stint at Bread Loaf, Kay was invited to offer a six-week course in the history of the short story at the University of Delaware in the summer of 1957, the first of her academic jobs. It was inconceivable that she should turn down the two-thousand-dollar fee. But, being Kay, she dramatized her sad fate as she offered James T. Farrell "a spirited lament for the plight of those who once rocked Paris and who now, with spectacles on their noses, try to teach teachers how to analyze a story instead of their own souls."

Kay said she didn't believe in such analysis. At the same time the idea of teaching at a university threw her into paroxysms of self-doubt. She feared she lacked "the academic patter"; she feared she knew nothing about the short story. "I can't talk the way they want me to," she told Malcolm Cowley. "You, and Daiches . . . have a fine academic background to resort to, and I haven't anything other than the conviction that all writing and everything else that is creative grows, develops in great part as unconsciously as the creature in the womb." She would, she decided right away, bring her strong social consciousness to the classroom. "You cannot grasp what human beings are like unless you understand the mechanics of power by which they move society and by which society moves them," she planned to say.

Few teachers can have prepared more assiduously than Kay Boyle. She scoured secondhand bookshops in New York, mindful that the dean at Delaware had told her to begin with the short story in Sanskrit and move through the New Testament to the present. "If I live through this," she moaned, "I'll never be the same." As she tried to review the books of friends whenever she could, so in class she was to teach their works: Bill March, Wolfgang Borchert, Emanuel Carnevali, James T. Farrell, Robert

McAlmon, of course. Nor, at the dawn of the civil rights movement, would she neglect "the Negro short story writers"; she lunched with Langston Hughes, but "even he was hard put to think of Negro short stories." It was now, in 1957, that Kay Boyle wrote to Samuel Beckett, whom she had met at only one dinner party since 1931.

She also sought the advice of critics, although she detested the New Criticism. She found the methods of analysis of Cleanth Brooks and Robert Penn Warren "shocking" and "a complete hoax" and developed a series of "hoax" lectures, parodies of the New Criticism, which she planned to expose for what it was. With its exclusive emphasis on the internal unities of the text, the New Criticism seemed almost designed to arouse the hostility of Kay Boyle. That it departed "drastically from the intentions of the writer whose work you discuss" offended her entire belief in the role of the poet as hero and prophet.

"The creative mind starts with an answer and ends with a question, while the critical mind does not," Kay told critic R. W. Stallman. Stallman replied that he was "hard-pressed to distinguish the creative mind from the critical." Charmed nonetheless, Stallman told Kay he was "delighted that you probe me." But when Stallman sent her his poems, she told him that "they frighten me with their coldness, with their unrelieved awareness of the intellect . . . I believe that all good writing is accomplished with the heart even more aware than is the mind." These were the notions of her youth, and they remained the credo of the woman. No less did they reflect her pride in how far her intuition and "heart" had brought her. Kay had sent Stallman her hoax New Critical analysis of James Joyce's "The Boarding House," and when he wrote her that she had contributed "invaluable critical material to Joyce-iana," she laughed at him behind his back.

At Delaware, Kay rented a noisy apartment across the street from the university (it had a garden she was not entitled to use) and remained by herself "about twenty-two hours a day." But her lectures were inspired and insightful; one she closed with the statement: "a renaissance in writing usually occurred when great social changes were in progress." She also worked on turning her hoax lectures into a textbook "intended to put Stallman . . . and other New Critics to shame." But Simon Michael Bessie at Harper's rejected the idea as lacking "the positive side."

A significant by-product of her Delaware experience was Kay's sharply reawakened sense of racism in America. Even as she taught, she explored the treatment of black people in Delaware. From firsthand knowledge came two *Nation* pieces. In "No Time to Listen" Kay is interrupted in her work on her novel by a man named Samuel Dodson. Dodson, who demands that she turn her attention to the suffering of black people in America, was principal of a Negro elementary school in Frankford, Delaware, a town which had not even begun to comply with 1954's *Brown* v. *Board of Ed-*

ucation. (The real-life Samuel Dodson read her manuscript, made some suggestions, gently told her how much the piece meant to him, and said, "If you wish to, you may use my name.") "City of Invisible Men" described black men transferred to Newark, Delaware's Plymouth plant from Detroit, only to be unable to find decent housing. "They were flesh and blood like any man," she wrote passionately, "and not to be willed away." A year later she published "The Long Dead Fathers," based on a lecture she had given at Delaware State College, a Negro school. It expressed her outrage that Delaware was a state with no civil rights law and demanded that writers "speak out loudly and clearly," in particular against voices like that of the superintendent of schools who had told her, "You've got to civilize them first."

Out of her observation of Delaware's bitter struggle to subvert *Brown* v. *Board of Education* and having heard Thurgood Marshall speak in a New Haven auditorium at a "civil rights for Negroes" conference, on which she reported for *The Nation,* Kay early raised her voice for civil rights. Marshall's call for every man to "respect the law as laid down by the highest court in the country," to honor the *Brown* decision, inspired Kay, who wrote about this "grave, dynamic man" whose "handsome, granite face seemed to bear an anguished scar." Before the freedom rides, before SNCC's voter registration drives and freedom schools, Kay Boyle had spoken, a writer who assumed moral responsibility, practicing what she preached. She was no longer the modernist writing her finely crafted stories of the twenties, thirties, forties, and early fifties. Out of her travails under McCarthyism, out of the personal tragedies of her life, which were only just beginning, she had shed that skin. In the late fifties she became a writer of social conscience as she never had been before.

Her causes were manifold, always humanitarian, on the side of peace, egalitarianism, and justice, and not at all sectarian, even if Communist front organizations had taken advantage of her willingness to stand up for the weak and the unforgiven. By the late fifties Kay Boyle had joined Dorothy Day in New York with a group of protesters refusing to take shelter during an air-raid drill. In 1958 she signed a petition "To the French People" urging an end to the Algerian war. Rushing into the fray, she mistakenly accused General Greenbaum's partner, Morris Ernst, of representing the dictator Trujillo. (In fact, in the notorious Galindez case, Ernst first spoke out for Trujillo's being entitled to the benefit of a trial before he was convicted of the Columbia professor's abduction and murder.) Kay Boyle saw a link between bohemian twenties Paris and the new protest movement, "against the bomb, against the total futility of drills and shelters, against nuclear attack, against war."

By the early sixties she was active in SANE and Women Strike for Peace. She marched against the H-bomb with Judith Malina and Julian Beck of New York's Living Theatre, singing and "embarrassing everyone on Fifth Avenue," and then publishing a story about the experience in

Liberation. With coeds at Penn in December of 1961 Kay Boyle discussed the freedom rides and the fallout shelters. In May of 1962 in New London she picketed Mrs. Kennedy, who was there to christen a Polaris submarine, no matter that a year earlier she had congratulated John F. Kennedy on his United Nations address in which he said that "mankind must put an end to war or war will put an end to mankind."

Out of the hospital after her gallbladder operation, Kay Boyle threw herself into a Connecticut campaign opposing the construction of a marina in Wilson Cove. And she took the time to write a long letter to François Mauriac about an article he had published in *The New Republic*. She pointed out that there was an America he had ignored, one offering "a tradition of courage and dissent of which we are deeply proud."

Even as she lectured at Southern Illinois University, and led fiction workshops at the New York City Writers' Conference at Wagner College on Staten Island, Kay struggled with that German history for which she had contracted. "Had I the money to live on, I feel sure I would abandon the German history," she admitted. It was an onerous task, and one for which she was little suited, as she decided she would write that Hitler was the logical result of all that had preceded him, going all the way back to Frederick the Great and Bismarck. To be paid the installments on her advance, she sent chapters to her new editor, Ken McCormick. Kay told a *New York Post* interviewer she had found "nothing" likable about the German people. To Kathryn Hulme, she admitted, "I *am* prejudiced against the Germans, but I don't want people to find out too soon or they won't go on reading the book."

In these years Kay Boyle presented herself as an expert on Germany. She complained of the absence of German voices acknowledging "the moral consequences of the *Wirtschaftswunder*" (economic miracle) and the presence of former Nazis in Adenauer's government. In a letter to the *Times* she attacked George N. Schuster for defending Hans Globke, a former Nazi and now "state secretary" in Adenauer's government. As she would frequently from now on, Kay quoted a new hero, Albert Camus: "have we the right to forgive who have merely survived?" In January of 1961 Kay Boyle appeared on *The Open Mind* with William L. Shirer, and aided by Shirer's recommendation, she received her second Guggenheim fellowship—to work on her history of Germany.

Kay also applied for a grant for her history of Germany from the American Jewish Committee. Instead, the Committee commissioned her to write a pamphlet for them to be called "Breaking the Silence: Why a Mother Tells Her Son About the Nazi Era." She chose a story form, a woman addressing her son as together they watch the trial of Adolf Eichmann on television. The father smokes his pipe and points out that even today "human rights need to be constantly guarded and improved." Kay invokes not only McCarthyism in this supposedly German-focused pamphlet but civil rights in America as well. "In certain sections of our country Negroes are still segregated and even barred from the polls," the boy is told.

This emphasis on the civil rights struggles of the present met with dismay from the American Jewish Committee, which rejected her effort. Samuel Fishzohn, the Committee's Director of Youth Services, complained that her style was "highly intellectual" and that she spent too much time discussing pre-Nazi Germany. She had received a thousand dollars on signing and was owed another thousand on acceptance. She revised her work four times before Fishzohn finally accepted it. Ironically, the Committee wanted James B. Conant, the Franckensteins' nemesis at HICOG, to write the introduction. Kay suggested Telford Taylor, the chief prosecutor at Nuremberg. Neither was chosen. Instead the executive vice president of the American Jewish Committee wrote a two-page foreword.

Kay Boyle was doing better with her publishers by the early sixties. Although he had been "offended and not a little hurt" when he learned that she had signed with Doubleday for her German history, Alfred Knopf in 1961 agreed to publish her *Collected Poems* and to reissue *The Smoking Mountain*, with a five-hundred-dollar advance, in the spring of 1963.

But if Knopf certainly stood by Kay Boyle through difficult times, there was no editor in her long career who was to be more sympathetic, supportive, and inspiring to her than Ken McCormick at Doubleday. When she entered the hospital for exploratory surgery in the summer of 1960, he told her, "We don't want this book at the expense of your health." The Martin Luther chapter, he told her, was "a masterpiece." She was "on the way to a tremendously exciting book." The chapter summarizing capitalism and Communism in Germany and the portrait of the plight of the Jews was "magnificent evidence of the great book you're doing for us." As the foreign rights were sold to Great Britain, Holland, and Spain, McCormick told Kay, "I can be patient with you to infinity, as long as you go on writing this remarkable book." Unbeknownst to McCormick, this was to be no exaggeration.

On her return to America in 1953 Kay had at once joined a world of discourse far beyond the narrow confines of family. By 1960 she sought quiet at the MacDowell Colony, feeling she could not "go on being all the things I am in the house and have energy left for the business of writing." It was a time of crisis for her immediate family and her older children as well. Only Kathe seemed content, Kathe who had played Juliet in *Romanoff and Juliet* opposite Peter Ustinov on the London stage. And one day Kay Boyle by herself took the train in from Rowayton to go to the movies in New York. "My daughter's in this movie!" she proudly told the ticket taker before she went in to see the Preston Sturges picture *The French, They Are a Funny Race* (1955), in which Kathe had a considerable role.

To put distance between herself and Laurence, Apple at twenty-seven had returned to the United States in 1956. Kay, Bobby had said, was Apple's "only hope now." Indeed, as she experienced the effects of long years of unresolved pain, Apple had become lost, unsure of herself, and alcoholic. "I worry without stopping over Apple," Kay had said. But her solution was that Apple remain with her and submit to a series of shock treatments to cure her alcoholism. Apple and her husband, Ted, fled to Miami as soon as they could. A few months later Laurence visited America, stopping by Rowayton. It was so trying a visit that on the day of his departure Kay was "seized with those terrible intestinal cramps."

Apple was even less able than her sisters to separate her own identity from Kay's. "We all miss you and are all so droopy at meals because you're not here," Apple wrote her mother from Miami, "those horrible chores of yours . . . should not be yours." Whatever Kay Boyle felt, it seemed, was mistaken by both Apple and Clover for their own feelings. The first project Apple planned upon her return to America was a set of murals depicting her mother's life.

In her twenty-ninth year, alcoholic and anorexic, Apple suffered a complete collapse. She threw a knife at Ted, and climbed a tree, taking with her a pack of cigarettes and a bottle of gin, and refused to come down. It took a group of hospital attendants to capture her before she was brought to the psychiatric ward at Jackson Memorial Hospital. There her psychiatrist, Dr. Selinsky, diagnosed her as "ambulatory schizoid."

Immediately, Laurence flew back to America, stopping again in Connecticut, where he appropriated Kay's typewriter for his own needs. She at once located an unsatisfactory substitute. "Conditions here are almost beyond bearing," she told friends, cautioning them not to telephone her as long as Laurence remained in the house.

Kay and Laurence now blamed each other for Apple's illness. Laurence accused Kay of never having liked girls. Kay attributed Apple's alcoholism and her collapse to Laurence's excesses, and was unsympathetic when Laurence complained that he couldn't afford four hundred dollars a week for Apple's care. Apple feared both parents now, Kay no less than Laurence, and her doctor urged Kay to postpone any trip to Florida. Amid their mutual accusations Kay and Laurence each feared being blamed by her doctors.

"Kay is not the best person to talk to doctors," Laurence told Djuna Barnes, "as she's apt to be somewhat hysterical, which would give the doctors another handle against the family, which is what they are looking for." Rooted as both Kay and Laurence were in surrealism and modernism, and their modes of depicting the subconscious, they nonetheless feared psychiatry, even as in their own lives they evaded self-examination. At the same time both were plagued by feelings of guilt toward the children. On one level Kay avoided introspection, and fled any consideration of the consequences of her actions; on another she believed she had harmed her older daughters greatly both by breaking up the family and by giving so much of her time to her work.

When Dr. Selinsky at last told Kay he would meet with her, the students and teachers at the Thomas School raised four hundred dollars to send her and Mousie to Florida. There Selinsky revealed to Kay his conviction that Apple had been abandoned as a child. Taking this statement literally, in keeping with her aversion to introspection, Kay professed herself dumbfounded. First she insisted that Apple had never been abandoned. Then she concluded that Apple must have been referring to those times when she had to move out of the room she shared with Bobby when Pegeen visited. But when Kay saw Apple and suggested this alternative, Apple immediately denied it had any bearing. She had been relieved to have a room of her own.

What Apple did remember was that day in Cortina when she had been left overnight while the others went skiing. She remembered Laurence and Kay going off to Paris while she lay sick, and herself standing outside her mother's door in Mégève, listening to the tap-tapping of the typewriter, wanting her mother, yet afraid to interrupt, so that she stood there immobile. She remembered the mountain hike when her mother walked ahead holding the hands of two other children while she had walked woefully behind. The child Apple had been sacrificed to meet the needs of others, especially Laurence, whom she had to nurture after he lost Kay. Never having felt nurtured, she could neither give love nor receive it.

Kay would not acknowledge Apple's sense that she had been abandoned psychologically. "If you go down too deeply, there's no way out again," Kay Boyle would say later, firm in her opposition to plumbing the depths of the psyche.

"You have to go down to find out who you are," an exasperated Clover would reply.

"You find out who you are by the people around you and by your actions," Kay insisted all her life. "That's how you're defined, not by all this soul-searching. It's a very destructive process." But although her children suffered for their mother's resistance to introspection, some reviewers praised her for it. In his review of her *Collected Poems* in 1963, Robert Knoll applauded how "unlike some of her contemporaries Miss Boyle's emotions do not turn inward, feeding on themselves; and she is not the object of her own speculation." Indeed, she was not.

As she had treated her daughters as reflections of herself, never to oppose her, always to pay her homage, Kay became more important to them than they were to themselves. Not surprisingly, she emerged from her visit with Apple believing that "her love for me, thank God, has not changed." Narcissistically, she thought of herself. Melodramatically, she described, to Ann Watkins, a trek through the tropical Everglades, "three hours of blistering heat each way." To James T. Farrell, she described herself lying awake "half the night going over and over and over what can be done. She [Apple] is so talented and wonderful, and so frail and frightened and lost."

By April, following Kay's visit, Apple was back in the hospital. Kay rationalized that she was "getting the care she has needed so desperately for so many years," and admitted that seeing Apple for her had been "a nightmare," and that she had been unable "to reach her in any final way." As Kay dissuaded Laurence from returning again to America, Dr. Selinsky forbade *her* from coming back to see Apple, even once a week for half an hour, as Kay suggested. It was clear to Apple's doctors that both parents had to be kept away. Certainly, Kay and Laurence both seemed to derive a certain pleasure from their children's dependency.

Kay had to take some comfort from an apologetic letter from Sindbad, who told her, "You raised me and took care of me more than a mother. I acted like a bastard with you in France after the war. I was too young and impulsive and crude. It's a bit late now Kay, but anyway I'd like to say I regret it." Sindbad visited Apple only to pronounce Dr. Selinsky "money grabbing" and to reiterate once more to Kay his appreciation for what she had done for him. "I am sure you civilized me; you taught me manners and how to act," he told his stepmother. "I don't think I'll ever forget that."

Eventually Apple began to recover, and even became pregnant. But she remained obsessed by her mother. In a favorite daydream, she held her mother's hand; then she placed her hand on Kay's head "because you used to hold my forehead when I was carsick and then also I remember feeling so helpless in Lisbon when you were so ill and the whole room was dark." When some years later Apple fell in love with a married ski teacher, she told Kay, "You fell in love with a ski teacher, so I had to have a ski teacher." The pattern of not being able to differentiate herself from her mother, her inability to forge a separate identity, had been established for life.

Kay's closest confidante was now her daughter Clover, to whom she admitted she blamed herself for Apple's illness. It was Clover who worried most about Kay's health, her chores, her schedule, and she must have known that Clover would absolve her of any blame for what had happened to Apple. Clover, who still could not bear to be separated from her mother, even when Kay went down to visit Apple, satisfied her mother's need to remain the parent of unblemished rectitude.

And indeed Clover assured her it was unjust for her to suffer because of what happened to someone else, even if it was her own daughter. Clover told her that it was with Laurence that the blame must lie, Laurence who thought of nothing but drink. Clover appears to have used Kay's concern about Apple to draw closer to her mother as she applauded Kay Boyle for the courage she gave her. Meanwhile Laurence wrote Clover frantically for news of Apple: "I want so much to know of her from you."

So distraught was Laurence over the collapse of his beloved Apple that his behavior became more eccentric than usual. One night in a hotel in Avallon, having gone to bed drunk, he suddenly awakened. Unable to find his way to the bathroom to "do pipi," as he put it, Laurence, ever the surrealist, decided to pee out the hotel window. But he leaned too far, and fell out the window into the courtyard, injuring his testicles, which at once swelled. Depressed, feeling himself "an object of disgust and inferior," Laurence spent three weeks at the American Hospital in Neuilly, uncomfortably urinating through an implanted tube.

It was perhaps in the wake of Apple's breakdown that Kay began to see herself as a lonely woman whose needs were not being met, one whose life was devoid of the solace a woman needed from a man. Her marriage to Joseph, never a marriage of equals, had long been unsatisfactory. As the years passed, even after he was cleared, Joseph was unable to find work appropriate to his talents and his considerable intellect. In his deepest soul he felt making money was beneath him, as indeed Laurence had, and spoke of people "in trade" as beneath contempt, an attitude traceable to his origins among the Austrian nobility. Kay had been left to cope virtually alone with overwhelming financial burdens.

Meanwhile, even as she kept up their badgering, bullying relationship, in which she controlled Joseph as if he were one more of her children, he had become sexually impotent, in part perhaps because of the brutalization he had suffered under McCarthyism. Now more than ever he seemed a younger brother rather than a husband to his wife. Certainly he never seemed to compliment her or to make much of her. Joseph remained loyal to his wife and continued to call her "Fifi," but he retreated ever more deeply into his own private world. Now Kay drew away from him in more profound ways. When she took up with other men, neither Faith (formerly Mousie) nor Clover was surprised, because they knew that intimacy between Kay and Joseph had ceased.

At fifty-seven, Kay by no means felt herself "old." She disliked it when her age was mentioned, and told Willard Maas, who was writing up the brochure for the Wagner College writers' conference, that he might mention her birthplace, but "my husband does not like me to mention the year," an unlikely fabulation, of course, given Joseph's subservience to her wishes. Soon she would dye her hair black. Now she wore dark makeup around her eyes and heavy blue eye shadow, even in the morning. "I hear she's dyed her silver curls a midnight black!" Solita Solano cattily told Djuna Barnes, "too rigorous a search for youth." And Louise Bogan spotted Kay Boyle at a MacDowell Colony admissions committee meeting wearing a large fur hat "with her usual load of eye-shadow and feminine charm." Bogan liked her, she said, but wished "she'd wash her face (meow! meow!)."

But it was the admiration of men rather than women that Kay Boyle sought now. She confessed to missing the old excitement she had shared with Laurence and began to bring men home to Rowayton, including a longshoreman she met at the writers' conference, who lived with the family until he became insulting and left. Kay now sought men unlike her gentle husband, men whom she could not control, men who aroused her by their unpredictability and violence.

In 1959 Kay met a painter named Arthur Deshaies, a short, hard-drinking, portly, madcap, red-haired man nineteen years her junior. Deshaies would sweep Kay into his arms and carry her from room to room. On his knees, he declared that she was the most magnificent person he had ever met. He adored her, he said. He sang operatic arias, to the younger children's delight, as they too joined in the mad spectacle.

Kay declared herself "in love" and covered the walls of Ann Watkins's cottage with photographs of Arthur Deshaies. That Deshaies had a wife and a new baby mattered to her not at all. It was more than just a new man who had aroused her, reawakened her, Kay said. Her writing itself was at stake. She could go on, she told herself, only by going back to "a time, and a passion and rage, and to the same people, however their names may have changed."

That place was Paris. With Arthur Deshaies, she could relive the time of her greatest accomplishment as an artist, and her fulfillment as a woman. When she went into the hospital to have her gallbladder removed, she left instructions that her diary "be destroyed." Ironically, all the while that she was in raptures over Arthur Deshaies, her mother-in-law was continuing in her efforts to rehabilitate her and Joseph in the eyes of the Catholic Church, so that to appease her Kay even contacted Richard Brault, who now lived in Algeria. But Brault wanted nothing to do with an annulment. Meanwhile Kay, who always hated to be criticized in the slightest way, was agitated that the Countess Esterházy believed she was "somehow to blame for the unalterable facts."

Indeed, there was more on Kay Boyle's mind than sanctifying her moribund marriage in the eyes of the Roman Catholic Church. Blissfully she now announced to many that she had fallen in love, as she embraced Deshaies in an orgy of physical closeness, dancing, touching. As Clover would remember, if there wasn't penetration, there was everything else. Flamboyantly Deshaies had entered Kay's life as one more in a long line of romantic figures. As if she didn't have a husband at all, he assumed the role of her companion.

During the summers of 1959 and 1960 Kay persuaded Joseph to take on the assignment of guiding a group of girls from the Thomas School on a tour of Europe. Tired and depressed, Joseph had no desire to make these trips. But Kay wanted him to go and so he did, although the second time only four girls signed up. To his young charges, Joseph seemed to be a wounded man. He was painfully thin, and he smoked incessantly. Sometimes in the evenings they spotted him in a bar or restaurant deeply engrossed in conversation with one young woman or another, and there was a definite romantic aura about these encounters. Nor were the girls surprised since Joseph seemed so young to them, and his grey-haired wife so old.

The first summer that Joseph was gone, Arthur Deshaies virtually moved in with Kay. They went about everywhere together. When Howard Nemerov visited, Arthur did the cooking, and later Kay gathered his recipes for an anthology to which she contributed her own "Ratatouille Rowayton." Deshaies described himself for the list of contributors as "Thoreauic, red-bearded and pipe-smoking." Kay Boyle professed herself, archly, as "loath to receive guests without my earrings on," and coyly listed the ingredients of her recipes without quantities or instructions.

Kay Boyle offered Arthur Deshaies help, and access to people who might help him. When he had too much work to do to get ready for a show, Kay decided to skip the annual Institute ceremonies rather than go without him. When one of his painter friends committed suicide, and Arthur was in "violent, tearful agony," Kay slept that night on the stone floor of his studio. It was not Joseph but Arthur Deshaies who accompanied her to her "tender and loving reunion" with William Carlos Williams in Rutherford, New Jersey. "This is the last time, Kay," Williams told her.

Clearly distraught and agitated by her new love, Kay wrote Howard Nemerov that Deshaies was only a "symbol," of the direction she wanted to take. Laurence, she fabulated, had asked her to come back to him, and she could not "do anything else but go." In fact, it was Kay who, confused by her own emotions, thought of returning to Laurence. When she wrote to Laurence comparing Arthur with his "shouts of rage as he destroys himself and his paintings day after day" with Laurence as she remembered him, Laurence Vail was irritated. "It's the way it was between you and me," Kay wrote her ex-husband at Christmas 1959. "I have met a man just like you!" She now announced to Laurence that she had discovered something new about herself: "I belong in this catastrophe. I have always belonged in it, and that other life is something that is not mine."

But Laurence had still not forgiven Kay for smashing the family. That her marriage to Joseph no longer worked gave him small satisfaction; he was not petty in those ways. When Kay wrote him that she loved him, including in her letter sentimental reminiscences of the two of them together in the mountains, he was disturbed.

His equilibrium shattered, Laurence paced his studio. "Your mother's going absolutely crazy," he told Kathe. Kathe in turn wrote Kay that it was shocking that she should be confiding her love affairs to Papa. "Your mother's a dreadful person. I can't bear her," Laurence was to tell Ian Franckenstein a few years later. He called Joseph a "lovely man" and repeated that he pitied him.

Not surprisingly, Joan Detweiler also took a dim view of her sister's behavior. Kay had a husband who "waited on her hand and foot," a man everyone admired. Yet she insisted upon having an affair with "this un-attractive fat artist" whose wife had just had a baby. Jo thought Kay had "broken Joseph's heart."

"To salvage my conscience I say that I am not needed in the other life," Kay told Howard Nemerov as she sought to justify her behavior. But what she was doing was not "a departure but a return. I have to live with the articulate," Kay added, and "the academic world is not articulate."

Faith saw her mother as happy only when she was in love. Then she was full of life, full of beauty, and intimate in a way she had not been with Joseph for years. She had been transformed into a person who was less austere. When Arthur was present, the children were permitted to do whatever they wanted. Deshaies had awakened her long-dormant desires and one night with Deshaies there was a party at which Kay got drunk for the first time in years. She and Faith then shed their clothes and in the pitch-dark night mother and daughter jumped naked together into the warm summer waters of Wilson Cove.

One night in April of 1960, after Kay had spent the day painting a picture in Arthur's studio, she regarded a drunken, sleeping, and snoring Deshaies and knew: "everything else as a way of living had come to an end." Kay's own art shaped her life, even as it autobiographically chronicled that life, for this was a line almost identical to one she had used in *Primer for Combat* describing the effect of her affair with Kurt Wick. She was fifty-eight years old, and she had discovered, she thought, a fundamental truth about herself: she belonged "with the lost and the terrified and the outcasts and the defeated—and, yes, even the drunks."

Kay was also saving this artist, she thought, as she could not save Laurence, offering him "calmness and unjudging love . . . constructive passion, instead of the destructive kind." When he exhibited his paintings at the Rowayton Art Center, she wrote an article about him called "Paintings in Flight" for the community magazine, exalting "the humor and pulse and energy of one man's personality," which she felt Deshaies had transferred to his art. She hung his prints in her workroom and wrote poems to accompany them. "I understand him and love him more each day," she told Fay Rappaport in January of 1961. Indeed, 1961, when they both received Guggenheim fellowships, Kay for her German history, Arthur for his paintings, was to be "our year . . . Arthur's and mine." The plan was for him to drive her up to the MacDowell Colony for the summer of 1961, which would give them another long stretch of time together.

Kay Boyle continued with Arthur Deshaies as long as she could. Even when, drunk, he would come into Faith's bedroom, even when he approached her daughters, Kay Boyle was not disturbed. "So many lone grieving poems have I / Written you," began one of her "Poems for a Painter," written in July of 1960. In another poem, having missed him, she sees his face in a landscape she has painted. "Poem for a Painter Who Drinks Wine" is strongly erotic: "interchangeable tongues . . . breasts as similar as stars . . . one man's restless bed . . . his hands and mouth at rest in tender hair . . . fable of anemone." A year later, "Seascape for an Engraver" reflects, however, not only Kay's passion for Deshaies but a suggestion of his ultimate inaccessibility: "you are the footprint filled with sea." Deshaies stands before her in this poem "engraving / The frail shadow of man's long prevailing with knife." Inspired by her passion, Kay produced fine poetry, finer than she had in years.

It was about romance and erotic energy and the exhilaration of existing in the maelstrom of a man's power. It was about sex in a way she had rarely written before, and not for years. As always, she turned the smallest details of her life to her art. "A Poem for Arthur" describes a New York evening when she lost an earring at Marianne Moore's. "You shook the liquid amber tree . . . and all my earrings fell . . . you shook the liquid amber . . . and the pods fell, / Raining their seeds into your scarlet beard." Deshaies called Kay "*belle poisson d'or*" and signed the telegram he sent her when she was in the hospital early that summer of 1960: "Love and So Much Love and Why Not." He compared her powers to those of nature and insisted he preferred "the kiss of the White Hair'd Goddess of Art."

After they spent a week together in March of 1961, and Arthur left, Kay was so "shattered" by his absence that she couldn't write, eat, or sleep. She told herself she should be "grateful for this great love," that she could "love anyone at my age so tremendously." It was all-encompassing, and to Kay Boyle, as did all her romances, it felt permanent. She was beginning anew with a man with whom she would spend the rest of her life, exactly as she had felt with Ernest Walsh, with Laurence, with Kurt Wick, with Joseph. Everything about the loved object delighted her: "his solicitude, his practical sense, his instinctive emotions about people."

All the details of this romance Kay shared with Clover, who said she pitied her mother for all that had been missing from her life with Joseph. When Arthur was silent or absent, Clover suffered with her. Clover told her that Arthur gave her courage. She comforted her mother when Deshaies was drunk, depressed, or silent, wishing only for calm and peace between the couple. Together with Kay, she mourned the fact that Deshaies behaved as if he were desperate even when he was with her. Clover told her mother she knew she had to find someone who loved her for what she was. Joseph, it was implied, had worshipped her as a goddess on a pedestal, and that was not what she needed. As Kay alternated between ecstasy and despair in her relationship with Deshaies, she continued to share her feelings with Clover.

Unlike Laurence, however, Deshaies really was a man without limits, and one night he did go too far, sleeping with Clover. Kay returned to MacDowell, calling it "essential that [Clover] become *me* for an interval, until she can work the whole relationship out." Still she saw no danger in a daughter's having become interchangeable with her.

But it was not yet over. When Deshaies fled to Greece, a trip Kay correctly perceived as an escape from her, she suffered bitterly. They wrote to each other constantly, and Deshaies even enlisted Kay to ask his wife to send him three hundred dollars for the fare home. In Paris, Deshaies had an affair with Bobby. Kay forgave him everything, and even planned to ask the admissions committee at MacDowell to allow him to return the following January.

At last, it did end. Deshaies finally pulled back. Kay accused him of taking her for granted, of being unable to express his love for her. But he was not able to give her the complete love she required from everyone. Arthur Deshaies chafed under Kay Boyle's insistence that things must be handled her way, as, indeed, Laurence had. He said he felt her "greatness." But he could not understand the way she lived, all the manifold contradictions.

The flamboyant shows of rapture ceased. Deshaies suddenly said he had to devote all his energy to his work.

Kay had made him stronger, built up his morale, done everything she could for him. But he was not ready to devote his whole life to her. Yet, five months after this confrontation, Kay was still insisting that her love for Deshaies "increases month by month" and had arranged a one-man show for him on Martha's Vineyard. But soon references to Joseph were sprinkled in Deshaies's letters, as they had not been before.

When they first met, Deshaies had appeared at Kay's house with his wife and baby. Now wife and baby reappeared. It was over. A chronic survivor, Kay Boyle knew how to cut her losses. The solution, as always, was work. "One must work hard and correct reality by creativity, as Camus says," she insisted, as if she were Katherine Evans Boyle incarnate.

27

Death of a Man

*You were laughing, saying: "Don't be angry, Joseph," and I fell
into a bottomless pit.*
JOSEPH FRANCKENSTEIN

Now Joseph will have his cross.
JANET FLANNER

In August of 1961 Clover, now twenty-two, attempted suicide. She
told her mother that Paul Robeson's rendition of the spiritual "Sometimes
I feel like a motherless child" kept reverberating obsessively in her consciousness. It was increasingly evident that her sense of self-worth had for
too long resided in sacrificing her own needs to those of her mother. Clover
had nursed Kay back to health after her gallbladder operation, had typed
up the newspaper editorials about Joseph for their friends, had gone to
Bread Loaf with her mother, had, in short, been amanuensis, confidante,
friend, and acolyte to Kay. In place of the heightened sexual atmosphere
of Laurence's world (one night in the mid-fifties Laurence had taken Clover
to sleep at a whorehouse) was Kay's imposing on this daughter all her
disappointment in her marriage, her loneliness, and her pain.

As she drew Clover closer to her, Kay repeated that Kathe and Faith,
the "blondes," were "the stupid ones." As extensions of their mother, they
did not measure up. But Clover was her alter ego.

There were warnings that such behavior might yield harmful effects.
One night, drunk, Clover had yelled furiously at Joseph, "You're not my
goddamned father," breaking dishes. Terrified, Faith had slapped her sister, only for Kay to turn furiously on her: "You used violence! You hit
her!" Then on the night before Faith was to leave for a trip to England,
Clover got up on the windowsill, threatening to throw herself into the icy
sound. Kay now attacked Clover more violently than Faith ever had, giving
her two black eyes.

Frightened by Clover's nearly fatal suicide attempt in August of 1961,
having obviously learned little from Apple's travail, Kay had Clover committed by force to a state hospital. According to Clover, she took this

extreme step on the advice of a local pediatrician, with no first recourse to conventional therapy. Rationalizing, Kay then told people there had been no alternative.

It was for Clover an "abandonment" far more overt than anything Apple had experienced, and a "ruthless" act. Laurence was opposed to the idea. But, far away, he bowed to his much stronger-willed ex-wife's judgment. By now Laurence had taken to tossing Kay's frequent letters to him in a brown envelope marked "War of Nerves with Kay."

By November, Kay was telling people that if "Clover would fall in love and marry *instantly*," she would be all right. She accepted Clover's dedication, making her mother the focus of her life, as her due homage; she had failed to perceive the dark meaning of her daughter's words, the fear, the plea that without her mother she felt as if she did not exist. Clover had been for her mother a virtual surrogate spouse, a role complicated by the advent of Arthur Deshaies. Trying to meet her own needs, for Clover, as for Apple, had come to mean risking the loss of the one parent she had. Expressing her own needs, in contradistinction to her mother's, made her fear further abandonment.

Kay had been proud when Clover, as a high school student, won a mural competition sponsored by the *Herald Tribune*. But now Clover perceived this pride as her mother's pleasure in how Clover's artistic success reflected on herself. Like all victims, Clover blamed herself for her troubles. Voluntarily she committed herself to Hillside Hospital in New York.

But even in the hospital Clover struggled to convince herself that her mother's view of things was the only one that made sense, that only her mother's praise could give her self-confidence, and that she was whole only when she was with Kay. Of all the daughters, it was only Faith who would grow up with a measure of personal power and confidence, in part because she had not been selected to be that surrogate spouse, that confidante. At the time Faith had been jealous that she had not been so chosen, but years later Clover would tell her that she was the only person in the entire family who had ever stood up to their mother.

By January of 1962, in the midst of Clover's illness, Kay had found a new admirer. He was a young writer named Herbert O. Kubly, whom she had met at the MacDowell Colony and who had won a National Book Award in 1956 for a nonfiction work, *American in Italy*. As soon as they met, Kay demanded that Caresse "*tell me all you know of Herbert Kubly*." Then she added: "very important, and, of course, between us two." Kay admitted to Caresse, "I am very fond of him." By February, he was "my beloved Nic." Following her pattern, Kay had again chosen a much younger man. When they met, Kubly was forty-seven years old and Kay was sixty.

Once more she was in love "desperately." Once more it was a love which would "last forever." As Joseph had all the qualities Kurt Wick lacked, so Kubly was "the exact opposite of Arthur." Unlike Deshaies,

Kubly helped Kay, she said, in her strengths rather than her weaknesses. He was "big and wise and protective" and his concern was to care for her and to spare her pain. He was a writer and "famous" yet unencumbered by family. And he shared her political beliefs, having shouted "vehemently about fall-out shelters" and Berlin.

It was, this time at last, a "great and understanding love." With "Nic," unlike Arthur, Kay predicted, there "could be no feeling of anguish," not even "if he should marry." Meanwhile they attended square dances in Connecticut, where Kubly made her feel as if she were "about sixteen." Kay Boyle was ecstatic. She considered herself "deeply, deeply lucky . . . to have been permitted to find him." So strongly did she feel that she was certain that there would "be no more infidelity to torture me," as there had been with Deshaies.

And so Herbert Kubly, calling Kay Boyle "Carissima," entered the sphere of Kay Boyle's narcissism in the place which had only recently been occupied by Arthur Deshaies. Kay took on the role once more of nurturer of a younger man's talent, and of his self-esteem. To help him with a novel in progress, she put aside her own history of Germany and would even list herself as co-author of *At Large* in her Gale autobiographical memoir. Meanwhile he assured her that their friendship was the most important thing in his life, more important to him even than his novel. He told her that she was the first great artist who had applauded his talent, that she was a courageous and gallant woman. Beset as she was by fears and problems of her own, she was always there for him. She had given him the gift of believing in him. He would love her forever.

Soon Kubly was sharing with her the most intimate of her problems. He had advised her not to commit Clover because the guilt would remain with her always. He offered his opinion that Clover should accept Laurence's money, which Clover's own sense of integrity did not permit her to do. Meanwhile, Kubly told Kay Boyle he thought Joseph was "noble." He worried about her health and attacked her latest bête noire, writer Tillie Olsen, author of *Tell Me a Riddle* (1960), who irritated Kay by pleading that household responsibilities had kept her from writing, whose "tragedy," Kay would later tell Doris Grumbach, was that she was "paralyzed." Once at a dinner party of Simon & Schuster authors, someone inquired who his editor was. Kubly stopped the party conversation dead by replying, "Kay Boyle."

For her part, Kay made untiring efforts for Kubly, as she had for Deshaies. She recommended to Willard Maas that he be invited to one of the evening discussions at the Staten Island writers' conference. There were theater engagements, lunches and dinners in New York. When she gave him two plants, they named them "Eloise" and "Abelard." There was an intense weekend in Connecticut. Kay confessed to Ken McCormick that they were in love.

Clover remained ill that summer of 1962, but Kay was wrapped up in her involvement with Kubly. There was gossip about them at the MacDowell Colony. Then, one night in Connecticut, there was a "ghastly saga," which Kubly termed "Joseph trauma." Kubly professed himself to be worried about Kay and protective toward Faith and Ian. But it was over. They agreed that her name would not appear on the dedication page of his novel, that there be only a private reference to his "Carissima." Later, after she had been disappointed, she again poured out her heart to Mc-Cormick. Rumors of Kubly's homosexuality had left her feeling as if she had been betrayed.

Still later, Kay Boyle attributed the cooling of their relationship to the fact that she knew "too much about his private life and he can no longer be the man he wanted to appear, and he is very defensive and unpleasant." Indeed, she had been as possessive with this lover as she had been with Joseph and the children. She had demanded the same reassurances she had of Deshaies, and had thus reduced Kubly to echoing his predecessor and insisting that he belonged to himself first.

Kay memorialized her passion for Kubly in a poem called "A Square Dance for a Square," which was published in the *Southern Review* in July of 1965. Kubly is the poet's "sweet partner / Of men's furtive nights." He is also a man with "each ankle dragging with it ball and chain." He is a man with "a curtain" dividing his life. Kay appears as "the illicit roomer with / Brief-case and lowered girlish lids who once, in sleep, had kissed / You on the mouth." Kay had wished "to enter the back bedroom" of his "despair." And as he removed his hand from hers, she cracked "my skull, my jaw, my knee."

Later Kay dismissed the entire relationship as "a rather intense mama—little boy friendship." Kubly, she decided, was the victim of "paranoic delusions," and she was no longer "disposed to take his part." By the time it was over with Kubly, Joseph was no longer living in America. Her emotions depleted by her relationships with Deshaies and Kubly, awaiting Clover's recovery, Kay at last made plans to resume some sort of life with her husband.

Kay's visits to Clover at Hillside Hospital in Queens remained disturbing. After she left, Clover could smell her mother's Chanel No. 5 on her hands where she had touched and held Kay. Yet so angry did she remain that one day in late March of 1962, as Kay was waiting to visit her and was sitting in the doctor's office, Clover slashed her wrists.

"What are you going to do now?" the doctor asked Kay Boyle.

"Hug her," Kay Boyle promptly said.

"You should smack her in the face," Kay said the doctor told her, asserting that Clover needed discipline; he went on to applaud her for having given her daughter those two black eyes. Kay would acknowledge only that she had grown too close to Clover, the two-year-old who had remained with her when she left Laurence. It had been a mistake for her to have allowed Clover to sleep in bed with her when Joseph wasn't there.

Clover's problem, Kay thought, was that she wanted to remain her mother's little girl, and "as soon as she is required to make a life of her own, as a mature person, everything collapses."

Still in the dark, many years later, Kay would tell Faith never to confide in her children; it was the worst thing a parent can do. Of the "contradictions" in Kay, perhaps none looms larger than that a writer who had spent forty years chronicling the emotions of men and women with sensitivity should perceive so little about her own children.

Clover remained at Hillside Hospital for thirteen months. When she emerged, her mother had ceased to be a goddess. Instead she had become someone who needed to be an "idol" for others, a person who had not listened to her own daughter's needs. Demoralized by Kay's cold perfection, which Laurence too had found so maddening, Clover had turned against herself. What hurt even more was that Kay did not even realize that she had not been a nurturing mother. She had violated important psychological boundaries, invading her children's sensibilities in unwholesome ways. Laurence may have refused to admit his own responsibility, and refused to take anything seriously. But Kay had been "cold, remote and perfect." Indeed, three of her daughters, not only Apple and Clover but Bobby too, had attempted to take their own lives, as did, more than once, her step-daughter, Pegeen.

Kay Boyle, never understanding why her children felt as if they had been abandoned, remained defensive. As late as 1970, she insisted to Clover, "You were never left alone at any time," hence had not been abandoned. Kay pointed to her books, "the story of my life," as proof that "I do not beat my children with my fists when they come to me for understanding, and I do not live insensible to the feelings of others." Unconvinced, Clover would bitterly ask her mother, "What is the sense of saving the children of Biafra if you can't save your own children?"

For challenging Kay Boyle so profoundly, Clover would not be forgiven. "You have GOT to see that your concern with your own feelings has all too often kept you from considering the feelings of others," Kay admonished Clover. Kay would admit only that she could be "reproached for divorcing Papa." But she could not be reproached for "abandoning" Clover. Of that she was certain.

Trying to help her daughter, Kay told her that it was "free will" which alone could save the "individual," that exalted individual whom Kay had worshipped since the days of her mother's admiration for John Cowper Powys. It was as if Kay had never heard of the unconscious. Indeed, it was as if Sigmund Freud had yet to be born.

Meanwhile Joseph had given up. He was only fifty-one years old, but he seemed aged and frail. Bone thin, he smoked endlessly, reaching for a cigarette even before breakfast. And had anyone cared enough to notice, he was very ill. Certainly Joseph was far too demoralized to consider a second career in the Foreign Service. Joseph was not, however, wholly disenchanted with his adopted country. In the 1960 presidential race, Joseph had disliked both Kennedy and Nixon. But when Kay refused to vote for either of them, Joseph had become enraged; still he cherished his participation in American democracy. "What happens if Nixon wins by one vote?" he demanded of Kay. "It will be all your fault."

In 1961, Kay insisted that Joseph reapply for another job with the American government. Knowing Joseph would do nothing to better his situation, she took matters into her own competent hands. Drawing on an old friendship, she enlisted Will Lang at *Time/Life* in Paris to help her husband "resume work for which his talents and preferences best fit him." Then Judge Clark's son, Blair, who worked for CBS himself, told her that, on his own strong recommendation, his classmate and friend John F. Kennedy had appointed Edward R. Murrow as head of the U.S. Information Agency. Kay decided that Joseph must write to Murrow inquiring about the possibility of his rejoining the Foreign Service.

Dispirited as he was, Joseph, as always, acceded to his wife's wishes. He wrote Murrow the story of how he had been cleared of loyalty and security charges, and expressed the hope that "with the more favorable climate in our country's political life," he might "return to government service." Murrow was making a point of hiring people who had been blacklisted during the darkest moments of McCarthyism. He read Joseph's file and at once accepted him.

Kay took it as a great victory. Once more they had "beaten McCarthy and Kohn [sic] and Schine." She pronounced herself "proud and happy for Joseph," telling friends he had been given "an important post." The reality, alas, was different. Joseph had gone from the high posts he had held in Germany to being a deputy cultural attaché in some remote outpost. Certain he would be posted to the Congo or Pakistan, he drew instead the job of deputy director of a binational center in Teheran. In reply to a question on his application as to whether his wife was "enthusiastic about possibility of accompanying you overseas," Kay wrote in her own hand: "yes." In fact, she planned to join him in Teheran with Ian only the following summer.

By October, Joseph was ready to depart for Teheran. It would be, as William L. Shirer puts it, "a cruel exile." On his passport photograph Joseph appears gaunt, his face deeply lined, his eyes anguished. He no longer seems younger than his wife, who was eight years older. "We'll see you at Christmas," Arthur Deshaies boomed at Joseph's farewell party thrown by the principal of the Thomas School.

Buried in the trauma of his disillusionment with America, Joseph had been so remote a father that now, as he departed, Faith and Ian were far closer to their mother than to him. Kay was "the most profound influence" on them both. At the University of Connecticut, Ian had applied for conscientious objector status, his beliefs in keeping with his mother's pacifism. Ian wrote his speech to the draft board himself, a fact which alone made

Kay proud. When asked whether he could under any circumstances carry arms, he replied, "If my mother or my country were invaded."

Dreading the moment when he had to inform his war hero father, who had been so proud of serving America under siege, of his decision, Ian had consulted the psychiatric social worker at Hillside Hospital. "You can give each other respect," he was told. Indeed, when Ian broke the news to Joseph, his father was silent for a long five minutes. But finally Joseph put his arm around his son and said, "I respect you too."

A courtly gentleman of a bygone world, Joseph demanded that his daughter be ladylike, never wear makeup, and stay good and pure. Faith rebelled. But when Kay spoke, she listened. "I don't like that color of lipstick on you," she might say. And Kay was understanding when, after scarcely a semester, Faith wanted to drop out of Boston College. She asked only that her daughter have a plan, and suggested Faith go to Europe using the thousand dollars she had earned teaching dancing. In Paris, Faith walked into the Coupole with a man in a velvet costume, one leg orange, one green, topped by a purple smoking jacket. Enjoying the knowing glances exchanged by all, Laurence Vail introduced Faith as his "step-daughter."

In January of 1963, Faith, now nineteen, became pregnant by a married man named David Gude. She had been planning to move to Teheran along with Kay and Ian the coming summer. Everyone now counseled her to have an abortion, everyone except Kay Boyle. Abortion was "terrible," Kay said, although she had had a few herself.

Faith should have the baby, but she also had to have a husband. Disingenuously, Kay attributed this view to Joseph. She told Faith she could not disgrace her father by appearing dishonorably in Teheran with a baby while still using her maiden name. Kay even told Faith that she and her child could not be counted by the Foreign Service as Joseph's dependents unless she was married—which was not true. Kay told Faith that Joseph's name would "suffer" if she were not married; it was as if she had forgotten entirely her own bohemian life. As always, Kay spoke for her husband, expecting Joseph to bend his will to hers.

When Faith went off to Europe in quest of an old boyfriend who might marry her, Kay said, "I'm so proud of you. I knew you were going to take care of this yourself." Kay, along with Clover and Ian, went to Hoboken to see her off. Standing at the ship's rail, Faith cried out, "Mama! Mama!"

When the boyfriend would not comply, Faith fled to France and her sisters, Bobby and Kathe. All the anger they felt at Kay, whom they believed had abandoned them as surely as she had Clover and Apple, erupted. But it was directed not at their self-righteous mother, but at Faith.

"You're exactly like Mama!" they admonished Faith. "You'll bring a child into the world just like she did, and then abandon it just like Mama did with all her children. You're selfish, just like Mama." Her sisters advised her to have an abortion.

"Marry me!" Laurence offered. "That would be fantastic. It would mean that all your sisters would become your stepdaughters. Your mother would never live it down!"

Kay soon summoned Faith home, informing her that Joseph didn't want her "living off my ex-husband." But when Faith wrote, telling her father she was pregnant, Joseph's reply was so warm that she doubted he could ever have said he didn't want her living off Laurence. He would always love her; she would always be his daughter, Joseph told Faith. But bending to her mother's wishes, Faith married a friend of Ian's named Jesse Ferland purely for his name. (Later Ferland wanted to be a real husband to Faith, and even attempted to gain custody of the child who was not his. These dilemmas Kay Boyle would leave to her daughter to resolve.)

Kay planned to take Clover, Ian, and Faith to Teheran, and now she ordered Joseph to find suitable universities in Iran for Ian. Whatever Faith or Clover might do, there was never any question of Ian's not going to Teheran with her, even when Joseph reported that Ian could not attend the University of Teheran without knowing Farsi.

By November of 1962, Joseph was already exhausted by his new assignment of running the American center. He lived in a hotel, and was too poor even to pay for a hunting license. Running the "queer shop" all by himself, Joseph found his work "nervewracking." He taught adult education courses at night and worked fourteen hours a day. Joseph also chafed under the USIA policy of attempting to convince local intellectuals that "Russia was bad." He violated the rules by discussing taboo topics, from Russia to the Shah, in his room late at night. For relaxation, he played chess at the Iran-America Society.

Joseph had also fallen ill within a month of his arrival. Constant diarrhea confined him to a diet of soup and oatmeal. He had a bad stiff neck, was losing weight, was very weak, and all his ailments were complicated by loneliness. "I feel lonely with no music, no Boo, no Mouse and no Fifi," he sweetly wrote his son. He reported that he attended a concert where many people in the audience were coughing—including himself.

Finally Kay noticed that the handwriting in Joseph's letters was shaky. "Do you think he's become an alcoholic?" she asked.

By December, having lost more weight, Joseph would still not see a doctor. But a viciously painful attack on Christmas Day suggested he might need to have his appendix out. The crisis passed. He wrote Kay that he lived for letters from his family. Mousie wrote how sad it made her to think of her poor father alone and sick in Teheran.

One night Joseph dreamed he was in a big hall. Thousands of people sat around him. Suddenly, in a double bed, he discovered Kay and Howard Nemerov together. Caught by her husband in this act of sexual betrayal, Kay laughed and said, "Don't be angry, Joseph!" Then Joseph "fell into a bottomless pit." That Joseph was hurt and bewildered by Kay's need for other men was apparent. "The men," as Faith called them, peopled his unconscious mind, and were actors in his nightmares, now exacerbated by fever and delirium. By March, Joseph was so ill that he agreed to fly to Tel Aviv to see a doctor about what he had concluded was arthritis. Then, ever the dreamer, he had his wallet stolen containing all his identity papers and three hundred and fifty dollars. Sending most of his money home to Kay, he had scarcely enough to survive.

Meanwhile, fellow-in-residence at Wesleyan University in Connecticut, Kay was awarded an honorary degree. "The Soldier Ran Away" was dramatized on *The U.S. Steel Hour* in April. Kay appeared on public television on *Books for Our Time* discussing *Babbitt*. Watching, her admirer Bill Shirer found her looking "very pretty." Kay also introduced a friend she had made at MacDowell, James Baldwin, at the Y. She taught one night a week at the New School. Her "mission" as a teacher at universities, she now said, was "to save the creative writer from academia." She, the least introspective of writers, told interviewers she wrote as "a process of self-analysis." But when people asked Kay if she had ever been psychoanalyzed, she replied, "After you've written thirty books, you don't need it." When friends wished to meet her in New York now, she told them they could find her on picket lines for integration or peace.

By the early sixties, Kay had come fully into her own as a political woman. Politics became in the sixties the perfect arena for her self-dramatization. On these picket lines she could become heroine of her own life. She was among the very first writers to declare herself against the Vietnam War. She was less the writer than the activist now.

In its January-February 1963 issue, *Story* magazine published "Should Be Considered Extremely Dangerous," which had been rejected so many times by commercial magazines. A careless melodrama about a boy living on a cove like Wilson Cove and a young "criminal" who takes him hostage, the story is ill-conceived and laden with improbability. Kay had given a lecture at La Salle College on the "vanishing short story," blaming the academic "analytical approach" for its demise. Reflecting her own new identity, she called for a renaissance of the short story in keeping with the social changes she saw developing in the early sixties. She seemed unperturbed by the distinct falling off of her art.

That spring of 1963 Malcolm Cowley wrote a text for *Esquire* to accompany a photograph of "The Last of the Lost Generation." Kay Boyle appears in that picture in her white earrings. Her hair is dyed black, her mouth open in laughter. She was, Cowley writes, "the baby of the group," looking "more Latin than Irish," and rather like "an admired diva who has passed in a moment from a fit of scorn to an outburst of hilarity." From Paris days, Cowley remembered Kay as "a rather elfin creature." Now he expressed astonishment at all she had accomplished.

In June of 1963, Kay and Ian sailed for Teheran. From the boat, Kay wrote Marianne Moore that she expected to be gone "a number of years."

The producer of a film she saw on board turned out to be a man named David Ffolkes, who owed her option money. Kay at once dashed off a letter to Mike Watkins, who had taken over the agency from his mother. Unlike Ann, however, he chafed under Kay's constant demands. When the SS *Exeter* docked in Marseilles, Kay was reunited with Bobby and Kathe, whom she had not seen for nearly a decade.

Arriving in Teheran, Kay was startled by the transformation in Joseph's appearance. At first she did not recognize him, so much did he resemble a "walking skeleton." Within a day of Kay's arrival, Joseph was hospitalized, having developed sudden paralysis in his right arm and leg. Nor could he find the appropriate words to express what he wanted to say. The Teheran doctors concluded he had had a mild stroke and ordered that he be sent to the U.S. Army hospital at Landstühl, in Germany.

In great pain, Joseph managed to tell his Fifi that he didn't like her hair dyed black. As soon as she could, Kay bought herself a grey wig.

Late into the night of the day of his arrival at Landstühl, Joseph's head was X-rayed. On July 5, he was operated on for three hours for a brain tumor. Kay settled in a room on the ground floor of a wooden barracks for transient guests. MP jeeps patrolled. Taps sounded in the mornings. She took her meals at a snack bar and discovered four of her books in the Army library.

As Joseph lay in the ward for the most serious cases, Kay saw him at mealtimes and fed him herself. Otherwise, she sat in the library and did research on her history of Germany. Soon Joseph seemed to be recovering, and his complexion grew more ruddy. His eyes cleared. Kay began to hope that the worst was over.

But a few days later, the doctors told her that the malignant brain tumor was merely "a cell cast off by another cancer somewhere in his body which travelled through the bloodstream to his brain." More X rays and tests were ordered. Now Kay returned to Teheran to pack up their belongings and collect Ian. Competent as always, she instructed Ian to arrange rabies shots for their cats Schnibby and Pinky and a box in which they could travel back to America by freight. Kay and Ian would return to America together and join Joseph, whom the Army was sending to Walter Reed Hospital in Washington, D.C.

By now Kay knew she must secure a teaching job in America for herself for the fall semester. She would be the sole support of her family. She enlisted Howard Nemerov to help her navigate the shoals of academe. Indeed, her courage grew with each frightful and lonely moment. She arranged for the Countess Esterházy to visit Joseph while he remained in Germany. "We will meet things as we come to them," she told Ian. "Life is beginning for all of us."

Waiting in Teheran for the plane that would carry her back to America, Kay sat up deep into the night typing children's stories about her cat, which would be published as *Pinky, the Cat Who Liked to Sleep* in 1966 and

Pinky in Persia in 1968. These charming stories revealed Kay Boyle's great affection for cats, as well as a capacity to imagine how animals think. It was an affection so deep that some years later a friend said that the only time he ever heard Kay Boyle cry was when her cat Dopey died, Dopey a cat she had hooked up for intravenous feeding when it could no longer eat, a cat she believed contained the soul of her dead mother.

By July 26 Kay had taken a furnished room in Washington across from Walter Reed Hospital. She fed Joseph his meals, and even berated him in the old way, complaining if he got egg on his pajama jacket. Concerned for his morale, she secretly sent friends his hospital address, knowing he loved to receive mail directly at the hospital. Still Joseph did not know the severity of his illness, and was not aware that some doctors had even suggested that Kay take him home because "time is so short."

Confined to her furnished room, Kay wrote a piece about skiing for *Glamour* to make a quick six hundred dollars. "I am keeping my sanity by working hard," she told her agent, as she accepted an assignment from *Holiday* on German writers. Kay and Ian both participated in the great civil rights march on Washington that August of 1963 and heard Martin Luther King give his "I have a dream" address. Kay pictured herself that Wednesday demonstrating, as she put it, "with all men of good will." Then she wrote an article about the march, which her agent tried, unsuccessfully, to sell to A. J. Muste at *Liberation* magazine.

Kay became depressed and anxious, however, when no teaching job materialized despite the efforts of Nemerov, Paul Horgan at Wesleyan, and John Malcolm Brinnin at Radcliffe. When Herbert Wilner at San Francisco State College offered Kay a job teaching creative writing, she could not afford to turn him down, although California was a long way for Joseph to travel. Her salary would be only $12,396, with full professor status. Nor, despite her rank and distinction, would her schedule be light at this jerry-built school which looked like a series of Quonset huts arbitrarily thrown down on an abandoned lot. Kay Boyle would teach three courses, one of which, short story writing, met in the evening. But on the faculty with her would be such distinguished writers as Wright Morris, Ray B. West, and Mark Harris. Ian could be admitted as the son of a faculty member.

Joseph had begun to walk on the hospital grounds and to swim in the hospital pool. Kay tried to believe he was holding his own. Her friends rallied and Kathryn Hulme sent her a check. Apple wrote in her *précieuse* way that "tragedy is trying to tell us that we must speak out to one another, and say all that we believe." Kay now viewed Apple as the daughter who was "so like Clover." Warmhearted Janet Flanner sent Kay a check to use for "*yourself*," writing in praise of "noble, good, kind, hardworking Joseph" who "did not merit what he has reaped."

By September, Kay knew that Joseph was not going to get well. She read aloud to her husband from Romain Gary's *The Roots of Heaven*, saying she loved the "absolutely limitless freedom of the thought that the elephants, not us, are the roots of heaven." Alone, she mourned Joseph. She was sixty-one years old. Carson McCullers and Marianne Moore had both praised her "stamina." But Kay felt she was "too old to start over again in a new place." Then, summoning her formidable will, she determined that this not be true.

Early that September, Kay and Joseph spent a few days at Clover's loft in New York, where Mousie awaited the birth of her baby. Herbert Kubly visited and was shaken when he saw how frail Joseph had become. On September 6, it was Kay and not Joseph who answered a telephone call from Memorial Sloan-Kettering Hospital, where he had undergone more tests. Joseph had cancer of the right lung and more brain tumors. No treatment was possible. He would not live out the year.

During a farewell party, amid the drinking and the attempts at cheer, Mousie whispered to Kay, "Mom, I'm in labor."

"Oh, you good girl," Kay said, "I knew you'd have this baby while I was in town." As Faith suffered excruciating pain, she asked Kay how she could have had so many children. "Because you forget," was the response. But then, it was as if Kay didn't believe her daughter really was in labor, because she turned back to the party, ignoring Faith. Faith had to ask Clover what to do, and finally she called the baby's father, David Gude, who was married to the daughter of the painter Thomas Hart Benton.

"Get him out of here! I don't want him staying here," Joseph demanded, hating the irresponsible man who had impregnated both Jessie Benton, his wife, and Mousie.

"It's her hour. Let her have what she wants," Kay said. But when Faith's water broke, and it seemed she would have her baby right there in the loft, Kay became hysterical. Frantic, as she prepared to head for the hospital, she clapped on her grey wig backwards. When the lights went out suddenly, Kay concluded that all the lights in New York City had gone out, and there would be no electricity for Faith's delivery. By the time Kay got to the hospital, at four in the morning that September 10, Geordie Gude had been born.

When Joseph suffered an attack of convulsions from his brain tumors, Kay was certain he would not survive. But two days later, on September 12, Kay and Joseph flew to San Francisco. An ambulance met the plane, carrying Joseph to the Army's Letterman Hospital.

Joseph Franckenstein's final days were spent in unendurable agony. He weighed only one hundred thirty pounds now and could no longer walk. He was, Kay mournfully reported, "like a dead bird to touch." Cancer of the larynx had closed his throat so that he could no longer eat. Feeding him, Kay said, was "the most refined of cruelties." His nasal passages closed.

Joseph was frightened now. He clung to Kay "like a lost child," she said. With every passing day, his pain became "more acute." In search of comfort for her desperately suffering husband, praying even that he would die before his suffering went beyond endurance, Kay wrote to his USIA colleague Keith W. Bailes. Kay urged that he write Joseph telling him that his colleagues missed him. "It would be a great happiness to him," Kay pleaded. (Bailes did write: "it would require entirely too much space to list the many friends who have inquired about you"—a letter dated the day of Joseph's death.)

Kay was shocked when Joseph, fearing damnation, suddenly asked for a priest. On Kathryn Hulme's recommendation, a Franciscan father came to see Joseph—only to tell him, Kay would report, that he had been living in sin for twenty-three years and was suffering so much because he had married a twice-divorced woman.

"But you will not go to hell," this priest reassured him. "God has punished you for this sin by giving you so much agony. But you have paid your debt and you will go to heaven." To Kay's astonishment, Joseph, returning to the beliefs of his youth, was comforted.

At ten o'clock on the night of October 7, Kay, exhausted, left the hospital. Joseph Franckenstein died alone, and later Kay berated herself for having "failed" Joseph, for not having been there all that night as he lay dying.

Kay saw to it that Joseph had a full military funeral, with many pallbearers, and farewell taps, which she said all but broke her heart. Ever conscious of the symbols of her husband's vindication, Kay requested that the State Department send a representative to the funeral. No one, she was told, was available. Joseph Franckenstein was buried in Golden Gate National Cemetery near San Bruno, deeply enough so that when the time came, his wife's coffin could be placed on top of his.

"Poor, sweet Joe," Ann Lochner wrote Kay, "with his smile, and his easy-going tolerant way." Bobby wrote to her mother of Kay's own courage: "through every pain you must always come out stronger and more admirable than before." Apple wept whenever her mother's name was mentioned. Kathe responded as Clover and Apple had before her: she wished she "could take some of your unhappiness on me," she wrote her Mimi. "I should want you to be my daughter instead of my mother." Mousie wrote a poem:

> *The day my father died I cut my hair.*
> *Sawing ruthlessly huge hunks*
> *'Till my feet seemed weightless*
> *Uplifted by blond clouds of childhood.*

When John Kennedy was assassinated that November, Kay watched the funeral on television, and "the throb of the drums" brought back to her all the "pain of Joseph's death and his funeral."

28

The Finished Woman

Perhaps when I'm in the sixties or seventies I can go in for
leisurely friendships and not just momentary glimpses.

I'm madly in love.

The best of Kay Boyle's writing life was over. Now, as a woman of age, her life became even more her art. There had, of course, never been any true distinction between the two: personal experiences had always been the stuff of her tales, while in her writing Kay attained a level of truth and honesty she did not always maintain in her life. Now she created a model of the woman of age living life fully and freely. She would make no concession to the fact that as a woman past sixty she was not expected to be sexually attractive. Moreover, she would live as a politically committed citizen with a deep social conscience, expecting her words and her actions to be heeded despite her age and gender.

Reed slim, her deep-set blue eyes expressing her serious interest in any companion, Kay Boyle moved into her sixties and seventies a beautiful, passionate, and vital woman, ageless in her energy, and with as full an appetite for risk as ever. While Peggy Guggenheim wrote nostalgically to Djuna Barnes of how she missed "the twenties and everything that reminds me of it," Kay had allied herself with her own and her country's future. Indeed, men were as drawn to her as ever.

You always knew where her center was, Leo Litwak, her colleague at San Francisco State, would say. She seemed a finished woman, neither weak nor clinging, but emotionally self-sufficient. Yet she also seemed vulnerable, as she warmed to a man's protectiveness. And she remained as accomplished a flatterer as Katherine Evans Boyle had been before her. She especially enjoyed telling the story of how once Dustin Hoffman had visited and drunk wine with her and Ian. At the end of the evening, standing on the stairs, he took her hands in his and said, "You're a beautiful woman. I'd like to make love to you." At the time she was nearly seventy.

Immediately she made Joseph an icon. She told James T. Farrell she didn't know "how one starts life over again after losing someone who was all that Joseph was." The reality of their last years was best forgotten.

Indeed, within a month of Joseph's death, Kay Boyle had rallied. In front of the children, she kept her grief to herself, although she told Caresse she could not "bear it that he is dead." Before October was out, she had organized a scholarship fund in Joseph's name at the Thomas School. With Joseph's insurance and death benefits, she purchased an elegant four-story house in San Francisco a few blocks from Haight Street. Not yet the gathering ground of sixties hippies, it was the "Negro section" and that, Kay said, was why she chose it. "Until the residential pattern changes in our country," she said, "there can be no true integration." Indeed, a week after Joseph's death, Kay Boyle appeared on the "Women Today" page of the *San Francisco Examiner*. Her hair dyed black, wearing a sleeveless pleated yellow dress, she announced that she hoped her purchase of a house in the "Negro quarter" would "give a shot in the arm to the cause of equality."

The house was lovely, a gingerbread Victorian with two sets of Corinthian columns flanking the front door, and a large bowed second-story window overlooking Frederick Street. There was stained glass, and floors inset with pink and mauve mosaic tiles. Kay would occupy the attic, which she converted to her private apartment, complete with a kitchen. Her windows overlooked the city roofs, she said, reminding her of Paris. Downstairs the place was partitioned into apartments, which she planned to rent out to students. Ian's quarters would be in the basement, Faith's on the second floor.

There, Kay hoped, Faith would live with David Gude, whom she referred to as Faith's "husband," although, of course, he was still married to someone else. Meanwhile she had begun teaching; at once she paid off the bills left from Clover's studies at Bennington. Her old admirer Dr. Lehfeldt sent Kay the message that she had "a great full life ahead of her." He needn't have bothered. Kay Boyle was a survivor.

Kay's seventy students the first semester discovered the anomaly of the elegant teacher in what looked like a black suit designed in Paris carrying a black leather attaché case, using always a fine fountain pen, and teaching in the shabby, low-slung barracks of their campus. She was the hardest-working, although the oldest, of all their teachers, and she shared the fruits of her long experience. "You should be both humble and proud," she told future editor and creative writing teacher Gordon Lish in 1963, "humility and pride should always go together, as Faulkner never ceased pointing out." It became an event to be in her class. There was only one requirement for creative writing students to earn her interest and her praise: you had to be politically committed in your stories.

As far as Kay was concerned, life was to be lived. A bout with pneumonia in the winter of 1964 didn't prevent her from agreeing to return for another Staten Island writers' conference. If her writing seemed didactic, she kept on writing. When she broke her ankle, she put her mattress on the floor and the typewriter next to it, and crawled to the typewriter to meet what she said was a deadline. And it was always action, not introspection, to which she turned to alleviate her loneliness and depression. When she was asked at a reading when one writes poetry, she replied, "When one is in love, or is moved by social injustice."

Apologetic, as always, for her poetry, admitting she was unable to "write about 'issues' and still keep it, or make it poetry," she persisted and wrote "A Poem About the Jews," dedicated to another of her heroes, A. J. Muste, the pacifist editor of *Liberation.* The poem culminates in the sailors dragging the Pearl River outside Philadelphia, Mississippi, in search of the bodies of James Chaney, a black, and two Jews, Andrew Goodman and Michael Schwerner, who had been murdered for their participation in civil rights work in Mississippi during the summer of 1964. "Can we say the history is done?" the poet demands to know. In 1965 Kay Boyle was to lead a campaign to garner the Nobel Peace Prize for Muste.

"A strange and rather exciting journey seems about to materialize," she told Howard Nemerov. "I do hope you haven't been hired by CIA to foment a free verse uprising in Dahomey, or disseminate bourgeois formalism behind the Bead Curtain," Nemerov teased her. She traveled in a chartered airplane to Neah Bay in Washington State with Marlon Brando, James Baldwin, Charlton Heston, and Paul Jacobs to participate in a "fish-in" on behalf of Indian fishing rights. Later Kay reported that Marlon Brando was "a sincere and dedicated man who does his homework on the issues he's involved in, and he's pretty attractive too."

By 1964 she was protesting against the American presence in Vietnam, picketing the mortuary, the California Funeral Service, where the bodies of dead American soldiers were being returned from Vietnam. Every morning for several weeks, dressed all in black, Kay Boyle walked slowly back and forth, outside the mortuary. She carried no sign, she said, because "this is not a protest, nor is it anything political; it is simply a vigil." Although she told reporters she marched alone, Kay liked always to have a male escort, and would often appropriate Herb Wilner. Wilner would don his blue suit, his wife Nancy remembers, and off they would go. Kay also enlisted Jessica Mitford, until a reporter wondered whether Mitford's presence as the author of *The American Way of Death* meant that this particular mortuary was found wanting.

She was even ready to take up the cudgel for a former lover. In an angry letter she decried *Time* magazine's review of Herbert Kubly's *The Whistling Zone* with its implication that the author "was a sexual pervert." It was, Kay Boyle declared, a "malicious attack . . . in no way prompted by incidents in the book itself."

With Cesar Chavez's farm workers, Kay marched from Delano to Modesto, one hundred fifty hot miles on a melting asphalt highway, wearing thin tennis shoes, never once complaining. As she believed a woman of any age would be most fulfilled to the degree that she was committed to something beyond the self, so, as ever, Kay Boyle had no patience for intellectual arguments. She knew what was right. She acted. In these years, she was fearless. When someone stole her yellow jeep, which she had left with the motor running on Haight Street, she ran after the car and, trying to block its way, was tossed up onto the hood. Later she marched into the neighborhood drug clinic in the hope of discovering exactly who that man was.

In the same spirit she organized the San Francisco chapter of Amnesty International. Every year there was to be a benefit on her birthday—February 19—at which writers read the work of political prisoners, or their own. It became one of the events of the San Francisco social season. "She doesn't teach us how to grow old. She teaches us how to live," her friend Hank McGuckin, a professor whose father had been a Wobbly and who sang the "Internationale" at those parties, said. Having visited a woman of ninety-two one day, Kay Boyle emerged saying, "If I ever talk about my health, shoot me. It's boring."

The contradictions to which Kay Boyle had always been prey multiplied, however. Always insisting that she was free of bourgeois expectations, Kay suddenly forbade Faith to live with David Gude until he was legally divorced from Jessie Benton. "I have his baby! What are you talking about?" Faith demanded of her mother.

"Absolutely not. You can't!" Kay insisted, as she got Faith her own apartment on Tenth Street in New York. The two had just driven cross-country so that Kay could attend the Wagner College writers' conference. As soon as her mother's back was turned, Faith did as she pleased. Meanwhile, her hair impeccable in a blue rinse, so that with the light from behind she seemed to have an aura, Kay was a dominant presence at the conference.

"You're going to love Kay. She's very flirtatious," poet Kenneth Koch told a twenty-two-year-old Ron Padgett. The first time Padgett saw Kay Boyle she was introducing a reading by one of the teachers, a "surprisingly tall, regal even," woman, with her head held high, "topped with a pale blue aureole."

"It gives me great *pleasure* to introduce today's reader," Kay Boyle said matter-of-factly. But she was sparkling, like a glass of champagne in a pale blue goblet, Padgett thought, a woman who expressed her pleasure in living simply in the way she stood, dressed up, a finished woman. One evening Koch gave her one of his poems to read. The next morning he found slipped under his door a note from Kay Boyle, an appreciative response.

Each day, her students wrote and each night she returned their manuscripts covered with comments in purple ink. Young David Shapiro thought she looked like Barbara Stanwyck in *The Lady Eve*. Koch concluded Kay had the effect of making people better than they were. If she had a high opinion of you, you became nobler because she thought you were good. Like most men, Koch responded to her aristocratic air of command, which came leavened with such ingratiating vulnerability. Kay seemed to be having a good time, and so others did too.

That same summer of 1964 she ran fortuitously into Samuel Beckett, who was in New York making a film with Buster Keaton, a twenty-minute short called *Film*, in a Spanish restaurant on Charles Street. Kay strode up to Beckett and introduced Koch as a "brilliant young poet." Nervously Beckett spilled his drink. "Sam is nervous with new people," Kay told Koch knowingly, although she had met the man only twice in her life. Keaton, who had silently drifted off to another table, seemed to Kay only a "very fat" man in red suspenders. (Keaton, now in his sixties, was hardly "fat," although he did have a little potbelly.)

With Herbert Kubly replacing her at San Francisco State, during the autumn of 1964 Kay was a fellow at the Radcliffe Institute. Her project was her German history, but she was at a loss, thinking she might try to follow Goethe's definition of history as "the voice of the people speaking through the centuries." Finally she sought the help of Erich Kahler at Princeton, who had written *Man the Measure*. When Ken McCormick asked for a manuscript by May of 1965 for the book that was now four years late, Kay's feelings were ruffled. At once McCormick apologized and they settled on July.

The woman who had grown up in luxury, and had lived well all her life in Europe, now eschewed the trappings of wealth. In Cambridge, Kay found herself in a rented apartment strewn with garbage and broken furniture; quickly she moved to a furnished room. From now on, most of what she earned would go to her grown children, as if she were attempting to compensate in money for what she had failed to offer in nurture. That June she had borrowed five hundred dollars from Nemerov, which went at once to Clover. Apple too was always in need. It was then that Kay Boyle, apparently forgetting the horror she had expressed when she examined McAlmon's papers at Yale, decided to sell her own, first to Syracuse, then to Yale. Finally she settled on Southern Illinois University, where her friend Harry T. Moore taught. In 1964, all her royalties earned her only a meager $4,993.93. It didn't matter. Her life had been pared down, and it was only for her children that she needed money.

That September, a misadventure of Kay's made all the New York newspapers. The original and two carbon copies of the first hundred pages of her history of Germany were stolen from her car along with her clothes, and her checkbooks in the glove compartment. She had been on her way to deliver copies to Watkins and McCormick. "I suspect Mary McCarthy!" her friend Nelson Algren wrote her mischievously, invoking a literary rival. Kay paid for an advertisement in the New York *Daily News*, which produced a telephone call from a man who had "found" the material beside a garbage pail in Chelsea. The papers were returned to the office of Mike Watkins, who paid the reward, no questions asked.

A memorial service was held at the Thomas School for Joseph Franckenstein on the first anniversary of his death. Kay related the story of his life, "in the far-off, barbaric days of the late forties and early fifties, known as the McCarthy era." Generously she praised Miss Thomas and Mrs. Opie for making the Thomas School "an American hearth and heart to him." She spoke too of Joseph's loyalty, how he was "not accustomed to seeing people change their houses, their cars, their clothes, their shoes, their hats, their schools, and, at times, their convictions, quite so frequently" as they did in America. "I believe it must be the concern of all of us who cherished what he was to see that his name and his spirit do not die," she concluded.

Her time at Cambridge was leavened by the visits of friends, including Bill Shirer, who one night got down on his knees and declared that he had loved her all his life.

"Get up, Bill," Kay ordered, amused, if not surprised. Then, to his embarrassment, Shirer discovered he could not quite get up. Amid peals of laughter, Kay related the incident to her children.

At Harvard too, Kay Boyle met Robert Lowell, whom she accused of "running a literary Gestapo," using *The New York Review of Books* with his wife, Elizabeth Hardwick, as a "weapon . . . damning and praising as they see fit, without objectivity." It was, of course, exactly what she had done and was doing with her own pantheon.

From the loneliness and depression she was feeling in the late fall of 1964, she was revived by the news of the eruption of the Free Speech movement on the Berkeley campus. "My heart is with them," Kay Boyle immediately responded. In a letter to *The New York Times* in response to an article by Sidney Hook, Kay defended the civil disobedience of the young radicals. "It is the old and the wise who must bear the greater share of the failure and the blame," she said.

Faith gave birth to her second child, whom she named Clotilde, accomplishing for Laurence what none of his own daughters had done, a memorializing of his beloved sister. Kay reconciled herself to her daughter's continuing unmarried state, addressing her as "Mrs. David Gude." Meanwhile her own career as a writer continued apace. Kindly Ken McCormick pushed forward the deadline of the history of Germany to January of 1966, while Kay's best story of the sixties, "One Sunny Morning," about integration, sold to *The Saturday Evening Post* for a healthy twenty-five hundred dollars. Harry T. Moore wrote a preface to the reissue of *Plagued by the Nightingale*, contrasting Kay with the proletarian writers of the thirties, and concluding that the social bias of the decade had prevented her novels from gaining widespread approval. Acknowledging that her reputation rested on the short stories, he argued, quixotically, that "Kay Boyle the novelist . . . be reevaluated," beginning with *Plagued*, "a first-rate novel that has been too long overlooked."

In May of 1965 Kay appeared on CBS's *Camera Three* in a discussion of "new German writing." Her face seemed long and thin, her cheekbones high and prominent; her hair remained black. She wore a white turtleneck and a dark suit, her only adornment seashell-white earrings. In a high-pitched girlish voice and affected accents (she pronounced "chance" as "chahnce"), Kay Boyle asked the young writers Günter Grass, Uwe Johnson, and Reinhard Lettau how politics affected their work. Emotionally, she declared that Madison Avenue corrupts our language just as the Nazis destroyed the German language. Gently, the young writers rejected the extremes of the analogy. But ingratiating, a beautiful woman of no certain age, Kay Boyle came across as deeply involved in the literary and political issues of her time, a woman seemingly devoid of vanity and egotism.

In June, still in the East, Kay Boyle joined a delegation of writers to confront Adlai Stevenson at the U.S. Mission to the United Nations on the subject of Vietnam. Their goal was to make Stevenson resign in protest against American policy. Stevenson's face was flushed, Kay later remembered, his jowls "bluish," as he seemed to be suffering. At the end of the meeting, Kay told Stevenson they had no one else to whom to turn in their "outrage and despair." President Johnson did not heed their voices; McNamara, Rusk, and Bundy were "totally deaf" to their pleas. As she spoke, emotional as always, Kay felt as if she were not going to be able to stop herself from crying. Then, looking into her eyes, Stevenson, who had only a short time to live, said, "I am going to act for you, here in my capacity as ambassador to the United Nations."

Disappointed, Kay Boyle was about to conclude that the diplomat had triumphed over the man when suddenly Stevenson looked at them, spread his hands out, and asked, "But how are we going to get out of Vietnam?" As soon as the meeting was over, Kay wrote to Stevenson, deploring his unwillingness "to act politically for us, for yourself, in this tragic moment in our country's history." No cause touched Kay as Vietnam did, as in that year she had ballots printed at her own expense which she urged friends to sign and mail to Lyndon Johnson expressing their horror of the war. "I cannot believe or bear what is happening in Vietnam," Kay told Nemerov.

In August, she set out for the MacDowell Colony to spend a quiet month completing the last two chapters of the history of Germany. But she was not to meet that long overdue obligation, not then or later. Instead, at age sixty-three, she fell in love.

Once more she was swept away; once more she had met a man who brought her happiness and a "freedom of feelings" she had not dreamed were possible. Within weeks Kay Boyle was certain that the new love she had found was permanent. Immediately she shared the news of her new love with Faith, who told her mother, "There must indeed be a very very very potent nectar in MacDowell soup."

Fifty-seven-year-old Robert Gessner was a brilliant man and writer, who, at twenty-three, had burst on the literary scene with *Massacre*, a powerful investigative book about Indian reservations in the genre of James Agee's *Let Us Now Praise Famous Men*. The year was 1931. By the late thirties, Gessner had become politically close to the Communist Party and was writing for *New Masses*. His politics were not all that different from Kay Boyle's when she had signed all those petitions. Gessner went on to write more books, *Treason*, a novel about Benedict Arnold, and *Some of My Best Friends Are Jews*, in 1935, another strong investigative report, this time about the plight of the Jews of Europe. He also wrote poetry and won a prize for a collection called *Upsurge*.

When he met Kay Boyle, Gessner was a professor at New York University, where he would go on to create their film studies program. A pioneer in the advocacy of film as an art form and in promoting it as an academic subject, he was the author of the seminal film study *The Moving Image*. To such brilliant students as Martin Scorsese, Gessner taught concepts like "visual literacy" and "shot awareness" and told them that their films "must not be theatrical." "Have a vision, have a philosophy of life," Scorsese remembers Gessner telling them. "If you have nothing to say, forget it!"

Gessner was a big, handsome man of enormous charm and worldliness, a man with a playful sense of humor, who enjoyed women. Indeed, he had the reputation of being something of a womanizer, being the veteran of affairs with the writer Martha Gellhorn and the actress Nina Foch. A marriage of three decades was finally ending.

He was unquestionably a man in Kay Boyle's style, a flamboyant, hard-drinking man, full of energy and vitality, a man with a history of political commitments, and one who remained immensely attractive. He had grown a bit portly, his curly brown hair having turned to salt and pepper. But he was still dynamic, a fast talker, and a worldly man who presented himself as being free and available.

Indeed, Kay was smitten. Gessner appealed to her as a man of ideas worth expressing. In the model of Arthur Deshaies, he was also a man a woman could not easily control. Flirtatiously, Gessner encouraged Kay's obvious interest in him. She had a penchant for visiting cemeteries. Together they knelt down and brushed aside a blanket of leaves from Willa Cather's tombstone. Kay Boyle was a renowned literary figure and Gessner was impressed.

Knowing she was no longer young, Kay attempted to seduce Gessner, as she had Kubly, by telling him she would help him with the novel with which he was struggling. She introduced him to her famous friends, like Caresse Crosby, to whose castle in Italy, Roccasinabalda, Kay urged Gessner to repair in October, as a houseguest if he couldn't pay, to complete his novel during a sabbatical leave. "There is a very pleasant film-writer here," Kay began in her first description of Gessner to Caresse. "He is extremely nice and is considered a brilliant man in experimental cinema." Kay encouraged Gessner to take himself more seriously, as she had Arthur Deshaies and Nic Kubly before him. She would rescue him, restore him to himself as a novelist, find him an agent, a publisher. Meanwhile she regaled him with stories of her exciting past as a veteran of twenties Paris, describing her first meeting with Ernest Walsh. Kay took to calling Gessner "Bobby."

Not since Laurence Vail had a man helped Kay Boyle with *her* work. Gessner at once offered to edit the foundering history of Germany. In the cocoon of MacDowell, they made love. "I'm madly in love," Kay confessed to Bill Shirer; as always, she announced to friends when she had fallen in love. "I know I shouldn't be." Shirer, who remained "a little bit in love" with Kay Boyle himself, was worried. But he held his tongue.

By the end of August, Kay had announced her forthcoming marriage. There was no more talk of Gessner's going off to Caresse's romantic Italian castle without her. Instead they would go there together the following summer. By September, Clover and Faith had blessed their mother's forthcoming marriage.

Then Gessner went off to Cork, where he was on the jury of the film festival, and Kay returned to San Francisco, where she was tear-gassed at a Berkeley teach-in. "I am exceedingly happy and quite foolishly in love," she confessed to Nemerov, revealing that after the fall semester she hoped to find a way of quitting teaching entirely. She and Bob would leave "for other parts," spending first the spring and summer again at MacDowell.

In New York in October, Gessner suffered a heart attack. Faith went to visit him in the hospital with flowers and a book of poetry Kay had lent her which she thought "Bob might enjoy . . . because it had your name written on it." Kay herself flew to New York on the twenty-second to celebrate Gessner's birthday the following day. They seemed ill-matched to some, she formal, reserved, a stern, regal figure with her hair tinted blue and her heavy white ceramic earrings, he a playful man with a strong Jewish sense of humor, while Kay seemed to many to have no sense of humor at all.

Kay had hoped he would soon join her in San Francisco; the doctors forbade it. But Kay and Gessner planned now to spend three months in the spring at Ossabaw Island off the coast of Georgia. There each would pursue his art; there they would live as man and wife. The trip to Ossabaw will "be the real beginning of our life," Kay exulted. Photographer Diane Arbus, Nemerov's sister, ran into the couple and reported that Gessner was "a most attractive man."

Kay had to return to San Francisco. But she planned to be back in New York in early December to marry Gessner. Meanwhile she wrote him poetry. In "A Poem of Love" she plants a palm tree for Gessner, and reminds him of it "once when we awoke," commemorating their sexual life.

In "Thunder Storm in South Dakota for R.G.," written during Gessner's trip to Cork, Kay awakens lonely, reaching out her hand in an "alien motel bed." She seeks "the pulse that skips so lightly in your wrist," suggesting Gessner's weak heart. The sounds of the South Dakota night seem distant from the rain, which is falling "gentle as tears, in Ireland where you are." The speaker is a woman deeply in love and bereft without her lover. In its passion this poem demands that a woman of sixty-three be accepted as sexually appealing, as vital, as loving, as a woman of any age.

Meanwhile Kay asked Mike Watkins to represent Gessner, cautioning him not to say anything about their relationship because it made "for complications with his wife," now ill. That there might be some ambiguity about Gessner's abandoning his sick, albeit estranged wife, and immediately remarrying, seems not to have occurred to her. In December, Kay still spoke of traveling the coming summer to Caresse's *castello* "with a man I love," worrying only about the stairs, given Gessner's heart condition.

But when Kay returned to New York after her classes were over, she discovered that Gessner had taken up with another woman. On December 27, Kay threw a party. Gessner never arrived. The following day he called with the lame excuse that he had been snowbound on Long Island with an eighty-five-year-old uncle. At once she told friends that they would not be going to Ossabaw Island because she had not yet finished her history of Germany. Kay now had no choice but to ask Herb Wilner to take her back at San Francisco State for the coming semester. To save face, she told everyone she and Gessner would return to MacDowell in the summer.

If she still entertained hopes, Gessner soon let Kay know not only that he had another woman but that she was a priority. Still, Kay did not relinquish the relationship easily. Realizing he had to make his position absolutely clear, Gessner now criticized her for her "excesses" and accused her of being "possessive and irrational." Diplomatically, however, he told her he needed time and she must wait until he saw things more clearly. Then he retreated. Nor was it long before Kay learned about the beautiful young English professor who had supplanted her.

It was clear to those who knew him that Gessner, who was still attractive to young women, could not realistically have been claimed by Kay. He had never been involved with women older than he. Although they were certainly intellectually and culturally compatible, being with the older Kay Boyle simply wasn't romantic enough for him. Some thought too that Gessner had even been alarmed by Kay's persistence as she pursued him and by her single-minded attempts to control him.

Meeting Bill Shirer at a party, Gessner denied the affair had been "all that serious," to Shirer's horror. To his son Peter, Gessner kept repeating, "She's too old, she's too old." He hadn't meant to hurt her, but he never had any intention of marrying her. "She wants to marry me and I can't do it," Gessner pleaded.

For Kay, however, the affair with Gessner had marked the start of a new life, one full of hope and promise. Feeling betrayed by what she experienced as his sudden rejection, she became bitter. The relationship "was doomed," Ken McCormick told her. Now she should hold her head high and resume her "wonderful, creative life." Other friends quoted remarks Gessner had made, suggesting he had a version of the truth different from Kay's, and she became even angrier, no matter that she was a seasoned fabulator herself. It got back to Kay that Gessner had called a briefly held plan of hers to join the Peace Corps "ridiculous." After Gessner "confided" that Doubleday had given him Kay's German history to "edit," Shirer pronounced him "like all Hungarians . . . highly critical and not loyal."

For her part, Kay began to tell people Gessner was having "some sort of a breakdown," for which he saw a psychiatrist twice a week. To those closest to her she had admitted that "everything with him was so happy and right—eating, drinking, talking, bed, everything." She never admitted that his philandering spirit kept him in search of younger women. Kay said her affair with Gessner had ended because his "despair about his work" had "shattered him." Some people were told that it was *she* who had broken with him.

Deeply angry now, she sought revenge. "He creates his own diabolical reality, in order to preserve his own self-image," Kay wrote Caresse, who had reported to Kay that Gessner actually still planned to go to Roccasinabalda. A woman scorned, Kay was not about to allow Gessner to use her friends. "I beg of you," Kay wrote Caresse, "to keep this lost and terrifying man from your door." Melodramatically, Kay told Shirer she had lost her integrity in the affair with Gessner. I don't like it that there has been "cruel rejection for you this year," May Sarton kindly wrote. Everyone knew.

They met again in March of 1966 when Doubleday paid Kay's way to New York for the National Book Award ceremonies, and they agreed to be "friends." Then, on his way to England to be with his English lover, Gessner wrote Kay what she considered so "insulting" a letter that she said he was "totally mad in an evil and vindictive way." With all the force of her bitterness, Kay declared Robert Gessner her "enemy." Ignoring her, Gessner indeed cabled Caresse that summer, asking to be received at the *castello* with his girlfriend. Kay demanded that Caresse "not . . . receive Robert Gessner under any circumstances," telling Caresse that Gessner had said "revolting things" about her. Her anger remained at a fevered pitch. Caresse, she said, was also to request of poet Gregory Corso "and other men of distinction whom I love, to throw Robert Gessner out if he turns up—and even to break his neck, if possible."

The following November, at a MacDowell Colony dinner, Gessner went up to Ken McCormick and told him that the poem Kay had read "made him cry." For her part, after its first appearance in the *Southern Review*, Kay Boyle removed the dedication "for R.G." from the title of "Thunderstorm in South Dakota."

Now truly unencumbered, free of her old romantic faith in love, Kay entered the turbulent mid-sixties. At sixty-four, she was to exhibit an appetite for commitment, a courage and a tenacity which would rival that of any woman her junior. Whatever Robert Gessner thought, Kay Boyle was decades away from counting herself out as "old."

Indeed, back in San Francisco, having survived the "hell" of the demise of her hope for a shared life with Robert Gessner, she became what her friend novelist Herbert Gold called "the holy mother of a certain kind of radical movement." She drove her jeep, cooked spaghetti dinners for politically minded students, longshoremen, and assorted radical friends, and spoke at antiwar teach-ins. She also affixed her name to more petitions than McCarthy and Cohn could have imagined, from a War Resisters League plea to the Soviet Union for dissenters Yuli Daniel and Andrei Sinyavsky to many protesting the continued American saturation bombing of Vietnam. She wrote the Society for the Prevention of World War III that, alongside their images of Jewish witnesses, they should include "accounts of Vietnamese parents screaming out at this moment in history as their children die before their eyes from our napalm attacks." Kay wrote such pieces as "The Battle of the Pagoda," about insurgent monks, for the antiwar *Liberation*, and for *The Catholic Worker* such political poems as "Dedicated to *Terre des Hommes*," about a Swiss organization which attempted to evacuate wounded children in Vietnam, "with their scarves of napalm," only to be refused American Air Force assistance.

Clover was married that February of 1966 in New York to poet and student of chiropractic Sidney Rosenblum, two years her junior. Kay Boyle did not attend the wedding. She was "the kind of mother I would have liked to have," Rosenblum would say, finding it a "privilege" to know her.

In June of 1966, Doubleday published Kay Boyle's final volume of short stories, *Nothing Ever Breaks Except the Heart*. This weakest of all her collections she had originally dedicated to Robert Gessner, only to change the dedication to read: "Ann Watkins Burlingame." "What the hell does she mean by that?" her sister Jo sputtered as she read the title. "Absolute gibberish." So the sisters maintained the uneasiest of truces. "She broke Joseph's heart with her affairs. That's what she broke," Jo said.

Nothing Ever Breaks Except the Heart, incorporating as it did four of the *Saturday Evening Post* potboilers, turned out to be the best-selling of all of Kay Boyle's collections. By the end of the year, nine thousand copies had been sold, testifying, in part, to the power of *The New York Times Book Review*. There Kay's friend Maxwell Geismar announced, incredibly, that with this volume Kay Boyle had finally become "a major writer in contemporary American fiction." Inventing literary history, obviously unacquainted with her earlier work, Geismar decided that Kay Boyle had now added to "her earlier vision of sensibility" what he called a "standard of human morality." What he was approving, of course, were her politics— the invocations of McCarthyism in "Fear," segregation in "One Sunny

Morning," and Vietnam in "You Don't Have to Be a Member of the Congregation."

Kay Boyle did remain, despite the falling off of her work, an important American literary personage. In the *Chicago Tribune* book section, Richard Sullivan wrote in a first-page spread that it was more important to consider Kay Boyle a literary figure whose work "deserves much more respect and gratitude than has been accorded it" than to define her by this one collection. On the other hand, Thomas Lask in the daily *New York Times* noted that sentimentality had taken over in Kay Boyle's work, and that she had adopted a "social worker's approach to her characters," so that "the lower you go on the social scale, the more likely you will find people with hearts of gold." Reviewing her in *Critique*, W. J. Stuckey suggested that readers turn back to "Effigy of War" and "The White Horses of Vienna" for the best of Kay Boyle, although she was certainly "to be found on the right side of every important conflict." Overall her politics so nicely matched the historical moment of the sixties that the good reviews overwhelmed the bad.

To a San Francisco interviewer, Kay Boyle scoffed at the view that her stories might be too sentimentally sympathetic to "people of the lower scale." "Without realizing it I brought up all the children to be afraid of the rich," she confided, slender as ever in an aqua linen suit and big white shell earrings from Paris. "I've made them my villains." Then, with a laugh, she admitted that "all of my daughters have married poor men." Impressing interviewers with her regal demeanor, she shared confidences as if she were speaking to an intimate friend, no matter that they were at her children's expense.

In August, a month after the publication of *Nothing Ever Breaks Except the Heart*, Kay Boyle received inoculations against cholera, plague, and typhoid. Then she joined Donald Duncan, a former Green Beret, Floyd McKissick of the Congress of Racial Equality, and Russell Johnson of the Friends on a fact-finding mission to Cambodia. American bombing of North and South Vietnam had spilled over into Cambodia and the Ho Chi Minh Trail, despite ruler Prince Norodom Sihanouk's having declared his country's neutrality. While the Americans denied that this was so, investigative trips were being undertaken by opponents of the war. Kay immediately asked Ken McCormick's permission to take "three weeks out of my life and my work" and go to Cambodia, although the German history remained "the great problem," and she still had not begun to work on her autobiographical addition to Robert McAlmon's memoirs, *Being Geniuses Together*, which had been due at Doubleday on the first of July.

By now in 1966 Kay was defining herself more by her political activism than by her writing. She called the invitation to Cambodia "one of the greatest opportunities of my life . . . for me to put into action my beliefs." Even Clover called Kay's trip to Cambodia "a great moving."

The group was sponsored by "Americans Want to Know Citizens Mission to Cambodia" and their purpose was to determine whether Cambodia was neutral or, as General Westmoreland insisted, was sympathetic to Communism, allowing the North Vietnamese and Vietcong to take refuge within its borders, the argument the American government gave for bombing the Ho Chi Minh Trail in Cambodia. Kay said she was going to Cambodia with an open mind. "We are really going without knowing what we will find," she said, admitting that Prince Sihanouk had put a helicopter at the disposal of the group so that they might inspect the area where it was charged by the American authorities that the Vietcong were entering the country. The group discovered that American and South Vietnamese planes had strafed a Cambodian village near the frontier, killing a pregnant woman. They concluded that Prince Sihanouk was "staunchly neutral," although Sihanouk himself had stated that while he didn't support the National Liberation Front or North Vietnam, "we do support and will always support the sacred principles for which they stand and fight," particularly that of national self-determination.

Kay returned to America with an infected hand, and a plenitude of energy. She also was utterly enchanted by Prince Sihanouk. She said he had confided privately to her that "one of the big powers will take over here one day." She also lauded Cambodia as "a matriarchal society" where "the women really prevailed," the Queen, and Sihanouk's mother, being "in charge." The Cambodians, she determined, were "non-violent people, but we taught them to be violent, when we got in there." She had to use toilets which were merely a hole in the floor and stay at military camps. But she said she didn't mind. She hated swank hotels, including the one they stayed at in Tokyo.

Always speaking in absolutes and full of emotion, Kay held a press conference in September after her return at the Sir Francis Drake Hotel. She called Lyndon Johnson "a vain, stupid, prejudiced man" who, she predicted, would "leave the White House as the most discredited President in history." Secretary of State Dean Rusk was "an obsessed, dangerous man." Asked whether she thought the Pentagon deliberately lied to the American people, she replied, "Yes." As to a report that the Americans planned to carve up Cambodia and "deliver the chunks to Thailand and South Vietnam," she said, "After what we've done in Vietnam, I believe our present Administration is capable of anything." Then she sat down and wrote a self-conscious poem called "The Lost Dogs of Phnom Penh," in which she contrasted herself back in America, "this land of packaged meats," with stray dogs in Cambodia scrounging for garbage, while crying out "as men cry out / Across the intricate frontier of broken, still unbroken, Vietnam." The poem could find no home but the first issue of a review out of Dublin called *Lace Curtain*, in 1969. She was also to include "The Lost Dogs of Phnom Penh" in her own collection *Testament for My Students* six years later.

Tactfully, Ken McCormick rejected the hundred pages of a Cambodia diary which Kay Boyle hoped might make a book. It offered, he told her, "the elements of a magazine article that would almost instantly be in readers' hands," while book publication would take eight to nine months. An account of Kay's trip to Cambodia appeared in the November issue of *The Progressive*. The piece contains much hero-worshipping homage to Prince Sihanouk, who appears in his white linen jacket and full black satin knickerbockers, a man "so dynamic that he seemed to be the only living person on this brilliant scene." Sihanouk's endorsement of the Chinese "respect for our independence, our sovereignty," goes unchallenged by Kay Boyle, who describes his particular brand of socialism as "imbued . . . with the humility and the serenity of the Buddha." No less embarrassing is her description of chanting monks as "a hymn of praise for a civilization in which the white man had never played a part."

What distinguishes Kay Boyle's "Assignment in Cambodia" are the images of herself, whether dressed all in white being feted at Sihanouk's court or as a game sixty-four-year-old slogging through the "sucking mud of the old logging road of the alleged Ho Chi Minh trail." Her assessment of the captured mercenaries she questioned is entirely persuasive; men of Cambodian ancestry, they had been trained by the CIA to invade a country they had never known. They too were patriots, Kay Boyle thought, men who wanted the same thing Sihanouk wanted: a free and independent nation whose sovereignty was respected by all foreign powers. Kay donated her small fee from *The Progressive* to "Americans Want to Know."

29

Commune, Redux

You are the only "parent" who has not sent a damnation on us.
FAITH GUDE

Kay Boyle—I wanted her kids and she wanted them. Eventually, I won.
MEL LYMAN

In the autumn of 1966, Faith and David Gude were among the sixties young who saw in communal life the road to "self-discovery." In communes they would resurrect the values of cooperation and unselfishness forgotten by parents who had constructed their lives on greed and carried America into Vietnam. Faith and David, to whom she was still not married, followed a harmonica player with the Jim Kweskin Jug Band named Mel Lyman, and moved with Geordie and Clotilde into a ramshackle house in the black ghetto of Roxbury, Massachusetts. The two houses the group occupied were near a Revolutionary War watchtower, which gave the name Fort Hill to the area. Forming their own spiritual "family," under Mel Lyman's tutelage, they would create music and art and live free from corrupting bourgeois influences. In this they resembled twenties youth like Kay Boyle, who had fled from the domination of her Republican grandfather, Jesse Peyton Boyle.

Faith cited as the inspiration for her choice of life in a commune those visits she had taken with her mother to German orphanages in search of children for Joan Detweiler to adopt. Now she proudly told her mother that, as "everyone's children," Geordie and Clotilde had begun to obey the other adults (there were about twenty) as well as their own parents. But it was a rough group Faith had entered, this "Lyman family." People who wanted to leave were accused of not being "ready to sacrifice, to strip, to begin to be what they are." They were also harassed and sometimes beaten.

Mel Lyman called the communards "his people," and he made all the decisions. With him they were gaining "internal freedom," he told them. Physically, he was an unprepossessing character, thin and small with tiny eyes and a protruding jaw; soon he had all his teeth pulled, so, he said, he could play the harmonica better. He was not talented and made mediocre music and amateur films; finally he told reporter David Felton, who published two devastating pieces about the group in *Rolling Stone*, that he was a creator "in the medium of people."

Meanwhile there were mandatory experiences with drugs, as Mel, a self-proclaimed "acid therapist," guided the chosen through their LSD trips. He was a master of sixties cant, as he talked of how adversity strengthened a man's character. He also said, shades of Kay Boyle, that the mind was the enemy; it was the heart that counted.

A cigarette dangling from his lips, he talked of himself as the returned Christ. Hero worship, which Faith had imbibed from her mother, as Kay had from Katherine Evans Boyle, fueled the group. Unlike other charismatic personalities of the sixties, however, Mel Lyman had little politics; this was no graduate of SDS, and it seems apparent that the aim of the "Lyman family" was largely to glorify Mel Lyman, and then to make money. Other than Mel, their hero was John F. Kennedy.

Faith promised Kay that she had no intention of living a "Beatnik existence" forever. To support the group, everyone worked, or contributed their parents' money, as David Gude's wife, Jessie Benton, did—all of course except Mel, a master at getting others to do all the work. Household duties were segregated by sex: the women, like Faith, were condemned to cleaning, cooking, and washing dishes, which, Mel said, was "women's work."

Needless to say, most parents were appalled. From the start, it was important to Faith that Kay Boyle approve of her participation in the Lyman family. By Faith's reasoning, Kay was "the happiest and free-est" of any of the parents. "You," Faith wrote her mother, "are the only 'parent' who has not sent a damnation on us." Having lived in Raymond Duncan's commune, Kay, Faith reasoned, would surely sympathize.

But it wasn't enough that Kay Boyle approve. She must come to Roxbury and see for herself. Mel Lyman thought so too. Kay Boyle's joining the group in Roxbury would validate the Lyman family commune, grant it a legitimacy. Faith pressed. Didn't Kay—out of money once more, having given away most of what she had to perpetually needy children, those children she had laughed at for having married poor men—need a place to work? Faith promised that, living with the Lyman family, Kay would find the peace and tranquility to fulfill the three-book contract she had committed herself to at Doubleday. The German history and Robert McAlmon's memoir, *Being Geniuses Together*, to which Kay would add her own chapters, would comprise two of those works.

Kay Boyle felt particularly pressed because Ken McCormick could not accept as the third book a reissue of *Three Short Novels*, since Beacon still had four thousand copies of its edition left. Even as this remaining book was left unspecified on her contract, the German history was stalled. Erich Kahler, uneasy with Kay Boyle's view that the "more than life-sized figures of Frederick II and Bismarck . . . served to dwarf and diminish the German people almost beyond recovery," had tried to tell her that Luther was a far more crucial figure. That April of 1966 Ken McCormick had offered Kahler one hundred dollars to evaluate 90,000 words of the manuscript.

Kahler was charmed by Kay Boyle, as she wrote a poem for him called "The Jew Among Nations," based on one of his own titles. So smitten was Kahler that when he saw her photograph by Man Ray, he said he had "loved" Kay Boyle before. But looking at that picture he had *fallen in love*, "plunging into your youth with my imagination." The German history, Kay said, now five years overdue, was hanging over her "like a death sentence." Kahler sympathized, but he could not sanction the publication of a work he found so deeply uninformed and eccentric. Only *Being Geniuses Together* seemed truly viable, although by no means was Kay yet ready to give up her German history.

Kay's living at the commune would be inexpensive. She need pay only for her food. Working in collaboration with Kahler, she still hoped she might finish this book at last. She would have to live among young people, but she had been doing that at Frederick Street. The other parents would all "flip," Faith exulted, "when they heard that 'Kay Boyle is coming to live here!' "

Faith and the others set to work at once painting a room for Kay, stripping the filthy linoleum from the floor, making curtains. "It will be peaceful here for you," Faith promised. At times, Faith had her doubts. Music sounded into every corner of the house until two in the morning. "We are open to change," Faith wrote Kay cryptically, but "you must believe in us for all our obvious differences." Often Faith reiterated that she was living as her mother had once done with Duncan. "I learned all this from you anyway," Faith said. Faith suggested Kay might get her own room to work in and return to the commune at night. She would even work at half pay as her mother's new "Aaron Fisch," the pseudonymous imaginary secretary Kay Boyle sometimes invoked to ward off unwelcome interruptions.

Back in San Francisco, Kay reached into her pocket and bought a washer and dryer for the commune. She also sent Faith, who, despite her yellow hair, was a virtual incarnation of her mother, with her heavily lidded blue eyes, rosebud mouth, and long slim body, a red dress of her own, since they were the same size. Faith told her mother she loved the dress because "it smells of you still." The scent of Kay Boyle's Chanel No. 5 for her daughters was their version of Proust's madeleine.

Kay planned to arrive in Roxbury for Christmas and remain until June. She would teach one day a week at Amherst and lecture wherever she could. By the end of the year, she hoped, the German history would be completed and she would have made considerable progress on *Being Geniuses Together*. At Thanksgiving, still in San Francisco, her hospitality now legendary, she stuffed two turkeys for sixteen people. Then she and Ian and a former student got into the car and began the long drive across the country.

In Roxbury, Faith's worst fears were immediately realized. Kay found the music blaring all night maddening. She shared her room with baby Clotilde. When she complained that the music woke the little girl, David Gude nastily told her, "I hope we kept you awake last night. That was the intention." One morning Kay came down to discover twenty people rolled up in blankets on the floor. In reply to her mother's question as to who they were, Faith told her, "I have no idea. The door was open and they just came in."

Kay found the house freezing cold and she feared for her grandchildren's health. That there wasn't enough food, no orange juice, no milk for the children, appalled her. One morning, referring to the commune's hefty telephone bill, Jessie Benton casually remarked, looking at Kay, "Granny will pay the bill!" At this, Kay sent a frying pan skittering across the floor at Jessie's feet.

But Faith sided with her friend, no matter that they both had shared David Gude's bed. Kay was hostile. She had to "learn to change," to become "more honest," as if, Ian reflected when he heard the story, she who had lived so much longer was expected to "fit into their pattern of living." By New Year's Eve everyone was down with intestinal flu. As for Mel Lyman, who Kay reported was "very insignificant looking and very weak looking," he seemed to have made a decision to ignore her completely.

One night, Kay related to David Felton, Faith was cooking supper while she enjoyed her usual Dubonnet in the living room. Suddenly Faith put on a tape, and then disappeared. What Kay heard were the cries of a woman in the throes of sexual intercourse while on an LSD trip, with, it seemed, both David Gude and Mel Lyman present. The girl screamed, "I love you, I love you, this is so marvelous. Oh, Mel, you are the most beautiful man." Kay thought Mel's chortling sounded like "a devil." Then the girl cried out, "Oh, don't go! Don't ever leave me. Oh, no!" And Kay thought she heard the woman imploring not just for Mel to sleep with her but "please, Mel, get me pregnant!"

"How did you like it?" Faith returned to ask. Then she revealed that she had been the woman on the tape.

"That was Jessie's voice. That wasn't you," Kay replied at once. She had found it "shocking," "ghastly," "awful." Surely the voice on the tape was not that of anyone she knew.

"Mama, that was me," Faith repeated. She thought that what she had done took guts, and here her mother couldn't stand it that anyone else should be the center of attention.

By early January, Kay had moved across the street to a room where she could write without distractions. One morning she went over to help

Faith dress the children only to discover that the heat had gone off entirely and the children were "literally blue with cold." Immediately she found herself in a confrontation with one of the members of the commune, who, in response to her indignation, told her, "Beautiful. It's just beautiful to see children like that. Children should be cold and hungry all the time—then they're close to reality." Once more Kay blew up.

Leaving the Lyman family commune, Kay Boyle resumed life as a writer. She went to Princeton to consult with Erich Kahler, and read her poetry at a memorial service for A. J. Muste in New York. Meanwhile she continued to send Faith money, for food, for the children. Parents who did not send money were accused of having stopped "growing." But soon, of all Kay's children, it was Faith who demanded that her mother stop driving herself, stop sending money, pleading that the others, Bobby in particular, needed more help than she did.

"God, I've never known such hatred, real hatred, in people as on this hill," Kay was to report to David Felton. If Faith had hoped her mother would applaud the commune as a worthy experiment, she was soon disappointed. On a visit a few years later, Kay discovered a photograph of Charles Manson in the children's playroom. When she asked Faith if they thought he was innocent, Faith told her, "It doesn't matter. He made a gesture against all the things we do not believe in."

Kay noticed they changed the flowers under Manson's picture every day. By then the Lyman family had armed itself. There were skirmishes with the police and a bank robbery. And in a dark concrete room in the basement called the "vault," family members who had misbehaved were placed in solitary confinement. It would all end, Kay was certain, in total noncommunication or even suicide.

Indeed, suicide was often on Kay Boyle's mind. If Bobby, Apple, and Clover had all attempted to take their lives, on March 1, 1967, Pegeen was finally successful with a combination of pills and alcohol, choking on her vomit. She was forty-one years old. Kay, predictably, blamed Peggy Guggenheim. "She did destroy her two children without pity," was Kay's judgment on her old adversary. Kay remembered Pegeen as "so beautiful, so foolish, so little more than a child herself." For a time she had been important to Pegeen, only to allow the contact to lapse. "Surely, something could have been done," Kay said now.

Having at last told Ken McCormick that the German history would not "work out," Kay proposed turning the project into a book about German women, who were the first to have a peace movement: "Many of them were against every war their men dragged them into." Ever her supporter, McCormick agreed to shift the advance over to this new project. It was only later that he, finally, shaken, concluded that "she was very good at having ideas that sounded absolutely terrific, but when she got down to doing them she didn't have all the material she needed."

In the wake of the fiasco at Roxbury, Kay immersed herself in activity. She renewed her attempt to get Carnevali's autobiography published, and supervised, without much success, serial sales of *Being Geniuses Together*, forbidding Mike Watkins to send the manuscript to either *The New Yorker* or *The Atlantic*. Unfortunately, Watkins had already received a rejection from *The Atlantic* on the ground that they had "no space." Always she needed money now, for Sharon, so she could continue painting, for the aged Countess Esterházy in Austria. She sold the one letter she had from James Joyce to Southern Illinois University for five hundred dollars, and requested assistance from the National Institute of Arts and Letters, which sent her a thousand dollars. Solita Solano sent her a check, as did Jo.

When Man Ray demanded one hundred dollars for the use of his extraordinary photograph of her in the Carnevali autobiography, Kay was indignant. Meanwhile she complained to friends that none of her children had read anything she had written. People observed that what she gave them was money. And she seemed in these days to talk more about her cats than her children, or her grandchildren. If once she had thought that the big house on Frederick Street would become a rallying place for her large family, as Laurence had made Mégève, that had not happened.

In these years Kay became even more disputatious. She had always manifested a certain hauteur. She had always divided the world into heroes and villains. But now she began a series of disagreements, misunderstandings, and vendettas with people. It began in 1967 with Edward Dahlberg. He had written to Kay hoping she would "rescue" him by reviewing two of his books. In his letter he engaged in no small amount of flattery, pointing out that Ernest Walsh "had a strong, passionate countenance." Dahlberg found her own verse "magical." When Kay did not respond quickly enough, he wrote another pleading letter. Generously, Kay obliged with extravagant praise in a *Nation* review, which she even showed Dahlberg before submitting it for publication.

But before long Kay discovered among Dahlberg's frequent letters "unpleasant rebukes." He had chided her, "You do alter your mind very often." He referred to Ethel Moorhead's charge that Kay had not given Walsh his hypodermic needle when he required it. "She hated you, and you abhor her," Dahlberg told Kay, "so how can I make any judgment as to who is correct or not?" He told her that she had "all the advantages, youth, beauty, and the passionate love of Ernest Walsh," and that Kay should forget her "hatred of a deceased woman" who had done so much for Walsh.

As if this weren't bad enough, Dahlberg attacked Joyce as "Jew-baiting," said William Carlos Williams had his own "antisemitic outbreaks," and called *Being Geniuses Together* "drossy," while McAlmon had become so paranoid at the end of his life that he had accused Dahlberg of trying to steal his work. Still later, Dahlberg accused Kay of calling him a "professional Jew." He also had unsolicited advice for her. "You are devouring yourself taking up one cause or another," he told her. She should "write, write and write." Worst of all was his charge that the six million Jews annihilated in the gas ovens were "a mere nothing to you, my darling celt."

Finally Kay called Dahlberg "a bitter and profoundly cruel man" whose "complete and quite vicious distortion" of her character prevented her from using his words in the foreword to Carnevali's autobiography, as she had originally agreed to do.

Late in 1967 Horizon Press published *The Autobiography of Emanuel Carnevali*. It received a rave review in *The New York Times Book Review*, where Kay's friend Yale professor Norman Holmes Pearson praised her "compilation" which brought Carnevali "excitingly alive with all his fierce tormented power." The "autobiography" had, of course, always been a compilation of separate pieces, from the time Kay had collected the fragments after her visit to Carnevali on her way to Austria. There had never been a manuscript of an autobiography. But Kay had fulfilled one important promise she had made long ago to the Italian poet whom Ernest Walsh and Robert McAlmon had admired so much.

Kay forgave Edward Dahlberg for his many harsh judgments and words. The following May she went ahead with her original plan and nominated him for membership in the National Institute of Arts and Letters. Their correspondence, of course, had come to an end. By March of 1968 Kay was offering Dahlberg's letters for sale to Andreas Brown at the Gotham Book Mart in New York, along with other papers of hers.

All his life, Kay thought, Ian had worshipped his sister Faith, less than a year older than he. She had fought all his battles; she had screamed in anger when in France a teacher had dared to separate them. As he reached adulthood, Kay observed that Ian had only blond girlfriends, which she attributed to his infatuation with his sister. Meanwhile Kay, in her relationship with the son for whom she had so longed, was a controlling mother. Once when Ian wanted to build a porch onto the Frederick Street house as a gift to her, Kay had insisted on paying him, until her friend Ted Keller, a professor at San Francisco State, had intervened. "Leave him alone," Keller advised. "He wants to make a gesture."

In October of 1967, still at loose ends over his status with the draft board, having failed so far to find a means of alternative service to fulfill his conscientious objector status, Ian decided to visit Faith at the Lyman commune in Roxbury. It was a step forward for Ian, away from Frederick Street, and toward independence. All Kay could do was wait, and consider how to bring him back home.

In New York, Ian shepherded his "stepfather," Laurence Vail, about town. A lonely, frail old man now, suffering from cancer, Laurence warmed to Ian's good nature. Ian, at twenty-two, enjoyed Laurence as "a real character," no matter that he spoke of Kay with bitterness. (Ever the surrealist, one night Laurence with his son-in-law Sidney Rosenblum pushed to the head of a movie line. "We're still back there," Laurence called to the irate patrons now behind him.)

Laurence was failing, but at sixty-five, Kay was full of vigor and purpose. Her friends had begun to die (Roger Burlingame and Ann Watkins within a week of each other). But Kay seemed to have been reborn. In 1967 she predicted a coming revolution for America. At one anti-Vietnam War rally in Berkeley, she spotted a Hell's Angel lying idly under a tree. At once she marched up and poked her finger into his considerable belly. "Why aren't you marching?" she demanded.

Kay would not attend a dinner sponsored by the National Endowment for the Arts because it was "impossible" now, given her opposition to the war, to attend any government-sponsored event. When a picture of Lady Bird Johnson and her grandchild appeared in the newspaper, Kay wrote urging her to help her husband "understand the shame of many, many American grandmothers—myself among them," who "apologize to those women who carry the shattered blood-drenched bodies of other babies in their hearts until they die." Her language had become even more extreme, intemperate. At a vigil at Port Chicago in Canyon, California, the port from which napalm shipments were made to Vietnam, she spent two days picketing the Naval Weapons Station.

"If it's Kay, tell her I'm dead," Herb Wilner called to his wife, Nancy, when the phone rang, fearing that he would be enlisted onto one more picket line. Kay had become an exhausting conscience. A colleague named Dan Weiss accepted a Fulbright fellowship to Greece, then under the dictatorship of the colonels. "I'm not interested in politics," he pleaded to Kay Boyle. She never acknowledged him as a friend again.

Her mode had become even more confrontational as she condemned a policeman in uniform who was served wine at a table near hers at an Italian restaurant in San Francisco: "Ask that gentleman if it's appropriate to be carrying that weapon and drinking that wine," she demanded of the waiter in a loud voice, insisting that the policeman either return the bottle or remove his weapon. Cringing, the policeman finally got up and left.

Sometimes these exchanges were friendly. When Howard Nemerov would not succumb to her exhortations to become an activist, he received a witty poem whose opening lines read:

I never thought that Zeus would come between us
Above all not disguised as L.B.J.

Nemerov would not budge, however. "I'm not going to lie down under tanks with you. You have more courage than wits, Mother Boyle," Nemerov told her. James T. Farrell was irritated too when Kay wanted him to agree to a "tax pledge" of writers and editors against the war. "When I want to, or do speak on Vietnam, I do not need your group and my voice would be more effective alone," he wrote her angrily.

She forged ahead. In *The Progressive* she published an ironic piece called "Seeing the Sights in San Francisco," in which all the "sights" have to do with the deaths inflicted in Vietnam, from cemetery to mortuary, to Travis Air Force Base, which, Kay wrote, "has the distinction of being the one base to receive all the containers flown in from Southeast Asia." When the civil rights movement entered its separatist stage, Kay Boyle endorsed that, writing a poem for *Liberation*, "On Black Power," and addressing "Stokely" Carmichael directly as the legatee of Mahatma Gandhi. Kay herself appears in the poem as an old woman with "rheumy, failing eyes," urging others as aged as she to see "that prophets wear cloaks of fire now." She was not going to be left behind. (When the poem was reprinted as "A Poem About Black Power" in the San Francisco State *Journal of Contemporary Revolutions*, Kay had removed all the references to Stokely Carmichael, reflecting her new allegiance to the Black Panther Party. But she had never been a stranger to disputes, sectarian or otherwise.)

If she had always fabulated and exaggerated, Kay Boyle did so with even more abandon in the late sixties, as she insisted that America had fallen prey to a dictatorship and that James Baldwin's phone was bugged (as indeed it might well have been). "We are truly living in a police state here," she said, "and it is growing worse." To Caresse, she wrote, "As you must realize, revolution is on its way. We are very close to it." These views were no doubt as much a means of feeling young, alive, and involved, and a means of living intensely in the present, as they were coherent responses to the reality.

October 16, 1967, inaugurated "Stop the Draft Week," a series of demonstrations in which students and the police met in violent confrontation. On the Monday there was a nonviolent sit-in outside the Oakland Induction Center, and bright and early Kay Boyle, sixty-five years old now, was there. The evening before, she had attended a War Resisters League meeting at which it had been decided they would not interfere with the inductees themselves. Kay sat with Joan Baez, and her daughter, the folksinger Joanie, blocking the entrance.

The inductees climbed over the demonstrators and went inside. But Kay was arrested, along with some one hundred others. She walked sedately to the paddy wagon, her back ramrod straight, a regal presence, explaining all the while to reporters that she had tried to protest against the war through legitimate means, such as signing petitions and writing to her representative. None of that had made any difference.

In court the next day, Kay informed the judge that it had been "a rather unique demonstration in that many older people and professionals such as myself are involved in it." She asserted that "the American people had the power, if they so wished, to stop this war." Fearlessly, as if she had nothing to lose, she urged that every American "commit civil disobedience" and continue to do so "until the war has been brought to an end." Nor would she allow the young to go to jail alone. Kay was sentenced to ten days in jail. The day she was arrested to part of the next afternoon counted as two days; she later served two four-day weekends to complete her sentence.

Kay's first visit to Santa Rita Prison was something of a lark. The Baez mother and daughters, Joanie and Mimi Fariña, embroidered the words "peace" and "love" on the seams of prison-issue shorts and pants. Martin Luther King came and talked over the wall to the imprisoned demonstrators, and Kay read aloud Howard Nemerov's poem about William Remington, who had suffered under McCarthyism. During this first incarceration, Kay was permitted to work in the overgrown prison garden, digging up irises and splitting them with blunt scissors, replanting them with a rusty trowel. She was also able to walk around the courtyard. Her goal was a mile a day.

"I will never voluntarily go to jail again," Kay Boyle announced when she was free. Then, ever the prisoner of her own contradictions, she did just that. "Come on, Kay," the Baezes implored, luring her back to the Oakland Induction Center for a second round. On an icy day, the week before Christmas, Kay joined a crowd of carol-singing, flower-bearing demonstrators, among them the City Lights poet Lawrence Ferlinghetti. Wearing a white scarf and her white earrings, Kay huddled in a corner for seven hours, blocking access until the police at last made their move.

As they were arrested, the demonstrators sang "We Wish You a Merry Christmas!" to the police. Kay took comfort in the fact that one of the policemen removed his jacket and cap and refused to make the arrests. This time, however, she received a forty-five-day sentence. Unwilling to spend the holidays in prison, she requested and received a continuance. The judge told her he had read two of her books. She could serve her time during Easter vacation.

Kay Boyle's final incarceration at Santa Rita came in April of 1968. She was placed not with the singing Baezes, but with the general population of women prisoners, sleeping, as they did, on a "pancake thin" mattress. She worked in the prison kitchen, priding herself on being the first to spring from her cot at five in the morning. Wearing a canvas cap, she boiled eggs, made toast, and stirred the oatmeal in its giant cauldron. She was still the heroine of her own life. "These are crucial times," she wrote, "and I am glad to be taking my part in the protest against armed authority."

"Mama's in jail!" Kathe blurted out when she ran into Janet Flanner one day on a Paris street.

"Good for her!" Flanner retorted sardonically. "Well, that's all she ever wanted."

In fact, it was not much fun. She wore a drab grey dress with a ripped hem and sneakers two sizes too big for her. Makeup was forbidden, which

Kay found "terrible." She was thrown into one lockup after another. Carrying her sheets, pillowcase, greyish towel, toothbrush, and sliver of soap, she moved from cell to cell until she found herself in a room adjacent to "the Hole" with three women of whom she was frightened. "Now, Kay, you've made enough trouble," she was told when she expressed her fears. "Just keep quiet."

A black woman who had killed her lover in a bar asked Kay to write a letter for her to the public defender which was "legally right," although all she seemed to want was the thirty dollars the victim had in his pocket, which she claimed was hers. "When I get out, I'm going to kill his wife too if she's got that thirty dollars," she vowed. Turning to Kay, she demanded, "What you in for?"

"Well, I'm just a demonstrator," Kay later wrote she told the woman, mentioning, as she recounted the incident, the time she ultimately served for both sentences. "I'm serving thirty-one days, weekends and holidays. That's so I won't lose my job."

"Demonstrating against what?"

When she heard that Kay Boyle had blocked the entrance to the Oakland Induction Center, according to Kay, the woman was indignant, and asked, "Ain't you never heard of national honor?"

It was in the prison shower that Kay Boyle first felt the lump in her breast. It was a tiny lump, really nothing, she thought. But when she felt for it later, it was still there. Then she asked to see a doctor, only to be refused.

When her lawyer, Robert Treuhaft, arrived to see her, Kay told him she had a lump "where ladies get lumps, the usual place." Treuhaft was nothing if not effective. Within an hour, Kay later wrote, he had her in the county hospital. But when the hospital clerk asked for her name, the deputy who had accompanied Kay said, "You don't need a name. Just put down number 2362." When her children were small, Kay had often told them of her fear that she might get breast cancer, since her own mother had it. Now her worst nightmare had come true.

Released from prison on April 9, having discovered that she had breast cancer, Kay wanted Ian back with her in San Francisco. But as she had worshipped that long line of heroes, so Ian, on whom she had so strong an influence, thought in the same way. Refusing to return, he called Mel Lyman "our better side" and wrote his mother that Mel was a person of "great feeling" and "compassion." Ian pointed out to his mother that at "the hill" they emphasized "feeling" above all else. Hadn't she done the same?

Although he knew he might sound "cruel, and even selfish," returning to Frederick Street would "be a step backward!" Kay had outlined to him her many obligations. But this time, Ian told her, "somehow these tasks must be, and can be done without me." Calling her illness a "minor" emergency, he argued that "nothing is temporary, as you well know."

That Kay had summoned Ian to San Francisco back in February for no such good reason made it easier for him to refuse her now. "I ask and pray that you may weather this horrible operation without me," Ian wrote. "I do all this for a greater love." He was satisfying a need inside himself, he begged his mother to understand, "like you and jail." He knew he "should be there to lend support." But he now had a commitment to himself. He had to endure the "pain" of not rushing to his mother's side, as he begged her not to use her illness to clip his wings. Ian tried to tell this woman who had longed all her life for a son at her side that a different kind of love was necessary if there were to be love at all. He urged his mother to keep on loving him, even if she could not accept "the hill" and Mel Lyman.

As she had been with husbands and lovers, so had Kay Boyle been possessive and controlling with her son. "You have needs that cry out to be fulfilled," Ian told his mother, "and I do too. Let us fulfill these needs for one another through understanding." He loved his mother, as he would all his life. But he must now become his own man. One of the ironies, of course, was that the Lyman family commune's authoritarianism made it the unlikeliest of venues for anyone to become his own man.

Laurence Vail died in his sleep in Cannes on April 16, 1968. "Hopelessness is a more satisfactory condition than hope," Laurence had written to Djuna Barnes two years earlier as he struggled vainly to recover from stomach cancer, which he had been told was only jaundice. Kathe sent off two telegrams, one to Kay and one to Peggy. "He was terrible but he was wonderful also," Apple said.

Kathe, Laurence's most devoted child, who took care of him up to the end, thought she loved her father so much because he had so many faults and because he was so honest. Kathe had decided too that the more Kay could admit her faults, "the more we can love her." Bobby, who had learned so horribly that Laurence was not her father, regretted not having been summoned to his funeral, saying "nobody seemed to have realized that it meant something to me to be there."

Laurence Vail died without forgiving Kay for the sorrow she had brought him. He had long since dismissed her as "the symbol of romantic hypocrisy." To the end he accused her not only of breaking up their marriage but of having turned Apple and Clover against him.

A week after Laurence's death, Kay was operated on for breast cancer at Kaiser Hospital on Geary Street in San Francisco. She handled the event with courage and aplomb. Friends took over her classes so that she would be paid for the spring semester, although San Francisco State managed to dock her for the month of May anyway. Neither Apple nor Kathe nor Bobby was told about the operation.

"Will I be pretty anymore after my breast is gone?" Kay coyly asked a young male colleague.

"Now I won't be able to admire my body in the mirror," Kay told Ted Keller.

"Have you been doing that?" he asked, incredulous. Told that she had, Ted advised that she "look from the navel down."

Kay Boyle's room was filled with the flowers of spring. Bouquets arrived from Erich Kahler, and from Frances Steloff, who sent roses, wild lilies, and peonies. Ira Morris and Janet Flanner also responded. Two days after her radical mastectomy for a cancer which had metastasized in the lymph nodes, Kay Boyle was sitting up in bed. Her makeup was impeccable, her white earrings in place. Now she served wine and hors d'oeuvres to her guests.

"Where's your roommate?" Nancy Wilner asked her.

"She's down the hall with a petition," Kay explained. She had enlisted the woman in one of her causes. From her hospital bed, Kay ordered a copy of Eldridge Cleaver's *Soul on Ice* and *Unspeakable Practices, Unnatural Acts* by Donald Barthelme, which she planned to use in class. That Clover was flying out to offer her "daughterly care," was a source of satisfaction too.

Clover found her mother so full of determination that she even wanted to dance a tango with her friend Reginald Major and then be photographed to show her daughters in Paris how well she was feeling. Only to close friends like Caresse Crosby did Kay confide that she could not "bear being so crippled and hideous." From the Lyman family commune came word from Faith and Ian that she had created her own pain, or so Kay interpreted their words. Angrily she replied that her breast cancer was not "the result of some kind of wrong thinking, or lack of love, on my part." Her illness could not have been caused by unresolved psychological pain because she did "not sit and brood over things which disturb me." Her concerns were with peace in Vietnam and race relations, rather than with "personal problems." Robert Kennedy had just been assassinated, and this was more important to her than her own pain. Faith wrote her back in no uncertain terms: "You have lost him and me."

Kay Boyle emerged unable to use her left arm. Doctors told her there was only a fifteen percent chance that they had got all the cancer. That was enough for Kay, who promptly told Ted Keller that she had been cured. "Everything is going to be all right," she said as she went on with her activist life. Neither old age nor, now, serious illness could dampen her spirit.

That same June of 1968 Robert Gessner died of a heart attack in the Hotel Chelsea while in the act of love with the young professor about whose existence Kay had so bitterly learned. He was discovered bent on one knee, poised on one foot, like a crow, his brother Harold said, paralyzed, his muscles having frozen. The woman seemed terrified, weeping uncontroll-ably, her nude snapshot stuck into the hotel room mirror. He was only sixty-one years old.

Only a few days earlier, Kay had mailed a fifty-dollar check to Gessner at the Chelsea as "final payment on money borrowed from him in 1966." He had died before it could be cashed. At once Kay instructed Mike Watkins to stop payment. "I believe my children need the $50.00 in question more than does the Gessner estate, which is a very prosperous one," Kay wrote Watkins in her haughtiest tones.

In the mid-seventies at a party for some political cause, Gessner's son Peter, who had directed *Time of the Locust*, an acclaimed antiwar film about Vietnam, was delighted to encounter Kay Boyle.

"Remember me? I'm Peter Gessner," the mild-mannered young man introduced himself.

Kay Boyle took one long look at Peter Gessner. Then she turned away, cutting him dead.

30

Fabulations

How do I know that I am telling the truth now about what I believed and wanted then?

I thought she fabulated.
MALCOLM COWLEY

In June of 1968 Kay Boyle at last published *Being Geniuses Together*. For this new edition of Robert McAlmon's original 1934 text, she deleted some passages. Then she alternated chapters of her own reminiscences of the decade 1920–30 with McAlmon's, prompting both her friend James Stern and London *Daily Telegraph* reviewer Anthony Powell to accuse her of riding on McAlmon's coattails. "One absolutely gasps at Boyle's including her own life. That she was there surely does not include the right to chop up his book and superimpose her own," Powell thought.

Kay's chapters were far superior to McAlmon's, as critics were swift to point out. Jean Stafford in *The New York Review of Books* called McAlmon's writing "repetitious and boring," while Kay's was "instinct with grace and gallantry." "The book's triumph is Miss Boyle's," Charles Poore wrote in the daily *New York Times*. "She writes rings around him," *Newsweek* said. Only Powell had done his homework sufficiently to be appalled by Kay Boyle's efforts "to clean it up" by excluding from McAlmon's original book stories which showed him in a less than favorable light.

Kay Boyle's chapters of *Being Geniuses Together* are often distressingly pretentious when they are not self-dramatizing. Once more she airs her prejudice against intellect, dismissing Evelyn Scott as "desperately intellectual, as these women I loved were not, and I decided this was because of her more formal education." The analogies are overblown: the 1968 rebellions of the young are compared with a broad sweep and little accuracy to those of Kay, McAlmon, and Jolas in Paris; Ernest Walsh searching for a hotel is linked to "the young men of the Irish Republican Army . . . on the run." Another unconvincing moment has Kay "weeping" at the age of nine or ten when listening to Bach because "the man who had found this vocabulary of courage had had to die." Even more discomforting is her assertion that her own promiscuity that summer of 1928 represented a disintegration of "the whole moral fabric" of society.

The 1968 *Being Geniuses Together* is riddled with Kay's errors of fact and of omission. Indeed, it appears as if she never even referred back to her own letters and papers. She was eleven, not ten, at the Armory Show; they lived at John Singer Sargent's house the following season; *New Masses* came into existence five years after she pictures herself entering its offices in search of a job; the ship she sailed on to France was called the *Suffren*, not the *De Grasse*; she never "studied to be an architect," but took a few courses in mechanical drawing at the Ohio Mechanics Institute; she began to wear white earrings as her trademark in the late thirties, not in 1923; her father did not graduate from Penn Law School; she was younger than sixteen when she took up with the married car salesman; Ernest Walsh was born in Detroit, not in Cuba; the Claridge was in Paris, not in London; Marguerite, according to her letters, was her favorite Brault sister, not Charlotte. And she married Laurence Vail in 1932, not in 1931, as she writes.

Nor, in matters of literary history, is Kay Boyle's account to be trusted. Nowhere in *Being Geniuses Together* does she even hint at the real conflict between Ernest Hemingway and Ernest Walsh, which had to do with Walsh's demand that Hemingway continue to do editorial and layout and copy-editing work on the second issue of *This Quarter*. The dialogue between Walsh and Pauline Pfeiffer, without the background of Walsh's break with Hemingway, seems absurd. Kay also has Pauline report on a conflict between Hemingway and McAlmon which occurred in 1929, three years after Pauline's visit. In a letter to Kay during her work on *Being Geniuses Together*, Bill Bird reminded her of this notorious twenties confrontation based on gossip Hemingway heard from Maxwell Perkins regarding what McAlmon said after they shared a bed together in Pamplona; Kay Boyle interpolated it into her memoirs, out of chronological order, as part of her lifelong grudge against Hemingway. She has Walsh tell Pauline that he and Hemingway were like "brothers," an unlikely Walsh comment since they had already come to a parting of the ways, not, as Kay Boyle suggests, over Hemingway's "betrayal" of Sherwood Anderson in *The Torrents of Spring*, but because Hemingway could no longer take the time to shepherd Walsh's magazine through publication in Paris. When Hemingway suggested to Walsh that for the second number he hire a friend named Bill Smith for one thousand francs a month (twenty dollars), Walsh accused him of trying to extort money from him and Moorhead.

There was another point of contention between Hemingway and Walsh, which Kay Boyle ignores and which she had to have known about. In a gush of extravagant prose, Walsh had compared Robert McAlmon to a host of masters from Shakespeare, Dickens, and Conrad to Mark Twain. Hemingway at once vowed to stop writing if Walsh seriously believed McAlmon had ever written anything that deserved to be mentioned in the same universe with *Huckleberry Finn*, and went on to accuse Walsh, correctly, of a grotesque form of hero worshipping. Walsh was furious at this challenge, and more so when Hemingway would not allow him to serialize *The Sun Also Rises* in *This Quarter*. In vengeance, Walsh then went on to circulate a nasty review of "The Cheapest Book I Ever Read." "Gentlemen," Hemingway implored, throwing up his hands in a play on a certain Ernest Walsh poem to which Kay Boyle had also taken a fancy, "I give you the Irish."

That quarrel, coupled with the chapter of *A Moveable Feast* called "The Man Who Was Marked for Death," in which Walsh appears as a charlatan promising both Joyce and Hemingway the same prize if only they would write for his magazine, made Hemingway Kay's lifelong enemy. Her fury was based on Hemingway's attack on her fallen lover and, the reader will recall, not on her outrage when she had learned Hemingway was having an affair with Pauline Pfeiffer while he was still married to Hadley, as all her life Kay would claim. At the very moment of Pauline's visit to Kay and Ernest Walsh, Kay was, of course, living with a man who was not her husband, nor later in her life did she place much stock in bourgeois morality. But even at the age of sixty-six Kay Boyle was not ready to return to the actualities of the conflict between Ernest Hemingway and Ernest Walsh.

Equally obfuscating was her omission of how Katherine Evans Boyle had categorically refused to welcome her home after Ernest Walsh's death when Kay was pregnant, penniless, alone but for Ethel Moorhead's ambiguous charity, and frightened. Her project was to idealize her mother, and in the service of that myth, she had to resort to serious distortion of the truth. Nor does Kay ever acknowledge that her mother's support was motivated by her need to fulfill her own abandoned dreams through her younger and more malleable daughter; certainly, as Joan Detweiler believes, it was not as disinterested and noble a maternal love as Kay Boyle insists.

If McAlmon in his pages flatly accused Kay of excessive romanticizing, she is far less honest about him in hers. Comparing his profile with John Barrymore's, she reveals that she remains a bit in love with him, or his memory. So she accepts McAlmon's Victorian-minded sister Victoria's insistence that McAlmon had been betrayed by Bryher in their marriage— that he had not known that it was to be a marriage of convenience and that Bryher was a lesbian. Yet the well-documented facts reveal that he knew all along. Indeed, he had written to William Carlos Williams that "the marriage is legal only, unromantic, and strictly an agreement." Kay quotes Victoria McAlmon as saying "the word 'love' was synonymous to 'lie' for him because one woman had made it seem that way," and Kay endorses that view.

Kay Boyle, it would appear, still had not come to terms with McAlmon's homosexuality. In the notes she made for her chapters of *Being Geniuses Together*, she wrote: "emotional frustrations, the stalemate, crises between

Bob and me . . . kept us from making a life together." (By 1975, still unable or unwilling to acknowledge that McAlmon had been predominantly homosexual, Kay had decided that his black moods in Paris in the twenties were caused by sexual impotence.) That she certainly knew that McAlmon was homosexual, however, is revealed not only in John Glassco's *Memoirs of Montparnasse*, in which the Kay Boyle character tells Buffy that McAlmon was so crazy about him that he would publish him. Her knowledge was also revealed in her reactions during the summer of 1931 when McAlmon appeared in the South of France and she was directly confronted with his homosexual choices. "All the filth about McAlmon," she wrote Jo at the time, "has so turned my stomach that I can't be civil to him." Fabulating, however, had become second nature. By 1968, believing perhaps that any admission of McAlmon's essential homosexuality would damage the reputation she was working so diligently to resurrect, Kay Boyle chose to deny it altogether.

Being Geniuses Together is best read as a work of fiction, as Kay Boyle's imaginative recall of long-ago Paris. There is much vivid and deeply felt writing in her chapters. The imagery is alight with felt life, from the cabbages of Harfleur to Ethel Moorhead in her pince-nez and clan plaids, to Joyce and Gertrude Stein icily ignoring each other in the Jolases' living room, to Stein turning girlish at the appearance of Raymond Duncan at the Dayang Muda's. Kay sits in her gold tunic on Bill Bird's knee, throws a stein of beer at McAlmon at the long Coupole bar, and refuses to romanticize Paris. Even as she fabulates about her own life, she does not perpetuate the myth that twenties Paris nurtured writers. This refusal to sentimentalize that time is her real homage to her friend Robert McAlmon, a stance of which McAlmon would indeed have been proud.

There are other moments of striking honesty in *Being Geniuses Together*. Kay Boyle admits that her rejection of Eugene Jolas's edict that writers should explore the subconscious may have been the result of her own fear of questioning where her writing was coming from. She acknowledges that she was viewing her own collapse into promiscuity in "dramatic and outsized terms." And she accepts McAlmon's judgment of her that "Kay, come hell or high water, had to romanticize every situation." This, Kay says, "may very well be true." It is the last line of her narrative, and it is startling in its sheer honesty.

In accomplishing the first American publication of Bob McAlmon's memoir, Kay Boyle was participating in a chain of loyalty. As Ernest Walsh had helped Carnevali, as McAlmon had fought Ethel Moorhead to help Kay find a publisher for Walsh's poetry, as Kay finally had published the compendium of pieces which she called Carnevali's *Autobiography*, and as she was now also working on getting René Crevel's *Babylone* back into print, so she re-created McAlmon's reputation as well. Tirelessly, and without the hope of great financial remuneration, she had made all this happen. She was paying homage in deed.

Malcolm Cowley devoted the entire first page of his front-page Sunday *New York Times* review of *Being Geniuses Together* to an assessment of why McAlmon had suffered so "spectacular" a neglect. He concluded it was because McAlmon "never in his life wrote so much as a memorable sentence." Only in the runover does Cowley get to Kay Boyle. Unlike McAlmon, Cowley writes, Kay had "mastered the craft of writing."

As she had with Edward Dahlberg, so now with Malcolm Cowley, Kay marched into a full-scale dispute. Cowley, of course, had come into direct conflict with her purpose, which was to grant McAlmon a recognition he had long been denied. Kay wrote Cowley she was "saddened" by the review, in which he had his "revenge on Bob" because McAlmon referred to him in the book as "a little slow on the uptake." She also had five "inaccuracies" to report in Cowley's review, four of which, however, were matters of opinion: Cowley had referred to Hemingway's "booklets," which were, in fact, books; McAlmon started a publishing house to publish his own work; McAlmon never wrote a memorable sentence, certainly an error, Kay Boyle contended, since Cowley had not mentioned which books of McAlmon's he had read (!). It was also "inaccurate" to quote Slater Brown, rather than people like Katherine Mansfield, Katherine Anne Porter, Joyce, and Eliot, all of whom admired McAlmon, Kay Boyle insisted. What might have been the one actual inaccuracy was Cowley's calling Ethel Moorhead Walsh's "mistress," although, by Kay's own account, she certainly behaved like one.

Showing some humor, Cowley told Kay Boyle that considering what McAlmon said about other people, being "a little slow on the uptake" amounted to "almost praise." Quietly he challenged Kay to quote for him a memorable sentence from one of McAlmon's books. Cordially he noted that Kay had been in jail, "the most honorable address in these times, for a conscientious citizen." (For the 1988 issue of *Twentieth Century Literature* devoted to Kay Boyle, Cowley contributed a paragraph saluting her "personal courage" and "long and brilliant career." On the subject of McAlmon, he was too honest not to admit that they did not agree. "I thought she fabulated," Cowley remembered.) Cowley's assessment of McAlmon's prose was in fact echoed by most people. Finding the review "not so bad," John Glassco wrote Kay that ninety percent of Bob's writing "*is* pretty slapdash."

Recovering as she was from a mastectomy, Kay took up Cowley's challenge. She enlisted friends to help her find memorable paragraphs and lines from McAlmon's writing. Glassco obliged and marked a few passages from *Miss Knight.* Loyally, he also called Cowley "rather sterile and Establishment." Jay Laughlin found her loyalty to McAlmon "beautiful . . . as it was with the Carnevali." Finally, that cooler head Howard Nemerov told Kay to "call it quits" in her quarrel with Cowley.

Later, relaxing, Kay played a game with her friend Studs Terkel in which Terkel cast the movie version of *Being Geniuses Together*: Peter O'Toole would play McAlmon; Vanessa Redgrave would be Kay Boyle.

Mario Puzo in his *Washington Post* review, however, had Audrey Hepburn in the role of the "hopelessly romantic" Kay Boyle.

Still sore from her mastectomy, sixty-six years old and the grandmother now of fourteen, Kay willed that she continue to be viewed as a woman in her prime. She obtained accreditation from *The Progressive* and moved to Jessica Mitford's house in Oakland that summer of 1968 to cover the trial of Black Panther Huey Newton, who had been charged with killing one policeman and wounding another. Kay Boyle, nothing if not partisan, took up the cause of the Black Panthers not out of radical chic, but because she believed they were playing an important role in exposing police brutality in the ghetto. With her usual hyperbole, she called Newton's "the most important trial of our time," certain as she was that it would "make history."

Unquestioningly, Kay Boyle accepted the group's view that the Oakland police were out to "get every Black Panther with or without pretext." The issue, she contended, was not whether Huey P. Newton shot Patrolman Frey, but "*why* he was stopped in the first place." With the zeal of the newly converted, Kay insisted it was "one more act of harassment in the organized plan to wipe the Black Panther Party leaders out of existence." For Kay Boyle, so recently granted a new lease on life, it was certain that the Black Panthers would "develop into the most constructive black liberation movement in America."

The piece she wrote for the October *Progressive*, "Notes on Jury Selection in the Huey P. Newton Trial," was sheer propaganda. The villain is seventy-two-year-old Judge Monroe Friedman with his "bleak-eyed furrowed mask," a man embittered, according to Kay, because President Eisenhower had not appointed him to the federal bench. Newton's lawyer, Charles Garry, on the other hand, is "brilliant" and "hard-hitting." In contrast to Friedman, who is "scrawny as a molting eagle," Garry looks "ten years younger than his fifty-nine years." As for the defendant, Huey P. Newton, he is a "warrior," an "articulate, slender young black man . . . self-assured and eagerly communicative," and one who has the masses on his side.

By the end of the article, Kay has argued that anyone who does not support the Black Panther Party and its solutions must be a racist. Indeed, one reader protested that her account of the jury selection process read like "the product of television westerns" in which she "labelled the good guys . . . and the bad guys." Undaunted, Kay wrote back that Huey P. Newton "was not, and could not be . . . tried before a jury of his peers!" As for her having offered only one-dimensional characters, she insisted that we must be "honest enough to admit that there are some pretty good guys around and a great many pretty bad ones as well."

On September 8, Huey P. Newton was found guilty of voluntary manslaughter in the shooting death of policeman Frey. The next day, ready to fight on, Kay Boyle wrote to Fay Stender, a member of the defense team, requesting stenographic records so she could expand her *Progressive* piece into a pamphlet. "It is only the first act that came to an end at ten o'clock last night," Kay closed. Never one in these later years of newfound activism to rely on words alone, Kay Boyle now joined the Black Panther Party herself.

As one of its closest white supporters, in October she introduced Eldridge Cleaver, the "Minister of Information," at a public meeting. Kay Boyle called Cleaver a "courageous artist," insisting that he and D. H. Lawrence were "blood brothers," as the language of *Soul on Ice* carried Lawrence's "dark, passionate searching for truths," no matter that, in fact, Cleaver's lawyer Beverly Axelrod had done most of the writing. She and Cleaver were in agreement, Kay said: all the white heroes, "their hands dripping with blood, are dead." She had bought the rhetoric wholesale. That night she announced that in November she would be casting her vote for Eldridge Cleaver for President of the United States. Kay also wrote a poem called "For James Schevill—On the Occasion of His Arrest," insisting again that America had become a police state: "the tongue that serves in courtroom is alien metal." Repeating her inevitable theme, she added, "Poets alone are summoned as witnesses."

Having read the piece in *The Progressive*, Joan Detweiler gently chided her sister. Kay could well have pointed out these injustices without rushing to the conclusion that America had become a police state. What society, Jo wondered, had proven itself "less sick, less power-dominated"? Grabbing her sword as she did so often in these years, Kay was incensed. Jo, in turn, was "stunned" that Kay could respond so angrily to a letter which had been written "with warmth, not heat," and she apologized. She had harbored "no feeling of disrespect" for her sister's work. But Kay Boyle could not be challenged, not by anyone, and certainly not by her lifelong antagonist, her older sister.

At Christmas, Kay flew off to spread the gospel in Paris, Frankfurt, and Innsbruck. In Paris, she spoke at the Sorbonne, and at the American Center for Students and Artists on the boulevard Raspail. She was paid only fifty dollars. But Kay Boyle was in her element. Announcing that the revolution was near, she presented herself in the vanguard of the struggle. In the audience sat Bobby. "I've always admired my mother," she later told Solita Solano. "But I'll never forget that evening!"

Three years from mandatory retirement, Kay Boyle was granted tenure at San Francisco State for the academic year 1968–69. Some noted that she always seemed to be giving tutorials, "directed reading" and writing, rather than undergraduate courses. But certainly she worked hard, always acting, her students thought as the years passed, much younger than she was. The postwar building which housed her office was dingy and decaying. But Kay kept a bottle of sherry in her desk and made the best of it. Her assignments too were eclectic, as she seemed always to be introducing her students to new writers, from John Hawkes to Charles Olson. One day she brought twenty copies of Richard Brautigan's *Trout Fishing in America* to class. What little money she had she spent generously and then scrambled to pay her bills.

Even as she revealed insecurity about her lack of academic degrees (she always wrote to Ted Keller as "Doctor"), Kay Boyle's suspicions of academe persisted. "The academic world really gives me nothing, absolutely nothing, and most professors are very alien to me," she said. There were ugly moments too. "That's not what you're supposed to have read," she told a young man in her course preparing students for their M.A. exams. At that, he picked up his book bag filled with books and threw it at her across the room. It hit her desk. At times she was autocratic in the classroom, calling the work of B. Traven, a student favorite in those years, "sentimental" junk.

With Keller and Hank McGuckin she team-taught a course called "Rebels and Reactionaries in Twentieth Century Literature." Kay Boyle would not discuss her own work, although Keller and McGuckin did; like others before them, they discovered the lesbian theme in "The Bridegroom's Body," only for Kay to profess dismay, even shock.

"I'm not pleased," Kay Boyle would say whenever Keller or McGuckin invoked one of her works. "I'm trying to rewrite that." When Keller assigned Jack London's *The Iron Heel*, Kay was irritated. "That's not literature!" she insisted, the proletcult not having got to her yet. For one of her "revolutionaries," she chose Chekhov.

Even as the years passed, she covered the students' stories with meticulous and constructive comments, writing so much, she laughed, that it became "a novel on that novel." Her comments were penetrating. "We will have to talk about why you write stories that stand like walls between you and the reader," she wrote to Dan Tooker. On legal pads she did line-by-line editing, neatly in the left margin listing page numbers, responding to virtually every sentence. "Is your typewriter ribbon very pale, or are my eyes worse than I thought?" she wrote at last. She signed her comments "KB." When her students' master's degree oral examinations came, she arrived with coffee and cake.

She was particularly skeptical about the value of teaching creative writing. Creative writing workshops, she thought, "should be absolutely abolished." What students needed, she believed, was a discipline, as she advised them to take astronomy or philosophy, or science or mathematics, doing for her students what she had not done herself or known how to do for her own children. They should get jobs as merchant seamen before they became writers, she advised. In each creative writing course, she begged the students never to take another workshop; workshops were "death to a would-be writer."

Her goal, she admitted, was to make "revolutionaries" of her students. She quoted, of course, Camus: "not by nature but through an effort of the will I tried not to separate myself from my time." Shawn Wong, who became a novelist and poet, remembered that "everything we wrote had to be relevant." Without convictions, she told them, they would fail as writers. In the same spirit, she opposed "the terrible emphasis on the first person singular," that perennial favorite of students.

Shawn Wong rented one of the available rooms at Frederick Street for seventy dollars a month. "I didn't hear your typewriter last night," Kay would tell him in the morning. She would start typing at 6 a.m. The first poem Shawn Wong published was called "A Letter to Kay Boyle," in homage, and when Paul Bowles, interviewing Kay, asked her to "name a student who will do something," she replied, "Shawn Wong." Wong was indeed the type of student Kay Boyle favored: he was a member of a minority, politically aware, an activist, and male.

Many years later she gave him her silver dessert spoons, forks, and ladles. "Here's part of the house you were a big part of, to remember," she told him fondly. Some of the silverware bore her mother's initials, some those of Mrs. Vail. "Use them every day and put them in the dishwasher!" Kay ordered. People were, as she did, to live for the moment, for the day. And some years after that when a reviewer gave Wong's novel *Homebase* something less than a rave, Kay was there to embarrass the man.

"Can you write a short story?" she demanded of Jesuit priest Jim Hietter, whom she said she was delighted to have in her class. "I was afraid you'd say it wasn't good and I was wasting my time with the Jesuits," Hietter told her. Kay Boyle looked him in the eye then. "You were hoping I would say it wasn't any good because writing is hard work," Kay admonished him. After Hietter took his orals, Kay made an imperial gesture: she stood up and threw her arms around him, preempting the other professors, who were supposed to confer as to whether he had passed. But when Hietter, a Southerner, wrote a story about a white woman and a black man, Kay was not pleased. "The white race has pretty much lost its energy," she said. "The black race is going to take over." That Hietter became one of Kay Boyle's "boys," is reflected in his appearance in her 1970 collection, *Testament for My Students:*

> There was Father Jim Hietter
> Muted laughter, muted grief, melodious student, saying to me
> That Christian hate had masqueraded for so long as Christian love
> The time had come to call it by its rightful name.

When Hietter wrote poetry with sexual imagery, however, Kay was distressed, as if this were unbecoming in a priest.

On her tour of Europe, Kay read aloud a poem by Hietter which concluded:

>*There is* POLICE ON EARTH
>*And Eichmann carols the countdown to the Child's birth.*

Kay told Hietter she had omitted a line, "Paste our eyes to the orgy of Bowl games," and changed that last line to the "*Christ* child's birth."

"That ruins it," Hietter told her.

"It makes it," Kay argued back. "The rhythm is better." (When Hietter published it in the *San Francisco Quarterly*, however, it was without "Christ.")

Kay did not confine her attentions to students for whom she predicted literary success. She took one Japanese-American student to AA meetings. She wrote long inspiring letters to students who simply told her that they couldn't hand their work in on time. "If you really want to write, you do," Kay Boyle said. A student named Gary Watkins thanked her for helping him regain his "sense of living" after the death of his mother. Some of her students joined the War Resisters League, others the chapter of Amnesty International which she had founded. She was such a strong motivator in part because she was, as one of her colleagues put it, a "pre-Freudian personality" who could demand strength of people without looking inward. No doubt thinking of her daughters, she told her students that delving deeply into oneself to find one's identity might end only in suicide.

The negative side of Kay Boyle as a teacher was that she could be cold, austere, and willful, and would never depart from a judgment, even one hastily made and proven incorrect. Sometimes she made foolish statements, such as that Clifton Fadiman had once given her a bad review because he was a Jew. She seemed uncritical of herself and opinionated, and she didn't respect views different from her own, as if, some thought, she had learned nothing from her own experience of McCarthyism. In the role of epic heroine she cut her wide swath, plunging into battle unburdened by either remorse or regret.

She viewed her role as teacher as extending far beyond the classroom. She tried to get her best students published, using her extensive New York contacts; indeed, in 1968 she got Victor Turks a four-hundred-dollar option contract for his novel from Harry Sions at Little, Brown. "I have been searching for someone who would think my writing is beautiful," Turks wrote her. "I have found that person in you." These students were invited to parties at Frederick Street, and there was a definite frisson of sexual energy between Kay Boyle and them. "When it was time for us to say goodnight, I embraced you and kissed you," Turks wrote, "it was lovely embracing you, darling Kay." One day she called out from her green Chevrolet to Dan Tooker, asking if he wanted a ride, and he felt as if it were not his teacher, but a woman in black leather boots, blue jeans, and a smashing shirt. It felt like an overture from a very attractive woman.

At the end of the day Kay Boyle enjoyed being seen to her yellow jeep with its canvas top and plastic windows by a young man. Stranded at

Sears one day, she called on Turks: "Victor, you've got to come quickly," Kay said. "I can't start the jeep!" Tooker invited a girlfriend to one of the parties at Frederick Street, and the young woman was amazed to discover that her hostess, nearing seventy, had by no means ruled herself out of the sexual wars. She still painted her toenails! "There's a woman still trying," the girl said in awe.

So confident was Kay in the strength of her appeal that she was upset when her colleague Charlotte Painter hadn't included her in a book called *Gifts of Age* about the lives of women seventy or over; in fact, Painter had asked her and she had declined. The contradictions, of course, were always there, as was the alternation in Kay Boyle between stately reserve, her customary hauteur, and a certain intimacy and frankness.

The light burned late in her attic room. Her life was, in fact, often now the life of a woman of age. She watched the evening news, fed the cats, did some gardening, hosed down the kitchen steps. One of the students living in the house on Frederick Street screened her calls. She visited Joseph's grave.

When she was sixty-six, however, an event occurred at San Francisco State which brought Kay Boyle once more back to the barricades she had first joined as a "flaming youth" in Cincinnati. As an outgrowth of the civil rights movement, in which Kay had taken so consistent a part, came the demand at American universities that they reconsider the profoundly Eurocentric curriculum. San Francisco State College was in 1968 a public institution with many aware black students, who now demanded a black studies program taught by black professors. It would be the first major black studies department in the country, representing the birth of multiculturalism, as, simultaneously, student leaders demanded an ethnic studies program to serve the many Asian students as well.

The undergraduate curriculum committee had tried to comply, and by the fall of 1968 had approved a Department of Black Studies based on a proposal authored by Nathan Hare. It included even a course called "Black Statistics." When a mathematician on the committee, who happened to be black, inquired what black statistics might be, Hare told him: "If you got three stores in the ghetto, and you burn one and loot another, how many have you got left? That's black statistics."

One black professor objected to the black studies proposal, arguing that he would have done so had it been "white" as well. It would have been "paternal racism" for him to have accepted an intellectually bankrupt idea. But such were the times, so thick had the polarized campus become with hostility, that the man abstained from voting out of fear that he might be beaten up. Heavily influenced by the Black Panthers, who had made their presence felt on campus, the Black Student Union called a student strike, despite the fact that the proposal for a black studies program had in fact passed.

The professors had been too slow for the Black Student Union, and for Kay Boyle, who during the academic year 1967–68 had been the sponsor of poet Sonia Sanchez, brought prematurely to campus to teach black studies. Sanchez taught a course in the evenings for black students, without credit, and Kay Boyle sat in. At first the black students resented her interventions, all those anecdotes about her own experiences. They were not "relevant." But Kay humbly behaved as if she were just another student in Sanchez's class, and she won them over.

When the disturbances began, Kay, her white hair a cloud of indignation, was ready to put her body on the line between police and students, ready to declare herself against authority, bureaucracy, and official academe.

31

Strike at

San Francisco State

Hayakawa Eichmann!

*The chisel of anti-rationalism driven by the hammer of moral
self-righteousness.*

JOHN H. BUNZEL

The upheaval began with a sit-in of several hundred students at the
administration building. A faculty member named John Gerassi had been
at the forefront of an "open campus" movement. Gerassi had declared that
if the ROTC and Dow Chemical could recruit on campus, so could Latin
American guerrilla movements, from Bolivia to Venezuela, as if guerrilla
movements would recruit publicly, like Pepsico, for peasant partisans of
an armed struggle. At one point Gerassi was boosted up to enter the
administration building through a window. Gerassi would claim that his
foot slipped and the glass shattered. But he could not dispute that he had
grabbed a bullhorn to urge the students on, promising they would not be
arrested.

Kay was having dinner at Herb Wilner's when Wilner received a call
to go to the campus to dissuade the vice president for academic affairs
from calling the police.

"I'm going with you," Kay said at once.

"Look, it's going to rain," Wilner told her. She was still feeling the
aftereffects of her mastectomy. It didn't seem like a good idea for her to
appear at a potentially violent scene.

"It's my college as much as yours," Kay replied. On that day she took
her stand on behalf of the students and black people she would term our
"redeemers." Students, she would say, were "the great and vital thing."
But Wilner and Kay were too late. Gerassi and ten students had been
arrested.

By the autumn of 1968 the Black Student Union was using fiery
rhetoric. Its members talked of revolution and of warfare against the police.
A black studies program at the school seemed a paltry demand given the

felt need to talk "revolution." They favored a strike that would pit them against the power structure and its repressive instrument, the "pigs." The issue of black and ethnic studies programs was merged with the desire for radical discourse about exploitation and imperial war, notably in Vietnam. How a student strike could, in itself, resolve these huge political questions went relatively unexplored by the third of the faculty which supported the strike, Kay included. There was no clear strategy for political organizing outside the campus or for how to win a wide base of support in the population at large. For most, the disparity between method and demand was mediated by raising the pitch of the rhetoric.

Several skirmishes preceded the strike. Black Panther Party "Minister of Education" George Murray, a graduate student teaching Special Admissions students remedial English, complained of racist reporting on the school paper. Instead of formulating appropriate demands and organizing student and faculty support, however, he and a group of others beat up the student editor and broke the finger of a journalism instructor. Such pseudo-revolutionary posturing was then presented as militance, and students and faculty were "tested" by the measure of their uncritical support for such tactics. In this climate Murray was permitted to continue to teach freshman composition in the English department.

At a campus rally, leading students in the chant "Fuck [Governor] Reagan," Eldridge Cleaver instructed them to "seize power," omitting any details as to how students without a political program, organization, or, as yet, mass support could take power from the "corporate elite." Middle-class students and faculty felt judged and intimidated if they did not match the revolutionary posturing with equivalent words and gestures of their own. Cleaver challenged Reagan to a duel, concluding his tirade with the line "Walk, chicken, with your ass picked clean." Kay Boyle continued in her unquestioning support for Cleaver. Soon Murray had announced that political power came through the barrel of a gun. One day he jumped up onto a table in the commons dining hall and urged all African-American students not only to support the strike but to carry guns at all times to defend themselves "from the murderous assault of the pigs."

This time Murray was fired. But now former SNCC activist Stokely Carmichael, temporarily a Black Panther, arrived on campus to address black students in an auditorium from which all whites were banned; those attempting to enter were beaten up and thrown out.

It was in this atmosphere that the Black Student Union now called its strike, issuing ten "nonnegotiable" demands, which included not only the black studies courses but open admissions and the rehiring of Murray. A "Third World Liberation Front" led the fight for a school of ethnic studies. They too demanded that Murray be rehired "as their teacher." At once members of the Black Student Union attempted to block and disrupt classes, and when some instructors refused to dismiss their students, fistfights broke out. Students were then bodily thrown out of classrooms, and professors were attacked. It wasn't long before the San Francisco Tactical Squad was called onto the campus. Bloody battles ensued.

Kay Boyle was an uncritical supporter of the strike from the start. The suspension of George Murray, she believed, was "just one more instance of effacing one more black individual from the record of those who are permitted to function as human beings in a white society." In her essay "The Long Walk at San Francisco State," Kay wrote: "as black and Third World students cleared building after building, lively and valuable dialogue took place, and there were teachers who temporarily relinquished their authority to the invaders and sat down as students themselves to listen to them speak." Whatever insight she might have gained into the rights of freedom of speech and opinion in her battle with McCarthyism, she now misappropriated Malcolm X's exhortation—"by any means necessary"— to apply to the students who disrupted classes as "education teams."

When the Black Student Union took over a faculty meeting and wouldn't even yield to the list of speakers, that was all right too. The threats came: should any of them teach, the black leaders told them, "we'll come with guns and get you. We'll get machine guns and get all of you. There ain't going to be any teaching!" Immediately the executive board of the teachers' union voted four to one to close the campus. Back came George Murray in sunglasses and an army field jacket denouncing the professors for not understanding the black man. The white radicals effaced their guilt with uncritical support. What if, Herb Wilner finally imagined himself asking Eldridge Cleaver, "*your* solution is part of the problem?" The question would not have occurred to Kay Boyle.

She saw herself at last as a heroine, her age no factor at all, part of a human wall protecting students from the justly hated Tactical Squad. At once she joined a Faculty Action Committee of thirty or forty people who agreed to be available whenever the Tactical Squad arrived to stand between police and students "as a buffer." Courageously, she told a reporter, "I don't mind dying for a worthy cause." Kay Boyle at sixty-six rose to the occasion as did few of her peers, even if she was uncritical in support of self-defeating tactics. She walked the picket lines several hours a day, pronouncing it "a very heartening experience." She also enjoyed the camaraderie of the picket lines; she was not a lonely widow feeding her cats, a writer whose best days were gone, but a member of a group fighting for a worthy cause. One day Kay picked up her sign for the day and it read: "All trustees are horse's asses."

"For God's sake, Kay, put that sign down," the group's lawyer told her.

In her zeal, however, Kay would brook no more opposition or disagreement than she ever had from husbands, lovers, or children. A professor named Joe Illick, who had in fact pioneered the first black studies course at San Francisco State in the spring of 1966, didn't join the strike because of the methods used and had crossed the picket line. When Herb Wilner tried to introduce him, Joe held out his hand, but Kay refused to take it, and stared through him as if he didn't exist. When she walked away, Wilner explained. "If you're not on strike, she won't talk to you."

Her rhetoric emulated that of the Black Panthers. In sweeping utterances delivered in her haughtiest of tones, she compared sixties America to Nazi Germany. Whether she was right on a given issue or not, however, Kay Boyle was always now the regal grande dame, and no one could tell her anything. Stuart Creighton Miller, who had chaired the curriculum committee, tried to tell her that the black studies proposal had in fact been approved and the ethnic studies program was about to be. Kay went on telling people it had not been done.

Some faculty members now called her conduct "deplorable, adolescent, and even unprofessional." But the sense that she was involved in worthy action, that, like Camus, she was putting her beliefs into practice, outweighed other considerations. Kay felt pride in putting herself between students and police. By her own account, she rescued one of her students, Eduardo Guerrero, who was about to throw rocks at the "plastic-masked faces of the Tactical Squad." Kay dropped her picket sign and flung her arms around Guerrero, threatening to "give him an F in the course if he stepped out of his rightful role."

On another occasion thirty police had been surrounded by four hundred students in a potentially violent situation. Kay and other faculty members proceeded to the scene. As Eric Solomon led his little band of faculty toward police and students, he hesitated. But Kay was right behind him. "Go *on!*" she insisted. For Solomon "it was like the Red Sea parting" as Kay Boyle, soldier in the ranks, led them all toward the commons, while students cheered. As the faculty demonstrators linked arms, they stood between students and police. It was war, a crusade. "Black, oriental, white, and Mexican," Kay later wrote, "we were resisting together the armed invasion of a territory we knew was entirely our own." She was a romantic heroine at war with the forces of reaction. In the midst of such physical danger, she had been rescued from the encroachments of old age.

For those faculty who did not wish to strike, let alone those who publicly deplored the tactics employed, life was made unbearable. A ticking bomb was placed outside Professor John Bunzel's office door. Still Kay Boyle expressed no disapproval. It seemed, rather, her heroes and villains firmly in place, she endorsed every disruption. She was, however, clear-sighted about the ruthlessness of the police special units, telling reporters she would not conduct her classes on the campus, even when it reopened, unless she was assured that her students "will not be killed by the police."

Kay continued to meet her students at her home. Later she admitted she gave A's to students who understood "the issues of the strike and wrote about those issues." She rewarded "comprehension of the realities of the struggle in which we were engaged" with the highest grade. When, later, during her lectures in Paris, an American told her, "That is not the subject you were hired for," which, of course, was teaching writing, Kay scathingly told him, "I would have had to give you an F for lack of comprehension." Kay Boyle saw herself as carrying the flame of revolution.

In the midst of the strike, in late November, S. I. Hayakawa, a linguist and popularizer of semantics and a faculty member who had opposed the strike, was named acting president. Hayakawa, a five-foot-six-inch Japanese-American with a little mustache and a trademark tam-o'-shanter, was no stranger to controversy. He had already defended the internment of his Japanese parents during World War II. "If he takes the job, we'll forgive him Pearl Harbor," Governor Ronald Reagan exulted condescendingly. Indeed, at once "Samurai Sam," as Hayakawa was nicknamed, filled the campus with police, leading to the injury of nine more students.

Following his appointment, Hayakawa called a press conference at the San Francisco Press Club. It was a Saturday and Kay was of course there. At once she rose from the audience to ask why Hayakawa hadn't chosen a faculty meeting instead of a press conference to inform the college of his plans. There have been too many faculty meetings already, he replied. Later when he tried to greet her, Kay locked her arms behind her back and told him he had betrayed the faculty.

On December 2, 1968, Kay Boyle arrived on the campus before eight in the morning to begin her picketing. A parked sound truck on Nineteenth and Holloway, not quite on the campus, exhorted students to stay out of class. Suddenly the voice was silenced. Hayakawa had leapt onto the back of the truck, jostling with its owner. Then, from his perch, he began to speak. In retaliation, the student turned his speakers back on in an attempt to drown the president out. Furious now, and out of control, Hayakawa found the wires and ripped them out.

"Private property!" cried the students.

In mockery, Hayakawa now began to lead the gathered students in the chant of "On strike! Shut it down!" He was so angry, one onlooker observed, that "you could see the foam on his mouth."

Suddenly Kay, in as loud a voice as she could muster, shouted up to the president.

"Hayakawa Eichmann!" Kay Boyle yelled. "Hayakawa Eichmann!"

"Kay Boyle, you're fired," Hayakawa shot back, pointing his finger directly at her. Later that day KPIX television accused Kay of "screaming curses like a fishwife."

When reporters gathered in his office, Hayakawa told them he had said, "Kay Boyle, you should be ashamed of yourself." He said he had no authority to fire a professor in any event. By March of 1969 Kay Boyle had joined with the owners of the truck and another professor in a suit against Hayakawa in which she demanded a public apology. Hayakawa, Kay said, her contradictions alive and well, had attacked "the right of freedom of speech." Indeed he had, but the behavior of the Panthers and their white counterparts undermined their own ability to invoke that argument.

It was only in March of 1969 that faculty and students settled their differences. Black studies would be taught; there would be no open admissions for Third World students. In jail for gun possession, George Murray did not get his job back. After one more confrontation with Hayakawa, Nathan Hare was fired. Kay completed her poem "Testament for My Students, 1968–69," in which she gave them her unstinting support without being able to help them transcend their serious limitations:

I am inclined
To agree with Eldridge Cleaver and the BSU
    that you are part of the problem
Or else you are part of the solution.

Kay had told people she was certain she would be fired, that she would need a new job for the academic year 1969–70. That did not happen. "It is not possible to teach at gunpoint," she melodramatically insisted, "and this is what Hayakawa and the trustees are demanding." The college did rule that she had "resigned" during the strike, thereby sacrificing her tenure. But Kay replied that she had met her classes, had turned in her grades. "Striking in a just cause," she said, "is far from resignation." Then she compared the dean of the School of the Humanities, James Wilson, to a "Nazi Party bureaucrat." January of 1969 was the first month she was not paid. Upset, she had her students write letters testifying they had attended her classes off campus during the strike.

In 1970 Grove Press published *The Long Walk at San Francisco State and Other Essays*, including her essay about Huey P. Newton and the one about seeing the sights in San Francisco. It was a paean to the strike and the strikers. Blacks and students, she proclaimed, were "two enormous and enormously historic figures who seem at times to be more alive than we are ourselves." She wrote as if a majority of the faculty had supported the strike, when, in fact, two-thirds had opposed it, as did many students.

When Kathe told her she thought the book was propagandistic, Kay Boyle was furious. She demanded that her daughter then call her books about the fall of France and the Germans and the Spanish propaganda too. "I find your letter a pretty severe indictment of all I am," she told Kathe. When John Bunzel's negative review, including the telling phrase "the chisel of anti-rationalism driven by the hammer of moral self-righteousness," appeared in the *San Francisco Sunday Examiner & Chronicle*, Kay wrote to the book review editor, Bill Hogan. She denounced Bunzel as an enemy of the students, a man so biased he had written his review in fulfillment of "a political grudge."

"May I add, dear Bill," she wrote, "that this is the first time I have written to an editor protesting a review of any book of mine." Hogan printed Kay Boyle's letter to him, including the "May I add, dear Bill" paragraph.

The politics of the late sixties and early seventies undoubtedly encouraged extreme attitudes like Kay's. The political finesse and courage and rationality of Bob Moses, who had selflessly risked his life in Mississippi so that black people might vote, had long since given way to the inflammatory tirades of Newton and Cleaver. To her friend Sonia Sanchez's distress, Kay continued to support Eldridge Cleaver. "Any man who is practicing on black women to rape white women—that's terrible for all women," Sonia told her. Considering him a "hustler," Sanchez refused to attend the parties Kay gave for Cleaver at her house. When Sanchez warned Kay that the Black Panthers were abusing young women adherents, she still would not listen.

Willfully she now began to denounce John Gerassi as an agent of the Central Intelligence Agency. Gerassi had been fired from San Francisco State following the demonstration at the administration building. Now Kay insisted there were violent demonstrations wherever Gerassi appeared, that far from being on the left, he was a CIA-financed provocateur. She told people he had insinuated himself with left-wing journalist Felix Greene; then he had proceeded to pump Greene for information about the war in Vietnam. Others, such as Ted Keller, noted that after he was fired, Gerassi disappeared and wasn't there for the strike, only to turn up in Paris in a very good situation, the "establishment" having taken him back. Kay Boyle insisted again and again that the CIA was known to plant provocateurs in the movement to foment violence and discredit the left. Gerassi, she was certain, was one of them. But she had no real proof that his behavior wasn't simply opportunism, infantile and self-aggrandizing perhaps but not necessarily the work of a paid government agent.

"How can you say that?" Herb Gold asked her when he saw that she had no real proof.

"I can tell. I can feel these things," Kay replied. Her intuition was enough. Later, when she went to teach at Hollins College in Virginia in 1970, the wife of one of the professors informed her that Gerassi, who had been at Hollins before her, had bragged that he had been with Che Guevara the day before he was killed—"more proof."

One day back in San Francisco, Kay got a call from Gerassi's lawyer, Charles Garry, who wanted to come and see her, bringing Gerassi with him. "He wants you to stop telling everybody he's a CIA agent," Garry told her.

"Well, he is," was the retort.

At the meeting Gerassi wore a beret, as if, Kay thought disapprovingly, he were trying to look like Che Guevara. She wore "her most capitalistic clothes," as she put it. Gerassi at once told her that people had started to become suspicious of him because of her statements. They had to stop. But Kay felt that Gerassi's own actions had engendered that view.

"I'm convinced that you are a CIA agent," Kay repeated. "What more can I say? And I'm not going to stop until you prove to me that you're not." (That she had only a decade before been required herself to prove a negative—that she was not a Communist—did not seem to occur to her.)

According to Kay Boyle, Gerassi then shouted at her, while Garry threatened to sue her for defamation of character.

"Sue me? I didn't call him a Communist, did I?" Kay replied.

A few weeks later, in the interest of resolving this dispute, Ted Keller and a lawyer friend of Gerassi's, Beverly Axelrod, the ghost collaborator on *Soul on Ice*, agreed on a strategy. Keller invited Kay to dinner. Afterwards, Gerassi and Axelrod arrived. Once more the subject was addressed. Axelrod indeed expected that Kay would have some facts they could counter. She offered nothing specific. Kay mentioned the names of those people who had told her Gerassi said he had been present at the execution of Che Guevara. She also accused him of having taken money from the Peace Corps.

Gerassi replied that he had never heard of these people, and had, in fact, been right there at San Francisco State at the time of Guevara's assassination, a fact Keller himself confirmed. It was true that he had lectured for the Peace Corps.

"I'd take money from anyone," Gerassi stated. "It's what you're doing that's important." Certainly the Peace Corps had never censored his remarks.

"My sources must be mistaken," Kay said, with respect to the murder of Guevara. But still she would not relent.

At this, Gerassi lost his temper.

"You're a congenital liar," he shouted. "You ought to be exposed yourself."

In the face of this opposition, and Keller's silence, Kay seemed to become almost hysterical. It was as if she had expected people to believe her on the strength of the fact that it was she who had made the accusations. As Gerassi continued to berate her, she walked out and didn't speak to Keller for some time. For his part, Gerassi attributed her motives to rivalry. "Nobody was paying any attention to her after I came," he said. "I really swept San Francisco to the left. The fact that I went on demonstrations, the fact that I got hit by cops, there were pictures of me with blood running down my face . . . Kay Boyle had to be jealous." Certainly Gerassi's behavior was counterproductive and undermined support for his professed views. He, like others, substituted disruption and stillborn rhetoric for the politics of creating a movement of people who shared his beliefs.

But Gerassi noted correctly that Kay "kept it up because she couldn't believe she had made a mistake." This was a familiar Kay Boyle stance, rushing to judgment and then defending the position before examining its inadequacies, never admitting she might have been wrong. She would continue to accuse Gerassi for years to come. In 1974 Kay had Maria Jolas check up on Gerassi in Paris. Jolas concluded he was a "mythomaniacal exhibitionist (the penis hanging out), poor, lost, *nut*," but not an agent of the American government. As Judge Clark might have put it, "God save the mark!"

Kay kept up her activist life even as age pursued her. A choking spasm on the boulevard St.-Germain turned out to be only sinus trouble. But late in 1969 she had her first bout with what would be chronic diverticulitis. In June of 1970, she had a slight stroke. She kept on. Ted Keller had to drag her away from a vigil for Eldridge Cleaver ("our beloved Eldridge Cleaver," Kay called him) at a church. A group of young people had followed her and Ted Keller back to the house on Frederick Street, where, about to serve coffee, she suddenly turned pale, fatigue washing over her. Then she threw her head back, stormed into the kitchen, and made the coffee. At a demonstration at Union Square an indigent white man struck a well-dressed black man, only for Kay Boyle to rush forward to stop the white man from retaliating after his victim had returned a glancing blow. A few months later, perhaps because the incident did not fulfill her politics, she astonished Ted Keller by forgetting it had ever taken place.

Her career edged forward too. Richard Huett at Laurel Editions of Dell agreed to publish a peace anthology she had compiled with Justine Van Gundy, to be called *Enough of Dying*. Unperturbed by her failure to produce a credible history of Germany, Ken McCormick now extended her to a four-book contract, including her new poetry collection, *Testament for My Students*. Many of the poems were homages to famous friends, like James Baldwin ("We are a race in ourself, you and I / Sweet preacher") and Marianne Moore. There were also those older homages to McAlmon, Harry Crosby, Robert Carlton Brown, and Laurence Vail. The fourth book would be a new novel. "This gives a whole new lease to life," Kay Boyle wrote McCormick gratefully. But she declined McCormick's offer that she write Carson McCullers's biography. She would only produce "an evil book," Kay told him. So disenchanted with McCullers had she become that she even felt guilty at having kept the silver baby cup Carson gave her when her godchild, Faith Carson, was born. That Carson's husband, Reeves, whom Kay "loved," had been the "lover of one of my beautiful daughters" made the project doubly impossible.

When *Esquire* wanted her list of "underrated and overrated" writers, Kay Boyle was ready. At the top of her list of the underrated was Marianne Moore, "who was never for an instant concerned in working on her image." Moore was followed by McAlmon, Grace Paley, William Carlos Williams, Langston Hughes, Eudora Welty, Maya Angelou, and Sherwood Anderson. Those overrated ranged from Pound and Eliot to lesser lights like Sinclair

Lewis, Sylvia Plath, and Norman Mailer. That she listed Lawrence Ferlinghetti among the overrated did not later prevent her from including his
name on her list for advance copies of *Testament for My Students* sent to
elicit favorable quotes.

There was time too for one more brouhaha; this time her victim was
a Long Island University professor named Jack Salzman, who had carelessly
described her as working in Germany for the "War Department" in 1943.
Kay rose up in indignation: the implication had to be that she was working
for the Nazis, since the only War Department there had to be the German!
Such a suggestion was not only damaging but "actionable." Jay Laughlin,
she decreed, must write Salzman demanding that his anthology of stories,
The Survival Years, be withdrawn at once from circulation. Even as in
October of 1969 Laughlin dutifully wrote to Salzman, he told her he doubted
they could succeed without a lawyer. But Kay's high-minded tones of moral
self-righteousness as conveyed by Laughlin worked. Salzman and his publisher, Pegasus, capitulated. Shipment of the books ceased. The entire
stock was returned to the bindery.

Kay spent Christmas of 1969 alone. Faith and Ian were at the Lyman
family commune in Roxbury, Clover in New York, Apple in Miami, Bobby
and Kathe in France. Having accused Clover of being "frightened of love,"
Kay was alienated from this daughter too. Clover longed to discuss their
relationship, but Kay refused. As Robert W. French, among others, noted
in his highly favorable review of *Testament for My Students*, "for Kay Boyle
the dominant movement has been outward rather than inward." Still she
argued that one would do well to repress one's feelings. Accusing Clover
of not having read her books, she brought up the financial hardship she
and Joseph had suffered sending her to Bennington.

Kathe too was alienated from her mother. "Love is acceptance and
indulgence and not constant judging," Kathe told her mother in sad dis-
affection. Kay Boyle immediately wrote back that her daughter was "judging" *her*. Kathe perceived that her mother's constant gifts and financial
help amounted to "interference." Kay replied that she was only wishing
"to help you lead the life you have chosen," in one more attempt to justify
herself. It was Kathe who seemed to feel the weight of her mother's judgments: about her smoking, her "complexes," and her "bourgeois values."
Her mother behaved, Kathe felt, as if she had "a right" to change her
daughter. At this, of course, Kay became angry, as she appealed to the
older children for sympathy for her having lost Faith and Ian to the commune. Failing to understand that her children were begging to be loved
for themselves, she defined a mother as "one who seeks to transmit to her
child her own love for all people, her own convictions about justice, her
own sense of freedom about the lives of others." Motherhood too, now, was
about politics. She sold her papers to Southern Illinois University, receiving
a check for $14,800, and including in the boxes she shipped off to Car-
bondale many very personal letters to her from her children.

On Christmas Day, Kay Boyle went to visit the Indians living in the abandoned prison on Alcatraz Island, bearing a gift of much-needed propane gas. She was to visit Alcatraz four times and write a short article for *The New Republic*. Rich friends like Ira Morris sent contributions to the Indians. "How any of us could ever complain about anything after seeing the conditions they are living under so courageously there is beyond imagination," she wrote Mike Watkins.

Caresse Crosby died of heart disease on January 24, 1970. "You are among the very, very few women that Caresse ever had any real affection for," her companion, Robert Boone, wrote Kay. When the *San Francisco Chronicle* obituary suggested that Caresse had "made a career of having her own way," the writer received a long indignant letter from Kay Boyle. There were few causes Kay overlooked in these years, from Anita Pollitzer's long effort to publish her biography of Georgia O'Keeffe to the fate of George Jackson, accused of murdering a guard in prison, and his brother Jonathan, who had stormed into the Marin County courthouse and shot a police officer. "The letters of George Jackson," Kay Boyle insisted, "could teach creative writing students more about writing, and about *thinking*, than any course I know."

Kay taught at Hollins College during the academic year 1970–71, and was paid a minimal salary of thirteen thousand dollars. At the cocktail party welcoming her, she confronted the president, John A. Logan, Jr.: why weren't there any black people in attendance at the event? In her poem "On Taking Up Residence in Virginia," dedicated to Joyce, she wrote that she now shared with him the experience of living on alien land. But Kay charmed many of the professors she met, including one man at the University of North Carolina at Greensboro, whom she startled by asking him to zip up her dress. To her host that day she seemed "an old lady of good breeding, charm and definite opinions who had embraced every left-wing cause."

That autumn Kay appeared in New York on a panel about the fate of the short story. "I don't think students should take writing courses," she repeated. Jean Stafford, whom Kay, her hair dyed black, her white earrings in place, treated as a rival, said she wrote "for myself and God and a few close friends." Kay Boyle's acerbic reply was: "I don't think God's going to hear you."

In October, Kay Boyle received a disturbing telephone call from the tenants in her house on Frederick Street. Members of the Lyman family commune had invaded the house, and the tenants were frightened. For years Kay had been attempting to persuade Ian to leave the commune. She took up the cause of a former girlfriend of Ian's, criticizing her replacement as "unstable." She accused Mel Lyman of "destroying the identity and the individual will of every man who becomes involved in the hill." She told Ian his life had no "enduring meaning," and that he was "callous," a "shattered man," who was "afraid of life." If having lost Faith hurt Kay Boyle, losing Ian, her favorite, was devastating.

Ian treated these imprecations as manifestations of his mother's possessiveness, but never broke off contact with her. He asked her to send him a gun since the neighborhood in Roxbury was dangerous. She refused. She did express her pleasure that some "hill people" knew some Black Panthers. But she urged Ian not to join the Panthers, as she had done. That would involve his once more "submerging" his will "in a communal decision." She offered him a trip to Austria, where his cousins needed him "to assure themselves that they are men." She told him he was "a rare and extraordinary person, and to refuse to accept the responsibility of your own character and your own gifts is a very destructive thing for you." As possessive parents will, she threatened Ian with her age. "I shall not be alive forever," she wrote.

One day Ian called Kay at Hollins to announce that he was returning to San Francisco to look for a job. Kay was elated. It meant that he was leaving the commune. "I'm very happy," she told him, reminding him that his apartment awaited him.

"Oh yes, I know that," Ian told her.

Kay added that the present tenants had rented the house until June. Then, suspicious as always of Mel Lyman, Kay called Ian back to emphasize that no changes were to be made in the house until her return.

"Don't you trust me, Mom?" Ian asked her.

32

Feminists

So I am again the abandoner and not the abandoned.

At seven one morning, Kay Boyle received a telephone call from one of her tenants. Arriving in the company of David Gude, Ian had informed the woman that she would have to leave immediately. Whatever agreement she had made with Kay was rendered null and void. Great changes were coming, Ian had announced to the small besieged group of tenants. He was taking over the house as a West Coast branch of the Lyman family commune. Immediately Gude and another commune member moved quantities of electronic equipment into the living room which was a common room shared by Kay's tenants. Chaos erupted.

Kay immediately telephoned. Gude, the man she called her "son-in-law," now accused her of "conventional morality" and of being "hide-bound by right conduct."

"We're going to have this house if we have to burn it to the ground," Gude told her.

After three frantic telephone calls from Kay Boyle, Ian and Gude still had not obeyed her instructions and moved out. Ian told his mother, "If you don't give me the entire house at once, this is the end of our relationship." Their taking the house was for Faith, Ian said. It was also Mel Lyman's wish.

Kay Boyle had a powerful ally, however, in a black neighborhood friend named Reginald Major, to whom James Baldwin had introduced her. The director of the Educational Opportunity program at San Francisco State, Major had written a book called *The Panther Is a Black Cat*. Although he was not a member of that organization, Major had friends among them. Now Major made his presence felt. Intimidated, Ian and his friend departed.

A month later, Ian and another commune member named Owen de

Long were back. Owen moved into one of the rooms. The living room was rearranged. Owen made his presence felt very specifically. One day he physically attacked one of the tenants, pinning her arms behind her back. "Is this what your family is like?" she demanded of Ian, whom everyone recognized as a gentle person. "But you made him angry," Ian told her.

Doors were now barricaded, furniture removed. Asked to wash his spoon, which he had thrown defiantly into the sink, Owen screamed and threw the spoon at one of the tenants. Kay was consulted on what exactly were Ian's privileges. In fact, Ian owned half of the house; his name was on the deed.

Kay sent Ian a telegram. "I beg of you not to have guests living in a house which is completely rented to others. This is a breach of my trust in you and if necessary I shall return to SF to make my meaning clear." Nothing worked. "I feel utterly lost and undone," she wrote to Jessica Mitford. "I want to leave the country and forget the past decades of my life, in which these two children were almost my entire existence."

Kay hoped Reggie Major might frighten Ian again, that through the tug-of-war between Ian's dread of Major and his fear that obeying his mother would lead to censure by Faith and Mel Lyman, she might solve her problem. "What's your philosophy?" Major demanded of the Lyman members. "Sounds like fascism." When Major left, one of the Lyman people said, "Well, we got rid of *that* nigger." But this wasn't the last the Lyman family would hear of Reginald Major.

It was, finally, Jessica Mitford's husband, the lawyer Robert Treuhaft, who saved Kay's house for her that November. Treuhaft told Ian that Kay had capitulated, and invited him to his office. Boasting of his knowledge of the law, Owen de Long accompanied him.

When they arrived, Treuhaft told them he had drawn up all the papers transferring the property to the commune; all Ian had to do was sign it. Treuhaft passed the document to Ian, who turned it over to the friend who had bragged he had taken some law courses. "We ought to read this over," Ian told him. "Oh, no, I'm sure it's all right," De Long said, impressed by Treuhaft's Harvard diploma. "He went to Harvard Law School. He must know what he's doing."

Without reading the document, Ian signed away his rights, transferring sole ownership of 419 Frederick Street back to his mother. Treuhaft then called Kay, and she suggested that Reggie Major handle the rest.

Ian was told that Kay had sold Reginald Major the house, and, indeed, Major soon appeared in the company of two Black Panther friends. "I have a piece of paper," he told Ian in his booming voice. Kay Boyle had sold the Black Panthers the house, and Ian and his friends had to get out.

"It's impossible," Ian said, as the Lymans now pleaded that they were merely encouraging the tenants to be more enlightened.

"We don't want you here. If you have any argument, discuss it with your mother," Major told Ian. Meanwhile, not only did he have a deed, but he also had, as Major puts it, "an absolute willingness to shoot them." It turned out that no blows were necessary. Ian and Owen de Long slunk off, and none of the Lymans returned. They were cowards, Major concluded. Soon they invaded the KPFA radio studios insisting that Mel Lyman's music be played. When their demands were not met, they wrecked the studio.

Forever after, in an effort to protect her beloved son from looking foolish, Kay Boyle propagated the story that she had sold her house on Frederick Street to a "Black Panther," Reginald Major, for one dollar. Major backed her up, explaining that Treuhaft had mailed the deed to Kay for her to sign and that he, in turn, quitclaimed it right back. It wasn't, of course, necessary for the property to be sold to Major once Ian's name had been removed from the deed. But the story of the sale to a Black Panther bore a romantic frisson of danger. In fact, Kay's real problem was different: she did not want to resort to the police to evict Ian and the Lyman family members. The solution had been a salutary one. Meanwhile Kay told the story to David Felton, who was then writing about cults and cultists, from Mel Lyman to Charles Manson, for *Rolling Stone*.

Proud that she was the only cult parent who had been willing to talk to the press, Kay told Felton exactly what she thought of Mel Lyman. After his articles appeared, Faith began to mail Kay Boyle's letters back to her unopened, marked "return to sender."

One Tuesday in July of 1971, Faith paid her mother a visit at 419 Frederick Street. Kay later told Kathe that Faith had worn black leather and had carried a whip; there was no doubt in her mind that Faith had come for a "confrontation." In fact, Faith arrived to talk. The tenants were present, as well as Ian and Jim Kweskin, the jug-band leader, who was also a Lyman family member.

"You're a cruel daughter," Kay accused Faith. "Did Mel Lyman send you here?"

By midnight, tempers had flared. "What crime am I on trial for?" Kay demanded. "What is the crime I've committed?"

Suddenly Faith slapped her mother so hard across the face that Kay lost her balance and fell. At once Faith was sorry. It was inexcusable. But Kay ran from the room, falling on her knees in her bedroom. When Faith rushed after her, and tried to put her arms around her mother, she pushed her away.

Yet on Christmas Day 1971, Faith appeared again at Frederick Street in the company of her four children. She felt betrayed by the Felton articles in which Kay had called the Lyman family "fascist monsters." She wanted her mother to make a public retraction. But not only did Kay say she would never take back her words, she called it her duty to speak publicly about the commune since it was the "only way to destroy Lyman's power." From her vantage, her daughter's privacy was less important than the exposure of a destructive cult.

At the moment when Faith struck her mother, the Lyman family lost its power over Ian Franckenstein, and he never returned to Roxbury. It was over. Years later, however, he revealed that he had not entirely accepted his mother's condemnation of Mel Lyman. Kay Boyle, he said, "has very little tolerance . . . and doesn't even begin to understand how a Mel Lyman functions, or why." Mel Lyman died in his late thirties, but the commune lives on to this day, his picture lovingly displayed in every room of the many houses the family now owns.

Kay now took the story of Faith and the commune, as well as her own imprisonment at Santa Rita, as the subject of her new novel. In 1975 Doubleday published *The Underground Woman*, which culminates in the commune's attempted takeover of the house on Frederick Street. Missing entirely from the story is Ian, as if the author could not bear to write about her son's effort to secure his independence from her.

Otherwise the book is as linearly autobiographical as most of Kay Boyle's fiction. Where events do not match the reality, they express needs, fantasies, and dreams of the author, as she once more uses her fiction to justify behavior about which she herself was in doubt. The heroine, Athena, is forty-two, not in her late sixties, but she is a professor who "got into the academic world by the back door." Kay also employs the real names of students Eduardo Guerrero and Shawn Wong.

Often Athena behaves as if she were a woman in her sixties, pleading that she is glad sexuality is gone from her life, the better to "be able to take action without suffering this inner drama of division." As Kay Boyle must have done, she mourns her lost "round throat" and "the exquisite brilliance of her eyes," pondering whether "they were presented as gifts to my daughters." So she revealed in her fiction, where she was often most honest, that she resented her daughters as women, as competitors, as Laurence had always accused her of doing. That the Faith character, Melanie, has two children, as Faith had when her mother was arrested, is "just one of the ways that the lives of daughters transcribe their mothers' lives." Daughters were collaborators with time, that enemy against which Kay Boyle would do combat all her life.

As the author vents her anger in this novel, Melanie is also a "witch," who has given "her will and her conscience into the bondage of idolatry." Safeguarding Ian's privacy was one thing. Faith's was another. Kay Boyle even depicts Faith as a child kleptomaniac (which she was) whose "saintly beauty" saved her from the consequences of her actions. Indeed, the older children thought their mother was jealous of Faith, this most beautiful of her daughters, who, as a child, when she wanted something would have Ian, their mother's favorite, whom she called her "saviour," do the asking.

"Beautiful as Venus riding the wave," Faith is the villain stalking *The Underground Woman*. The tape of Faith on her LSD trip is here, minus the sexual element, as is Kay's throwing that frying pan at Jessie Benton.

Here Kay pictures herself throwing it at Mel Lyman. Accusing the commune of seeking only "fame and fortune," she writes about Faith as if she were lost to her forever. Often, however, her language is static and rhetorical with a tedious overlay of mythological parallels; the only one which works, and then only partially, is the story of Demeter and Persephone, an obvious analogue to Kay's relationship with Faith.

Yet even in so weak a novel as *The Underground Woman* there are those insights into herself which Kay reserved for her fiction. A fellow prisoner says that what every young woman fears is becoming "not like her mother, but exactly the same woman her mother was," as if Kay Boyle, now seventy-three years old, had at last caught a glimpse into the insidious nature of Katherine's control over her. A young woman is urged to leave home, as Kay Boyle justifies once more her own decision to abandon her hapless father, Howard; late in life she ponders whether she might have "made something else out of the silence between us simply by asking him to allow me a choice."

It is her own father's love, and his long absence from her life, which strangely whispers through *The Underground Woman*. Otherwise, as always, Kay Boyle defends herself against the charge that she was not a sufficiently nurturing mother; her character wishes she could touch her children's hands again. If Joseph is so idealized as Rory that he seems not like a real man at all, she reveals a glimpse into her own loneliness as she returns from prison to the empty house on Frederick Street. There is a sexual kiss with Luchies McDoniel, the Reginald Major figure. Robert Treuhaft has become an African-American. He need not trick Ian, since, for once in her fiction, there is no son at all.

It is one of the boys from the commune who "raised his right hand and struck her hard across the face . . . struck her twice with his open palm and she stumbled back against the sink." Kay could not bear to write that it was Faith who had so struck her. But Kay adds, "I knew it wasn't Lucky's hand striking me. I couldn't bear it any more because it was Melanie's hand." If only figuratively, the truth does out.

Kay herself called *The Underground Woman* "practically unreadable." But for this final and weakest of her novels, she was fortunate in her reviews. *The New York Times Book Review*, *The Nation*, and *The New Republic* all reviewed her on her good intentions and moral fortitude. *The Nation* praised her "worthy" effort, her "attempt to enlighten her fellow citizens." Admitting the novel was "imperfect," the *Times* said it spoke "to all sensitive and conventional women with bad consciences," offering them "a way toward self-respect." In *The New Republic* Doris Grumbach commented almost exclusively on Kay Boyle's politics, praising her for "her activity on behalf of amnesty, and for the freedom of political prisoners everywhere." Others wrote more objectively. *Newsweek* suggested that Kay was "too close to her prison experience and her daughter's ordeal . . . to turn either into good fiction." But Blanche H. Gelfant in the *Hudson Review*, despite the outdated "machinery of the novel," warmly praised the author for the courage she embodied, which was not routine at all.

For Kay it had been more important to tell the story of the commune once more than to repair her tattered relationship with Faith. "She brought me up to live this life and once I started living this life she hated me for living this life," Faith concluded, remembering her mother's foray into Raymond Duncan's commune, which was as much a cult as Mel Lyman's family was. Faith said that Kay "was extremely possessive of her children and Mel was a rival," particularly with Ian. "He challenged her authority over her son," Faith says, "and that was insupportable." It would be twenty years before Kay and Faith were to meet again.

If Kay Boyle endorsed most of the radical movements of the sixties and seventies, there was one cause of which she wanted no part. That was feminism. Socially, despite her having close women friends like Joan Baez and Jessica Mitford, she preferred men overwhelmingly to women. Indeed, many women at San Francisco State, discovering how much more kindly disposed she was toward male students, refused to sign up for her classes. "A book by a man almost always offers the full-length portrait of its author," Kay Boyle wrote in one of her book reviews. "Women writers, on the other hand, are frequently on the defensive." She concluded in that review that "competency in a woman or a woman writer can be appealing as long as there is also present the charm of hesitancy and uncertainty."

In the early seventies, when women were protesting their virtual exclusion from the literary canon, Kay Boyle persisted in her view that being a woman had never been an obstacle to her. "On the contrary," she told one interviewer, "people love women writers—sometimes too much." Perhaps still recoiling from her competition with her older sister, she cast a cool eye on her female competition.

One day Herb Gold brought to tea at Frederick Street a woman friend who was writing a doctoral dissertation on the poet Philippe Soupault. Kay had told Gold that she would agree to an interview and would tell the woman what she knew. But taking one look at the young and beautiful graduate student, Kay became curt and abrupt; she would say nothing.

"Did you know him?" the woman began.

"Yes, I knew him very well," Kay admitted.

"Can you tell me about him?" the poor woman persisted.

"He was a good friend of mine," Kay replied coldly, refusing to offer the young woman even a crumb of her reminiscences. It wasn't even graceful, Gold thought. It was funny. It was clear to him that as soon as the beautiful younger woman had walked in, Kay had decided she wasn't going to help her.

As by the mid-seventies the women's movement gained momentum, Kay revealed definite hostility to women and their aspirations. Interviewed by Merla Zellerbach for the *San Francisco Chronicle* on the subject of women of wealth who worked, Kay Boyle argued that the trend was not all that positive because "certain people get jobs not because of their ability but because of their fame." Her examples were Lynda Robb, Lyndon Johnson's daughter, and Jacqueline Onassis, who didn't strike Kay Boyle as "being either practical or well-organized." Always she was harder on women than on men. "I don't think women should try to write like men but I think they should try not to write like women," she had said in 1964, before the movement had taken shape. "What I mean by that is presenting the woman's instead of the human point of view."

Feminism to Kay was mistakenly synonymous with separatism, as she persistently revealed a lack of sympathy with the efforts of women to transcend their traditional social role. Nor would she ever change her mind. She had not had to make that exhausting effort to be taken seriously, thanks in part to her mother. Perhaps out of some unconscious revulsion at what her mother had made her, Kay held out long and hard against supporting women struggling to live independent creative lives.

When the women graduate students at San Francisco State demanded that they be permitted to include Tillie Olsen among the three writers whom they chose to study in depth for their master's degree orals, Kay Boyle objected vehemently. Tillie Olsen hadn't accomplished enough, wasn't good enough. She had only written "three short stories." The student who made the request went over Kay Boyle's head to Herb Wilner, who, supporting Kay, told her there were forty significant women writers, but Tillie Olsen wasn't one of them. Then he told his wife, Nancy, "We'll be up all night. We have to think of forty women writers."

Kay liked to tell the story of how her women students refused to read Samuel Beckett and Bertolt Brecht because they were men. "Why do you want to study with me? What is it that you've read?" she would demand of women students. If one might be ill-advised enough to tell her, "I've never read anything you've written, but you're a woman," Kay would be very angry. If she had forgiven the Black Panthers their excesses, she would not extend the same courtesy to young women forging their own way. *The Nation* had been grateful that *The Underground Woman* was "not a feminist novel, in the tendentious sense," implying that there was no other. That line could not but have pleased Kay Boyle.

Kay wrote the publisher that she had enjoyed *Sexual Politics*, Kate Millett's groundbreaking study of the image of women in literature written by men. She said she had been "impressed by [Millett's] clarity, simplicity, and astuteness." Yet she never wavered in insisting that women be offered no special dispensations merely because they were women. And she began to oppose their demands for greater power, greater voice, and more equity. Exaggerating her case as always, she reported that her feminist students had been distressed when they learned that at a peace march in Belfast women had walked hand in hand with their husbands. "We all know there are awful, terrible women, and there are awful terrible men. And though women as a group have been disadvantaged, so have men," she said.

Repeatedly she declared that she didn't "want to be in a separatist group. It's doing to the men what men have done to the women through the years." The feminists were those women who "had had terrible conflicts with their fathers," as if their behavior, and no one else's, was motivated by early childhood pain. The sympathy she had afforded students and African-Americans was unavailable to members of her own sex.

Through the seventies, she kept up a drumbeat of opposition to the women's movement: "I think the women's movement is a reactionary movement, and they want what the man has, and I don't happen to want what that man has . . . I don't want a good paying job in a bank . . . I want a total revolution where everybody is equal." It was, Kay granted, "a man's world." But she believed that what was required was "the liberation of all people, both women and men." The enemy was "the social system," not men. Asked by interviewer Barbaralee Diamonstein whether she preferred the company of men or women, Kay Boyle replied, "Both equally"; it was "the spirit, the mind, the temperament" that interested her, "not the mere fact of their maleness or their femaleness." Yet it was also obvious that she was irritated by what she called the "soul-searching" of women; the slightest weakness expressed by women in the movement provoked her scorn.

In her classes she waged war against many women writers, among them Anaïs Nin. "Art is NOT the submersion in oneself," she repeated, as if hers were the only way to write, as if now, at her age, she feared introspection all the more. Sylvia Plath, the favorite of many women students, also invited her scorn. "I am convinced that if Anaïs Nin were to commit suicide, she would outstrip Plath in popularity," Kay said, neatly slaying her two birds.

Yet some women students at San Francisco State considered her approach salutary, like Jana Harris, who wrote Kay that teachers and students with too strong a feminist consciousness were afraid that "any critical comments" might be "too harsh" and "dampen my spirits," while men considered her work "a little too powerful and violent for a girl." Kay Boyle made neither of these errors. To another woman student, Kay wrote that at moments of desperation in her life she used to say that "to be a woman writer you *had* to be a Lesbian; in other words, you had to have someone (as did Gertrude Stein) to do the urgent daily household things for one." As she confounded the issues of gender, sexuality, and class, she chose to ignore now, of course, that she herself over the years had had many servants. "Above all," Kay told the student, as she offered her motivation, "*write*, create, don't analyze too much. That can destroy everything you are." It was her lifelong antirationalist credo.

That Kay Boyle so set herself against the new women's movement might well have accounted for the fact that the new women's studies teachers excluded her from their syllabi. For a Rutgers University course entitled "The Woman Writer in the 20th Century," feminist literary critic Elaine Showalter did not even include Kay Boyle in a unit called "expatriates and rebels," or in one devoted to "women living politically." Showalter says it did not even occur to her to choose her. Nor did a *College English* article called "The New Feminist Criticism," by Annis Pratt, examining how women writers dealt with "the heroine's entanglement with patriarchal norms," even mention the author of *Plagued by the Nightingale*, although it deals with just that conflict. When she should have been rediscovered by women seeking recognition for those of their sex whom cultural bigotry had deemed inferior to male writers, Kay Boyle was repaid for her attacks on their fledgling movement by being virtually ignored. Nor, of course, would she raise her voice in protest. When the Feminist Party of the USA awarded her their annual Media Workshop Award in 1974, Kay was astounded. "How did that ever happen?" she wondered. "I'm not a feminist!"

As a woman in her seventies Kay Boyle remained loyal to Ernest Walsh's distinctly antifeminist insistence that her role in life would be as one who paid homage to the great. "I served and gave homage to others in the traditional feminine role," she said, echoing Walsh's words in 1976. "It was a role to which I was well suited, and still am today." Sympathy with feminism, any rebellion against the "traditional feminine role," would amount to disloyalty to Ernest Walsh's memory.

That autumn, the women students at San Francisco State finally became fed up with both what they perceived as male domination of the creative writing department and a male-oriented curriculum. On the advice of the director of the Poetry Center, the poet Kathleen Fraser, they formed a Women's Caucus and threatened to go on strike unless a full-time tenured woman full professor was hired. They also demanded that the curriculum include certain women authors now unavailable to them for study as "major authors" on the M.A. orals examination. Among them, of course, was Tillie Olsen.

When she had been "forced into retirement" in 1973, Kay Boyle had been the only female professor in the department. But she continued to teach as a professor emeritus, receiving, as she said, "the magnificent sum of two hundred and seventy-seven dollars a month." Her political role in the department also continued.

Kay vehemently opposed the Women's Caucus. The department didn't have the money to hire any more full professors, she argued. Kathleen Fraser, now teaching in the department, was an obvious candidate. Before long, Kay had set herself against Fraser's advancement. This was in direct contradiction to her vote a year earlier, in February of 1975, when she had urged that Fraser be promoted to assistant professor and had praised her as "a fine poet." For a low position, a young woman might be tolerated.

Kay now wrote a sharply negative letter urging that Fraser not be retained in the creative writing department at all. At first, her ground was that Fraser did not "have the scholarly expertise" to teach the 820 course in "major authors," although she was a widely published poet and critic and the recipient of many awards. But the letter makes it clear that it was Fraser's feminism which caused Kay to urge that the younger woman be fired.

Kay condemned what she called the "restrictions" Fraser had placed on herself "concerning male authors." She had encouraged and attended "segregated lectures and meetings," something "strictly taboo on any campus in our country," a posture which was "sexist, prejudicial, and totally at variance with enlightened teaching." It was all right with Kay when Stokely Carmichael, who had declared that the position of women in the movement should be "prone," spoke before a student audience at an event to which no whites were admitted. But when feminists gave readings from which men were excluded—or even met in the absence of men to discuss their agenda—Kay bitterly excoriated them. Nor was Kay Boyle above including trivial rumor in her denunciation. She had heard that Fraser had called a "number of fellow professors . . . male chauvinist pigs." Not only did Kay Boyle vote against Fraser's reappointment, but she urged others to do so as well.

Many saw Kay's stance as irrational, and noticed that she had excused the Panthers for what she wouldn't tolerate in women seeking their own voice. Linda Ferguson, a young friend of Kay's and editor of the literary supplement of the weekly *Pacific Sun*, wrote her that she knew Kay must have had a good reason for voting as she did. "Now," she asked Kay, "what is it?"

It seemed inexplicable. "I'm sick and tired of talking to middle-class women. I don't want to waste my time on any middle-class women," Kay had told a woman student. It was perhaps the bias of which Laurence had long ago accused her: her old prejudice against girls which made her as hidebound a victim of the social era into which she had been born as any reactionary. It had accounted for her obsessive need to bear a son, and to demonstrate her womanhood by bearing as many children as her body could endure. Now her acceptance of the higher value the culture placed on men, this prejudice, had surfaced in her single-minded opposition to the concerns of the women's movement of the 1970s.

Professor Stan Rice wrote in defense of Kathleen Fraser, with whom he had worked at the Poetry Center. Fraser had opposed the idea that men be excluded from the reading, he said; she had invited male poets to read, and when she retired from her directorship she had recommended both a man and a woman to replace her. That she had acted as a "bridge" between women students and the creative writing faculty did not make her responsible for the women's views. In an impassioned plea, Rice wrote that to punish Kathleen Fraser for attending a reading which excluded men amounted to "guilt by association," a line of reasoning by Kay Boyle which threw "the icy shadow of McCarthyism" over the proceedings.

Indeed, Kay Boyle's attack on Kathleen Fraser for "separatism" ignored the principle of self-determination and the right of those suffering oppression to organize themselves around issues, to work out their program, and to develop a political movement specific to their particular case. Imputing sexism to women banding together to fight their oppression was a classic instance of blaming the victim. To seek allies might be a later step to be taken after women had worked out their own needs, agenda, and political expression. About blacks, Kay Boyle was clear that this was necessary. Women she granted no such opportunity.

Over Kay Boyle's objections, the creative writing department did reappoint Fraser. But then the provost objected to the department's decision on the ground that they had not given Kay Boyle's concerns "sufficient attention." Fraser was forced to defend herself directly.

This she did, correcting Kay Boyle's statement about "segregated lectures and meetings" and pointing out that there had been only one such event. The speaker, poet Adrienne Rich, had herself requested that she meet only with women students and faculty. Learning that this was illegal on campus, Fraser had notified her students that they were to allow male guests. That women had every right to meet together to discuss their common problems was another matter, and perfectly acceptable. As for the charge of "separatism," Fraser wrote, "I abhor such attitudes as much as she and only wish she had chosen to check out the facts before writing a letter based on speculation."

In her courses, Fraser explained, she assigned male as well as female authors. "I have *never* been a separatist in principle or in action," Fraser pleaded. "I do not find it a useful or humanistic principle." Kay Boyle had argued she was not qualified to teach the "820 Selected Major Authors" course. Now Fraser had to tell the provost: "Professor Boyle never visited the class, nor did she at any time ask to discuss with me my teaching approach to the class." If Fraser was unqualified on the ground that she was not a "trained scholar" with a Ph.D., so was Kay Boyle and so was most of the creative writing faculty.

Kathleen Fraser requested a private meeting with Kay Boyle, and she was invited to tea at 419 Frederick Street. Kay did not turn on the lights, and the two women sat together in the gathering dusk. In her best manner as the grande dame, she poured tea. Politely she asked whether Kathleen took sugar or cream. It was as if nothing had happened, as if Kay Boyle had not jeopardized Fraser's entire academic career with false accusations and innuendo, based largely on guilt by association.

Kay told Fraser she needed to become more articulate at faculty meetings. Listening, Fraser felt that Kay Boyle as the powerful token woman in the department had neither understanding nor sympathy for how difficult it had been for her as a new young female in the department, only the second woman ever, untenured and unempowered. Meanwhile a majority of the student poets were women who had discovered that there were few women writers on their reading list.

Kay Boyle had assumed that Fraser was against men, that she had no male students. When Fraser denied this was so, Kay seemed to listen, and seemed to be surprised. Fraser had hoped that their discussion would result in Kay's voluntarily withdrawing her damaging letter, although she could make no such request. This did not happen. But Kay wrote no more attacks, and when Fraser came up for tenure, she did not object. At the end, Fraser concluded, it seemed that Kay had enjoyed being the one powerful woman, the heroine in a sea of men. Having other women around who might challenge that role did not please her.

Combat continued to keep Kay Boyle young. When she attacked Marshall Windmiller of the international relations department, he accused her of hurling "accusations without first ascertaining the facts." Kay rushed to judgment as well when Lawrence Ferlinghetti broke with his City Lights bookstore partner, "Shig" Murao, who had managed the shop for him. There had been widespread shoplifting and disastrous financial losses. Ferlinghetti had suggested he needed another manager. Offended, Shig had insisted they part company entirely. Hearing of the dispute, Kay Boyle leapt to Shig's defense without even asking Ferlinghetti what had happened. Even as, that fall of 1975, she organized a "Celebration for Shig Murao" at the house on Frederick Street at which famous writers donated valuable manuscripts, she only made matters worse.

Eldridge Cleaver remained a hero; in 1971 Kay Boyle had visited him in Algiers, bringing, at Cleaver's request, baby food and a pair of knee-high leather boots "for one of the sisters." From Paris that same winter, she returned bearing with her tapes Jane Fonda had made with American pilots in prison in Hanoi and a large piece of an exploded fragmentation bomb given her by left-wing Australian journalist Wilfred Burchett. Now, unlike during the Black Panther period, when she compared America to Nazi Germany, her arguments were grounded in fact. American saturation bombing exceeded in nine months the total tonnage used in the Pacific theater in World War II; the Phoenix program executed thousands of peasants, students, and trade union figures. Strategic hamlets, free-fire zones, and the use of bacteriological weapons had been part of a total warfare which killed two million Vietnamese. "Well, how do American manufacturers of napalm and antipersonnel fragmentation bombs differ from the German businessmen of the Nazi years?" Kay Boyle demanded on KPFA radio.

A student in the "Rebels and Reactionaries" course objected to the "fervent revolutionary posturing that is the style in class" and suggested to Kay that she add to the reading list Freud's *Civilization and Its Discon-*

tents. In return, he received an angry letter from Kay accusing him of distortion and lecturing him on the "near annihilation of an entire country," Vietnam. She wrote to Harper & Row objecting to their having published a book which stated, accurately, that George Jackson had beaten that guard to death in Soledad Prison. Kay's argument hinged not on whether Jackson was guilty, but on the betrayal of confidence by the writer, who, since he had been allowed to visit Jackson as a "legal researcher," had violated the lawyer-client relationship of confidentiality in what he wrote.

There were many Kay Boyles in these years. She was the grande dame when she opened the door to former student Dan Tooker, now interviewing her for a book, with a postcard from Nelson Algren in her hand, as if it were a fetish. She could be censorious, admonishing Bob Dunn, a student living in her house, for drinking milk out of the carton from the tenants' refrigerator instead of using a glass. "Didn't your mother teach you manners?" Kay demanded.

To his surprise, Dunn discovered that 419 Frederick Street was not a happy house. Dunn was also disconcerted as he watched the owner of Serendipity Books appraising, buying, and so dismantling Kay Boyle's splendid library; it seemed a travesty. On a practical level what bothered Dunn more than Kay Boyle's admonitions about his manners or about his playing music too loud was that she objected to his use of a space heater, although his room, adjacent to the garden, which he was expected to tend, was not heated. An aspiring writer, Dunn comforted himself with the thought that he was, after all, sleeping in Marcel Duchamp's old bed.

The birthday parties which were fund raisers for Amnesty continued, and even Ferlinghetti came once. But when columnist Herb Caen, a San Francisco institution himself, wrote that one of these parties was a gathering of "old Lefties," he received a long indignant letter from Kay Boyle. She took a course in astronomy at the planetarium in Golden Gate Park and on Friday nights, sometimes wearing blue jeans, she went folk dancing with Joan Baez, explaining, "I used to be a mountain climber, but at my age, folk dancing is about all I can undertake." She received honorary degrees in these years, from Columbia College in 1971 and from Skidmore.

There was also a Kay Boyle who was down to earth and unpretentious. Driving Kay back to California after a lecture at Southern Illinois, rare books librarian David Koch was amazed when, after the car got stuck in the salt flats, she squatted down on the open prairie in her long trench coat and urinated. At a truck stop she took out her bottle. Then she poured the water from her glass and added the booze. Local rednecks stared. "Is everything all right?" the owner, nonplussed, asked her.

"Fine," Kay Boyle said.

"You grow more attractive as the years slip by," her old admirer Shirer wrote her, "and that is something—to one who first knew you when you were one of the most attractive women Paris had in the twenties." Kay Boyle was not old yet.

Although her peace anthology, *Enough of Dying*, had sold twenty thousand copies by the end of December of 1972, Kay was still always short of money. In that year she earned from her writing only slightly more than nine hundred dollars; in 1973, six hundred. Fattened by the advance for *The Underground Woman*, her earnings reached three thousand dollars in 1974. To earn more money, she attempted to market her papers to Southern Illinois on an annual basis, until they finally could afford no more. She wrote "Report from Lock-up" for a book called *Four Visions of America*, a meditation on being arrested at Santa Rita, on her visits to Alcatraz Island, on Alexander Berkman, and on Puss's meeting with Alice Paul. But her translation of Crevel's *Babylone* would not be published until 1985.

In her seventies it was as if age had honed her, extending her prominent nose and her high cheekbones and her heavily lidded eyes, even as she grew ever more strident in the expression of her views. But her love of life gave her energy when the body faltered. Into her seventies too she wore blue eye shadow and mascara as her white earrings framed her image. She wore, she freely confessed, "the bigger ones when I'm feeling particularly inadequate or depressed, the smaller when I'm happy and self-assured . . . like Emily Dickinson always dressing in white after a certain age." She was never far from self-promotion. One reporter noted that there was "more fervor in her voice" when she talked about her students than when she discussed her children.

She now had energy only for poetry, polemical essays, and occasional reviews, which she wrote only on hundred percent recycled paper. Thirteen pages of her German history were published in 1971 in a journal called *Prose*, all that would ever appear of that long effort. It was easier now to write articles for the newsletter of the Committee for Artistic and Intellectual Freedom in Iran (CAIFI), of which she was an honorary chairperson. In particular, she took up the cause of Vida Hadjebi Tabrizi, an Iranian woman tortured in the Shah's prisons for making a sociological study of conditions in the Iranian countryside. Kay enlisted Jessica Mitford to appear with her at a CAIFI meeting which was broken up by Maoists with gratuitous attacks upon Iranian poet Reza Baraheni, with whom, although he was opposed to the Shah, they had political differences. "Kay, how could you get me into this!" Mitford asked exasperatedly.

There was energy for a multiplicity of causes. The death of a student inspired one of Kay's most heartfelt poems, "On the Death of My Student, the Poet Serafin":

> *Serafin return*
> *I say return I cry it under the tall campus trees*
> *there are questions I need the answers to:*
> *how many poems were in your veins that night*
> *and did you for a moment recognize*

behind the surgeons' masks
the grinning harlequin of death's disguise . . .

Asked to write an introduction to an *American Poetry Review* selection of
young Filipino poets, she gladly complied. And in November of 1976 Kay
Boyle requested her voluminous files from the FBI under the Freedom of
Information Act. Meanwhile she refused to pay the federal tax, which she
called a "war" tax, on her telephone bill, picturing herself to Nelson Algren
as "sitting waiting for the Internal Revenue agents to come and seize my
house." On one typical morning she telephoned friends urging them to
send telegrams to the House Judiciary Committee opposing Nelson Rock-
efeller's confirmation as Vice President because of his brutal suppression
of the Attica rebellion.

Dare offer the slightest skepticism concerning one of Kay Boyle's
pantheon now and be sure her scorn would follow. In his *Black Sun* (1976),
Geoffrey Wolff had revived the moribund reputation of Harry Crosby. But
that his book contained less than adulatory descriptions of the Crosbys'
nihilistic lifestyle infuriated her. She accused Wolff of sensationalism and
of taking digs at her when she would not cooperate. Wolff had described
Harry Crosby's "yellow metal ring" bought in Egypt as having been
"stomped flat" in the room where Harry took his mistress's life and then
his own. It was a story Caresse Crosby had long insisted was not true. Kay
now declared that the ring was on her own very finger!

Malcolm Cowley fared no better than Wolff as she attacked him for
failing to do justice to Marianne Moore in a piece called "Reconsideration
of the Thirties" he had written for *The New Republic*. What of Gertrude
Stein and Djuna Barnes, Kay demanded, writers of "greater interest to
present-day students than are Dos Passos and Hemingway?" That she
abhorred the efforts of women students to read women writers did not
restrain her from this argument. William Carlos Williams, who had also,
in her opinion, been given short shrift by Cowley, was "probably the greatest
writer we have had in this century." Her pantheon was always the best. It
was another form of fabulation.

Samuel Beckett, Kay Boyle decided in this period, was her "closest
and oldest friend." Of course, until 1957, when Kay wrote to Beckett,
addressing him, appropriately, as "Mr. Beckett," they had met only those
two previous times by chance. It was in 1957, after *Waiting for Godot* had
made Beckett famous, that Kay wrote to him requesting his opinion of the
"hoax" exegesis of Joyce's "The Boarding House" she planned to use in
her course at Delaware. In a brief note, Beckett wrote back saying the
allegory was "not only unnecessary but perhaps an injustice to him." Appalled that she had offended someone she was courting, Kay Boyle immediately wrote back to make it "adequately clear" that she was "trying

to show how evil the allegory-symbol-seeking of the lifeless, bloodless, academically paralyzed 'new critics' of our time can be."

So it began. Over the next thirty years, through the mails, Kay Boyle seduced Samuel Beckett. She was solicitous, seductive, and always flattering, as Katherine Evans Boyle had taught her to be. She was also aggressive as she bombarded Beckett with letters, her many books, and even her photographs. Beckett's replies were brief and polite. She wrote at least two letters to his one. They met again briefly in New York in 1964, when he came to Clover's house for dinner. Beckett sat, withdrawn, drinking heavily and talking little. It was clear that he and Kay shared no common history and had little to say to each other. Later Beckett apologized to Kay for not having been very sociable. There were a few later meetings in Paris. That was all.

At first, appropriately, Beckett signed his letters "Yours sincerely, Samuel Beckett." "It's no business of mine," he wrote of her Joyce criticism. "Whether I agree or disagree with what you say is of no importance." But, undaunted, Kay Boyle began to share with Beckett the intimate details of her life, becoming injured when he would not join her in equal intimacy. In 1961 she had even requested that he see Arthur Deshaies. By her birthday in 1963 Kay Boyle had made progress, and Beckett was signing his letters "affectionately," as he succumbed to her relentless siege.

Kay Boyle well knew how to alternate strength with vulnerability and helplessness and how to call upon a man to succor and protect her, even through the mails. When Joseph fell ill, Kay Boyle wrote Beckett all the details. "May this dreadful pain soon be past, for him and for you and for your children," Beckett replied, obviously affected. When Joseph died, Beckett wrote, "I bow my head and am full of compassion and great wonder at your bravery." Every detail was now retailed to Beckett. "So glad you like your new house," he wrote politely when she bought 419 Frederick Street.

Indeed, soon Beckett was writing that he was thinking of her. "Don't kill yourself marching. Give yourself a little peace," he urged in the late sixties. Her powers of flattery were accomplishing their end. "You have the capacity to break the heart in the most subtle and personal and distressingly intimate ways," Kay wrote him. "No one else has it." Beckett succumbed. By the late seventies he was writing that he longed to see her "before the curtain rattles down." He had begun to look forward to her visits to Europe.

Through the mails, as Kay pursued the fantasy of her "closest and oldest friend," they grew old together. Beckett was safely thousands of miles away in Paris; there need be none of the diurnal disappointments which had so withered her relationship with Joseph Franckenstein. They gossiped. He ran into Maria Jolas, "her mien more purposeful than ever." He confided he was suffering life "as it dribbles away." "The trouble with tragedy," Beckett wrote Kay, "is the fuss it makes over life & death & other halfpenny aches."

Like a disappointed lover, she complained when he did not write as often as she would have liked, as in Le Havre she had lamented when William Carlos Williams would not stay the night. "You see, you don't miss much, dear Kay, when I fail or delay to reply," Beckett pleaded. His life was not interesting. And after fifteen years, his letters began to read like love letters, as hers long had. When he read *The Underground Woman*, he "found again your dear unflinchingness of eye & spirit & word & bowed to it again."

Interviewed by Deirdre Bair for her biography of Beckett, Kay used the term "intimate."

"Intimate can mean many things," Bair remarked.

In what William L. Shirer called her "golden voice with the cultivated accent," Kay now tried to face Bair down.

"Intimate in every sense of the term," Kay declared haughtily, with the clear implication that they had been lovers.

Later Bair asked Beckett himself about Kay. Beckett was chivalrous and wouldn't reveal whether he had been her lover. But he did say he remembered her as a strong-willed woman with a "predatory" quality. Later Kay complained that "that Deirdre person" was going to write that she had a love affair with Beckett, as if Bair would have been concocting some falsehood. The biographer, of course, wrote no such thing.

When Kay's truly long-standing friend Bessie Breuer died in 1975, Howard Nemerov was left as Kay's sole literary executor. Ian was her sole heir. Should Ian die before her, Clover would inherit what she had. Apple, Bobby, and Kathe were not mentioned; Faith, of course, had ceased to exist. "They're going to bury me in a cardboard box without benefit of undertaker, which is as it should be," Kay Boyle said.

33

Vesna

Little girls' tales.
SINDBAD VAIL

Let's not ever talk about the past.

Kay Boyle borrowed money on the house on Frederick Street so that she could go to Europe during the summer of 1972. One of her grand-daughters now had leukemia. In Paris, Bobby and her new husband, John Cowling, met with Kay's approval, as did Sindbad, who came armed with flowers. Kay charmed them all by cooking quail for dinner and telling stories about her teaching. She told her students to write something they felt strongly about, she related. At this the students picked up their pens. Then, dramatically, Kay Boyle paused in her instructions. "Except your mother." At this, she reported, all her students put down their pens. Motherhood was always a sore point with her now, ambiguous, fraught with tension and unresolved guilt.

Visiting Bobby in Vendras, a town an hour from Avignon, during the summer of 1974, Kay wrote a poem called "The Ruined Village" about all the old ladies in black in the village waiting to die. Kay said she told those women one should change one's life every ten years; she strongly disap-proved of their apparent view that women's lives ended with the deaths of their husbands. Kay Boyle, that enemy of the feminists, was leading a life which embodied the feminist ideal: it was a full and productive life devoted to good works and to her art.

In Vendras, she locked herself into her room. "My mother's door is closed," Bobby would tell people, just as she had all those long years ago in Mégève. "She's working." Kay wrote letters home dramatizing herself "writing poems in a four hundred year old farmhouse near Nîmes." To her chagrin, there was no post office in the town. Later she told people she was glad to get home.

When she visited Kathe at her house in Tunisia during these years, she found her daughter living in a world of movie celebrities, "the international movie and Paris fashions, homosexual, hard-drinking set" favored by Kathe's husband, Edgar Kuhn, who had been fired from Columbia Pictures. Kay was depressed by them all, down to their "Arab robes with their tanned belly-buttons revealed, and nothing underneath, except their jockstraps." She added that she was "not objecting to their homosexuality, but to the empty, hard-drinking uselessness of their lives." On one of these visits, oppressed by the heat, Kay even consented to wear one of Peggy Guggenheim's abandoned dresses.

Throughout her visit in 1972 Kay remained sharply disapproving. She objected to Kathe's having named her house "The Five Children" in Arabic, and having the maids set the table for the children's breakfast the night before, as she herself had done in Mégève. No more now than earlier with Apple did she perceive how poignantly her daughters had borrowed her own identity. Kathe, Kay accused, was living in the past, even clinging to Man Ray, who lived in the neighborhood, "because he knew Papa and me in years gone by." When Kathe expressed her longing for a visit from Apple, Kay moralistically told her "it was not realistic to think of such a thing, for the drinking scene was very far from [Apple's] way of life." Taken aback by her mother's harshness, Kathe murmured that she and Edgar "were sociable drinkers." Kay seemed always to be passing judgment, even on Pegeen's son, Sandro, whom Kathe was raising. The game of chess, Kay decided, would "teach him patience and thoughtfulness," and on her way home she mailed him a set from Paris.

Taking care of Clover's children, Devin and Ariel, in New York, Kay was equally censorious. Dyslexic, Ariel had trouble spelling the word "bicycle."

"If you get out of your seat, I'll hit you," Kay threatened. "You can't get up until you spell 'bicycle.' " When the child apologized, Kay turned her head away.

Only Ian could do no wrong. In Paris, Kay and Ian had together met Samuel Beckett. Kay proudly reported that Beckett had been "impressed" that Ian, who had pursued a career on the stage, had once acted the part of Estragon in *Waiting for Godot*. When Kathe and Bobby visited her from Europe, it was still only Ian, who lived nearby, whom Kay was excited about seeing. "Ian has arrived!" she told her daughters. "Aren't you going out to greet him?"

"Isn't he coming inside?" Kathe had to ask.

As harsh as she sometimes seemed, however, Kay Boyle's politics had grown more moderate by the late seventies. She was not afraid to criticize the Soviet Union and was not intimidated by the argument that this would amount to a reheating of the Cold War. She vociferously protested against the censorship of Solzhenitsyn's works in his own country and participated in a "permanent vigil" at the Soviet consulate. She also protested against the torture of Soviet political prisoners. And she signed a petition condemning the Vietnamese invasion of Cambodia.

There was a touching innocence at times about Kay Boyle now as she responded with "great astonishment" to a standing ovation at a talk before the College English Teachers of California. She was disarming too as, her hair dyed black once more, she read in December of 1975 before the San Francisco State Poetry Center. She told the audience that when she wrote "Testament for My Students" during the strike, she became so excited that she mistakenly put prose right in the middle of the poem—no matter that she had been doing that for years. Even as she said, "I think of myself as a revolutionary," Kay Boyle now publicly admitted that she had become disenchanted with Eldridge Cleaver, who had returned to America no longer a revolutionary and was soon to be a born-again Christian. One of the poems she read was called "Poets." It began:

> Poets, minor or major, should arrange to remain slender,
> Cling to their skeletons, not batten
> On provender, not fatten the lean spirit
> In its isolated cell, its solitary chains . . .

So indeed she had done. So was she doing.

By 1976, Kathe had been married for fifteen years to Edgar Kuhn. Back in the fevered days when war loomed over Europe, it had been Kuhn who seduced a still-virginal Pegeen on the banks of Lake Annecy. "My little Kay," Kuhn had patronizingly dismissed her views when she visited Tunisia. "You don't know enough about the politics here." Kuhn had brought teenaged girls to Paris from Tunisia to work for him and Kathe, and wound up seducing them all. One committed suicide; another became pregnant. Kay hated him, and later would accuse him of having seduced "all my daughters" at one time or another.

Kuhn and his crowd of unsavories had done more sinister things than turn Kay Boyle's stomach in Hammamet. In Paris, Edgar Kuhn had raped one of Bobby's daughters, who then tried to kill herself. Bobby had discovered her daughter lying on the kitchen floor. A note addressed in part to Edgar, in part to her father, Michel Sciama, was found as well. Bobby had bundled her daughter into a taxi and saved her life.

In her note, the girl had implicated her aunt's husband. But Kuhn, slippery-tongued, had no trouble replying to a desperate fifteen-year-old's accusation. She hero-worshipped me since she was seven years old, he insisted; she needed a father. "Don't worry, me too," Pegeen had then consoled her niece, "when I was your age I too was in love with Edgar."

At the time Kathe staunchly denied that Edgar could have done such a thing. If it were really true, she demanded, why did Bobby continue to see them, even sending the children for visits?

The horror, in fact, had just begun. Edgar had also been molesting Kathe's daughter, his eighteen-year-old stepdaughter, Vesna, since she was ten years old. She and her cousin both had tried to tell. But Sindbad brushed off their words as "little girls' tales." Living in a state of denial, Kathe would not allow herself to believe it. When Vesna left home, Kathe explained to Kay that she wanted to be with her real father.

Eventually Vesna confessed to her mother about the things Edgar had done to her. When Kathe confronted her husband, he wept and cried and accused Vesna of trying to separate them. He denied everything. Vesna was such a little girl, he said. He could never imagine doing such a thing. Meanwhile Kathe and Vesna met only in cafés. During one of her visits, Kay learned what Vesna had told Kathe. So too had Vesna's Yugoslav father, Velya, who begged Kay to intervene. But she would not. "I'm here for a week or two," she told him. "You live here."

Eventually Vesna moved to a room of her own, boarding with a family. Raped by Kuhn, she wrote a nine-page letter full of self-blame. To my granny in San Francisco, Vesna had written, please forgive me for what I'm about to do. I'm ashamed. Then one day in March of 1976 she jumped from the sixth story of the building to her death in the courtyard below. At the funeral, Kay learned, to her rage, Vesna's father had actually shaken Edgar Kuhn's hand.

In her pain, Kay volunteered for the San Francisco suicide hot line. But to be a volunteer, she was told, she would have first to take a six-week course. Kay told them she didn't have the time.

In her niece Vesna's suicide, Clover saw her own suicide attempts. Edgar's overtly incestuous behavior had been paralleled by Laurence's quasi-sexual overtures. It was as if the incestuous feelings of fathers toward daughters were part of the secret identity of the whole family. In some way, Clover believed, just as Kay had not protected her children, so she had also not intervened for her granddaughter. At first, Kay Boyle said, she blamed herself "because we were very close . . . if only I'd been there." But later she thought that "as much as I loved her, hers was a vengeful act too . . . she did it so calmly and extraordinarily, but it was revenge." Meanwhile Kathe simply and without guile took all the blame on herself. "I made him credible for others," she lamented.

As always, Kay went back to work. When her history of German women did not prove viable, Ken McCormick suggested a book about "extraordinary women in the history of the west." Kay, however, decided to write a book about the women of Ireland. She had come from a family of strong women, and a book about the politically and socially conscious women of Ireland would be homage to her own heritage.

In the late seventies, Kay Boyle assumed so overtly Irish a persona that she was described in a journal of Irish poetry as "the first lady of Irish-American letters." If Ernest Walsh's entry into her life had made useful the Irishness of the hated Boyles, now at seventy-three she transformed herself into a full-blown "Irish" writer. Indeed, at a peace demonstration during the spring of 1978, she carried the Irish flag.

Kay Boyle made her first visit to Ireland in the summer of 1976 following Vesna's suicide. Her guide was Liadain O'Donovan-Cook, the daughter of the writer Frank O'Connor, who traveled with her from San Francisco. Kay wanted to meet Irish women who had been jailed for their beliefs. She was also interested in women like Terence MacSwiney's wife, who in 1920 had seen him through his long hunger strike to his death, women who were "help-meets," as she had been.

"My stepmother thinks she may have met you," Liadain told Kay.

"Nobody thinks they've met me. They *know* they've met me," was Kay's reply.

The women about whom she planned to write included a Dominican nun named Sister Benvenuta, who called herself a "law-abiding subversive" and supported the Irish woman's right to both divorce and abortion, a political activist named Hilary Boyle, no relation, and a woman named Mary Grant, who was a cousin of Ken McCormick's. On Mary Grant's farm Kay took the goats out to pasture.

One night at a Dublin pub called O'Donohue's there was much singing and talking until a begging gypsy entered with a baby. When the owner asked the gypsy to leave, Kay rose indignantly out of her seat.

"I won't stay in a place where a gypsy woman has been asked to leave," she said. Liadain, who knew Ireland well, tried to explain that in the desperate economy where many were out of work, and the price of one beer stood between a man and his sanity, beggars could not be allowed to disturb the patrons of a pub, themselves not much better off. But furious with the pub owner, Kay refused to accept these arguments. It was apparent that she knew little about Ireland, which she was calling "land of my forebears."

There were other difficulties. Liadain had brought her young son with her; Kay became irritated when Liadain had to leave her alone for as long as two hours, and she then had to deal with the money and other irritations of foreign travel. She seemed to Liadain inordinately vain as she said that when she put her stockings on in the morning she wore white gloves so that the edges of her nails would not pull the stockings. In the evenings Liadain was reluctant to leave her little boy alone at the bed-and-breakfast. But Kay always wanted to go out, to see and be seen.

"Leave him with the woman of the house," Kay told Liadain. So hostile did Kay seem to the child that when one of her subjects, "Faysie," a woman who ran a small shop-factory making clothes, offered the boy a boiled egg, Kay made her displeasure obvious. Liadain returned from the trip feeling angry and used, and she concluded that one problem might have been that they were seeing only women, whereas Kay clearly preferred men, especially adoring younger ones. Back home Kay sent Liadain letters urging her to attend the meetings of Amnesty International held on Thursday evenings at 419 Frederick Street, only to receive no reply.

Kay Boyle professed to have no idea why Liadain had dropped out of touch. "I am sorry you have not responded to my letters and suggestions that we meet, and I find it difficult to understand why you have not," she wrote. "Is it possible that I did not work out our accounts accurately and that I am still in your debt?" It wasn't, of course, about money at all. That Christmas, the little boy whom Kay had ignored in Ireland received a Christmas card. "You would love all the seashells on the beach," Kay wrote from Florida, where she was visiting Apple.

Edgar Kuhn was arrested at the Place Pigalle in Paris and jailed for drug trafficking, for which he was soon serving ten months in prison. Needing desperately to unravel the financial labyrinth in which Kuhn had placed her, Kathe called on her mother. "The only thing I am asking of you is not to triumph," she wrote. Early in 1977, Kathe told Kay that she had "forgiven her all." Kathe reminded her mother of her admonition: "Let's not ever talk about the past."

Desperate, alone, and with four children to care for, Kathe pleaded: "I have not your intelligence or talent or many things, but I do have some of you, some of Papa, a little of myself, of course." Of her childhood, Kathe remembered that Kay had her truth, Papa his, and Kay "didn't budge really." If, when she was a child, she had believed Kay was "unfaithful" to Papa, now she saw that at least Kay had done it "openly." Once Kathe had felt that her mother had "betrayed" her. But she didn't any longer.

Kay responded with whatever financial resources and legal contacts she had. Edgar had not put his wife's name on their Tunisian property; to avoid community property laws he had managed to declare himself a resident of the state of Massachusetts. Released from jail, he had disappeared. Kay enlisted lawyers Robert Treuhaft and Joseph Rauh to help her daughter, sending four thousand dollars at once to Kathe in Tunis. Kay would borrow. She would never refuse, she said, although she was "semi-retired" and was earning less than four hundred dollars a month now from teaching and little from her writing. During the summer of 1977 Kathe and her youngest daughter travelled from Paris to Hammamet, where they discovered Edgar in residence, in the company of his prison cellmate. Kathe's nightmare was far from over.

This was not a good year. Stepping off a curb on New Year's Day, Kay broke her foot and was immobilized for six weeks. From her bed, she wrote irritably to a woman at Stanford who was writing a book about twentieth-century women poets. "No," Kay wrote angrily, " 'a room of our own in which our voices can resonate' is not a goal with which I can sympathize . . . I don't think I have the patience to hear one more time about Tillie standing there ironing," referring, of course, to Olsen's story

"I Stand Here Ironing," which had been praised by many feminists. Indeed, hadn't William Carlos Williams, a full-time doctor, also been plagued by interruptions? Still she insisted that no special allowance be made for women. Soon Kay began to hobble about the house on crutches while Ian took care of her and cooked her meals. By March she was ready to shepherd through publication a reissue of her favorite novel, *Monday Night*.

Then, in April, cancer "raised its ugly head again." Undaunted, she rushed off to receive her honorary degree from Skidmore, where she told the audience she had been "spared any formal schooling," and picked up a seven-hundred-dollar fee. A week later Kay was subjected to her second mastectomy. This time the anesthetic tube kept in her throat for four hours during surgery so dislocated her swallowing apparatus that she could not eat solid food for a long time; the pain was excruciating. Ian brought honey to the hospital, but that only made it worse. Her voice was hoarse and she could barely speak. Even taking liquids produced coughing fits. She was unable to choke down codeine pills. Later, to her horror, the doctor told her the damage might have been caused by assistants "leaning on" her throat during the operation.

The already rail-thin Kay lost twenty pounds, as into May still she could not take solid food. Ian continued to care for her. Then, in the midst of her pain, Apple wrote with news that one of her children was involved with drugs, and she was afraid he might smash the mosaic on which she had been working for months. When she tried to call the police, her son and his friends ripped out the phone wires. Into the third generation, children reacted self-destructively to that bohemian and undisciplined existence of the Vail Sanger's circus.

That month Kay's good friend Herb Wilner died after open-heart surgery. Kay had now to struggle with another "old enemy," her diverticulitis; adding a major irritant was the fact that Paul Appel, the publisher of *Monday Night*, had not sent out the review copies she had requested. Kay wrote Martin Peretz at *The New Republic* requesting a review by a critic "sympathetic to my work." It was the first time, she said, she had ever asked such a favor of an editor.

Refusing to yield to the rebellions of her body, wearing now artificial breasts of liquid silicone, in June Kay boarded a plane for Europe. She would go to Paris, and then back to Ireland. But she tired easily, and was unable to do much work. Helga Einsele joined her, and, as Einsele put it, they frequented the pubs "while on the trail of the Irish women's movement." After a week on the Bantry Peninsula, Kay grew restless and complained that she was losing time. She saw the Grants, those cousins of Ken McCormick, again, but they were no longer politically active, and Kay let them know she didn't think this was right. Afterwards Einsele brought a young released prisoner to San Francisco. The woman drank too much and proved to be difficult and disruptive. But Kay, Einsele noted, became angry "only rarely."

Sitting down to write about the Irish women, Kay discovered she had arrived at an impasse. "Isn't it the women more than the politics who are important?" her friend Joan Baez asked her when Kay seemed blocked by the fact that their politics were less than satisfactory. Kay didn't see it. But Ireland was now, she insisted, home to her. "I cannot live without Ireland," she told her agent, Mike Watkins, as she talked about buying a house and spending part of each year there.

Although she would work on a book about Ireland for the next decade, Kay published only one story out of the experience, "St. Stephen's Green," which appeared in the June 1980 *Atlantic Monthly*. It was an autobiographical vignette in which Kay, sitting on a bench at St. Stephen's Green, wearing her familiar long trench coat, meets an Englishman; he is blind to Ireland, to the fact that "injustice is the air they breathe every day of their lives." Kay Boyle's only other writing about Ireland was a respectful review of a biography of Maud Gonne.

If the illnesses of the late seventies threatened to bring her low, she did not complain. When Doris Grumbach asked her during an interview whether she was in pain, Kay replied, "Oh, you know, it's there." Later she would tell Shawn Wong never to ask anyone of her age how they were. They were *never* "fine." New ailments like bursitis and disintegration of the spinal vertebrae had joined her other chronic complaints. But in 1977 she was still not ready to think of herself as "old." When a salesperson called her "dear" one day, she thought, "God, so I look that old! Am I that old?"

Combativeness kept her going, as she took umbrage even at her good friend Joan Baez, who had arrived at Frederick Street with a culinary offering, but late. "I can't use it," Kay said. She wouldn't even say goodbye. Later she insisted she was the one who was "hurt." Jay Laughlin angered her when he decided not to reprint *Thirty Stories*. As for the "hard financial realities" New Directions had invoked, wasn't Laughlin, Kay sputtered, a "steel millionaire"? With money scarce, she sold for three thousand dollars her magnificent Black Sun edition of "Mr. Knife, Miss Fork," that section of René Crevel's *Babylone* she had translated.

"I have become a non-writer," she lamented in January of 1978. Her energy would now go to "fighting for others." Yet she was still the daughter of Katherine Evans Boyle. "I am filled with stories and poems and the longing to write," she said helplessly on another occasion. She had grown weak, but she had not lost her zest for life. The 1978 birthday party in honor of Amnesty featured belly dancers.

In March, the *San Francisco Chronicle* asked several well-known authors to send in sketches of how they saw themselves. Kay drew herself as an angel flying nude in the heavens. Her hair is black and curly, her arms outstretched. In each hand she carries a smoldering bomb. "Since receiving several volumes of censored data through the Freedom of Information Act," Kay wrote, "I see myself as a dangerous 'radical' cleverly disguised as a perfect lady. So I herewith blow my cover." The quotation marks around "radical" were inserted by the *Chronicle* editors. As Kay and her lawyer Jerome Garchik demanded from the government full disclosure of her files, they were amused to discover an FBI decision in June of 1976 to drop their investigation "in view of the background of the subject, her advanced age, and lack of asset potential." Mystified by what they meant by "background," Kay Boyle and Jerry Garchik persisted into the 1980s in demanding from the government the thousands of pages of the Franckenstein files.

In April of 1978, Kay appeared at Rutgers University at a conference honoring women writers of the twenties in Paris and New York. Kay pleaded with Djuna Barnes to join her: "you and I could hold our ancient hands all the way from New York to New Brunswick," she urged. "I know that Laurence, looking down from his cloud on high—or maybe looking up from his bed of coals—would like us to do that." They were "only a few left," Kay said. But Djuna refused, and later Kay remarked she had declined because she weighed three hundred pounds and would not allow herself to be seen.

According to Kay, as she sat on the podium beside Lillian Hellman, Hellman turned to her and asked whether she should have a face lift.

"Lillian, we get old. There's not much we can do."

"I don't want to be old," Lillian told her.

"Why did they put a microphone in front of me? I'm not going to say one word," photographer Berenice Abbott muttered.

"Oh, look at all those students," Kay replied.

"Not one word," Abbott repeated.

As they were being introduced by a young male professor, Blanche Wiesen Cook, later to become Eleanor Roosevelt's biographer, standing in the back, yelled, "You sit down. We want to hear from the women, not from you!"

At that, Berenice Abbott grabbed her microphone. "What's the matter with you people back there?" she demanded. "Why don't you work the way we did when we were young? You really make me sick, you feminists."

Immediately, Kay Boyle remembered, the whole place applauded. Her own sympathies, of course, were entirely with Abbott. Still she misconstrued feminism as "separatism"; still she was unsympathetic with the women's movement.

Kay Boyle had not lost her appetite for honors, and she was grateful when Howard Nemerov proposed her name for membership in the American Academy of Arts and Letters, the elite group modeled on the French Academy, drawn from the ranks of the Institute of Arts and Letters. "I don't know why I care," she wrote him simply, "but I somehow do, about that particular promotion." Nemerov immediately informed the Academy of her dire financial circumstances, and she was awarded a grant. But when the Authors' League also sent Kay Boyle a check, she promptly and proudly returned it, "as the National Institute had sent me money," referring to her Institute of Arts and Letters grant.

When combativeness receded, pride took over. Kay ran into Archibald MacLeish, who suggested that they write a letter to each other every month for the rest of their lives. "He must be very lonely. He must be really sad," Kay concluded. To neither of these emotions would she succumb. Then she directed her energies to the details of Joseph's memorial scholarship, in jeopardy now that Thomas had merged with the Low-Heywood School in Stamford.

Bedeviled by Kuhn, who had appealed their divorce judgment in an effort to evade any financial responsibility, Kathe bought a small house in a village outside Paris with her mother's help. Kay urged her daughter to fight, to face things. Locked in battle with her ex-husband, Kathe sent her daughters Myrine, aged eleven, and Yannick, aged fifteen, to San Francisco for the summer of 1978. With their grandmother, Kathe hoped, there would be a relationship of "*sagesse*." "Yannick admires you, the way Vesna did," Kathe wrote. Knowing her mother was a "good pusher," Kathe hoped Kay would add "order and organization" to the children's lives. When Kay praised her daughter for having lived for others, that gave Kathe strength.

The visit of Myrine and Yannick Kuhn to 419 Frederick Street proved, sadly, to be a failure. For Kay, survival now meant maintaining the life she had created for herself. She was also ill. Just before the girls arrived, she had recovered from a bout with walking pneumonia, and was now spending an hour in traction every day for severe arm pain which cortisone injections had not relieved.

To the children, it seemed all Kay could do was correct their manners. "Don't say you're full when you've finished eating," she instructed. The girls should shake hands when they were introduced to someone. They must not walk ahead of people. Most of the time they didn't see their grandmother at all. She remained in her attic apartment, appearing for dinner only twice a week. They were even more uncomfortable when Kay tried to confide in them, as once she had confided in Clover and Faith. "Your poor mother, you must help her," Kay said. "Your poor mother has no money." When one of the girls remarked that she hadn't visited the dentist, Kay rushed to judgment. "Oh, your poor mother. She couldn't afford to send you to the dentist." The girls knew it wasn't true, and they resented it. Kathe had given them spending money, but Kay at once confiscated it, as Kathe had instructed her to do. But the children didn't like that either. "Your mother is so poor," Kay repeated. She asked often about their brother, Kolia, and about their cousin, Pegeen's son, Sandro. There was no physical affection, no hugs, no kisses. "She's not really human," Yannick decided.

When Myrine and Yannick departed, Kay returned the money Kathe had entrusted to them. By now the pain in her arm was so severe that she could no longer type. She had a high fever. But it was also true that the role of traditional grandmother was alien to her. Once Bobby said, pointing to Michel Sciama's mother, "You see that woman? *She's* a real grandmother." And Sandro had noticed that Kay talked ceaselessly about herself, her trip to Ireland, but she never got around to asking her grandchildren about their own lives. As between Kay and his other grandmother, Peggy Guggenheim, Sandro would say, "To tell you the truth, I wouldn't choose either of them." Her grandchildren were proud of her being "the writer Kay Boyle," but they were also disappointed when she did not behave like a loving grandmother.

Back in France, Yannick and Myrine announced to their mother that they did not like Kay Boyle. All that redeemed their visit was their young uncle Ian, who did take the trouble to spend time with them. They had no desire ever to return to Frederick Street. "I know how much you gave of yourself and how much time it took away from your writing," Kathe wrote her mother, no doubt mindful of her own childhood when her mother's writing always had priority. "It was a wonderful thing that you managed it, with what sacrifices!"

Kay knew she had been strict. But, aware of the children's antipathy, she defended herself; she had only done what Kathe had urged her to do. Kathe reassured Kay Boyle that "it has done them a world of good," and they would "appreciate it for the rest of their lives." But more than a decade later, Myrine remembered only her grandmother's unremitting strictness, and Kathe had to say that if she had sent two boys, things might have been entirely different.

Kay Boyle was too ill to attend the ceremony inducting her into the Academy. When her name was read out by architect I. M. Pei, he quoted Alfred North Whitehead on style as the ultimate morality of the mind. Applause rang through the auditorium. Two standing ovations came to Kay Boyle when she attended the Modern Language Association meeting in December of 1979. A National Endowment for the Arts Creative Writing Fellowship for $15,000 in 1980 kept her going financially.

For her arthritis, Kay was taking Motrin. Cataracts now began to form over both her eyes. Still she managed a poem and two reviews in 1979, excerpts from a poem dedicated to Beckett in 1982, and a poem "for the Teesto Diné of Arizona" in 1983. Her occasional writings included her memoir for the Gale *Contemporary Authors Autobiography Series*, which was a paean to saintly Katherine Evans Boyle, and that letter about Ezra Pound in Rapallo which appeared in *The New York Review of Books* in 1987. Her introduction to Anita Pollitzer's biography of Georgia O'Keeffe was published in 1988.

If Laughlin had allowed *Thirty Stories* to slip from print, in 1980 Doubleday issued its own *Fifty Stories*, with *The New York Times Book Review* running a front-page homage by Vance Bourjaily. Bourjaily counted up Kay's oeuvre: twenty-nine books in fifty years of publication. "Looked at as a whole," Bourjaily argued, her stories were "notably free of a compulsion to romanticize," whatever McAlmon had thought. It was in the craft of the short story that Kay had distinguished herself, in particular through her employment of "the technique of surrealism," which ran through stories as varied as "Wedding Day," "Maiden, Maiden," "Defeat," and even "The Ballet of Central Park," as Bourjaily selected a story from each decade. It was a long-overdue summary appreciation of Kay Boyle as the master writer of the short story she had been for fifty years.

The publication of *Fifty Stories* created further reassessment of Kay Boyle and her achievement. *The Saturday Review*, while calling her "one of our finest minor writers," praised the stories themselves as "true classics of the genre," with *Fifty Stories* "Kay Boyle's best book, and it is pure, sweet cream." *The Christian Science Monitor* found in the stories "the stylistic equivalent of grace under pressure." *The Nation* applauded "the diligence, the persistent quality of caring and the integrity of a long lifetime of work." "The second rank is a very high rank indeed," Lillian Hellman once told her student Fred Gardner. In Kay Boyle's case, this is certainly true.

The publication of *Fifty Stories* led a new generation to discover Kay Boyle. In the decade that followed, many of her works were reissued. Far from abandoning her, the "steel millionaire" Jay Laughlin issued a small collection of her stories called *Life Being the Best and Other Stories* in 1988, *Death of a Man* in 1989, *Three Short Novels* in 1991, and *The Crazy Hunter* in 1993. In 1991 Capra Press reissued *Gentlemen, I Address You Privately*, which the author had so revised in her eighty-eighth and eighty-ninth years that *The New York Times* found in the new version "not only a more explicit rendering of erotic emotion, but also a more profound confrontation of Munday's anguish as he struggles between the priestly and the passionate aspects of his character." North Point Press would publish her essays in *Words That Must Somehow Be Said* and the complete translation of René Crevel's *Babylone* in 1985, the same year that Sun & Moon Press brought out some of her occasional poems in *This Is Not a Letter*. The *Collected Poems* would be issued by Copper Canyon Press in 1991. Meanwhile the feminists finally had discovered her, with Virago Modern Classics reissuing *Year Before Last* and *My Next Bride* in 1986 and then under Penguin's imprint *Plagued by the Nightingale* in 1990. In the summer of 1992, with the Penguin paperback edition out of print, *Fifty Stories* was reprinted by Jay Laughlin.

Nor was Kay now ignored in Europe. In 1991 *Der rauchende Berg* (*The Smoking Mountain*) rose to No. 6 on "Die Bestenliste," the best-seller list in Baden-Baden, as the new Germany sought in Kay Boyle's stories an understanding of the Nazi past. So delighted was her German publisher, Verlag Neue Kritik, after several printings, that they brought out a new collection in 1991, *Wedding Day and Other Stories*.

The letter had become Kay's chief medium of political expression. She wrote to her old adversary, S. I. Hayakawa, now a member of the U.S. Senate, on the issue of nuclear energy. When Quentin L. Kopp, a member of the San Francisco Board of Supervisors, would not sign a document for world disarmament, he received an angry rejoinder. That he had praised her short stories brought no mitigation of Kay Boyle's fury. "I deeply regret that in reading my short stories while you were in high school," she told him, "you failed to absorb some insight into compassion and moral integrity." Angrily she accused *The Nation* of publishing without her permission a letter she had written to Barbara Grizzuti Harrison complimenting her for an attack on Joan Didion; it was "inexcusable." That Kay's own agent, now Gloria Loomis, who had taken over for Mike Watkins, had granted that permission, telling *The Nation* not to bother Kay, was beside the point.

The most courageous political stand Kay Boyle took in these years was not even her appearances at those tumultuous CAIFI meetings. Rather, it was her signing Joan Baez's "Open Letter" to the government of Vietnam attacking its abuses of human rights. For this she was attacked by many of her old friends on the moribund Stalinist left, sometimes in New Left disguise, who believed that you do not publicly criticize a Communist government because that would give comfort to the real enemy, the capitalists. But Kay believed now that the "socialist state" was to be held to the same moral standards as any other. There were political prisoners, in particular Buddhist priests, in prison in Vietnam, and they had to be supported, she thought. Furthermore, it was no more correct in Stalin's era to stifle one's criticism of his atrocities than it would be now to ignore Vietnamese injustices.

Jane Fonda sent a letter to each of the signers of Joan Baez's "Open Letter" (they included the Berrigans, Daniel Ellsberg, Ed Doctorow, William Styron, and James A. Michener) accusing them of coming around to the position of Cardinal Spellman and John Foster Dulles that "Communism is worse than death." The effect of this letter would be "a new cold war with Vietnam." Presumably the fate of the Buddhist priests was a small enough price to pay.

Under attack by Jane Fonda and the Women's International League for Peace and Freedom, Kay Boyle defended herself nobly. She believed "in no government and in no political party," she said, echoing the words of her beloved friend Alexander Berkman. Of course she had not become an anarchist; the issue was "the lives and the liberty of people." She also could not help but wonder, she told the Women's International League, whether they were disappointed in "Izzy Stone, and Cesar Chavez, and Daniel Berrigan as well," since they had also signed the "Open Letter." The supposedly antifeminist Kay Boyle was not about to be attacked in sexist guise.

Kay Boyle spoke out publicly as well. "That we *must not* criticize *any* socialist country," she believed, was "a terrifying premise." In one of her strongest political letters of this period, she wrote to the Women's International League: "I am as disappointed in you as an organization as you are in me as a person." *Her* disappointment dated back to the time when they had "made no protest about the Vietnam government's invasion of Cambodia."

This was one of Kay Boyle's finest hours. Principle overcame special interest as she asserted the right of all people on the planet to the same freedom and self-determination. She reminded the League of the "old, old days when it was considered treason if any true American leftist criticized Josef Stalin." Many of the signers of the "Open Letter" had served prison terms for their opposition to "America's brutal invasion in Vietnam," as she herself had done. Now men and women were "dying in the 're-education centers' in Vietnam." The "normalization of trade" with that country, which the signers of the letter were accused of sabotaging, would not "give them back their lives."

Turning to the fate of the imprisoned Buddhist monks in Ho Chi Minh City, Kay Boyle wrote that "the *truth* must be made public at any cost." She went on to insist: "No ideological or political doctrine should be considered more important than life and love for our fellow human beings."

Whatever her reliance on letters, she had not ceased to appear at political demonstrations. When Joan Baez organized a demonstration against the absence of democracy in North Vietnam, Kay Boyle sat crouched in a three-foot "tiger cage" in Union Square. With Daniel Ellsberg she traveled to Livermore, "where the bombs begin," to picket the nuclear plant there. She read a poem dedicated to assassinated Mayor George Moscone at the Glide Memorial Church. She was seventy-seven years old and suffering the effects of two hours of surgery on an impacted wisdom tooth that day. Later Joanie Baez drew a cartoon of Kay with her big earrings and her face stitched together, holding a drink.

"Dr. says I can have Dubonnet on Friday," Kay Boyle says in the caption. "God Dammit, isn't it Friday?"

34

Do Not Go Gentle

Lady Lazarus, she's coming back!
STUDS TERKEL

*anyway what was the use of my having come from Oakland it was
not natural to have come from there yes write about it if I like or
anything if I like but not there, there is no there there.*
GERTRUDE STEIN

By October of 1979 Kay had decided to sell 419 Frederick Street. She talked again of moving to Ireland, where there was no income or property tax. "I want to start my life over again in Ireland," she said, following her own formula: a new life every ten years. She made a new will, leaving everything to Ian. Should he die before her, however, all was to go, not to Clover, as in the previous document, but to "Apple-Joan (Goeser) Vail, and only if she were not available, to Sharon Cowling, Kathe (Kuhn) Vail and Clover (Rosenblum) Vail." She requested that selections from Verdi's *Requiem* be played at her funeral; Ian was to read aloud James Joyce's poem which began: "I hear an army charging upon the land."

Nearly seventy-eight years old now, she was far from ready to die. She did at last retire permanently from San Francisco State, now "University," in December of 1979, after sixteen years of service. Suffering from the flu, she appeared at her farewell party, and cried, she reported to William L. Shirer, when "people said nice things about me." The dean of the School of Humanities, Nancy G. McDermid, said Kay Boyle had taught her that "nothing can ever make me believe that we are helpless as individuals."

Kay gave away or sold her furniture and her books, stripping her life bare. She wrote to Faith at the Lyman family commune: "I have carried you inside me always, through the pain and the heartbreak." Faith replied: "You were my center always." Kay sent Faith a silver tray and pitcher from the house.

An infusion of capital arrived when Austrian-born film director Fred Zinnemann bought "Maiden, Maiden"—for ten thousand dollars. The resulting film, called *Five Days One Summer*, distorts Kay's brilliant story even more than most adaptations. Zinnemann turned "Maiden, Maiden" into the story of an obsession of a girl for her older uncle (played by Sean Connery), whom she ruthlessly pursues without any guilt toward his wife. Their marriage is impossible because of the incest taboo, and not, as in the story, because, having long tired of her older doctor lover, the girl has fallen in love with her Austrian guide.

In 1980 Kay took up the case of novelist Gwen Davis, being sued by her publisher, Doubleday. Davis had lost on appeal a libel suit by a psychologist named Paul Bindrim, who argued that she had signed an agreement not to portray him or his nude encounter group therapy sessions in a novel, only to do just that. Kay Boyle had, of course, been the most autobiographical of novelists, and she rose to defend Gwen Davis, a writer she had never met—against her own publisher. She went on to assert that she would not be published by a firm which sued its authors, despite her long friendship with Ken McCormick. She returned, not the thousands advanced to her by Doubleday for the German history which she never completed, but one thousand dollars which she argued "represented the advance paid on the Irish book alone." Of the rest of the money which she knew she owed Doubleday, Kay insisted that "morally and legally" she no longer owed it.

One of Doubleday's demands during its settlement conferences with Davis was that she "stop doing things like asking Kay Boyle to do what she did." Yet they had never spoken, even on the telephone. "You seem to know a great deal more about bravery and cowardice . . . than anyone I have encountered," Davis wrote Kay gratefully.

The house on Frederick Street was sold in the summer of 1980. Kay sent Frank Detweiler a check for $30,000 as repayment for all he had done for her. But Detweiler returned it, according to Kay Boyle, telling her it would change the way she lived, but it would not alter his life. Kay used part of the money to finance Kathe's case against Edgar Kuhn.

It was as if she really were starting anew, as she told Leah Garchik, who was interviewing her for the *Chronicle*, "I'm not at all interested in the past. It bores me to death." She favored immaculate white blouses now; her hair, grey at last, was coiffed and puffed about her regal-looking head. "One does every day what comes up," Kay said. If she had not become "a better writer," she reflected, it was the result of her political activism, never putting "a rein on myself." At a book party at Minerva's Owl, she signed copies of the new Doubleday edition of *Fifty Stories*, and bade her friends farewell.

Kay had given Ian half the proceeds of the sale of the house on Frederick Street. Ian then moved to Oregon to pursue a career as a radio disc jockey. Before long, however, Kay had followed her son to Cottage Grove, Oregon. "We have always stimulated each other," she told people. "He is very devoted." She began to tell friends that as long as she was alive, Ian would never marry.

"It's a whole new life. I'm starting life again," Kay proclaimed, a determined stranger from now on to self-pity or fear of loneliness. Cottage Grove was no worse than Le Havre, Harfleur, or Stoke-on-Trent, she decreed. In this logging town twenty miles from Eugene, the trucks bore bumper stickers like "Don't tread on me. I'm an American," and "I'm a fighter, and a lover, and a wild bullrider." Kay Boyle was now "far from civilization," in a town which had no library.

But Kay colored her hair dark once more, and looking ten years younger than she was, rented a house for herself not far from Ian's. There she lived with her two cats, Tassi and Dopey, who had become television addicts, touching the screen with their paws as they watched the animated cartoons. Kay noted disapprovingly—she as slender as she demanded that poets be—that most of the inhabitants of Cottage Grove were "monstrously overweight," having gorged themselves on "biscuits with gravy" and looking "like nothing so much as hogs." The Hot Spot, the local café, she reported, was "socially the Deux Magots or Coupole of Cottage Grove, except that there was no alcohol."

By February of 1981, Cottage Grove had turned into "an icy spot." Kay Boyle felt "mixed up. I don't know that I have any identity anymore." She tore a two-dollar bill in half and sent her friend Joan Baez one half in the hope that soon they would be together again to join their two halves. Making the best of her "monastic life," she wrote an article on whales and porpoises for Greenpeace, and hurried back to San Francisco for her annual birthday party. At seventy-nine, her hair now bluish grey, wearing a blue-grey suit, she read aloud "St. Stephen's Green." On that trip she lunched with Hank McGuckin at Tommy's Joint, where Kay said she could not understand how neo-Nazis could deny that the Holocaust had actually occurred. When McGuckin told her they don't want to believe and so reject the source, Kay mistakenly jumped to the conclusion that McGuckin himself was somehow denying that six million people had died during the Holocaust.

Brave as she was, Kay was beset by ailments in Oregon. One day she fell on the pavement of Main Street, landing on her wrists and face. Cataracts, now full-blown in both eyes, awaited removal. When Joan Baez and then William Shirer visited, they were appalled by the bleakness and the cultural wasteland in which Kay was trapped.

As they took a walk along the river one day, Shirer confessed to Kay Boyle: "Kay, I'm awfully sorry. I never could stand Bob McAlmon. He was a faker."

"Let me tell you," Kay retorted. "He never liked you either."

Of Ian's current girlfriend, Kay, as usual, did not approve. "Leave him alone," Shirer advised. Shirer thought Ian would "probably like to live his own life." But when he said that, Kay became annoyed.

"You know, all these years I've been claiming I'm two years younger than you," Kay confessed. "I'm two years older." Later Kay called McGuckin and made Shirer come to the phone to explain that the Holocaust really had occurred. McGuckin was annoyed, and embarrassed. Intellectual arguments, he concluded, were beyond her. By the time she moved to Oregon, McGuckin was forced to concede, Kay had become dogmatic, unnuanced, and rigid in her views.

In January and February of 1982, Kay was writer-in-residence at Eastern Washington University in Cheney, Washington, not far from Spokane. She hoped that by teaching two courses, for ten thousand dollars, she could afford to return to Ireland the following summer. About to be eighty, she announced she did not "feel that old for a moment."

Eastern Washington appalled Kay, not least its ill-mannered students. One woman ate potato chips in class, and when the teacher objected, the student had the temerity disrespectfully to answer back: "I have hypoglycemia and I have to eat all the time." Few of her students shared her political convictions. Worse, she had to live in a dreary graduate student dorm room with a cracked linoleum floor. When she complained, the president would see her only while his portrait was being painted.

In an interview in the local paper, Kay frankly expressed her negative views of the creative writing program. The story appeared under the headline "Teacher Gives Creative Writing Program an F." One of the local poets, enlisted to defend the school, replied that teachers might say creative writing programs are a waste of time, but they're willing to take the money. Meanwhile Kay gave one of her students, Andrew Poliakoff, a sour look when he told her he had not gone to Spokane to hear Maya Angelou speak. ("What are *you* doing way out here?" Angelou had demanded of her. "What *am* I doing here?" Kay echoed.)

Later Kay generously gave Poliakoff inscribed copies of her books. Written inside *Avalanche* was: "Remember this book was written for a noble purpose—and written in a language the multitude would understand." In *1939*, that undiscovered masterpiece among her *oeuvre*, which of all her novels would wait the longest for reissue, Kay wrote: "I have an attachment to this book. It is the only one I ever wrote which I might try re-reading one day."

With fifteen hundred dollars from Eastern Washington, which was supposed to be used to invite five prominent women writers, Kay brought to Eastern Washington one writer of note—Grace Paley. Kay was so straight, pale, and old. Paley doubted that they would have much to say to each other. Instead, they became very good friends, as Paley tried to change Kay Boyle's mind about the women's movement. When Kay insisted that her mother had been a strong woman, Paley said this was what the movement was trying to do, write about such women. Paley found, to her amazement and great admiration, that Kay had no regrets about any of the decisions of her life. And Paley thought: People with full sexual lives do not have regrets.

Money was ever a problem, and to earn enough to pay her taxes, Kay had to teach again in April of 1982, this time at the University of Colorado.

Ian "has persuaded me that I need him, and that he needs me," she explained her decision to remain in Oregon for another year.

Beckett had told her, Kay said, "I can do without 1982." It was then that she wrote her poem to Beckett, exhorting him not to welcome death:

> *I'll not discuss with you by any name, however gently, soberly you ask.*
> *When the spectacle of it comes downstage, well off-center, "white hair,*
> *White nightgown, white socks," let humor lead the onslaught decked out*
> *In coat of mail . . .*

It was "not really poetry," Kay knew, but prose. Considering herself Irish now, Kay wrote out the names "Pearse, Connolly, McBride" into her poem, begging Beckett to identify with her. The words were "remnants of a better time." She urged them both now "tottering on the brink, gripping canes in our mottled claws / To hold the enemy at bay." In 1983 the Amnesty party for Kay Boyle at the Café du Nord was her "Irish party."

When Nelson Algren died suddenly in 1981, Kay immediately decided to establish "some kind of memorial in his name." With Algren's friend Studs Terkel, she established the Nelson Algren Award, to be administered through PEN in New York. Terkel had visited Kay in San Francisco as she struggled with the aftereffects of her second mastectomy. "Lady Lazarus, she's coming back!" Terkel had exclaimed. The recipients of the Algren Award were to be writers "unable to complete an already partly written novel or collection of stories because of lack of money on which to live," the only PEN-administered award of its kind. It was in keeping, Kay Boyle believed, with Algren's contempt for literary snobbery, and for the "New York mandarins" in particular, with his rebellious spirit and his refusal to put on airs. Indefatigably, Kay proceeded to raise the money, enlisting John Cheever, Peter Mathiessen, and Babette Deutsch. In gratitude to Kay, Gwen Davis sent one thousand dollars.

Quietly in late 1982, Kay had a hysterectomy. The following summer she took Clover and Apple to Paris. They stayed in Sindbad's guest house just outside the Bois de Boulogne. Before Kay arrived, Sindbad promised Kathe, "I won't say anything. But she was a bitch to leave Papa." On the very night of Kay's arrival, however, Sindbad, unable to restrain himself, confronted his now aged stepmother.

"When did you decide to divorce my father?" he demanded. "When did you fall in love with Joseph?" It was a *dégringolade*, as Laurence would have put it, of grievances; the old feelings of childhood still had not been resolved for the sixty-year-old man.

The next morning, Sindbad apologized to Kay. "I didn't want to do that," he told her. "You're the only one in my life who was a mother to me, the only mother I've had. I hated to lose you."

On this particular return to Paris, Kay Boyle faced the unresolved emotions of more than one child. One night when Sindbad and his wife were out, Clover and Apple together attacked Kay about their childhoods, and they would not relent. Bitterly they told their mother they could never measure up to what she expected of them. Deep into their own middle age, her children felt they had been somehow abandoned and betrayed. Kay kept murmuring "my darling Clover," but it did her no good. Finally, Sandro Rumney, Pegeen's son, intervened. "If you're going to talk this way to Kay, just walk out," he ordered.

Later Kay wept as she told the story to Kathe. "They cornered me last night," she said. As Kathe drove her down a country road on a visit to Maria Jolas, Kay began to air her grievances against Clover; as always, she disparaged one child to another. Finally Kathe slammed on the brakes so hard that Kay almost went through the windshield.

"Will you shut up!" Kathe told her mother. "It's between you and her. I don't want to hear about it!"

On that trip, Kay telephoned Samuel Beckett and dinner was proposed. "It's complicated," Kay said. She had no way of getting there without Sindbad's help, and so Beckett told her to bring everybody. (But Clover suggests that Kay Boyle dragged them all along because she was uneasy being alone with Beckett, the two really having so little shared experience, so little in common.) Sindbad's sons brought their cameras. But that wasn't the worst of it.

"How did you enjoy your love affair with my mother?" Sindbad began his siege of Samuel Beckett, as one of his sons began to snap pictures. "You cannot take pictures," Kay protested. Meanwhile both Sindbad and Clover, irritated at finding themselves at this awkward dinner, demanded to know whether Beckett and *Kay* had ever been lovers. Kay and Beckett looked at each other, while the rest of the group sat there with bated breath.

Beckett was too chivalrous to deny it. Kay said nothing, clearly enjoying the idea, and looking extremely pleased with herself.

At the end of the dinner, Kay tried to put a five-thousand-franc note into Beckett's hand. At first he thought she was trying to hold his hand. But when he saw the money, he refused. Later he wrote their mutual friend Ruby Cohn of his displeasure with the entire evening. After Kay, Clover, and Apple had returned to America, Kathe concluded that she must be the only one of Kay's daughters who could get along with her.

Back in rainy Oregon, and the "cold, grey misery of Cottage Grove," Kay restlessly moved from house to house, using always as her address Ian's house on North K Street. Kay was now writing an imaginary conversation with René Crevel to be included in her translation of *Babylone*, which had at last found a publisher in North Point Press. She enlisted the help of David Rattray, a poet, who had translated Crevel's *La Mort Difficile* (*Difficult Death*). As collaborator and friend, Kay took great pains to help Rattray get his Crevel manuscript published, sending it herself to Bill Turnbull, the owner of North Point.

The imaginary conversation was to take place at the Coupole bar, the dialogue drawn from quotations from Crevel's writings. Those sitting at the table with Crevel, Kay planned, would be "filled with love and tenderness for him," as she offered one more homage. It would be a conversation between people who shared a belief in "a path of freedom," and would close with Crevel picking up the brown paper parcel of the translation of *Babylone* and placing it under his arm. But when he would open his mouth to speak, no sound could be heard because Crevel, of course, had taken his life in June of 1935. Late into the night, with only Tassi and Dopey for company, Kay pored over xeroxes of Crevel's works. Despite her ill health, she worked "all the harder so as not to dwell on that," trying to make the quotations from Crevel sound like natural conversation.

When *Babylon* was published in 1985, critics agreed that Kay Boyle had revived a major work of surrealist writing. *The New York Times*, however, found her translation laden with "a certain starched quality" which limited "Crevel's resonance." They criticized as well her use of "much archaic language," and her "attempt to clarify Crevel's elliptical and often obscure phrases."

As Kay kept indefatigably on, her work reflected considerable weariness. In its review of her essays, *Words That Must Somehow Be Said*, the *Chronicle* noted that "she can't respond to sensibilities fundamentally different from her own"; the *Los Angeles Times*, however, in a far more favorable review, persisted in finding in her essays a person who was "clear-thinking, direct, sometimes tart, concerned both with fine distinctions and larger meanings. The point of view is principled, liberal, vigorous: wrongs can be righted through action; let us take action now." Both views can be seen to reflect fundamental truths about Kay Boyle.

Kay blithely told Rattray she was so busy that when publishers asked her for blurbs now, she told them she was about to enter the hospital. Then she would drive to the local hospital and stand in the waiting room for five minutes so as to convince herself she hadn't told a lie. An actual visit to the intensive-care unit turned out not to involve a heart attack, but acute arthritis of the chest. A botched operation on her leg in Eugene during the summer of 1984 left the nerves in her leg badly damaged. Now she was immobilized "with a leg that won't work anymore." "I have one foot in the grave and am writing like mad with the other," she joked.

At seven in the morning one day in January of 1985, Kay went out into the backyard to empty the cat box. Suddenly she stepped into a hole and fell, hitting her head against a tree and breaking two bones in her left foot. "So I now have a black eye, and crutches, and am already disappointed in 1985," she reported with her customary pluck and irony.

It turned out she had fractured her spine as well. Doctors buckled her into a surgical corset and forbade her to work sitting up. To write she stood at a stand. "Hemingway had a stand and typed standing up," she said, forgetting, for the moment, her old animosity. To read she lay flat on her back, strapped into what she called "an iron contraption." Vertigo plagued her.

Kay had already been so unhappy in Oregon that Ian had been looking for a job in California. Now Kay's accident made remaining in Oregon impossible. In May of 1985, Kay returned "to civilization," lying in the back seat of the car while Ian drove. "I have the privilege of taking care of and being with my old mother, of which privilege my sisters deprive themselves," Ian told his father's old friend George Popper. He had tried to enlist Faith's help, but she still wanted her mother to recant her condemnation of the commune.

Instead Kay gave another interview about the Lyman family, this time to David Johnston, then writing for the *Los Angeles Times*. "Fame and fortune, fame and fortune, that's all they care about," she had muttered. When Johnston informed her that his middle name was "Cay Boyle," his father having been a great admirer, Kay demanded to know why it was spelled "Cay." Nor was she pleased. "They had no right to name you that, to take my name," she said coldly. As far as the members of the commune were concerned, they remained "fascists." When Johnston, having visited the commune for his story, disagreed, explaining that they had become sedate even, Kay refused to accept the idea that over the years the members of the Lyman family might have changed. Indeed, Johnston concluded that she seemed bewildered that a daughter of hers had an identity in any way different from her own.

Kay Boyle settled now in Oakland, where she rented a downstairs floor-through apartment in a house on Yosemite Avenue off Piedmont Street. "I equate depression with cowardice," she told an interviewer that year, "and courage with optimism, and I think to give in to depression at this time . . . would be a great act of cowardice. So as best I can I keep on fighting."

Testy now and in great pain, unable to walk for months, Kay Boyle proved to be a difficult author for her editor at North Point Press, Jack Shoemaker. She blamed Shoemaker for the uncertainties involved with the publication of *Difficult Death*, and finally wrote telling him she had heard he had accused her of "telling anyone that will listen" that North Point is "dragging its feet" and treating David Rattray "abusively." This she denied. "I only know that my good friend David Rattray was in despair over the situation, and wanted me to find out what was taking place," she defended herself.

Meanwhile she had grievances of her own, which included her dismay that the catalogue copy "had little to do with the book itself." There was also what she termed a serious error: the "owl-ghost" of the grandmother's dead sister did not speak "to a number of characters," but only to the "grandmother and her." Worse even was that North Point had announced it was publishing "her first book of essays," which was not true. And still worse was that she had requested in writing that galleys or advance copies be sent to Doris Grumbach, Bill Shirer, and Studs Terkel, and they had received their copies of the finished book only when bookstores received theirs. North Point had also mislaid the list of friends to whom Kay Boyle wished—at her own expense—copies to be sent.

Shoemaker was responsible for it all, including the North Point catalogue's stating that *Babylon* had been translated "for North Point Press," so that, Kay Boyle exaggerated, a number of people had asked how she had managed to do it so quickly. In fact, she had done the translation, she said, in 1930, and had been revising it for fifty years. Shoemaker corrected the error on the dust jacket. But still she was not appeased. That she was dealing with a small independent publisher without the resources of a Doubleday seemed not to occur to her.

"No, Jack, I never said to anyone that you were 'incompetent,' " Kay wrote the beleaguered editor, "although you certainly are the most difficult publishers I have ever dealt with."

Shoemaker never found, he said, a greater discrepancy in character between the public and the private personality than he did with Kay Boyle. At first impression he found her someone you want to take care of. Soon he discovered she could be "disputatious and cruel." Offering no apologies, she was "abusive" to his staff. You could never do enough for her, Shoemaker found, and "I'm sorry" was not in her vocabulary. Particularly infuriating to Shoemaker were the many interviews Kay Boyle gave insisting that Crevel was not homosexual, in order, by some reasoning of her own, to protect his reputation, and in direct contradiction with North Point's own releases. She had, of course, done the same thing for McAlmon. Her first concern, then as now, was to protect someone she admired from what she was certain would be societal displeasure. That her concealment of Crevel's homosexuality was contradicted by her radicalism, and her belief in individualism, was simply another of the many disparities between belief and practice in her life.

In her eighties Kay Boyle became not only "disputatious" but also litigious. Soon she began a lawsuit against Paget Press, a Canadian publisher, who, with biographer Hugh Ford's collaboration, was reissuing Harold Stearns's autobiography. Kay often said she admired Ford's *Published in Paris*, and he had depicted her respectfully in his *Four Lives in Paris*. Ford had shown her the manuscript in advance, and she had made three sets of corrections. Kay Boyle had even disputed points for which Ford had written documentation. Confronted, she would reply, "Did I say that?"

Yet they had become friends, and together with Ford, she saw Ingmar Bergman's film *Autumn Sonata*. Ingrid Bergman had played a concert pianist in her final years confronted by her past, and in particular by a daughter she had neglected. "You think this is my story, but it's not," Kay told Ford. When he got to know Apple and Clover, he found them both far warmer in recalling Laurence than Kay.

At first Kay told Ford she was delighted he was getting Stearns back into print. When his publisher, Peter Brown, asked for permission to use her description of Harold Stearns from *Being Geniuses Together*, Kay agreeably told him to get in touch with her agent. She told Ford there would be no problem. When Brown failed to hear from Gloria Loomis, however, he went ahead with the book. It was in print when he finally received a letter of permission from Loomis, requesting a fifty-dollar fee. At once Brown sent off his check.

In the finished book, *Confessions of a Harvard Man*, Brown used Kay Boyle's paragraph about Stearns, which took up a page, under the heading "Preface." In all innocence, he sent a copy of the book to Kay Boyle. In a rage, she instructed Loomis not to cash the fifty-dollar check, and went on to sue Paget Press and Brown for using her words as a "preface" without her permission. The whole edition amounted to fifteen hundred copies, but Kay persisted and won a judgment of ten thousand dollars plus her attorney's fees of two thousand dollars. Soon she discovered that it would cost several thousand dollars to collect this money in a Canadian court, and she had to forgo pursuing it any further.

"You knew it and condoned it and are as guilty as Brown," Kay accused Ford. "I almost included you in the suit." When Ford pleaded that Brown had not consulted him about calling the paragraph a "preface," Kay insisted, "I've seen correspondence in which you agreed." It wasn't so. Years later Kay said she was sorry she had not included Hugh Ford personally in the suit. A gentle, forgiving, and reasonable man, Ford attributed the dispute to "dementia" and went on to write a favorable review of *Words That Must Somehow Be Said*.

Her disputatiousness continued. Reading the galleys of Janet Flanner's letters to Natalia Murray, soon to be published as *Darlinghissima*, she came upon a line of Flanner's referring to Bobby: "I don't know who the father was of this daughter and by this time I don't think Kay knows either." Kay demanded that the publisher excise this, as well as several passages about Laurence Vail, or she would sue. Random House capitulated.

When Brenda Wineapple came to interview Kay for her biography of Flanner, *Genêt*, Kay lay on her bed staring up at the ceiling as she talked. "Don't write that down!" Kay periodically called. Nor, of course, was Wineapple to use a tape recorder. It was about control, about Kay Boyle's need to mythologize, Wineapple concluded. What interested her in particular was the relationship between Ernest Walsh and Flanner's sister, Hildegaard, with whom he had been in love.

Life had become hard for Kay, determined still to maintain her independence. Having spent so much of her money on Kathe's case, she had to borrow money now from Shirer. Scrupulous as ever, she paid him back swiftly. Grace Paley visited her in Oakland and found her still immobilized. Nor had she come around to sympathy for the women's movement.

"Well, I could do it, with my children," Kay insisted, referring to her writing. The movement, she complained, had taken up the women who said "I can't," rather than the ones who, like herself, had said "I did." Kay took physical therapy three times a week involving Rolfing and it hurt. But by Thanksgiving she was visiting the McGuckins, wearing white earrings made from chicken bones, and seated firmly on a hard chair.

A fire broke out in the basement of her Oakland house. Kay became frightened of staying alone. When young Kate Moses, working for North Point, offered to sleep over, Kay gratefully accepted. "When you first sleep in a new house, you should go to bed and look in every corner of the room, then make a wish," Kay told her sweetly. "And when you wake up in the morning, you should remember which corner your eyes first turn to, and that is the wish that will come true."

Kay was not defeated yet. Her 1986 Amnesty party had to be held in December of 1985, a party which her friend Frances Steloff, aged ninety-nine, attended from New York, because Kay was rising from what she termed her "bed of pain" to move for the semester to Bowling Green University in Ohio. Kay was the last important survivor of twenties Paris, a legend, and universities still wanted her. Friends warned it was "the Siberia of our United States." Kay Boyle needed the money, more than twenty thousand dollars, and an extra thousand for a lecture, and an honorary doctorate. Having written an antiwar essay for a volume called *Voices of Survival in the Nuclear Age*, in which she suggested that "as long as violent sports like football and ice hockey remained popular, the majority of Americans would not engage in actions on behalf of peace," she moved to flat, brown Bowling Green. She took her cat Dopey with her.

The head of the writing program, Philip O'Connor, went to meet Kay at the Toledo airport. He had been waiting for some time when suddenly he saw walking toward him a magnificent person. He was fifty-three, and she was about to be eighty-four, and it was as if he had fallen in love. Kay Boyle in her movements had "animal qualities." She was like a "severe blade," and it was never in her motherly mode that she approached men. As always, she was as cool, as aloof as her mother had been with Puss. "She will go on doing a number on men until she dies," Eric Solomon had predicted.

Kay had been given to understand she should not discuss politics in class. This she ignored. Nor was her political activity confined to the classroom. When American planes bombed Libya, Kay marched with twenty-some others in protest. "Bomb Libya! Bomb Libya!" fraternity boys called, only to be taken aback by the sight, Kay remembered, of the old lady with white hair marching with the others. She later said she thought the old had "a responsibility" to give meaning to such protests so that it wouldn't seem that "just kids" were involved.

She had tried to enlist O'Connor for one of these marches. He refused, arguing that if it wasn't the war in Vietnam or peace in Central America, they would find something else. Their relationship deteriorated after that.

But later she wrote him, "We don't go at it the same way, but we get the same results." Back home, however, she remained unforgiving. O'Connor, Kay insisted, had supported the Contras, for which he could not be excused.

In the classrooms of Bowling Green, Kay, with her Chanel No. 5 perfume, white earrings, wool pants, and bright red lipstick, came on like a baroness. Of her own work, she discussed only McAlmon's *Being Geniuses Together*. She also taught and championed her friends: Algren, Grace Paley, McAlmon, assigning *A Hasty Bunch*, and Nemerov. Critics had read too much into her works, she insisted, citing this time a Jungian interpretation of her much-anthologized story "Astronomer's Wife," which she termed "ridiculous." Probing the students for lines of poetry they knew by heart, she went on to recite entire poems from memory.

Some had wondered whether, at her age, she could handle two courses. But a week after her arrival, she complained to O'Connor that the students weren't giving her enough writing. Soon a student objected to the amount of work she assigned: "She's killing us." They still had to write their papers over if they were not acceptable; still their manuscripts bore her copious marginal notes.

Her public readings were triumphs as she read aloud from her continuing poem to Samuel Beckett, who was "only eighty, and with his whole youth yet before him." Beckett was frightened of death, Kay Boyle confided to her Bowling Green audience. As his senior, she was trying to comfort him. She wore a ruffled white blouse and a black pantsuit that night, and, as always, was impressive.

When her diverticulitis flared up, Kay was hospitalized for a week. Friends back home wondered whether they should rush to Ohio. "Pish-posh," Kay said then, "I don't need anybody." There would be no whining, no complaining, as age tightened its stranglehold. Even with magnified new glasses, she found it painful to read, and the ophthalmologist told her she should not be using her eyes at all. But the students' papers awaited her. Diligently too she did her back exercises on a chinning bar.

At Bowling Green, Kay charmed many. Wittily she explained that she didn't like snow "at this elevation." Mégève was one thing, Bowling Green another. She was strident now too about living a nonmaterialistic life. Eating little, in restaurants she passed her food to others. Magazines must go to hospitals. It was frivolous to send flowers. A graduate student drove her to the laundromat, where she washed her own pajamas and sheets.

She loved to gossip now, even at the expense of the family. Telling about how Peggy Guggenheim's sister had thrown her children off a roof was one thing. But Kay also talked about Clover's troubles, revealing how her daughter was now writing her letters about how awful her childhood had been. Clover had been in a mental hospital, Kay confided to virtual strangers, as if somehow she were removed from the situation. Later she told the McCords, a couple she met at Bowling Green, that Ian had not grown up as much as he should have.

To others it seemed that Clover's letters so upset her that they caused the diverticulitis attack. She pleaded with Clover to see her side: "I understand your resentment," Kay wrote, "but please try to understand how difficult it has been to reconcile all the various demands that were made during the past fifty years. I believe that love for, and protection of, my children never faltered." Yet Clover's alienation persisted.

To some, she was "just plain Kay"; to others, she was the Queen Bee demanding special treatment, a person deaf to the perspectives of others. Her hostess, Virginia Platt, a retired professor of history, earned Kay's contempt when she did not respond appropriately, as Kay saw it, to the story of how Kay had been protected by that black soldier at Verdun. Kay also disapproved of Platt's not giving her books to charity. At first they drank sherry together at Platt's kitchen table. Gertrude Stein craved attention, especially from men, Kay confided. Later Platt became upset by Dopey's shedding, and put a board across the upstairs landing. Indignant, Kay said she had not been informed of this insult to her cat in advance.

"You know, I think that cat's my mother," Kay said in all apparent seriousness. "She seems to understand the way my mother understood."

There was more trouble. The graduate student who had been assigned to drive her about objected to one of Kay's demands, and let her know she had to swim every morning at a certain time. The demands accelerated. Kay asked the student to do some typing, which was not part of their agreement. "I am not your secretary," the young woman informed her. Nor was the student happy about driving her car up onto the sidewalk so that Kay wouldn't have to walk on the ice. At their moment of parting, the student slammed the car door hard, and the relationship ended. Kay got along no better with a male assistant. He had confessed to wanting to write commercial novels. "We're writing serious fiction," Kay told him indignantly.

In May, Ian arrived, rented a red Thunderbird, and with Kay napping on the reclining seat, and Dopey settled in the back, they drove back to California. For sustenance, Kay nibbled on bran muffins. "I'm never going to do that again," she vowed.

Thin as ever, her hearing now impaired, Kay packed up that summer of 1986 and was off once more to Ireland to work on her book about Irish women. A male graduate student accompanied her, as they stayed at bed-and-breakfasts and took buses and trolleys. Once more Kay saw Faysie, and Mary Grant in Cork. There was no sense of her needing luxury or regretting not having it.

Frail now, Kay managed to get to Valparaiso, Indiana, in November to attend a writers' conference on "Prosperity and Hardship: Life in the 1920s and 1930s." She was the keynote speaker, being paid two thousand dollars. She could not refuse.

That November, Kay Boyle received the Robert Kirsch Award from the *Los Angeles Times* for an outstanding body of work by an author from the West. Kate Moses accompanied her to Los Angeles for the party, where she ran into Noel Young, of Capra Press, which had published *Four Visions of America*. Young felt the urge to take Kay Boyle protectively in his arms, as once Jack Shoemaker had felt. Now Kay seemed overwhelmed by the crowd at the huge cocktail reception.

As he made his way across the room, Young was shocked by how Kay had aged. But she looked as chic as ever in her black suit with a blue satin scarf, even if she was now a little hunched. Young held out his hand, and also leaned forward. Would she respond by leaning forward as well, signaling he was to kiss her?

Flirtatiously, Kay offered her cheek and took Young's arm, leading him to a place, she said, where they could be alone together, where it was quiet so they could talk. He put his arm around her shoulders, and she felt like a small bird. But she still knew how to make a man feel male and in command.

"I want to do a book with you," Young said. "Is there anything you can think of, something new, or even something to revive?"

"I think I have an idea for you," Kay began, and then she was interrupted. So it happened as a result of that meeting that Capra Press agreed to reissue *Gentlemen, I Address You Privately*, although Young had imagined he would be reshooting the old pages, not publishing an entirely new book. But Kay had revisions in mind, especially rewriting the ending so that it would not seem as if the ex-priest, Munday, were returning to heterosexuality. Kay said that she had to revise the book to sharpen her point that sex was genderless, and eroticism was based on the same type of attraction, for both sexes alike.

Kay seemed to enjoy her companion Kate Moses's parents, and even her six-year-old stepsister, who told her she wanted to be a football player, or a juggler in front of the La Brea tar pits, when she grew up. She liked so "specific" a reply, Kay said, and it seemed to Kate Moses that Kay had a better time with her family than she had at the ceremony honoring her. Later at lunch with Doug Messerli of the Sun & Moon Press, Kay spoke animatedly of Djuna Barnes, and of the Hayakawa episode, always one of her favorite anecdotes. Frankly she admitted she had been "mistaken" about the Black Panthers, as she now called Huey P. Newton "a murderer." Kay had come too far to hesitate about changing her position about something so important as that. It was one of her rare admissions of error.

35

Surviving

It is reassuring to know that you will have the endurance
to become ninety.
HERBERT O. KUBLY, c. 1963

Old age has finally succeeded in getting me down.

One day as she was sitting on a bench in Oakland, Kay Boyle met an elderly woman who told her she was overcome by a sense of hopelessness.

"Why should I go on living? I'm eighty-five," the woman told her.

"*I'm* eighty-five," Kay said.

The woman lived in a retirement home in the neighborhood; the place was comfortable, but she wondered why she kept on living.

"Well, you have to get interested in things outside yourself. You have to think of something beyond the self," Kay advised.

At eighty-five, Kay still drove her dull green 1965 Chevrolet. Its only fault, she insisted, was that it lacked power steering. Surviving with her was Tassi, now eighteen years old, her yellowish fur mangy, her bones poking through her coat here and there. Kay made friends with her young neighbors, one with a punk haircut dyed purple, and served them dinner, driving from market to market in search of a particular brand of canned Spanish rice.

Her closet now offered a sparse array of clothes, freshly laundered crisp white blouses, and sensible shoes. A perky blue-and-aqua quilted suit she had ordered from a catalogue. From the furnishings of the house on Frederick Street, she had kept a plaster sculpture with outstretched hands which she had purchased on a jaunt with Marcel Duchamp on New York's Third Avenue in the 1940s for fifty cents.

It was largely with Ian's help that she maintained her independence. He balanced her checkbook, but, Kay said, did not allow her to "feel dependent." Kay took comfort in the loyalty and devotion of her son, while Ian compassionately saw his mother as suffering from "a tremendous amount of guilt having been both a mother and a career person" while leading "a rather tempestuous love life." He said he felt the same way about her that she felt about her own mother, Katherine Evans Boyle.

In 1987 Kay began to edit her diaries, revising her life as she went along. "You see, I am cheating a bit on my entries," she confessed to Jimmy Stern, a survivor like herself. As an Irishman, he was somewhat skeptical of her recently acquired Irish identity. She was also still struggling with her portraits of Irish women. "I simply can't get a handle on the book I'm supposed to be writing," she admitted. "I haven't even thought of a title for it." The idea of resting from those labors Katherine had devised for her eighty years before remained inconceivable.

The local French restaurant gave her a discount, as Kay invariably insisted on picking up the check. Principle prevailed in every corner of her life. She refused to patronize the Metro cab company because she had heard one of the drivers say, "I hate old people." She still withheld the federal tax on her telephone bill. Indefatigably soliciting contributions for the Nelson Algren Award, she remained impatient with those who turned her down. "If you can't give money," she said, "you can't give love."

About other women, even virtual strangers, she often spoke competitively. She referred to that eighty-five-year-old woman she had met on the street as "very big," whereas Kay herself remained "slender." She had read Diane Johnson's *Vanity Fair* article about Lillian Hellman and Dashiell Hammett, stressing, Kay thought, how many lovers he had and claiming that she wasn't very important to him. I don't think it should have been published, Kay said in 1987, "because the only thing Lillian had to hold on to in life was that love." There was distinct condescension in her voice then, she who had had so many loves.

There remained, as age stalked her, two Kay Boyles. She could be the charming, motherly mentor to Kate Moses and Shawn Wong. She could also be capricious and pursue old vendettas. Hugh Ford, whose work she had so admired, now was guilty of "flights of imagination in his writing about the twenties," having given her love affairs she did not have in his *Four Lives in Paris*. Although she had read and corrected Sandra Whipple Spanier's manuscript for *Kay Boyle: Artist and Activist*, Kay now decided that "she's a very academic young woman and she thinks of me as completely wild and without principles because she's never had any kind of life of her own." Fabulating her own history, she came into conflict with writers and scholars. But she broke also for a time with her lawyer and with her young assistant, Emily Zukerberg. She'd get a bee in her bonnet, Jessica Mitford observed, and it was hard to dislodge it. A certain callousness also surprised people, and some remembered how when her San Francisco State colleague Antoinette Willson was ill, Kay had gone to her apartment and taken clothes and jewelry, remarking, "She's going to die anyway."

Kay spoke proudly now of having managed to arrange for two of Apple's stories to be published in Sallie Bingham's magazine, *The American Voice*, published out of Kentucky, in one of which a son asks his mother why she and his father broke up. So her children could never, into their own late middle age, transcend that moment in their lives of the shattering of Les Six Enfants. Apple, who as a child had so resented taking her mother's heavy packet of letters to the post office every day in Mégève, now frequented the post office herself.

A heavy smoker and recovering alcoholic, Apple was diagnosed with lung cancer when she was fifty-seven. Surgery went well, only for Apple to suffer an aneurysm and fall into a deep coma. That Bobby and her husband had separated added to Kay's anguish. She unexpectedly sided with her daughter against "that ardent Catholic, that ex-priest," her husband; usually sons-in-law were in the right. Kay invited Clover to join her in a visit to Apple in Miami in July of 1987.

At the hospital, Kay suggested that they sing to the comatose Apple in French. Clover then glared at her with what Kay experienced as "absolute hatred."

"I am here on my own terms, not on yours," Kay says Clover told her. Kay then retaliated with accusations that Clover had been "absolutely awful" to her husband.

"Supermom, who understands everybody and never loses her temper!" Clover taunted her mother, throwing the alarm clock across the room, as Laurence had so often thrown crockery, the radio, the typewriter.

In the nursing home where Apple was brought, she lived in the world of the past. She mistook Ted Goeser for Laurence, and was unable to believe that her father was dead. Sometimes she spoke as if Kay and Laurence were still in the process of becoming divorced. Apple announced that she had made her decision: she would live with Kay rather than with Laurence.

Back in Oakland, Kay joined a demonstration at the Concord Naval Weapons Station and a silent walk to the place where Brian Willson, once an Air Force intelligence officer in Vietnam and now an antiwar activist, had sat on the tracks in protest against the "death trains" carrying arms to Central America. Willson had been struck by a munitions train and lost both legs. Now Kay Boyle sat down on the tracks just a foot away from where Brian Willson had been hit. Joanie Baez sang.

Suffering a severe case of the "Taiwan flu," Kay rose from her sickbed to lecture at the San Francisco State University Poetry Center. Her voice high and shrill, she spoke once more about the responsibilities of the writer. "There are times," Kay told her young audience, "when I sit down at the typewriter and on the clean white page I've inserted in the roller I can see only the senseless streamings of the black man's blood." She remained opposed, she said, to the "intellectual system which fosters intellect and ambition and competition at the expense of emotion, instinct and the soul of man." So the influence of John Cowper Powys continued to reverberate through her life.

By now her arthritis had spread from her spine and neck to her skull.

Christmas of 1987 brought what Kay called "a little bit of a heart attack." More attacks of angina followed. Soon Kay could no longer cook for herself, and the chef at the Bay Wolf restaurant made dinners, or Ian or Kate Moses would prepare her meals. Still Kay felt she must work harder than ever to "help pay the staggering hospital and doctors' bills" for Apple. Working was a way of keeping herself "from thinking about my beloved child." She wrote that Apple's illness had "shattered" her. "I can only cry out her name in silence," Kay said.

Yet Apple's illness could not shatter the habits of a lifetime. Bobby visited, and Kay was bossy, talking only about the past, critical still of Laurence, talking about returning to Oregon, where she had been so unhappy. Bobby concluded they had "nothing to say to each other." Then as soon as Bobby was gone, Kay confided all the details to Jimmy Stern, adding that "Bobby always had a very serious inferiority complex." Kay also expressed her irritation that Bobby would not discuss taking her estranged husband back.

To earn money, Kay agreed to be a judge for the PEN Syndicated Fiction Project, but an assistant had to read the stories to her aloud. KPFA radio ran an all-day birthday tribute for Kay Boyle in February of 1988, only for music director Charles Amirkhanian, who had organized the event, to be offended by her imperiousness, her failure to listen to any of the program, and her behaving as if it had all been her due. He emerged from the event feeling used, as if, having served her, he had ceased to exist. It was a charge Doris Grumbach had leveled against her as well.

Appearing on *The Today Show* in 1988, Kay Boyle said, "I never understood what 'Lost Generation' meant." Modestly, she expressed her surprise that she should be an entry in the *Encyclopaedia Britannica*. Wearing an ivory cable-knit Irish cardigan over a starched white blouse with a Victorian high neck, her carved white earrings in place, she seemed a happy and composed woman at peace with herself.

Among the petitions she signed that year was one calling for an end to aid to "Apartheid Israel," in support of the "heroic people of Palestine," and for a "democratic and secular Palestine." Among her fellow signers were Lawrence Ferlinghetti and Nathan Hare, who had once been so instrumental in agitating for the black studies program at San Francisco State.

Apple died in May of 1988. "She was on the threshold of a great writing career," Kay told people. Almost simultaneously, Apple's son Bruno committed suicide, joining the many members of Kay Boyle's family for whom the only option seemed self-destruction. Kay promised to pay Apple's daughter Emily's college tuition as "Apple's share."

"You had many problems with Apple," Kathe remarked when she visited her mother that year. Kathe had in mind all the many letters she had received over the years from Apple complaining bitterly about their mother.

"I don't know what you're talking about," Kay said. When Kathe went through Apple's possessions, she discovered many loving letters to their mother which Kay had returned to her when she sold her papers. These letters were written at the same time as she was writing bitterly to her sisters that she of all the children had been most damaged by Kay and Laurence's divorce.

In April, Kay suffered another coronary attack, only to return home from the hospital "a good deal weaker and more disillusioned about her physical well-being." But soon she was back in her sunny Oakland kitchen, at her "desk," a white-painted kitchen table. She wrote letters on the paper of her electrocardiogram, and still managed to make her way to post office, bank, and market. For relaxation, she drank her favorite Dubonnet. By June, Kay found it difficult to use her right leg; but she would not walk with a cane. She was trying, she said valiantly, "not to be entirely eighty-six years old." In September, she had a cataract operation. As hard as Kay Boyle fought, old age closed in mercilessly.

But renewed once more, she bought Rockport shoes, known for their orthopedic qualities, and insisted that Samuel Beckett send her a tracing of his feet so that she could buy him Rockport shoes too. When he was placed on a breathing machine, Beckett told her to forget about the shoes, but she sent them anyway. Did he like them? Kay was asked by the McGuckins. "He's getting used to them," she said evasively. In fact, they didn't fit. "They'll improve with wearing," Beckett wrote graciously. "Already I feel they'll help keep one upright." Beckett was indeed facing his own death with trepidation. " 'Time gentlemen please,' as they used to say in the Dublin pubs coming up to 10 p.m. 'Ochone Ochone Dead and not gone,' " he wrote Kay, calling her by 1989 "indomitable Kay."

Asked if she was writing her autobiography, Kay replied, without irony, "How boring to write about oneself." She stood as tall as she could in spite of the pain. She discarded her pain. Thanksgiving at the McGuckins' found her, as Hank's wife, Jackie, put it, "very, very verbal."

At her 1989 birthday party for Amnesty, Kay sat at a table in a navy-blue suit and signed and sold her books. Later when IWW songs were sung, Kay sang along. When a photographic portrait of her was auctioned off, it fetched $325. Hank McGuckin closed the evening by singing "Solidarity Forever." In a clear, strong voice, Kay thanked everyone for coming.

As always in her last years, conflict invigorated her. At eighty-seven she discovered in writer Dorothy Bryant a new adversary. *Twentieth Century Literature* had devoted an issue to Kay; Sandra Whipple Spanier, the guest editor, had invited Kay's closest friends, and her children, to supply personal reminiscences to accompany scholarly essays about her work. Ian wrote a poem, picturing himself watching his mother asleep at night in her bedroom, and invoking her life as a young woman when she was "like a long-legged colt," when she was "radiant to men, to children too." None of the other children wrote, but Spanier used a piece of one of Kathe's letters, and Bobby's 1942 poem, "To Mama." There was nothing from Faith or Clover. Samuel Beckett also declined to contribute, even a paragraph.

But among those who did agree to write a tribute was Bryant, who had been a friend since 1984 and one of the readers at Kay's 1989 Amnesty party. Wanting to please Kay and to convey a sense of her forcefulness, Bryant turned to the subject herself for guidance.

"Oh, make something up," Kay told her. "You wouldn't refuse to do something for me, would you?"

Bryant then created a fictitious anecdote based on an incident related to her by one of Kay's students. Asking her for a recommendation for a grant, the student had simultaneously admitted that the money would be used not to produce fiction, but for a trip. "Kay yelled at me and threw me out," Bryant was told, as the woman seemed more admiring than angry. "She told me I was wasting my time and talent and threw me out of her office." This, Bryant believed, was Kay Boyle at her uncompromising best.

From this anecdote, Bryant invented an incident in which she placed herself outside of Kay's office, waiting for a *male* friend, who had confided in her that he planned to get Miss Boyle to sign a grant application, then "submit some old stories as evidence of work done" and go off on a trip. Bryant hears Kay's voice, "like a bird, a very angry bird," ordering the student: "Get out of my office! I'm sorry I ever wasted any of my time on you!" To Bryant, standing there, Kay seemed "like a white hawk, with her thin, beak-like nose," and her "sharp eyes, and her grey-white hair swept back as if she were diving down upon my retreating friend."

In Bryant's second anecdote, Kay visits her home only to stop and, horrified, cry out, "Dorothy!" She had spotted "grapes" on the table, despite the Chavez boycott, and her look at Bryant was the same "hawk-like stab" the student had received. Bryant ended her affectionate tribute: "Bless Kay Boyle for showing us the unswerving integrity without which neither art nor humanity will survive."

Furious at Dorothy Bryant's fictionalizing, Kay wrote a scathing letter. The episode about the grapes was fine. But Kay was "a bit disturbed" about being depicted as "ordering a student friend of yours out of my office and accusing him of wasting my time." She insisted she "had *never* ordered anyone" out of her office, "not even Hayakawa," or accused "*anyone*" of wasting her time. "I look on every encounter," she wrote irrelevantly, "as a potentially valuable experience." Having forgotten that she had suggested to Bryant that she make something up, she said she was curious about why Bryant cared enough about this person to accompany him to her office and wait outside for him since she considered him dishonest. Or, Kay concluded, "did you dream up this totally inaccurate story, dear Dorothy?" In a note at the bottom of the page, Kay added, her feelings obviously injured, "I'm very sorry you see me as a sharp-eyed hawk. I don't feel like one."

Well aware of how litigious Kay had become, Bryant immediately wrote what she herself would term "an abject apology . . . it really was groveling." But it was also sincere. Bryant pleaded that if she had offended Kay, it was the opposite of her intention. She explained how the episode had been fictionalized from an anecdote a woman had recounted to her. Acknowledging, for the record, that she should have shown Kay the article first, she added that she regretted ever writing such words.

Unappeased, Kay Boyle behaved as if she were going into battle. At once she sent the correspondence to her lawyer, Robert Treuhaft. "I really don't know this woman," she told Treuhaft, although she had known her for years. When Kay accused Bryant of xeroxing her letter and showing it to others, Treuhaft reminded her that she had done the same thing.

With legal avenues closed to her, Kay now launched a virtually world-wide attack on Dorothy Bryant. She mailed copies of her own letter and Bryant's apology to friends far and wide. She accused Bryant of being "demented," and a person who disliked women writers who "had" publishers because she had to publish her own books. Jay Laughlin, James Stern, Ken McCormick, many received such diatribes along with their packets, as Kay instructed them to attach the two letters to their copies of the "Kay Boyle Issue" of *Twentieth Century Literature*. The episode embarrassed her friends, but inevitably most forgave her. Jessica Mitford, however, could not.

As if her quarrel with Dorothy Bryant had worn her out at last, by the spring of 1989 Kay Boyle admitted that she could no longer manage life alone. She applied to a retirement community called The Redwoods. She had first to submit to a two-day geriatric exam, which inquired into her state of mind as well as testing her motor skills. "Do you get depressed often?" she was asked. References were required. William Shirer read the questionnaire he was sent with indignation. Will this person fit in well with others? he read. Does she like the company of many different people?

"You mustn't answer it," Kay told him, clearly embarrassed.

"You have in your midst a distinguished writer with a sterling character," Shirer wrote. "You ought to be glad to have somebody like that."

Soon, however, Kay was ensconced at The Redwoods. It was a "blessing," she told everyone, denying herself, as always, the empty solace of self-pity. Free of housework, laundry, cooking, shopping, taking out the garbage, and standing in line at the post office, she could "become a writer again." This was important, she said, since her total earnings from her writing in 1988 had been only two thousand dollars.

In her one-room studio, piled high with books, were displayed photographs of William Carlos Williams and Samuel Beckett, as well as many of Joseph Franckenstein. In 1990 Samuel Beckett signed his last letter to Kay "with sixty years of love," as he finally had entered into her fabulation of their long friendship, he now grateful and dependent, hers the much stronger will. As soon as he died, she sold all his letters to the University of Texas.

On her bureau at The Redwoods were also pictures of lawyer Charles
Garry and Joan Baez. Soon Ian's acting posters began to decorate the walls,
as he resumed his career in the theater, playing roles from Shakespeare
to *The Wizard of Oz*. There was no space for a couch. Kay now slept on
Marcel Duchamp's old narrow iron bed, which she had covered with a
blue-and-white quilt.

"Not very comfortable," Hank McGuckin remarked.

"But this is Marcel Duchamp's bed," Kay told him. "He gave it to
me. Can you imagine how many acts of love were consummated on this
bed?" No matter if she was an old lady now; she could still remember
sexual desire and wanted you to know it.

From her studio balcony, she could look out over a salty marshland
of weeping willows and blue herons and egrets, wild geese and gulls. As
soon as she was settled at The Redwoods, Kay Boyle told people she was
"working non-stop." She wrote writer Louise Erdrich: "I've been doing
nothing but work all day, can you imagine? It's marvelous. I should have
moved here years ago." She insisted it was "rather wonderful."

Shortly after her arrival at the home, Kay Boyle accosted a fellow
resident in the dining room with a familiar gesture of supplication.

"Bob, I'm thinking of starting an Amnesty group here," Kay said. "I
have four people. Will you join?"

Bob hesitated.

"Come on, Bob. You're not dead yet. Don't you realize people are
suffering?"

When Bob still proved recalcitrant, Kay Boyle became angry. "What
kind of character do you have?" she demanded.

It was, as always, part pose and part conviction. It was who she was.
In June of 1989, political activist Ralph Schoenman called to read Kay
Boyle a statement urging support for the Chinese students and workers of
the democracy movement, in defense of the veterans of the demonstrations
at Tienanmen Square.

"Well, you know, I'm at an old people's home," Kay explained. "It's
rather dreadful. You can imagine the opinions of the people here. The only
thing they know about the Chinese is they're against them." She was "proud"
to sign the document.

Kay Boyle would not be defeated by an alien or reactionary environment. She arranged for a group from The Redwoods to join her in a demonstration against the death penalty. She was brought to San Quentin in a
wheelchair.

When San Francisco journalist Cyra McFadden came to visit Kay
Boyle, Kay appeared for lunch smartly outfitted in one of her pants suits
and wearing her white earrings. Complaining about the Wasp uptightness
of The Redwoods, she confessed that she was inviting black friends to the
dining room to stir things up. She found many of the women in the home
supporting Oliver North for President. "They don't understand American

534]   K A Y B O Y L E / *Author of Herself*

policy," Kay complained to her visiting granddaughter, Clover's Ariel. "Everyone is so selfish. They can't put the self aside for the greater good."

Sometimes close friends like Ted Keller now perceived traces of unusual self-doubt in Kay. Ted concluded it may have provided a clue as to why she had to do all that writing, so people would admire "the writer Kay Boyle" rather than be required to appreciate Kay for herself. It was an insight he arrived at independently of any knowledge of how Katherine had programmed Kay to be that writer, and it was true. "I suppose you can't stay much longer," Kay wistfully asked Ted during one of his Sunday visits. It was as if she were saying: What do I have to offer you now? Ted assured her it wasn't a chore to visit her at all.

By 1990 the infirmities of age renewed their hold. One day she fell in the parking lot of the Safeway supermarket where Ian had driven her, and loosened some teeth. Her hearing faltered. "What?" she'd ask Ian again and again. Now when friends from San Francisco visited, as soon as they were gone Kay complained that they had stayed too long.

"You should have told them to leave," Ian said.

"I couldn't," Kay answered. Once she asked a visitor to write a poem. She too would write one. Then they would read each other's poems, embrace, and the visitor would go home.

Her doctor, Tom Stone, advised her to walk a mile a day for her circulation, and although she was notorious for refusing to heed medical advice, she took visitors to the marsh, where they could walk among the egrets and the great blue herons.

"I always felt marvelous when I was pregnant," Kay told Kate Moses, herself now pregnant. "Those are the great days."

One of her most devoted visitors was her colleague Leo Litwak, who found that after a while you forgot she was an old lady, so centered a woman was she, even now.

"How are things?" Leo asked one day.

"Oh, well, you get old," Kay said simply. "The 'golden years' are a crock."

With Dr. Tom Stone, a vigorous, athletic man in his sixties, married to a younger woman, Kay began to behave like an infatuated schoolgirl in a parody of the days when she had been the belle of Paris. Ian accused her of falling in love, and she became cross. But Kay was in earnest as she insisted that she was the woman Stone preferred to his wife. Kay demanded that Stone take her out to dinner at one of the local restaurants at least once a week, that he take her for walks, that he even take her shopping, that he behave indeed as if he were a suitor, or a husband. Toward Stone's absent wife, Kay was unrelentingly critical. "You don't think he really likes her?" she asked friends skeptically.

Once when Stone was fifteen minutes late, she became as flustered as an adolescent. "He's never done this before," she said, flushed with anxiety. At eighty-seven, she had decided that Stone had found the woman of his life; it was one more recapitulation of all those times when she was convinced that men, her doctors, fellow writers, husbands of friends, the husband of her sister, were in love with her. And, of course, some of them had been.

She dedicated a poem, "December 1989," to "my beloved Dr. Thomas Stone." Her art, poetry, was the one arena in which she could best Stone's younger wife. "Tom, I will do anything you recommend and do it / Happily, without protest or argument," she wrote in humorous violation of the truth. Mocking her "myriad geriatrical infirmities," she promised to obey him even if he advised her to walk at least "seventy times eighty miles a day."

Five of Kay's children were alive and well. But it was Ian, the forty-six-year-old son for whom she had so craved, who tended to her needs. "You took care of Papa," Ian told Kathe, as if, indeed, Laurence had been a relative of his too, "now I'm taking care of Mama." Fulfilling his mother's prophecy, Ian had not married. "So I've got something to look forward to," he said lightly. Ian perceived that his mother could be dogmatic and argumentative, but, lovingly, he forgave her. "It's instinctive in her," he said. "She's not even aware that she's doing it."

Kathe maintained an interested distance, persuaded still that the more Kay admitted her faults, the more the children could love her. "She was more positive about work, actions, and ideals," Kathe remembered. The parent she loved, however, was Laurence, who never let her down. Kay didn't need the children so much, Kathe concluded. She had so many other people.

It was only Clover, now fifty and a painter living in New York, however, who penetrated Kay Boyle's fantasy about her own mother. She wouldn't treat her daughters as she did if her mother had been so nurturing, Clover thought. Katherine Evans Boyle had been a hard-driving, fiercely ambitious woman, and Kay's children and grandchildren had paid the price.

To Ian's chagrin, Kay would not forgive Clover her intransigence. His mother was a warm woman, Ian thought. Only in her not finding a kind word to say for Clover did Ian, her strongest advocate, perceive a hardness she shared with her sister, Joan.

During granddaughter Ariel's visit to The Redwoods, she discovered, to her chagrin, that Kay would have preferred to see her brother, Devin, whom she called "a genius." He was not a better student than Ariel, but he was a male. To young Ariel, it was perplexing that Kay, who praised her mother and her grandmother so much in her writing, had so unfair a preference for men. Kathe remained amused when Kay sent good wishes to her son Kolia, while barely listening when Kathe told her that her daughter Yannick had cancer.

Was it having been enlisted without her permission to fulfill her mother's dream that had tilted Kay against women? Was it that unfair competition Katherine created between Kay and Joan which had led Kay Boyle all her life to distrust women as competitors? Or was it that she remained a victim of her time, she a woman born into a Victorian home at the turn of the century into a society which overwhelmingly supported and nourished the aspirations of men, and relegated women to the role of "helpmeets," as critic Margaret Lawrence had accused Kay Boyle of being, domestic enablers of the creative potential of men?

To bury her resentment against her mother, Kay Boyle had glorified Katherine in both *Being Geniuses Together* and her Gale autobiographical sketch, as a character full of force and purpose; she had created a Katherine Evans Boyle recognizable to no one who knew the pallid, retiring woman so clearly under the thumb of her two very strong-willed daughters. But Kay, living her mother's dream, had been indeed powerless as a child before Katherine's indomitable will, and that servitude to her mother's ambition for her remained with her all her life. Kay Boyle had lived a role set by her mother in other ways too. As Katherine had been a manipulative woman, a flatterer of men who knew how to win their favor, so her daughter had practiced these arts. She had pitied her mother for her devalued role in the Boyle household, while simultaneously she adopted Katherine's strategies for surviving.

Visiting Kay in September of 1990, Kathe found her mother weak and frail. Arthritic pain in her neck made it difficult for her even to stand. When she tried to write, her hands hurt. She had survived disease of the gallbladder, diverticulitis, breast cancer and two mastectomies, a hysterectomy, broken bones, and angina attacks. But she was still capable of being the hostess, inviting guests so that Kathe would not be bored.

Bemused, Kathe observed her mother's infatuation with Dr. Stone. How it would hurt her, Kathe thought, should Kay hear Dr. Stone speak of her, as he did, as a frail old lady who had led too sedentary a life. The subject of regrets surfaced.

"I should never have divorced Papa," Kay admitted to Kathe now, relinquishing at last the myth of Joseph as her great love.

"What do you mean?" Kathe protested. "You couldn't have stayed together. And you wouldn't have had Ian."

But even this reference to her beloved son did not move Kay Boyle to relent.

"I don't see why you say that," she bristled.

Pain had at last defeated her. "It's too long," Kay murmured. She wrote a poem called "A Poem on Getting Up Early in the Morning (Or Even Late in the Morning) When One Is Old." Immediately, the poet hears "Tom's voice across the wire." But Tom, younger than she, is unaware that "rising in the morning is the final chapter of despair."

This poem was very different from Kay Boyle's "Advice to the Old (Including Myself)," written when she was in her seventies. Then she could valiantly exhort herself not to "speak of yourself (for God's sake) even when asked" and not to

> *. . . dwell on other times as different from the time*
> *Whose air we breathe; or recall books with broken spines*
> *Whose titles died with the old dreams . . .*

In her seventies Kay Boyle had been able to conceal her pain, "take the old fury" in her "empty arms" and "bear it fiercely, fiercely to the wild beast's lair." Now the pride of keeping her suffering muted had been sacrificed to the breakdown of her physical being. Her afflictions had taken the gloss off the ambiguous gift of longevity.

When Kathe arrived back in Paris, she found a letter from her mother. "You drink too much. You're out of shape," Kay scolded, accusing this kindest of her daughters of setting a bad example for her children. Her mother had withheld her approval one more time, forcing her middle-aged daughter to struggle still for her love. In tears, Kathe telephoned Clover.

"We're such a disappointment to Mama," Kathe said mournfully.

"Well, she's a disappointment to me," Clover replied indignantly, well aware of her mother's inability to love her daughters for themselves, as Katherine had been unable to love her. If Katherine had turned little Kay into a vessel for her own abandoned dreams, so that the child produced an outpouring of poems and stories, Kay had made her own daughters do the same for her, although never with the hope that they might succeed in reaching beyond where she had been able to go.

Still she remained largely unaware of self. Kay Boyle, who courageously had survived every physical challenge to her body, and who spiritually had survived McCarthyite harassment, who had risen to the political and moral needs of her time, who had survived the deaths of husbands, and a child, could never bear the pain of the examined life. Finally it diminished her as an artist. And always it diminished her as a mother, so that, approaching her ninetieth year, she remained emotionally recalcitrant and unbending, still withholding her approval. At such times she resembled the old woman she had written about in *Death of a Man* half a century before, "a hard, bitter, cold-eyed old woman, a tight fisted witch, unasking and ungiving."

In October of 1990, Kay was suddenly seized by excruciating pain. Scar tissue from her 1982 hysterectomy had caught in the large intestine, blocking the passage. Ian saw her through once more. The ensuing operation weakened her. She weighed only eighty-five pounds, and had shrunk from her former five feet seven inches, the tall lean figure of her prime. Her blue eyes were sunk deep into her head, her nose more prominent. She still resembled the exquisite photograph Man Ray had made of her sixty years earlier, but one hundred years older.

Still she would not give up her Redwoods studio, with its independence, its telephone, and her books, and move into the hospital wing. "I'm going to hang in," Kay told Ian. If, often quiet and depressed now, she sometimes said she was ready to die, she soon had an assistant and was dictating revisions of her diaries, cutting and shaping her life story. She had even reestablished contact with her sister Joan in Florida, now confined to a wheelchair. Kay suggested that Jo move to the Redwoods, so they could end their lives together, as they had begun. But Jo declined her offer.

Coda

I haven't changed much since I was ten years old.

Let it be courage that our tongues compose,
There being no refuge from the hurricane that blows.

It had been more than twenty years since Kay had seen Faith. Yet of all the daughters, she was the most affirming of her mother. Even if Kay had seemed to Faith like "a Queen in exile" in America, even if her own work always came first, Faith liked the idea of her mother having a gift and pursuing it. The mother Clover found a "grande dame" and "neglectful," Faith, who had fewer expectations, chose to remember as a woman who had gone out and lived by her own lights. She was not to be viewed by ordinary standards. Of course, as the fifth daughter, Faith had never hoped to be primary in her affections.

Yet Faith felt she was the child most like her mother. If she had devoted her life to building a commune, hadn't Kay too been attracted by Raymond Duncan's cult? Didn't she find her fulfillment as a woman in bearing children, having five of her own to match Kay's six? "My childhood prepared me for the life I live today," Faith believed. Her mother had exposed her to a bigger life, a larger sense of the world than an ordinary woman could have done. For that she was "eternally grateful."

Twenty years after their break, Faith acted. "I don't want her to die hating me," she said.

In February of 1991, the week of her mother's eighty-ninth birthday, Faith wrote to her: "Somehow there must be a way for us to talk to one another." She also told her mother: "It was you who taught me and prepared me to live this life I do by teaching me how to live with different people and to accept with love what life offered. Can you forgive me?" she added.

"Your letter has changed my whole life and brought me much happiness and I long to see you more than ever," Kay immediately replied.

"I am now eighty-nine years old, and it is not pleasant to get old, but the love of my children makes it less difficult."

But as Faith considered when she might be reunited with her mother, Kay complained privately that she still had not left the commune. To Kathe, it seemed that even now Kay would be satisfied with nothing less than Faith's declaring, "You were right and I was wrong." It was that trait which so infuriated Bobby, Kay's bad-mouthing one sister to another, or to other people. Meanwhile, that the commune had sustained itself and become economically self-sufficient, that her daughter had found some measure of fulfillment, did not permit Kay to temper her original judgment, as if there were some principle involved in not changing her mind.

There were times now, alas, when she became confused. By mistake, she sent to Faith Bobby's "Forever France" scarf, reminding her of the day she had sailed back to France to begin her adult life alone. "We admired your bravery," Kay wrote. Then, realizing she had confused one daughter with another, she mailed Faith a check for six dollars so she could send the scarf on to France. Chilled when she saw that check, Faith returned the scarf to California. It reminded her too much of how her mother had so often seen her children as extensions of herself. If now she was getting them mixed up, so all her life she had played them off against each other.

Kay had been able to establish relationships which were far less emotionally ambiguous with her students. "She was something," Kathe would grant. But Shawn Wong could declare that he "loved" her. When Copper Canyon Press decided to issue Kay Boyle's *Collected Poems*, she chose to dedicate that volume to Shawn Wong.

"I don't know why you want to do that," he protested.

"Poetry didn't mean anything to me until I met you," she told him. During the political ferment of the late sixties, she had stopped writing poetry; he had then inspired *Testament for My Students*. Kay apologized to him for changing her will and not leaving him her old green Chevy, which would go to the person who ran errands for her at The Redwoods.

"Come and see me. You know I'm not going to live forever," Kay urged, and Shawn Wong responded because he considered her a surrogate grandmother. "You tell Frank [Chin] he's on my death list for not coming to see me," Kay joked, and Chin, who had never actually been her student, went. She ran into former student Victor Turks at the Wells Fargo Bank in Mill Valley, and he began weekly visits to The Redwoods.

When Wong learned in 1990 that Kay Boyle was out of money (she told him she had to sell her jewelry), he recommended to the Lannan Foundation that they offer her their Outstanding Literary Achievement award, and she received thirty-five thousand dollars. In March of 1992, the Northern California Booksellers Association awarded her the Fred Cody Award for Excellence of a Body of Work, this award a thousand dollars.

She was too frail to attend the ceremonies, and Ian was appearing on the stage that night.

Burton Weiss, rare-book dealer, who accepted for her, recounted to the audience how Kay had once told him, "It's a pity we were never arrested together." Weiss confided to the audience that Kay had advised him to "open with a joke." ("What would you like me to say?" Weiss had in fact asked. Kay gave him "carte blanche," telling him to "just do it." But when he read her his text, she protested: "No, that's all wrong." Finally he decided to devote his remarks to their relationship, and to how he came to speak for her.)

Weiss described how he proofread Kay's collected poems with her. Weiss sat at Kay's worktable, reconciling various editions; Kay lay dozing in her bed. When he needed to consult her, he woke her. Instantly Kay gave "firm writerly answers." Then she would fall back to sleep to regain her energy for the next round.

The praise Kay said meant most to her came in a letter from a young professor at Wuhan University in China, who told her she represented the best of modern American literature, not only for what she wrote but for how she had lived her life. She meant more to the Chinese than Ernest Hemingway, Gui Juo-ping wrote, because "we don't necessarily appreciate all of his life, especially the ending." She was a "model," in her works as in her "progressive activities." She was always on the side of the young; she was "always young" herself. Gui Juo-ping then invited her to come to China and lecture. "I wish you a long life," he closed. All her life, at the end as at the beginning, she was being discovered, and rediscovered.

In response Ian was enlisted to mail tapes of her poetry readings to China. Kay was defining the terms of her own fulfillment. She did it at twenty-four when she joined Ernest Walsh, and she did it now as she approached her ninetieth birthday.

Her spirits were "good," and "she continued to work," Kay wrote Blair Clark in a letter dictated to an assistant because her eyesight was failing. Unable to read, she wanted high school students with reading problems to be brought to The Redwoods so she could ask them to read good books to her. Kay Boyle said she would tell them what to expect from life so they wouldn't make the same mistakes she did. Her visitors now had to be organized carefully: the McGuckins one day, Leo Litwak another, Daniel Ellsberg. Visiting every day, Ian took charge.

"I have things to do," Kay told Kathe, anxious to get off the telephone and back to some writing "about the children." It must be something about Apple, Kathe concluded. "I suddenly realize you and Apple were very close," Kay told her, an odd comment, Kathe thought, since she and Apple had gone together with Laurence after the breakup.

By the fall of 1991, Kay Boyle's demands had proven to be too much for kindly Dr. Tom Stone. In an aggressive manner, she had overburdened him, he felt. His patience exhausted, he found himself even repelled by her manipulativeness, her attempts to make him feel guilty if he did not agree to do what she wanted. She had tried to make him feel he was abandoning his responsibilities. He had retired from the practice of medicine, and it was not to him as a doctor that she was making her demands, but to him as a man. She was accusing Dr. Stone of emotional defection.

Stone found that her conversation now consisted of gossip and name dropping, which he found boring. He had come to see her as a woman who had been a strong, manipulative personality all her life, one who used people for what she could get from them, and was now continuing in that pattern. Now she had created a fantasy in which she expected far more of him than was realistic. No longer able to behave as if he were her admirer, to flatter her ego, he was forced to act. Unlike her son Ian, whom Stone perceived as her prey, "a mouse in her hands," he was free to do something about the situation.

Stone was not unsympathetic. He saw Kay as "lonely as heck" and fastening on anyone to satisfy her craving to have someone in her life. But the fantasy that he was that man had become "utterly intolerable."

He attempted to let her down gently.

"Come up and have dinner at our house. I hate this restaurant scene," he invited her. But Kay insisted on tête-à-têtes; she did a lot of posing, he realized, and needed an audience, one which assuredly did not include Mrs. Stone. In the fall of 1991 Kay and Dr. Stone parted company. Kay pretended that it was she who had rejected him and that the relationship had dissolved because Mrs. Stone had been jealous of *her*. "How can a forty-five-year-old woman be jealous of me?" she demanded of Ian.

"I'm like a boat without oars," Kay mournfully told Bobby. A woman of the world, she needed something in which to believe. This was as essential a component of Katherine's legacy as her need to write. But Kay Boyle's beliefs always came to her through the medium of an engaging man. In this she remained a member of a generation of women who came of age believing that men were their superiors, necessary to their sense of themselves not only as women but as human beings. For all her radicalism, Kay Boyle still remained a woman for whom her own was the devalued sex.

Nearing ninety, Kay befriended Father Gerry O'Rourke, a craggy-faced, handsome white-haired Irish priest who had been born in the old country and spoke with a resonant brogue. Before long she had made the decision to enter the Catholic Church. As a child Kay Boyle had attended no church. And she had joked about Faith and Ian dutifully learning their catechism as Joseph attempted to make them Catholics. "What does he think is going to happen in heaven?" Kay had laughed. "That I'll meet Richard Brault and Ernest Walsh?"

Now, as a Catholic, Kay would join Joseph, her mother-in-law the

Countess Esterházy, who had died in the late sixties, and Apple, who had also converted to Catholicism before her death. Father O'Rourke baptized Kay Boyle in a ceremony which Ian filmed, and which Kay interrupted by threatening to tell a joke about Adolf Hitler. Regularly, she attended Mass. When she became too weak, she took Communion from her bed. But if Father O'Rourke were the priest officiating on a particular Sunday, Kay could be found in the chapel.

Only when Father O'Rourke urged her to be more forgiving did Kay become irritated with him. She sent him little notes despite the arthritis which made the physical act of writing excruciating. As Katherine had called the younger men she gathered to her table "son," so now did Kay. "Dearly beloved son Jerry [sic] O'Rourke," she wrote, requesting that he read her novel *Gentlemen, I Address You Privately*, so that he might tell her whether her portrayal of the priest Munday was in fact authentic. "I was with you in spirit, if not in the flesh," she apologized for falling asleep at services.

Nor was her conversion an affectation for Kay Boyle, as she wrote Father O'Rourke, "Your voice has always been the voice of my beloved mother telling me of the sanctity of tenderness and love. And now that I am ninety years old it is your voice that rocks me into slumber, and thus continues the lullaby of confidence, of re-assurance of eighty-five years ago (or more)." The Catholic priest now offered continuity with her past, returning her to the relationship which had made her what she was, that with her mother. Struggling despite her failing health to remain Kay Boyle, she wrote, "Thank you dear Father for taking me into the fold . . . but I have one question: now that I am a Catholic should I not *do* more for my belief? Are there not traditional ways that I could express and serve this belief?" A complete human being lived fueled by convictions, made authentic only through action: this was Kay Boyle's best legacy.

Yet religion proved to be an insufficient refuge. Still she complained, "I can't get down to my work"; still she was not free of her need to fulfill Katherine's long-ago dream. But in fact her labors had ceased.

Kay was now in contact with Heidi and Bruce, those children she had sent from Germany to be raised by her sister. When Kay had asked Jo for Wolfgang's address, her sister had denied knowing it. But Kay found him. He told Kay they had never forgotten her, that they had thought of her all their lives. Kay told people that on the telephone "Wolfgang" had cried. It was a "great moment" for her. She had not seen him for thirty years.

She was frequently in the infirmary now, calling Ian to come, and then falling asleep as soon as he arrived. She could relax and feel safe only when he was there, just as in his last days Laurence had telephoned Kathe, and then irritated her by falling asleep as soon as she was in the door.

Doctors told Kay that she had less than a year of eyesight remaining to her. Many other residents in this "retirement residence" are blind, she said, "so I deserve no special sympathy, and I'll survive as the others do." She rarely saw people now, retreating to the richly peopled world of her past.

On her ninetieth birthday, Wolfgang, Bruce Detweiler, and his wife celebrated with her and Ian. "I always felt Kay was my true mother, my *Mütie*," Wolfgang says. When he left, she threw herself on him, weeping, "Don't leave. My family. My family. I wish I could be with my family. Why can't we live together?" Then she wept some more.

In March of 1992, Kay and Faith were reunited at last. Their first moment was their finest. Faith feared that her mother might not recognize her. But as soon as Faith entered the room, Kay smiled. At once Faith put her arms around her now gaunt and shrunken mother and cradled her gently.

"Oh, I'm so glad you came to see me!" Kay said. Faith then introduced her to her seventeen-year-old daughter, Tucia, one of the grandchildren Kay had never met.

"Yes, you've written me about her," Kay said graciously.

"How dare you get taller than your mother!" Kay chided statuesque Faith. Then Kay turned to Tucia. "How dare *you* get taller than *your* mother!" If a sense of humor was never among her strongest qualities, she could still joke.

Kay gestured in the direction of the aged residents of The Redwoods.

"See these people. They are so narrow-minded!" she told Tucia. "I go from table to table with a petition to abolish the death penalty, and an old lady screamed at me. Can you imagine their faces when I walked into the dining room with a black man!" Kay told Tucia that her only friends at The Redwoods were the waiters. Not once during the visit did she mention the Lyman family commune.

After a while, Kay asked Faith to write her name on a piece of paper so she could remember whom she was with. Although Faith knew she was being irrational, that her mother was old and failing, her feelings were injured. Oblivious, Kay chatted on about a man she called her "boyfriend," whose photograph she showed Faith, a man who had disappeared.

Darker moments followed. Kay sat down on Marcel Duchamp's old bed in her studio room. She held Ian's hand.

"Now, his side of the family is Austrian," she told Faith, forgetting that Faith and Ian shared the same father. More upsetting to Faith was how Kay now went on about Bruce, who had come to see her on her ninetieth birthday.

Bruce wasn't even a child she had raised, Faith thought. He had only lived with her for six months. The moment came as an epiphany. Family for her mother had been all show: it hadn't meant anything to her. She was now like a child, just as in years gone by she had been no more than a little girl bringing up children who were "accessories" to her.

Once Kay had complained that Faith showed no emotion when her mother was leaving after a visit to her boarding school in Connecticut. Now, as Faith departed, Kay Boyle expressed no emotion. She was small and helpless. But there was also something evil, Faith felt. (Nor did a visit from Bobby and her daughter Constance proceed without misunderstandings.)

In July of 1992, Kay fell and broke her pelvis. Surgery was impossible. Codeine, she complained to Leo, clouded her mind, and she refused to take it. Briefly she moved into the "health care" wing of The Redwoods, its hospital with twenty-four-hour care. She had great difficulty in walking, but Ian felt mentally she did not yet belong there. Kay Boyle's great solace remained her son, who continued to make his life in the area so that he could be near her. Ian was now with the Marin Shakespeare Company. Having quit his job as bartender at the No-Name in Sausalito, he was devoting himself to acting.

More insistently, Kay began to refuse to eat. "If I don't eat, I die," she remarked matter-of-factly. "I don't want to live."

"I love you," Leo told her one day, speaking from his heart. But Kay eyed him skeptically, her head cocked, as if she didn't believe it, or didn't believe she deserved it. The German publisher who had seen *The Smoking Mountain* rise on the best-seller lists in 1991, and had gone on to publish *Wedding Day and Other Stories*, planned to bring out eight more of her books. "I was out of money until a German publisher bought all my works," Kay said. Then she looked puzzled. "I don't know whether it really happened or I imagined it," she added helplessly.

One day she sat down on her bed and cried. "I want to die," she told Ian, "but I can't let go of you. I'm holding on to you. I don't want you to live without me." A nurse advised Ian to tell her, "It's all right to let go." But he couldn't bring himself to do it.

Yet in September, Kay told Ian he must call her agent, Gloria Loomis, and announce that she would write another book. It would be called "Two Imprisonments" and would contrast Santa Rita with The Redwoods. At Santa Rita, Kay insisted, there had been genuine feeling between the recidivist prostitute prisoners and the deputies. At The Redwoods there was "no compassion." When she was irritated, she would call The Redwoods "this place." As Leo Litwak would put it, her second great imprisonment was "old age."

Moving to "personal care," independent living an impossibility now, Kay endured new indignities. "Don't dawdle," a nurse impatiently demanded. "I've written almost forty books. I don't dawdle," Kay answered angrily. A black male nurse insisted that she take a shower. Kay said she didn't want to. Later Kay told Leo the man had "hosed her down" naked. He should complain on her behalf. Doubting whether such things could happen, Leo inquired of other residents, only to learn that they did indeed.

Kay also complained about one of her roommates who had Alzheimer's disease. No matter her infirmity, Kay was furious when the woman revealed racist sentiments.

The presidential election of 1992 found Kay rallying her energies to become a staunch supporter of Bill Clinton. She contributed money and received a photograph of Clinton and Gore, which she told people had been sent to her personally. Ian must write to Clinton, Kay ordered, informing him that she would help with local arrangements for a speaking engagement in Mill Valley. When the local Democrats sent her a plant, Kay reported that Clinton himself had sent her flowers.

Just before Thanksgiving, a meal she did not eat, Kay told Ian, "I'd love to see Clover." She also longed to see Faith, she said. It was Ian who was seeing her through, who sat alone beside her bed as Kay slept, eating his own skimpy turkey dinner and then her untouched plate.

During the holiday season, Kay managed to attend a performance of *Oliver!* in which Ian played a small role, although it was difficult for her to distinguish her son from the other actors. She surprised everyone by remaining awake throughout the performance. But one day when Leo made his Wednesday visit, she left him to retrieve something from her room, and did not reappear. It was, he thought, as if, at last, she were turning her back.

There had been small skirmishes in her final year. Obsessed by money, as she had been for so long, she was persuaded by her Alzheimer patient roommate that since she was now occupying only half a room, she was entitled to a refund. Ian must see to it. She urged Ian to sell some of her books, including an inscribed and annotated copy of Samuel Beckett's poems. These were Beckett's French poems translated into English. In one poem Beckett had crossed out a line and made a change, an annotation Kay had suggested after she read the inscribed volume and then returned it to him. There was a slip of paper in the book on which Kay had described the incident in her own hand.

But after Ian sold it to Burton Weiss, and Weiss in turn offered it to a client, a university library, Kay demanded that it be returned to her, that there had been a misunderstanding. "Tell them I'm crazy and I made a mistake. I'm an old lady," she insisted.

"I'm not supposed to be offering books I'm not sure of," Weiss protested. But he returned it to her out of love. Then, according to Ian, she accepted it ungraciously with a curt "thank you." Later, with no basis in fact, she told Ian, "It's worth more than the seven hundred and fifty dollars Weiss paid." Weiss continued to visit her every week; the Beckett book was never referred to again. Their friendship continued.

Two weeks into December, Kay clenched her lips tight when a nurse tried to feed her. Only morphine could ease her pain. On Christmas Day, when Burton Weiss visited her, Kay opened her eyes, said either "You and Ian are great" or "You and Ian are mad," and then was dreaming again before Weiss could ask which she had said. When as part of a "holiday project" a family visited her, and there was a baby, Kay from her bed urged the mother to bend down. She had something to say. "Tell her when she grows up Kay Boyle loved her," Kay whispered.

At Christmas, Kay fell into a coma. Father O'Rourke, having performed the "Sacrament of the Sick" for her many times, did so again. Ian asked her to make a sign to indicate that she heard him, but there came back no sign. For three days she lay in a coma. On Sunday, December 27, Father O'Rourke saw her at eleven in the morning and performed the final rites. Ian held the oil, while Kay lay there snoring. Then, in unison, the two men recited the Lord's Prayer. Later, reassured by the nurses that his mother's vital signs were good, Ian went to dinner.

It was 8 p.m. The wind howled, a ferocious storm of hailstones and sheets of rain ending San Francisco's seven-year drought. The nurse stopped Ian when he returned at 9:28. Kay had stirred, taken two breaths, and expired. Ian entered the room, and it seemed that his mother was still alive. Her mouth had fallen open, and her "beautiful" gnarled and veined hands were folded on her slightly bloated stomach. Only that she had turned very yellow pronounced the end. He touched her forehead, her nose, her ears. Then he made the telephone calls. "Your baby sister died," he told Joan Detweiler, forsaking now the long pretense that Kay was the elder. Mrs. Detweiler burst into loud sobs.

On the morning of Kay Boyle's funeral, the sun shone defiantly over San Francisco Bay. At the Russell and Gooch funeral home in Mill Valley, her body waited to make its final journey to Golden Gate National Cemetery near San Bruno, where Joseph had been buried in 1963. Ian had her dressed in the blue-jean jacket with its many insignias made by Amnesty International, the turkey-bone white earrings she had worn on *The Today Show*, her bracelets, her wedding ring, and her mother's wedding ring. He chose as well the plum-colored socks which had been distributed for Christmas at The Redwoods by the Salvation Army and which had delighted her. On the morning of her funeral, he tied on her white shoes and gave her a final kiss. She had requested that the casket be closed.

There were only six cars driving behind the hearse, Ian directly behind in Kay's old green Chevrolet, which she had promised to so many. Ian would be alone, without his "quarterback," as he put it. The tiny group included Leo, of course, Leah and Jerry Garchik, Hank and Jackie McGuckin, Burton Weiss, and a visibly bereaved Cosette Thompson of Amnesty. Among her tiny group of mourners as well was entrepreneur and social activist Peter Cunningham, who in her last days had read to Kay from James Joyce's *Ulysses* ("Would you go back two lines and read that again," Kay would ask) and helped her with her correspondence; Cunningham's mother, Kathleen McEnery, had been the youngest artist to exhibit in the Armory Show of 1913 where once Kay Boyle had walked; her mentor was Robert Henri, an influence as well on Kay Boyle's aunt, Nina Allender. Kay reminded Cunningham of his mother, who, in Paris, had been her admirer. Apple's daughter Emily hung back so shyly it didn't seem she was one of the family. Emily was, however, the only one of Kay's seventeen grandchildren present.

Kay Boyle's coffin was made of pressed wood, sawdust, and sawdust chips. "It was what she wanted," Ian told Jerry and Leo apologetically as the three carried her inside the tiny chapel. Looking every inch the actor, Ian recited the poem by James Joyce which began: "I hear an army charging upon the land," and concluded: "my love my love my love why have you left me alone." Only at the end did he press his lips together to suppress his emotions. Father O'Rourke spoke of "forgiveness" and called Kay a "great warrior." Then Ian asked that the little group, numbering fewer than twenty, stand, join hands in a circle, and recite together the Lord's Prayer.

It was Kay Boyle's wish that she be buried in the same grave as Joseph, a wish she had expressed in 1963, so that he had been placed nine feet down. Now her coffin would be placed at six feet, directly on top. "Kay B. Franckenstein" read the tag attached to the back of his monument, "his wife." Ian planned to change the inscription later so that the writer Kay Boyle might be remembered by future generations.

Ten days later, on January 9, 1993, a memorial service was held at the Chinese-pagoda-shaped Our Lady of Mount Carmel Church in Mill Valley, where Kay Boyle had been baptized. Several hundred people gathered in the circular, chilly church, Shawn Wong and Frank Chin among the first to arrive. Dorothy Bryant too was there, and Reggie Major, who had once saved her house from the commune. Joan Baez came with her daughter Mimi Fariña, who would sing a song about leaving "this lonesome town," her full clear voice filling the church, although she had to admit that Kay wouldn't have liked the song because it "wallows in feeling."

Of all Kay Boyle's children Ian stood there alone. He read an old fortune cookie he had discovered in Kay's bedside table after her death: "Your road will be made smooth for you by good friends." Father O'Rourke held up Kay's certificate of baptism and begged Kay's forgiveness for never having found the time to read her novel *Gentlemen, I Address You Privately*. "She lived with the big questions," he told her former students, her colleagues in Amnesty, her former tenants. "She's with God now." It was Kay, Father O'Rourke quipped, who must have planned that the church have no heat this day "so we would be alert." He praised her for battling "the savage attacks humans made on humans," and he told her friends and her son that "in God's presence Kay is loved unconditionally . . . and forgiven unconditionally . . . she forgives each and every one of us unconditionally." For he knew that Kay Boyle did not find it easy to forgive. "I thank Ian for the extraordinary devotion he has shown his mother," the priest said graciously.

Kay's wish to have excerpts from Verdi's *Requiem* played was honored; Ian chose the recordings, and the speakers: Leo, her most devoted friend, came first, wearing his long trench coat. He spoke rapidly and full of emotion, although he had not anticipated he would be so overcome. She dreamed an angel came to her and she'd be gone at the end of the month and she felt relieved, Leo confided. Hank McGuckin spoke of "this slender ramrod-straight figure of incredible dignity" with whom he had marched from Delano to Modesto never once whimpering about her blistering feet, and who told him in the final month of her life that she was composing a poem in her head about the mistreatment, in prison, of the IRA at the hands of the British, integrating official documents into her poem, although she could no longer see or write. "How are things at the college, Hank?" she had asked ten days before her death. Told that the struggle went on, she had nodded in contentment.

There were Ruby Cohn, Sandra Whipple Spanier, and David Koch, director of special collections at Southern Illinois University, who revealed that Kay called him "her keeper" because he was the curator of her papers. Ted Keller told of two French students who had come to San Francisco seeking revolutionaries and whom Kay had brought to him and Hank. So disappointed had they been that they returned home to firebomb a jail. "He's a fascist," Kay had whispered to Ted at a demonstration about a man of whom neither had heard; it had been Jim Jones, ten months before Jonestown.

When Ian asked friends to come forward, Shawn Wong revealed that when he had termed himself an orphan, Kay was there to argue, "I was there to call you mine," the unlikely landlady who had complained because he was *not* typing. "Too much power" in one person, Wong remarked affectionately. Nancy McDermid of San Francisco State recalled Kay asking, "But did you really try to make a difference?" Burton Weiss quoted movingly from the Book of Psalms in Hebrew and in English, a passage about seeking peace and pursuing it, as Kay had done. Most humorous was David Ryan's story of how Kay had told him she had considered becoming a nun, but did not want to struggle through the novitiate. "Do you suppose they accept people as Mother Superiors?" she wanted to know.

Of her daughters, only Kathe sent a message. She remembered her mother dressed in khaki leaving for Europe in the middle of the war (Kay as that "simulated captain," Kathe the only one of her children not too angry to say goodbye, but none of that is mentioned now). She remembered her mother saying that "crying was feeling sorry for one's self," and resolving, herself, not to cry. She closed with a quotation from *The Youngest Camel*: "And love's invisible it is true and still has the shape and smell of you."

As for Ian, he stood and said that the word which came to his mind was "gratitude . . . deep gratitude for all she gave to all of us." His refrain, "Thank you, Mom," was for "her work, her care, her financial and moral support, for finding your own way when you had to." He said he honored and respected "the way you lived and worked which were one and the same, your devotion to life itself." Ian, the son for whom she had always longed, thanked Kay Boyle for her anger at injustices, her pride when one of her children took a stand, and, finally, for her "plain hard work." She gave him "the strength to go on." And now once more he recited "I hear an army charging upon the land." In his final benediction, Father O'Rourke told Kay Boyle's friends, "What I'm left with is a woman of profound humility with the desire for forgiveness." He could see, he said, Kay "marching in" to the "new and eternal Jerusalem."

Each heart holds locked tightly its secret, which, once unlocked, might challenge the very wellsprings of one's existence, the premise by which the psyche survives intact. The relentless quest for recognition as "the writer Kay Boyle" imposed on her by her mother, left unexamined, as it was, brought her considerable accomplishment, for she was a woman of enormous imagination, talent, and energy. It also brought with it the anxiety that accompanied the feeling of never having done enough, and a "ruthless" (Clover's term) need to push aside husbands, children, grandchildren, whoever would stand in the way of her fulfillment of her mother's ancient dream. While her own children cried out that she had left them no identities of their own, she had herself become so like her own mother, Katherine, that she gravitated toward weak men as husbands, men like her father, men who could not support her and her children.

Fearing the exposure of so disturbing a truth, Kay Boyle all her life not only avoided but politically opposed self-examination. She made a fetish of action, calling our deeds the only means by which we are ever known to ourselves, or to others. It was a compulsion as unconscious as her writing, and she approached it with as little analytic power. This glorification of "action" led her carelessly to support Stalinist front organizations, and the Black Panthers, and to decide that Cambodia was a matriarchy. After a lifetime of avoiding organized religion, she could even accept the rituals of the Roman Catholic Church.

The Cassandra of her daughters pleaded: How can you save the children of Biafra when you can't save your own? But no daughter's voice could counter the hold Katherine's urgent need had imposed on Kay Boyle when she was a very little girl. Even before Kay had learned to read, Katherine was insisting that little Kay was writing "poetry," as she copied down her daughter's every childish utterance. No wonder, then, that Kay Boyle as a child resisted learning to read for as long as she could!

Katherine's dream for this daughter came true. Kay Boyle became a literary figure of consequence. If she was not of the very first rank, then certainly she was not far behind. In the history of the American short story, few were her equal. As a woman she sought as well to live by the most progressive values she could, echoes themselves of Katherine's early socialist leanings.

With valor, Kay Boyle lived the last decades of life fortified by courage and principle. If she did not always understand, still she endured. She created myths around who she had been, so that her work became her one truth, her life a gossamer web, half fantasy, half reality. Yet in the merging of her life with her work she became a credit to the woman who, in her quiet self-effacing way, had done so much to make her an artist.

"I haven't changed much since I was ten years old," Kay Boyle frequently told interviewers. Sometimes the ten even became a five. At such moments it may have occurred to her that her path through life had been chosen for her when she was very young. But ever more vociferously would she picture her mother as that savior who had selflessly encouraged her. It may be too that Kay Boyle drove off would-be biographers, a professor named Ian MacNiven after years of their working together, as well as writer Hugh Ford, lest that central myth of her life be shattered. She had even written to Stephen Joyce in defense of his decision to burn his Aunt Lucia's letters.

As with most of us, Kay Boyle's greatest strength became her underlying flaw. As she sought to reach the heights which would make her mother proud (and how often she used that phrase—making someone proud of her), a frenetic, compulsive, and uncritical approach to her work undermined the very effort. Her work became less fine, less coherent, as fragmented as the strands of an unexamined life.

Over the years, Kay Boyle's reputation declined from its apogee in the thirties and forties for a host of reasons, some to her credit, others not. Her failure to please critics in search of "proletarian literature" irritated some in the thirties; her turning to potboilers in the forties, as she tried to support the many children she had in part as a rebellion against her servitude to her mother's dream, led critics like Edmund Wilson to undervalue the fine work she had done. The anti-intellectualism of America in the fifties, when people refused to read stories of historical conflict set in Europe in their *Woman's Home Companion*, made Kay Boyle seem a relic of the best-forgotten past. As she was an opponent of the women's movement, feminists of the seventies ignored her in favor of women writers who were willing to blame their failure to achieve adequate recognition on their sex, an excuse to which Kay Boyle proudly would not stoop. She abandoned her premier form, the short story, because her stories stopped selling, only for the feverish attempt to live someone else's dream to weaken the internal coherence of her long fiction. Her abhorrence of psychological insight finally rendered her poetry and her nonfiction alike didactic and preachy.

Through all the many trials of her life, historical and personal upheaval, she wrote prodigiously. A body of excellent work remains, the legacy of Kay Boyle's considerable talent. As Thomas Mann's Gustav von Aschenbach knew well, art exacts its sacrifices, those accepted and those repressed. Kay Boyle made her share of sacrifices in full and tragic measure.

A biographer can offer but one observer's impression of a life. Amid all the contradictions, the paradoxes, one is left admiring the writer Kay Boyle for that creative energy her mother lovingly nurtured. Even more, one is left in awe of the strength which allowed Kay Boyle to do what few women in American literature had: to carve out for herself an indubitable and significant place in the literary history of her century.

NOTES

SELECTED BIBLIOGRAPHY

WORKS BY KAY BOYLE

INDEX

NOTES

SOURCES

Works frequently cited are abbreviated as follows:

KBP: The papers of Kay Boyle, housed at the Morris Library at Southern Illinois University, Carbondale, IL. Also included within this collection are the papers of the Ann Watkins agency.

BERG: Kay Boyle papers housed at the Berg Collection at the New York Public Library, New York, NY.

BSA: The papers of Caresse Crosby are housed in the Black Sun Archive at the Morris Library at Southern Illinois University, Carbondale, IL.

RCBP: The papers of Robert Carlton Brown are housed at the Morris Library at Southern Illinois University, Carbondale, IL.

ASP: The papers of Alfred Stieglitz are housed at the Beinecke Library at Yale University, New Haven, CT.

HLP: The Firestone Library, Princeton University, Princeton, NJ, houses the papers of Harold Loeb.

BGT: Kay Boyle and Robert McAlmon, *Being Geniuses Together* (San Francisco: North Point Press, 1984).

Gale memoir: Kay Boyle, "Kay Boyle," *Contemporary Authors Autobiography Series*, ed. Dedria Bryfonski (Detroit: Gale Research, 1984).

HRHRC: Harry Ransom Humanities Research Center, University of Texas at Austin, houses many collections used here, among them: Evelyn Scott, William Carlos Williams, Katherine Anne Porter, Bill Bird, Robert McAlmon, Edward Dahlberg, and Marcel Duchamp.

The letters of Lola Ridge are quoted here courtesy of Elaine Sproat.

The letters and papers of James Laughlin are quoted courtesy of James Laughlin.

Laurence Vail's letters and his unpublished memoir, *Here Goes*, are quoted courtesy of Kathe Vail.

INTRODUCTION: PLACE NAMES

3 "I do not believe": KB to Caresse Crosby, 25 October 1933, BSA.

3 "a record of our age": KB to Walter Lowenfels, 15 August 1930, KBP.

3 "Good afternoon": Noel Young interview with JM, 10 December 1990.

4 "to be over eighty": Ian Franckenstein phone conversation with JM, 1991.

4 "youthful excesses": Noel Young interview with JM.

4 "it's too long": Kathe Vail phone conversation with JM, 1992.

5 "put only my talent into my works": Richard Ellman, *Oscar Wilde* (New York: Vintage, 1988) 371.

5 "love of my life": Faith Gude interview with JM, 7 December 1989.

5 "a fierce integrity": KB to Lola Ridge, 12 January 1927.

6 "Sappho Jane Austen Kay Boyle": Edward Germain, ed., *Shadows of the Sun: The Diaries of Harry Crosby* (Santa Barbara: Black Sparrow Press, 1977) 267.

6 Farrell scrawls: James T. Farrell to KB, undated poem [c. February 1958], KBP.

6 "run-down Paris hotel": KB in an April 1977 speech given at Skidmore College when receiving a Doctor of Humane Letters degree. All quotes within this paragraph are from the Skidmore speech.

7 "among the strongest": Katherine Anne Porter, "Example to the Young," *New Republic* April 1931: 279.

7 "Hemingway's successor": Mary H. Colum, "Life and Literature: In Favor of Best Sellers," rev. of *Monday Night*, by Kay Boyle, *Forum* October 1938: 166.

7 "a Queen in exile": Faith Gude to JM, 18 December 1989.

9 "Isn't Vail a Jewish name?": Natalie Robins, interview with JM, summer 1990.

9 "You're just like Mama!": Faith Gude, interview with JM, 8 December 1989.

9 "liberation of all people": KB interviewed by Barbaralee Diamonstein, *Open Secrets: Ninety-four Women in Touch with Our Time* (New York: Viking, 1972) 24.

9 "overwhelmingly male": Mary Gordon, "Surviving History: For Many American Writers, Italy's Natalie Ginzburg Is a Literary Icon," *New York Times Magazine* 25 March 1990: 42. Nor is Kay Boyle mentioned in either Ellen Moers's *Literary Women: The Great Writers* (New York: Anchor Books, 1977) or Elaine Showalter's *Women's Liberation and Literature* (New York: Harcourt Brace Jovanovich, 1971).

10 "My life can be known": Hugh Ford, *Four Lives in Paris* (San Francisco: North Point Press, 1987) 137.

1. A LITTLE GIRL IN A HAT

11 "I force myself": Marcel Duchamp, *Salt Seller: The Writings of Marcel Duchamp* eds. Michel Sanouillet and Elmer Peterson (New York: Oxford UP, 1973) 129.

11 "I was there to kill": Gertrude Stein, *The Geographical History of America* (1936; New York: Vintage, 1973) 6.

11 "drooping like ferns": Kay Boyle, "I Remember Philadelphia," *Philadelphia Sunday Bulletin* 21 October 1962: 6–7.

11 "Where are the girls' hats?": KB interview with Hugh Ford, 1978.

11 so "weak, so useless": Kay Boyle and Robert McAlmon, *Being Geniuses Together* (1968; San Francisco: North Point Press, 1984) 20. Further references to *Being Geniuses Together* will be noted by the abbreviation *BGT*. Unless otherwise noted, all future references will be to this edition.

12 Katherine might have been telling the truth: KB interview with JM, August 1987.

12 "no bigger than a hummingbird": KB to Kathe Vail, 1 February 1970.

12 "the apotheosis of an ostrich plume": Milton W. Brown, *The Story of the Armory Show: The New Spirit* (Washington: Joseph H. Hirshhorn Foundation, 1963) 133.

12 "everything he painted into satin": Martin Green, *New York 1913: The Armory Show and the Paterson Strike Pageant* (New York: Scribner's, 1988) 133.

12 Katherine became a fervent supporter. KB interview with JM, August 1987.

12 "Take them!" James Weinstein, *The Decline of Socialism in America: 1912–1925* (New York: Random House, 1969) 8–11.

12 "one of the most Christ-like men": Green, *New York 1913* 190–91.

12 "no life without change": Frederick James Gregg, preface, *The Armory Show Catalogue*. See Green 176.

12 "The dry bones of a dead art": Green, *New York 1913* 184.

13 "a great fire, an earthquake": Ibid.

13 "Set up your own darkroom": Alfred Stieglitz to Katherine Evans Boyle, undated letter, ASP.

13 Jesse Peyton Boyle had laid down the law: KB interview with JM, August 1987.

13 something "precious": Katherine Evans Boyle to Alfred Stieglitz, 4 January 1915, ASP.

13 "a firm foundation for my belief": Ibid.

13 "I am frankly anxious over their future": Katherine Evans Boyle to Alfred Steiglitz, 6 April [no year], ASP.

13 "Have the young ladies done any drawing": Alfred Stieglitz to Katherine Evans Boyle, 4 November 1915, ASP.

13 "honored." Katherine Evans Boyle to Alfred Stieglitz, undated letter, ASP.

13 "on your hands and knees": KB interview with JM, August 1987.

14 "hungry young men": Joan Detweiler to JM, 2 February 1989.

14 "giddy with joy": William Carlos Williams, *The Autobiography of William Carlos Williams* (New York: Random House, 1948) 134.

14 "I laughed out loud": Ibid.

14 "explosion in a shingle factory": Brown, *Story of the Armory Show* 168.

14 "contradicting itself": "History of Modern Art at the International Exhibition Illustrated by Paintings and Sculpture," *New York Times* 23 February 1913: Sec. 6, p. 15.

14 "Art is the only form": Duchamp, *Salt Seller* 133.

14 "the battle cry of freedom": Brown, *Story of the Armory Show* 152.

15 "the precision and sensitiveness of an instrument": Green, *New York 1913* 266.

16 lifelong love of Shakespeare: Joan Detweiler to JM, 20 February 1989.

16 "sacrificed at the Shrine": *Berks & Schuylkill Journal*, obituary of Jacob Bower.

17 "fearless of Indians": Kay Boyle, "Kay Boyle," Gale memoir 105.

17 "ancient grandmother": KB to Howard Nemerov, 23 April 1960, Washington University Libraries, St. Louis.

18 "a good deal older": KB interview with JM, August 1987.

18 "hullabalooing out": Kay Boyle, "Episode in the Life of an Ancestor," *Fifty Stories* (Garden City, NY: Doubleday, 1980) 17–23. All subsequent references are to this edition.

19 "really only squatters": KB interview with JM, August 1987.

19 an organization whose conservatism offended her: Joan Boyle Detweiler to JM, 15 March 1989.

19 "to remind them of Paris": KB interview with JM, August 1987.

19 Eva Evans kisses the black servants: Ibid.

20 Nina Allender called herself a "widow": Ibid.

20 "a total, total egoist": Ibid.

20 "A woman's place is in the home!": Kay Boyle, "The Family," *Words That Must Somehow Be Said*, ed. Elizabeth Bell (London: Chatto & Windus–Hogarth Press, 1985) 9.

21 happy as a professor: Joan Boyle Detweiler to JM, 20 February 1989.

21 "I won't have you running down your chin": Howard Peyton Boyle to Katherine Evans Boyle, KBP.

21 "more than you ought": Howard Peyton Boyle to Katherine Evans Boyle, 14 January 1899, KBP.

21 "No, little wife": Howard Peyton Boyle to Katherine Evans Boyle, undated, KBP.

21 "It was not that he did not know about books": Gale memoir 101.

21 would reply, "Nothing": KB interview with JM, August 1987.

21 a "frustrated person who couldn't communicate his feelings": KB interview with Dan Tooker.

21 "speak to Puss": KB interview with JM, August 1987.

21 "I knew from my father and grandfather what I didn't want to be": KB interview with Charles Amirkhanian. Courtesy of Charles Amirkhanian.

22 a "rigid one": KB interview with JM, August 1987. See also Gale memoir.

22 "What do you want for Christmas?": KB interview with JM, August 1987.

22 "belly pouting": Kay Boyle, "Black Boy," *Fifty Stories* 50–54.

22 "Come in!": Kay Boyle, "Security," *Fifty Stories* 89–94.

22 "Go up to the attic": Kay Boyle, "Ben," *Fifty Stories* 38–43.

22 "As a capitalist": KB, "Souvenir City," *Harper's Bazaar* March 1944: 121.

23 patted him on the head. KB interview with JM, August 1987.

23 a strict Presbyterian: Joan Boyle Detweiler to JM, 20 February 1989.

23 call her "Mother Boyle": KB interview with JM, August 1987.

23 "You're a wonderful cook": Susan Hager interview with JM, 6 June 1988.

24 "her doctor's thesis on the status of women": Kay Boyle, "Report from Lock-up," *Four Visions of America: Erica Jong, Thomas Sanchez, Kay Boyle, Henry Miller* (Santa Barbara: Capra Press, 1977) 32.

24 "just completely negative": KB interview with Charles Amirkhanian.

24 "How can I help my father and mother like each other": Gale memoir 106.

24 "Why doesn't Dad speak very much?": KB interview with JM, August 1987. See also Gale memoir.

24 "all that enchanted her": Kay Boyle, "The Family," *Words That Must Somehow Be Said* 6.

25 "gentlemen at the next table are smoking": Kay Boyle, "I Remember Philadelphia," 7.

25 "not until years later": Joan Boyle Detweiler to JM, 20 February 1989.

2. MOTHER AND DAUGHTER

26 "Mother's untroubled and intuitive knowledge": Gale memoir 98.

26 until New Year's Eve 1999: Gale memoir 106.

26 Katherine was sympathetic: Gale memoir 98.

27 something of a family disgrace: Susan Hager interview with JM, 6 June 1988.

27 Kay pronounced "dull": *BGT* 19.

27 "My grandfather was too outspoken": KB interview with Charles Amirkhanian.

27 "ladies of fashion": See Kay Boyle's childhood notebooks in KBP.

28 "Have you read this one of Katherine's?": Katherine Evans Boyle to Mrs. Harold S. Cook. Undated, BERG.

28 "dying of shame": Maxine Block, ed., *Current Biography: Who's Who and Why, 1942* (New York: H. W. Wilson Company, 1942) 102.

28 Kay's was as original: Gale memoir 104. See also *BGT* 20.

28 "everyone on the porch": Gale memoir 108.

28 "desperately ill": See Gale memoir and KB interview with JM, August 1987.

28 "Maybe at vacation time": KB interview with JM, August 1987.

29 "beautiful night moth": Gale memoir 105.

29 "to be disciplined": Gale memoir 107–8.

29 "If you were colored, there wouldn't be any tomorrow afternoons": Gale memoir 110.

29 lecture on *Coriolanus*: Kenneth Hopkins, *The Powys Brothers: A Biographical Appreciation* (Rutherford, NJ: Farleigh Dickinson UP, 1967) 28.

30 "Dinner is served!": Gale memoir 99.

31 Puss submits a serial to *The Blue Heron*: See Kay Boyle, "Security," *Fifty Stories* 89–95.

32 "If my writing is good": Ibid.

32 "shaking for joy": Ibid.

33 "Cad! Hypocrite!": Ibid.

33 "no respect at all": KB interview with Charles Amirkhanian.

34 his "amanuensis": Gale memoir 110.

34 "Dear Mary": Ibid.

35 Kay Boyle's childhood poems are preserved in KBP.

35 "The girls are so well grounded": Eva Evans to Katherine Evans Boyle, "Monday Evening," 1 October [no year], KBP.

35 Kay became notorious: Richard R. Centing, "Kay Boyle," *Ohioana Quarterly* Spring 1972: 11–13.

36 one day the man's wife arrived: Susan Hager interview with JM, 6 June 1988, and KB interview with JM, August 1987.

36 "telegraph pole": KB interview with JM, August 1987.

36 attempted to sabotage: Ibid.

37 with "biting venom": *BGT* 13.

37 "you're going to be all right": KB interview with JM, August 1987.

38 "You should be crying because of your failures": Gale memoir 113 and KB interview with JM, August 1987.

38 "shiverings and shakings": Gale memoir 114.

38 "the little fairy in the home": KB to Joan Boyle, 5 March 1920, KBP.

38 "what's happening now in the back seats of those cars": KB interview with JM, August 1987.

38 "string" of admirers: KB to Joan Boyle, 14 June 1920, KBP.

38 "Mack Sennett bathing girl": Ibid.

39 "act in the manner": KB to Joan Boyle, 14 June 1920, continuation of letter marked "Tuesday," KBP.

39 "rather down on myself": KB to Joan Boyle [1920], KBP.

39 "you don't sound sorry": KB to Joan Boyle, 19 January 1920, KBP.

40 his complexion was a "disaster": *BGT* 69.

40 "vile looking jew with a bald head": KB to Joan Boyle, 14 June 1920, continuation of letter marked "Tuesday," KBP.

40 "everyone in the near vicinity": Ibid.

40 "If I object, he'd get his feelings hurt": KB to Joan Boyle ["Jo"], 21 January 1920, KBP.

40 "the other kind": Ibid.

40 he "would only be right": Ibid.

40 "Why should pretty": KB to Joan Boyle [1920], KBP.

40 "I suppose one must marry a sort of common-place man": KB to Joan Boyle, 21 December 1921, KBP.
40 "what do you want me to do?": KB to Joan Boyle, 21 January 1920, "Monday morning," KBP.
41 "willing to give up anything": KB to Joan Boyle, 21 January 1920, KBP.
41 "He either flops or fizzles": Ibid.
41 "grumpy . . . how one can loathe": KB to Joan Boyle, 14 June 1920, KBP.
41 "What in hell is the matter?": Ibid.
41 "a big kid": KB to Joan Boyle, 14 June 1920, continuation of letter marked "Tuesday," KBP.
42 "vile disposition": KB to Joan Boyle, 14 June 1920, KBP.
42 "marvellous . . . a god": KB to Joan Boyle, 11 July 1920, KBP.
42 "one perfect man in the whole, wide world": KB to Joan Boyle, 14 June 1920, KBP.
42 "Rotarian" wholesale jeweler: *BGT* 14.
42 "we can count on your support": KB to Joan Boyle, 9 November 1921, KBP.
42 "becoming more radical": Ibid.
42 Katherine too timid: KB interview with JM, August 1987.
42 "delicate and gentle": Duane Swift to KB, 31 March 1966, BERG.
43 "so romantic": KB to Joan Boyle, 27 June 1919, KBP.
43 "Forget us": Duane Swift to KB, 31 March 1966, BERG.
43 "I have heard so damned": Lois Gordon and Alan Gordon, *American Chronicle: Seven Decades in American Life* (New York: Crown, 1990) 23.
43 "a free spirit" . . . "flaming youth": Fragment among the Malcolm Cowley papers, Newberry Library, Chicago.
44 "refuse heap": KB to Joan Boyle, 16 June 1921, KBP.
44 "weather-beaten type of man": KB to Joan Boyle, 3 October 1921, KBP.
44 "too bristly": KB to Joan Boyle, 22 August 1921, KBP.
44 "This is my wife": KB to Joan Boyle, 16 June 1921, KBP.
44 "adorably impossible": KB to Joan Boyle, 3 October 1921, KBP.
44 "We have been talking": Ibid.
44 "sheets of iron": Ibid.
45 "because of the uniform he wears": KB interview with JM, August 1987. See also Gale memoir and KB unpublished interview with Hugh Ford.
45 "reactionaries": Kay Boyle, "Reactionary Composers," *Poetry* 49.2 (November 1921) 104–6.
45 "Meanwhile": Ibid.
45 The moderns . . . "*are* ourselves": Ibid.
45 "you with your Crowninsheild [sic]": KB to Joan Boyle, 12 December 1921, KBP.
45 "I'm not discouraged yet": Ibid.
45 "utter professionality": KB to Joan Boyle, 27 March 1922, KBP.
45 "Kay planning to do": Joan Boyle to Katherine Evans Boyle, undated letter, BERG.
45 "all my sweetness and good will": KB to Joan Boyle, 12 December 1921, KBP.
45 "sweet and forbearing silence": Ibid.
46 "people starving in America": Ibid.
46 "I want to get married": KB interview with Hugh Ford, 1978, and KB interview with JM, August 1987.
46 "I hate the name of Boyle": KB to Joan Boyle, 12 December 1921, KBP.

3. SHE WAS A ROLE MODEL

47 "I'd give a year of France": KB to Evelyn Scott, 28 March 1927, HRHRC.
47 "I believe in the world they are making": *BGT* 12.
48 "Would I be writing reviews": KB to Katherine Evans Boyle, "Thursday," June 1922, KBP.
49 "l'art pour l'art": KB to Joan Boyle, "Wednesday," undated letter, KBP.
49 "a good stenographer": Lola Ridge, quoted in Harold Loeb, *The Way It Was* (New York: Criterion, 1959) 124.
50 "Censored lies": First published in *Ghetto*, c. 1918. Courtesy Elaine Sproat.
50 Socialism was the new dawn: For Lola Ridge's poems "To Alexander Berkman" and "To Emma Goldman," see Lola Ridge, "Reveille," *Dial* 3 May 1919: 551.
50 "Woman is not and never has been man's natural inferior": William Drake, *The First Wave: Women Poets in America, 1915–1945* (New York: Macmillan, 1987) 194.

50 "I shall watch for Kay Boyle": Marianne Moore to Lola Ridge, 27 November 1922, Marianne Moore Archives, Rosenbach Museum and Library, Philadelphia.

50 "there is nothing to discover in me": KB to Joan Boyle, 19 November 1923.

50 "enormous charm and grace": Ibid.

51 "the petty gossip": Harold Loeb to KB, 15 December 1922, HLP.

51 "it doesn't look like any American they ever saw": KB to Harold Loeb, 29 December 1922, HLP.

51 "his modesty, his simplicity, his generosity": KB interview with Kay Bonetti for American Audio Prose Library, March 1985. Courtesy of Charles Amirkhanian.

51 "wild and daring": *BGT* 22.

51–52 "Resign on inclusion": Lola Ridge's telegram to Harold Loeb is recounted in Loeb 143.

52 "Eyes shining above her scimitar nose": Loeb 153.

52 "some excellent verse": Loeb 136.

52 "Kay Boyle, young, unprinted": Lola Ridge to Harold Loeb, handwritten note on submission of Kay Boyle's poem, "Morning," later published in *Broom*.

52 "I am afraid": Kay Boyle, "Morning," *Broom* January 1923: 121–22.

52 "that comradeship which has brought me to the many realizations": KB to Lola Ridge, 26 January 1923.

52 "printed matter": KB to Harold Loeb, 7 March 1923, HLP.

53 "I am sorry you felt you had to let *Broom* die": KB to Harold Loeb, 12 March 1923, HLP.

53 "to plunge hardily": Quoted in Frederick J. Hoffman, *The Twenties: American Writing in the Post-War Decade* (New York: Collier, 1962) 290.

53 "I am not entering any of the March shipments in the books": KB to Harold Loeb, 12 March 1923, HLP.

53 "ever so grateful": Harold Loeb to KB, 26 March 1923, HLP.

54 "miscarriage" . . . "torture": KB to Lola Ridge, 11 May 1923.

54 "idea of contact": *BGT* 23.

54 "the brave spirit": KB to Katherine Evans Boyle, 26 May 1923, KBP.

54 "I shall hope to see you for a moment then": KB to Harold Loeb, 3 June 1923, HLP.

55 "certain strokes that are so completely Lawrence": KB to Katherine Evans Boyle, 26 May 1923, KBP.

55 "there is NO time but YOUTH": Nina Allender quoting Kay Boyle back to herself, letter of Nina Allender quoted in KB to Katherine Evans Boyle, 26 May 1923.

55 "rebels" who "really live": KB to Lola Ridge, 28 May 1923.

55 "only each other": KB interview with Hugh Ford, 1978.

55 "the entire Brault family": KB to Katherine Evans Boyle, 26 May 1923.

55 "an uncertain person": Ibid.

55 "gorgeous": KB to Lola Ridge, 4 June 1923.

55 "Any rain on the voyage?": *BGT* 41.

56 "So if you don't have a grey suit": *BGT* 42.

56 "have to get her a hat": *BGT* 44.

56 "Ladies don't put paint on their mouths": *BGT* 47.

56 "nest of reactionary stagnation": KB to Lola Ridge, 31 December 1923.

56–57 "dear and devoted": KB to Lola Ridge, 20 June 1923.

57 "They love me because": KB to "Tante," 23 July 1923, KBP.

57 "a red": KB to Katherine Evans Boyle, 19 June 1923, KBP.

57 "most awfully good-natured": Ibid.

57 "How it is to be done, we don't yet know": KB to Katherine Evans Boyle, 21 June 1923, KBP.

57 "realizes the futility": KB to Katherine Evans Boyle, 12 December 1923, KBP.

57–58 "to purify linen and soul and flesh": *BGT* 65.

58 "dogmatic eyebrows": KB to Howard Boyle, 10 March 1924, KBP.

58 "American lice": *BGT* 71.

58 "fine figure of a rebel": *BGT* 68.

58 "What time is it in New York now?": *BGT* 67.

59 "stumbling along slowly with this painful language": KB to Nina Allender, 23 July 1923, KBP.

59 "a separate entity": *BGT* 69.

59 "two cases of abortion": KB to Lola Ridge, 24 July 1923.

59 "Poor defeated Dad": Ibid.

59 "drifting mercilessly" . . . "his so-needed philosophy": KB to "Tante, Dear Person," 23 July 1923, KBP.

59 "I want a million dollars": Ibid.

60 "convenient deafness": KB letter "To Muddie," 11 August 1923, KBP.
60 "the unequal chance of youth against pull and graft": Ibid.
60 "All Brault need do is stick by you": Ibid.
60 "more flowing than before the 'miscarriage,' ": KB to Katherine Evans Boyle, August 1923, KBP.
60 "thrown in our lot together": KB to Joan Boyle, 20 August 1923, KBP.
60 "a choice between Paris and a miserable salary": Ibid.
60 "You will love me so much the better": Ibid.
61 "laden with brilliant paintings": Ibid.

4. BUTTOCKS AND THIGHS

62 "Paris doesn't mean for me 'The Dôme' ": KB to Evelyn Scott, 11 August 1924, HRHRC.
62 "At thirty I'll be dead": KB to Louise Theis, 5 October 1925. The papers of Louise and Otto Theis are housed in the Berg Collection, New York Public Library.
62 "We will go away": *BGT* 83.
62 "surprisingly many people": KB to "Tante," 23 July 1923, KBP.
62 "Richard is to be job-hunting": KB to Harold Loeb, 22 August 1923, HLP.
62 "I'm ready to work": KB to Lola Ridge, 12 September 1923.
63 "heat and bitterness": KB, undated letter to Lola Ridge, from "Les Brossis, Pleudihen" [c. September or October 1923].
63 "one has no belief in him": KB to Joan Boyle, 19 November 1923, KBP.
63 "smeared with make-up": *BGT* 85.
64 "God's got to be a good poet": *BGT* 87.
64 "the *Broom* outfit": *BGT* 31.
64 "wasted months at St.-Malo": *BGT* 105.
64 "as the French were poor": *BGT* 109.
65 "burst into tears": KB to Joan Boyle, 21 November 1923, KBP.
65 "It's my fault we took this place": KB to Katherine Evans Boyle, 25 October 1923, KBP.
65 "unbent his ego": KB to Joan Boyle, 12 December 1923, KBP.
65 "You can't be free and yourself": KB to Lola Ridge, 8 November 1923.
65 "protruding personalities—no babies": KB to Katherine Evans Boyle, 4 December 1923.
65 "I know how to have my next miscarriage": KB to Katherine Evans Boyle, Ibid.
66 "Joan will never think of it": KB to Katherine Evans Boyle, 25 October 1923, KBP.
66 "How I *loathe* it": KB to Katherine Evans Boyle, 4 December 1931, KBP.
66 "unless I am in action": Ibid.
66 "no matter *what* has come": Ibid.
66 "most horrible to my limited nature": KB to Katherine Evans Boyle, 4 December 1923, KBP.
66 "If it wasn't that Richard is Richard": KB to Lola Ridge, 8 November 1923, KBP.
66 "It's what we appear to build our lives on": *BGT* 140.
66 "table crashed over": KB to Joan Boyle, 19 November 1923, KBP.
66 pronounced "wonderful": Ibid.
67 "one of the most beautiful signs": Emanuel Carnevali, *The Autobiography of Emanuel Carnevali* (New York: Horizon, 1967) 117.
67 "thin as a rake": *BGT* 129.
67 "difficult to set down": *BGT* 129.
67 "a very peculiar sort of faith I had in circumstances": KB to Lola Ridge, 31 December 1923.
67 "almost speaking real French now": KB to Lola Ridge, 8 November 1923. See also KB to Lola Ridge, 11 August 1924: "Now that I can speak French with actual ease, I feel more independent."
67 "stroke of protest": KB to Lola Ridge, 31 December 1923.
67 "used to pile into that car to the breaking point": Mary D. Brite to Katherine Evans Boyle, 5 April 1924, KBP.
67–68 "Puss is the actually *poor* one among us": KB to Joan Boyle, 21 November 1923, KBP.
68 "Wouldn't I rather shiver": KB to Joan Boyle, 21 November 1923, KBP.
68 "I really want to write": KB to Katherine Evans Boyle, 12 December 1923, KBP.
68 "why you choose to winter in Le Havre": Quoted in KB to Lola Ridge, 31 December 1923, KBP.
68 "two gorgeous bunches of paper": KB to Katherine Evans Boyle, 12 December 1923, KBP.
68 "Poor girl": William Carlos Williams, *The Autobiography of William Carlos Williams* (New York: Random House, 1948) 187.
69 "not to be dragged by the hair of their heads": *BGT* 144.

69 "Tomorrow I shall be twenty-one": KB to David Lawson, 18 February 1924. Courtesy of Elaine Sproat.
69 "I think you splendid": KB to Howard Peterson Boyle, 10 March 1924, KBP.
69 dropped into the ocean: KB to Howard Peterson Boyle, 10 March 1924.
69 "I do not want to come to New York": KB to Lola Ridge, 1 April 1924.
69 "He seems to me very fine": KB to Lola Ridge, 8 November 1923.
69 "We could live in sandals": KB to Lola Ridge, 1 April 1924.
69 "assertion of a new faith": Ibid.
69 "I shall be free!": KB to Lola Ridge, 1 April 1924.
70 "remove with my thumbnail": *BGT* 149.
70 "see my husband rarely": KB to Katherine Evans Boyle, 13 June 1924, KBP.
70 "I ever want to see America again": KB to Lola Ridge, 12 May 1924.
70 "Once I wrote a book": KB to Katherine Evans Boyle, 11 June 1924, KBP.
70 "want you wholly free": KB to Joan Boyle, 21 July 1924, KBP.
70 "Yvonne's lovely long dark hair was unwound": KB to Joan Boyle, 21 July 1924 [?], KBP.
71 "such hideous people": KB interview with Hugh Ford, 1978, and KB interview with Charles Amirkhanian.
71 "all those years in France": KB interview with Hugh Ford, 1978.
71 For "Harbor Song," see *Poetry* 25 (February 1925): 250–51. See also "Summer," *This Quarter* 3 (1927): 117.
71 "I knew that because I felt it necessary to put them in here . . . there is something wholly wrong": KB to Lola Ridge, 30 May 1924.
71 "too personal": Ibid.
71 "I don't understand it": Recounted in KB to Katherine Evans Boyle, 13 June 1924, KBP.
71 "shoulders" was completely "wrong": KB to Lola Ridge, 11 August 1924.
71 Kay was gratified to be praised: KB to Lola Ridge, 22 August 1924.
71 "My people are not real": KB to Lola Ridge, 11 August 1924.
71–72 "a sense of definition": D. A. Callard, *Pretty Good for a Woman: The Enigmas of Evelyn Scott* (London: Jonathan Cape, 1985) 89.
72 "one of the great artists of her generation": Evelyn Scott to Lola Ridge, ibid.
72 "our coming novelist": Evelyn Scott quoted in KB to Lola Ridge, 15 December 1924.
72 "pain in the heart": *BGT* 151.
72 "too constricted" . . . "whimper": Ibid.
72 "I'd love to introduce you to a young writer named Ernest Hemingway": KB interview with JM, August 1987.
72 "I've read his first book": Ibid.
72 "for infinity": KB to Katherine Evans Boyle, 17 September 1924, KBP.
72 "I weep profusely": Ibid.
72 "a strong labor woman": KB to Lola Ridge, 30 January 1925.
72 "the Paris of Harold Loeb": KB to Evelyn Scott, 11 August 1924, HRHRC.
73 "One was aware at every instant": *BGT* 152.
73 "desperately intellectual": Ibid.
73 "alien and cold, remote like a homosexual": *BGT* 153.
73 "sensitive, intelligent and talented girl": Callard 89.
73 "a rapport for friendship": Ibid.
73 "Evelyn is very fine": KB to Lola Ridge, 25 September 1924.
74 "smiling giant": Vyvyan Holland, *Son of Oscar Wilde* (New York: E. P. Dutton, 1954).
74 He was a *rouspéteur*: KB interview with Hugh Ford, 1978.
74 "best I have read in years": Quoted in KB to Lola Ridge, 30 January 1925.
75 "hectic outburst of untrammeled youth": Quoted in KB to Lola Ridge, 12 March 1925.
75 "I notice you changed the word 'buttocks' ": Ernest Walsh, "From Ernest Walsh to Harriet Moore," *This Quarter* 1.2 (1925): 305–6.
75 "his voice in firm and muscular retreat": Kay Boyle, "Flight," *This Quarter* 2 (1925): 161–71.
76 "I grow ten years older every year": KB to Katherine Evans Boyle, 10 October 1925, KBP.
76 "Russia is the eclectic creator": KB to Katherine Evans Boyle, 11 October 1925, KBP.
76 "You don't realize, Louise, what it is to have no one": KB to Louise Theis, 5 October 1925, Berg Collection, New York Public Library.
76 "know anyone within a thousand miles": KB to Louise Theis, 20 October 1925, Berg Collection.
76 "a very sick man": KB to Katherine Evans Boyle, 24 November 1925, KBP.
76 "I am not myself ": Ibid.

76 Kay began to dream: *BGT* 155.
77 "Is there any place you think it would be good for you to go?": Ibid.
77 "But into the intellectual and sexual turmoil of her life": Ibid.
77 "I don't want to go ahead": Ibid.
77 "spoil" her . . . "perfume sprayer": KB to Katherine Evans Boyle, 2 January 1926. KBP.

5. THE MAN SHE LOVED

78 "And I, who had preached fidelity": *BGT* 179–80.
78 "She talked about him": Faith Gude interview with JM, December 1989.
78 "angelic Ernest Walsh": KB to Katherine Evans Boyle, 2 January 1926, KBP.
78 "hence my present condition": Ibid.
78 it is dull and lonely: Ibid.
78 "the most humane person": Ibid.
79 eyes "burning": Kay Boyle, *Year Before Last* (London: Penguin Books–Virago Press, 1988) 21. All subsequent references are to this edition.
79 "Everything hangs largely on me": KB to Katherine Evans Boyle, 2 January 1926, KBP.
79 "I *hate* to leave R.": Ibid.
79 "tall and slender and ivory-skinned": *BGT* 174. See also Kay Boyle, *Year Before Last.*
79 "his head was beautiful": Kay Boyle, *Year Before Last.*
79 "an air of authority": *BGT* 174.
79 "an acrimonious mouth": Edward Dahlberg, *The Confessions of Edward Dahlberg* (New York: Grosset & Dunlap, 1971) 191.
80 "wait until the poor girl has caught her breath": *BGT* 174.
80 "a little mad": Ethel Moorhead, memoir, *Ernest Walsh: Poems and Sonnets* (New York: Harcourt, Brace, 1934) xvi.
81 "dark, intense, faultlessly Irish": Ernest Hemingway, "The Man Who Was Marked for Death," *A Moveable Feast* (New York: Bantam, 1965) 122–23.
81 "My debt to her is too great to ever repay": Ernest Walsh to Kate Buss, 12 November 1922. The papers of Ernest Walsh are housed in the Morris Library at Southern Illinois University, Carbondale, IL.
82 "It's bad for your health": *BGT* 177.
82 "To be a genius": Ernest Walsh, "What Is Literature?" *This Quarter* 1.3 (c. 1926–27) 59–87.
82 "I haven't written one single thing since I first started going down to Clarke's": Ernest Hemingway to Ernest Walsh [March 1925], University of Virginia.
83 "There is no death": Emanuel Carnevali, *The Autobiography of Emanuel Carnevali* (New York: Horizon, 1967) 231 ff.
83 "suffused with poetry": Ibid.
83 "I felt he had become ill": Ernest Walsh, *This Quarter* 2.2 [Cannes] 1927. Quoted in "Preface" by Kay Boyle to *The Autobiography of Emanuel Carnevali* 15.
83 "That's me!" Walsh cried: *BGT* 176.
83 "I *wish* you were here": KB to Richard Brault, fragment of letter dated 17 January 1926.
84 Kay feasted on American food: KB to "Dearest People," 11 February 1926, KBP.
84 "poisons": KB to Jesse Peyton Boyle, 23 February 1926, KBP.
84 "charming people": KB to "Dearest People," 11 February 1926, KBP.
84 "gave not a thought": *BGT* 180.
85 "homage-giver to the great": *BGT* 214.
85 "Anger and Silence": See Walsh, *Poems and Sonnets.*
86 "solitude is not a virtue": KB to Jesse Peyton Boyle, 23 February 1926, KBP.
86 "It is a long time that I have not heard from you": Ibid.
86 "a profound contentment": Ibid.
86 "another great Irishman": Ibid.
86 "spasmodically": KB to "Dearest People," 11 February 1926, KBP.
86 "the end of the world": Ibid.
87 "living the dream of protest": KB, notes dated 13 May 1967, KBP.
87 "climate is not good": Ernest Walsh quoted in KB to "Dearest People," 11 February 1926.
87 "I take to my bed": KB to Jesse Peyton Boyle, 23 February 1926, KBP.
87 "time and space are like the mist in the morning": Jesse Peyton Boyle to KB, 20 February 1926, KBP.

87 "Coresponse suspended herwith": *BGT* 188.

87 "such two wrecks of humanity": KB to [?], c. March 1926, KBP.

88 "bigger and better man": Ibid.

88 "unshaken moral certainty": *BGT* 180.

88 "You are what there is to beleive [sic] in": KB to Alfred Stieglitz, 16 March 1926, ASP.

88 "rather too Arts Décoratif": Ibid.

89 "moral turpitude" . . . "lied": KB to Joan Boyle, undated letter, c. 1926, KBP.

90 feasting on one hard-boiled egg, rice, and peanut butter: KB to Katherine Evans Boyle, 16 March 1927, KBP.

90 asked the Picabias for help: KB to Alfred Stieglitz, 16 March 1926, ASP.

90 in his "smoking": KB to Joan Boyle, undated letter, c. 1926, KBP.

90 "unhappy as hell": KB to Joan Boyle, undated letter, c. 1926, KBP.

91 "the most exciting and authentic publication": KB to Lola Ridge, 12 June 1926.

91 "I think Michael is with Steiglitz [sic] and Carnevali": KB to Lola Ridge, 12 June 1926.

91 "I have the first number": *BGT* 186.

91 "A delightful Monroe Wheelerish fairy": KB to Katherine Evans Boyle, 15 July 1926, KBP.

92 "rather dull and commonplace": KB to Jesse Peyton Boyle, 7 August 1926, KBP.

92 "what we were going to do with our lives": *BGT* 190.

92 "a hard woman": Kay Boyle, *Year Before Last.*

92 "Maman and Papa and the sisters": *BGT* 190.

93 Jo looked very much fatter: KB to Katherine Evans Boyle, 15 July 1926, KBP.

93 "Good as a doctor": Ibid.

93 For Richard Brault's efforts to help Ernest Walsh, see KB to Katherine Evans Boyle, 15 July 1926, KBP.

93 "solicitous" and "understanding": KB interview with Charles Amirkhanian.

6. "HE *MUST* BE PERFECT"

94 "I'll never look at another man again": Faith Gude interview with JM, December 1989.

94 Kay screamed back: KB to Katherine Evans Boyle, 15 July 1926, KBP.

94 she planned to join Richard: KB to Katherine Evans Boyle, 15 July 1926, KBP.

95 vaginal discharge: KB to Evelyn Scott, 5 November 1926, HRHRC.

95 "start the blood again": Kay Boyle, *Year Before Last.*

95 "a thread of blood": Ibid.

95 "I'll see you in Monte Carlo": Gladys Palmer Brooke, *Relations and Complications: Being the Recollections of H. H. the Dayang Muda of Sarawak,* ghostwritten by Kay Boyle (London: Lane–Bodley Head, 1929) 207. All subsequent references are to this edition.

96 "You have danced with your hard feet": Kay Boyle, "For an American," *Collected Poems* (New York: Knopf, 1962) 88. All subsequent references are to this edition.

96 "What will you do now": *BGT* 191.

96 "this rotten France": KB to "My dear Lola and Davy" [Lola Ridge], undated, c. 1927.

97 her mother's response came as a thunderbolt: KB to Lola Ridge, 12 January 1927.

97 "My kid will have his own family": Ibid.

97 "a Christ": Ibid.

97 "a rare artist" . . . "damned glad of the kid": Evelyn Scott to KB, undated, KBP.

97 Michael "re-born": KB to Evelyn Scott, 5 November 1926, HRHRC.

97 "he was something to have gone on with": Ibid.

97 "no one in America": KB to Lola Ridge, 12 January 1927.

97 "anything would make me feel like agreeing with Michael Gold": KB to "My beloved Lola and Davy," undated letter.

97 "do great things": KB to Lola Ridge, 12 January 1927.

97 "thumb [her] nose": Ibid.

98 "fly-by-night": *BGT* 209.

98 "walk down the street the way you do": *BGT* 192.

98 "I'll never understand it": *BGT* 211.

98 "abstract tradgedy": KB to Katherine Evans Boyle, undated letter, c. 1927, KBP.

98 "for the sake of literature": KB to Evelyn Scott, 31 January 1927, HRHRC.

98 "the Righteous": Ibid.

99 "He approaches the divine": KB to Lola Ridge, 12 January 1927.

99 "I want never to forget": KB to Evelyn Scott, 31 January 1927, HRHRC.
99 "I feel that I have lost you": KB to Katherine Evans Boyle, 2 January 1927, KBP.
99 "one experience I've not had": KB, undated fragment, KBP.
99 "dry regret": KB to Katherine Evans Boyle, undated fragment, c. 1927, KBP.
99 "given him everything at once": Ibid.
99 "First impressions are the only ones of any value": Ibid.
99 "a worse hell than anything that can ever happen to me": KB to Katherine Evans Boyle, 2 January 1927, KBP.
99 "You should have eloped with your Italian": KB to Katherine Evans Boyle, undated letter, c. 1927.
99 "All he wanted was to live with someone he loved": KB, undated fragments, KBP.
99 "the fairy who is all kinds of comfort": KB to Evelyn Scott, 31 January 1927, HRHRC.
99 "the home and devotion of a distinguished and elderly man": KB to Katherine Evans Boyle, 2 January 1927, KBP.
100 "He *must* be perfect": KB to Katherine Evans Boyle, c. 1927, KBP.
100 "What can I feed his son": KB to "My beloved Lola and Davy" [Lola Ridge], undated letter, c. 1927.
100 Michael Francis for Picabia: KB to Lola Ridge, 8 March 1927.
100 "I think the world is good to me": KB to Katherine Evans Boyle, 10 March 1927, KBP.
100 "you are the most important man in America": KB to Alfred Stieglitz, 8 March 1927, ASP.
100 "a signal to us": KB to Lola Ridge, 8 March 1927.
100 "one can't accept labor": KB to Evelyn Scott, 28 March 1927, HRHRC.
100 "You are a poet": KB to Alfred Stieglitz, 8 March 1927, ASP.
101 "You are my family": KB to Lola Ridge, 8 March 1927.
101 "one cannot ask it of strangers": KB to Jesse Peyton Boyle, 10 March 1927, KBP.
101 "weep and be weak": KB to Katherine Evans Boyle, undated fragment, c. 1927, KBP.
101 "able to speak and reason and discourse": KB to Jesse Peyton Boyle, 10 March 1927, KBP.
101 "enough racket to wake the town of Nice": KB to Katherine Evans Boyle, 11 March 1927, KBP.
101 everything she "didn't want": Ibid.
101 "the sound of Sharon Walsh": KB to Katherine Evans Boyle, 16 March 1927, KBP.
101 "beastly" hemorrhoids: Ibid.
101 "the image of Stieglitz": KB to Katherine Evans Boyle, 16 March 1927, KBP.
101 "every woman over twenty": *BGT* 209.
101 imaginary advertisements: KB to Katherine Evans Boyle, 24 March 1927, KBP.
102 "girl-girly off-moments of Harriet's crew": KB to Evelyn Scott, 18 March 1927, HRHRC.
102 "so little credit": KB to Evelyn Scott, 28 March 1927, HRHRC.
102 the Braults dispatched a friend to call on Kay: KB interview with Hugh Ford, 1978.
102 "damned noisy affair": KB to Katherine Evans Boyle, undated fragment, c. 1927.
102 "nose seems small": KB to Katherine Evans Boyle, 4 April 1927, KBP.
102 "I did want a son": KB to Alfred Stieglitz, 10 April 1927, ASP.
102 "quailed before his icy gaze": *BGT* 210.
102 "a youth, agile and attractive": From Emanuel Carnevali's review of Robert McAlmon's book of poems, *Explorations*, quoted in Hugh Ford, *Published in Paris: A Literary Chronicle of Paris in the 1920s and 1930s* (New York: Collier, 1975) 37.
102 "honest and sensitive": KB to Joan Boyle, 4 May 1927, KBP.
102 "hard, obdurate": Ibid.
103 "Ask her opinion on anything": *BGT* 210.
103 "So that should give you a hint": *BGT* 209.
103 "perfectly peeled eye": KB to Joan Boyle, 4 May 1927, KBP.
103 "You don't belong there": *BGT* 211.
103 "inadvertently" . . . "in error": KB to Edward Dahlberg, 24 January 1967. See also KB's undated notes for *Being Geniuses Together*, KBP.
103 "off somewhere by myself with Sharon": KB, undated fragment, c. 1927, KBP.
103 "arrogant pride": KB to Joan Boyle, 4 May 1927, KBP.
103 "I'll spend the rest of my life paying him back": KB to Evelyn Scott, 19 May 1927, HRHRC.
103–4 "obstinacy to believe in my own importance": KB to Evelyn Scott, 28 March 1927, HRHRC.
104 "You and Lola and me doing that is a sin": KB to Evelyn Scott, 18 March 1927, HRHRC.
104 "to be neither right nor wrong": KB to Evelyn Scott, 19 May 1927, HRHRC.
104 "Tell the baby's father": *BGT* 211.
104 "there was not a promise": *BGT* 212.

104 "color coming back": KB to Katherine Evans Boyle, 16 February 1927, KBP.
104 "hard" and "unmoving": KB to Evelyn Scott, 18 July 1927, HRHRC.
104 her "chastity": KB to Evelyn Scott, 18 July 1927, HRHRC.
104 "the color of spring": *BGT* 215.
105 "Boyle influence": KB to "dearest mommy," "Friday" [Stoke-on-Trent] [1927], KBP.
105 "disagreed on the subject of motherhood": KB to Katherine Evans Boyle, undated letter, c. 1927.
105 affairs "all over the place": KB interview with JM, August 1987.
105 "walk the continent": KB to Evelyn Scott, 18 July 1927, HRHRC.
105 "dementalized": KB to Katherine Evans Boyle, 18 July 1927, KBP.
105 "an anything which pays enough": KB to Louise Theis, 26 July 1927, Berg Collection, New York Public Library.
105 "boundless energy": Ibid.
105 "my sister is about as much help as Sharon": KB to Louise Theis, Friday [1927], Berg Collection.
105 "entangling" teas: KB to Katherine Evans Boyle, 15 June 1927, KBP.
105 "Why Richard selected Stoke and me": KB to Louise Theis, 17 November 1927, Berg Collection.
105 "I cannot inflict a platonic wife upon Richard": KB to Lola Ridge, 29 November 1927.
105 "live on someone else all my life": KB to Louise Theis, 17 November 1927, Berg Collection.
106 Bobby "for my own": KB to Joan Boyle, 27 July 1927 ("Dearest Girl"), KBP.
106 "was the gayest": KB to Lola Ridge, 29 November 1927.
106 "inevitable times": KB to Joan Boyle, 27 July 1927, KBP.
106 For the incident of Kay Boyle's aborted protest against the impending execution of Sacco and Vanzetti, see *BGT* 217–19.
106 "a sad month": KB to Jesse Peyton Boyle, 4 October 1927, KBP.
106 "emotional prejudice" . . . "aura": KB to Evelyn Scott, undated from "London," c. 1927, HRHRC.
106 "considered Carnevali": KB to Evelyn Scott, 22 October 1927, HRHRC.
106 "ceased being an honest writer": KB to Lola Ridge, 29 November 1927.
106 "You are a cold brute": KB to Evelyn Scott, 22 November 1927, HRHRC.
107 "Hasn't Mrs. Scott perhaps an emotional prejudice herself?": Quoted in KB to Katherine Evans Boyle, undated letter titled "Friday," KBP.
107 "I'd walk a million": KB to Evelyn Scott, 27 November 1928, HRHRC.
107 "a story about Grandma": KB to Katherine Evans Boyle, undated fragment, KBP.
107 "with the rain": For "Richard's poems," see *Poetry* February 1927.
107 "pet peeves": "Unrecommended List," *This Quarter* (Spring 1927) 272–73.
107 "big rough hairy": Wyndham Lewis, *Time and Western Man* (Boston: Beacon, 1957) 46.
108 "gather his seed": For "To America" and "For an American" and "Comrade," see *This Quarter* 3 (1927), 111–18.
108 "his face soft": Kay Boyle, serial version of *Plagued by the Nightingale*, *This Quarter* 3 (1927), 165–203.
108 "full of a running sap": Lola Ridge quoted in KB to Katherine Evans Boyle, 22 June 1927, KBP.
108 "superbly written": William Carlos Williams quoted in KB to Katherine Evans Boyle, 18 July 1927, KBP.
108 "what could any good": Kay Boyle, "Summer," in *Calendar: A Literary Review* 4 (April 1927) 38–43.
109 "woman of habits": Kay Boyle, "Theme," *transition* April 1927: 31–35.
109 "approach to America": Kay Boyle, rev. of *In the American Grain*, by William Carlos Williams, *transition* April 1927: 139–41.
109 "My blood is a long lament for you": Kay Boyle, "And Winter," *transition* August 1927: 139–41.
109 "Jesus Jesus remember this man": Kay Boyle, "A Sad Poem," *transition* January 1928: 169.
109 "I've been waiting for months to tell the world": KB to Katherine Evans Boyle, 16 September 1927, KBP.
109 art "seems to me to be a much simpler thing": KB to Louise Theis, 27 January 1928, Berg Collection.
109 "after Crane America has no poets": Dougald McMillan, *Transition 1927–1938: The History of a Literary Era* (New York: George Braziller, 1976) 127.
109 "explosive boil": Hart Crane to Slater Brown, quoted in John Unterecker, *Voyager: A Life of Hart Crane* (New York: Farrar, Straus & Giroux, 1969) 527.
110 "my grandmother and her grandson's poems": Hart Crane to Isidor Schneider, quoted in ibid. 527–28.
110 "as for Hart Crane": KB to Evelyn Scott, 27 January 1928, HRHRC.

110 "means anything to me": Ibid.
110 "hero-worship business of Stein and Joyce": Ibid.
110 "Don't talk *transition*": KB to Louise Theis, 27 January 1928, Berg Collection.
110 For "Portrait," see Kay Boyle, "Portrait," *transition* June 1927: 29–31.
110 "I'll be something more": Kay Boyle, "Polar Bears and Others," *transition* September 1927: 52–56.
110 "I took a cigaret": Kay Boyle, "Bitte Nehmen Sie die Blumen," *transition* December 1927: 88–93.

7. AT LAST, PARIS

112 "abandoning of Bobby": KB to Evelyn Scott, 27 February 1928, HRHRC.
112 "for toilet paper": Kathe Vail interview with JM, June 1990.
112 "every intention of being present at the birth": KB to Jesse Peyton Boyle, 18 January 1928, KBP.
112 "appall[ed]" her: KB to Jesse Peyton Boyle, 20 February 1928, KBP.
112 "it's fresher": KB to Evelyn Scott, 27 February 1928, HRHRC.
112 "That to me means that I must have failed": KB to Louise Theis, 27 January 1928, Berg Collection.
112 hated to "abandon": KB to Evelyn Scott, 27 February 1928, HRHRC.
113 "to weed Bobby": KB to Katherine Evans Boyle, 8 March 1927, KBP.
113 "counting Bobby out": Ibid.
113 "I want my kid all the time": Ibid.
113 "to have one's own work": KB to Jesse Peyton Boyle, 11 January 1928, KBP.
113 "If women have children": Ibid.
113 "at once wise": John Glassco, *Memoirs of Montparnasse* (New York: Oxford UP, 1970) 14.
114 Kay wore an orange panne velvet dress: *BGT* 238.
114 Archibald MacLeish stops to tie his shoelaces. See fragment, BERG. See also *BGT* 239.
114 Kay Boyle meets James and Nora Joyce: See *BGT* 240–42 and KB to Hugh Ford, 18 July 1975, BERG.
114 She was not much of a reader: KB interview with JM, August 1987.
114 "Harold Loeb complained": Loeb, *The Way It Was* 62.
114 "Irish colleen": *BGT* 241.
115 "the kidney": *BGT* 259.
115 "the machine": Advertisement in *transition* Summer 1928.
115 "undoubtedly the greatest quarterly arts": Brooke, *Revelations and Complications* 205.
115 Kay Boyle haughtily stalked off: *BGT* 265.
116 "a Hittite princess": Jay Allen to KB, undated letter, KBP.
116 "madder than hatters": Kay Boyle, "Afterword" to the Black Sun catalogue, unpublished manuscript, p. 2, KBP.
116 "I like girls when they are very young before they have any minds": Geoffrey Wolff, *Black Sun: The Brief Transit and Violent Eclipse of Harry Crosby* (New York: Random House, 1976) 209. All subsequent references are to this edition.
116 "mad party": Harry Crosby, *Shadows of the Sun* 188.
116 "silver-green . . . like a blade . . . neat as a needle . . . Seminole maiden": Caresse Crosby, *The Passionate Years* (Carbondale: Southern Illinois UP, 1968) 248. All subsequent references are to this edition.
116 "How good of you both": KB to Harry Crosby, undated letter, Black Sun Archive, Morris Library, Southern Illinois University, Carbondale, IL.
116 "If you wrote out what is there churning": KB to Harry Crosby, undated letter, Morris Library.
117 "Testament of the Sun": KB to Harry Crosby, undated letter, BSA, Morris Library.
117 "(Saint Leger . . .)": Crosby, *Shadows of the Sun* 193.
117 "best girl writer since Jane Austen": Harry Crosby to Henrietta Crosby, in Wolff 251.
117 "a dull book": Crosby, *Shadows of the Sun* 209.
117 "McAlmon is in Paris": *BGT* 270.
117 "corn-fed": William L. Shirer, interview with JM, 22 May 1989.
117 "Bob," she began: For a description of this evening with Kay Boyle and Robert McAlmon, see *BGT* 270.
118 "You're a provincial": Quoted in KB to William Carlos Williams, 8 November 1930, Beinecke Library, Yale University.
118 "crazy enough about you": Glassco, *Memoirs of Montparnasse*.

118 "knew everything": Billy Kluver and Julie Martin, *Kiki's Paris* (New York: Harry N. Abrams, 1989) 167. All subsequent references are to this edition.
118 "what's the matter with me": Kay Boyle, "I Can't Get Drunk" *Life Being the Best and Other Stories* (New York: New Directions, 1988) 35–41. All subsequent references to *Life Being the Best* are to this edition.
119 "If only Djuna Barnes or Mina Loy turned up": *BGT* 288.
119 "the nights Bob and I spent looking for you all over Paris": *BGT* 290.
119 "cold hilariousness": Brooke, *Relations and Complications* 229.
119 "I have waited so badly": Kay Boyle, "Spring Morning," *Wedding Day and Other Stories* (New York: Jonathan Cape and Harrison Smith, 1930).
120 Joan Boyle laughed at Kay's lifelong belief: Susan Hager interview with JM, 6 June 1988.
120 Bobby's tantrums: KB interview with Hugh Ford, 1978.
120 as middle-class as Hemingway: KB to Sandra Whipple Spanier, 29 May 1981, KBP. See also *BGT* 296.
120 Archie wanted to keep Gertrude Stein: KB to Sandra Whipple Spanier, 29 May 1981, KBP.
120 For the account of the tea at the Dayang Muda's, see *BGT* 262–64 and Brooke, *Relations and Complications*.
121 "if only she had stuck": *BGT* 290.
121 "I knew you when you drank sherry": *BGT* 263.
121 "All your troubles": *BGT* 292.
121 "We hope to make a big thing of it": KB to Jesse Peyton Boyle, 8 May 1928, KBP.
122 "in his community conditions": KB to Katherine Evans Boyle [? June 1928], KBP.
122 Little Bobby was punished: Jacqueline Ventadour Hélion, interview with JM, June 1990.
122 "far from forgotten me": KB to Katherine Evans Boyle [? June 1928], KBP.
122 "If only he would join the Duncan colony": Ibid.
122 "I shall do great things": KB to Jesse Peyton Boyle, 15 June 1928, KBP.
122 "McAlmon is the third corner in every triangle": *BGT* 312.
122 "I am interested": KB to Katherine Evans Boyle, "Tuesday" [July ? 1928], KBP.
123 her satiric portrait of Duncan: See Kay Boyle, *My Next Bride* (London: Penguin Books–Virago Press, 1986). All subsequent references are to this edition.
123 "*Je ne suis pas sculpteur*": *Remembering Paris: Catalogue for the Paintings of Arthur Deshaies* 1960.
123 "I am sick for a sight": Kay Boyle, "Letter for Archibald Craig," *transition* Summer 1928.
123 For "The United States" and "Written for Royalty," see *transition* Summer 1928.
124 "That's what I think": *BGT* 316. See also Sanford J. Smoller, *Adrift Among Geniuses: Robert McAlmon Writer and Publisher of the Twenties* (Pennsylvania State UP: University Park and London, 1975).
124 "mad with despair": Gale memoir 116.
124 "a Jewish fellow": Kay Boyle, "Vacation-Time," *transition* Fall 1928.
124 "events for Kay were too hectic:" *BGT* 274.
125 "modelled after you": John Glassco to KB, 2 December 1968, papers of John Glassco, National Archive of Canada. For the account of May Fry during the summer of 1928, see Glassco papers.
125 she was not driven by sexual desire: Kathe Vail interview with JM, June 1990.
125 "distortion": KB to John Glassco, 6 February 1969, National Archive of Canada.
126 "I've come here for one reason": KB interview with Hugh Ford, 1978.
126 "Do you know who I am?": Kathe Vail interview with JM, June 1990.
126 "from eternal damnation": KB to Caresse Crosby, undated letter, BSA.
126 "I'd have been preparing a Jewish cradle": KB to Caresse Crosby, undated letter, BSA.
127 "deep fecund green" privy: Kay Boyle, *My Next Bride* 275.
127 "never been a sister": KB interview with Hugh Ford, 1978.
127 "psychological disorders": *BGT* 322.
127 "You are the honey": Hugh Ford, *Four Lives in Paris* (San Francisco: North Point Press, 1987) 89. All subsequent references are to this edition.
128 "sane and healthy living": KB to Louise Theis, undated letter, Berg Collection.
128 "the beautiful Sharon": KB to Alfred Stieglitz, 30 September 1928, ASP.
128 "Explanations . . . collection of words as important as a lace handkerchief": Kay Boyle, "Why Do Americans Live in Europe?" *transition* Fall 1928: 102–3.
128 "to be a saner person": KB to Louise Theis, 30 September 1928, Berg Collection.

8. KAY AND LAURENCE

129 "when I walked down the street with him": Peggy Guggenheim, *Out of This Century: Confessions of an Art Addict* (New York: Universe Books, 1987) 34. All subsequent references are to this edition.

129 "Bear with me": *BGT* 324.

129 "*You* may go": Ibid. See also Kay Boyle, *My Next Bride* 254.

130 "Come and have a drink": Ford, *Four Lives* 188.

131 "You'd better wash": *BGT* 326.

131 "what a nursery": Crosby, *The Passionate Years* 235.

131 "and a squeaking": Crosby, *Shadows of the Sun* 220.

131 "It's too damn depressing": *BGT* 328.

131 "six years saying the same poem": *BGT* 328.

133 lifelong alliance with his sister: Kathe Vail interview with JM, June 1990.

133 "the feeling that they were made for incest": Guggenheim, *Out of This Century* 40–41.

133 "yellow manes": Kay Boyle, "Wedding Day," *Fifty Stories* 24–30.

133 "I'm here to save you": Kathe Vail interview with JM, June 1990.

134 "a brother and sister relationship": KB discussion notes, 1964, KBP.

134 "always a liar": Laurence Vail to Malcolm Cowley, in Jacqueline Bograd Weld, *Peggy: The Wayward Guggenheim* (New York: E. P. Dutton, 1986) 86. All subsequent references are to this edition.

134 Laurence Vail, *Piri and I* (New York: Lieber & Lewis, 1923). All subsequent references are to this edition.

134 throwing "bottles": Laurence Vail, *Murder! Murder!* (London: Peter Davies, 1931) 65. All subsequent references are to this edition.

134 "security of family life": Sandra Whipple Spanier, *Kay Boyle: Artist and Activist* (Carbondale and Edwardsville: Southern Illinois UP, 1986) 3. All subsequent references are to this edition.

134 Laurence was patient: KB interview with JM, August 1987.

134 "Can't you keep your eyes open?": Ibid.

135 "your breasts must be made of diamonds": Henry Miller, foreword to the catalogue of the Black Sun Press, KBP.

135 "murder of Max Eastman good job": KB telegram to Caresse Crosby, 24 June 1929, BSA.

135 "poetry of social comment": See John Glassco, "Conversation Between Robert McAlmon and Self," Nice (France) [1929], papers of John Glassco, National Archive of Canada.

135 "a wooly-brained incoherent posturing fraud:" Katherine Anne Porter, marginal notes on p. 299 of her copy of *BGT*, McKeldon Library, University of Maryland Libraries.

135 "I feel as though my heart would break open": KB to Caresse Crosby, undated letter, BSA.

135 hadn't "been in love": Ibid.

135 "you'd like Laurence Vail's paintings": KB to Alfred Stieglitz, 2 February 1929, ASP.

136 "write and write": KB to Caresse Crosby [winter 1929], BSA.

136 "But I'm going to": Ibid.

136 "poets and pederasts": Crosby, *Shadows of the Sun* 237.

136 "magnificently intoxicated": Crosby, *The Passionate Years* 251.

136 "makes fun": Crosby, *Shadows of the Sun* 237.

136 "(including Kay Boyle and Laurence Vail)": Hart Crane to Malcolm Cowley, 4 February 1929, in Hart Crane, *The Letters of Hart Crane, 1916–1932*, ed. Brom Weber (Berkeley: University of California Press, 1965) 335.

136 "Kay Boyle (who has decided she likes me)": Hart Crane to Isidor Schneider, 1 May 1929, ibid. 341.

136 "marvelous picture": Crosby, *Shadows of the Sun* 239.

136 Jonathan Cape's wife: KB interview with Hugh Ford, 1978.

136 "I loathed her": Weld, *Peggy* 86.

136 ended "disastrously": KB to Joan Boyle, 28 February 1930, KBP.

137 "nervy and peculiar": KB to Caresse Crosby, undated letter from "La Rue Louis David," BSA.

137 "family is insane": Laurence Vail to Eleanor Fitzgerald, 7 December 1928, Apple Vail's collection of the papers of Laurence Vail.

137 "in every way": Ford, *Four Lives* 193.

137 "Too bad he wasn't frightened of you": Guggenheim, *Out of This Century* [1987 edition] 145.

137 Bobby was scarcely to remember her Aunt Coco: Sharon Cowling interview with JM, June 1990.

137 "We can't fight her": KB to Caresse Crosby, 30 June 1930, BSA.

137 "such easy rich lives": Guggenheim, *Out of This Century* 110.

138 "that I have a roof": KB to Jesse Peyton Boyle, 9 May 1929, KBP.

138 "I think a great deal these days of Kay": Jesse Peyton Boyle to Joan Boyle, 7 July 1929, KBP.

138 "not exactly right": Kathe Vail interview with JM, June 1990.

138 "The mystery is not mine to touch": Kay Boyle, "An Open Letter to René Crevel," *transition* June 1932: 262.

138 "easy motoring distance": KB to Jesse Peyton Boyle, 17 March 1929, KBP.

138 "trained nurses": KB to Caresse Crosby [November 1929], KBP.

138 "poor baby alone": Ibid.

138 "nothing better calculated": KB to Caresse Crosby, undated letter [c. 1929], BSA.

139 "Sappho Jane Austen Kay Boyle," Harry Crosby, *Shadows of the Sun* 267.

139 "assault our sleep": William Carlos Williams, "The Somnambulists," rev. of *Short Stories*, by Kay Boyle, *transition* November 1929: 147–51.

139 "a turning point in the evolution": Eugene Jolas, "glossary," rev. of *Short Stories*, *transition* June 1929: 326–28.

139 "amaze and cut and make one cry out": Charles Henri Ford, rev. of *Short Stories*, *Blues* 2.7 (1929): 45.

139 "I believe in her": Archibald MacLeish to Harry Crosby, 22 April 1929, in Archibald MacLeish, *Letters of Archibald MacLeish: 1907–1982*, ed. R. H. Winnick (Boston: Houghton Mifflin, 1983) 229. All subsequent references are to this edition.

139 "were by no means as good": Hugh Ford, *Published in Paris: A Literary Chronicle of Paris in the 1920s and 1930s* (New York: Macmillan, 1975) 194. All subsequent references are to this edition.

139 "no field for revolt": Kay Boyle, "A New Mythology," *Paris Tribune* 10 March 1929. Reprinted in *The Left Bank Revisited: Selections from the Paris Tribune, 1917–1934*, ed. Hugh Ford (University Park: Pennsylvania State UP, 1972) 249–50.

140 "revolution in the English language": For "The Revolution of the Word," see *transition* June 1929: n.p. See also *BGT* 236.

140 called for acceptance of a uniquely American syntax: KB to Harry Goldgar, 26 May 1987, KBP.

140 "Mumbo Jumbo": See *BGT* 252 and Ford, *Four Lives* 179.

140 Hart Crane pleaded that he had been drunk: Malcolm Cowley, *Exile's Return: A Literary Saga of the Nineteen Twenties* (New York: Viking, 1961) 277. All subsequent references are to this edition.

140 "Paper Sir REVOLUTION": Laurence Vail, "Caspar Loot," *transition* March 1932: 318–19.

140 "didn't even read it before I signed it": KB interview with Charles Amirkhanian.

140 "loved the stuff": William L. Shirer interview with JM, 22 May 1989.

140 "we" distributed . . . "experimental school": Kay Boyle, lecture, San Francisco State University Poetry Center, 11 February 1987.

141 "No one pays attention to Hemingway anymore": KB interview with Katherine Heineman, undated notes, Beinecke Library, Yale University.

141 Apple-Jack, Apple-Joan: KB interview with JM, August 1987.

141 "a girl for Papa": Weld, *Peggy* 85.

141 Laurence so took over Apple: Clover Vail interview with JM, 20 February 1991.

141 Peggy headed for the park: Kathe Vail interview with JM, June 1990.

142 "no one who ever lived more consistently": Kay Boyle, "Homage to Harry Crosby," *transition* June 1930: 221–22.

142 "not a poem to appear in print": KB to Caresse Crosby, 26 September 1930, BSA.

142 "forgotten / In the government office": Kay Boyle, "Valentine for Harry Crosby," *Blues* 2.9 (Fall 1930): 35–37.

142 "proud of everything Harry ever did": KB to Caresse Crosby, undated letter [June 1930], BSA.

142 "Harry Crosby took each day as a new challenge": Kay Boyle, "A Paris Letter for Charles Henri Ford," *Blues* Spring 1930: 32–33.

142 Caresse had to apologize: Caresse Crosby to KB, 7 October 1931, BSA.

142 "not one of us": Kay Boyle, unpublished preface to *Shadows of the Sun*; see Wolff, *Black Sun* 299–300.

143 "a very cruel": KB to Geoffrey Wolff, 23 January 1973. Cited in Wolff 299.

143 "I loved him from the depths of my heart": KB to Caresse Crosby, 17 December 1929, BSA. There are three letters dated 17 December 1929. Only one is signed.

143 "a fiery little steed": KB to Caresse Crosby, 17 December 1929, BSA.

9. THE WRITER KAY BOYLE

144 "If she goes the right way": Katherine Anne Porter to Josephine Herbst, 11 February 1931, Beinecke Library, Yale University.

144 "I write my short stories too quickly": KB to Robert Carlton Brown [August 1931], RCBP.

144 "It marks an epoch": Kay Boyle, "A Paris Letter for Charles Henri Ford," *Blues* Spring 1930: 19–20.

144 "worried" by Cagnes: KB to Bob Brown, 28 March 1931, RCBP.

145 "I wrote that story": KB to James Stern, 16 September 1974, KBP.

145 "I like your energy": KB to Robert Carlton Brown [undated], RCBP.

145 "Sat smoking cigarettes": Kay Boyle, "Change of Life," RCBP. For a description of Robert Brown's reading machine, see Ford, *Four Lives* 202; Ford, *Published in Paris* 310–11; and Wambly Bald, "Tues. May 19, 1931," *On the Left Bank: 1929–1933*, ed. Benjamin Franklin (Athens: Ohio UP, 1987) 67.

145 "perfectly sober": KB to Bob Brown, 15 April 1931, RCBP.

145 "I gillespie": KB to Bob Brown, "Wednesday" [August 1931?], RCBP.

145 "write, or care": KB to Caresse Crosby, "Saturday," undated letter, BSA.

145 "fine humor": For an account of Caresse Crosby's visit to the Vails, see Caresse Crosby, *The Passionate Years* 302–3.

146 "Oh, darling, I shall die": KB to Caresse Crosby, 2 October 1931, BSA.

146 "great and courageous man": KB interview with Hugh Ford, 1978.

146 "I've been in prison too": Ibid.

146 "Anarchism is more demanding": Leo Litwak, "Kay Boyle—Paris Wasn't Like That," *New York Times Book Review* 15 July 1984: 1+.

146 "didn't seem to me to have the integrity that Sasha had": KB interview with Hugh Ford, 1978.

147 "You know, dearest comrade": Kay Boyle, "Alexander Berkman: A Memory," *Phoenix* 6.1–2 (Summer–Fall 1977) 161.

147 "There is Kay and there are other friends": Ibid.

147 a "grand girl" . . . "Stein, Carnevali": KB to Bob Brown, 9 December 1931, RCBP.

148 "viscounts and princes": KB to Caresse Crosby, 7 July 1931, BSA.

148 "in their eyes": Caresse Crosby to KB, 10 September 1931, BSA.

148 "the rejoicing": KB to Caresse Crosby, 2 October 1931, BSA.

148 no point in being jealous: Sharon Cowling interview with JM, June 1990.

148 "he would have loved it": KB to Caresse Crosby, 6 November 1931, BSA.

148 "All the filth about McAlmon": KB to Joan Boyle, 8 August 1931, KBP.

149 Kay called Bobby "happy": Ibid.

149 "I'm always a victim": Sharon Cowling interview with JM, June 1990.

149 "Fortunately the whole house": KB to Bob Brown [March 27, 1932], RCBP.

149 "wash my mouth out with soap": KB interview with JM, August 1987.

149 "to keep us company": KB to Bob Brown, "Saturday" [7 November 1931], RCBP.

149 "hard at baby love": KB to Caresse Crosby [June 1930], BSA.

149 For the account of Kay Boyle's meeting with Samuel Beckett, see Kay Boyle, "All Mankind Is Us," *Samuel Beckett: Waiting for Godot, a Casebook*, ed. Ruby Cohn (London: Macmillan, 1987) 176–80. Also KB interview with JM, August 1987.

150 "I brought back the baby clothes": KB interview with Hugh Ford, 1978.

150 "everything I have ever read of yours": Kay Boyle to James T. Farrell, 15 November 1931, Charles Van Pelt Library, University of Pennsylvania.

150 Kay's "bodyguard": KB interview with Hugh Ford, 1978.

150 "all the sentimental, childish ones": KB to Caresse Crosby, 6 November 1931, BSA.

150 "pompous decision": KB to William Carlos Williams, 8 November 1930, Beinecke Library, Yale University.

150 "obsequiously rubbing his hands saying 'Miss Boyle' ": Ibid.

150 "such nice blonde Germanic babies": Ibid.

151 "leave that gay Rapallo": KB to "Dear Ezra," undated handwritten note of 1930, Beinecke Library, Yale University.

151 "organized opinion": Ernest Walsh, "An Open Letter to Mike Gold," *New Masses* December 1926: 23.

151 "wonderful writer": Mike Gold, "A Note on Ernest Walsh," *New Masses* December 1926: 23.

151 "terribly low ebb": KB to Caresse Crosby [June 1930], BSA.

151 "a stenographer again": Ibid.

151 Peggy asked Laurence how much money: KB interview with Hugh Ford, 1978.

151 "for consolation": KB to Bob Brown, "Friday" [January 1932], KBP.

151 "Laurence won't get over this week": KB to Bob Brown, 2 February 1932, RCBP.

151 John Holms so lusted: KB interview with JM, August 1987.

152 "something human": KB to Caresse Crosby, 2 February 1932, BSA.

152 typing eleven pages: KB to Caresse Crosby, 10 October 1931, BSA.

152 "If only I can work hard and long enough": KB to Caresse Crosby, 10 October 1931, BSA.

152 "doing the best I can": KB to Bob Brown, "Wednesday Morning" [August 1931], RCBP.

152 "days of work": Ibid.

152 "going to hell and rack and ruin": KB to Bob Brown, "Thursday" [October 1931], RCBP.

152 "women's fiction": See KB to Bob Brown [after May 1931?]: "As long as I write nice girlish novels and short stories about the English, everything will be all right." RCBP.

152 "Vagina" was "most aggravating": KB to Bob Brown, "Tuesday March first" [1932], RCBP. See also KB to Bob Brown, 29 April 1932, RCBP, and KB to Bob Brown, "Tuesday" [December 1931?], RCBP.

152 "The speech that suits": Kay Boyle, "A Glad Day for Laurence Vail," *transition* March 1932: 157–58.

153 "Tact and complacency have long been women's attributes": KB interview with Evelyn Harter; see Evelyn Harter, "Kay Boyle: Experimenter," *Bookman* June–July 1932: 249–52.

153 did "not write simply or violently enough": Ibid.

153 "how women miss being great": For Kay Boyle's description of Edith M. Stern's article, "Men the Best Writers," see KB to Bob Brown, 2 February 1932, RCBP.

153 "I miss in high society": KB to Bob Brown, 2 February 1932, RCBP.

153 work of a "lady writer": see Kay Boyle to Bob Brown, "Monday" [October 1931], RCBP.

153 "hot from the heart": KB to Bob Brown, "Friday" [August 1931], RCBP.

153 "lady novelist": Ibid. See also KB to Bob Brown, "Monday" [October 1931], RCBP.

153 "back to the gutter": KB to Bob Brown, "Friday" [August 1931], RCBP.

153 "write a record of our age": KB to Walter Lowenfels, 15 August 1930, KBP.

153 "The present day reader is not worth a ha'penny bit": Ibid.

153 "for posterity": Ibid.

153 "mere lower case revoltée": Gerald Sykes, "Too Good to Be Smart," rev. of *Wedding Day and Other Stories, Nation* 24 December 1930: 711–12.

153 letting "the subconscious out": "Kay Boyle's Experiments," rev. of *Wedding Day and Other Stories, New York Times Book Review* 16 November 1930: 8.

153 "the impression made": E. B. C. Jones, rev. of *Plagued by the Nightingale, Adelphi* 1 October 1931: 68.

154 "everyone was an individual": Kay Boyle, *Plagued by the Nightingale* (Carbondale: Southern Illinois UP, 1966). All subsequent references are to this edition.

154 "a better book before I dragged in a love interest": KB to Bob Brown, 14 October 1931, RCBP.

154 Kay's novel, *Plagued by the Nightingale*, impressed . . . Hart Crane: Hart Crane to Caresse Crosby, 31 April 1932, in *Letters of Hart Crane, 1916–1932* 405.

154 "the splendor of the stars in her writing": quoted in KB to Bob Brown, 31 May 1931, RCBP.

154 "one cannot complain": Charles Hansen Towne, "Kay Boyle's Novel," rev. of *Plagued by the Nightingale, New York Times Book Review* 5 April 1931: 7,20.

154 "too self-conscious": L. A. G. Strong, rev. of *Plagued by the Nightingale, Spectator* 18 July 1931: 94.

154 "They are very gorgeous": Katherine Anne Porter to Josephine Herbst, 11 February 1931, Beinecke Library, Yale University.

155 "good almost in spite of herself": Ibid.

155 "a magnificent performance": Katherine Anne Porter, "Example to the Young," *New Republic* 22 April 1931: 279–80.

155 "shout and wave": KB to Katherine Anne Porter, in Joan Givner, *Katherine Anne Porter: A Life* (New York: Simon & Schuster, 1982) 231.

155 "invented techniques": Vance Bourjaily, "Moving and Maturing," *New York Times Book Review* 28 September 1980: 9.

156 "simply live before us": See Harter, "Kay Boyle: Experimenter."

156 "All human misery can be seen as the failure of love": KB to Sandra Whipple Spanier, 4 June 1981, KBP.

156 "going in for magic this season": KB to Bob Brown, 16 January 1932, RCBP.

156 Kay Boyle, "Black Boy," *Fifty Stories* 50–55.

156 "a knot of black gleaming serpents": Kay Boyle, "One of Ours," *New Yorker* 17 October 1931: 17–19.
156 too "indelicate": T. S. Eliot quoted in KB to Bob Brown, "Saturday" [October 1931], RCBP.
156 new story on July 8: KB to Bob Brown, 9 July 1931, RCBP.
156 "Pretty English": Ibid.
156 "too quickly": KB to Bob Brown [August 1931], RCBP.
156 "a lamentable idea": Ibid.
156 "going to drink myself under the table": KB to Bob Brown, 9 July 1931, RCBP.
157 "a prolific writer": KB to Bob Brown, 18 July 1931, RCBP.
157 "write ten novels": KB to Bob Brown [August 1931], RCBP.
157 "I *have* to write short stories": KB to Caresse Crosby, "Evening" 2 October [1931], BSA.
157 "the ship afloat with short stories": KB to Caresse Crosby, 27 July 1931, BSA.
157 "too dark loinsy": KB to Bob Brown [July 1931], RCBP.
157 "an intellectual": KB to Bob Brown, "Wednesday" [August 1931?], RCBP.
157 the line "I'll say you do": KB to Bob Brown, "Wednesday Night" [August 1931], RCBP.
157 "fairy book": KB to Bob Brown, "Monday" (marked [October 1931], but more likely July or August 1931), RCBP.
157 "out of pushing": KB to Bob Brown, "Wednesday" [October 1931], RCBP.
157 "the only way to get things done": Ibid.
157 "sly and foxy and obscene": KB to Caresse Crosby, 2 October 1931, BSA.
157 "felt like taking cold douches": Ibid.
157 "that horrid Cape": KB to Bob Brown, "Saturday" [November 1931], RCBP.
157 "a couple of half-wits": KB to Joan Boyle, 8 August 1931, KBP.
158 Kay plotted: KB to James Hamilton, 7 November 1931, RCBP.
158 "What's a girl to do?": KB to Bob Brown, "Saturday" [7 November 1931], RCBP.
158 "pay back the advance": Virginia Rice quoted in KB to Bob Brown, 9 December 1931, RCBP.
158 "with no strings attached": Ibid.
158 "Tell her I'm not satisfied": KB to Bob Brown, "Monday," [14] December 1931, RCBP.
158 "bad businesswoman": KB interview with Hugh Ford, 1978.
158 "hard-boiled baby": KB to Caresse Crosby, undated letter, BSA.
158 "quaint Polish-Jewish": KB to Caresse Crosby, 16 November 1931, BSA.
158 Poetry remained her first passion: KB to William Carlos Williams, 17 November 1930, Beinecke Library. See also KB to William Carlos Williams, 8 November 1930, Beinecke Library.
158 "fictionalizing": Telephone conversation with Joan Detweiler, 18 February 1993.
159 "Have the moon shine": KB interview with Kay Bonetti, 1988.

10. "IF IT WERE NOT FOR THE CHILDREN"

160 "a picture in the Paris paper": William L. Shirer interview with JM, 22 May 1989.
160 "travel on the same passport": KB interview with Hugh Ford, 1978.
160 "Just do it privately": Ibid.
160 She's always telling me what to do: Ibid.
160 "stupid to make a special celebration": Alexander Berkman to Emma Goldman, 31 March 1932, in Alexander Berkman and Emma Goldman, *Nowhere at Home: Letters from Exile of Emma Goldman and Alexander Berkman*, eds. Richard and Anna Maria Drinnon (New York: Schocken Books, 1975) 217.
160 "MAY LOVE LAST": Telegram of Alexander Berkman to Kay Boyle, KBP. "Wedding bells": Bald, *Left Bank, 1929–1933* 103. For an account of the wedding, see also Bald's *Paris Tribune* piece, "Laurence Vail and Kay Boyle Wed in Simple Ceremony," 3 April 1932, reprinted in Ford, *The Left Bank Revisited* 130. See also Ford, *Four Lives* 211.
160 "for some morbid reason": Guggenheim, *Out of This Century* 110.
161 "Where are the children?": KB interview with JM, August 1987.
161 "You'll only make a fool of me because everyone knows": KB to Bob Brown, 29 April 1932, RCBP.
161 "mind and heart are wide, wide open": Kay Boyle, "Writers Worth Reading," *Contempo* 4 (5 July 1932) 4.
161 "If allowed to enter New York, I must recite": KB to Virginia Rice, letter titled "This Is For Yale Review," undated, Beinecke Library, Yale University.
162 Dr. B. Hogden: For Kay Boyle's birth records, see copy of the card on file at the Department of

Health, City of St. Paul, Minnesota, filed on February 22, 1902, and citing the birth of a girl, Katherine Boyle, on 19th of February, 1901, which is crossed out to read, in parentheses above, "(1902)." The card was marked "altered per suppl. February 3, 1932," and again on August 6, 1968. Kay Boyle's date of birth, February 19, 1902 in Ramsey County, St. Paul, was also filed with "Vital Statistics Registration," Minnesota Department of Health, in Minneapolis.

162   "gave a dignity to the heart": Kay Boyle, "The Man Who Died Young," *Yale Review* 21 (June 1932) 785–809.

162   "soft and filled with love": Kay Boyle, "Friend of the Family," *Harper's* 165 (September 1932) 396–401.

162   "too eager for love": Kay Boyle, "Three Little Men," *Criterion* 12 (October 1932) 17–23.

162   "I simply cannot": KB to Bob Brown, 16 January 1932, RCBP.

162   "The Riviera's fine for everything but work": KB to Bob Brown [1932], RCBP.

163   Kay "willfully . . . kidnapped" . . . two screens: KB to Caresse Crosby, 8 February 1932, BSA.

163   "I don't think it matters": Ibid.

163   "cries of the offspring": KB to Bob Brown, "Thursday" [March 1932], RCBP.

163   "lonely for the sound of the other's machine": Ibid.

163   "I wish I could give a leg or an arm": KB to Bob Brown [March 1932], RCBP.

163   For the incident of Apple in Cortina d'Ampezzo, see KB interview with Hugh Ford, 1978.

163   "pie-eyed": KB to Bob Brown, "Thursday" [March 1932], RCBP.

163   "You have no sex appeal": Ibid.

164   "an ordeal" to write: KB to Bob Brown, 2 February 1932, RCBP.

164   "the literary value of stripping oneself naked": KB to Caresse Crosby, 27 February 1932, BSA.

164   too "sexually frank": Recounted in KB to Bob Brown, "Saturday" [October 1931], RCBP.

164   "as near perfect": Waverly Lewis Root, "Kay Boyle Writes Novel of Quality Too Rarely Found," rev. of *Year Before Last, Paris Tribune* 4 July 1932.

164   "predicament of the exile": Robert Cantwell, "American Exile," rev. of *Year Before Last, Nation* 20 July 1932: 60–61.

164   "limited to readers of literary tastes": Rev. of *Year Before Last, Booklist* November 1932: 73.

164   "near preciosity": Myra Marini, "The Romantic Temper," rev. of *Year Before Last, New Republic* 13 July 1932: 242.

164   "a subject which is organically her own": Philip Rahv, "Improvisations of Reality," rev. of *The Crazy Hunter, Nation* 23 March 1940: 396.

165   "If this writer goes on being ignored": E. B. C. Jones, rev. of *Year Before Last, Adelphi* July 1932: 718–20.

165   "reach the larger public": Gladys Graham, "Inescapable End," rev. of *Year Before Last, Saturday Review of Literature* 9 July 1932.

165   "I have not seen such beautiful writing": Clare Boothe Brokaw to Kay Boyle, 8 July 1932, KBP.

165   "dead great men": Kay Boyle, "Lydia and the Ring-Doves," *Vanity Fair* 39 (November 1932) 36, 62, 66.

165   "live too much from hand to mouth": KB to Caresse Crosby, 19 April 1932, BSA.

165   "keep at short stories": KB to Caresse Crosby, 19 April 1932, BSA.

165   "why he should be expected to give a photographic view": KB to Robert McAlmon, 17 December 1932, Beinecke Library, Yale University.

165   "I picked out the ones I wanted": KB to Robert McAlmon, 5 June 1933, Beinecke Library.

165   "what they feel is necessary for the reader": Ibid.

165   "People too lazy to examine the facts": Ezra Pound to Robert McAlmon, 2 February 1934, in Ezra Pound, *The Letters of Ezra Pound,* ed. D. D. Paige (New York: Harcourt, Brace, 1950) 252.

166   "I'm trying to be important": KB to Robert McAlmon, 17 April 1932, Beinecke Library.

166   "stripped sentences": Kay Boyle, letter, *Paris Tribune* 17 December 1932. Kay Boyle's letter, addressed to "Mr. Root," is reprinted in Ford, *The Left Bank Revisited* 276–77.

166   "Something rather grand ought to be done about McAlmon": KB to Caresse Crosby, 11 May 1932, BSA.

166   "what an unusual and vigorous feeling for the language": *BGT* 337–38. See also KB to Robert McAlmon, 13 February 1933, Beinecke Library.

166   "insensitive dismissal of the work and value": Kay Boyle, letter, *New English Weekly* [c. November 1932]. See also August Warren, "Some Periodicals of the American Intelligentsia," *New English Weekly* [6 October 1932] 331.

166   "Some kind of poetic form has to be found": KB to William Carlos Williams, 17 November 1930, Beinecke Library. Quoted in a letter Williams addressed to Kay Boyle, but destined for publication

in *Contact: The Selected Letters of William Carlos Williams*, ed. John C. Thirwall (New York: McDowell, Obolensky, 1957) 129–36.

166 "how sad I am": KB to Evelyn Scott, 19 May 1933, HRHRC.

166 "He was a dear": KB to Caresse Crosby, 19 May 1932, BSA.

166 "Do you think Bergery will be too busy now": Alexander Berkman quoted in KB to Caresse Crosby, 2 June 1932, BSA.

166 "The poor darling is almost destitute": KB to Caresse Crosby, 26 July 1932, BSA.

167 "too non-committal": KB to Caresse Crosby, 10 June 1932, BSA.

167 "I would give you anything": KB to Caresse Crosby, 30 March 1933, BSA.

167 "something for Sasha": See KB to Caresse Crosby, 10 May 1933, KBP. See also KB to Evelyn Scott, 19 May 1933, HRHRC.

167 "heart is like a hawk's flight": Kay Boyle, "A Comeallye for Robert Carlton Brown," *Americans Abroad: An Anthology*, ed. Peter Neagoe (The Hague: Servire Press, 1932).

167 forcing her into the car: Clover Vail interview with JM, February 20, 1991.

167 "the thing that was very wonderful about Laurence Vail": KB interview with Hugh Ford, 1978.

167 "a son of a bitch": William L. Shirer interview with JM, 22 May 1989.

167 "I have done nothing": Laurence Vail, *Murder! Murder!*

168 "To know that you and Rose doubt Laurence": KB to Bob Brown, 21 May 1932, RCBP.

168 "If you need it": Ibid.

168 "Of the lot of us": Ibid.

168 "disloyal": Ibid.

168 "It is a great": Ibid.

168 "lost and homeless": KB to Caresse Crosby, 21 March 1933, BSA.

169 "Miss Boyle has not yet quite mastered": Louis Kronenberger, "The Short Stories of Kay Boyle," rev. of *The First Lover and Other Stories*, *New York Times Book Review* 26 March 1933: 7.

169 "precious": Rev. of *The First Lover and Other Stories*, *Forum* May 1933: vi.

169 "artifice": Rev. of *The First Lover and Other Stories*, *Nation* 19 May 1933: 453.

169 "match her manner": Hazel Hawthorne, "Kay Boyle," rev. of *The First Lover and Other Stories*, *New Republic* 3 May 1933: 342.

169 "then have O'Brien's remarks left blank": KB to Milton Abernethy, 17 March 1933, HRHRC.

169 "never, never, never write the name of George Davis": KB to Caresse Crosby, 30 March 1933, BSA.

169 "exile bathes the vision clear": Kay Boyle and Laurence Vail, rev. of *Americans Abroad: An Anthology*, by Peter Neagoe, *Contempo* 15 (March 1933): 1+.

170 "to wangling advances": Samuel Putnam, "Americans Abroad," *Contempo* 15 May 1933: 2.

170 "I wondered why you printed Putnam's libel": KB to Milton Abernethy, 13 July 1933, HRHRC.

170 "stone hearts": Kay Boyle, "Convalescence," *Story* 2 (April 1933): 34–40.

170 For "Life Being the Best," see *Harper's* November 1933, and Kay Boyle, *Life Being the Best and Other Stories* (New York: New Directions, 1988).

171 a "passing fad": Kay Boyle, "In Defense of Homosexuality," *New Review* April 1932: 24–25.

171 "utterly unwarranted paragraph about me": Ezra Pound to KB, *New Review* April 1932: 24–25.

171 "The Meeting of the Stones," in *Life Being the Best* 69–80.

171 "the womanly": Kay Boyle, *Gentlemen, I Address You Privately* (New York: Harrison Smith and Robert Haas, 1933). All subsequent references are to this edition.

172 "sole survivors": Kay Boyle, *Gentlemen, I Address You Privately*.

172 "undue theatricality," Louis Kronenberger, "Kay Boyle's Story of a Moral Crisis," rev. of *Gentlemen, I Address You Privately*, *New York Times Book Review* 12 November 1933: 9.

172 "another of those orgies": "Shorter Notices," rev. of *Gentlemen, I Address You Privately*, *Nation* 29 November 1933: 630.

173 "a world made up of insulated groups": Robert Cantwell, "Exiles," rev. of *Gentlemen, I Address You Privately*, *New Republic* 13 December 1933: 136–37.

173 "virtuosity is this writer's curse": Henry Seidel Canby, "Style Without Design," rev. of *Gentlemen, I Address You Privately*, *Saturday Review of Literature* 4 November 1933: 233.

173 "Kay Boyle's style is more perverse": Clifton Fadiman, rev. of *Gentlemen, I Address You Privately*, *New Yorker* 4 November 1933: 66–67.

173 came away with sixty dollars: KB interview with JM, August 1987.

173 "more commercial": KB to Caresse Crosby, 16 February 1933, BSA.

173 Nice was "abominable": KB to Evelyn Scott, 2 July 1933, HRHRC.

173 "a cheaper and more difficult country": Ibid.

173 "at long intervals": Ibid.

173 "two blond-headed infants": Ibid.
173 "keep the pennies dribbling in": Ibid.
174 "the first time": KB to Milton Abernethy, 13 July 1933, HRHRC.
174 "Which one of these country towns": Carnevali, *The Autobiography of Emanuel Carnevali* 207.
174 "like a pinned butterfly": KB to Caresse Crosby, 18 July 1933, BSA.
174 "detach Kay Boyle's head from the body": Carnevali, *The Autobiography of Emanuel Carnevali* 50.
175 "I don't know what to do": KB to Caresse Crosby, 18 July 1933, BSA.
175 "You do not need to tell me": Ibid.
175 "move heaven and earth": Ibid.
175 "or I will never write again": KB to Caresse Crosby, 25 August 1933, BSA.
175 For the scene of Caresse Crosby at the offices of Simon & Schuster, see Crosby, *The Passionate Years* 326–27.
175 "isolate in himself ": KB to Milton Abernethy, 2 August 1933, HRHRC.
176 "if I die in the attempt": KB to William Carlos Williams, 24 November 1933, Beinecke Library.
176 "I could get you enough": KB to Milton Abernethy, 12 August 1933, HRHRC.
176 "I hope your high hopes": Carnevali quoted in KB to Caresse Crosby, 8 September 1933, BSA.
176 "Is it possible": Carnevali quoted in KB to Caresse Crosby, 25 October 1933, BSA.

11. NAZIS AS HEROES

177 "a sneaking admiration for fascism": Tania Stern interview with JM, June 1990.
177 "The gods of the North": Mark Van Doren, "Under the Swastika," rev. of *Death of a Man*, *Nation* rpt. in *The Private Reader: Selected Articles and Reviews, 1942* (New York: Kraus Reprint Co., 1968) 241–44.
177 hating Vienna: See KB to William Carlos Williams, 24 November 1933, Beinecke Library, Yale University, and KB to Evelyn Scott, undated letter, December 1933, HRHRC.
177 "without hope or promise": KB to William Carlos Williams, 24 November 1933, Beinecke Library.
177 "an Austrian club": Dr. Robert Hecht, quoted in F. L. Carsten, *Fascist Movements in Austria: From Schönerer to Hitler* (Sage Studies in 20th Century History, Volume 7) (London and Beverly Hills: Sage Publications, 1977) 29.
178 "bewildering love": KB to Caresse Crosby, 25 October 1933, BSA.
178 "what is to come": Ibid.
178 "I wish you would write": KB to Caresse Crosby, 30 September 1933, BSA.
178 "absolutely heartbroken": Ibid.
179 "destitute, barefooted families": *BGT* 338.
179 "The breath of the white horses of Vienna was smoke": KB to James Stern, "On His Birthday," KBP.
179 "I was more to him than she ever was": Moorhead's anger is detailed in Robert McAlmon to KB, 11 December 1933, KBP.
179 "lonely sex-starved and thwarted old gal": Ibid.
179 "fight it out": Ibid.
179 "The moment she knows": Ibid.
179 she tore the manuscript: Ford, *Four Lives* 219.
180 "frightful" months: Ford, *Four Lives* 217–18.
180 "magnificent blizzard": Ibid.
180 "no talk, for the lips are closed": Kay Boyle, "Maiden, Maiden," *Fifty Stories* 130–50.
180 "ecstatic": Ford, *Four Lives* 217–18.
180 "Send me some names of boys": KB to Evelyn Scott, 29 December 1933, HRHRC.
180 "queer inward feelings": Ibid.
180 "to the point of tears": Ibid.
180 "I'm in a state of nerves": KB to Ann Watkins, in Ford, *Four Lives* 218.
181 "white slave trade": See Bettina Bedwell, *Yellow Dusk*, ghostwritten by Kay Boyle (London: Hurst & Blackett, 1937). All subsequent references are to this edition.
181 "Harry's spirit will supply the wind": KB to Caresse Crosby, 7 May 1931, BSA.
181 "go much further": Evelyn Scott, recommendation included with letter of KB to Evelyn Scott, 29 December 1933, HRHRC.
181 "The baby can come": KB interview with Hugh Ford, 1978.
181 "Being pregnant": Ibid.

181 "a nice kind of relaxation": Ibid.

181 "stay forever": KB to Bob Brown, 11 May 1931, RCBP.

181 "pay you so much an hour": KB interview with Hugh Ford, 1978.

182 "we were fascists": C. Earl Edmondson, *The Heimwehr and Austrian Politics: 1918–1936* (Athens: University of Georgia Press, 1978) 260.

182 For accounts of the political situation in Austria during Kay Boyle's sojourn there, see Edmondson, *The Heimwehr.*

182 "It's awful for him": Ford, *Four Lives* 221.

182 "five years of my life": KB to Joan Boyle, 25 March 1934, KBP.

182 "lazy-go-lucky": KB notebook for 1934, KBP.

182 See Kay Boyle, Laurence Vail, and Nina Conarain, eds., *365 Days* (New York: Harcourt, Brace, 1936). All subsequent references are to this edition.

183 "equate . . . sexuality with vulgarity": KB "Afterword" to the Black Sun catalogue (1975) 5, KBP. Published as "The Crosbys: An Afterword," *ICarbS* 3 (1977) 121.

183 "kind of puritanical or twilighty romantic": Ibid.

184 For an account of the attempted bombing of the *Tyrolia*, see "Dynamitanschlag auf unsere Druckerei" (Dynamite Attack on Our Printing Works), *Tiroler Anzeiger* 28 June 1934: 1, and "Der Schaden des Anschlages auf die Tyrolia-Druckerei" (The Damage of the Attack on the *Tyrolia* Printing Works), *Innsbrucker Zeitung* 29 June 1934: 2.

184 "they drifted slowly down around us like flower petals": Kay Boyle, *Primer for Combat* (New York: Simon & Schuster, 1942). All subsequent references are to this edition.

185 Kay and Laurence are interviewed by the Heimwehr: KB to Ann Watkins, 3 July 1934. See also Edmondson, *The Heimwehr.*

185 She was no one's favorite: Kathe Vail interviews with JM, June 1990 and November 1991.

185 "We wanted a boy": KB to Bob Brown, 19 November 1934, RCBP.

185 "Everything much exaggerated": KB to Katherine Evans Boyle, 30 July 1934, KBP.

185 "That's the way it is": KB interview with JM, August 1987.

186 "I've never met a Jew": Ibid.

186 Kathe raised her arm in the "*Heil Hitler*" salute: Kathe Vail interviews with JM, June 1990.

187 See "Count Lothar's Heart," *Harper's Bazaar* May 1935, and Kay Boyle, *Fifty Stories* 166–80.

187 "the powder chest of European politics": Kay Boyle, "December 16—Saar," *365 Days* 396.

187 "the doctor": Kay Boyle, "The White Horses of Vienna," *Harper's* April 1935. See also Kay Boyle, *The White Horses of Vienna and Other Stories* (New York: Harcourt, Brace, 1936) 3–27.

188 "an October-fest fling": Crosby, *The Passionate Years*, 317.

188 "a gimlet-eyed man": Ibid. 319.

188 "*Guten Tag*": KB interview with JM, August 1987. See also KB to Sandra Whipple Spanier, 4 June 1981, KBP.

188 "a history of women": KB to Ann Watkins, in Ford, *Four Lives* 223.

188 "material inequality": KB to Sandra Whipple Spanier, 30 November 1984, KBP.

188 "last expatriate novel": Clifton Fadiman, "Remember Your Alice—The Vegetarian Novel—The Women Who Did," rev. of *My Next Bride, New Yorker* 10 November 1934: 110–11.

189 "dates hopelessly": Rev. of *My Next Bride, Christian Century* 5 December 1934: 1564.

189 "trivial material": Edith Walton, "Miss Boyle's Irony," rev. of *My Next Bride, New York Times Book Review* 11 November 1934: 6.

189 "exaggerated attention to detail": Mary McCarthy, "The Romance of Paris," rev. of *My Next Bride, Nation* 26 December 1934: 746–47.

189 "how glad we should be": George Dangerfield to KB, 30 January 1934, KBP.

189 "extremely anxious": Cleanth Brooks to KB, 23 March 1935, Beinecke Library.

189 Janet Flanner: Brenda Wineapple interview with JM, 18 December 1990.

189 "way above, distant": Sharon Cowling interview with JM, June 1990.

189 "efficient nurse": Guggenheim, *Out of This Century* 140–41.

189 "How can you possibly take on the responsibility": Ibid.

190 "I didn't know Santa Claus was so thin": Sharon Cowling interview with JM, June 1990.

190 "strangely thrilling": KB to Bob Brown, 13 January 1935, RCBP.

190 "disgusting—all finance and big promises": Ibid.

190 "not *against* America": KB to "Robos" [Bob Brown], 10 March 1935, KBP.

190 "go directly to the west or south": KB to Mabel Dodge Luhan, 3 February 1935, Beinecke Library.

190 "I prefer the emotional thing": KB to Bob Brown, 13 January 1935, RCBP.

190 "I could not believe my ears": KB to Sandra Whipple Spanier, 4 June 1981, KBP.

191 "ready to faint": KB to Katherine Evans Boyle, 21 March 1935, KBP.

191 "That's what I do with orders!": Kay Boyle, *Death of a Man* (New York: New Directions, 1989). All subsequent references are to this edition.

193 "Novelist she is not": Helen Moran, rev. of *Death of a Man, North American Review* Winter 1936: 443–45.

193 Clifton Fadiman: Alan M. Wald, *The New York Intellectuals: The Rise and Decline of the Anti-Stalinist Left from the 1930s to the 1980s* (Chapel Hill: University of North Carolina Press, 1987) 49.

193 "The glamour which Miss Boyle casts": Rev. of *Death of a Man, Times Literary Supplement* 3 October 1936: 788.

193 See "Nazi Idyll," rev. of *Death of a Man, Time* 12 October 1936: 87.

193 "to hypnotize the reader": Mark Van Doren, "Under the Swastika," rev. of *Death of a Man, Nation* rpt. in *The Private Reader* 241–44.

193 "case for the Nazi spirit": Otis Ferguson, "The Brown Blouses of Vienna," rev. of *Death of a Man, New Republic* 21 October 1936: 322.

193 "the impulses that have driven so many plain folk": Alfred Kazin, "Kay Boyle's New Novel," rev. of *Death of a Man, New York Times Book Review* 11 October 1936: 8.

194 "agonized American girl": KB interview with Erik Bauersfeld for KPFA.

194 "that virtuous American woman stalking": KB interview with Kay Bonetti, 1985.

194 "sympathetic to the Nazis!": KB interview with JM, August 1987, and Susan Hager interview with JM, 6 June 1988.

194 "the true artist": Katherine Evans Boyle quoted in KB to Sandra Whipple Spanier, 4 June 1981, KBP.

12. KITZBÜHEL-DEVON-MÉGÈVE

195 "I would not give in": Laurence Vail, *Here Goes*, unpublished memoir, c. 1945. Courtesy of Kathe Vail.

195 "She said 'his father' ": Kay Boyle, *Monday Night* (1938; Mamaroneck, NY: Paul P. Appel, 1977). All subsequent references are to this edition.

195 "my first legitimate child": KB to "Dearest Robos," 3 March 1935, RCBP.

195 "Kay and I are not professional typists": KB interview with Charles Amirkhanian.

196 "all their many little daughters": Guggenheim, *Out of This Century* 144.

196 "I want to become a boarder": Sharon Cowling interview with JM, June 1990.

196 "a good place for work": KB to Robert McAlmon, 26 October 1935, Beinecke Library.

196 Kay was convinced that because they had rented: KB to Robert McAlmon, 26 October 1935, Beinecke Library: "Having a house here, one is expected to be a millionaire at the least."

196 "always avoided them": Ibid.

196 "the utter dullness": Ibid.

196 "Life's too short": Ibid.

196 "livable place": Ibid.

196 "typewriter ribbon is soaking": KB to Joan Boyle, 2 October 1935.

196 For an account of the card game Family, see the papers of Kay Boyle, undated reminiscences, BERG: "Laurence and I and the children were playing cards. It was a game we had invented called 'Family.' " See also Katherine Evans Boyle to Alfred Stieglitz, 13 February 1936, ASP.

196 "It is good for me": Katherine Evans Boyle to Alfred Stieglitz, 13 February 1936, ASP.

196 "Christopher": Kay Boyle, "Education," *New Yorker* 17 October 1936: 23–24.

197 "Let's save him": Kay Boyle, "Declaration for 1955," *Nation* 29 January 1955: 102–4.

197 "the wonderful home": Howard Peterson Boyle to Joan Boyle, 26 September 1935, KBP.

197 "desperate that I cannot be generous as I want to be": KB to Joan Boyle, 2 October 1935, KBP.

197 Laurence would never recover: Kathe Vail interviews with JM.

197 "snow and sports": KB to Robert McAlmon, 17 January 1936, Beinecke Library.

197–98 "the lily-souled Emanuel": Ezra Pound to Harriet Monroe, 24 October 1931, in Pound, *The Letters of Ezra Pound* 228.

198 the "instrument": Ezra Pound to KB, 3 December 1935, Beinecke Library.

198 "the same bank swine who have been starving England": Ibid.

198 "The sanctions thing is part of the whole, filthy scheme": KB to Ezra Pound, 8 December 1935, Beinecke Library.

198 "this pederast": KB to Ezra Pound, 21 April 1936, Beinecke Library.

198 "Good God, haven't we all had them?": KB to Ezra Pound, 10 June 1936, Beinecke Library.

198 twenty-nine different types of hors d'oeuvres: KB to "Dearest Browns," 19 February 1937, RCBP.
198 "a consummate artist": Nathan L. Rothman, "Kay Boyle's Stories," rev. of *The White Horses of Vienna, Saturday Review of Literature* 8 February 1936: 6.
198 "sea bird": Archibald MacLeish, "The Lost Speakers (For Kay Boyle)," *Saturday Review of Literature* 8 February 1936: 6.
199 "at her near-best": Edith H. Walton, "Kay Boyle's Stories," rev. of *The White Horses of Vienna, New York Times Book Review* 9 February 1936: 7.
199 "most interesting": Harlan Hatcher, *Creating the Modern American Novel* (New York: Russell & Russell, 1935) 258–60.
199 "blush with shame": KB to Evelyn Scott, 7 June 1936, HRHRC.
199 "Helpmeets": See Margaret Lawrence, *The School of Femininity: A Book For and About Women As They Are Interpreted Through Feminine Writers of Yesterday and Today* (1936; Port Washington, NY: Kennikat Press, 1966).
199 "I am not a Communist": KB to James Laughlin, 12 May 1936.
199 "the prevalent Red fad": KB to Robert McAlmon, 31 May 1936, Beinecke Library.
199 "useless": See Richard Drinnon, *Rebel in Paradise: A Biography of Emma Goldman* (Chicago: University of Chicago Press, 1961) 299. See also Alexander Berkman to Emma Goldman, 23 March 1936, in Drinnon, *Nowhere at Home* 257: "I have lived my life and I am really of the opinion that when one has neither health nor means and cannot work for his ideas, it is time to clear out."
200 "rage against such Communists as Bob Brown": KB to Robert McAlmon, 31 May 1936, Beinecke Library.
200 "perfectly sound": Ibid.
200 "I just don't believe": Ibid.
200 "miserly" Uncle George Vail: KB to "Dearest People" [Bob Brown], 14 October 1938, RCBP.
200 "a country housewife": KB to Robert McAlmon, 31 May 1936, Beinecke Library.
200 "Yes, Kline": See Laurence Vail, *Here Goes.*
201 "How could she": Ibid.
201 She longed to knock: Ted Goeser telephone interviews with JM, 12 March 1991 and 16 March 1991.
201 "that one woman in ten": Vail, *Here Goes.*
201 "fed up with mountain climbing": Jacqueline Ventadour Hélion interview with JM, June 1990.
202 "Use your imagination!" Faith Gude interview with JM, December 1989.
202 "Child, thou art loving": For copies of the *Vails' Family Almanach*, see KBP.
203 "See, you did sleep": Jacqueline Ventadour Hélion interview with JM, June 1990.
203 "They're the happiest family": Ibid.
203 "Pegeen can scarcely spell her own name": KB to "Dearest People" [Bob Brown], 14 October 1938, RCBP.
204 "for rain": KB to James Laughlin, 6 August 1938.
204 For Kay Boyle's "A Complaint for M and M" (Mary Reynolds and Marcel Duchamp), see *transition* 27 (Spring 1938) 34–40.
204 her efficiency annoyed her husband: James Stern interview with JM, June 1990.
204 "worshipper of Poe": Laura Riding, "Jamais Plus," *transition* 7 (October 1927) 141.
204 "vindicative [sic] bitch": KB to William Carlos Williams, 19 January 1939, Beinecke Library.
205 savage absent friends: Jacqueline Ventadour Hélion interview with JM, November 1991.
205 "Oh, it was nothing": Ibid.
205 "I was the only bastard": Sharon Cowling interview with JM, June 1990.
205 all she found to praise was their appearance: Ibid.
206 "such a slender, fastidious looking person": Katherine Evans Boyle to Joan Boyle, 5 February 1939, KBP.
206 "how I can get rid of Tania": Katherine Evans Boyle to Joan Boyle, 5 February 1939, KBP.
206 "Do you know Henry Miller?": David Gascoyne, *Paris Journal 1937–39* (London: Enitharmon Press, 1978) 106.
206 "To grow old is the greatest horror": Katherine Evans Boyle to Joan Boyle, 5 February 1939, KBP.
206 "feigned an affectionate nature": Cited in Andrew Field, *The Formidable Miss Barnes* (Austin: University of Texas Press, 1985) 157. See also Gascoyne, *Paris Journal.*
206 "Maidened by constant springtime": Kay Boyle, "Angels for Djuna Barnes," *Delta* 2 (April 1938) 3–4.

206 "inexpressive": Anaïs Nin, *The Diary of Anaïs Nin*, Vol. 3: *1939–1944*, ed. Gunther Stuhlmann (New York: Harcourt Brace Jovanovich, 1969) 158.
206 "to join or enter": KB interview with Hugh Ford, 1978.
207 "Not girls or men": Kay Boyle, "A Communication to Nancy Cunard," *New Republic* 9 June 1937: 126–27.
207 "Sanger's circus": See Margaret Kennedy, *The Constant Nymph* (New York: A. L. Burt–Doubleday, 1925) 3.
207 "She gave us symbols": Kathe Vail interview with JM, June 1990.
207 "vivid little face": Yvonne Hagen interview with JM, 15 November 1990.
207–8 incidents of Apple's feeling abandoned in Mégève: Ted Goeser telephone interviews with JM, 12 March 1991 and 16 March 1991. Also KB interview with Hugh Ford, 1978.
208 "Tyrolean Gretchen": Vail, *Here Goes.*
208 "your father": Sharon Cowling interview with JM, June 1990.
208 "inferiority complex": James Stern interview with JM, June 1990.
208 "One galaxy after another": Kathe Vail interview with JM, June 1990.
209 Grandma Coco hangs cellophane stockings with money: Sharon Cowling interview with JM, June 1990, and Kathe Vail interview with JM, June 1990.
209 It's because I'm not a Vail: Sharon Cowling interview with JM, June 1990.
209 Laurence threw a full-scale tantrum: Kathe Vail interview with JM, June 1990.

13. "DOSTOIEVSKY IN A SKI SUIT"

210 "Liked him more than I ever have": KB to James Laughlin, 16 September 1938.
210 "self-control was never my forte": Vail, *Here Goes.*
210 "I always take my husband's judgment on wines": See the book jacket of the British edition of *The White Horses of Vienna* (London: Faber and Faber, 1937).
210 "If she does things so well": Vail, *Here Goes.*
210 "She's a writing machine": James and Tania Stern interview with JM, June 1990. See also Vail, *Here Goes*: "She'll write on two chairs, or in bed even, this typewriter digging into her stomach, so close down to her work sometimes that the paper must tickle her in the chin."
210 "romantic novels": See Vail, *Here Goes*: "She liked living in the country, didn't care much what sort of country so long as she had time to pound out her romantic novels on the typewriter."
211 "just a whiff": Ibid.
211 Peggy's "peddling": Ibid. Vail talks of Peggy doing "what she liked best . . . peddling," and calls her "Pigeon Peddleheim."
211 Kay compared herself to the mother in D. H. Lawrence's story: KB to Joan Boyle Detweiler, 18 April 1939, KBP.
211 For the scene with the jam, toast, and tea: Yvonne Hagen interview with JM, 15 November 1990.
211 Kay locked herself in the bathroom: Faith Gude interview with JM, December 1989.
212 "depressing little place": *BGT* 297.
212 Kay Boyle's debate with James Joyce: James Joyce to "Dear Mrs. Vail" [Kay Boyle], 1 September 1937, KBP.
212 He had sexual intercourse with the corpse: KB interview with JM, August 1987.
212 "effectively do what the other systems have not done": KB to James Laughlin, 12 May 1936.
212 "one can see only the rich Jews": KB to Joan Boyle Detweiler, 29 June 1938, KBP.
212 "the Japanese are justified": KB interview with the Federal Bureau of Investigation in 1943. See FBI file 151-2369, Kay Boyle Franckenstein.
212 "loved him except the professional anti-fascists": James Laughlin to KB, 9 June 1939.
213 "Just a few straight words from you": KB to Ezra Pound, 5 November 1938, Beinecke Library.
213 "appalled" by his views: FBI file 151-2369.
213 "almost hysterical on the subject of the international Jewish conspiracy": KB interview with Charles Amirkhanian, 1971.
213 "I disliked him then": KB lecture/discussion at the San Francisco State University Poetry Center, 11 February 1987.
213 "I'll feel obliged": James Laughlin to KB, 6 April 1939, KBP.
213 "alters every feeling": KB to James Laughlin, 26 April 1939.
213 "blue maternity gown": Gascoyne, *Paris Journal* 106.
213 "If he hasn't a son": Kay Boyle, "The Bridegroom's Body," *Southern Review* 4 (Summer 1938) 58–100.

214 "isn't too disappointed": KB to Joan Boyle Detweiler, 29 June 1938, KBP.

214 "won't have to be French": KB to "Dearest People" [Bob Brown], 14 October 1938, KBP.

214 "waiting in the garden of Eden": KB to Robert McAlmon, 18 March 1939, Beinecke Library.

214 "dying" in Cannes: KB to Robert McAlmon, 22 March 1939, Beinecke Library.

214 "writing friend": Quoted in KB to Robert McAlmon, 4 April 1939, Beinecke Library.

214 "You should never have told her": Ibid.

214 "peculiar" position: Ibid.

214 "Of course it's a girl": Ibid.

214 "hard to bear": KB to James Laughlin, 26 April 1939.

214 "luckier and had a boy": KB to Robert McAlmon, 4 April 1939, Beinecke Library.

214 "in some queer fashion": KB to Joan Boyle Detweiler, 27 June 1939, KBP.

215 "sounds manly enough": KB to Robert McAlmon, 4 April 1939, Beinecke Library.

215 "Where's the baby?": For this incident, see Clover Vail interview with JM, 20 February 1991.

215 "so many months to make up for": KB to Joan Boyle Detweiler, 30 June 1939, KBP.

215 "the women [wore] her out": KB to Joan Boyle Detweiler, 27 June 1939, KBP.

215 "making millions": KB to Joan Boyle Detweiler, 18 April 1939, KBP.

215 "sharp, icy Boston eye": See Kay Boyle, "War in Paris," *New Yorker* 26 November 1938: 18–20, and Kay Boyle, "Major Engagement in Paris," *American Mercury* August 1940: 450–56.

215 Manifesto in the *Partisan Review*: League for Cultural Freedom and Socialism, "Statement of the L.C.F.S.," *Partisan Review* 6 (Summer 1939) 125–27.

215 drafted by Leon Trotsky: George Novack interview with JM, 4 January 1991.

216 Having seen Laughlin's signature: KB to James Laughlin, 8 August 1939.

216 "in large part because I saw your name": Ibid.

216 "they're not offering me enough money": Ibid.

216 "proud and pleased": Ibid.

216 "confuse literature and party politics": John Wheelwright, "To the Editors of the 'Socialist Appeal' in *Partisan Review*," *Partisan Review* 3 (February 1938) 63.

216 "a very excellent magazine": KB to Charles Henri Ford, 23 August 1939, HRHRC.

216 "fascism as the chief enemy": League for Cultural Freedom and Socialism, "War Is the Issue!" *Partisan Review* 5 (Fall 1939) 125–27.

216 "As the war had not then been declared": Kay Boyle, "Note from Kay Boyle," with response by Dwight Macdonald, *Partisan Review* 7 (January–February 1940) 79.

217 "the general manifesto of common political aims": Ibid.

217 "the best thing I've ever done": KB to Joan Boyle Detweiler, 27 June 1939, KBP.

217 For *Three Short Novels*, see Kay Boyle, *Three Short Novels: The Crazy Hunter, The Bridegroom's Body, and Decision* (Boston: Beacon, 1958). All subsequent references are to this edition.

217 "I am sure *Monday Night*": KB to Sandra Whipple Spanier, 23 July 1981, KBP.

217 endorsement of *The Unvanquished*: See Kay Boyle, "Tattered Banners," rev. of *The Unvanquished*, by William Faulkner, *New Republic* 9 March 1938: 136–37. Reprinted: Kay Boyle, "The Unvanquished," *The Critic as Artist: Essays on Books, 1920–1970*, ed. Gilbert A. Harrison (New York: Liveright, 1972) 38–44.

217 "unhappy little stories": Kay Boyle, "Katherine Mansfield: A Reconsideration," *New Republic* 20 October 1937: 309.

217 "exceedingly": KB to Charles Henri Ford, 23 August 1939, HRHRC.

217 couldn't "see the sense": KB to Robert McAlmon, 29 May 1939, Beinecke Library.

217 "I knew how incompetent a critic he was": KB to Robert McAlmon, 18 March 1939, Beinecke Library.

218 "the greatest testing-ground": Hugh Ford, preface to Harold Stearns, *Confessions of a Harvard Man: Paris and New York in the 1920s & 30s* (Sutton West and Santa Barbara: Paget Press, 1984) xix.

218 For Kay Boyle's "Life Sentence," see *Harper's Bazaar* 71 (June 1938) 42–43, 102–7.

218 "a very grand book": Dylan Thomas to "Dear Kay Boyle," undated letter from "Blashford, Ringwood, Hants," KBP: "I thought that was a very grand book indeed, and I wrote a review of it . . . This is a fan letter. You haven't got a greater admirer than me."

218 "manikins who walk through her books": Alfred Kazin, "The Tormented People of Kay Boyle," rev. of *Monday Night*, *New York Times Book Review* 31 July 1938: 7.

218 "all the people here are from the deep fringe": Otis Ferguson, "The Lost, to the Lost," rev. of *Monday Night*, *New Republic* 3 August 1938: 369.

218 "puzzling neurotics": Rev. of *Monday Night*, *Time* 8 August 1938: 51.

219 "fragility of her themes": Philip Rahv, "Improvisations of Reality," rev. of *The Crazy Hunter: Three Short Novels, Nation* 23 March 1940: 396.

219 "hard to sell": James Laughlin to KB, 11 November 1938 [?], KBP.

219 "the most talented": Mary Colum, "Kay Boyle's Special Talents," *Forum* 150:12 (June 1940) 324.

219 Howard Nemerov remembered: Howard Nemerov interview with JM, 13 September 1990.

219 "one of the best short-story writers in America": Peter Monro Jack, rev. of *The Crazy Hunter: Three Short Novels, New York Times Book Review* 17 March 1940: 5.

219 "very beautiful indeed": Clifton Fadiman, rev. of *The Crazy Hunter: Three Short Novels, New Yorker* 4 March 1940: 76–77.

219 Apple remembered unhappily . . . "it was sexual, the way Laurence looked at us": See Weld, *Peggy* 229, 313. See also Clover Vail interviews with JM, 19 January 1991 and 20 February 1991, and Kathe Vail interviews with JM, June 1990 and November 1991.

219 "Didn't you see the way he looked at us?": Clover Vail interview with JM, 20 February 1991.

220 "never for a moment" suggested that "a lesbian affair": KB to Sandra Whipple Spanier, 20 June 1981, KBP.

221 "an aspect of love that I was never moved to experiment with": Ibid.

221 Kay Boyle, *A Glad Day and Other Poems* (Norfolk, CT: New Directions, 1938).

221 "I've truly never seen such carelessly done": KB to James Laughlin, 21 December 1937.

221 "as much as a woman can": "Nine and Two," rev. of *A Glad Day and Other Poems, Time* 26 December 1938: 41–43.

221 "great talent for language": Louise Bogan, "Verse," rev. of *A Glad Day and Other Poems, New Yorker* 22 October 1938: 83–84.

221 "Thick blood-filled livers": For Louise Bogan's parody, see *Nation* 10 December 1938.

222 "I never had an idea": KB to James Laughlin, 9 May 1938.

222 "imagist": Reuel Denny, "Fine Workmanship," rev. of *A Glad Day and Other Poems, Poetry* 54 (September 1939) 347–49.

222 "dwell on my sensibility": KB to James Laughlin, 9 May 1938.

222 "My book on flight": KB to James Laughlin, 21 December 1937.

222 For fragments of Kay Boyle's air epic, see "Two Fragments from an Aviation Epic," *Vertical: A Yearbook for Romantic-Mystic Ascensions,* ed. Eugene Jolas (New York: Gotham Book Mart Press, 1941) 20–29.

222 "born writer": Bogan, "Verse" 83–84.

222 "I simply haven't sold": KB to Joan Boyle Detweiler, 30 June 1939, KBP.

222 "for the advance": KB to Caresse Crosby, 6 May 1939, BSA.

222 "I always loathed writing novels": Ibid.

222 "cheap story": KB to "Jo Boyle" [Joan Boyle Detweiler], 27 June 1939, KBP.

222 See Kay Boyle, "How Bridie's Girl Was Won," *Harper's* 172 (March 1936) 393–400; Kay Boyle, "The King of the Philistines," *New Yorker* 13 March 1937: 22–25; and Kay Boyle, "The Herring Piece," *New Yorker* 10 April 1937: 24–28.

222 "stick to short stories": KB to "Jo Boyle" [Joan Boyle Detweiler], 27 June 1939, KBP.

222 "the magazines": Ibid.

222 "afford to put a year's labor into a novel": KB to Caresse Crosby, 19 April 1939, BSA.

222 "aviation" novelette: KB to James Laughlin, 21 December 1937. See also KB to Caresse Crosby, 19 April 1939, BSA.

223 the love between an aging mother camel: See Kay Boyle, *The Youngest Camel* (Boston: Little, Brown, 1939).

223 "a good book": Clifton Fadiman, rev. of *The Youngest Camel, New Yorker* 25 November 1939: 73.

223 "one of her failures": "Kay Boyle: Nine Years," rev. of *Monday Night, Newsweek* 1 August 1938: 29.

223 "Dostoievsky in a ski suit": Alfred Kazin, "The Tormented People of Kay Boyle," *New York Times Book Review* 31 July 1938: 7.

223 "so nice when you are sunburned": KB interview with Erik Bauersfeld and Lee Jenkins, 1975.

223 "When I like someone": KB to James Laughlin, 21 December 1937.

224 "a frail girl from Minnesota": "Kay Boyle: Nine Years," rev. of *Monday Night, Newsweek* 1 August 1938: 29.

224 "Hemingway's successor": Mary Colum, "In Favor of Best Sellers," includes rev. of *Monday Night, Forum* October 1938: 162–67.

224 "one of the few women": "Kay Boyle: Nine Years," rev. of *Monday Night, Newsweek* 1 August 1938: 29.

224 "She does not merely write": Clifton Fadiman, rev. of *The Crazy Hunter: Three Short Novels, New Yorker* 4 March 1940: 76–77.

14. BRONZED APOLLO

225 "I thought of him and I couldn't work": Kay Boyle, *Primer for Combat* (New York: Simon & Schuster, 1942) 31.

225 "The gods of the North": Van Doren, "Under the Swastika," rev. of *Death of a Man, Nation* 24 October 1936: 494.

226 "see other people's faces": Kay Boyle, "The Baron and the Chemist," *New Yorker* 26 February 1938: 19–20.

226 "enough of my life can be known through my work": KB interview with Hugh Ford, 1978.

226 "This is the way life goes on": Kay Boyle, "Anschluss," *Harper's* April 1939: 474–83.

226 "bronzed flat-bellied Apollo": Kay Boyle, *1939* (New York: Simon & Schuster, 1948) 42. All subsequent references are to this edition.

227 "You've got the legs": Yvonne Hagen interview with JM, 15 November 1990.

227 "a darling man . . . beautiful on skis": KB to James Laughlin, 26 April 1939.

228 "I shall miss her": KB to Katherine Evans Boyle, 11 February 1940, KBP.

228 "People overrate principles": Yvonne Hagen interview with JM, 15 November 1990.

228 "red ties, blue shirts": Vail, *Murder! Murder!* 151.

228 "Mooslini-Hoodini": Ibid. 23.

228 "that joke of jokes": Ibid. 197: "Where have I perceived that thin turned-up nose, those self-conscious pimples? If it isn't . . . If it isn't . . . Why it is the Individual, that joke of jokes."

228 "the Radicals, the Communists, the anarchists": Ibid.

228 "that individuals could not affect the unending cycle": Gale memoir 117.

228 "large bare posterior": Vail, *Murder! Murder!* 198.

228 "I must think of something": Ibid. 234.

229 "whores and prostitutes": See Vail, *Here Goes.*

229 it seemed to them so unjust: James and Tania Stern interview with JM, June 1990.

229 "Effortlessly": Kay Boyle, "Diplomat's Wife," *Harper's Bazaar* 73 (February 1940) 48–49, 110, 113–14, 116, 120, 122, 124.

230 Laurence was convinced that Kay did not like sex: Kathe Vail interviews with JM, June 1990 and November 1991.

230 For the scene at the Mégève pool, see Faith Gude interview with JM, December 1989.

231 "eloquent background": Kay Boyle, *Primer for Combat* 149–50.

231 "Life only seems possible in this place": KB to James Laughlin, 16 July 1939.

231 "It is interesting to be here and live through it": KB to Joan Boyle Detweiler, 15 October 1939, KBP.

231 "Half the world is ski-ing": KB to Caresse Crosby, 16 February 1940, BSA.

231 "her house, her cooking": See *John O'London's Weekly* 29 March 1940.

231 "Everything is very quiet": KB to James T. Farrell, 10 December 1939, Charles Van Pelt Library, University of Pennsylvania.

232 "sun-blacked, blond-head": Kay Boyle, "Effigy of War," *New Yorker* 25 May 1940: 17–19.

232 "monstrous charges": KB to Katherine Evans Boyle, 11 February 1940, KBP.

233 "Bored people are heavy": Vail, *Piri and I* 242.

233 Kay Boyle leaves a note on Laurence's pillow: Kathe Vail interviews with JM, June 1990 and November 1991.

233 "What's the matter with her?": Sharon Cowling interview with JM, June 1990.

233 "You know where she's gone": Ibid.

233 "You think my mother is so terrible": Ibid.

234 "Not a nation but a class has won": Kay Boyle, *Primer for Combat* 33.

234 "*un chef* . . . a direction, a faith": KB to Charles Henri Ford, 20 July 1940, HRHRC.

234 "those men who might have been expected to know": Ibid.

234 "decided to make a life together": KB to Katherine Evans Boyle, 25 June 1940, KBP.

234 "This more or less happy family life goes on": Ibid.

234 "we will have to get to America": Ibid.

234 "He is financially independent": KB to James Laughlin, 7 July 1940.

235 "the kind of life I like": KB to James Laughlin, 17 June 1940.
235 "You almost make America sound good and right": Ibid.
235 "Can't you work a miracle for me?": KB to James Laughlin, 7 July 1940.
235 "Laurence and I will take care of the money side": KB to Caresse Crosby, 26 August 1940, BSA.
235 "I'm obsessed by this matter of the civil status": KB to James Laughlin, 2 August 1940.
235 "Some country must do something": Ibid.
235 "I do feel that if anyone wants anything": Ibid.
236 "changed so much in the things I had begun to write": KB to Caresse Crosby, 26 August 1940, BSA.
236 "a lot of money—and I MUST do so": Ibid.
236 "Sindbad has never been to America": KB to James Laughlin, 2 August 1940.
236 "the one completely definite thing I know about my life": KB to Katherine Evans Boyle, 25 June 1940, KBP.

15. MY BARON

238 "It's so easy to be unselfish": KB, undated fragment, KBP.
238 "I have not the endurance for regret": Kay Boyle, *Primer for Combat* 245.
238 "change one's life every ten years": KB, reading at the San Francisco State University Poetry Center, 10 December 1975.
239 "manipulative, industrious": Frederic Morton, *A Nervous Splendor: Vienna 1888–1889* (Boston: Little, Brown, 1979) 7.
239 the "Red Baron": See FBI file 123-3915, Joseph Maria Franckenstein, document 7, November 1950: V1-15455: "In Traunregg, Austria, Subject's birthplace, Subject was called the 'Red Baron.' This was not because of communistic tendencies, but because he did not live up to the standards set by his title."
239 it was committed to strengthening Austrian independence: Testimony of Joseph Maria Franckenstein for the Hennings Committee, FBI file 123-3915, Joseph Maria Franckenstein.
239 "to arouse the Tyrolean people": Joseph Maria Franckenstein, "Curriculum Vitae," in FBI file 123-3915, Joseph Maria Franckenstein.
240 "I've never forgiven myself": George Popper interview with JM, 20 June 1988.
241 "strong man": Kay Boyle, "Men," *Harper's Bazaar* 75 (February 1941): 45, 102, 104–5. See also *Fifty Stories* 275–87.
241 "Are you still a virgin?": Weld, *Peggy* 205–7. For these scenes of the Vail children at Mégève, I am indebted to Jacqueline Weld.
241 "little whores": Apple Goeser to Kay Boyle, 4 June 1959, KBP.
242 "lily-white prince": Weld, *Peggy* 208.
242 one thing she doesn't have is a title: KB interview with JM, August 1987.
242 "guilty of certain activities": Kay Boyle, *Primer for Combat* 240.
242 "*Bleue Augen*": For this incident, see KB interview with JM, August 1987, and Sharon Cowling interview with JM, June 1990.
242 "*au revoir*": quoted in KB to Katherine Evans Boyle, 6 January 1941, KBP.
242 "The day your first letter came": This moment is rendered in Kay Boyle's diary for 1940, KBP. The diary later became the novel *Primer for Combat*. For this incident, see *Primer for Combat* 195.
243 "not to want to see things in an exalted way": KB to "Oh, darling mother" [Katherine Evans Boyle], undated letter, c. 1940, KBP.
243 "symbol, the figurehead": Ibid.
243 "the one woman . . . the one person": Ibid.
243 "this rotten, rebellious professor": Ibid.
244 "My Baron is something that scarcely ever happens": KB to "Oh, darling mother" [Katherine Evans Boyle], undated fragment, c. 1940, KBP.
244 "being gay enough and unegotistical enough": Ibid.
244 "out of white thread": Joan Boyle Detweiler to Robert McAlmon, 15 January 1941, Beinecke Library.
244 "Joseph, Joseph, won't you make up your mind?": Jacqueline Ventadour Hélion interview with JM, November 1991.
244 "impatient with his humility": Kay Boyle, *Primer for Combat* 193–94.
244 "blue with snow": Ibid. 173.

244 "I am terribly, hopelessly in love": KB to Ann Watkins, 1 April 1944, KBP.

245 "Get out. Just get out": Kathe Vail interviews with JM, June 1990 and November 1991. See also Faith Gude interviews with JM, December 1989.

245 "I cannot work": KB to Katherine Evans Boyle, 6 January 1941, KBP.

245 "This is not a breaking up": Ibid.

245 "presentable": KB to James Laughlin, 8 January 1941.

246 "What do you think of her going?": Incident recounted by Joseph Franckenstein to Kay Boyle, and quoted in KB to Katherine Evans Boyle, 6 January 1941, KBP.

246 "mad American writer": George Popper interview with JM, 20 June 1988.

246 "When I'm with you": Quoted in KB to Katherine Evans Boyle, 6 January 1941, KBP.

246 "I only know how to say 'I want' ": Ibid.

246 "proud" of her: Ibid.

246 Laurence pours glue on Kay's clothes: KB interview with JM, August 1987. See also Faith Gude interviews with JM, December 1989.

247 "a permanent and good thing for Joseph": KB to Katherine Evans Boyle, 6 January 1941, KBP.

247 "lots of material for short stories": KB to James Laughlin, 18 January 1941.

247 "so wonderfully poetical when you write": Sharon Vail to KB, 17 April 1941, KBP.

247 "ugly sad subject": Pegeen Vail to KB, 20 April 1941, KBP.

247 "Oh, Kay do come back": Ibid.

247 "that thing": Weld, *Peggy* 229.

248 "I guess there's nothing": Guggenheim, *Out of This Century* [1946 ed.] 267.

248 "She's so stupid": Sharon Vail to KB, 20 April 1941, KBP.

248 "the way she talks": Ibid.

248 "looking daggers": KB interview with JM, August 1987.

248 you could avoid the police checkpoint: Ibid.

248 Clover wouldn't understand: Kathe Vail interviews with JM, June 1990 and November 1991.

249 "The boat on which": Guggenheim, *Out of This Century* [1946 ed.] 269.

249 Laurence grabbed the marble top: KB interview with JM, August 1987.

249 "It was the only brave act": Ibid.

249 "Why must you leave me?": Ibid.

250 "I hugged my father": Kathe Vail interview with JM, June 1990.

250 The American embassy was conspiring with Vichy: Varian Fry, *Surrender on Demand* (New York: Random House, 1945).

250 "intense, emotional": Ibid. 185.

250 "undeniable form of cruelty": KB to Varian Fry, 1 May 1941, KBP.

251 "violent perfume": See Kay Boyle, "The Canals of Mars," *Harper's Bazaar* 77 (February 1943) 56–57.

16. GOING HOME

252 "She deserted a great number of children": James Stern interviews with JM, June 1990.

252 "She was a bitch to leave Papa": Kathe Vail interview with JM, June 1990.

252 "So you see even I, Bob darling": KB to Robert McAlmon, 9 August 1941, Beinecke Library.

252 The allies needing ships: Kay Boyle to Sandra Whipple Spanier, July 1981.

253 "sinus trouble": Weld, *Peggy* 234–39.

253 you could hear the sound of Laurence weeping: Jacqueline Ventadour Hélion interview with JM, June 1990. For these scenes in Lisbon, see also Laurence Vail, *Here Goes*, and Weld, *Peggy* 236 ff.

253 Kay now requested that Laurence send telegrams: Guggenheim, *Out of This Century* 277–88.

254 "high tension": Jacqueline Ventadour Hélion interview with JM, June 1990.

254 "you'll marry a nice, fat Italian cook": Kathe Vail interview with JM, June 1990.

254 "She's a monster": Sharon Cowling interview with JM, June 1990.

254 For a depiction of the Vail family boarding the Clipper to America, see Kay Boyle, "Les Six Enfants," *Harper's Bazaar* 74 (October 1941) 73, 122.

254 "You're the only mother I've ever had": KB interview with JM, August 1987.

254 she had made many people very unhappy: James Stern interview with JM, June 1990.

255 "as though she were answering a challenge": Robert Van Gelder, "Kay Boyle, Expatriate," *New York Times Book Review* 3 August 1941: 2.

255 she was writing a novel based on the lives: See "Return from France on the Maiden Voyage of the Clipper," New York *World-Telegram* 15 July 1941.

256 "Kay Boyle's Was the Largest Family": Marianne Hauser, rev. of *Primer for Combat, New York Times Book Review* 8 November 1942: 6.

256 "Story of the Family": KB notebook for 1941, KBP.

256 psychologically incapable: Jacqueline Ventadour Hélion interview with JM, June 1990.

256 "simply cannot do it": KB to Jacqueline Ventadour Hélion, 3 November 1942. Courtesy of Jacqueline Ventadour Hélion.

257 she had lost a frightened two-year-old: See Agnes Adams, "Kay Boyle and Six Children Back Home Again," *New York Post* 31 July 1941.

257 "I couldn't possibly concentrate in a dress": See Adams, "Kay Boyle and Six Children," and Robert Van Gelder, "An Interview with Kay Boyle, Expatriate," *New York Times Book Review* 3 August 1941.

257 "We'd stand in line": Van Gelder, "Kay Boyle, Expatriate." See also Adams, "Kay Boyle and Six Children Back Home Again."

258 "two-piece suit": *Town and Country* January 1942.

258 "deep in domestic smash-up": Laurence Vail to Eleanor Fitzgerald, 26 July 1941, quoted in Weld, *Peggy* 247.

258 "Djuna with her maternal quality": Vail, *Here Goes.*

258 "There was a young man from Thistlehurst": Rob Cowley interview with JM, 7 December 1990.

259 Kay withheld sex: Jacqueline Weld telephone interview with JM, 15 May 1989.

259 "last time I saw her": Muriel Cowley interview with JM, 30 July 1990.

259 "She's mine!": Kathe Vail interview with JM, June 1990.

259 "Diane wants you": Diane Vail to KB, undated letter, c. 1942, KBP.

259 there was beautiful Nancy: See Kay Boyle, "Nancy Cunard," in *Nancy Cunard: Brave Poet, Indomitable Rebel,* ed. Hugh Ford (Philadelphia: Chilton Book Co., 1968) 78–80.

259 "Régiment de Marche des Volontaires Étrangères": Hans Habeat to KB, 8 October 1941, KBP.

260 "to get a ranch": KB to Robert McAlmon, 9 August 1941, Beinecke Library.

260 "and Carlos Williams": Warren Miller to KB, December 1941, KBP.

260 "men of that tragically unarmed": Kay Boyle, "Defeat," *New Yorker* 17 May 1941: 18–22.

260 "the State Department": KB to Robert McAlmon, 6 December 1941, Beinecke Library.

260 "absolutely non-politically": KB to Bob Brown, 6 December 1941, RCBP.

260 "my talk is neither for intervention": Ibid.

261 "hating" the faces looking up at her: See diary of Kay Boyle [1941], KBP. See also KB interview with JM, August 1987, and materials shown to the author by KB.

261 "just or unjust": Kay Boyle, "Two and Carry One," *New Republic* 3 November 1941: 596.

261 "as good a set of standards": Kay Boyle, "Full Length Portrait," *New Republic* 24 November 1941: 707.

262 "see my love": KB to Bob Brown, 4 December 1941, RCBP.

262 "and he feels": KB to "My Darlings Robob, Bobro" [Bob Brown], undated letter, RCBP, KBP.

262 "keep sane": Kay Boyle, unpublished diary for 1941. Boyle records that she wrote to Joseph on December 10, telling him she realized how wrong they had been in their decision for him to go to California: "I said I could not keep sane under the present circumstances." Courtesy of Kay Boyle.

262 "I am writing hard": KB to Bob Brown, 26 November 1941, RCBP.

262 "brief, quick record": KB to Roger Burlingame, 4 January 1942, KBP.

262 "against this sort of dishing up": Statement by Kay Boyle concerning *Primer for Combat,* KBP.

262 "In case you need": Joseph Franckenstein wrote to his draft board on December 7, 1941: "In case you need my service, I am ready." The letter is found in FBI file 123-3915, Joseph Maria Franckenstein. Joseph had actually enlisted in 1941, only for his physical examination to reveal spots on his lungs. A year later he was examined again on Governors Island and pronounced physically fit for service.

262 "I hate thinking of you now, Kay": Pegeen Vail to KB, December 1941, KBP.

262 "at last accepted me": Ibid.

263 "I think of them": Nina Conarain to KB, undated note, KBP.

263 "he is—perhaps completely—a poet": KB to Caresse Crosby, 10 January 1942, BSA.

263 "hybrid ménage": Carson McCullers to Newton Arvin, c. 1941. The papers of Carson McCullers are housed at the William Allan Neilson Library, Smith College.

263 pull up her underpants: KB interview with JM, August 1987.

263 "Marcel remains for all of us": KB to Charles Henri Ford, fragment, c. 1941, HRHRC.

263 "It seems to be stupid": Charles Henri Ford to William Carlos Williams, 20 February 1942, Beinecke Library.

263 "the indignity of an immigrant's visa": KB to William Carlos Williams, 28 February 1942, Beinecke Library.

263 "one of the dearest people I have ever known": KB to Robert McAlmon, 3 November 1942, Beinecke Library.

263 "Marcel's night": KB interview with JM, August 1987.

264 *"Arrête! Arrête!"*: Kathe Vail interview with JM, June 1990.

264 one wild ride: George Popper interview with JM, 20 June 1988.

264 Bobby appreciated her mother's great abilities: Sharon Cowling interview with JM, June 1990.

264 "spelling doesn't matter": Kathe Vail interviews with JM, June 1990 and November 1991.

265 Apple never mentioned Kay to the other children: Rob Cowley interview with JM, 7 November 1990.

265 "very very nice": Kathe Vail to KB, undated letter, c. 1941, KBP.

265 "You must be so lonely": Pegeen Vail to KB, July 1942, KBP.

266 "we arrived in this huge dump": Pegeen Vail to KB, from Gaylordsville, CT, July 1942, KBP.

17. BABIES

267 "My own darling went over": KB to Robert McAlmon, 27 August 1944, Beinecke Library.

267 "artists as dissimilar": Maxine Block, ed., *Current Biography* (New York: H. W. Wilson Co., 1942) 101–2.

267 Kay Boyle's "The Ten Books Which Have Most Influenced Me" may be found in BERG.

268 "propaganda bit": KB to Robert McAlmon, 18 September 1942, Beinecke Library.

268 "pretty broke": KB to James Laughlin, 22 April 1942.

268 "Typing like mad": KB to Caresse Crosby, 15 September 1942, BSA.

268 "policy of appeasement": Kay Boyle, letter, "Dossier on Pétain," *Nation* 16 December 1944: 750.

268 evenhanded review: See Kay Boyle, "Hollywood Paris," rev. of *The Last Time I Saw Paris*, by Elliot Paul, *Nation* 25 April 1942: 490–91.

268 "the worst book ever written": KB to Robert McAlmon, 3 November 1942, Beinecke Library.

268 "unmistakeably . . . exciting accents of truth": Kay Boyle, "The Steel of Victory," rev. of *The Edge of the Sword*, by Vladimir Pozner, *Nation* 23 May 1942: 604–5.

268 "heedless little volume": Kay Boyle, "Occupied France," rev. of *First Harvest*, by Vladimir Pozner, *New York Times Book Review* 2 May 1943: 18.

269 "courage, of unshaken loyalty": Kay Boyle, "The Fall of France," rev. of *A French Officer's Diary*, by D. Barlone, *New York Times Book Review* 30 May 1943: 5, 17.

269 "the cautious subtleties of Gide": Kay Boyle, "The Jew Is a Myth," rev. of *Stepchildren of France*, by Charles Jean Odic, *Nation* 13 October 1945: 368, 372. This review also may be found in Kay Boyle, *Words That Must Somehow Be Said: The Selected Essays of Kay Boyle*, ed. Elizabeth Bell (London: Chatto & Windus–Hogarth Press, 1985) 162. All subsequent references are to this edition.

269 she fell short: See Kay Boyle, "A 'Good' German in a Poetic Setting," rev. *The Silence of the Sea*, by Vercors (Jean Bruller), *New York Times Book Review* 27 February 1944: 12.

269 "uncompromising patriots": Kay Boyle, "Biography of a Misunderstood Leader," rev. of *The Truth About De Gaulle*, by André Riveloup, *New York Times Book Review* 23 July 1944: 7.

269 "not a Frenchman": Kay Boyle, "The French Retreat," rev. of *War Diary*, by Jean Malaquais, *New York Times Book Review* 6 February 1944: 12.

269 See Kay Boyle, "The New Novels," rev. of *The Real Life of Sebastian Knight*, by Vladimir Nabokov, *New Republic* 26 January 1942: 124–25. This article also contains reviews of the following: Hilda Abel, *Victory Was Slain*; Arthur Meeker, Jr., *The Ivory Mischief*; Upton Sinclair, *Dragon's Teeth*.

269 Kay reviewed friends: See Kay Boyle, "The Poetry of Walter Mehring," rev. of *No Road Back*, by Walter Mehring, *New York Times Book Review* 3 September 1944: 4.

269 "The Austrian aristocracy": Kay Boyle, "The New Novels," *New Republic* 26 January 1942: 124–25.

270 "their attack on popular prejudice": Ibid.

270 "imaginary people": Kay Boyle, "Elizabeth Bowen," rev. of *Bowen's Court* (and, in passing, *To the North, House in Paris, Death of the Heart*, and *Look at All Those Roses*), by Elizabeth Bowen, *New Republic* 21 September 1942: 355–56.

270 "just a simple party": KB to Caresse Crosby, 17 August 1942, BSA.

270 "wild" to join him: KB to James Laughlin, 29 October 1942.

270 "damnable" serial: Ibid.

270 "Always coming out smelling like a rose": Letter from Kathe Vail to JM, 26 December 1990. See also Clover Vail interviews with JM, 19 January 1991 and 20 February 1991.

271 "incisive portrait of France": Marianne Hauser, "Kay Boyle's *Primer for Combat*," rev. of *Primer for Combat, New York Times Book Review* 8 November 1942: 6.

271 "nothing better has been written on France": Raoul de Roussy de Sales, rev. of *Primer for Combat, Atlantic* December 1942: 152.

271 "the cold determined need": KB to Josephine Herbst, 16 December 1942, Beinecke Library.

271 "again the bird profile": Anaïs Nin, *The Diary of Anaïs Nin*, Vol. 3: *1939–1944*, ed. Gunther Stuhlmann (New York: Harcourt Brace Jovanovich, 1969) 158.

271 "I want a son so badly": KB to James Laughlin, 29 October 1942.

271 "pray for a boy": KB to Robert McAlmon, 3 November 1942, Beinecke Library.

271 "Think of it!": Carson McCullers to Kay Boyle, 3 December 1942, Smith College.

271 "*so* nice": Weld, *Peggy* 314.

271 "That's a long-distance call!": Ibid.

271 no saint had ever been named Fay: Faith Gude interview with JM, December 1989.

272 "Incredible as it may seem": KB to James Laughlin, 6 December 1942.

272 "I'm counting on her": Ibid.

272 "let me love you always": Carson McCullers to KB, 3 December 1942, KBP.

272 "I think it very beautiful": KB to Alfred Kreymborg, 17 March 1942. The Alfred Kreymborg papers are housed by the libraries of the University of Virginia.

272 For Sharon Vail, *Four Poems* (Gemor Press of New York: Christmas, 1942), see KBP.

273 "Laurence would *want* to": KB to Robert McAlmon, 18 February 1943, Beinecke Library.

273 asked Bob Brown to mail some of her letters: KB to Bob Brown, 18 January 1943, RCBP.

273 "fully legitimate": See KB to Bob Brown, 13 January 1943, RCBP, and KB to Bob Brown 18 January 1943. See also KB to Joan [Boyle] Detweiler, 7 February 1943, KBP.

273 "love and confidence in me": Sharon Vail to KB, 26 January 1943, KBP.

273 "I don't think many people have such mothers as you": Sharon Vail to KB, 1 February 1943, KBP.

273 "marvellous brilliant lady": Ibid.

273 "I'm glad you're coming out on top": Katherine Evans Boyle to KB, quoted in KB to "Jo" [Joan Boyle Detweiler], "Saturday Morning," from Reno [1943], KBP.

273 "by typing until three in the morning": Ibid.

273 "please to pay": KB to Joan Boyle Detweiler, 9 February 1943, KBP.

274 "for an instant": KB to Robert McAlmon, 7 February 1943, Beinecke Library.

274 "it's such a relief to have you here": KB interview with Kay Bonetti, 1985.

274 "my biddy": KB to Joan Boyle Detweiler, 7 February 1943, KBP.

274 For all references to the FBI's investigation of Kay Boyle, see FBI file 151-2369, Kay Boyle Franckenstein, available from the Department of Justice under the Freedom of Information Act.

274 "She has the loveliest nature of any child": KB to Joan Boyle Detweiler, 9 February 1943, KBP.

275 "What the hell is this?": Quoted in KB to "Darling Jo" [Joan Boyle Detweiler], "Saturday Morning. Later" [1942 or 1943], KBP.

275 "her husband, like mine": See Kay Boyle, *American Citizen: Naturalized in Leadville, Colorado* (New York: Simon & Schuster, 1944).

275 "Kay, you have more life": Carson McCullers to KB, 2 April 1943, KBP.

275 Katherine sets her hat on fire: See KB to Joan Boyle Detweiler, "Sunday" [24? May 1943], KBP.

276 "take charge": Ibid.

276 "Mother has been incredibly selfish": KB to Joan Boyle Detweiler, 10 July 1943, KBP.

276 "write to Julia about the church's": Ibid.

276 "Is Kay anything like her?": KB to Joan Boyle Detweiler, "Sunday" [24? May 1943], KBP.

276 sharing a house in Carmel: Eva Mayer interview with JM, 1987.

276 found in his happiness: For a description of Joseph Franckenstein in the Aleutian Islands, see "Extracts from Letter of Burton Pierce," June 1944, KBP.

277 they had been cautioned not to touch: Clover Vail interview with JM, 20 February 1991.

277 "talented mother": See *Harper's Bazaar* November 1943.

277 small penis: Weld, *Peggy* 313.

277 For an account of Pegeen in Mexico, see ibid., 318–19.

278 "I am willing to accept any mission": Joseph Franckenstein's application to the OSS found in FBI file 123-3915.

278 "mixing up of people": Kay Boyle, "World Harmony," *Saturday Evening Post* 23 October 1943: 4. For Kay Boyle's *Avalanche*, see *Avalanche: A Novel of Love and Espionage* (New York: Simon & Schuster, 1944). All subsequent references are to this edition.

278 "mother of several children": Biographical note on Kay Boyle contained in the archives of *Story* magazine, Princeton University Library.

278 "Making yourself free": KB to Pegeen Vail, 18 January 1944, KBP.

279 "the most revolting sight I have ever seen": KB to Joan Boyle Detweiler, 11 March 1944, KBP.

279 For an account of Kay Boyle's life in Colorado, see KB interview with Kay Bonetti, 1985.

280 "I suppose you are too busy": Apple Vail to KB, undated letter, KBP.

280 "I wish I could hear your voice": Apple Vail to KB, undated letter. KBP.

280 "fiendish": Sharon Vail to KB, 11 March 1944, KBP.

280 "Diane just kissed you": Kathe Vail to KB, undated letter, KBP.

281 Kay Boyle's miscarriage in New York: Kathe Vail interviews with JM, June 1990 and November 1991. See also Faith Gude interview with JM, December 1989.

281 certain that her doctor was in love with her: Faith Gude interview with JM, December 1989.

281 For documents of the OSS investigation, see FBI file 151-2369, Joseph Maria Franckenstein.

281 He looks just like Kay: Nina Conarain to KB, 22 August 1944, KBP.

282 "He's the most comfortable understanding person": Ibid.

282 who marveled at how serene: Telephone interview with Natalia Murray, 1991.

282 "moral courage to a degree": Unpublished memoir written in 1976 for Roy Simmonds, who was embarking on a biography of Bill March, BERG.

282 For the evening with Mr. Kantor, see FBI file 151-2369, Kay Boyle Franckenstein, and the sworn statement of Kay Boyle Franckenstein, dated 6 July 1954 and addressed to Mr. John W. Sipes, Security Counsel, Department of State.

282 "a worse bitch": KB to Robert McAlmon, 27 August 1944, Beinecke Library.

283 "the moral fiber of the French people": Kay Boyle, letter, "Canard by Cannell," *Nation* 23 September 1944: 363.

283 "about the gremlins": KB to Robert McAlmon, 27 August 1944, Beinecke Library.

283 surreal department-store mirrors: See Kay Boyle, "Battle of the Sequins," *Nation* 23 December 1944: 770–71. Kay Boyle's "Vocabulary of Courage" appeared in *Harper's Bazaar* October 1944: 65.

283 For the account of "Laurence's tragedy," see Kathe Vail interviews with JM, June 1990 and November 1991. See also Faith Gude interview with JM, December 1989.

18. SIMULATED CAPTAIN

284 "I hope my dreams will sometime leave me": Joseph Franckenstein to KB, 19 June 1945, included in KB to Robert McAlmon, 19 July 1945, Beinecke Library.

284 "I picked out Kay Boyle's *Avalanche*": Edmund Wilson, "Kay Boyle and *The Saturday Evening Post*," *New Yorker* 15 January 1944: 66 +. All subsequent references are to this article.

284 were so upset: Kathe Vail interviews with JM, June 1990 and November 1991.

284 taught how to salute: KB interview with JM, August 1987.

285 "How in the world did we get on the side of authority?": Brenda Wineapple, *Genêt: A Biography of Janet Flanner* (New York: Ticknor & Fields, 1989) 233.

285 "*Bon soir*": KB interview with Hugh Ford, 1978.

285 "but you can't sit at this table": KB interview with JM, August 1987.

285 entire French nation with contempt: Gale memoir 119.

285 "He deserved better": *BGT* 312.

285 she suddenly needed a toilet: KB interview with JM, August 1987.

285 Boostie had no idea: KB to Frances Steloff, 19 April 1945, BERG: "My son did not know me for about 24 hours."

286 For the accounts of Joseph's exploits during his missions for the OSS, see FBI file 123-3915, Joseph Maria Franckenstein, and KB interview with JM, August 1987. See also Donald Muntz telephone interviews with JM, 6 June and 12 June 1989, and Ian Franckenstein interview with JM, August 1987. See also Joseph E. Persico, *Piercing the Reich: The Penetration of Nazi Germany by American Secret Agents During World War II* (New York: Viking, 1979).

286 with fellow OSS officer Fritz Molden: See Fritz Molden, *Exploding Star: A Young Austrian Against Hitler* (London: Weidenfeld & Nicolson, 1978).
286 "You too?" Donald Muntz telephone interviews with JM, 6 June and 12 June 1989.
286 *"Das Schwein ist tot"*: KB interview with JM, August 1987.
288 "bringing all the babes along": Joseph Franckenstein to KB, 19 June 1945, Beinecke Library.
288 "the answer . . . to all our hopes": KB to Caresse Crosby, 21 April 1945, BSA.
288 "Tell Sartre not to come": KB interview with JM, August 1987, and Kathe Vail interviews with JM, June 1990 and November 1991.
289 For Kay Boyle's two articles for "How America Lives," see Kay Boyle, "Family with Nine Kids," *Ladies' Home Journal* March 1946: 165–70, and Kay Boyle, "Meet a United Nations Family in the U.S.A.," *Ladies' Home Journal* December 1946: 181–86.
289 "I can't afford it": Sharon Cowling interview with JM, June 1990.
290 "deliberately turned your face": Carson McCullers to Newton Arvin, 16 September 1946, Smith College.
290 "with babes, animals": KB to Robert McAlmon, 19 July 1945, Beinecke Library.
290 "too good to lose": Vail, *Here Goes*. For scenes at Truro, see Vail, *Here Goes*, and Kathe Vail interviews with JM, June 1990 and November 1991.
290 "She's the only wife": Vail, *Here Goes*.
290 *coup de foudre*: Jacqueline Ventadour Hélion interviews with JM, June 1990 and November 1991.
290 "Run over and hug him": Faith Gude interviews with JM, December 1989.
290 "an important role in postwar reconstruction": Douglas Gilbert, "Ski Trooper Husband Aided Kay Boyle's Book," New York *World-Telegram* 24 August 1944.
291 Kay Boyle's potboilers: See Kay Boyle, "Frenchman's Ship," *Saturday Evening Post* 21 November 1942: 14–15; Kay Boyle, "The Ships Going to Glory," *Saturday Evening Post* 5 August 1944: 26–27, 62, 64, 66; and Kay Boyle, "The Last Aviator Left Flying," *American Magazine* December 1943: 44–45, 114–18.
291 A young American woman: See Kay Boyle, "Listen, Munich," *New Yorker* 19 August 1939: 17–19. Reprinted: *John O'London's Weekly* 15 September 1939: 793–94.
291 "if there was going to be a war": Kay Boyle, "Wanderer," *Accent* 2 (Winter 1942) 85–91.
291 *chair à canon*: See Kay Boyle, "They Weren't Going to Die," *New Yorker* 12 October 1940: 21–22.
291 class loyalties forged: See Kay Boyle, "Hilaire and the Maréchal Pétard," *Harper's* 185 (August 1942) 284–96.
291 "the tattered, exiled army of despair": Kay Boyle, "Let There Be Honour," *Saturday Evening Post* 8 November 1941: 12–13, 104–5, 107.
291 Kay Boyle, "Poor Monsieur Panalitus," *New Yorker* 20 January 1940: 19–22; Kay Boyle, "Their Name Is Macaroni," *New Yorker* 3 January 1942: 16–19; and Kay Boyle, "This They Carried With Them," *Harper's Bazaar* 75 (October 1942): 100–1, 136–38.
291 "I couldn't believe": Kay Boyle, "Let There Be Honour."
292 "Some were written for love": Kay Boyle, "Foreword," *Thirty Stories* (New York: Simon & Schuster, 1946).
292 See Kay Boyle, "Nothing Ever Breaks Except the Heart," *New Yorker* 4 October 1941: 18–21.
292 privileged little American girl: Kay Boyle, "Winter Night," *New Yorker* 19 January 1946: 19–23.
292 jingoistic pieces: See Kay Boyle, "The Little Distance," *Saturday Evening Post* 6 March 1943: 22–23, 74 +, and Kay Boyle, "Luck for the Road," *Woman's Home Companion* 71 (January 1944) 17, 38, 40, 42, 45.
292 "We need you": Kay Boyle, "Hotel Behind the Lines," *Nation* 9 June 1945: 642–45.
292 archly romanticized: See Kay Boyle, "The Canals of Mars," *Harper's Bazaar* 77 (February 1943) 56–57.
293 for Jean Gabin: KB to Caresse Crosby, 17 August 1942, BSA.
293 "Bobby and I worship him beyond measure": Pegeen Vail to KB, 14 July 1942, KBP.
293 "this blasted serial": KB to Bob Brown, 18 January 1943, RCBP.
293 "stop being a precious, careful writer": Ibid.
293 "dragged him in every twenty pages": KB interview with Dan Tooker.
294 "written with greater simplicity": KB to Ann Davidon, 17 June 1987, presented to the author courtesy of Kay Boyle.
294 "not for an instant 'propaganda' ": Ibid.
294 See Kay Boyle, *A Frenchman Must Die* (New York: Simon & Schuster, 1946). All subsequent references are to this edition.

295 "the intellectual": Bernardine Kielty, "Under Cover Stuff: Kay Boyle's New Novel," rev. of *A Frenchman Must Die, Ladies' Home Journal* March 1946: 5.
295 "with an eye to the demands of Hollywood": Edmund Wilson, "Kay Boyle and *The Saturday Evening Post*," *New Yorker* 15 January 1944: 66+.
296 "italicized passages": Diana Trilling, "Fiction in Review," *Nation* 22 January 1944: 105.
296 "Pot-Boyler," rev. of *Avalanche, Time* 17 January 1944: 357.
296 "a person like Miss Boyle hasn't a right": Struthers Burt, "Kay Boyle's Coincidence and Melodrama," *Saturday Review of Literature* 15 January 1944: 6.
296 likened Kay Boyle to romance writers: Catherine Maher, "Alpine Adventure," rev. of *Avalanche, New York Times Book Review* 16 January 1944: 4.
296 Gary Cooper rather than Charles Boyer: See Kate O'Brien, "Fiction," *Spectator* 22 December 1944: 584.
296 "while she can understand people seeking escapist": Gilbert, "Ski Trooper Husband Aided Kay Boyle's Book."
296 "plain melodrama": Burt, "Kay Boyle's Coincidence and Melodrama."
296 "clichés": Laurence Lee, "Manhunt," rev. of *A Frenchman Must Die, New York Times Book Review* 7 April 1946: 43.
296 "very slight": Rev. of *A Frenchman Must Die, Booklist* April 1946: 247.
296 "one of the best": Struthers Burt, "The Mature Craft of Kay Boyle," rev. of *Thirty Stories, Saturday Review of Literature* 30 November 1946: 11.
296 "unmistakeable honesty": Edith R. Mirrielees, "Stories to Remember," rev. of *Thirty Stories, New York Times Book Review* 1 December 1946: 9, 72.
296 See Margery Barrett, "Tour in Technicolor," rev. of *Thirty Stories, New Masses* 31 December 1946: 23–24. All subsequent references are to this article.
297 "fishermen, soldiers": Kay Boyle, letter, *New Masses* 15 April 1947: 21–22. See also Margery Barrett's "Reply to Kay Boyle" in the same issue.
298 "how all that was simple": KB to Sandra Whipple Spanier, 4 June 1981, KBP.
298 "exceedingly stupid": KB to Sandra Whipple Spanier, 27 July 1981, KBP. See p. 22 of this long letter, which continues over several dates.
298 "was simply not literature": Ibid.
298 "without apology": KB to Sandra Whipple Spanier, 20 June 1981, p. 11 of the continuing letter, KBP.
299 "dry-as-dust intellectual": KB to Ann Davidon, 17 June 1987.

19. FOREIGN CORRESPONDENT

300 "some bright beautiful herald": Kathryn Hulme to KB, 26 January 1947, sent from Wildflecken, KBP.
300 "a good person to remember": Bernardine Kielty, "Under Cover Stuff: Kay Boyle's New Novel."
300 "undefiled": KB to James Laughlin, 24 May 1946.
300 "If a political man no longer stands": Kay Boyle, "Farewell to New York," *Nation* 8 March 1947: 271–72.
301 Joseph plays "Touchy": Kathe Vail interviews with JM, June 1990 and November 1991.
301 "Poor man": Ibid.
301 "fiction out of Germany": See Kay Boyle's dedication to Harold Ross in *The Smoking Mountain* (New York: McGraw-Hill, 1951).
301 "Oh, Mama's Kleenexes!": Apple Vail to KB, undated letter, KBP.
301 she must burn all of Kurt Wick's letters: Clover Vail interview with JM, 19 January 1991.
301 "reconstruction of Democratic Germany": FBI file 123-3915, Joseph Maria Franckenstein. See Walter R. Owens, "To whom it may concern," 14 April 1947, "Training Unit: Group 'B' 7742: Civil Censorship Division, European Command."
302 "strong feelings" about the German people: KB to Sandra Whipple Spanier, 27 July 1981, KBP.
302 "cowboy outfit": Eugene Jolas, "Kay Boyle, Journalist," *New York Times Book Review* 24 November 1946: 8.
302 For Kay Boyle's life at the Hôtel de France et Choiseul, see KB to Ann Watkins, 27 November 1946, KBP.
302 "I want to go home": KB interview with JM, August 1987.
303 "exploited, betrayed": *BGT* 313.
303 Kay was stunned: KB interview with Hugh Ford, 1978, and KB interview with JM, August 1987.

303 poor Clover struggling: Clover Vail interviews with JM, 19 January 1991 and 20 February 1991.
303 "the German bitterness": Kay Boyle, 27 March 1947, notebook for 1947, KBP.
304 "If you knew me": See Kathryn Hulme to KB, 26 January 1947, and Kathryn Hulme to KB, 22 March 1947, both from Wildflecken, KBP. See also Kay Boyle, "Monument to Hitler," *Nation* 12 April 1947: 417–19.
304 "unaccompanied children": Kathryn Hulme to KB, 22 September 1946, KBP.
304 "revolutionize" the world: Jolas, "Kay Boyle, Journalist."
304 See Kay Boyle, "The Lost," *Tomorrow* March 1951: 10–17.
304 "I'll simply die": Kathryn Hulme to "My darlings," sent from Wildflecken, 26 January 1947.
304 "Nazism has not been destroyed": Kay Boyle, "Monument to Hitler."
304 "very like Alexander Berkman": KB to Nancy Cunard, 16 March 1947, HRHRC.
305 See Kay Boyle, "Isabelita Has Lost Her Reason," *Nation* 24 May 1947: 628–29, and Kay Boyle, "Faces of Spain," *Nation* 12 July 1947: 35–38.
305 See Kay Boyle, "Decision," in *Three Short Novels* 211–62. "Decision" was originally published as "Passport to Doom," *Saturday Evening Post* 15 May 1948: 20 +.
305 her "own to write": KB to Ann Watkins, 22 June 1947, KBP.
305 "one of the most interesting things I have written": KB to Ann Watkins, 16 June 1947, KBP.
305 Kay Boyle at her sister Joan's New Jersey farm: Kay Boyle, "Miracle Goat," *Woman's Home Companion* January 1947: 25, 83–85. See also Susan Hager interview with JM, 6 June 1988.
305 See Kay Boyle, "One Small Diamond, Please," *Woman's Home Companion* August 1947: 22, 113, 115–17; Kay Boyle, "The Searching Heart," *Woman's Home Companion* January 1948: 18–19, 66, 69, 71; and Kay Boyle, "Dream Dance," *Saturday Evening Post* 13 December 1947: 32–33, 139 +.
305 Kay Boyle, "Evening at Home," *New Yorker* 9 October 1948: 26–32.
306 "didn't want to take a chance": Harold Ross to KB, 16 June 1947, KBP.
306 For Kay Boyle's "Army of Occupation," see *New Yorker* 7 June 1947: 29–34.
306 "it might have been better if the Germans had won": Kay Boyle, "French Harvest," *Tomorrow* May 1948: 5–12.
306 "holding a tin cup out": Kay Boyle, "Fire in the Vineyards," *Saturday Evening Post* 2 July 1966: 76–77, 79–81.
306 "an improbably picturesque": "Briefly Noted," rev. of *1939*, *New Yorker* 13 March 1948: 123–24.
306 "little more than a glamor-boy": Nona Balakian, "Two Cards at a Time," rev. of *1939*, *New York Times Book Review* 15 February 1948: 22.
306 "Why is it that Kay Boyle's novels": "Intensity in the Alps," rev. of *1939*, *Time* 1 March 1948: 92.
307 "hasn't done for you the sort of job": Richard Simon, fragment of note to KB, KBP.
307 a title to which Aswell at once objected: Edward Aswell to KB, 22 January 1948, KBP.
307 "My faith in you is unwavering": Ibid.
307 "This is a great book": Edward Aswell to KB, 25 February 1948, KBP.
307 "a new period": Edward Aswell to KB, 16 March 1948, KBP.
307 "12 million interruptions": KB to Ann Watkins, 7 November 1947, KBP.
307 "to resign his foul job": KB to Nancy Cunard, 16 March 1947, HRHRC.
308 "Any one of those conditions": KB interview with JM, August 1987.
308 "But, Momi": Ibid.
308 "Don't be angry": Kathe Vail to KB, undated letter [1948], KBP.
308 "Amazing . . . a daughter who prefers her dog": Kathe Vail telephone interview with JM, 1991.
308 sexually frigid: Ted Goeser telephone interviews with JM, 12 March 1991 and 16 March 1991.
309 Mousie refused to go to the dentist: Faith Gude interviews with JM, December 1989.
309 "Don't ever do that again": KB interview with JM, August 1987, and Clover Vail interviews with JM, 20 February 1991.
309 For accounts of Joseph Franckenstein's encounters with Franz Borkenau and Ernest Knoblauch, see FBI file 123-3915, Joseph Maria Franckenstein. See also Donald Muntz telephone interviews with JM, 8 June 1989 and 12 June 1989.
310 "politically undesireable": KB to Richard Wright, 26 April 1949, Beinecke Library. See also KB to Richard Wright, 22 April 1949, Beinecke Library.
310 None of the male members of his family: Donald Muntz telephone interviews with JM, 8 June 1989 and 12 June 1989.
310 "could not thrive on introspection": Katherine Evans Boyle to KB, 14 February 1948, BERG.

310 Laurence had made her feel sexual: Ted Goeser telephone interviews with JM, 12 March 1991 and 16 March 1991.
310 "She wrote potboilers": Ibid.
310 "flung far and wide": See Kay Boyle, *Generation Without Farewell* (New York: Knopf, 1960). All subsequent references are to this edition.
310 "speechless at the sight": KB to Ann Watkins, 11 May 1948, KBP.
311 they dropped their pajamas: Faith Gude interviews with JM, December 1989.
311 "a conqueror, well-fed": KB to Ann Watkins, 11 May 1948, KBP.
311 "hard bitter population": Ibid.
311 "turn into rude aggressive little Americans": KB to Sharon Vail, 26 May 1948, KBP.
311 "no possible gentleness": Ibid.
311 "with the cold north German thing": Ibid.
311 "democratic force": Harvey Breit, "Talk with Kay Boyle," *New York Times Book Review* 23 April 1951: 26.
311 not once did the words "liberty": KB to Sharon Vail, 26 May 1948, KBP.
311 "tactful, to be careful": KB to Nancy Cunard, 8 September 1948, HRHRC.
311 "stubborn refusal to admit": KB to James Laughlin, 2 November 1948.
311–12 "the most monstrous national crime in history": Ibid.
312 "the appearance of a figure": KB to Sharon Vail, 26 May 1948, KBP.
312 "Why not a leader": Ibid.
312 "show of uniforms": KB to Ann Watkins, 16 December 1948, KBP.
312 "all these niggers": KB to Sharon Vail, 26 May 1948, KBP.
312 "sitting down at table with a nigger": Ibid.
312 "road that all free men must share": See *Generation Without Farewell* and Donald Muntz telephone interviews with JM, 8 June 1989 and 12 June 1989.
313 Knoblauch invoked a "list": For this incident, see FBI file 123-3915, Joseph Maria Franckenstein.

20. THE SMOKING MOUNTAIN

314 "I have done a book": KB to James Laughlin, 20 July 1950.
314 it was gratifying for Joseph: KB to Edita Morris, 23 July 1948, KBP.
314 "to be considered (by Germans and Americans alike)": Ibid.
314 "What's the cause of Kay Boyle's misery?": Robert McAlmon to James Stern, 9 October 1948, University of Maryland Libraries.
314 "what it is to have the interests": KB to Edward Aswell, 28 May 1948, KBP.
315 "In my position": KB to Nancy Cunard, 30 November 1948, HRHRC.
315 "I'd rather be dead than Swiss": Donald Muntz telephone conversation with JM, 14 July 1991.
315 "Silly man": Ibid.
316 "little crabs": For the visit of Hannah Reitsch, see Kay Boyle, introduction, *The Smoking Mountain* (New York: Knopf, 1963) 41–42.
316 "another face of Germany": Ibid. 4. The line in Kay Boyle's introduction reads: "painstaking and almost completely loveless search for another face of Germany."
316 the street cleaner: KB interview with Hugh Ford, 1978.
316 "in this bigoted little town": KB to Ann Watkins, 1 October 1948, KBP.
316 "Why do we pee": Faith Gude interviews with JM, December 1989.
317 "She does not": Jeannie Vail, *A Voyage of the Vails in Italy*, unpublished memoir, c. 1948. Courtesy of Kathe Vail.
317 He was kindly but distant: Faith Gude interviews with JM, December 1989.
317 "you're the worst child": Clover Vail interview with JM, 20 February 1991.
318 "This is the kind of evil": KB to Nancy Cunard, 29 November 1948, HRHRC.
318 "as near to living in suburbia": KB to Ann Watkins, 16 December 1948, KBP.
318 she was astonished: KB to Edward Aswell, 12 February 1950, KBP.
318 her "life-termers": KB to Ann Watkins, 8 June 1950, KBP.
318 "one of the greatest living writers in the world": KB to Ann Watkins, 27 March 1950, KBP.
319 "perhaps because Joseph is one of the principal men": KB to Ann Watkins, 29 March 1944, KBP.
319 "really ridiculous": KB to Ann Watkins, 6 December 1947, KBP.
319 "truth and loyalty": Ibid.

319 "the capacity for lightness": Kay Boyle, *His Human Majesty* (New York: Whittlesey House–McGraw-Hill, 1949). All subsequent references are to this edition.

319 "signal failure": Nathan Rothman, "Foreign Legion in Colorado," rev. of *His Human Majesty, Saturday Review of Literature* 9 April 1949: 13.

319 "her characters become simply projections": Nona Balakian, "The War in Colorado," rev. of *His Human Majesty, New York Times Book Review* 10 April 1949: 21.

319 "if any good publisher": Peter White, rev. of *His Human Majesty, Commonweal* 20 May 1949: 155–56.

319 "I probably write to escape": Ralph Thompson, "In and Out of Books," *New York Times Book Review* 10 April 1949.

319 "I want to write stories": KB to Ann Watkins, 11 May 1948, KBP.

320 her "superficiality": KB to Ann Watkins, 16 January 1950, KBP.

320 "in comfort, wealth": Ibid.

320 "departmental intrigues": KB to Roger Burlingame, 13 October 1949, KBP.

320 "try to articulate all the despair": KB to Nancy Cunard, 30 November 1948, HRHRC.

320 "to Harold Ross": See the dedication in Kay Boyle's *The Smoking Mountain.*

320 "devastating fire": Helga Einsele, "A Friendship Across Two Continents," *Twentieth Century Literature* [Special Kay Boyle Issue], ed. Sandra Whipple Spanier, 34.3 (Fall 1988) 273.

321 See Kay Boyle, "Frankfurt in our Blood," *Nation* 15 October 1949: 364–66.

321 "not going to write stories that sell": KB to Ann Watkins, 20 December 1949, KBP.

321 "re-adjustment to life": Ibid.

321 See Kay Boyle, "The Lovers of Gain," *Nation* 24 June 1950: 615–18.

321 See Kay Boyle, "A Reporter in Germany—The People with Names," *New Yorker* 9 September 1950: 37–42, 44–52, 55–56, 58–61, 64–70, 73–77.

321 "the *other* face of Germany": KB to Ann Watkins, 29 April 1950, KBP.

321 "We Germans have never fought on the barricades": Heinz Pol to KB, 5 June 1950, KBP.

321 "it does not seem humanly": KB to Ann Watkins, 2 June 1950, KBP.

322 "a terrifying document": John K. Hutchens, "On the Books . . . On an Author," *New York Herald Tribune Book Review* 22 April 1955: 3.

322 several critics compared her to Rebecca West: See Lewis Gannett, "Books & Things," rev. of *The Smoking Mountain, New York Herald Tribune* 30 April 1951.

322 "very strongly. . . . I love Ross": KB to Ann Watkins, 19 May 1950, KBP.

322 "NO ONE is being allowed": Ibid.

322 Hans Jahn: See Kay Boyle, "Hans Jahn Fights Rearmament," *Nation* 173 (15 December 1951): 519–21.

322 "giving enough support": Harvey Breit, "Talk with Kay Boyle," *New York Times Book Review* 29 April 1951.

323 "would be the wrong time": KB to Ann Watkins, 30 December 1951, KBP.

323 "Our impression . . . is that it belongs pretty much": Gus Lobrano to Ann Watkins, 24 February 1950, KBP.

323 "a sharp focus": Gus Lobrano to Ann Watkins, 28 April 1950, KBP.

323 "the German people nostalgic for the Nazi regime": Ann Watkins to KB, 1 March 1950, KBP.

324 "typing ten and twelve hours a day": KB to Ann Watkins, 8 May 1950, KBP.

324 "a bit rambling": KB to Ann Watkins, 16 January 1950, KBP.

324 "wonderful foreign coverage": KB to Ann Watkins, 28 March 1950, KBP.

324 "dispenser of white-skinned charity": Kay Boyle, "Home," *Harper's* 202 (January 1951): 78–83.

324 "it isn't really clear why the G.I.": Gus Lobrano to Ann Watkins, 17 March 1950, KBP.

324 See Kay Boyle, "A Disgrace to the Family," *Saturday Evening Post* 223 (23 September 1950): 22–23.

324 "So much for Lobrano's criticism": KB to Ann Watkins, 26 April 1950, KBP.

324 "too cumbrous": Gus Lobrano to Ann Watkins, 9 November 1950, KBP.

324 See Kay Boyle, "Cabaret," *Tomorrow* 10 (April 1951): 57–67.

324 "this is the sort of story we should have published in 1947": William Maxwell to Ann Watkins, 17 August 1950, KBP.

324–25 "the subject of European orphan children": *Today's Woman* to Ann Watkins, 28 August 1950, KBP.

325 "I think that it is unlikely": Knox Burger to Ann Watkins, 21 June 1950, KBP.

325 "I know how futile": KB to Ann Watkins, 30 June 1950, KBP.

325 "what Kay had in mind": Gus Lobrano to Ann Watkins, 5 March 1951, KBP.

325 "Miss Boyle is going backwards": *American Mercury* to Ann Watkins, 6 April 1951, KBP.

325 "If you don't sell it to 'The New Yorker' ": KB to Ann Watkins, 2 July 1951, KBP.

325 "a good deal less effective": Gus Lobrano to Ann Watkins, 18 July 1951, KBP.

325 "almost only a sketch": Whit Burnett to Ann Watkins, 26 July 1951, KBP.

325 "not up to her usual level": Louisa Dalcher to Ann Watkins, 17 September 1951, KBP.

325 "this particular story just doesn't fit": Carey McWilliams to Ann Watkins, 26 September 1951, KBP.

325 "How I was deceived in this talent": See Joan Givner, *Katherine Anne Porter: A Life* (New York: Simon & Schuster, 1982) 231.

325–26 "might break the spell": KB to Ann Watkins, 26 April 1950, KBP.

326 For the manuscript of Kay Boyle's unpublished article about the animal poisoning trial in Frankfurt, see BERG.

326 "a rather vast amount of German stuff": Harold Ross to KB, 29 August 1950, KBP.

326 See Kay Boyle, "Summer Evening," *New Yorker* 25 June 1949: 20–24.

326 See Kay Boyle, "Diagnosis of a Selfish Lady," *Saturday Evening Post* 224 (5 April 1952) 24, 119–24.

326 "glad to have it": Ann Watkins to KB [c. September 1951], KBP.

326 "God knows what's happened": KB to Ann Watkins, 24 January 1951, KBP.

326 "All I seem to do is shop for food": Ibid.

326 "background HAS to be German": KB to Ann Watkins, 2 July 1951, KBP.

326 "character sketch": KB to Ann Watkins, 5 August 1951, KBP.

326 "having everything rejected recently": KB to Ann Watkins, 5 August 1951, KBP.

326 "the figure which emerges—the eternal 'I' ": KB to Ann Watkins, 6 January 1951, KBP.

327 "a story of action": Ann Watkins to KB, 14 August 1951, KBP.

327 "cheap sordid stories": KB to Ann Watkins, 19 April 1950, KBP.

327 "I'm your baby for bad stories": KB to Ann Watkins, 26 April 1950, KBP.

327 "invitations to lunch": "Kay Boyle," *New York Herald Tribune* 7 October 1951: 6, 28.

327 "expensive places": Ibid.

327 "in a small room where no current of air": Ibid.

327 "in a very cavalier way": Ann Watkins to KB, 14 September 1950, KBP.

327 "lovely": KB to Ann Watkins, 23 September 1950, KBP.

327 "I'll have to write another novel quick": KB to Ann Watkins, 27 June 1951, KBP.

327 "a big love story": KB to Ann Watkins, 19 July 1951, KBP.

327 "a certain latent hostility": Edward Aswell to KB, 28 January 1952, KBP.

327 "one of the last people": KB to Ann Watkins, 27 June 1951, KBP.

327 "I would leave for Hollywood": KB to Ann Watkins, 22 May 1951, KBP.

328 "too close a margin financially": KB to Ann Watkins, 2 March 1952, KBP.

328 "the romance, the fire, the sense of justice": KB to Ann Watkins, 13 January 1952, KBP.

328 "I'm just NOT going to let everything": KB to Ann Watkins, 28 April 1952, KBP.

328 "It became necessary": KB to Stuart Rose [May 11 1952], KBP.

21. GUILT BY MARRIAGE

330 "character, reputation": J. Edgar Hoover to SAC, Washington Field Office, 25 October 1949, FBI file 123-3915, Joseph Maria Franckenstein, Sections 1 and 2, Serials 1–78.

330 "you can not imagine": Heinz Pol to KB, 28 March 1949, KBP.

330 "a popular fiction authoress": See FBI file 123-3915, Joseph Maria Franckenstein, New York office report dated 11-15-49.

330 "somewhat unconventional": Ibid.

330 "a follower of Henry Wallace": See FBI file 100-381638, Kay Boyle Franckenstein, Sections 1 and 2, Serials X to NR Memo 11/9/72, New Haven report dated 11-14-49, RE: Joseph Maria Franckenstein: Special Inquiry—State Dept., "Voice of America," 123-3915-16 (2), page 13. See also FBI file 123-3915, Joseph Maria Franckenstein.

330 "of a Bohemian nature": See FBI file 123-3915, Joseph Maria Franckenstein, page 4 of nine-page Washington, D.C., report dated 12-5-49.

330 "careless in dress": See FBI file 123-3915, Joseph Maria Franckenstein, New York report and letter to Washington, D.C., field office dated 10-25-49 and headed "Neighborhood."

331 "not [being] attentive": Ibid.

331 "a highly intelligent person": FBI file 100-381638, Kay Boyle Franckenstein, New York report

dated 11-28-49. See also page 5 of the summary on Kay Boyle Franckenstein in the State Department Referral for Joseph Maria Franckenstein.

331 "a temperamental and impulsive woman": FBI file 100-381638, Kay Boyle Franckenstein, New York report dated 11-28-49. This phrase appears throughout the FBI material on Kay Boyle. For example, FBI file 123-3915, Joseph Maria Franckenstein, New York report and letter to Washington, D.C., field office dated 10-25-49 and headed "Neighborhood."

331 "looked into the cause": FBI file 100-381638, Kay Boyle Franckenstein, New York report dated 11-28-49.

331 "shocked" to discover: See the transcript of the proceedings of the Loyalty Security Board: In the Matter of: Joseph Franckenstein, October 20, 1952, and October 21, 1952, the U.S. High Commission, page F-46.

331 "not a Communist or Fascist": Joseph Franckenstein, signed Appointment Affidavit, October 1949, FBI file 123-3915, Joseph Maria Franckenstein.

331 "an unevaluated allegation": Office Memorandum: To: Mr. Fletcher; From: J. W. Amshey; letter dated 1-12-50; FBI file 123-3915, Joseph Maria Franckenstein.

331 "of the activities of subject and wife": Conrad E. Snow to James E. Hatcher, Chief Investigations Division, United States Civil Service Commission, Washington, D.C., FBI file 123-3915, Joseph Maria Franckenstein.

331 "beautiful son": KB to James Laughlin, 22 March 1950.

331 "when I try to regulate": KB to Ann Watkins, 29 December 1950, KBP.

332 "filled with light, strength, and vitality": Katherine Evans Boyle to KB, 20 January 1950, BERG.

332 "Be well, you are so important": Katherine Evans Boyle to KB, 27 May 1950, BERG.

332 "persuaded to go to New Jersey": KB to Katherine Evans Boyle, 17 July 1950, BERG.

332 "the death of my mother": KB to Ann Watkins, 17 July 1950, KBP.

332 "furious that Mother has to be treated": KB to Ann Watkins, 30 July 1950, KBP.

332 "Mother is far better off": KB to Joan Detweiler, 31 July 1950, KBP.

332 "and you had helped her in so many ways": Katherine Evans Boyle to KB, 19 August 1950, BERG.

332 "I think her courage": KB to Robert McAlmon, 18 November 1951, Beinecke Library.

332 "My feelings are steady": Katherine Evans Boyle to KB, 4 July 1951, BERG.

332 "Jo is jealous of you": Ibid.

332 "a real flood": Ibid.

332 "How close you and I are": Katherine Evans Boyle to KB, 23 November 1951, BERG.

332 "quite sober and very worried": KB to Ann Watkins, 14 July 1950, KBP.

332 "she and Reeves are apparently drinking gin, and wine": KB to Ann Watkins, 31 July 1950, KBP.

333 "In giving all this attention to Honey Chile": KB to Joan Detweiler, 5 October 1950, KBP.

333 "senseless interruptions": KB to Ann Watkins, 27 September 1950, KBP.

333 "dreadful . . . her little rain-and-tear streaming face": KB to Ann Watkins, 6 January 1951, KBP.

333 "I just hate Mousie going there": KB to Ann Watkins, 8 January 1952, KBP.

333 "absolutely heart-sick": KB to Ann Watkins, 10 December 1950, KBP.

333 "really violent and meaningful protest": KB to James Laughlin, 11 September 1950.

333 "in our country we can speak our protest": Ibid.

334 "start marching to the Atlantic": James Laughlin to KB, 27 September 1950, KBP.

334 "I didn't know anyone—except McCarthy": KB to James Laughlin, 18 October 1950.

334 "regimes we can only despise": Ibid.

334 "with Franco, the puppet regime in Greece": Ibid.

334 "a pink": Page 7 of Complaint Investigation D261009, III-1448, x-661, dated 10-10-50, FBI file 123-3915, Joseph Maria Franckenstein.

334 "one hundred per cent pro-Soviet": FBI file 123-3915, Joseph Maria Franckenstein, page 1 of report dated 6-11-51. See also "Results of Investigation," page 2, in the State Department Referral for Joseph Maria Franckenstein.

334 "pro-French": This phrase appears throughout the FBI material on Kay Boyle. See Agent Report Re: Franckenstein, Kay Boyle, 1-9-52, FBI file 100-381638, Kay Boyle Franckenstein, and Agent Report, 9-28-51, FBI file 123-3915, Joseph Maria Franckenstein.

334 "a Liberal": Complaint Investigation dated 4-11-51, FBI file 123-3915, Joseph Maria Franckenstein.

334 "a kind person": FBI file 100-381638, Kay Boyle Franckenstein. See also Complaint Investigation D201009, 3-30-51, FBI file 123-3915, Joseph Maria Franckenstein.

334 "a Liberal who would probably vote for a candidate": Complaint Investigation D201009, 3-30-51, FBI file 123-3915, Joseph Maria Franckenstein.

334 "slightly left of center": Ibid.

334–35 "I can only conclude that the air mail service": KB to Ann Watkins, 14 February 1951, KBP.

335 "Why do you talk to him like that?": For this incident, Kathe Vail interview with JM, June 1990.

335 "Be nice to your granny": Ibid.

335 "Judy Holliday and Jose Ferrer": *New York Herald Tribune* 5 April 1951: 1, 39.

336 "It's preposterous": KB interview with JM, August 1987.

336 her name appeared in the *Daily Worker*: See "6 Protestant Bishops, Other Notables Fight Franco Aid," *Daily Worker* 17 May 1951: 2, 9.

336 "make Stalin's job": FBI New York office, report 100-350512-409 (1), FBI file 100-381638, Kay Boyle Franckenstein.

336 "She'll just jump": Susan Hager interview with JM, 6 June 1988.

336 "because I'm not a Communist": KB to Robert McAlmon, 18 November 1951, Beinecke Library.

336 "does not believe I am a Communist": KB to Caresse Crosby, 8 July 1951, BSA.

336 "Have we become so frightened": quoted in Heinz Pol to KB, 10 September 1950, KBP.

336 "so frightened that": Ibid.

337 "Stalin's most effective representatives": Louis Budenz, *The Cry Is Peace* (Chicago: Henry Regnery, 1952) xi–xii.

337 "Sometime in the early 1940's": Testimony of Louis Budenz's interview with the FBI, report dated 2-26-53, FBI file 100-381638, Kay Boyle Franckenstein, and FBI file 123-3915, Joseph Maria Franckenstein.

337 "CP member or CP sympathizer": FBI report dated 7-25-51, FBI file 100-381638, Kay Boyle Franckenstein.

337 everyone would know her true age: Kathe Vail interview with JM, June 1990.

338 Frank Detweiler was in bed with her: KB interview with JM, August 1987.

338 "I've been dashing between hospital, school, prison": KB to Ann Watkins, 2 March 1952, KBP.

338 "so very much our kind of child—blond and blue eyed": KB to Joan Detweiler, 3 March 1952, KBP.

338 "I would like to have him myself": Ibid.

338 "many misgivings as to my qualities as a foster mother": KB to Ann Watkins, 28 April 1952, KBP.

338 "of a gentleness": Ibid.

338 "orgy of spending": KB to Ann Watkins, 28 April 1952 [received by Watkins on 2 May 1952], KBP.

338 "all I have missed in not having a young one": Ibid.

339 "How come those men": Faith Gude interviews with JM, December 1989.

339 "handsome little Wolfgang": KB to Ann Watkins, 28 April 1952 [received by Watkins on 2 May 1952], KBP.

339 set fire to the Christmas tree: Susan Hager interview with JM, 6 June 1988.

339 "I was sorry I hadn't kept them": KB interview with JM, August 1987.

339 "Of all farcical things, in white veils": KB to Ann Watkins, 5 May 1952, KBP.

339 "Why did she do such a thing?": Susan Hager interview with JM, 6 June 1988.

339 "I got out of my marriage": Laurence Vail to KB, quoted in KB to Ann Watkins, 4 March 1953, KBP.

340 "a liberal interested in the 'under dog' ": FBI New York office report dated 1/29/52, FBI file 100-381638, Kay Boyle Franckenstein, Sections 1 and 2, Serials X to NR Memo 11/9/72.

340 "fellow traveller": Heinz Pol to KB, March 6, 1950, KBP.

340 "Nobody knows about it": Heinz Pol to KB, 31 July 1951, KBP.

341 "Subject's wife is stated": Addendum Summary of Information, security background report dated 10-27-53, FBI file 123-3915, Joseph Maria Franckenstein, and State Department Referral of Joseph M. Franckenstein.

341 "out of the blue": KB to Ann Watkins, 28 April 1952, KBP.

341 "I know Pol is not": Ibid.

341 "the consistently pro-Soviet": Clement Greenberg, "The Nation Censors a Letter of Criticism," *New Leader*, March 19, 1951, 16–18. *The New Leader* published Greenberg's letter after *The Nation* had refused and in fact had threatened to sue for libel were it printed elsewhere.

341 "defending all writers": Kay Boyle refused to join James Burnham, Sidney Hook, Norman Thomas, Peter Viereck, Elliot E. Cohen, and William White in their defense of *The New Leader*, against which *The Nation* and Julio Alvarez del Vayo had filed a libel suit for $200,000, as threatened.

Kay Boyle wrote: "I am convinced that Mr. Greenberg's letter concerning Mr. del Vayo's unfitness to be foreign editor of '*The Nation*' was not written in any spirit of detached political criticism, but with the deliberate intent to smear a fine and forthright man." She favored, she said, *The Nation*'s "defending all writers from irrelevant [sic] and irresponsible attack."

22. LOYALTY HEARING

342 "a long time to believe": Transcript of the proceedings of the Loyalty Security Board: In the Matter of: Joseph Franckenstein, October 20, 1952, and October 21, 1952, the United States High Commission, page F-11. See also KB to Ann Watkins, 17 February 1953, KBP.

342 "Kay darling, you could never be a member": KB interview with JM, August 1987.

342 "that the many fine letters": Katharine White to KB, 13 June 1952, KBP.

342 "encouraging": KB to Ann Watkins, 12 June 1952, KBP.

343 "I do not know Mr. Franckenstein": William Shawn to Shepherd Stone, 11 June 1952, FBI file 100-381638, Kay Boyle Franckenstein, Sections 1 and 2, Serials X to NR Memo 11/9/72.

343 "make critical comments about our government": Gus Lobrano, "To Whom It May Concern," 3 October 1952, letter of endorsement, ibid.

343 "unable to betray her country": Roger Burlingame, "To Whom It May Concern," 10 June 1952, letter of endorsement, ibid.

343 "a true patriot": Stuart Rose, "To Whom It May Concern," 23 May 1952, letter of endorsement, ibid.

343 "makes one proud": Edward C. Aswell, "To Whom It May Concern," 20 May 1952, letter of endorsement, ibid.

343 "a courageous American liberal": Janet Flanner, "To Whom It May Concern," 3 June 1952, letter of endorsement, ibid.

343 You told me your letters were opened: Sharon Cowling interview with JM, June 1990.

343 "Kay Boyle Franckenstein has endorsed": Joseph Franckenstein to Conrad E. Snow, 15 September 1952, FBI file 123-3915, Joseph Maria Franckenstein, Sections 1 and 2, Serials 1–78.

344 "guilt by association so much favored": Ibid.

344 "I'm going to have to lean on you": Benjamin Ferencz telephone interview with JM, 2 October 1991.

344 "energetic, soft-spoken": KB to General Edward Greenbaum, 28 October 1952, HRHRC.

344 "A tiny little Hungarian Jew": Janet Flanner to Natalia Murray, 11 October 1952, in *Darlinghissima: Letters to a Friend*, ed. Natalia Danesi Murray (New York: Harcourt Brace Jovanovich, 1985) 174.

344 "more gravely accused": KB to General Greenbaum, 28 October 1952, HRHRC.

345 "ghastly": Janet Flanner to Natalia Murray, 11 October 1952, in *Darlinghissima* 172.

345 "He is forty": Ibid. 173.

345 "Oh, alas, alas, her need for money": Ibid. 174.

345 "a wonderful woman": Ibid.

345 "How could one ask for warmth": KB to William Shawn, 21 March 1953, KBP.

345 "I'm sorry. I can't stop it": Benjamin Ferencz telephone interview with JM, 30 September 1991.

346 "associated with persons": Memorandum: From: Herbert L. Sultan, Assistant Legal Officer—Loyalty Security Board, HCIOG Panel, 10-17-52, FBI file 123-3915, Joseph Maria Franckenstein, and FBI file 100-381638, Kay Boyle Franckenstein.

346 the government had to keep its sources confidential: Ibid.

346 "a display of temper": Ibid.

346 "Have learned Franckenstein": Classified Telegram, Donnelly to Sipes, 10-17-52, FBI file 123-3915, Joseph Maria Franckenstein.

346 "raise questions of civil liberties": Ibid.

346 This description of the hearing of Joseph and Kay Franckenstein before the Loyalty Security Board in Bad Godesberg is based largely on the transcript of the proceedings, published by the U.S. High Commissioner for Germany as a confidential document and later declassified. A copy is also available in KBP.

347 so harassed and pressured: Benjamin Ferencz telephone interview with JM, 30 September 1991.

348 Clark could be obstreperous: For the description of Judge William Clark, I have relied on interviews with his children, Blair Clark and Anne Martindell.

349 Terrified that he might lose his American citizenship: Benjamin Ferencz telephone interview with JM, 30 September 1991.

354 Kay Boyle, "The Daring Impersonation," *Saturday Evening Post* 226 (8 August and 15 August 1953): 17–19, 68–70, 74, 76; 36–37, 96–99, 101.
355 "meekly": KB to General Edward Greenbaum, 28 October 1952, HRHRC.

23. THE NINETEENTH FLOOR

356 "Our whole investment": Janet Flanner to KB, 3 February [1953], KBP.
356 "nervous, white and thin": Janet Flanner's "report" on the trial of Joseph Franckenstein and Kay Boyle is found in *Darlinghissima* 173–77.
356 "paralyzed melancholy": Ibid. 174.
357 they had never heard of Harold Ross: Ibid. 175.
357 "wooden" . . . "cement": Ibid. 174.
358 "semi-Europeanized": Ibid. 177.
358 Herbert Sultan wept: Benjamin Ferencz telephone interview with JM, 30 September 1991. See also KB to General Edward Greenbaum, 28 October 1952, HRHRC.
358 "I feel like joining": KB to General Edward Greenbaum, 28 October 1952, HRHRC.
359 "the best way out": Ibid.
359 Houston Lay "not too well satisfied": Houston Lay to John Sipes, 10-27-52, FBI file 123-3915, Joseph Maria Franckenstein, Sections 1 and 2, Serials 1–78.
359 "outstanding and heroic": Rationale, HICOG Loyalty Security Board, ibid.
359 "parlor pink": Houston Lay to John Sipes, 12-3-52, ibid.
359 "McCarthy's man": KB to Nancy Cunard, 1 June 1953, HRHRC.
359 "was a little bit sympathetic": Walter J. Donnelly, U.S. High Commissioner, Bonn, quoted in Houston Lay to John Sipes, 12-3-52, FBI file 123-3915, Joseph Maria Franckenstein.
360 "until the security": Office Memorandum: From: John W. Sipes, dated 12-11-52, ibid.
360 "political or controversial subjects": Telegram: Donnelly to Secretary of State, 12-2-52; see also Acheson to HICOG, 12-4-52, FBI file 123-3915, Joseph Maria Franckenstein, and FBI file 100-381638, Kay Boyle Franckenstein.
360 "for clearance": KB to General Greenbaum, 18 January 1953, HRHRC.
360 "good fiction": Robert L. Thompson, Chairman, Committee on Unofficial Publication, to Peter Regis, U.S. Government Memorandum dated 19 January 1953, FBI file 100-381638, Kay Boyle Franckenstein.
360 "a highly sensitive and volatile personality": Jack B. Minor, Chief Security Officer, ibid.
360 "consistent and credible": Office Memorandum, U.S. Government, From: Conrad Snow, Chairman Loyalty Security Board; To: Mr. Humelsine, 31 December 1952, FBI file 123-3915, Joseph Maria Franckenstein.
360–61 "clearance of Mr. Franckenstein on security": Office Memorandum, U.S. Government, From: S. D. Boykin; To: Humelsine, 13 January 1953, ibid.
361 "depressing" Bad Godesberg: KB to Caresse Crosby, 21 December 1952, BSA.
361 "would be in bars": Laurence Vail to KB, 18 November [1952], BERG.
361 "I do believe": Ibid.
361 "I know that one must live": Kathe Vail to KB, 2 February 1953, KBP.
361 All the children believed: Clover Vail interviews with JM, 19 January 1991 and 20 February 1991.
361 "kind of flat": *New Yorker* to Ann Watkins, 16 January 1953, KBP.
361 "Inasmuch as the *New Yorker* does not accept": KB to Ann Watkins, 7 January 1953, KBP.
361 "first-reading fiction agreements": See, for example, R. Hawley Truax, Treasurer, New Yorker Magazine, Inc., to KB, 27 December 1948, KBP.
361 "jeopardized the reputation": KB interview with JM, August 1987. See also KB interview on Katharine White, 1981, available in KBP.
362 "wept for hours": KB interview with JM, August 1987. See also KB interview on Katharine White, 1981, KBP.
362 "Have I been completely mistaken in the character of Bill?": Janet Flanner to KB, 3 February [1953], KBP.
362 "that this sudden action": KB to William Shawn, 1 February 1953, KBP.
362 "its obvious honesty": William Shawn to KB, 11 March 1953, KBP.
362 "so goddam many kids": Katharine White to Janet Flanner, 20 March 1953, Library of Congress.
362–63 "constitutionally" prevented from signing: William Shawn to Janet Flanner, 24 April 1953, Library of Congress.

363 "deception of our government": Katharine White to Janet Flanner, 20 March 1953, Library of Congress.

363 "disloyalty" . . . "intimate friend": William Shawn to Janet Flanner, 24 April 1953, Library of Congress. See also Wineapple, *Genêt* 231.

363 "write to Heidelberg": KB to Ann Watkins, 15 March 1953, KBP.

363 "why the accreditation was being withdrawn": KB to William Shawn, 21 March 1953, KBP.

363 "weakening over-statement," Katharine White to Janet Flanner, 20 March 1953, Library of Congress.

364 "warm-heartedness": William Shawn to Janet Flanner, 24 April 1953, Library of Congress.

364 "would think that the *New Yorker*": Janet Flanner to Kay Boyle, "Sunday Night," undated letter, KBP.

364 "I have always felt married to *The New Yorker*": Janet Flanner to KB, 3 February [1953], KBP.

364 "who broke a lance for Kay Boyle": Note written on Janet Flanner to Katharine White, 12 May 1953, Library of Congress.

364 "You have a husband": KB interview with JM, August 1987. See also KB interview on Katharine White, 1981, KBP.

364 "This is a fine thing": KB to Ann Watkins, 9 May 1953, KBP.

364 "*cannot withdraw*": Ibid.

364 "my last piece": Ibid.

364 "What could I do?": KB interview with JM, August 1987.

364 "if Kay Boyle had actually": Natalie Robins, "The Defiling of Writers: The FBI and American Literature," *Nation* 10 October 1987: 372.

365 "unconvinced of the woman's": *Harper's Bazaar* to Ann Watkins, 6 February 1953, KBP.

365 "too much a woman's point of view": *Collier's* to Ann Watkins, 4 March 1954, KBP.

365 "her characters are dreadful dopes": MacLennan Farrell to Ann Watkins, 16 June 1954, KBP.

365 "I shall keep a completely open mind": Edward Aswell to Ann Watkins, 5 March 1953, KBP.

365 "the big magazine market will be closed to me": KB to Ann Watkins, 27 April 1953, KBP.

365 "All indications are that all is well": Ibid.

365 "not ONLY by the Communists": KB to Ann Watkins, 17 February 1953, KBP.

365 "senseless policy": Ibid.

366 "the alliance of a strong": Ibid.

366 "to build on": KB to Ann Watkins, 4 March 1953, KBP.

366 "added ordeal of facing zero": Ibid.

366 "limited-service appointment": See letter dated 2 April 1953, and Joseph Franckenstein to Theo Hall, 9 April 1953, FBI file 123-3915, Joseph Maria Franckenstein.

366 "unable to accept the terms": Joseph Franckenstein to Theo Hall, 9 April 1953, ibid.

366 "outraged a lot": Nicholas von Hoffman, *Citizen Cohn: The Life and Times of Roy Cohn* (New York: Bantam, 1988) 170.

367 "brought about by Cohn": KB to Sandra Whipple Spanier, 29 April 1982, KBP.

367 "McCarthy's assistants": KB interview on Katharine White, 1981, KBP.

367 "distempered Jackals": *London Financial Times*, c. April 1953, Hoffman, *Citizen Cohn* 167.

367 "was not due to any security or loyalty considerations": Confidential document, 28 May 1953, FBI file 123-3915, Joseph Maria Franckenstein. See also FBI file copy of letter, Joseph Franckenstein to James B. Conant, 31 May 1953.

367 "openly to prove my loyalty": Confidential document, 28 May 1953, FBI file 123-3915, Joseph Maria Franckenstein.

367 "would never get a decent job anywhere again": KB to Roger Burlingame, 15 April 1953, KBP.

367 "designated": See letter dated 2 April 1953, FBI file 123-3915, Joseph Maria Franckenstein.

367 "Kay shouldn't have got herself into this mess": Kathe Vail interviews with JM, June 1990.

367 See "The Easy Out," *Washington Post* 25 May 1953.

368 "We wish we could celebrate": KB to Roger Burlingame, 15 April 1953, KBP.

368 Kay typed legal documents: KB to Ann Watkins, 9 May 1953, KBP.

368 John Sipes was delighted: John W. Sipes, memorandum, 22 May 1953, FBI file 123-3915, Joseph Maria Franckenstein.

368 "result in his knowingly": "Confidential—Security Information/Summary and Recommendations," 23 May 1953, ibid.

368 "moral courage": Joseph Franckenstein to James B. Conant, 31 May 1953, ibid.

368 Joseph wanted to remain in Europe: Faith Gude interview with JM, 2 March 1991.

369 "one of the times in history": Kay Boyle, "Farewell to Europe," *Nation* 177 (24 December 1953) 526–28.

369 "Ah God, how one must fight the evil": KB to Nancy Cunard, 24 May 1953, HRHRC.
369 "strong forces at work": Ibid.
369 "I didn't fail him": KB to Ann Watkins, 24 May 1953, KBP.
369 she had a sexual dream: Ibid.
369 "Write to us about the other America": Kay Boyle, "Farewell to Europe."
369 James B. Conant told John Foster Dulles: Telegram, From: Bonn; To: Secretary of State, 1 June 1953, FBI file 123-3915, Joseph Maria Franckenstein.
369 a "temporary refuge": KB to Ann Watkins, 9 May 1953, KBP.
369 See Kay Boyle, "Carnival of Fear," *Saturday Evening Post* 227 (11 December and 18 December 1954) 20–21, 102–5; 34–35, 50, 52–53.

24. LAND OF THE FREE

370 "Thin, old, and nerve-wracked": *Darlinghissima* 199.
370 The fighting began: Faith Gude interviews with JM, December 1989, and Ian Franckenstein interview with JM, August 1987.
370 "I hate you, I hate you": Ian Franckenstein interview with JM, August 1987.
370 a bit of a martinet: Howard Nemerov interview with JM, 13 September 1990.
371 "It's hopeless": Ian Franckenstein interview with JM, August 1987, and Faith Gude interviews with JM, December 1989.
371 "so goddamned ashamed": William L. Shirer interview with JM, 22 May 1989.
371 "I would have been very tempted": Benjamin Ferencz to Kay and Joseph Franckenstein, 14 September 1953, KBP.
371 "Your entire life will change now": Faith Gude interview with JM, 2 March 1991.
371 "Nobody around here says good morning": Ibid.
372 "This is Joseph's and my bed": KB interview with JM, August 1987.
372 "organized and passionate resistance to McCarthy": KB to Nancy Cunard, 28 July 1953, HRHRC.
372 "Please don't work": Faith Franckenstein to Kay Boyle, 10 November 1953, KBP.
372 "come home": Faith Franckenstein to KB, December 1953, KBP.
372 "Mousie doesn't miss me": Faith Gude interviews with JM, December 1989 and 2 March 1991.
372 "I wish you were a little girl here in Cherry Lawn": Faith Franckenstein to KB, 18 November 1953, KBP.
372 she threatened to throw herself under the wheels of the car: Faith Gude interviews with JM, December 1989 and 2 March 1991.
373 "you were not tolerated": Clover Vail quoted in Weld, *Peggy* 429.
373 "How can you just sit there listening?": Faith Gude interviews with JM, December 1989 and 2 March 1991.
373 she was amazed: KB interview with JM, August 1987.
373 "a security risk": Faith Gude interviews with JM, December 1989 and 2 March 1991.
374 "Get your father to help you": Faith Gude telephone interview with JM, June 1991.
374 *"La silence de la mer"*: Marsha Torkelson interview with JM, January 1992.
374 "singularly little known": Richard C. Carpenter, "Kay Boyle," *College English* 15.2 (November 1953) 81.
374 "of so unnational": KB quoted in Ray B. West, Jr., "The Pre-World War II Group (1930–1940)," *The Short Story in America* (New York: Books for Libraries Press, 1968) 69. Originally published in 1952 by Henry Regnery Company, Chicago.
374 "Is one not to write about foreign countries": KB to Sandra Whipple Spanier, 30 December 1984, KBP.
374 See Kay Boyle, "The Kill," *Harper's* 211 (August 1955) 43–51.
374 four of her short pieces: See "Declaration for 1955," *Nation* 180 (29 January 1955) 102–4; "A Puzzled Race," *Nation* 180 (4 June 1955) 481–83; "Spain Divided," *Nation* 180 (11 June 1955) 506–7; and "They Sing of Love: A German Vignette," *Nation* 181 (10 September 1955) 224–25.
375 "France was never more greatly in need": KB to Edward Aswell, 15 November 1953, KBP.
375 "Innocence and Corruption": Ibid.
375 "for no party": Ibid.
375 "The characters seem to be stock figures": Edward Aswell to KB [December 1953], KBP.
375 "Frankly, if this book is published": Edward Aswell to Ann Watkins [December 1953], KBP.
375 "physical action": Stuart Rose to Ann Watkins, 29 December 1953, KBP.
375 "written to sell": KB to William Manchester, 2 February 1955, KBP.

375 "to be satisfactory": Ibid.

375 "thinking hard of my accumulation": Ibid.

375 "in all its lack of balance": Ibid.

376 "They can fight their war in Indo-China": See Kay Boyle, *The Seagull on the Step* (New York: Knopf, 1955). All subsequent references are to this edition.

376 "She liked me the way she liked Joseph." Interview with Michel Sciama, November 1991.

377 "She has the most marvelous husband, Michel Sciama": Kathe Vail interviews with JM, June 1990 and November 1991.

377 "Oh, Joseph will get those!": Jacqueline Ventadour Hélion interview with JM, November 1991.

377 "wonderful story": Paul Engle, "Hope Out of France," rev. of *The Seagull on the Step*, *New Republic* 132.20 (16 May 1955) 38–39.

377 "love letter to France": Lewis Gannett, rev. of *The Seagull on the Step*, *New York Herald Tribune* 9 May 1955.

377 "exact and true": rev. of *The Seagull on the Step*, *New Yorker* 17 September 1955: 177.

377 "the parable . . . too self-conscious": Sidney Alexander, "The Gulf Between," rev. of *The Seagull on the Step*, *New York Times Book Review* 8 May 1955: 2.

377 "Your intensity": Janet Flanner to KB, 10 June 1955, KBP.

378 One winter, she related: See the Fay and Herman Rappaport papers, in KBP. Kay repeatedly thanked the Rappaports for their help: for example, KB to Herman Rappaport, 15 February 1958.

378 "your associations": Robert C. Cartwright to Joseph Franckenstein, 5 May 1954, FBI file 123-3915, Joseph Maria Franckenstein.

379 "the individual": KB to James Laughlin, 8 May 1954.

379 the "moral responsibility of the writer": See Kay Boyle, "A Declaration for 1955," *Nation* 180 (29 January 1955) 105, and Kay Boyle, "Intellectuals Are Failing America," *St. Louis Post-Dispatch* 2 December 1956: part II, page 1.

379 "temporary" rather than a permanent: See Robert C. Cartwright to Joseph Franckenstein, 5 May 1954, and Confidential Memo, Scott McLeod to Thruston B. Morton, Subject: Leave-Without-Pay Status of Joseph Franckenstein, FBI file 123-3915, Joseph Maria Franckenstein.

379 "There is nothing that can be done until": Joseph Alsop to KB, 9 August 1954, KBP.

379 "cleared by the Democrats": KB to Nina Conarain, 12 May 1954, KBP.

379 "When I have had a set task": Laurence Vail to KB, 17 May 1954, KBP.

379 "affidavit from another subversive": Ira Morris to KB, 8 June 1954, KBP.

380 "cruel. . . . were Pol a Communist": KB to Walter Mehring, 20 June 1954, KBP.

380 "on a strong, fearless statement": KB to Edward Greenbaum, 12 June 1954, HRHRC.

380 "that the Communists made propaganda": The original drafts of Kay Boyle's and Joseph Franckenstein's statements are available in KBP.

380 "the principles of American democracy": See pamphlet dated 6 July 1954, addressed to John Sipes, FBI file 123-3915, Joseph Maria Franckenstein. A copy of the pamphlet and drafts of Joseph's and Kay's statements may be found in KBP.

381 "purely personal": Joseph Franckenstein to John Sipes, 5 July 1954, FBI file 123-3915, Joseph Maria Franckenstein.

381 "publicize the Department's action": Mr. Seluk to Mr. Ryan, 27 October 1954, Office of Security, Department of State, ibid.

381 "high level": KB to Freda Kirchwey, 7 August 1954, KBP.

381 "October": Kay Boyle, "October 1954," *Nation* 179.18 (30 October 1954) 383.

381 "consistent with the interests of national security": John Sipes, "Limited Official Use—Opinion of Security Council: Sufficiency of Answer to Charges," FBI file 123-3915, Joseph Maria Franckenstein, and FBI file 100-381638, Kay Boyle Franckenstein.

382 "a kick in the teeth": KB to Edward Greenbaum, 26 October 1954. See FBI file 100-381638, Kay Boyle Franckenstein.

382 "commercial writing markets": Ibid.

382 "it is the writers": Kay Boyle, "A Declaration for 1955" 105.

382 see Kay Boyle, "A Puzzled Race" 482.

382 See Kay Boyle, "Intellectuals Are Failing America."

382 "It's the American government": For this account of how Maurice J. Magner invaded Kay Boyle's house at Rowayton, see KB interview with JM, August 1987. See also Faith Gude interviews with JM, December 1989 and 2 March 1991.

383 Magner was unhappy: KB interview with Charles Amirkhanian, 1988. See also Department of State, Office of Security, report dated 22 April 1955, FBI file 100-381638, Kay Boyle Franckenstein.

383 "alleged Communist": See "Refusal," signed R. B. Shipley, 6 April 1955, FBI file 100-381638, Kay Boyle Franckenstein: reason for refusal is stated as "Alleged Communist." In Kay Boyle's FBI file, see also Kay Boyle's testimony before the Hennings Committee, pp. 1555–57, and Sturgis Warner to J. L. Franzmathes, Passport Division, 8 June 1955. See also Willis H. Young to Joseph M. Franckenstein, 29 March 1955, FBI file 123-3915, Joseph Maria Franckenstein.

383 Frances Knight, director of the passport office, even asked the Assistant Attorney General: See Frances G. Knight to William F. Tompkins, 8 December 1955, FBI file 100-381638, Kay Boyle Franckenstein.

383 there wasn't enough evidence that Kay had been a party member: William F. Tompkins to Frances G. Knight, 6 January 1956, ibid.

383 "good sign . . . that yr bad luck is over": Janet Flanner to KB, 10 June 1955, KBP.

383 Kay Boyle wrote to the National Council of the Arts, Sciences, and Professions: See KB letter to the National Council, 14 April 1953, KBP.

384 "personal liberty": KB to Dr. Harlow Shapley, 24 April 1955, KBP.

25. VINDICATION

385 "I have simply lived": KB to James Laughlin, 8 May 1954.

385 "Our moral tradition": Senator Thomas C. Hennings, Jr., to John Foster Dulles, 8 March 1956, FBI file 100-381638, Kay Boyle Franckenstein, Sections 1 and 2, Serials X to NR Memo 11/9/72.

385 "lone operator": Roger Baldwin to KB, 30 December 1954, KBP.

385 "been a swimming instructor": William Clark to Honorable Robert Murphy, 28 October 1955, KBP.

386 "to be able to speak": Gale memoir 122.

386 "was completely anti-Communist": Karl Gruber to Joseph Franckenstein, 25 November 1955. The letter is cited in Joseph's testimony before the Hennings Committee, p. 1522, FBI file 123-3915, Joseph Maria Franckenstein, Sections 1 and 2, Serials 1–78.

386 "Are you or have you ever been a Communist?": Kay Boyle testifying before the Hennings committee. Found in the transcript of the Hennings hearings, p. 1544, FBI file 100-381638, Kay Boyle Franckenstein.

386 "a disgrace to the Senate": Joseph McCarthy, quoted in the *Daily Worker*, 29 November 1955. A clipping of the *Daily Worker* article may be found in FBI file 100-381638, Kay Boyle Franckenstein.

387 "Red" . . . "anti-Communist": *Chicago Daily Tribune*, 22 April 1957, 2:4.

387 "subversive connections": Mrs. F. H. Detweiler, letter, "Not on Trial," *Plainfield Courier-News*, c. 1955.

387 "We don't want to sound vindictive": "Treasury Man Facing Quiz on Facts in 'Risk' Firing," *New York Post* 25 November 1955.

387 "so that my life as a writer": KB to R. W. Stallman, 17 July 1957, University of Virginia Library.

387 "It must be the publicity": KB to Caresse Crosby, 27 January 1956, BSA.

387 "one of the most flagrant violations": Thomas C. Hennings to Joseph Franckenstein, FBI file 123-3915, Joseph Maria Franckenstein. See also Thomas C. Hennings to John Foster Dulles, 23 January 1956, ibid.

387 "on the question of guilt-by-kinship": Thomas C. Hennings to John Foster Dulles, 5 December 1955, FBI file 100-381638, Kay Boyle Franckenstein.

387 "in a position of apologizing": See Scott McLeod to Dennis A. Flinn, 10 May 1956, FBI file 123-3915, Joseph Maria Franckenstein. See also John Sipes to Scott McLeod, 21 December 1955, ibid.

387 "anxious to have the department's views": Thomas C. Hennings to John Foster Dulles, 10 January 1956, FBI file 100-381638, Kay Boyle Franckenstein.

387 "The matter of an employee's association": Thruston Morton to Thomas C. Hennings, 23 December 1955, ibid.

387 "grave doubts in the mind": Thomas C. Hennings to John Foster Dulles, 23 January 1956, ibid.

388 "unfavorable publicity": Judge William Clark to Robert Murphy, 26 January 1956, ibid.

388 their flirtatious relationship: Anne Martindell interview with JM, 1989.

388 "he has not been allowed": Thomas C. Hennings to John Foster Dulles, 8 March 1956, FBI file 100-381638, Kay Boyle Franckenstein.

388 "A very great wrong" has been done: See "Confidential Memorandum of Conversation: Edward

S. Greenbaum, John W. Hanes, Jr.," 2 March 1956, FBI file 100-381638, Kay Boyle Franckenstein.

388 Henderson told McLeod to cut off all communication: Loy W. Henderson to Mr. McLeod, memorandum, 22 March 1956, FBI file 100-381638, Kay Boyle Franckenstein.

388 they need only "vacate": Ibid.

389 "the incorrectness of the original decision": Memorandum of Conversation, 7 May 1956, Edward
S. Greenbaum, John W. Hanes, John W. Sipes, FBI file 100-381638, Kay Boyle Franckenstein.

389 "vindication": Ibid.

389 "additional intervention": Ibid.

389 "fight the bastards": Ted Kaghan to KB, 9 December 1956, KBP.

389 "Only litigation can bring about full clearance": Joseph Franckenstein to Rowland Watts, 31 May
1956, KBP.

389 the organizations he worked with provided funds for victims of *Nazi*: Benjamin Ferencz to Joseph
Franckenstein [Kay and Joe], 22 March 1960, KBP.

389 "security status had been favorably resolved": State Department to Joseph Franckenstein, 1 April
1957, and Loy W. Henderson to Joseph Franckenstein, 4 February 1957, FBI file 123-3915,
Joseph Maria Franckenstein.

390 Sipes and company agreed among themselves: See Mr. Lyerly to Mr. Henderson, 26 October
1956, and Scott McLeod to Dennis A. Flinn, 10 May 1956, ibid.

390 "the Department has finally recognized the injustice": Joseph Franckenstein to Loy W. Henderson,
Deputy Under Secretary, Department of State, 5 April 1957, ibid.

390 "factual inaccuracies" . . . "constitute acquiescence": John W. Sipes, Memorandum, 9 April
1957, ibid.

390 the State Department had indeed "cleared" Joseph: See Herbert Foster, "Pair Cleared in 'Risk'
Case," *Washington Post* 22 April 1957.

390 "grudging and inadequate reparation to a citizen": "Franckenstein," editorial, *Washington Post*,
23 April 1957.

390 "innocent victims": Ibid.

390 "security risk charges": *Chicago Tribune* 22 April 1957.

391 "at your and your husband's final clearance": Alfred A. Knopf to KB, 23 January 1957, KBP.

391 a "new beginning": KB to Sheila St. Lawrence, 19 April 1957, KBP.

391 "Isn't it a glorious day?": Ibid.

391 "part-time dependent": See Kay's 1961 statement to the Guggenheim Foundation.

391 "very popular misconception of German education": Siegfried Maruhn to KB, 14 February 1959,
KBP.

391 "pictured the spirit": Ibid.

391 "an honor undeserved": Ibid.

391 "public songs and dances": KB to Howard Nemerov, 2 March 1960, Washington University
Libraries, St. Louis.

391 "You immerse yourself completely in her glancing prose": John Barkham, "This Time the Germans
Were Receiving Orders," rev. of *Generation Without Farewell*, New York *World-Telegram & Sun*
25 January 1960.

391 "paralysis of plot": "One Novelist's Germany," rev. of *Generation Without Farewell*, *Newsweek*
January 1960: 92.

391–92 "difficult but fascinating": Gene Baro, "Novelist's Vision of Post-War Germany," rev. of
Generation Without Farewell, *Herald Tribune Book Review* 17 January 1960: 5.

392 "Kay Boyle's distinguished prose": Martha McGregor, "Kay Boyle's Thirteenth Novel: Occupied
and Occupier," rev. of *Generation Without Farewell*, *New York Post* 12 January 1960: 17.

392 "too mannered": Granville Hicks, "The Light and the Dark," rev. of *Generation Without Farewell*,
Saturday Review of Literature 43.3 (16 January 1960) 59.

392 "Kay Boyle has never written more poignantly": Virgilia Peterson, "There Is No Armistice," rev.
of *Generation Without Farewell*, *New York Times Book Review* 17 January 1960: 4.

392 "voice has been one of the few": George Steiner to KB, 19 March 1960, KBP.

392 "an interesting novel": William Carlos Williams to KB, 9 February 1960, HRHRC.

392 "a very meaningful story of the aftermath": Rev. of *Generation Without Farewell*, *McCall's* January
1960.

392 "statuesque and elegant": Ibid.

392 "phenomenal feat": "In and Out of Books," *New York Times Book Review* 17 January 1960: 8.

392 "bring her some of the recognition": Harry T. Moore, "Kay Boyle's Fiction," *Kenyon Review* 22
(Spring 1960) 323–24.

392 "I don't know a damn thing about history": KB interview with Dan Tooker and Roger Hofheins, *Fiction! Interviews with Northern California Novelists* (New York: Harcourt Brace Jovanovich and William Kaufmann, 1976) 28.

392 "lack of candor": Alfred A. Knopf to KB, 11 February 1960, KBP.

393 "pay grocer, milk": KB to Ann Watkins, 16 June 1956, KBP.

393 "so violent that I didn't care": KB to Herman Rappaport, 17 March 1957, KBP.

393 "comes more from worry": KB to Ann Watkins, 3 April 1956, KBP.

393 "so hard I'm dizzy": KB to Ann Watkins, 22 June 1954, KBP.

393 "like any other day": KB to Fay Rappaport, 12 December 1958, KBP.

393 "getting a story by Kay Boyle": Elliot W. Schryver to Ann Watkins, 17 July 1956, KBP.

393 "seems to have no real reason for being": Stuart Rose to Ann Watkins, 21 April 1955, KBP.

393 "each man is a country": Kay Boyle, "Spring," *Ladies' Home Journal* 74 (March 1957) 211.

393 "a Kay Boyle vogue": Harry T. Moore to KB, 12 June 1956, KBP.

394 Rust Hills at *Esquire* rejected: See Rust Hills to Ann Watkins, 20 August 1958, KBP.

394 "A hex on Rust Hills": KB to Ann Watkins, 28 August 1958, KBP.

394 "it's as if she were trying to say so many things": Katherine Jackson to Ann Watkins, 29 September 1958, KBP.

394 "Nobody's jumping up and down with joy": KB to Ann Watkins, 9 August 1955, KBP.

394 See Kay Boyle, "The Ballet of Central Park," *Saturday Evening Post* 237 (28 November 1964) 44–48, 50–51.

394 "this way of story-telling": Franchot Tone to KB, 28 January 1961, KBP.

394 "a distinguished and representative writer": Jerry Wald to KB, 12 October 1955, KBP.

394 "a soggy plodding drama": Rev. of CBS television presentation of "The Crazy Hunter," *Herald Tribune* 30 December 1958.

394 "authors shouldn't look at their own works": KB to Mike Watkins, 4 January 1959, KBP.

395 "I'm going to go over and tell Langston Hughes": KB interview with JM, August 1987.

395 "the big function": KB to Howard Nemerov, 28 March 1960, Washington University Libraries.

395 "it was suggested that I be thrown out the window": Ibid.

395 "Wouldn't it be a shock": KB to Bob Brown, 8 August 1958, RCBP.

395 "an enchanter": Marianne Moore to KB, 22 December 1958, KBP.

395 "How like a man": KB to Bernie McDonald, 29 May 1957, KBP.

395 "My God, what a shock": KB to Malcolm Cowley, 29 May 1957, Newberry Library.

396 "dearest Argie-Bargie": Nelson Algren to KB, 25 November 1958, KBP.

396 "Blessing on your pointy pen": Ibid.

396 "Where are you?": KB to Robert McAlmon, 24 May 1955, Beinecke Library.

396 "inadequate": KB to Howard Nemerov, 31 January 1959, Washington University Libraries.

396 "There was never anyone quite like McAlmon around": Kay Boyle, "Brighter Than Most," rev. of *McAlmon and the Lost Generation*, by Robert E. Knoll, *Prairie Schooner* 34 (Spring 1960) 1–4.

396 "It seemed disturbingly wrong": KB to William Carlos Williams, 19 November 1960, Beinecke Library.

396 "the unjudging, undamning": Kay Boyle, "In Memoriam, Bob Brown," editorial, *Village Voice* 26 August 1959: 4.

396 "a vitally important contribution": Kay Boyle, letter, *Herald Tribune* 16 October 1960.

396 "A curse on Gordon Abominable Craig": KB to William L. Shirer, 17 October 1960, KBP.

397 Kay pleaded she had not known: KB to Simon Michael Bessie, 10 October 1957, KBP. See also Kay Boyle, "Living Up to the Part," rev. of *The Actress*, by Bessie Breuer *New York Times Book Review* 6 October 1957: 4.

397 Kay Boyle, "For a Friend Whose Eyes Were Operated On in May," KBP.

397 Kay Boyle, "A Poem of Gratitude—for Caresse," *Poetry* 93 (March 1959) 376.

397 Kay Boyle, "Two Twilights for William Carlos Williams" and "A Dialogue of Birds for Howard Nemerov," *Poetry* 95 (March 1960) 356–57.

397 Kay Boyle, "Two Poems for a Poet," *Poetry* 97 (February 1961) 300–1.

397 "Kenneth Rexroth makes me wax wrath": Kay Boyle, letter, *New York Times Book Review*, 23 January 1961, KBP.

397 a letter from Kay went off at once: Kay Boyle, letter, *Nation* 23 January 1961.

397 "Irreplaceable As Treasures": KB to Marianne Moore [1958], KBP.

397 "had an instinctive and belligerent loyalty": KB to Karl Shapiro, 13 December 1959, KBP.

397 "put an end to all that petrified poetry": Karl Shapiro to KB, 9 January 1960, KBP.

397 "descended into orthodoxy": William Carlos Williams to KB, 20 January 1960, HRHRC.

397 "One of the main things wrong with my poetry": KB to Howard Nemerov, 10 August 1959, Washington University Libraries.
397 "progressed a lot in the art": William Carlos Williams to KB, 7 October 1959, HRHRC.
397 "poetic metres or feet": KB to William Carlos Williams, 13 October 1959, Beinecke Library.
398 "What a hypocrite": KB to Ann Watkins, 2 February 1954, KBP.
398 Kay waxed indignant when Walter Lowenfels: KB to Nancy Cunard, 27 February 1955, HRHRC.
398 "Mr. O'Connor's ill-mannered": KB to Francis Brown, 10 September 1958, KBP.
398 "as a gesture": KB to Ann Watkins, 16 June 1956, KBP.
398 "marred by her tendency to preach": Herbert Weinstock to Ann Watkins, 13 June 1956, KBP.
398 "a lot of preaching needs to be done": KB to Ann Watkins, 16 June 1956, KBP.
398 "We don't drink": Ibid.
398 "Mrs. Trilling was opposed": Robert M. MacGregor memo to James Laughlin, typed onto the top of a copy of a letter to Kay Boyle, September 1956, courtesy of James Laughlin.
398 "advocates of a regime": Diana Trilling to JM, 18 November 1991.
399 It was too cool: See Harry T. Moore to KB, 17 March 1957, KBP.
399 "He did say you were one of the best": Ibid.
399 "just about the worst book of mine": KB to R. W. Stallman, 17 July 1957, University of Virginia Libraries.

26. ABANDONED

400 "I should be grateful": KB to Fay Rappaport, 30 March 1961 [?], KBP.
400 "that words have a shape": KB Christmas card to James Laughlin, 1954.
400 "the black of a student's writing": Kay Boyle, "Kay Boyle," *Women Writers of the West Coast*, ed. Marilyn Yalom (Santa Barbara: Capra Press, 1983) 107.
400 "I can edit manuscripts": KB to Caresse Crosby, 1 June 1956, BSA.
401 "obviously considered": KB to Sheila St. Lawrence, 11 November 1956, KBP.
401 "thousands in readings": KB to Malcolm Cowley, 29 May 1957, Newberry Library.
401 "series of pamphlets": KB to Richard Wright, 5 October 1956, Beinecke Library.
401 "working with the State Department": Ibid.
401 "a spirited lament": KB to James T. Farrell, 28 April 1957, Charles Van Pelt Library, University of Pennsylvania.
401 "the academic patter": KB to Herman Rappaport, 13 January 1957, KBP.
401 "I can't talk the way they want me to": KB to Malcolm Cowley, 22 February 1957, Newberry Library.
401 "what human beings are like": KB to Herman Rappaport, 2 February 1957, KBP.
401 "If I live through this": KB to Bob Brown, 14 February 1957, RCBP.
402 "Negro short story writers": KB to Herman Rappaport, 15 February 1957, KBP.
402 "even he was hard put": KB to Herman Rappaport, 13 April 1957, KBP.
402 "shocking" and "a complete hoax": KB to Padraic Colum, 1 April 1957, KBP.
402 "drastically from the intentions of the writer": KB to R. W. Stallman, 29 April 1957, University of Virginia Libraries.
402 "The creative mind starts with an answer": KB to R. W. Stallman, 24 May 1957, KBP.
402 "hard-pressed to distinguish": Ibid.
402 "delighted that you probe me": Ibid.
402 "they frighten me with their coldness": KB to R. W. Stallman, 18 September 1957, University of Virginia Libraries.
402 "invaluable critical material": KB to Jerome Weidman, 6 August 1957, HRHRC.
402 "about twenty-two hours a day": KB to Roger Burlingame, 14 July 1957, KBP.
402 "a renaissance in writing usually occurred": KB to Roger Burlingame, 23 June 1957, KBP.
402 "intended to put Stallman and West and other New Critics": KB to Simon Michael Bessie, 2 January 1958, HRHRC.
402 "the positive side": Simon Michael Bessie to KB, 17 January 1958, HRHRC.
402 See Kay Boyle, "No Time to Listen," *Nation* 185 (16 November 1957) 341–42.
403 "If you wish to": Samuel Dodson to KB, undated, KBP.
403 "They were flesh and blood": Kay Boyle, "City of Invisible Men," *Nation* 185 (21 December 1957) 475–76.
403 "speak out loudly and clearly": Kay Boyle, "The Long Dead Fathers," *Progressive* 22 (September 1958) 35–37.

403 "respect the law as laid down": Kay Boyle, "So Slowly We Move," *Nation* 184 (4 May 1957) 390–93.

403 "To the French People": A petition against the Algerian war, dated 28 May 1958 and available in KBP: " 'To the French People' we, your friends and allies, are prompted to address you by our deep concern over the lengthening tragedy of the Algerian war. Do not, we beg you, straightaway dismiss this as an unasked interference in your affairs . . ." The twenty-eight signers of this petition included not only Kay Boyle but also Eleanor Roosevelt, Roger N. Baldwin, Paul Bowles, Erich Fromm, Sidney Hook, Norman Thomas, Marianne Moore, Upton Sinclair, William Carlos Williams, and Ralph Ellison.

403 "against the bomb": Kay Boyle, "Triumph of Principles," *Words That Must Somehow Be Said: The Selected Essays of Kay Boyle, 1927–1984*, ed. Elizabeth Bell (London: Chatto & Windus–Hogarth Press, 1985) 190.

403 "embarrassing everyone on Fifth Avenue": Kay Boyle, "January 29, 1962," *Liberation* 7 (March 1962) 8.

404 With coeds at Penn: Kay Boyle, "Life with Penn's Coeds," Philadelphia *Sunday Bulletin* (25 March 1962) 6–7.

404 Kay Boyle had congratulated John F. Kennedy: KB to John F. Kennedy, 25 September 1961, KBP. See also FBI file 100-381638, Kay Boyle Franckenstein, Sections 1 and 2, Serials X to NR Memo 11/9/72.

404 "a tradition of courage": KB to François Mauriac, 22 November 1959, Beinecke Library.

404 "Had I the money to live on": KB to Howard Nemerov, 22 August 1960, Washington University Libraries.

404 "nothing" likable about the German people: Beverly Gary, "Close-up: Student of Germany," *New York Post* 1961.

404 "I *am* prejudiced against the Germans": KB to Kathryn Hulme, 8 August 1959, Beinecke Library.

404 "the moral consequences of the *wirtschaftswunder*": Kay Boyle, "Has Germany Changed?" *Foreign Policy Bulletin* 39.15 (15 April 1960) 117.

404 "have we the right to forgive": Kay Boyle, letter, *New York Times*, 27 February 1960, KBP.

404 "human rights need to be constantly guarded": Kay Boyle, "Breaking the Silence: Why a Mother Tells Her Son About the Nazi Era." Published by Institute of Human Relations Press, The American Jewish Committee.

405 "highly intellectual": Samuel S. Fishzohn to KB, 24 November 1961, KBP.

405 "offended and not a little hurt": Alfred A. Knopf to KB, 11 February 1960, KBP.

405 "We don't want this book": Ken McCormick to KB, 15 August 1960, KBP.

405 "a masterpiece": Ken McCormick to KB, 9 February 1961, KBP.

405 "a tremendously exciting book": Ibid.

405 "magnificent evidence of the great book": Ken McCormick to KB, 4 April 1961, KBP.

405 "I can be patient": Ken McCormick to KB, 16 June 1961, KBP.

405 "go on being all the things I am": KB to Roger Burlingame, 14 February 1960, KBP.

405 "My daughter's in this movie": Kathe Vail interviews with JM, June 1990 and November 1991.

406 "only hope now": Clover Vail to KB, 13 September 1955, KBP. The text of the letter reads: "Bobby said: the best thing for Apple was you. That you were her only hope now."

406 "I worry without stopping over Apple": KB to Fay Rappaport, 2 April 1956, KBP.

406 a series of shock treatments: Ted Goeser telephone interviews with JM, 12 March 1991 and 16 March 1991.

406 "terrible intestinal cramps": KB to Herman Rappaport, 31 January 1957, KBP.

406 "We all miss you": Apple Goeser to KB, 21 August 1961, KBP.

406 She threw a knife at Ted: Ted Goeser telephone interviews with JM, 12 March 1991 and 16 March 1991.

406 "ambulatory schizoid": KB to Herman Rappaport, 7 February 1958, KBP.

406 "Conditions here are almost beyond bearing": KB to Herman Rappaport, 6 January 1958, KBP.

406 Kay and Laurence now blamed each other: Kathe Vail interviews with JM, June 1990.

406 her doctor urged Kay to postpone any trip: KB to "dear Fay, dear Herman" [Rappaport], 7 February 1958, KBP.

406 "Kay is not the best person to talk to": Laurence Vail to Djuna Barnes, 3 March 1958, University of Maryland Libraries.

406–7 she believed she had harmed her older daughters: Ian Franckenstein interview with JM, August 1987.

407 his conviction that Apple had been abandoned: KB interview with Hugh Ford, 1978.

407 she insisted that Apple had never been abandoned: Ibid.

407 "If you go down too deeply": KB unpublished interview with Debbie Linton, San Francisco State University, 1979.

407 "You have to go down to find out who you are": Ibid.

407 "You find out who you are by the people around you": Ibid.

407 "unlike some of her contemporaries": Robert E. Knoll, "Love Poems," rev. of *Collected Poems*, by Kay Boyle, *Prairie Schooner* 37.1 (Spring 1963) 176–78.

407 "her love for me": KB to Fay and Herman Rappaport, 6 March 1958, KBP.

407 "three hours of blistering heat": KB to Ann Watkins, 5 March 1958, KBP.

408 "half the night going over and over": KB to James T. Farrell, 6 March 1958, Charles Van Pelt Library, University of Pennsylvania.

408 "You raised me": Sindbad Vail to KB, 2 February 1958, KBP.

408 "money grabbing": Sindbad Vail to KB, 4 July 1958, BERG.

408 "you used to hold my forehead": Apple Goeser to KB, 14 September 1959, BERG.

408 "You fell in love with a ski teacher": KB interview with Hugh Ford, 1978.

408 "I want so much to know of her from you": Laurence Vail to Clover Vail, 18 April 1958, KBP.

409 "do pipi": Laurence Vail to KB, 19 October 1958, BERG.

409 "an object of disgust": Laurence Vail to Djuna Barnes, undated, University of Maryland Libraries.

409 "in trade": Donald Muntz interview with JM, 30 March 1990, and Donald Muntz phone conversation with JM, 14 July 1991.

409 "my husband does not like me to mention the year": KB to Willard Maas, 31 January 1962, HRHRC.

409 "I hear she's dyed her silver curls a midnight black!": Solita Solano to Djuna Barnes, undated, University of Maryland Libraries.

409 "with her usual load of eye-shadow": Louise Bogan to Ruth Limmer, 7 March 1963, in Ruth Limmer, ed., *What the Woman Lived: Selected Letters of Louise Bogan 1920–1970* (New York: Harcourt Brace Jovanovich, 1973) 350–51.

410 until he became insulting and left: Faith Gude interviews with JM, December 1989 and 2 March 1991.

410 Deshaies would sweep Kay into his arms: Ibid.

410 "in love": KB to William Carlos Williams, 30 June 1960, Beinecke Library.

410 "a time, and a passion": KB to Howard Nemerov, 23 April 1960, Washington University Libraries.

410 "be destroyed": KB to Howard Nemerov, 9 July 1959, Washington University Libraries.

410 "somehow to blame for the unalterable facts": KB to Kathryn Hulme, 28 October 1959, Beinecke Library.

410 if there wasn't penetration: Clover Vail interview with JM, 20 February 1991.

410 Joseph seemed to be a wounded man: Marsha Torkelson interview with JM, January 1992.

411 "Ratatouille Rowayton" . . . "Thoreauic, red-bearded": See Beryl Barr and Barbara Turner Sachs, eds., *The Artists and Writers Cookbook* (Sausalito: Contact Editions, 1961) 222.

411 "violent, tearful agony": KB to Fay Rappaport, 11 May 1961, KBP.

411 "tender and loving reunion": KB to Fay Rappaport, 20 March 1961, KBP.

411 "symbol" . . . "do anything else": KB to Howard Nemerov, 23 April 1960, Washington University Libraries.

411 "shouts of rage": Ibid.

411 Laurence Vail was irritated: Kathe Vail interviews with JM, June 1990 and November 1991.

411 "It's the way it was between you and me": Ibid.

411 "I belong in this catastrophe": Ibid.

411 "Your mother's going absolutely crazy": Kathe Vail interviews with JM, June 1990 and November 1991.

411 "Your mother's a dreadful person": Ian Franckenstein interview with JM, August 1987.

411 "waited on her hand and foot": Susan Hager interview with JM, 6 June 1988.

411 "To salvage my conscience": KB to Howard Nemerov, 4 December 1961, Washington University Libraries.

412 Kay got drunk: Faith Gude interviews with JM, December 1989 and 2 March 1991.

412 "everything else as a way of living": KB to Howard Nemerov, 23 April 1960, Washington University Libraries.

412 "with the lost and the terrified": Ibid.

412 "calmness and unjudging love": KB to Fay Rappaport, 7 January 1961, KBP.

412 "the humor and pulse": Kay Boyle, "Paintings in Flight," *Mark* [the community magazine serving Norwalk and its environs] 7 (30 July 1960) 9–10.

412 "I understand him": KB to Fay Rappaport, 12 January 1961, KBP.

412 "our year . . . Arthur's and mine": KB to Fay Rappaport, 26 April 1961, KBP.
412 he would come into Faith's bedroom: Faith Gude interviews with JM, December 1989 and 2 March 1991.
412 "So many lone grieving poems": Kay Boyle, "A Poem for a Painter," May 1960, KBP.
412 she sees his face in a landscape: Ibid.
412 "interchangeable tongues": Kay Boyle, "Poem for a Painter Who Drinks Wine," *Nation* 192 (14 January 1961) 38.
413 "you are the footprint": Kay Boyle, "Seascape for an Engraver," *Poetry* 99 (January 1962) 214.
413 "You shook the liquid": Kay Boyle, "A Poem for Arthur," *Southern Review* n.s. 1 (July 1965) 607.
413 "Love and So Much Love": Arthur Deshaies telegram to KB, 22 June 1960, BERG.
413 "White Hair'd Goddess of Art": Arthur Deshaies to KB, 5 March 1961, BERG.
413 "shattered" by his absence: KB to Fay Rappaport, 20 March 1961, KBP.
413 "grateful for this great love": Ibid.
413 "his solicitude": Ibid.
413 "essential that": KB to Fay Rappaport, 19 October 1961, KBP.
414 her "greatness": Arthur Deshaies to KB, 20 August 1962, BERG.
414 "increases month by month": KB to Caresse Crosby, 29 July 1961, BSA.
414 "One must work hard": KB to Ian Franckenstein, 30 September 1962, BERG.

27. DEATH OF A MAN

415 "You were laughing": Joseph Franckenstein to KB, undated fragment, KBP.
415 "Now Joseph will have his cross": Janet Flanner to KB, 25 September 1963, KBP.
415 the "blondes": Clover Vail interviews with JM, and 20 February 1991.
415 "You're not my goddamned father": Faith Gude interviews with JM, December 1989 and 2 March 1991.
415 Kay had Clover committed: Clover Vail interview with JM, 19 January 1991.
416 "War of Nerves with Kay": Kathe Vail interviews with JM, June 1990 and November 1991.
416 "Clover would fall in love": KB to Fay Rappaport, 14 November 1961, KBP.
416 *"tell me all you know of Herbert Kubly"*: KB to Caresse Crosby, 31 January 1962, BSA.
416 "I am very fond of him": KB to Caresse Crosby, 9 February 1962, BSA.
416 "my beloved Nic": KB to Fay Rappaport, 2 February 1962, KBP.
416 "desperately": KB to Fay Rappaport, undated, KBP.
416 "last forever": Ibid.
416 "the exact opposite of Arthur": KB to Fay Rappaport, 14 November 1961, KBP.
417 "big and wise": Ibid.
417 "famous": Ibid.
417 "vehemently about fall-out shelters": Ibid.
417 "could be no feeling of anguish": Ibid.
417 "about sixteen": Ibid.
417 "deeply, deeply lucky": Ibid.
417 "be no more infidelity": Ibid.
417 and would even list herself as co-author: Gale memoir 124. Listed under Kay Boyle's fiction, the entry reads: "At Large, with Herbert Kubly. London: Gollancz, 1963; Garden City, N.Y.: Doubleday, 1964."
417 There was an intense weekend: Ken McCormick interview with JM, 15 March 1989.
418 "ghastly saga": Herbert Kubly to KB, 8 August 1962, KBP.
418 "too much about his private life": KB to Ian Franckenstein, 30 September 1962, BERG.
418 "sweet partner": Kay Boyle, "A Square Dance for a Square," *Southern Review* n.s. 1 (July 1965) 608–11.
418 "a rather intense mama–little boy friendship": KB to Herbert Wilner, 24 January 1965, KBP.
418 "paranoic delusions": Ibid.
418 "What are you going to do now?": KB interview with JM, August 1987.
419 remain her mother's little girl: Ibid.
419 "required to make a life of her own": KB to Fay Rappaport, 2 February 1962, KBP.
419 "cold, remote and perfect": Clover Vail telephone interview with JM, 8 December 1990.
419 "You were never left alone": KB to Clover Vail, 7 February 1970, BERG.
419 "What is the sense of saving the children of Biafra?": Clover Vail to KB, 6 January 1970, BERG.

419 "You have GOT to see": KB to Clover Vail, 7 February 1970, BERG.

419 "reproached for divorcing Papa": Ibid.

419 "free will": Ibid.

419 Joseph had given up: Faith Gude interviews with JM, December 1989 and 2 March 1991.

420 "What happens if Nixon wins": Ian Franckenstein interview with JM, August 1987.

420 "resume work": Will Lang to Donald Wilson, 23 February 1961, FBI file 123-3915, Joseph Maria Franckenstein.

420 "with the more favorable climate": Joseph Franckenstein to Edward R. Murrow, 12 April 1961, ibid.

420 "beaten McCarthy": KB to Howard Nemerov, 14 June 1962, Washington University Libraries.

420 "proud and happy for Joseph": Ibid.

420 "enthusiastic about possibility": Ibid.

420 "a cruel exile": William Shirer, *Twentieth Century Journey: A Memoir of the Life and Times, Vol. 1: The Start—1904–1930* (New York: Simon & Schuster, 1976) 176.

420 "We'll see you at Christmas": Quoted in Herbert Kubly to KB, undated, KBP.

420 "the most profound influence": Ian Franckenstein interview with JM, August 1987.

421 "If my mother or my country were invaded": KB interview with JM, August 1987.

421 "You can give each other respect": Ian Franckenstein interview with JM, August 1987.

421 Joseph demanded that his daughter: Faith Gude interviews with JM, December 1989 and 2 March 1991.

421 Abortion was "terrible": Ibid.

421 "I'm so proud of you": Ibid.

421 "You're exactly like Mama": Ibid.

422 "living off my ex-husband": Ibid.

422 "queer shop": Joseph Franckenstein to Ian Franckenstein, 5 January 1963, BERG.

422 "Russia was bad": Joseph Franckenstein to KB [1963], KBP.

422 "I feel lonely": Joseph Franckenstein to Ian Franckenstein, 19 November 1962, BERG.

422 "Do you think he's become an alcoholic?": Kathe Vail interviews with JM, June 1990 and November 1991.

422 "Don't be angry": Joseph Franckenstein to KB, undated fragment, KBP.

423 "very pretty": William L. Shirer to KB, 19 March 1963, KBP.

423 "to save the creative writer from academia": John B. Jarzavek, "Kay Boyle: Missionary and Scholar," *Wesleyan Argies* [February–March 1963].

423 "a process of self-analysis": "Never Stop Learning," *Register* 21 April 1963.

423 "After you've written": Ibid.

423 a young "criminal": See Kay Boyle, "Should Be Considered Extremely Dangerous," *Story* 36 (January–February 1963) 54–71.

423 "vanishing short story": Kay Boyle, "The Vanishing Short Story," *Story* 36 (July–August 1963) 108–19.

423 "the baby of the group": Malcolm Cowley, "The Last of the Lost Generation," *Esquire* 60 (July 1963) 77.

423 "a number of years": KB to Marianne Moore, 13 June 1963, HRHRC.

424 "walking skeleton": KB interview with JM, August 1987.

424 "a cell cast off by another cancer": KB to Ian Franckenstein, 8 July 1963, BERG.

424 "We will meet things": KB to Ian Franckenstein, 11 July 1963, BERG.

424 See Kay Boyle, *Pinky, the Cat Who Liked to Sleep*, illustrated by Lillian Obligado (New York: Crowell-Collier, 1966), and Kay Boyle, *Pinky in Persia*, illustrated by Lillian Obligado (New York: Crowell-Collier, 1968).

425 the only time he ever heard Kay Boyle cry: Herbert Gold interview with JM, 22 December 1988.

425 complaining if he got egg: Susan Hager interview with JM, 6 June 1988.

425 "time is so short": KB to Howard Nemerov, 2 August 1963, Washington University Libraries.

425 a piece about skiing: See Kay Boyle, "Skiing," *Glamour* 50 (November 1963) 130, 174–75.

425 "I am keeping my sanity": KB to Mike Watkins, 8 August 1963, KBP.

425 "with all men of good will": KB to Kathryn Hulme, 24 August 1963, Beinecke Library.

425 "tragedy is trying": Quoted in KB to Howard Nemerov, 18 August 1963, Washington University Libraries.

425 "so like Clover": Ibid.

425 *"yourself"* . . . "noble": Janet Flanner to KB, 25 September 1963, KBP.

425 "absolutely limitless freedom": KB to Nancy Cunard, 6 September 1963, HRHRC.

426 "stamina": Marianne Moore to KB, 22 December 1962, KBP. See also Carson McCullers to

Newton Arvin, "Sunday" [1942], Smith College: "She [Kay Boyle] is expecting her baby this week-end. The letter was written yesterday and she is still working hard at still another book. Think of it!"; and Carson McCullers to KB, 2 April 1943, KBP: "Kay, you have more life and vigor and courage in you than anyone I know."

426 "too old to start over": KB to Howard Nemerov, 23 August 1963, Washington University Libraries.
426 "Mom, I'm in labor": Faith Gude interviews with JM, December 1989 and 2 March 1991.
426 "like a dead bird": KB to Kathryn Hulme, undated, Beinecke Library.
426 "the most refined of cruelties": KB to Howard Nemerov, 4 October 1963, Washington University Libraries.
426 "like a lost child": KB to Kathryn Hulme, 20 September 1963, Beinecke Library.
427 "It would be a great happiness": KB to Keith W. Bailes, FBI file 123-3915, Joseph Maria Franckenstein. See also FBI file 100-381638, Kay Boyle Franckenstein.
427 "it would require entirely": Keith W. Bailes to Joseph Franckenstein, 7 October 1963, FBI file 123-3915, Joseph Maria Franckenstein.
427 "But you will not go to hell": KB interview with JM, August 1987.
427 having "failed" Joseph: KB to Fay Rappaport, 18 October 1963, KBP.
427 all but broke her heart: KB to Howard Nemerov, 19 October 1963, Washington University Libraries.
427 "Poor, sweet Joe": Ann Lochner to KB, October 1963, KBP.
427 "through every pain": Sharon Cowling to KB, October 1963, KBP.
427 "could take some of your unhappiness on me": Kathe Vail to KB, 29 November 1963, KBP.
427 "The day my father died": Untitled poem by Faith Gude, BERG.
427 "the throb of the drums": KB to Fay Rappaport, 24 November 1963, KBP.

28 THE FINISHED WOMAN

428 "Perhaps when I'm in the sixties": KB to Louise Theis, 16 October 1965, BERG.
428 "I'm madly in love": William L. Shirer interview with JM, 22 May 1989.
428 "the twenties and everything": Peggy Guggenheim to Djuna Barnes, 19 April 1962, University of Maryland Libraries.
428 You always knew where her center was: Leo Litwak interview with JM, 14 December 1989.
428 "You're a beautiful woman": Ian Franckenstein interview with JM, August 1987; Hank McGuckin interview with JM, 15 December 1989; and Gwen Davis telephone interview with JM, 1992.
429 "how one starts life over again": KB to James T. Farrell, 30 January 1964, Charles Van Pelt Library, University of Pennsylvania.
429 "bear it that he is dead": KB to Caresse Crosby, 25 October 1963, BSA.
429 "Until the residential pattern changes": See "Kay Boyle: Champion of Understanding," *San Francisco Examiner* 12 October 1963: 6. Quotes from this article are also included in FBI file 100-381638, Kay Boyle Franckenstein.
429 "Negro quarter": Ibid.
429 reminding her of Paris: KB to Ann [Watkins] and Roger Burlingame, 13 December 1963, KBP.
429 Faith's "husband": Faith Gude interviews with JM, December 1989 and 2 March 1991.
429 "a great full life": Clover Vail to KB, 27 October 1963, BERG.
429 For this picture of Kay Boyle in the classroom, I have drawn on the following interviews: Dan Tooker with JM, 18 October 1989 and 20 November 1989; Shawn Wong with JM, 3 June 1991; and Victor Turks with JM, 13 December 1989.
429 "You should be both humble and proud": KB to Gordon Lish, 3 November 1963, HRHRC.
430 "When one is in love": "Sketch of a Poet" [article printed after Kay Boyle's reading at the San Francisco Museum of Art], *San Francisco Chronicle* 12 April 1964.
430 "write about 'issues' ": KB to Howard Nemerov, 18 November 1964, Washington University Libraries.
430 "Can we say the history is done?": Kay Boyle, "A Poem About the Jews," *Harvard Advocate* 100 (Fall 1966) 21–23.
430 "A strange and rather exciting journey": KB to Howard Nemerov, 9 February 1964, Washington University Libraries.
430 "I do hope you haven't been hired by CIA": Howard Nemerov to KB, 13 February 1964, KBP.
430 "a sincere and dedicated man": Horace Schwartz, "Writer Kay Boyle," *San Francisco Examiner* 31 May 1964.

430 "this is not a protest": Herb Caen, "Oh What Lovely War," *San Francisco Chronicle* 12 July 1966.

430 Wilner would don his blue suit: Nancy Wilner interview with JM, 14 December 1989.

430 "was a sexual pervert": KB to Raphael Paganelli of *Fact* magazine, 18 October 1963, KBP.

431 "She doesn't teach us": Hank McGuckin interview with JM, 15 December 1989.

431 "If I ever talk": Ted Keller interview with JM, 15 December 1989.

431 "I have his baby": Faith Gude interviews with JM, December 1989 and 2 March 1991.

431 "You're going to love Kay": Ron Padgett telephone interview with JM, January 1990.

431 "surprisingly tall": Ron Padgett, "The First Time I Saw Kay Boyle," *Twentieth Century Literature* [Special Kay Boyle Issue], ed. Sandra Whipple Spanier, 34.3 (Fall 1988) 293.

431 Koch gave her one of his poems: Kenneth Koch interview with JM, 24 January 1990.

431 she looked like Barbara Stanwyck: David Shapiro telephone interview with JM, 26 January 1990.

432 "brilliant young poet": Kenneth Koch interview with JM, 24 January 1990.

432 "very fat": KB to Howard Nemerov, 22 July 1964, Washington University Libraries.

432 "voice of the people": KB to Nancy Cunard, 29 November 1963, HRHRC.

432 "I suspect Mary McCarthy": Nelson Algren to KB, 22 September 1964, KBP.

433 "in the far-off, barbaric days": Talk by Kay Boyle given 9 October 1964, at the Thomas School, "On the Occasion of the First Memorial Assembly for Joseph M. Franckenstein," KBP.

433 "Get up, Bill": Faith Gude interviews with JM, December 1989 and 2 March 1991.

433 "running a literary Gestapo": KB to Howard Nemerov, 26 November 1964, Washington University Libraries.

433 "My heart is with them": KB to James Laughlin, 13 December 1964.

433 "It is the old and the wise": Kay Boyle, letter to *New York Times*, 3 January 1965, KBP.

433 See Kay Boyle, "One Sunny Morning," *Saturday Evening Post* 238 (3 July 1965): 61–62, 64.

434 "Kay Boyle the novelist": Harry T. Moore, introduction, *Plagued by the Nightingale* (1931; Carbondale and Edwardsville: Southern Illinois UP, 1966).

434 "bluish": KB to Mr. Walton, 25 September 1967, KBP.

434 "to act politically": KB to Adlai Stevenson, 28 June 1965, KBP.

434 "I cannot believe or bear what is happening in Vietnam": KB to Howard Nemerov, 24 March 1965, Washington University Libraries.

434 "freedom of feelings": Faith Gude to KB, 29 August 1965, KBP.

435 "very potent nectar": Ibid.

435 "visual literacy": Martin Scorsese interview with JM, 14 February 1990.

435–36 "There is a very pleasant film writer here": KB to Caresse Crosby, 8 August 1965, BSA.

436 "a little bit in love": Ibid.

436 "I am exceedingly happy": KB to Howard Nemerov, 22 September 1965, Washington University Libraries.

436 "Bob might enjoy": Faith Gude to KB, 4 October 1965, KBP.

436 no sense of humor at all: Peter Gessner interview with JM, 13 December 1989.

436 "be the real beginning": KB to Howard Nemerov, 6 October 1965, Washington University Libraries.

436 "a most attractive man": Diane Arbus, quoted in Howard Nemerov to KB, 25 September 1965, KBP.

436 "once when we awoke": Kay Boyle, "A Poem of Love," *Love* [no vol.] [c. 1966] 25. (*Love* is edited by Al Young and published in Berkeley. This issue has a cover by Roald Dahl.)

437 "alien motel bed": Kay Boyle, "Thunder Storm in South Dakota for R.G.," *Southern Review* n.s. 3 (October 1967) 951.

437 "for complications": KB to Mike Watkins, 19 December 1965, KBP.

437 "with a man I love": KB to Caresse Crosby, 9 December 1965, BSA.

437 "excesses": William Shirer to KB, 24 January 1965, KBP.

437 "possessive and irrational": KB to Caresse Crosby, 27 January 1966, BSA.

437 clear to those who knew him: See Harold Gessner interview with JM, 6 June 1989; Stephen Gessner interview with JM, Peter Gessner interview with JM, 13 December 1989; and Carolyn Burke telephone interview with JM, 8 March 1990.

437 "all that serious": William L. Shirer interview with JM, 22 May 1989.

437 "She's too old": Peter Gessner interview with JM, 13 December 1989.

438 "was doomed": Ken McCormick to KB, 17 January 1966, KBP.

438 "ridiculous": "Wink & Ernie" to KB, 2 February 1966, BERG.

438 "like all Hungarians": William L. Shirer to KB, 24 January 1965, KBP.

438 "some sort of a breakdown": KB to Howard Nemerov, 10 January 1966, Washington University Libraries.

438 "everything with him was so happy and right": Ibid.

438 "He creates his own diabolical reality": KB to Caresse Crosby, 22 January 1966, BSA.

438 "I beg of you to keep this lost and terrifying man": KB to Caresse Crosby [1966], BSA.

438 "cruel rejection": May Sarton to KB, 23 March 1966, KBP.

438 "friends": KB to Caresse Crosby, 3 May 1966, BSA.

438 so "insulting" a letter: Ibid.

438 "not . . . receive": KB to Caresse Crosby, 23 August 1966, BSA.

438 "made him cry": Ken McCormick to KB, 23 November 1966, KBP.

439 the "hell" of the demise: KB to Howard Nemerov, 5 March 1966, Washington University Libraries.

439 "the holy mother of a certain kind of radical movement": Herbert Gold interview with JM, 22 December 1988.

439 "accounts of Vietnamese": Kay Boyle, letter to the Society for the Prevention of World War III, 15 December 1966, KBP.

439 See Kay Boyle, "The Battle of the Pagoda," *Liberation* 11 (August 1966) 28–29.

439 "with their scarves of napalm": Kay Boyle, "Dedicated to *Terre des Hommes,*" *Catholic Worker* 33 (December 1966) 8.

439 "What the hell does she mean by that?": Susan Hager interview with JM, 6 June 1988.

439 See Kay Boyle, *Nothing Ever Breaks Except the Heart* (Garden City, NY: Doubleday, 1966). All subsequent references are to this edition.

439 "a major writer": Maxwell Geismar, "Aristocrat of the Short Story," rev. of *Nothing Ever Breaks Except the Heart, New York Times Book Review* 10 July 1966: 4, 16.

440 "deserves much more respect": Richard Sullivan, "Twenty Stories from a Worker in Words," rev. of *Nothing Ever Breaks Except the Heart, Chicago Tribune* 10 July 1966: "Books Today" section, 1.

440 "social worker's approach": Thomas Lask, "May Good Prevail," *New York Times* 21 June 1966: L1.

440 "on the right side": W. J. Stuckey, "The Heart Is Not Enough," rev. of *Nothing Ever Breaks Except the Heart, Critique* 9.2 (1967) 85–88.

440 "people of the lower scale": Kay Boyle quoted in Mildred Schroeder, "Author Kay Boyle Spurs New Kind of Integration," *San Francisco Examiner* 1 July 1966: 20.

440 "three weeks out of my life and my work": KB to Ken McCormick, 30 May 1966, KBP.

440 "one of the greatest opportunities": Ibid.

440 "a great moving": Clover Vail to KB, 10 June 1966, KBP.

441 "We are really going without knowing what we will find": "Kay Boyle to 'See for Self' in Cambodia," *San Francisco Examiner* 12 July 1966.

441 "staunchly neutral": "5 Cambodia Trippers Bring Back Same Views," *San Francisco Examiner* 11 August 1966.

441 "one of the big powers will take over here one day": Kay Boyle, "Assignment in Cambodia," *Progressive* 30 (November 1966) 17–20.

441 "a matriarchal society": KB interview with Erik Bauersfeld, 1975.

441 "a vain, stupid, prejudiced man": "Kay Boyle's Bitter View of Johnson," *San Francisco Examiner* 15 September 1966: 15.

441 "land of packaged meats": Kay Boyle, "The Lost Dogs of Phnom Penh," *Lace Curtain* 1 (Winter 1969–70) 8.

442 "the elements of a magazine article": Ken McCormick to KB, 7 October 1966, KBP.

442 "so dynamic": Kay Boyle, "Assignment in Cambodia."

29. COMMUNE, REDUX

443 "You are the only 'parent' ": Faith Gude to KB, 14 October 1966, BERG.

443 "Kay Boyle—I wanted her kids": Mel Lyman, quoted in David Felton, "The Lyman Family's Holy Siege of America," *Rolling Stone* 98 (23 December 1971) 40–58; 99 (6 January 1972) 40–60.

443 "everyone's children": Faith Gude to KB, 21 November 1966, KBP.

443 "ready to sacrifice": Faith Gude to KB, 19 October 1966, KBP.

443 "his people" . . . "internal freedom": Felton, "Lyman Family's Holy Siege of America," *Rolling Stone* 99 (6 January 1972) 58.

444 "in the medium of people": Ibid.

444 "Beatnik existence": Faith Gude to KB, 16 September 1966, KBP.

444 "women's work": Felton, "The Lyman Family's Holy Siege of America," *Rolling Stone* 98 (23 December 1971) 40–58.

444 "the happiest": Faith Gude to KB, 14 October 1966, KBP.

444–45 "life-sized figures of Frederick II and Bismarck": KB to Erich Kahler, 25 June 1966, KBP.

445 Kahler was charmed by Kay Boyle: Lily Kahler interview with JM, 19 April 1988.

445 "loved" Kay Boyle . . . "plunging into your youth": Erich Kahler to KB, 20 December 1967, Erich and Evelyn Kahler papers, Morris Library, Southern Illinois University, Carbondale, IL.

445 "like a death sentence": KB to Erich Kahler, 23 November 1966, KBP.

445 "flip . . . when they heard that 'Kay Boyle is coming to live here!' ": Faith Gude to KB, 14 October 1966, KBP.

445 "It will be peaceful here for you": Faith Gude to KB, 16 September 1966, KBP.

445 "We are open to change": Faith Gude to KB, 14 October 1966, KBP.

445 "I learned all this from you": Ibid.

445 "it smells of you still": Faith Gude to KB, 7 December 1966, KBP.

446 "I hope we kept you awake": KB interview with JM, August 1987; and Felton, "The Lyman Family's Holy Siege of America," *Rolling Stone* 98 (23 December 1971) 45.

446 "I have no idea": Ibid.

446 "Granny will pay the bill": KB interview with JM, August 1987.

446 "learn to change": Ian Franckenstein to KB, 25 January 1967, BERG.

446 "fit into their pattern of living": Ibid.

446 "very insignificant looking": Felton, "The Lyman Family's Holy Siege of America," *Rolling Stone* 98 (23 December 1971) 44.

446 "I love you": KB interview with JM, August 1987; and Faith Gude interviews with JM, December 1989 and 2 March 1991.

446 what she had done took guts: Faith Gude interviews with JM, December 1989 and 2 March 1991.

447 "literally blue with cold": Felton, "The Lyman Family's Holy Siege of America," *Rolling Stone* 98 (23 December 1971) 45.

447 "Beautiful": Ibid.

447 "I've never known such hatred": Ibid.

447 "It doesn't matter": Ibid.

447 "She did destroy her two children": KB to Sandra Whipple Spanier, 23 July 1981, KBP.

447 "so beautiful, so foolish, so little more than a child herself": KB to Edward Dahlberg, 13 April 1967, HRHRC.

447 "work out": Ken McCormick interview with JM, 15 March 1989. See also KB to Ken McCormick, 4 July 1970, KBP.

447 "she was very good": Ken McCormick interview with JM, 15 March 1989.

448 "no space": See KB to Mike Watkins, 10 November 1967, KBP.

448 she complained to friends: Nancy Wilner interview with JM, 14 December 1989.

448 "rescue" him: Edward Dahlberg to KB, 3 January 1966, HRHRC.

448 For Kay Boyle's review of Edward Dahlberg, see "A Man in the Wilderness," rev. of *Epitaph of Our Times, Letters of Edward Dahlberg*, and *The Edward Dahlberg Reader*, by Edward Dahlberg, *Nation* 204 (29 May 1967) 69, 94.

448 "unpleasant rebukes": KB to Edward Dahlberg, 23 April 1967, HRHRC.

448 "You do alter your mind": Edward Dahlberg to KB, 10 April 1967, HRHRC.

448 "She hated you and you abhor her": Edward Dahlberg to KB, 26 April 1967, HRHRC.

448 "Jew-baiting" . . . "antisemitic outbreaks": Edward Dahlberg to KB, 14 January 1967, HRHRC.

448 "professional Jew": Edward Dahlberg to KB, 2 February 1967, HRHRC.

448–49 "You are devouring yourself taking up one cause or another": Edward Dahlberg to KB, 26 April 1967, HRHRC.

449 "bitter and profoundly cruel man": KB to Edward Dahlberg, 28 April 1967, HRHRC.

449 "compilation": Norman Holmes Pearson, rev. of *The Autobiography of Emanuel Carnevali*, *New York Times Book Review* 10 December 1967: 32.

449 Ian had worshipped his sister: KB interview with JM, August 1987.

449 "Leave him alone": Ted Keller interview with JM, 15 December 1989.

449 still at loose ends: Ian Franckenstein interview with JM, August 1987.

449 "a real character": Ibid.

450 "Why aren't you marching?": Leo Litwak interview with JM, 14 December 1989.

450 "impossible" now: KB to Carolyn Kizer, 11 February 1967.

450 "understand the shame": KB to Lady Bird Johnson, 8 August 1967, KBP.

450 "If it's Kay": Nancy Wilner interview with JM, 14 December 1989.

450 "I'm not interested in politics": Leo Litwak interview with JM, 14 December 1989.

450 "Ask that gentleman": Ibid.

450 "I never thought that Zeus": KB to Howard Nemerov, 12 September 1967, Washington University Libraries.

450 "I'm not going to lie down under tanks": Howard Nemerov interview with JM, 13 September 1990.

450–51 "When I want to, or do speak on Vietnam": James T. Farrell to KB, 26 September 1967, KBP.

451 the "sights" have to do with deaths: See Kay Boyle, "Seeing the Sights in San Francisco," *Progressive* 31 (December 1967) 19–21.

451 "rheumy, failing eyes": Kay Boyle, "On Black Power," *Liberation* 11 (January 1967) 23.

451 When the poem was reprinted: See Kay Boyle, "A Poem About Black Power," *Journal of Contemporary Revolutions* Winter 1967–68.

451 "We are truly living in a police state": KB to James Stern, 25 February 1968. Courtesy of James Stern.

451 "revolution is on its way": KB to Caresse Crosby, 2 November 1967, BSA.

451 the evening before, she had attended: Seldon Osborne interview with JM, 13 December 1988.

451 explaining all the while to reporters: See "Jail Terms Given 104 Defendants," *Oakland Tribune*, 18 October 1967, in which KB states: "I have signed petitions. I have written to my representative. I finally found the one way left to end war and the Vietnam war is to back the young Americans who refuse to fight there." See also "Reporter's Transcript of Excerpts of Proceedings: October 17, 1967, The People of the State of California, Plaintiff, vs. Joan Baez, Kay Boyle, and many others, Defendants," in which KB says: "To this end I did everything I possibly could to help. I signed petitions, wrote presidents, called on Mr. Stevenson to act for us as a peace candidate."

451 "unique demonstration": "Reporter's Transcript of Excerpts of Proceedings: October 17, 1967."

452 For accounts of Kay Boyle's visits to Santa Rita Prison, see KB interview with JM, August 1987; and Ted Keller interview with JM, 15 December 1989.

452 "I will never voluntarily go to jail again": Seldon Osborne interview with JM, 13 December 1988.

452 "Come on, Kay": KB interview with JM, August 1987.

452 Kay took comfort in the fact that one of the policemen: KB interview with Charles Amirkhanian, 1976.

452 she received a continuance: See "Draft Protesters Stay in Jail," *San Francisco Examiner* 20 December 1967.

452 "pancake thin" mattress: Kay Boyle, "Report from Lock-up," *Words That Must Somehow Be Said*, 118–51.

452 priding herself on being the first to spring from her cot: See KB interview with JM, August 1987.

452 "These are crucial times": KB to Caresse Crosby, 2 November 1967, BSA.

452 "Mama's in jail!": Kathe Vail interview with JM, June 1990.

452 Makeup was forbidden: See "Report from Lock-up" 149 and KB interview with JM, August 1987.

453 "Now, Kay": KB interview with JM, August 1987.

453 "legally right" . . . "When I get out": Kay Boyle, "Report From Lock-up" 136, and KB interview with JM.

453 "where ladies get lumps": Ibid. 149.

453 "You don't need a name": Ibid. 151.

453 "our better side": Ian Franckenstein to KB, 7 June 1968, KBP.

453 "great feeling" and "compassion": Ibid.

453 "cruel, and even selfish": Ian Franckenstein to KB [March 1968], KBP.

453 "somehow these tasks": Ibid.

453 "nothing is temporary": Ibid.

454 "that you may weather this horrible operation": Ian Franckenstein to KB, 1 May 1968, KBP.

454 "You have needs": Ian Franckenstein to KB [March 1968], KBP.

454 "Hopelessness is a more satisfactory condition than hope": Laurence Vail to Djuna Barnes, 31 December 1966, University of Maryland Libraries.

454 "He was terrible but he was wonderful also": Apple Vail to KB, 6 May 1968, KBP.

454 "the more we can love her": Kathe Vail interviews with JM, June 1990 and November 1991.

454 "nobody seemed to have realized": Sharon [Vail] Walsh to KB, 6 May 1968, KBP.

454 "symbol of romantic hypocrisy": Laurence Vail to Djuna Barnes, 2 April 1966, University of Maryland Libraries.

455 "Will I be pretty": Hank McGuckin interview with JM, 15 December 1989.

455 "Now I won't be able to admire my body": Ted Keller interview with JM, 15 December 1989.
455 "Where's your roommate?": Nancy Wilner interview with JM, 14 December 1989.
455 "bear being so crippled": KB to Caresse Crosby, 1 June 1968, BSA.
455 "the result of some kind of wrong thinking": KB to Ian Franckenstein, 5 June 1968, KBP.
455 "You have lost him and me": Faith Gude to KB, 14 June 1968, KBP.
455 "Everything is going to be all right": KB to Caresse Crosby, 16 May 1968, BSA.
455 discovered bent on one knee: Harold Gessner interview with JM, 6 June 1989.
456 "final payment": KB to Robert Gessner, 12 June 1968, KBP.
456 "I believe my children need the $50.00": KB to Mike Watkins, 19 June 1969, KBP.
456 "I'm Peter Gessner": Peter Gessner interview with JM, 13 December 1989.

30. FABULATIONS

457 "How do I know": *BGT* 103.
457 "I thought she fabulated": Malcolm Cowley, "Personal Views," *Twentieth Century Literature* [Special Kay Boyle Issue], ed. Sandra Whipple Spanier, 34.3 (Fall 1988) 271.
457 prompting both her friend James Stern: James Stern interview with JM, November 1991.
457 "One absolutely gasps": Anthony Powell, "Knocking Around the Latin Quarter," *London Daily Telegraph* 9 April 1970: 6.
457 "repetitious and boring": Jean Stafford, "Spirits," *New York Review of Books* 24 April 1969: 28.
457 "The book's triumph": Charles Poore, "Expatriates en Brochette," *New York Times* 18 July 1968.
457 "She writes rings": Saul Maloff, "Again the Lost Ones," *Newsweek* 8 July 1968: 70.
457 "desperately intellectual": *BGT* 152.
458 The correspondence between Ernest Walsh and Ernest Hemingway is available at the University of Virginia.
459 "Gentlemen . . . I give you the Irish": Ernest Hemingway to F. Scott Fitzgerald, 7 September 1926, in Carlos Baker, *Ernest Hemingway: Selected Letters 1917–1961* (New York: Scribner's, 1981) 217–18.
459 as all her life Kay would claim: KB interview with JM, August 1987.
459 See Joan [Boyle] Detweiler to JM, 2 February 1989, and Joan [Boyle] Detweiler to JM, 15 March 1989.
459 "the marriage is legal only": Robert McAlmon to William Carlos Williams, quoted in *BGT* 45. The complete letter is available in KBP.
459 "emotional frustrations": See Kay Boyle's undated notes for *Being Geniuses Together*, KBP.
460 his black moods in Paris: KB, unpublished interview with Katherine Heineman, notes available in the Beinecke Library.
461 so "spectacular" a neglect: Malcolm Cowley, "Those Paris Years," rev. of *Being Geniuses Together*, *New York Times Book Review* 9 June 1968: 1.
461 "saddened" by the review: KB to Malcolm Cowley, 22 June 1968, KBP.
461 amounted to "almost praise": Malcolm Cowley to KB, 25 June 1968, KBP.
461 "personal courage": See Cowley, "Personal Views" 271–72.
461 "not so bad": John Glassco to KB, 9 September 1968, National Archive of Canada.
461 "rather sterile": John Glassco to KB, 9 July 1968, National Archive of Canada.
461 "beautiful . . . as it was with the Carnevali": James Laughlin to KB, 5 September 1968, KBP.
461 "call it quits": Howard Nemerov to KB, 21 July 1968, KBP.
462 "hopelessly romantic": See Mario Puzo, "That's How It Used to Be in Camelot," *Washington Post Book World* 9 June 1968: 1. Studs Terkel's casting for *Being Geniuses Together* is available in KBP.
462 "the most important trial": KB to Fay and Herman Rappaport, 30 July 1968, KBP.
462 "get every Black Panther": Kay Boyle letter to the editors of *The Nation* 11 August 1968, BERG.
462 "bleak-eyed furrowed mask": See Kay Boyle, "Notes on Jury Selection in the Huey P. Newton Trial," *Progressive* 32 (October 1968) 29–35.
462 "product of television westerns": James N. Miller, letter, *Progressive* 32 (October 1968).
462 "was not, and could not be": KB letter to the editors of *The Progressive*, 26 October 1968, BERG.
463 "It is only the first act": KB to Fay Stender, 9 September 1968, BERG.
463 Kay Boyle joined the Black Panther Party: KB interview with JM, August 1987. See also KB to Ian Franckenstein, 14 September 1969, BERG.
463 "courageous artist": Kay Boyle introducing Eldridge Cleaver, 13 October 1968, BERG.

463 "the tongue that serves": Kay Boyle, "For James Schevill, on the Occasion of His Arrest," *Poem* 3–4 (November 1968) 1.
463 "less sick, less power-dominated": Joan [Boyle] Detweiler to KB, 26 October 1968, BERG.
463 Kay was incensed: Ibid.
463 "stunned": Ibid.
463 "I've always admired my mother": Sharon Cowling quoted in Solita Solano to KB, 12 January 1969, KBP.
463 Kay kept a bottle of sherry: Charlotte Painter interview with JM, December 1988.
464 "The academic world really gives me nothing": KB interview with Doris Grumbach, July 1977, available from the manuscripts department of the University of Virginia.
464 "That's not what you're supposed to have read": KB interview with JM, August 1987.
464 "sentimental": Dan Tooker interviews with JM, 18 October 1989 and 20 November 1989.
464 only for Kay to profess dismay: Hank McGuckin interview with JM, 15 December 1989; and Ted Keller interview with JM, 15 December 1989.
464 "a novel on that novel": KB interview with Erik Bauersfeld and Lee Jenkins, 1975.
464 "Is your typewriter ribbon very pale?": KB written comments on the manuscript of *Celibate Nights*, by Jim Hietter, dated 16 October 1968, KBP.
464 "absolutely abolished": KB interview with Erik Bauersfeld and Lee Jenkins, 1975.
464 "death to a would-be writer": KB lecture given at the San Francisco State University Poetry Center, 11 February 1987.
464–65 "not by nature but through an effort of the will": Ibid.
465 "everything we wrote": Shawn Wong interview with JM, 3 June 1991.
465 "the terrible emphasis": KB interview with Kay Bonetti, 1985.
465 "I didn't hear your typewriter last night": Shawn Wong interview with JM, 3 June 1991.
465 "Here's part of the house": Ibid.
465 "Can you write a short story?" Jim Hietter interview with JM, 15 April 1989.
465 "There was Father Jim Hietter": Kay Boyle, "Testament for My Students, 1968–69," *Southern Review* 6 (January 1970) 149–50. The poem is also found in *Testament for My Students and Other Poems* (Garden City, NY: Doubleday, 1970).
466 "There is POLICE ON EARTH": See Jim Hietter, "Advent Song," *San Francisco Quarterly* 6.1 (Winter 1970).
466 "If you really want to write, you do": KB to Peter Levitt, 8 January 1968, KBP.
466 "sense of living": Gary Watkins to KB, undated, KBP.
466 "pre-Freudian personality": Stan Rice interview with JM, 14 April 1989.
466 Clifton Fadiman had once given her a bad review: Dan Tooker interviews with JM, 18 October 1989 and 20 November 1989.
466 "I have been searching": Victor Turks to KB, 2 August 1968, KBP.
466 "When it was time for us to say good-night": Victor Turks to KB, c. fall 1968, BERG.
466 he felt as if it were not his teacher: Dan Tooker interview with JM, 18 October 1989.
467 "Victor, you've got to come quickly": Victor Turks interview with JM, 13 December 1989.
467 "a woman still trying": Dan Tooker interview with JM, 18 October 1989.
467 she was upset when her colleague: Charlotte Painter interview with JM, December 1988.
467 For the account of the strike at San Francisco State in this and the following chapter, I have drawn on interviews with Arthur Chandler, Stuart Creighton Miller, Eric Solomon, Leo Litwak, Ted Keller, Hank McGuckin, Herbert Gold, Joseph Illick, John Bunzel, John Gerassi, and others. See also Leo Litwak and Herbert Wilner, *College Days in Earthquake Country* (New York: Random House, 1971), and Kay Boyle, *The Long Walk at San Francisco State and Other Essays* (New York: Grove Press, 1970).
467 what black statistics might be: Stuart Creighton Miller interview with JM, 13 December 1988.
468 not "relevant": Sonia Sanchez interview with JM, 10 November 1988.

31. STRIKE AT SAN FRANCISCO STATE

469 "Hayakawa Eichmann!": KB interview with JM, August 1987. See also Kay Boyle, "Long Walk," *The Long Walk at San Francisco State and Other Essays* (New York: Grove Press, 1970).
469 "the chisel of anti-rationalism driven by the hammer": John Bunzel, "Saga of the Strike at San Francisco State," *San Francisco Sunday Examiner & Chronicle* 24 January 1971.
469 Gerassi had declared: John Gerassi interview with JM, 28 September 1989.
469 "I'm going with you": Nancy Wilner interview with JM, 14 December 1989.

469 "redeemers" . . . "the great and vital": *Long Walk* 6–7.

470 "seize power": Litwak and Wilner, *College Days in Earthquake Country* 75–77.

470 "Walk, chicken": Ibid.

470 "from the murderous assault of the pigs": Ibid. 90.

471 "effacing one more black": *Long Walk* 13

471 "as black and Third World students cleared": Ibid.

471 "education teams": Ibid. 21.

471 "we'll come with guns": Litwak and Wilner, *College Days* 174.

471 "*your* solution": Ibid. 45.

471 "as a buffer": Bob Haesler, "Kay Boyle Assesses San Francisco State," *San Francisco Chronicle* 16 November 1968: 13.

471 "I don't mind dying": Ibid.

471 "a very heartening experience": KB to John Glassco, 6 February 1969, John Glassco papers, National Archive of Canada.

471 "All trustees are horse's asses": KB interview with JM, August 1987.

472 "If you're not on strike": Joe Illick interview with JM, 19 December 1988.

472 Kay went on telling people: Stuart Creighton Miller interview with JM, 13 December 1988.

472 "deplorable": Stuart Creighton Miller to JM, 27 June 1988.

472 "plastic-masked faces": *Long Walk* 15.

472 "Go *on!*": Eric Solomon interview with JM, 20 December 1988.

472 "Black, oriental": *Long Walk* 47.

472 A ticking bomb was placed: John Bunzel telephone interview with JM.

472 "will not be killed": Haesler, "Kay Boyle Assesses San Francisco State."

472 "the issues of the strike": *Long Walk* 36.

473 "If he takes the job": Bill Snyder, "Former Prof. Evolved from Semanticist to Scholar," *Oakland Tribune* 28 February 1992: a-13.

473 Kay Boyle locked her arms: KB interview with JM, August 1987.

473 "Private property!": KB interview with JM, August 1987, and *Long Walk* 50.

473 "screaming curses" . . . "Kay Boyle, you should be ashamed": James R. Wilson to KPIX television, 2 December 1968, BERG: "I strongly protest the outrageous observation of your reporter on today's noontime news broadcast that Kay Boyle was 'screaming curses' at a Mr. Hayakawa this morning . . . to accuse her of 'screaming curses' like a fishwife is grossly defamatory and an infamous libel."

473 "the right of freedom of speech": *Long Walk* 60.

474 "I am inclined / To agree with Eldridge Cleaver": Kay Boyle, "Testament for My Students, 1968–69," *Southern Review* 6 (January 1970) 149–50.

474 "It is not possible to teach at gunpoint": KB to Mike Watkins, 19 January 1969, KBP.

474 "Striking in a just cause": KB to James Wilson, 9 February 1969, KBP.

474 Upset, she had her students write: See, for example, KB to Jim Hietter, 22 March 1969. Courtesy Jim Hietter.

474 "two enormous": *Long Walk* 65.

474 Kathe told her she thought the book was propagandistic: Quoted in KB to Kathe Vail, 4 February 1971, BERG.

474 "I find your letter a pretty severe indictment": Ibid.

474 "a political grudge": KB to Bill Hogan, 2 February 1971, BERG.

475 "Any man who is practicing on black women": Sonia Sanchez interview with JM, 10 November 1988.

475 a "hustler": Ibid.

475 Kay began to denounce Gerassi: KB interview with JM, August 1987.

475 after he was fired, Gerassi disappeared: Ted Keller interview with JM, 15 December 1989.

475 "How can you say that?": Herb Gold interview with JM, 22 December 1988.

475 "Well, he is": Beverly Axelrod telephone interview with JM, 1992.

475 "her most capitalistic": KB interview with JM, August 1987.

476 "Sue me?": John Gerassi interview with JM, 28 September 1989.

476 For the scene at Ted Keller's with John Gerassi, I have drawn on interviews with KB, John Gerassi, Ted Keller, and Beverly Axelrod.

476 "Nobody was paying any attention to her": John Gerassi interview with JM, 28 September 1989.

477 "mythomaniacal exhibitionist": Maria Jolas to KB, 13 July 1974, BERG.

477 Ted Keller had to drag her away: Ted Keller interview with JM, 15 December 1989.

477 "our beloved Eldridge": KB to Caresse Crosby, 28 November 1968, BSA.

477 "We are a race": Kay Boyle, "For James Baldwin" [1969].
477 "new lease to life": KB to Ken McCormick, 22 February 1969, KBP.
477 "an evil book": KB to Ken McCormick, 14 November 1969, KBP.
477 "who was never": Kay Boyle's list for *Esquire* magazine of the most overrated and underrated writers may be found in BERG.
478 For Kay Boyle's quarrel with Jack Salzman, see KB to James Laughlin, 15 October 1969; James Laughlin to KB, 21 October 1969; KB to James Laughlin, 26 October 1969; New Directions records dated October 27, 1969; KB to James Laughlin, 28 October 1969; James Laughlin to KB, 10 November 1969; and KB to James Laughlin, 17 November 1969.
478 "frightened of love": Clover Vail to KB, 6 January 1970, BERG.
478 "for Kay Boyle the dominant movement has been outward": Robert W. French, rev. of *Testament for My Students, Nation* 8 June 1970: 696.
478 "Love is acceptance and indulgence": Kathe Vail quoted in KB to Kathe Vail, 4 February 1971, BERG.
478 "judging" *her*: KB to Kathe Vail, 6 February 1971, BERG.
478 "interference": KB to Kathe Vail, 4 February 1971, BERG.
478 "to help you lead": Ibid.
478 "one who seeks to transmit": Ibid.
479 "How any of us could ever complain": KB to Mike Watkins, 25 December 1969, KBP.
479 "You are among the very, very few women": Robert Boone to KB, 18 February 1970, KBP.
479 "made a career of having her own way": KB to Charles McCabe, 31 January 1970, KBP.
479 "The letters of George Jackson": KB to Howard Nemerov, 15 September 1970, Washington University Libraries.
479 why weren't there any black people: KB interview with Richard Centing, 11 December 1971.
479 she now shared with him the experience: Kay Boyle, "On Taking Up Residence in Virginia," *Hart* (c. 1970–71) [16]. The poem is also found in Kay Boyle, *This Is Not a Letter and Other Poems* (Los Angeles: Sun & Moon Press, 1985) 23–24.
479 "old lady of good breeding": H. T. Kirby-Smith to JM, 7 February 1988.
479 "I don't think students should take writing courses": See Thomas Collin, "Short Story Dead? Yes, no, maybe," *Newsday* 1 December 1970: 13.
479 "for myself and God": Ibid.
479 "unstable": KB to Ian Franckenstein, 3 August 1969, BERG.
479 "destroying the identity and the individual": Ibid.
479 "enduring meaning": Ibid.
480 "submerging" his will: KB to Ian Franckenstein, 14 September 1969, BERG.
480 "to assure themselves that they are men": KB to Ian Franckenstein, 6 December 1969, BERG.
480 "a rare and extraordinary person": KB to Ian Franckenstein, 14 September 1969, BERG.
480 "not be alive forever": KB to Ian Franckenstein, 15 December 1969, BERG.
480 "I'm very happy": See David Felton, *Mindfuckers: A Source Book on the Rise of Acid Fascism in America* (San Francisco: Straight Arrow Books, 1972) 253.
480 "Don't you trust me": KB to Jessica Mitford, 11 November 1970, KBP.

32. FEMINISTS

481 "So I am again the abandoner": Kay Boyle, *The Underground Woman* (Garden City, NY: Doubleday, 1975) 212. All subsequent references are to this edition.
481 Great changes were coming: See Adda Helus to KB, 8 November 1970, BERG.
481 "conventional morality": KB to Jessica Mitford, 11 November 1970, KBP.
481 "If you don't give me the entire house": Quoted in ibid.
481 Major had friends: Reginald Major telephone interview with JM, 1990.
482 "Is this what your family is like?": Adda Helus to KB, 8 November 1970, BERG.
482 "I beg of you not to have guests": KB to Ian Franckenstein, telegram, BERG.
482 "I feel utterly lost": KB to Jessica Mitford, 11 November 1970, KBP.
482 "Well, we got rid of *that* nigger": Felton, *Mindfuckers* 254.
482 "We ought to read": Robert Treuhaft interview with JM, 14 December 1989.
483 "absolute willingness": Reginald Major telephone interview with JM, 1990.
483 sold her house to a "Black Panther": KB interview with JM, August 1987.
483 "You're a cruel daughter": For this incident, Faith Gude interviews with JM, December 1989 and 2 March 1991.

483 "only way to destroy Lyman's power": KB to Bessie Breuer, 18 March 1970 [sic] [actually 1971], BERG. See also Felton, *Mindfuckers* 253–55.

484 "very little tolerance": Ian Franckenstein interview with JM, August 1987.

484 "got into the academic world by the back door": See Kay Boyle, *The Underground Woman.*

485 "fame and fortune": David Cay Boyle Johnston telephone interview with JM, 2 January 1990.

485 "practically unreadable": KB interview with Kay Bonetti, 1985.

485 "worthy" effort: Phillip Corwin, "The Telling of the Story," rev. of *The Underground Woman, Nation* 22 March 1975: 347.

485 "to all sensitive and conventional women": J. D. O'Hara, rev. of *The Underground Woman, New York Times* 2 February 1975: 4.

485 "her activity on behalf of amnesty": Doris Grumbach, "Fine Print: Kay Boyle et al.," rev. of *The Underground Woman, New Republic* 8 February 1975: 33.

485 "too close to her prison experience": Peter S. Prescott, "Life with Daughter," rev. of *The Underground Woman, Newsweek* 13 January 1975: 67A.

486 "machinery of the novel": Blanche H. Gelfant, "Fiction Chronicle," rev. of *The Underground Woman, Hudson Review* 28.2 (Summer 1975) 316.

486 "She brought me up": Faith Gude interviews with JM, December 1989 and 2 March 1991.

486 "A book by a man": Kay Boyle, "The Far East and Fiction," *American Scholar* 26.2 (Spring 1957) 223.

486 "people love women writers": Betty Burroughs, "3 Novelists Speak of Involvement in Art," *Evening Journal* [Wilmington, DE] 18 February 1965: 3.

486 "Did you know him?" For this incident, see Herb Gold interview with JM, 22 December 1988.

487 "certain people get jobs": Merla Zellerbach, "BP's Who Work for Money" ["My Fair City" column], *San Francisco Chronicle.* A clipping of the article is available in KBP.

487 "I don't think women should try to write like men": "Kay Boyle," *Talks with Authors,* ed. Charles F. Madden (Carbondale and Edwardsville, IL: Southern Illinois UP, 1968) 235.

487 "three short stories": KB interview with Erik Bauersfeld and Lee Jenkins, 1975.

487 "We'll be up all night": Nancy Wilner interview with JM, 14 December 1989.

487 "Why do you want to study with me?": KB interview with JM, August 1987.

487 "impressed by . . . clarity": KB to Ken McCormick, 22 April 1970, KBP.

487 "We all know": KB interview with Marilyn Yalom, published in *Women Writers of the West Coast Speaking of Their Lives and Careers,* ed. Marilyn Yalom (Santa Barbara: Capra Press, 1983) 119.

488 "in a separatist group": KB interview with Doris Grumbach, July 1977. The transcript is available in the Doris Grumbach papers, University of Virginia.

488 "had terrible conflicts with their fathers": Ibid.

488 "I think the women's movement": Ibid.

488 "a man's world": KB interview with Barbaralee Diamonstein, published in *Open Secrets: Ninety-four Women in Touch with Our Time,* ed. Barbaralee Diamonstein (New York: Viking, 1972) 26–27.

488 "the liberation of all people": Ibid.

488 "Both equally": Ibid.

488 "soul-searching": Ibid.

488 "Art is NOT the submersion in oneself": KB to Max Steele, 28 May 1972, KBP.

488 "I am convinced that if Anaïs Nin were to commit suicide": KB to Kenneth Koch, 22 September 1972, KBP.

488 "any critical comments": Jana Harris to KB, 5 June 1972, KBP.

488 moments of desperation: KB to Nancy Flynn, 1 February 1974, KBP.

489 For "The Woman Writer in the 20th Century," see Elaine Showalter, "Women and the Literary Curriculum," *College English* 32.8 (May 1971) 855–62.

489 Showalter says it did not even occur to her: Elaine Showalter telephone interview with JM, 6 June 1992.

489 "the heroine's entanglement with patriarchal norms": See Annis Pratt, "The New Feminist Criticism," *College English* 32.8 (May 1971) 872–78.

489 "How did that ever happen?": KB to Howard Nemerov, 26 August 1974, Washington University Libraries.

489 "I served and gave homage": Transcript of KB telephone interview, 22 October 1976, KBP.

489 "forced into retirement": KB interview with Erik Bauersfeld and Lee Jenkins, 1975.

489 "the magnificent sum of two hundred": Ibid.

489 "a fine poet": KB to "Whom It May Concern," 17 February 1975. Courtesy of Kathleen Fraser.

490 "the scholarly expertise": KB to Leo Litwak, 12 October 1976.

490 Many saw Kay's stance as irrational: Stan Rice interview with JM, 14 April 1989.

490 "Now, what is it?": Linda Ferguson to KB, 12 December 1975, KBP.

490 a "bridge": Kathleen Fraser to JM, 19 December 1989.

491 "sufficient attention": Memo: Donald L. Garrity, Provost, to Leo V. Young, 25 May 1977.

491 "segregated lectures": See KB to Leo Litwak, 12 October 1976; and memorandum dated 7 June 1977 to William Dickey, Chairman, Creative Writing, and Leo Litwak, Chairman, HRT, from Kathleen Fraser.

491 For the meeting between Kay Boyle and Kathleen Fraser at Frederick Street, see Kathleen Fraser interview with JM, 15 December 1989.

492 "accusations without first": Marshall Windmiller to KB, 14 December 1971, BERG.

492 For the incident between Lawrence Ferlinghetti and his partner, see Lawrence Ferlinghetti interview with JM, 14 December 1989; Herb Gold interview with JM, 22 December 1988; and a brief talk with Shig Murao. See also the correspondence between KB and Lawrence Ferlinghetti available at BERG.

492 "for one of the sisters": KB to Fay Stender, 14 January 1971, KBP.

492 "American manufacturers": 1976 transcript of KB interviewed by Erik Bauersfeld on KPFA radio.

492 "fervent revolutionary": Richard Hendry to KB, 18 October 1973, KBP.

493 "near annihilation of an entire country": KB to Richard Hendry, 20 October 1973, KBP.

493 "legal researcher": Eileen Lottman, "George Jackson Confession," *Village Voice* 16 May 1974: 1, 35.

493 Kay Boyle with a postcard from Nelson Algren: Dan Tooker interviews with JM, 18 October 1989 and 20 November 1989.

493 "Didn't your mother teach you manners?": Bob Dunn interview with JM, January 1990.

493 "old Lefties": Quoted in KB to Herb Caen, 26 February 1975, BERG. See also Herb Caen to KB, 27 February 1975, BERG.

493 a long indignant letter from Kay Boyle: See KB to Herb Caen, 26 February 1975, BERG.

493 "I used to be a mountain climber": Kathy Drew, "Kay Boyle Dedicates Self to Human Dignity," *Lost Generation Journal* 4.1 (Winter 1976) 23.

493 "Is everything all right?": David V. Koch interview with JM, 1 June 1988.

493 "You grow more attractive": William L. Shirer to KB, 28 May 1973, KBP.

494 "when I'm feeling particularly inadequate": Blake Green, "Kay Boyle—A Study in Paradox," *San Francisco Chronicle* 17 February 1975 ["People" section] 12.

494 "more fervor in her voice": Ibid.

494 Thirteen pages of her German history: See Kay Boyle, "Introduction to a Modern History of Germany," *Prose* 3 (Fall 1971) 5–18.

494 "Kay, how could you": Jessica Mitford interview with KB, 14 December 1988.

494 See Kay Boyle, "On the Death of My Student, the Poet Serafin," *Wind* 11 (Spring 1974) 10–12.

495 Asked to write an introduction: See Kay Boyle, "A Selection of Young Filipino Poets," *American Poetry Review* 3 (July–August 1974) 47–48.

495 "sitting waiting": KB to Nelson Algren, 19 November 1973, KBP.

495 infuriated her: J. M. Edelstein, rev. of *Black Sun*, by Geoffrey Wolff, *New Republic* 6 November 1976. For Kay Boyle's response, see KB to J. M. Edelstein, 13 November 1976, BERG.

495 "greater interest to present-day students": KB to Malcolm Cowley, 29 November 1976, BERG.

495 "closest and oldest friend": KB to Henry Miller, 22 May 1972, KBP.

495 "not only unnecessary": Samuel Beckett to KB, 28 May 1957, HRHRC.

495 "adequately clear": KB to Samuel Beckett, 1 June 1957, HRHRC.

496 Beckett sat, withdrawn: Clover Vail telephone conversation with JM, October 1992.

496 "It's no business of mine": Samuel Beckett to KB, 29 August 1960, HRHRC.

496 "May this dreadful pain soon be past": Samuel Beckett to KB, 8 August 1963, HRHRC.

496 "I bow my head": Samuel Beckett to KB, 22 November 1963, HRHRC.

496 "So glad you like your new house": Samuel Beckett to KB, 29 February 1964, HRHRC.

496 "Don't kill yourself marching": Samuel Beckett to KB, 4 December 1969, HRHRC.

496 "You have the capacity to break the heart": KB to Samuel Beckett, 27 June 1965, HRHRC.

496 "before the curtain rattles down": Samuel Beckett to KB, 10 July 1978, HRHRC.

496 "her mien more purposeful than ever": Samuel Beckett to KB, 27 August 1971, HRHRC.

496 "as it dribbles away": Samuel Beckett to KB, 8 August 1973, HRHRC.

496–97 "The trouble with tragedy": Samuel Beckett to KB, 22 August 1973, HRHRC.

497 "You see, you don't miss much": Samuel Beckett to KB, 22 February 1974, HRHRC.

497 "your dear unflinchingness": Samuel Beckett to KB, 9 August 1975, HRHRC.

497 "intimate in every sense": Deirdre Bair interview with JM, 1992.

497 "They're going to bury": KB to Howard Nemerov, 25 January 1976, Washington University
     Libraries.

33. VESNA

498 "little girls' tales": Quoted in Sharon Vail to KB, 11 December 1976, KBP.
498 "Let's not ever talk about the past": Kathe Vail to KB, 22 July 1977, BERG.
498 "Except your mother": Sharon [Vail] Cowling interview with JM, June 1990.
498 Kay said she told those women one should change: Videotape of Kay Boyle speaking before the
     San Francisco State University Poetry Center, 10 December 1975.
498 "My mother's door": Ibid.
498 "writing poems in a four hundred year old farmhouse": KB to William L. Shirer, 12 December
     1974, KBP.
499 "the international movie and Paris fashions, homosexual": KB to Apple [Vail] Goeser, 9 September
     1972, BERG.
499 Kay even consented to wear one of Peggy Guggenheim's: Kathe Vail interviews with JM, June
     1990 and November 1991.
499 She objected to Kathe's having named: KB to Apple [Vail] Goeser, 9 September 1972, BERG.
499 "because he knew Papa": Ibid.
499 "were sociable drinkers": Ibid.
499 "teach him patience": Ibid.
499 "If you get out of your seat, I'll hit you": Ariel Rosenblum interview with JM, 9 March 1991.
499 Beckett had been "impressed": KB to Apple [Vail] Goeser, 9 September 1972, BERG.
499 "Ian has arrived": Kathe Vail interviews with JM, June 1990 and November 1991.
500 "great astonishment": KB to Howard Nemerov, 9 October 1976, Washington University Libraries.
500 "I think of myself as a revolutionary": Videotape of Kay Boyle speaking before the San Francisco
     State University Poetry Center, 10 December 1975.
500 "Poets, minor or major, should arrange to remain slender": See Kay Boyle, "Poets," *Pacific Sun
     Literary Quarterly* 21–27 (May 1976) 7.
500 "My little Kay": KB interview with JM, August 1987. For much of this account of Edgar Kuhn
     and how he had hurt her family, I have relied on my August 1987 interviews with Kay Boyle.
500 She hero-worshipped me: Kathe Vail to KB, "Sometime in February—1977," KBP.
500 "Don't worry, me too": Ibid.
500 If it was really true: Ibid.
501 Vesna was such a little girl: Ibid.
501 "I'm here for a week": KB interview with JM, August 1987.
501 Vesna's father had actually shaken: Ibid.
501 "because we were very close": Ibid.
501 "I made him credible": Kathe Vail to KB, "Sometime in February—1977," KBP.
501 "extraordinary women": Ken McCormick to KB, 23 March 1976, KBP.
501 "the first lady of Irish-American letters": "Contributors" in *Aisling* 1 (Summer 1975). This issue
     of *Aisling* includes Kay Boyle's article "A Talk Given Here and There." See pp. 8–13.
502 "My stepmother thinks she may have met you": Liadain O'Donovan-Cook interview with JM,
     19 December 1988.
502 "law-abiding subversive": Ibid.
502 "I won't stay": Ibid. I am indebted to Liadain O'Donovan-Cook for much of this account of Kay
     Boyle's 1976 trip to Ireland.
503 "I am sorry": KB to Liadain O'Donovan-Cook, 4 October 1976. Courtesy of Liadain O'Donovan-
     Cook.
503 "all the seashells": KB Christmas card to Liadain O'Donovan-Cook and son, December 1976.
     Courtesy of Liadain O'Donovan-Cook.
503 "The only thing I am asking of you is not to triumph": Kathe Vail to KB, "Sometime in
     February—1977," KBP.
503 "forgiven her all": Ibid.
503 "I have not your intelligence": Kathe Vail to KB, 22 July 1977, BERG.
503 "semi-retired": KB to Clover Vail, 7 March 1977, BERG.
503 " 'a room of our own' ": KB to Lynda Koolish, 2 February 1977, BERG.
504 "raised its ugly head": KB to Mike Watkins, 6 April 1977, KBP.
504 "spared any formal schooling": Kay Boyle, address at Skidmore College, April 13, 1977.

504 "leaning on": KB to Dr. Leonard Rosenman, 13 May 1977, BERG.

504 "old enemy": KB to Mike Watkins, 8 June 1977, KBP.

504 "sympathetic to my work": KB to Martin Peretz, 29 September 1977, BERG.

504 "while on the trail": Helga Einsele, "Personal Views," *Twentieth Century Literature* [Special Kay Boyle Issue], ed. Sandra Whipple Spanier, 34.3 (Fall 1988) 275.

504 "only rarely": Helga Einsele to JM, 7 October 1989.

505 "Isn't it the women": Joan Baez to KB [1977], BERG.

505 "cannot live without Ireland": KB to Mike Watkins, 17 August 1977, KBP.

505 "injustice is the air": See Kay Boyle, "St. Stephen's Green," *Atlantic* 245 (June 1980) 41–44.

505 a respectful review: See Kay Boyle, rev. of *Lucky Eyes and a High Heart: The Life of Maud Gonne*, by Nancy Cardozo, *New Republic* 179 (28 October 1978) 36–38.

505 "Oh, you know": KB interview with Doris Grumbach, July 1977, Doris Grumbach papers, University of Virginia.

505 They were *never* "fine": Shawn Wong interview with JM, 3 June 1991.

505 "God, so I look that old!": KB interview with Doris Grumbach, July 1977, University of Virginia.

505 "I can't use it": KB quoted in Joan Baez to KB, 17 November 1977, BERG.

505 "hard financial realities": KB to Mike Watkins, 29 April 1978, KBP.

505 "become a non-writer": KB to Ken McCormick, 14 January 1978, KBP.

505 "I am filled with stories": Ibid.

505 "Since receiving several volumes of censored data": Kay Boyle quoted in Merla Zellerbach, "When Writers Give Themselves Away," *San Francisco Chronicle* 15 March 1978: 15.

506 "in view of the background": San Francisco Office report 105-40724, dated 8 June 1976, in FBI file 105-299129, Kay Boyle Franckenstein.

506 "you and I could hold our ancient hands": KB to Djuna Barnes, 11 March 1978, University of Maryland Libraries.

506 weighed three hundred pounds: KB to George Gutekunst [1978], BERG.

506 "Lillian, we get old": KB interview with JM, August 1987.

506 "I don't know why I care": KB to Howard Nemerov, 5 July 1978, Washington University Libraries.

507 "as the National Institute had sent me money": KB to Authors' League, 31 July 1978, BERG.

507 "He must be very lonely": KB interview with Hugh Ford, 1978.

507 "*sagesse*": Kathe Vail to KB, 24 May 1978, KBP.

507 "Yannick admires you": Ibid. See also Kathe Vail to KB, 9 June 1978, KBP.

507 "Don't say you're full": Kathe Vail interviews with JM, June 1990 and November 1991; and Yannick Kuhn interview with JM, November 1991.

508 "You see that woman?": Sharon Cowling quoted in Kathe Vail interviews with JM, June 1990.

508 she never got around to asking her grandchildren: Sandro Rumney interview with JM, November 1991.

508 "I know how much you gave of yourself ": Kathe Vail to KB, 30 August 1978, KBP.

508 Kay knew she had been strict: See Kathe Vail to KB, 18 September 1978, KBP, and Kathe Vail to KB, 25 September 1978, KBP: "I am so proud of you because you were 'aware' of your strictness (*your* words) and you did it so—because it is *exactly* what I wanted you to do." See also Kathe Vail interviews with JM, June 1990 and November 1991; and Myrine Kuhn interview with JM, November 1991.

508 "a world of good": Kathe Vail to KB, 25 September 1978, KBP.

508 See "Excerpt from a Long Poem in Progress—for Samuel Beckett," *Conjunctions* 2 (Spring 1982) 113–14; "A Poem for the Teesto Diné of Arizona," *Malahat Review* 65 (July 1983) 96–97; "Reincarnation—excerpt from a long poem to Samuel Beckett," *Rolling Stock* 5 (1983) 3; Gale memoir 97–125; "Pound in Rapallo," *New York Review of Books* 7 May 1987: 47; and "Heroines and Also Heroes," introduction, *A Woman on Paper: Georgia O'Keefe*, by Anita Pollitzer (New York: Simon & Schuster–Touchstone, 1988) ix–xx.

509 "Looked at as a whole": Vance Bourjaily, "Moving and Maturing," rev. of *Fifty Stories*, *New York Times Book Review* 28 September 1980: 9, 32.

509 "one of our finest": Carole Cook, "Fiction: Fifty Stories," rev. of *Fifty Stories*, *Saturday Review of Literature* September 1980: 70.

509 "the stylistic equivalent": Beth Ruby, "Power and Delicacy from Kay Boyle," rev. of *Fifty Stories*, *Christian Science Monitor* 10 November 1980: B6.

509 "the diligence": Earl Rovit, "Distant Landscapes," rev. of *Fifty Stories*, *Nation* 27 February 1980: 287.

509 "a more explicit rendering": Lauren Belfer, rev. of *Gentlemen, I Address You Privately*, *New York Times Book Review* 5 October 1991: 25.

510 wrote to her old adversary: See S. I. Hayakawa to KB, 21 May 1979, BERG.

510 "I deeply regret that in reading my short stories": KB to Quentin L. Koop, 3 April 1979, BERG.

510 "inexcusable": KB to the editors of *The Nation*, 20 November 1979, BERG.

510 Joan Baez's "Open Letter" to the government of Vietnam, dated 1 June 1979, may be found in BERG.

510 Kay believed now that the "socialist state": KB to Daniel Ellsberg, 8 June 1978, BERG.

510 "Communism is worse than death": Jane Fonda to KB, 30 May 1979, BERG.

510 "in no government": KB to Alan Snitow, 19 June 1979, BERG.

510–11 "That we *must not* criticize *any* socialist country": KB to William L. Shirer, 16 June 1979. Courtesy of William L. Shirer.

511 "I am as disappointed in you as an organization": KB to Melva Mueller, 9 June 1979, BERG.

511 "where the bombs begin": KB to William L. Shirer, 4 May 1979. Courtesy of William L. Shirer.

511 "Dr. says I can have Dubonnet on Friday": Cartoon in BERG.

34. DO NOT GO GENTLE

512 "Lady Lazarus": Studs Terkel telephone interview with JM, 24 February 1990.

512 "anyway what was the use of my having come from Oakland": Gertrude Stein, *Everybody's Autobiography* (New York: Random House, 1937) 289.

512 "I want to start my life over again in Ireland": KB unpublished interview with Deborah Linton, October 1979.

512 "Apple-Joan (Goeser) Vail, and only if": Kay Boyle's will of 27 October 1979, KBP. See also KB to Howard Nemerov, 25 January 1976, Washington University Libraries.

512 "people said nice things": KB to William L. Shirer, 18 December 1979. Courtesy William L. Shirer.

512 "nothing can ever make me believe that we are helpless": Nancy G. McDermid, dean, School of Humanities, San Francisco State University, speaking at a party honoring Kay Boyle, 18 December 1979.

512 "I have carried you inside me always": Faith Gude to KB, 24 March 1980, KBP.

512 "You were my center": Faith Gude to KB, 10 April 1980, KBP.

513 "represented the advance": KB to Ken McCormick, 9 May 1980, KBP.

513 "stop doing things like asking Kay Boyle": Gwen Davis to KB, 27 December 1980, BERG.

513 "You seem to know a great deal more about bravery": Ibid.

513 it would change the way she lived: KB interview with JM, August 1987.

513 "I'm not at all interested": KB quoted in Leah Garchik, "A Friend and Fighter Is Moving On," *San Francisco Chronicle* 19 October 1980: 9.

513 "We have always stimulated": KB to William L. Shirer, 10 January 1981. Courtesy William L. Shirer.

513 Ian would never marry: KB interview with JM, August 1987.

514 "It's a whole new life": See Barbara Venton, "Kay Boyle Has Led a Remarkable Life," *Siesta Key Pelican* 18 December 1980, B4. See also KB to Howard Nemerov, 6 February 1981, Washington University Libraries.

514 "far from civilization": KB to Doris Grumbach, 8 October 1981, Doris Grumbach papers, University of Virginia.

514 "monstrously overweight": KB to Howard Nemerov, 6 February 1981, Washington University Libraries.

514 "socially the Deux Magots": Ibid.

514 "an icy spot": KB to Olga Titelbaum, 7 February 1981. Courtesy of Olga Titelbaum.

514 "mixed up": Linda Ferguson interview with KB, published in *Bloomsbury Review* January–February 1981: 15.

514 "monastic life": KB to Howard Nemerov, 5 June 1981, Washington University Libraries.

514 she could not understand how neo-Nazis: Hank McGuckin interview with JM, 15 December 1989.

514 "I'm awfully sorry": William L. Shirer interview with JM, 22 May 1989.

515 Intellectual arguments were beyond her: Hank McGuckin interview with JM, 15 December 1989.

515 "feel that old": KB to Doris Grumbach, 8 October 1981, University of Virginia.

515 "I have hypoglycemia": Andrew Poliakoff telephone interview with JM, 21 July 1990.

515 For Kay Boyle at Eastern Washington, I am indebted to Andrew Poliakoff for his reminiscences. See ibid.

515 "What are *you* doing": Ibid.

515 Kay was so straight: Grace Paley interview with JM, 4 December 1989.

516 "persuaded me that I need him": KB to William L. Shirer [1982], KBP.

516 "I can do without 1982": Yalom, *Women Writers of the West Coast* 112.

516 "I'll not discuss with you by any name": Kay Boyle, "Excerpts from a Poem for Samuel Beckett," *This Is Not a Letter and Other Poems* (Los Angeles: Sun & Moon Press, 1985) 7.

516 "not really poetry": KB to Howard Nemerov, 20 January 1981, Washington University Libraries.

516 "some kind of memorial": KB to Howard Nemerov, 5 June 1981, Washington University Libraries.

516 "unable to complete an already partly written novel": KB to Doris Grumbach, 8 October 1981, University of Virginia. See also *News from PEN*, 18 August 1987: "PEN/Nelson Algren Fiction Award Announced for 1987."

516 "I won't say anything": For Kay Boyle's 1983 trip to Paris, I have drawn from previously cited interviews with KB, Kathe Vail, and Clover Vail.

517 "cold, grey misery": KB to David Rattray, 1 November 1983, East Hampton Library, East Hampton, NY.

518 "filled with love": KB to David Rattray, 5 July 1984, East Hampton Library.

518 "all the harder so as not to dwell on that": KB to David Rattray, 6 October 1984, East Hampton Library.

518 "a certain starched quality": Clayton Eshleman, "The Maid Drinks Kerosene," rev. of *Babylon*, by René Crevel, *New York Times Book Review* 22 September 1985: 31.

518 "she can't respond": Emily Leider, "The Writer as Moral Force," rev. of *Words that Must Somehow Be Said*, *San Francisco Chronicle* 7 July 1985: 3.

518 "clear-thinking, direct": Susan Slocum Hinerfeld, rev. of *Words That Must Somehow Be Said*, *Los Angeles Times* 29 September 1985: 10.

518 Kay blithely told Rattray: KB to David Rattray, 5 July 1984, East Hampton Library.

518 "with a leg that won't work anymore": KB to David Rattray, 19 April 1984, East Hampton Library.

518 "I have one foot in the grave": Ibid.

518 "So I now have a black eye": KB to David Rattray, 16 January 1985, East Hampton Library.

518 "Hemingway had a stand": David Rattray telephone interview with JM.

519 "an iron contraption": KB to David Rattray, 16 June 1985, East Hampton Library.

519 "to civilization": KB to Doris Grumbach, 10 April 1985, University of Virginia.

519 "I have the privilege": George Popper interview with JM, 20 June 1988.

519 "They had no right": David Cay Boyle Johnston telephone interview with JM, 2 January 1990.

519 "I equate depression with cowardice": KB interview with Kay Bonetti, 1985.

519 "telling anyone that will listen": KB to Jack Shoemaker, 8 September 1985, East Hampton Library.

519 "I only know that my good friend David Rattray": KB to Jack Shoemaker, 5 October 1985, East Hampton Library.

519 "had little to do with the book itself": Ibid.

519 the "owl-ghost": Ibid.

520 "No, Jack": Ibid.

520 a greater discrepancy in character: Jack Shoemaker telephone interview with JM, November 1989.

520 "Did I say that?": Hugh Ford interview with JM, 27 February 1989.

521 "You knew it": KB interview with JM, August 1987, and Hugh Ford interview with JM, 27 February 1989.

521 she was sorry she had not included Hugh Ford: KB interview with JM, August 1987.

521 "Don't write that down!": Brenda Wineapple interview with JM, 18 December 1990.

521 "Well, I could do it": Grace Paley interview with JM, 4 December 1989.

522 "When you first sleep in a new house": Kate Moses interview with JM, 14 December 1989.

522 "bed of pain": KB to Doris Grumbach, 19 November 1985, University of Virginia.

522 "the Siberia of our United States": Ibid.

522 "as long as violent sports like football": See "Kay Boyle," *Voices of Survival in the Nuclear Age*, ed. Dennis Paulson (Santa Barbara: Capra Press, 1986) 99–100.

522 "animal qualities": Philip O'Connor telephone interview with JM, January 1990.

522 "She will go on doing a number on men": Eric Solomon interview with JM, 20 December 1988.

522 "Bomb Libya!": Kay Mills, "Kay Boyle: A Writer's Duty to Speak for the Disenfranchised," *Los Angeles Times* 12 October 1986: 3, 6.

522 "a responsibility" to give meaning: See the Kay Boyle papers from Bowling Green, BERG: "I think older people taking part is very important. We marched all around, and as we passed the fraternity houses, the young men came out and yelled 'Bomb Libya.' " See also ibid.

523 "We don't go at it": Philip O'Connor telephone interview with JM, January 1990.

523 O'Connor had supported the Contras: KB speaking at the San Francisco State University Poetry Center, 11 February 1987.
523 like a baroness: Jennifer McCord telephone interview with JM, 15 January 1990.
523 "ridiculous": Ibid.
523 "She's killing us": Philip O'Connor telephone interview with JM, January 1990.
523 "only eighty, and with his whole youth yet before him": Quoted in Ruth Bauerle, "Kay Boyle's Promises Are for Keeping," *Columbus Dispatch* 16 March 1986, BERG.
523 "Pish-posh, I don't need anybody": KB to Joan Baez, 18 April 1986, BERG.
523 "at this elevation": Maryellen Rump telephone interview with JM, January 1990.
523 talked about Clover's troubles: Howard McCord telephone interview with JM, 5 January 1990, and Jennifer McCord telephone interview with JM, 15 January 1990.
524 "I understand your resentment": KB to Clover Vail, undated fragment sent from Bowling Green, BERG.
524 "just plain Kay": Anne McCormick interview with JM, 24 May 1989.
524 Virginia Platt did not respond appropriately: KB interview with JM, August 1987.
524 At first they drank sherry: Virginia Platt telephone interview with JM, 18 January 1990.
524 "I think that cat's my mother": Ibid.
524 "I am not your secretary": Philip O'Connor to Maryellen Rump, 22 February 1986, BERG.
524 "We're writing serious fiction": Howard McCord telephone interview with JM, 5 January 1990.
524 "I'm never going to do that again": Ibid.
524 no sense of her needing luxury: KB interview with JM, Summer 1986.
525 Young felt the urge: Noel Young interview with JM, 10 December 1990.
525 so "specific" a reply: Kate Moses interview with JM, 14 December 1989.
525 "mistaken" about the Black Panthers: Doug Messerli telephone interview with JM, 1991.

35. SURVIVING

526 "It is reassuring": Herbert O. Kubly to KB, undated letter [c. 1963], KBP.
526 "Old age has finally succeeded in getting me down": KB to JM, 16 March 1988.
526 "Why should I go on living?": KB interview with JM, August 1987.
526 "feel dependent": Ibid.
526 "a tremendous amount of guilt": Ian Franckenstein interview with JM, August 1987.
527 "I am cheating a bit on my entries": KB to James Stern, 5 February 1989. Courtesy of James Stern.
527 "can't get a handle": KB interview with JM, August 1987.
527 "If you can't give money": Ibid.
527 "the only thing Lillian had": Ibid.
527 "flights of imagination": KB to Harry Goldgar, 15 February 1987. Goldgar reviewed Hugh Ford's *Four Lives in Paris* for *The New York Times Book Review*.
527 "a very academic young woman": KB interview with JM, August 1987.
527 "She's going to die anyway": Olga Titelbaum interview with JM, 17 December 1988.
528 "that ardent Catholic": KB to James Stern, 30 November 1987. Courtesy of James Stern.
528 "absolute hatred": KB interview with JM, August 1987.
528 mistook Ted Goeser for Laurence: Ted Goeser telephone interviews with JM, 12 March and 16 March 1991. See also Kathe Vail interviews with JM, June 1990 and November 1991.
528 "There are times when I sit down at the typewriter": Kay Boyle speaking at the San Francisco State University Poetry Center, 11 February 1987.
529 "bit of a heart attack": Kate Moses interview with JM, 14 December 1989.
529 "help pay": KB to JM, 10 December 1987.
529 "from thinking about my beloved child": Ibid.
529 "I can only cry": KB to JM, 13 April 1988.
529 "nothing to say to each other": Kathe Vail interviews with JM, June 1990 and November 1991. See also James Stern interviews with JM, June 1990 and November 1991, and Sharon Cowling interview with JM, June 1990.
529 "Bobby always had a very serious inferiority complex": KB to James Stern, 20 April 1988. Courtesy of James Stern.
529 He emerged from the event feeling used: Charles Amirkhanian telephone interview with JM, 1988.
529 "She was on the threshold of a great writing career": KB to JM, 17 May 1988.

529 "You had many problems with Apple": Kathe Vail interviews with JM, June 1990 and November 1991.
530 "a good deal weaker": Ian Franckenstein to JM, 27 April 1988.
530 "not to be entirely eighty-six years old": KB to James Stern, 23 June 1988. Courtesy of James Stern.
530 "He's getting used to them": Jackie McGuckin telephone interview with JM, January 1990.
530 "They'll improve with wearing": Samuel Beckett to KB, 23 May 1989, HRHRC.
530 " 'Time gentlemen please,' ": Samuel Beckett to KB, 2 January 1989, HRHRC.
530 "How boring to write about oneself": Jackie and Hank McGuckin telephone interviews with JM, January 1990, and Hank McGuckin interview with JM, 15 December 1989.
530 "very, very verbal": Jackie McGuckin telephone interview with JM, January 1990.
530 "like a long-legged colt": Ian Franckenstein, "The Mailbox," *Twentieth Century Literature* [Special Kay Boyle Issue], ed. Sandra Whipple Spanier, 34.3 (Fall 1988) 279.
531 "Oh, make something up": Dorothy Bryant interview with JM, December 1989.
531 "submit some old stories": Dorothy Bryant, "Personal Views," *Twentieth Century Literature* [Special Kay Boyle Issue], ed. Sandra Whipple Spanier, 34.3 (Fall 1988) 263–64.
531 "a bit disturbed": KB to Dorothy Bryant, 11 April 1989.
531 "an abject apology": Dorothy Bryant interview with JM, December 1989.
532 she regretted ever writing: Dorothy Bryant to KB, 13 April 1989. Courtesy of Dorothy Bryant.
532 "I really don't know this woman": Dorothy Bryant interview with JM, December 1989.
532 "demented": KB to Dorothy Bryant, 13 April 1989. Courtesy of Dorothy Bryant.
532 "You mustn't answer it": William L. Shirer interview with JM, 22 May 1989.
532 It was a "blessing": KB telephone conversation with Ralph Schoenman, June 1989.
532 "with sixty years of love": Samuel Beckett to KB, undated and quoted in KB to James Stern, 3 April 1990: "Dearest. I am feeling too poorly to write more. With sixty years of love. Sam." Courtesy of James Stern.
533 "Not very comfortable": Hank McGuckin interview with JM, 15 December 1989.
533 "working non-stop": Louise Erdrich, "Kay Boyle: Power vs. Love," *Lear's* 4.2 (April 1991) 79.
533 "I've been doing nothing but work all day": Ibid.
533 "Bob, I'm thinking of starting an amnesty group": Leo Litwak interview with JM, 14 December 1989.
533 "an old people's home": Interview with Ralph Schoenman.
533 she was inviting black friends: Telephone interview with Cyra McFadden, 1991.
533–34 "They don't understand American policy": Interview with Ariel Rosenblum.
534 Ted concluded it may have provided a clue: Interview with Ted Keller, December 1989.
534 "You should have told them to leave": Telephone conversation with Ian Franckenstein, 1990.
534 "I always felt marvelous when I was pregnant": Kate Moses interview with JM, 14 December 1989.
534 "Oh, well, you get old": Leo Litwak telephone interview with JM, 1992.
534 Kay demanded that Stone take her out: Dr. Tom Stone telephone interview with JM, 1992.
534 "You don't think he really likes her?": Kathe Vail interview with JM, November 1991.
534 "He's never done this before": Ibid.
535 "my beloved Dr. Thomas Stone": See Kay Boyle, "December 1989," *Collected Poems of Kay Boyle* (Port Townsend, WA: Copper Canyon Press, 1991) 164.
535 "You took care of Papa": Kathe Vail interview with JM, November 1991.
535 "So I've got something to look forward to": Ian Franckenstein interview with JM, August 1987, and telephone interviews with JM, 1990 and 1991.
535 "She was more positive about work": Kathe Vail interview with JM, November 1991.
535 She wouldn't treat her daughters as she did: Clover Vail telephone conversation with JM, 12 November 1990.
535 Only in her not finding a kind word: Ian Franckenstein telephone conversations with JM, 1990 and 1991.
536 How it would hurt her: Kathe Vail interview with JM, November 1991.
536 "It's too long": Ibid.
536 "Tom's voice across the wire": Kay Boyle, "A Poem on Getting Up Early in the Morning (Or Even Late in the Morning) When One Is Old," *Collected Poems of Kay Boyle* 167.
536 "speak of yourself": Kay Boyle, "Advice to the Old (Including Myself)," ibid. 145.
537 "You drink too much": Clover Vail interview with JM, 19 January 1991.
537 For this account of Kay Boyle's illness, I have drawn on telephone conversations with Ian Franckenstein, November 1990.

537 "I'm going to hang in": Ibid.
538 Kay had suggested that Jo move: Kathe Vail interview with JM, November 1991.

CODA

539 "I haven't changed much since I was ten": KB interview with Hugh Ford, 1978.
539 "Let it be courage": Kay Boyle quotation printed on the program for her memorial service, 9 January 1993.
539 "a Queen in exile": Faith Gude to JM, 18 December 1989.
539 "grande dame" . . . "neglectful": Clover Vail telephone conversations with JM, 12 November 1990, 5 December 1990, and 6 December 1990.
539 "My childhood prepared me for the life I live today": Faith Gude interviews with JM, December 1989.
539 "I don't want her to die hating me": Faith Gude telephone interview with JM, 1992.
539 "Somehow there must be a way for us to talk": Faith Gude to KB, 23 February 1991. Courtesy of Faith Gude.
539 "Your letter has changed my whole life": KB to Faith Gude, 10 March 1991. Courtesy of Faith Gude.
540 "You were right": Kathe Vail interview with JM, November 1991.
540 "We admired your bravery": For the incident of the "Forever France" scarf, Faith Gude interview with JM, 2 March 1991.
540 he "loved" her: Shawn Wong interview with JM, 3 June 1991.
541 "It's a pity": Burton Weiss accepting the award for Kay Boyle. From the notes of Deborah Linton.
541 "we don't necessarily": Gui Juo-ping to KB, undated. Courtesy of James Stern.
541 spirits were "good": KB to Blair Clark, 23 September 1991. Courtesy of Blair Clark.
541 "I have things to do": Kathe Vail telephone interview with JM, 12 July 1991.
542 "a mouse in her hands": Dr. Tom Stone telephone interview with JM, 16 December 1991.
542 Kay pretended: Kathe Vail interview with JM, November 1991, and telephone interviews, 12 July 1991 and 6 January 1992.
542 "I'm like a boat without oars": Kathe Vail telephone interview with JM, 6 January 1992.
542 "What does he think is going to happen in heaven?": KB interview with JM, August 1987.
542–43 For Kay Boyle's conversion to Catholicism, see Ian Franckenstein telephone conversations with JM.
543 "Dearly beloved son": KB to Father Gerry O'Rourke, 10 December 1991. Kay Boyle's letters to Father Gerry O'Rourke appear courtesy of Father O'Rourke.
543 "with you in spirit": KB to Gerry O'Rourke, 26 May 1992.
543 "Your voice has always": KB to Gerry O'Rourke, 9 February 1992.
543 "Thank you dear father": KB to Gerry O'Rourke, 16 January 1992.
543 "I can't get down to work": Kathe Vail telephone interview, 6 January 1992.
543 "Wolfgang" had cried: Faith Gude telephone interview with JM, 17 March 1992.
544 "I always felt Kay was my true mother": Bruce Detweiler telephone interview with JM, November 1993.
544 "so I deserve no special sympathy": KB to JM, 7 March 1991.
544 "Oh, I'm so glad you came to see me": For the reunion of Kay Boyle and Faith Gude, Faith Gude telephone conversation with JM, 17 March 1992.
545 Ian felt mentally: For this account of Kay Boyle at The Redwoods, see Ian Franckenstein to JM, June 2, 1992, and July 7, 1992.
545 "I want to die": Ian Franckenstein interview with JM, 2 January 1993.
545 "Don't dawdle": Leo Litwak interview with JM, 30 December 1992.
546–47 For the account of Kay Boyle's last months, I have drawn on interviews in December 1992 and January 1993 with Ian Franckenstein, Leo Litwak, Herbert Gold, Peter Cunningham, Burton Weiss, and Father Gerry O'Rourke.

SELECTED

BIBLIOGRAPHY

Aaron, Daniel. *Writers on the Left.* New York: Discus Books, 1961.

Abel, Lionel. *The Intellectual Follies: A Memoir of the Literary Venture in New York and Paris.* New York: W. W. Norton, 1984.

Adams, Agnes. "Kay Boyle and Six Children Back Home Again." *New York Post* 31 July 1941.

Alexander, Sidney. "The Gulf Between." Rev. of *The Seagull on the Step,* by Kay Boyle. *New York Times Book Review* 8 May 1955: 2.

"All-American Parley on Peace Called Sept. 5." *Daily Worker* 29 July 1949: 5.

Allen, Frederick Lewis. *Only Yesterday: An Informal History of the Nineteen-Twenties.* New York: Bantam, 1950.

———. *The Big Change: America Transforms Itself, 1900–1950.* New York: Harper & Row, 1952.

Alsop, Joseph. "The Strange Case of Louis Budenz." *Atlantic Monthly* April 1952: 29–33.

Amirkhanian, Charles. "An 86th Birthday Valentine." *Kay Boyle: Writer of Conscience. KPFA Folio* (program guide for KPFA and KFCF, San Francisco) February 1988.

Anderson, Sister J. M. "The Underground Woman." *Choice* 12.5–6 (1975) 680.

Andreas, Alfred Thayer, and William G. Cutler. *The History of the State of Kansas.* Two vols. Chicago: A. T. Andreas, 1883.

Armory Show of 1913, 50th Anniversary Exhibition. Catalogue. Proctor Institute, Utica, NY: Henry Street Settlement and Munson-Williams, 1963.

Ashley, Beth. "Kay Boyle: A Long and Eloquent Life." *Marin Independent Journal* 3 December 1989: E1, 8.

"Atchison, Topeka and Santa Fe Time Table," September 1881.

"Atom Scientist to Address Peace Parley." *Daily Worker* 28 February 1949: 2, 9.

Rev. of *Avalanche,* by Kay Boyle. *Booklist* 15 January 1944: 183.

Bair, Deirdre. *Samuel Beckett.* New York: Harcourt Brace Jovanovich, 1978.

Baker, Carlos. *Ernest Hemingway: A Life Story.* New York: Scribner's, 1969.

Balakian, Nona. "Two Cards at a Time." Rev. of *1939,* by Kay Boyle. *New York Times Book Review* 15 February 1948: 22.

———. "The War in Colorado." Rev. of *His Human Majesty,* by Kay Boyle. *New York Times* 10 April 1949: 21.

Bald, Wambly. *On the Left Bank: 1929–1933.* Ed. Benjamin Franklin V. Athens: Ohio UP, 1987.

Barkham, John. "This Time the Germans Were Receiving Orders." Rev. of *Generation Without Farewell,* by Kay Boyle. New York *World-Telegram & Sun* 10 April 1949: 21.

Baro, Gene. "Novelists's Vision of Post-War Germany." Rev. of *Generation Without Farewell,* by Kay Boyle. *New York Herald Tribune Book Review* 17 January 1960: 5.

Barrett, Margery. "Tour in Technicolor." Rev. of *Thirty Stories*, by Kay Boyle. *New Masses* 31 December 1946: 23–24.

————. Reply to Kay Boyle. *New Masses* 15 April 1947: 21–22.

Barrows, Herbert. *Suggestions for Teaching Fifteen Stories*. Boston: D. C. Heath, 1950. Pp. 23–26.

Barth, Alan. *The Loyalty of Free Men*. New York: Pocket Books, 1952.

Bauerle, Ruth. "Kay Boyle's Promises Are for Keeping." *Columbus Dispatch* 16 March 1986.

Baughman, Robert W. *Kansas Post Offices, 1828–1961*. Topeka: Kansas Postal History Society, 1961.

Bedwell, Bettina. *Yellow Dusk*. Ghostwritten by Kay Boyle. London: Hurst & Blackett, 1937.

Rev. of *Being Geniuses Together*, by Kay Boyle and Robert McAlmon. *Virginia Quarterly Review* 44 (1968) CLX.

Belfrage, Cedric. *The American Inquisition, 1945–60*. Indianapolis: Bobbs-Merrill, 1973.

Bell, Elizabeth S. "Call Forth a Good Day: The Nonfiction of Kay Boyle." *Twentieth Century Literature* [Special Kay Boyle Issue], ed. Sandra Whipple Spanier, 34.3 (Fall 1988) 384–91.

Bendersky, Joseph W. *A History of Nazi Germany*. Chicago: Nelson-Hall, 1985.

"Bergery, Gaston Frank." *Dictionnaire de la Politique Française*. Ed. Henry Couston. Paris: La Librairie Française, 1967.

Bernikow, Louise, ed. *The World Split Open: Four Centuries of Women Poets in England and America, 1552–1950*. New York: Vintage, 1974.

Blackmore, R. L. "John Cowper Powys." *Dictionary of Literary Biography*. Vol. 15. Detroit: Gale Research, 1983. Pp. 448–64.

Bogan, Louise. Rev. of *A Glad Day*, by Kay Boyle. *New Yorker* 22 October 1938: 83–84.

Boucheron, Robert. "The Surprise of the Floor." Rev. of *Babylon*, by René Crevel. Trans. by Kay Boyle. *New York Native* 26 August–1 September 1985.

Bourjaily, Vance. "Moving and Maturing." Rev. of *Fifty Stories*, by Kay Boyle. *New York Times Book Review* 28 September 1980: 9, 32.

Boyd, A. C. "Miss Kay Boyle." Rev. of *Death of a Man*, by Kay Boyle. *London Mercury* October 1936: 562.

"Boyle, Kay." *Current Biography: Who's News and Why, 1942*. Ed. Maxine Block. New York: H. W. Wilson Co., 1942. Pp. 101–4.

Breuer, Bessie. *The Actress*. New York: Harper & Brothers, 1957.

Brickell, Herschel. "Kay Boyle's Queer Folk." Rev. of *Gentlemen, I Address You Privately*, by Kay Boyle. *North American Review* 12 November 1933: 93.

"Bronowski, Jacob." *Current Biography Yearbook, 1958*. New York: H. W. Wilson Co., 1958.

Brooke, Gladys Palmer. *Relations and Complications: Being the Recollections of H. H. the Dayang Muda of Sarawak*. Ghostwritten by Kay Boyle. London: Lane–Bodley Head, 1929.

Brooks, V. E. "Miss Kay Boyle." Rev. of *The White Horses of Vienna*, by Kay Boyle. *London Mercury* February 1937: 425.

Brown, Milton W. *The Story of the Armory Show: The New Spirit*. Washington: Joseph H. Hirshhorn Foundation, 1963.

Bryant, Dorothy, et al. "Personal Views of Kay Boyle." *Twentieth Century Literature* [Special Kay Boyle Issue], ed. Sandra Whipple Spanier, 34.3 (Fall 1988): 263–312.

Bryher, Winifred. *The Heart to Artemis: A Writer's Memoirs*. New York: Harcourt, Brace, 1962.

Budenz, Louis F. *This Is My Story*. New York: McGraw-Hill, 1947.

————. *Men Without Faces*. New York: Harper & Brothers, 1950.

————. *The Cry Is Peace*. Chicago: Henry Regnery, 1952.

Bullett, Gerald. Rev. of *Year Before Last*, by Kay Boyle. *New Statesman and Nation* 9 July 1932: 43.

Burra, Peter. Rev. of *Death of a Man*, by Kay Boyle. *Spectator* 2 October 1936: 560.

Burt, Struthers. "Kay Boyle's Coincidence and Melodrama." Rev. of *Avalanche*, by Kay Boyle. *Saturday Review of Literature* 15 January 1944: 6.

————. "The Mature Craft of Kay Boyle." Rev. of *Thirty Stories*, by Kay Boyle. *Saturday Review of Literature* 30 November 1946.

Callaghan, Morley. *That Summer in Paris*. New York: Coward-McCann, 1963.

Callard, D. A. *Pretty Good for a Woman: The Enigmas of Evelyn Scott*. London: Jonathan Cape, 1985.

Canby, Henry Seidel. "Style Without Design." Rev. of *Gentlemen, I Address You Privately*, by Kay Boyle. *Saturday Review of Literature* 4 November 1933: 233.

————. "Kay Boyle's Sketch of a Likeable Nazi." Rev. of *Death of a Man*, by Kay Boyle. *Saturday Review of Literature* 10 October 1936: 12.

Cantwell, Robert. "American Exile." Rev. of *Year Before Last*, by Kay Boyle. *Nation* 20 July 1932: 60–61.

————. "Exiles." Rev. of *Gentlemen, I Address You Privately*, by Kay Boyle. *New Republic* 13 December 1933: 136–37.

Carey, Glenn O. Rev. of *Being Geniuses Together*, by Kay Boyle and Robert McAlmon. *Library Journal* 15 May 1968: 1998.

Carnevali, Emanuel. *The Autobiography of Emanuel Carnevali*. Prefaced and compiled by Kay Boyle. New York: Horizon, 1967.

Carpenter, Humphrey. *Geniuses Together: American Writers in Paris in the 1920s*. Boston: Houghton Mifflin, 1988.

————. *A Serious Character: The Life of Ezra Pound*. Boston: Houghton Mifflin, 1988.

Carr, Virginia Spencer. *The Lonely Hunter: A Biography of Carson McCullers*. Garden City, NY: Doubleday, 1975.

Carsten, F. L. *Fascist Movements in Austria: From Schönerer to Hitler*. Sage Studies in Twentieth Century History. Vol. 7. London and Beverly Hills: Sage Publications, 1977.

————. *The Rise of Fascism*. 2nd ed. Berkeley and Los Angeles: University of California Press, 1980.

Census Report. Kansas State, City of Topeka, Shawnee County, 1875.

————. United States. 1880.

Centing, Richard R. "Kay Boyle." *Ohioana Quarterly* 15 (Spring 1972): 11–13.

Cheney, Sheldon. *The Story of Modern Art*. New York: Viking, 1941.

"Chief Justice of Utah Rips Trial of '12.' " *Daily Worker* 28 February 1949: 1, 9.

Churchill, Allen. *The Literary Decade*. Englewood Cliffs, NJ: Prentice-Hall, 1971.

Clark, Suzanne. "Revolution, the Woman, and the Word: Kay Boyle." *Twentieth Century Literature* [Special Kay Boyle Issue], ed. Sandra Whipple Spanier, 34.3 (Fall 1988): 322–33.

Coates, Robert M. Rev. of *Don Juan*, by Joseph Delteil. Trans. by Kay Boyle. *New Yorker* 2 May 1931: 74.

Cogley, John. *Report on Blacklisting*. I: *Movies*. Fund for the Republic, 1956.

————. *Report on Blacklisting*. II: *Radio and Television*. Fund for the Republic, 1956.

Cohn, Roy. *The Autobiography of Roy Cohn*. Ed. Sidney Zion. New York: St. Martin's Press, 1988.

Coleman, John. "Big Gleeful Hood." Rev. of *Generation Without Farewell*, by Kay Boyle. *Spectator* 8 July 1960: 73.

Rev. of *Collected Poems of Kay Boyle*. *Publishers Weekly* 28 June 1991: 97.

Colum, Mary H. "In Favor of Best Sellers." Includes rev. of *Monday Night*, by Kay Boyle. *Forum* October 1938: 162–67.

————. "Poets and Psychologists." Includes rev. of *The Crazy Hunter*, by Kay Boyle. *Forum* June 1940: 322–26.

"The Coming Writers Congress." *Partisan Review* 11.6 (January–February 1935) 94–96.

Conover, Anne. *Caresse Crosby: From Black Sun to Roccasinabalda*. Santa Barbara: Capra Press, 1989.

Cook, Carole. Rev. of *Fifty Stories*, by Kay Boyle. *Saturday Review* September 1980: 70.

Cooper, Louise Field. "Averted Hearts." Rev. of *The Smoking Mountain*, by Kay Boyle. *Saturday Review of Literature* 21 April 1951: 17–18.

Corwin, Phillip. "The Telling of the Story." Rev. of *The Underground Woman*, by Kay Boyle. *Nation* 22 March 1975: 347.

Cosman, Max. "Novel About the Occupation." Rev. of *Generation Without Farewell*, by Kay Boyle. *Commonweal* 8 January 1960: 425.

Cowley, Malcolm. "The Last of the Lost Generation." *Esquire* July 1963: 77–79.

————. "Those Paris Years." Rev. of *Being Geniuses Together*, by Kay Boyle and Robert McAlmon. *New York Times Book Review* 9 June 1968: 1+.

————. *Exile's Return: A Literary Saga of the Nineteen Twenties*. New York: Viking, 1961.

————. *A Second Flowering: Works and Days of the Lost Generation*. New York: Viking, 1973.

Crane, Hart. *The Letters of Hart Crane, 1916–1932*. Ed. Brom Weber. Berkeley: University of California Press, 1965.

Crosby, Caresse. *The Passionate Years*. 1953; Carbondale and Edwardsville: Southern Illinois UP, 1968.

Crosby, Harry. *Shadows of the Sun: The Diaries of Harry Crosby*. Ed. Edward Germain. Santa Barbara: Black Sparrow Press, 1977.

Dahlberg, Edward. *The Confessions of Edward Dahlberg*. New York: Grosset & Dunlap, 1971.

Davenport, Basil. "Walpurgisnacht." Rev. of *Monday Night*, by Kay Boyle. *Saturday Review of Literature* 30 July 1938: 13.

Davidon, Ann Morrissett. "Head Over Heart." Rev. of *Kay Boyle: Artist and Activist*, by Sandra Whipple Spanier. *Progressive* February 1987: 44–45.

Davis, John H. *The Guggenheims (1848–1988): An American Epic.* New York: Shapolsky Publishers, 1988.

de Sales, Raoul de Roussy. Rev. of *Primer for Combat*, by Kay Boyle. *Atlantic* December 1942: 152.

Dean, Virgil W. "Great Bend, Barton County, Kansas, and Rail Travel East." Unpublished report. Kansas State Historical Society, 1990.

Rev. of *Death of a Man*, by Kay Boyle. *Times Literary Supplement* 3 October 1936: 788–89.

Rev. of *Death of a Man*, by Kay Boyle. *Forum* 96 (December 1936) ix.

Denny, Reuel. "Fine Workmanship." Rev. of *A Glad Day*, by Kay Boyle. *Poetry* 54 (September 1939) 347–49.

Dewey, John, et al. "A Letter to the L.A.W." *Partisan Review* 6 (Fall 1939) 127–28.

Diamonstein, Barbaralee. *Open Secrets: Ninety-four Women in Touch with Our Time.* New York: Viking, 1972.

Dobree, Bonamy. Rev. of *Gentlemen, I Address You Privately*, by Kay Boyle. *Spectator* 9 February 1934: 208.

Donner, Frank. "The Informer." *Nation* 10 April 1954: 302–6.

Dos Passos, John. Reply to questionnaire, "Whither the American Writer?" *Modern Quarterly* 6 (Summer 1932) 11–12.

Drake, William. *The First Wave: Women Poets in America, 1915–1945.* New York: Macmillan, 1987.

Drinnon, Richard. *Rebel in Paradise: A Biography of Emma Goldman.* Chicago: University of Chicago Press, 1961.

Duchamp, Marcel. Notes for a lecture, "Apropos of Myself," 1964. With *Nu Descendant un Escalier.* Philadelphia Museum of Art.

––––––. *Salt Seller: The Writings of Marcel Duchamp. Marchand du Sel.* Eds. Michel Sanouillet and Elmer Peterson. New York: Oxford UP, 1973.

"Dynamitanschlag auf unsere Druckerei" (Dynamite Attack on Our Printing Works). *Tiroler Anzeiger* 28 June 1934: 1.

Eastman, Max. "The Cult of Unintelligibility." *Harper's Monthly Magazine* April 1929: 632–39.

––––––. "The Tendency Toward Pure Poetry." *Harper's Monthly Magazine* June 1929: 222–30.

"The Easy Out." Editorial. *Washington Post* 25 May 1953.

Edel, Leon. Introduction. *Memoirs of Montparnasse*, by John Glassco. New York: Oxford UP, 1970. Pp. vii–xi.

Edmonson, C. Earl. *The Heimwehr and Austrian Politics, 1918–1936.* Athens: University of Georgia Press, 1978.

Ellman, Richard. *James Joyce.* New York: Oxford UP, 1959.

––––––. *Oscar Wilde.* New York: Vintage, 1988.

Engle, Paul. "Hope Out of France." Rev. of *The Seagull on the Step*, by Kay Boyle. *New Republic* 16 May 1955: 38–39.

Erdrich, Louise. "Power vs. Love: Author Kay Boyle." *Lear's* April 1991: 76–79.

Ernst, Jimmy. *A Not-So-Still Life: A Child of Europe's Pre-World War II Art and His Remarkable Homecoming to America.* New York: St. Martin's–Marek, 1984.

Eshleman, Clayton. "The Maid Drinks Kerosene." Rev. of *Babylon*, by René Crevel. Trans. by Kay Boyle. *New York Times Book Review* 22 September 1985: 31.

Fadiman, Clifton. Rev. of *Gentlemen, I Address You Privately*, by Kay Boyle. *New Yorker* 4 November 1933: 66–67.

––––––. "Remember Your Alice?—The Vegetarian Novel—The Woman Who Did." Rev. of *My Next Bride*, by Kay Boyle. *New Yorker* 10 November 1934: 89–90.

––––––. Rev. of *The Youngest Camel*, by Kay Boyle. *New Yorker* 25 November 1939: 73.

––––––. Rev. of *The Crazy Hunter*, by Kay Boyle. *New Yorker* 4 March 1940: 76–77.

"Farmer-Labor Party, The." *World Book Encyclopedia.* 1955 ed.

Farrell, James T. "Thirty and Under." *New Freeman* 1 (2 July 1930) 373–74.

––––––. "The Last Writers' Congress: An Interim Report on Its Results." *Saturday Review of Literature* 5 June 1937: 10, 14.

Federal Bureau of Investigation. Subject: Joseph M. Franckenstein. File no. 123-3915.

––––––. Subject: Kay Boyle Franckenstein. File no. 100-381638, sections 1 and 2, and file no. 151-2369, section 1.

Feld, Rose. "France: Strong, Exciting and Unconquerable." Rev. of *Avalanche*, by Kay Boyle. *New York Herald Tribune Book Review* 9 January 1944: vi.

Feldman, Paula R. "Margaret Anderson." *Dictionary of Literary Biography.* Vol. 4: 3–10.

Felton, David. *Mindfuckers: A Sourcebook on the Rise of Acid Fascism in America.* San Francisco: Straight Arrow Books, 1972.

Ferguson, Otis. "The Brown Blouses of Vienna." Rev. of *Death of a Man*, by Kay Boyle. *New Republic* 21 October 1936: 322.

———. "The Lost, to the Lost." Rev. of *Monday Night*, by Kay Boyle. *New Republic* 3 August 1938: 369.

Field, Andrew. *Djuna: The Formidable Miss Barnes*. Austin: University of Texas Press, 1985.

Rev. of *The First Lover and Other Stories*, by Kay Boyle. *Nation* 19 April 1933: 453.

Rev. of *The First Lover and Other Stories*, by Kay Boyle. *Contempo* 15 May 1933: 7.

Rev. of *The First Lover and Other Stories*, by Kay Boyle. *Forum* May 1933: vi.

Flanner, Janet. *Darlinghissima: Letters to a Friend*. Ed. Natalia Danesi Murray. New York: Harcourt Brace Jovanovich, 1985.

"Flashes of Dementia." Rev. of *Monday Night*, by Kay Boyle. *Time* 8 August 1938: 51.

Flint, Lucy, and Thomas M. Messer. *The Peggy Guggenheim Collection: Handbook*. New York: Harry N. Abrams, 1983.

Ford, Charles Henri. Rev. of *Short Stories* by Kay Boyle. *Blues* 2.7 (1929) 45.

Ford, Hugh, ed. and introduction. *The Left Bank Revisited: Selections from the Paris Tribune, 1917–1934*. University Park: Pennsylvania State UP, 1972.

———. *Published in Paris: A Literary Chronicle of Paris in the 1920s and 1930s*. New York: Macmillan, 1975.

———. *Four Lives in Paris*. San Francisco: North Point Press, 1987.

Foster, Herbert. "Pair Cleared in 'Risk' Case." *Washington Post* 22 April 1957.

Fracchia, Charles. "Kay Boyle: A Profile." *San Francisco Review of Books* April 1976: 7–9.

French, Robert W. " 'I' Poems and 'You' Poems." Rev. of *Testament for My Students*, by Kay Boyle. *Nation* 8 June 1970: 695–98.

Rev. of *A Frenchman Must Die*, by Kay Boyle. *Booklist* 1 April 1946: 247.

Friedman, Mickey. "A Literary Legend Who Refuses to Rest on Her Laurels." *San Francisco Examiner* 27 September 1978: 21.

"From Mont Blanc to Matunuck by Clipper Plane: The Vail Youngsters Wish They Had Snow for Skiing." *Providence Sunday Journal* 3 August 1941.

Fry, Varian. *Surrender on Demand*. New York: Random House, 1945.

Gannett, Lewis. Rev. of *The Smoking Mountain*, by Kay Boyle. *New York Herald Tribune* 30 April 1951.

Garcia, Ken. "Kay Boyle: Victim of a Witch Hunt." *Phoenix* 9 March 1978: 4.

Gascoyne, David. *Paris Journal 1936–7*. London: Enitharmon Press, 1980.

———. *Paris Journal 1937–9*. London: Enitharmon Press, 1978.

Geismar, Maxwell. "Aristocrat of the Short Story." Rev. of *Nothing Ever Breaks Except the Heart*, by Kay Boyle. *New York Times Book Review* 10 July 1966: 4, 16.

Gelfant, Blanche H. "Fiction Chronicle." Rev. of *The Underground Woman*, by Kay Boyle. *Hudson Review* 28.2 (Summer 1975) 309–20.

Rev. of *Gentlemen, I Address You Privately*, by Kay Boyle. *Nation* 29 November 1933: 630.

Gessner, Robert. *Massacre: A Survey of Today's American Indian*. 1931; New York: Da Capo Press, 1972.

———. *Some of My Best Friends Are Jews*. New York: Farrar & Rinehart, 1936.

———. *Here Is My Home*. New York: Alliance, 1941.

———. *Treason*. New York: Scribner's, 1944.

———. *Youth Is the Time*. New York: Scribner's, 1945.

———. *The Moving Image: A Guide to Cinematic Literacy*. New York: E. P. Dutton, 1968.

Gibbs-Smith, Charles H. *The Aeroplane: An Historical Survey of Its Origins and Development*. London: Her Majesty's Stationery Office, 1960.

Gilbert, Douglas. "Ski Trooper Husband Aided by Boyle's Book." *New York World-Telegram* 24 August 1944.

Gilbert, James Burkhart. *Writers and Partisans: A History of Literary Radicalism in America*. New York: Wiley, 1968.

Gill, Brendan. *Here at The New Yorker*. New York: Random House, 1975.

Gitlin, Todd. *The Sixties: Years of Hope, Days of Rage*. New York: Bantam, 1989.

Givner, Joan. *Katherine Anne Porter: A Life*. New York: Simon & Schuster, 1982.

Glassco, John. *Memoirs of Montparnasse*. New York: Oxford UP, 1970.

Gold, Mike. "A Note on Ernest Walsh." Reply to letter of Ernest Walsh. *New Masses* 2 (December 1926) 23.

Goldman, Emma. *My Disillusionment in Russia*. Garden City, NY: Doubleday, Page, 1923.

———. *My Further Disillusionment in Russia*. Garden City, NY: Doubleday, Page, 1924.

————. *Living My Life.* Vol. 1. New York: Knopf, 1931.

————. *Living My Life.* Vol. 2. 1931; New York: Dover, 1970.

———— and Alexander Berkman. *Nowhere at Home: Letters from Exile of Emma Goldman and Alexander Berkman.* Eds. Richard and Anna Maria Drinnon. New York: Schocken, 1975.

Gordon, Mary. "Surviving History: For Many American Writers, Italy's Natalia Ginzburg Is a Literary Icon." *New York Times Magazine* 25 March 1990: 42–46, 62.

Gould, Jean. *American Women Poets: Pioneers of Modern Poetry.* New York: Dodd, Mead, 1980.

Graham, Gladys. "Inescapable End." Rev. of *Year Before Last,* by Kay Boyle. *Saturday Review of Literature* 9 July 1932: 827.

————. "Artistic Fiction." Rev. of *The First Lover,* by Kay Boyle. *Saturday Review of Literature* 25 March 1933: 501.

Green, Blake. "Kay Boyle—A Study in Paradox." *San Francisco Chronicle* 17 February 1975: 12, 14.

Green, Martin. *New York 1913: The Armory Show and the Paterson Strike Pageant.* New York: Scribner's, 1988.

Gross, Theodore L. "Where Have All the Children Gone?" Rev. of *Nothing Ever Breaks Except the Heart,* by Kay Boyle. *Saturday Review of Literature* 16 July 1966: 35.

Grumbach, Doris. "Fine Print: Kay Boyle et al." Rev. of *The Underground Woman,* by Kay Boyle. *New Republic* 8 February 1975: 33.

Guggenheim, Peggy. *Out of This Century: The Informal Memoirs of Peggy Guggenheim.* New York: Dial Press, 1946.

————. *Out of This Century: Confessions of an Art Addict.* New York: Universe Books, 1987.

Gutman, Israel. "Anschluss." *Encyclopedia of the Holocaust.* Ed. Israel Gutman. 4 vols. New York: Macmillan, 1990.

Haesler, Bob. "Kay Boyle Assesses San Francisco State." *San Francisco Chronicle* 16 November 1968: 13.

Hallock, Joseph. "Choice of Love or War." Rev. of *1939,* by Kay Boyle. *New York Herald Tribune* [?] 7 March 1948: 3, see KBP.

Hamilton, Mildred. "Kay Boyle: Genius at Large." *San Francisco Examiner & Chronicle* 23 June 1968.

Hansen, Arlen J. *Expatriate Paris: A Cultural and Literary Guide to Paris of the 1920s.* New York: Arcade Publishing, 1990.

Harlow, Gail. "The Underground Woman." *Library Journal* 1 February 1975: 309–10.

Harrison, Gilbert A. *The Critic as Artist: Essays on Books, 1920–1970.* New York: Liveright, 1972.

Hart, Elizabeth. Rev. of *My Next Bride,* by Kay Boyle. *Books* 11 November 1934: 4.

Harte, Barbara, and Carolyn Riley, eds. *Contemporary Authors: Bio-bibliographies of Selected Leading Writers of Today with Critical and Personal Sidelights.* Detroit: Gale Research, 1969.

Harwood, H. C. Rev. of *Plagued by the Nightingale,* by Kay Boyle. *Saturday Review of Literature* 8 August 1931: 185.

Hatcher, Harlan. *Creating the Modern American Novel.* New York: Russell & Russell, 1935.

Hatlen, Burton. "Sexual Politics in Kay Boyle's *Death of a Man.*" *Twentieth Century Literature* [Special Kay Boyle Issue], ed. Sandra Whipple Spanier, 34.3 (Fall 1988): 347–62.

Hauser, Marianne. Rev. of *Primer for Combat,* by Kay Boyle. *New York Times Book Review* 8 November 1942: 6.

Havighurst, Walter. "Avalanche in the Haute-Savoie." Rev. of *1939,* by Kay Boyle. *Saturday Review of Literature* 28 February 1948: 12–13.

Hawthorne, Hazel. Rev. of *The First Lover and Other Stories,* by Kay Boyle. *New Republic* 3 May 1933: 342.

Haynes, Michael A. Rev. of *Fifty Stories,* by Kay Boyle. *Library Journal* 1 October 1980: 2103–4.

Heller, Lee. "Lifetime Anti-fascist Writer Speaks Her Piece." *People's Daily World* 25 June 1986: A-11.

Hellman, Lillian. As quoted in "Sees Finnish Aid Imperiling Peace." *New York Times* 21 January 1940: L + 27.

Hemingway, Ernest. *The Sun Also Rises.* 1926; New York: Scribner's, 1954.

————. "The Man Who Was Marked for Death." *A Moveable Feast.* New York: Bantam, 1965. Pp. 119–27.

————. *Selected Letters, 1917–1961.* Ed. Carlos Baker. New York: Scribner's, 1981.

Hicks, Granville. "The Light and the Dark." Rev. of *Generation Without Farewell,* by Kay Boyle. *Saturday Review of Literature* 16 January 1960: 59.

Hinerfeld, Susan Slocum. Rev. of *Words That Must Somehow Be Said,* by Kay Boyle. *Los Angeles Times Book Review* 29 September 1985: 10.

Hoey, Reed A. Rev. of *The Seagull on the Step*, by Kay Boyle. *Library Journal* 1 March 1955: 560.

Hoffman, Frederick. "A New Enterprise in Publishing." Rev. of *Plagued by the Nightingale*, by Kay Boyle. *Los Angeles Times*, see KBP.

———, Charles Allen, and Carolyn F. Ulrich. *The Little Magazine: A History and a Bibliography.* Princeton: Princeton UP, 1947.

Hoffman, Nicholas von. *Citizen Cohn: The Life and Times of Roy Cohn.* New York: Bantam, 1988.

Hoffman, Paul. Rev. of *The White Horses of Vienna*, by Kay Boyle. "The Atlantic Bookshelf" section, *Atlantic* April 1936.

Hofstadter, Richard. *The American Political Tradition.* New York: Vintage, 1955.

Holland, Vyvyan. *Son of Oscar Wilde.* New York: E. P. Dutton, 1954.

"Hollywood Thriller." Rev. of *Avalanche*, by Kay Boyle. *Commonweal* 39 (21 January 1944) 357.

Hopkins, Kenneth. *The Powys Brothers: A Biographical Appreciation.* Cranbury, NJ: Farleigh Dickinson UP, 1967.

Hoyenga, Betty. "A Question of Fiction." Rev. of *Nothing Ever Breaks Except the Heart*, by Kay Boyle. *Prairie Schooner* 40.4 (Winter 1966) 370–71.

Hutchens, John K. "On the Books, On an Author." Rev. of *The Smoking Mountain*, by Kay Boyle. *New York Times Book Review* 22 April 1951: 3.

"Intensity in the Alps." Rev. of *1939*, by Kay Boyle. *Time* 1 March 1948: 92.

Jack, Peter Monro. Rev. of *The Crazy Hunter*, by Kay Boyle. *New York Times Book Review* 17 March 1940: 5.

Jolas, Eugene. Rev. of *Short Stories*, by Kay Boyle. *transition* 16–17 (June 1929) 326.

———. "*Transition*: An Epilogue." *American Mercury* 23 (June 1931) 185–92.

———. "Kay Boyle, Journalist." *New York Times Book Review* 24 November 1946: 8.

Jones, E. B. C. Rev. of *Plagued by the Nightingale*, by Kay Boyle. *Adelphi* 1 October 1931: 68.

———. Rev. of *Year Before Last*, by Kay Boyle. *Adelphi* July 1932: 718–20.

———. Rev. of *Wedding Day and Other Stories*, by Kay Boyle. *Adelphi* 1 October 1932: 73–76.

———. Rev. of *Gentlemen, I Address You Privately*, by Kay Boyle. *Adelphi* May 1934: 155.

Joost, Nicholas. *Scofield Thayer and the Dial.* Carbondale: Southern Illinois UP, 1964.

Josephson, Matthew. *Life Among the Surrealists.* New York: Holt, Rinehart and Winston, 1962.

"Judy Holliday and Jose Ferrer Named on House Red-Front List: Academy Award Winners Reported as Sponsors of 1949 'Peace' Rally; Both Deny Party Ties." *New York Herald Tribune* 5 April 1951: 1, 39.

Kansas. Department of Public Instruction. *Fourteenth Annual Report of the Department of Public Instruction of the State of Kansas.* Topeka: George W. Martin, 1874.

Kansas Historical Collections 8 (1903–4).

Kay Boyle: Writer of Conscience. KPFA *Folio* (program guide for KPFA and KFCF, San Francisco). February 1988.

"Kay Boyle's Experiments." Rev. of *Wedding Day and Other Stories*, by Kay Boyle. *New York Times Book Review* 16 November 1930: 8.

Kazin, Alfred. Rev. of *Death of a Man*, by Kay Boyle. *New York Times Book Review* 11 October 1936: 6–7.

———. "The Tormented People of Kay Boyle." Rev. of *Monday Night*, by Kay Boyle. *New York Times Book Review* 31 July 1938: 7.

———. *On Native Grounds: An Interpretation of Modern American Prose Literature.* New York: Harcourt, Brace, 1942.

———. *Starting Out in the Thirties.* Boston: Little, Brown, 1965.

Kee, Robert. Rev. of *1939*, by Kay Boyle. *Spectator* 23 July 1948: 122–24.

Kelly, James. "Behind the Façade." Rev. of *The Seagull on the Step*, by Kay Boyle. *Saturday Review of Literature* 14 May 1955: 16.

Kennedy, Margaret. *The Constant Nymph.* New York: A. L. Burt–Doubleday, 1925.

Kettmann, Steve. "Old Novel Offers Insights into Nazism." Rev. of *Death of a Man* (reissue), by Kay Boyle. *San Francisco Chronicle* 14 September 1989.

Kielty, Bernardine. "Kay Boyle's New Novel." Rev. of *A Frenchman Must Die*, by Kay Boyle. *Ladies' Home Journal* March 1946: 5.

Kindermann, Gottfried-Karl. *Hitler's Defeat in Austria, 1933–1934.* Trans. by Sonia Brough and David Taylor. Boulder: Westview Press, 1988.

Kingery, Robert E. Rev. of *His Human Majesty*, by Kay Boyle. *Library Journal* 1 April 1949: 546.

Klausler, A. P. "A Summer's Dozen." Rev. of *Generation Without Farewell*, by Kay Boyle. *Christian Century* 31 August 1960: 998.

Kluver, Billy, and Julie Martin. *Kiki's Paris: Artists and Lovers, 1900–1930.* New York: Harry N. Abrams, 1989.

Knoll, Robert E., ed. *McAlmon and the Lost Generation: A Self-Portrait*. Lincoln: University of Nebraska Press, 1962.

———. "Love Poems." Rev. of *Collected Poems*, by Kay Boyle. *Prairie Schooner* 37.1 (Spring 1963) 176–78.

Koch, David V. "Kay Boyle." *Dictionary of Literary Biography*. Vol. 4. Detroit: Gale Research, 1980. Pp. 46–56.

Kokotailo, Philip. *John Glassco's Richer World: Memoirs of Montparnasse*. Toronto: ECW Press, 1988.

Kraditor, Aileen S. *The Ideas of the Woman's Suffrage Movement, 1890–1920*. New York: Columbia UP, 1965.

Kramer, Dale. *Ross and The New Yorker*. Garden City, NY: Doubleday, 1951.

Kronenberger, Louis. Rev. of *The First Lover and Other Stories*, by Kay Boyle. *New York Times Book Review* 26 March 1933: 7.

———. "Kay Boyle's Story of a Moral Crisis." Rev. of *Gentlemen, I Address You Privately*, by Kay Boyle. *New York Times Book Review* 12 November 1933: 9.

"Kronenberger, Louis," *Notable Names in the American Theatre*. Clifton, NJ: James T. White & Co., 1976.

Kuehl, John. *Write and Rewrite: A Study in the Creative Process*. New York: Meredith Press, 1967.

Lacouture, Jean. *De Gaulle: The Rebel 1890–1944*. New York: W. W. Norton, 1990.

Lask, Thomas. "May the Good Prevail." Rev. of *Nothing Ever Breaks Except the Heart*, by Kay Boyle. *New York Times* 21 June 1966: L 41.

Lawrence, Margaret. *The School of Femininity: A Book For and About Women as They Are Interpreted Through Feminine Writers of Yesterday and Today*. 1936; Port Washington, NY: Kennikat Press, 1966.

League for Cultural Freedom and Socialism. "Statement of the L.C.F.S." *Partisan Review* 6 (Summer 1939) 125–27.

———. "War Is the Issue!" *Partisan Review* 6 (Fall 1939) 125–27.

Lebel, Robert. *Marcel Duchamp*. Trans. by George Heard Hamilton. New York: Grossman, 1967.

Lee, Lawrence. "Manhunt." Rev. of *A Frenchman Must Die*, by Kay Boyle. *New York Times Book Review* 7 April 1946: 43.

Leider, Emily. "The Writer as Moral Force." Rev. of *Words That Must Somehow Be Said*, by Kay Boyle. *San Francisco Chronicle* 7 July 1985: 3.

———. "Kay Boyle's Poetic Commentary." Rev. of *Collected Poems*, by Kay Boyle. *San Francisco Chronicle* 22 December 1991: 8.

Leland, John. *A Guide to Hemingway's Paris*. Chapel Hill: Algonquin Books, 1989.

Lewis, Wyndham. *Time and Western Man*. Boston: Beacon Press, 1957.

Linkous, Robert. "Strictly San Francisco." Rev. of *Words That Must Somehow Be Said*, by Kay Boyle. *San Francisco Review of Books* Fall–Winter 1985.

Littell, Robert. Rev. of *Primer for Combat*, by Kay Boyle. *Yale Review* 32.2 (Winter 1943) viii.

Litwak, Leo. "Kay Boyle—Paris Wasn't Like That." *New York Times Book Review* 15 July 1984: 1+.

——— and Herbert Wilner. *College Days in Earthquake Country*. New York: Random House, 1971.

Loeb, Harold. *The Way It Was*. New York: Criterion, 1959.

Rev. of *The Long Walk at San Francisco State*, by Kay Boyle. *Choice* 8.3 (May 1971) 434.

Lottman, Eileen. "George Jackson Confession." *Village Voice* 16 May 1974: 1, 35.

Lowe, Sue Davidson. *Stieglitz: A Memoir/Biography*. New York: Farrar, Straus & Giroux, 1983.

Loyalty Security Board, U.S. High Commissioner for Germany. *In the Matter of Joseph Maria Franckenstein*. Transcript of proceedings. 20–21 October 1952.

Luža, Radomír. *Austro-German Relations in the Anschluss Era*. Princeton: Princeton UP, 1975.

Lyons, Eugene. *The Red Decade: The Stalinist Penetration of America*. Indianapolis: Bobbs-Merrill, 1941.

MacGregor, Martha. "Kay Boyle's Thirteenth Novel: Occupied and Occupier." Rev. of *Generation Without Farewell*. *New York Post* 17 January 1960.

MacLean, David. "In the City of Flesh." Rev. of *Babylon*, by René Crevel. Trans. by Kay Boyle. *Body Politic* August 1985: 37.

MacLeish, Archibald. "The Lost Speakers (For Kay Boyle)." *Saturday Review of Literature* 8 February 1936: 6.

———. *Letters of Archibald MacLeish: 1907–1982*. Ed. R. H. Winnick. Boston: Houghton Mifflin, 1983.

MacNiven, Ian S. "Kay Boyle's High Country: *His Human Majesty*." *Twentieth Century Literature* [Special Kay Boyle Issue], ed. Sandra Whipple Spanier, 34.3 (Fall 1988): 363–374.

Maddox, Brenda. *Nora: The Real Life of Molly Bloom*. Boston: Houghton Mifflin, 1988.

Maher, Catherine. "Alpine Adventure." Rev. of *Avalanche*, by Kay Boyle. *New York Times Book Review* 16 January 1944: 4.

Malin, Irving. Rev. of *Babylon*, by René Crevel. Trans. by Kay Boyle. *Review of Contemporary Fiction* Fall 1985.

Maloff, Saul. "Again the Lost Ones." Rev. of *Being Geniuses Together*, by Kay Boyle and Robert McAlmon. *Newsweek* 8 July 1968: 70.

Mangione, Jerre. "Nearly Every Page Rings with Protest: Kay Boyle at San Francisco State." Rev. of *The Long Walk at San Francisco State*, by Kay Boyle. see KBP.

Mariani, Paul. *William Carlos Williams: A New World Naked*. New York: McGraw-Hill, 1982.

Marini, Myra. "The Romantic Temper." Rev. of *Year Before Last*, by Kay Boyle. *New Republic* 13 July 1932: 242.

Matusow, Harvey. *False Witness*. New York: Cameron & Kahn, 1955.

McAlmon, Robert. *Post-Adolescence*. 1920; Paris: Contact Publishing Co., n.d.

———. *A Hasty Bunch: Short Stories*. Carbondale and Edwardsville: Southern Illinois UP, 1977.

McAlmon, Victoria. "Free—For What?" *These Modern Women: Autobiographical Essays from the Twenties*. Ed. and introduction by Elaine Showalter. New York: Feminist Press, 1978. Pp. 109–15.

McCarthy, Mary. "Romance of Paris." Rev. of *My Next Bride*, by Kay Boyle. *Nation* 12 December 1934: 746–47.

McMillan, Dougald. *transition: The History of a Literary Era, 1927–1938*. New York: George Braziller, 1976.

McWilliams, Carey. Rev. of *The Long Walk at San Francisco State*, by Kay Boyle. *Nation* 26 April 1971: 540.

"Meals by Fred Harvey." Advertisement. *Kansas City Star* 29 March 1914.

Mechem, Kirke, compiler. *The Annals of Kansas, 1886–1925*. Two vols. Topeka: Kansas State Printer, 1954–56.

Melia, Tamara Moser. "Winfield Scott." *Research Guide to American Historical Biography*. Vol. 3. Ed. Robert Muccigrosso. Washington, DC: Beacham Publishing, 1988.

Meynell, Viola. Rev. of *Plagued by the Nightingale*, by Kay Boyle. *New Statesman and Nation* 1 August 1931: 144.

Millay, Edna St. Vincent. *Collected Lyrics*. New York: Harper Colophon, 1981.

Millett, Fred B. *Reading Fiction: A Method of Analysis with Selections*. New York: Harper & Row, 1950.

Mills, Kay. "At 84, Writer Kay Boyle Still Speaks for the Disinherited." *Norfolk Virginia Pilot* 17 October 1986. See also Mills, "Kay Boyle: A Writer's Duty to Speak for the Disenfranchised," *Los Angeles Times* 12 October 1986: 3, 6.

———. "Still a Rebel at 84." *Houston Chronicle* 17 October 1986: sec. 5, p. 3.

Mirrielees, Edith R. "Stories to Remember." Rev. of *Thirty Stories*, by Kay Boyle. *New York Times Book Review* 1 December 1946: 9, 72.

"Missouri Pacific Time Tables," 1881 and 1890. Library of the Kansas State Historical Society.

Modelski, Andrew M. *Railroad Maps of North America: The First Hundred Years*. Washington, DC: Library of Congress, 1984.

Molden, Fritz. *Exploding Star: A Young Austrian Against Hitler*. London: Weidenfeld & Nicolson, 1978.

Rev. of *Monday Night*, by Kay Boyle. *New Yorker* 30 July 1938: 44.

Rev. of *Monday Night*, by Kay Boyle. *Newsweek* 1 August 1938: 29.

Rev. of *Monday Night*, by Kay Boyle. *Christian Century* 12 October 1938: 1233–34.

Moore, Harry Thornton. "Psychology and Symbolism." Rev. of *The Crazy Hunter*, by Kay Boyle. *Saturday Review of Literature* 23 March 1940: 10.

———. "In Germany the Ruins Still Smolder." Rev. of *The Smoking Mountain*, by Kay Boyle. *New York Times Book Review* 22 April 1951: 5.

———. "Kay Boyle's Fiction." *Age of the Modern and Other Literary Essays*. Carbondale and Edwardsville: Southern Illinois UP, 1971. Pp. 32–36.

Moran, Helen. Rev. of *Death of a Man*, by Kay Boyle. *North American Review* Winter 1936: 443–45.

Morris, Edwin T. *Fragrance: The Story of Perfumes from Cleopatra to Chanel*. New York: Scribner's, 1984.

Morse, Deborah Denenholz. "*My Next Bride*: Kay Boyle's Text of the Female Artist." *Twentieth Century Literature* [Special Kay Boyle Issue], ed. Sandra Whipple Spanier, 34.3 (Fall 1988): 334–46.

Morton, Brian N. *Americans in Paris: An Anecdotal Street Guide*. Ann Arbor: Olivia & Hill Press, 1984.

Morton, Frederic. *A Nervous Splendor: Vienna 1888–1889*. Boston: Little, Brown, 1979.

Moses, Kate. "Personal Portrait." *Kay Boyle: Writer of Conscience. KPFA Folio* (program guide for KPFA and KFCF, San Francisco) February 1988.

Mosse, George L. "Racism." *Encyclopedia of the Holocaust.* Ed. Israel Gutman. 4 vols. New York: Macmillan, 1990.

Rev. of *My Next Bride*, by Kay Boyle. *Saturday Review of Literature* 24 November 1934: 318.

Rev. of *My Next Bride*, by Kay Boyle. *Christian Century* 5 December 1934: 1564.

"Nazi Idyll." Rev. of *Death of a Man*, by Kay Boyle. *Time* 12 October 1936: 87.

Nichols, Lewis. "In and Out of Books: Miss Boyle." *New York Times Book Review.* 17 January 1960: 8.

Nightingale, Benedict. "Fred Zinnemann Distills a New Film from an Old Dream." *New York Times* 7 November 1982: 1, 16.

Nin, Anaïs. *Diary of Anaïs Nin*, Vol. 3: *1939–1944.* Ed. Gunther Stuhlmann. New York: Harcourt Brace Jovanovich, 1969.

"Nine and Two." Rev. of *A Glad Day*, by Kay Boyle. *Time* 26 December 1938: 41–43.

Rev. of *1939*, by Kay Boyle. *Booklist* 1 March 1948: 233.

Rev. of *1939*, by Kay Boyle. *New Yorker* 13 March 1948: 123–24.

Rev. of *Nothing Ever Breaks Except the Heart*, by Kay Boyle. *Library Journal* 15 September 1966: 4366.

Oboler, Eli M. Rev. of *Nothing Ever Breaks Except the Heart*, by Kay Boyle. *Library Journal* August 1966: 3763.

O'Brien, Kate. Rev. of *The Crazy Hunter*, by Kay Boyle. *Spectator* 29 March 1940: 457.

———. Rev. of *Avalanche*, by Kay Boyle. *Spectator* 22 December 1944: 584.

Oetter, Joanna. "Literary Rebel Sees the Poet as a 'Sentient Harpsichord.' " Rev. of *Babylon*, by René Crevel. Trans. by Kay Boyle. *St. Louis Post-Dispatch* 14 December 1985.

O'Hara, J. D. Rev. of *The Underground Woman*, by Kay Boyle. *New York Times* 2 February 1975: 4.

O'Keeffe, Georgia, and Anita Pollitzer. *Lovingly, Georgia: The Complete Correspondence of Georgia O'Keeffe and Anita Pollitzer.* Ed. Clive Giboire. New York: Simon & Schuster, 1990.

Olsen, Tillie. *Silences.* New York: Dell, 1979.

O'Neill, William L. *The Last Romantic: A Life of Max Eastman.* New York: Oxford UP, 1978.

Pach, Walter. *Queer Thing, Painting: Forty Years in the World of Art.* New York: Harper & Brothers, 1938.

Packer, Herbert L. *Ex-Communist Witnesses.* Stanford: Stanford UP, 1962.

Pass, Sylvia. "What Is It All About?" Rev. of *The White Horses of Vienna*, by Kay Boyle. *Christian Century* 4 March 1936: 368.

Persico, Joseph E. *Piercing the Reich: The Penetration of Nazi Germany by American Secret Agents During World War II.* New York: Viking, 1979.

Peterson, Virgilia. "There Is No Armistice." Rev. of *Generation Without Farewell*, by Kay Boyle. *New York Times Book Review* 17 January 1960: 1.

Pick, Robert. "The War After the War." Rev. of *A Frenchman Must Die*, by Kay Boyle. *Saturday Review of Literature* 20 April 1946: 16.

Pickrel, Paul. Rev. of *The Seagull on the Step. Yale Review* 44.4 (Summer 1955) 638–39.

Rev. of *Plagued by the Nightingale*, by Kay Boyle. *New York Times Book Review* 5 April 1931: 7, 20.

Rev. of *Plagued by the Nightingale*, by Kay Boyle. *Nation* 6 May 1931: 509.

Rev. of *Plagued by the Nightingale*, by Kay Boyle. *Booklist* June 1931: 453.

"Politics and *Partisan Review.*" Editorial. *Partisan Review* 4 (February 1938) 61–62.

Poore, Charles. "Expatriates en Brochette." Rev. of *Being Geniuses Together*, by Kay Boyle and Robert McAlmon. *New York Times* 18 July 1968: 31.

Porter, Katherine Anne. "Example to the Young." *New Republic* 22 April 1931: 279–80.

———. *Letters of Katherine Anne Porter.* Ed. Isabel Bayley. New York: Atlantic Monthly Press, 1990.

"Pot-Boyler." Rev. of *Avalanche*, by Kay Boyle. *Time* 17 January 1944: 96+.

Pound, Ezra. Letter (9 April 1928) accompanying Kay Boyle's "In Defense of Homosexuality." *New Review* 2 (April 1932) 24–25.

The Letters of Ezra Pound, 1907–1941. Ed. D. D. Paige. New York: Harcourt, Brace, 1950.

Pratt, Annis. "The New Feminist Criticism." *College English* 32.8 (May 1971) 872–78.

Prescott, Peter S. "Life with Daughter." Rev. of *The Underground Woman*, by Kay Boyle. *Newsweek* 13 January 1975: 67+.

Rev. of *Primer for Combat*, by Kay Boyle. *Newsweek* 2 November 1942: 72.

Rev. of *Primer for Combat*, by Kay Boyle. *New Yorker* 14 November 1942: 70.

Putnam, Samuel. Letter. *Contempo* 15 May 1933: 2.

————. *Paris Was Our Mistress: Memoirs of a Lost and Found Generation.* New York: Viking, 1947.

Puzo, Mario. "That's How It Used to Be . . . in Camelot." Rev. of *Being Geniuses Together*, by Kay Boyle and Robert McAlmon. *Washington Post Book World* 9 June 1968: 1, 4.

Quenell, Peter. Rev. of *The White Horses of Vienna*, by Kay Boyle. *New Statesman and Nation* 16 January 1937: 86–88.

Radge's Biennial Directory: City of Topeka for 1872–1873.

Radiguet, Raymond. *The Devil in the Flesh.* Trans. by Kay Boyle. Paris: Crosby Continental Editions, 1932. New York: Harrison Smith, 1932.

Rahv, Philip. "Two Years of Progress—From Waldo Frank to Donald Ogden Stewart." *Partisan Review* 4 (February 1938) 22–30.

————. "Improvisations of Reality." Rev. of *The Crazy Hunter*, by Kay Boyle. *Nation* 23 March 1940: 396.

Ramsey, Nancy. "A Genius Alone." *Vogue* December 1986: 174, 176.

Riding, Laura. "Jamais Plus." *transition* 7 (October 1927) 139–56.

Rogers, W. G. "An Old Welcome Style: Kay Boyle's Stories." Rev. of *Nothing Ever Breaks Except the Heart*, by Kay Boyle. *New York Herald Tribune* [?], 10 June 1966, see KBP.

Rollyson, Carl. *Lillian Hellman: Her Legend and Her Legacy.* New York: St. Martin's Press, 1988.

Root, Waverly Lewis. "Kay Boyle Writes Novel of Quality Too Rarely Found." Rev. of *Year Before Last*, by Kay Boyle. *Paris Tribune* 4 July 1932. Rpt. in *The Left Bank Revisited: Selections from the Paris Tribune, 1917–1934.* Ed. Hugh Ford. University Park: Pennsylvania State UP, 1972. Pp. 273–74.

————. "Kay Boyle Writes Best Novel of Real Imaginary Character." Rev. of *My Next Bride*, by Kay Boyle. *Paris Tribune* 12 November 1934.

Rosenfeld, Paul. *Port of New York.* New York: Harcourt, Brace, 1924.

Rothman, Nathan L. "Kay Boyle's Stories." Rev. of *The White Horses of Vienna*, by Kay Boyle. *Saturday Review of Literature* 8 February 1936: 6.

————. "Foreign Legion in Colorado." Rev. of *His Human Majesty*, by Kay Boyle. *Saturday Review of Literature* 9 April 1949: 13.

Rovit, Earl. "Distant Landscapes." Rev. of *Fifty Stories*, by Kay Boyle. *Nation* 27 September 1980: 286–87.

Ruby, Beth. "Power and Delicacy from Kay Boyle." Rev. of *Fifty Stories*, by Kay Boyle. *Christian Science Monitor* 10 November 1980: 86–87.

Saunders, Lelia. Rev. of *Generation Without Farewell*, by Kay Boyle. *Library Journal* 1 February 1960: 674.

"Der Schaden des Anschlages auf die Tyrolia-Druckerei" (The Damage of the Attack on the *Tyrolia* Printing Works). *Innsbrucker Zeitung* 29 June 1934: 2.

Schroeder, Mildred. "Kay Boyle, Champion of Understanding." *San Francisco Examiner* 13 October 1963.

Scott, Evelyn. *Escapade.* New York: Thomas Seltzer, 1923.

Rev. of *The Seagull on the Step*, by Kay Boyle. *New Yorker* 17 September 1955: 171.

Shirer, William L. *Twentieth Century Journey: A Memoir of the Life and Times*, Vol. 1: *The Start— 1904–1930.* New York: Simon & Schuster, 1976.

————. *A Native's Return: 1945–1988: A Memoir of the Life and Times.* Boston: Little, Brown, 1990.

"Shostakovich to Visit U.S. for Peace Parley." *Daily Worker* 21 February 1949: 2, 9.

Showalter, Elaine. "Women and the Literary Curriculum." *College English* 32.8 (May 1971) 855–62.

"Sight and Sound." Rev. of *Generation Without Farewell*, by Kay Boyle. *McCall's* January 1960.

"6 Protestant Bishops, Other Notables Fight Franco Aid." *Daily Worker* 17 May 1951: 2, 9.

Socolofsky, Homer E., and Huber Self. *Historical Atlas of Kansas.* Norman: University of Oklahoma Press, 1972.

Solomon R. Guggenheim Museum. *Works from the Peggy Guggenheim Foundation.* New York: Solomon R. Guggenheim Foundation, 1969.

"Song of Songs." Bible, King James Version. New York: Simon & Schuster, 1957.

Spanier, Sandra Whipple. *Kay Boyle: Artist and Activist.* Carbondale and Edwardsville: Southern Illinois UP, 1986.

————, ed. *Twentieth Century Literature* [Special Kay Boyle Issue] 34.3 (Fall 1988).

————. "Kay Boyle: 'No Past Tense Permitted.' " *Twentieth Century Literature* 34.3 (Fall 1988): 245–57.

Spector, Shmuel. "Franz Novak." *Encyclopedia of the Holocaust.* Ed. Israel Gutman. 4 vols. New York: Macmillan, 1990.

"The Spirit at Bay." Rev. of *Year Before Last.* *New York Times Book Review* 26 June 1932: 7.

Stafford, Jean. "Spirits." Rev. of *Being Geniuses Together*, by Kay Boyle and Robert McAlmon; *Those Remarkable Cunards, Emerald and Nancy*, by Daphne Fielding; and *Nancy Cunard: Brave Poet, Indomitable Spirit*, ed. Hugh Ford. *New York Review of Books* 24 April 1969: 26–29.

Stearns, Harold. *Confessions of a Harvard Man: Paris and New York in the 1920s and 30s*. Sutton West and Santa Barbara: Paget Press, 1984.

Steffens, Lincoln. *The Autobiography of Lincoln Steffens*. New York: Harcourt, Brace, 1931.

Stein, Gertrude. *Tender Buttons*. 1914; New York: Gordon Press, 1972.

———. *Everybody's Autobiography*. New York: Random House, 1937.

Steiner, George. "The Problem of Powys." Rev. of *John Cowper Powys: Letters 1937–1953*. *Times Literary Supplement* 16 May 1975: 541.

Stone, Stephen L. "A Journey of Stephen Stone: Observations on Kansas in 1881." Eds. Gerald Gaither and John R. Finger. *Kansas Historical Quarterly* 37 (Summer 1971) 148–54.

Strachey, Richard. Rev. of *Wedding Day and Other Stories*, by Kay Boyle. *New Statesman and Nation* 24 September 1932: 347.

Straus, Dorothea. *Palaces and Prisons*. Boston: Houghton Mifflin, 1976.

Strong, L. A. G. Rev. of *Plagued by the Nightingale*, by Kay Boyle. *Spectator* 18 July 1931: 94.

Stuckey, William. Rev. of *Generation Without Farewell*, by Kay Boyle. *Minnesota Review* 1.1 (October 1960) 115–21.

———. "The Heart Is Not Enough." Rev. of *Nothing Ever Breaks Except the Heart*, by Kay Boyle. *Critique* 9.2 (1967) 85–88.

Sullivan, Richard. "Lyric, Symbolic Tale of Post-War Germany." Rev. of *Generation Without Farewell*, by Kay Boyle. *Chicago Sunday Tribune* 17 January 1960: 3.

———. "Twenty Stories from a Worker in Words." Rev. of *Nothing Ever Breaks Except the Heart*, by Kay Boyle. *Chicago Sunday Tribune* 10 July 1966, "Books Today" section: 1.

Sutherland, Fraser. *John Glassco: An Essay and Bibliography*. Ontario: ECW Press, 1984.

Suval, Stanley. *The Anschluss Question in the Weimar Era: A Study of Nationalism in Germany and Austria, 1918–1932*. Baltimore: Johns Hopkins UP, 1974.

Sykes, Gerald. "Too Good to Be Smart." Rev. of *Wedding Day and Other Stories*, by Kay Boyle. *Nation* 24 December 1930: 711–12.

Tempel, Gudrun. *The Germans: An Indictment of My People; A Personal History and a Challenge*. New York: Random House, 1963.

Thielen, Benedict. Rev. of *Death of a Man*, by Kay Boyle. "The Atlantic Bookshelf" section, *Atlantic* February 1937.

Rev. of *Thirty Stories*, by Kay Boyle. *Booklist* 1 January 1947: 132.

"34 Notables Sign Appeal for JAFRC 11." *Daily Worker* 18 October 1948: 4.

Rev. of *Three Short Novels*, by Kay Boyle. 1958; rpt. 1991, with an introduction by Doris Grumbach. *Publishers Weekly* 21 December 1990: 49.

Tooker, Dan, and Roger Hofheins, eds. *Fiction! Interviews with Northern California Novelists*. New York: Harcourt Brace Jovanovich, 1976.

Topeka City Directory, 1874–1875.

Trilling, Diana. Rev. of *Avalanche*, by Kay Boyle. *Nation* 22 January 1944: 105.

Uehling, Edward M. "Tails, You Lose: Kay Boyle's War Fiction." *Twentieth Century Literature* [Special Kay Boyle Issue], ed. Sandra Whipple Spanier, 34.3 (Fall 1988): 375–83.

Rev. of *The Underground Woman*, by Kay Boyle. *New Yorker* 20 January 1975: 97.

Vail, Jeannie. *A Voyage of the Vails in Italy*. Unpublished memoir, 1948.

Vail, Laurence. "Little Birds and Old Men." *Broom* 3.2 (September 1922) 95–96.

———. *Piri and I*. New York: Lieber & Lewis, 1923.

———. *Murder! Murder!* London: Peter Davies, 1931.

———. "Caspar Loot." *transition* 21 (March 1932) 318–19.

———. "Fragment from a Novel." *transition* 27 (April–May 1938) 138–41.

———. *Here Goes*. Unpublished memoir, c. 1945.

Van Doren, Mark. "Beauty and the Beast." Rev. of *The White Horses of Vienna*, by Kay Boyle. *Nation* 4 March 1936: 286–88.

———. "Under the Swastika." Rev. of *Death of a Man*, by Kay Boyle. *Nation* 24 October 1926: 494. Edited and reprinted in *The Private Reader: Selected Articles and Reviews, 1942*. New York: Kraus Reprint Co., 1968. Pp. 241–44.

"Vercors, 89, Author Who Wrote of Nazi-Occupied France, Is Dead." *New York Times* 13 June 1991: D24.

"Victors and Vanquished." Rev. of *Generation Without Farewell*, by Kay Boyle. *Time* 25 January 1960: 94, 96.

Wald, Alan M. *The New York Intellectuals: The Rise and Decline of the Anti-Stalinist Left from the 1930s to the 1980s*. Chapel Hill: University of North Carolina Press, 1987.

Waldo, J. Curtis. *J. Curtis Waldo's Illustrated Missouri Pacific Gazetteer*. New Orleans and St. Louis: J. Curtis Waldo, 1882.

Walker, Mildred. "Mind, Spirit of the German People Today." Rev. of *The Smoking Mountain*, by Kay Boyle. *Chicago Sun-Tribune* 29 April 1951: 5.

Walsh, Ernest. "*This Quarter* Gets Reviewed." *This Quarter* 1.2 (1925) 305–6.

———. "From Ernest Walsh to Harriet Monroe." *This Quarter* 1.2 (1925) 307–10.

———. "An Open Letter to Mike Gold." *New Masses* 2 (December 1926) 23.

———. *Poems and Sonnets*. With a Memoir by Ethel Moorhead. New York: Harcourt, Brace, 1934.

Walton, Edith H. "Miss Boyle's Irony." Rev. of *My Next Bride*, by Kay Boyle. *New York Times Book Review* 11 November 1934: 6.

———. Rev. of *My Next Bride*, by Kay Boyle. *Forum* 92 (December 1934) ix, x.

———. "Kay Boyle's Stories." Rev. of *The White Horses of Vienna*, by Kay Boyle. *New York Times Book Review* 9 February 1936: 7.

Weeks, Edward. "The Sitzmark." Rev. of *1939*, by Kay Boyle. *Atlantic Monthly* April 1948: 108.

Weinstein, James. *The Decline of Socialism in America, 1912–1925*. New York: Random House, 1969.

Weld, Jacqueline Bograd. *Peggy: The Wayward Guggenheim*. New York: E. P. Dutton, 1986.

West, Anthony. Rev. of *The Crazy Hunter*, by Kay Boyle. *New Statesman and Nation* 16 March 1940: 371–72.

West, Ray B., Jr. *The Short Story in America, 1900–1950*. Freeport, NY: Books for Libraries Press, 1968. Originally published in 1952 by Henry Regnery Company, Chicago.

White, Peter. Rev. of *His Human Majesty*, by Kay Boyle. *Commonweal* 20 May 1949: 155–56.

Rev. of *The White Horses of Vienna*, by Kay Boyle. *Time* 17 February 1936: 70.

Wilder, Daniel Webster, compiler. *Annals of Kansas: New Edition, 1541–1885*. Topeka: T. Dwight Thacher, Kansas Publishing House, 1886.

Williams, William Carlos. Letter in response to Laura Riding's "Jamais Plus." *transition* 10 (January 1928) 145–46.

———. "The Somnambulists." Rev. of *Short Stories*, by Kay Boyle. *transition* 18 (November 1929): 147–51.

———. *The Autobiography of William Carlos Williams*. New York: Random House, 1948.

———. *Selected Essays of William Carlos Williams*. New York: New Directions, 1954.

———. *Selected Letters of William Carlos Williams*. Ed. and introduction by John C. Thirlwall. New York: McDowell, Obolensky, 1957.

Wilson, Edmund. "Kay Boyle and *The Saturday Evening Post*." *New Yorker* 15 January 1944: 66 + .

———. *The Shores of Light: A Literary Chronicle of the Twenties and Thirties*. New York: Vintage, 1961.

———. *The Triple Thinkers*. New York: Farrar, Straus & Giroux, 1976.

Wilson, Ted. Rev. of *Year Before Last*, by Kay Boyle. *Contempo* 25 October 1932: 5.

Wineapple, Brenda. *Genêt: A Biography of Janet Flanner*. New York: Ticknor & Fields, 1989.

"[Kay Boyle] Wins O. Henry Prize for Best Short Story." *New York Times* 7 November 1941.

Wolff, Geoffrey. *Black Sun: The Brief Transit and Violent Eclipse of Harry Crosby*. New York: Random House, 1976.

Wright, William. *Lillian Hellman: The Image, the Woman*. New York: Simon & Schuster, 1986.

Rev. of *Year Before Last*, by Kay Boyle. *Booklist* 29 (November 1932) 73.

Zellerbach, Merla. "When Writers Give Themselves Away." *San Francisco Chronicle* 15 March 1978: 15.

OBITUARIES

Folkart, Burt A. "Kay Boyle; Novelist, Anti-War Activist." *Los Angeles Times*, 29 December 1992: Metro section, 8.

"Kay Boyle, writer and poet, is dead," *San Francisco Examiner*, 29 December 1992: A-15.

Pace, Eric, "Kay Boyle, 90, Writer of Novels and Stories, Dies," *The New York Times*, 29 December 1992: A-13.

"Kay Boyle—Author, Teacher, Crusader," *San Francisco Chronicle*, 29 December 1992: A-20.

WORKS BY KAY BOYLE

"Reactionary Composers." *Poetry* 49 (November 1921) 104–6.

Unsigned. Rev. of *Mr. Antiphilos, Satyr*, by Remy de Gourmont. *Dial* August 1922: 233.

Unsigned. Rev. of *An Outline of Wells*, by Sidney Dark. *Dial* October 1922: 457.

"Collation." *Calendar of Modern Letters* 3 (October 1926). Rpt. Edgar Richmond and Douglas Garman, eds. New York: Barnes & Noble, 1966. Pp. 171–74.

"Mr. Benét Looks at the Civil War." *transition* 15 (February 1929) 169–70.

"A New Mythology." *Paris Tribune* 10 March 1929. Rpt. in *The Left Bank Revisited: Selections from the Paris Tribune, 1917–1934*, ed. Hugh Ford. University Park: Penn State UP, 1972. Pp. 249–50.

"Confession to Eugene Jolas." *Blues* 1.6 (July 1929) 140–43.

"Dedicated to Guy Urquhart." *transition* 18 (November 1929) 85.

Trans. "Mr. Knife, Miss Fork," by René Crevel. *transition* 18 (November 1929) 242–51.

Short Stories. Paris: The Black Sun Press, 1929.

"The Only Bird That Sang." *transition* 19–20 (June 1930) 261–63.

"Episode in the Life of an Ancestor" (1930). In *Fifty Stories* (1981) 17–24.

"A Valentine for Harry Crosby." *Blues* 2.9 (Fall 1930) 35–37.

"A Statement for El Greco and William Carlos Williams." *Morada* 5 (December 1930) 21–25.

"Wedding Day" (1930). In *Fifty Stories* (1981) 24–30.

Plagued by the Nightingale. 1931; Carbondale: Southern Illinois UP, 1966.

"One of Ours." *New Yorker* 17 October 1931: 17–19.

"Christmas Eve." *New Yorker* 26 December 1931: 13–15.

Year Before Last. 1932; London: Penguin Books–Virago Press, 1986.

"A Comeallye for Robert Carlton Brown." *Americans Abroad: An Anthology*, ed. Peter Neagoe. The Hague: Sevire Press, 1932. Pp. 38–41.

"In Defense of Homosexuality." *New Review* 2 (April 1932) 24–25.

"Friend of the Family" (1932). In *Fifty Stories* (1981) 55–64.

"To the Pure." *Scribner's Magazine* June 1932: 341–44.

"Black Boy" (1932). In *Fifty Stories* (1981) 50–55.

"The Man Who Died Young." *Yale Review* June 1932: 785–809.

"Writers Worth Reading." *Contempo* 5 July 1932: 4.

"Three Little Men." *Criterion* October 1932: 17–23.

"Lydia and the Ring-Doves." *Vanity Fair* November 1932: 36 + .

"McAlmon's *Indefinite Huntress*." *Paris Tribune* 17 December 1932. Rpt. in *The Left Bank Revisited: Selections from the Paris Tribune, 1917–1934*, ed. Hugh Ford. University Park: Pennsylvania State UP, 1972. Pp. 276–77.

Gentlemen, I Address You Privately. New York: Harrison Smith and Robert Haas, 1933.

The First Lover and Other Stories. New York: Harrison Smith and Robert Haas, 1933.

"Keep Your Pity" (1933). In *Fifty Stories* (1981) 73–89.

With Laurence Vail. "Americans Abroad." *Contempo* 15 March 1933: 1+.

"The Sky Is Woven of the Wind's Four Directions" (published as "The Sky Is Woven of the Four Directions of the Wind"). *Seed* 1 (April and July 1933) 3–7.

"Flight of Fish." *Nation* 16 August 1933: 190.

"White as Snow." *New Yorker* 9 (5 August 1933) 20–22, 26–28.

"Flying Foxes and Others." *Nation* 18 October 1933: 444–45.

My Next Bride. 1934; London: Penguin Books–Virago Press, 1986.

"First Offence." *New Yorker* 5 January 1935: 19–20.

"Count Lothar's Heart." *Harper's Bazaar* 68 (May 1935) 84–85, 124, 126, 128.

"I'm Ready to Drop Dead." *New Yorker* 6 July 1935: 23.

"Security" (1936). In *Fifty Stories* (1981) 89–95.

Death of a Man. 1936; New York: New Directions, 1989.

The White Horses of Vienna and Other Stories. New York: Harcourt, Brace, 1936.

"Rondo at Carraroe." *Spectator* 28 February 1936: 340–41.

"Volunteer." *New Yorker* 16 May 1936: 25–26.

"Education." *New Yorker* 17 October 1936: 23–24.

With Laurence Vail and Nina Conarain, eds. *365 Days.* New York: Harcourt, Brace, 1936.

"The King of the Philistines." *New Yorker* 13 March 1937: 22–25.

"Katherine Mansfield: A Reconsideration." *New Republic* 20 October 1937: 309.

"A Communication to Nancy Cunard." 1937; *Testament for My Students and Other Poems.* Garden City, NY: Doubleday, 1970. Pp. 64–69.

"The Unvanquished." 1938; *The Critic as Artist: Essays on Books 1920–1970,* ed. Gilbert A. Harrison. New York: Liveright, 1972. Pp. 38–41.

A Glad Day. Norfolk, CT: New Directions, 1938.

Monday Night. 1938; Mamaroneck, NY: Paul P. Appel, 1977.

"Ben" (1938). In *Fifty Stories* (1981) 38–44.

"The Baron and the Chemist." *New Yorker* 26 February 1938: 19–20.

"A Complaint for M and M" (Mary Reynolds and Marcel Duchamp). *transition* 27 (Spring 1938) 34–40.

"Life Sentence." *Harper's Bazaar* June 1938: 42–43, 104–7.

"Big Fiddle." *Phoenix* 1 (Autumn 1938) 112–146.

"War in Paris." *New Yorker* 26 November 1938: 18–20.

The Youngest Camel. Boston: Little, Brown, 1939.

"Anschluss." *Harper's* April 1939: 474–83.

"World Tour." *Seven* 4 (Spring 1939): 2–3.

"Listen, Munich." *New Yorker* 19 August 1939: 17–19.

"Poor Monsieur Panalitus." *New Yorker* 20 January 1940: 19–22.

"Note from Kay Boyle," with response by Dwight Macdonald. *Partisan Review* 7 (January–February 1940) 79.

"Effigy of War," *New Yorker* 25 May 1940: 17–19.

"The Most Unforgettable Character I Ever Met." *Reader's Digest* September 1940: 46–50.

"T'en Fais Pas." *Harper's Bazaar* December 1940: 122.

"They Weren't Going to Die" (1940). In *Fifty Stories* (1981) 288–93.

"Major Engagement in Paris" (1940). In *Fifty Stories* (1981) 239–46.

"Defeat" (1941). In *Fifty Stories* (1981) 294–304.

"Men" (1941). In *Fifty Stories* (1981) 275–87.

"Two Fragments from an Aviation Epic." *Vertical: A Yearbook for Romantic-Mystic Ascensions,* ed. Eugene Jolas. New York: Gotham Book Mart Press, 1941. Pp. 20–29.

"Les Six Enfants." *Harper's Bazaar* October 1941: 73, 122.

"Nothing Ever Breaks Except the Heart." *New Yorker* 4 October 1941: 18–21.

"Full-Length Portrait." Rev. of *A Curtain of Green,* by Eudora Welty; *House of Fury,* by Felice Swados; *Strangers Are Coming,* by I. A. R. Wylie; and *Saratoga Trunk,* by Edna Ferber. *New Republic* 24 November 1941: 707–8.

"Two and Carry One." Rev. of *On Troublesome Creek,* by James Still; *Anything Can Happen,* by Edward Newhouse; and *The Penguin New Writing Six,* ed. John Lehmann. *New Republic* 3 November 1941: 596–98.

"Let There Be Honour" (1941). In *Fifty Stories* (1981) 305–27.

"The New Novels." Rev. of *The Real Life of Sebastian Knight,* by Vladimir Nabokov; *Victory Was*

Slain, by Hilde Abel; *The Ivory Mischief*, by Arthur Meeker, Jr.; and *Dragon's Teeth*, by Upton Sinclair. *New Republic* 26 January 1942: 124–25.

"Hollywood Paris." Rev. of *The Last Time I Saw Paris*, by Elliot Paul. *Nation* 25 April 1942: 490–91.

"The Steel of Victory." Rev. of *The Edge of the Sword*, by Vladimir Pozner. *Nation* 23 May 1942: 604–5.

"The Eternal Train." *Harper's Bazaar* June 1942: 40, 46–47.

"Hilaire and the Maréchal Pétard." *Harper's* August 1942: 284–96.

"Elizabeth Bowen." Rev. of *Bowen's Court*, by Elizabeth Bowen. *New Republic* 21 September 1942: 355–56.

"Frenchman's Ship." *Saturday Evening Post* 21 November 1942: 14 + .

"Wanderer." *Accent* 2.2 (Winter 1942) 85–91.

"This They Took with Them" (1942). In *Fifty Stories* (1981) 328–38.

"Their Name Is Macaroni" (1942). In *Fifty Stories* (1981) 339–48.

Primer for Combat. New York: Simon & Schuster, 1942.

"The Canals of Mars" (1943). In *Fifty Stories* (1981) 577–86.

"The Loneliest Man in the U.S. Army" (1943). In *Fifty Stories* (1981) 587–96.

"The Little Distance." *Saturday Evening Post* 6 March 1943: 22 + .

"Occupied France." Rev. of *First Harvest*, by Vladimir Pozner. *New York Times Book Review* 2 May 1943: 8, 18.

"The Fall of France." Rev. of *A French Officer's Diary*, by D. Barlone. *New York Times Book Review* 9 May 1943: 5.

"The Sword of Fighting France." Rev. of *The Fighting French*, by Raoul Aglion. *New York Times Book Review* 30 May 1943: 5, 17.

"World Harmony." *Saturday Evening Post* 23 October 1943: 4.

"Cairo Street." *Accent* 3.2 (Winter 1943): 95–99.

"The Last Aviator Left Flying." *American Magazine* December 1943: 44–45, 114–18.

"Luck for the Road." *Woman's Home Companion* January 1944: 17 + .

"The French Retreat." Rev. of *War Diary*, by Jean Malaquais. *New York Times Book Review* 6 February 1944: 12.

"A 'Good' German in a Poetic Setting." Rev. of *The Silence of the Sea*, by Vercors. *New York Times Book Review* 27 February 1944: 5, 22.

"Souvenir City." *Harper's Bazaar* March 1944: 120–21, 170–72.

"Where the National Hero Is an Outlaw." Rev. of *Army of Shadows*, by Joseph Kessel. *New York Herald Tribune Book Review* 18 June 1944: 1.

"Biography of a Misunderstood Leader." Rev. of *The Truth About De Gaulle*, by André Riveloup. *New York Times Book Review* 23 July 1944: 7.

"The Ships Going to Glory." *Saturday Evening Post* 5 August 1944: 26 + .

"The Poetry of Walter Mehring." Rev. of *No Road Back*, by Walter Mehring. *New York Times Book Review* 3 September 1944: 4.

"Notebook of Paris a Decade Ago." Rev. of *Fair Fantastic Paris*, by Harold Ettlinger. *New York Herald Tribune Book Review* 17 September 1944: 2.

"Canard by Cannell." Letter. *Nation* 23 September 1944: 363–64.

"Through Four Years' Darkness." Rev. of *Imaginary Interviews*, by André Gide. *New York Herald Tribune Book Review* 29 October 1944: 5.

"Vocabulary of Courage." *Harper's Bazaar* October 1944: 65.

"Dossier on Pétain." *Nation* 16 December 1944: 748, 750.

"Battle of the Sequins." *Nation* 23 December 1944: 770–71.

Avalanche: A Novel of Love and Espionage. New York: Simon & Schuster, 1944.

American Citizen Naturalized in Leadville, Colorado. New York: Simon & Schuster, 1944.

"Reaping Enemy Harvest." Rev. of *I Lied to Live*, by Alexander Janta-Pokczyski. *New York Herald Tribune Book Review* 7 January 1945: 10.

"The Jew Is a Myth." Rev. of *Stepchildren of France*, by Charles Jean Odic. *Nation* 13 October 1945: 368, 372.

"Stranger in the Snow." *Mademoiselle* December 1945: 131, 211–13.

"Family with Nine Kids." *Ladies' Home Journal* March 1946: 165–70, 191–92.

"Meet a United Nations Family in the U.S.A." *Ladies' Home Journal* December 1946: 181–86 + .

"An Interview with Kay Boyle, Expatriate." With Robert van Gelder. *Writers and Writing*, ed. Robert van Gelder. New York: Scribner's, 1946.

A Frenchman Must Die. New York: Simon & Schuster, 1946.

"Miracle Goat." *Woman's Home Companion* January 1947: 25, 83–85.

"Farewell to New York." *Nation* 8 March 1947: 271–72.

"Monument to Hitler." *Nation* 12 April 1947: 417–19.

"Kay Boyle Challenges *NM* Review." Letter. *New Masses* 15 April 1947: 21.

"Isabelita Has Lost Her Reason." *Nation* 24 May 1947: 628–29.

"Army of Occupation." *New Yorker* 7 June 1947: 29–34.
"Faces of Spain." *Nation* 12 July 1947: 35–38.
"One Small Diamond, Please." *Woman's Home Companion* August 1947: 22 + .
"Isabelita's Trial." Letter. *Nation* 11 October 1947: 393–94.
"Dream Dance." *Saturday Evening Post* 13 December 1947: 32 + .
"French Harvest" (1948). In *Fifty Stories* (1981) 348–65.
"Evening at Home" (1948). In *Fifty Stories* (1981) 607–20.
"Passport to Doom." *Saturday Evening Post* 15 May 1948: 20 + .
1939. New York: Simon & Schuster, 1948.
"The Criminal." *New Yorker* 5 March 1949: 31–36.
"Aftenvagt." *Illustrenet Famille Journal* 19 April 1949.
"Begin Again." *New Yorker* 7 May 1949: 32–34.
"Summer Evening." *New Yorker* 25 June 1949: 20–24.
"Adam's Death." *New Yorker* 10 September 1949: 29–34.
"Fife's House." *New Yorker* 15 October 1949: 32–36.
"Frankfurt in Our Blood." *Nation* 15 October 1949: 364–66.
His Human Majesty. New York: Whittlesey House–McGraw-Hill, 1949.
"Lovers of Gain." *Nation* 24 June 1950: 615–18.
"A Reporter in Germany—The People with Names." *New Yorker* 9 September 1950: 37 + .
"A Disgrace to the Family." *Saturday Evening Post* 23 September 1950: 22–23.
"Home." *Harper's* January 1951: 78–83.
"The Lost." *Tomorrow* March 1951: 10–17.
"Aufwiedersehen Abend." *Harper's* April 1951: 57–67.
"Cabaret." *Tomorrow* April 1951: 10–17.
"Talk with Kay Boyle." With Harvey Breit. *New York Times Book Review* 29 April 1951: 26.
"Kay Boyle." *New York Herald Tribune Book Review* 7 October 1951: 6, 28.
"Hans Jahn Fights Rearmament." *Nation* 15 December 1951: 519–21.
The Smoking Mountain. New York: McGraw-Hill, 1951.
"Diagnosis of a Selfish Lady." *Saturday Evening Post* 5 April 1952: 24, 119–24.
"The Soldier Ran Away." *Saturday Evening Post* 28 February 1953: 20–21, 115–19.
"The Daring Impersonation." *Saturday Evening Post* 8 and 15 August 1953: 17 + and 36 + .
"Farewell to Europe." *Nation* 12 December 1953: 526–28.
"Fear." *New Statesman and Nation* 25 September 1954: 352 + .
"October." *Nation* 30 October 1954: 383.
"Carnival of Fear." *Saturday Evening Post* 11 and 18 December 1954: 20 + and 34 + .
"Declaration for 1955." *Nation* 29 January 1955: 102–4.
"A Puzzled Race." *Nation* 4 June 1955: 481–83.
"Spain Divided." Rev. of *The Cypresses Believe in God*, by José María Gironella. *Nation* 11 June 1955: 506–7.
"The Kill." *Harper's* August 1955: 43–51.
"They Sing of Love: A German Vignette." Rev. of *We Shall March Again*, by Gerhard Kramer. *Nation* 10 September 1955: 224–25.
The Seagull on the Step. New York: Knopf, 1955.
"Evidence of Conscience." Rev. of *They Fell from God's Hands*, by Hans Richter; *The Burnt Offering*, by Albrecht Goes; and *The Revolt of Gunner Asch*, by Hans Hellmut Kirst. *Nation* 14 April 1956: 316–18.
"Education on the East Front." Rev. of *Cross of Iron*, by Villi Heinrich, and *The Train Was on Time*, by Heinrich Böll. *Nation* 14 July 1956: 43–44.
"The New Emigration." *Nation* 22 September 1956: 246.
"A Breach of Satire." Rev. of *The Tribe That Lost Its Head*, by Nicholas Monsarrat. *Nation* 24 November 1956: 462–63.
"The Intellectuals Are Failing America." *St. Louis Post-Dispatch* 2 December 1956: sect. II, p. 1.
"Spring." *Ladies' Home Journal* March 1957: 211.
"Creative Writing." *The Dolphin* [of the Thomas School] 9 March 1957: 1–2.
"The Far East and Fiction." Rev. of *The Frontiers of Love*, by Diana Chang; *The Setting Sun*, by Osamu Dazai; and *The Sound of Waves*, by Yukio Mishima. *American Scholar* 26 (Spring 1957) 222 + .
"So Slowly We Move." *Nation* 4 May 1957: 390–93.
"Wit, Humor, and a Dash of Kafka." Rev. of *Tiger in the Kitchen and Other Short Stories*, by Villy Sorenson. *New York Times Book Review* 12 May 1957: 30.
"Living Up to the Part." Rev. of *The Actress*, by Bessie Breuer. *New York Times Book Review* 6 October 1957: 4.
"No Time to Listen." *Nation* 16 November 1957: 475–76.

"City of Invisible Men." *Nation* 21 December 1957: 475–76.

"The Imposed Revolution." Rev. of *Forced to Be Free: The Artificial Revolution in Germany and Japan*, by John D. Montgomery. *Nation* 4 January 1958: 14–15.

"The Long Dead Fathers." *Progressive* 22 (September 1958) 35–37.

Three Short Novels: The Crazy Hunter, The Bridegroom's Body, and Decision [replacing *Big Fiddle*]. Boston: Beacon, 1958. Rpt. Norfolk, CT: New Directions, 1991.

"The Seventh Day." Rev. of *The Seventh Day*, by Hans Hellmut Kirst. *Venture* 3.3 (1959) 62–63.

"A Poem of Gratitude—For Caresse." *Poetry* March 1959: 376.

"Dreams Dreamed." *Saturday Review* 4 April 1959: 24.

"Big Books on the Bonn Side." Rev. of *The Forsaken Army*, by Heinrich Geriach; *Stalingrad*, by Theodore Plevier; *The Seventh Day*, by Hans Hellmut Kirst; and *Tidings*, by Ernst Weichert. *Saturday Review* 30 May 1959: 21–22.

"In Memoriam, Bob Brown." Editorial. *Village Voice* 26 August 1959: 4.

"The Aesthetics of the Future." *Syracuse* December 1959: 32–35.

"Two Twilights for William Carlos Williams." *Poetry* March 1960: 356.

"A Dialogue of Birds for Howard Nemerov." *Poetry* March 1960: 357.

"Brighter Than Most." Rev. of *Robert McAlmon, Expatriate Publisher and Writer*, by Robert E. Knoll. *Prairie Schooner* 24 (Spring 1960) 1–4.

"Has Germany Changed?" *Foreign Policy Bulletin* 15 April 1960: 117–18.

"The Triumph of Principles." *Liberation* 5 (June 1960) 11.

"Paintings in Flight." *Mark* [Norwalk] 30 July 1960: 9–10.

"Hitler's Inferno." Rev. of *The Rise and Fall of the Third Reich*, by William L. Shirer. *New York Post Sunday Magazine* 16 October 1960: 11.

Generation Without Farewell. New York: Knopf, 1960.

"Poem for a Painter Who Drinks Wine." *Nation* 14 January 1961: 38.

"Two Poems for a Poet." *Poetry* February 1961: 300–1.

"Print from a Lucite Block." *Outsider* 1 (Fall 1961) 85.

Rev. of *The Tin Drum*, by Günter Grass. *The Griffin* 12 (1962) 7–8.

"Seascape for an Engraver." *Poetry* January 1962: 214.

"Rendezvous." *Poetry* January 1962: 215–16.

"January 29, 1962." *Liberation* March 1962: 8.

"Life with Penn's Coeds." *Sunday Bulletin Magazine* [Philadelphia] 25 March 1962: 6–7.

"The Room, the Siege, the Escape, of a Versatile Man." *Contact* June 1962: 25–29.

"The Exile Who Couldn't Return." Rev. of *McAlmon and the Lost Generation*, by Robert E. Knoll. *New York Times Book Review* 5 August 1962: 5, 25.

"The Writer in Our Time." *News* [MacDowell Colony] September 1962: 1–2.

"I Remember Philadelphia." *Sunday Bulletin Magazine* [Philadelphia] 21 October 1962: 6–7.

Collected Poems. New York: Knopf, 1962.

"Story of a Man: His Bitter Ordeal." Rev. of *The Sand Pebbles*, by Richard McKenna; *The Street Where the Heart Lies*, by Ludwig Bemelmans; and *That Summer in Paris*, by Morley Callaghan. *Cosmopolitan* January 1963: 33.

"Should Be Considered Extremely Dangerous." *Story* 36 (January–February 1963) 54–71.

"Where It Is Always Spring." *Glamour* March 1963: 148–49, 206–8.

"The Vanishing Short Story." *Story* 36 (July–August 1963) 108–19.

"Tragedy Became Commonplace." Rev. of *Other Winters, Other Springs*, by Flora Sandstrom. *New York Times Book Review* 7 October 1963: 5.

"Skiing." *Glamour* November 1963: 130, 174–75.

Introduction. *The Germans: An Indictment of My People; A Personal History and a Challenge*. By Gudrun Tempel. New York: Random House, 1963.

"Raymond Whearty." *Genesis West* 2 (Winter–Spring 1964) 113–14.

"A Cry in the Dusk of Nightmare." Rev. of *Blood from the Sky*, by Piotr Rawicz. *New York Times Book Review* 19 January 1964: 5.

"The Teaching of Writing." *NEA Journal* 53 (March 1964) 11–12.

"A Voice from the Future." *Holiday* October 1964: 12 +.

"The Ballet of Central Park." *Saturday Evening Post* 28 November 1964: 44–48, 50–51.

"A Short Poem in Color." *Southern Review* July 1965: 606.

"A Poem for Arthur." *Southern Review* July 1965: 607.

"A Square Dance for a Square." *Southern Review* July 1965: 608–11.

"One Sunny Morning." *Saturday Evening Post* 3 July 1965: 61–62, 64.

The Youngest Camel: Reconsidered and Rewritten. Boston: E. M. Hale, 1965.

"A Poem of Love." *Love* (c. 1966) 25.

"You Don't Have to Be a Member of the Congregation." *Liberation* April 1966: 26–28.

"The Wild Horses." *Saturday Evening Post* 9 April 1966: 60–65.

"Fire in the Vineyards." *Saturday Evening Post* 2 July 1966: 76–77, 79–81. In *Fifty Stories* (1981) 366–75.

"The Battle of the Pagoda." *Liberation* August 1966: 28–29.

"A Poem About the Jews." *Harvard Advocate* 100 (Fall 1966) 21–23.

"Assignment in Cambodia." *Progressive* November 1966: 17–20.

"Dedicated to *Terre des Hommes*." *Catholic Worker* December 1966: 8.

"On Black Power." *Liberation* January 1967: 23.

"A Man in the Wilderness." Rev. of *Epitaph of Our Times, The Letters of Edward Dahlberg*, and *The Edward Dahlberg Reader*, by Edward Dahlberg. *Nation* May 1967: 693–94.

"Thunderstorm in South Dakota for R.G." *Southern Review* October 1967: 951.

"Seeing the Sights in San Francisco." *Progressive* December 1967: 19–21.

"Letter from Joyce." *Tri-Quarterly* 8 (Winter 1967) 195–97.

Ed. and preface. *The Autobiography of Emanuel Carnevali*. New York: Horizon, 1967.

"For Marianne Moore's Birthday, November 15, 1967." *Twigs* [Pikeville College, KY] 4 (c. 1968) 4.

"A Poem in One Sentence." *Twigs* 4 (c. 1968) 5.

"Notes on the Jury Selection in the Huey P. Newton Trial." *Progressive* October 1968: 29–35.

"Policemen as Suicides." *Progressive* October 1968: 30.

"For James Schevill, on the Occasion of His Arrest." *Poem* November 1968: 1.

With Robert McAlmon. *Being Geniuses Together, 1920–1930*. Garden City, NY: Doubleday, 1968.

"Nancy Cunard." *Nancy Cunard: Brave Poet, Indomitable Rebel, 1896–1965*, ed. Hugh Ford. Philadelphia: Chilton, 1968. Pp. 78–80.

Interview. *Talks with Authors*, ed. Charles F. Madden. Carbondale and Edwardsville: Southern Illinois UP, 1968. Pp. 215–36.

"Bohemian Journey to a State of Mind." *This World* [book section of *San Francisco Examiner & Chronicle*] 2 March 1969: 34, 39.

"The Syllabic Sound Refused to Stay Still." *This World* 25 May 1969: 39, 41.

"Nothing New Here About Paris of the 1920s." *Chicago Sun Times Book Week* 21 September 1969: 4.

"The Lost Dogs of Phnom Penh." *Lace Curtain* 1 (Winter 1969–70) 8.

"Testament for My Students, 1968–1969." *Southern Review* January 1970: 149–50.

"Day on Alcatraz with the Indians." *New Republic* 17 January 1970: 10–11.

"The Long Walk at San Francisco State." *Evergreen Review* March 1970: 21–23, 69–80.

"The Voice of the Poet Speaks Quickly." *This World* 24 May 1970: 31.

"Jazz Is the Pulse of Harper's Poetry." Rev. of *Dear John, Dear Coltrane*, by Michael Harper. *This World* 24 May 1970: 31.

"No One Can Be All Things to All People." *Evergreen Review* August 1970: 62–66.

"On Taking Up Residence in Virginia—For James Joyce and James Liddy." *Hart* (c. 1970–71) 16.

"This Is Not a Letter." *Twigs* 7 (1971) 1–2.

"For an Historian, Following an Operation on His Eyes." *Twigs* 7 (1971) 3–5.

"So Vividly Alive." *Sunday Bulletin* [Philadelphia], "Books and Art" section, 10 January 1971: 3.

"The Long Walk at San Francisco State—A Rebuttal." *This World* 14 February 1971: 39.

"The Winter Soldiers." *Cargoes* [of Hollins College] (Spring 1971) 45–46.

"Was the Issue Black Studies?" Rev. of *Blow It Up! The Black Student Revolt at San Francisco State and the Emergence of Dr. Hayakawa*, by Dikran Karagueuzian. *Ararat* 12 (Summer 1971) 40–42.

"Writers in Metaphysical Revolt." *Proceedings of the Conference of College Teachers of English of Texas* September 1971: 6–12.

"A New Name for Peace." *Liberation* September 1971: 28–30.

"Branded for Slaughter—for Shawn Wong." *Antaeus* November 1971: 75–76.

"Introduction to a Modern History of Germany." *Prose* 3 (Fall 1971) 5–18.

"Saluting Kings and Presidents." Rev. of *Stories, Fables, and Other Diversions*, by Howard Nemerov. *Nation* 7 February 1972: 184, 186–87.

"Our Lower Depths." Rev. of *Absolutely Nothing to Get Alarmed About*, by Charles S. Wright. *Mercury Book Review* 6 December 1972: 12–13.

"A Fictional Triumph of the Survival Struggle." Rev. of *The Cell*, by Horst Bienek. *This World* 4 February 1973: 40, 45.

"Excerpts from Novel in Progress, *The Underground Woman*." *ICarbS* 1 (Fall–Winter 1973) 3–9.

"A Dialogue with Victor Ourin." *Pembroke Magazine* March 1974: 3–4.

"Some Thoughts on Writing." *New School Letter on Human Conflict* 11 March 1974: 1.

"Nolo Contendere." *Antaeus* 13–14 (Spring 1974) 253–65.

"On the Death of My Student, the Poet Serafin." *Wind* 11 (Spring 1974) 10–12.

"A Poem for Rosemary and Timothy Leary." *New School Letter on Human Conflict* 28 May 1974: 2.

Introduction. "A Selection of Young Filipino Poets." *American Poetry Review* July–August 1974: 47–48.

"I Am Furious (Yellow)." Rev. of *AIIIEEEEE: An Anthology of Asian-American Writers. Rolling Stone* 29 August 1974: 64–65.

"A Poem for the Students of Greece." *New York Quarterly* 17 (1975) 44–46.

"A Talk Given Here and There." *Aisling* 1 (Summer 1975) 8–13.

Rev. of *Published in Paris: American and British Writers, Printers, and Publishers in Paris, 1920–1930*, by Hugh Ford. *New York Times Book Review* 14 September 1975: 6.

"I'm Not Solzhenitsyn." Rev. of *Cry of the People and Other Poems*, by Kim Chi Ha. *Pacific Sun Literary Quarterly* Fall 1975: 6–7, 17.

The Underground Woman. Garden City, NY: Doubleday, 1975.

"All Mankind Is Us." 1975; *Samuel Beckett: Waiting for Godot, a Casebook*, ed. Ruby Cohn. London: Macmillan, 1987. Pp. 176–80.

"The Genius of Robert McAlmon." *Pembroke Magazine* 7 (1976) 324–27.

"Dialogue with Indian Women." Rev. of *Indian Women of the Western Morning: Their Life in Early America*, by John and Donna M. Terrell. *Pacific Sun Literary Quarterly* 5–12 March 1976: 7.

"Sisters of the Princess." *CAIFI Newsletter* March 1976: 11.

"Poets." *Pacific Sun Literary Quarterly* 21–27 May 1976: 7.

"An Open Letter to Vida Hadjebi Tabrizi." *CAIFI Newsletter* March 1977: 8–10.

"The Crosbys: An Afterword." *ICarbS* 3 (Spring–Summer 1977) 117–25.

"March in the Cove." *Perma Frost* April 1977: 8.

"Walking Through the Fire." *New York Times Book Review* 12 June 1977: 6.

"Alexander Berkman: A Memory." *Phoenix* 6 (Summer–Fall 1977) 158–71.

"Report from Lock-up." *Four Visions of America: Erica Jong, Thomas Sanchez, Kay Boyle, Henry Miller.* Santa Barbara: Capra Press, 1977. Pp. 9–40.

Afterword. *A Hasty Bunch: Short Stories*, by Robert McAlmon. Carbondale and Edwardsville: Southern Illinois UP, 1977. Pp. 287–99.

"For Paul Jacobs." *San Francisco Review of Books* March 1978: 23.

"Conquered People Are Afraid to Be Themselves." *KPFA Folio* July–August 1978: 6.

Rev. of *Lucky Eyes and a High Heart; The Life of Maud Gonne*, by Nancy Cardozo. *New Republic* 28 October 1978: 36–38.

"No on 6: A Personal Opinion." *New West* 6 November 1978: 57–61.

Rev. of *Figures of Thought*, by Howard Nemerov. *San Francisco Review of Books* March 1979: 12.

"A Poem for George Moscone, Assassinated November 27, 1978." *Letters Magazine* [Maine Writers' Workshop] April 1979: 2–3.

"Strictly San Francisco." Rev. of *Awake in the River: Poems and Stories*, by Janice Mirikitani. *San Francisco Review of Books* July 1979: 5.

"St. Stephen's Green." *Atlantic* June 1980: 41–44.

"A Friend and Fighter Is Moving On." Interview with Leah Garchik. *San Francisco Chronicle* 19 October 1980.

Fifty Stories. New York: Penguin Books, 1981.

"Excerpt from a Long Poem in Progress—for Samuel Beckett." *Conjunctions* 2 (Spring 1982) 113–14.

"A Poem for the Teesto Diné of Arizona." *Malahat Review* July 1983: 96–97.

"Reincarnation—excerpt from a long poem to Samuel Beckett." *Rolling Stock* 5 (1983) 3.

Interview. *Women Writers of the West Coast Speaking of Their Lives and Careers*, ed. Marilyn Yalom. Santa Barbara: Capra Press, 1983. Pp. 105–20.

"Kay Boyle." *Contemporary Authors Autobiography Series*, ed. Dedria Bryfonski. Vol. 1. Detroit: Gale Research, 1984. Pp. 97–125.

Words That Must Somehow Be Said: The Selected Essays of Kay Boyle, 1927–1984, ed. Elizabeth Bell. London: Chatto & Windus–Hogarth Press, 1985.

"Pound in Rapallo." *New York Review of Books* 7 May 1987: 47.

Life Being the Best and Other Stories. New York: New Directions, 1988. Includes: "Life Being the Best" 3–26, "I Can't Get Drunk" 35–41, "Art Colony" 53–61, "The Meeting of the Stones" 69–80, "Peter Foxe" 81–91, and "Convalescence" 93–102.

"The Spirit of a Woman of Letters: An Interview with Kay Boyle." With Linda Ferguson. *Living in*

Words: Interviews from the Bloomsbury Review, 1981–1988, ed. Gregory McNamee. Portland: Breitenbush Books, 1988.

"Heroines and Also Heroes." Introduction. *A Woman on Paper: Georgia O'Keeffe*, by Anita Pollitzer. New York: Simon & Schuster–Touchstone, 1988. Pp. ix–xx.

Collected Poems of Kay Boyle. Port Townsend, WA: Copper Canyon Press, 1991.

INDEX